UNIVERSITY CASEBOOK SERIES

BATTERED WOMEN AND THE LAW

by

CLARE DALTON
Professor of Law
Matthews Distinguished University Professor
Northeastern University School of Law

ELIZABETH M. SCHNEIDER
Professor of Law
Brooklyn Law School

NEW YORK, NEW YORK

FOUNDATION PRESS

2001

11 Penn Plaza, Tenth Floor
New York, NY 10001
Phone Toll Free 1–877–888–1330
Fax (212) 760–8705
fdpress.com

ISBN 1–56662–480–0

To Bob Reich, and Adam and Sam Dalton Reich
— from C.D.

To Harry M. Schneider, Anna and Matthew Schneider-Mayerson
and Tom Grunfeld,
and in memory of Natalie Usdan Schneider
— from E.M.S.

But also
to the many activists and scholars
who have labored to create this field,
and to the women whose experiences are recorded here,
and whose courage and resilience are reflected on every page
— from both of us.

*

PREFACE

When I first taught a course in Battered Women and the Law, Liz's teaching materials provided the foundation on which I built. A few years later, she was the one to propose that we combine our efforts to produce a casebook. I thank her for her partnership in the project, and for her dual convictions: that this was a book whose time had come, and that it was a goal within our reach. There have been times when I questioned the second, but I have never doubted the first.

The book has emerged out of materials adapted and refined over the course of several years. I want to thank the Northeastern law students who have participated in my Battered Women and the Law course during those years, expanding and challenging my vision, and often contributing new ideas and materials through their research and service projects. There are several Northeastern students who have done even more; as my research assistants they have made important contributions to the book in its final form. I would like in particular to acknowledge the exceptional work of Hillary Weingast, Mindy Levinson, Elizabeth Tobin Tyler, Gina Gill, Christie Getto Young and, most recently, Miriam Barcimanto. I am grateful to Sara Shepard, then a student at American University's Washington College of Law, for her case study of Curtis v. Firth, which appears in Chapter 11. Karin Raye, then a student and now a fellow and colleague at the Domestic Violence Institute at Northeastern, educated me about the unique aspects of domestic abuse as it affects people with disabilities; that education is reflected in Chapter 3.

Three of my law school colleagues at Northeastern deserve particular thanks for patiently lending an ear, and a hand; Mary O'Connell, whose sound advice in matters of family law and the relationship between children and the state has been invaluable; Dan Givelber, who has steered me away from both error and prejudice in matters of criminal law and the criminal justice system, and Jim Rowan, whose quietly principled existence has provided a steady reminder of life's priorities, and whose support and understanding has carried me through many rough patches. The law school library staff, especially Jon Fernald, were unfailingly helpful, no matter how arcane the request. My final and most heartfelt thanks are reserved for my partners at the Domestic Violence Institute, Lois Kanter and Pualani Enos. My commitment to this project has had a concrete impact on our work together, and I thank them for their patience, and their willingness to pick up the pieces I have dropped along the way. More than that, however, much of what I have come to understand about domestic violence I have learned through and with them, and when I am tempted to turn away from the pain of that understanding, what keeps me in the work is the knowledge that I share it with them.

— *C.D.*

This casebook emerged from a joint vision of the importance of teaching law students about domestic violence. However, although the conception, structure and planning of the book over several years has been shared, I want to acknowledge Clare's greater contribution to the writing, revising and production of the final manuscript. Without her work this book would never have seen the light of day. I am deeply grateful to her for making the project a reality, for her friendship and support over many years, and last, but hardly least, for her patience and understanding through many bumps in the road.

I also want to acknowledge the support and encouragement of many other friends and colleagues, particularly Martha Minow, Sylvia A. Law, Nan Hunter, Minna Kotkin, Susan N. Herman and Stacy Caplow who have cheered this project on for many years. Without Charles Krause, my talented and devoted assistant, June Parris, and Rose Patti my portions of the book would not have been completed. Many students at Brooklyn Law School over the long life of this project provided helpful research assistance and helped to shape the content of the book, Kara Koski, Melissa Gable, Catherine Paszkowska, Lina Del Plato, Tracy Peterson, Kristin Bebelaar, Jodi Golinsky, Pamela Garas, Ami Mehta, and Alexandra Derian were particularly helpful. I am also grateful to all of my students in the Battered Women and the Law courses and seminars that I have taught, first at Harvard Law School, then at Brooklyn Law School and Florida State University School of Law and most recently at Columbia Law School, who shared their reactions to these developing materials. Sara Robbins and the entire library staff at Brooklyn Law School were responsive to my every research need.and incredibly patient. Dean Joan G. Wexler generously supported my work over many years with summer research grants.

— *E.M.S.*

ACKNOWLEDGEMENTS

Foundation Press and the authors gratefully acknowledge the authors and publishers that permitted us to reprint excerpts of copyrighted works. They are:

APA Presidential Task Force on Violence and the Family, VIOLENCE AND THE FAMILY, REPORT OF THE APA PRESIDENTIAL TASK FORCE ON VIOLENCE AND THE FAMILY, pp.39-41. Copyright (c) 1996 by the APA Presidential Task Force on Violence and the Family. Reprinted by permission.

Ashe, Marie; Cahn, Naomi, *Child Abuse: A Problem for Feminist Theory*, 2 Texas Journal of Women and the Law 75, pp.76, 84-88, 90, 93-96, 100, 104-05, 108, 111-12 (1993). Reprinted by permission.

Atterbury, Jennifer, *Employment Protection and Domestic Violence: Addressing Abuse in the Labor Grievance Process,* 1998 Journal of Dispute Resolution 165, pp.169-74 (1998). Reprinted by permission.

Blaisure, Karen R.; Geasler, Margie L., *Results of a Survey of Court-Connected Parent Education Programs in U.S. Counties,* 34 Family and Conciliation Courts Review 23, pp.24-35 (1996). Copyright (c) 1996 by Sage Publications, Inc. Reprinted by permission of Karen R. Blaisure and Margie L. Geasler.

Borgmann, Caitlin E., *Battered Women's Substantive Due Process Claims: Can Orders of Protection Deflect DeShaney?* 65 New York University Law Review 1280, pp.1290-93 (1990). Reprinted by permission.

Bowermaster, Janet M., *Relocation Disputes Involving Domestic Violence,* 46 Kansas Law Review 433, pp.433-35, 445-47 (1998), reprinted by permission of Kansas Law Review and Janet M. Bowermaster.

Bowker, Lee H.; Arbitell, Michelle; McFerron, Richard J., *On the Relationship Between Wife Beating and Child Abuse,* in FEMINIST PERSPECTIVES ON WIFE ABUSE 158, pp.159-66 (K. Yllo & M. Bograd, eds.). Copyright (c)1990 by Sage Publications, Inc. Reprinted by permission of Lee Bowker; Richard McFerron.

Braver, Stanford L.; Salem, Peter; Pearson, Jessica; DeLuse, Stephanie R., *The Content of Divorce Education Programs: Results of a Survey*, 34 Family and Conciliation Courts Review 41, pp.41-43, 48-50 (1996). Reprinted by permission of Sanford L. Braver.

Browne, Angela, WHEN BATTERED WOMEN KILL pp.38-48, 52-53. Copyright (c) 1987 by the MacMillan Free Press. Reprinted by permission of The Free Press, a Division of Simon & Schuster, Inc.

Buzawa, Eve S.; Austin, Thomas L.; Buzawa, Carl G., *The Role of Arrest in Domestic Versus Stranger Assault: Is There a Difference,* in DO ARRESTS AND RESTRAINING ORDERS WORK? (E.S. Buzawa & C.G. Buzawa, eds.) 150, pp.153-154, 156-163, 169-170. Copyright (c) 1996 by Sage Publications, Inc. Reprinted by permission.

Buzawa, Eve S.; Buzawa, Carl G., *The Scientific Evidence is Not Conclusive: Arrest Is No Panacea,* in CURRENT CONTROVERSIES ON FAMILY VIOLENCE (E.S.Buzawa & C.G. Buzawa, eds.) 337, pp.348-351. Copyright (c) 1993 by Sage Publications, Inc. Reprinted by permission.

Cahn, Naomi, *Innovative Approaches to the Prosecution of Domestic Violence Crimes,* in DOMESTIC VIOLENCE: THE CHANGING CRIMINAL JUSTICE RESPONSE (E.S. Buzawa & C.G. Buzawa, eds.) 161, pp. 162-75. Copyright (c) 1992 by Greenwood Publishing Group, Inc. Reprinted by permission of Greenwood Publishing Group, Inc. and Naomi Cahn.

Carlson, Bonnie E., *Questioning the Party Line on Family Violence*, 7 Affilia: Journal of Women & Social Work 94, pp. 97-100 (1992). Reprinted by permission of Sage Publications, Inc. and Bonnie E. Carlson.

Copelon, Rhonda, *Recognizing the Egregious in the Everyday: Domestic Violence as Torture,* 25 Columbia Human Rights Law Review 291, pp.292-98, 306-15, 319 (1994). Reprinted by permission.

Crenshaw, Kimberle, *Mapping the Margins: Intersectionality, Identity Politics, and Violence Against Women of Color,* 43 Stanford Law Review 1241, pp.1244-62 (1993). Reprinted by permission.

Dalton, Clare, *Domestic Violence, Domestic Torts, and Divorce: Constraints and Possibilities,* 31 New England Law Review 319, pp.324-30, 352-53, 364-70, 374-94. Copyright (c) 1997 by New England School of Law, all rights reserved. Reprinted by permission of the New England School of Law and Clare Dalton.

David and Lucile Packard Foundation, 9 The Future of Children, Executive Summary 4. Copyright (c) 1999 by the David and Lucile Packard Foundation, all rights reserved. Reprinted by permission.

Davis, Martha, *Domestic Violence and Welfare Reform: A Status Report,* Sojourner: The Women's Forum 32 (May 1998). Reprinted by permission of Martha F. Davis.

Dobash, Russell P; Dobash, R. Emerson; Cavanagh, Kate; Lewis, Ruth, *Separate and Intersecting Realities: A Comparison of Men's and Women's Accounts of Violence Against Women,* 4 Violence Against Women 382, pp.405-07. Copyright (c) 1998 by Sage Publications, Inc. Reprinted by permission of Sage Publications, Inc. and Russell P. Dobash.

Domestic Abuse Intervention Project, Power and Control and Equality Wheels. Reprinted by permission of Domestic Abuse Intervention Project.

Doyle, Roddy, THE WOMAN WHO WALKED INTO DOORS pp.175-86. Copyright (c) 1996 by Roddy Doyle. Reprinted by permission of Viking Penguin, a division of Penguin Putnam Inc.

Dutton, Donald, THE BATTERER: A PSYCHOLOGICAL PROFILE pp.24-30, 33-35, 61-62, 64-77, 96-100, 114-16, 120-24. Copyright (c) 1995 by Basic Books, a member of Perseus Books, L.L.C. Reprinted by permission.

Dutton, Mary Ann, *Understanding Women's Responses to Domestic Violence: A Redefinition of Battered Woman Syndrome,* 21 Hofstra Law Review 1191, pp.1194-96, 1198-1201, 1216-27, 1231-32 (1993). Reprinted by permission of the Hofstra Law Review Association.

Easterling, Michelle W., *For Better or Worse: The Federalization of Domestic Violence,* 98 West Virginia Law Review 933, pp.933-38, 940-46 (1996). Reprinted by permission.

Ellis, Desmond; Stuckless, Noreen, MEDIATING AND NEGOTIATING MARITAL CONFLICTS pp.1-2. Copyright (c) 1996 by Sage Publications, Inc. Reprinted by permission of Desmond Ellis and Noreen Stuckless, Ph.D.; La Marsh Research Centre on Violence and Conflict Resolution, York University, Toronto, Canada.

Emerge, Violent and Controlling Behaviors Checklist. Reprinted with permission of Emerge, a Counseling Program for Batterers, Cambridge, Massachusetts.

Enos, V. Pualani, *Prosecuting Battered Mothers: State Laws' Failure to Protect Battered Women and Abused Children,* 19 Harvard Women's Law Journal 229, pp.240-46, 249-51, 253-61 (1996). Copyright (c)1996 by the President and Fellows of Harvard College and V. Pualani Enos. Reprinted by permission.

Erickson, Nancy, *Battered Mothers of Battered Children: Using Our Knowledge of Battered Women to Defend Them Against Charges of Failure to Act,* in CURRENT PERSPECTIVES IN PSYCHOLOGICAL, LEGAL AND ETHICAL ISSUES, Vol. 1A, CHILDREN AND FAMILIES: ABUSE AND ENDANGERMENT (S.A. Garcia & R.Batey, eds.)197, pp.204-08. Copyright (c) 1991 by Jessica Kingsley Publishers Ltd. Reprinted by permission.

Family Violence Project of the National Council of Juvenile and Family Court Judges, *Family Violence in Child Custody Statutes: An Analysis of State Codes and Legal Practice,* 29 Family Law Quarterly 197, pp.208-210, 212-222 (1995). Copyright (c) 1995 by the American Bar Association. Reprinted by permission of the National Council of Juvenile and Family Court Judges.

Feeney, Kate L. S., *The Jurisdictional Juggle of Child Custody: An Analysis of the UCCJA, PKPA, UMEA and Massachusetts Law,* 16 Massachusetts Family Law Journal 35, 35-38 (1998). Reprinted by permission.

Findlater, Janet; Kelly, Susan, *Child Protective Services and Domestic Violence*, 9 The Future of Children 84, pp.87-93. Copyright (c)1999 by the David and Lucile Packard Foundation, all rights reserved. Reprinted by permission of the David and Lucile Packard Foundation, Janet Findlater and Susan Kelly.

Fineman, Martha; Opie, Ann, *The Uses of Social Science Data in Legal Policymaking: Custody Determinations at Divorce*, 1987 Wisconsin Law Review 107, pp.113, 115-17. Reprinted by permission of Wisconsin Law Review and Martha Fineman.

Finn, Peter; Colson, Sarah, Civil Protection Orders: Legislation, Current Court Practice, and Enforcement, pp.10-11, 19-27, 60-61. National Institute of Justice, March 1990. Reprinted by permission.

Fischer, Karla; Vidmar, Neil; Ellis, Rene, *The Culture of Battering and the Role of Mediation in Domestic Violence Cases,* 46 Southern Methodist University Law Review 2117, pp. 2119-33, 2136-41, 2157-65 (1993). Reprinted by permission of the Southern Methodist University Law Review, the Southern Methodist University School of Law, and Neil Vidmar.

Flitcraft, Ann, *The AMA Guidelines One Year Later,* Preventing Violence to Women: Integrating the Health and Legal Communities, pp.21-24. Copyright (c) 1993 by the Association of Trial Lawyers of America. Reprinted by permission of West Group.

Ford, David A.; Reichard, Ruth; Goldsmith, Stephen; Regoli, Mary J., *Future Directions for Criminal Justice Policy on Domestic Violence,* in DO ARRESTS AND RESTRAINING ORDERS WORK? (E.S. Buzawa & C.G. Buzawa, eds.) 243, pp.258-261. Copyright (c) 1996 by Sage Publications, Inc. Reprinted by permission of Sage Publications, Inc.

Ford, David A.; Regoli, Mary J, *The Preventive Impacts of Policies for Prosecuting Wife Batterers,* in DOMESTIC VIOLENCE: THE CHANGING CRIMINAL JUSTICE RESPONSE (E.S. Buzawa & C.G. Buzawa, eds.) 181, pp.182, 184-89, 192-95, 197-205. Copyright (c) 1992 by Greenwood Publishing Group, Inc. Reprinted by permission.

Fuhrmann Geri; McGill, Joseph C., PARENTS APART: PARENTS' HANDBOOK, pp.16-18. Reprinted by permission of The University of Massachusetts Medical Center, Family Services of Central Massachusetts and Joseph C. McGill.

Fuhrmann Geri; McGill, Joseph C.; O'Connell, Mary, *Parent Education's Second Generation: Integrating Violence Sensitivity,* 37 Family and Conciliation Courts Review 24, pp.31-32 (1999). Reprinted by permission of Geri Fuhrmann.

Gamache, Denise; Asmus, Mary, *Enhancing Networking Among Service Providers: Elements of Successful Coordination Strategies,* COORDINATING COMMUNITY RESPONSES TO DOMESTIC VIOLENCE: LESSONS FROM DULUTH AND BEYOND (M.F. Shepard & E.L. Pence, eds.) 65, pp.73-86. Copyright (c) 1999 by Sage Publications, Inc. Reprinted by permission.

Ganley, Anne, *Integrating Feminist and Social Learning Analyses of Aggression: Creating Multiple Models for Intervention with Men Who Batter,* in TREATING MEN WHO BATTER: THEORY, PRACTICE AND PROGRAMS (P.L. Caesar & L.K. Hamberger, eds.)196, pp.198-99, 217, 223-24. Copyright (c) 1989 by Springer Publishing Company, Inc. Reprinted by permission.

Gelles, Richard J.; Schwartz, Ira, *Children and the Child Welfare System,* 2 University of Pennsylvania Journal of Constitutional Law 95, pp. 96-99 (1999). Reprinted by permission of University of Pennsylvania Journal of Constitutional Law and Ira Schwartz.

Goldfarb, Sally F., *Violence Against Women and the Persistence of Privacy,* 61 Ohio State Law Journal 1, pp.7-8, 46-54 (2000). Reprinted by permission of the Ohio State Law Journal.

Goldner, Virginia; Penn, Peggy; Sheinberg, Marcia; Walker, Gillian, *Love and Violence: Gender Paradoxes in Volatile Attachments,* 29 Family Process 343, pp.356-57, 359-61 (1990). Copyright (c) 1990 by Family Process, Inc. Reprinted by permission.

Gondolf, Edward W.; Fisher, Ellen R., BATTERED WOMEN AS SURVIVORS: AN ALTERNATIVE TO TREATING LEARNED HELPLESSNESS pp.11-22. Copyright (c) 1988 by Lexington books, an imprint of Macmillan, Inc. Reprinted by permission of Edward W. Gondolf.

Gorelick, Jamie; Litman, Harry, *Prosecutorial Descretion and the Federalization Debate,* 46 Hastings Law Journal 967, pp. 968-77 (1995). Copyright (c) 1995 by University of California, Hastings College of Law. Reprinted by permission of Hastings College of Law, Jamie Gorelick, former Deputy Attorney General, and Harry Litman, U.S. Attorney, Western District of Pennsylvania.

Graham-Bermann, Sandra A., *The Impact of Woman Abuse on Children's Social Development: Research and Theoretical Perspectives,* in CHILDREN EXPOSED TO MARITAL VIOLENCE: THEORY, RESEARCH AND APPLIED ISSUES, (G.W. Holden, R. Geffner & E.N. Jouriles, eds.) 21, pp.32-45. Copyright (c) 1998 by the American Psychological Association. Reprinted by permission of Sandra A. Graham-Bermann, Ph.D.

Grillo, Trina, *The Mediation Alternative: Process Dangers for Women,* 100 Yale Law Journal 1545, pp. 1547-48, 1551-55, 1594-96 (1991). Reprinted by permission of The Yale Law Journal Company and William S. Hein Company.

Groves, Betsy McAlister, *Mental Health Services for Children Who Witness Domestic Violence*, 9 The Future of Children 122, pp. 125-27. Copyright (c) 1999 by the David and Lucile Packard Foundation. Reprinted by permission of the David and Lucile Packard Foundation and Betsy McAlister Groves.

Gwinn, Casey G.; O'Dell, Sgt. Anne, *Stopping the Violence: The Role of the Police Officer and the Prosecutor*, 20 Western State Law Review 298, pp.300-03, 308-09 (1993). Reprinted by permission of Western State Law Review, Casey Gwinn and Sgt. Anne O'Dell.

Halikias, William, *The Guardian Ad Litem for Children in Divorce: Conceptualizing Duties, Roles and Consultative Services,* 32 Family and Conciliation Courts Review 490, pp. 494, 497-99 (1994). Copyright (c) 1994 by Sage Publications, Inc.

Hamberger, L. Kevin; Lohr, Jeffrey M., *Proximal Causes of Spouse Abuse: A Theoretical Analysis for Cognitive-Behavioral Interventions,* in TREATING MEN WHO BATTER: THEORY, PRACTICE AND PROGRAMS (P.L. Caesar & L.K. Hamberger, eds.) 53, pp.57-58, 63-67, 69-71. Copyright (c) 1989 by Springer Publishing Company, Inc. Reprinted by permission of Springer Publishing Company, Inc. and L. Kevin Hamberger.

Hanna, Cheryl, *No Right to Choose: Mandated Victim Participation in Domestic Violence Prosecutions*, 109 Harv. L. Rev. 1849, pp.1867, 1869-72, 1882-85, 1888, 1890-91 (1996). Reprinted by permission of the Harvard Law Review.

Hanna, Cheryl, *The Paradox of Hope: The Crime and Punishment of Domestic Violence,* 39 William & Mary Law Review 1505, pp.1513, 1517-25, 1563-66 (1998). Reprinted by permission of the William & Mary Law Review.

Harrell, Adele; Smith, Barbara E., *Effects of Restraining Orders on Domestic Violence Victims,* in DO ARRESTS AND RESTRAINING ORDERS WORK? (E.S. Buzawa & C.G. Buzawa, eds.) 214, pp.223-225. Copyright (c) 1996 by Sage Publications, Inc. Reprinted by permission of Sage Publications, Inc. and Adele Harrell. Based on research funded by the State Justice Institute.

Hart, Barbara J., *State Codes on Domestic Violence: Analysis, Commentary and Recommendations*, 1992 Juvenile and Family Court Journal 3, pp.14-19, 23-24. Reprinted by permission of the National Council of Juvenile and Family Court Judges.

Hart, Barbara J., Safety Planning for Children: Strategizing for Unsupervised Visits with Batterers. Pennsylvania Coalition Against Domestic Violence, 1990. Reprinted by permission.

Hart, Barbara J., *Lesbian Battering: An Examination,* in NAMING THE VIOLENCE, SPEAKING OUT ABOUT LESBIAN BATTERING (K. Lobel, ed.) 173, pp.174-82. Copyright (c) 1986 by the National Coalition Against Domestic Violence. Reprinted by permission.

Harway, Michele, *Battered Women: Characteristics and Causes,* in BATTERING AND FAMILY THERAPY: A FEMINIST PERSPECTIVE (M. Hansen & M. Harway, eds.) 29, pp. 29-31, 35-36. Copyright (c) 1993 by Sage Publications, Inc. Reprinted by permission.

Herman, Judith Lewis, TRAUMA AND RECOVERY pp.133-54. Copyright (c) 1992 by BasicBooks, a division of HarperCollins Publishers. Reprinted by permission.

Hofford, Meredith; Harrell, Adele V., Family Violence, Interventions for the Justice System, 1993. Reprinted by permission of Adele Harrell. This document was created under a grant awarded by the Bureau of Justice Assistance, Office of Justice Programs, U.S. Department of Justice. The opinions, findings, and conclusions or recommendations expressed in this document are those of the authors and do not necessarily represent the official position or policies of the U.S. Department of Justice.

Holden, George W., *Introduction: The Development of Research Into Another Consequence of Family Violence,* in CHILDREN EXPOSED TO MARITAL VIOLENCE: THEORY, RESEARCH AND APPLIED ISSUES (G.W. Holden, R. Geffner & E.N. Jouriles, eds.) 1, pp.6-11. Copyright (c) 1998 by the American Psychological Association. Reprinted by permission.

Holden, George W.; Stein, Joshua D.; Ritchie, Kathy L.; Harris, Susan D.; Jouriles, Ernest N., *Parenting Behaviors and Beliefs of Battered Women,* in CHILDREN EXPOSED TO MARITAL VIOLENCE: THEORY, RESEARCH AND APPLIED ISSUES (G.W. Holden, R. Geffner & E.N. Jouriles, eds.) 289, pp.325-30. Copyright (c) 1998 by the American Psychological Association. Reprinted by permission.

Island, David; Letellier, Patrick, MEN WHO BEAT THE MEN WHO LOVE THEM pp.236-39, 245-47. Copyright (c) 1991 by the Haworth Press, Inc. Reprinted by permission.

Jacobs, Michelle, *Requiring Battered Women Die: Murder Liability for Mothers Under Failure to Protect Statutes,* 88 Journal of Criminal Law and Criminology 579, pp. 613-15 (1988). Reprinted by special permission of Northwestern University School of Law, Journal of Criminal Law and Criminology, and by permission of Michelle Jacobs.

Jacobson, Neil S.; Gottman, John M., WHEN MEN BATTER WOMEN: NEW INSIGHTS INTO ENDING ABUSIVE RELATIONSHIPS pp.36-39. Copyright (c) 1998 by Neil Jacobson and John Gottman. Reprinted by permission.

Jones, Ann, NEXT TIME SHE'LL BE DEAD: BATTERING AND HOW TO STOP IT pp.199-206. Copyright (c) 2000 by Ann Jones. Reprinted by permission.

Klein, Catherine F., *Full Faith and Credit: Interstate Enforcement of Protection Orders Under the Violence Against Women Act of 1994*, 29 Family Law Quarterly 253, pp. 254-57, 263-66 (1995). Copyright (c) 1995 by the American Bar Association. Reprinted by permission of the American Bar Association and Catherine F. Klein.

Klein, Catherine F.; Orloff, Leslye E., *Providing Legal Protection for Battered Women: An Analysis of State Statutes and Case Law*, 21 Hofstra Law Review 801, pp.814-17, 820-25, 827-41, 1122-24 (1993). Reprinted by permission of the Hofstra Law Review Association, Catherine F. Klein and Leslye Orloff.

Lawrence, Liza; Kugler, Lisa, *Selected Voir Dire Questions,* in WOMEN'S SELF-DEFENSE CASES: THEORY AND PRACTICE (E. Bochnak, ed.) 256-65 (1981). Reprinted by permission.

Lehrmann, Federica L., DOMESTIC VIOLENCE PRACTICE AND PROCEDURE, §§ 6:23-6:26, 10:26-10:30. Copyright (c) 1997 by West Group. Reprinted by permission.

Lennett, Judith, *Like Ships That Pass in the Night: AFDC Policy and Battered Women,* 19 Law and Policy 191, pp. 194-95 (1997). Copyright (c) 1997 by Blackwell Publishers Ltd. Reprinted by permission.

Loseke, Dorileen, R., THE BATTERED WOMAN AND SHELTERS pp.20-21, 27-28, 149-51, 154. Copyright (c) 1992 by State University of New York Press. Reprinted by permission of the State University of New York Press and Dorileen Loseke.

Maguigan, Holly, *Battered Women and Self-Defense: Myths and Misconceptions in Current Reform Proposals,* 140 University of Pennsylvania Law Review 279, pp.382-87, 439-43 (1991). Reprinted by permission.

Manning, Peter K., *The Preventive Conceit: The Black Box in Market Context,* in DO ARRESTS AND RESTRAINING ORDERS WORK? (E.S. Buzawa & C.G. Buzawa, eds.) 83, pp. 83-84, 92-93. Copyright (c) 1996 by Sage Publications, Inc. Reprinted by permission of Sage Publications, Inc. and Peter Manning.

Marcus, Isabel, *Reframing "Domestic violence": Terrorism in the Home,* in THE PUBLIC NATURE OF PRIVATE VIOLENCE (M.A. Fineman & R. Mykitiuk, eds.)11, pp.20-23. Copyright (c) 1994 by Routledge. Reprinted by permission.

McConnell, Joyce, *Beyond Metaphor: Battered Women, Involuntary Servitude and the Thirteenth Amendment,* 4 Yale Journal of Law and Feminism 207, pp.207-09, 219-20 (1992). Reprinted by permission.

Meier, Joan, *Domestic Violence, Character and Social Change in the Welfare Reform Debate*, 19 Law & Policy 205, pp.220-25, 227-30 (1997). Copyright (c) 1997 by Blackwell Publishers Ltd. Reprinted by permission.

Meier, Joan, *Notes From the Underground: Integrating Psychological and Legal Perspectives on Domestic Violence in Theory and Practice,* 21 Hofstra Law Review 1295, p.1361 (1993). Reprinted by permission.

Muhlhauser, Tara L.; Knowlton, Douglas D., *Exploring the Concept of a Guardian Ad Litem Team*, 71 North Dakota Law Review 1021, pp.1023-35 (1995). Reprinted by permission of the North Dakota Law Review.

National Council of Juvenile and Family Court Judges, Model Code on Domestic and Family Violence, January 1994. Reprinted by permission of the National Council of Juvenile and Family Court Judges.

Pleck, Elizabeth, DOMESTIC TYRANNY: THE MAKING OF AMERICAN SOCIAL POLICY AGAINST FAMILY VIOLENCE FROM COLONIAL TIMES TO THE PRESENT pp.7-11. Copyright (c) 1987 by the Oxford University Press.

Rabin, Bonnie, *Violence Against Mothers Equals Violence Against Children: Understanding the Connections*, 58 Albany Law Review 1109, pp.1109-10 (1995). Reprinted by permission of the Albany Law Review.

Raphael, Jody, SAVING BERNICE: BATTERED WOMEN, WELFARE AND POVERTY pp.25-28, 143-48. Copyright (c) 2000 by Jo Ann Raphael. Reprinted by permission of Northeastern University Press and Jo Ann Raphael.

Reihing, Katherine M., *Protecting Victims of Domestic Violence and Their Children After Divorce: The American Law Institute's Model,* 37 Family and Conciliation Courts Review 393, pp.398-402 (1999). Copyright (c) 1999 by Sage Publications, Inc. Reprinted by permission.

Richie, Beth, COMPELLED TO CRIME: THE GENDER ENTRAPMENT OF BATTERED BLACK WOMEN, pp. 63-68, 97-102. Copyright (c) 1996 by Routledge. Reprinted by permission of Routledge and Beth Richie.

Schechter, Susan, WOMEN AND MALE VIOLENCE: THE VISIONS AND STRUGGLES OF THE BATTERED WOMEN'S MOVEMENT, pp.20-24, 29-68, 81-87, 93-98, 103. Copyright (c) 1982 by South End Press. Reprinted by permission of South End Press and Susan Schechter.

Scherer, Douglas, *Tort Remedies for Victims of Domestic Abuse,* 43 South Carolina Law Review 543, pp.557-62 (1992). Reprinted by permission.

Schmidt, Janell D.; Sherman, Lawrence W., *Does Arrest Deter Domestic Violence,* in DO ARRESTS AND RESTRAINING ORDERS WORK? (E.S. Buzawa & C.G. Buzawa, eds.) 43, pp. 45-46, 48-49, 50-53. Copyright (c) 1996 by Sage Publications, Inc. Reprinted by permission of Sage Publications, Inc.

Schneider, Elizabeth M., BATTERED WOMEN AND FEMINIST LAW-MAKING pp. 20-27, 53-56, 112-40, 143-47. Copyright (c) 2000 by the Yale University Press. Reprinted by permission.

Schulman, Joanne; Pitt, Valerie, *Second Thoughts on Joint Child Custody: Analysis of Legislation and Its Implications for Women and Children,* 12 Golden Gate Law Review 538, pp. 546-53 (1982). Reprinted by permission.

Shalleck, Ann, *Theory and Experience in Constructing the Relationship Between Lawyer and Client: Representing Women Who Have Been Abused,* 64 Tennessee Law Review 1019, pp.1023-38 (1997). Reprinted by permission of the Tennessee Law Review Association, Inc., and Ann Shalleck.

Sharp, Paula, CROWS OVER A WHEATFIELD pp. 254-58. Copyright (c) 1996 by Paula Sharp. Reprinted by permission of Hyperion.

Siegel, Reva B., *The Rule of Love: Wife Beating as Prerogative and Privacy,* 105 Yale Law Journal 2117, pp.2118-20, 2197-2206 (1996). Reprinted by permission of the Yale Law Journal and Reva B. Siegel.

Silvern, Louise; Kaersvang, Lynn, *The Traumatized Children of Violent Marriages*, 68 Child Welfare 421, pp.427-30 (1989). Reprinted by permission of the Child Welfare League of America, Inc., Lynn Kaersvang and Louise Silvern.

Sinden, Amy, *"Why Won't Mom Cooperate?": A Critique of Informality in Child Welfare Proceedings,* 11 Yale Journal of Law & Feminism 339, pp. 344-50 (1999). Reprinted by permission.

Stark, Evan, *Mandatory Arrest of Batterers: A Reply to Its Critics,* in DO ARRESTS AND RESTRAINING ORDERS WORK? (E.S. Buzawa & C.G. Buzawa, eds.) 115, pp.122-24. Copyright (c) 1996 by Sage Publications, Inc. Appeared originally in 36(5) American Behavioral Scientist, May/June 1993. Reprinted by permission of Sage Publications, Inc. and Evan Stark.

Straus, Murray, *The Controversy Over Domestic Violence by Women: A Methodological, Theoretical and Sociology of Science Analysis,* in VIOLENCE IN INTIMATE RELATIONSHIPS (X.B. Arriaga & S. Oskamp, eds.) 17, pp. 22-39 (1999).

Straus, Robert B., *Supervised Visitation and Family Violence,* 29 Family Law Quarterly 229, pp. 230-49 (1995). Copyright (c) 1995 by the American Bar Association.

Thomas, Dorothy Q; Beasley, Michele E, *Domestic Violence as a Human Rights Issue,* 58 Albany Law Review 1119, pp.1119-33, 1140-47 (1995). Reprinted by permission of the Albany Law Review.

Toronto Forum Report, 33 Family and Conciliation Courts Review 63, 72-74 (1995). Copyright (c) 1995 by Sage Publications, Inc.

United States Department of Justice, Stalking and Domestic Violence: The Third Annual Report to Congress Under the Violence Against Women Act (1998). Reprinted by permission. This document was created by the Violence Against Women Office of the United States Department of Justice. The opinions, findings, and conclusions or recommendations expressed in this document are those of the authors and do not necessarily represent the official position or policies of the United States Department of Justice.

Waits, Kathleen, *Battered Women and Their Children: Lessons from One Woman's Story*, 35 Houston Law Review 29, pp. 46-50, 52-56, 59-62 (1998). Reprinted by permission of the Houston Law Review and Kathleen Waits.

Walker, Lenore E.A., *The Battered Woman Syndrome is a Psychological Consequence of Abuse,* in CURRENT CONTROVERSIES ON FAMILY VIOLENCE (R.J.Gelles & D.R. Loseke, eds.) 133, pp.138-44. Copyright (c) 1993 by Sage Publications, Inc. Reprinted by permission.

Walker, Lenore E.A., Terrifying Love: Why Battered Women Kill and How Society Responds, pp.42-45. Copyright (c) 1990 by Lenore E. Auerbach Walker. Reprinted by permission of HarperCollins Publishers, Inc.

Wang, Karin, *Battered Asian Women: Community Responses from the Battered Women's Movement and the Asian American Community*, 3 Asian Law Journal 151, pp.161, 167-71 (1996). Reprinted by permission of the Asian Law Journal.

West, Robin, *Toward an Abolitionist Interpretation of the Fourtenth Amendment,* 94 West Virginia Law Review 111, pp. 129-32, 140-44, 146-47 (1991). Reprinted by permission.

Weyrauch, W.O., Katz, Sanford N., Olsen, Fran, CASES AND MATERIALS ON FAMILY LAW: LEGAL CONCEPTS AND CHANGING HUMAN RELATIONSHIPS pp.838-43 (1994). Reprinted by permission of Sanford N. Katz and Fran Olsen.

White, Lucie, *No Exit: Rethinking Welfare Dependency from a Different Ground*, 81 Georgetown Law Journal 1961, pp.1986-90, 1997-2000 (1993). Reprinted by permission of Georgetown University, Georgetown Law Journal and Lucie White.

Williams, Lucy, *The Ideology of Division: Behavior Modification Welfare Reform Proposals*, 102 Yale Law Journal 719, pp. 719-21(1992). Reprinted by permission of the Yale Law Journal and Lucy Williams.

Zorza, Joan, *The Criminal law of Misdemeanor Domestic Violence, 1970-1990*, 83 Journal of Criminal Law & Criminology 46, pp.48-50, 53-60 (1992). Reprinted by permission of the Journal of Criminal Law and Criminology and Joan Zorza.

Zorza, Joan, *Must We Stop Arresting Batterers?: Analysis and Policy Implications of New Police Domestic Violence Studies*, 28 New England Law Review 929, pp.930-31, 965-67, 973-74 (1994). Reprinted by permission of Joan Zorza.

*

SUMMARY OF CONTENTS

*

TABLE OF CONTENTS

TABLE OF CASES

Principal cases are in bold type. Non-principal cases are in roman type. References are to Pages.

BATTERED WOMEN AND THE LAW

*

INTRODUCTION

Although domestic violence, or battering, or woman abuse, has a long history in this country and around the world, as recently as the early 1960s there was in the United States no legal recognition of the systematic violence done to women by their partners. By 1992, almost thirty years later, the United States Supreme Court was ready to recognize the pervasiveness and severity of domestic violence for the first time in *Planned Parenthood v. Casey*, 505 U.S. 833 (1992). In 1994 Congress passed the Violence Against Women Act, creating for the first time at the federal level both criminal and civil causes of action addressing domestic violence.

Feminists in the United States had argued for more than two centuries that women's legally sanctioned subordination within the family denied them equality and citizenship. They saw violence as an important vehicle for this subordination. Feminists claimed that domestic violence threatened not only women's right to physical integrity, and perhaps even to life itself, but also women's liberty, autonomy, and equality. Yet it was only in the late 1960s, at the prompting of feminist activists and lawyers, that any aspect of this link between violence and equality began to be reflected in culture and in law.

Since then, the rebirth of a women's rights movement in the United States has had a substantial impact in changing attitudes and defining public issues. Law has been a critical component of this process of change and feminist lawyers have played a central role in shaping it. Feminist activists and lawyers have challenged assumptions about gender roles, the family, and the workplace. Through a process of feminist lawmaking they have given name and visibility to harms experienced by women, such as domestic violence and sexual harassment, that were previously buried by cultural complicity.

The development of a battered women's movement has been one of the most important contributions of the women's rights struggle. This movement constructed a theoretical framework around the practice of battering, and the issue has now moved from social invisibility as a "private problem" to an important public concern. There is hardly a day when a domestic violence story does not appear in the media. The O.J. Simpson case, with its subtext of battering, held public attention for several years. There has been an explosion of innovative efforts in both state and federal legislative arenas. Organizations have founded shelters or networks of "safe homes," set up telephone hotlines, challenged police practices that leave battered women at risk, drafted protective order legislation, and stimulated reforms in the criminal justice and family law systems. Lawsuits and legislation have produced improved police and court practices. Activists have worked alongside practitioners and educators to develop teen-dating violence programs, child witness to violence programs, batterers' intervention programs, and specialized training programs for professionals in a variety of disciplines. Government reports, legal and social science literatures, and media coverage have proliferated. Advocates and scholars continue to formulate new legal approaches to violence against women. Work in the

United States is linked to a feminist human rights campaign addressing gender violence around the world.

This casebook on battered women and the law examines violence against women in intimate relationships, and the ways in which this violence shapes law and is shaped by the law. It is a product of the recent explosion of feminist lawmaking. Although intimate partner violence has been an issue that has always been implicated in law and in law school courses on family law, criminal law, torts, property, and civil rights, to name just a few, it has usually been invisible. It is only in the last decade that there have been lawyers sensitive to this issue, specialized law school courses and clinical programs addressing the problems that women who are battered face in the legal system, and serious efforts to integrate legal issues regarding domestic violence into traditional law school courses. Indeed, even a few years before *Casey* was decided, the issue of domestic violence and its link to reproductive choice might never have been argued.

The book draws on materials developed for courses taught by authors Clare Dalton and Elizabeth Schneider beginning in 1990 at Northeastern University Law School and Harvard Law School. It is intended for specialized offerings in domestic violence, but could also be used as a supplement for courses in family law, criminal law, and the range of other law school courses which address issues of domestic violence.

Part I, An Introduction to Abuse, examines the history of domestic violence as a legal and social problem; the dynamics of abusive relationships; and how the experience of abuse is shaped by the race, cultural identity, sexual orientation, economic status, and physical and mental health status of both abuser and abused. This part also introduces the reader to the ways in which, as the law has begun to recognize domestic violence, battered women have been depicted in legal contexts. In Part II , Battered Women as Mothers, we explore the ways in which battering affects children, and how the child welfare system, criminal justice system and family law system affect the relationships between battered mothers and their children. Part III, Holding Batterers Accountable, examines the primary legal remedies that have been developed to impose responsibility on batterers and keep battered women safe: the civil protective order and criminal prosecutions. Part IV, Self–Defense and Beyond, looks first at battered women's self-defense claims, the area of law for which battered women's syndrome testimony was first developed, and in which courts first wrestled with the nature of battering relationships. This part also includes other issues specific to battered women as criminal defendants. Part V, Newer Legal Frameworks, looks at domestic violence as a basis for tort claims, at the potential third party liability of police and employers, at civil rights claims, and at claims based on violations of international human rights. Part VI rounds out the book with a look at the unique challenges involved in advocacy on behalf of battered women, and at cutting edge approaches to combating domestic violence, both within and outside the legal system. The book is interdisciplinary, drawing on literature, history, the social sciences and journalism, as well as primary and secondary legal sources.

A caveat is in order. The book is titled BATTERED WOMEN AND THE LAW, but that choice was not an easy or an inevitable one. Its principal merit is that it acknowledges the origins of legal activism and legal reform on behalf of women who have suffered abuse in the grass roots battered women's movement. But there are those who argue that to call a woman "battered," as if that single adjective summed her up, inappropriately limits both her description and our understanding of her situation. Unless or until she pays the ultimate price, and dies at the hands of her partner, she is also, and importantly, a survivor. She may be a cellist, a salesperson, a lawyer, secretary or truck driver, or bake the best cookies on the block. She may be a woman others would describe as sexy, or funny, or tough, before they would describe her as battered.

Would it have been better, given these concerns, to call the book DOMESTIC VIOLENCE AND THE LAW? Domestic violence has certainly become a popular label for the issues the book addresses. But some argue that the very adjective "domestic" seems to "domesticate" the problem, making it sound as if this violence is somehow less threatening, less lethal, than violence between strangers, or violence on the street. Too many women know that this is not the case. Others dislike the gender neutrality of the term "domestic violence," pointing out that it appears to support the controversial claim (one we pay attention to in due course) that abusive partners are as often female as they are male. Still others are concerned that because of the strong cultural association between "domesticity" and families headed by heterosexual partners, the label "domestic violence" helps us overlook the extent to which "intimate partner violence" is as endemic to same-sex partnerships as it is to heterosexual ones. BATTERED WOMEN AND THE LAW has the same problem; historically it refers to women battered by men, not women battered by other women, and it definitively screens from our view men battered by men, as well as the men (for there are certainly some) who are battered by women. Even the term "battering" to describe abuse has its limitations, limitations it shares with "violence," as a description of the problem. Both accentuate physical injury, and threats of physical injury, while "abuse" more easily accommodates the full range of power and control tactics used by abusive partners, including physical, sexual and emotional abuse. One of the recurring themes of the book is the tendency of law to focus on physical violence and physical injury at the expense of a fuller and richer understanding of the dynamics and the impact of abuse.

After pondering all these issues, and choices, we came back to BATTERED WOMEN AND THE LAW, as an appropriate title for a book that seeks to acknowledge its past as well as point to the future. But the issues that title may seem to suppress are in fact fully represented in the pages that follow.

PART I

An Introduction to Abuse

CHAPTER ONE

Domestic Violence in Historical and Social Context

A. A Contemporary Picture of Domestic Violence

We open with data on domestic violence; its pervasiveness and scope, and its impact on the lives of women and children. Our first capsule picture of domestic violence is taken from the Supreme Court's decision in *Planned Parenthood v. Casey*, 505 U.S. 833 (1992).

Casey is widely known as the decision in which the Supreme Court narrowly upheld constitutional protection for women's right to reproductive choice, not as a case about domestic violence. But the restrictive Pennsylvania abortion statute challenged in *Casey* included a mandatory "spousal notification" provision. Battered women's advocacy organizations argued that enforcement of this provision would mean that women who lived with violent partners would be unable freely to exercise their reproductive choice, because they could not tell their partners that they were pregnant, or that they wanted an abortion, without fear of reprisal. The Court struck down the spousal notification provision as unconstitutional on these grounds. It relied on the following statistics to support its conclusion that domestic violence was a serious and widespread problem, with a severe impact on women's reproductive freedom:

> The American Medical Association (AMA) has published a summary of the recent research in this field, which indicates that in an average 12-month period in this country, approximately two million women are victims of severe assaults by their male partners. In a 1985 survey, women reported that nearly one of every eight husbands had assaulted their wives during the past year. The AMA views these figures as "marked underestimates," because the nature of these incidents discourages women from reporting them, and because surveys typically exclude the very poor, those who do not speak English well, and women who are homeless or in institutions or hospitals when the survey is conducted. According to the AMA, "researchers on family violence agree that the true incidence of partner violence is probably *double* the above estimates; or four million severely assaulted women per year. Studies on prevalence suggest that from one-fifth to one-third of all women will be physically assaulted by a partner or ex-partner during their lifetime." AMA Council on Scientific Affairs, Violence Against Women 7 (1991) (emphasis in original). Thus on an average day in the United States, nearly 11,000 women are severely assaulted by their male partners. Many of these incidents involve sexual assault.

> *Id.*, at 3–4; Shields & Hanneke, Battered Wives' Reactions to Marital Rape, in The Dark Side of Families: Current Family Violence Research 131, 144 (D. Finkelhor, R. Gelles, G. Hotaling, & M. Straus eds. 1983). In families where wife beating takes place, moreover, child abuse is often present as well. Violence Against Women, *supra*, at 12.
>
> Other studies fill in the rest of this troubling picture. Physical violence is only the most visible form of abuse. Psychological abuse, particularly forced social and economic isolation of women, is also common. L. Walker, the Battered Women Syndrome 27–28 (1984). Many victims of domestic violence remain with their abusers, perhaps because they perceive no superior alternative. Herbert Silver, & Ellrd, Coping With an Abusive Relationship: I. How and Why do Women Stay?, 53 J. Marriage & the Family 311 (1991). Many abused women who find temporary refuge in shelters return to their husbands, in large part because they have no other source of income. Aguirre, Why Do They Return? Abused Wives in Shelters, 30 J. Nat. Assn. of Social Workers 350, 352 (1985). Returning to one's abuser can be dangerous. Recent Federal Bureau of Investigation statistics disclose that 8.8 percent of all homicide victims in the United States are killed by their spouses. Mercy & Saltzman, Fatal Violence Among Spouses in the United States, 1976–85, 79 M. J. Public Health 595 (1989). Thirty percent of female homicide victims are killed by their male partners. Domestic Violence: Terrorism in the Home, Hearing before the Subcommittee on Children, Family, Drugs and Alcoholism of the Senate Committee on Labor and Human Resources, 101st Cong., 2d Sess., 3 (1990).

Id. at 891–892.

There are an increasing number of sources of data concerning violence against women. Pursuant to the Violence Against Women Act of 1994, the first major federal legislation on domestic violence, the newly created Violence Against Women Office within the United States Department of Justice gathers statistics from federal, state and private sources. The American Bar Association's Commission on Domestic Violence also gathers statistics. Many other federal agencies have also conducted studies and gathered information. Here are some other preliminary statistics to consider:

- Among all female murder victims in 1998, 33 percent were slain by husbands or boyfriends. Four percent of male victims were killed by wives or girlfriends. Bureau of Justice Statistics, U.S. Dep't of Justice, NCJ–178247, Special Report: Intimate Partner Violence 2 (May, 2000).
- In 1994, 37% of women injured by violence and treated in an emergency room were injured by an intimate; less than 5% of men injured by violence and treated in an emergency room were injured by an intimate. Bureau of Justice Statistics, U.S. Dep't of Justice, NCJ–156291, Special Report: Violence–Related Injuries Treated in Hospital Emergency Room Departments 5 (1997).

- Roughly 85% of reported victimizations by intimate partners in 1998, or about 876,340, were against women. Bureau of Justice Statistics, U.S. Dep't of Justice, NCJ–178247, Special Report: Intimate Partner Violence 2 (May, 2000).
- Each year, an estimated 3.3 million children are exposed to violence by family members against their mothers or female caretakers. Violence and the Family: Report of the American Psychological Association Presidential Task Force on Violence and the Family, 11 (1996).
- About 4 of 10 female victims of intimate partner violence lived in households with children under age 12. Population estimates suggest that 27% of all U.S. households were home to children under 12. Bureau of Justice Statistics, U.S. Dep't of Justice, NCJ–178247, Special Report: Intimate Partner Violence 6 (May, 2000).

Despite the proliferation of studies and statistics about domestic violence in the last decade, many of the findings remain highly contested, and many are misleading unless carefully interpreted. Statistics drawn from criminal justice sources, for example, catch only those instances of violence that are reported to, and recorded by, the police—and that are reported and recorded as incidents of domestic violence. Reporting practices still vary widely from state to state, and even community to community. And many of those who experience violence at the hands of a partner do not report; sometimes out of fear, sometimes because they do not want to set the criminal justice machinery in motion, and sometimes because they do not interpret what has happened to them as a crime. Many of the social science studies, on the other hand, depend on self reporting, raising issues about the reliability of the numbers generated. For an interesting analysis of the extent to which reporting by victims matches reporting by perpetrators, and some provocative hypotheses about how to interpret discrepancies, see R. Dobash et al., *Separate and Intersecting Realities: A Comparison of Men's and Women's Accounts of Violence Against Women,* 4 VIOLENCE AGAINST WOMEN 382 (1998). These are issues to which we will return in subsequent chapters. An excerpt from the Dobash article appears in Chapter 2, below, at pp. 126–27.

The National Crime Victimization Survey (NCVS), which began in 1973, is conducted by the U.S. Census Bureau using a nationally representative sample of U.S. households. The NCVS collects information on incidents characterized by household members as crimes whether or not they were reported to law enforcement. At least one commentator has suggested that the reason why domestic violence statistics gleaned from this source record such a large percentage of ex-husband or ex-boyfriend perpetrators is that women are more likely to experience the continued stalking, harassment and violence of these men, with whom they have broken off relationships, as criminal. M. Straus, *The Controversy Over Domestic Violence By Women: A Methodological, Theoretical, and Sociology of Science Analysis,* VIOLENCE IN INTIMATE RELATIONSHIPS, 17 (X.B. Arriaga & S. Oskamp, eds., 1999). See pp. 128–31, below.

B. THE SOCIAL RESPONSE TO BATTERING: A HISTORICAL PERSPECTIVE

Introductory Note

Abuse of one intimate partner by another is a practice with a long historical pedigree, and global reach. But every age and culture has its own terminology, its own understandings and explanations, and its own set of private and public responses. In fact, things may not even be as tidy as this suggests. In our own culture, for example, quite divergent terminologies, understandings and responses co-exist, and compete. There is no societal consensus about what amount of violence exists in intimate relationships, who does it to whom, who is to blame for it, and what should be done about it. These issues will surface over and over again in the chapters that follow. To some extent, however, the disagreements are rooted in history, with older understandings surviving even as newer ones develop. In this section, therefore, we look at the history of public understandings of, and responses to, partner abuse in this country, from the mid-nineteenth century to the present, to gain a better understanding of the current situation.

Bradley v. State (MS, 1824)

The readings open with an old case, *Bradley v. State*, from Mississippi in 1824. *Bradley* represents the understanding of the era that woman abuse is legal as long as the husband's "correction" of his wife is "reasonable."

Next come two different historical overviews, by historians Elizabeth Pleck and Linda Gordon. They share an understanding that responses to domestic violence are historically contingent; not just in the sense that the problem will surface as a matter of public concern in one era, only to disappear from view in the next, but also in the sense that how the problem is understood, and what are felt to be appropriate responses, will depend on which constituencies are interested, and what they have to offer, or to gain, by their involvement. Pleck and Gordon ask us to pay attention to the vocabulary employed in discussing domestic violence, and to identify which public or private agencies were deemed to have relevant expertise or authority in addressing it. They pursue the question of how vocabulary, understanding and prescription fit together, and which constituency or constituencies seem to drive the choices in each era they examine. A third historical perspective, focusing on the period immediately prior to the birth of the battered women's movement, is provided by Susan Schecter.

Legal historian Reva Siegel adds a different and discomforting perspective. Her argument is that what passes for "change" or "reform," at least in the legal arena, is often merely reformulation that provides more current and culturally acceptable justifications for old practices oppressive to women. The last reading is an excerpt from the Missouri Supreme Court's opinion in *Townsend v. State*, 708 S.W.2d 646 (1986). In *Townsend* the court finally abolished Missouri's interspousal tort immunity; but documented more than a hundred years of judicial prevarication; providing strong support for Siegel's thesis.

Bradley v. State

1 Miss. 156, Walker 156.
Supreme Court of Mississippi, 1824.

■ Opinion of the Court, by the HON. POWHATTAN ELLIS.

This cause was tried in the circuit court before the honorable judge Turner, at the April term of 1824. The defendant was indicted for a common assault and battery, and upon his arraignment, pleaded not guilty, . . . and that Lydia Bradley was his lawful wife & c. Issue was taken upon all the pleas. After the evidence was submitted, and before the jury retired, the counsel for the defendant moved the court to instruct the jury. If they believed the person named in the bill of indictment, and upon whom the assault and battery was committed, was the wife of the defendant, at the time of the assault and battery,—that then and in such case they could not find the defendant guilty. The court refused to give the instructions prayed for by the defendant, and charged the jury, that a husband could commit an assault and battery on the body of his wife, to which opinion of the court, a bill of exceptions was filed, and the case comes up by writ of error upon petition.

The only question submitted for the consideration of the court, is, whether a husband can commit an assault and battery upon the body of his wife. This, as an abstract proposition, will not admit of doubt. But I am fully persuaded, from the examination I have made, an unlimited licence of this kind cannot be sanctioned, either upon principles of law or humanity. It is true, according to the old law, the husband might give his wife moderate correction, because he is answerable for her misbehaviour; hence it was thought reasonable to intrust him with a power necessary to restrain the indiscretions of one for whose conduct he was to be made responsible. Strange, 478, 875; 1 H. P. C. 130. Sir William Blackstone says, during the reign of Charles the First, this power was much doubted. Notwithstanding, the lower orders of people still claimed and exercised it as an inherent privilege, which could not be abandoned without entrenching upon their rightful authority, known and acknowledged from the earliest periods of the common law down to the present day. I believe it was in a case before Mr. Justice Raymond, when the same doctrine was recognised, with proper limitations and restrictions, well suited to the condition and feelings of those who might think proper to use a whip or rattan, no bigger than my thumb, in order to enforce the salutary restraints of domestic discipline. I think his lordship might have narrowed down the rule in such a manner as to restrain the exercise of the right, within the compass of great moderation, without producing a destruction of the principle itself. If the defendant now before us, could shew from the record in this case, he confined himself within reasonable bounds, when he thought proper to chastise his wife, we would deliberate long before an affirmance of the judgment.

The indictment charges the defendant with having made an assault upon one Lydia Bradley, and then and there did beat, bruise, & c.—and the jury have found the defendant guilty. . . . However abhorrent to the feelings of every member of the bench must be the exercise of this remnant of feudal authority, to inflict pain and suffering, when all the finer feelings of the heart should be warmed into devotion, by our most affectionate regards, yet every principle of public policy and expediency, in reference to the domestic relations, would seem to require the establishment of the rule we have laid down, in order to prevent the deplorable spectacle of the exhibition of similar cases in our courts of justice. Family broils and dissentions cannot be investigated before the tribunals of the country, without casting a shade over the character of those who are unfortunately engaged in the controversy. To screen from public reproach those who may be thus unhappily situated, let the husband be permitted to exercise the right of moderate chastisement, in cases of great emergency, and use salutary restraints in every case of misbehaviour, without being subjected to vexatious prosecutions, resulting in the mutual discredit and shame of all parties concerned. Judgment affirmed.

NOTE

1. *Bradley* was overruled in *Harris v. State,* 71 Miss. 462, 14 South. 266 (1894). As the next reading from Elizabeth Pleck describes, this change of heart occurred during the nation's first feminist assault on women's subordination in the home, and on domestic violence.

Elizabeth Pleck
Domestic Tyranny: The Making of Social Policy Against Family Violence From Colonial Times to the Present, 3–13 (1987)

Many people think that family violence was discovered in the 1960s. It is true that the scale of effort on behalf of victims has been greater since that period than ever before. Yet there were two earlier periods of reform against family violence in American history. From 1640 to 1680, the Puritans of colonial Massachusetts enacted the first laws anywhere in the world against wife beating and "unnatural severity" to children. A second reform epoch lasted from 1874 to about 1890, when societies for the prevention of cruelty to children (SPCC) were founded and smaller efforts on behalf of battered women and victims of incest were initiated. The third era of interest began in 1962, when five physicians published an article about "the battered child syndrome" in the *Journal of the American Medical Association*. In the early 1970s, the women's liberation movement rediscovered wife beating and, somewhat later, marital rape. Since then many other types of family violence, from abuse of the elderly to sibling violence, have come to light.

. . .

Why did family violence become a matter of public policy in these three periods of American history? One explanation is that the incidence of it was rising, thus contributing to public alarm. But not all historical statistics support this. The Puritans of Massachusetts Bay Colony were the first to pass laws against family violence, although the domestic murder rate in their settlement was the lowest ever reported in American history. On the other hand, during the 1870s a violent crime wave made the public fearful. The family homicide rate was rising then, too, so an increase in the incidence of family violence may have been one reason for noticing "child cruelty." But the rediscovery of battered children in the early 1960s was not prompted by an epidemic of family murder. In 1962 the rate of domestic murder, by twentieth-century standards, was quite low. (However, unprecedented levels of it were soon reached, a decade or more *after* the battered child syndrome had already become public knowledge.)

Reform against family violence has mainly occurred as a response to social and political conditions, or social movements, rather than to worsening conditions in the home. The Puritans of Massachusetts Bay drafted a criminal code that reflected their religious principles and humanitarian ideas about the treatment of women and children rather than any assessment of current domestic disarray. The SPCC, as we have noted, were in part a response to public outcries for sterner measures against a rising crime wave. In the late 1950s and early 1960s, new programs against family violence developed out of the general atmosphere of social reform and the belief that government should protect minority rights. The civil rights movement, along with the growth in women's employment and education, eventually led to the rebirth of the women's movement in the 1960s. In turn, the burgeoning of the radical wing of feminism contributed to the rediscovery of wife beating a decade later.

In all the reform periods, small organizations and dedicated individuals—ministers, millionaires, physicians, temperance activists, and women's liberationists—have made family violence a social issue that demanded public attention. Some have tried to pass legislation against domestic violence; others have also founded institutions—from SPCC in the 1870s to shelters for battered women in the 1970s—on behalf of the victims of abuse. . . .

. . . [T]he history of [reform] efforts is not simply one of humanitarianism triumphing over prejudice and indifference. Altruism was rarely unalloyed, and many of the reformers had motives other than helping the victims. The Puritans, for example, wanted to stamp out family violence because they felt it, along with other forms of wicked behavior, threatened to disrupt their divinely sanctioned settlement. In the 1870s reformers sought to control dangerous and violent lower-class men. Even in contemporary times, the desire to deter and prevent crime has been one reason for creating social policies against family violence—a stronger motive in the battered women's movement than in programs on behalf of abused children. Leaders of the battered women's movement in the 1970s also wanted to demonstrate the importance of feminist ideas as well as aid the victims. Along with helping to alleviate human suffering, the pediatricians and radiologists who rediscovered child abuse helped enhance the reputation of their professional specialties and strengthen medical control of social problems.

Mixed motives have been characteristic of reformers in periods of interest in family violence; nonetheless, lack of concern about the issue has been the normal state of affairs. Inattention to the problem of domestic abuse lasted from about 1680 to 1874 and from 1890 to 1960. The first signs of declining attention are easy to detect: ministers, writers, or judges would urge a return to a more private family life or argue that the state should refrain from interfering in the family. Greater suspicion of government intrusion or increased respect for family privacy would diminish support for social policies against family violence.

During the two long periods of inattention, laws from the previous reform epoch remained but were unlikely to be enforced. Victims still appealed to outside agencies for help; the police and the courts continued to receive complaints. But the level of social resources and general notice of the problem declined. Some institutions or policies begun during the reform era remained, but the priorities of courts or other social organizations responsible for enforcing laws against family violence changed. Domestic abuse came to be thought of as a problem of the past; the methods once appropriate in dealing with it were viewed as outmoded. New, more "modern" ways of thinking made family violence seem a less serious matter. At the lowest point of interest, there was a denial it existed at all, except in a few highly unusual instances.

. . . [T]he first American reform against family violence [involved] unique laws enacted in the New England colonies beginning in 1641. After the decline of the Puritan experiment, no significant public reform against family violence emerged until the formation of the first SPCC in 1874. Yet the American family was undergoing a reordering of its power relations. By the 1830s writers for women's magazines and authors of family advice books declared the private sphere of the family a female zone of influence. . . . [G]reater maternal authority in the home led to a decline in whipping as an acceptable form of corporal punishment among the educated middle class. . . . Mothers were assumed to be able to govern their children without resorting to the rod. Later on, ideas about proper mothering and child nurture helped to define the standards of parental care that social welfare institutions sought to enforce. But in the early nineteenth-century the curtain was drawn on family life, closing off private troubles from public view. The feminist movement of the 1850s . . . exposed the abuses that occurred at the domestic fireside and sought women's entrance into the public world. In the 1850s Elizabeth Cady Stanton and Susan B. Anthony, leaders of the woman's rights movement, sponsored but failed to pass legislation to add physical cruelty as grounds for divorce in New York state.

The punitive approach toward family violence reached its apex in the last third of the nineteenth-century. The three reform efforts against domestic violence of that era defined it as a crime requiring stern punishments. The largest and most successful of these resulted in the formation of the SPCC; . . . smaller-scale feminist and temperance programs . . . protect[ed] battered women and victims of incest. . . . [M]ale lawyers, district attorneys, and other law enforcement officials . . . wanted to protect battered women by punishing abusers. They believed that fines and imprisonment had failed to reduce wife beating, and called for corporal punishment of batterers. . . . [S]pecialized tribunals for children or families [were] founded in the early twentieth century. These courts introduced a new, noncriminal approach to family violence and furthered the decline of interest in it already under way. Psychoanalytic thought influenced American clinical practice beginning in the 1920s. These ideas . . . relegated abuse to the world of childish fantasy. When the reality could not be denied, clinicians were trained to inquire into the victim's complicity. In the 1960s, after more than seventy years of neglect, private family troubles again became an important social issue. . . . [T]he largest single reform against family violence [was] . . . the feminist battered women's movement, and [its] significant innovation, shelters for abused women and their children.

The history of reform against family violence is not unlike that of other social movements in the United States. Campaigns against poverty, alcoholism, drug addiction, and mental illness have all gone through periods of sustained attention followed by periods of apathy. Highly educated people have frequently offered solutions for social problems that did not directly affect them. Proposed changes often combined the desire to control the lower classes with humanitarian compassion. The under funding of programs made it difficult for reformers to achieve their objectives. But the campaign against family violence, although similar in some respects to many other efforts, has had one aspect that necessarily limited it and made it more controversial.

The single most consistent barrier to reform against domestic violence has been the Family Ideal—that is, unrelated but nonetheless distinct ideas about family privacy, conjugal and parental rights, and family stability. In this ideal, with origins possibly extending into antiquity, the "family" consists of a two-parent household with minor children. Other constellations, such as a mother and her children, were seen not as a family but as a deviation from it.

One crucial element of the Family Ideal was belief in domestic privacy. The family, it was held, should be separate from the public world. . . . A seventeenth-century Englishman, Sir Edward Coke, coined the phrase "a man's home is his castle." Because the privacy of the family was believed to be valuable yet fragile, government was to refrain from interfering in it. Notions of family privacy did not appeal to the English Puritans who migrated to the New World, however. They believed that neighbors and the church had a duty to regulate family life. Nonetheless, although the Puritans did not have a modern notion of family privacy, they believed divorce or removal of children from abusive parents was justified only in unusual circumstances.

By the 1830s the private sphere came to acquire a deeply emotional texture; it became a refuge from the hard, calculating dealings of the business world. Relations between family members were seen as qualitatively different—more affectionate, lasting, and binding than those between strangers. Nothing was more sacred and socially useful than mother love—it made children righteous and responsible. Even more than before, intervention in the family was viewed as problematic, a violation of family intimacy. Although there have been many periods of American history since the 1830s when family privacy declined in importance, belief in it has persisted to the present day. . . .

A second element of the Family Ideal is a belief in conjugal and parental rights. In ancient times, the head of the household had the power to compel obedience from his wife, children, and servants and maintain domestic harmony. A husband also the "right" to demand sexual intercourse with his wife at his pleasure. Traditionally, the husband and father possessed the "right of correction" (physical discipline) over his wife, servants, apprentices, and children. He was permitted, even expected, to use the rod or the whip in a moderate fashion. A mother, whose power to punish was delegated by her husband, could also use force in disciplining her children. Although abuse has always been separate from correction, the right of discipline has served as a justification for virtually all forms of assault by parents and husbands short of those that cause permanent injury.

. . .

A third element of the Family Ideal is belief in the preservation of the family. Marriage was supposed to be life long, for religious reasons and for the responsibility of raising children. Conservatives in the nineteenth-century argued that women were dependent on the family for their happiness. They were tethered to it because of their children and in order to make the home a place of affection.

Thus—for the sake of their children, or the redemption of their husbands—wives have traditionally been urged to renounce their personal liberty. Many women have been bound to marriage and the family by this sense of duty and obligation. It follows, then, that the desire for personal autonomy, especially among women, would threaten family stability. Since the nineteenth-century, but especially in modern times, feminism and the more generalized quest for self-realization have encouraged women to question the sacrifices they made automatically in the past.

In sum, reform against family violence is an implicit critique of each element of the Family Ideal. It inevitably asserts that family violence is a public matter, not a private issue. Public policy against domestic violence offers state intervention in the family as a major remedy for abuse, challenges the view that marriage and family should be preserved at all costs, and asserts that children and women are individuals whose liberties must be protected.

The fate of proposed legislation against family violence has depended to a large extent on how reformers regarded the Family Ideal. Those who criticized it most directly and vehemently were defeated. Nineteenth-century advocates of women's rights, for example, attacked the Family Ideal as a hypocritical belief that denied the seriousness of abuse. They posed the issue of divorce for battered women as a choice between the Family Ideal and women's rights to freedom and autonomy. By thus making divorce reform a referendum on the politics of Family, they ensured legislative failure. In the 1970s as well, feminist espousal of divorce for battered women and a conservative backlash against the women's movement led to initial Congressional defeats of domestic violence legislation.

The more successful reformers have been politically circumspect. Conservative feminists and female advocates of temperance after the Civil War avoided criticizing power relations in the family and presented their remedies as a means of preserving the home.... In the 1970s modern feminists, after their first defeat, were far more successful than their nineteenth-century counterparts. Their early encounters with the political process taught them to mute their rhetoric; some feminists claimed they were helping to restore the family, and other tried to conceal or sidestep the controversy....

... [T]he use of personal influence, intriguing new definitions of family violence, and unusual reform coalitions have contributed to legislative success. The Puritans buried provisions against wife beating and child abuse in a highly popular criminal code. Although some of its provisions provided for the liberties of women and children, others safeguarded parental authority. Founders of the SPCC succeeded partly because they were wealthy and politically well-connected. While deliberately reassuring the public that they supported "good wholesome flogging of children," they also capitalized on public concern about the plight of helpless, innocent children.... In the 1960s the physicians who discovered "the battered child syndrome" successfully defined child abuse as a public health problem and quickly focused public attention on it, with the aid of television and the press.

... The women's movement of the 1970s succeeded in passing new state laws because it relied on a coalition with representatives who favored other women's rights issues. It employed the same strategy in Congress, but found success, after incurring several defeats, through compromise with conservatives.

Before the founding of the SPCC, no formal institutions other than secular or church courts aided the victims of family violence. Beginning in the 1870s, concerned groups established new organizations. Thereafter reform against family violence became part of the history of social welfare. The SPCC of the late nineteenth-century were private institutions staffed by semiprofessionals and volunteers. The juvenile and family courts founded in the early twentieth-century received public funds and employed probation officers, social workers, and psychiatrists. They regarded domestic violence as a family problem, not a violation of the criminal law. In the 1920s, another layer of institutions was added. Mental health and child guidance clinics and family service associations provided individual or marital therapy. Like the family courts, these services were not designed to meet the needs of victims of family violence, although some of their clients were families where abuse was occurring. In the 1960s pediatricians and social workers helped to establish hospital treatment teams for battered children and new social services for abusive and neglectful parents. Women's groups a decade later founded shelters for battered women and their children.

. . .

Families in which abuse occurs need the protection offered by the police or outside agencies. Yet assistance has also been accompanied by efforts at social control and class domination. Still, some policies and programs have worked better than others. Those that blamed the victim for having caused abuse added psychic damage to the original injury; those that attempted family reconciliation at any price left victims in danger. The most successful efforts were those that made protection of victims their highest priority and offered them concrete resources, emergency housing, relief or welfare, legal aid for divorce, child support agreements, foster care leading to permanent adoption. By these criteria, the policies against family violence established since the 1960s receive the highest marks.

The polices before the 1960s deserve more criticism. Yet historical study provides more than a scoreboard for evaluating past programs, and more than a repository of past cruelties and barbarities. It also reveals inherited domestic ideals, and their impact in shaping and distorting social policy regarding family violence.

* * *

NOTES

1. When you read Susan Schechter's account of the contemporary battered women's movement, you will have the opportunity to decide whether you agree with the parallels and contrasts Pleck draws between this era of feminist-inspired change and the last.

2. Historian Linda Gordon reinforces Pleck's argument about the historical variability of responses to family violence, and focuses her attention on the periods in which the problem disappeared from public attention as well as the periods in which it was visible. The 1988 book from which the next excerpt is drawn, HEROES OF THEIR OWN LIVES: THE POLITICS AND HISTORY OF FAMILY VIOLENCE, is based on a study of "how Boston-area social-work agencies approached family-violence problems, from 1880 to 1960." Id. at 7. Here is her "rough periodization" of that history:

   1. The late nineteenth century, approximately 1875–1910, when family violence agencies were part of the general charity organization and moral reform movement, influenced by feminism.
   2. The Progressive era and its aftermath, approximately 1910–1930, when family violence work was incorporated into professional social work and a reform program relying heavily on state regulation.
   3. The Depression, when intrafamily violence was radically de-emphasized in favor of amelioration of economic hardship.
   4. The 1940s and 1950s, when psychiatric agencies and intensely "pro-family" values dominated the social work approach to family problems.

5. The 1960s and 1970s, when feminist and youth movements began a critique of the family which forced open the doors of closets that hid family problems.

Id. at 19–20.

The following excerpt introduces Gordon's theoretical orientation; provides a picture of the late nineteenth century feminist assault on domestic violence that interestingly and provocatively differentiates between the ideology and agenda of reformers, on the one hand, and their "clients" on the other; and then looks at the period between 1930 and the rebirth of feminism in the 1960s, seeking to explain the "woman-blaming" approach to domestic violence that dominated during that period.

Linda Gordon
Heroes of Their Own Lives: The Politics and History of Family Violence, 2–5, 257–260, 271, 281–284 (1988)

The changing visibility of family violence is, in my opinion, the leading indicator of the necessity of an historical approach to understanding it. Concern with family violence has been a weathervane identifying the prevailing winds of anxiety about family life in general. The periods of silence about family violence are as significant as the periods of concern. Both reveal the longing for peaceful family life, the strength of the cultural image of home life as a harmonious, loving, and supportive environment. One response to this longing has been a tendency to deny, even suppress, the evidence that families are not always like that. Denying the problem serves to punish the victims of family violence doubly by forcing them to hide their problems and to blame themselves. Even the aggressors in family violence suffer from denial, since isolation and the feeling that they are unique make it difficult to ask for the help they want.

. . .

[F]amily violence has been historically and politically constructed. I make this claim in a double sense. First, the very definition of what constitutes unacceptable domestic violence, and appropriate responses to it, developed and then varied according to political moods and the force of certain political movements. Second, violence among family members arises from family conflicts which are not only historically influenced but political in themselves, in the sense of that word as having to do with power relations. Family violence usually arises out of power struggles in which individuals are contesting real resources and benefits. These contests arise not only from personal aspirations but also from changing social norms and conditions.

The historical developments that influenced family violence—through the behavior of family members and the responses of social-control agencies—include, prominently, changes in the situation of women and children. Another major argument ... therefore, is that family violence cannot be understood outside the context of the overall politics of the family. Today's anxiety about family issues—divorce, sexual permissiveness, abortion, teenage pregnancy, single mothers, runaway or allegedly stolen children, gay rights—is not unprecedented. For at least 150 years there have been periods of fear that "the family"—meaning a popular image of what families were supposed to be like, by no means a correct recollection of any actual "traditional family"—was in decline; and these fears have tended to escalate in periods of social stress. Anxieties about family life, furthermore, have usually expressed socially conservative fears about the increasing power and autonomy of women and children, and the corresponding decline in male, sometimes rendered as fatherly, control of family members. For much of the history of the family-violence concern, moreover, these anxieties have been particularly projected onto lower-class families. Thus an historical analysis of family violence must include a view of the changing power relations among classes, sexes, and generations.

Yet family-violence policy is mainly discussed today without an historical dimension, and with its political implications hidden. The result has been a depoliticization of family-violence scholarship, as if this were a social problem above politics, upon which "objective" scientific expertise could be brought to bear. The questions raised by proposed remedies cannot be answered by "neutral" experts, but only by public decisions about the extent and limits of public responsibility.

A few examples may offer an introductory sense of what it means to call family violence a political problem. For over a century there has been a consensus that there must be some limits placed on treatment family "heads" can mete out to their dependents. But setting and enforcing those limits encounters a fundamental tension between civil liberties and social control. . . . Moreover, social control of family violence is made difficult by our dominant social norm that families ought to be economically independent. There is a consensus that children ought to have some minimal guarantees of health and welfare, no matter how poor their parents. Yet there is a consistent tendency to insist that social welfare be a temporary expedient, made uncomfortable, and its recipients stigmatized. These dilemmas must be confronted by political choices; they cannot be ironed out by expert rationalization.

The political nature of family violence is also revealed in the source of the campaign against it. . . . Concern with family violence usually grew when feminism was strong and ebbed when feminism was weak. Women's movements have consistently been concerned with violence not only against women but also against children. But this does not mean that anti-family-violence agencies, once established, represented feminist views about the problem. On the contrary, anti-feminism often dominated not only among those who would deny or ignore the problem but also among those who defined and treated it. In some periods the experts confronted wife-beating and sexual assault, male crimes, while in others they avoided or soft-pedaled these crimes and emphasized child neglect, which they made by definition a female crime. In some periods they identified class and in others gender inequalities as relevant, and in still others ignored connections between family violence and the larger social structure.

Political attitudes have also affected research "findings" about family violence. For example, in the last two decades, experts on the problem have tended to divide into two camps. A psychological interpretation explains the problem in terms of personality disorders and childhood experience. A sociological explanatory model attributes the problem primarily to social stress factors such as poverty, unemployment, drinking and isolation. In fact, these alternatives have been debated for a century, and the weight of opinion has shifted according to the dominant political mood. More conservative times bring psychological explanations to the foreground, while social explanations dominate when progressive attitudes and social reform movements are stronger.... Social diagnoses imply social action and demand resources; psychological diagnoses may point to the need for psychotherapy but also justify criminal penalties and remove family violence from the range of problems called upon to justify welfare spending.... But both sides have often ignored the gender politics of family-violence issues, and the gender implications of policy recommendations, not only when women or girls were the victims of men, but also when women were the abusers.

Political attitudes have determined the very meanings of family violence. Family violence is not a fixed social illness which, like tuberculosis, can have its causal microorganism identified and then killed. Rather, its definitions have changed substantially since it first appeared as a social problem. Most of the discussion of family violence today assumes that what makes it problematic and requires social action is self-evident. Yet what was considered spanking a century ago might be considered abusive today, and the standards for what constitutes child neglect have changed greatly.

. . .

What was new in the nineteenth-century middle-class reform sensibility was the notion that wife-beating was entirely intolerable. Family reformers proposed, like abolitionists toward slavery and prohibitionists toward drink, to do away with physical violence in marriage altogether.... By contrast, many poor battered women had a more complex view of the problem than their benefactors: welcoming all the help they could get in their individual struggles against assault, they also needed economic help in order to provide a decent family life for children. Given a choice, they might have preferred economic aid to prosecution of wife-beaters.

. . .

By far the most striking and consistent women's complaint ... through the 1930s focused on their husbands' non-support rather than abuse.... The 1930s were the divide in this study, after which the majority of women clients complained directly rather than indirectly about wife-beating....

Wife-beating accusations stood out even more because of the virtual disappearance of non-support complaints. This striking inverse correlation between non-support and wife-beating complaints stimulates an economistic hypothesis: economic dependence prevented women's formulation of a sense of entitlement to protection against marital violence, but it also gave them a sense of entitlement to support; by contrast, the growth of a wage labor economy, bringing unemployment, transience, and dispersal of kinfolk, lessened women's sense of entitlement to support from their husbands, but allowed them to insist on their physical integrity. It is a reasonable hypothesis that the Depression, by the leveling impact of its widespread unemployment, actually encouraged women regarding the possibilities of independence.

An oblique kind of supporting evidence for this process of consciousness change is provided by wife-beaters' defenses. Men did not often initiate complaints to agencies, but they frequently responded with counter-complaints when they were questioned. Their grievances were usually defensive, self-pitying, and opportunistic. They remain, however, important evidence of a consensus among men about the services they expected from wives–or about what complaints might be effective with social workers. Men accused of wife-beating usually countered that their wives were poor housekeepers and neglectful mothers, making themselves the aggrieved parties. The men's counter-accusations were, of course, a means of seeking to reimpose a threatened domination. Yet they simultaneously expressed a sense of an injustice, the violation of a traditional and/or contractual agreement, and their dismay at the historical changes that made women less able or willing to meet these expectations.

. . .

While the first-wave women's movement had asserted women's rights to personal freedom even in marriage, it had not provided any organized, institutional means for poor women to secure and defend that right, a power which was necessary for women really to believe in their own entitlement. Until the revival of feminism and the establishment of battered-women's shelters in the 1970s, wife-beating victims had three resources: their own individual strategies of resistance; the help of relatives, friends, and neighbors; and the intervention of child-welfare agencies. None was adequate to the task. The first two were easily outweighed by the superior power of husbands and the sanctity of marriage itself, and the last did not well represent the interests of the women themselves....

. . .

For several reasons a woman-blaming response to wife-beating became more pervasive after the 1930s. Changes in social work procedures created a structural imperative to map the problem onto the client who was present and influenceable. In the early years of child protection, caseworkers tried to reform men. The unembarrassed moralism of the earlier period, combined with the wider range of pre-professional techniques, gave agency workers a choice of tactics to influence male behavior: they hectored, threatened, and cajoled; they used short jail sentences, frequent home visits, including surprise visits, visits to employers and relatives; and they dunned non-supporting men for money. As professionalized casework concentrated on office visits, fewer men were seen. Moreover, women were more introspective and self-critical–more productive in casework. Men infrequently originated cases, were rarely willing to meet with caseworkers, and were more defensive about their own behavior. In search of any ways to influence troubled families, social workers not unnaturally focused on those most open to influence.

More fundamentally, blaming family problems on women was part of a change in family and gender ideology evident by the 1930s.... "Instead of aligning our agency with the mother," the MSPCC [Massachusetts Society for the Prevention of Cruelty to Children] reported in 1959, "we felt it only proper to have the father present his side of the picture.... The mother was seen and, instead of encouraging her laments about her husband, efforts were made to help her to understand his needs and the strains he was under."

After world War II a particularly intense anxiety about wifely sexual and gender maladjustment became evident. Nor was there parallelism: if men suffered similar maladjustment, no one noticed. Freudian thought influenced many caseworkers in their direction, with its story that women's maturity required self-sacrifice and renunciation. But the social workers' concern about maladjusted women was also an observation of the stresses of actual social and economic change, the conflicts women were experiencing between earning and housekeeping, raised aspirations and continued constriction of opportunity, public rights and continued subordination. They had to counsel women to perform in contradictory ways.

This was the era of the "feminine mystique," not of Victoria. Divorce was a common occurrence. The marital counsel offered by the child protectors and marriage experts combined woman-blaming with toleration for marital separation. A standard social work manual on women in marital conflict categorized problems under the headings: excessive dependence, the need to suffer, rejection of femininity, sex response, interfering relatives, cultural differences, and economic factors; four of the seven referred to women's faults, none to men's faults, and three to extramarital pressures. A classic" feminine mystique" document, the book expresses the contradictions of the age, condemning both excessive dependence, a quality acknowledged to be culturally encouraged ... and women's employment. It blamed women for provoking abusive men and then for staying with them....

. . .

The denial of wife-beating was expressed in the language. By the 1940s gender-neutral euphemisms like marital discord and marital disharmony began to dominate. Where the violence was directly named by the women, social workers sought to probe "deeper." ... These analyses became psychologized, or psychiatric.... Masochism was a repeated diagnosis.... These kinds of diagnoses emerged even in cases in which workers were obviously sympathetic to the women....

* * *

NOTE

1. Susan Schechter, in the next excerpt, offers further evidence of the woman-blaming and psychologizing tendencies of the period between the

1930s and the 1970s, an account that both supports Linda Gordon's, and suggests that those tendencies did not disappear with the birth of the contemporary battered women's movement.

Susan Schechter
Women and Male Violence: The Visions and Struggles of the Battered Women's Movement, 20–24 (1982)

From its inception in 1939 through 1969, the index of the *Journal of Marriage and the Family* contained no reference to "violence." In other forums, when battered women were discussed, conjecture passed for evidence. A 1964 article in the *Archives of General Psychiatry*, a journal of the American Medical Association, unselfconsciously reveals professional attitudes toward battered women. In "The Wifebeater's Wife: A Study of Family Interaction," Snell, Rosenwald and Robey speculate about the wives of thirty-seven men charged with assault and battery. The women, who are seen in a psychiatric clinic attached to the court, first turn to the police after 12–20 years of marriages marked by abuse, and the psychiatrists want to know "why now?" They discover that the intervention of an adolescent child into the violence often leads the worried mother to search for help. This "discovery," however, is interpreted as a disturbance of "a marital equilibrium which had been working more or less satisfactorily."

> Snell *et al.* cite a case in which an older son intervenes to stop the violence inflicted by a husband who drinks too much and then makes heavy sexual demands on his wife. The wife enters psychotherapy. The psychiatrists concur with her husband that she is in control of her family's life, including the violence.
>
> The husband stopped drinking shortly after his wife began treatment, and the violent arguments practically stopped. This improvement, *while not lasting* (emphasis added), was impressive to him and his wife, and they both felt, for different reasons, that it was due to her treatment. He took it as confirmation that she had been the "cause" of his behavior: she felt that it was because she was learning how to "handle" his behavior. We felt that the initial improvement was due to the venting of the wife's hostility and manipulative behavior out of the marriage, taking pressure off the husband.
>
> The authors report that the wife later dealt with her "frigidity."
>
> It was about this time that the wife began dealing in treatment with her great hostility toward her husband, alcoholic brothers, and men in general. She talked more about her alcoholic father and his pattern of violence in the home, but it remained difficult for her to translate the hostility she so clearly felt toward other men into terms of her feelings toward her father.

Perhaps the authors believe there is no good reason for her hostility toward an assaultive, alcoholic husband who demands sex when he is drunk. To them it is her feelings toward her father which are most significant.

At no point in the article are the authors outraged by the violence directed against battered women. They suggest that, like the wives of alcoholics, these wives have a masochistic need that their husbands' aggression fulfils.

> The essential ingredient seems to us to be the need both husband and wife feel for periodic reversal of roles; she to be punished for her castrating activity; he to reestablish his masculine identity.

According to the authors, these women were generally "aggressive, efficient, masculine, and sexually frigid." As evidence, they note that all but one of them later regretted taking legal action, and the one woman who said she would do it again was "the most masculine of all."

. . .

By 1974, although writings on battered women had become less overtly hostile, they were still permeated with sexism. In an article that originally appeared in *Medicine, Science and the Law,* M. Faulk, a psychiatrist, describes twenty-three men who are in custody for seriously assaulting their wives. He categorizes their five types of marital relationships: 1. dependent passive husband; 2. dependent and suspicious husband; 3. violent and bullying husband; 4. dominating husband; and 5. stable and affectionate group. Some of these categories seem to suggest that men are now held accountable for their violence. However, a description of the most common type, the dependent passive husband, reads:

> In this type of relationship the husband characteristically gave a good deal of concern and time to trying to please and pacify his wife, who often tended to be querulous and demanding. The offense was an explosion which occurred after a period of trying behavior by the victim. There was often a precipitating act by the victim.

The author adopts, without question, the husbands' perspective on the marital dynamic. According to this view, the husband loses control because of his wife; he has neither the will to resist her "provocation" nor responsibility for his behavior. The author colludes in this justification of violence and leaves the reader sympathizing with the man and blaming the woman for causing the problem.

Only nine of the twenty-three men went to jail, while five, including two who had been charged with murder, were placed on probation. Informing us that most of these men were responding to strain or were severely mentally ill, Faulk notes the courts' sympathy for them and their "tragic situations." The extraordinary fact that two women died and their murderers were placed on probation goes almost unnoticed.

These articles are part of a growing body of sociological, psychological and criminology literature focusing on the woman's participation in her own victimization.... In this literature, the families involved are often described as problematic or exceptional. In a totally unsupported thesis, it is proposed that victims and victimizers display unique characteristics or personality problems that lead them to find or provoke one another.

. . .

Victim provocation theories are not confined to academic journals and psychotherapy. Their assumptions are echoed by medical, law enforcement, and social service institutions.... In 1976, researchers examined the entire medical histories of all women who came to the surgical emergency room at a large metropolitan hospital in December of 1976. This pilot study, analyzing the medical records of 481 women, found that "of the more than 1400 injuries these women had ever brought to this hospital, physicians had identified 75 abusive incidents, although an additional 340 or 24 percent fell into the 'probable' or 'suggestive' categories of this methodology."

The findings suggest that battering is perhaps ten times more frequent than physicians acknowledge. Equally disturbing is the response to battered women when, for example, their x-rays and lab tests are normal, but their complaints persist. [The researchers] found they were "labeled 'neurotic,' 'hysteric,' 'hypochondriac,' or 'a well-known patient with multiple vague complaints.' One non-battered woman in 50 leaves with one of these labels; one battered woman in 4 does, and is given tranquilizers, sleeping medication, or further psychiatric care." This study is important not only because it suggests how widespread battering is, but also because it traces how the real issue—violence—is hidden, and the woman herself labeled the problem. Especially before 1975, this response was common....

* * *

NOTES

1. The widespread influence of the woman-blaming, psychological approach to domestic violence is important for domestic violence lawyers to keep in mind, because of the continuing influence of psychology and psychologists in areas of the law central to domestic violence practice. Family law may be the area where that influence is strongest, but criminal law is another important example. Bear in mind that if the authors of the articles Schecter describes were in their thirties when they wrote, they are probably still in practice. Even if they had been in their fifties, they, or others of their generation who probably shared their general orientation, would have trained many of the professionals in practice today.

2. With the next reading we turn back to the legal history of domestic violence, and the sobering reminder that sometimes superficial change can mask a rearguard effort to uphold the status quo.

Reva B. Siegel
"The Rule of Love": Wife Beating As Prerogative and Privacy, 105 Yale Law Journal 2117, 2118–2120 (1996)

The Anglo-American common law originally provided that a husband, as master of his household, could subject his wife to corporal punishment or "chastisement" so long as he did not inflict permanent injury upon her.

The persistence of domestic violence raises important questions about the nature of the legal reforms that abrogated the chastisement prerogative. By examining how regulation of marital violence evolved after the state denied men the privilege of beating their wives, we can learn much about the ways in which civil rights reform changes a body of status law. In the nineteenth century, and again in the twentieth century, the American feminist movement has attempted to reform the law of marriage to secure for wives equality with their husbands. Its efforts in each century have produced significant changes in the law of marriage. The status of married women has improved, but wives still have not attained equality with their husbands—if we measure equality as the dignity and material "goods" associated with the wealth wives control, or the kinds of work they perform, or the degree of physical security they enjoy. Despite the efforts of the feminist movement, the legal system continues to play an important role in perpetuating these status differences, although, over time, the role law plays in enforcing status relations has become increasingly less visible.

[E]fforts to reform a status regime do bring about change—but not always the kind of change advocates seek. When the legitimacy of a status regime is successfully contested, lawmakers and jurists will both cede and defend status privileges—gradually relinquishing the original rules and justificatory rhetoric of the contested regime and finding new rules and reasons to protect such privileges as they choose to defend. Thus, civil rights reform can breathe new life into a body of status law, by pressuring legal elites to translate it into a more contemporary, and less controversial, social idiom. I call this kind of change in the rules and rhetoric of a status regime "preservation through transformation," and illustrate this modernization dynamic in a case study of domestic assault law as it evolved in rule structure and rationale from a law of marital prerogative to a law of marital privacy.

As the nineteenth-century feminist movement protested a husband's prerogatives, the movement helped bring about the repudiation of chastisement doctrine; but, in so doing, the movement also precipitated changes in the regulation of marital violence that "modernized" this body of status law. A survey of criminal and tort law regulating marital violence during the Reconstruction Era reveals that the American legal system did not simply internalize norms of sex equality espoused by feminist critics of the chastisement prerogative; instead, during the Reconstruction Era, chastisement law was supplanted by a new body of marital violence policies that were premised on a variety of gender-, race-, and class-based assumptions. This new body of common law differed from chastisement doctrine, both in rule structure and rhetoric. Judges no longer insisted that a husband had the legal prerogative to beat his wife; instead, they often asserted that the legal system should not interfere in cases of wife beating, in order to protect the privacy of the marriage relationship and to promote domestic harmony. Judges most often invoked considerations of marital privacy when contemplating the prosecution of middle-and upper-class men for wife beating. Thus, the body of formal and informal immunity rules that sprang up in criminal and tort law during the Reconstruction Era was both gender- and class-salient: It functioned to preserve authority relations between husband and wife, and among men of different social classes as well.

These changes in the rule structure of marital status law were justified in a distinctive rhetoric: one that diverged from the traditional idiom of chastisement doctrine. Instead of reasoning about marriage in the older, hierarchy-based norms of the common law, jurists began to justify the regulation of domestic violence in the language of privacy and love associated with companionate marriage in the industrial era. Jurists reasoning in this discourse of "affective privacy" progressively abandoned tropes of hierarchy and began to employ tropes of interiority to describe the marriage relationship, justifying the new regime of common law immunity rules in languages that invoked the feelings and spaces of domesticity. Once translated from an antiquated to a more contemporary gender idiom, the state's justification for treating wife beating differently from other kinds of assault seemed reasonable in ways the law of chastisement did not.

As the history of domestic violence law illustrates, political opposition to a status regime may bring about changes that improve the welfare of subordinated groups. With the demise of chastisement law, the situation of married women improved—certainly, in dignitary terms, and perhaps materially as well. At the same time, the story of chastisement's demise suggest that there is a price for such dignitary and material gains as civil rights reform may bring. If a reform movement is at all successful in advancing its justice claims, it will bring pressure to bear on lawmakers to rationalize status-enforcing state action in new and less socially controversial terms. This process of adaptation can actually revitalize a body of status law, enhancing its capacity to legitimate social inequalities that remain among status-differentiated groups. Examined from this perspective, the reform of chastisement doctrine can teach us much about the dilemmas confronting movements for social justice in America today.

* * *

NOTE

1. In the case that follows the Supreme Court of Missouri finally and definitively repeals that state's interspousal tort immunity, for intentional torts. A companion case decided at the same time, S.A.V. v. K.G.V., 708 S.W.2d 651 (Mo. 1986), did the same for the tort of negligence. What is even more illuminating than the fact that interspousal immunity survived in Missouri until 1986 is the history of how the state courts had contrived for almost a hundred years to keep it alive, despite the legislature's passage in 1889 of a Married Women's Act that gave a woman broad rights to sue and be sued, with or without joining her husband as a party. In its 1986 opinion the court says explicitly that it is belatedly recognizing the legislature's 1889 intent to abrogate the fiction of marital unity, and leave the way clear for spouses to sue one another in tort, as well as in contract or with respect to property rights.

Townsend v. Townsend

708 S.W.2d 646.
Supreme Court of Missouri, 1986.

■ En Banc. ALBERT L. RENDLEN, J., HIGGINS, C.J., BILLINGS and WELLIVER, JJ., concur. ROBERTSON, J., concurs in result. BLACKMAR, J., concurs in separate opinion filed. DONNELLY, J., dissents in separate opinion filed.

■ Opinion by RENDLEN, J.

The principal issue for resolution is whether the common law doctrine of interspousal immunity shall remain a bar against claims for personal injuries inflicted by one spouse against the other during marriage.

Appellant Diana Townsend filed action against her husband seeking damages for personal injuries suffered when he shot her in the back with a shotgun as he attempted to enter her residence. It was alleged the shooting was "intentional and malicious in that defendant acted with a purpose to seriously injure or kill the plaintiff by means of a deadly weapon," causing injuries which entitled her to compensatory and punitive damages.[1]

Respondent moved for summary judgment, raising as a bar the doctrine of interspousal immunity and on the issues thus framed the trial court entered the summary judgment for respondent. Appeal was taken to the Court of Appeals Eastern District and prior to opinion, transfer was granted that we might examine the issue presented which is both of general interest and special importance....

Long established common law principles authorize courts to compel tort-feasors to compensate those they intentionally or negligently injure.... Finding insufficient support remaining for the proposition that tort-feasors should escape liability for injuries they inflict because the victim happens to be their spouse, we today abolish the doctrine of interspousal immunity as a bar to claims for intentional torts. This step, though a departure from earlier Missouri case law, recognizes that the doctrine from its origin had been a rule in search of a rationale and that the bases advanced in prior years for its support have been substantially diluted or simply disappeared.

Interspousal tort immunity flowed as a by-product from the common law concept of oneness or the "identity of spouses." "By marriage, the husband and wife are one person in law: that is, the very being or legal existence of the woman is suspended during the marriage, or at least is incorporated and consolidated into that of the husband." 1 W. Blackstone Commentaries 442. Suspension of the wife's personal and property rights meant "that she lost the capacity to contract for herself, or to sue or be sued without joining the husband as plaintiff or defendant." W. Prosser, The Law of Torts 859–860 (4th ed. 1971).[2] This concept made suits between

1. Counsel in oral argument informed this Court, although outside the record, that the shooting occurred in the period following the trial and submission of a suit for dissolution but prior to the entry of final judgment in that separate action.

2. It would serve little purpose to inquire further "at this late date as to how far the historical basis of these rules is a mixture

husband and wife virtually impossible; because if either was plaintiff in suits against the other it was deemed that the husband sued himself.

Missouri, as did other states in varying degrees, modified the rule in 1855 by granting a married woman her legal identity. This was first accomplished through exception to joinder rules in our civil procedure statutes. Thirty-four years later the Married Women's Act more substantively defined the scope of a married woman's legal identity. [T]he act deemed a married woman a "femme sole" for the purposes of "transact[ing] business . . . to contract and be contracted with, *to sue and be sued*, and to enforce and have enforced against her property such judgments as may be rendered for and against her, and may *sue and be sued at law* or in equity, *with or without* her husband being joined as a party. . . ."(emphasis added).[1]

. . .

The crucial question never squarely addressed by the Court was whether that language abrogated the common law unity fiction for purposes of interspousal torts. In Rogers v. Rogers, 265 Mo. 200, 177 S.W. 382 (1915), the act was only nominally construed in dismissing a wife's false imprisonment action against her husband. . . . [T]he entrenched unity doctrine played a continuing role in the narrow "statutory construction" resulting in this Court's refusal to depart from the archaic doctrine absent express legislative authority. "Whether the absence of this authority is due to the doctrine of the unity created by the marriage relation, or to any effort on the part of legislatures and courts to promote harmony or at least lessen the cause of controversy between the husband and wife, the nonexistence of the husband's [and thus the wife's] right in this regard uniformly prevails." 177 S.W. at 384.

The narrow statutory construction of *Rogers*, flowing from the unity fiction, persists in Missouri, despite a thirty-year trend away from strict application of interspousal immunity. . . . [L]egislative inaction in the face of *Rogers*, was in the end analysis given as justification for the decision. . . .

However, in Mullally v. Langenberg Bros. Grain Co., 339 Mo. 582, 98 S.W.2d 645 (1936), a wife was allowed to sue her husband's employer for her injuries suffered as a result of acts by the husband in the course of his employment. Quoting Judge Cardozo, the Court found the negligent or willful acts upon the person of a wife did not cease to be unlawful because the law exempted the husband from liability. . . .

In Hamilton v. Fulkerson, 285 S.W.2d 642 (Mo. 1955), the narrow statutory construction of *Rogers* was again circumvented to allow a wife to sue her husband for injuries sustained by his negligent operation of an automobile *before* their marriage. There the Court construed a Married

of the Bible and mediaeval metaphysics, the position of the father of the family in Roman law, the natural law concept of the family as an informal unit of government with the physically strong person at the head, or the property law of feudalism." W. Prosser, The Law of Torts 860 (4th ed. 1971).

1. The language of the 1889 statute has remained unchanged and is currently denominated § 451.290, RSMo 1978.

Women's Act provision making rights of action possessed by a woman at marriage separate property as an abrogation of the unity doctrine for antenuptial torts. "Irrespective of statutes, any common law rule based on the fiction of the identity of husband and wife, long since contrary to the fact, should not be applied to any 'first impression' fact situation arising in this state." 285 S.W.2d at 645.

The unity fiction was also found inapplicable where a wife sought to sue the administrator of her deceased husband's estate for the negligent acts of her husband during their marriage. Ennis v. Truhitte, 306 S.W.2d 549 (Mo. banc 1957) (overruled in Ebel v. Ferguson, 478 S.W.2d 334, 336 (Mo. banc 1972)). With the husband dead, there was no marital relationship to disturb and thus no policy basis for applying the rule.

The trend toward liberalization came to a halt in Brawner v. Brawner, 327 S.W.2d 808 (Mo. banc 1959), cert. denied, 361 U.S. 964, 4 L. Ed. 2d 546, 80 S. Ct. 595 (1960). Distinguishing earlier cases of interspousal tort recoveries as special circumstances, the Court found itself "in [no] better position to interpret the legislative intent of these statutes than the courts that decided the *Rogers* case in 1915. . . ." . . . Against the confusing backdrop of the *Rogers, Hamilton, Ennis* and *Brawner* cases, this Court in its most recent decision on the issue retreated further, refusing to "*create* a cause of action" where, due to the unity fiction, "no cause of action [comes] into existence during the marriage." Ebel v. Ferguson, 478 S.W.2d 334, 336 (Mo. banc 1972).

. . .

Today we reject the archaic doctrine embraced in *Ebel* and *Rogers*. Those decisions as well as related cases employing the doctrine of interspousal immunity in intentional tort actions are disapproved and are no longer to be followed. It "belies reality and fact to say there is no tort when the husband either intentionally or negligently injures his wife" or vice versa. Brawner, 327 S.W.2d at 819–20 (Hollingsworth, J., dissenting).

For the reasons discussed we conclude that the plaintiff-appellant should not be limited in recovery to the damage to her clothing (personal property) caused by the shotgun blast, but may also be compensated for the damage to her person. It does not suffice to refuse this remedy because the cause of action fails to fit a precise formula of common law. . . . Missouri "did not adopt the English common law as a substantive statute but rather as decisional law" of which this Court is custodian, with authority to alter or abrogate a common law doctrine absent contrary statutory direction by our legislature. . . . We find no such contrary direction. . . .

Turning to the specific statute at issue, the expansive language is plain, deeming a married woman a "femme sole" so that, among other things, she "may sue and be sued" at law or in equity. Section 451.290, RSMo 1978. "The broad and all inclusive language of the statute is not limited in any respect, and does not directly or by inference provide that she may be sued by everyone except her husband." 327 S.W.2d at 821 (Hollingsworth, J., dissenting). . . . With due consideration of those cases which have previously spoken to this issue, we believe their statutory analysis was limited less by the legislature than by the initially flawed construction in *Rogers* and the narrow view stemming from so-called "public policy" considerations inherent in the unity fiction.

Turning to the unity fiction itself, our construction today does not *create* a right but rather constitutes an overdue *recognition* that our General Assembly attempted to abrogate this common law doctrine in the Married Women's Act. The derivative sections of the act by their terms authorize married women to transact business, convey property, contract, sue and be sued in the same manner as a single woman.... A husband is relieved of liability for his wife's torts.... Spouses may contract between themselves and each sue the other for contractual breach. They may own property separately, convey property to the other and sue the other to protect those rights.... This panoply of rights has been confirmed in a variety of cases, including suits sounding in tort. *See Brawner,* 327 S.W.2d at 817 (cases cited); Nebbitt v. Nebbitt, 589 S.W.2d 297 (Mo. banc 1979) (interspousal tort immunity inapplicable where tort was conversion of spouse's separate property). The unity concept has also been diluted by the fact that spouses can sue for dissolution of marriage merely on grounds of irreconcilable differences ... and by limits placed on privileged communications between spouses....

As to public policy, it is little comfort to the victim of an intentional shooting at the hands of her husband that her recovery is barred by a common law doctrine having as its basis "her protection and benefit: so great a favorite is the female sex in the laws of England." 1 W. Blackstone, Commentaries 445. By the same token, we no longer indulge the notion that this doctrine is needed to preserve the sanctity of the home. In cases such as this, there can be little sanctity remaining when the relationship becomes the source of wanton violence. Nor can we foresee that personal injury suits between spouses will be any more damaging to marital harmony than the multiplicity of property and contract actions currently permitted. Indeed, to frustrate recovery where warranted arguably contributes to violent domestic disturbances.

Accordingly, because the rationale for the holding of the *Rogers* and similar cases can no longer be justified, we hold that a spouse may maintain an action against the other for an intentional tort. Our holding today shall be applicable to all actions in which a final order, decree or judgment has not been entered as of the date of issuance of this opinion.

The judgment is reversed and the cause remanded to the trial court with direction to reinstate plaintiff's petition.

. . .

■ Concurring Opinion: Blackmar, J.

. . .

Based on the assurances in S.A.V. v. K.G.V., 708 S.W.2d 651(1986) (Mo. banc 1986), that the principal opinion does not foreclose further consideration of "unwanted kiss" and "rolling pin" cases, I join in the principal opinion.

■ Dissenting Opinion: DONNELLY, J.

. . .

... I do not argue that this Court is without power to abrogate interspousal immunity in Missouri. I do argue that the power should be exercised with some evidence of restraint. I merely submit that the question of abolishing interspousal immunity should be decided by the people or by their elected representatives and not by this Court.

I respectfully dissent.

NOTE

1. For further material on the interspousal tort immunity, and on the gradual development of recovery for interspousal torts since the abolition of the immunity, see Chapter 11, below.

C. RECENT HISTORY

This last set of readings focuses on the most recent historical period, which is to say, from the mid 1970s to the present. It begins with an excerpt from Elizabeth M. Schneider's BATTERED WOMEN AND FEMINIST LAWMAKING (2000), briefly describing the birth of the battered women's movement and its political and theoretical underpinnings, but also documenting some of the sources of continued resistance to a feminist account of battering relationships. The next reading is from Susan Schechter's WOMEN AND MALE VIOLENCE: THE VISIONS AND STRUGGLES OF THE BATTERED WOMEN'S MOVEMENT (1982). Schechter's book, and hopefully even this brief excerpt, depicts in rich detail the social and political activism that resulted in the development of both the battered women's movement and the shelter movement (indeed, the terms are often used interchangeably).

It is important to maintain the same kind of critical distance from contemporary accounts that we achieve much more easily with respect to historical ones. In reading these excerpts, ask yourself what the governing vocabulary is, how the problem of partner abuse is understood and described, and how those choices of terminology and explanation might shape law's response. The excerpt from Dorileen Loseke's THE BATTERED WOMAN AND SHELTERS (1992) promotes just this kind of critical appraisal of contemporary approaches to partner violence.

The section ends with another excerpt from Schneider documenting the recent movement to make the legal system more responsive to issues of partner violence. These efforts began, with the shelter movement, in the late sixties and early seventies. The 1990s, and the election of a Democratic President whose own family of origin was marked by domestic violence, have brought some further changes which will be the subject of later chapters.

Elizabeth M. Schneider
Battered Women and Feminist Lawmaking, 20–27 (2000)

It took the rebirth of feminism in the 1960s for the "rediscovery" of battering. With a new spotlight on intimate violence and the ensuing development of a battered women's movement, many reforms designed to protect women from marital violence have been secured.

In both England and the United States, the focus of feminist consciousness raising about domestic violence was on intimate violence in the context of heterosexual relationships. The term first used to describe the problem was "wife-abuse," which revealed that it was viewed primarily through the lens of a marital relationship. Domestic violence was seen as part of the larger problem of patriarchy within the marital relationship.

Feminist activism around issues of domestic violence was highly diffuse and took many different forms. One focus was the development of battered women's "refuges," "shelters," or "safe houses." These houses, women-run and women-centered, were established to give battered women a place to go when they left a violent home, and to provide safety for them and their children. The idea of temporary residences for battered women was devised by a group of women in London who established a neighborhood center, Chiswick, that offered child care and a refuge for homeless women; many of those who needed the help of the center were women who had been abused. Police, social workers, social service agencies, and doctors wouldn't help them, but Chiswick admitted any woman who wanted to stay. Soon, women began to arrive from all over, and the center received wide publicity. Other shelters were set up around the country.

Many Americans visited the English shelters during their first years. In the United States, however, the only available models were safe houses for the wives of alcoholics. One of the first American shelters for battered women was Women's Advocates in St. Paul Minnesota, founded in 1974 by Women's Advocates, a consciousness-raising group that had previously written a divorce rights handbook and organized a phone service to provide legal information to women. When battered women called the group's telephone hotline for assistance, they were housed at first in the staff's own apartments, then in a one-bedroom apartment, then in the dining room of a private house, and then in a three-story, five-bedroom house. Eventually, a twenty-four hour crisis telephone operated from the house, which could accommodate twelve women and their children at a time. There was a paid staff as well as volunteers, but Advocates operated as a collective and divided administrative responsibilities; they opposed hiring professionally credentialed staff. Pleck quotes a founder of the shelter as saying, "A shelter is not a treatment center, residents are not described as clients, battering is not described as a syndrome. Women are not thought of as victims of a crime requiring redress."

Battered women's organizations were important sites of political activism and organizing—in communities, college campuses, and national women's rights organizations. As statewide task forces and national coalitions were formed, the battered women's movement began to shape public debate.

The theoretical approach to battering that developed from the battered women's movement was explicitly political. Its dimensions were not made explicit; they were never listed as part of a social program but functioned as precepts of activist literature and work. First, "battered women" were set forth as a definable group or category, with battering regarded within the larger context of "power and control"; physical abuse was a particular "moment" in a larger continuum of "doing power," which might include emotional abuse, sexual abuse and rape, and other maneuvers to control, isolate, threaten, intimidate, or stalk. Battering, and the problem of power and control, were understood within a systematic framework as part of the larger dilemma of gender subordination, which included gender role socialization; social and economic discrimination in education, workplace, and home; and lack of access to child care. Battered women and battered women's experiences were the focal point of strategies for change; battered women were viewed as "sisters," actors, participants in a larger struggle. Their needs for safety, protection, refuge, and social and economic resources drove the movement.

In her book on the early contributions of the battered women's movement, Susan Schechter describes the political content of the movement. "Feminists," she says, "defined violence against women as a political problem to be solved with political solutions." She cites the movement's commitment to women's self-determination, self-organization, and democratic participation. Within the shelters, Schechter says, "women have learned to think differently about male-female relationships, sex-roles and the meanings behind the violence." She quotes one women's expression of this change: "Do or die I will raise my children with the understanding that no matter how much of what kind of physical abuse man has perpetrated on his subordinates, it is not and cannot be used to make another being do what you want them to do, nor is it humane to use another person as a punching bag to take your frustrations out on." She tells us that activists had learned that "violence restricts women's ability to move freely and confidently into the world and therefore hinders their full development. The fear of violence robs women of possibilities, self-confidence, and self-esteem. In this sense, violence is more than a physical assault; it is an attack on women's dignity and freedom." She concludes that "the movement [has] ... challenged the idea that the family is always a safe haven from a brutal world.... The seemingly private sphere of the family and the public sphere of social and work life will never be quite so separate again.... Male privilege and domination are further eroded as violence is redefined from appropriate chastisement directed toward an inferior, to criminal abuse. This radical redefinition signifies how deeply male domination, even within its hidden bastion, is under attack."

Today, some of this has changed. In the United States the trend within battered women's organizations has been toward a service orientation and away from explicitly feminist organizing. Although many groups that began as feminist organizations are still actively involved in battered women's work, many newer groups that have organized around battering see themselves primarily as service providers. They do social service work and perceive battered women as "clients," not "sisters"—as persons to be helped, not participants in a larger struggle.

. . .

The battered women's movement defined battering within the larger framework of gender subordination. Domestic violence was linked to women's inferior position within the family, discrimination within the workplace, wage inequity, lack of educational opportunities, the absence of social supports for mothering, and the lack of child care. Traditionally, however, intimate violence had been viewed from a psychological perspective. This approach, which predated the feminist analysis of the 1960s, had been concerned with how violence is linked to specific pathology in the individual's personality traits and psychological disorders.

Significantly, even since the advent of the battered women's movement, this psychological perspective has not focused primarily on the pathology of male batterers. Although violent men are commonly labeled "sick" or "emotionally disturbed," in the public mind this perspective of pathology focuses largely on the woman who is battered. Those who are battered and who remain in battering relationships are regarded as more pathological, more deeply troubled, than the men who batter them....

. . .

A second perspective, a sociological approach, rests on the premise that social structures affect people and their behaviors. This approach, which exploded as a focus of research on battering in the early 1980s, focuses on the problem of family violence—the way the institution of the family is set up to allow and even encourage violence among family members. Proponents of this view look at violence as a result of family dysfunction and examine how all participants in the family may be involved in perpetuating the violence.

Research on family violence further deflected attention from the crucial link to gender, and shifted focus onto research tools that deeply challenged feminist approaches. In a review of the family violence literature in 1983, Wini Breines and Linda Gordon perceived the dangers in this approach: "First, all violence must be seen in the context of wider power relations; violence is not necessarily deviant or fundamentally different from other means of exerting power over another person. Thus, violence cannot be accurately viewed as a set of isolated events but must be placed in an entire social context. Second, the social contexts of family violence have gender and generational inequalities at heart. There are patterns to violence between intimates which only an analysis of gender and its centrality to the family can illuminate."

. . .

... [B]oth psychological and sociological perspectives have done much to shape the context of research and the nature of public views of violence. Evan Stark has observed: "For fifty years or more, the realities have been concealed behind images that alternatively 'pathologize' family violence or else 'normalize' it, making it seem the inevitable byproduct of some combination of predisposition—because the abuser was mistreated as a child, for example—and environmental 'stress.' The use of violence is abstracted from its political context in gender and generational struggles, and its varied meanings in different cultures and classes are simply glossed over. Static conceptions posit aggression as inherent in (male) human nature or as inevitable given poverty, 'violence prone' cultures or personalities, and intergenerational transmission." Advocates of psychological and sociological perspectives recognize the significance of the "alternate" perspective and acknowledge that both psychological and social factors are significant variables. Yet both these approaches minimize the role and the impact of gender and are grounded in gender-neutral explanations.

. . .

This politicization of social "knowledge" by "experts" on battering has a long history. In 1983 Evan Stark and Anne Flitcraft identified "the sudden social science concern with family violence in the 1980's" as part of the "same self-righteous puritanism that reappears in the very upper-class campaign to abolish 'sin' (prostitution, alcoholism, 'dirty homes' and wife beating) among the working classes." They argued that "just behind the cycle of concern about abuse lies a new ideological affinity between those who document the evils at the heart of family life, those who 'treat' these evils, and those who, like the ideologues supporting the current Family Protection Act, would unhesitatingly restore traditional patriarchal authority whatever the costs in individual freedom, an alliance between those who locate the principles of violence in 'private' life and those who would leave violence against women to private solutions." Contested sources of knowledge about battering highlight the deeply political nature of the descriptive stakes.

* * *

Susan Schechter
Women and Male Violence: The Visions and Struggles of the Battered Women's Movement, 29–68, 81–87, 93–98, 103 (1982)

Raised Consciousness

In the early 1970s, it sometimes seemed as if the issue of battered women came out of nowhere. Suddenly feminist lawyers, therapists, and women's crisis and anti-rape workers were reporting hundreds of calls and visits from abused women desperately in need of housing and legal assistance. No mere accident, this groundswell was the result of the changing political consciousness and organizing activity of women. The emerging feminist movement painstakingly detailed the conditions of daily life that would allow women to call themselves battered. A fundamental assertion of the movement, women's right to control their bodies and lives, and one of its practical applications, women's hotlines and crisis centers, provided a context for battered women to speak out and ask for help. . . . Later, larger informal feminist networks and state and national meetings, like the 1976 International Women's Year Conference in Houston, provided the settings in which women found one another and created a national battered women's movement.

. . .

The influence of the women's liberation movement on the battered women's movement is illustrated concretely in hundreds of shelters and women's crisis centers in the United States. In St. Paul, Minnesota, Women's Advocates, one of the oldest shelters solely for battered women, began as a consciousness raising group in 1971. Later wanting to move beyond their own small group experience, these women dreamed of opening a house for themselves and for any woman who needed a place to go. This house was to be a liberating, utopian community. Their early vision of a home never encompassed a battered women's shelter, although this is what it would become.

The first Boston shelter, Transition House, was also influenced by women's liberation ideas. Although the two women who started the shelter were former battered women, they were soon joined by two members of Cell 16, one of Boston's earliest radical feminist groups. Women using the house were encouraged to explore their personal lives, learning the political parameters of "private" problems. For the activists at Transition House, physical abuse was not an isolated fact of daily existence. Battering was an integral part of women's oppression; women's liberation its solution.

The Influence of the Anti-Rape Movement

. . .

Although many activists in the battered women's movement never did rape crisis work, the battered women's movement maintains a striking and obvious resemblance to the anti-rape movement and owes it several debts. The anti-rape movement articulated that violence is a particular form of domination based on social relationships of unequal power. Through the efforts of the anti-rape movement it became clear that violence is one mechanism for female social control. Today this sounds obvious; ten years ago it was a revelation. The anti-rape movement changed women's consciousness and redefined the parameters of what women would individually and collectively tolerate.

The feminist anti-rape movement has not only laid the foundation to change public consciousness, but also has built organizations and networks of politically sophisticated and active women. The anti-rape movement has unmasked the domination that violence maintains, has torn away a veil of shame, and shown that women can aid one another, transforming individual silence and pain into a social movement. Such work handed ideological tools, collective work structures and political resources to the battered women's movement. Without this precedent, the new movement might have faced far greater resistance and hostility from bureaucracies, legislatures, and the general public. By 1975, it was clear that since rape and battering had the same effects upon their victims and depended upon similar sexist mythology, battering had to be declared socially, not privately, caused.

Ideological and Personal Diversity Within the Movement

Women who started battered women's programs were motivated by diverse ideological and personal experiences.

. . .

Those who entered the battered women's movement from a woman's rights perspective often came with a social work or legal background. They assumed that equality with men would be gained through reforming the existing social system. While some women's rights activists defined their goals more broadly, most were primarily committed to ending discrimination. Questions of organizational structure and process were secondary: most often hierarchy was the preferred model in order to perform tasks quickly.

Unlike women's rights activists, radical feminists articulated a theory in which specific non-hierarchical organizational forms and self-help methods were a logical outcome of an analysis of violence against women. In many programs, locally and nationally, radical feminists organized first, setting the style and practice that continues to dominate in much of the battered women's movement. Radical feminists believe that historically and structurally the division of labor and power between men and women became the basis for other forms of exploitation, including class, ethnic, racial and religious ones. . . .

. . .

Socialist feminists who worked within the battered women's movement joined an analysis of male domination to one of class and race oppression. They grounded women's oppression within material reality: the unequal division of labor between the sexes inside and outside the home, female responsibility for childbearing, and women's work maintaining home and family. For socialist feminists, although male domination predated capitalism, class and race oppression could not be reduced to or explained by patriarchy. Each form of oppression had its unique historical foundations. . . . Socialist feminists urged an explanation of the changing nature of the family and the state under capitalism, refusing to label all women as one class and asserting that differences among women by class and race were as important as similarities.

. . .

In many locations, lesbian feminists were among those initiating battered women's services. Committing themselves to help women and children live free from terror and pain was their goal. As one woman said: "Lesbians were able to look at violence and its political ramifications and not freak out about its meaning for their relationships with men. If you live with men and work with battered women, you have to find a way to deal with anger and rage."

. . .

Third world feminists brought their own diverse experiences and political ideologies to the battered women's movement. . . . Their unique histories of cultural and racial oppression shaped their politics. The Combahee River Collective—a black feminist group whose members have worked on diverse projects and issues including sterilization abuse, abortion rights, rape, health care, and battered women—defines its goal as developing "a politics that was antiracist, unlike those of white women, and antisexist, unlike those of black and white men."

. . .

Other black feminists had different analyses and different politics. However, almost all third world women with the battered women's movement asserted that their experiences as women were different from those of white women. Some also explained third world male violence in a different way:

> . . . This country has systematically discriminated against, humiliated, and degraded certain of its people. These battered people, the poor and powerless, the ethnic minorities, the disenfranchised, are the real abused children of the white patriarchy. . . . These powerless men inflict violence on women and children, the only people who are even more powerless than themselves.

Feminist ideology and diverse experiences of women in the movement were not all that determined practice. Circumstances influenced the form the battered women's movement took in different locales, and how it expressed its politics. Some rural, more conservative communities translate feminism into "women who just want to break up families." Rural women had to tread even more carefully than their urban counterparts who were forced to exercise substantial caution but who, at least, had more potential allies. It is a stark understatement to suggest that circumstances forced feminists to work in less than ideal environments and to downplay, if not modify, their politics.

. . .

The First Positive Responses

In the 1970s, feminists, community activists, and former battered women increasingly responded in a new way, providing emotional support, refuge, and a new definition of "the problem."

Feminist women's centers, like Women's Center South in Pittsburgh, sometimes offered a safe place for women in crisis. This women's center, with a kitchen, a place to sleep, a reading room, and an information center, had someone in the house 24 hours a day. In an 11 month period in 1975, "the center logged 191 women sheltered, 86 children, and 839 visitors arriving to talk, create, nap, plan, work, or just be themselves. . . ."

Former battered women or women who had seen violence in their families of origin were among the first to reach out. In Boston in 1976, "Chris Womendez and Cherie Jiminez opened up their five room apartment as a refuge for battered women.... Cherie Jiminez' earlier stay at Interval House, a Toronto program primarily for battered women, influenced her decision to found the Boston shelter. 'I had never seen a place like that before ... I had never seen women helping each other out like that.' " ...

Marta Segovia Ashley, whose mother was murdered by her stepfather, describes the earliest discussions among the six women, both feminists and violence victims, who founded San Francisco's La Casa de Las Madres.

> In sharing the violence in our lives, we began to see that we were equally oppressed. There would be no separation between staff and resident.... We did not want the social worker/white missionary establishment to run La Casa. We wrote into the original proposal that the residents would, hopefully by the end of the first year, become staff at La Casa and that we would work ourselves out of jobs.

. . .

Shelter Life

From the beginning, shelters for battered women have assumed a variety of forms. Perhaps 20% share space in YWCA residences or use institutional settings, like motels or abandoned orphanages. Most often, shelters are old houses with many bedrooms where battered women and their children can stay for a few days or a few months. Although the buildings are often run-down, shelter staff become expert at repairing almost anything, valiantly attempting to keep them homelike. Capacity is usually five to ten families although size varies. Many women bring two or more children. Together women residents divide house chores, cook, and clean. Women may rotate tasks; for example, each woman chooses one or two meals that she will prepare for the entire group during the week. In many settings, each woman and her children share one bedroom; in others, because of severe space shortages, families double up in one room. Each shelter has rules about safety, drugs, curfew, care of children, and attendance at house meetings to discuss problems and chores. Often, length of stay agreements are made with residents.

. . .

Many women describe the shelter's assumed but most significant advantages as time and safety to think, free from coercion and violent interruption.

Support from staff and other residents sustains women during moments of doubt. Although there is rapid turnover in residents, relationships among women form quickly, based on similar experiences, common living spaces, and the necessity of accomplishing major tasks. Support often comes through sharing food or coffee at the kitchen table. At a discussion with residents at Women's Survival Space in Brooklyn, one woman remarked, "Being here—you feel safe and that's *very* important. But you also don't feel alone. Group sessions help you relieve things that build up inside of you. It feels good inside.''

. . .

Receiving more than courage from one another, women transform their understanding of why they were beaten. They hear repeatedly that the beatings were not their fault, and some take the first step toward freedom by rejecting responsibility for male violence. ''Liberation'' describes the experience of watching one shelter resident after another nod her head in recognition of another woman's plight, confusion, and eventual rage.

. . .

Because American society is so racially segregated, a shelter may be one of the few places women live interracially. Battering, living in a shelter, and starting over with nothing are the common experiences among sheltered women; racial and ethnic lines are crossed through mutual aid. Because no one escapes the racism in this society, differences and tension are common.

. . .

Shelter Philosophy and Structure

. . .

Women's Advocates' philosophy had been hammered out early in practical debates about whether a hotline worker should tell a caller what to do. Battered women's rights to self-determination, including the decision to leave or stay with their husbands, were to be respected; if sexism robbed women of control over their lives, Women's Advocates would work on methods for returning it, even if no one knew quite how. Outside agencies also forced a clarification of values. When the first funding sources suggested that Women's Advocates change its name to something ''less inflammatory,'' the collective refused to compromise on its basic philosophy.

> We have never called women needing help ''clients'' or ''cases,'' and this has not prevented effective communication with the professional community. When we were told that only trained and certified professionals could run the house, we insisted that professional credentials not be included as job requirements. We asserted our belief that women in need of shelter were not sick or in need of treatment, emphasizing instead their need for safety, support, and help with practical problems.

. . .

One of the central issues for many shelters is whether the shelter belongs to staff or residents. Often this question surfaces in discussions of rules. When Women's Advocates' opened in 1974, they had no house rules. Immediately, however, they found they had to set limits. The first rules centered around mandatory house meetings, signing up for jobs so that the house could function, and a ''no drugs'' policy. One founder commented, "on the first day we declared that there were no pets, on the second, no drugs, and on the third, no furniture storage." Rules were made on the basis of experience, often negative ones, and sometimes the collective had to remind itself or be reminded by the residents that it had created too many restrictions.

. . .

From the beginning, Transition House has emphasized women's opportunities to share with and support one another. The growth of all women who pass through the house, battered women and staff, is seen as important. As one staffer explained, "we are part of a liberating process of women helping each other. We are all sharing pain and through that similarity we grow. Often we forget to share our lives and become objects of services. When we share, there is a continual transformation of our own lives." Transition House staffers understood that the process of giving to others makes women feel stronger. Resident strengthening resident, a primary goal of the shelter, was considered more potent than staff helping resident.

. . .

> We were not providing social services. As staffers, we were not different from the women except that they were in crisis. We only gave people safety and information. We emphasized women have to make their own decisions.... Our advocacy model was a woman who went to welfare yesterday taking another woman today.... If you caretake, you don't give a woman what she needs. Shelters where women went back to their husbands were often shelters where they had been taken care of as opposed to being helped to develop survival skills. This didn't prepare the woman for living on her own in an often hostile world.

. . .

Through redefining a social "problem" into a social movement, women from Transition House and Women's Advocates helped other shelters begin and served as catalysts for state, regional, and national coalitions. Using the self-help method, egalitarian philosophy, and collective organizational structures developed within the women's liberation movement, these two groups discovered and then articulated a grassroots, non-professional view of battered women's needs. Through their struggle to define a feminist "shelter," they gave birth to one more alternative, a democratic women's institution. Although their efforts and ideology were not always replicated in other cities, Transition House and Women's Advocates became respected and often copied pioneers.

. . .

Shelter Services Expand

Battered women's shelters, safe home projects, counseling, and hotline services appeared in hundreds of locations after 1976. Rarely, however, did services exist for all who needed them. A 1977 survey of 163 programs revealed that "46,838 battered women were served by these programs ...

approximately four times as many of the clients were served on a nonresidential basis as were housed. During that same period, 14,473 children were sheltered in program facilities. Unfortunately, the average capacity of a shelter program was 15 persons, including women and children, and program directors report that they often have to turn women away because of lack of space." According to a 1979 survey, in the state of Minnesota, 70% of the women requesting shelter had to be turned away because of lack of space.

The less than ideal circumstances under which service was provided are as noteworthy as the statistics. In one study, "of the 138 programs which responded to this question, 93 . . . indicated that at least half of their workforce was comprised of volunteers. Without CETA funding and extensive volunteerism, many programs either would not exist or would be unable to offer the surprisingly wide range of services currently available." Volunteers outnumbered paid staff by almost three to one in these programs. Services included twenty-four hour crisis hotlines, counseling, medical or job assistance, legal and welfare advocacy, and child care, often for sheltered and non-sheltered women alike.

. . .

As new programs were born, old programs expanded their services by acquiring more substantial government or foundation support. The Domestic Violence Service Center (DVSC) in Wilkes–Barre, Pennsylvania, finally gained a breathing space after two years of subsisting with no secure funding base. In 1979, "the DVSC, with the support of the United Services Agency and United Way of Wyoming Valley, was able to obtain its first Title XX grant." One activist recalls, "this marked a milestone in our agency's history: our grass roots struggle had found community support and acceptance. Battered women in Luzerne County would be assured a safe refuge. . . ." After operating on so little, the agency's $50,000 a year budget seemed a windfall. . . .

Almost every project contended with renewable grants, guaranteed for no more than one or two years. At any time, limited foundation or government funds might be allocated to other pressing problems. Many shelters watched their funding come and go.

. . .

Shelters, old and new, flourished nevertheless, and by 1982 estimates place the number of shelters and safe homes projects somewhere between 300 and 700. There is enormous variation from state to state in the number of shelters; in 1980, for example, Arkansas had four shelters and California sixty-eight. While Maine had five shelters and three safe homes projects, Kansas had three of each and New Hampshire had four refuges and five safe homes networks. Minnesota reported seventeen shelters, all of which provided hotline services, as well as four separate crisis hotlines for battered women. Across the country, the labor of thousands of women had made possible the development and expansion of essential services.

The Search for Legitimacy and Funding

As the movement grew, shelters with diverse philosophies and goals faced some common tasks and problems. Local groups had to convince sometimes skeptical communities and funding agencies that their shelter legitimately represented battered women. Maneuvers to gain credibility reveal a flexible, strategically astute movement aware of the odds it faced.

. . .

Throughout the country, women's groups tell animated stories about efforts to legitimate their activities. Some groups moved into buildings, declared their need, and squeaked by for months on courage, hard work, and the intense energy they generated. Their efforts moved people to respond. Others, the majority, spent years lobbying, testifying, and writing grants. Almost all relied heavily on educational forums, public hearings, radio, and television to reconceptualize the issue and explain its parameters, stressing that woman abuse was a community responsibility rather than an interpersonal "problem." Often, months or years were spent gathering allies among legislators, agency directors, and foundation staff and convincing them that a problem and a constituency existed. Elected officials and the many state and local Commissions on the Status of Women held hearings which legitimated the issue. Battered women came forward along with activists and professionals to testify repeatedly to the desperate need that mandated shelter funding. In many cities, women's clubs, the Junior League, or the National Council of Jewish Women responded as needed allies during hearings and supplied small grants or volunteers.

For change to occur, strategies had to be matched by persistence, skill, unpredictable luck, and even tragedy. In one state, feminists spend three years constantly lobbying their Public Welfare Department for funding with no results; the next year, a supportive woman became director and substantial funding was granted immediately to programs statewide. In another, as legislators debated the first domestic violence bill and women lobbied around the clock, two battered women were murdered by their husbands. Legislation was enacted rapidly. As one activist recalls, "Our local Junior League had a member whose husband killed her right after she had complained about him at a Junior League meeting. They became immediate supporters of the shelter, helping us enormously."

Because women's groups established services long before other agencies offered any help to battered women, many funding agencies and community institutions were moved, sometimes begrudgingly, to trust them and use their programs. In huge numbers, battered women also turned to these new organizations which, unlike other agencies, provided the concrete assistance needed. The fact that most shelters stayed full from the first day they opened spoke most eloquently in the search for legitimacy and funding that continues to this day.

. . .

In addition to providing room and board for victims of abuse, shelters worked to protect battered women's rights, a more difficult and elusive task than it would seem. Advocates were forced to know more than the local welfare or police bureaucrats who often ran circles around uninformed clients, denying them their legal rights through technicalities. Any shelter resident might find herself in Family, Criminal, or Divorce court; she might need welfare benefits or have to sign up on a waiting list for a low-cost apartment from the Housing Authority. At any moment, if criminal charges were pressed or injuries noted, the police, the Bureau of Child Welfare, and a hospital might also become involved. Staff and volunteers were extensively trained in advocacy and spend a substantial amount of time accompanying battered women through court or welfare centers, writing letters for them or making phone calls. As one advocate said, "You have to do a million things to get one woman help."

Once activists mastered the details of various bureaucracies, they worked to convey the information to battered women, shelter advocates, and the constant stream of professionals who called for advice. Literally, hundreds of legal rights, welfare rights, and counseling manuals were written, revised constantly, and distributed through battered women's shelters.

. . .

Not only did women in the movement help individuals through the bureaucratic maze, they also spent much time attempting to change regulations and establish new procedures. Shelter staff have negotiated with and lectured to thousands of personnel in hospitals, police departments, and social service agencies.

. . .

Money, the Mixed Blessing

. . .

Money . . . was not the unmixed blessing it originally seemed. A larger funding base sometimes undermined important movement principles. Shelters that chose to expand often saw themselves transformed in unpredictable, unwanted ways.

. . .

Changes sometimes occurred because there was too much to be done and hierarchical structures appeared to be the solution to overwork. At other times, however, funding sources explicitly influenced organizational and structural changes. . . .

In approaching funders and community groups, activists encountered charitable and professional values that emphasized helping the "needy" and often unwittingly assigned to women the permanent status of helpless "victim." The pervasive influence of psychological explanations for social problems was seen as funding agency after funding agency defined battered women as a mental health issue.

As funding increased, even the most politically sophisticated programs noted subtle changes in their treatment of women residents. For example, when individual shelters fought for and won welfare or Title XX reimbursements, they also had to fill out forms and account for "units of client services." Many of these "units" are credited according to the individual counseling and advocacy sessions provided. As a result, worker after worker has commented that she slowly and unconsciously started to call battered women "clients." Greater attention was paid to the individual woman's counseling needs and less to group sharing, peer support, and teaching battered women to advocate for one another.

In many cases, the funding agencies downplayed or discouraged social change. Federal Title XX funds can be used for services only, not for community education. Helping victims was tolerable, while changing the social conditions that created these victims was far less desirable, measurable, or fundable.

In the constant search for legitimacy and credibility, hiring professionals seemed like one way to placate the funding sources. And in some states funding agencies required that a social worker with a master's degree supervise all paid staff. Other states are beginning to demand similar qualifications, although in many areas such requirements have not been placed on battered women's programs.

It was easy for external pressures to become internal ones. Many shelters decided that social workers and lawyers not only had needed group and organizational skills, but also might make funding negotiations less arduous. Many women felt bullied by bureaucracies or their own boards of directors or worried about their competence in working with battered women or their legitimacy within the social service "community." Uncertain about how to proceed, they gave in, changed their structures, or hired more professionals, sometimes later regretting these choices.

Usually, funding agencies did not consciously intend to undermine the work of the battered women's movement. They simply expected battered women's programs to respond like every other social service organization. The movement held different views, and clashes and compromises from both sides would occupy significant movement energy for the next several years.

. . .

In some states, individual shelters still face these kinds of struggles alone; in others, like Pennsylvania and Illinois, statewide women's coalitions now receive grants that they distribute to their member programs. In still others, like Massachusetts, grants are made to individual shelters, but the statewide coalitions serve as strategy making bodies and as negotiating buffers. In all these cases, the fear and reality of cutbacks have forced grassroots groups to mobilize every year. At any time, one conservative legislator or bureaucrat can introduce damaging fiscal or regulatory amendments that might undermine shelter autonomy. In many states, hundreds of hours are spend strategizing as well as establishing and maintaining relationships with state agencies.

. . .

Decisions About Structure

. . .

Despite the pressures that come with growth, some shelters have retained egalitarian work structures even after major expansion; women's political commitments have helped them through hard times. Transition House and Women's Advocates are still collectives; within them, old-timers worry about specialization or staff's assumption of too much control, but equality is still the goal. Here too, funding and daily crisis occupy too much time and sometimes community outreach and education efforts suffer. Yet these shelters continue to serve as models, and in the 1980s, throughout the country, women are again talking about the feminist roots of the movement and how their vision was sometimes shoved aside in the push to provide essential services, build organizations, and endure.

* * *

NOTES

1. Schechter's account ends in the 1980s. Since then, shelter services for battered women and their children have continued to expand and to gain in legitimacy. A big boost was provided by the Violence Against Women Act, which authorized the expenditure of $325,000,000 in federal dollars over five years to the states for allocation to shelters. While one priority continues to be increasing the availability of beds, another is to expand the range of services to women and children who for a variety of reasons cannot, or are not willing, or would not be served by, moving into a shelter. These services include groups for both women and children, individual counseling for women, and a range of advocacy services to secure needed legal relief or public benefits. For example, the STOP (Services Training Officers Prosecutors) Violence Against Women Formula Grants Program provides law enforcement grants to the States, who in turn must use 25% percent of their grants to support nonprofit, nongovernmental victims services. The states then release subgrants to individual organizations. Through February 1998, states reported awards of 2,473 STOP subgrant awards for the 1995–1997 period, totaling $95,875,206. Of these subgrants, 1,333, for a total of $39,174,372, went to organizations providing "victims services," including crisis centers, stalking hotlines and shelters for battered women. Martha R. Burt, Lisa C. Newmark, Lisa K. Jacobs, Adele V. Harrell, *1998 Report: Evaluation of the STOP Formula Grants Under the Violence Against Women Act of 1994*, The Urban Institute 1922 (July, 1998).

2. The rhetoric of the battered women's movement has emphasized the "discovery" of abuse; and the new possibilities created by the women's movement for battered women to tell their stories, both to one another and to the public. This rhetoric is a rhetoric of "truth," and of "reality," and indeed, the wrenching stories you will read throughout the book bear the undeniable stamp of authenticity. Nonetheless, if we subscribe to the notion that reality is always, in part, constructed; that stories are always

shaped by the historical and social context in which they occur, and the purposes they are designed to serve, then we must pay attention to the ways in which even these new "tellings" may be incomplete, or may be "interpretations" of a more complex reality. One author who has analyzed the new rhetoric of abuse in this way is Dorileen Loseke, in her book The Battered Woman and Shelters, written in 1992.

Loseke argues that the need to compel public sympathy for abused women, and to secure both necessary funding and meaningful legal reforms, constrained the ways in which feminist activists presented battered women and their situations. She argues specifically that this constrained image then limited access to shelter for women who did not fit the "public" image of a battered women, and required that women who did access shelter conform their behavior to fit the public image. But her argument has broader implications, as she points out in the excerpt below. The extent to which opponents of the feminist agenda have exploited the incompleteness of this image, and the ways in which it has limited the ability of lawyers to argue on behalf of battered clients whose reality is messier than the image allows, are themes to which we will return in a variety of contexts. The strength of Loseke's account is that it grounds these problems in the historical necessity of drawing public attention the problem of domestic violence, and securing support for the needs of its "victims."

Dorileen Loseke
The Battered Woman and Shelters, 20–21, 27–28, 149–151, 154 (1992)

... In the composite image, wife abuse is a label for severe, frequent, and continuing violence that escalates over time and is unstoppable. Such violence is that in which unrepentant men intentionally harm women and where women are not the authors of their own experience which they find terrifying.

Such a collective representation was successful in overcoming popular public interpretations that violence by husbands against wives was not serious, was victim-precipitated and limited to poor and/or minority women. In defining such traditional interpretations as "myths of wife abuse," what had been previously interpreted as personal troubles were transformed into a public problem. At the same time, the construction raises its own question: Why is such abuse repeated.

... The collective representation of wife abuse leads to the common sense conclusion that a woman *should* leave such a relationship, and this prescription is part of the collective representation: A woman experiencing wife abuse must leave her relationship....

... [I]f she stays because she does not mind the abuse, indeed, if she stays because she *chooses* to stay for any reason, then claims about the content of this public problem are challenged. In the process of accounting for a woman's behavior of staying in a relationship containing wife abuse, claims construct a new type of person—a "battered woman"—a woman whose unexpectable behavior of staying in a relationship containing wife abuse supports rather than challenges claims about the content of this public problem.

. . .

. . . The fully described ideal type would be a woman of any age, race, social class, or marital status who was in the social roles of wife and mother. Such a woman would want to leave—or would want to leave if she was not so confused as the result of her victimization—but she would be trapped within her continuing and brutal victimization by economic and emotional dependence, by friends and social service providers who refused to help, and by her traditional beliefs. Such a woman would be isolated from others, overwhelmingly fearful and emotionally confused; she would have little faith in herself and she would suffer from a range of physical and emotional illnesses that were understandable reactions to her terrible plight. . . .

Such a collective representation deflects challenges to the wife abuse problem posed by the behavior of women who "stay." Simultaneously, this representation furnishes a warrant for public intervention. Indeed, the representation furnishes a *mandate* for intervention since, in the final analysis, a battered woman type of person *requires* help if she is to be able to remove herself from her plight. . . .

. . .

. . . To be viable, social problems claims must convince enough social members that a condition at hand is intolerable and constructing the image of extreme conditions has the best chance of attaining this viability. Thus, just as *stranger rape* yields more public concern than does *date rape*, and just as *homelessness* is more compelling than *poverty*, which is more compelling than the problems of the *near poor*, as socially constructed, the public problem of *wife abuse* yields more concern than *normal violence* and this is more compelling than *marital troubles*.

. . .

. . . [I]t is easy to see why this *particular* construction was publicly viable. Merely consider the possibility that many Americans would offer sympathy and services to a type of woman characterized as experiencing "normal violence," to a woman who was aggressive, domineering, or nagging. Probably not. Indeed, until the 1970s this *was* the image of victimized women. The public believed such a woman's victimization was not severe and that she "deserved" to be hit. No sympathy was forthcoming until the image of the victimized woman was changed, until the image of the "battered woman" was constructed.

. . .

There are implications to this fact that social problems are constructed out of the heterogeneity and complexity of lived realities. At the level of social policy, for example, there is a tendency for policy to reflect the constructed images of problems rather than the heterogeneity of lived realities. For the case at hand, the image of wife abuse as severe, frequent, consequential and unstoppable violence has led to a focus on shelters for women who should and who must leave such a relationship; it has led to a focus on promoting police arrest and criminal prosecution of wife abusers.... It makes sense that a woman experiencing the type of violence known as wife abuse would need a shelter; it makes sense to argue she should permanently leave her relationship; it makes sense that her abuser should be arrested and prosecuted since such violence obviously and clearly is criminal. But what about a woman who is "slapped" once or twice? Should *she* necessarily leave her relationship? Should police arrest, prosecute, and jail her abuser?

. . .

[There] is another reason why the specific content of collective representations is important.... Is it likely that a woman experiencing not-so-extreme, not-so-frequent and not-so-consequential violence will label herself or be labelled by others as a "battered woman?" Will a man who pushes around his wife define himself or be defined by others as a "wife abuser?" At the level of individual sensemaking, the extreme images of social problem conditions likely discourage practical actors from incorporating heterogeneous experience into these categories. Furthermore, collective representations painting images of persons in situations of most dire need ... might prevent persons from incorporating themselves into these categories for another reason. The image of the battered woman is the case in point. Such an image does indeed encourage sympathy for such a woman but what woman would want to be known as such a person? As constructed, a battered woman is incompetent; she is unable to assist herself; she is out of touch with her own emotions.... The identity is discrediting, so it is no wonder that many women resist it.

* * *

NOTE

1. Feminist lawyers have been a part of the battered women's movement from its inception; innovative and imaginative legal efforts to protect women from abuse developed alongside the shelters and safe home networks that offered material safety. The next reading offers both a history of battered women's assertions of a "right" to be free from violence, and the briefest of sketches (to be filled in in subsequent chapters) of how that vision has translated into legal action in the seventies, eighties and nineties.

Elizabeth M. Schneider
Battered Women and Feminist Lawmaking, 42–45 (2000)

Claims regarding women's right to be free from battering did not begin in the 1960s. Linda Gordon has detailed the experiences of battered women in the early twentieth century who, through their interactions with social workers, began to define an affirmative entitlement not to be hit. Gordon has subsequently suggested that these stories of battered women "show how deeply notions of rights were at times able to intensify and solidify their grievances and sense of purpose in taking action against them."

Gordon is interested in exploring "how forms of resistance emerge from a variety of historical influences: what conditions are necessary for an extremely subordinated group to talk of rights?" She notes that "these battered women present a good example for examination because they are in a uniquely difficult position. Disproportionately poor and oppressed, they were also unusually isolated in their victimization because wife beating occurs in private and because they had to deal with a dominant culture that has rendered this problem unspeakable."

Gordon examines how the very discovery or invention of family violence in the 1870s was conditioned by the women's rights movement. The women's movement looked at violence shaped by the temperance movement and the feminist campaign for divorce. Feminists also saw violence within a child raising discourse in which the harm to the mother was inextricably linked with harm to the child. She observes that "when feminists condemned wife beating they did so in a chivalric mode, positioning women as vulnerable and men who would abuse their wives as monstrous and depraved, lacking in true manhood. Some spoke of a woman's ownership of her body, but not her right to freedom from violence." Gordon suggests that it was not until after 1930 that a new tactic was discernable in women's struggles against abusive men and women's complaints to social workers. "This new discourse claimed an entitlement to absolute freedom from physical molestation and was grounded in terms of a 'right' ... [It] meant that clients felt entitled to ask for help in leaving their abusive marriages." She explores how the assertion of rights emerged from "changing social possibilities and aspirations" but led to many forms of resistance as women met obstacles in enlisting assistance from social workers and police, fighting with their partners, and seeking to end their marriages.

Gordon suggests that right claims concerning battering seem to emerge under conditions of social and economic possibility: assertion of rights claims were avoided while social and economic conditions made it difficult for married women to become independent of their husbands. At the same time, she concludes that talk of rights was problematic and did not capture the complexity of women's experiences and needs. Rights talk seemed to fit with absolute claims—no physical coercion, for example—which did not reflect the constrained life experiences of many women "for whom putting up with a husband's fists might not be worse than the poverty and loss of one's children attendant to separation," or who "might have preferred economic aid to prosecution of wife beaters." Gordon's historical perspective and insight on rights assertion by battered women are useful in considering contemporary developments of rights claims concerning battering.

From the beginning of the battered women's movement in the 1960s, legal work played an important role in activist efforts on battering. Activists saw the law as a necessary and important tool in obtaining safety and protection for battered women. It was also an essential way in which the battered women's movement asserted "claims" and defined the social problems of intimate violence. Many local legal groups and national organizations were formed to do legal work and advocacy on issues of violence against women, including the National Center on Women and Family Law in New York and the Center for Women's Policy Studies in Washington, D.C. The focus of much of this work was the development or expansion of legal remedies to protect women and stop the abuse and to assert battered women's right to be free from violence.

One of the first and most important legal issues that came to the fore was the failure of police to protect battered women from assault. In the early 1970s, class-action lawsuits were filed in New York City and Oakland, California, which challenged police's failure to arrest batterers. This litigation raised the dramatic notion that domestic violence was criminal, sanctionable activity that was a harm against the "public," the state, not just an individual woman, and should be treated the same as an assault against a stranger. The New York case, *Bruno v. Codd*, was the focus of much national attention. Development of injunctive remedies to keep the batterer away, known as civil protective or restraining orders, was also an important area of work. These orders were first sought in the late 1960s, and during the late 1960s and early 1970s many states passed statutes to provide for civil protective remedies.

Since that time, domestic violence has been the focus of an extraordinary degree of legal activity in the context of both law reform and litigation. New state statutes have required mandatory arrest by the police, developed complex civil protection order provisions, and enacted special rules regarding child custody where there is evidence of domestic violence. Federal legislation, such as the Violence Against Women Act of 1994, which was passed as part of the Violent Crime Control and Law Enforcement Act of 1994, asserts federal power to remedy violence. Feminist advocates on battering have begun to draw important interconnections between battering and economic discrimination and poverty, linking issues of homelessness, insurance, workplace violence, and immigration to battering. In conjunction, they are proposing new federal and state legislative initiatives and working to protect battered women's interests in current welfare "reform" legislation. Much of this law reform activity and litigation has been premised on the link between gender discrimination and violence.

Struggles over meaning in law are important sites of definition and resistance. We live within particular cultures that reflect both legal structures and legal interpretation. Women's lives, culture, and law are in a state of continuing interaction. As feminist legal scholar Martha Mahoney explains, "Cultural assumptions about domestic violence affect substantive law and methods of litigation in ways that in turn affect society's perceptions of women; both law and societal perceptions affect women's understanding of our own lives, relationships and options; our lives are part of the culture that affects legal interpretation and within which further legal moves are made." Historically, serious harm to women has resulted from the ways law and culture have distorted women's experiences. Feminist lawmaking seeks to transform the way both law and culture describe these experiences.

* * *

NOTES

1. The recent article by Linda Gordon referenced in the excerpt above is *Women's Agency, Social Control and the Construction of 'Rights' by Battered Women,* in NEGOTIATING AT THE MARGINS 126 (S. Fisher & K. Davis, eds., 1993). Bruno v. Codd, the New York case challenging police failure to respond to domestic violence can be found at 47 N.Y.2d 582, 393 N.E.2d 976 (N.Y. App. Ct. 1979), and is discussed further in Chapter 12 A, below.

2. Although feminist precepts have shaped the evolution of legal work on domestic violence, it is important to understand that these views are contested. Conservative political organizations have rallied to create a significant backlash against domestic violence advocates and victims. Leading conservative political groups, such as the Family Research Council, attack domestic violence statistics, saying they are "overblown." They contend that "men are more likely to be victims of assault than women" and that "the safest place in America for a woman is to be married and living in a household headed by a man." Robert Maginnis for the Family Research Council, *The Myths of Domestic Violence* 7/94. The particular issue of domestic violence statistics and violence against men is discussed in depth in the next chapter.

3. While the legal profession has taken the lead in combating domestic violence, lawyers are no longer the only group of professionals who participate in domestic violence intervention, prevention and education. Many professionals are making efforts aimed at integrating the assessment and treatment of domestic violence into the specific missions and responsibilities unique to their areas of expertise.

In the 1990s several groups within the healthcare professions formulated policies and guidelines acknowledging the need to address domestic violence, and establishing an agenda for action. In 1993, for example, the American Medical Association (AMA) sponsored the National Coalition of Physicians Against Family Violence. Then, in 1996, the AMA adopted a resolution in support of the education of medical students and residents in domestic violence by advocating that:

> . . . medical schools and graduate medical education programs educate students and resident physicians to sensitively inquire about family abuse with all patients, when appropriate and as part of a comprehensive history and physical examination, and provide information about the available community resources for the management of the patient.

AMA Resolution H–295.912 (1996). The American Psychological Association (APA) published a *Resolution on Male Violence Against Women* in 1999, and sponsors the APA Presidential Task Force on Violence in the Family, which was convened to bring psychological research and clinical experience to bear on the problems of family violence, including partner abuse. The American Nurses Association sponsors the Family Violence Protection Fund, which is involved in efforts to promote routine screening of every woman who is hospitalized or comes to a nurse practitioner's or doctor's office. Patricia Underwood, PhD, RN, at Media Briefing on ANA Family Violence Protection Fund (Oct. 14, 1999). Finally, the American Academy of Pediatrics issued a pediatric guide, *Diagnostic and Treatment Guidelines on Domestic Violence*, in 1996, and in 1998 issued a resolution on *The Role of the Pediatrician in Recognizing and Intervening on Behalf of Abused Women*, in which they recognized that "the abuse of women is a pediatric issue." American Academy of Pediatrics, Policy Statement RE9748 (June, 1998).

Nor are these domestic violence initiatives limited to the health care professions. The National Education Association, for example, urges school districts and communities to provide preventive training and educational programs for education employees, students, and parents/guardians/care givers. National Education Association, Resolution C–8: Family/Domestic Violence (1999). They also encourage ongoing communications regarding domestic violence issues between social service agencies and education employees. National Education Association Resolution C–9: Standards for Family/Domestic Crisis Care (1999).

Evolving contemporary responses to domestic violence are also discussed in Chapter 15 B, below.

CHAPTER TWO

The Dynamics of Abusive Relationships

Introductory Note

The previous chapter stressed the "systemic" nature of partner abuse—the ways in which men's abuse of women, through tactics of power and control that include physical violence, is enabled by a cultural context that makes women available for abuse. You might sketch the outlines of this systemic understanding, crudely enough to be sure, by saying that a patriarchal society will always organize itself to enforce the superior position of men, and women's subordinate status. In part, this arrangement is likely to be supported by public regulation. But in addition, the hierarchy is likely to be enforced by enabling individual men to control individual women, even, in some cases, when that involves inflicting physical injury. It goes without saying that in such a society women will not have the same freedom to exert control over, or exact services from, men.

American society has never been completely tolerant of woman abuse, of course. Throughout American history, when a man killed or injured or sexually assaulted a woman with whom he had no intimate relationship, it was still, in the eyes of the law, homicide, or assault, or rape, unless, perhaps, the woman was a slave, and the man her owner. In the period in which men were licensed to chastise their wives, that privilege was technically available only within marriage. If the relationship was intimate, but not marital, the man's privilege was only informal, operative when law enforcement looked the other way, or witnesses could not be found to testify. That same informal privilege continues to operate today, when the laws on the books prohibit the use of violence even within marriage, and yet enforcement lags behind. The one substantial area of continuing legal privilege for a husband's violence is sexual access,—where many states continue to differentiate between a stranger's rape or sexual assault, and a husband's.

If we were to look not at legal sanctions, but social ones, we would find a somewhat similar pattern; clear disapproval of certain extreme forms of violence, but lesser and greater degrees of tolerance in other circumstances, where the man is viewed as having the "right" to exert discipline or insist on sexual access, or as having an excuse for his "loss of control," either because of his relationship with the woman, or because of her behavior towards him.

Much of the history you read in the previous chapter gave a richer and more textured account of exactly how the balance between tolerating and prohibiting violence was struck in each era, and what specific understandings of men, women, the relationships between them, and the relationship between the state and its citizens, structured that balance. Subsequent chapters will return to these questions in more specific legal contexts.

This chapter takes on a different task. However persuaded we are that partner abuse is governed by underlying social forces, the fact remains that the individual man battering his partner will not usually understand himself as a bit actor in the large historical drama of patriarchy. Nor is his partner likely to interpret his actions in that light, or her own as a voluntary or coerced submission to the demands of patriarchy. Rather, the abusive relationship will have its own internal dynamic, and the partners will understand the violence as a problematic, or perhaps an unproblematic, aspect of that dynamic. Similarly, many of those with whom the batterer and his partner will interact—family members, friends and neighbors, teachers and pastors, social service providers and law enforcement personnel, lawyers and judges—will see the problem as lodged in the couple's relationship, rather than any larger social or political framework. Throughout these materials, we will be seeking to refine our understanding of both the broad social context which enables and condones woman abuse, and the interpersonal dynamics of abusive relationships. But in this chapter, we introduce contemporary understandings of the internal dynamics of abusive relationships, and some of the controversies currently animating discussions of those dynamics in the sociological and psychological literatures.

Why should lawyers struggle to understand the psychodynamics of abusive relationships? Why is it not enough to take a stand against partner abuse, insist that the legal system eradicate any residual tolerance for abuse or resistance to those who would challenge it, and offer legal assistance to women who seek to hold their batterers accountable? First, because unless we understand the subjective experience of battering or being battered, we are unlikely to create laws, or implement them, in ways that serve our clients. Second, because if our understanding of the problem is at odds with our clients' understandings, it will be hard to represent them effectively, even within the existing legal system. Third, because we will encounter misunderstandings among the social service providers, the law enforcement personnel and the lawyers, judges and jurors who will have power over our clients' lives, and must be able to advocate for our clients in non-legal as well as legal settings.

Most of the readings in this chapter deal explicitly with heterosexual relationships, and do not differentiate based on race or culture. The next chapter asks what is the same and what is different if the abusive relationship is between partners of the same sex, and how the particulars of race, culture, or socio-economic or immigrant status, or physical, mental or emotional disability, may influence the experience of abuse. This chapter and the next focus almost exclusively on the batterer and his partner, while Part Two explores what it means for a woman who is being battered to be a mother of young children, as so many are.

The chapter opens with a look at the behaviors that make a relationship abusive. The focus here is on the whole spectrum of behaviors through which an abusive partner exerts power and control—not all of which involve physical violence. Although the law's concern is largely with violence, violence is only one of many strategies an abuser may use to impose his will on his partner, and the threat of violence alone, or a rare exercise of violence combined with more frequent threats and emotional abuse, may be enough to ensure her subjugation. As advocates for women, therefore, we need to understand the broader context of abuse within which physical violence plays a part.

The next readings address the question of why men become abusers. Is abuse just a caricatured version of "normal" male behavior in this society, as some believe? Is it instead always symptomatic of pathology, as others have argued? Or is the truth somewhere in between?

What about the women who find themselves becoming victims or targets of abuse in their relationships? Once we have dispelled old myths about women's masochism, what can we say about how and why women are drawn into relationships that become violent, and why they stay even once the violence has begun, or is escalating to dangerous levels? In this context we have to pay close attention to the distinction between who these women were before their abusive relationships began, what they may become after a period of exposure to the trauma of physical and emotional abuse, and the potential they may have for an entirely different life once the violence ends. There is disagreement here within the community of those seeking to develop a feminist understanding of woman abuse, and its consequences. Some members of that community have stressed the debilitating consequences of abuse, and the "learned helplessness" of those exposed to random violence over which they seem incapable of exercising control, while others have emphasized the strength and resourcefulness of women seeking to protect themselves and their children from abuse.

The goal of this chapter is to introduce these themes as they appear in the academic literature, and as they inform our generic understanding of the dynamics of abuse. There is a different inquiry to which we will turn in chapter four, and again in subsequent chapters, which is the inquiry into how the legal system filters and selects information about men who batter, women who are battered, and abusive relationships, to inform legal decision-making in the many different arenas in which such information may play a crucial part; for the woman who is charged with killing her batterer, for example, or for the mother who is seeking to limit her partner's access to their children, or for the woman who seeks damages in a tort action for intentional infliction of emotional distress.

A. ABUSIVE BEHAVIORS

What makes a relationship abusive? One of the issues that has bedeviled social scientists attempting to assess the prevalence of domestic violence is the question of what measure to use. Surveys that use a single incidence of physical violence, from a slap or a push to a shooting or stabbing, as a test of abuse, may overestimate the number of genuinely abusive relationships, as well as overestimating the abuse of men by women. The same emphasis on incidents of physical violence, independent of the broader context in which they occur, has tended to characterize the legal framework within which crimes of domestic violence are adjudicated. This limited legal focus often results in an underestimation of the danger posed by a batterer, and the imposition of an inadequate sanction, which leaves his partner vulnerable to continued abuse.

Focusing on the relational context of abuse, however, does not automatically produce a more accurate understanding of domestic violence. Another frequent mistake is to understand the relationship as "conflictual," as if the abuse grew out of disagreement, and the inability of the partners to communicate, and resolve their differences, by other means. The notion that couples counseling is appropriate for an abuser and his partner often grows out of this vision. So does the insistence on the part of family courts that an abuser and his partner can profit by mediating the issues that have brought them to court.

Instead, this text is premised on understanding abusive relationships as relationships in which one partner systematically seeks to exert control over the other through a range of strategies which may well include but are certainly not limited to physical abuse. Evan Stark has called this the "coercive control" model of domestic violence, and Karla Fischer, Neil Vidmar and Rene Ellis, in the excerpt below, emphasize the "culture of battering" within which individual incidents of violence occur. Within that culture, an abuser is likely to use a range of behaviors to impose his will—a range suggested both by the "Power and Control Wheel" reproduced below, and the list of abusive behaviors provided by the batterers' treatment program EMERGE.

Karla Fischer, Neil Vidmar and Rene Ellis
The Culture of Battering and the Role of Mediation in Domestic Violence Cases, 146 Southern Methodist University Law Review 2117, 2119–33, 2136–41 (1993)

Much of the research on domestic violence has tended to divide itself along disciplinary lines, with substantial bodies of literature in psychology, sociology, criminal justice, nursing, and other disciplines. It has also fragmented according to the subjects under study. The bulk of work has focused on battered women, typically those seeking assistance through formal help sources, or on abusive men, typically those ordered by the court to engage in counseling. The literature tends to center on the individual psychology of abused women or that of their abusers or on the various social and economic factors that constrain escape from abusive relationships. Very little research has attempted to study abusive couples or abusive families by conceptualizing the abuse as occurring within a broader relationship or family context.

The concept of "culture" as applied to battering is our first attempt to describe this relationship context, as it helps us to move beyond the individuals and understand the important dynamics of abusive relationships. One definition of culture, "shared information or knowledge encoded in systems of symbols," captures an element of the relationship context that exists even in normal, non-abusive relationships. Through daily interaction and shared history every couple develops idiosyncratic modes of communication, such as single word phrases, facial expressions, gestures, tones of voice, and private jokes, that may be mysterious or unnoticed to outsiders but which convey clear meaning to the couple themselves. Consequently, we use culture as the paradigm through which to view battering for two reasons. First, we emphasize that the appropriate level of analysis for understanding the problem of domestic violence is not that of individual decisions, motivations, or behaviors, but the dyadic interaction that transcends them—the relationship context. Second, culture is not only descriptively accurate but also is intended to convey an explicit rejection of pathological terminology such as "battered woman syndrome," instead highlighting similarities of the dynamics between normal and abusive relationships.

In battering relationships these cultural components become an extension of the pattern of domination itself, whether it be a nose scratch signal devised specifically for a mediation session, a drawn line gesture used repeatedly over the course of the relationship, or perhaps a fleeting facial change. A gesture that seems innocent to an observer is instantly transformed into a threatening symbol to the victim of abuse. It is a threat that carries weight because similar threats with their corresponding consequences have been carried out before, perhaps many times.

. . . [T]he shared knowledge represented by these private symbols arises out of deeper elements of the culture of battering. The process by which such information becomes shared knowledge to the couple is best explained by a description of the elements of the culture of battering. The first essential element of the culture is the abuse itself, including any or all of the multiple forms of abuse: emotional, physical, sexual, familial, and property. The second element is the relationship context in which the abuse is folded into a systematic pattern of control and domination by the abuser. Our emphasis on this cultural aspect of battering is intended to highlight what we believe is a fundamental misinterpretation of abusive relationships by many scholars and practitioners. Our view rejects the dominant explanation of battering as conflict; we suggest that in many relationships, conflict has little, if anything, to do with the causes of battering. Rather, when conflict is a triggering event it tends to be only an expression of an attempt to control. The third element involves the tendency, on both the part of the victim and the abuser, to hide, deny, or minimize the abuse and the total control that the abuser attempts to exert on the victim.

Definitions of Abuse

Researchers in the field of domestic violence have not agreed on a uniform definition of what constitutes violence or an abusive relationship. It is important to briefly consider this literature in order to, first, expand the definition of abuse beyond physical assault, and, second, to distinguish relationships that are characterized by a culture of battering from those involving isolated acts of physical assault or other forms of abuse. Acts of assault and abuse occur in many domestic disputes and while they might incur criminal charges, relationships involving a culture of battering are of another order (they are qualitatively and perhaps quantitatively different as well).

Richard Gelles and Murray Straus, the authors of two national studies that assessed the prevalence of domestic violence, limited their definition to physical abuse: "specific, definable acts of omission and commission that are harmful to individuals in families." Gelles and Straus surveyed over 3,000 individuals in American homes, measuring the frequency and severity of physical violence such as slapping, hitting, pushing, beating, or using weapons.

While the bulk of research on domestic violence has implicitly or explicitly followed the lead of Gelles and Straus by focusing on physical assaults, there is growing professional recognition that emotional and sexual forms of abuse should fall under the rubric of "domestic violence." The reasons for labeling these as domestic violence run along two lines: 1) emotional and sexual forms of abuse are commonplace in battered women's experiences, frequently accompanying the physical assaults—i.e. they are an integral part of being battered; and 2) emotional and sexual abuse are harmful to women.

As sociologist Liz Kelly has noted, the prevailing stereotype about domestic violence is that assaults are "physical, frequent, and life threatening." Yet, the reality of battered women's lives does not conform solely to this image. Advocates for battered women have long noted that financial abuse and property abuse are forms of emotional abuse inflicted upon women. Abusers frequently restrict women's access to money and destroy their personal property in an effort to gain control over them or keep them in a state of fear. Emotional and sexual abuse may be even more common. Forms of emotional abuse include acts that do not constitute overt threats of injury or violence, such as constant humiliation, insults, degradation, and ridicule. Of course, explicit threats to harm or kill, including those attached to vivid descriptions of the method the abuser would use to carry it out, also have emotional consequences. The abuser may extend threats of harm to the victim's extended family or her children....

Researchers who have investigated the phenomenon find that rates of battered women who have been sexually assaulted consistently fall in the thirty-three percent to sixty percent range. Sexual abuse frequently involves acts that could also be classified as physical assaults, blurring the line between physical and sexual abuse, such as the insertion of objects into the woman's vagina, forced anal or oral sex, bondage, forced sex with others, and sex with animals. Sexual violence sometimes marks the end of a physical abusive incident; for others, the sexual violence begins the assault. Some of the abuse involves the use of pornography, as batterers may force their partners to look at or watch pornographic materials and/or act out pictures or scenes from these materials.

Emotional, familial, and sexual abuse have also been recently labeled as domestic violence because these forms of assault harm women, both psychologically and physically. Some battered women have described psychological degradation and humiliation as the most painful abuse they have experienced. The impact of this kind of abuse can be long lasting and harmful to women's psychological health. Emotional, familial, and sexual abuse may also affect women's physical health. Physical symptoms such as high blood pressure, ulcers, chronic back pain, chronic fatigue, and tension headaches may manifest as a result of physical abuse or as a result of the stress produced by the other forms of violence. Research on the psychological impact of rape suggests that sexual abuse, particularly when the assailant is known to the woman, has deleterious mental health effects including depression, anxiety, suicidal ideation, and a loss of self esteem and self worth.

Several researchers have developed measures of emotional abuse that correspond to the physical abuse scale developed by Gelles and Straus. For example, Marshall includes behavior such as "shook a fist at you" and "made threatening gestures." Follingstad and colleagues define six categories of emotional abuse, including ridicule, jealousy, and property abuse. Tolman developed an inventory that includes items such as "my partner tried to make me feel like I was crazy" and "my partner yelled and screamed at me." Finally, Sullivan's index contains items like "lied to you or deliberately misled you" and "ridiculed or criticized you in public."

Gelles and Straus' physical abuse measure has received heavy criticism that could also be applied to the emotional abuse scales described above. Abstracted from their social reality, the reports of abuse that result from these quantitative scales lack a description of the relationship and family context in which the abusive behaviors are occurring. For example, a woman involved in an emotional divorce might respond affirmatively to many of the scale items, such as denigration, outbursts of anger and perhaps even physical assault, but this would not necessarily capture the fear, domination, and control that characterizes the culture of battering relationships.

. . .

THE SYSTEMATIC PATTERN OF CONTROL AND DOMINATION

1. *The Context of Rule–Making*

. . .

a. *The Ruler and the Ruled*: Battered women have frequently reported that abusers are extremely controlling of the everyday activities of the family. This domination can be all encompassing: as one of the batterers from Angela Browne's study was fond of stating, "[y]ou're going to dance to my music . . . be the kind of wife I want you to be." Charlotte Fedders' account of the escalating rules imposed by her husband over the course of their seventeen year, extremely violent marriage is particularly illuminating about the range of control that abusers can exert. Her husband insisted that no one (including guests and their toddler children) wear shoes in the house, that the furniture be in the same indentations in the carpet, that the vacuum marks in the carpet be parallel, and that any sand that spilled from the children's sandbox during their play be removed from the surrounding grass. Charlotte was not allowed to write checks from their joint checking account. Any real or perceived infraction of these rules could result in her husband beating her, or at the very least, the expression of his irritation that was frequently a harbinger to a beating.

Typically, battered women talk to the men about the abuse, partly as an attempt to concretize the rules that are connected to the absence of abuse. In turn, many abusers promise to stop the abuse. One abuser in Browne's study formalized such discussions into a written document, where he set forth a list of conditions that his victim was to agree to in exchange for cessation of his violence. These conditions were: 1) the children were to keep their rooms clean without being told; 2) the children could not argue with each other; 3) he was to have absolute freedom to come and go as he wished, and could have a girlfriend if he wanted one; 4) she would perform oral sex on him anytime he requested; and 5) she would have anal sex with him. He enforced this document shortly after she "agreed" to it and continued to sexually assault her until his death. This abuser simply made explicit the rules in the relationship and made it obvious that abuse was the punishment for violating the rules.

. . .

b. The Internalization of Rules over Time: The Process of Self–Censorship

SELF-CENSORSHIP

As time goes on in a battering relationship, as in the Fedders' case, specific rules and their attached consequences give way to a general climate of increasingly subtle control, where the batterer needs to do less and less to structure his family's behavior. Caught up in the day to day fight for survival, the victims may not even be aware of this censorship process:

> I would do anything for him. I would cook, clean, you know, pick up his shit, whatever. He could have said, drop off the face of the earth, and, sure, I would have done it. . . . I was so stressed out that I was scared from one day to the next of what was going to happen with him. When I first moved in things were pretty happy-go-lucky. In the second year I was starting to . . . I wouldn't go out, I'd make excuses to people. I got to understanding that he didn't want me telling a lot of people where I lived, who I was seeing . . . That started clicking in . . . I wouldn't let my family come over to the house because I didn't know what kind of a mood he was going to be in, if he would want company. I was living a lie for two and a half years.
>
> I suppose you might be able to prevent [the abuse] by suppressing so much of yourself, learning to avoid the kind of behaviour that precipitates it. But then that in itself is a form of violence.

What fuels this self censorship process is the responsibility the victim feels, both as a woman socialized into believing that making relationships work is her job, and the responsibility added by the abuser, who blames her for the "failure" of the relationship, as evidenced by the occurrence of abuse. Women are taught in our society to care for others, to make decisions around what is best for other people, even if it denigrates their own needs. Batterers reinforce this societal message by consistently blaming women for everything that goes awry in their lives. The end result is manifested in frantic attempts by the woman to be the perfect wife, mother, and homemaker.

c. The Enforcement of Rules by Punishment

The rules that battered women try desperately to follow become established in a pattern of domination and control by the enforcement mechanism used by the batterer. Batterers may either simply respond with abuse when a rule is broken, or they may make it clear that the abuse is punishment for violations....

d. Cementing the Connection Through Fear, Emotional Abuse, and Social Isolation

At the core of these types of systematic control and domination is the fear that battered women have about future violence. This fear can be a result of past beatings or threats of physical or sexual abuse. The fear may also be triggered by any verbal or nonverbal symbol associated with the onset of an abusive incident. In some cases, threats of harm against the victim's extended family or against her children may be as effective in controlling her behavior as physical violence itself....

Control is also maintained, and fear is intensified, through the extensive use of humiliation, ridicule, criticism, and other forms of emotional abuse; financial abuse; and social isolation. It is undoubtedly easier to control someone if they think less of themselves. It is difficult for victims to leave their abusers when they do not have access to money. Similarly, limiting victims' interactions with other people enhances the batterers' domination over the family by both cutting off potential sources of support and by making the boundary between the family culture of battering and the outside world more defined.

2. Rebellion and Resistance

The pattern of rule-making and rule-enforcing, nested within the control and domination exerted by the batterer over his family, is frequently interspersed with episodes of rebellion by the victims. Expanding on Hannah Arendt's argument that force is only used when power is threatened, Liz Kelly suggested that the victim's resistance strategies forces the abuser to make his coercive power explicit. Any threat, however small, to the abuser's authority within the family is likely to be met with violence: "I think because I was sticking up for myself the hidings got harder. I think that's what it was, he wanted to show that he was still my governor." These resistance incidents are not initiated with ignorance on the part of victims, as they are very much aware that any type of challenge to the batterer is likely to result in further, perhaps escalating, violence.

. . .

It is important to distinguish episodes of rebellion and resistance (of which helpseeking is one example), which depart from the victim's usual active attempts to follow the rules, from the consequences of those episodes. The fact that battered women seek help for the abuse, a process that increases over time, and periodically rebel against their abusers' rule structures does not mean that they escape punishment for doing so. That battered women continue to resist the domination and control asserted against them even in the face of brutality is further evidence of their resilience and courage. As illustrated by the narratives above, they risk further and heightened violence each and every time they resist. Resistance breaks the most fundamental rule in the relationship: do not rebel against any of the rules.

3. *The Pretext of Conflict or Disputes*

Our argument that abuse occurs within a relationship context of control and domination is an explicit rejection of the popular belief that abuse is simply a logical extension of a heated argument or disagreement. Richard Gelles and Murray Straus, authors of the major assessment tool in the field, the Conflict Tactics Scale (CTS), clearly identify conflict as the cause of family violence. In their perspective, all violence flows from conflict, captured particularly well in the instructions for the CTS:

> No matter how well a couple gets along, there are times when they disagree . . . or just have spats or fights because they're in a bad mood or tired or for some other reason. They also use many different ways of trying to settle their differences. I'm going to read some things that you and your partner might do when you have an argument. I would like you to tell me how many times . . . in the past 12 months you. . . .

The CTS has been criticized for precisely the reason that Gelles and Straus designed it: that it seeks only to identify violence that occurs in the context of conflict, leaving out violence that occurs "out of the blue," although actually as a result of a broken rule, or other context. Battered women's narratives of the context of the abuse suggests quite the opposite of conflict. Women are typically beaten in a variety of situations that could hardly be classified as conflict: while sleeping, while using the toilet, and while in another room that the batterer suddenly entered to begin his beating. The usual scenario women describe is that at one moment all is calm and in the next, there is a major, seemingly untriggered explosion. . . .

In addition to the information about context, batterers' behavior during abusive incidents does not support an image that these are men out of control with anger. Women have reported deliberate, calculating behavior, ranging from searching for and destroying a treasured object of hers to striking her in areas of her body that do not show bruises (e.g. her scalp) or in areas where she would be embarrassed to show others her bruises.

Anger and conflict may be frequently confused with violence because both can be a proxy for abuse. The abuser may in fact be angry when he beats his victim or a conflict over what she has served for dinner may have developed before the incident of violence. But this simple coexistence in time does not mean that the anger or conflict has caused the violence. Lurking underneath the surface anger or conflict is the batterer's need to express his power over his victim. . . .

4. Separation Abuse: Heightened Risk for Abuse Following Separation

The most dangerous time for a battered woman is when she separates from her partner. Many attacks are precipitated in retaliation for her leaving, some as part of an escalation of violence following separation. Separation tends to increase, not decrease the violence, and many of the women who are murdered by their partners are killed after separation. As Martha Mahoney has argued, women who leave their partners may commit the ultimate act of rebellion, which triggers the fatal control/domination response from the abuser, the final episode of violence. As separation abuse illustrates, the victim's attempt to end the relationship does not ensure that the control and domination will end; indeed, it may escalate.

HIDING, DENYING, AND MINIMIZING THE ABUSE

This third element of the culture of battering involves the shame and embarrassment battered women feel, particularly when their injuries are visible to others. It is typical for women to remain inside their homes until their bruises and other injuries fade away....

Even when it becomes impossible to hide the abuse from others, battered women may engage in extreme forms of denial or minimize the seriousness of the abuse or the abuser's intent to harm....

... The coping strategy of minimization, like denial, allows women to escape temporarily from the pain and trauma of the violence. Women may not identify themselves as battered, citing a lack of physical abuse or examples of women who have been more severely abused. Minimizing the abuse also may involve attending to the positive aspects of the relationship, reducing the impact of the abuse on the victims' lives. As Liz Kelly wrote, minimization is fostered by the cyclical nature of domestic violence: "Where there were long gaps between violent episodes, women tended to minimize the violence by choosing [to] focus on the time when it was not occurring and by hoping that it would not occur in the future."

* * *

NOTE

1. No account of battering behaviors would be complete without addressing the "cycle of violence;" a pattern of abusive behavior first identified and described by Lenore Walker, an early pioneer in battered women's research. Walker first wrote about the cycle of violence in her 1979 book, THE BATTERED WOMAN, but the account excerpted here comes from a later work, published in 1989. In Walker's own research, the cycle of violence was reported to occur in two-thirds of sixteen hundred battering incidents studied; others have suggested that it is characteristic of some but by no means all batterers, and caution against assuming that it will be present in all abusive relationships. For a description of the cycle of violence from the perspective of the batterer, see the excerpt from Donald Dutton, below, at pp. 76–80. Judicial enthusiasm for the cycle of violence as a reliable indicator of a battering relationship is explored in Chapter 4, below.

The Cycle of Violence from Lenore Walker, Terrifying Love: Why Battered Women Kill and How Society Responds, 42–45 (1989)

I break the Cycle of Violence into three phases: the tension-building phase; the acute battering incident; and the tranquil, loving (or at least non-violent) phase that follows.

During the tension-building phase, minor battering incidents occur; slaps, pinches, controlled verbal abuse, and psychological warfare may all be part of this phase. The women's attempts to calm the batterer can range from a show of kind, nurturing behavior to simply staying out of his way. What really happens in this phase is that she allows herself to be abused in ways that, to her, are comparatively minor. More than anything, she wants to prevent the batterer's violence from growing. This desire, however, proves to be a sort of double-edged sword, because her placatory, docile behavior legitimizes his belief that he has the right to abuse her in the first place. Any unexpected circumstance that arises may catalyze a sudden escalation of violence, an explosion; in the initial part of the tension-building phase, battered women will do almost anything to avoid that.

... As the cycle progresses, the battered woman's placatory techniques become less effective. Violence and verbal abuse worsen. Each partner senses the impending loss of control and becomes more desperate, this mutual desperation fueling the tension even more. Many battered women say that the psychological anguish of this phase is its worst aspect. (Some will even provoke an acute incident, just to "get it over with" and, at the cost of grave physical injury, save themselves from real insanity or death.) But, sooner or later, exhausted from the unrelenting stress, the battered woman withdraws emotionally. Angry at her emotional unavailability and, because of that anger, less likely to be placated, the batterer becomes more oppressive and abusive. At some point and often not predictably, the violence spirals out of control, and an acute battering incident occurs.

During the acute phase—set apart from minor battering incidents by its savagery, destructiveness, and uncontrolled nature—the violence has escalated to a point of rampage, injury, brutality, and sometimes death. Although the battered woman sees it as unpredictable, she also feels that the acute battering incident is somehow inevitable. In this phase, she has no control; only the batterer may put an end to the violence.... Usually, the battered woman realizes that she cannot reason with him, that resistance will only make things worse. She has a sense of being distant from the attack and from the terrible pain, although she may later remember each detail with great precision. What she is likely to feel most strongly at the time is a sense of being psychologically trapped.

Many battered women don't seek help during an acute battering incident. They often wait for several days afterward before seeking medical attention, if they do so at all. And, like other survivors of trauma and disaster, they may not experience severe depression or emotional collapse until days or even months later.

. . .

When the acute battering incident ends, the final phase in the Cycle of Violence Begins. In this phase, usually all tension and violence are gone, which both members of the couple experience as a profound relief. This is a tranquil period, during which the batterer may exhibit warm, nurturing, loving behavior toward his spouse. He knows he's been "bad," and tries to atone; he promises never to do it again; he begs her forgiveness....

During the third phase, the battered woman may join with the batterer in sustaining this illusion of bliss. She convinces herself, too, that it will never happen again; her lover can change, she tells herself. This "good" man, who is gentle and sensitive and nurturing toward her now, is the "real" man, the man she married, the man she loves. Many battered women believe that they are the sole support of the batterer's emotional stability and sanity, the one link their men have to the normal world. Sensing the batterer's isolation and despair, they feel responsible for his well-being....

It is in this phase of loving contrition that the battered woman is most thoroughly victimized psychologically. Now the illusion of absolute interdependency is firmly solidified in the woman's psyche, for in this phase battered women and their batterers really are emotionally dependent on one another—she for his caring behavior, he for her forgiveness. Underneath the grim cycle of tension, violence, and forgiveness that make their love truly terrifying, each partner may believe that death is preferable to separation. Neither one may truly feel that she or he is an independent individual, capable of functioning without the other.

* * *

Power and Control and Equality Wheels Domestic Abuse Intervention Project, Duluth, Minnesota

The "power and control wheel" is a particularly helpful tool in understanding the patterns of abusive and violent behaviors used by batterers to establish and maintain control over their partners. Very often, one or more violent incidents are accompanied by an array of these other types of abuse, less easily identified, but firmly establishing a regime of intimidation and control. The "equality wheel," by contrast, describes the kind of "negotiated" relationship in which neither partner tries to control the other.

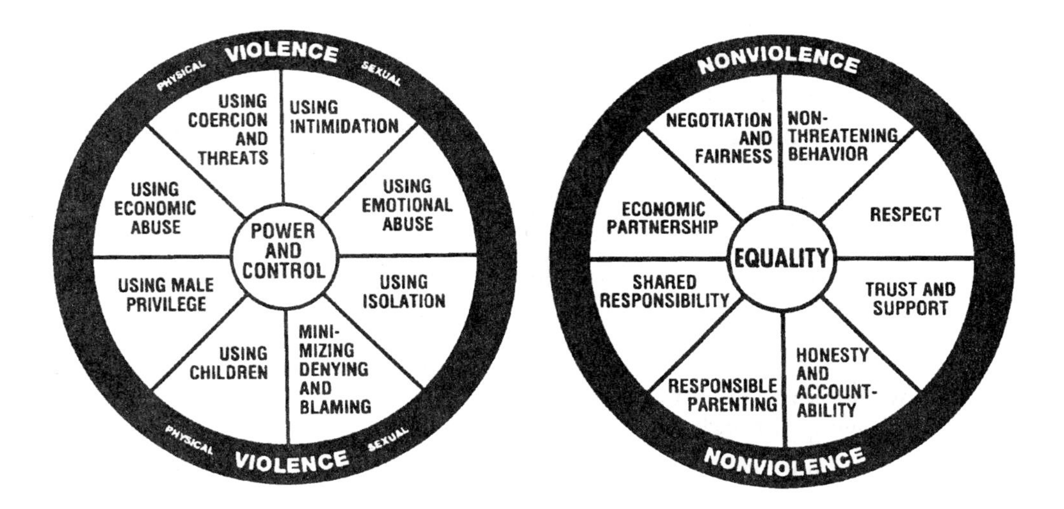

Violent and Controlling Behaviors Checklist Prepared by EMERGE, a Counseling Program for Batterers, Cambridge, Massachusetts

[The checklist is used by counselors at EMERGE to help batterers identify and take responsibility for their behaviors.]

Physical Violence:

___ Slap, punch, grab, kick, choke, push, restrain, pull hair, pinch, bite.

___ Rape (use of force, threats or coercion to obtain sex).

___ Use of weapons, throwing things, keeping weapons around which frighten her.

___ Abuse of furniture, home furnishings, pets, destroying her possessions.

___ Intimidation (standing in the doorway during arguments, angry or threatening gestures, use of size to intimidate, standing over her, outshouting, driving recklessly).

___ Threats (verbal or nonverbal, direct or indirect).

___ Harassment (uninvited visits or calls, following her around, checking up on her, embarrassing her in public, not leaving when asked).

___ Isolation (preventing or making it difficult for her to see or talk to friends, relatives or others).

___ Other. Please list.

Psychological and Economic Abuse:

___ Yelling, swearing, being lewd, raising your voice, using angry expressions or gestures.

___ Criticism (name-calling, swearing, mocking, put downs, ridicule, accusations, blaming, use of trivializing words or gestures).

___ Pressure Tactics (rushing her to make decisions, using guilt or accusations, sulking, threatening to withhold financial support, manipulating the children, bandwagoning, abusing feelings).

___ Interrupting, changing topics, not listening, not responding, twisting her words, topic stringing.

___ Economic Coercion (withholding money, the car, or other resources; sabotaging her attempts to work).

___ Claiming "The Truth," being the authority, defining her behavior, using "logic."

___ Lying, withholding information, infidelity.

___ Withholding help on child care or housework. Not doing your share or following through on your agreements.

___ Emotional withholding (not expressing feelings, not giving support, validation, attention, compliments, respect for her feelings, opinions and rights).

___ Not taking care of yourself (not asking for help or support from friends, abusing drugs or alcohol, being a "people-pleaser").

___ Other forms of manipulation.

NOTE

1. The next reading breathes life into the abstract accounts of abusive behaviors with which this section opens. It is excerpted from a recent novel by the Irish writer Roddy Doyle, a novel remarkable in its ability to capture the reality of abuse, and the nuances of the relationship between the perpetrator and his target. The narrator of the story escapes from the relationship only when her partner is killed by the police, as they pursue him for an unrelated crime.

Roddy Doyle
The Woman Who Walked Into Doors, 175–186 (1996)

Ask me. Ask me. Ask me.

Here goes.

Broken nose. Loose teeth. Cracked ribs. Broken finger. Black eyes. I don't know how many; I once had two at the same time, one fading, the other new. Shoulders, elbows, knees, wrists. Stitches in my mouth. Stitches on my chin. A ruptured eardrum. Burns. Cigarettes on my arms and legs. Thumped me, kicked me, pushed me, burned me. He butted me with his head. He held me still and butted me; I couldn't believe it. He dragged me around the house by my clothes and by my hair. He kicked me up and he kicked me down the stairs. Bruised me, scaled me, threatened me. For seventeen years. Hit me, thumped me, raped me. Seventeen years. He threw me into the garden. He threw me out of the attic. Fists, boots, knee, head. Bread knife, saucepan, brush. He tore out clumps of my hair.

Cigarettes, lighter, ashtray. He set fire to my clothes. He locked me out and he locked me in. He hurt me and hurt me and hurt me. He killed all of me. Bruised, burnt and broken. Bewitched, bothered and bewildered. Seventeen years of it. He never gave up. Months went by and nothing happened, but it was always there—the promise of it.

. . .

For seventeen years. There wasn't one minute when I wasn't afraid, when I wasn't waiting. Waiting for him to go, waiting for him to come. Waiting for the fist, waiting for the smile. I was brainwashed and brain-dead, a zombie for hours, afraid to think, afraid to stop, completely alone. I sat at home and waited. I mopped up my own blood. I lost all my friends, and most of my teeth. He gave me a choice, left or right; I chose left and he broke the little finger on my left hand. Because I scorched one of his shirts. Because his egg was too hard. Because the toilet seat was wet. Because because because. He demolished me. He destroyed me. And I never stopped loving him. I adored him when he stopped. I was grateful, so grateful,

I'd have done anything for him. I loved him. And he loved me.

. . .

I loved him. He was everything and I was nothing. I provoked him. I was stupid. I forgot. I needed him.

I buried a baby because of him.

He burned money in front of me.

— How will you cope?

He slashed my good coat.

— Where'll the money come from for a new one?

He picked me up off the ground. And I loved him. He picked me up and held me. He cried on my head. I needed him. For years I thought that I needed him, that I could never recover without him; I was looking for everything I got. I provoked him. I was useless. I couldn't even cook a fry properly, or wash a good shirt.

I promise!

I was hopeless, useless, good for fuckin' nothing. I lived through years of my life thinking that they were the most important things about me, the only real things. I couldn't cope, I couldn't earn, I needed him. I needed him to show me the way; I needed him to punish me. I was hopeless and stupid, good for only sex, and I wasn't even very good at that. He said. That was why he went to other women.

— Can you fuckin' blame me?

I could smell them off him. He called me other names when we were in bed. He rubbed me and called me Mary and Bernie. He laughed. He closed his eyes and called me Chrissie. I could see him looking at them. Knackers and dirtbirds. Bleach and false teeth. He came home with their smell on him and then he had me. For afters. He even came home with lipstick on his collar. It must have been deliberate. The lousy bitch, whoever she was. The lousy cheap bitch, kissing his collar. She must have known.

I lost a child because of him.

There were days when I didn't exist; he saw through me and walked around me. I was invisible. There were days when I liked not existing. I closed down, stopped thinking, stopped looking. There were children out there but they had nothing to do with me. Their dirty faces swam in front of me. Their noises came from miles away. There were rooms, food, clothes—nothing. There was a face in a mirror. I could make it smile and not smile. There was a warped, bruised face. There was a red-marked neck. There was a burnt breast.

. . .

There were days when I couldn't even feel pain. They were the best ones. I could see it happening but it meant nothing; it wasn't happening. There was no ground under me, nothing to fall to. I was able not to care. I could float. I didn't exist.

The second time he hit me he grabbed my hair and pulled me to him. I saw him changing his mind as he hauled me in. His grip loosened. He stared at me and let go. Another mistake; he hadn't meant it. I saw it in his eyes; that wasn't Charlo. Charlo was the one who let go, not the one who'd grabbed me. I can't remember why; I can't remember exactly when. I was still pregnant. Sunday morning, before we went to mass. I can't remember why. Something to do with breakfast, but I'm not sure. He was talking to me, giving me a lecture or something. I looked away, began to raise my eyes to heaven. (That was a habit he beat out of me.) I felt the rush and the sting on my ear, the air exploded and I was yanked forward. I stepped quickly to stay on my feet. My ear was hot and huge. I might have screamed. My skin was coming off the side of my head. I stepped forward, and looked at him. My hands—the palms landed on his chest. His face changed. He let go of my hair. I said nothing. I watched his face. I wasn't scared now; I hadn't time to be. He took his fingers out of my hair. He might have wiped them on his trousers. I watched him. He looked caught, cornered. He said nothing. He backed off. The side of my head settled into a throb. The left side; I can still feel it. He went into the kitchen. He said nothing. No sorrys, no excuses. I wish I could remember it all; it doesn't matter. I could make it up and it would still be true. He'd hit me again. We went to mass together. He bought me a Flake on the way home. I used to break them before I unwrapped them. Then I'd open the wrapper very carefully, slowly and I'd take out the bigger pieces, then the smaller ones. Then I'd make a funnel of the wrapper and empty the chocolate dust into my mouth. He watched me while I did it. I didn't offer him any. He smiled. I was making a fool of myself. He liked that. I was his little fool. I didn't care. His smile meant lots of things. I smiled back. Over and done with; another mistake. We went to my parents' house. It was Sunday. He helped me off the bus. I was his pregnant wife. He walked at my pace, crawled along beside me. We walked side by side. We talked.

. . .

He once asked me how I'd got my black eye. I didn't know why, what he was up to. It scared me. We'd just been talking, about something on the telly. We used to watch the News; this was years ago. I think it was during the Hunger Strikes. Charlo was big into the H Blocks. He knew all the names, how many days they'd gone without food; he was an expert. He'd have loved to have been in there with them. I said that to him.

— Yeah, he said back.

He didn't even know I was slagging him. He wore a black armband all around the place, put it on before his trousers every morning. He still ate like a pig, though, and drank like one. We were watching the News, commenting on it, and he asked me where I'd got my black eye. I kept looking at the telly. I was being tested; I was sure I was. There was a right answer. But this came out of nowhere. There hadn't been a row. There wasn't any tension. We'd been getting along fine, chatting away about the world and the H Blocks. It was nice; the trick was to agree with everything he said. Then he came out with it.

— Where'd you get that?

— What?

— The eye.

It was a test. I was thumping inside. He was playing with me. There was only one right answer.

— I walked into the door.

— Is that right?

— Yeah.

— Looks sore.

— It's not too bad.

— Good.

He was messing with me, playing. Like a cat with an injured bird. With his black armband, the fucker. Keeping me on my toes, keeping me in my place. Pretending he didn't remember. Pretending he'd never seen black and red around and in that eye before. Pretending he cared. I didn't believe he'd forgotten, not even for a second. He wanted me to think that—or that he was sick, having blackouts, that he was like Doctor Jekyll and Mister Hyde, a schizophrenic, that I should feel sorry for him and try to understand. I didn't believe it. He was playing with me. Ruining the night because it was getting too cosy. Only playing. He had me; I could say nothing. I could never fight back. When he wasn't hitting me he was reminding me that he could. He was reminding me and getting me ready. Like the cat playing with the bird, letting it live a bit longer before he killed it.

He put one of his fingers on the bruise. I made sure I stayed absolutely still. I looked ahead, at the telly. The tip of his finger was freezing. He rested it gently under my eye.

— You must have walked right into it, did you?

— Yeah; I wasn't looking.

— Which door?

— Bedroom.

He took his finger away. I could still feel it on my cheekbone.

— Were you drinking?

— No.

— Sure?

— Yeah.

— Just careless.

— Yeah.

— Okay.

I waited for more. I sat beside him and waited.

— I saw you.

— You didn't.

— I fuckin' saw you.

— You didn't, Charlo.

He's making it up as he goes along, making himself believe it; working himself up, building up his excuse. He's getting ready to let go. He's going to beat me; there's no pont in arguing, nothing I can do. I should say nothing. But I never learn. I always defend myself. I always provoke him.

— I know what I fuckin' saw, righ'.

He's seen me looking at a man. In the pub; we're just back from the pub, just in the door.

— I didn't look at anyone, Charlo.

His open hand. The sting and the shock, the noise, the smack. He's too fast.

— Say that again.

You never get used to it. Predicting it doesn't matter. Nothing I can do; he has complete control. It's always fresh, always dreadful.

Again.

Always a brand new pain.

The skin doesn't get any harder.

Stay out of the corners; I have to make sure that I don't get caught.

Again.

Buzzing. Things swim and dive. My husband is beating me. A horrible fact. A stranger. Everything collapses.

— Say it.

Again.

A stranger.

— Cunt! Say it.

The back of his hand. Too scared to expect it. Shapes are changing. My hair is grabbed as the hand comes back. Stay out of the corner.

— You fuckin' cunt!

Pulls my head down.

— You fuckin'-

Pushes me, drops me into the corner. Hair rips. A sharper pain. His shoe into my arm, like a cut with a knife. His grunt. He leans on the wall, one hand. His kick hits the fingers holding my arm. I lose them; the agony takes them away. Leans over me. Another grunt, a slash across my chin. My head thrown back. I'm everywhere. Another. Another. I curl away. I close my eyes. My back. Another. My back. My back. My back. My back. Back shatters.

The grunting stops. Breaths. Deep breaths. Wheezing. A moan. I wait. I curl up. My back screams. I don't think, I don't look. I gather the pain. I smooth it.

Noises from far away. Creaks. Lights turned on, off. Water. I'm everywhere. I'm nothing. Someone is breathing. I'm under everything. I won't move; I don't know how to. Someone's in pain. Someone is crying. It isn't me yet. I'm under everything. I'm in black air. Someone is crying. Someone is vomiting. It will be me but not yet.

Do I actually remember that? Is that exactly how it happened? Did my hair *rip*? Did my back *scream*? Did he call me a cunt? Yes, often; all the time. Right then? I don't know. Which time was that anyway? I don't know. How can I separate one time from the lot and describe it? I want to be honest. How can I be sure? It went on for seventeen years. Seventeen years of being hit and kicked. How can I tell? How many times did he kick me in the back? How many times did I curl up on the floor? How can I remember one time? When did it happen? What date? What day? I don't know. What age was I? I don't know. *It will be me but not yet.* What is that supposed to mean? That I was nearly unconscious; that the pain was unbearable? I'm messing around here. Making things up; a story. I'm beginning to enjoy it. Hair *rips.* Why don't I just say He pulled my hair? *Someone is crying. Someone is vomiting.* I cried, *I* fuckin' well vomited. I choose one word and end up telling a different story. I end up making it up instead of just telling it. *The sting and the shock, the noise, the smack.* I don't want to make it up, I don't want to add to it. I don't want to lie. I don't have to; there's no need. I want to tell the truth. Like it happened. Plain and simple. *My husband is beating me up. A horrible fact. A stranger.* Did any of this actually happen? Yes. Am I sure? Yes. *Absolutely sure, Paula?*

I have a hearing problem, a ruptured eardrum. A present from Charlo. It happened. A finger aches when it's going to rain. Little one on the left; he pulled it back till it snapped. It happened. I have places where there should be teeth. There are things I can't smell any more. I have marks where burns used to be. I have a backache that rides me all day. I've a scar on my chin. It happened. I have parts of the house that make me cry. I have memories that I can touch and make me wake up screaming. I'm haunted all day and all night. I have mistakes that stab me before I think of them. He hit me, he thumped me, he raped me. It happened.

. . .

He'd bring me a cup of tea. Or a Flake. That was all it took. A tiny piece of generosity—a kiss, a smile, a joke. I'd grab at anything. And I'd forget. Everything was fine. Everything was normal. He'd put the Flake in the fridge and let me find it. That took planning; the kids always had their heads in the fridge, especially at night—his timing had to be perfect. That was all it took. I still break them before I unwrap them. I sometimes cry when I eat them.

* * *

B. THE BATTERER

Our contemporary attention to, and concern with, the problem of domestic violence grows out of the battered women's movement. That movement, in turn, grew out of the recognition that violence against women in their homes was a much larger problem than had previously been appreciated, and that women, isolated in abusive relationships, lacked any kind of social, legal or emotional support to assist them in ending the violence in their lives. Shelter for women, legal redress for women, counseling services for women—women's safety and independence—these were the movement's goals. Viewed from this perspective, the batterer was not someone on whom attention should be lavished—not someone it was important to understand or help. As Lynn Caesar and Kevin Hamberger say in the preface to their book TREATING MEN WHO BATTER: THEORY, PRACTICE AND PROGRAMS, xv (1989):

> "All of us who have worked with, known, or been battered may question why a man who violates the civil liberties of a woman in a violent, humiliating and dehumanizing fashion should engender empathy, concern, or special attention. To offer help to a man who beats his wife suggests that we will share the problem. Assisting a man who rapes, beats and infringes upon the rights of his female partner arouses strong emotions within anyone who cares enough about the problem of wife battery to get involved. To feel moral outrage when a battered woman reveals her blackened eyes but to contain the anger to get close enough to the batterer to whom the woman may soon return is, at times, an exercise in emotional gymnastics."

To the extent that advocates and activists within the battered women's movement did focus on the batterer, it was to wake the public up to the very real danger he posed to his partner. The goal here was to shift public understanding from the view of the batterer as someone provoked beyond endurance by a shrewish wife, or as someone who occasionally lost control, perhaps after having "one too many," to a view of the batterer as someone who systematically set out to control his partner's every movement and every thought, and would stop at nothing, including extreme physical violence, to achieve that end. To win public funding for battered women's programs, and support for new legal mechanisms of protection, the batterer was portrayed as a monster from whom his partner had to be rescued. Within the context of the criminal justice system in particular, battered women's advocates sought to ensure that men accused of violence against their intimate partners were treated like other violent criminals. They should be arrested, not merely walked around the block to "cool off." They were rational and instrumental in their use of violence, not mentally ill, and should be prosecuted, not merely diverted into treatment programs without ever standing trial or facing conviction. They should be incarcerated for serious violence, not merely put on probation.

As with any stereotype, this view of the batterer has severe limitations. While to some extent it did indeed serve as a corrective for earlier myths and misconceptions, it falls far short of explaining who batterers are, what motivates them to behave as they do, and why women make and sustain strong emotional commitments to them. And while this deeper understanding may once have seemed irrelevant for purposes of raising public consciousness about domestic violence, or insisting on its recognition as a crime, there are weighty reasons today to move beyond the "monster" stereotype. First, not all batterers are alike, and the less monstrous any individual man appears to a judge, or an untrained therapist, the less likely they are to appreciate the danger he poses, and to exercise proper caution in their dealings with him. Second, domestic violence is not a problem that could be solved by incarcerating all batterers, even if the criminal justice system were a lot more willing than it is today to invoke that sanction. Thus, while it remains crucial to use the tools currently available to us to keep individual women and their children safe, we must be looking in the longer-term to forms of treatment that can help at least some batterers become non-violent partners, and to learn what makes a batterer, so that we can focus on raising non-violent men.

Finally, and perhaps most important, women in relationships with abusive men rarely understand them as monsters, pure and simple. Unwittingly, when we portray them as such, we fuel the persistent question "Why did she stay?" When we respond to that question only by stressing the debilitating effects of violence, or the external social and economic constraints which make it hard or impossible to leave, or the fear of retaliatory violence, we deny, and may seem to delegitimate, the ongoing emotional connection that may prompt a woman, for at least some period of time, to endure the violence in the hopes that it can be ended without the relationship itself coming to an end. Ironically, then, increasing our understanding of the batterer may leave us with a greater understanding of, and respect for, the woman he is abusing, and assist us in supporting her without undermining her self-respect.

The most useful contemporary work on batterers grows out of the clinical experiences, and related research, of those involved in batterers' treatment. An account of the different forms of treatment available, and the debates about the theoretical underpinnings of those modalities is postponed for a later chapter. What follows here are two readings that offer "typologies" of batterers, one drawn from the work of Donald Dutton, and one from the work of collaborators Neil Jacobson and John Gottman. Dutton is a psychology professor at the University of British Columbia, and director of the Assaultive Husbands Program in Vancouver. His most recent book, from which these excerpts are drawn, grows out of twenty years of experience as both a researcher and a clinician. Jacobson and Gottman are both professors of psychology at the University of Washington. Jacobson is a pioneer in the scientific study of marital therapy, and Gottman has also been studying marriages for more than twenty years.

What is a Batterer?
Donald G. Dutton, with Susan K. Golant, The Batterer: A Psychological Profile, 24–30, 33–35 (1995)

Psychopathic Wife Assaulters

. . . Lenny had nine relationships with women in the previous three years. He'd been violent in at least three relationships that I knew of. His criminal career started with stealing his mother's jewelry. He said he had never really known her. He left home at fifteen. "The people I stole from were insured anyway,' he explained. "They never suffered. The only one who suffered was me. The woman I hit had it coming. She had a bad drug habit and was sleeping around. I warned her to quit the drugs. I was trying to go straight, and she was stopping me. Now she's not around to get in my way . . ."

And on and on it went. No remorse. No looking back. Only a relentlessly unrealistic view of the future.

About forty percent of the men who come to our treatment groups meet the diagnostic criteria for antisocial behavior—that is, they have a history of criminal activities. Antisocial behavior was once thought to be indicative of psychopathy, but in his book *Without Conscience: The Disturbing World of the Psychopaths Among Us*, my colleague Robert Hare, who has studied psychopaths for more than twenty years, has noted that while they do typically engage in criminal activities, they also have a more central and psychological defining feature: a lack of emotional responsiveness that sets them apart from other criminals.

Hare describes this as missing conscience. Conscience is the ability to punish the self for violating one's own standards of conduct. Most normally socialized men who are not psychopathic do go through some remorse for hurting their wives. The pangs of guilt are painful, so they find ways to neutralize the self-punishment by mentally reconstructing the reprehensible action—often by blaming the victim for having provoked it ("I told her not to make me angry. If she hadn't nagged me . . . ") or an outside factor such as alcohol. Sometimes they will minimize the act through the language they employ to describe it ("the night we had our little incident") or they'll make comparisons to others ("Most men are as violent as I am").

But psychopaths have no such pangs. In fact, Hare has found that their brains do not function like those of normal people when they are observing emotionally provocative events. MRI (magnetic resonance imaging) brain scans performed on psychopaths and normal men shows dramatically different processing. The MRI for psychopaths looks as though nothing is happening—just a bit of bright color in the brain stem area toward the back of the brain, indicating glucose metabolism and brain activity. . . .

By contrast, the scans of the normal men revealed huge color patterns radiating from the brain stem forward to the temporal lobes—an indication of extensive brain activity.

The psychological syndrome of psychopathy includes the loss of the ability to imagine another person's fear or pain or the dreadful consequences that might follow abuse. Other key signs of psychopathy include shallow emotional responses and an unrealistic future scenario . . . accompanied by an unwillingness to examine past problems.

How are psychopaths created? That's unclear. Hare . . . theorizes that it's a genetic condition. Others believe, however, that it has a psychological basis. Psychiatrist John Bowlby, for example, thought of psychopathy as a form of extreme "detachment" resulting from an infant having its early needs for intimacy and closeness chronically frustrated. And psychologist Dan Saunders of the University of Michigan has found that generally violent men who have been the most severely abused when growing up are the most extremely abusive toward their wives.

Unlike cyclical abusers, however, psychopathic batterers such as Lenny are often violent with others as well as their partners. Moreover, they are frequently arrested for nonviolent crimes such as forgery, passing bad checks, or confidence rackets. These actions are hallmarks of a so-called antisocial lifestyle.

When psychopaths are referred to treatment groups for wife assault, they are considered a poor bet for improvement. Psychopaths don't look back. As a result, they never learn from past mistakes.

Psychologist Neil S. Jacobson has identified a subgroup of psychopathic men whom he calls "vagal reactors." (*Vagal* refers to the vagus nerve, which conducts impulses between the brain and the muscles of the throat, heart, and abdomen.) Usually when we're upset, we experience an autonomic response: our hearts race, our palms become sweaty, our breathing turns quick and shallow, our stomachs churn. Vagal reactors don't respond in this way. In fact, their internal reactions become cool and controlled when they are engaged in heated arguments with their wives.

As Jacobson put it in his 1993 keynote address to the American Association of Marriage and Family Therapy,

> . . . the batterers who showed this heart rate decrease were the most belligerent and contemptuous toward their wives. . . . The "disconnected" group showed the highest rates of violence outside the marriage, and were the most likely to have reported violence in their family of origin.

According to Jacobson, about twenty percent of all batterers and half of all antisocial personalities are vagal reactors.

Overcontrolled Wife Assaulters

About thirty percent of assaultive males are designated *overcontrolled*. These men appear to be somewhat distanced from their feelings and on psychological tests show a strong profile of avoidance and passive-aggression. These are they guys who say they just want to be working on their cars; they can't understand what the fuss is all about. Their anger—usually a buildup of frustration to external events—can suddenly erupt in violence after long periods of seething but unexpressed rage.

For these reasons, overcontrolled wife assaulters have the lowest profile; they simply lack the flamboyant characteristics that attract media reports of violence. They are, in many ways, the mirror opposite of the stereotypical wife beater.

Two kinds of overcontrolled men exist. The *active type* is sometimes characterized as a "control freak" who extends his need for extreme domination to others. Wives of these men describe them as being meticulous, perfectionistic, and domineering. The *passive type* simply distance themselves from their wives, and the couple usually argue over the attainment of some emotional contact. Both types show up for treatment as apparently "good clients"—they are compliant and try hard to please the therapist.

On psychological tests that measure the maltreatment of women, overcontrolled men generate extremely high scores on one factor of abusiveness called dominance/isolation and on a second scale used most often to measure emotional abusiveness. Dominance/isolation includes behavior in which the husband requires rigid observance of sex roles ("He becomes upset if the household work is not done when he thinks it should be"), demands subservience ("He acts like I'm his personal servant"), and isolates his wife from resources ("He refuses to let me work outside the home," "He restricted my use of the telephone," "He was stingy giving me money").

The emotional abuse includes verbal attacks ("He insults or shames me in front of others"), and the denial of emotional resources ("He withholds affection from me"). All forms of emotional abuse are coercive techniques to generate submission.

. . .

Cyclical/Emotionally Volatile Wife Abusers

... About thirty percent of all habitually assaultive men ... are ... cyclical/emotionally volatile abusers.

These men are not constantly violent, but periodically so. Many of their partners describe their recurring metamorphosis: they transform from a kindly Dr. Jekyll personality to a terrifying Mr. Hyde. Although they are frequently buddies with men and unlikely to display any anger with them, their predominant rage is with the woman to whom they're emotionally connected. Indeed, this woman becomes a lightning rod for all the emotional storms in their lives. Others describe a specific triggering event that brings on the beating—a real or imagined move toward leaving the relationship, even a pregnancy.

Furthermore, these men are abusive only within the confines of the relationship and the abuse occurs repeatedly in spite of what the women may do; pleading, cajoling, reasoning, fighting back make little difference. Nevertheless, according to Murray Straus's surveys, about one-third of the men who assault their wives stop spontaneously, without police involvement. Why this happens is unknown. Perhaps some women convince their husbands they will leave, or perhaps the men have become too upset about their actions.

. . .

I once read in a magazine the following statement attributed to a male movie star: A man wants to keep a woman like a snake on a stick with a noose around its neck so that he could move her closer or further at will. The sense of danger from too much closeness or distance struck me. The phrase spoke to the fear that cyclical/emotionally volatile abusers experience around intimacy: they feel either abandonment or engulfment.

My earliest work with these men focused on their ability to describe their feelings and their extreme need to control intimacy. We all need power in our lives but we don't all generate it by dominating others. I wondered if an inner sense of powerlessness created this preoccupation with external power—with control of another whom the abuser simultaneously views as essential and abhorrent. . . .

I started to think about emotional distance as the most crucial issue to intimately violent men. Why, I still didn't know. . . . But if these men were so afraid of intimacy, why were they in relationships at all? What kept drawing them back? I frequently asked them these questions but they would only shrug and say, "I don't know." When they did offer an explanation, it was usually in terms of reliability and creature comforts.

Over the years, however, I discovered that the cyclical/emotionally volatile abusers experience a constellation of feelings involving rage and jealousy. They find ways of misinterpreting and blaming their partners, holding them responsible for their own feelings of despondency, making impossible demands on them, and punishing them for inevitably failing. These men are held in the grip of cyclical moods that ebb and flow with a fearful rhythm.

Perhaps that is why their wives describe them as having dual personalities. I don't remember how many times I heard it before it dawned on me. But as I look now at the interview notes I took from partners of my clients, the phrases jump off the pages: "He's like two people." "His friends never see the other side of him. They just think he's just a nice guy, just one of the boys." "I never know which one is coming in the door at night." I have more than two hundred files with the same statements, all offered spontaneously to my request for a description.

* * *

Myth #2: All Batterers Are Alike
Neil S. Jacobson and John M. Gottman, When Men Batter Women: New Insights into Ending Abusive Relationships, 36–39 (1998)

Although there is still a tendency for professionals to talk about batterers as if they were all alike, there is growing recognition that there are different types of batterers. There are at least two distinguishable types that have practical consequences for battered women, and perhaps more. Each type seems to have its unique characteristics, its own family history, and perhaps different outcomes when punished by the courts or educated by groups for batterers. Based on our findings of a distinction between the Cobras and the Pit Bulls, and the work of Dr. Amy Holtsworth–Munroe and Gregory Stuart, we think a compelling case can be made for at least two subtypes, roughly corresponding to our distinction between the Cobras and the Pit Bulls.

Cobras

Cobras appear to be criminal types who have engaged in antisocial behavior since adolescence. They are hedonistic and impulsive. They beat their wives and abuse them emotionally, to stop them from interfering with the Cobras' need to get what they want when they want it. Although they may say that they are sorry after a beating, and beg their wives' forgiveness, they are usually not sorry. They feel entitled to whatever they want whenever they want it, and try to get it by whatever means necessary. Some of them are "psychopaths," which means they lack a conscience and are incapable of feeling remorse. In fact, true psychopaths have diminished capacity for experiencing a wide range of emotions and an inability to understand the emotions of others: they lack the ability to sympathize with the plight of others, they do not experience empathy, and even apparent acts of altruism are actually thinly veiled attempts at selfishness. They do not experience soft emotions such as sadness, and rarely experience fear unless it has to do with the perception that something bad is about to happen to *them*.

But not all Cobras are psychopaths. Whether psychopathic or merely antisocial, they are incapable of forming truly intimate relationships with others, and to the extent that they marry, they do so on their terms. Their wives are convenient stepping stones to gratification: sex, social status, economic benefits, for example. But their commitments are superficial, and their stance in the relationship is a "withdrawing" one. They attempt to keep intimacy to a minimum, and are most likely to be dangerous when their wives attempt to get *more* from them. They do not fear abandonment, but they will not be controlled. Their own family histories are often chaotic, with neither parent providing love or security, and they were often abused themselves as children.

As adults, they can be recognized by their history of antisocial behavior, their high likelihood of drug *and* alcohol abuse, and the severity of their physical and emotional abuse. Their wives fear them, and are often quite depressed. But fear and depression do not completely explain why the women are unlikely to leave the relationship. Nor is it simply that they lack economic and other resources: indeed, Cobras are often economically dependent on their wives. Despite the fact that they are being severely abused, it is often the women rather than the men who continue to fight for the continuance of the relationship. It is these couples where the men exude macabre charisma.

(2) *Pit Bulls*

The Pit Bulls are more likely to confine their violence to family members, especially their wives. Their fathers were likely to have battered their mothers, and they have learned that battering is an acceptable way to treat women. But they are not as likely as the Cobras to have criminal records, or to have been delinquent adolescents. Moreover, even though they batter their wives and abuse them emotionally, unlike the Cobras the Pit Bulls are emotionally dependent on their wives. What they fear most is abandonment. Their fear of abandonment and the desperate need they have *not* to be abandoned produce jealous rages and attempts to deprive their partners of an independent life. They can be jealous to the point of paranoia, imagining that their wives are having affairs based on clues that most of us would find ridiculous.

The Pit Bulls dominate their wives in any way they can, and need control as much as the Cobras do, but for different reasons. The Pit Bulls are motivated by fear of being left, while the Cobras are motivated by a desire to get as much immediate gratification as possible. The Pit Bulls, although somewhat less violent in general than the Cobras, are also capable of severe assault and murder, just as the Cobras are. Although one is safer trying to leave a Pit Bull in the short run, Pit Bulls may actually be more dangerous to leave in the long run. Cobras strike swiftly and with great lethality when they feel threatened, but they are also easily distracted after those initial strikes, and move on to other targets. In contrast, Pit Bulls sink their teeth into their targets; once they sink their teeth into you, it is hard to get them to let go!

It is not clear how Cobras and Pit Bulls are apportioned within the battering population. In our sample, 20 percent of the batterers were Cobras. Interestingly, Dr. Robert Hare, an internationally renowned expert on psychopaths, estimates that 20 percent of batterers are psychopaths. This correspondence is provocative. However, our guess is that Cobras constitute a larger percentage of the clinical or criminal population of batterers than the 20 percent found in our study. The Cobras fit the profile of the type of batterer who comes into contact with the criminal justice system much more than the Pit Bulls do. The profile of the Cobra also describes those referred by judges to treatment groups much better than the profile of the Pit Bull.

* * *

NOTES AND QUESTIONS

1. The work of Amy Holtzworth–Munroe and Gregory L. Stuart to which the authors refer is *Typologies of Male Batterers*, 116 PSYCHOLOGICAL BULLETIN 476 (1994). The article provides a survey of the literature, and a summary of the different typologies offered by different researchers. One important question is how to understand the relationship between one typology and another. For example, is the "cobra" of Jacobson and Gottman's typology the "psychopath" of Dutton's typology? And is the "pit bull" the "cyclical/emotionally volatile" abuser? If these parallels seem convincing, then where do we put Dutton's third category, the "overcontrolled" abuser?

2. Even given some ongoing uncertainty about the categories, the identification of batterers with different behavior profiles is an important contribution to those who work in the field of domestic violence. It helps us resist stereotypes, and easy assumptions about who is and who is not likely to abuse a partner. It may also contribute to the development of more accurate tools for threat and lethality assessment. The next level of question is then how boys become batterers of one type or another; what genetic predisposition, what physical or emotional injuries, what societal or familial influences create batterers out of children. The next readings, again drawn from the work of Dutton and Jacobson and Gottman, present and critique some contemporary theories, and provide some additional suggestions.

The Creation of a Cyclical Batterer
Donald G. Dutton with Susan K. Golant, The Batterer: A Psychological Profile, 61–62, 64–77, 92–93, 96–100, 114–16, 120–24 (1995)

The Brain Damage Theory

Experts have divided aggression into two categories: "normal," which is directed toward an enemy, and "abnormal," which is directed toward a stranger or a loved one—the act of a madman. Like Dr. Frankenstein's cursed monster who was implanted with a "criminal" brain, medical science believed that wife assaulters committed violence because of an aberration in the brain structure. At a 1977 international forensic psychiatry conference I attended, for example, all the research papers on wife assault focused exclusively on its neurological causes.

Frank Elliott, a psychiatrist at the Pennsylvania Hospital, one of the leading proponents of this theory, believed that occurrences of explosive rage, or *episodic dyscontrol*, were caused by an electronic micro storm in the limbic system, the "ancient" part of the brain situated in the brainstem that is believed to be the seat of emotion.

He described dyscontrol as periods of intense rage "triggered by trivial irritations and accompanied by verbal or physical violence." The individual usually has a "warm, pleasant personality," but may have "a history of traffic accidents resulting from aggressive driving."[2]

According to Elliott, the most common "organic" condition associated with intimate violence is temporal lobe epilepsy (an uncontrolled electrical discharge in the area of the brain that regulates strong emotions). This condition, in turn, could have been caused by any early trauma to the brain such as an interruption to the oxygen supply during birth or infancy or other traumatic scars. . . . In addition, he believed metabolic disorders such as hypoglycemia could also trigger intimate rage.

. . .

Intimate violence is a complex action, filled with rich symbolism of the woman as lover/savior/mother/betrayer. It is awash with obsessions and revulsions, tensions, jealousy, and rage. How can one reduce it to a simple perturbation in the limbic system? How does scar tissue lead one to attack only one's wife and only in private? Clearly, some higher order of mental association that relates the victim to the perpetrator and the context of the violence must direct and influence the assault.

. . .

The Genetic Mandate

In the 1970s, another way of understanding human aggression, sociobiology, became popular. This discipline studies how human social behaviors may be genetically encoded and are inherited through a process of natural selection. Spurred by the influential work of E.O. Wilson, a biologist at Harvard University, sociobiology began to influence thinking about behavior in general, and wife assault in particular.

Sociobiologists see abuse as a man's way to dominate an intimate female in order to guarantee reproductive and sexual exclusivity. In their view, a man hits his intimate partner in order to satisfy the biological imperative that his genes be passed along to the next generation.

. . .

The logic of sociobiology raises many questions. Is violence toward an intimate partner the product of a million years of evolution? If it is part of "human nature," why aren't all men assaultive? Are men who punch and kick their wives simply playing out a sociobiological mandate handed down through natural selection? If it is inevitable, why should we punish individual transgressors? Would it be possible to stop the violence through short-term treatment? Could we stop in sixteen weeks what it took hundreds of thousands of years to develop? The implications are staggering.

. . .

Also, why are the rates so high for physical violence directed toward pregnant women? That makes no sense from a sociobiological perspective. Why would a man bent on passing along his genes endanger his progeny and the source of future descendants? Yet researchers have found that 58 percent of women reporting some form of violent victimization were pregnant when the abuse began.

While the neurological view is too narrow, the sociobiological explanation for abuse is so broad that it too fails to take into account another obvious fact: that only a small percentage of men physically assault their wives.

Male Tyranny: The Feminist View

. . .

To feminists, a man batters because he expects to have all the power and be the boss. These expectations develop from the way boys are raised in our culture—their male sex role identification—which prepares them for "male privilege." Men have been socialized to dominate. They learn to exercise this privilege through violence. What's more, this control is always directed outward. They are woefully inept at monitoring what is within, emotions such as anger or jealousy.

. . .

The feminist view focuses on society rather than individuals as the cause of male abusiveness: Domination of women is a cultural prescription, and violence against a means to that end. This emphasis on the cultural is reflected in the feminist distrust of psychological causes of male violence.

In fact, much feminist analysis argues that it is misguided to emphasize psychopathology to explain wife assault because violence results from "normal psychological and behavioral patterns of most men." All too often, we use a damaging childhood or drug abuse to exonerate an individual perpetrator, simultaneously absolving him of his crimes and precluding a hard look at the society that fostered his behavior.

This analysis shone a light into the abandoned social context of male abusiveness and found the power, domination, and male privilege that male psychiatrists had conveniently overlooked. Feminists were also uncomfortable with sociobiology, which made male jealousy, domination, abuse, and philandering sound like some inevitable biological blueprint.

. . .

Eventually though, research data began to accumulate that called for a more complex view of wife assault. . . .

. . . Men hold widely dissimilar beliefs about women, have diverse individual levels of personal power with them, and act in varied ways toward them. The abusive-domineering male "created" by socialization and historical forces is, in fact, in the minority. The broad-based feminist theory makes such global statements that it fails to explain these individual variations in actions occurring in intimate relationships.

Social Learning Theory

. . .

Social learning theory examines how habitual actions, such as violence, are acquired through observation of others, and how these are maintained by social payoffs called rewards. . . . These theorists examine individuals' unique learning experiences to discover opportunities the subjects might have had to observe actions they would eventually perform.

From this perspective, wife assaulters are believed to copy, or model, violence they observed in their families of origin. Research has shown that watching their fathers hit their mothers did make men more likely to assault their wives. Furthermore, there are built-in instant rewards for battering: Men "win" arguments that may have been going badly. Faced with what they believe are their wives' superior verbal and emotional skills, they fall back on their one advantage: physical superiority. They feel *agentic*; that is, they act out and control the situation the way they think real men are supposed to.

Social learning theory has advantages over the other explanations of wife assault: It accounts for individual variations in behavior, and it relates wife assault to a large body of general studies on aggression.

However, there are still problems. For one thing, according to this theory, violence is always triggered by an external event. . . . But partners of assaultive men typically report that the men themselves generate tension. They become irritable for no apparent reason. Rather than passively responding to incidents in their environment, these men inevitably and repeatedly create the event that triggers their violence.

In addition, observational learning doesn't lead to violence in the linear fashion that this theory predicts. Aggression by either parent toward the other can increase violence and victimization by sons and daughters. In other cases, as in my own father's, the witness of interparental abuse defines himself in opposition to his model. He does everything he can to avoid becoming like the violent parent.

Something more complex than mere copying of actions is going on. Abusive men experience profound depressions, delusional jealousy, and disproportionate rage—all in an intimate context. How does one model the inner experience of depression? A deeper, more pervasive form of personality disturbance seems to be at work than what social learning theory would describe.

A Telling Clue

None of these theories answered all my questions about cyclical abusers, and some raised new ones. I was dissatisfied, and decided to pursue my own research into the origins of their personalities. . . . [A]fter I had engaged in this study for some time, I stumbled upon a feature I had not expected. And this clue indicated not a genetic, physiological, societal, or socially learned theory but rather a psychological basis for abuse that originated in early development.

The clue to an earlier origin was that cyclically assaultive men experienced the symptoms of post-traumatic stress disorder (PTSD), the normal reaction anyone would have to a highly disturbing situation such as an attack or natural disaster. PTSD symptoms include depression (crying, sadness, feelings of inferiority), anxiety (tension, trouble breathing, panic attacks), sleep disturbance (restlessness, nightmares, early morning awakenings), and dissociation (spacing out, flashbacks, dizziness, out of body experiences.)

. . .

At first, this was confusing to me. Common sense dictates that only victims suffer trauma symptoms—not perpetrators. Were batterers also victims? Because they were abusive and aggressive, we don't usually think so. Besides, most of these men were unwilling or unable to describe their past. They had great difficulty talking about their emotions. Further analysis and study was needed.

In 1987, Harvard psychiatrist Bessel van der Kolk described how children who had been traumatized experienced rage reactions and difficulties modulating their aggression. There was a link here. I had to wonder which traumas occurred regularly in the childhoods of the men I had been studying that might underlie their fury. The PTSD-like symptoms they reported and their chronic anger and abusiveness all pointed to a common early source.

In an attempt to understand the connection between early trauma and wife assault, I gave groups of assaultive and nonabusive men a questionnaire that assessed their childhood memories. I wanted to know if their parents were warm or cold, accepting or rejecting. I found that those who reported cold, rejecting parents experienced more severe, extensive, and frequent trauma symptoms. I developed a different questionnaire to measure shaming actions that parents might have used against the men when they were boys. Again, those who had been shamed as children also had intense trauma symptoms.

These results suggested that chronic adult trauma symptoms and abusive behavior might originate in childhood experiences. With further investigation, I found that they were related to painful experiences of shaming, rejection, and abusiveness in the men's upbringing. Mike, for example, eventually opened the Pandora's box of his childhood, revealing that he had been severely and randomly beaten by his alcoholic father. Although abusive men can't express it verbally, they seemed to experience some early form of trauma that has numerous effects beyond just modeling abusive actions. These effects manifest themselves globally in their sense of self, their inability to trust, their delusional jealousy, their mood cycles, their view of the world. They form what I have come to call the abusive personality.

I theorized that as the adult batterer cycles through the phases of abuse, he becomes not one personality but two. Just as a woman's dissociation may help her cope with the inescapable terror of sexual abuse, so may men have learned other aspects of trauma reaction, such as emotional volatility and rage, to cope with being victimized. They may use and eventually misuse these mechanisms, as with any other trauma response, long after the original terror is gone, and when conditions no longer call for them. Now they are inappropriate, even destructive.

As I gathered research results, I could see how early experiences can have lasting effects that go far beyond the copying of violent actions. They influence every aspect of the man's "intimate personality": how he sees his wife, how he feels, how he thinks about the causes of his problems.

I found that the psychological seeds of abusiveness are sown very early in life—even during infancy. The development of the abusive personality is a gradual process that builds over years. . . . [T]he seeds come from three distinct sources: being shamed, especially by one's father; an insecure attachment to one's mother; and the direct experience of abusiveness in the home. No one factor is sufficient to create the abusive personality; these elements must exist simultaneously for the personality to develop. They create a potential for abusiveness that is shaped and redefined by later experiences, but that potential develops early in life.

. . .

SHAME: THE FATHER'S CONTRIBUTION

. . .

Shame and the Abusive Personality

Early upbringing plays a major part in formation of the self. At young, vulnerable ages, children are open and susceptible to the vicissitude of family function and dysfunction. The impact of experiences such as violence between parents, angry divorce, rejection, and shaming can take a toll on every part of the child, from his self-concept, to his ability to self-soothe or tolerate aloneness, to his capacity to modulate anger and anxiety, to the elaboration of opiate receptors in the brain, and finally to his compulsive need to externalize blame because accepting responsibility reactivates the mortification.

At every level, from the physiological-neurological to the psychological, the abused/rejected boy is primed to use violence. This is not merely the learning or copying of an action that occurs in violent families, it is the configuration of an entire personality.

That configuration lays the foundation for the abusive personality. It creates certain pathways, ways of responding that will lead to further reinforcement for abuse: rage with girlfriends, possessiveness, selection of male friends who tolerate or even praise the violent streak.

As the "preabusive" boy enters his teen years, he passes from a latency period, when girls are irrelevant, to a new phase of life with peer groups and messages from the culture and his subculture about what it means to be a man. I believe that abused/rejected boys interpret and accept this information differently, even seek out different information. The message they want to hear is the one that tells them they're all right, that their anger is justified, that women are the problem. As the adolescent moves from failed relationship to failed relationship, he creates a self-fulfilling prophesy filled with fear and loathing that leads him to expect women to be disloyal, untrustworthy, and in need of control.

There is a pool of rage and shame in such an individual that can find no expression—that is, until an intimate relationship occurs, and with it the emotional vulnerability that menaces his equilibrium, the mask he has so carefully crafted over the years. Perhaps it is the mask of a "tough guy," or a "cool guy," or a "gentlemen." Whatever identity he had created is irrelevant. Now a woman threatens to go backstage and see him and his shame without the makeup. Then, to his own surprise, the rage starts. He feel it like an irritation, and sometimes like a tidal wave.

He is shocked and surprised. He may apologize and feel shame immediately after, but he can't sustain that emotion; it's too painful, too reminiscent of hurts long buried. So he blames it on her. If it happens repeatedly with more than one woman, he goes from blaming her to blaming "them." His personal shortcomings become rationalized by an evolving misogyny. This misogyny then feeds on itself, contributing further to his rage with women.

At this point the abusiveness is hardwired into the system. The man is programmed for intimate violence. No woman on earth can save him, although some will try.

AMBIVALENT AND ANGRY ATTACHMENT: THE MOTHER'S CONTRIBUTION

. . .

Normal Separation and Individuation

. . .

According to object relations theory, as we wander for the first time from our mother's embrace, our basic notions of selfhood develop. It gradually dawns on us that we are a separate entity from our mother. Mahler has described this awareness as the "psychological birth of the human infant." It is also not a coincidence that rage is born and temper tantrums appear during this period.

When an infant becomes a toddler and can walk away from his mother (at age ten to fourteen months), some dramatic changes occur in his emotional world. He begins to exhibit a growing awareness of separation; he realizes that he is on his own. As this awareness flourishes during the next period (between fifteen and twenty-four months), the infant seems to have increased need for his mother to share with him every one of his new skills and experiences. His need for closeness, held in abeyance throughout the previous developmental period, becomes evident at the very time he is developing the capability to create physical distance between himself and his mother.

. . . At this stage, the infant alternately searches for and avoids body contact with his mother. He shadows her, incessantly watching and following her every move, and then scampers away.

With this behavior, the child indicates his deep ambivalence: He wants to reunite with the one he loves but at the same time fears she will re-engulf him.... The toddler begins to learn that he is not omnipotent, but instead small and dependent. Yet, since his newfound autonomy is so exciting, he denies or suppresses his dependency. And so, as Mahler explains, this period is "characterized by the rapidly alternating desire to push mother away and to cling to her."

... In truth, [this] is [the toddler's] first experience with the paradoxical demands of intimacy—to be oneself and yet be part of a relationship—with all the ambivalence that this engenders.

A toddler's ability to tolerate separation from his mother depends on his developing inner representations of her. If his inner image is of a warm, nurturing mother, that is sufficient to sustain ordinary periods of separation. When he wanders afield, he holds this internal image of her and knows he can safely return to her whenever he wants. This stable inner representation of mother is called *object constancy*. When properly attained, the child develops a secure, consistent, positive sense of a mother soothing him. Later on he is able to soothe himself by activating this inner representation. Because of this ability, he can keep tension from building.

If, however, the mother is unavailable, the toddler invests too much energy in "wooing her" and doesn't have enough left for the next developmental steps. Conversely, if she is too anxious and begins shadowing *him*, she intrudes upon him and he cannot separate. He literally forces his attention to the outside world to avoid this intrusion and cannot easily return to mother. In either case, the inner notion of a stable lovable self is impaired.

This is a normal impulse. But I wonder how a mother, abused by her husband, can possibly proffer all of the crucial and sensitively tuned responses that her baby requires. She may, for example, find "optimal emotional availability" difficult to provide constantly. This developmental aspect of abusiveness has been generally overlooked, despite its important ramifications for the development of a rageful self.

Around twenty-one months "the clamoring for omnipotent control, the extreme periods of separation anxiety, the alternation of demands for closeness and autonomy," subside and each child begins to find an *optimal distance* from his mother.... It is a compromise between separation anxiety (if too far from mother) and engulfment (if too close).

Mahler extended this concept to the human lifespan by viewing life as a dance between the desire for autonomy and the desire for fusion. Put somewhat differently, relationship issues become those of optimal distance. Too little distance carries a threat of re-engulfment and identity loss; too much carries abandonment and loss of the other.

Compare these notions of optimal distance with my research on wife assaulters. The men I studied reacted with unbridled anxiety and anger to videotaped scenarios of "abandonment" that seemed innocuous to other men. Departures from their comfort zones for optimal distance produced the most extreme rage in assaultive men—literally off the scale. They also have personality deficits that render them most susceptible to dependency on their intimate partners, their panic and hysterical aggression are the psychological result of perceived loss of the female.

I believe the roots of such emotional patterns may be found during this separation-individuation phase. My hunch is that a consequence of an assaultive husband is a mother who cannot possibly balance the difficult demands of this process. In this way, the father's physical abusiveness, even when not directed at the son, has important ramifications for the boy's personality, not just his behavior.

Moreover, since an incomplete rapprochement task plagues abusive men, there are certain similarities in their childhood and adult behaviors. These include the inability to use language in a way that produces a sense of control.... Instead, these men are either extremely unassertive, leading to occasional explosions (like the over controlled batterer ...) or they become dominators who use every form of control (financial, emotional, physical) instead of negotiation.

... [A]dults with remnants of rapprochement conflict tend to lose sight of themselves in intimate relationships. They experience anxiety about closeness and separation, poor spouse-specific assertiveness, and poor tolerance of aloneness (or conversely high dependency).

Assaultive men present this very profile. They search for women they can dominate, especially in the sense of dictating the emotional distance in the relationship, perhaps as a way of finally managing the original trauma of a failed rapprochement. When we try to control something, usually anxiety and anger lie behind our behavior....

. . .

Abusiveness and Fearful Attachment

. . .

It was my belief that fearful attachment and adult abusiveness are related. Along with my colleague Kim Bartholomew, I set out to empirically verify this idea. We tested groups of men for attachment styles and compared those scores with others measuring the potential for intimate violence and their wives' reports of domestic abuse. I was most interested in the men whose profiles indicated a fearful attachment. They experienced strong and unresolvable push-pulls in intimacy and were hypersensitive to rejection.

Interestingly, we found that the fearful men reported their relationships with their mothers to be high on both warmth and rejection. This is obviously a contradiction, but it points to the ambivalent relationship these men had with their mothers. They learned to want her and that she could fulfill their needs; on the other hand, they learned that she could be absent or unavailable or rejecting. They experienced a constant contest between clinginess and distancing.

The fearful men were the ones I thought would be most abusive, but I thought it was a misnomer to call them fearful. While fear might have been at the core of their reaction to anticipated rejection, anger was the prominent feature of their emotions and behavior. Whether this anger was a male cover-up for underlying fear or a vestige of what Bowlby called "the anger born of fear" didn't really matter. These men were "angrily attached," as if they were infants, *seeking proximity to mother and simultaneously arching angrily away*—a prototype of lifelong reactions to women.

As I suspected, these fearfully (angrily) attached men scored high on my measures of abusive personality. Their profiles also indicated high levels of chronic anger and jealousy and frequent post-traumatic stress symptoms: They didn't sleep well, became depressed and anxious, and experienced dissociative states when things seemed "unreal." Their fearful attachment scores were more highly associated with reports of abuse by their female partners than any other attachment style. In fact, from the men's attachment profiles, we were able to predict adult abusiveness with eighty-eight percent accuracy.

In our earlier videotape studies, we had found that physically abusive males demonstrated greater arousal, anxiety, and anger while viewing conflicts in which a woman expresses her need for greater independence from the man. At the time I referred to this as abandonment anxiety; however, I had made no attempt to discern if some assaultive men showed this pattern more than others. In retrospect, I believe that fearfully (angrily) attached men would have exhibited it the most.

Fearfully attached men had the highest levels of depression, anxiety, dissociative states (sometimes accompanied by rageful acting out), and sleep disturbances. They have been traumatized, probably by extreme attachment disruptions, and react with rage whenever they are in intimate relationships. As adults, they experience high levels of trauma symptoms. They have little insight into the causes of this constellation of problems and avoid seeking help, believing it will only make things worse.

Fearfully attached men experience extreme chronic anger as an inevitable by-product of attachment yet have great difficulty living without a woman. Intimacy inevitably produces anger in them. They cannot conceive of and do not understand the anger in attachment terms. They blame it instead, especially during their dysphoric phases, on their wives. "Why can't she make me feel better?" they wonder. In reality, the feeling stems, at least in part, from the inescapable emotional consequences of their own disturbed attachment. What remains in their development profile are the responses or action patterns through which they learn to express this anger.

LEARNING THE WAYS OF VIOLENCE

. . .

Is it Society's Fault?

Several books on male abusiveness have made the mistake of trying to explain it solely as a product of socialization—male expectations of privilege and power. . . .

From my point of view, however, abusiveness can't be explained away by socialization. Too many men, socialized in the same culture as abusive men, remain nonabusive. Socialization had to be combined with psychological influences that precede it developmentally. . . .

. . . It is only after the personality originates that culture exerts its influence—and it exerts it unevenly on secure and insecure boys.

The boy whose early experiences have been dysfunctional, whose sense of personal identity has not been buttressed by his mother's warmth and his father's presence, is the one who is most susceptible to cast about desperately for aspects of the culture that will reaffirm or justify his abusiveness. Society can provide negative attitudes toward women and an acceptance of violence as a means of resolving conflict. Society helps mold aggression—it teaches the means, points to the target. Aggressive role models far outnumber creative ones. Power, control, and violence become the prevalent modes of resolving conflicts.

Nevertheless, attachment style, interest, and competing social influences take many boys away from the more aggressive mode. Boys who do have a secure attachment and identity take the cultural influences as they come, rejecting some outright, picking up parts of others. Their persona or social identity is a melange of many sources. It is for this reason that not every boy emulates Rambo, and most of those who do, do so only as part of a stage. They develop and move on.

. . . With the supportiveness of a close male relationship, men in our research samples were less likely to have abusive personalities and were also less likely to hold negative beliefs and hostile attitudes toward women.

. . .

From Father to Son?

. . . Violence in the family . . . is the third key factor in the formation of the abusive personality. . . .

In his national survey data, sociologist Murray Straus found that boys who witnessed their parents attack one another were more than three times as likely to assault their wives or become the victims of their wives' violence than boys who had not experienced those family disturbances. Straus's survey, however, simply reported an association between home life and assault. There might have been other potential causes for adult abusiveness, such as emotional support being unavailable to the boys or the fact that they had been struck by parents themselves. Also, for reasons we don't fully understand, some sons of abusive fathers become adamantly nonviolent, perhaps defining themselves in opposition to their hurtful parent. These confounding factors make it difficult to isolate the cause of spousal abuse from survey research.

Moreover, if we study adult abusers and trace the violence back into their childhoods, we are likely to find a history of brutality. But such methods do not allow us to trace all of the cases in which an abused child does not go on to be violent himself—the so-called false positives.

To correct for this problem, scientists investigating the transmission of family violence have, instead, followed groups of previously identified abused children for years as they matured into adulthood. They discovered that abused children do have higher subsequent rates of violent crime. Indeed, my colleague Steve Hart and I found the type of abuse in the family was strongly related to the types of crimes federal prisoners committed. Violent men had been physically abused, sex offenders had been sexually abused.

We can draw two conclusions from these findings. The first is that firsthand abuse experiences or even the witnessing of abuse increases one's chances of becoming violent. The second is that the majority of abused children do not go on to become abusive themselves. This is not a contradiction. It simply means that modeling or observation has an influence on later life, but doesn't totally determine one's behavior....

There are numerous other experiences that can break the chain of abusiveness from one generation to another. Many abused children may not have had the need or the adult opportunity to engage in violence. Others may have come under the influence of what we call protective factors—positive events that could mitigate against early negative consequences. One of these factors is having at least one supportive adult in an otherwise hostile early environment. Another is being in an emotionally supportive family as an adult. Involvement in psychotherapy as an adolescent or young adult is also helpful in breaking the cycle of violence. Still others have had their violence punished, ending its use as a behavioral strategy.

* * *

NOTES AND QUESTIONS

1. Dutton's account focuses on the background of "cyclical/emotionally volatile" batterers, who seem to correspond, although perhaps not completely, with the "pit bull" category described by Jacobson and Gottman. In their work, these two authors describe the following differences in the backgrounds of the "cobras" and "pitbulls" they studied:

> In many ways, we were left with the impression that Cobras had come from backgrounds that more seriously crushed something very fragile that every child begins life with, a kind of implicit trust that, despite all their limitations, parents have the child's best interest at heart. Our image was that this horrible childhood background had somehow led the Cobras to vow to themselves that no one would ever control them again....
>
> Cobras came from more chaotic family backgrounds than Pit Bulls, although the Pit Bulls were more likely to have had batterers as fathers. Specifically, 78 percent of the Cobras in our study came from families where there was some kind of violence in the home when they were children, compared to 51 percent of the Pit Bulls. Even this 51 percent figure is high, since in the population at large (a still alarming-

> ly high) 20 to 25 percent of children grow up in violent homes. So both types of batterers are more likely than members of the general population to have grown up in violent homes.
>
> Twenty-three percent of the Pit Bulls came from families in which their fathers beat up their mothers and the violence went only one way. The Cobras almost invariably came from childhoods that were quite traumatic, with violence manifesting itself in a variety of ways including having very violent mothers who abused them.

Neil S. Jacobson & John M. Gottman, WHEN MEN BATTER WOMEN: NEW INSIGHTS INTO ENDING ABUSIVE RELATIONSHIPS, 94–95 (1998).

2. For an account of the different models of treatment programs available for abusers, see Chapter 9 D., below.

3. Where does Roddy Doyle's batterer, Charlo, fit in the two typologies you have been introduced to in this section? What characteristics determined your choice?

C. WOMEN AS VICTIMS OF ABUSE

If we can postulate one or more theories that explain why men batter, is there an equivalent theory to explain why women find themselves being battered? For many years, such theories abounded. Women in battering relationships were masochistic, depending psychologically on abusive treatment; provocative, or self-defeating. Recent studies have found no empirical basis for such claims. The authors of one such study suggested in 1986 that battered women differ from nonbattered women only in the extent of violence in their families of origin. Others have suggested that while there is no "personality profile" for the victim of domestic violence, many women are rendered susceptible to abuse both by gender-role socialization that encourages them to adapt and submit to male demands, and by childhood experiences—whether personal or familial—of violence and sexual molestation or assault. These findings and discussions are the topic of the first reading excerpted below, from an essay by psychologist Michele Harway. These recent studies also caution against confusing the psychological state of the woman who has been subjected to prolonged abuse, and who may well be suffering from an array of symptoms including those grouped under the heading "post traumatic stress disorder," with the "personality" of that same woman before the abuse began.

If there is no psychological predisposition on the part of the woman to choose an abusive partner, then it becomes important to ask how it is that women find themselves in such relationships. Angela Browne has written movingly about the "courtship" of batterers, recounting stories that illustrate how the most violent partner can appear an ideal suitor at the start of the relationship, when his possessiveness masquerades as attentiveness, and his obsessive focus can be a welcome change from others' seeming carelessness. An excerpt from her 1987 book WHEN BATTERED WOMEN KILL is included here.

It is equally important to ask why it is that many women find it difficult or impossible to leave their abusive relationships—to the extent we think that question is not fully answered by the credible threats of retribution from their batterers, or the intimidating economic and social barriers they face. This question marches us right into the midst of a lively dispute within the growing academic field of domestic violence studies—the validity, and the usefulness, of the concept of learned helplessness, and of battered woman syndrome, in explaining the behavior and choices of battered women. These issues are taken up in the next section of this chapter, which discusses the impact of abuse.

Michele Harway
Battered Women: Characteristics and Causes; Battering and Family Therapy: A Feminist Perspective, 29–31, 35–36 (M. Hansen & M. Harway, eds. 1993)

PSYCHOANALYTIC THEORY

Psychoanalytic theory holds that the individual's personality (developed early in life) predisposes him or her to be violent or to submit to violence. These personality characteristics are often reported as psychiatric diagnoses. In particular, in the Diagnostic and Statistical Manual of Mental Disorders, third edition (DSM–III) the diagnosis of a dependent personality disorder is explained using an example of a woman who tolerates an abusive marriage.... The DSM–III–R appendix includes a description of self-defeating personality disorder (SDPD) as one of a handful of proposed "new" diagnoses. Some of the diagnostic criteria for SDPD are as follows: a persistent pattern of self-defeating behavior, including choosing people and situations leading to disappointment or failure; rejecting attempts of others to help; inciting angry or rejecting responses from others and then feeling hurt, defeated or humiliated; failing to accomplish tasks crucial to personal objectives despite the ability to do so; and engaging in self-sacrifice unsolicited by the recipients of the sacrifice.... The self-defeating personality disorder has been critiqued ... "as an unwarranted pathologizing of traditional, socialized 'feminine' behavior" ... , as describing as maladaptive those behaviors that battered women and other victims of interpersonal violence adopt to keep themselves from serious harm, ... as a diagnostic category with very little empirical evidence to support its existence, and ... as a label that could lead "to serious harm to women by declaring certain normative, post-traumatic responses to such violence, as indicative of a serious, deeply rooted characterological flaw...."

Consistent with the pathological label applied to battered women by the psychoanalytic approach, some writers from this camp describe battered women as having a basic need to provoke violence, as displaying passive hostility that contributes to the violence, and as having a masochistic motivation that promotes continued violence.... However, no empirical support for these postulates exists. Hotaling and Sugarman ... who reviewed more than 400 studies, found no support for personality traits such as masochism, passivity, and low self-esteem occurring more often in battered women than in any other group. Indeed, some studies suggest that battered women demonstrate particularly ingenious powers of survival. . . .

More recently, Root . . . has delivered a stinging critique of approaches to understanding battering (and other situations of trauma) that involve applying diagnostic labels. The conceptualization of posttrauma responding as a personality disorder (based on the diagnosis of post-traumatic stress disorder [PTSD] or of borderline personality disorder, commonly given to battered women) comes from a belief that such posttrauma response is an individual's *pathological* reaction to battering, rather than, as Root sees it, behavior designed for survival. When [these] diagnoses (or the beliefs that underlie them) are used to guide treatment, the therapist deals with the battered woman from the perspective of a "personal deficit model," rather than looking at her behavior as the result of an interaction between the woman and the context within which she is traumatized. Moreover, her functioning is seen as the result of "coping skills deficits or characterological weaknesses." The treatment (which may be seen as blaming the victim) may serve to retraumatize the woman by denying her experience of reality and by failing to shore up her self-confidence during her recovery.

. . .

Characteristics of Battered Women

What are battered women like? Hotaling and Sugarman . . . conclude that battered women are different from nonbattered women only in the extent of violence in their families of origin. No psychological predisposing traits were found: "There is no evidence that the status a woman occupies, the roles she performs, the behavior she engages in, her demographic profile or her personality characteristics consistently influence her chances of intimate victimization". . . . Their analysis concludes that risk markers for being battered do not consistently include impaired cognitive functioning, traditional sex role adherence, or lack of assertiveness (although much research, including Walker's, suggests that these factors may be the *result* of battering). Nor do battered women, more often than other women, appear to be diagnosable as having dependent personalities. Hotaling and Sugarman conclude that "these findings do not augur well for theoretical models of victimization that focus on characteristics of victims". . . .

That battered women are not demonstrably different from other women is supported by [Lenore] Walker's . . . research. She interviewed 403 self-identified battered women, 17–59 years old, in the Rocky Mountain region. The women were all intelligent, well-educated people holding responsible jobs and quite successful in appearing to be like everyone else. Maintaining appearances of normality in order to cover up the violence often exacted a heavy psychological cost from these women, leaving them isolated from others and often psychologically vulnerable. Walker's research, however, shows no specific personality trait that suggests a victim-prone personality for the battered women. In support of this finding, battered women who left their abusive situations were less likely to go into new relationships, and when they did, they were rarely violent ones.

Walker and [Angela] Browne . . . present data demonstrating that although gender has an impact on the experience of being a victim of an intimate's violence, no particular personality pattern leads to a person's becoming a victim. Rather, they suggest that women—who are socialized to adapt and submit and who are likely to become victims of men's sexual violence or physical abuse—may not develop adequate self-protection skills as children, especially if they come from childhood homes in which females are victimized. Walker has described this factor as susceptibility to violence (based on reported events occurring with some regularity in the lives of the subjects). Events suggesting a susceptibility factor include early and repeated sexual molestation and assault, substantial violence by members of the individual's family of origin, perceptions of critical or uncontrollable events in childhood, rigid sex role socialization, and experience of other conditions that put the individual at high risk for depression.

This susceptibility factor could interfere with a woman's ability to become free of violence. The women interviewed for Walker's study believed that their batterers could kill them; however, even though they were cognizant of the danger, they also felt confident that they could help the batterers change. This form of denial and other psychological sequelae that constitute the battered woman syndrome are described by Walker as symptoms adopted as survival techniques in situations that are filled with violence. Findings also support the appropriateness of the terror experienced by the women in the face of the violence and validate the women's fears that separation will make the violence worse.

* * *

NOTE

1. For the research cited in this excerpt, see: G.T. Hotaling & D.B. Sugarman, *An Analysis of Risk Markers in Husband to Wife Violence: The Current State of Knowledge,* 1 VIOLENCE & VICTIMS 101 (1986); Lenore E.A. Walker, THE BATTERED WOMAN SYNDROME (1984); L.E.A. Walker & A. Browne, *Gender and Victimization by Intimates,* 53 J. OF PERSONALITY 179 (1985). Root's attack on using diagnostic labels to describe responses to trauma can be found in M.P.P. Root, *Reconstructing the Impact of Trauma on Personality,* in PERSONALITY AND PSYCHOPATHOLOGY: FEMINIST REAPPRAISALS, 229 (L.S.Brown & M.S. Ballou, eds. 1992).

If personality characteristics do not determine women's entry into abusive relationships, what does attract women to, and hold them in relationships with, abusive partners? The next reading offers some insight into those questions.

Courtship and Early Marriage: From Affection to Assault
Angela Browne, When Battered Women Kill, 38–48, 52–53 (1987)

Molly met Jim Johnson in the fall of 1978, when she was twenty-nine. Jim was thirty-five, tall and muscular, and strikingly good-looking. Friends indicated he had had a long string of relationships with women and never wanted to settle down, but with Molly it was different. Jim's interest in Molly began at their first meeting and never abated. He was dependable and attentive, rearranging his schedule to be with her and dropping other activities and even former friends with whom she felt uncomfortable.

In the following months, Jim was with her every moment Molly would allow. He occasionally spent time away from her and went drinking with old friends, but when he came back was as gentle and considerate as ever and he never drank heavily around her. Most of the things they did they did alone together. Jim said Molly was too fragile for his male world, and that he found relief from the daily pressures of life just being around her. And he did seem at peace; his friends said he was the happiest they had ever seen him, and Molly was glad to be a part of that. From what she knew of his past, she felt like he'd had a hard life.

Thinking back on that time, Molly remembers that she just felt fortunate Jim had noticed her. He didn't seem to mind her shyness; wasn't always pushing her to talk more or to party with him, like other men she had dated. And was always attentive and there—something that was important to her, after the long absences of her first husband. In May 1979, Molly married Jim in a quiet ceremony by a justice of the peace with two of Molly's employers in attendance.

There wasn't any abuse during the first few months Molly and Jim were married. Jim was working steadily and was good to Molly. At his urging, Molly quit work and stayed home; she enjoyed setting up a household again. But then Jim quit his job during a fight with his boss and couldn't get another one. He wouldn't hear of Molly going back to work, telling her he had married her and would support her. They stayed in the apartment another month, and then Jim put everything in storage and he and Molly moved into his van. They were living at the coast and would move the camper from rest stop to rest stop. Jim usually left in the truck during the day to look for work; Molly waited for him to come home, then fixed supper on the camp stove and they'd move to another location for the night.

Molly tried hard to be supportive; Jim was a proud man and she knew it was a difficult time for him. He was very quiet and moody, but most of the time they got along alright. The only serious arguments they had were when Molly attempted to persuade him to let her look for work, even if just on a temporary basis. The first time Jim yelled at Molly was over this issue, and Molly never brought it up again. Jim refused to let her go with him into town, and persuaded her not to tell her family and friends where she was until they got themselves settled. Molly knew Jim was embarrassed about the change in his circumstances and complied. It seemed to her that it rained all fall; she read a lot, and tried not to let herself get depressed.

As the weeks went by, Jim began coming back later at night, often drunk. When drinking, Jim was different than Molly had ever seen him—yelling at her, calling her names, accusing her of not loving him or of wanting to leave him. And sometimes, he raped her. Molly didn't think you could call it rape, when it was your own husband, but he was very rough during lovemaking—pinching and biting and treating her with anger. At these times, he was like another person; he didn't seem to know her or realize what he was doing. Molly began to have constant bruises and bite marks. But Jim was always cold sober by morning—quiet and depressed and terribly sorry. He would apologize and stroke her face, and drink less and spend more time with her for the next several days. Molly prayed he'd find work soon. She kept telling herself things would be alright once he got a job and they moved out of that van.

The First Beating

Jim found employment just before Christmas, and they moved from the van to an old house in town. He was gone most of the time now, getting things in order and working overtime to pay back bills. But Molly was ecstatic; so glad to have a home again and to be moving things into shelves and closets. After unpacking, she began fixing the house for Christmas. Jim didn't want her to spend much money, but she put up a tree and made some decorations. She also made a couple of presents for Jim.

When Jim came home from work on Christmas Eve, he seemed alright. But suddenly he became very irritated, angry that she hadn't reminded him to get her a Christmas gift. The more Molly tried to reassure him, the more angry Jim became. He tore the tree down, then began to hit Molly in the head with his fists. Molly attempted to pull away, but Jim grabbed her by the hair and slammed her head back against the wall with all his force. Molly came to with Jim throwing water on her. When he saw that she was conscious, he hit her in the stomach, carried her to the bedroom and had sex with her, and then fell asleep. Molly slipped into the bathroom and cried. Jim had never beaten her like that and she could not understand it. She thought maybe it was because his brother had been killed the month before in Viet Nam.

The next day, Molly had black eyes, a swollen nose, and bruises on her face and stomach. Jim said he was sorry, but added that if she had reminded him to buy her something for Christmas, it wouldn't have happened. He made her put makeup on her face so he wouldn't have to look at the bruises, and while she was doing that, he fixed the tree. But Molly hid the presents, for fear of making him angry again. For the next few weeks, Molly just felt numb, realizing that Jim had hit her. She'd go up to the attic and sit staring out of the window for hours. They had an income and a house. This is when things were supposed to be getting better.

FIRST IMPRESSIONS

Molly's initial impressions of Jim were similar to those reported by the majority of women in the homicide group about their mates. Women noted that these men were, in the first weeks and months they knew them, the most romantic and attentive lovers they'd ever had. Such characteristics as early and intense interest; a constant concern with the woman's whereabouts and activities; a desire to be with them all the time; wanting to do everything together, often alone; and major changes in the men's life-styles were mentioned over and over again. The women remembered that the men showed a particularly intense concern with what they were thinking and feeling, watching them closely and responding strongly to any perceived shifts; and this the women also saw as evidence of sensitivity and love.

The women often perceived these men as unusually communicative and open as well; the men's need for an early commitment and their expressed fears of being hurt seemed endearingly honest and vulnerable. In the early stages of a relationship, with all the attendant insecurities and unknowns, neediness can be a charming quality in a partner. A man who wants you so would never turn around and leave you; a man who cares so deeply and is so aware of your moods seems unlikely to later treat you badly.

One woman, raised in an abusive family, remembered that her partner was "a wonderful man" when she first met him, "very observant and gentlemanly." She did know he "liked women" and that he was used to "stepping out"; she caught him in an affair once and nearly left him. But he was so sorry and so charming; his intensity over her convinced her she was really the one he cared for. He pressed her to move in with him, and then to marry him, and she felt they had worked through their problems. In those early days, he laughed easily and drank lightly; it was three years before she realized he was an alcoholic. His temper started to change in the second year: You could say one thing and he would laugh at it, and then later become angry over the same thing. She learned that much of the time he was lying to her about his past and his activities; he quit his job two months before she found out he wasn't going to work. The third year they were married he began "dating"; the physical abuse started soon after.

Even with some indications of prior trouble, women often believed the men had changed, and they made their commitment to the men as they were when they met them.

. . .

Early Warnings

. . . Typically—in 72 percent to 77 percent of the cases—violence occurs only after a couple has become seriously involved, is engaged, or is living together; rather than in the early, more casual stages of dating. Victims have difficulty interpreting assaultive behavior from someone they thought they knew so well. Violent episodes are attributed to specific circumstances (or even to love . . .), and the relationships continue despite the outburst. Although many respondents report that their relationships worsened or terminated after the violence, in 26 percent to 37 percent of the cases, respondents report that their relationships "improved" or became more committed after an assault. (It is interesting to note that, in at least one study, men were twice as likely as women to say that their relationships improved after the use of violence, whereas women were more likely to say the relationships deteriorated.) The longer the couple is involved and the more serious their commitment, the more likely they are to remain together after a physical attack.

It is sometimes difficult to separate the warning signs of future violence from more typical romantic interactions. Couples newly in love do think primarily of one another, want to spend time together and, in the process, often isolate themselves from other acquaintances. Verbal expressions are intense and emotions easily triggered. Since our romantic tradition is based on gender stereotypes and premises of possession, characteristics of a partner that suggest a potential for future violence are often hidden within behaviors culturally sanctioned as appropriate for men who are in love. A clustering of these behaviors, however, particularly in the areas of intrusion and possessive control, should be carefully evaluated for the history that might underlie their outward expressions.

Intrusion

Many of the behaviors that women in the homicide group initially thought so romantic, over time became the triggers that led to their assault. The men's constant desire to know their whereabouts, for example—which at first made the women feel missed and cared for—stiffened into a requirement that they account for every hour and led to violent reprisals when their partners were not satisfied with their explanations. Women reported being followed to work or to friends' houses, constant phone calls to make sure they were where they said they would be, and sudden appearances to check up on them. The early interest in their activities became confounded with suspicion and distrust, and arriving home a few minutes late could mean a beating.

Isolation

This need for constant knowledge of the woman's whereabouts, combined with a preference for not letting the woman interact with people other than themselves, led in most cases to severe restrictions of the women's activities, especially once a commitment had been established. Men in the homicide group cut their partners off from friends and family, refused to let them work outside the home, and treated activities the women wanted to pursue without them as a personal affront. There had usually been some indication of this tendency to isolate the woman from outside contacts in the early days of the relationships: Women remembered that their partners had often not wanted them around their friends and had shown little interest in, or even expressed jealousy of, the women's friends. In the first stages of the relationships, however, this unwillingness to be a part of a larger network had gone unnoticed in the intensity of being together. Such isolation left the women at great risk once the abuse began, reducing their resources and the chance that others would be aware of their plight or intervene.

Possession

The dynamics of touch and intimacy also changed for these women, from the gentle but persistent persuasion reported as characteristic of the early experiences with the abusers to forceful possession without regard for the women's wishes or well-being. For many women in the homicide group, physical intimacy changed from a joy to the most threatening part of the relationship. They found they were unable to predict when lovemaking would be affectionate and when assaultive; consequently, they felt at risk any time intimate contact was initiated. Now women remembered that, even in the good days, there had been something determined about the way the man guided them through a room at a party or indicated by touch that they were his. In the early days of courtship, this had seemed more protective than controlling.

That the women should be confused about the meanings of touch is not surprising. Possession is an accepted part of romantic interactions between men and women, and many of these behaviors would be hard to distinguish from more normal ways of relating until they began to degenerate over time. In our present culture, even the violent forcing of physical intimacy is frequently seen as an indication of true love: In the popular genre of Harlequin romance novels, for instance, dashing "heros" tear women's clothing and leave bruises on the bodies, thus alerting the reader that they really love them and will probably marry them by the end of the tale. Ironically, such unions are presented as stroke of immense good fortune for the women involved: Marriage to an assaultive man *is* the "happy ending" to the story.

Jealousy

Another factor woven throughout our tradition of romantic love is the expression of jealousy. From the "chivalry" of dueling to folklore and ballads about crimes of passion, jealousy has been used not only as a yardstick by which to gauge affection, but as a justification for violence. In the homicide group, the men's tendencies toward extremes of jealousy were often masked by an initial emphasis on the positive dimensions of being along, or were only implicit in their constant inquiries about the women's activities and thoughts. Yet all the women reported that this became a serious problem in their relationships with their abusers. Many violent incidents were triggered by a partner's jealous rage and, in almost all cases, the men's jealous suspicions far exceeded all bounds of possibility by the end of the relationships.

Prone to Anger

Reports of women in both the homicide and comparison groups suggest other warning signs, less confounded with our concepts of romantic love, although still supported by cultural stereotypes for male behavior. Even before their partners became physically assaultive, the women noticed that many of these men seemed easily angered. Their mood could change from laughter to fury without warning, and what might set them off was hard to predict. More importantly, this anger was often completely out of proportion to the circumstance that occasioned it, and it was this pattern that later left women victims of violent attacks for something so minor as forgetting to turn off the oven or leaving the checkbook in the car.

Early outbursts of violence were frequently directed at objects or against pets, rather than against persons. Women reported watching their men rip pictures off walls or smash furniture, when the reasons for their distress were not exactly clear. An aggressive approach to life was frequently displayed in driving behavior as well. Women recounted occasions of recklessness in which the men seemed to deliberately put both their lives in danger, and reported them deliberately running into things such as stop signs or parked cars, or using the car as a weapon or threat. These behaviors demonstrate a man's willingness to do damage. . . .

Unknown Pasts

Many of the women knew almost nothing about the pasts of their men when they first became involved with them, or even at the point at which they made major commitments. Most had spent relatively little time with their partner's friends early in the relationship and few had mutual acquaintances who knew the man well. Thus, their impressions were based almost exclusively on their own interactions and on the sides of the man they were allowed to see. The women were often so blinded by the men's intense interest and desire to know about *their* pasts that they didn't notice how little they knew about the men's.

Such knowledge might have helped them. The majority of men in the homicide group had a history of violent interactions, if not with prior female partners, then with peers or family members. . . .

While other warning signs may be hard to separate from more typical romantic interactions, a prior history of violence is a factor that should not be ignored. Even if prior assaults were not directed at female partners, it is very hard to keep repeated violence compartmentalized in one area of one's life. . . .

. . .

Women's Responses to Early Assaults

Women reacted to initial assaults with shock and disbelief; sometimes attempting to discuss the incidents with their partners, often withdrawing into silence and confusion and attempting to avoid any further confrontations while they thought it out on their own. As one woman, who had not had any exposure to physical abuse prior to her marriage, described the sequence of shock and denial: "You wonder if it's something wrong with you that is causing him to behave this way; what the fact that your partner is violent with you says about you. You tell yourself things might be better if he wasn't so unhappy at his job, if you lived in another house, if you weren't working, or if you were. You begin to question if it really is as bad as you are making it out; if you're exaggerating, if you're going crazy. You wonder if anyone would believe you if you told them. But you keep it all inside, so you never do find out how others might judge the situation if they knew. Sometimes you wonder if it ever happened. In an odd way, you attempt to protect your sanity by denying your own reality."

Most women in the homicide group did not attempt to seek help after the first incidents of violence—or refused outside intervention if it was offered—as a result of their shock, confusion, and shame. Again, this is typical of women's reactions to assault by their intimate partners. A few women attempted to leave the men after the onset of violence.... However, most of these women were talked into returning by the men's assurances that the violence would not occur again, and by their own sense that they should give the relationship another chance. In some cases, even when women made serious escape attempts, the very sources they turned to for help persuaded them to return.

* * *

NOTE

1. In *Love and Violence: Gender Paradoxes in Volatile Attachments,* 29 FAMILY PROCESS 343 (1990), the authors, Virginia Goldner, Peggy Penn, Marcia Sheinberg and Gillian Walker, report on a study growing out of their couples counseling with partners whose relationships were marked by violence, but who expressed a desire to stay together. These individuals, in other words, wanted to end the violence in their relationships, but not to end the relationships themselves. Many have been critical of using couples counseling in the context of domestic violence, fearing for the safety of the abused partner, and doubting that the process can be a productive one in the presence of such a disparity of power between the two individuals. The authors of this study felt that with appropriate safeguards, and within a framework in which the abusive partner was asked to take responsibility for his violence, useful work could be done.

As they explored the violent relationships of their clients, they came to understand them as deeply influenced by the assumptions the partners brought to the relationship about gender, and the tensions associated with the partners' contradictory needs to meet traditional expectations associated with their gender, on the one hand, and escape the straightjackets imposed by those expectations, on the other. Among the issues they explore is the one we are discussing here—why it is that women form emotional attachments to violent men, and sometimes have difficulty severing those attachments, even when the relationships become highly dangerous.

Virginia Goldner et al.
Love and Violence: Gender Paradoxes in Volatile Attachments, 29 Family Process 343, 356–57, 359–61 (1990)

The mysterious "stickiness" of these relationships was all the more intriguing when we discovered that these women, contrary to what we had imagined, were not timid, self-deprecating, fragile victims. They were victims, but they were, in nearly every case, women of substance who had strong opinions and conveyed a sense of personal power. . . .

Our thinking owes much to the revisionist theories of female development and psychology that have become increasingly influential in recent years. . . . The central tenet in all the new work about women is the idea that women form a sense of self, of self-worth, and of feminine identity through their ability to build and maintain relationships with others. This imperative is passed to daughters from mothers whose view of feminine obligation has been to preserve both family relationships and the family as a whole, no matter what the personal cost. Thus, the daughter, like her mother, eventually comes to measure her self-esteem by the success or failure of her attempts to connect, form relationships, provide care, "reach" the other person.

Sarah, who as a child was beaten (as was her mother) by an alcoholic father, and who now is being battered by her husband Mike, put it like this: "From the time that Mike and I got involved, I got the sense that he was like a hurt child. I felt the best way of working on our relationship was to try to build him up and make him feel better about himself." Thus, even in the context of her own victimization, Sarah, against her own best interests, can humanize her abuser and devote herself to his care.

With this idea alone we have the beginning of a positive re-description of the meanings of staying in a bad relationship. For Sarah or women like her, staying put is not about weak character, morbid dependency, or masochism, but is better understood as an affirmation of the feminine ideal: to hold connections together, to heal and care for another, no matter what the personal cost. . . .

Put another way, staying protects the woman against the guilt engendered by giving up her caretaking role. More specifically, since women learn to be acutely attuned to the needs of others, their gendered capacity for empathy gives them a subliminal knowledge of the batterer's fragile dependency. Often this means they cannot escape the feeling that in leaving they betrayed the terms of the relationship.

. . . Thus, a woman who walks out must contend with the meanings and consequences of having claimed the male prerogative of putting herself first.

. . .

It has been hard to assume that the irrationality of violence has its reasons and that those reasons are powerful enough to hold a couple together in a sometimes fatal attraction. But to react only to the violent "face" of the behavior without viewing its other face, the face of atonement and redemption, is to deny the power of the bond that fully possesses the couple. In the wake of the irrefutable logic that compels the couple to separate, the next wave of that logic breaks, and they are caught in the powerful tides of reaffiliation. This redemptive moment in the couple's cycle, which we are calling "the alliance," is as complexly structured as the violent tide that produced it. Both parts of this cycle must be deconstructed, their elements unpacked and critiqued, if the violence is to stop.

The alliance is a unique aspect of the couple's relationship because it acts to sustain and preserve reconnection after a violent rupture has occurred. It is experienced by both partners as a bond; but, since it is a bond termed by others as shameful, sick, and regressive, it remains a secret, hidden from the world.

. . .

The life stories of these men and women, his and hers, are narratives filled with pain and disappointment. Yet, when the couple tells the story of their relationship, especially how it began, the cloud lifts. It is as though an electrical connection had been made between them, a bond that keeps them attached despite the crazy violence.

Initially, and implicitly, the couple's bond is positioned against their families of origin and against the world at large. Tracing the history of this theme through the reconstructions of both partners led us to speculate that each of them was looking for a magical rescue from the loyalty binds and gender injunctions they experienced in their original families. They were looking for a deus ex machina, and, like many of us, they found it in the extravagent illusions of romantic love. Each partner believed that they had found a perfect match, and together they formed a complementary, reparative bond premised on the fantasy of a yin/yang "fit" between them.

For our purposes, the most intriguing aspect of their initial attraction was the way in which it seemd to represent, at least in part, an attempt to escape the rigid strictures of gender conformity that had been enforced by their families of origin. For the men who had to deny or suppress any sign of need or vulnerability, the relationship represented the chance to reclaim these affects without dishonor. As one man put it, "Alice accepts my weaknesses and my sensitivity. With my mother, I had to be always strong, never weak." And, for the women who were raised to submit and be silent, the relationship gave early dignity to their voice. In Sarah's words, "Mike respects by opinion as no one else has."

. . .

It should be no surprise that this bond, premised on the hope that love can provide reparation for the injuries of the past and freedom from the constraints of the culture, cannot survive the ordinary insults of daily life. A reparative experience is inherently a critique that cannot be sustained. In this case, it is a challenge to family loyalty and to conventional gender dichotomies.

With regard to gender, insofar as the bond is based on an acknowledgement of repressed similarities, the very desire to loosen gender-incongruent prohibitions pushes the man toward an intolerable feeling of similarity to the woman. Eventually, this collapse of difference will become too compromising, and he will have to reassert his masculine difference from her by becoming menacing or even violent.

* * *

D. THE IMPACT OF ABUSE

Harway, in the article excerpted above, was careful to distinguish between what women bring to a relationship with an abusive partner, and the emotional damage that may be inflicted over the course of that relationship. Again, Lenore Walker was an enormously influential early contributor to research, and reporting, on the impact of abuse; coining both the psychosocial construct of "learned helplessness," and the related diagnostic category of "battered woman syndrome." Walker has used the theory of learned helplessness to help explain the psychological component of battered women's inability to leave their relationships, and this application has proved very important in many battered women's self-defense cases. Why so? Chiefly because it has offered judges and juries an explanation of how the violence can have been as bad as the woman says it was, and how her fear of the batterer could be justified to the point of her using deadly force against him, even though she has been in the relationship for some period of time, and there is no recent evidence of her trying to end it.

Without denying the potential for abuse to leave emotional scars, Edward Gondolf, in the work excerpted below, suggests the dangers involved in imagining that all battered women respond in similar ways to abuse, and counteracts the stereotype of the "helpless" battered women by documenting the strength and resilience that many victims of abuse bring to their situations. He also asks society to look at the way it responds to victims, and ask some hard questions about whether women who seem trapped in violent relationships are trapped by their own lack of resources, or by the failure of helping institutions and professions to meet them half way in their efforts to free themselves from violence.

In her most recent work, Lenore Walker responds to her critics. The final excerpt in this section captures the flavor of this response.

Survivor Theory
Edward Gondolf, with Ellen Fisher, Battered Women as Survivors: An Alternative to Treating Learned Helplessness, 11–22 (1988)

re-examines theory of learned helplessness

Our assertion that battered women are active survivors raises a fundamental theoretical issue. It appears to contradict the prevailing characterization that battered women suffer from learned helplessness. According to learned helplessness, battered women tend to "give up" in the course of being abused; they suffer psychological paralysis and an underlying masochism that needs to be treated by specialized therapy. Our survivor hypothesis, on the other hand, suggests that women respond to abuse with helpseeking efforts that are largely unmet. What the women most need are the resources and social support that would enable them to become more independent and leave the batterer. . . .

In this chapter, we examine in more detail the theoretical basis for these two contrasting characterizations of battered women. First, the assumptions of learned helplessness are discussed. We consider also the experimental research underlying learned helplessness and its application to battered women. Second, we present the basis of a survivor theory with an overview of our survivor hypothesis, a summary of the supportive empirical research, and a redefinition of the symptoms of learned helplessness.

. . .

Learned Helplessness

The Prevailing Characterization

The battered woman has been typically characterized as a helpless and passive victim. Lenore Walker's ground-breaking book, *The Battered Woman* (1979), noted that the battered woman becomes "psychologically paralyzed" as a result of learned helplessness. As animal experiments have demonstrated, there is a tendency to become submissive in the face of intermittent punishments or abuse. Similarly, the battered woman is immobilized amidst the uncertainty of when abuse will occur. She begins to feel that she has no control over her experience. No matter what she does, she "gets it." In the process, the victim begins to blame herself for the abuse. This self-blame implies some recourse or control over the otherwise unpredictable abuse. "If only I change myself, then the abuse will stop."

. . .

Battered women, therefore, appear to need specialized counseling to address their debilitated psychological state. A number of clinical studies have in fact, prescribed treatment for the battered woman's lack of self-esteem and fragmented identity . . . , feelings of loss and inadequacy . . . , or isolation and anxiety that is traced to abuse as a child. . . . Feminist critics, however, have strongly objected to the implication that battered women provoke or prolong abuse and generally require psychological counseling. . . .

The Experimental Basis

The prevailing notion of learned helplessness is drawn from the extensive laboratory research of Martin Seligman of the University of Pennsylvania. . . . During the late sixties, Dr. Seligman led a team of researchers experimenting with dogs in studies that would raise the ire of today's animal rights activist. The animals, after a series of intermittent electric shocks, eventually became immobilized. They would not escape from their cages even when an open route was provided for them. There is even evidence that this learned helplessness could immobilize a victim to the point of death.

. . . Since then, the notion of learned helplessness has gained a broad currency. Seligman alluded to prisoners of war, political prisoners, concentration camp detainees, and institutionalized patients as vulnerable to learned helplessness. Learned helplessness has also been used to explain the low motivation among some welfare recipients, the fatalism evident among many Third World peasants, and the persistent economic failure of some industrial towns....

Explanations of Battered Women

It is not surprising, then, that the notion of learned helplessness has become a fixture in the domestic field as well. Battered women, as the theory goes, typically are conditioned to tolerate the abuse as a result of persistent and intermittent reinforcement from the batterer. The community lack of response to the abuse, and frequent accusation that the woman contributed to the abuse, further the helplessness. The cage door is shut, so to speak, and the women have no apparent way out.

Additionally, studies have suggested that learned helplessness may be rooted in childhood exposure to violence. Exposure to violence as a child may, in fact, predispose a woman to an abusive relationship as an adult.... She may grow up thinking that abuse is normal, or feel such shame and rejection that she expects and accepts the worst. The relationship between abuse as a child and as an adult may, however, be spurious or inevitable given the amount of violence in and around our homes.... Perhaps a more acceptable position is that the batterers appear to be "violence prone," and not battered women....

Another popular explanation for what appears as learned helplessness is the "brainwashing" that a woman experiences in an abusive relationship as an adult. The batterer's manipulation and control of the woman has, in fact, been likened to the tactics used by brainwashers in prisoner-of-war camps. Eventually the captive is psychologically broken down to the point of relinquishing any sense of autonomy and complying to all the wishes of the captor.

Psychologist Donald Dutton and Susan Painter ... have similarly applied the theory of "traumatic bonding" to battered women. They point out that the abuse leaves the victim emotionally and physically drained and in desperate need of some human support or care. She is therefore likely to respond to the batterer's apologies and affection after the abuse. In this vulnerable state, she may sympathize and overidentify with the batterer, much as some prisoners of war or concentration camps have become sympathetic toward their guards. In essence, the trauma makes the woman prone to a kind of masochism.

Helplessness as Masochism

Although the initial application of learned helplessness to battered women was not intended to implicate masochism, it has been explicitly extended to do so. Several clinicians have viewed women's inclination to stay in violent relationships as evidence of their desire for abuse.... These "experts" suggest that there is some emotional or existential exhilaration in being a victim. That is, women look for trouble and bring some of it on themselves. Some victims simply don't feel like they deserve any better and are not satisfied until that self-perception is fulfilled.

The legacy of Freud, in particular, has much of the psychology field still asserting that women are predisposed to masochism. As Barbara Ehrenreich and Deirdre English (1979) wrote in their book, *For Her Own Good: 150 Years of the Experts' Advice to Women*, the psychoanalytic view has shaped the medical and psychological treatment of women with mounting acceptance. In this view, women innately tolerate and even welcome more pain than men, in part because of their destiny to receive forceful penetration during sexual intercourse. . . . Also, women's aggressions are turned inward and expressed in self-blame and shame, because society limits their outward expression.

Natalie Shainess . . . revises and extends the psychoanalytic notion of masochism to contemporary women. She insists that women contribute to their victimization by acting indecisive and vulnerable. She describes what she terms the "masochistic personality" of women who tend to seek out and exacerbate their abuse.

Dr. Shainess . . . argues, in fact, that learned helplessness is really another term for masochism. . . . In Shainess's conception, however, masochism is learned developmentally and culturally, rather than predestined as the Freudians suggest. This may in part be related to growing up in abusive homes and thinking, as a result, that abuse is normal, or to internalizing the persistent subjugation and degradation of women in society at large. The masochism can be unlearned, therefore, by being more assertive and decisive in interpersonal relations. . . .

Reformulations of Helplessness

The learned helplessness theory has admittedly been critiqued and reformulated in recent years. . . . Its earlier versions reflected the assumptions of behaviorist conditioning. Like the animals in Seligman's experiments, humans appeared to be "trained" into submission and learned helplessness. Their situation appeared to determine their behavior. In sum, learned helplessness was a conditioned reaction to the unpredictable punishments one received.

The advent of cognitive psychology has introduced the role of individual expectations and attributions in mediating learned helplessness. . . . In this view, one's *perceptions* of the environment are what most influence one's reaction to it. If an individual perceives a series of punishments or failures as outside of his or her control, then learned helplessness is more likely.

Similarly, several qualitative studies of battered women have shown that their assumptions about their social environment contribute to their reactions to abuse. . . . However, rather than confirm learned helplessness, these studies actually open the door to alternative explanations. The women, rather than being passive recipients of the violence, appear instead as participants in the definition of the relationship and of themselves. If anything, the battered women *learn*, as the abuse escalates, that the self-blame associated with learned helplessness is inappropriate.

Interviews with self-identified battered women show that the women are more likely to blame themselves for the abuse after the first incident.... Consequently they may attempt to change their behavior to please their batterers and avoid further abuse. As is usually the case, the violence recurs and escalates despite the women's efforts to please their batterers. They begin, therefore, to increasingly blame the batterer (that is, attribute the cause to him) and seek ways to change him. When these fail, the women then seek more decisive intervention and means to establish their own safety.

There is some suggestion, however, that there is a limit to this initiative. After repeated unsuccessful attempts to control the battering, some women may then begin to give up and lessen their helpseeking.... This resignation, after an intermediate phase of active helpseeking, differs from the conventional notion of learned helplessness in which there is a progression toward total brainwashing....

Another interview study ..., with a small sample of shelter residents, suggests that the women experience a loss of self; for example, they mention feeling like a zombie, a robot, or simply numb amidst the violence. They begin to lose their "observing self" as well, in that they doubt and question their judgment and interpretation of events. However, the battered women continue to have "insights" about their relationship and their batterers' definition of the situation. They occasionally act on these insights by seeking verification of or response to them. The women also creatively and valiantly develop coping strategies intended to reduce the severity of the abuse. Eventually, with sufficient confirmation of the insights, they begin to define themselves as "survivors,"—as individuals who are aware of their strength in enduring the abuse. They muster self-respect for that endurance and attempt to improve their situation.

This shift in perception begins to occur after any one of a variety of catalysts: a change in the level of violence, a change in resources, a change in the relationship, severe despair, a change in the visibility of the violence, and external interventions that redefine the relationship. Any of these [may] prompt a rejection of the previous rationalizations or denials of abuse....

Not only are the women's perceptions seen as basic to their reaction, these perceptions also evolve and change. In fact, the tentative findings suggest that battered women are rational in their response. They hold to societal conceptions of their duty in a relationship until that conception is no longer plausible. The catalysts for change are not "treatment" of the symptoms of learned helplessness but rather a change in situational evidence or events that necessitates an adjustment in one's perceptions and attribution. As has been argued about other oppressed or victimized people, the women's "grievance" has to be confirmed ... and resources made available ... in order for them to become "mobilized."

Toward a Survivor Theory

The Survivor Hypothesis

The alternative characterization of battered women is that they are active survivors rather than helpless victims.... As suggested above, battered women remain in abusive situations not because they have been passive but because they have tried to escape with no avail. We offer, therefore, a survivor hypothesis that contradicts the assumptions of learned helplessness: Battered women increase their helpseeking in the face of increased violence, rather than decrease helpseeking as learned helplessness would suggest. More specifically, we contend that helpseeking is likely to increase as wife abuse, child abuse, and the batterer's antisocial behavior (substance abuse, general violence, and arrests) increase. This helpseeking may be mediated, as current research suggests, by the resources available to the woman, her commitment to the relationship, the number of children she has, and the kinds of abuse she may have experienced as a child.

The fundamental assumption is, however, that women seek assistance in proportion to the realization that they and their children are more and more in danger. They are attempting, in a very logical fashion, to assure themselves and their children protection and therefore survival. Their effort to survive transcends even fearsome danger, depression or guilt, and economic constraints. It supersedes the "giving up and giving in" which occurs according to learned helplessness. In this effort to survive, battered women are, in fact, heroically assertive and persistent.

Empirical Research

There are at least a few empirical studies that substantiate this hypothesis that battered women are survivors. The studies by Lee Bowker (1983), Mildred Pagelow (1981), and Lenore Walker (1984) indicate quantitatively that the helpseeking efforts of battered women are substantial.

Perhaps the most significant of these empirical works is Walker's *The Battered Women's Syndrome* (1984), designed to verify the author's original learned helplessness and "cycle of violence" theorization. Walker found, however, that the women in her Rocky Mountain sample were not necessarily beaten into submissiveness; rather, helpseeking increased as the positive reinforcements within the relationship decreased and the costs of the relationship in terms of abusiveness and injury increased. . . .

Furthermore, the battered women in the Walker sample did not score significantly lower on psychological tests for the externalized control, weak self-esteem, or depression associated with learned helplessness than did a control group of women not in abusive relationships. . . .

The Myth of Masochism

The implications of female masochism raised with learned helplessness have been similarly challenged. As the empirical studies suggest, battered women do not appear to be "victim prone." Women contribute to the violence only in the fact that they are female. . . .

Furthermore, it is highly debatable that assertiveness and carefulness in themselves can lessen one's vulnerability. Numerous studies have shown that male violence is for the most part indiscriminate and unpredictable. Gloria Steinem . . . poignantly alludes to this in reevaluating the severely abused porno star, Linda Lovelace. She likens looking for some predisposition or inclination for abuse to asking, "What in your background led you to a concentration camp?"

The reinforcements for male violence against women ... supersede women's efforts to resist or avoid abuse. There is a social system of patriarchy that denies women a way out. To be the autonomous person, which Shainess ... prescribes as an antidote to masochism, requires financial support, job training, dependable child care, adequate housing, and personal transportation that are not available to the majority of battered women—or women in general, for that matter.

The notion of female masochism focuses on deficiencies in the women and may be responsible for the research preoccupation with why women stay with their batterers....

In light of the feminist challenge to female masochism, the more appropriate question may be "Why do so many men get away with woman battering?"....

The Female Survivor Instinct

How then do we explain the survivor tendency of battered women? Anthropologists have long argued that females have an instinctual tendency to attempt to preserve life through their nurturing and cooperative habits.... According to the biological determinist view, these characteristics are rooted in the physiological differences that enable females to bear children and the more muscular male to hunt game for the family or fight to defend it. Sociologists, on the other hand, see the differences reinforced, if not generated, by the social roles ascribed to women as domestic servants and men as public servants....

Some modern feminists have redefined the biological determinism of the past in their rendition of social biology. They argue, rather impressively, that the woman's unique capacity for birthing and mothering has given women an appreciation for life that men can only emulate. Menstruation and other bodily changes, furthermore, link women with "nature" in ways that broaden their conceptions of the world. In other words, the female worldview is more in touch with life processes and reveres them more. It is consequently more global, inclusive, and harmonizing.

Feminist psychologists have asserted the moral superiority of this female reasoning process as well. Mainstream psychology, according to the feminists, has evaluated the female experience as deficient because it has assessed women with a male norm. Most notably, Carol Gilligan (1982), in her revision of developmental psychology *In a Different Voice*, identifies the female tendency to resound to moral issues with collaborative and accommodating solutions, as opposed to the more competitive and discriminating solutions of males. Women value most their personal relationships, rather than the instrumental ends that appear to preoccupy men in an "ends justify the means" mentality.

. . .

Self-transcendence in Helpseeking

These assertions about women survivors may reflect a more fundamental philosophical assumption about human nature in general. The survivor tendency we see in battered women is more than self-assertion, self-actualization, or self-determination.... An inner strength, yearning for dignity, desire for good, or will to live appears despite one's previous conditioning and present circumstances. Even in the midst of severe psychological impairment, such as depression, many battered women seek help, adapt, and push on. This is not to say that we should expect battered women, or other survivors of misfortune, to bounce back on their own. Rather, by receiving the proper supports, one's inner strength can be realized, resiliency demonstrated, and a new life made.

This process is one that must be supported by helpers rather than invoked by them. This is accomplished by what some call a reflexive approach; that is, helpers accentuate the potential for self-transcendence in others by displaying it in themselves. The challenge is, therefore, for helpers to express resiliency, determination, and optimism, rather than succumb to the learned helplessness of so many bureaucratized help sources. As a result, so-called clients are more likely to discover and express their own resiliency.... It is a matter of community building—that is, creating a place where positive role models promote mutual support.

Shelters have afforded one of the most promising experiments in this regard. Women and children, by virtue of their circumstances, are joined in a kind of intentional community where not only emotions and experiences are shared but also the common tasks of daily life. The "muddling with the mundane" in the communal living arrangements of shelters—the negotiating and even haggling over food, shelter, and children—potentially teaches much in itself.... If managed effectively, shelter life may encourage women to assert themselves in new ways, clarify issues and fears, and collaborate with other women in need. In the process, the intimidating isolation that so many battered women experience is broken and an internal fortitude released.

Redefining the Symptoms

This is not to deny the observations of shelter workers that some battered women do experience severe low self-esteem, guilt, self-blame, depression, vulnerability, and futility—all of which are identified with learned helplessness. Some battered women may even appear to act carelessly and provocatively at times, as the proponents of masochism argue. But cast in another light, these "symptoms" take on a different meaning, as well as a different proportion.

The so-called symptoms of learned helplessness may in fact be part of the adjustment to active helpseeking. They may represent traumatic shock from the abuse, a sense of commitment to the batterer, or separation anxiety amidst an unresponsive community. All of these are quite natural and healthy responses.... Not to respond with some doubts, anxiety, or depression would suggest emotional superficiality and denial of the real difficulties faced in helpseeking.

First, the symptoms of learned helplessness may be a temporary manifestation of *traumatic shock*. Many of the women arriving at shelters have suffered severe physical abuse equivalent to what one might experience in a severe auto accident. What appears as physical unresponsiveness or psychological depression may therefore be more an effort of the body and mind to help themselves. The women, rather than being passive and withdrawn personalities, are going through a necessary healing process. They need not so much psychotherapy as time and space to recuperate.

Second, the symptoms may reflect an effort by battered women to *save the relationship*. Seeking help represents, in some sense, an admission of failure to fulfill the traditional female role of nurturing and domesticity. It appears to some women, too, as a breach of the marriage vow to love and honor one's spouse. As several of the interview studies show . . . , battered women do initially blame themselves for not being nurturing, supportive, or loving enough to make the marriage work. It is important, however, to distinguish this initial sense of failure from the sense of an uncontrollable universe which underlies learned helplessness. . . .

Third, the depression and guilt in some shelter women . . . may be an expression of *separation anxiety* that understandably accompanies leaving the batterer. The women face tremendous uncertainty in separating even temporarily from the batterer. They fear reprisals for leaving, loss of custody of the children, and losing their home and financial support. The unknown of trying to survive on one's own can be as frightening as returning to a violent man. The prospects of obtaining employment sufficient to support oneself and children are minimal for most shelter women, especially considering their lack of previous experience and education. This coupled with the feminization of poverty in contemporary America . . . makes a return to the batterer the lesser of the two evils. At least there is a faint hope that the batterer will change, whereas the prospects for change in the larger community seem less favorable.

Treating the Helpers

Helplessness among Helpers

In sum, many battered women make contact with a variety of helping sources in response to their abuse. As the abuse becomes more severe and the batterer more apparently beyond change, the diversity of the woman's contacts actually increases. We argue that this represents a survivor tendency of strength and resiliency. Depression, guilt, and shame may accompany a battered woman, but these should not be used to characterize battered women in general or to label them as victims of learned helplessness.

The prevailing notion of learned helplessness may, in fact, be misleading. Learned helplessness suggests that it is the woman who needs to be diagnosed and treated. Admittedly, some women do need tremendous emotional support and mental health care in the wake of devastating abuse.

However, we believe that there is a more important side to consider: the insufficient response of community help sources.

* * *

NOTE

1. The debate about the usefulness of "battered woman syndrome" and "learned helplessness" as labels for how women are affected by abuse continued in CURRENT CONTROVERSIES ON FAMILY VIOLENCE (R.J.Gelles and D.R. Loseke, eds. 1993), with researcher Lee Bowker taking the position that "A Battered Woman's Problems are Social, Not Psychological" (pp. 154–65), and Lenore Walker defending the position that the "The Battered Woman Syndrome Is a Psychological Consequence of Abuse" (pp. 133–53). In her contribution, Lenore Walker argued that:

> (a) the syndrome is part of a recognized pattern of psychological symptoms called *post-traumatic stress disorder* (PTSD) reported in the psychological literature to be produced by repeated exposure to trauma such as the physical, sexual, and/or serious psychological assault experienced by battered women; (b) the syndrome is consistent with feminist theoretical explanations of abuse of women; (c) the syndrome is useful in developing appropriate intervention programs that assist battered women to recover from their victimization; and (d) the syndrome is accepted by others who can offer battered women assistance, such as those in the medical, psychological, and legal communities.
>
> The alternative argument . . . seems to deny that a woman may be psychologically affected in a particular and recognizable way by the abuse she experiences, that she may adopt certain psychological symptoms that assist her in coping with the "crazy-making" situation she experiences, and that she may be unable to cease using these coping strategies even when they are no longer useful. The point of view [adopted by Walker] recognizes these coping strategies as part of the clinical symptoms observed in BWS [battered woman syndrome], which is a legitimate psychological construct that can affect different women in different ways, depending upon a particular woman's previous exposure to other oppressors, mental health status, available support systems, frequency and severity of the abuse, and a quality best described as "hardiness" of the individual woman.
>
> As with many other clinical syndromes, all symptoms are not observable in all situations, and many are evident only under certain kinds of stress. Some symptoms are more likely to be potentiated when battering interacts with other forms of oppression, such as racism, poverty, homophobia, physical debility, or other mental illnesses. It is easy to confuse a clinical syndrome with theoretical explanations for the dynamics of abuse, such as the cycle theory of violence and the psychosocial construct of learned helplessness, both of which can precipitate coping strategies that are then labeled as clinical responses by psychologists. Although some find this labeling process stigmatizing

> and unhelpful, I would argue that placing the psychological impact from abuse into the context of other stress responses actually avoids the typical victim blaming that frequently blocks women from receiving appropriate community assistance.

Lenore Walker, *The Battered Woman Syndrome Is a Psychological Consequence of Abuse,* CURRENT CONTROVERSIES ON FAMILY VIOLENCE 133, 133–34 (R.J. Gelles & D.R. Loseke, eds. 1993).

Walker goes on to clarify the meaning of "learned helplessness:"

> One consequence for those who develop learned helplessness is the loss of their belief that they can reliably predict that a particular response will bring about their safety. This is called a lack of response-outcome contingencies, in behavioral psychology language, and describes the loss of ability to predict normally expected contingent outcomes when a particular response is made. In the case of battered women with learned helplessness, they do not respond with total helplessness or passivity; rather, they narrow their choice of responses, opting for those that have the highest predictability of creating successful outcomes. Even if learned helplessness were another way of labeling the BWS, which it is not, the process does not suggest the alleged helplessness or inherent weakness of battered women.

Id. at 135.

In the same piece, Walker offers a contemporary definition of BWS, as a subcategory of PTSD. It will be important to compare this clinical account with the sometimes quite different definitions that emerge in legal contexts, and will be explored at other points in this text. Indeed, it could be argued that much of the disapproval directed at Walker by Gondolf, Bowker and others is unfair, to the extent that it focuses less on what she has said than on the uses, and abuses, of her work by others. While her early work may have been framed in ways that facilitated its abuse, she has certainly worked to correct misperceptions and to define her terms with increasing precision as others' responses to her work have demanded.

Lenore Walker
The Battered Woman Syndrome Is a Psychological Consequence of Abuse; Current Controversies on Family Violence 133, 138–44 (R.J. Gelles & D.R. Loseke, eds, 1993)

[Walker first explains the connection between PTSD and the "fight or flight" response to experiences of danger and fear.]

The notion that human beings systematically prepare in the particular way for "fight or flight" when feeling scared in a dangerous situation was first proposed in the early days of psychology by classic theorists such as William James. Many of the earliest psychologists attempted to measure such responses to danger and looked at the cost such preparation might have for victims' other functions. In this context, *fight* refers to the body's and mind's preparedness to take on a challenging and dangerous situation, often included in the study of the high arousal of the autonomic nervous system. Recent studies of stress and its impact on mental and physical health include the study of the effects of such high arousal on anxiety, panic disorders, phobias, hypertension, and other physiological components of stress and anxiety.... Although battered women do cope with their abuse, often protecting themselves and their families, sometimes the cost is an almost constant state of high arousal that keeps their bodies and minds running at full speed.

Flight refers to running away; physically, if possible, or mentally, when physical escape is impossible. The typical psychological flight coping responses of high avoidance of further harm and pain include depression and other often very sophisticated ways to keep the batterer as calm as possible for as long as possible. The psychological defenses or avoidance techniques of denial, minimization, repression, and dissociation ... are also avoidance coping strategies....

. . .

PTSD first appeared as a diagnostic category in the DSM–III in 1980 and was slightly revised for the DSM–III–R in 1987. For a clinician to make a BWS diagnosis, he or she must also find that the subject meets the PTSD criteria that are minimal in nature; a woman with BWS often has more than the minimum symptoms required for PTSD. A recent study of more than 4,000 trauma victims, including a large sample of battered women, found that only 4% could not be diagnosed using the present PTSD criteria.... Many of these women had been misdiagnosed with more serious personality disorders as well as separate diagnoses of depression and anxiety disorders that really were associated with the PTSD....

There are five criteria for the diagnosis of PTSD using the DSM system:

1. presence of a stressor that could cause a traumatic response (battering)
2. symptoms lasting for more than a month
3. measurable cognitive and memory changes
4. at least three measurable avoidance symptoms
5. at least two measurable arousal symptoms

The first two of these are threshold criteria; the last three are specific patterns of symptoms that correspond to the expected fight or flight trauma reaction.

Threshold criteria. First, the traumatic event must be of sufficient magnitude that it would be expected to cause similar symptoms in almost any normal person who experienced it. Second, the symptoms must last for more than one month. The first is important as it differentiates the PTSD from other diagnoses of mental illness by insisting that a normal person can develop it as a result of adaptation to survive abnormal experiences. The second category assures that someone who is having a difficult emotional reaction to a traumatic event but recovers spontaneously within four weeks will not be mislabeled as having PTSD.

Symptoms corresponding to fight or flight trauma. Cognitive and memory distortions make up the first group of symptoms listed in the PTSD criteria. *Cognitive distortions* take many forms, including difficulty in concentration and confused thinking. The insistence of the batterer that he monopolizes the woman's perceptions may result in her believing his twisting of the truth. The pessimistic thinking style of those who develop learned helplessness ... is another example of a cognitive disorder than can result in poor judgment.

. . .

Memory distortions in PTSD can take two major forms: *intrusive* memories of the trauma that frighten the woman and magnify her terror, and *partial psychogenic amnesia* that causes her to forget much of the painful experiences.... Often those battered women who have also been victims of child sexual abuse learn to dissociate from the experience to reduce their ability to feel the pain. Those who dissociate, or split their minds from their bodies, may also develop psychogenic amnesia for parts of the abuse. Although there is much discussion today in the literature concerning the role of memory acquisition, integration, and retrieval in PTSD, most clinicians ... and researchers ... document memory changes in abuse victims.

Intrusive memories can occur spontaneously, without any conscious thoughts about the abusive incidents. They often occur when the woman is quietly at rest and may cause her to engage in frenetic, hysterical types of activities or obsessive thinking to avoid the frightening spontaneous thoughts. [One researcher] found that the single factor that best predicted female alcohol and drug abusers is whether or not they were abuse victims. He suggests that the chemical substances are used by such women to continue to keep away the intrusive memories that prolong the experience of terror, abuse, and its subsequent pain. The memories can also intrude during the woman's dreams, whether they specifically reenact parts of past battering incidents or re-create her feelings of vulnerability and terror.

Some intrusive memories are so vivid that the woman believes that the abuse is reoccurring, usually reexperienced through *flashbacks* or *dissociative* experiences in BWS. It is common for a battered woman to have flashbacks to fragments of some previous abusive incidents when she senses that the batterer is about to begin another acute battering incident. This magnifies the fear and causes the woman to perceive each successive battering incident as more dangerous than if it were the first one to occur. Dissociation, or the ability to separate one's mind from the experiences of one's body, is a psychological defense mechanism that protects abuse victims from cognitively knowing the full experience of the trauma. Some liken it to a trance experience.... When the intrusive memories of the abuse become too overwhelming, the battered woman, particularly if she has also been sexually abused, if often able to dissociate from the reexperience, too. Intrusive memories may also be recognized when there is actual physiological discomfort at the memories elicited by a conditioned-like response to something that serves as a reminder to the battered woman of the abuse. . . .

High avoidance, depression, and other flight symptoms make up the second set of BWS symptoms that measure avoidance responses and numbing of feelings. They include a variety of ways of avoiding the situation, including physically leaving whenever possible and, when this is not possible, using psychological defense mechanisms, usually unconsciously, to leave the situation mentally. Most battered women are aware that leaving the man does not stop the violence. . . . Many battered women try to avoid thinking about the violence by conscious efforts not to deal with it other than by keeping the man as calm as possible as well as unconscious attempts through coping strategies such as minimization, denial, repression and dissociation. . . . Some battered women become so mentally confused that they cannot concentrate on the extent of their fears; others become obsessed about trying to reduce the probability that they will be seriously hurt. . . .

The woman with BWS demonstrates less interest in significant activities that she used to like, has begun to feel different from, and estranged from, other people, and believes that she will not live as long as others. She no longer experiences the same range of feelings as she did prior to the abuse. In some cases, a more serious depression occurs that may receive a separate clinical diagnosis. . . . As described earlier, some women use alcohol and other drugs to numb their feelings, another form of avoidance that blocks pain. In most cases these symptoms can clear up spontaneously, sometimes prior to or at the point of separation; other times, they are reduced after the woman becomes safe from the abuser. . . .

High arousal, anxiety based symptoms, and other fight symptoms make up the third set of symptoms that often develops in women trying to protect themselves from further abuse. *Sleep problems*, such as too little or too much sleep and difficulties in falling asleep and in staying asleep, are common. . . . Sometimes this pattern has been established by the batterer, who won't let [his partner] go to sleep as he forces her to pay attention to him or else he wakes the sleeping woman when he isn't sleeping. . . . *Eating problems* are also present, whether the battered woman can't eat because of the high stress or because the man actually controls what kind of food and how much of it she eats. . . .

Hypervigilance to cues of danger and *exaggerated startle response* are two other high-arousal PTSD criteria that are commonly found in battered women. . . . Sometimes they are able to use this early warning system as a signal to better protect themselves. Other times they are likely not to pay attention to it (using avoidance symptoms described earlier). . . . Both the startle response and hypervigilance to danger cues are the most resistant to change; long after the woman has found safety, she may still react with hypervigilance and startle when she is scared. . . .

Irritability and even *angry responses* by a battered woman are also included in this list of high-arousal symptoms. Some have suggested that someone with BWS must behave consistent with the stereotype of the passive and ineffective battered woman, which is not part of the criteria.... [M]any battered women do block th[eir] legitimate angry feelings so that they often come out slowly, in indirect ways, or through irritability at times when it is less dangerous to express such angry feelings....

. . .

Physiological reactivity, especially when situations remind the woman of prior violent episodes, is commonly seen in most battered women with BWS.... [One researcher] found that post-assault victims made twice as many visits to physicians as did non-victims.... Chronic pelvic pain, headache, back pain, facial pain and TMJ, gastrointestinal complaints, and chronic illnesses are all reported after abuse. These high-anxiety symptoms may also appear as panic reactions in which the woman's psychological terror is expressed in body symptoms that mimic suffocation, heart palpitations and other indications of a heart attack, and general debilitation of an emergency nature. Women who have been sexually as well as physically abused are more likely to have such serious physiological and panic reactions.

* * *

NOTES AND QUESTIONS

1. For a powerful and persuasive account of the ways in which battered women's responses to abuse parallel the responses of other trauma victims, particularly veterans of combat and prisoners of war, see Judith L. Herman TRAUMA AND RECOVERY (1992). Both Judith Herman and Mary Ann Dutton, in EMPOWERING AND HEALING THE BATTERED WOMAN (1992) offer descriptions of effective clinical interventions with battered women, of the healing process, and of how women's experiences of abuse affect their relationships with mental health providers. The extent to which there are lessons here for advocates and lawyers who serve battered women will be discussed below in Chapter 15.

2. In a more recent essay, written with Angela Browne, Edward Gondolf continues to urge those working with battered women not to overlook their strengths. The authors urge mental health clinicians to conduct a "strengths assessment" with their clients, to use the resulting inventory to assist women in applying their strengths to "difficulties and problems related to past or current abuse," and to "communicate information on the strengths of victims and survivors to other service providers or referrals as actively as clinicians now communicate information on the negative outcomes of abuse and trauma." At the same time, Gondolf and Browne acknowledge the toll that abuse takes on its victims, and the reality of both posttrauma effects and, in some cases, mental illness that is either precipitated by abuse or a chronic underlying condition. Edward Gondolf with Angela Browne, *Recognizing the Strengths of Battered Women,* ASSESSING WOMAN BATTERING IN MENTAL HEALTH SERVICES 95 (E. W. Gondolf, ed. 1998).

3. Going back to the protagonist's account of her abuse in the excerpt from Roddy Doyle's novel, above at pp. 68–74, do you think that she is

suffering from PTSD, or BWS, according to Walker's definition? What symptoms can you identify? Do they in any way undermine her credibility as a narrator? Might they undermine her credibility as a witness in a legal context?

Gender/Sexual Orientation

E. WOMEN'S VIOLENCE TOWARDS MEN

One question not yet asked is whether women abuse their male partners in the same ways that men abuse their female ones, and if so, how often, and to what extent? This is a subject of significant controversy, informed by conflicting theoretical perspectives, and conflicting interpretations of available data.

Certainly women are capable of violence in intimate and family relationships. We know that some women abuse their children, both physically and emotionally; we know that the incidence of abuse in lesbian relationships is in all probability as great as its incidence in heterosexual relationships (a topic explored in more depth in the next chapter), and we have all read the highly publicized cases in which women do violence to, or kill, their male partners. In the context of heterosexual relationships, the argument about women's capacity for violence gains intensity from the suspicion that those who accuse women are politically motivated—by the desire to minimize, or even justify, male violence, and by the desire to undermine women's claims to have used violence in self-defense. For those who see men's use of violence against their women partners as an enforcement of patriarchal norms, still to some extent socially condoned, evidence of relationships in which men are abused by women is also theoretically inconvenient.

It is possible, however, to embed male violence towards women in a larger theoretical framework that accommodates a recognition of women's violence without denying the particular susceptibility of women to male violence in a society that has traditionally been, and to some extent still is, governed by patriarchal norms. Such a larger theory would incorporate the psychological factors that drive some but not other individuals to control and abuse those with whom they are in relationship, and the cultural, political and economic factors that render certain groups, and individuals within those groups, more vulnerable to abuse (because more dependent or less socially valued, for example) than others.

Bonnie E. Carlson
Questioning the Party Line on Family Violence, 7 Affilia 94, 97–100 (1992)

Although it can be persuasively argued that much of wives' violence toward their husbands consists of justifiable fighting back, this argument explains the violent behavior only of women toward their abusive husbands. Women who are violent toward their nonviolent husbands may be as large a group as those with abusive husbands. For example, 23 percent of the respondents who admitted using violence in Straus, Gelles, and Steinmetz's (1980) national survey were wives who used violence toward nonabusive husbands. The existence of such a group was corroborated in Margolin's (1987) and Szinovacz's (1983) studies of 103 couples each. Nine wives, 14 husbands, and 18 couples in Margolin's study and 4 husbands, 14 wives and 12 couples in Szinovacz's study (both mutually exclusive counts) reported that the wives engaged in violence but the husbands did not. This violence cannot be justified by self-defense or retaliation.

Why are these women violent toward their nonviolent husbands, and does their violence constitute abuse? . . .

Setting aside the debate about gender, many scholars, researchers, and practitioners in the field of wife abuse, including those with a feminist perspective, agree that *control and power—specifically, the attempt to maintain them or compensate for the lack of them—play a central role in wife battering.* Perhaps this observation can contribute to an understanding of the instances in which women are perpetrators, not victims, of family abuse.

Interpersonal power can be defined as the ability to exert influence over other people. In the context of the family, it can be viewed as access to and control over a variety of difference kinds of resources, insofar as control over resources is a major way of influencing people. Whereas gender is one basis for personal power (some may consider it to be virtual proxy for power), it is not the only basis for power in a relationship. Other factors also influence access to resources. As [one commentator] noted: "Personal power is based on [differences in] education, income and economic security, employment skills and marketability, class, age, religious experience, physical power, [strength], health, social skills and networks." Some of these commodities may be more valued in a relationship than are others. Thus men may value physical strength more than do women, who may value superior verbal skills more. [Other commentators have] observed that "individuals in our society *inherit* [italics added] different degrees of power depending on their sex, class, race, and age. These differences are acted out in intimate relationships." However, other bases for power are *acquired* and many compensate for the lack of inherited power based on gender, class, or ethnicity. Thus a well-educated white woman from a wealthy family may have much more interpersonal power than may her black, poorly educated male partner.

There is widespread agreement that men have greater access to resources and power in the context of the family because of the history of patriarchy and the way in which this culture is structured. Furthermore, men may generally be more accustomed to expecting that they will be more powerful in a relationship than will women as a result of their sex role socialization.

However, the desire to feel powerful and to be in control is more a human than a male attribute, and between any pair of individuals in a family, resources may be distributed in such a way that gender is not the primary factor that determines who is more powerful. In parent-child and lesbian relationships, for example, power differentials also exist and may contribute (along with other factors) to abuse but do not derive from gender differences. . . .

Thus the evidence suggests that a subgroup of women use violence toward nonviolent husbands, although why they do so and the impact of the violence are unclear. That much of this violence may not be physically injurious raises several important questions: If physical injury does not result from the use of violence, is the violence acceptable or excusable? Does it constitute abuse? Must one have superior power in a relationship to be abusive? How often are wives in that position? How these questions are answered is important. Women, too, desire interpersonal power, and although gender is one basis for power in a relationship it is not the only one. Violence by wives that is not defensive is no more justified than is violence by husbands, irrespective of whether it causes injury, physical or otherwise. But this violence must be acknowledged before it can be understood. The dynamics of power may well be at the root of this violence and should be explored further. . . .

* * *

NOTES AND QUESTIONS

1. Carlson's account suggests a desire for power in a relationship that is both conscious and rational. To what extent is this inconsistent with Dutton's explanation of how men come to batter their intimate partners? Could Dutton's theory—based as it is in the early dynamics of parent-child relationships—be adapted to accommodate the possibility of a woman abusing her male partner?

2. Even if we accept Carlson's suggestion that women's violence (actual or threatened) towards men may in at least some cases be motivated by the same desire for power and control that characterizes male violence towards women, her use of statistics from the Straus, Gelles and Steinmetz 1980 survey raises a red flag. That survey, as well as the other surveys she cites, were based on the administration of a tool called the Conflict Tactics Scale, developed by Murray Straus in the late seventies. As its title suggests, the Conflict Tactics Scale assesses violence in the context of conflict, not in the context of control. Desmond Ellis and Noreen Stuckless explain the difference in the following excerpt.

Definitions
Desmond Ellis and Noreen Stuckless, Mediating and Negotiating Marital Conflicts, 1–2 (1996)

Conflict-Instigated Abuse

Conflict-instigated abuse refers to acts engaged in by male or female partners with the intention of injuring or hurting their partners, thereby resolving the conflict that motivated the intentional use of the abusive acts in the first place.

This definition builds on the one formulated by Murray Straus.... It is relevant to note that the Straus definition deals only with acts and not *injuries*. In this specific sense, it is similar to legal ... definitions of assault. The crime of assault can be injury free. Conflict-instigated abuse is always injury free because the actual infliction of injury or pain is not part of the definition, although it may imply it.

The Conflict Tactics Scale (CTS) is used as one measure of spousal abuse because conflict is associated with the process of separating, and abuse has been found to be associated with conflict. In the Ellis ... study, the CTS was not used as the only measure of spousal abuse for two reasons. First, a significant amount of the abuse that male partners direct towards their wives may not be conflict instigated.... Second, it provides a misleading account of the patterning of spousal abuse. That is to say, the CTS routinely yields findings indicating that male and female partners are equally likely to abuse each other, not because they really are, but because this instrument itself elicits a symmetrical pattern of responding, and its users equate spousal abuse, generally, with one particular form of abuse: conflict-instigated spousal abuse. By using the CTS as well as other measures of abuse, we are in a position to demonstrate this.

Control–Instigated Abuse

Non-conflict-instigated abuse refers to physical, verbal, and emotional abuse as well as the intentional infliction of pain or hurt that is not associated with conflict. A number of feminist writers have defined this form of abuse as *social control motivated.* Social-control-motivated abuse refers to intentionally inflicted physically or psychologically painful or hurtful acts (or threats) by male partners as a means of compelling or constraining the conduct, dress, or demeanor of their female partners. Feminist writers such as Dobash and Dobash ... restrict the definition of social-control-motivated abuse to male partners. In the Ellis ... study, the definition applies to both male and female partners.

Measures of non-conflict-instigated abuse are used because they uncover a significant amount of abuse that is not revealed by use of the CTS. In addition, they indicate an asymmetrical pattern of abuse that is not shown by the CTS. Third, they include measures that focus on the *consequences* of abuse (e.g., hurting), not on a series of apparently consequence-free acts, as the CTS does. Last, the use of non-conflict-instigated measures, and questions associated with them, provides information on meanings and motives for abuse. The CTS does not.

* * *

NOTES

1. Using these definitions, and reviewing all the surveys of spousal violence published in Canada between 1981 and 1994, Ellis and Stuckless concluded that whereas "[a]pproximately equal proportions of male and female partners engage in conflict-instigated violence," "a significantly

higher proportion of male partners engage in control-instigated violence." Id. at 46.

2. The British feminist writers Russell and Emerson Dobash, along with coauthors Kate Cavanagh and Ruth Lewis, expand on the Ellis and Stuckless critique of the Conflict Tactics Scale. They point out, for example, that it does not address "the contextual and interactional sequences associated with the onset of violence." In addition:

> [I]t sharply delimits the set of acts defined as violent in the 11–item scale ... and excludes sexual violence; the scale itself and specific items within it conflate significant forms of violence with potentially trivial gestures (e.g., "Hit, or tried to hit with something" may mean a husband punching his wife and a wife swinging a pillow); and restricting the measurement of violence to acts results in a failure to adequately distinguish what makes violence distinct from other physical acts, such as malevolent intent....
>
> Additional problems occur when CTS-derived results are translated into specific findings. For example, it is necessary to confirm the use of only one act of violence (as specified in the CTS list) to define a person as violent. With this operational transformation, the woman who reports she threw something at her partner and the man who admits he beat up his partner are both assessed as violent.

Dobash et al., *Separate and Intersecting Realities: A Comparison of Men's and Women's Accounts of Violence Against Women,* 4 VIOLENCE AGAINST WOMEN 382, 385–86 (1998).

The Dobash article also raises a concern about the accuracy of measures like the Conflict Tactics Scale, which depend on men's and women's self-reporting. In a study which included 95 couples, they discovered significant discrepancies between the accounts of abuse given by the two partners.

Russell P. Dobash et al.
Separate and Intersecting Realities: A Comparison of Men's and Women's Accounts of Violence Against Women, 4 Violence Against Women 382, 405–07 (1998)

... [T]he disparities in men's and women's accounts of violence and injuries are highly pertinent. The results show vast and often statistically significant differences in the accounts of men and women; it is only at the lower end of violence—pushing and restraining—that there is much congruence in their respective reports of violence. Similarly, men's and women's accounts of injuries were also at considerable odds. Generally, much lower proportions of men reported ever inflicting any specific type of injury (prevalence), and their reports of frequent injuries were even more discordant with those of women.

With respect to men's controlling and intimidating behaviors, women and men also reported a wide range of such behaviors and, in contrast to their reports of violence and injuries, there was a fair degree of concordance between them about the prevalence of these acts. Accounts are reasonably congruent regarding men's perpetration of at least one incidence of shouting, swearing, threatening, criticizing, nagging, and calling women names, as well as on men's feigning to hit women and questioning their movements. Men's and women's accounts were not congruent, however, on other controlling behaviors, such as men's attempts to control family resources, restrict women's lives, and check up on their movements. . . .

. . . Although accounts sometimes overlap and intersect when considering the prevalence of physical abuse and the coercive control of women, they often reflect distinct and separate realities and interpretations. . . . Other studies examining couples' accounts of men's threats and use of violence have also found that men's reports are likely to be lower than those of women partners. . . .

. . . Some have suggested that both men and women underreport their own violence and overreport their victimization, whereas others suggest that women's accounts of men's violence and of their own may be more reliable. . . . Some of those who have examined men's and women's accounts of women's violence argue in favor of women's reports, stating that women may be more likely to remember their own aggression because it is deemed less appropriate and less acceptable for women than for men and thus takes on the more memorable quality of a forbidden act or one that is out of character. . . . For this research, with its focus on men's and women's accounts of men's violence, the literature is less well developed, although the results presented here, as well as evidence from the fieldwork and the transcripts from the interviews, indicate that women provide much more detailed and lengthy accounts than men, usually enter the narrative at a much earlier point in the violent event, and extend the narrative beyond the acts of violence to include injuries and other consequences. This would seem to be a fruitful area for further investigation.

The evidence presented here stands in stark contrast to the claim that men's and women's accounts of violence are unproblematic and/or that men's accounts of their own violence can stand alone as a valid assay of those acts.

* * *

NOTE

1. Other measures, which do not depend on self-reporting, show a much less symmetrical pattern of partner abuse. One incontrovertible statistic is that more than 90% of heterosexual partner violence reported to and recorded by law-enforcement authorities is perpetrated by men. See, e.g., Demie Kurz, *Physical Assaults by Husbands: A Major Social Problem,* CURRENT CONTROVERSIES ON FAMILY VIOLENCE 89–90 (R.J. Gelles & Dorileen R. Loseke, eds. 1993). But any statistic that depends on reports to law enforcement is likely to reflect only the more serious levels of violence or threat, or the behaviors most clearly understood by those against whom

they are directed as unlawful. Official reports will also underrepresent any victim constituency reluctant to seek official intervention. It has often been claimed that domestic violence by men is significantly under-reported, although this may be changing as the problem, and the availability of services for victims, become more widely publicized. In a society that stresses male self-reliance, however, it may be even more difficult for a man to call the police to report that his female partner is abusing him. See Murray A. Straus, *Physical Assaults by Wives: A Major Social Problem,* Current Controversies on Family Violence 71–73 (R.J. Gelles & Dorileen R. Loseke, eds. 1993).

Supporting the conclusion that serious male violence is much more prevalent than serious female violence are consistent findings that men injure women at much higher rates than women injure men. See, for example, the seven to one ratio reported in J.E. Stets and M.A. Straus, *Gender Differences in Reporting of Marital Violence and Its Medical Consequences,* Physical Violence in American Families: Risk Factors and Adaptations to Violence in 8,145 Families, 151 (M.A. Straus & R.J. Gelles, eds. 1990).

Murray Straus has recently himself contributed to the debate about how to reconcile these very discrepant findings.

Murray A. Straus
The Controversy Over Domestic Violence by Women: A Methodological, Theoretical, and Sociology of Science Analysis; Violence in Intimate Relationships 17, 22–39 (X.B. Arriaga & S. Oskamp, eds. 1999)

The low rate of assaults by both husbands and wives found by crime studies . . . probably results from a number of situational and unintended "demand characteristics" . . . . These surveys were presented as a study of crime. . . . Unfortunately, when a survey of crime, violence, or injury is the context for estimating rates of domestic assault, the contextual message can take precedence over specific instructions to include all assaults, regardless of the perpetrator and regardless of whether injury resulted. This can lead some respondents to misperceive the study as being concerned only with assaults that are experienced as a crime or as violence, or only assaults that resulted in injury. However, only a small percentage of assaults are experienced as a crime or as a threat to personal safety or violence. For example, while people experience being slapped or kicked by their partner as a horrible experience, it takes relatively rare circumstances to perceive the attack as a "crime" . . . . One such circumstance is an injury. Injury serious enough to need medical attention occurs in only one to three percent of domestic assaults on women and one half of one percent of domestic assaults on men. . . . To the extent that it takes injury for a respondent in a crime survey to perceive there is something to report, the low injury rate is part of the explanation for the extremely low rate of partner assaults found by the crime studies. This does not mean that all respondents misperceived what was expected in this way. Indeed, crime surveys include substantial numbers of assaults without injury . . . but still a fraction of the 97% to 99% found in family conflict surveys. . . .

. . .

Another similar process probably accounts for the extremely high rate of assaults by *former* partners in crime studies. That is, one of the circumstances leading a respondent in crime studies to report an assault by a partner is if the attack is by a former spouse. That makes it a "real crime" because a former spouse "has no right to do that." Even with the revisions, intended to avoid this problem, the NCVS [National Crime Victimization Survey] found 25 times more assaults by former partners in the previous 12 month period than by current partners. . . . Given the vastly greater time exposure to current spouses during the 12 month referent period, that ratio does not seem plausible.

In summary, assaults by a partner are most likely to be experienced as a crime if the attacks result in injury or if it is an attack by a former partner. To the extent that this is correct, it helps explain the drastically lower prevalence rate for intimate partner assaults in crime studies because those circumstances are relatively rare.

. . . [T]he same "demand characteristics" of a crime study that produced the extremely low rates for both men and women, also produce the high ratio of male to female offenders. Assuming that one of the circumstances that leads a respondent to experience being hit by a partner as a crime, or one of the circumstances that leads a police officer to make an arrest, is an injury that needs medical attention, if assaults resulting in injury are much more likely to occur when a man is the offender, it follows that men predominate in statistics based on crime surveys or crime reports. . . .

. . .

Another consideration that may lead to under reporting of assaults on partners by women as crime or a threat to safety is that such attacks are often discounted as a joke. In one of my initial exploratory interviews on domestic assaults, I asked one of the men if his wife had ever hit him. He stood up and shoved his shoulder toward me as if I were his wife. He said "Yeah, I told her, go ahead and hit me." For still another group, the idea of being assaulted by one's wife may be so threatening to their masculine identity that they would be ashamed to report it. . . .

. . .

A Sociology of Science Analysis of the Controversy

[M]uch of the controversy over violence by women occurs as a result of each side using "violence" to refer to something different. I will call these two approaches broad and narrow definitions. . . .

. . . [T]he narrow definition restricts violence to the act of assault, regardless of injury, whereas the broad definition defines violence to include multiple modes of maltreatment and the resulting injury. One reason each of these definitions is unacceptable to those who adhere to the other is that more than scientific issues are at stake. Each definition also reflects an underlying moral agenda and professional role. Consequently, to abandon one or the other definition is tantamount to abandoning that agenda and professional role.

. . . [T]hose following the broad definition tend to be service providers and feminist activists. It would be ridiculous and unethical if service providers such as shelters, batterer treatment programs, or marital therapists, restricted their focus to physical assaults and ignored the psychological assaults, sexual coercion, subjugation, and economic situation of battered women, or the behavior of men who engage in these other forms of degradation. On the other hand, those who use a narrow definition tend to be academics and researchers. They tend to focus on investigating one specific type of maltreatment, such as physical assaults, because each type is complex and difficult to investigate. Much can only be learned by a concentrated research focus. I believe that most of those who focus on just one form of maltreatment also recognize the need for research that takes into consideration multiple forms of maltreatment, even though they themselves do not conduct that type of research.

The difference in emphasis on injury reflects the different needs of service providers and researchers. For a service provider, it is essential to know if the assault resulted in injury because different steps are needed to deal with cases involving injury. For a researcher investigating such things as the type of family or type of society in which partner assaults are most likely to occur, injury may not be a crucial issue because it can be assumed that injury occurs in a certain proportion of cases. Moreover, for some purposes it is necessary to exclude injury as a criterion. One of these is research that seeks to estimate the prevalence of domestic assaults. If injury is one of the criteria, it restricts the data to more serious assaults and, as we have seen, the overall prevalence rate is vastly underestimated. Thus, the widely cited figure from the National Family Violence Survey of 1,800,000 women severely assaulted each year becomes only 188,000 when the criteria for a severe assault includes injury. . . . Of course, this is a false dichotomy. . . . [B]oth figures are needed. Feminist activists, for example use both figures. . . . They have made extensive use of the 1,800,000 figure (often presented as a woman is battered every 15 seconds) to mobilize resources. At the same time they also use police, crime survey, and emergency room statistics to show that there are many more women victims (in the sense of injured) than male victims.

. . . [U]nderlying the differences just discussed is a deep seated difference in moral agenda. Those who use a broad definition tend to be primarily concerned with the well being of women. They are, of course, also concerned with physical assaults regardless of who is the victim, but their primary concern is ending maltreatment of women. Moreover, as is to be expected, they are hostile to research that might be used by critics of feminism, and this includes research on assaults by women. On the other hand, those defining violence as a physical assault tend to place ending physical violence at the top of their agenda, regardless of whether the offender is a man, woman, or child. Of the two evils, physical violence and the oppression of women, physical violence tends to take priority, even though (as in my case) they are also concerned with ending all types of gender inequality and maltreatment.

. . . [R]esearch using a broad definition and emphasizing injury, may be most useful for informing programs designed to treat offenders or help victims. By contrast, research focusing on the act of assault, most of which does not involve injury but does involve millions of couples, may be most useful for informing programs of "primary prevention," i.e., steps that will prevent physical assaults from ever happening. The former tends to be highest on the agenda of service providers and feminist activists, whereas primary prevention tends to be highest on the agenda of other professions and interest groups.

* * *

NOTE

1. In its careful effort to explain the differences and bridge the divide between those who focus on partner abuse, and its "multiple forms of maltreatment" and those who focus on physical assault between family members, or what is often called "family violence," Straus's essay is a determined attempt at peacemaking. From a theoretical standpoint, it seems reasonable enough to acknowledge that both problems deserve sustained attention, and to welcome both bodies of research as advancing our understanding of family relationships. The debate becomes bitter and the gulf widens, however, when data generated by one "camp" is used to discredit policy arguments made or positions taken by the other, or when in an individual case decision makers with important power over the lives of family members are asked to make potentially dangerous choices between two different interpretations of the situation presented to them. You will have many opportunities in subsequent chapters to see these tensions in action.

CHAPTER THREE

DIMENSIONS OF THE BATTERING EXPERIENCE

A. INTRODUCTION

In the previous chapter we examined, as the paradigm of an abusive relationship, the relationship between a male abuser and a female target. While we did ask whether the roles are sometimes reversed, we did not ask whether partners in same sex couples are also vulnerable to abuse. We did not ask whether our paradigm couple was white, of color, or interracial; what socio-economic class the partners belonged to; whether they were new immigrants to the United States or came from families who had been in the country for generations; whether English was their primary language; or whether they identified with a particular racial, cultural or religious subcommunity.

In this chapter we ask what difference these differences make, within a four factor framework. One possibility is that difference will change the subjective experiences of the abusive and abused partners in the relationship. Patrick Letellier, for example, talks about the difficulty gay men have in acknowledging, even to themselves, that they have been abused by their partners, a difficulty he attributes to the firm grip of an ideology that views victimization as inconsistent with male identity. A second possibility is that differences will isolate the partners within a community in which support or assistance is not available. Many new immigrants to the United States, for example, could not conceive of survival outside the immigrant community that harbors, and possibly condones the behavior of, their abusers. Victims of abuse in small rural communities may find it much harder to access resources, and perpetrators in such communities may have closer ties to the very people who might otherwise take responsibility for intervening, such as the police.

A third possibility is that specific features of the abuser's or the target's identity will affect the willingness or the ability of the partners to reach out for support or assistance to those in the broader society who are in a position to provide it. New arrivals to the country, for example, often will not willingly risk the ostracism by their immigrant community that might result from their calling the police to intervene in an abusive episode. It has been frequently argued that many African–American women are too aware of the ways in which African–American men have been abused by white police officers to be comfortable delivering their partners into the hands of a white police force. Physically or mentally disabled victims may be unable to communicate their victimization, or lack credibility when they do. Economic or cultural factors may preclude recourse to mental health services. Dietary restrictions may preclude the use of shelter services. A fourth possibility is that the identifying characteristics of the abuser or the target will affect the responses of those in the broader society who are either charged with a responsibility to intervene, or who have the capacity to intervene. Homophobia, for example, may leave police with the attitude that the female or male victim of a same-sex partner deserves everything she or he gets in the way of abuse. The smooth-looking and talking middle class abuser may be treated more deferentially than his poorer counterpart.

The previous chapter posited a psychological dynamic within abusive relationships that may remain operative across the lines of race, culture, sexual orientation or class. Paying attention to differences among abusers and their victims, and the difference they make, however, involves acknowledging that abuse has social and systemic dimensions, and that gender is not the only relevant dimension, nor patriarchy the only relevant social system. One commentator has proposed that individual psychological factors within a context of cultural tolerance produce individual incidents of domestic violence, while cultural, political and economic factors may produce increases in the frequency and severity of domestic violence at the societal level.[1] This understanding does not negate the value of feminist theory in explaining why women are abused by men, but asks that we broaden our understanding to include the influence of other ideologies, social practices, and social conditions on the experience of partner abuse.

The specific "differences" taken on in this chapter include sexual orientation, race, culture and ethnicity, poverty, and disability. There are two necessary caveats. First, none of these dimensions can be fully isolated out for analysis; in the life of any given individual the influence of any one factor is intertwined with the influence of all the others. We need, as Kimberle Crenshaw describes in the excerpt you will read later in this chapter, an "intersectional" understanding of how individuals become vulnerable to abuse, and how their responses to it, and others' responses to them, are conditioned by the particularities of their identity and situation. The second is that this provisional list of influential factors is, and probably always would be, incomplete. There is no section here on the differences between experiencing battering in an urban and a rural setting, for example, and no section on the differential distribution of battering across the life span. However, you are invited to apply the framework suggested here to those and other dimensions of the battering experience; and to keep a look out in the developing literature for material to expand your understanding and refine your analysis.

1. Jaquelyn Campbell, *Prevention of Wife Battering: Insights from Cultural Analysis,* 14 RESPONSE TO THE VICT. OF WMN. & CHN. 18, 18 (1992).

B. Battering in Same-Sex Relationships

Amy Edgington
Anyone But Me, Gay Community News, July 16, 1989

I am a survivor and a victim of lesbian battering. I am proud to have come through a trial that might have taken my life, but I recognize that my survival is partly due to luck: others just as strong and brave have died.... Battering leaves deep, mostly invisible scars and I may never be the woman I was before I was battered. Nevertheless, I don't want the pity or contempt victims often receive.

... I was in a battering relationship between 1977 and 1981. My lover and I fought once a day on average: the rare "good days" were canceled out by marathons of abuse. Severe verbal abuse was part of every fight, and many of them escalated to threats of violence or abandonment in extremely difficult or potentially dangerous circumstances. My lover had a gun and threatened to use it on herself, me, her children and others. I tried everything I could think of to stop the abuse—therapy, confrontation, appeasement, reasoning, ignoring it—but nothing worked consistently or for very long. Her demands frequently placed me in double-bind, no-win situations. She held me responsible for other people's behavior, for things that had happened in the distant past, for her own mistakes. Behavior that she criticized severely in me, she might praise the next day in someone else or in herself. Actual physical violence was much less frequent than the threat of it, insults, humiliation, isolation and crazy-making mind games.

Soon after my escape I began to read accounts of political prisoners and concentration camp survivors. Although my experience was not comparable to theirs, I gained my first comprehension of what had happened to me. Bruno Bettleheim ... explains that the most feared guards at the camps were the ones who gave beatings rarely and unpredictably and who mostly engaged in verbal threats and other psychological abuse. A year or two later I ran across some articles on post-traumatic stress disorder, and I realized I was suffering the same symptoms that so often plague war veterans and disaster victims: heightened anxiety, painful flashbacks, guilt, and difficulty adjusting to the "normal" world and to a damaged self I could scarcely recognize. In 1985, when I finally began to read about battering, I recognized examples of abuse I had experienced, but still had not been able to name.

I think now that my difficulty (and also your difficulty) in accepting what happened to me is part of a larger climate of denial that enables battering to continue. My denial started long before I was battered and it lulled me into a false sense of security. I had been around lesbians since I was a teenager, and although some of them had troubled relationships, I was unaware of any battering. I attached myself to the comfortable myth that lesbians don't batter. Much later, when I was "out" enough to go to gay bars in a town that was liberal enough to tolerate them, I saw that some lesbians did indeed batter. However, I thought they were all of a type—drunks, sexist butches or apolitical lesbians—so I decided that feminist lesbians don't batter. I thought that relating to other radical feminists was safe, and I saw battering as a limited problem that would be solved by politicizing all lesbians.

Even when I discovered evidence of battering among feminists, I still thought I was personally too smart and too tough to be battered. I believed in the myth of a "victim personality": that some women with a history of abuse or alcoholism or destructive behavior patterns wear a semi-visible "Kick Me" sign and attract those who will do just that. At the time I met my batterer, I did not fit my own stereotype of a victim in any way. I was very public as a lesbian: I led women's problem-solving groups and worked at a women's center. Now I know that anyone can be battered and that no one can spot every batterer. They can be charming and charismatic: they can somehow reconcile battering with feminist politics and even use politics to justify abuse. I think anyone could have fallen in love with the woman who battered me. There is no such thing as a typical batterer or a typical victim. In fact, I believe that batterers are like vampires—they are most likely to choose *strong* victims; then, over the course of the relationship, the battered woman grows progressively weaker as the batterer sucks off every resource and strength the victim has.

A batterer will use everything she can to increase her control and your dependence. When I acknowledge that my batterer manipulated my best qualities, not just weaknesses, to keep me in the relationship, it counteracts some of the shame I feel. I have made the following list of my vulnerabilities and strengths in this situation:

Vulnerabilities

1. *Fear of the consequences of leaving.* I knew that if I left, I would lose all contact with my lover's children, live in terror of retaliation, and receive little sympathy from other lesbians.

2. *Lack of resources.* I had very little money and no transportation. I was isolated from family and friends. I had no information about lesbian battering and little hope I could get protection in a shelter advertised as "open to all women."

3. *Denial.* Each time the violence escalated, I escalated my denial: "She doesn't mean it when she insults me," became "She was out of control when she hit me" and then "She wouldn't really kill me."

4. *Lack of perspective.* Staying so long appeared stupid, but actually I needed all my smarts to survive each crisis and try to anticipate and avoid the next. I couldn't afford to feel the full horror of what was happening to me: this is probably a healthy response to danger, but it doesn't work well when danger is continual.

5. *Shame.* Nothing was as acutely painful as my admission that I was being battered. I blamed myself for "stupidity," and began to feel all the hurt, rage and humiliation I had suppressed during actual fights.

Strengths

1. *Love.* I loved this woman and her children. Everything about her was admirable and appealing except her battering behavior, which only gradually developed into a form I could recognize. I kept waiting for the wonderful woman I loved to reappear in place of the screaming monster. I thought my love and forgiveness could save her from her "bad side."

2. *Willingness to work hard.* I didn't expect a good relationship to come easy. I was eager to cooperate and adapt to my lover's needs, but they became increasingly contradictory and impossible to fulfil, and I was punished for having any needs myself.

3. *Feminism.* My politics told me the last thing I should do was abandon a woman in trouble. I failed to see that battering was working for my lover, and that I was a woman in serious danger.

4. *Lesbian identity.* A lesbian's relationship with her lover is supposed to be the piece of cake that makes all the oppression worthwhile. It was devastatingly hard to admit that my lover was my worst enemy.

. . . I thought no woman could terrorize me the way a man could, even though this contradicted all the rest of my Amazon credo about the superior powers of lesbian women. In fact, lesbian batterers can do anything male batterers can do, and I think the extreme intimacy of lesbian relationships increases the damage. We tend to assume relationships between women will automatically be more equal than heterosexual relationships. But once battering starts, equality goes out the window. No matter how much or how little political power the batterer has in comparison with her lover, she immediately gains the upper hand in her home by battering. A battered lesbian may be equal to her partner in size or larger, and she may be more likely to fight back than a heterosexual woman, but that does not make her a batterer: feminists do not lay this label on straight women who defend themselves. Battering, by definition, can't be mutual. Battering is not violence alone: it is the use of violence (including threats) to maintain absolute control over your lover. Don't count and compare the bruises on two women. Listen to their stories and you will begin to hear that one woman is fearful, isolated, and gives ground to the other's needs and demands. Don't let yourself be influenced by how much you like a particular woman—a battered lesbian may have all the charisma of a squashed toad. If oppression hasn't made women noble, don't expect battering to make a lesbian appealing.

The consequences of battering may be worse for lesbians. I doubt we'll ever have accurate statistics about lesbians—but I think the numbers would be largely irrelevant anyway. Our choice of lovers is limited. If there's even one batterer in a small community, we stand a greater chance of getting involved with her, and for every batterer, there's likely to be a string of victims.

If she has a job, a battered lesbian may have more economic resources than a housewife, but a few phone calls from her vengeful lover can cost her the job, her apartment, and any family she has. If she's in the closet, she may have to isolate herself from the only lesbian she knows in order to be "free." If she's out (particularly if she's engaged in political networking with lesbians in other communities), all the resources she's worked so hard to build can be used against her by a lesbian batterer who wants to find her. A man would have to spend a lot of money for detective services the lesbian grapevine provides.

. . .

Ultimately, it is the task of lesbian communities to see that lesbian battering stops. Leaving saves individual lives, but it does not keep the abuser from battering her next lover and her next. We need safe houses and safe communities. We do enough hiding in the straight world: what freedom do we have left if we must also hide from lesbians who beat us, who don't believe we were beaten, who defend the women who beat us, who think such a thing could never happen to them, who automatically pass on our names, phone numbers and addresses to any lesbian seeking them, since danger from another woman does not occur to them? With friends like these, do we need enemies? . . .

The simple fact is, if we don't exclude battering from our midst, we exclude the battered. . . .

. . .

Each lesbian must begin to realize that she herself could be a batterer's victim and that this possibility is violence against her. Furthermore, while battering exists, the lesbian community can never be a "safe house" inside the patriarchy. Battering undermines the revolutionary potential of lesbianism and tolerating it invalidates our feminist politics. How can we talk seriously about struggling against racism, classism, anti-Semitism, homophobia, etc.—all of which lead women to inflict damage on other women—when we hesitate to take a firm stand against women who batter other women?

* * *

The Story of David Begor
1997 Report on Lesbian, Gay, Bisexual, Transgender Domestic Violence, The National Coalition of Anti–Violence Programs, Appendix A: Three Survivor Stories

I never thought I'd be saying that I was a victim of domestic violence but it's true.

I met my now ex-boyfriend at the gym in early 1996, and we began dating shortly thereafter. A few months later he moved into my apartment. I loved him very much, and more than anything I wanted our relationship to work.

The problems began almost immediately. He didn't pay his second month's rent, he would go out all night and not return, and he began calling me names such as "whore" and telling me I was not enough to keep him satisfied.

I remember being really confused about what was happening. I had never been in this kind of situation before, and nothing made sense. We agreed that a couple's counselor might be able to help and began seeing one. In the meantime, I just kept hoping and trying to make things better.

Unfortunately, his verbal and physical abuse became more and more scary. At one point he told me that I was ugly and the only reason people liked me is because they felt sorry for me. As I became more afraid, I also became more angry at how he treated me. On one occasion when he cornered me in the apartment, I even threw a pan at him in self-defense, something he later used against me to prove I was the one with the problem.

With the counselor's assistance, I got him to agree to move out, but that did not stop the violence and harassment. He repeatedly showed up at my place of work, verbally abusing me and pushing me around. He followed me to my gym and threw his bicycle at me and then struck me.... In the last incident he struck and kicked me and ripped my shirt right off me. He then threatened to call the police and tell them that I had assaulted him. Since I am significantly bigger than he is, I was afraid they would believe him.

With help from Community United Against Violence in San Francisco, I obtained a civil restraining order against my ex, and believe it or not, I haven't heard from him since.

* * *

NOTE

In the next excerpt, Barbara Hart addresses two questions: why lesbians batter, and whether it is possible to develop a "profile" for the lesbian who batters. As you read, ask yourself how much of what she has to say could be applied to heterosexual battering relationships, and how much to abusive relationships between gay men.

Barbara Hart
Lesbian Battering: An Examination; Naming the Violence, Speaking out About Lesbian Battering 173, 174–82 (Kerry Lobel ed., 1986)

Why do lesbians batter?

Like male batterers, lesbians who batter seek to achieve, maintain and demonstrate power over their partners in order to maximize the ready accomplishment of their own needs and desires. Lesbians batter their lovers because violence is often an effective method to gain power and control over intimates.

Lesbians, like their non-lesbian counterparts, are socialized in a culture where the family unit is designed to control and order the private relationships between members of the family. Men are assigned the ultimate power and authority in family relationships. This is true despite the fact that there is nothing inherent in the male gender which would render them the appropriate wielders of power. Rather, this attribution of "legitimate" power is given to men based on a system of beliefs and values that approves and supports men's power and control over women—sexism.

. . .

Lesbians, like non-lesbians, often desire control over the resources and decisions in family life that power brings and that violence can assure when control is resisted. The same elements of hierarchy of power, ownership, entitlement and control exist in lesbian family relationships. Largely this is true because lesbians have also learned that violence works in achieving partner compliance. Further, lesbian communities have not developed a system of norms and values opposing power abuse and violence in our communities.

Which lesbian will batter?

Perhaps the partner who is physically stronger and perhaps not.

We know that part of the effectiveness of men's violence as a tactic of control is that their size and physical strength, compared to women, is such that men's violence has the potential to inflict serious bodily harm on women. Non-lesbian women will often acquiesce in the demands of violent partners because of the knowledge that noncompliance may be followed by violent attacks that could result in injury.

But just as men choose to batter and also choose to not batter because they are physically strong, so also with lesbians.

. . .

[O]ne lesbian might choose not to be violent because she concludes that it would not work by virtue of her lack of physical power relative to her partner. Another could choose to be violent because she concludes violence will intimidate her partner and because she believes she can handle any violent response safely. Another lesbian with years of street or bar fighting experience might choose not to use violence to control her partner because she believes that it would be unfair and morally wrong. Yet another lesbian might choose to use violence to control by employing a weapon to eliminate her comparative weakness and to overcome the physical power possessed by her partner.

Thus, even though superior strength can render violence a more effective tactic of control, many choose not to use it.

Perhaps the partner who has more personal power and perhaps not.

Men who batter usually possess more personal power in their lives than the women they victimize. Personal power is based on education, income and economic security, employment skills and marketability, physical power, health, social skills and networks, etc. Each partner possesses a

Personal power

particular amount of every attribute of power. Some attributes, like income or employment skills, may be more significant measures of personal power than others in any particular relationship.

But men do not batter because they have more personal power than their partners. Nor do they batter because they happen to have less. Violence is not a necessary outgrowth of differential power.

. . .

Many lesbians who batter, regardless of their portion of personal power, demonstrate strong powers of coercion and intimidation, such that members of the couple's friendship network or their immediate lesbian community may defer to or pacify the batterer to avoid confrontation or humiliation.

Perhaps the partner who experienced violence as a child and perhaps not.

Many female children are physically or sexually abused by family members or friends as children. As victims of violence, young women certainly learn the power that violence grants. Violence can terrorize, immobilize and render fearful the most competent and extroverted, as well as the weak and powerless. Children, whether or not they are victims, observers or perpetrators, learn early that violence eliminates the recipient's control over her own life. Children learn the perverse pleasure they may derive from dominating others. Children learn that there may be few adverse consequences to violence.... Children who grow up in families where there is no model for negotiating over scarce family resources or for strategizing for maximizing the need and wish fulfillment of each family member, may lack ethical concepts of sharing and fairness and skills for problem-solving.

Surely, many girl children also learn that violence is not appropriate female behavior. Additionally, girl children who grow up as victims of violence often strongly reject violence as a tactic of control. This is particularly true for women who perceive the childhood violence as unjust and unnecessary.

Unfortunately, there is not any research data that answers the question of how many lesbians who were violated as children choose to be violators as adults. The fact that a woman was abused as a child is not a reliable indicator that she will batter her partner.

Perhaps the lesbian who is acutely homophobic and perhaps not.

All lesbians feel vulnerable and endangered to some extent because of the reality of the virulent prejudice and coercive, punitive power that has been brought to bear against us. To the lesbian who greatly fears exposure or self-hatred, an understanding of the risks of exposure may create a chronic emotional crisis where self-protection and self-validation consume exhausting amounts of energy.

. . .

But this does not precipitate violence or abuse of her partner. Although the lesbian experiencing homophobia or internalized homophobia copes with inordinate stress and rage, these do not override her capacity to choose to be violent. Nor does the fact that she lives in terror due to injustice determine her decision to act justly or unjustly towards others.

Perhaps the lesbian who holds contempt for women or who identifies with men and perhaps not.

Misogyny is the hatred of women. A misogynist attitude is one that devalues, discredits or disparages women. Young women are taught in this culture not to trust or respect women, to believe that women are less competent than men. The media, purveyors of cultural norms and values, constantly reinforce this inferiority of women. It is, therefore, not surprising that women harbor contempt and hatred for women. Women who have worked diligently to be rid of self-hatred will never totally succeed in that endeavor in a society where women-hating is endemic.

Lesbians who have been battered often report that a seemingly integral part of the pattern of violence inflicted upon them is derogatory, women-hating tirades by the batterer.

Does the lesbian who uses women-hating verbal attacks as a tactic of control hate herself as a woman, or does she hate other women, distinguishing herself somehow from them, or does she permit herself to ventilate women-hating attitudes because she knows this type of assault will be a particularly effective tactic of control over the woman she is abusing?

It has been suggested that lesbians who batter do so because they are identifying with men, the powerful gender.

The process of identification with men is rarely a denial of the lesbian batterer's womanhood. It is not usually conscious self-hatred of herself as a woman. It may involve devaluing her partner based on her "lesser worth" because she is a woman. Sexually pejorative salvos may be used because they are most shameful and debilitating—most powerful. Identification may include an assessment that the lesbian batterer has the physical and personal power to batter successfully without adverse consequences—akin to men. It may entail a strong sense of ownership of the partner which brings with it the right to use her at will.

But identification with men or hatred of women does not compel violence, although it may allow the lesbian batterer to conclude that violence as a tactic of control will be successful or to feel justified in her actions.

Perhaps the lesbian who perceives herself to be victimized by the world and misused or controlled by her victim and perhaps not.

Most men who batter are said to feel controlled by people and circumstances other than themselves. . . .

Not only do male batterers describe themselves as the accidental or intentional victims of others' neglect or injury, they also see themselves as "henpecked"—controlled by their partners.

Lesbian batterers also express feelings of powerlessness and helplessness in their relationships and assert they are controlled and victimized by their partners. Lesbian assailants invariably utilize every disagreement by the partner, every failure to meet the batterer's needs, every independent/self-caring action by the partner as a violation or external control imposed by the victim.

. . .

But there is no evidence to suggest that the lives of batterers are actually less rich or more fraught with injustice than lesbians who do not choose to batter. Furthermore, there is strong evidence from battered lesbians that they have persistently worked very hard to fulfill their partner's expectations and to nurture them through difficult times.

And many lesbians who meet with very trying circumstances and who are treated unkindly by their partners do not batter.

Perhaps the lesbian who has anger control or communications problems and perhaps not.

Many lesbian batterers speak of the inordinate anger that is generated by their partners. They acknowledge that identical behavior by another person would not propel them into th[at] rage. . . .

. . .

Batterers are not aware of the reasons behind the "triggering." . . . Lesbians who batter, like male batterers, strongly believe that once anger emerges, it becomes uncontrollable, and that violence subsequently erupts—the batterer having no control over either.

Battered lesbians report that batterers often appear to be looking for something about which to become angry to provide rationalization for battering. They also find that the batterer many times becomes angry only after she assaults to control and assault does not produce the desired result.

. . .

Battered lesbians are often told by partners who have sought help from therapists not informed about battering that she batters because she is not adequately able to communicate her needs and feelings, nor able to express herself. She somehow short-circuits and becomes violent, with violence being a reflection of frustration, not a tactic of control.

Underlying this claim is a misconception that better communication would produce a better understanding of needs and feelings which would, in turn, result in the partner working harder to accommodate the batterer and violence being thereby averted. This assumes that the batterer is a person whose needs are not well understood and that the battered lesbian has a responsibility to go the additional distance to respond positively to the batterer's needs.

Both assumptions are often false. Many batterers are excellent communicators. Batterers who have worked in therapy to increase their communication skills, without first achieving the termination of violence or threats of violence, become more skillful, sophisticated controllers of their partners—better terrorists.

Many lesbians who are not articulate or do not have a clear sense of their feelings and needs are not violent. Most lesbians striving to improve communication skills and to better identify and actualize their needs and feelings have never considered violence as appropriate activity in relationships.

* * *

NOTES

1. Hart argues strongly that there is no reliable "profile" for a lesbian batterer, and it seems that her argument would apply equally for gay male batterers. One of the issues this raises is how to distinguish the batterer from the victim in an incident of same-sex battering when both parties claim victim status, and both may be bruised or scratched, if the battered partner has tried to defend herself. Of course, this problem is not limited to same-sex relationships. Increasingly it seems that male batterers claim violence on the part of their female partners when the police come to the door, prompting mutual arrests and the issuance of mutual restraining orders, even in situations in which a modest inquiry would reveal which partner was the aggressor, and which aggressed against. In a sense it is a problem built into the language of restraining order legislation, and into definitions of assault and battery in criminal law, where what is condemned is physical violence, or the threat of physical violence, and the law does not separately define or condemn "abuse," or focus specifically on violence that is part of a pattern of abuse. Nonetheless, the problem may well be exacerbated in same-sex relationships, both because the partners may more often be physically matched, and because of an assumption that "fighting" or "mutual combat" is a typical, or at least not a surprising aspect of a gay or lesbian relationship.

Those assumptions can be exploited by gay and lesbian batterers:

> ... [G]ay and lesbian batterers frequently perpetuate their abusive behavior by exploiting the "myth of mutual battering," the assumption that "most abusive intimate relationships are characterized by reciprocal violence in which each partner is both a perpetrator and a victim of abuse." This myth—that "s/he likes it," or "it's a two-way street"—is also common in heterosexual relationships. But the myth of mutual battering is particularly invidious for same-sex couples, since a common misconception in both the heterosexual and the homosexual communities is that any violence between two men or two women is by its very nature "just fighting," which is actively initiated by both parties.
>
> Moreover, since abused lesbians and gay men tend to use physical force to defend against their batterers more frequently than abused heterosexual women do, the victim him/herself might believe the assertion of

the batterer, and even friends and counselors, that such self-defensive fighting constitutes abuse, and that the victim is the aggressor, and does not deserve help or consideration. "Often batterers use the survivor's self-doubt to their advantage. Batterers are notorious for labeling the survivor 'mutually abusive' in order to avoid taking responsibility for their actions."

In a variation on the myth of mutual abuse, the lesbian or gay batterer often claims to be the actual victim of abuse, thus seeking to exploit the fact that in same-sex relationships identifying the batterer often is more difficult than in heterosexual situations, particularly if the couple is about the same age, size, etc. Gay and lesbian batterers who claim themselves to be the victims often obtain restraining orders against the real victims, thereby enlisting the police and the courts in perpetuating the battering.

In short, same-sex batterers often use the myth of mutual battering to disguise their abuse as mutual, consensual combat; alienate the victim from sources of assistance; reinforce the victim's guilt and self-doubt; and allow the abusive relationship to continue without challenge. The myth of mutual abuse, which at bottom is founded on sexist and heterosexist assumptions about how people behave, thus becomes a potent tool of control in many abusive same-sex relationships.

Sandra Lundy, *Abuse That Dare Not Speak Its Name: Assisting Victims of Lesbian and Gay Domestic Violence in Massachusetts,* 28 New Eng. L. Rev. 273, 283–284 (1993).

The New York City Gay and Lesbian Anti–Violence Project has offered guidelines and assessment information for police responding to incidents of same sex violence:

1) Listen Carefully to the Client's Narrative.

People who are abused tend to minimize the violence that they've experienced. They may also assume a lot of the blame.... Conversely, an abusive person will often place blame on their partner for the incident, and focus their attention on what that person did to 'provoke' the incident.

2) Ask Open–Ended Questions.

"Then what happened?" "Could you talk more about that?" "What were you feeling when s/he did that?" Another way to help people talk about their experience is to reflect back to them what they are saying to you. "She took your keys away and said you weren't going anywhere ..." The client will then pick up the story and continue.

3) Use the Power and Control Wheel to Help the Client Identify Acts of Abuse.

Give the client a copy of the wheel and go over it with her/him. They may identify acts of abuse they did not realize were abusive, for example emotional abuse, economic abuse or intimidation. Sometimes a partner may be abusing economic or skin privilege and being manipulative and emotionally abusive to control their partner, and eventually the partner may lash out physically, in an isolated incident. It is important to assess the dynamics of power in the relationship.

4) WHO SEEMS TO BE MORE IN CONTROL OF THE OTHER PERSON?

Who makes most of the decisions? Who seems to get their way most of the time? Has the client had to modify their behavior in any way? For example, changed jobs, friends, activities, in response to the other person's requirements? Ask her/him to describe the differences they see in themselves now and before this relationship began. What parts of themselves do they feel they have lost? Often times the isolation of the client will become evident, as well as the low self-esteem they may be experiencing as a result of the abuse.

5) IS THIS A PATTERN OF BEHAVIOR?

Is the client saying the abuse happened more than once? Explain the cycle of domestic violence; most people being battered will relate and respond to the dynamic, and identify the pattern in their own relationship.

6) ARE THEY AFRAID OF THEIR PARTNER?

Is the client indicating fear of her/his partner? Are they afraid to disagree with their partner?

7) LOOK FOR "MISPLACED COMPASSION".

Many times victims of domestic violence are unduly concerned with the wellbeing of their abuser. They will be reluctant to "get them in trouble," or worried about their health and well being before their own. Sometimes victims will spend a great deal of time trying to understand and justify the abuser's actions ... "they had a terrible childhood"; "they are under a lot of stress at work." "It is the alcohol, they can't help it," ... are examples of this.

How would you expect a police officer to respond to the situation suggested in 3) above, where an individual lashes out physically, "in an isolated incident," in response to ongoing emotional abuse or intimidation? Does the "provocation" for the violence excuse it? Isn't this exactly the kind of victim-blaming argument domestic violence advocates have been working to discredit, both within the legal system and in the culture at large? Otherwise, do you find these guidelines helpful?

2. Just as the myth of mutual battering reflects a homophobic assumption that can be exploited by a gay or lesbian batterer, so too can other societal manifestations of homophobia be used by gay or lesbian batterers against their partners:

> Society's fear and hatred of homosexuality causes isolation and increases the vulnerability of gay men and lesbians to domestic abuse. The same-sex batterer frequently uses homophobia as a powerful tool to maintain the control and power imbalance in the relationship in a

variety of ways. For example, the batterer may threaten "to out" the victim to family, friends, co-workers and ex-spouses who are not aware of and will not accept his or her sexuality. When forced "out of the closet," victims may lose child custody, prestigious careers, and valued personal relationships. Since there are few positive gay and lesbian role models, batterers may convince "newly out" partners that their relationship is normal and abuse occurs in all gay or lesbian relationships. They may also take advantage of their partners' own internal homophobia and guilt to convince them that they do not deserve any better because they are homosexual.

. . .

A victim's prior unpleasant experiences with members of heterosexual society often lend credibility to batterers' claims. For example: a shelter may have refused to admit or help the gay man; a restraining order clinic advocate may have asked the battered lesbian for her husband's name; the hot line worker may not have believed that the male caller is really a domestic violence victim; or the police officers may have referred to the gay male victim as "she". . . .

As a result of homophobia, some people believe that gay and lesbian victims are less deserving of assistance and intervention because their lifestyles are immoral. Victims are reluctant to report violence that will only reinforce the homophobic attitudes that all "unnatural relationships" have such problems because gay men and lesbians have worked so hard to validate their relationships to heterosexual society. Other people mistakenly believe that because gay men and lesbians are not as emotionally committed as heterosexual partners, it should be easier to leave the abusive relationship, especially since they are not legally married and usually do not have children. Such beliefs demonstrate a serious lack of understanding about homosexuality and the dynamics of domestic violence.

In addition to the typical characteristics of a domestic violence situation, "the fact alone of being lesbian or gay tends to increase one's distance from the larger society and from its resources." Gay and lesbian victims often do not have a strong support system, causing them to feel they do not have many options to help them stop the violence. People with AIDS or who are HIV positive particularly may feel they have no viable alternatives to staying with their abusive partners. If victims are geographically separated from other gay men and lesbians, they may think their partners are the only ones who can understand and accept their sexuality. The gay man or lesbian may be concealing his or her sexual orientation or facing disapproval from other people, including his or her own family. Both gay men and lesbians are less likely than heterosexual women to turn to family members for emotional support.

. . .

. . . [V]ery few support services for gay and lesbian victims or treatment programs specifically for gay and lesbian batterers exist anywhere with the exception of San Francisco, Seattle, Minneapolis and New York.

Kathleen Finley Duthu, *Why Doesn't Anyone Talk About Gay and Lesbian Domestic Violence,* 18 THOS. JEFF. L. REV. 23, 31–33 (1996).

3. The less able a victim of gay or lesbian violence feels to reach out for support, the more vulnerable he or she will be to ongoing abuse. When homophobic attitudes on the part of law enforcement derail effective intervention, the danger can be acute, or even deadly:

> "He's buck naked. He has been beaten up ... he is really hurt ... he needs some help," said concerned neighbors in a telephone call to 911 emergency services, reporting the alarming presence of a young man on the street. Police officers responding to the call dismissed emergency services personnel from the scene and forcibly returned the young man to the apartment of an older male, who persuaded them that the incident was nothing more than "a homosexual tiff." In a radio report from the scene, the officers laughingly described the result of their cursory investigation of the home: "Intoxicated Asian, naked male, was returned to his sober boyfriend." When one local woman called the police station to protest this casual disregard for the younger man's safety and offered additional information, she was told by another officer, "I can't do anything about somebody's sexual preferences in life." Thirty minutes later, fourteen-year-old Konerak Sinthasomphone became the thirteenth of seventeen young men tortured, killed, mutilated and sometimes eaten by his supposed companion, Jeffrey Dahmer.

Nancy E. Murphy, *Queer Justice: Equal Protection for Victims of Same–Sex Domestic Violence,* 30 VAL. U. L. REV. 335, 335 (1995).

According to Sandy Lundy's assessment:

> [L]esbian and gay violence is largely unreported, in part because of an expectation of hostile responses from those in authority. When the battered same-sex partner does take the extraordinary step of disclosing her or his situation to persons in authority, s/he is likely to be subjected to a devastating, institutionalized re-victimization. S/he may find, for instance, that s/he is excluded from protection under the state's domestic violence laws. Not all states protect victims of same-sex domestic violence, and the abuse protection laws of several states specifically exclude such victims from their protection. Same-sex victims who are nominally protected by the law may not fare much better. [One commentator] notes that "at every point in the system, [gay men are] more afraid to identify themselves as a victim," and that their pleas for help are often met by police, district attorneys' offices, and even their own attorneys with demeaning, abusive remarks such as, "Why aren't you defending yourself? You're a man. Stand up for yourself." Negative reactions by the police also were overwhelmingly common in one study of lesbians who reported abuse. Often, for example, police failed to take any action once they realized that a domestic dispute involved two women. As one interviewee told Profes-

> sor Renzetti, "I called the police, but nothing was done about it. I kept thinking, 'No one cares because I'm a lesbian.' The police basically took the attitude, 'So two dykes are trying to kill each other; big deal.'" One gay man reported to Island and Letellier that he was repeatedly referred to as "she" by police officers to whom he reported an incident of domestic violence.

Sandra Lundy, *Abuse That Dare Not Speak Its Name: Assisting Victims of Lesbian and Gay Domestic Violence in Massachusetts,* 28 NEW ENG. L. REV. 273, 290 (1993).

4. While fear of a hostile reaction may be one reason the victim of gay or lesbian violence does not report abuse, solidarity with his or her partner in the face of the broader society's homophobia may be another. The next excerpt draws both these lessons from an account of abuse in a gay male relationship.

The Neighbors Call the Police
David Island and Patrick Letellier, Men Who Beat The Men Who Love Them, 236–39, 245–47 (1991)

... *He is livid now. The blow to my mouth comes fast and direct—POW! He hits me so hard he cuts both my lip and his knuckle; we are both bleeding. I turn my head quickly to avoid the next punch, and blood is smeared on the wall. We continue to struggle and grapple with each other, and Stephen is relentlessly punching me, in the face, in the stomach, on the side of my head, in the chest. It is all I can do to defend myself. I know that somehow I have to get out of the apartment. I literally throw him across the room, using every ounce of my strength, and bolt for the front door. Next to the front door is a coat closet and its door is open. As I run for the front door, Stephen pushes me hard from behind, and I land face down in the closet on top of some suitcases with my legs sticking out into the hall.*

Instantly Stephen is there behind me, kicking me in the shins. Kicking, kicking, kicking, with all his might, as hard as he can. From where I am I can see his face. For the first time I can see the expression on his face as he batters me.... The intensity, the deliberation, the concentration....

Then, suddenly, it is over. His rage has passed. The shouting and screaming that had been going on has stopped, and the apartment is quiet. Stephen walks away, going ... I don't know where. I go into the bathroom and look at my lip. "It's a small cut," I think. "Maybe nobody will notice it." I feel my shins. I know they are bruised and will hurt even more later. And then I remember blood on a wall somewhere. I wet a facecloth, wipe my face and cut lip, and go into the bedroom to look for blood stains. As I'm wiping them off the wall, the doorbell rings. Stephen, looking out of a window, mutters, "Oh my God. There's a police car out front." Then he directs me, "Pull yourself together." Remarkably, he looks worse than I.

I listen from the bedroom as Stephen talks to the police. I hear only fragments. "No, no problems here. We were just having an argument, that's all . . ." And then I hear the policewoman say something about "not leaving until we see the other party." Stephen politely calls out, "Patrick, will you come here please. They want to see you."

I quickly check my appearance in the mirror (I look okay. "Good enough," I think) and go to the door. "Everything is fine," I hear myself say. "We were just having an argument, that's all. . . ." I smile weakly.

. . . I stand there, numbly staring at those two officers, wondering if they think I've been beating Stephen, because he looks absolutely terrified right now. I hear them something about intervening, "if it gets physical." They leave. . . .

"Neighbors" . . . shows how reluctant a victim may be, even when the opportunity is present, to tell the police the truth about the violence and to file a complaint against the batterer. There are many reasons for victim reluctance. Fear is at the top of the list. Fear of recrimination from the batterer may prevent victims from saying anything to the police, particularly in the presence of the batterer. Gay male victims may also be understandably afraid of homohating police officers. Patrick has no way of knowing what the police may do if he identifies Stephen as a lover who beats him. They may decide the abuse is "mutual combat" and arrest them both. They may ridicule Patrick as a "fag" who deserves to get beaten up. They may tell both Patrick and Stephen that they are "sissies who should learn to fight like real men." (Both of the above scenarios were reported by victims of gay men's domestic violence when the San Francisco police arrived at their homes.) The police may also arrest Stephen and book him on spouse abuse, as they should, but Patrick has no way of knowing what they will do. At such times, victims may believe that silence is their safest option.

The most important lesson of this narrative is about complicity. Patrick has now inadvertently joined Stephen as a "partner in crime." Patrick colluded with Stephen to lie to the police and to "cover up" the violence. They are now joined together as partners in violence against the world "out there," including the police. This act of complicity will make it even more difficult for Patrick to extricate himself from the relationship and much more difficult for him to convince Stephen that he wants no part of the violence.

. . .

Reasons gay male victims do not call the police more frequently than they do include their valid fear of retaliation . . . and homophobic or abusive treatment by the police. But those are not the only reasons. An analysis of the American family also supplies a reason.

In a family, such as a gay couple, the members are bound to each other by emotional, economic, and psychological bonds. Solidarity develops, which explains why and how a family rallies to form an united front when a tragedy occurs. Old disputes are put aside and the family functions as "one" to overcome a problem or fight outside forces.

. . . High solidarity means personal closeness in which family members identify with each other and can easily put themselves in each other's shoes, and it means longstanding and strong emotional connections. High solidarity, then, resists family break-up.

Furthermore, in gay relationships solidarity may be abnormally high. Living in a homohating society such as the United States, many gays, cut off from family, church, and other traditional forms of societal support, may place a greater value on their own relationship. Often gay couples hold an "us against the world" view, obviously intensifying the solidarity between the members of the couple. Homophobia may also play a more direct role in increasing solidarity in gay couples. Gay couples with children may understandably fear police involvement and the accompanying heterosexist custody laws that may destroy their families. Fear of bigotry and police brutality may unite victims and batterers on one side, as members of an oppressed and hated minority, and police on the other side, as oppressors and gay-haters. For many gay men of color, trusting the police may simply be out of the question.

. . .

. . . This discussion of solidarity has important messages for victims. First, it is important for gay victims to understand that their reluctance to turn in their batterers may have its roots in a healthy and normal human phenomenon: high solidarity with family. However, in relationships with violent men, high solidarity can be lethal, inhibiting victims from effectively dealing with a life-threatening situation. Victims must acknowledge, then put aside, their feelings of solidarity in order to survive.

Second, a batterer's pathological dependence may have the illusion of solidarity, but much more is involved, and their dependence should be recognized as extremely unhealthy. In fact, acknowledging batterer obsession may help victims put aside their own feelings of solidarity, as they see the disparity between the two forces.

* * *

NOTES

1. Solidarity between the abuser and his or her victim is the theme of this last excerpt, but a final important factor increasing the vulnerability of gay and lesbian victims of partner violence is the solidarity within their respective communities; the reluctance to acknowledge abuse, and the reluctance to sanction internally (through ostracism, for example), or to report abusers to external authorities.

In her article *Lavender Bruises: Intra-Lesbian Violence, Law and Lesbian Legal Theory,* 20 GOLDEN GATE U. L. REV. 567, 583 (1990), Ruthann Robson reports the story of one battered lesbian:

> The response of the local lesbian community to the arrest of my former lover was demoralizing. Lesbians were upset—even angry—that I had called the police. "I can see turning in a batterer and calling the

cops," said one woman. "But a lover? What does that say about your ability to be intimate with anyone?" ... Several women put a lot of pressure on me to drop the charges. They said things like: "Oh, come on. Haven't you ever hit a lover? It wasn't all that bad." "You're dragging your lover's name through the mud. It was in the newspapers." "Do you realize that the state could take away her children because of what you have done?" They suggested setting up a meeting between my former lover and me. They volunteered to mediate so we could reach an "agreement."

I can think of few crueler demands on a woman who has been attacked than to insist she sit down with her attacker and talk things out. I would guess that none of the lesbians who wanted me to do that would consider demanding such a thing from a straight woman who had just been attacked by her boyfriend.... The lowest blow came when a friend called me the day before a pre-trial hearing. "You should drop the charges," she said. "We in the lesbian community can take care of our own." "But what about me? Who's going to guarantee my safety and see that my house doesn't get trashed?" She had no response.

Sandy Lundy confirms that "[t]he lesbian and gay communities historically have failed to support or shelter abused same-sex partners," although she sees differences in the two communities:

Activist Ann Russo notes that battered lesbians "continue to face the denial and passivity of the battered women's movement and the feminist and lesbian communities." While denial and passivity also plague battered heterosexual women, they seem particularly entrenched in the lesbian community. Lesbian communities, for instance may be reluctant for ideological reasons to acknowledge that women can batter other women, because to do so would mean shattering a utopic vision of a peaceful, women-centered world. Or lesbians may discourage the battered lesbian from seeking help because they may believe that the lesbian community should not "air its dirty laundry" in public or participate in patriarchal institutions such as the courts. As a result, women who choose to report the abuse may be ostracized or isolated from her lesbian friends.

Moreover, the lesbian batterer may be a prominent person in the lesbian community or the battered women's community, thus providing what Leventhal calls the "perfect coverup" to cast doubt on the victim's account and allow the battering to go unchallenged. As a result, Russo notes, "[b]attered lesbians continue to face comments from other lesbians and feminists that their experiences don't constitute abuse, that their batterers have hard lives and so can't be expected to be perfect, and the abuse isn't that bad." These comments and attitudes, which would be roundly condemned by many lesbians if directed towards battered heterosexual women, are routinely inflicted on battered lesbians by women who purport to be their allies.

For gay male victims of partner abuse, community awareness and response are far more muted. According to Steven Taylor, a victim advocate who has counseled many abused gay men, the topic of male domestic violence is almost completely ignored by the gay male community. Sandra Moore–Pope, a Texas therapist who has counseled battered gay men, surmises that one reason for this avoidance may be that gay men wish to maintain the illusion that "they are somehow more evolved [than heterosexual men], . . . [that] they have left the paternalistic dominant society, and they would certainly never do something like that." Or the victim's gay male community might cling to the masculinist idea that men are never victims and may consider the battered gay male as a threat to certain ideas about sexual freedom and masculinity. In other words, in the gay male community, unlike in the lesbian community (where considerable controversy rages about how to define lesbian battering and what to do about it), there is little controversy about the issue of domestic violence because there is almost no discussion of it. As Letellier and Island put it, "[o]ne very important reason why it is so hard to find out how many gay men are battered by their mates is that the gay community would rather not know."

Sandra Lundy, *Abuse That Dare Not Speak Its Name: Assisting Victims of Lesbian and Gay Domestic Violence in Massachusetts,* 28 NEW ENG. L. REV. 273, 286–87 (1993).

2. An important new resource in this area is SAME SEX DOMESTIC VIOLENCE: STRATEGIES FOR CHANGE (B. Leventhal & S.E. Lundy, eds., 1999).

C. RACE, CULTURE AND THE EXPERIENCE OF ABUSE

This group of readings addresses partner violence in communities of color, communities with a specific minority ethnic or cultural identity, and immigrant communities. Of course, some of the stories we have already read have been about relationships, and violence, experienced by people of color; not all of the women about whom Angela Browne writes, for example, are white. But now it is time to ask how battering may be experienced differently, and responses to battering may be different, both on the part of those involved in the relationships, and on the part of others in the society, when the batterer and/or his victim is black, or Asian, or Latino/a, or American Indian, or Eastern European. Even to use these labels is to risk minimizing potential differences, and overlooking relevant nuances. We are, after all, talking about women, and men, who are, by birth or family origin, African American, Caribbean, Haitian, Vietnamese, Sri Lankan, Hawaiian, Cuban, Mexican, Portuguese, Romanian, Croatian, Navajo or Sioux, just to name a few possibilities. Moreover, even if they hail from the same country, they may be part of radically different political, cultural or religious subcommunities. They may be new immigrants, or born and raised in the United States.

These few pages cannot do justice to the multitude of issues these differences raise. Instead, we will offer examples of thoughtful writing about some of them, within the framework offered in the introduction to this chapter. We ask, that is to say, how issues of race, culture, ethnicity and immigrant status might affect:

(a) individuals' subjective experiences of abuse;

(b) their own community's understanding of abuse, in the context of community norms about family structure and gender role expectations;

(c) their ability to reach out from their own community to the larger society for assistance; and

(d) the larger society's responses to their abuse—

while not losing sight of the ways in which these questions are profoundly interrelated.

The section opens with a look at differences in how women understand or interpret their own experiences of abuse. The first reading is drawn from a book by Beth Richie, COMPELLED TO CRIME: THE GENDER ENTRAPMENT OF BATTERED BLACK WOMEN (1996), in which she reports on a study of women incarcerated on Riker's Island, for criminal activity that she discovered was often related, directly or indirectly, to the abuse they suffered at the hands of an intimate partner. Her study included African American battered women, white battered women, and non-battered African American women. In looking at their backgrounds, at their expectations of themselves and their partners, and at their experiences, she uncovered some important and thought provoking differences among the three groups. This excerpt suggests some ways in which women's subjective experiences of abuse—and of the "gender entrapment," in Richie's words, that results in abuse—may differ in ways that are, if not determined by race, then at least influenced by race.

Richie's study provides a wonderful example of the kind of highly contextual and nuanced inquiry necessary to an understanding of the ways in which numerous aspects of women's lives "intersect" to influence their vulnerability to abuse, how they understand or interpret their abuse, and their responses to it. She is not writing about all African American women, but about a specific subgroup—incarcerated African American women, all of whom come from economically deprived backgrounds. Even within this sample, she is at pains to demonstrate that generalizations about her subjects are misleading; rather, their backgrounds and experiences, while inevitably influenced by race as well as economic status, fall into quite distinct patterns, with importantly different consequences.

Beth Richie
Compelled to Crime: the gender entrapment of battered black women, 63–68, 97–102 (1996)

Gender–Identity Development

Several features generally characterize all of the families of origin of the three subgroups in this study. Despite slight variations in income level, all of the women's families lived close to the social and economic margin. Even those women who described their lives as "comfortable" experienced their economic status as fragile. Most of the families depended on multiple incomes from unstable jobs to support the family, and even those who accumulated extra material possessions were vulnerable to changes in employment status, health problems, and other unexpected family crises. In both subgroups of African American women, the women's mothers worked outside of the homes, while the white women did so only on occasion. In all of the families, the women were primary caretakers of the children, and all of the women worked in their households, performing routine household tasks that were usually organized around gender. Only the white families were highly organized by generation; in the African American families the distinctions between children and adults were less rigid.

Of the seven themes that emerged about the families, childhood roles, and the construction of female identities, the findings indicated that the three subgroups in this study were distinct. The African American women who were battered were distinguished by their racial/ethnic identity and by their early childhood experiences....

* In terms of their positions in their households, the African American battered women described childhoods that were distinguished from other childhoods by more privileges, material possessions and attention. With this elevated status came a symbolic burden on the women to *maintain* the privileged status through emotional, academic, household, and other "*work.*" This unusual position and their efforts to maintain status were the initial circumstance that left the African American battered women vulnerable to gender entrapment.

In contrast, the African American women who were not battered recalled being average children, feeling a sense of commonality with the other children with whom they grew up. As such, they were less concerned with differentiating themselves from others. Of the three groups, the white children typically described childhood experiences that were the most deprived relative to other children in their families. They tended to be scapegoated and ignored, and their burdens were more concrete than emotional in nature. They almost came to expect degrading treatment and recognized it as such.

* The second theme that emerged from the data as an important finding for the gender-entrapment theory was the images the women had of adult women and men. The African American battered women recalled a paradoxical relationship with their female caretakers. On the one hand, they tended to idealize them, and, on the other hand, they described feeling distant and, at times, disappointed in their mothers' lack of emotional and physical availability to them as children. The African American battered women adopted their mothers' tendency to feel sorry for men in their lives, tolerating their irresponsibility, their limitations, their indiscretions, and, ultimately, their violence....

The African American women who were not battered had a more realistic sense of who their mothers were. This subgroup tended to identify with their mothers in more ways than the African American battered women, including taking on their mothers' dismissal or disdain for men. Their mothers were less generous with their tolerance and more discounting of men's roles in their lives. In this way, they were significantly less vulnerable to men's violence as adults. The white women were generally more distant from adults as children than the other two groups, and they tended to feel sorry for their mothers and avoid interaction with their fathers. However, as children, the white battered women developed an understanding of the relative power that men and boys held in their families and, indeed, in the world.

* The findings from this theme were related to a third theme that emerged from the data as relevant to gender entrapment: the women's experiences and observation of abuse during their childhood. In each subgroup, the women tended to internalize and draw meaning from their mothers' responses to abuse if they observed it. The African American battered women's' mothers who were battered themselves tended not to leave abusive relationships, while the African American non-battered women's' mothers tended to resist and leave right away. The white women's mothers responded to being abused by planning to leave and attempting to leave. However, in the end, they were not able to stay away permanently for a number of reasons. In each case, the decision to stay or leave was related to the mother's sense of herself in relationship to the man by whom she was abused, as well as the availability of concrete options.

For those women in this study who themselves experienced abuse as children, the effect was significant, albeit different, for each subgroup. The African American battered women were less often physically abused as children, and more often abused sexually, which is a significant element in their gender entrapment. The role of protecting the adults who committed this heinous act was added to the burden of being "special" children.... The African American non-battered women experienced some physical and sexual abuse, but were not targeted as victims any more than other children in their families.... All of the white women in this sample were abused as children, and, like the African American battered women, internalized some of the consequences. For them, the situation was compounded by serious childhood neglect.

* As the African American battered women grew up and began to encounter the subtle messages and overt pressures from the social world to conform to "appropriate" gender and racial/ethnic roles, they began to engage in self-limiting behavior in order to more consistently fit within their sense of expected behaviors. The African American battered women were surprised that they did not command the same respect from teachers, employers, and peers that they did from their families, and they began to work even harder to please others rather than themselves. They tended to avoid risks, and some even sabotaged their opportunities for social advancement. Instead, they focused on their domestic relationships, becoming overconfident of their abilities to effect change in the private sphere of their lives.

At the other extreme from the African American battered women, the African American non-battered women in the sample were the most likely to ignore expectations and to take symbolic and concrete risks while they were growing up. When they felt discriminatory treatment in the public or private sphere that limited their choices or constricted their behavior, they defied regulations despite the threat of punishment. The women in this subgroup were much more peer-identified than the other two groups, and they did not censor themselves. Instead, they sometimes acted incautiously and engaged in behaviors that resulted in negative sanctions. The white battered women in the sample tried to avoid rejections, as did the African American battered women, but they had come to expect it and had learned to cope more effectively with it. . . .

* All of the women in this study initially desired traditional, heterosexual nuclear families, especially the African American battered women. In this subgroup, the women's motivations were, in part, in response to their sense of family loyalty, their sense of family life needing strong women (such as the ones they thought they would become), and their desire to rest and be taken care of in response to negative experiences in the public sphere, which they felt was hostile to them.

The African American women who were not battered also wanted family lives that were consistent with the dominant form; however, they expressed a pessimistic view of the likelihood that they would be able to accomplish this goal. The non-battered African American women abandoned their desire to fit the ideological norm at a very early age. They were prepared to have their relationships fail and were open and willing to establish alternative family forms.

The white women remained highly attached to the dominant ideology about family, and they imagined that the hegemonic family would answer the problems they faced as relatively deprived children. The dreams of the women in this subgroup had an escapist tone. These findings are relevant to the gender-entrapment theoretical model inasmuch as the African American battered women worked the hardest and the longest and, indeed, with the most conviction, to create and maintain a hegemonic nuclear family, even when the violence began and they became involved in illegal activities.

* The meaning of the women's gender roles, as expressed through the question, "How would your life have been different were you a boy?" was consistent with the overall patterns that emerged from the three subgroups. African American or white, all of the women felt that their lives had been negatively influenced by the constraints placed on them because of their gender. The differences among the three subgroups lay in the developmental stage and in the social moment that the women *felt* the gender constraints. The African American battered women felt vulnerable as women but not as girls. . . . This finding was ironic given the extent of sexual abuse they experienced. It suggested how significant denial was to their gender entrapment, for even as young girls the women sensed that by sacrificing themselves, they were serving a greater cause in their families—men's need for power, the sexual satisfaction of their abuser or preserving the families' integrity by not disclosing the abuse.

The African American women who were not battered expressed awareness of a more concrete set of limiting factors that were gender related. The white battered women also acknowledged their gender liability in concrete terms; however, their consciousness of limitations began much earlier in their lives than for either subgroup of African American women.

* The last theme that emerged . . . was the importance of racial/ethnic identity and solidarity in the women's overall sense of themselves. As the cases illustrated, the African American women in both groups expressed a keener sense of their racial/ethnic identity than the white battered women. However, for the African American battered women, loyalty was directed to their families and, by implication, to African American men in their families. This factor was a key element in their emotional interest, every-day work, and identities as "Black women trying to create families with Black men," which was changing to "battered women," "victim," or "female offenders." In contrast, the African American women who were not battered constructed their racial/ethnic identities more in terms of the African American community as a whole, including African American women. They consider the contemporary issues that limit women's lives as central and important. Their identities were less gender-bound and relationship-bound. The white battered women did not indicate that race/ethnicity was a critical element of their identities, and it did not overtly influence their behaviors, thoughts, or feelings as much as it did the African American battered women.

. . .

Trapped by Violence

. . . The African American battered women entered into their intimate relationships with optimism that resulted from their heightened status in their households of origin. As their experiences in the public sphere were disappointing, they became more strongly committed to establishing a respectable and successful domestic life , which, for them, included arranging their lives in accordance with the dominant ideology about gender roles in nuclear families. This desire and their efforts towards this goal posed a particular challenge for them; their African American male counterparts were excluded from opportunities that characteristically lead to male privilege (like earning more money than women), and the African American battered women themselves felt forced to participate actively in the public domain.

Feeling sorry for the men they were involved with, the women denied their vulnerability and tolerated the abuse, which, in turn, became worse while the women disbelieved that they were being hurt and humiliated by the men for whom they were caring. When they realized that their domestic lives were failing them, they isolated themselves out of shame and embarrassment and in order to protect the image of their family. The African American battered women were, therefore, increasingly vulnerable to the abuse and domination of their violent male partners.

The circumstantial and emotional factors that characterized the white battered women's adult households were different. They entered their intimate relationships with lower self-esteem and fewer expectations. That their relationships were unsatisfying and, indeed, abusive from the onset did not surprise or confuse them. Their identity was not as damaged by the abuse, and they did not become as immobilized as the African American battered women. When they were hurt, afraid and humiliated, they planned to or attempted to get help. Even when their attempts were unsuccessful, they *felt* less trapped by the abuse and by their feelings about the men with whom they were involved.

These differences in vulnerability led to different consequences for the African American and the white women who were battered. First, the effects of the abuse varied considerably in terms of race/ethnicity. . . . [T]he African American women suffered particularly degrading forms of physical abuse from their male partners while the white battered women's [experiences] were more consistent with the national average; the abuse was of a more controlled nature. An important difference between the two subgroups on this item was the degree to which the African American battered women were permanently disfigured and suffered chronic pain from the physical abuse. This overt, public manifestation of being abused had a profoundly effective role in the gender-entrapment process—it furthered the African American women's deep loss of dignity, given their previously heightened sense of themselves.

In terms of emotional abuse, the women I interviewed in both subgroups described the horrific, damaging effect of regular psychological victimization. When combined with physical assaults, both groups of battered women were made further vulnerable by the damage caused by the insulting, dishonest, controlling behavior of their male partners. Women from each group described how the isolation, shame, loss of dignity and the fear created an interlocking pattern of vulnerability and violence that kept many women immobilized in the abusive relationships. The African American battered women experienced this pattern as far more disorienting than did the white battered women, most of whom were quicker to recognize it as abusive. In some ways the white battered women were more pessimistic and were emotionally hurt earlier in their lives, and, therefore they were less affected by the emotional abuse of their adult intimate partners. Furthermore, the social and familial stigma that the African American women anticipated or experienced was a complicating factor for them, given their privileged status in their households of origin and family-loyalty issues. In contrast, the white battered women were more estranged from their families of origin. . . .

In terms of those women who experienced sexual abuse, the life-history interviews revealed little difference between the two subgroups. Both the African American battered women and the white battered women found the marital rape and other forms of sexual violence extraordinarily hard to bear, and they suffered long-term negative consequences. The effects were not affected by the presence or absence of sexual abuse as children.

The women's increased vulnerability to violence from their intimate partners and the consequence of the abuse affected their practical responses, influencing a distinct pattern of concrete behavior from the two groups of battered women in this study. The African American battered women's stories show how they attempted to conceal the abuse and avoided use of public services, while the white women tended to reach out to more individuals and to social-service programs. This finding is particularly noteworthy in terms of use of the criminal justice system for crisis-intervention services given that the women were, indeed, victims of a crime. Unlike most of the white women, the African American battered women had a distinct and vehement opposition to calling the police; they avoided pressing criminal charges against their abusive partners or otherwise becoming involved in a criminal justice solution to the violence. The extent to which mistreatment by law-enforcement officials, biased criminal justice practices, and the knowledge of the disproportionate incarceration rates of men of color consciously influenced the African American battered women's response to the abuse in their intimate relationships was significant. . . .

* * *

NOTES

1. While we may not have parallel in-depth studies to guide our understanding of how women of other races, ethnicities, cultures and classes may experience abuse, Richie's work demonstrates the need to avoid making assumptions about those experiences, and suggests the kinds of questions we might want to ask to test our starting hypotheses.

2. Richie's account also suggests the power of community norms, often transmitted through families, but also through other community institutions and through peer culture, to shape the experience of abuse, even as she reminds us that competing norms can coexist, even in relatively cohesive communities. These next readings take up this question of the culturally specific community norms that shape understandings of, and responses to, abuse.

Karin Wang
Battered Asian American Women: Community Responses from the Battered Women's Movement and the Asian American Community, 3 Asian Law Review 151, 161, 167–71 (1996)

Discussing how Asian American women are differently situated from white women implies that all Asian American women are similarly situated with respect to each other. I do not intend to assert an essential Asian American identity, as there is no singular Asian culture or nation. "Asian American" as an identity is socially constructed and created out of political and social necessity, in recognition of the need to embrace commonalities among diverse Asian Americans. It is in this vein that I discuss battered Asian American women. . . .

. . .

Because most Asian Americans are immigrants, most Asian American communities retain, at least in part, the culture of their country of origin.

Although treating all Asian American communities as fungible can be dangerous, the diverse Asian American subgroups do share certain cultural commonalities which have important implications for battered Asian American women....

The Importance of Family and Gender Roles

> *"I didn't sense the danger because I was so focused on the shame my daughter's actions would bring in the Cambodian community. And I was thinking about my daughter's children and the importance of their having a family." Kim Leang is remembering her daughter Kim Seng, killed by her abusive husband, Sartout Nom. A week before Kim Seng's murder, Kim Leang had organized a family meeting, where both sides of the family urged the young couple to stay together and asked Nom to stop beating Kim Seng. Says Kim Leang, "Sometimes because we value our cultural conditions, we try to get families reunited at whatever cost."*

Asian cultures are group-oriented. A person's identity and worth are not measured individually, but are instead reflected by the group as a whole. Consequently, the family is the most important social unit. A person is regarded as an extension of the family and is expected to subjugate individual needs to family interests....

To the extent that individualism does matter in Asian cultures, male individuals are valued over females. While men are highly respected and valued by the family, women are considered inferior. The secondary status of women is illustrated by their traditional role in marriage and family. Marriages, which were frequently pre-arranged, often involved an exchange of money from the groom's family to the bride's family, so that essentially, the wife was owned by and subject to the desires of the husband. The man governed and supported the family while the woman stayed home. Within this traditional family structure, power was vested vertically in the male head. A woman was not given an identity outside the family, and was always subordinate to the various men in the family; her father, her husband, her sons. As followers and never leaders, women were expected to be dependent, to suffer, and to persevere.

These traditional cultural beliefs about family and gender roles have important implications for battered Asian American women.... First, the group focus of Asian cultures protects family reputation at the expense of the individual. In many Asian cultures, "keeping face" is an important social rule. Because the individual is viewed as an extension of the group, one family member's guilt or shame transfers to the rest of the family. The individual must "keep face" and minimize public attention to her and, by extension, to her family's problems. For a battered Asian American woman, publicly admitting that she is battered would often be "synonymous with condemning herself to isolation and ostracization." The pressure to "keep face" prevents many battered Asian American women from seeking assistance from outsiders or even from other family members. Furthermore, the emphasis on "keeping face" also pressures the batterer and other members in the family to hide any abuse from non-family and non-community members. By avoiding external intervention or public acknowledgment of battering, the battered Asian American woman, her abuser, and their families keep the violence hidden inside the family, which complicates the already frustrating problem of general under reporting of domestic violence incidents.

Second, the emphasis on family cohesion eliminates divorce as a realistic option for many battered Asian American women.... [B]ecause the family is all-important in Asian cultures, marriage may be viewed as being too sacred an institution to destroy. The emphasis on family may keep the family together, but at great personal cost to the woman. In a culture where individual rights are deemphasized and where a woman's identity is rooted in her family, a battered Asian American woman has little incentive to escape battering and indeed is often tacitly discouraged by her culture from doing so.

Third, the traditional gender roles ascribed to men and women in Asian cultures create problems which clash with modern-day gender roles. The cultural expectation that a woman should stay at home and care for the family often collides with American social and economic reality. Because recent immigrants are often relegated to low-paying, menial jobs not taken by non-immigrants, immigrant families often need the combined income of both the husband and the wife in order to survive. Immigrant Asian men cannot realistically be the sole breadwinners in America and many immigrant Asian women must work to help support their families. It is not uncommon for immigrant women to find work before or more easily than immigrant men, since low-paid, unskilled labor readily exists for immigrant women in garment sweatshops and other dangerous, unregulated industries. The woman's role in supporting the family changes the traditional family structure and gender roles. These changes, which Asian American women may perceive as liberating, simultaneously threaten their husbands, especially in a society hostile toward Asian American men. The shift in gender roles and subsequently in power within the family establishes an environment where battering may be more likely and may even be considered justified.

* * *

NOTES

1. See also Nilda Rimonte, *A Question of Culture: Cultural Approval of Violence Against Women in the Pacific–Asian Community and the Cultural Defense,* 43 STANFORD L. REV. 1311 (1993). There are some striking parallels between Karin Wang's account of women's expected role within Asian American cultures, and the following account of Latino culture:

> Within the Latino community, Latinas' identities are defined on the basis of their roles as mothers and wives. By encouraging definitions of Latinas as interconnected with and dependent upon status within a family unit structure, the Latino patriarchy denies Latinas individuality on the basis of gender. For Latinas, cultural norms and

myths of national origin intersect with these patriarchal notions of a woman's role and identity....

This intersection of gender, national origin, and race denies Latinas a self-definitional, experiential-based, feminist portrait. Those within the Latino community expect Latinas to be traditional, and to exist solely within the Latino family structure. A Latina must serve as a daughter, a wife, and a parent, and must prioritize the needs of family members above her own. She is the foundation of the family unit. She is treasured as a self-sacrificing woman who will always look to the needs of others before her own. The influence of Catholicism throughout Latin America solidifies this image within the community, where Latinas are expected to follow dogma and to be religious, conservative, and traditional in their beliefs.

Jenny Rivera, *Domestic Violence Against Latinas By Latino Males: An Analysis of Race, National Origin, and Gender Differentials,* 14 B.C. THIRD WORLD L.J. 231, 241(1994). Like Karin Wang in her use of the term "Asian American," Jenny Rivera is careful to acknowledge that the "Latino community" is in fact made up of people from many different communities:

"Latinas" ... refers to women of Latin American, Caribbean, and mixed ethnic origin, as well as women who consider themselves Latina, based on their country of national origin. This includes women born in Latin America or the Latin American Caribbean, as well as women born in the United States or elsewhere outside Latin America whose ancestral roots are in Latin America. For example, Puerto Rican women who migrated to this country, and their United States-born daughters, would fall within this definition of Latina.

Linguistic and cultural knowledge or familiarity are not essential for identification as Latina. It is often the social, political, and cultural reality of members of distinct ethnic groups in the United States that, generationally, they evidence a distancing from familial, ethnic, and regional origins. As a result, each generation strives to overcome ignorance and misinformation about its own language and culture.... This "cultural distancing," however, does not always result in complete ignorance of language or culture, nor in a feeling of exclusion from one's ethnic group. In fact, such distancing can be the basis for strong feelings of ethnic solidarity and pride. Cultural distancing can instill deep desires to connect with the group's culture and to learn about one's past heritage.

Id. at 232, n.10.

2. Locating women's vulnerability to violence in particular community norms may be essential to shaping interventions and services that "fit" women's self-definitions, situations and needs. At the same time, we have to use this information with caution. In specifying what it is in "other" cultures that makes women targets for abuse, we should not let "mainstream" American culture off the hook, or indeed allow ourselves to fall into unwarranted negative stereotypes about those "other" cultures. Leti Volpp makes this point in the specific context of immigrant cultures, but what she says has equal applicability to minority community cultures here in the United States:

> Selectively blaming culture leads to the misapprehension that certain ... cultures are fundamentally different from "our" culture. Ethnic difference is equated with moral difference, with which we must struggle in a multicultural state. Specifically, commentators depict the sex-subordinating practices of certain immigrants as creating an irreconcilable tension between the values of feminism and multiculturalism. The presumed existence of this conflict leads to policy proposals and theoretical conclusions that exaggerate differences between "us" and "them." Such misreadings prevent us from seeing, understanding and struggling against specific relations of power—both within "other" cultures and our own.

Leti Volpp, *Blaming Culture for Bad Behavior,* 12 YALE J. L. & HUMAN. 89, 90–91 (2000).

This tendency to "blame culture," and the conflict it can create between members of the cultural subcommunity and mainstream advocates and activists is well illustrated by reactions to the case of Dong Lu Chen, a Chinese American man sentenced by a New York judge to only five years probation for the murder of his wife. The judge based his decision on testimony that Chen's state of mind at the time of the murder was dictated by traditional Chinese values; Chen had learned of his wife's infidelity and was driven to kill her, he claimed, by culturally specific attitudes about adultery and loss of manhood. While this did not exonerate him, it led to a verdict of manslaughter rather than murder, and permitted the lenient sentence. Although cultural arguments on behalf of criminal defendants have been loosely called "cultural defense" arguments, they are in fact arguments that support other defenses, or support a reduction in the severity of the charges, or in the sentence, as in Chen's case.

Although Asian American community activists and feminists came together briefly to protest the judge's decision, the coalition quickly fell apart. White feminists argued that it was altogether inappropriate to allow defense arguments based on culture. The District Attorney, Elizabeth Holtzman, said: "There should be one standard of justice, not one that depends on the cultural background of the defendant. There may be barbaric customs in various parts of the world, but that cannot excuse criminal conduct here." What outraged Asian American activists about the verdict, by contrast, was the assumption that the depiction of Chinese culture as tolerating such a killing was accurate. Barbara Chang, from the Asian Women's Center in New York, said firmly: "Chinese culture does not give a man permission to kill his wife regardless of what the situation was at home." For the Asian American activists, on the other hand, the argument that culture should be routinely excluded from the courtroom was nonsensical. In the words of Monona Yin of the Committee Against Anti–Asian Violence, "Culture informs everything each person does." For further discussions of the Chen case, and of cultural defense arguments in domestic violence cases more generally, see Karin Wang, *Battered Asian American Women: Community Responses from the Battered Women's Movement and the Asian American Community*, 3 ASIAN L. REV. 151, 161, 167–71 (1996); Leti Volpp, *(Mis)identifying Culture: Asian Women and the Cultural Defense,* 17 HARV. WMN'S L.J. 57 (1994); Nilda Rimonte, *A Question of Culture: Cultural Approval of*

Violence Against Women in the Pacific–Asian Community and the Cultural Defense, 43 STANFORD L. REV. 1311 (1993).

3. American Indian history and traditions offer a vision of male-female relationships quite different than the patriarchal model common to European, Asian and Latin American cultures. Here is a collection of testaments to that alternative, taken from the introduction to Gloria Valencia Weber and Christine P. Zuni, *Domestic Violence and Tribal Protection of Indigenous Women in the United States,* 69 ST. JOHN'S L. REV. 69, 69–70 (1995):

> A man who battered his wife was considered irrational and thus could no longer lead a war party, a hunt, or participate in either. He could not be trusted to behave properly.... He was thought of as contrary to Lakota law and lost many privileges of life and many roles in Lakota society and the societies within the society.
>
> What we do know is that in most Native American societies men's and women's roles were delineated in such a way that violence against women among their own groups did not seem to be a common and regular practice.
>
> We were always taught that women were sacred and that everything in the home belonged to the women. Our extended families used to live together and no one would have ever thought of abusing women and children. It wasn't until families started to move into town or to move away from each other that we started to hear stories about someone beating up his wife.

Further evidence comes from the Navajo common law, summarized here by James W. Zion and Elsie B. Zion in *Hozho' Sokee'—Stay Together Nicely: Domestic Violence Under Navajo Common Law,* 25 ARIZ. ST. L.J. 407, 413–15 (1993):

> ... Navajo marriage ceremonies use the clan as an institution to teach the law of marriage. During the course of the ceremony, elders and clan relations teach the rights and duties of spouses. They include admonishments such as, "Don't get mad at each other;" "Don't talk back to each other;" "Don't divorce each other;" and "Stay together nicely." The ceremony specifically addresses spousal abuse, and grooms learn the rule that a man "should never take his hand to his wife (i.e. beat her)."
>
> A common American Indian social practice which irritated non-Indians and "proved" the "barbaric" nature of Indians was polygamy. In Navajo society, one of polygamy's purposes was to "obviate dissension and to insure conjugal fidelity" through marriage to a wife's sisters. A man's potential spouses also included a widow, or divorced woman, and her daughters by the prior union. This was a woman-controlled family arrangement, where a man would have difficulty abusing a tight-knit women's group.... [W]here a woman left her protective family, polygamy was sometimes a marital condition.
>
> The family is a legal institution which enforces these rules. One of the first things an outsider learns about Navajos is that they trace their ancestry through their mothers, and that they are members of their mother's clan....

Traditionally, Navajos practiced matrilocal residence after marriage; the husband went to live with the wife's mother's group. A woman's family had a corresponding duty to protect her if her husband became abusive. Navajo's men's life histories show that they understood both the prohibition against domestic violence and the role of the family as an institution to prevent it. While not all couples lived with the wife's family, there was a protective custom whereby couples did not live alone during their first year of marriage.

Another rule of Navajo common law, which is reinforced in the family and clan as an institution, is that it is best for couples to reconcile their differences. Navajos use a family meeting to make arrangements for an effective reconciliation or an agreed divorce. Another Navajo practice, although fading, is the arranged marriage, entered into for economic benefit and relationships between clans. It shamed clan elders for their children to disrupt family and inter-clan survival by domestic violence. Accordingly, there was strong familial interest in preserving peace among married couples.

James and Elsie Zion argue that the rise of domestic violence among the Navajo is a consequence of the disruption of traditional norms and practices caused by forced assimilation and the imposition of mainstream values and culture: "it exists in a climate of institutionalized violence, where traditional values of equality and harmony have been broken down, and new forces have caused people to lose hope and replace it with dependence and disharmony." Id. at 408. The question posed by these authors is whether sufficient vitality remains in traditional Navajo institutions and cultural norms to promote culturally specific responses to domestic violence.

4. The next reading takes us to the consideration of whether women are able to reach out from their particular communities to the larger society for assistance in dealing with intimate partner violence; and how the larger society responds to those requests. The author, Kimberle Crenshaw, describes how gender, race and culture intersect to produce contextualized responses to abuse. Crenshaw first developed the concept of "intersectionality" to describe how race and gender interact to shape the employment experiences of Black women. Kimberle Crenshaw, *Demarginalizing the Intersection of Race and Sex,* 1989 U. CHI. LEGAL FORUM 139 (1989). In the excerpt below, she applies that analysis to the experience of domestic violence.

Kimberle Crenshaw
Mapping the Margins: Intersectionality, Identity Politics, and Violence Against Women of Color, 43 Stanford Law Review 1241, 1244–62 (1993)

Structural Intersectionality and Battering

I observed the dynamics of structural intersectionality during a brief field study of battered women's shelters located in minority communities in

Los Angeles.... Many women who seek protection are unemployed or underemployed, and a good number of them are poor. Shelters serving these women cannot afford to address only the violence inflicted by the batterer; they must also confront the other multilayered and routinized forms of domination that often converge in these women's lives, hindering their ability to create alternatives to the abusive relationships that brought them to shelter in the first place. Many women of color, for example, are burdened by poverty, child care responsibilities, and the lack of job skills. These burdens, largely the consequence of gender and class oppression, are then compounded by the racially discriminatory employment and housing practices women of color often face, as well as by the disproportionately high unemployment among people of color that makes battered women of color less able to rely on the support of friends and relatives for temporary shelter.

When systems of race, gender and class domination converge ... interventions based solely on the experiences of women who do not share the same class or race backgrounds will be of limited help to women who because of race and class face different obstacles....

... [C]ultural barriers often ... discourage immigrant women from reporting or escaping battering situations. Tina Shum, a family counselor at a social service agency, points out that ... "Just to find the opportunity and courage to call us is an accomplishment for many." The typical immigrant spouse, she suggests, may live "[i]n an extended family where several generations live together, there may be no privacy on the telephone, no opportunity to leave the house and no understanding of public phones." As a consequence, many immigrant women are wholly dependent on their husbands as their link to the world outside their homes.

Immigrant women are also vulnerable to spousal violence because so many of them depend on their husbands for information regarding their legal status. Many women who are now permanent residents continue to suffer abuse under threats of deportation by their husbands. Even if the threats are unfounded, women who have no independent access to information will still be intimidated by such threats. And ... there are countless women married to undocumented workers (or who are themselves undocumented) who suffer in silence for fear that the security of their entire families will be jeopardized should they seek help or otherwise call attention to themselves.

Language barriers present another structural problem that often limits opportunities of non-English-speaking women to take advantage of existing support services. Such barriers not only limit access to information about shelters, but also limit access to the security shelters provide. Some shelters turn non-English-speaking women away for lack of bilingual personnel and resources.

These examples illustrate how patterns of subordination intersect in women's experience of domestic violence. Intersectional subordination need not be intentionally produced; in fact, it is frequently the consequence of the imposition of one burden that interacts with preexisting vulnerabilities to create yet another dimension of disempowerment....

Political Intersectionality

The concept of political intersectionality highlights the fact that women of color are situated within at least two subordinated groups that frequently pursue conflicting political agendas. The need to split one's political energies between two sometimes opposing groups is a dimension of intersectional disempowerment that men of color and white women seldom confront. Indeed, their specific race and gendered experiences, although intersectional, often define as well as confine the interests of the entire group. For example, racism as experienced by people of color who are of a particular gender—male—tends to determine the parameters of antiracist strategies, just as sexism as experienced by women who are of a particular race—white—tends to ground the women's movement. The problem is not simply that both discourses fail women of color by not acknowledging the "additional" issue of race or of patriarchy but that the discourses are often inadequate even to the discrete tasks of articulating the full dimensions of racism and sexism. Because women of color experience racism in ways not always the same as those experienced by men of color and sexism in ways not always parallel to experiences of white women, antiracism and feminism are limited, even on their own terms.

. . . The failure of feminism to interrogate race means that the resistance strategies of feminism will often replicate and reinforce the subordination of people of color, and the failure of antiracism to interrogate patriarchy means that antiracism will frequently reproduce the subordination of women. These mutual elisions present a particularly difficult political dilemma for women of color. Adopting either analysis constitutes a denial of a fundamental dimension of our subordination and precludes the development of a political discourse that more fully empowers women of color.

A. The Politicization of Domestic Violence

That the political interests of women of color are obscured and sometimes jeopardized by political strategies that ignore or suppress intersectional issues is illustrated by my experiences in gathering information for this article. I attempted to review Los Angeles Police Department statistics reflecting the rate of domestic violence interventions by precinct because such statistics can provide a rough picture of arrests by racial group, given the degree of racial segregation in Los Angeles. L.A.P.D., however, would not release the statistics. A representative explained that one reason the statistics were not released was that domestic violence activists both within and outside the Department feared that statistics reflecting the extent of domestic violence in minority communities might be selectively interpreted and publicized so as to undermine long-term efforts to force the Department to address domestic violence as a serious problem. I was told that activists were worried that the statistics might permit opponents to dismiss domestic violence as a minority problem and, therefore, not deserving of aggressive action.

The informant also claimed that representatives from various minority communities opposed the release of the statistics. They were concerned, apparently, that the data would unfairly represent Black and Brown communities as unusually violent, potentially reinforcing stereotypes that might be used in attempts to justify oppressive police tactics and other discriminatory practices. These misgivings are based on the familiar and not unfounded premise that certain minority groups—especially Black men—have already been stereotyped as uncontrollably violent. Some worry that attempts to make domestic violence an object of political action may only serve to confirm such stereotypes and undermine efforts to combat negative beliefs about the Black community.

1. Domestic violence and antiracist politics.

Within communities of color, efforts to stem the politicization of domestic violence are often grounded in attempts to maintain the integrity of the community. The articulation of this perspective takes different forms. Some critics allege that feminism has no place within communities of color, that the issues are internally divisive, and that they represent the migration of white women's concerns into a context in which they are not only irrelevant but also harmful. At its most extreme, this rhetoric denies that gender violence is a problem in the community and characterizes any effort to politicize gender subordination as itself a community problem. . . .

. . .

. . . People of color often must weigh their interests in avoiding issues that might reinforce distorted public perceptions against the need to acknowledge and address intracommunity problems. Yet the cost of suppression is seldom recognized in part because the failure to discuss the issue shapes perceptions of how serious the problem is in the first place.

The controversy over Alice Walker's novel The Color Purple can be understood as an intracommunity debate about the political costs of exposing gender violence within the Black community. One critic lambasted Walker's portrayal of Celie, the emotionally and physically abused protagonist who finally triumphs in the end. Walker, the critic contended, had created in Celie a Black woman whom she couldn't imagine existing in any Black community she knew or could conceive of.

The claim that Celie was somehow an unauthentic character might be read as a consequence of silencing discussion of intracommunity violence. Celie may be unlike any Black woman we know because the real terror experienced daily by minority women is routinely concealed in a misguided (though perhaps understandable) attempt to forestall racial stereotyping. Of course, it is true that representations of Black violence—whether statistical or fictional—are often written into a larger script that consistently portrays Black and other minority communities as pathologically violent. The problem, however, is not so much the portrayal of violence itself as it is the absence of other narratives and images portraying a fuller range of Black experience. . . .

The political imperatives of a narrowly focused antiracist strategy support other practices that isolate women of color. For example, activists who have attempted to provide support services to Asian- and African-American women report intense resistance from those communities. At other times, cultural and social factors contribute to suppression. Nilda Rimonte, director of Everywoman's Shelter in Los Angeles, points out that in the Asian community, saving the honor of the family from shame is a priority. Unfortunately, this priority tends to be interpreted as obliging women not to scream rather than obliging men not to hit.

Race and culture contribute to the suppression of domestic violence in other ways as well. Women of color are often reluctant to call the police, a hesitancy likely due to a general unwillingness among people of color to subject their private lives to the scrutiny and control of a police force that is frequently hostile. There is also a more generalized community ethic against public intervention, the product of a desire to create a private world free from the diverse assaults on the public lives of racially subordinated people. The home . . . may . . . function as a safe haven from the indignities of life in a racist society. However, but for this "safe haven" in many cases, women of color victimized by violence might otherwise seek help.

There is also a general tendency within antiracist discourse to regard the problem of violence against women of color as just another manifestation of racism. In this sense, the relevance of gender domination within the community is reconfigured as a consequence of discrimination against men. Of course, it is probably true that racism contributes to the cycle of violence, given the stress that men of color experience in dominant society. It is therefore more than reasonable to explore the links between racism and domestic violence. But the chain of violence is more complex and extends beyond this single link. Racism is linked to patriarchy to the extent that racism denies men of color the power and privilege that dominant men enjoy. When violence is understood as an acting-out of being denied male power in other spheres, it seems counterproductive to embrace constructs that implicitly link the solution to domestic violence to the acquisition of greater male power.... [W]hile understanding links between racism and domestic violence is an important component of any effective intervention strategy, it is also clear that women of color need not await the ultimate triumph over racism before they can expect to live violence-free lives.

2. Race and the domestic violence lobby.

. . .

Efforts to politicize the issue of violence against women challenge beliefs that violence occurs only in the homes of "others." While it is unlikely that advocates and others who adopt this rhetorical strategy intend to exclude or ignore the needs of poor and colored women, the underlying premise of this seemingly universalistic appeal is to keep the sensibilities of dominant social groups focused on the experiences of those groups. Indeed, as subtly suggested by the opening comments of Senator David Boren (D–Okla.) in support of the Violence Against Women Act of 1991, the displacement of the "other" as the presumed victim of domestic violence works primarily as a political appeal to rally white elites. Boren said:

> Violent crimes against women are not limited to the streets of the inner cities, but also occur in homes in the urban and rural areas across the country.
>
> Violence against women affects not only those who are actually beaten and brutalized, but indirectly affects all women. Today, our wives, mothers, daughters, sisters, and colleagues are held captive by fear generated from these violent crimes—held captive not for what they do or who they are, but solely because of gender.

Rather than focusing on and illuminating how violence is disregarded when the home is "othered," the strategy implicit in Senator Boren's remarks functions instead to politicize the problem only in the dominant community.... The experience of violence by minority women is ignored, except to the extent it gains white support for domestic violence programs in the white community.

... The point here is not that the Violence Against Women Act is particularistic on its own terms, but that unless the Senators and other policymakers ask why violence remained insignificant as long as it was understood as a minority problem, it is unlikely that women of color will share equally in the distribution of resources and concern.... As long as attempts to politicize domestic violence focus on convincing whites that this is not a "minority" problem but their problem, any authentic and sensitive attention to the experiences of Black and other minority women probably will continue to be regarded as jeopardizing the movement.

* * *

NOTES

1. The reluctance on the part of women from immigrant or minority communities to summon police to their homes in response to domestic violence is widely documented. In part that reluctance may have to do with community norms of honor and shame, but distrust of law enforcement is another strong and widely held sentiment. One of the African American women Beth Richie interviewed for her study, Kim, provided a powerful, but representative statement:

> Call the police? Never! Everyone I knew spent all of our time running from the police! The cops are the worst people to get involved in a family problem, probably because they beat up on women too! I know it because my girlfriend's old man is a cop, and he is an abuser himself. The station house is full of drug-using, prostitute-using, woman-hating men. *That's* why they are called pigs. Seriously, though, I just never could really trust that they would help me and not just use my 911 call as one more excuse to beat up a Black man. They were never that decent to me or anyone I knew. I just couldn't do it. I learned early in my life that the cops were dangerous to my people. They were to be avoided at all costs.

Beth Richie, COMPELLED TO CRIME: THE GENDER ENTRAPMENT OF BATTERED BLACK WOMEN, 95 (1996).

Here is Jenny Rivera talking about the experience of the Latino community:

> ... The idealized image of the police officer as a kind, governmental guardian ... is not a common experience among either ethnic groups or whites in this country. The violence perpetrated against people of color and the double standard applied in law enforcement were dramatically exemplified in the beating of Rodney King by Los Angeles police officers. Cases involving Latino victims of police abuse include the Jose Garcia case in Washington Heights and the Federico Pereira case in Queens, New York.
>
> Latinos in the United States have had a long, acrimonious history of interaction with local police and federal law enforcement agencies. This history is marked by abuse and violence suffered at the hands of police officers who have indiscriminately used excessive physical force against Latinos.... The history of racism and current racial tensions affects the success of any domestic violence enforcement strategy. For example, Latinas are suspicious of police who have acted in a violent and repressive manner toward the community at large. In addition, a Latina must decide whether to invoke assistance from an outsider who may not look like her, sound like her, speak her language, or share any of her cultural values.

Jenny Rivera, *Domestic Violence Against Latinas by Latino Males: An Analysis of Race, National Origin and Gender Differentials,* 14 B.C. THIRD WORLD L.J. 231, 245–46 (1994).

For Asian American women, particularly recent immigrants, the distrust of police may have additional dimensions:

> ... Asian Americans distrust law enforcement authority for a number of reasons. Many, particularly recent immigrants and refugees, distrust authority as a result of bad experiences with homeland government or law enforcement officials. In this country, police insensitivity to and misconduct toward Asian Americans has heightened both community and individual distrust of law enforcement officials. Common examples of police insensitivity and misconduct towards Asian Americans include brutal treatment of innocent Asian Americans, harassment of Asian American youths suspected of belonging to youth and criminal gangs, and the use of Asian "facebooks" by police departments.
>
> Furthermore, the police often encounter both a linguistic and a cultural gap in dealing with Asian Americans. For instance, few police realize that some Asian cultures traditionally discipline their children physically. Police unaware of this practice are likely to view these parents as child abusers, not understanding that the children are loved and protected and are simply being disciplined. Such misunderstandings have led to disastrous consequences. As a result of these and similar incidents, Asian Americans perceive the police as an entity to be feared and distrusted.

> The fear of law enforcement and other authority has particular ramifications for battered immigrant Asian American women. Undocumented Asian American women are extremely unlikely to report domestic violence to the police out of fear of deportation. The passage in California and the impending proposals of other state and federal laws requiring police, teachers and service providers to report suspected undocumented immigrants to the INS is likely to exacerbate underreporting and heighten immigrant fear of authority. Both legal and undocumented immigrants already fear that they will be reported to the INS. Even if these fears are unfounded, they nonetheless keep many immigrants from seeking help or calling police. Many Asian American women's distrust of the police and other authority figures bars access to basic police protection, as well as other services such as medical care, shelter, legal advice, counseling, public assistance, and child care.

Karin Wang, *Battered Asian American Women: Community Responses from the Battered Women's Movement and the Asian American Community*, 3 ASIAN L. REV. 151, 172–73 (1996).

2. Just as language and cultural barriers may play a part in the failure of women to seek police assistance, so too, as the last passage from Karin Wang's article suggests, may they prevent women from seeking other services. Shelters may not have multilingual capacity, and may offer living or eating arrangements that are culturally alien, or violate cultural or religious norms. An Orthodox Jewish woman, to give just one example, may not be able to keep kosher in the shelter. Common shelter rules that preclude women from having contact with anyone outside the shelter for an initial period (often 72 hours) may leave a woman whose sense of herself is embedded in extended family and community more thoroughly disoriented and traumatized than did the violent incident that brought her to shelter. Mainstream American culture is a good deal more conversant and comfortable with the therapeutic paradigm than other cultures, which may depend more heavily on informal support networks. Ironically, of course, taking advantage of those informal networks may require staying within the community, and not "betraying" it, or the abuser, by disclosing abuse to the authorities.

Can you identify other possible ways in which language and cultural barriers might impede access to medical and legal assistance, as well as to public benefits?

3. Materials in this section have already alluded to some of the particular problems faced by recent immigrants to the country who are trapped in abusive relationships. Adaptation of immigration laws and regulations to take account of abuse, and offer protection to battered women and their children, has been an ongoing project since at least 1990. The Immigration Act of that year amended the marriage fraud rules to accommodate immigrant women who were battered or exposed to extreme cruelty by the United States citizens or permanent residents these women entered the United States to marry. Prior to that amendment, anyone entering the country to marry had to remain "properly" married for two years before he

or she could apply for permanent resident status, and the application for permanent status had to be filed by both parties. As Kimberle Crenshaw reports:

> Predictably, under these circumstances, many immigrant women were reluctant to leave even the most abusive partners for fear of being deported.... Reports of the tragic consequences of this double subordination put pressure on Congress to include in the Immigration Act of 1990 a provision ... allow[ing] for an explicit waiver for hardship caused by domestic violence. Yet many immigrant women, particularly immigrant women of color, have remained vulnerable to battering because they are unable to meet the conditions established for a waiver. The evidence required to support a waiver "can include, but is not limited to, reports and affidavits from police, medical personnel, psychologists, school officials, and social service agencies." For many immigrant women, limited access to these resources can make it difficult for them to obtain the evidence needed for a waiver....

Kimberle Crenshaw, *Demarginalizing the Intersection of Race and Sex,* 1989 U. CHI. LEGAL FORUM 139, 1247–48 (1989).

In 1994 further reforms were instituted through the Violence Against Women Act, Subtitle G of which extended protections for battered immigrant women and their children. The Act permits women and children of U.S. citizens and legal residents to self-petition for legal resident status once the woman has been residing with, and legally married to her abuser, in the United States, for three years. The woman must show that her spouse has not filed a petition on her behalf. She must also demonstrate that she has been abused, but the Attorney General is directed to consider "any credible evidence" of abuse, a measure that was intended to ease the evidentiary burden created by the 1990 legislation. In addition, the Act provides for the "suspension of deportation" of battered immigrant women, which may address immigrant women's fears of immediate deportation if they report abuse to the authorities.

Despite these reforms, however, many of the problems Kimberle Crenshaw identified in her article remain. If battered immigrant women depend on their batterers for information about their status, and if batterers mislead their partners in order to hold them in the relationship, they will not take advantage of reforms. If the abusive man is not a U.S. citizen or legal resident, but undocumented, the reforms do not apply; both the abuser and his spouse will still be vulnerable to deportation. If the relationship is not one of marriage, the reforms also have no application. In short, while the law is moving in the right direction, it leaves many battered immigrant women still at grave risk. For a fuller account of the legislative history and its implications, see Tien Li Loke, *Note: Trapped in Domestic Violence: The Impact of United States Immigration Laws on Battered Immigrant Women,* 6 B.U. PUB. INT. L.J. 589 (1997). Loke also considers the impact of the Illegal Immigration Reform and Immigrant Responsibility Act of 1996, which exempted battered immigrant women from some of the restrictions placed on receipt of public benefits by non-citizens, and also from an earlier 1996 provision prohibiting undocumented immigrants from receiving legal assistance from legal services.

4. Crenshaw talks extensively about "political intersectionality;" the ways in which stereotypes held by the majority culture about racial and cultural minorities increase pressure from inside the community to deny the existence of a problem, like domestic violence, that would reinforce the stereotype. Members of the community who violate the community's "privacy" by publicizing information about violence, she suggests, are frequently ostracized or subject to other sanctions. She also talks about the domestic violence movement's unwitting complicity in diverting attention away from the problem in minority communities—a complicity that arguably resulted precisely from the movement's challenge to the stereotypes that assigned the problem to "other" groups and cultures.

Another way in which mainstream prejudice and stereotyping works, however, is to condition the response of law enforcement personnel and other service providers to perpetrators and victims of abuse. Ironically enough, *both* stereotypes that assume the likelihood of abuse *and* stereotypes that assume its absence can operate to preclude intervention. Writing in the 1980s, Rosemarie Tong reported that: "police trainees are frequently told that physical violence is an acceptable part of life among 'ghetto residents.'" Rosemarie Tong, *Black Perspective on Women, Sex, and the Law,* in WOMEN, SEX AND THE LAW, 153 (1984). In other words, suggests Linda Ammons, "blacks are 'normal primitives,' or violence prone." Linda Ammons, *Mules, Madonnas, Babies, Bathwater, Racial Imagery and Stereotypes: The African American Woman and the Battered Woman Syndrome,* 1995 WISC. L. REV. 1003, 1019 (1995). With respect to domestic violence in African American communities, this can result in desultory enforcement. Police might decide that behavior considered normal by those engaging in it does not warrant attention from outsiders. They might also feel reluctance to get involved and risk injury themselves when the participants themselves see the altercation as normal. To the extent that the African American woman is considered violent, it can also result in the reinterpretation of abuse as mutual combat. This might mean that domestic-violence-specific responses, such as mandatory arrest, are not triggered, or that police fall back on mutual arrests and courts on mutual restraining orders, which implicate the woman in her own abuse. Another commentator who writes about perceptions of African American women in the criminal justice system is Shelby Moore, *Battered Woman Syndrome: Selling the Shadow to Support the Substance,* 38 HOWARD L.J. 297, 331–36 (1995).

Jenny Rivera suggests that mainstream culture may harbor the same assumptions about domestic violence as a "normal" feature of family life in the Latino community. Jenny Rivera, *Domestic Violence Against Latinas by Latino Males: An Analysis of Race, National Origin and Gender Differentials,* 14 B.C. THIRD WORLD L.J. 231, 247 (1994). Certainly the Latino male is portrayed as violent:

> Latino males are believed to be irrational and reactive. The standard description of Latino males as hot-blooded, passionate, and prone to emotional outbursts is legendary. "Macho" is the accepted—and ex-

> pected—single-word description synonymous with Latino men and male culture. Consequently, it is natural to expand and apply this construct to the entire Latino community, and thereby justify the assumptions that Latinos are violent.

Id. at 240. While the Latina is often constructed as docile and domestic, it is also assumed that to satisfy her partner, she must be sensual and sexually responsive. She too, in other words, can have the reputation of being hot-blooded. It is not hard to imagine that a police officer harboring this construct would have an easy time sympathizing with a Latino abuser accusing his partner of sexual infidelity, and downplaying violence committed out of sexual jealousy—missing the truth that many, many abusers, regardless of their culture, display inordinate jealousy in situations where their partner has done nothing to warrant it.

A different kind of problem is created when law enforcement and service providers operate out of stereotypes that make it impossible for them to imagine that a man accused of violence has in fact committed it. Karin Wang talks about the "model minority" myth, and its "dangerous assumptions that all Asian Americans have achieved economic, academic and social success...." Karin Wang, *Battered Asian American Women: Community Responses from the Battered Women's Movement and the Asian American Community*, 3 ASIAN L. REV. 151, 174 (1996). The myth, which includes an image of stable family life, may make "stories of battered Asian American women seem unrealistic or exaggerated." Id. at 175. Similarly, myth has it that Jewish men are "family men," and make wonderful husbands, making it harder for Jewish women to convince outsiders that they are victims of abuse. Beverly Horsburgh, *Lifting the Veil of Secrecy: Domestic Violence in the Jewish Community,* 18 HARV. WMN'S L.J. 171 (1995). Mainstream denial of domestic violence among white middle and upper income families created, and surely still creates, a similar hurdle for the wives and girlfriends of stockbrokers, doctors, lawyers and judges.

5. Crenshaw is not the only legal scholar to have challenged the reluctance on the part of both minority communities and mainstream domestic violence activists to collect and publish community-specific statistics about the incidence of domestic violence. Here is Karin Wang, writing about the relative "invisibility" of the experiences of battered Asian–American women:

> In our numbers-oriented society, the absence of specific empirical data on battered women of color marginalizes non-white domestic violence victims. One manifestation of this marginalization is the difficulty in obtaining or justifying the funding of specific services for battered Asian–American women. By presenting color-blind and race-less domestic violence statistics, the anti-domestic violence movement affirms the status quo of white domination.

Karin Wang, *Battered Asian American Women: Community Responses from the Battered Women's Movement and the Asian American Community*, 3 ASIAN L. J.151, 160 (1996).

The most recent report published by the Bureau of Justice Statistics on intimate partner violence does begin to provide some racially specific information, although Asian Americans' experiences with domestic violence are grouped together with the experiences of Alaskan natives and American Indians. For example, according to information collected through the National Crime Victimization Survey, both Black and Hispanic women were more likely to report domestic violence to the police than white women, Asian American and Native American women, or men. The overall percentage of victims reporting was 50% (53% of women, and 46% of men). But 67% of Black women reported, and 65% of Hispanic women, while only 50% of white, Asian American and Native American women reported. This is puzzling information, because it appears inconsistent with the assertions many have made, and you have sampled in previous pages, that women of color, and specifically Black and Latina women, are less likely to report victimization than whites because of their greater distrust of law enforcement.

In the same report, the Bureau of Justice Statistics indicated that the rate of intimate partner violence against women had dropped by 21% between 1993 and 1998. That rate, however, was still higher (11.1 per thousand) among Black than among white women (8.2 per thousand) or among Asian American, American Indian and Alaska native women (4.1 per thousand). The reported rate among Hispanic women was 7.7 per thousand. Here it may be important that the rate is measured by asking women, in their homes, whether they have experienced abuse meeting the legal definitions of rape, sexual assault, robbery, or aggravated or simple assault. The woman who is afraid to answer, does not have the privacy to answer confidentially, or who does not categorize the behavior of her abuser as criminal, might well not report her victimization, thereby skewing the results.

Another recent report is based on the National Violence Against Women Survey, a national telephone survey conducted between 1995 and 1996, during which period 8,000 men and 8,000 women were interviewed. The National Institute of Justice (NIJ) and Centers for Disease Control (CDC) jointly sponsored the study. Interview subjects were asked to report whether they had experienced rape, physical assault or stalking by a partner over the course of their lifetime. 24.8% of white women said yes, compared with 29.1% of African American women, 15% of Asian and Pacific Islander women, and 37.5% of American Indian and Alaska Native women. Women who identified themselves as of "mixed race" reported victimization at the rate of 30.2%. Patricia Tjaden and Nancy Thoennes, *Extent, Nature and Consequences of Intimate Partner Violence: Findings from the National Violence Against Women Survey,* 25–28 (NCJ 181867, July 2000). One of the key lessons here is the misleading nature of the results obtained by the BJS when it lumps together Asian American women, who consistently *report* the lowest figures (recognizing that this may not mean they *experience* such a low incidence of abuse), with American Indian and Alaska native women, who report the highest rates of abuse.

The Bureau of Justice Statistics also reports on the number of individuals killed by intimate partners, using statistics generated from the Supplementary Homicide Reports of the Uniform Crime Reporting Program, an FBI operation. The number of domestic-violence related deaths remained stable between 1976 and 1993, but then dropped significantly between 1993 and 1998—except among white women. Among black women it dropped 45%, among black men a whopping 74%, and among white men, 44%.

The problem, of course, is that these statistics raise as many questions as they answer. It is surely tempting to say that the overall reduction in both lethal and non-lethal violence is a consequence of all the efforts, private and public, state and federal, to address domestic violence over the last 30 years. It is further tempting to suggest that this new information about the willingness on the part of women of color to report abuse, about the reduction in its incidence among all women, and in particular about the reduction in domestic violence homicides among women and men of color, indicate that societal responses are not, or are no longer, as "white-focused" as some of their critics have argued. However, a good deal more information would be necessary before any firm conclusions could be drawn, especially since reliable front-line reports from around the country, some of which you have read in these pages, caution against any overly optimistic assessment.

6. Many battered women in immigrant communities, communities of color, and other minority ethnic communities are also struggling with economic hardship. The next section takes up the question of poverty, and its relationship to domestic violence.

D. BATTERED WOMEN AND POVERTY

Are poor women more battered than other women? Does battering make or keep women poor? Does being poor hold women more firmly in abusive relationships? Are poor men more likely to inflict domestic violence than men with more economic resources at their disposal? In the political climate of the battered women's movement of the seventies and eighties these questions were out of bounds; activists and advocates alike stressed the universality of abuse, and its origins in gender, not class, oppression. Ironically, only a sustained conservative attack on the poor, and on public programs attempting to mitigate the most extreme consequences of poverty, has promoted new interest in these questions. The materials below document the discovery of new connections between poverty, welfare policy and domestic violence, and the forging of new alliances between anti-poverty and domestic violence activists. Finally, these materials also sketch the current reality faced by battered women seeking public assistance, in the post "welfare-reform" world in which federal welfare funds provide Temporary Assistance for Needy Families (TANF) rather than Aid to Families with Dependent Children (AFDC).

Making the Connections: Poverty, Welfare and Domestic Violence

In the article excerpted below, Lucie White challenges welfare policy makers to develop new narratives about poverty incorporating new understandings of the lives of the constituencies their proposals affect. "Traditionally," she suggests, liberal welfare discourse "seeks to avoid blaming either poor people themselves, or welfare, for entrenched poverty." Yet at the same time, this tradition values the work incentive and views prolonged welfare dependency as a bad thing. Within that framework, it is difficult to answer conservative charges about welfare recipients' laziness, or apparent disregard of their own self-interest, or their drift through cycles of dead-end jobs and welfare. White proposes a harder look at the "widely advertised exit corridors of education, work and marriage." This scrutiny, she suggests, would reveal those corridors to be "blocked by threats of violence." Lucie White, *No Exit: Rethinking "Welfare Dependency" from a Different Ground,* 81 GEO. L.J. 1961, 1974 (1993).

White tells an extended story about the life of one welfare recipient, Elaine Preston, to illustrate her argument:

> When she is "laying low"—by drawing down welfare to support her children and watching a lot of TV—Ms. Preston's life is fairly quiet. But when she starts on the routes out of poverty . . . she opens herself up to a heightened risk of physical, sexual, and psychic injury.

Id. at 1975.

By documenting the indignities and harassment suffered by many women, and particularly poor women and women of color, in educational and workplace contexts, as well as the physical and sexual abuse of intimate relationships, Lucie White reminds us that a welfare policy which does nothing to remove these barriers to economic self-sufficiency, and yet penalizes women who do not leap over them, is destined to be both punitive and ineffective. It turns out, then, that the question "why doesn't she leave the welfare rolls?" is just another version of the question "why doesn't she leave her abuser?" Both assume, erroneously, that exit is always possible, and both assume, erroneously, that exit will make her better off, ignoring the difficulty and danger of an independent existence in a society organized around the hierarchies, and vulnerabilities, of race, class and gender.

Lucie White
No Exit: Rethinking "Welfare Dependency" from a Different Ground, 81 Georgetown Law Journal 1961, 1986–90, 1997–2000 (1993)

Whenever I listen intently to poor women talk about their lives, I hear stories of violence: the violence of racism and class bias that they remember—and expect—from school; the violence of industrial hazards, brain-deadening routines, repressive discipline and sexual harassment that they face in the few available jobs; and the violence inherent in the bargain when they seek to secure their children's futures through a man. Poor women are thus trapped in a no-win predicament. They face shame if they stay on welfare. Yet the "exits" they are offered are really traps, for rather than providing opportunities, these exits repeatedly expose them to violence.

Mainstream welfare discourse has been silent about this dilemma. Even progressive welfare scholars have too often failed to look for patterns in the multiple stories of violence that poor women tell. Even feminists have failed to locate that violence precisely at the gates of "opportunity" that women on welfare are badgered to pass through, or to link that violence to unjust routines of power within those institutions. Even feminists have failed to protest the injustice of the choice between shame and violence that poor women are compelled to make, and remake, throughout their lives. Rather than exposing the institutional practices that produce this double bind, welfare scholars have too often either randomized poor women's experiences of violence into repeating spates of bad fortune, or ignored them altogether.

Like the social science and legal literatures that refuse to address domestic violence in the first person, our sanitized discourses about welfare condone the violence that they refuse to name. Thus, through this silence, women like Elaine Preston are left to stand up against a conservative consensus condemning welfare and its takers more or less on their own. To break out of this silence, we must first relocate our scholarly and policy discourses on welfare precisely at the center of the double binds that poor women face,—"On the edge of hell." Once there, we must refuse to turn back to those old conversations, even when our own talk about "welfare" moves us away from topics like work requirements and child support enforcement in AFDC, and toward topics like grassroots democracy in schools, factories, and social programs, and androgynous, fuzzy-bordered families whose homes bridge the "public" and the "private" spheres. If we can be more bold about staking out such a counterhegemonic academic and political discourse about welfare, then women like Ms. Preston might not feel quite so alone, as they continue the interpretive—and physical—battles they cannot escape in their own lives. They might then find it possible, on occasion, to defy the normative and institutional presumptions on which their poisoned choices are premised, rather than merely absorbing the blame for the tragic costs that either making—or evading—those choices entails.

. . .

Find a Man

The third exit from poverty that is pushed on poor women is marriage. The notion that marriage provides economic security is grounded in an often noted demographic trend: the chance that an American family will be poor is many times greater if that family is headed by a woman, particularly a woman of color, than if it is headed by a man. Furthermore, over the last decade, the correlation between female-headed families and poverty has become dramatically more pronounced. But the statistics neither reveal the historical and social causes behind the trend, nor specify the appropriate policy responses. Yet in a kind of voodoo logic that has often been invoked over the last decade, the numbers have been cited by male welfare pundits to convince women that their best route off of welfare is a trip to the altar. For conservative moralist Dan Quayle, the point is beyond debate; in a speech berating the television character Murphy Brown, Quayle announced that "marriage is probably the best anti-poverty program there is." Others, like sociologist William Julius Wilson, have written about the link between female-headed families and extreme poverty in ways that make the same conclusion all too easy to draw.

But the numbers do not necessarily lead to the conclusion that marriage is a successful route off of poverty. As feminist scholars have repeatedly pointed out, we might conclude from the same numbers that poverty in America is linked to the dismal work options of single mothers, and to the striking absence in our country of the kind of universal family policy that shields most children from poverty in other industrial countries. We might seek social policies that bring wages above subsistence in traditionally female jobs, and that require quality on-site childcare, health coverage, and family leave as conditions of every job. We might also design enforcement mechanisms that ensure that every workplace is free from the physical, psychic, and sexual hazards that drive poor women to quit their jobs. We might use the numbers about poverty among single mothers to show that the need for such policies is beyond debate, and then put our heads and our purses together to cover their substantial costs. But instead of facing this hard fiscal question, it has seemed easier for armchair moralists to point a finger at poor women and accost them to escape poverty by catching a man.

When women seek to heed this advice, they are likely to confront violence. Elaine Preston did not talk to me much about her own father, the fathers of her children, or other men that might have passed through her life. But other women in her community have shared their experiences in some detail. Barbara Sutton, another mother in Ms. Preston's Head Start program, for instance, gave the following account.

After having a child on her own, Ms. Sutton tried for two years to make ends meet as a single mother. Finally, she met a man who seemed both eligible and responsible, and she dutifully fell in love. Her story, in her own assessment, then began to sound like a worn-out cliche. First, there was a whirlwind romance, with lots of roses and a church wedding that made her parents proud. After a few weeks, with no warning, there was an occasional slap, a few vile words. Then the cursing got fierce and the slaps became blows. There were outbursts of jealousy that led him to search through her things, hide her birth control pills so she could not cheat on him, and take her car keys so she would not leave the house.

She tried hard to calm his anger—by talking less or cooking better or avoiding "those looks" that he didn't trust. But it didn't always work. Once he put his intent bluntly. "I'm going to break you, break your spirit," she recalls him telling her, "even if I have to kill you first." Still she tried to hold the marriage together—because she loved him, and in order to give a future to her child. She explained how, "you're taught, as a woman, that it is your job to keep the family together, and that if it breaks up—no matter what he did to you—it's your fault."

Finally, after the beatings got so bad that her mother started asking questions about her swollen face, Barbara Sutton went to the courthouse for a restraining order. At the time, she was pregnant with his child. In court, she had to answer to a magistrate who called her "honey" and asked her what she had done to get on his nerves. Then the magistrate told her to "go on home and tell him you're sorry," but she would not follow his advice. Instead, she got a restraining order and a judicial separation. The sheriff moved her husband out of their mobile home. Though she grieved for the end of her marriage, she thought she had gotten away.

Three months later he came back with a box cutter to slit her throat. She crouched in a corner of her trailer, shielding her face with her hands. When he fled, vowing to come back to finish the job, her three year-old daughter sought refuge in her mother's lap. When the ambulance came, the medics had to pull the child away. With her tendons slashed, Barbara Sutton's hand is now permanently disabled; her face is disfigured in ways that plastic surgery can only partially repair. Her daughter is in counseling for emotional trauma. Her husband was convicted of assault, rather than attempted murder, and given a twelve year sentence with a possibility of early parole.

Stories like Ms. Sutton's—a rape, routine verbal and physical beating, a week in the hospital for a broken jaw—have repeatedly surfaced in interviews that began with innocent open questions about Head Start. Welfare scholars and advocates have not generally considered domestic violence "their" problem, for it is not unique to women who are poor. Yet when their silence about this problem is coupled with direct or implicit advice that poor women should get married, those women are left with a grim choice. They can get treated "like dirt" on welfare, or they can try to beat the odds of injury from a spouse.

Distanced from the Pain

For the most part, even progressive welfare advocates have echoed reactionary formulas chiding poor women to get an education, get a husband, get a job, and so on, without squarely addressing themselves to the violence that threatens women who are badgered to follow that advice.

. . .

Why ... has even the most well-meaning of mainstream welfare discourse consistently failed to document this pain, even at the cost of colluding in rhetoric that compels poor women through cycles of shame and violence? This section suggests two reasons for the failure.

The first is that it is profoundly difficult—if not impossible—to author a text that "documents" another person's experience of extreme pain....

A further reason ... is that if those accounts are taken seriously, they will raise hard questions about mainstream welfare policy. Both conservative and liberal welfare discourse take for granted, and indeed rely on, the fundamental institutional structure of work, family, and education. In its rhetoric and policy proposals, that discourse endorses and seeks to expand those institutions, in order to give the women who are driven off of welfare somewhere to go.

Thus welfare reformers have devised AFDC rules to force young women to stay in school. But those reformers have not required changes within the schools that might keep young women from wanting to drop out. Reformers have sought to draw low-end jobs into high welfare areas, often with promises of cheap labor or a union-free environment. But those reformers have not acknowledged that, for workers, "cheap labor" translates into job hazards and low wages, and a "union-free environment" means a totalitarian work culture that stifles workers' initiative, imagination, and hope. Welfare reformers have responded to the recent sea change in family structure by touting marriage as the best way for women with children to beat the demographic odds. But those reformers are then compelled to deny the centrality of violence to nuclear family life....

Consequently, the reform agenda that is endorsed by mainstream welfare scholarship depends on the very institutions—education, family, and work—in which the violence that maintains race, class, and gender domination is most at home. Therefore, mainstream welfare reformers cannot join a project that names this violence without complicating their own agenda.

* * *

NOTE

1. In 1993, Lucie White's integration of issues of poverty and domestic violence, let alone discrimination and harassment on the job and in educational settings, was unusual. In general, the poverty movement and the battered women's movement were disconnected, for reasons that Joan Meier explores in the next reading. Only recent welfare "reform" initiatives, culminating in the wholesale Republican attack on welfare entitlements that produced the federal Personal Responsibility and Work Opportunity Reconciliation Act of 1996, have brought the two constituencies together, and stimulated some important learning on both sides.

Joan Meier
Domestic Violence, Character, and Social Change in the Welfare Reform Debate, 19 Law and Policy 205, 220–25, 227–30 (1997)

The fact that domestic violence has not been a part of either progressive or feminist discussions of poverty/welfare reform is due in part to the historical disconnection between practitioners in the poverty and battered women's movements. For instance, Peter Margulies ... argues that family law and domestic violence work have been marginalized in legal services programs, pointing primarily to a traditional sexism which undervalues "women's" issues, and a preference for "public" over "private" litigation. In contrast, while many battered women's activists have worked with poor people in legal services, state coalitions and shelters, law school clinics, and other pro bono or non profit programs, with the exception of a handful of legal services lawyers, such advocates have typically specialized in domestic violence, not offering other traditional "poverty" advocacy.... Indeed, many domestic violence activists have traditionally avoided welfare advocacy in particular, because the welfare bureaucracy was perceived as deeply disempowering and stigmatizing for battered women....

. . .

Of course it is also true that many battered women's activists, and several state coalitions, have worked simultaneously as anti-poverty activists, for example, working with legal services offices on poverty and domestic violence cases, lobbying against welfare reform proposals which harm battered women and other poor people, and banding together with legal service and other non-profit entities facing devastating cuts and burdens from increasingly hostile state and federal legislatures....

However, in general, collaboration between domestic violence and poverty activists has been fairly local and isolated as a political matter.... Institutionally, and more importantly, philosophically, integrating the "causes" of domestic violence and of fighting poverty has remained problematic....

At the heart of the disconnection between progressive discussions of poverty and feminist discussions of domestic violence is a fundamental clash of ideologies and philosophies between the domestic violence and anti-poverty movements, one which parallels the clash between the ideologies of conservative reformers and poverty activists in the welfare reform debate. On the poverty side, the feminists' emphasis on the values and attitudes which lead to abuse and the need for moral education of perpetrators in order to change their beliefs and behavior, is anathema to anti-poverty activists who preach the structural and socioeconomic causes of the ills of the poor and who see any talk of moral or dysfunctional behavior of the poor as a form of blaming the victim. On the domestic violence side, battered women's activists have strenuously avoided discussing battering as a problem related to poverty in order to avoid its marginalization and to further the understanding that domestic violence is a reflection of fairly universal norms of a sexist society.... At first glance, the perspectives are quite incompatible. This potential clash has caused even feminist poverty analysts to separate out the domestic violence issue and pigeonhole it as a "feminist"—but not particularly a "poverty" issue.

The Battered Women's Movement's Historic Avoidance of the Poverty Issue

... [M]any active in the [battered women's] movement ... felt that a discussion of domestic violence and poverty in the same breath would only lead to furthering racist and classist prejudices rather than greater understanding of the problem.... Hence, the battered women's movement has long claimed that domestic violence "occurs among all races and socio-economic groups"....

. . .

Nonetheless, perhaps ironically, critiques of the intentionally "universalist" thrust of the battered women's movement have challenged it as "essentialism" or "privilege".... Kim Crenshaw ... notes that the "domestic violence lobby's" emphasis on the "universality" of domestic violence is intended to focus society's attention on white middle-class victims, precisely because poor people of color are less valued by dominant society. Her perception of this political choice as suspect is supported in part by the tainted history of both the women's movement's and the battered women's movement's treatment of women of color and their concerns.... However, the fact remains that had the new paradigm of battering been explicitly connected to poverty before battering was broadly understood and accepted as a serious and widespread social problem, it would have merely contributed to the demonization of poor people, and would not have advanced societal understanding of battering *or of poor people of color.* Thus, one member of the federal government involved in developing federal policy on domestic violence in the late 1970s later stated "there was a federal response because the problem cuts across class and race. If domestic violence affected only poor women, it would have been dismissed."

The Incompatibility of the Battered Women's Movement's Ideology with the Premises of the Anti–Poverty Movement

While the battered women's movement has, in the context of welfare reform, begun to address the link between poverty and domestic violence, the anti-poverty movement has yet to do so. This may be in part because the movement itself is currently so weak and lacks a powerful voice on behalf of poor people.... However, in greater part it is because the integration of the issue of domestic violence into poverty activism poses a far deeper challenge to the nature and ideology of poverty activism than the integration of poverty concerns poses to domestic violence activism....

. . .

... [M]ost battered women's advocates believe that criminal sanctions, which provide new "moral education" for both batterers and society, are necessary to counter both the moral righteousness of batterers and the centuries of social and cultural conditioning which have inculcated those values.

However, it is this very moral message which is anathema to those with strong anti-poverty convictions. The fundamental ideology of the progressive anti-poverty movement has been a belief that the poor are, as a class, victims of an unjust social, economic, and political order. Such "poverty progressives" are fueled by their belief that both the causes and cures for poverty are social, economic and political, *but not behavioral.* ... In contrast to the battle for social and economic "justice" on behalf of the poor against more powerful institutions, litigation by a wife against a husband is litigation by one poor person against *another poor person*, a family member. Certainly, in pitting the poor against each other, it might be said that there is "no net gain" for the poor community.

. . .

Not surprisingly, the preferred perspective of advocates for the poor is to frame battering in poor communities as another product of poverty; a tragic expression of poor, often African–American men's rage and frustration at racism and their own oppression by white, dominant society....

The problems with this paradigm of domestic violence among the poor are twofold: It exacerbates social denial about battering, and it feeds into the view that domestic violence is "caused" by poverty. The poverty advocate's paradigm provokes sympathy for the batterer and invites us to feel sorry for him because he is victimized on a larger level. To those of us who believe that poverty and racism are terrible social injustices which have profoundly harmed many people, there is a kernel of truth in this portrayal. However, invoking that sympathy or concern in the context of domestic abuse unfortunately plays directly into abusers' denials of responsibility, supporting the trap that battering typically lays for its victims: "I beat you because *I* am hurting, *I* am the victim, and *you* have failed to treat me right." It is precisely this dynamic which has kept many women "loyal" and victimized, and has encouraged both society's and their belief that the women's failures, inadequacies or provocations are responsible for the battering.

... This view essentially explains battering as not goal-oriented or gender-based but merely an untargeted explosion of the pain and rage caused by poverty and racism. Recognition that battering is intentional and goal-oriented, aimed at keeping its victim under the perpetrator's control and possession, is the most profound and radical element of the battered women's movement, for it demonstrates that battering is simply the logical extension of the sexist belief that men have the right to dominate women.... Thus, treating battering as an outgrowth of poverty rather than a behavior motivated by malevolence and sexism, allows anti-poverty advocates to remain morally engaged with their clients and cause. Sadly, it also contributes to the deep denial about the nature of battering which still seems to exist in poor communities of color, and sacrifices women and children in the name of "enlightened" dedication to the poor.

* * *

NOTE

1. Under the pressure of welfare reform, and the fear that as benefits were reduced, and new conditions imposed, many poor women would be rendered even more vulnerable to abuse, and even less capable of breaking free of violence, domestic violence researchers and advocates took on the task of demonstrating just how strong the connection is between welfare receipt and victimization at the hands of an intimate partner. This in turn has led to the recognition that in fact poor women *are* more likely to be battered than their wealthier counterparts, and that poor men *are* more

likely to abuse their partners than their wealthier counterparts. While it is still true that battering occurs across all economic lines, and still true that poverty is not a "cause" of battering, it is time to recognize the strength of that connection, as we craft both welfare and domestic violence policies at the state and national level. The next reading addresses first, the strong correlation between welfare receipt and abuse, and second, developing understandings of the relationship between poverty and abuse.

Jody Raphael
Saving Bernice: Battered Women, Welfare and Poverty, 25–28, 143–48 (2000)

National surveys estimate that domestic violence is a factor in approximately 6 percent of all U.S. households. During the past five years researchers have consistently found that 20 to 30 percent of women receiving welfare benefits are current victims of domestic violence, and approximately two-thirds are former victims. With approximately two million women on welfare during fiscal year 1998 . . ., as many as 400,000 women could be affected nationwide.

Bill Curcio developed a sample of 846 women on welfare, all mandatory participants in education, training and jobs-related activities in Passaic County, New Jersey. These participants were confidentially surveyed during the course of an eight-week life skills program at a time when they had been in the program for over a week, when security and mutual support had been established, and participants had already shared their life experiences with the class. Curcio cautions that respondents in this sample are those who showed up and remained in the program for the first two weeks. Those who didn't come or dropped out are probably those women with the most problems of one kind or another, and it can be assumed that a number of them are domestic violence victims prohibited from attending. Curcio's study found that approximately 15 percent of the entire sample were current victims of domestic violence, defined as physical violence. An additional 25 percent reported current verbal or emotional abuse.

The University of Massachusetts Boston Center for Survey Research designed a survey representing the first scientific sampling of one state's entire welfare caseload that measures both current and past prevalence of domestic violence. Seven hundred and thirty-four women, a representative sample of women on welfare in the state, were confidentially interviewed in all welfare department offices throughout Massachusetts between January and June of 1996. Using the definition of domestic violence in the Massachusetts Abuse Prevention Act, the study found 19.5 percent of the entire sample reporting physical violence at the hands of an intimate partner within the previous twelve months.

Susan Lloyd, a researcher, affiliated with the Northwestern University/University of Chicago Joint Center for Poverty Research, conducted a random survey of 824 women in one low-income neighborhood in Chicago, Illinois. Between September 1994 and May 1995 Lloyd's researchers randomly selected and screened the women in both English and Spanish in their homes for approximately fifty-five minutes. Lloyd's study enables us to compare the prevalence of domestic violence within the smaller sample of those women on welfare to the entire sample as a whole.

Although the study does not find any appreciable differences in the rates of violence among women differentiated by race or ethnicity, women in the lowest income levels, including those on welfare, experienced all forms of abuse at higher levels than the women in the highest income group. When incidence of physical aggression over the last twelve months was measured, women on welfare had experienced nearly three times the amount of violence experienced by nonwelfare women in the neighborhood (31 percent compared to almost 12 percent). Using a definition measuring more severe aggression within the past twelve months, which includes rape or threatening with or using a weapon, almost 12 percent of the entire sample had been so abused, compared with almost 20 percent of the welfare sample.

Two other studies also found a higher prevalence of domestic violence within households of women on welfare. In a survey of one thousand women residing in the state of Utah during April and May 1997, one in five respondents claimed that their children currently witness or hear verbal abuse, while one in fourteen stated that their children witness or hear physical abuse. Utah women who qualify for welfare had a greater tendency to say that their children hear or witness physical abuse: about 28 percent of welfare-eligible women, compared to 7 percent of noneligible women. In addition, welfare qualifiers were more inclined to report being victims of isolation (defined as someone controlling what others do and to whom they talk; limiting outside involvement; and using jealousy to justify actions). About four in ten (41 percent) of welfare eligible women said they experience some isolation, compared to 11 percent of noneligible women.

Moreover, welfare qualifiers were more inclined than the average respondent to have obtained a civil protective order and to have dealt with the courts regarding domestic violence situations. Twenty-eight percent of welfare-eligible women said yes, compared to 7 percent of noneligible women, to a question whether they had ever obtained a civil protective order. . . .

In 1993 the Commonwealth Fund's Survey on Women's Health undertook a national telephone survey of over more than two thousand women over the age of eighteen. Researchers asked whether certain behaviors occurred within the last five years with the partner with whom the respondent was currently living. Although twenty-four percent of the women on welfare reported domestic violence in the past five years with their current partner, only 7 percent of other respondents reported domestic violence.

Similar and equally sobering statistics come from the Worcester Family Research Project, a five-year study of 436 women, most of whom were welfare recipients, both homeless and housed in Worcester, Massachusetts, conducted by the Better Homes Fund between August 1992 and July 1995. Respondents took part in three to four face-to-face interview sessions lasting over ten hours. The Worcester Study found that nearly one-third of the women had experienced severe violence from their current or most recent partner within the last two years. One-third reported that an intimate partner had threatened to kill them. Moreover, about two-thirds had experienced severe physical assault by a parent or other caretaker while growing up, and over 40 percent had been sexually molested before reaching adulthood.

. . .

In a recent study involving a random sample of 753 women on welfare in a medium-size city in Michigan undertaken by the University of Michigan Research Development Center on Poverty, Risk and Mental Health, when defining physical abuse as either moderate physical violence or severe violence, nearly a quarter (23 percent) of the women in the sample experienced physical abuse in the past twelve months, and 63 percent encountered abuse in their lifetime in intimate relationships.

In 1997 Lisa Brush of the University of Pittsburgh interviewed 122 incoming enrollees at six sites of the briefest welfare-to-work program serving those participants deemed job-ready by the county. Thirty-eight percent of that sample disclosed physical violence or injury in their current or most recent relationship; 27 percent of the sample were seriously physically abused, and over two-thirds (almost 69 percent) reported domestic violence ever in their lives. . . .

Although differing definitions of domestic violence were employed in the research, the emerging data are remarkably consistent. It would appear that at least 20 to 30 percent of women on welfare are current domestic violence victims, meaning that the number of women . . . trapped by poverty and abuse, is quite high. . . .

. . .

. . . It is now time to fully consider the relationship between violence and poverty. Estimates from the redesigned National Crime Victimization Survey between 1992 and 1996 clearly demonstrate that the rate of intimate violence against women generally decreases as household income levels increase. Households with less than $7,500 in annual income, for example, suffer five times the amount of domestic violence as households with income above $50,000, and those with incomes between $7,500 and $15,000 experience three times the amount of domestic violence as households with income above $50,000.

When Susan Lloyd analyzed the data in her neighborhood survey . . . she also found that women in the lowest income level experienced all forms of abuse at higher levels than women in the highest income group. Women with annual incomes between $2,500 and $7,000 reported almost three times the amount of severe violence of those with income between $13,751 and $27,500, and those with incomes over $27,500. A recent study by the New York City Department of Health on homicides in New York City found that the majority of the murders were committed by husbands or boyfriends, but that the murdered women were disproportionately from the poorest boroughs of the city.

This relationship between violence and income has held true in other surveys in Cambodia, Peru, Chile, and Thailand. In a multilevel model of partner violence in inner-city Baltimore, several neighborhood-level factors, including the rate of unemployment, emerged as predictors of domestic violence. Anecdotal evidence from around the world suggests that violence against women increases as the economic situation of the family decreases.

. . .

Recently, multiple explanations have been advanced, and many factors may account for the connection between poverty and domestic violence. One obvious simple explanation, of course, is that poor women, lacking financial resources, are unable to escape the violent relationship to the extent that their better-off counterparts can.... Others have suggested that our efforts to eradicate domestic violence may have been more effective to date for middle-class women. The greater stress of unemployment, community violence, and racism have also been cited as factors.

Some analysts believe that low-income men, unable to support their families and dominate them through the paycheck, will attempt to control women by other means.... This theory, however, has been recently undercut by fairly persuasive evidence that abusers deliberately employ violence to prevent women from becoming economically self-sufficient, suggesting that the differential between the economic power of men and women in these relationships is at the heart of the issue.

... It is the woman's economic potential, as compared to that of her male partner, that might be the trigger for the violence. The fewer the economic resources of the male partner, the more intense the response that can be expected. The abuser therefore works overtime to maintain the economic imbalance that leans in his favor. As we have seen, women on welfare who have not steadily worked are the perfect matches for extremely low-income men.

Most recently a number of studies have discovered a correlation between imbalance of resources and domestic violence. In Lisa Brush's Pittsburgh sample, women who had less than a high school diploma or its equivalent reported significantly lower rates of work-related jealousy than those with these credentials. Hotaling and Sugerman found that domestic violence increased when the wife had more education or a higher income than her husband. In a sample of 365 women in Arizona, researchers found that total family income per se had no influence on domestic violence, but income disparity did. Violence against women increased as the interspousal income gap closed; the less disparity in income, or the more resources the woman had in relation to her husband, the more frequent and escalated the violence. Analysis of a sample of 102 women in California recently found that receipt of no income from the male partner was significantly correlated with increased relationship abuse within the preceding three months.

. . .

. . . It seems that when women have even a limited material advantage over the men they have relationships with, this in itself may in fact provoke those men to assert their male authority literally with a vengeance, through violence. This dynamic suggests that the frustration felt by men who are unable to confirm to patriarchal standards manifests itself in misogynistic behaviour towards the women they live off. Thus we can see that socio-economic jealousy may operate in a way that parallels sexual jealousy and often links up with it.

Looking at the situation in another way, we would also expect to see such a backlash during times of economic and social change. Full acceptance of women in the workplace has surely been hampered by the high rise of male unemployment. Betty Friedan, pointing out instances in which domestic violence escalated in the wake of community dislocation, argues that in times of economic stress women become the scapegoats.

Then along comes welfare reform, insisting that all low-income women must work, and in some instances providing resources, education, training, and other supportive services to them. Welfare reform marks a radical acceleration of this process of social and economic change in the general society and can be expected to cause a backlash in poor neighborhoods. One thoughtful analyst sees how welfare reform puts the low-income abuser in a bind. On one hand, he understands that his partner's working will put the household ahead financially, which would be a good thing. On the other hand, if she works, he fears, she will be out of his control and might leave him. If the abuser lets this latter fear guide his actions, the household will lose welfare benefits and be even poorer than before. Opting for control consigns the family to poverty, and he knows it. From the point of view of the abuser, all the choices are poor, and the conflict within him can cause considerable stress and hostility as the walls close in. . . .

Absent from this analysis, however, is a convincing explanation for the use of violence aimed at intimate partners. One might expect coercion, sabotage, or general turmoil, but why violence? One author posits that low occupational standing may index a number of other descriptors, including low educational achievement, low self-esteem, lower social skills, and alcohol or drug problems that may contribute toward the use of violence. Based on his many years of interviewing incarcerated males, the psychiatrist James Gilligan identifies the issue of shame that turns to hate and violence. His analysis seems especially persuasive because it integrates the issue of class and provides a convincing rationale for why men turn to violence and stalking, especially after women leave the relationships.

Gilligan says that batterers experience a "life-death dependency" on their partners and an overwhelming shame because of it. These men do everything they can to make their wives dependent on them, so that the women cannot possibly leave or abandon them. When their wives do leave them, "it intensifies the feelings of shame it causes; it increases the intensity of violence that such shame stimulates:

> "The horror of dependency is what causes violence. The emotion that causes the horror of dependency is shame. Men, much more than women, are taught that to want love or care from others is to be

> passive, dependent, unaggressive and unambitious or, in short, womanly; and that they will be subject to shaming ridicule, and disrespect if they appear unmanly in the eyes of others...."

Shame, which consists of a deficiency of self-love, says Gilligan, causes hate, which becomes violence, usually directed at other people. Given the horror of dependency in the United States, especially dependency of men, is it any wonder that we have so much male violence? The economic needs of men must be gratified. By not helping men to meet these needs we shame them for having the desire that all people have. To prevent domestic violence, then, we must work to eliminate relative poverty and race discrimination.

* * *

NOTES AND QUESTIONS

1. Jody Raphael's book, from which this excerpt is taken, tells the story of Bernice, her longstanding relationship with the abusive Billy, and her struggle to free herself and her children from his violence and carve out an independent life. Raphael asks Bernice why she thinks Billy turned into an abuser. Bernice's answer demonstrates her own conviction that his abuse was closely tied to his feelings of inadequacy, and his inability to meet the societal expectation that, as a man, he should be able to provide for his family:

> All he wanted was to take care of his family. When he went out there and looked for jobs and couldn't get enough money, he got frustrated. He always felt he should have a better job than what he had. These boys want to work and there is no program for them. He would have gone to training. He wants to be responsible for his children.
>
> . . .
>
> He said, "Bernice, that was one of your biggest problems. I felt so useless as a man, because I never could have taken care of you and the kids, and here you are, out there doing it by yourself. I don't even know how to begin apologizing to you for all the things I have done. That is why I don't try."
>
> . . .
>
> He may want to go on vacation, but the money that he makes only takes care of his survival needs, and so he works three years and he can never go on vacation. He gets frustrated, and he starts to tear himself down. He becomes unmotivated, he can't wake up early enough in the morning to be on time to work, he doesn't see change coming. He never gets ahead. So he gets so tired of not getting ahead that he gets depressed and sabotages himself.
>
> . . .
>
> Any time he is unemployed he has low self-esteem, he is frustrated, and he has more time on his hands. He is really upset that I'm going to leave, I'll meet someone else and want to be with someone else. He's

> very aggressive, he's always close to home when he is unemployed. He lives as a person who is very depressed, watching me so I don't leave. You're not going to leave him when he is at his lowest. That has proven to be very dangerous when you leave him at his lowest. I did it. When I left Billy for good in 1993, he wasn't working. I left him when it was the most dangerous time for me.
>
> . . .
>
> One time Billy had a good job for eleven months. I could go out, I could have friends, I could dress the way I wanted. When Billy is employed, he has more to offer....
>
> . . .
>
> ... I thought that they just abused their partners, but they have the same isolation, it affects them too. You're so scared and isolated and you can't move, and neither can they. We're both in prison. I broke out of it and he is still in it.

Id. at 140–42.

If you think back to Donald Dutton's account of the role of shame in creating a batterer, do you see a way to link the individual and psychological explanation with broader explanations based both on social conditions (like poverty and unemployment), and gender roles and expectations (as they affect both men and women)?

2. Research supports the common sense hypothesis that women with more economic resources, or more potential for economic independence, will be better able to extricate themselves from violence. In two studies by researchers Michael Strube and Linda Barbour, women's employment status was the strongest predictor of which women would make a permanent break from their abusers. In a Florida study of 426 women, the most prominent variables influencing whether women left their abusers included the victims' annual income and employment status, along with the severity of the abuse and the victims' level of self-esteem. In a large-scale study of 6,000 battered women in Texas, the best predictor of whether a woman would stay away from her abuser was again her degree of economic independence. Finally, in a recent Michigan study, only 12% of 141 women who had stayed at a shelter returned to their abusers—and they were the women most economically dependent on their abusers. For further accounts of and cites to these studies, see Susan James and Beth Harris, *Gimme Shelter: Battering and Poverty*, in FOR CRYING OUT LOUD: WOMEN'S POVERTY IN THE UNITED STATES, 60–61 (1996).

Welfare Reform and the Current Welfare Climate

These next materials depict the climate in which the "welfare reform movement" took root and flourished; offer the briefest of glimpses at the state experiments that preceded federal "reform" efforts, and provide highlights of the 1996 Personal Responsibility and Work Opportunity Reconciliation Act, Pub. L. No. 104–193, 110 Stat. 2105. They focus in particular on the provisions with the greatest potential impact on battered women, and what has been learned in the brief period during which those provisions have been implemented.

Lucy Williams
The Ideology of Division: Behavior Modification Welfare Reform Proposals, 102 Yale Law Journal 719, 719–21 (1992)

During their Administration and throughout the 1992 Presidential campaign, President Bush and Vice President Quayle claimed that the welfare initiatives of the 1960's are responsible for the persistence of poverty in the United States and the urban problems demonstrated so graphically by the Los Angeles riots [of that] spring. Their statements are part of a disturbing effort to divert attention from the structural problems of our society and to focus instead on the so-called deviance of the poor. The rhetoric of the current "welfare reform" debate goes something like this: Aid to Families with Dependent Children (AFDC) recipients are themselves responsible for their poverty because they have not "pulled themselves up by their bootstraps"; they are dysfunctional mothers incapable of fitting into mainstream society, and they are economically and emotionally atrophied because of their "dependence" on welfare. Proponents of "welfare reform" further argue that by withholding AFDC benefits, the government can transform present recipients into productive members of society, thereby solving the intractable problems of poverty. Consistent with this rhetoric, the current "welfare reform" proposals condition AFDC eligibility on conformity with putative moral norms of society. Underlying the proposals is the belief that the receipt of assistance is debilitating.

These concepts, always an undercurrent in American history, surfaced with new vigor in the work of conservative scholars in the early 1980's. The conservatives' ideas engendered several state demonstration projects, including Learnfare (loss of benefits if a child misses a certain number of days of school or fails to average a certain grade), Family Cap (loss of benefits for additional children), Bridefare or Wedfare (small monetary incentives given to a mother to marry the father of her child combined with the loss of benefits for additional children), incentives for recipients to use Norplant contraception, and benefit reductions if the mother pays her rent irregularly or fails to obtain medical treatment for her children. . . .

Because projects that condition eligibility on behavior contravene the mandated eligibility requirements set forth in the Social Security Act, they require the United States Department of Health and Human Services (HHS) to waive [the Act's] entitlement provisions. . . . Through this administrative mechanism, President Bush embraced the use of welfare laws to attempt to modify behavior.

* * *

NOTE

1. After the election of 1994, the new Republican majority entered a "Contract with America," promising to implement reforms to "restore accountability to Congress," and "be the beginning of a Congress that respects the values and shares the faith of the American family." Pursuant to this contract, the House passed the Personal Responsibility Act in 1994. The Act proposed to end the current AFDC program, and instead provide states with block grants to administer their own welfare programs with little federal oversight and no requirement that the states provide matching funds. Under this new structure there was to be no federal entitlement to welfare. The Act implemented time limits after which women would be barred from receiving welfare ever again, no matter what their family circumstances. Teenage women who became pregnant would be barred from receiving public assistance under many circumstances. Women who were unable or unwilling to establish paternity, permitting child support enforcement against the fathers of their children, would not, under most circumstances, qualify for benefits. Under the act all recipients of public assistance would be required to work, without any provision for childcare or education. The Act proposed to exclude most immigrants from most public assistance programs, even if they had legal status. President Clinton vetoed the first welfare reform act presented to him by Congress, and the second. Nonetheless, the third and final version of the legislation, embodied in the 1996 Personal Responsibility and Work Opportunity Act, still contained essentially all these restrictive features. Like its predecessors, it sought to impose marriage, reduce out-of-wedlock births, promote child support, and require employment, as well as reducing the costs of the federal welfare program by excluding those not born in the United States, and imposing rigid time limits on all recipients.

In the following excerpt, Judith Lennett summarizes those provisions of the 1996 Act with most immediate relevance to battered women.

Judith Lennett
Like Ships That Pass in the Night: AFDC Policy and Battered Women, 19 Law and Policy 191, 194–95 (1997)

Of the many changes made by this historic law, several are especially relevant to battered women and their children. These include the loss of a statutory entitlement to assistance; a maximum five-year lifetime limit on receipt of assistance (42 USC § 608(a)(7)) unless she meets the definition of a battered woman contained in section 103 of the act (42 USC § 608(a)(7)(C)(iii)); a requirement that most women participate in welfare-to-work activities that include working off their cash assistance in community-based "jobs" (42 USC § 607(d)); and expansions in women's obligation to provide information aimed at increasing child support payments (42 USC § 654). Two additional provisions of the act pose serious potential problems for battered women and others whose circumstances make transitioning from AFDC to work problematic. Under the first of these, unless a state opts out, it must require AFDC recipients to participate in community service employment after two months of receiving assistance, with minimum hours per week and tasks to be determined by the state. Under the second, a state will face several fiscal penalties if it fails to meet monthly work participation rates. For example, by 1997, 25% of families must be participating in work, with the percentage increasing to 50% by the year 2002 (42 USC § 607(a)(1)). While work, workfare, and community services all count as "work," education, literacy classes, GED preparation, English as a second language courses, and other pre-work activities do not. Job search is limited to six weeks (42 USC § 607(c)(2)(C)).

In order to meet these participation rates, states will have to force large numbers of women, regardless of their circumstances, into workfare. For many battered woman, these requirements could spell disaster. The Wellstone/Murray Domestic Violence Amendment (42 USC § 602), which allows states to waive all of the above mentioned program requirements, including the monthly work participation rate if they undertake to identify and respond to the needs of battered women, may be the only provision of the new statute offering an opportunity to minimize the potential damage facing battered women in need of government assistance.

... [H]ow states pick and choose among these provisions, and, most important, whether they choose to invoke the provisions of the Wellstone/Murray Family Violence Amendment, will be critical to battered women and their children....

* * *

NOTES

1. As Lennett notes, there are two separate references to domestic violence in the Act. One occurs in the context of the "hardship" exception to the 60–month limit on assistance. In general, states cannot use federal Temporary Assistance for Needy Families (TANF) funds to assist families who have already received 60 months of assistance. States *may* develop exceptions to the limit, but those exceptions cannot exceed 20% of the state's federally-funded caseload. Exceptions can be granted if the limit would create a hardship, *or* if the family includes an individual who has been battered or subjected to extreme cruelty, which is to say, subjected to:

(I) physical acts that resulted in, or threatened to result in, physical injury to the individual;

(II) sexual abuse;

(III) sexual activity involving a dependent child;

(IV) being forced as the caretaker relative of a dependent child to engage in nonconsensual sexual acts or activities;

(V) threats of, or attempts at, physical or sexual abuse;

(VI) mental abuse; or

(VII) neglect or deprivation of medical care.

Personal Responsibility and Work Opportunity Act, Section 103. The principal limitation of this provision is that needy individuals and families are competing for exemptions, in a situation in which states cannot grant more than 20% without jeopardizing their receipt of federal funds.

The second explicit reference to domestic violence is the Wellstone/Murray Family Violence Amendment, otherwise known as the Family Violence Option. Personal Responsibility and Work Opportunity Act Section 402(a)(7). In 1998, Martha Davis, legal director of the NOW Legal Defense and Education Fund, gave this synopsis of the Family Violence Option, and its implementation in the states.

Martha F. Davis
Domestic Violence and Welfare Reform: A Status Report, Sojourner: The Women's Forum 32 (May 1998)

The Family Violence Option, sponsored in Congress by Senators Patty Murray (D–WA) and Paul Wellstone (D–MN), gives states the option of adopting programs to address the impact of domestic violence on welfare recipients. Under the Option, states may create programs to confidentially identify and refer domestic violence victims who may be eligible for counseling and other services. When necessary, states may waive rigid program requirements in favor of flexible work goals and time limits, taking into account the individual needs of battered women. The federal agency monitoring states' compliance with the welfare law, the U.S. Department of Human Services, has alerted states that they will not be penalized by the federal government for granting such waivers.

The federal enactment of the Family Violence Option is only half the battle, however—and the easy half, at that, since few federal legislators proved willing to openly oppose measures to address domestic violence. First, every state must be convinced to adopt the Option. Second, and most importantly, the Option must be implemented in a way that will really help women.

As to the first point, advocates around the country have been working at the state level to secure adoption of the Option, resulting in a glass that is both half full and half empty. Given that two years ago, not a single state had such a provision, the progress is remarkable: to date, nearly half of the states have included the Family Violence Option in their state plans. However, many of the remaining states are reluctant to adopt a comprehensive approach, still resisting the plain truth that domestic violence is a triggering factor for women's poverty, and that their highly touted welfare-to-work plans will simply not succeed if they fail to address that issue.

In those states where the Option has been adopted, advocates face perhaps the most challenging and creative task—ensuring that the Family Violence Option is not simply a piece of paper, but is really available to women who need it. Implementing the Option entails developing screening and identification mechanisms that will encourage women experiencing domestic violence to come forward; developing referrals to sensitive, appropriate services; and crafting procedures for ensuring that waivers are available to those who need them. At this point, states' track records on implementation vary widely.

Perhaps the most critical issue at this stage is to ensure that women know about the Family Violence Option and understand that, under the Option, they need not choose between stalking and violence or a severe financial sanction for failing to comply with work requirements. Further, women need to be assured that they will not be penalized for revealing that they are domestic violence victims, and that their privacy will be respected. Sound, responsible initial screening is critical in order to save women from this dangerous dilemma. Yet Minnesota, New Jersey and Oregon provide that screening will be simply done by regular welfare caseworkers. Even with some modicum of training on domestic violence—which should be routinely required of all caseworkers—these welfare eligibility specialists are not likely to have sufficient expertise or time to properly handle the sensitive issue of domestic violence. Other states, such as New York and Maryland, involve a domestic violence expert employed by the state agency as a second level of screening. However, Rhode Island may have the best model, since its draft regulations provide for initial screening by an independent domestic violence expert, thus removing the potential deterrent effect of asking welfare recipients to reveal this sensitive information to a government representative in the first instance.

Further, if the Family Violence Option is to be effective, states must make a serious effort to ensure that possible victims of family violence are identified and, if appropriate, exempted from program requirements such as time limits or mandatory work. In Maine, New Jersey, Rhode Island and Washington, all welfare applicants are required to be notified of their ability to waive these requirements on the basis of domestic violence. In Maine, the notice must be given both orally and in writing. To date, however, the data on how many women have sought and been granted waivers is dismal—in the single digits in most states. At the same time, in the states that have collected the information, the overall number of individuals subject to sanction for failing to comply with welfare work requirements has risen dramatically.

* * *

NOTES

1. The program requirements that may be waived for battered women include time limits, residency requirements, child support cooperation requirements and family cap provisions, in cases where compliance with these requirements would: "make it more difficult for individuals receiving assistance under this part to escape domestic violence, or unfairly penalize such individuals who are or have been victimized by such violence, or individuals who are at risk of further domestic violence." For purposes of the Option, domestic violence is given the same definition as in the hardship exemption. The Department of Health and Human Services has indicated, although not definitively ruled, that waivers offered under the

Family Violence Option do not count against the 20% limit imposed on hardship exemptions; earlier doubt with respect to this issue inhibited the adoption of the Option in a number of states.

2. As Lennett suggests, knowing that a state has adopted the Family Violence Option does not, in and of itself, guarantee that battered women will know of its existence, or be able to take advantage of it—either to secure waivers from programmatic restrictions, or to take advantage of resources made available by the state. It is also important to note that the fact that a state has *not* availed itself of the Option does not preclude it from adopting other measures to ease the path of battered women from welfare to work, since the federal legislation gives each state great flexibility in developing its own programs. A year after Martha Davis published her preliminary assessment, the Taylor Institute, at the request of the Department of Health and Human Services, published an updated report on state experience with the Family Violence Option (FVO). The report's authors were Jody Raphael and Sheila Haennicke. *Keeping Battered Women Safe Through the Welfare to Work Journey: How Are We Doing? A Report on the Implementation of Policies for Battered Women in State Temporary Assistance for Needy Families (TANF) Programs* (Taylor Institute, September 1999).

As of May 1999, thirty-six states had formally adopted the Option., although only thirty-two had policies and procedures in place to implement it. Another five states reported that they were in the process of adopting the FVO and implementing procedures, while another six had not adopted the FVO but had other policies and procedures allowing battered women temporary deferrals from work-related activities. Wisconsin and Illinois had not adopted the FVO, and had no specific domestic violence policies in place, although battered women were allowed to obtain domestic violence services as a work activity. South Carolina had not adopted the FVO, and reported that domestic violence policies were "in development."

The report documented three different approaches to assessing welfare recipients or applicants for domestic violence; 39% notify women of the availability of temporary waivers from work requirements, and ask questions about the presence of domestic violence; 32% make an assessment before notifying applicants or recipients of the waiver possibility, and 29% notify, but then rely on women to self disclose, and do not follow up with any further questions about domestic violence. The report's authors found that 20 states had notice and assessment protocols that were wholly inadequate to the task of identifying and assisting women faced with domestic violence in their homes; information about the availability of waivers was brief, in small print, buried amongst a lot of other information, and not connected to any further effort to identify women who could benefit from the waiver. In other states the notices were too vague, or used language—such as the label domestic violence—with which women might not identify. The authors were particularly critical of the fact that most FVO forms failed to mention paternity or child support enforcement as program requirements that could be waived, because of a general failure of coordination between child support enforcement programs and welfare-to-work programs. On the other hand, the authors praised states that were clear in their presentation of the information, used easy-to-understand language, and provided a complete list of all the requirements that the FVO could temporarily waive. They also offered examples of language with which women could more easily identify. Oregon, for example, tells recipients: "No family is the same, so we have many different types of services ... Some families have things happening that keep them from being able to go directly to work ... If working, looking for a job or going to school might put you or your family in danger, we can ..." Report at 10. Rhode Island's notice reads: "If working, looking for a job or going to school may put you or your children in danger of physical, emotional or sexual abuse, we may be able to excuse you from these activities until the situation is resolved." Id.

Assessing clients for domestic violence has proved both sensitive and complex. Preliminary evaluations suggest that assessment works better when the interviewer departs from the formal script offered by an assessment instrument (usually posing just five or six questions about abuse), but without an instrument, it is hard to be sure that workers are discussing domestic violence with their clients. The other preliminary finding is that clients and workers respond better when the questions have obvious and immediate relevance to the welfare-to-work process, rather than seeming to pry into clients' private lives. The report offers Rhode Island's protocol as a model:

> Has paternity been established for your child(ren)? If no, would it cause problems or put you in danger if paternity were established?
>
> Is the absent parent(s) paying child support?
>
> If not, what do you think would happen if s/he were required to pay child support?
>
> The Family Independence Program wants everyone to have educational, job, or training opportunities if it is safe for them. Would this situation cause serious problems for you to participate in education or work requirements?

Id. at 13. The authors conclude that: "All questions about domestic violence should therefore be linked to potential sabotage and danger around education, training, work, and child support enforcement; there is no need to ask general and intrusive questions about their partner's abusive behavior ... that will appear as entirely too personal or shaming." Id.

In obtaining information about clients' domestic-violence related needs, one key choice is whether to train regular welfare case workers to identify and respond appropriately, or whether to involve domestic violence specialists. As of May 1999 fourteen states had chosen to involve outside domestic violence service providers in the assessment or waiver process. While the protocols vary, many include using these domestic violence specialists to verify clients' claims of abuse, as well as to perform assessments, and help develop safety and service plans. Id. at 14. The failure to integrate welfare-to-work and child support enforcement activities within welfare departments, mentioned above in the context of providing effective notice to clients of available waivers, has also resulted in a training failure; 29 states had not, as of May 1999, provided any training for their child support enforcement staff in basic domestic violence awareness, and in another 14 states the training had not been mandated for the entire staff.

There are two different time clocks that affect welfare receipt; the "work clock" that requires recipients of welfare to participate in work activities after 24 months, and the "benefit clock" that shuts off benefits altogether after 60 months of welfare receipt. Of the 44 states with FVO policies and procedures in place when the report was written, 20 provided up-front waivers that stopped the "work clock," while another 14 instead extended the work clock at the end of the 24 month period. 15 of the 44 states also offered waivers that would stop the "benefit clock." Ten states did not provide exemptions or deferrals, but counted participation in social services as a work activity for battered women. States vary widely in how long an initial waiver is good for (in 8 states it is indefinite, for example, while in another it is good for only 30 days, and in others for 3, 4, or 6 months); whether and under what conditions it can be renewed; and what level of corroboration is needed to trigger it. There is an important distinction between states that will accept a woman's sworn statement, or that statement endorsed by a domestic violence service provide or agency, and states that require verification from police, court or medical records. Only one state insists on that level of verification without creating an alternative for situations in which it is not available. The welfare caseworker is usually authorized to grant the waiver, although some states have review processes in place either for the initial decision or for subsequent renewals.

All but 12 states will grant waivers only if a welfare applicant or recipient is working actively with a domestic violence service provider, whether that provider has been brought into the welfare office to work with clients, or clients are referred out to community providers. The report ends with accounts of innovative welfare-to-work programming being offered to women affected by abuse in partnerships between state welfare offices and community service providers in Massachusetts; Topeka, Kansas; Orlando, Florida; Chicago; Rhode Island; San Antonio, Texas and Modesto, California. Id. at 25–31.

3. The "upside" of welfare reform has been the creation of new theoretical, political and practical linkages between those working against poverty and those working against domestic violence. The wealth of new thinking and new learning generated in the last decade has the potential to create valuable new approaches to helping women escape the double bind of poverty and abuse. The danger is that the many new reform initiatives will offer more in theory than they deliver in practice, unless their implementation is supported by ongoing education and training, and financial resources. This next critical period will determine whether women like Bernice, or Elaine Preston, will have different stories to tell.

E. Individuals with Disabilities as Victims of Domestic Violence

It has been only very recently that the domestic violence community has paid separate and special attention to the particular vulnerability of abused women who suffer from physical, mental or emotional disabilities. New studies document the ways in which women with disabilities are more vulnerable to abuse by their partners than other women, and new documentation of the incidence of abuse in this population confirms that increased vulnerability.

At the same time, the abuse of women with disabilities raises at least two important new questions. First, when such a woman is abused by her partner, are we seeing the by now familiar "power and control" dynamic at work, or might there be a competing interpretation—could the abuse be the result of "caregiver stress," as is often argued when the abuser is not a partner, but a parent, or child, or other caregiver? If the disability is itself the consequence of prior abuse, the question may be easy to answer. But if the disability predates the abuse, or its origins are distinct from the abuse, the question may take a little more investigation. Once we have answered it, we need then to determine how our answer affects our response to the situation, and what legal remedies we would want to see available.

The second question is whether, in this context, our definition of "domestic" violence should expand to include non-family members, either in those cases in which we see "coercive control" as the motivation for abuse, or more generally. Individuals with disabilities often have expanded "families" of caregivers, who have the kind of intimate access usually reserved for partners or other family members. Should the restraining order mechanism, to take one very concrete example, be available to an individual who claims that she, or he, is being abused by an unrelated caregiver? Illinois is the one state to have comprehensively revised its abuse protection legislation to cover this situation. In other states, coverage may depend on such arbitrary factors as whether the caregiver is living in the same household as the abused individual.

Prevalence of and Vulnerability to Abuse

Karin Raye
Individuals with Disabilities as Victims of Domestic Violence, 9–11, 19–20 (unpublished paper, 1998)

Physical and sexual abuse has emerged as a critical issue of concern within the disability community. In the 1995–1996 Delphi Survey conducted by Berkeley Planning Associates, women with disabilities were asked to rank service areas in order of overall importance. Abuse and violence emerge as the highest ranked priority area receiving eighty-five percent (85%) of the vote as "very important" while another ten percent (10%) of the survey group ranked it "important." The Delphi Survey also discovered that "women with disabilities share with non-disabled women the fact that their intimate partners may physically, emotionally or verbally abuse them. However, [women with disabilities] can also be subject to types of abuse that are not issues for non-disabled women, such as denial of medications, withholding of attendant services, or preventing use of assistive services."[1]

Berkeley Planning Associates is not alone in its findings. In 1985, a survey conducted by the DisAbled Women's Network (DAWN) in Canada found that violence and fear of violence were the most critical issues facing women with disabilities. It is estimated that women with disabilities are one and one half (1.5) to ten (10) times as likely to be abused as non-disabled women, depending on whether they live in institutions or in the community. The Colorado Department of Health reports that incidents of domestic abuse among disabled women may be as high as eighty-five percent (85%). Empirical evidence suggests that an individual with a disability is more likely to become a victim of assault or abuse than other people of similar age and gender.... [D]ue to the frequency with which people with disabilities are subjected to multiple or chronic abuse, the risk of abuse increases to at least twice as high and possibly five or more times higher than the risk for the general population.[2]

The prevalence of sexual abuse also has been documented among women and children with disabilities. A study of women with a variety of disabilities reported that they were about one and one half times as likely to have been sexually abused as children compared to non-disabled women. In addition, a recent Congressionally-mandated study conducted by the National Center on Child Abuse and Neglect documented physical and sexual abuse twice as often in children with disabilities compared to other children.

. . .

Disability-related factors may intensify methods of control by the abuser

Isolation, dependence and control are all common factors in abusive relationships of women with and without disabilities. A person's disability and subsequent reliance on others for daily basic needs may furnish an abuser with additional tools to effectuate his or her control and prevent escape by his victim. Financial exploitation, neglect, willful deprivation and other forms of abuse profoundly affect the health and safety of an individual with a disability. A woman with a disability ... may be less likely to physically protect herself from a physical attack. For example, a mobility impairment can prevent quick escape from dangerous situations, speech or communication impairments can make reporting difficult, and visual impairments or intellectual disabilities may affect a person's ability to discern danger. Moreover, methods of control used by the abusive partner, caregiver or family member can be designed specifically to prevent any possibility of escape and intensify the dependence upon the batterer. A batterer may destroy a prosthetic device, cancel a doctor's appointment, dispose of medication, over-medicate the individual or destroy a telecommunications device for the deaf (TDD).

1. Ann Cupolo Freeman et al., *Priorities for Future Research: Results of SPA's Delphi Survey of Disabled Women* 3 (1996).

2. Dick Sobsey, VIOLENCE IN THE LIVES OF PEOPLE WITH DISABILITIES: THE END OF SILENT ACCEPTANCE, xiv, 35 (1994).

Each ... act serves to cut the individual off from the outside world and prohibit her from leaving. Threats of reinstitutionalization are used to force the individual with a disability into submission. While these control dynamics are familiar to advocates who work with battered women, the power held by the batterer of a person with a disability may be even more complete and inescapable. Finally, medical complications are much more likely to occur when an individual with a disability is beaten, particularly when a physical disability is involved. As a result, the nature of one's disability may make a person more susceptible to forms of abuse or neglect designed to exploit disability-related vulnerabilities.

* * *

NOTES

1. Girls and women with disabilities may in addition be particularly vulnerable to sexual abuse, and to forming relationships with men who abuse them sexually:

> When a young woman reaches dating age, she may have fewer opportunities because of her difference, to experience a healthy process of learning what she likes and dislikes sexually, and how to set boundaries that are pleasing for her; she may not have dates, go to parties, or engage in any sexual activity appropriate to people her own age. Rejection may be her education, leaving her to first encounter sexual experience at a later age than her able bodied friends. Delaying the pleasure of progressive intimacy may cause her to be confused when the opportunity for any sort of sexual relationship arises. There are questions: Is this sexual activity suitable even though I am not enjoying it? Should I do what my partner demands because that person knows more about sex than I do? Should I do whatever s/he wants, because sex, pleasant or not, makes me feel more "normal"? Should I go along with it because *I have no idea* how to begin a relationship?
>
> ... If we use the example of the disabled woman who is naive about sexuality and has no experience with courtship, but is now confronted with a real situation, in addition to the fear of the unknown, she may also be excited by the attention. Her desire to be a "normal" woman, means she must repress that fear and let her partner lead her into unfamiliar territory. If she is lucky, that person will be caring and sensitive to her needs ... or instead may do what s/he pleases. This may not be the beginning of emotional battering, but unwillingness to pay attention to the woman's concerns can set up an unhealthy model that can lead to physical abuse if that person is inclined to such behavior. If she frees herself from this person, she may be left with the belief that only people who want to control her or to hurt her are those ... whom she will be able to have as sexual partners. She may feel she is left with one choice: celibacy or potentially violent sexual encounters....

Chris Womendez and Karen Schneiderman, *Escaping from Abuse: Unique Issues for Women with Disabilities* 9 SEXUALITY AND DISABILITY 273, 274 (1991).

2. The vulnerabilities women with disabilities suffer within their intimate relationships are compounded by the difficulties they face accessing services to assist them in escaping from abuse. A woman with a communication or physical impairment may be unable, without assistance, to contact police or find her way to a shelter. Appropriate and affordable transportation may not be available. At the shelter, she may find that the physical facilities do not meet her needs, or that shelter workers lack the training and sensitivity to help her manage those needs. Many courthouses are old and architecturally inaccessible. Although TDDs are more widely available than they used to be, few shelters, courts or law enforcement agencies have them, or are trained to use them effectively. The absence of sign language interpreters in shelters, hospitals and police stations prevents Deaf individuals from communicating with service providers. Personal assistance for completing forms, complaints or affidavits may not be readily available to a person who because of an intellectual disability or vision impairment cannot read or write.

Beyond these practical limitations, however, are others produced by society's continuing ignorance about, and prejudice against, individuals with disabilities. A 1995 report by L'Institut Roeher, *Harm's Way: The Many Faces of Violence and Abuse Against People with Disabilities,* documents the attitude that individuals with disabilities "are stupid and can be taken advantage of," and that they are "lesser beings." Along with these negative assumptions come others about the unreliability of individuals with disabilities, and a tendency to "doubt their story or blame them" for alleged incidents of abuse. Speech impairments, hearing impairments, mental, physical and other disabilities may all reduce the credibility of victims in the eyes of police, judges, attorneys, juries and the community at large.

State Responses to Individuals with Disabilities

Several states have responded to the barriers to access faced by individuals with disabilities seeking legal protection from abuse. The most common provision is one allowing a third party to apply for a protection or restraining order on behalf of a person prevented by physical or mental capacity from taken that step themselves. See, for example, Ariz. Rev. Stat. Ann. § 13–3602 (1989 & Supp. 1997); W. VA. CODE § 48–2A–4 (1996). In addition, some states allow hearings to be scheduled by telephone in order to accommodate a disability (see, e.g., WASH. REV. CODE ANN. § 26.50.050 (1997)), or require court appointment of an interpreter for an individual who has a hearing or speech impairment (WASH. REV. CODE ANN. § 26.50.055 (1997)).

These measures attempt to make traditional domestic violence protections available to a constituency that otherwise might be denied relief . Illinois has gone much further; revising its Domestic Violence Act, in 1989, to expand both its categories of protected individuals and its definition of abuse, in order to offer more meaningful protection to people with disabilities. These provisions, however, raise the question whether the statute remains a "Domestic Violence" Act, or whether the legislature has simply used the Domestic Violence Act as a handy vehicle for addressing a rather different problem.

Prior to the 1989 Amendments, the statute recognized "domestic violence as a serious crime against the individual and society which produces family disharmony in thousands of Illinois families, promotes a pattern of escalating violence which frequently culminates in intra-family homicide, and creates an emotional atmosphere that is not conducive to healthy childhood development." The amendments added as an additional purpose recognizing "domestic violence against high risk adults with disabilities," who are particularly vulnerable due to impairments in ability to seek or obtain protection, as a serious problem which takes on many forms, including physical abuse, sexual abuse, neglect, and exploitation, and facilitate accessibility of remedies under the Act in order to provide immediate and effective assistance and protection. ILL. REV. STAT. Ch. 40, § 2311–2 (1989). An adult with disabilities is defined as either an elder adult with disabilities—an adult prevented by advanced age from taking appropriate action to protect himself or herself from abuse by a family or household member—or a high-risk adult with disabilities—a person aged 18 or over whose physical or mental disability impairs his ability to seek or obtain protection from abuse, neglect or exploitation. It is not necessary that the person be adjudicated incompetent. ILL. REV. STAT. Ch. 40, § 2311–3 (1989).

The original 1986 statute governed abuse, defined as physical abuse, harassment, intimidation of a dependent, interference with personal liberty or willful deprivation, but excluding reasonable direction of a minor child by a parent or person in loco parentis. Even this early version of the statute recognized the particular vulnerability of individuals with disabilities in its definition of willful deprivation: "wilfully denying a person who because of age, health or disability requires medication, medical care, shelter, food, therapeutic device, or other physical assistance and thereby exposing that person to the risk of physical, mental or emotional harm, except with regard to medical treatment when the dependent person has expressed an intent to forgo such medical care or treatment," and its definition of intimidation of a dependent: "subjecting a person who is dependent because of age, health or disability to participation in or the witnessing of: physical force against another or physical confinement or restraint of another."

The 1989 amendments added two categories of prohibited conduct, exploitation and neglect. Exploitation is defined as "the illegal, including tortious, use of a high-risk adult with disabilities or of the assets or resources of a high-risk adult with disabilities. Exploitation includes, but is not limited to, the misappropriation of assets or resources of a high-risk adult with disabilities by undue influence, by breach of a fiduciary relationship, by fraud, deception, or extortion, or the use of such assets or resources in a manner contrary to law." Id. Neglect is defined as "the failure to exercise that degree of care toward a high-risk adult with disabilities which a reasonable person would exercise under the circumstances and includes but is not limited to: (i) the failure to take reasonable steps to protect a high-risk adult with disabilities from acts of abuse; (ii) the repeated, careless imposition of unreasonable confinement; (iii) the failure to provide food, shelter, clothing, and personal hygiene to a high-risk adult with disabilities who requires such assistance; (iv) the failure to provide medical and rehabilitative care for the physical and mental health needs of a high-risk adult with disabilities; or (v) the failure to protect a high-risk adult with disabilities from health and safety hazards." Id.

The family or household members against whom protective orders could be sought under the original legislation included spouses, former spouses, parents, children, stepchildren and other persons related by blood or marriage, persons who share or formerly shared a common dwelling and persons who have or allegedly have a child in common. The amendments added: "In the case of a high-risk adult with disabilities, 'family or household members' includes any person who has the responsibility for a high-risk adult as a result of a family relationship or who has assumed responsibility for all or a portion of the care of a high-risk adult with disabilities voluntarily, or by express or implied contract, or by court order." Id.

In addition to extending the protective order mechanism to individuals with disabilities experiencing abuse, exploitation or neglect at the hands of family or household members or other caregivers, the amendments took other steps to facilitate access on the part of those with disabilities to the legal system. One provision authorizes law enforcement agencies to assist individuals seeking access to the legal system in obtaining a search warrant or an ex parte injunctive order against those seeking to prevent that access, on a showing of probable cause that the individual is being abused in a manner that constitutes a criminal offense. If the individual is at risk of either death or great bodily harm, law enforcement officers are authorized to enter the premises where the individual is without a warrant. Ill. Rev. Stat. Ch. 40, § 2312–1 (1989). It seems unlikely that this provision actually increases the existing authority of law enforcement officers in these situations, but it throws the legislature's weight behind the proactive use of that authority. Another provision creates a hearsay exception in circumstances where the individual with a disability is unable to testify. Ill. Rev. Stat. Ch. 40, § 2312–13.1 (1989). Another provides for the appointment of independent counsel and temporary substitute guardians for high-risk adults with disabilities whose guardians are the subject of petitions for protective orders. Ill. Rev. Stat. Ch. 40, § 2312–13.3 (1989).

For a detailed analysis of the 1989 amendments see the publication produced by Protection and Advocacy, the organization responsible for drafting the amendments. *The 1989 Amendments to Illinois' Domestic Violence Act: Ensuring Access of High-risk Adults with Disabilities to Remedies and Services—A Guide for Judges and Attorneys* (April 1990).

QUESTIONS

1. What do you think is the practical impact of making restraining orders available against caregivers who are not otherwise family or household

members? How else might an individual with a disability take action against, for example, a neglectful caregiver, or one who was exploiting the individual financially? Does your assessment of the utility of the restraining order mechanism depend on the range of relief it authorizes? For a more detailed look at the remedies authorized under state restraining order legislation, see Chapter Eight, below.

2. What about the different scenario where the abuser is a partner, but also a caregiver? Under what circumstances might a restraining order be an effective remedy for abuse in that situation? What might make it a less effective remedy for an individual with a disability than for one without?

3. Do you have concerns about stretching the definition of domestic violence to cover financial exploitation of an individual by a paid caregiver? How would you articulate those concerns—are they concerns for the conceptual integrity of the legislation, or for the potential political consequences of extending the protective reach of the statute? What might those consequences be, do you think? Are they more likely to be negative than positive? As an Illinois legislator, which aspects of the 1989 amendments would you have supported, and which not?

4. In the context of same-sex partner violence, and in looking at issues of race and ethnicity, we looked at four factors; the partners' subjective experiences of abuse; particular community norms about family relationships, gender, or the use of violence; aspects of the particular community that made it harder to reach out beyond the community for help, and attitudes in society at large that affected the behavior of those in a position to provide assistance. Is that same framework applicable, or useful, in considering how individuals with disabilities experience, and cope with, abuse?

CHAPTER FOUR

LEGAL CHARACTERIZATIONS OF BATTERED WOMEN AND THEIR EXPERIENCES

Introductory Note

As you have seen in the earlier chapters on the dynamics and dimensions of abuse, there are many differing perspectives on battering. When abuse is presented in legal cases, these differing perspectives are reflected in legal argumentation, in the admission of evidence, and in judicial decision-making, as well as in the framing of legal remedies.

This chapter is intended to introduce you to some generic issues concerning the way that battered women's experiences—what battering is, and what it does—are reflected in law. We address these issues here because they pervade all the different legal contexts in which issues of woman abuse are implicated. In that sense, this chapter is a bridge between the previous chapters, which have presented the historical and social context of domestic violence and the dynamics and dimensions of abuse, and the rest of the book which examines in considerable detail the various ways in which domestic violence is understood and treated in and by the legal system.

Characterizations of battering by feminists early in the development of the battered women's movement explicitly articulated a broad view—of violence as a "moment" in, or part of, a relationship of power and control. That understanding has been reinforced by research in the fields of both psychology and sociology, as you read in Chapter 2. Responding to the legal system's tendency to deny or minimize abuse in intimate relationships, and to focus on single incidents of violence rather than grappling with the broader context in which these incidents occur, legal theorists have taken on the task of "explaining" abuse to the legal profession; the lawyers who will argue cases to the courts, and the judges who will decide them, or instruct the juries who will decide them.

Evan Stark, for example, emphasizes the batterer's pattern of coercion and control rather than his violent acts or their effect on the psyche of the victim. Evan Stark, *Re-Presenting Woman Battering: From Battered Woman Syndrome to Coercive Control*, 58 ALB. L. REV. 973 (1995). Stark's description draws on the traditional feminist interpretation of intimate violence: "The coercive control framework shifts the basis of women's justice claims from stigmatizing psychological assessments of traumatization to the links between structural inequality, the systemic nature of women's oppression in a particular relationship, and the harms associated with domination and resistance as it has been lived." Id. at 976. The framework emphasizes "restrictions on 'liberty,' highlighting a class of harms that extends beyond psychological or physical suffering to fundamental human rights." Id. Deprivation of liberty results from a process of ongoing intimidation, isolation, and control.

Martha Mahoney, to provide just one more example, takes on the particular question so often asked of battered women by the legal system: "Why didn't she just leave?" Mahoney describes battering in terms of the concept of "separation assault," the way the woman's effort to assert her independence and separate from her abuser triggers battering, and often an escalation of violence. Martha Mahoney, *Legal Images of Battered Women: Redefining the Issue of Separation*, 90 MICH. L. REV. 1 (1990). Mahoney maintains that the struggle for power and control is at the heart of the battering relationship. At the moment of separation or attempted separation—for many women the first encounter with the authority of law—the batterer's quest for control often becomes acutely violent and potentially lethal. Separation assault is "the particular assault on a woman's body and volition that seeks to block her from leaving, retaliate for her departure, or forcibly end the separation." Id. at 6. Mahoney emphasizes that naming "separation assault" as the harm is crucial to a broader understanding of power and control:

> As with other assaults on women that were not cognizable until the feminist movement named and explained them, separation assault must be identified before women can recognize our own experience and before we can develop legal rules to deal with this particular sort of violence. Naming the particular aspect of the violence then illuminates the rest. For example, the very concept of "acquaintance rape" moves consciousness away from the stereotype of rape (assault by a stranger) and toward a focus on the woman's volition (violation of her will, "consent"). Similarly, by emphasizing the urgent control moves that seek to prevent the woman from ending the relationship, the concept of separation assault raises questions that inevitably focus additional attention on the ongoing struggle for power and control in the relationship.

Id. at 7.

Whether the issue is understanding what battering is, or what it does to women—the strategies it forces them to deploy in order to survive, and the emotional toll it takes—the legal system has struggled, as the larger culture has struggled, to understand what it means to live in an abusive relationship. For those who represent battered women in court, the problem of making their abuse visible has three distinct aspects. First, the abuse must be understood as relevant to the proceedings—evidence of abuse will not be admitted unless it has a bearing on the legal issues in the case. In battered women's self defense cases, for example, treated in depth in Chapter 10, a restrictive definition of self defense might, and indeed often did, prevent the battered woman defendant from introducing evidence of any incident prior to the one in which she killed her batterer. Yet without understanding the background of her relationship with her batterer, a jury could not find her fear credible, or her actions to defend herself reasonable. In custody cases, as long as a father's behavior toward his partner was felt to be legally irrelevant to the quality of his fathering, his partner abuse was irrelevant to the question of whether he should be granted sole or joint custody of his children.

Second, evidence of the abuse must become a part of the case. Storytelling—using the "stories" of clients as the factual matrix of the case—has always been an essential part of good lawyering. But that assumes lawyers who are capable of listening and hearing battered women's experiences and then translating them into law. Bias and ignorance have had a substantial impact on the way many lawyers have understood and presented arguments based on battered women's experiences. Although intimate partner violence is a widespread problem that affects almost every aspect of legal practice, most lawyers are unfamiliar with its dynamics. They have not been adequately trained to consider this issue or to deal with clients who may have been abused. Many women who have been battered have been reluctant to talk about their experiences, particularly to lawyers, and many lawyers do not know how to pick up signals concerning possible battering. Moreover, lawyers may have been personally involved in violence and have ethical conflicts in representation.

As a result, in almost every field, cases continue to proliferate in which battering may be an issue but is not made visible in either the factual development or the legal argumentation in the case—because the client did not tell the lawyer, because the lawyer did not ask, or because the lawyer was not aware of how abuse might affect the particular legal issue that might need resolution. Lawyers who are sensitive to issues of abuse or have experience representing battered women frequently discover that some case on which they are working involves issues of abuse that were not raised by previous counsel. Often it is too late to raise them.

Third, the evidence must be sufficient to support the weight of the argument it has been introduced to bolster. Sometimes that means supplementing the testimony of the battered woman herself with the testimony of others; she herself may be too traumatized to be able to testify or to testify credibly; she may have been terrorized by her batterer into staying silent or recanting an earlier incriminating statement; she may on prior occasions have lied to medical or social workers so that there is no corroboration of her claims; she may have been too isolated to confide in friends or family. In some cases there will be other witnesses; neighbors, friends, doctors or emergency medical technicians, or police. But in other cases there may be none.

Expert testimony, by a psychologist, or social worker, or other professional knowledgable about domestic violence, was developed, first in battered women's self defense cases, but then in a variety of other legal contexts, to address each of these three aspects of making domestic violence visible to law. First, it was designed to assist judges in understanding the relevance of abuse to the legal issues raised by the case. When you read the *Kelly* case, in Chapter 10, for example, you will watch the judge coming to grips with the relevance of Gladys Kelly's prior abuse by her husband to the reasonableness of her belief that when she killed him he was about to kill her. Second, expert witnesses can work with (often less expert) lawyers to ensure that the client's story of abuse, and its implications for her case, is fully understood and presented. Third, expert testimony can supplement the testimony of the woman herself, and shore up her credibility: reassuring the jury that her experiences, which might seem outlandish, were in fact not unusual within the context of battering relationships; or explaining why she might have complained to the police on one occasion, but then refused to press charges; or even why she might have never sought relief from her batterer's abuse in ten years of marriage, but raise it for the first time in the context of a divorce, in which the custody of her children was at issue.

Since the early cases in which expert testimony on battering and its effects was first proffered, state and federal courts have wrestled with the question of its admissibility. In most states those issues have been dealt with under existing case law and legislation, but in a handful of states special legislation has been adopted. This is a topic addressed in Chapter 10, below, in the context of battered women's self-defense claims.

With the benefit of hindsight we can acknowledge that the particular framework developed for the introduction of expert testimony on battering—"battered women's syndrome testimony"—was perhaps unfortunate. On the one hand, it allowed psychologists specializing in domestic violence, like pioneer Lenore Walker, to claim that the growing body of knowledge about abuse and its impact met standards of scientific credibility, and allowed them to qualify as experts in that recognized field. On the other hand, it exacerbated the tension between describing women's responses to violence as rational reactions to the extreme demands of an abusive relationship, and describing them in psychological terms that imply abnormality and illness. That tension, to which you were introduced in Chapter 2, has been particularly acute in the legal context, where the difference between "reasonable" behavior and behavior that is excusable but based on "impaired" judgment can have important legal consequences. In the self-defense context, for example, it can mean the difference between a verdict of justifiable homicide, and a manslaughter conviction based on diminished capacity. But in other contexts too, a defense that is understood as a "state of mind" defense may have more limited application than a defense asserting the reasonableness of the defendant's conduct.

This first case demonstrates the use of battered women's syndrome testimony to explain the victim's recantation of a statement she made supporting the prosecution of her abuser. The Supreme Court of Connecticut demonstrates a sound understanding of both the nature and the purposes of the testimony. In particular, the court resists the defendant's efforts to define the testimony in purely psychological terms, but accepts it as helpful in understanding a range of otherwise puzzling behaviors battered women deploy in response to violence, including apparent inconsistency in their efforts to invoke the criminal justice system.

Connecticut v. Borrelli

629 A.2d 1105, 227 Conn. 153.
Supreme Court of Connecticut, 1993.

■ Judges: Peters, C.J., Callahan, Borden, Berdon and Katz, Js.

Opinion: Berdon, J.

The defendant, Anthony J. Borrelli, raises two issues on appeal: (1) whether the trial court improperly admitted a prior inconsistent statement of the victim for substantive purposes; and (2) whether the trial court improperly allowed expert testimony on battered woman's syndrome for the purposes of impeaching the victim's trial testimony and providing a possible explanation for her recantation.

The defendant was charged in an information with kidnapping in the first degree ..., assault in the second degree ..., criminal mischief in the third degree, ... unlawful restraint in the first degree, ... and threatening.... He was also charged with breach of the peace.... The defendant pleaded not guilty to all charges and elected a jury trial. Prior to trial, the defendant filed a motion to dismiss all charges, except for the breach of the peace charge, on the ground that there was insufficient evidence.[1] The trial court denied the motion after a full evidentiary hearing and consolidated all charges for trial. After a jury verdict of guilty on all charges, the defendant was sentenced to an effective term of imprisonment of twenty years, suspended after ten years, with five years probation. The defendant appealed to this court.... We affirm the judgment of the trial court.

The following evidence was presented at trial. On December 30, 1990, the victim, the wife of the defendant, accompanied by three of her children, went to the Torrington police department in the evening hours and spoke to police officer Dale Olofson. She gave Olofson a written statement alleging that the defendant had physically abused and detained her the previous evening. She read and signed the statement. Her statement reveals the following: The defendant smoked some cocaine in the late evening hours of December 29, 1990, and then began accusing her of cheating on him. He cut up her clothing, underwear, driver's license and social security card with a knife. He held a pillow over her face so she could not breathe, and then tied her hands and feet together with rope behind her back. While she was bound, he threw a knife into the bedroom walls a number of times. He repeatedly threatened to kill her and members of her family, cut her lips with a knife, and held a cigarette lighter near her genital area. At approximately 6 a.m., he released her by cutting the ropes with a knife, and ordered her to give him a ride to Waterbury to buy drugs. They returned at 9 or 9:30 in the morning. She was tired but he would not

1. At the hearing on the motion to dismiss, the defendant argued that there was insufficient evidence to bring the charges to trial due to the victim's recantation and stated unwillingness to testify at trial. The motion was denied by the trial court, Susco, J., on the ground that the victim's prior inconsistent statement was more credible than her testimony at the hearing. The admissibility of the prior inconsistent statement is an issue before this court in the present appeal.

let her sleep. He also would not let her cancel dinner plans they had made, so she began cooking.[2]

At the hearing on the motion to dismiss, the victim testified that the events alleged in her statement had not happened. At trial, she again recanted. During cross-examination by the defendant at trial, she testified for the first time that it was actually she who had tied up and physically abused the defendant. She also testified that she had made up her initial story in the hopes that the defendant would be arrested and given drug treatment.

I. The defendant's first claim is that the trial court improperly admitted into evidence for substantive purposes the victim's written, sworn statement to the police, in which she had described in detail the physical abuse that the defendant had inflicted upon her that morning....

[T]he victim was asked by the state's attorney if the words in her statement were "the truth as to what took place between you and your husband on December 30, 1990." She responded that the statement was not accurate. After questioning the victim as to some of the specific facts contained in her statement, the state offered the statement into evidence. The trial court admitted the statement for both impeachment and substantive purposes pursuant to State v. Whelan, 200 Conn. 743 (1986).

In *Whelan*, we adopted an exception to the hearsay rule allowing the substantive use of a prior inconsistent written statement of a nonparty witness if the declarant: (1) signed the statement; (2) had personal knowledge of the facts set forth in her statement; and (3) testifies at trial and is subject to cross-examination.... We reasoned that prior inconsistent statements made under circumstances providing a reasonable assurance of reliability should be admitted to advance the truth finding function of the jury....

The defendant argues, however, that the statement should have been excluded because the particular circumstances of this case undermine the reliability of the victim's prior inconsistent statement. Specifically, the defendant argues that in *Whelan*, the homicide eyewitness' claimed inability to remember the incident in question established the foundation for the admission of his prior statement. The defendant argues that *Whelan* is limited to this context, and does not stand for the proposition that the written statement of a victim who later asserts that the statement is not true is admissible for substantive purposes. We disagree.

It is true that the witness in *Whelan* testified in court that he was unable to remember the event because he had been intoxicated at the time

2. The following evidence was presented in support of the breach of the peace charge. A neighbor of the victim's testified that an April 9, 1991, he looked out his window and saw the victim and the defendant arguing loudly on the street. When he was not looking, he heard a woman yell for help and called 911. He looked out the window again and saw the defendant block the victim as she tried to get into her car. He then saw the defendant push the victim up against another car, with his hands around her face and neck area. Police officers arrested the defendant, who was crouching dawn behind the stairs leading into the house. Both officers testified that the victim had red marks on her neck.

and because he had been in an automobile accident that had left him in a coma. Id., 746. Our analysis in *Whelan*, however, did not focus on the circumstances surrounding the witness' statements in the courtroom. Rather, we carefully examined the circumstances surrounding the out-of-court statement, in order to determine if the statement was made under conditions providing a reasonable assurance of reliability....

. . .

In the present case, the trial court reasonably found sufficient indicia of reliability in the circumstances surrounding the victim's statement to uphold its admission for substantive purposes. First, the victim gave her statement to a police officer on the day of the incident described in the statement. The statement was made "long before the witness' memory [of such an event] might have faded." ... She also signed the statement after reading it, and swore to its accuracy under oath. She confirmed at trial that the words in the statement were the words that she had spoken to Olofson. Most importantly, the victim's statement was not "given in response to leading questions, which are laden with facts to which the witness has merely answered with a yes or no." ...

Furthermore, there was ample corroborative evidence in the present case.... Olofson testified that after she had taken the statement from the victim, she asked to see the marks that the victim had claimed were on her body. Olofson testified that the victim had had visible marks on her ankles, and had also showed Olofson marks on her wrists and cuts on her top and bottom lips. Olofson accompanied the victim to her house where she viewed pieces of cut up lingerie, a rope, and two knives. Finally, Olofson testified that there were "narrow vertical marks" in the walls of the bedroom. Olofson's observations corroborated the victim's statement, and thereby enhanced its reliability, preventing the specter of a prosecution based solely on an out-of-court inconsistent statement. "It is the trial court's responsibility to weigh the reliability of each statement on a case-by-case basis." ... In the present case, the trial court properly found that the out-of-court statement given by the victim had sufficient indicia of reliability to be admitted for both impeachment and substantive purposes.

. . .

II. The defendant next claims that the trial court improperly admitted the testimony of an expert witness concerning battered woman's syndrome. The state in its case-in-chief offered into evidence the expert testimony of Evan Stark, a sociologist, on the subject of that syndrome. The evidence was offered for the purpose of providing a possible explanation for the victim's recantation and to impeach her subsequent testimony that she had lied in the statement to get the defendant drug counseling. After a preliminary examination of Stark outside of the presence of the jury and briefing and argument by counsel, the trial court allowed the testimony over the defendant's objection.

The defendant raises three objections to Stark's testimony. First, the defendant claims that battered woman's syndrome has not gained the general acceptance in the scientific community that the defendant asserts is required for its admission. Second, the defendant argues that Stark was not an expert on the subject of battered woman's syndrome. Finally, the defendant claims that the expert testimony should have been excluded because it invaded the province of the jury, inasmuch as the jury has the sole prerogative of assessing and determining the credibility of witnesses. We will treat these claims seriatim.

A. The defendant first claims that the subject of battered woman's syndrome does not meet the test for admissibility of scientific evidence articulated in Frye v. United States, 54 App. D.C. 46 (D.C. Cir. 1923). The Frye test requires that when scientific expertise is offered, the subject matter of the testimony "must be sufficiently established to have gained general acceptance in the particular field in which it belongs."[1] ...

This court does not apply the Frye test to all types of expert testimony, even if technical or scientific concepts are involved.... We have found the Frye test appropriate when the experimental, mechanical or theoretical nature of the scientific evidence had the "potential to mislead lay jurors awed by an aura of mystic infallibility surrounding scientific techniques, experts and the fancy devices employed." ...

Nevertheless, expert testimony need not satisfy the Frye test in cases where "the jury is in a position to weigh the probative value of the testimony without abandoning common sense and sacrificing independent judgment to the expert's assertions based on his special skill or knowledge.... Furthermore, where understanding of the method is accessible to the jury, and not dependent on familiarity with highly technical or obscure scientific theories, the expert's qualifications, and the logical bases of his opinions and conclusions can be effectively challenged by cross-examination and rebuttal evidence." ... For example, without even discussing the Frye test, we upheld the admissibility of expert testimony on the behavioral characteristics of child sexual abuse victims. ...

In the present case, Stark did not examine the victim. He did not offer any opinion as to whether she was a battered woman or whether she exhibited the typical behavioral characteristics of a battered woman.... Instead, Stark's testimony was based on his observations of a large group of battered women through the lens of his educational background and experience. The state offered Stark's testimony in order to provide an interpretation of the facts that a lay jury might not have perceived because of its lack of experience with battered women.... We conclude that satisfaction of the Frye test is not a necessary precondition for the admission of expert testimony on battered woman's syndrome.

1. "Just when a scientific principle or discovery crosses the line between the experimental and demonstrable stages is difficult to define. Somewhere in this twilight zone the evidential force of the principle must be recognized, and while courts will go a long way in admitting expert testimony deduced from a well-recognized scientific principle or discovery, the thing from which the deduction is made must be sufficiently established to have gained general acceptance in the particular field in which it belongs." (Internal quotation marks omitted.) State v. Hasan, 205 Conn. 485, 489 (1987). We recognize that the United States Supreme Court in Daubert v. Merrell Dow Pharmaceuticals, 125 L. Ed. 2d 469 (1993), has cast some doubt on the continued viability of the Frye test. We need not, however, address this issue here.

B. The defendant also challenges Stark's qualifications to testify as an expert witness on battered woman's syndrome. "Generally, expert testimony is admissible if (1) the witness has a special skill or knowledge directly applicable to a matter in issue, (2) that skill or knowledge is not common to the average person, and (3) the testimony would be helpful to the court or jury in considering the issues." . . .

The defendant claims that Stark was not qualified to testify as an expert witness about battered woman's syndrome because he did not hold degrees in psychology or psychiatry, was not licensed to do psychological testing, had not published in psychiatric or psychological journals, and had never before testified as an expert before a jury. "The determination of the qualification of an expert is largely a matter for the discretion of the trial court. . . . The trial court's decision is not to be disturbed on appeal unless that discretion has been abused, or the error is clear and involves a misconception of the law. . . . In order to testify as an expert, an expert must demonstrate a special skill or knowledge, beyond the ken of the average juror, that, as properly applied, would be helpful to the determination of an ultimate issue." . . .

Stark testified that his qualifications included a master's degree in social work from Fordham University and a doctorate in sociology from the State University of New York. He was a tenured associate professor of public administration at Rutgers University and director of a domestic violence training project in New Haven. He also indicated that, at the time of trial, he was a visiting professor of social work at the State University of New York at Stonybrook.

As to his experience in the area of domestic violence, Stark testified that he was codirector of a Yale School of Medicine project funded by the National Institutes of Mental Health that had reviewed the medical histories of approximately 3600 women who had come to the hospital complaining of injury. He also testified that he was codirector of several other projects that had examined the relationships between domestic violence and child abuse, domestic violence and pregnancy, and the correlation between women who had attempted suicide and domestic violence. He was cochair of the United States Surgeon General's working group on domestic violence and health, and had also published approximately fifty book chapters and professional journal articles.

We have previously upheld a trial court's determination that Stark was qualified as an expert on battered woman's syndrome and that his testimony was relevant in the context of a family matter to determine the issue of custody of a minor child. . . . In light of Stark's extensive educational background, work experience, and research in the area of battered woman's syndrome, we conclude that the trial court did not abuse its discretion in determining that Stark was qualified as an expert on battered women's syndrome.

Not only was Stark qualified to testify, but his testimony focused on a subject that is beyond the knowledge and experience of the average juror. . . . Commentators have noted that "the research data indicates that potential jurors may hold beliefs and attitudes about abused women at variance with the views of experts who have studied or had experience with abused women. In particular, males are likely to be skeptical about the fear the woman feels in an abusive relationship and about her inability to leave a setting in which abuse is threatened." N. Vidmar & R. Schuller, "Juries and Expert Evidence: Social Framework Testimony," 52 Law & Contemp. Probs. 133, 154 (1989); see State v. Hennum, 441 N.W.2d 793, 798 (Minn. 1989) (applying similar "beyond the understanding of the average person" test and allowing expert testimony on battered woman's syndrome).

In the present case, Stark presented a general description of battered woman's syndrome, based on his experience with battered women and research and study in the area of domestic violence. Stark defined the term "battered woman's syndrome" as referring "to the behavioral and psychological consequences that many victims, but by no means all victims, experience as a consequence of living in domestic violence situations."

Stark explained that there are certain characteristics that are commonly found in relationships involving domestic violence. First, there is the "cycle of violence," in which "there's a period of tension build up in the relationship and then there's what we call the abusive episode where the batterer explodes and there's violence maybe combined with other forms of force and harassment ... and it's at that point or soon after that point that the battered woman may be quite clear about her danger and quite forthright in seeking help. But the next phase is what we call the honeymoon phase or where the batterer either says he'll never do it again or ... enters some kind of treatment program.... And she doesn't want the relationship to end, she wants violence to end. And she believes maybe this time it will be different. So at that point she's likely to believe that, in fact, it won't happen again. And she may at that point then either change her story or try to ... do what she needs to do ... in order to survive and to feel safe in the relationship."

Stark testified that some battered women develop a "learned helplessness" from repeated failures to take control of the relationship. The result of such learned helplessness is that battered women fail to take advantage of subsequent opportunities to seek help and escape the battering situation.

Stark also testified: "Now, the battered woman's syndrome includes a lot of behaviors which don't make any sense when you understand them as an outsider, but only make sense when you understand them from the standpoint of survival and safety;" Stark testified that battered women may stay in a relationship with an abuser despite the abuse. Battered women commonly fail to report their problems or delay reporting them to the authorities or others. Such women, who have suffered extraordinary harm, commonly minimize or even deny the harm that they have suffered. Finally, there is the "paradoxical situation ... where a woman will come in on one occasion and present a very clear and concise picture of danger that she's in, either explaining it to her health provider or to a police officer, and then a week later completely change her story." Stark testified that this last pattern "is one of the most common things that we see in the field."

Stark's testimony was consistent with the theory of battered woman's syndrome as it has been presented and discussed in scholarly commentary. See L. Walker, The Battered Woman Syndrome (1984) pp. 86–94, pp. 95–104; R. Schuller & N. Vidmar, "Battered Women Syndrome Evidence in the Courtroom: A Review of the Literature," 16 Law & Human Behavior 273, 274–77 (1992); C. Ewing, Battered Women Who Kill: Psychological Self-Defense as Legal Justification (1987) pp. 7–21; see generally L. Walker, The Battered Woman (1979).[1]

Moreover, expert testimony concerning battered woman's syndrome has been accepted by many courts when the testimony was offered by a criminal defendant to bolster a claim of self-defense.... Such expert testimony has also been accepted if offered by the prosecution to explain the recantation of the complaining witness; Arcoren v. United States, 929 F.2d 1235 (8th Cir.); and if offered to explain the victim's delay in reporting the abuse and remaining with the defendant after the abuse. State v. Frost, 242 N.J. Super. 601, 614, 577 A.2d 1282 (1990); State v. Ciskie, 110 Wash.2d 263, 272 (1988); see generally J. Schroeder, "Using Battered Woman Syndrome Evidence in the Prosecution of a Batterer," 76 Iowa L. Rev. 553 (1991). We conclude that the subject of battered woman's syndrome is "beyond the ken of the average juror," and therefore meets the threshold test for admissibility of expert testimony in this state....

Finally, Stark's expert testimony in this case was helpful to the jury. The most important issue in this case was the credibility of the victim. Her written, signed statement alleged that she had been the victim of egregious abuse. Before the jury, the victim testified that she had not been abused and that indeed it was she who had tied up the defendant and abused him. The defendant, through cross-examination of Olofson, questioned the credibility of the victim's written statement in view of her eighteen hour delay in making the complaint. The victim testified that she had made up the statement in order to get her husband into drug treatment. The state offered a different explanation, one beyond the knowledge and understanding of the average juror—that the statement was true, and the victim's recantation was a pattern of typical behavior consistent with battered woman's syndrome.

1. The defendant also argues that expert testimony concerning battered woman's syndrome should not be admitted because the American Psychiatric Association's Diagnostic and Statistical Manual of Mental Disorders (3d Ed. 1987), an important diagnostic treatise in the medical, psychiatric, and psychological fields, does not contain any reference to the syndrome. Stark specifically disclaimed, however, that the "syndrome" is an illness or mental disorder, but instead testified that battered women are "focusing on survival and safety ... [which] leads to these paradoxical behaviors and attitudes." See Bechtel v. State, 840 P.2d 1, 7 (Okla. Crim. App. 1992) (rejecting a similar argument and stating that the syndrome is a mixture of both psychological and physiological symptoms but is not a mental disease); Commonwealth v. Craig, 783 S.W.2d 387, 389 (Ky. 1990) (syndrome was not mental condition and expert could qualify to testify about it although not a psychiatrist or clinical psychologist); R. Schaller & N. Vidmar, "Battered Women Syndrome Evidence in the Courtroom: A Review of the Literature," 16 Law & Human Behavior 273, 281 (1992) (despite the label, battered woman's syndrome is not a diagnosable mental disorder, but is rather a descriptive term that refers to the effects of abuse on a woman).

In a case directly on point, the Eighth Circuit Court of Appeals upheld the admission of expert testimony on battered woman's syndrome to impeach an abuse victim's recantation at the criminal prosecution of the abuser. Arcoren v. United States, supra, 1241. In *Arcoren*, a victim of rape and assault described the defendant's violent sexual and physical assaults to a criminal investigator with the Bureau of Indian Affairs. Id., 1237. The victim also testified as to the assaults before a grand jury. At trial, however, the victim recanted her prior testimony and denied that the defendant had beaten and raped her. Id., 1238. The Circuit Court of Appeals noted that, as in the present case, the jury was then "faced with a bizarre situation." Id., 1240. "A jury naturally would be puzzled at the complete about-face she made, and would have great difficulty in determining which version of [the victim's] testimony it should believe. If there were some explanation for [the victim's] changed statements, such explanation would aid the jury in deciding which statements were credible." Id. Like the expert testimony in *Arcoren*, Stark's testimony provided the jury in the present case with an explanation for the victim's changed statements.

On the basis of the foregoing, we conclude that Stark was qualified to testify as an expert witness, that his testimony focused on a subject not familiar to the average person and that his testimony was helpful to the jury. Accordingly, his expert testimony was properly admitted.

C. The defendant's final claim is that the expert testimony in this case was actually opinion testimony as to the credibility of a witness, and therefore should have been excluded because it improperly invaded the province of the jury. The defendant relies on two recently decided cases; United States v. Whitted, 994 F.2d 444 (8th Cir. 1993); State v. Cheeks, 253 Kan. 93 (1993); in which convictions were reversed because physician experts testified that, in their opinions, the child victims were in fact sexually abused by the respective defendants....

Certainly, the jury had the right to consider Stark's testimony in determining whether to believe the victim's prior statement or her testimony at trial. Stark did not testify, however, that the victim was in fact battered and therefore did not comment, directly or indirectly, on her credibility.... [T]here is a "critical distinction between admissible expert testimony on general or typical behavior patterns of ... victims and inadmissible testimony directly concerning the particular victim's credibility." ... In the present case, the purpose of Stark's testimony was to present to the jury possible explanations for why a victim of abuse would completely recant her accusations, explanations that in all likelihood were beyond the jury's experience and knowledge. Stark neither presented opinion testimony as to the credibility of any witness nor indicated whether the out-of-court statement was credible.... Stark's testimony was relevant to describe the behavior patterns typically ascribed to battered women's syndrome. The trial court also cautioned the jury that expert testimony "is [not] binding upon you and you may disregard such testimony either entirely or in part. It is for you the triers of the facts to consider the testimony and with the other circumstances in this case, use your best judgment to determine whether or not you give any weight to the testimony and, if so, what weight you will give to it."

. . .

. . . We conclude that the expert testimony did not invade the province of the jury in determining the credibility of witnesses.

The judgment is affirmed.

In this opinion the other justices concurred.

NOTES AND QUESTIONS

1. In Michigan v. Christel, 449 Mich. 578, 537 N.W.2d 194 (Mich. 1995), the Supreme Court of Michigan took a very similar approach to the *Borrelli* court:

> Generally, battered woman syndrome testimony is relevant and helpful when needed to explain a complainant's actions, such as prolonged endurance of physical abuse accompanied by attempts at hiding or minimizing the abuse, delays in reporting the abuse, or recanting allegations of abuse. If relevant and helpful, testimony regarding specific behavior is permissible. However, the expert may not opine whether the complainant is a battered woman, may not testify that defendant was a batterer or guilty of the instant charge, and may not comment on the complainant's truthfulness. Moreover, the trial court, when appropriate, may preclude expert testimony when the probative value of such testimony is substantially outweighed by the danger of unfair prejudice.

449 Mich. at 580; 537 N.W.2d at 196. Note the court's emphasis on testimony with respect to "specific behavior." This provides more flexibility than an insistence that the testimony describe and explain a full-fledged clinical "syndrome." Note also the court's careful distinction between the expert witness providing the jury with a context for their decision-making, and the expert witness usurping the jury function by engaging in "fact finding" in areas in which the jury, informed by the expert testimony, is competent to exercise its own judgment. With respect to the expert being precluded from testifying that the complainant, in a prosecution of her batterer, or the defendant, in a self-defense case, is herself a battered woman, the *Borelli* and *Christel* courts are in a minority—only 20% of states have so ruled, while more than 75% have found expert testimony admissible on the question of whether the complainant or defendant is a battered woman or suffers from battered woman syndrome. To support such testimony, of course, the expert would need to make an individual assessment of the woman, and on a practical level this might significantly increase the cost of the testimony.

In *Christel*, the state introduced expert testimony to bolster the credibility of its assertion that even though the victim had tolerated abusive behavior from the defendant for some time, she had ended their relationship prior to the incident on which the criminal charges were based, and that she was not a willing participant in his subsequent forced entry into her apartment and rape, as the defendant sought to argue. The court determined that in the specific circumstances of the case, the testimony was insufficiently relevant, since:

> Complainant did not remain in the relationship until the date of the assault and try to hide or deny the abuse, did not delay reporting this incident, and did not later retract the claim of abuse. Instead, complainant testifies that the relationship ended one month before the assault, explained that she immediately reported the sexual assault, and has consistently maintained that the abuse occurred.

449 Mich. at 580–81, 537 N.W.2d at 196. Ultimately, however, the court deemed the admission of the evidence harmless error, "in light of the limited nature of the testimony and the other physical and testimonial evidence of abuse."

2. The issues that arise with respect to the admission of expert testimony differ with the context, as well as differing from state to state. Compare with the *Borrelli* decision, for example, the Massachusetts Supreme Judicial Court's decision in Commonwealth v. Lazarovich, 410 Mass. 466 (1991). Despite the admission of battered woman syndrome testimony, the defendant, Janice Lazarovich, was convicted of committing mayhem and assault and battery on her two year old daughter, and sentenced to 11 to 16 years in prison. Mayhem is a specific intent crime in Massachusetts; it requires showing that the defendant has committed certain disabling or disfiguring acts on another person "with malicious intent to maim or disfigure." Id. at 474.

The Commonwealth's theory was that the defendant either abused the child herself, or engaged in a joint venture with her husband, Roger Lazarovich, to abuse the child. The defendant's trial strategy was to persuade the jury that it was her husband, and not herself, who had injured the child. She testified that, except for a couple of spankings, she had never hit the child. The defendant testified about the nature of her relationship with her husband, and his with the child:

> Her testimony was that she married Roger in November, 1983. The child was born in August, 1984.... One month after the child was born, the defendant left the child alone with Roger for the first time in order to run an errand. On her return, she found the child "fussing in her crib," with red marks on her face. The defendant took the child to the hospital where she was diagnosed as having a fractured skull. A few months later, the defendant saw Roger "squeezing" the child's leg. After Roger left for work, the defendant took the child to the hospital where she was diagnosed as having a fractured left tibia and a second skull fracture.
>
> The defendant described how Roger became infuriated when the child wet herself. Sometimes when the child woke up wet, he placed her under a cold shower, yelled at her, and sometimes struck her in the face. Another time, when the child refused to eat, Roger shoved food

down her throat with his fingers, not caring "if it hurt her or if she cried."

The defendant also testified how, from the very beginning of their marriage, Roger hit her and forced her to have sex with him. One day, when the defendant was pregnant with her second child, Roger kicked her in the stomach, slapped her, and forced her to engage in oral sex. A few months later, when the defendant was seven months pregnant, he hit her on the head with a tire iron, and, when the defendant tried to call the police, he ripped the phone out of the wall and choked her with the cord.

Roger once locked the defendant in a closet for two hours. While trapped in the closet, the defendant heard him hitting the child while the child called her mother for help. The defendant also testified how one night Roger arrived home drunk. The couple had a fight, and Roger threw the defendant on the floor. He then went to the children's room, and the defendant called the police. After the police left, Roger picked up a knife with one hand and the child's younger brother with the other, and told the defendant that if she ever called the police again, "he would cut [the boy's] f__ head off." Roger then put the boy down, and threw the defendant against a wall, rendering her unconscious. When the defendant woke up, the child was sitting next to her and "[the child] was hurt herself because he had beaten her up.

The defendant also testified regarding the events leading up to the visit to the Center on January 24, 1987. On January 23, 1987, at approximately 9:00 p.m., the defendant was tending to her two boys in their bedroom when she heard Roger in the bathroom yelling at the child. The defendant left the boys and walked to the bathroom. When she arrived, she saw Roger hit the child. Roger then told the defendant to go back to the boys. The defendant did so; shortly thereafter, she once again heard Roger yelling at the child, followed by a "thud" on the floor of the bathroom and a "bang" as Roger walked out the door of the trailer. When the defendant walked into the bathroom, the child was lying unconscious on the floor. As the defendant had told the DSS investigator Harrington, Roger and she attempted to revive the child. The defendant, however, admitted that, unlike what she told Harrington, the child was injured on January 23, not on January 24. She stated that she had lied to Harrington because she was afraid of what Roger would do if she told the truth; she waited until the next day to take the child to the hospital because she was afraid of leaving the other two children with Roger....

Id. at 469–71.

Dr. Charles Ewing was the expert witness who testified about the cycle of abuse, and the development of learned helplessness. He explained that "women who are abused 'respon[d] with depression, with feelings of learned helplessness, feelings of being psychologically trapped in the relationship. That, of course, explains why many battered women stay in these relationships despite the fact [that] they are being abused.' Dr. Ewing explained how abused women lose their self-esteem, and how most women who suffer from the syndrome are too ashamed to seek help." Id. at 471. Ewing was also permitted to testify that, in his expert opinion, the defendant suffered from battered woman syndrome. He conducted a four hour examination, and reported that the defendant's response to the abuse "was also typical of that of women suffering from this syndrome. She became depressed, fearful, suffering from learned helplessness, felt that there was no way out, contemplated suicide, but couldn't see that as a way out because she feared what would happen if she left her kids—the situation that it would leave her children in. She felt trapped in the relationship." Id. at 471–72.

Defense counsel argued, at a side bar conference during the trial, that Dr. Ewing's testimony was relevant on the issue of intent, both on the question of whether the defendant had herself intended to hurt the child, and on the question of whether she had been a joint venturer with her husband in inflicting the injuries. The prosecutor argued that since the defense was claiming that the defendant had never herself injured the child, the intent issue was relevant only to the joint venture theory. Eventually the judge instructed the jury that "they could consider the battered woman syndrome if it is 'of assistance to you in deciding why the defendant did not leave the husband in this case. If that is a factor in your deliberations, you may consider it on that aspect of the case. And secondly, you may consider it on the aspect as to whether or not the defendant here was a joint venturer or had a joint enterprise in sharing her husband's criminal specific intent and his maliciousness.' " Id. at 472. Defense counsel did not object to the instruction at the time, but based an appeal on the argument that the jury should have been instructed that the expert testimony was also relevant to the question of whether the defendant harbored the requisite intent to commit mayhem on her own account, as well as with her husband. The Supreme Judicial Court upheld the judgment of the trial court, concluding that:

> The fact that the defendant might have suffered from battered woman syndrome, and that the syndrome might have impaired the defendant's ability to form the required specific intent, cannot be claimed to create a substantial risk of a miscarriage of justice where it is not relevant to the defendant's chosen trial strategy. Counsel may not try a case on one theory of law, and then obtain appellate review on another theory which was not advanced at trial. Id. at 476.

The decision in *Lazarovich*, and the opinion, raise many questions. First, what do you make of the Supreme Judicial Court's interpretation of defense counsel's "revised" strategy—namely, that the defendant's "syndrome" prevented her from forming the requisite intent to commit mayhem? The court is explicit that it understands this defense as a "state of mind" defense, and a claim that the defendant suffered from a "mental impairment." Is that really the import of Dr. Ewing's testimony? Isn't the defendant's story that she didn't hurt the child, or want to see the child hurt, but was powerless to stop it?

Second, even in saying that "learned helplessness" prevented her from acting to protect the child, aren't we discounting too readily the many times she did seek help for the child or for herself, despite the risks. How is it that the hospital twice diagnosed the child's skull fractures, without the child welfare authorities being alerted to intervene in the family situation? How is that the police responded to a domestic violence call, saw that there were young children in the home, and yet left Roger in place to threaten his son with a knife, hurl his wife against a wall, and abuse his daughter while his wife was unconscious? These are issues we will address in subsequent chapters.

Finally, how would you allocate responsibility for the ineffectiveness of the expert testimony in this case? Could defense counsel have argued its relevance differently or better, or were the courts to blame in interpreting its relevance in too restrictive a fashion? Was counsel, or were the courts, handicapped by an overly "clinical" understanding of the testimony? In the final analysis, was the defendant's conviction really the result of judicial error, or rather of the jury's horror at the injuries done the child, and determination to hold the mother accountable? For more analysis of cases in which mothers fail to protect their children from abuse, see Chapter 6, below.

3. In *Borrelli*, the court noted that: "Expert testimony on the subject of battered woman's syndrome is not relevant unless there is some evidentiary foundation that a party or witness to the case is a battered woman, and that party or witness has behaved in such a manner that the jury would be aided by expert testimony providing an explanation for the behavior." 629 A.2d 1105, 1115, n.15 (1993). This can create a catch–22 situation, in which, in the absence of other corroborating evidence, the expert testimony may be the only way to convince the court that the woman has been abused, but at the same time she is required to make that showing before the testimony can be admitted. This will be particularly problematic when the behavior she needs to explain as a consequence of, or a response to, abuse, is open to an alternative interpretation that the court is all too ready to adopt. The same problem attaches in self defense cases, where defendants are often required to make some preliminary showing that they acted in self-defense before evidence of their prior abuse, or battered woman syndrome testimony, is admissible. This creates serious problems for the woman whose reaction to the incident in which she killed her abuser is hard to interpret as self-defense until you know the history of her abusive relationship. This is a topic covered in more detail in Chapter 10.

4. As even these few examples illustrate, counsel and judges continue to struggle with the appropriate nature and scope of battered woman syndrome testimony. The case law is convoluted, and becomes only more so as the testimony escapes from its original self-defense context, and asserts its relevance in a wider variety of legal contexts. One disquieting judicial tendency, in the face of this chaos, is for courts to impose order through a new formalism—the development of rigid requirements about who "counts" as battered, and what symptoms "count" as legitimate reactions to abuse. The article from which the next reading is drawn offers an entirely sensible response to these problems. Mary Ann Dutton suggests that it is time for a "redefinition" of battered women's syndrome, one that

will refocus us on the range of battered women's experiences, and remind us that not all women respond in the same way to the realities of living in a battering relationship.

5. Although the court in *Borrelli* found it unnecessary to apply the Frye test to the testimony of Evan Stark, many courts have required that expert testimony about battered women's syndrome, or battered women's experiences, meet a test of scientific reliability. As the *Borrelli* court indicated, however, since its decision in *Frye* the U.S. Supreme Court has suggested alternative criteria under the Federal Rules of Evidence, first in Daubert v. Merrell Dow Pharmaceuticals, 509 U.S. 579 (1993), and then in General Electric Co. v. Joiner, 522 U.S. 136 (1997). The *Daubert* court described the Frye test, which demands general acceptance in the scientific community, as "austere." *Daubert* and *General Electric* propose instead an assessment based on multiple factors, including testability, peer review, publication, rate of error, and general acceptance. This is widely understood as a more flexible, and thus generous, standard. As the Supreme Court said in *Daubert:*

> "Vigorous cross-examination, presentation of contrary evidence, and careful instruction on the burden of proof are the traditional and appropriate means of attacking shaky but admissible evidence.... Additionally, in the event the trial court concludes that the scintilla of evidence presented supporting a position is insufficient to allow a reasonable juror to conclude that the position more likely than not is true, the court remains free to direct a judgment ..., and likewise to grant summary judgment.... These conventional devices, rather than wholesale exclusion under an uncompromising 'general acceptance' test, are the appropriate safeguards where the basis of scientific testimony meets the standards of Rule 702."

509 U.S. at 596.

In a yet more recent decision, the Court took a position on the very question addressed in *Borrelli,* extending the inquiry into scientific validity into the "soft" sciences. Kumho Tire v. Carmichael, 526 U.S. 137 (1999). The *Borrelli* court is by no means alone, however, in deciding that psychological testimony is less likely to overwhelm the common sense of the average juror than "hard science" expertise, and that it is therefore often unnecessary to subject that testimony to any rigorous test of scientific validity. See, for example, United States v. DiDomenico, 985 F.2d 1159, 1171 (2d Cir. 1993), cert. den. 519 U.S. 1006 (1996).

Expert Testimony

Mary Ann Dutton
Understanding Women's Responses to Domestic Violence: A Redefinition of Battered Women's Syndrome, 21 Hofstra Law Review 1191, 1194–96, 1198–1201, 1216–27, 1231–32 (1993)

Rationale for Redefining "Battered Woman Syndrome"

. . .

1. Testimony Concerning the Experiences of Battered Women Refers to More Than Their Psychological Reactions to Domestic Violence

Typically, the testimony offered in forensic cases is not limited to the psychological reactions or sequelae of domestic violence victims, and this has led to confusion about what is encompassed by the term "battered woman syndrome." Expert witness testimony may also be offered to explain the nature of domestic violence in general, to explain what may appear to be puzzling behavior on the part of the victim, or to explain a background or behavior that may be interpreted to suggest that the victim is not the "typical" battered woman or that she herself is the abuser.

These and other elements of the battered woman's experiences may be more or less relevant depending upon the legal context in which testimony is required. That is, the battered woman's psychological reaction to violence may be less relevant than other factors, such as her prior responses to violence, the outcome of those responses, and the context within which those responses were made.

. . .

2. The Psychological Realities of Battered Women Are Not Limited to One Particular "Profile"

. . .

Originally, battered woman syndrome was defined as the psychological sequelae to domestic violence. The definition emphasized "learned helplessness,". . . . By incorporating the theory of learned helplessness, expert testimony concerning battered women can better explain why some battered women do not perceive that they have certain options available to protect themselves, and may thus help to explain why they do not exercise those options.

Early stages of expert testimony concerning battered women's experiences focused heavily on the cognitive perceptions that followed directly from their actual experiences with domestic violence. More recently, the term "battered woman syndrome" has been used to refer to a particular subset of psychological reactions to violence: PostTraumatic Stress Disorder ("PTSD"). A battered woman's psychological reactions to domestic violence may meet most or all of the diagnostic criteria for PTSD: she may have flashbacks or other intrusive imagery or memories that may be experienced as highly distressful; she may experience anger, an inability to concentrate, and sleep disturbances; she may engage in conscious and unconscious efforts to avoid anything that may remind her of the prior violence, and these efforts may include dissociation from her affective experience or emotional feelings related to the abuse.

However, several problems arise in the legal context when battered woman syndrome is defined exclusively as PTSD. First, PTSD may or may not be the aspect of the battered woman's psychological reactions to violence that is most relevant to the immediate legal context. . . . [D]efining battered woman syndrome as PTSD frames the issue before the finder of fact as solely a "clinical" phenomena. Even though the traumatic stressor that leads to PTSD is one which is "usually experienced with intense fear, terror, and helplessness" by "almost anyone," and thus the psychological reaction to trauma is somewhat normalized, this may not always be clearly understood....

Second, even when PTSD is part of the psychological aftermath of violence, its relevance to the key legal issues may be minimal.... Unless it is the most relevant link to the legal question at hand, focusing the attention of the finder of fact primarily toward a clinical "syndrome" may be unnecessarily confusing, and even misleading. When a battered woman's reactions to violence are framed within a "clinical" context, the unintended result may be that the expert witness constructs for the finder of fact an image of pathology, clinical disorder, or diminished capacity when this construct may not only be inaccurate, but may be the opposite of what is intended.

Third, a diagnosis of PTSD requires the battered woman to meet a specific set of criteria in each of three symptom categories.... When a battered woman fails to meet these criteria, a diagnosis of PTSD is not warranted, and thus, a diagnosis of battered woman syndrome defined as PTSD cannot be supported. Nevertheless, when a battered woman meets partial, but not full, criteria for PTSD, those criteria that she does meet (e.g., amnesia regarding some parts of the abusive experience) may still be relevant....

... Even when an expert witness is permitted to testify about partial criteria, testimony that the battered woman did not meet full criteria for battered woman syndrome may create a misleading impression for the factfinder.

Finally, PTSD, as currently defined ..., describes only a subset of the possible range of reactions that result from exposure to traumatic experiences, and that range includes those reactions that are not defined as "clinical" phenomena as well as those that are so defined. Moreover, where the violence and abuse has been chronic and continual, the victim's psychological reactions may be even more complex than those described by PTSD as it is currently defined.

. . .

Thus, a battered woman who demonstrates identifiable psychological reactions to the violence and abuse she has experienced may nevertheless fail to meet full criteria for PTSD, for one or more of the following reasons: (1) her reactions are not considered "clinical" phenomena, and thus do not appear within diagnostic nomenclature; (2) her reactions are either more circumscribed than the full spectrum PTSD diagnosis, or are not characteristic of PTSD per se; and/or (3) her reactions are indicative of an even more complex clinical picture than that suggested by PTSD.

This Article proposes a redefinition of battered woman syndrome in three ways. First, descriptive references should be made to "expert testimony concerning battered women's experiences," rather than to "battered woman syndrome" per se. Second, the scope of the testimony concerning battered women's experiences should be framed within the overall social context that is essential for explaining battered women's responses to violence. Third, evaluation and testimony concerning battered women's psychological reactions to violence should incorporate the diverse range of traumatic reactions described in the scientific literature, and should not be limited to an examination of learned helplessness, PTSD, or any other single reaction or "profile."

. . .

The Question: What Are the Battered Woman's Psychological Reactions to Domestic Violence?

. . .

Typically, expert testimony concerning the battered woman's psychological reactions to violence has been used to address a number of different issues, including the reasonableness of the victim's perception of danger (where the victim is a criminal defendant claiming to have acted in self-defense); the psychological damage resulting from the domestic violence (where the victim is a plaintiff seeking damages in a civil tort action); the basis for sole child custody or restriction of visitation rights; and the battered woman's reasons for engaging in seemingly puzzling behaviors.

It is, of course, necessary to establish that the particular aspects of a battered woman's experience of violence (and its aftermath) toward which the testimony is addressed are directly relevant to the specific legal issues at hand. If this link is not made explicit to the factfinder, the relevance of the expert witness testimony may not be clearly understood, or may be missed altogether.

The nature and extent of violence and abuse experienced by battered women differ widely, as do women's reactions to the violence and abuse. Thus, a number of different psychological sequelae to battering may be relevant to a legal case involving a battering victim.

Further, the psychological impact of violence and abuse on women's lives (and on the lives of trauma victims generally) goes beyond those reactions generally considered to be symptom-focused, such as depression, anxiety, or nightmares. Psychological reactions to violence also include the ways in which battered women have come to think about the violence, themselves, and others as a result of their experiences. Finally, psychological reactions to violence also influence ways in which battered women relate to others.

As discussed previously, not all responses to trauma generally, or to domestic violence specifically, rise to the threshold of "clinical" or "pathological" conditions. A particular battered woman may exhibit both clinical and nonclinical reactions simultaneously. The distinction between battered women's "clinical" and "nonclinical" psychological reactions is more relevant to some kinds of legal action than it is to others. For example, the distinction is largely irrelevant to a battered woman's claims of self-defense, or to her argument for custody based on a history of domestic violence—understanding the battered woman's fear may be most relevant in these cases. Alternately, a claim of personal injury may rest, in part, on the psychological damages resulting from victimization that rise to the threshold of "clinical" phenomena. Thus, although exposure to domestic violence results in psychological symptomatology for some of its victims, that psychological symptomatology may or may not be relevant to the key legal issues at hand.

. . .

1. Cognitive Reactions to Violence and Abuse

Exposure to trauma, including violence and abuse, can change the way in which people view themselves, others, and the world. Specific beliefs, perceptions, and other cognitions identified in the scientific literature include reference to perceptions of safety or vulnerability; expectations regarding future violence (e.g., the expectation that violence or abuse will recur, or the expectation that future violence could be more serious); viewing oneself as negative or blameworthy (e.g., having low self-esteem, feeling responsible for the violence); perceiving that the violence or abuse is uncontrollable; perceiving a lack of alternatives available to oneself as compared to others; developing an increased tolerance for violence or abuse; changes in beliefs about others (e.g., trustworthiness, powerfulness); and perceptions of meaninglessness. It is important to note that, contrary to the assertion that these beliefs are necessarily distorted or pathologic, they may reflect accurate, or at least "reasonable" perceptions of reality based on the particular history of traumatic experience.

The battered woman's perception of viable options for stopping the violence and abuse by any means is not only shaped by her own prior experience with violence, but also influences her future actions in response to violence. The perception or understanding of whether there are options available that would end the violence is based largely on what has actually been learned through experience. One example is a battered woman who called the police on numerous occasions. The officers responded in a supportive manner and the batterer was arrested during some of those incidents. However, on each occasion he was released from jail quickly, and returned to continue his barrage of violence against the woman, her mother, and her children. Based on a combination of factors, this woman "learned" that police are a viable option for stopping the violence in an immediate situation. She also "learned" that, despite the support and interest of the police, they were not particularly effective in stopping the violence in the long-run. Another woman "learned" during childhood that the police were not a viable option to stop the violence even in an immediate situation: she observed her mother call the police on many occasions when her father beat her mother, only to hear them say that since the situation was "a domestic," they could not intervene. This woman never called the police when she had been beaten.

Some women who have been involved in prior abusive relationships may have a perception that they lack viable alternatives, because the problem is as bad or worse elsewhere. This may be based on their own prior abusive intimate relationships, on witnessing violence in their families of origin, on recognizing violence in the homes of their friends and family members, or on knowing of violence committed by persons who would not be expected to act that way. Further, the alternative of living without an intimate relationship may be unacceptable or impractical to the woman.

For many reasons, some battered women "tolerate" abuse for a period of time, in the sense that they make excuses or generate "understandable" reasons for it, or in some way come to believe that there is a "good" reason to give the batterer another chance to stop the violence. This "tolerance" may be explained as a function of the "cognitive dissonance" created by living in an abusive relationship from which the battered woman is unable to extricate herself: she may attempt to resolve that internal struggle or "dissonance" by focusing on reasons to remain. The "tolerance" may also derive from a battered woman's prior experience of even more severe violence elsewhere.

. . .

Regardless of the "reasons" a battered woman might previously have remained, or of her attempts to "live with" the violence, there often comes a point where she no longer chooses or is able to do so. It is at this point that a battered woman may react to a particular violent episode or threat as intolerable. This may occur even in cases where serious violence may have gone unchallenged in the past. Battered women's level of tolerance (or intolerance) may fluctuate at any given point in time and should be carefully evaluated in order to inform an understanding of the basis of her behavior. In sum, understanding these and other cognitions of a particular battered woman requires a careful analysis of the information and experience—especially regarding violence and abuse—available to her which may have shaped that learning.

2. Psychological Distress/Dysfunction

Numerous indicators of psychological distress and dysfunction have been identified as sequelae to physical and sexual violence. These include fear and terror; depression and grief; nightmares and flashbacks; avoidance and/or physiological reactivity to violence-related stimuli; anxiety; anger and rage; difficulty concentrating, or memory problems such as amnesia and dissociation; hypervigilance; feelings of shame; lowered self-esteem; somatic complaints; sexual dysfunction; morbid hatred; addictive behaviors; and other forms of impaired functioning. Nevertheless, these responses may occur in the immediacy of an acute violence episode or following its occurrence. Few of these indicators of distress or dysfunction are specific only to trauma or victimization.

Some battering victims meet the full criteria for PTSD, including intrusion (e.g., nightmares, flashbacks), avoidance (e.g., avoiding reminders of violence, trying to remove memory of violence), and arousal (e.g., difficulty concentrating, increased anger, sleep disturbances) symptoms. Some battering victims may also exhibit symptoms characteristic of other disorders (e.g., depressive or anxiety disorders), since meeting the criteria for several disorders simultaneously is not uncommon among persons with PTSD.

Identification of current psychological reactions to trauma, or even a clinical diagnosis of PTSD, while consistent with a history of violence and abuse, does not prove that domestic violence actually occurred, that it occurred at the hands of the particular perpetrator in question, or that the psychological effects are, in fact, sequelae to domestic violence. Ultimately, that determination rests with the factfinder, although the testimony of expert witnesses may assist the factfinder in reaching that determination.

. . .

Recognizing post-traumatic reactions of psychological distress or dysfunction may be helpful in explaining a battered woman's actions while responding to a subsequent episode of violence. The situation at issue may trigger certain intrusive images, affective responses such as fear or anger, or memories that may influence the course of the battered woman's behavior. For example, when a batterer begins to act out his threat to beat, rape, or kill the battered woman, she may experience rage and fear based on her (conscious or unconscious) memory of prior episodes when the batterer beat her severely, actually raped her, or attempted to kill her. Her actions in that immediate situation may be influenced by both the actual events occurring in the immediate situation and the triggered responses related to prior abusive experiences.

Understanding the nature of post-traumatic reactions may also help explain battered women's reactions to persons within the legal, social services, and health and mental health professions, especially when their posture is one of authority, dominance, and control. Even when an individual is acting within the norms of his or her profession, that individual may not recognize the powerful impact that even inadvertent gestures may have on someone experiencing post-traumatic effects resulting from violence and abuse at the hands of someone thought to be trustworthy.

3. Relationship Disturbances

Victimization by violence and abuse, especially by someone who is an intimate, can have an impact upon one's present and future relationships. When the victimization occurs during childhood, one may be especially vulnerable to re-victimization. Vulnerability to re-victimization appears to result from exposure to long-term victimization by violence and abuse. A battered woman with a history of childhood abuse may be even more vulnerable to the efforts of others to control and abuse her, and thus less able to protect herself from others. The battered woman may be re-victimized by subsequent intimate partners, and may even be re-victimized by professionals to whom she has turned for help.

Problems that battered women may experience within relationships include attachment to or dependency upon the abusive partner. The battered woman's attachment to her abusive partner reflects both the attachment that is characteristic of love relationships in their early stages, as well as the attachment that develops as a function of the abusive dynamic in the relationship. A battered woman's decreased sense of self-worth and the increased isolation associated with a forced dependency upon the abuser as the violence escalates over time can actually increase the battered woman's attachment to her abusive partner. In essence, the extreme imbalance of power between abuser and victim can actually lead to the development of a strong emotional bonding, accomplished primarily through the abuser's threats to harm the victim, the victim's perception of the abuser's ability to do so, the victim's inability to escape and social isolation, and the victim's perception of some degree of kindness shown by the abuser.

. . .

4. Diversity of Women's Psychological Reactions to Violence

All women exposed to violence and abuse in their intimate relationships do not respond similarly, contradicting the mistaken assumption that there exists a singular "battered woman profile." Like other trauma victims, battered women differ in the type and severity of their psychological reactions to violence and abuse, as well as in their strategies for responding to violence and abuse.

. . .

In order to develop an individual case formulation relevant to a specific legal context, a comprehensive psychological assessment is necessary to identify those psychological responses that are relevant with regard to a particular battered woman and to provide an understanding of those responses within the context of the scientific literature.

. . .

The Question: What Strategies Has the Battered Woman Used (Or Not Used) in Responding to Domestic Violence?

Perhaps the most commonly asked question about the battered woman (especially in a forensic context) is, Why didn't she leave? The question, to some extent, suggests that the battered woman, by remaining in (or returning to) an abusive relationship, is deviant, odd, or blameworthy in some way. Further, the question assumes not only that there are viable options for alternative behavior, but that she should have employed them, and that doing so would have lead to her safety. However, in the criminal context, this common perception is contrary to a fundamental legal premise: "The law has always been clear ... that a person has no obligation to rearrange her ... entire life, or even inconvenience herself, in order to avoid a situation in which the need to act in self-defense might arise." When a battered woman has not left (or has returned to) a battering relationship, it might inaccurately be presumed that she was falsely claiming abuse, that she was responsible for the violence in the first place, that she enjoyed the violence (especially if it included sexual abuse), or, at least, was not bothered by it. Gaining an understanding of what a battered woman did (or did not do) during and after prior incidents of violence and of the basis for her actions (or inactions) can inform the factfinder regarding key elements of a legal argument as well as other issues relevant to the case at issue.

Thus, the third key question reframed for the legal context is, what are the strategies previously used (or not used) by the victim in responding to the domestic violence? This question addresses a far more complete picture of the battered woman's efforts than the simple question, Why didn't she leave? The reframed question suggests that what the victim did is as important as what she didn't do, and that the consequences of actions taken (and the anticipated consequences of actions not taken) are relevant towards understanding her behavior.

. . .

The Question: What Contextual Factors Influenced Both the Battered Woman's Psychological Reactions to Domestic Violence and Her Strategies for Responding to that Violence?

In order to provide an adequate understanding of the battered woman, it is necessary to examine the context in which she lives. Numerous intervening factors may influence and thus help explain individual differences or variations in the battered woman's psychological reactions to the violence, the strategies she used (or did not use) in response to the violence, and, in cases where the battered woman is herself charged with a crime, her behavior in the situation that led to criminal charges. An inquiry regarding these contextual or intervening factors specific to a particular battered woman ... may shed some light on the reasons why the battered woman responded to violence and abuse in the way that she did.

Contextual influences may be based on current or historical events or circumstances. Some contextual factors (e.g., the personal or psychological) are strongly influenced by or originate within other contextual factors (e.g., the social, cultural, or economic). Specific intervening factors—the attachment the battered woman has to her children, the economic resources required to support them, the cultural value placed on caring for them, her own childhood history—may cut across several dimensions, and may influence the battered woman in a number of ways.

Specific contextual factors that influence the battered woman include: (1) fear of retaliation; (2) the economic (and other tangible) resources available to her; (3) her concern for her children; (4) her emotional attachment to her partner; (5) her personal emotional strengths, such as hope or optimism; (6) her race, ethnicity, and culture; (7) her emotional, mental, and physical vulnerabilities; and (8) her perception of the availability of social support. This list is not meant to be exhaustive; in the evaluation of a particular battered woman, there may be other specific contextual factors that should be considered.

* * *

NOTES

1. Dutton is careful to point out that not all women respond to battering in the same way. She is responding to the tendency of judges to understand battered woman syndrome testimony as offering a "profile" that will fit all women who have suffered from abuse. One danger with this approach is

that the "stereotypical" battered woman will be defined as both helpless and impaired. In the words of Elizabeth Schneider:

> " '[B]attered woman syndrome' carries with it stereotypes of individual incapacity and inferiority which lawyers and judges may respond to precisely because they correspond to stereotypes of women which the lawyers and judges already hold. Battered woman syndrome does not mean, but can be heard as reinforcing stereotypes of women as passive, sick, powerless and victimized."

Elizabeth M. Schneider, *Describing and Changing: Women's Self-Defense Work and the Problem of Expert Testimony on Battering*, 9 WMNS. RTS. L. RPTR. 195 (1986). Dutton's account undercuts this stereotype in part by insisting that looking at women's experiences with abuse must include looking at the strategies they have used, as well as the ones they have not, to cope with, or contain, the violence.

2. A second aspect of this problem is that women who do not fit the stereotype of the passive and powerless battered woman may be denied the benefit of expert testimony; since they do not appear to be suffering from the "syndrome," testimony about the "syndrome" is surely not relevant to their cases. This point has been made with particular poignancy in the context of African American women's self-defense claims, since the "battered woman" stereotype contradicts other cultural stereotypes about the "tough" black woman:

> The looking glass experience of black women is one of being trapped between sub- and super-human imagery and expectations. In addition to the negative stereotypes African-American women encounter, [even] attributes that in their truest sense should be considered positive, when applied to black women, can be detrimental. For example, ... African-American women have been characterized as strong and independent. They are blamed for the breakup of their families. Often the strength of black women to survive and progress despite the almost insurmountable obstacles and odds is labeled as pathological at one extreme and disloyal at the other. Sociologist Calvin Herton attributes the black woman's drive (a character flaw) to the historical treatment of African-American women. If these stereotypes can affect public policy, routine transactions, and normal discourse, to what extent is the African-American female defendant at a disadvantage when she is brought to trial for a violent crime—even if she claims that she acted in self-defense because she was being battered?

Linda L. Ammons, *Mules, Madonnas, Babies, Bathwater, Racial Imagery and Stereotypes: The African-American Woman and the Battered Woman Syndrome,* 1995 WISC. L. REV. 1003, 1054–55 (1995).

The negative stereotypes against which African-American women must defend themselves include "the hostile Sapphire, the wanton Jezebel, and the strong and assertive Sojourner Truth." Sharon Angella Allard, *Rethinking Battered Woman Syndrome: A Black Feminist Perspective*, 1 UCLA WMNS. L. REV. 191, 196 (1991). As Lenore Walker acknowledged in her 1984 book TERRIFYING LOVE: WHY BATTERED WOMEN KILL AND HOW SOCIETY RESPONDS:

> The ratio of Black women to white women convicted of killing their abusers is nearly two to one in one of my studies. My feeling is that this is the result of our society's misperceptions of Black people in general, of women in general, and of Black women in particular. The "angry Black woman" is a common stereotype in many white minds; subtly, but no less powerfully, white society in America fears "Black anger."

Id. at 206.

Ammons makes the indisputable argument that battered African-American defendants are entitled to "no less" than their white counterparts, when it comes to recognizing the impact of the abuse they suffer at the hands of their partners. Another commentator, Shelby Moore, makes the slightly different point that all women ultimately suffer from having to conform to a "victim" stereotype, and that all women must therefore struggle against the gender essentialism embodied in that stereotype, while acknowledging that African-American women have paid a particularly high price for not conforming, or not being viewed as conforming, to the stereotype. Shelby Moore, *Battered Woman Syndrome: Selling the Shadow to Support the Substance,* 38 HOWARD L. J. 297 (1995).

3. In 1996 the U.S. Departments of Justice and Health and Human Services issued a report on *The Validity and Use of Evidence Concerning Battering and Its Effects in Criminal Trials*, under a mandate contained in the 1994 Violence Against Women Act. REPORT RESPONDING TO SECTION 40507 OF THE VIOLENCE AGAINST WOMEN ACT, NCJ 160972 (May 1996). One aspect of the report was a summary of the current "state of play" with respect to expert testimony. The summary was based on a study of state and federal court decisions, as well as state legislation, originally commissioned by the National Association of Women Judges from the National Clearinghouse for the Defense of Battered Women in Philadelphia. The first key finding was that:

> With respect to admissibility, expert testimony on battering and its effects is admissible, at least to some degree, or has been admitted (without any discussion of the standards for admissibility), in each of the 50 states plus the District of Columbia.
>
> > 1. Of the 19 federal courts that have considered the issue, all but three have admitted expert testimony on battering and its effects in at least some cases.
> >
> > 2. Twelve states, moreover, have enacted statutes providing for admissibility of expert testimony, although in two states, the courts have interpreted these statutes in a restrictive fashion, limiting the admissibility of expert testimony to cases in which self-defense is claimed.
> >
> > 3. However, 18 states have excluded expert testimony in some cases. Only in Wyoming is there still doubt under case law as to the testimony's admissibility, but Wyoming provides for the admissibility of expert testimony by statute.

> While the types of cases in which expert testimony on battering and its effects is admitted can vary, it is most readily accepted by state courts (i.e., in 90 percent of the states) in cases involving traditional self-defense situations.

The report also summarized the impact of expert testimony in the cases in which it had been admitted:

> With respect to case disposition on appeal, the appeals of 152 battered women defendants were analyzed ... ; 63 percent resulted in affirmance of the conviction and/or sentence, even though expert testimony on battering and its effects was admitted or found admissible in 71 percent of the affirmances
>
> 1. These findings are considered strong evidence that the defense's use of, or the court's awareness of, expert testimony on battering and its effects in no way equates to an acquittal on the criminal charges lodged against a battered woman defendant.
> 2. Moreover, of those appeals in state courts that resulted in reversals, less than half were reversed because of erroneous exclusion of, limitation of, or failure of counsel to present, expert testimony.
> 3. Of the 22 appeals of battered women's cases heard in federal courts, more than three-quarters resulted in affirmances of convictions and/or sentences.

"Researchers consider this strong evidence that, contrary to the contention of some critics, admitting expert testimony on battering and its effects was not tantamount to an acquittal," the researchers concluded.

Overall, the report was upbeat, noting that:

> Judges, prosecutors, and defense attorneys interviewed concerning the impact of such evidence in criminal trials said that, within the courtroom, it has increased recognition of the broader problem of domestic violence and that its introduction can assist judges and juries to better understand the issues and/or dispel myths and stereotypes related to battered women.

However, the reports' authors cautioned in strong terms against using the label "battered woman syndrome" to describe expert testimony. Confirming the analysis of Mary Ann Dutton, whose article you have just sampled, and who was one of the report's principal researchers and writers, the report foreward states:

> Among the most notable findings was the strong consensus among the researchers, and also among the judges, prosecutors, and defense attorneys interviewed for the assessment, that the term "battered woman syndrome" does not adequately reflect the breadth or the nature of the scientific knowledge now available concerning battering and its effects. There were also concerns that the word "syndrome" carried implications of a malady or psychological impairment and, moreover, suggested that there was a single pattern of response to battering. Equally important is the clear statement that there is not a

"battered women's defense" per se. Expert testimony in these cases, when introduced by the defense, should be used to support a battered woman's claim of self-defense or duress, not to replace it.

4. The focus on expert testimony should not distract us from the other ways in which women can tell their stories of abuse in courtrooms. There is an obvious need, in some circumstances, for expert testimony to provide a framework establishing the relevance of the woman's story; or to fill gaps in the evidence; or to enhance the woman's credibility. Nonetheless, feminist theorists and lawyers worry that relying on expert testimony can be just one more way of disempowering women, and robbing them of their own voices. This tension is one to keep in mind as we move on to consider in more detail the various legal arenas in which stories of abuse are told.

*

PART TWO

Battered Women as Mothers

CHAPTER FIVE

The Children of Battered Women and Battered Women as Mothers

A. Introduction

When women are abused by their partners, it seems natural to assume that their children are also at risk. But what exactly are the risks? And how, and to what extent, does the legal system acknowledge or respond to them? This chapter looks at the ways in which children who live with mothers who are being abused are marked by that experience, and at the impact of abuse on the parenting they receive. The two subsequent chapters examine the legal system's response; Chapter Six looks at the child welfare system and at criminal prosecutions brought against parents who fail to protect their children from abuse, while Chapter Seven looks at the family law system.

One risk for children whose mothers are being abused by their partners is that they too will become victims of physical or sexual abuse at the hands of the abuser. The opening reading, from Paula Sharp's 1996 novel Crows Over A Wheatfield, offers a poignant example. Just how strong is the correlation between partner abuse and child abuse? When the abusive partner is also the one who abuses the children, is the motivation the same, or different? Are abused women more likely than women who are not abused to abuse their children? If so, is it only while they are in the abusive relationship, or even when it ends? Is the motivation for this abuse the same, or different? There is not, as yet, a body of research sufficient to provide definitive answers to many of these questions. But the accumulating data suggests, at a minimum, that where women are abused, there is a thirty to sixty percent likelihood that children also living in the household will be subject to physical abuse at the hands of the adult abuser. An even higher correlation is reported in the article by Bowker, Arbitell and McFerron excerpted below.

A newer discovery is that children do not have to suffer physical or sexual abuse themselves to be adversely affected by violence in their homes. Merely witnessing violence directed against a parent, or, as some researchers in the field prefer to say, being exposed to that violence, has potentially severe psychological sequelae, which are only now being documented in a rigorous way through research. Here we need to look at the ways in which this damage manifests itself. What are the symptoms children display—how does their exposure to violence affect their own behavior and functioning?

Are boys and girls affected to the same extent? In the same ways? Does the age of the child at the age of exposure make a difference? Will these children grow up to be abusers, or victims of abuse? We also need to ask about the process that produces the damage. Why, precisely, can exposure result in such negative consequences? Excerpts from essays by George Holden and Sandra Graham–Bermann take on these two inquiries; Holden describes the effects of exposure, and Graham–Bermann presents three interlocking theoretical explanations for the impact of domestic violence on children's development. A final excerpt in this section brings the research to life through the story of one child's exposure to a single incident in which his father used violence against his mother, and the dramatic consequences of that exposure.

Women who abuse their children are harshly judged by a society which idealizes motherhood, while providing very little in the way of support for mothers who are struggling to parent in circumstances made difficult by past or present abuse, economic hardship, the incompatible demands of work and family, or psychological impairment. It often seems that society judges equally harshly women who "allow" their children to be abused by a biological father or substitute father figure, or to witness his abuse, even when the women themselves live in fear of that man, and have been threatened by him with violence or death if they intervene. It seems that we expect women to keep their children safe, even when they have been unable to do the same for themselves. Many women meet those expectations, suffering violence at the hands of men as long as they are the only victims, but fighting back by involving the authorities, or fleeing, or using force themselves, when their children are threatened. How we judge women who cannot or do not protect their children, and what feminist theory teaches us about managing the tension between our empathy for mothers and our empathy for children, is the topic of the article by Marie Ashe and Naomi Cahn, *Child Abuse: A Problem for Feminist Theory*, 2 TEXAS J. WMN. & L. 75 (1993), excerpted below. How the courts address these issues is a subject to which we will return in subsequent chapters.

Even those who seek to enlarge our understanding of the dynamics of battering relationships, and our sympathy for mothers trapped in them, have made assumptions about how the abuse is likely to diminish the parenting abilities of the battered parent. In Section D, below, a report of new research in this area challenges these assumptions, suggesting instead that there may be much less difference between the parenting of battered and non-battered mothers than is commonly supposed. At the same time, this report offers some useful new evidence about how mothers, and others, may be able to assist children in processing the experience of exposure to abuse.

As suggested earlier, two subsequent chapters address the question of how the legal system responds to children who have been abused or exposed to abuse in the context of abusive adult relationships. But legal responses, while they can do much to protect children if they are properly conceived and implemented, are clearly only one part of a much larger picture. A final excerpt in this chapter lists the recommendations made by the David and

Lucile Packard Foundation in its recent report, *Domestic Violence and Children*, to indicate just how multi-faceted, and multi-disciplinary, a truly proactive response to children affected by domestic violence would be.

B. THE CONNECTION BETWEEN PARTNER ABUSE AND CHILD ABUSE

Paula Sharp
Crows Over A Wheatfield, 254–58 (1996)

[Ben is the child of Mildred and Daniel. Daniel is an abusive partner, and Mildred has recently separated from him. The narrator is Melanie, a friend of Mildred's and Ben's, who volunteers to drive Ben to and from his mandated visits with his father. The others in the story are also friends of Mildred and her family.]

At nine o'clock I knocked on Daniel's door, but he refused to answer. I returned to the van, warmed up the motor, and played the radio loudly. Mr. Eklund's face appeared behind the gas station window, swam backward, and then reappeared and hovered there.

At ten Daniel came outside. He put Ben down in the snow in front of the blue house and returned inside, without speaking. Ben stayed where he was, looking at his feet. I picked him up, and he did not fight or hug me. I belted him in the back seat. On the ride home Ben at first eluded every attempt I made to talk with him.

"Ben, did you have a good time?"

"I don't know."

"What did you do?"

"I don't know."

"Did you play checkers?"

"No."

"Did you go outside?"

"No."

"Did you stay inside?"

"No."

"Did you eat lunch?"

"No."

"Do you like saying no?"

"Yes," Ben answered, and tilted his head back against his seat. He looked weary, like an adult after a long week.

"Matt and Stretch Rockefeller made you icicles out of Kool–Aid," I said. "They hung a can from a hot-water pipe on the roof, and it dripped down Kool–Aid all night."

"Will it give me chicken pops?"

"You can't get chicken pox from things," I said.

"Daddy says all the presents will give me chicken pops."

"Daddy made a mistake. You can't get chicken pox from things. Believe me, I know. I've had chicken pox, and worse."

Ben didn't answer.

"The icicles are green and purple," I said. "Everybody missed you. You were gone so long."

"Daddy took away my sword," Ben said miserably.

When I looked in the rearview mirror, Ben was crying quietly. His head tilted forward and he whimpered. "Oh, oh, oh!" he said. "Oh, oh, oh."

I pulled over the car. I crawled in the back and put Ben on my lap. His clothes smelt like stale urine, and his hair was acrid. "What's wrong, honey? What is it?"

Ben kept sobbing, in that way children have, where their chests convulse and they hiccough as they cry. I could not help him stop. After a while he exhausted himself and curled sideways in my lap. I stroked his hair and felt his forehead. It was hot and soaked with tears. I held him until he relaxed in my arms, and then I drove him home.

When I carried him into the Steck's, Mrs. Shove was there.... She wore an auburn pantsuit and a new hairstyle that made me think of a bantam.

Mildred rushed to the door, lifted Ben, and said, "Sugarbeet, you're back." She whispered to me, "He smells like an old drunk."

He roused, pressed his face into her shoulder, and said, "I do not!"

"He feels a little hot," I said.

Mrs. Shove walked over to Mildred and touched Ben's cheek. "It's not really a fever," she told me. "He's probably just overtired. It seems like ninety-nine or a hundred. I used to give my boys a sponge bath when they were like that."

"That's just what I'll do," Mildred told her. "This boy needs fumigating." She kissed Ben's hair.

"Well, let me help," Mrs. Shove said. She followed Mildred up the stairs, to the bathroom, talking. I heard Ben cry out, and Mrs. Shove say, "Why, his pants look like he pooped in them a day ago. Look at this rash!"

I reached the top of the stairs as Mildred was settling Ben into the bathtub.

"Hey you," Mildred was saying. "Hey you, hey you."

Mrs. Shove sat on the toilet lid and poured bubble bath into the tub. I picked up Ben's soiled pants and ran them under the sink tap. They reeked.

I reached under the sink for soap, filled the basin with soapy water, and scrubbed at them.

"Try this, Sugarbeet," Mildred said, and handed Ben two orange aspirin tablets.

"They taste like candy," Ben said.

"How was the interview?" I asked her.

"I don't know," Mildred answered. "It was awkward. The doctor is sort of full of himself. He's not going to ask to see Ben. Don't you think that's strange? That he wouldn't want to see how Ben acts around Daniel?"

"What did that Munk man do, run him around in those wet clothes?" Mrs. Shove asked, peering at the sink.

"Do you have a penis?" Ben asked Mrs. Shove.

Mrs. Shove raised one plucked eyebrow and answered, "Not that I know of."

Ben looked at the bubbles rising around him, and said, "I took a bath last night."

"Well, it looks like you need another one," Mildred told him.

"Daddy made me take a bath, and then he made me sleep in dirty clothes!"

John poked his head inside the bathroom. "How's it going up here?"

"Oh, we ladies are having a to-do," Mrs. Shove answered.

"Everyone's in the bathroom!" Ben said.

"Matt and Stretch Rockefeller sent Ben this," John said, holding up a long icicle, striped green and purple. "It's lime and grape flavored."

"You can't come in!" Ben told him. "There's no more room in the bathtub."

"I'm not getting in the bathtub," John said. "I'm just handing you your icicle."

Ben reached for the icicle and said "It's hot!" and withdrew his hand.

"I'll take it," Mrs. Shove said, and wrapped a washcloth around the base. "Hold it here, honey." John's footsteps receded down the stairs.

"Daddy made me take a bath with him, too."

"Daddy took a bath with you?" Mildred asked.

"Why, he's too big for that! There wouldn't be enough room," Mrs. Shove said.

Ben took the icicle, stirred the bubbles with his free hand to clear a circle in the water, and stuck the icicle's point into it. "It turns the water purple," he said.

"It's melting," Mrs. Shove told him.

"Do you have a penis?" Ben asked Mildred.

"No, sweetheart," she answered. "I'm a lady, so I don't have a penis."

"*I* have a penis. Daddy has a big penis. A big penis that gets bigger when you touch it."

Mrs. Shove frowned. I stopped wringing the clothes in the sink.

Mildred drew a breath and asked, "Did Daddy let you touch his big old penis?"

Ben looked at his mother's face, puzzled, and said, "I don't know."

"Christ," I said.

"He got into the bathtub with me!" Ben answered.

"He did?" Mildred asked.

"It was my bathtub!" Ben said. "I hit him with my sword."

"You had your sword in the bathtub?" I said.

Ben smiled. "Yes." Then he frowned. "He took my sword! He hit me back with it."

"He did? Which sword?" Mildred asked. "The wood one with the red handle?"

Ben nodded. "It's my sword," he said.

"Where did he hit you?"

"He smattered the side of my head."

"Did he hit you on the head?"

"He *smattered* it. It made noise right through my neck." Ben touched his ear. Then he repeated, "It's my sword." Almost as an afterthought, he added, "And then he punched me on the side."

Mildred wiped the bubbles from Ben's shoulders and pulled his hands up.

"Show me where," she said.

"Here," Ben answered, touching the fold of his upper arm. And then we all saw it, on the right side of his rib cage, high up, a yellow bruise like an enamel rose on china.

Mildred would not release Ben for further visitation. "Daniel found something that would force me to keep Ben away. Now he'll accuse me of interfering with visitation," Mildred said. "His lawyer will use this to argue that I shouldn't have custody, won't he? And it won't matter to the judge that Daniel hit Ben, or did anything else to him, will it?"

When Mildred asked me this, she was seated in Ottilie's peacock-blue armchair. The hair in Mildred's braid had unwoven in feathery tufts, as if she had been pulling on it out of nervousness. Her flannel shirt was buttoned wrong, the collar slanting on the left side to meet a low buttonhole. Ben lay asleep in her lap. After the Saturday visit Ben clung to her as if he feared she would disappear if he strayed so far as another room by himself.

Vogelsang had filed a new petition in court the Monday after Ben's overnight visit, asking to terminate unsupervised visitation and attaching affidavits from all of us, and a letter from Ben's pediatrician. ("I assured the mother that there is no evidence of a concussion," he wrote, "and the hearing is intact. But the bruises on the upper torso and behind the ear are large.") Judge Bracken sat on the papers. He did not want extra work, and set the return date for the new petition on the same day he had originally scheduled for us to appear in court.

Even before this result, I thought the judge would merely find the further suggestion of Daniel's lack of sexual boundaries with his son distasteful, and shun our papers, and dismiss the evidence of Daniel's violence. Daniel was too hard to assemble into a picture, and an understanding of Daniel's motives would never be within the grasp of Judge Bracken's court: Daniel's love of brinksmanship, his desire to know that he could get away with anything. Even now it is unnerving for me to remember how effectively a man like Daniel, who subverted every code, fit the law into his hand like a well-worn tool. It was as though the law had been designed specifically for him all along.

* * *

NOTES

1. Daniel's abuse of Ben has several dimensions. In part, it appears that Daniel is seeking to punish Mildred for separating from him, by abusing and neglecting their son in ways that he knows will be intolerable to her. In part he is also showing her that he still has the power to control her, through her attachment to Ben, even though she has sought to break free of his control. In addition, however, it seems that his physical and sexual abuse of Ben demonstrates an inability or unwillingness to respect boundaries in his relationships; he treats others as instruments to his own ends. Finally, it may be that his need to control is as strong in his relationship with his son as it was in his relationship with his partner.

2. If Mildred's and Melanie's fears about how the legal system will respond to Daniel's abuse of Ben seem farfetched, you may decide after reading the next few chapters that truth is stranger than fiction. CROWS OVER A WHEATFIELD is a damning but not unrealistic indictment of the family law system, showing how three factors combine to put mothers and children at risk; judicial lack of understanding of battering relationships and batterers; judicial distrust of women's testimony and motives, and abusers' abilities to manipulate the system (witnesses as well as judges) to serve their own ends. The same three factors also serve to put mothers and children at risk within the child welfare system, and at the hands of prosecutors pursuing charges of failure to protect.

Lee H. Bowker, Michelle Arbitell and J. Richard McFerron
On the Relationship Between Wife Beating and Child Abuse, Feminist Perspectives on Wife Abuse 158, 159–166 (K. Yllo & M. Bograd, eds. 1990)

Research evidence suggests links between child abuse and wife beating; specifically, that husbands and wives who assault each other tend to hit their children. Straus (1978) found that almost one-third of the families in which there was a violent incident between spouses also reported the presence of child abuse. A total of 58% of the respondents reported using some form of violence against their children during the year prior to their participation in the study, and 16% of the couples also admitted directing violence toward each other at least once during the survey year (Gelles & Straus, 1979). Gelles (1980) also found a direct relationship between spousal violence and child abuse. Of a sample of college students, 16% acknowledged that they knew of at least one incident during their last year at home in which one of their parents had physically abused the other and nearly half of these parents had also used physical force against their children. Finally, the U.S. Department of Health, Education and Welfare (1980) has reported that children from homes where the wife is battered are at very high risk to receive their father's abuse.

The link between wife beating and child abuse may be related to the power inequality between husband and wife as well as that between parents and children. Children in a family often become their father's victims at the same time that he is abusing their mother.... Half of the women interviewed in the HEW survey (1980) admitted that their children were physically or psychologically abused. These children frequently witnessed wife beating incidents between their parents. Moore (1975) coined the phrase "yo-yo" children to label how children are often used as pawns in arguments by parents who are unable to discuss any rational solution to their difficulties. Woman battering and child abuse typically occur to spite the wife in these marriages.

In an attempt to establish the actual relationship between child abuse and battering in families, 116 mothers of children "darted" or flagged in a single year for abuse or neglect at a metropolitan hospital were studied by Stark and Flitcraft (1984).... These examinations revealed that 45% of the abused children had mothers who themselves were being physically abused and another 5% had mothers whose relationships were "full of conflict," although abuse was not verified. Children whose mothers had been battered were more likely to be physically abused and less likely to be "neglected" than children whose mothers had not been battered.

We know that children are often present during wife-beating incidents because of the frequency with which they appear in court as witnesses: Of the 1,014 witnesses who testified in 928 wife assault cases, 50% were children (Dobash, 1977)....

. . .

The present study portrays child abuse as one of the products of male domination of the family based on the following hypotheses:

(1) Children of battered wives are commonly abused by their fathers.

(2) The more severe the wife abuse, the more severe the child abuse.

(3) The higher the degree of husband-dominance in a violent marriage, the more severe the child abuse.

(4) The more extensive the father's experiences with violence in his family of origin, the more likely he is to move from wife abuse to child abuse.

These hypotheses reflect a feminist perspective suggesting that child abuse is one of the ways by which men increase their dominance over family members. This approach differs from other views of child abuse by highlighting the male struggle for interpersonal dominance and deemphasizing psychopathological factors, unpremeditated events, and general family dysfunctions. Child abuse is linked to other forms of male dominance in families, including wife beating, punitive economic deprivation, marital rape, coerced social isolation, incest, psychological brainwashing, and deliberately induced fetal death.

. . .

Of the 1,000 battered women in the study, 225 did not have children with the batterer. Wife beaters abused children in 70% of the families in which children were present....

Child abuse was generally less severe than wife abuse in these families. Batterers were five times more likely to beat up thoroughly or use weapons against their wives than to inflict these levels of abuse upon their children. Yet, 41% of the batterers slapped (not to be confused with mere spanking) one or more of their children. Lesser proportions of the batterers kicked, hit, or punched (16%), thoroughly beat up (more severe than kicking, hitting, or punching, but excluding weapons—4%), or used weapons (9%) against their children....

... The more children there are in a family, the more likely one of them is abused. The prevalence of child abuse increases from 51% with one child to 92% with four or more children.

Previous exposure of the parents to violence was a minor factor in child abuse. The strongest relationship ... was between the husband's own physical abuse by his parents and his abusing his own children.... The husband's previous experiences with violence were stronger predictors of the severity of wife beating than they were of his abusing both wife and children.

... Abuse was more likely to be present where there were frequent separations (including trips to battered women's shelters), the wife's low marital satisfaction apart from the violence, and high husband dominance.... Child abuse was most likely to occur where problems were generally solved to suit the batterer during the couple's most recent year together, less likely in egalitarian marriages, and much less likely when the wife generally won arguments.

The worse the wife beating, the worse the child abuse. The strongest correlations in this area were between child abuse and severity of wife beating, frequency of wife beating, and frequency of marital rape.... The absence of child abuse was more than four times as likely when the wife was never raped by her husband as it was in marriages within which she was raped more than a hundred times. An important finding is that the rise of weapons involvement in child abuse correlates with increasing frequency of marital rape....

... The use of all help-sources was higher where child abuse was present than where it was absent, which constitutes strong evidence of the wife's efforts to protect her children. The effectiveness of these help-sources was generally inversely related to child abuse.

All four of the hypotheses with which we began this study are substantiated by the data. Children of battered wives are very likely to be battered by their fathers. The severity of the wife beating is predictive of the severity of child abuse. Husband-dominance is also a predictor of child abuse. Wife beating is more likely to be accompanied by child abuse in families where the husband was beaten by his parents, although the evidence in support of this hypothesis is weaker than the evidence for the other three hypotheses.

Although 70% appears to be a high figure for the proportion of wife beaters who physically abuse their children, this may still underestimate the true correspondence between these two forms of male domestic violence. First, we noticed that many of the women we interviewed ... were extremely reticent to talk about child abuse even though they did not hesitate to relate the most intimate details of their own abuse, degradation and torture. Second, the women were able to report only the child abuse they knew about. They may not have been aware of many other incidents of their husbands' abuse of the children. Finally, there are many categories of child abuse that were not included in the study, including child sexual abuse, child neglect, and the torture and killing of pets.

The most intriguing finding is the ... relationship between husband dominance in the most recent year together and spousal child abuse.... [V]iolent and previolent men have high needs to dominate their wives and children. They achieve and maintain the level of dominance they consider appropriate by a variety of oppressive strategies, including wife beating, child abuse, marital rape, psychological abuse, punitive economic deprivation, and coerced social isolation. We do not know very much about the interaction of these dominance-enhancing strategies with each other or about how they combine to increase the level of family dominance by men....

* * *

NOTE

1. The seventy percent overlap between partner abuse and child abuse reported in this study is at the high end of results derived from other empirical studies. One recent review, summarizing results from a number of studies, reported overlap in between thirty and sixty percent of cases. J.L. Edelson, *The Overlap Between Child Maltreatment and Woman Battering,* 5 VIOLENCE AGAINST WOMEN 134 (1999). Another review reported a wider range—from 20% to 100%, with a median of 59%. A.E. Appel, M.J. Angelelli and G.W. Holden, *The Co-occurrence of Spouse and Physical Child Abuse: A*

Review and Appraisal, (1997). Obviously a lot depends on who asks the question, who answers it, how the question is framed, and the context in which it is asked. In 1991 a Massachusetts study by the Department of Social Services, reviewing 200 cases in which child abuse had been substantiated, found domestic violence in 33% of the case records. By 1994, however, a new DSS protocol required screening of all families for domestic violence, and a new study identified domestic violence in 48% of ongoing cases.

The Bowker et al. study recruited 146 subjects through advertising an investigation of wife beating, and then added another 854 women by publishing some of its preliminary findings in an article in *Woman's Day* magazine, and asking for additional volunteers. The data therefore consist of self-reports from battered women, and are not corroborated by other sources. The authors, in discussing their methodology, conclude: "The battered wives contributed vignettes that leave little doubt in our minds regarding what occurred, yet we should not mistake these vignettes as scientific reports." L.H. Bowker, M. Arbitell and J.R. McFerron, *On The Relationship Between Wife Beating and Child Abuse*, FEMINIST PERSPECTIVES ON WIFE ABUSE 158, 162 (K. Yllo & M. Bograd, eds. 1990). What would count as a "scientific report" of co-occurring partner and child abuse?

C. THE IMPACT ON CHILDREN OF EXPOSURE TO PARTNER VIOLENCE

George Holden
Introduction: The Development of Research Into Another Consequence of Family Violence; Children Exposed to Marital Violence: Theory, Research and Applied Issues 1, 6–11 (G.W. Holden, R. Geffner & E.N. Jouriles, eds. 1998)

Children in maritally violent homes have been called the "forgotten," "unacknowledged," "hidden," "unintended," and "silent" victims. When these children are compared with other victims of family violence and maltreatment, such as battered women or children who have been physically or sexually abused, these labels are indeed accurate. The children exposed to marital violence have received insufficient attention for far too long.

. . .

The corpus of empirical literature clearly establishes that children who live in maritally violent homes are at risk for a wide variety of problems. Associating marital violence with children's emotional and behavioral problems has been the primary question in most of the research published to date. In studies that are sometimes referred to as "first generation" research on the topic, numerous investigators have successfully linked children's exposure to family violence with a range of behavior and adjustment problems.

. . . Many of these children show a wide range of externalizing and internalizing problems, such as noncompliance, aggression, anxiety, and depression. . . . There is also evidence for long-term effects of childhood exposure to marital violence, including depression, low self-esteem, and various trauma-related symptoms. . . . Depending on the study, anywhere from 25% to 75% of these children may have problems that are considered severe enough to warrant clinical intervention. . . .

In addition to internalizing and externalizing problems, a wide array of mental health problems has been identified. A list of these problems . . . is provided in Exhibit 1. . . . The exhibit indicates that the negative consequences from exposure to marital violence are not limited to compromised mental health functioning. There is at least preliminary evidence for a range of other behavioral, health, school, and social interaction problems that these children commonly experience. Interestingly, many of the same problems (e.g. anxiety, depression, fears, hostility, somatization) also appear in adults who are victims of violent crimes. . . .

Exhibit 1
Children's Problems Associated With Exposure to Marital Conflict

Attention Deficit Disorder
Externalizing Problems
- Aggression
- Alcohol and/or drug use
- Anger
- Conduct Disorder
- Cruelty to animals
- Destructiveness
- Noncompliance
- Oppositional

Internalizing Problems
- Anxiety
- Depression
- Excessive clinging
- Fears
- Low self-esteem
- Passivity, withdrawal
- Sadness
- Self-blame
- Shyness
- Suicidality

Posttraumatic stress disorder symptoms (anxiety, flashbacks, hyperalertness, guilt, nightmares, numbing of affect, sleep disturbances)
Separation Anxiety
Social behavior—Competence Problems
- Beliefs in violence in relationships
- Deficits in social skills
- Low Empathy
- Poor problem-solving skills

Exhibit 1-continued

School Problems
- Academic Performance
- Poor conduct
- Truancy

Other
- Intergenerational transmission of violence
- Obsessive-compulsive
- Somatic problems (headaches, enuresis, insomnia, ulcers)
- Temperamentally difficult

Note: From *Family Violence Across the Lifespan* (pp. 141–142) by O.W. Barnett, C.L. Miller–Perrin, and R.D. Perrin, 1997, Thousand Oaks, CA: Sage. Copyright 1997 by Sage. Adapted by permission.

Although there is no typical pattern of problems manifested by children exposed to marital violence, the particular problem or problems exhibited may be governed to some degree by the children's age and gender. With regard to age, younger children are more likely to exhibit somatic complaints and experience greater distress than older children who may take on one or more specific externalizing or internalizing problems....

More studies have addressed the issue of how a child's gender affects his or her reaction to the violence. Given that fathers typically perpetrate violence and mothers are the victims, it is commonly thought that boys may react differently than girls. To date, the data on gender of child affects have been inconsistent. Some studies have found that girls are more negatively affected than boys ..., but other studies only find that difference on internalizing problems.... In contrast, some studies have found that boys have more externalizing problems ..., and still other investigators report no gender differences.... Part of the problem may be caused by the relatively small sample sizes that are common in this difficult research area. Nevertheless, whether (and if so, how) children's gender interacts with exposure to marital violence remains to be determined.

One or more studies have identified or proposed several variables that may moderate or mediate the effects of marital violence on the children, such as (a) the nature of the violence (e.g., severity and chronicity); (b) ethnicity; (c) the level of stress experienced by the mother; (d) the quality of mothering; (e) whether the child was also the recipient of verbal or physical abuse; and (f) child characteristics (self-esteem, personality characteristics) that may buffer the child.

... [O]ne potential moderator deserves more discussion. It is increasingly being recognized that children who are exposed to marital violence (and who are being traumatized just by living in that environment) are also at increased risk of being victimized in other ways as well. Most commonly, such children are at risk for being physically abused by one or both of their parents.

... Presumably some children who are both exposed to marital violence and are physically assaulted themselves are more likely to have problems, but this is not always the case.... There is also some evidence that children in maritally violent homes are also at increased risk for sexual abuse....

* * *

NOTES

1. The first two published articles on children exposed to domestic violence appeared in 1975, and the third not until 1980. In all, some 56 empirical articles were published between 1975 and 1995, along with a few review articles, and three books focusing on the children of battered women. The first of these, by Peter Jaffe, David Wolfe and Susan Wilson, THE CHILDREN OF BATTERED WOMEN, was published in 1990. The other two both appeared in 1995; ENDING THE CYCLE OF VIOLENCE: COMMUNITY RESPONSES TO CHILDREN OF BATTERED WOMEN (E. Peled, P.G. Jaffe & J.L. Edleson, eds. 1995), and E. Peled and D. Davis, GROUPWORK WITH CHILDREN OF BATTERED WOMEN: A PRACTITIONER'S MANUAL (1995). A fourth book, CHILDREN EXPOSED TO MARITAL VIOLENCE: THEORY, RESEARCH AND APPLIED ISSUES (G.W. Holden, R. Geffner & E.N. Jouriles, eds. 1998), an edited collection including Holden's article from which the above excerpt is drawn, appeared in 1998. As the interest in these issues increases, and the body of empirical and theoretical work grows, child victims of exposure to domestic violence become more visible, and the legal system, albeit slowly and somewhat grudgingly, more attentive to their plight.

Notable among legal responses have been a report published by the American Bar Association in 1994; Howard Davidson, *The Impact of Domestic Violence on Children*, and two publications of the National Council of Juvenile and Family Court Judges; *Effective Intervention in Domestic Violence and Child Maltreatment Cases* (1999), and *Emerging Programs for Battered Mothers and Their Children* (1998).

For additional moving fictional accounts, see, e.g., Roddy Doyle, PADDY CLARKE, HA, HA, HA (1993) (winner of the Booker Prize) and Andrea Ashworth, ONCE IN A HOUSE ON FIRE (1998).

Sandra A. Graham-Bermann
The Impact of Woman Abuse on Children's Social Development: Research and Theoretical Perspectives; Children Exposed to Marital Violence: Theory, Research and Applied Issues 21, 32–45 (G.W. Holden, R. Geffner & E.N. Jouriles, eds. 1998)

... I review and consider three possible theoretical explanations for the impact of domestic violence on children's social development. These are not mutually exclusive theories. Although they have developed from different traditions, there are conceptual overlaps and even ways of melding them so as to explain more comprehensively the ways in which children are affected by domestic violence.

Social Learning Theory

Explanations

... Behavior patterns that are overlearned in early childhood interactions with others are automatically used by the child when adapting to new circumstances and situations. The social learning explanation has been used to describe the ways in which children from violent families learn aggression tactics.... Although the focus of domestic violence research has been on the physical violence to the mother, research on battered women would suggest that the behavior of children raised in woman-abusive families reflects the entire complex of behaviors, meanings, intentions, and actions by those whose purpose is subduing and controlling the woman.... These behaviors are conveyed to the child through direct modeling and reinforcement....

Thus, in addition to aggression tactics, children may learn to manipulate, to cajole, and to coerce others to have their needs met—in essence, to show the beginnings of antisocial personality. These children may identify with the aggressor (their father or their mother's partner). Other children may learn that the only way to coexist with others is to submit, to blame oneself, or to give up in the face of difficulty.... [S]ocial learning theory posits that these lessons are "hard-wired" into the child's behavioral repertoire because they are performed by people the child loves and they are reinforced with violence and trauma.

. . .

Future Studies With a Social Learning Perspective

In future studies, the kinds of social behaviors expected to be associated with learning both physical aggression and control tactics should be distinguished depending on the age of the child. Hence, infants might show problems in emotion regulation, from clinging behavior to an inability to inhibit negative affect. Preschoolers might evidence more aggression in the form of temper tantrums, whereas others might exhibit withdrawal or a difficulty in relating to their siblings and peers. In studies of children during middle childhood, those exposed to domestic violence have significantly more problems with aggression, anxiety and depression.... Nonetheless it is expected that their social development also is impeded by their inadequate repertoire of social skills and by their learned expectations of the behavior and intentions of others. Learned behaviors that may find expression in the preadolescent years could take the form of early antisocial behavior (e.g. stealing) or avoidance of social situations. As demonstrated by studies of dating violence, researchers must examine (a) the problems with intimate relationships experienced by adolescents who as children have seen their mothers physically or psychologically maltreated and (b) the differential impact of exposure to violence on what different children in the family have learned, depending on their age, their identities, and their relationships with one another.

Trauma Theory

Explanations

Studies of social learning theory suggest that children have learned and incorporated the lessons of violence and that, without intervention, they tend to grow up and tend to repeat those lessons or behaviors. On the other hand, trauma theory offers explanations for behaviors not necessarily referenced or predicted by social learning theory. These behaviors include traumatic arousal, avoidance of people or places associated with the violence, and intrusive memories or flashbacks of the traumatic events.

Several factors affect the way the child copes with exposure to a traumatic event, such as the abuse of the mother. These include the child's perception of the danger of the event and his or her estimation of protection from harm either for the self or others.... The meaning of the event to the child and the immediate response of caretakers also influence the degree of trauma that the child may experience.... Too frequently the child is left to construct his or her own meaning or interpretation of violent events. To date, few researchers have inquired about how often children receive information regarding the violence in the family and from whom the information, if given, is received. The import of such questions is highlighted in one study ... in which more than half of 120 battered women with children ages 7–12 reported that they did not tell their children anything by way of explanation following the worst violent episode of the previous year and that when they did offer an explanation, approximately 10% blamed the child for the violence. What male batterers say to children has yet to be systematically researched, though clinical reports suggest that they are given to denial, minimization, and externalization of blame.

. . .

How, then, do children react to witnessing the abuse of their mothers? The construct of complex traumatic stress was described by Herman ..., who viewed responses to extreme stress along a continuum, rather than as a single disorder.... This may also be appropriate for describing the effects of spouse abuse on children, because children exposed to such violence most often are not reacting to a unitary event and hence may show a variety of symptoms. Children may also be subject to revictimization at any time, as when they view additional assaults or are reminded of them. Studies of television violence show that children are exposed to many images of violent incidents each day—images that can remind the child of a previous battering event.... Over time, many children may learn that they are powerless to do anything to stop domestic violence. Further, woman abuse often escalates and may be worse on one occasion than on the preceding occasion.... For the child, a persistent atmosphere of intimidation and threat can repeatedly stimulate posttraumatic play involving family members.... For instance, a child who has observed the father slamming the mother's arm in the car door may perseverate in playing out the same scene every day with a toy car and dollhouse figures.

Children in families of domestic violence may be further damaged and harmed by the lack of available support and abundant negative role and relational models, that is, the available relational models are the very ones children may wish to reject but are often doomed to repeat.... Moreover, children often do not have even one parent who is able to respond reasonably in ways to inoculate them against the further negative effects of traumatic abuse.... Whereas the positive attachment with a parent often mediates distress for children in other stressful circumstances ..., children in families with domestic violence may not have access to such support. Hence, the child exposed to domestic violence may be vulnerable to the effects of unrelenting distress.

. . .

Future Studies Assessing Trauma in Children of Abused Women

How can one begin to decipher or disentangle these phenomena? We ... designed a study to identify the range of trauma symptoms found in 64 children who were exposed to the physical and emotional maltreatment of their mother by their father or mother's partner during the past year. Unlike most studies of the children of batterers, this sample consisted of families living in the community.... We measured 17 posttraumatic symptoms in the child, each experienced directly in conjunction with the violence. In addition, posttraumatic stress symptoms were related to other indices of the individual child's adjustment. Results showed that more than half of the children had the symptoms of intrusive reexperiencing, and 42% experienced traumatic arousal symptoms. Fewer children evidenced avoidance reactions to the violence. However, 13% qualified for a complete diagnosis of PTSD.

... The specific links of trauma and children's social behavior have yet to be made. For example, the child may avoid either specific people in the family or potentially conflictual situations, or the child may experience reminders of traumatic events at inopportune times, such as when playing with others. Traumatic intrusions may interfere with attentional focus and concentration at school and ultimately may influence school achievement. A traumatized mother may be less available to provide bonding, protection, and support to the developing child. Given that more than half of the children in the study just cited showed the symptoms of "intrusive reexperiencing," it is clear that, for many children, the devastating effects of domestic violence continue well beyond the time frame of the violent events themselves. Future studies are needed to address these issues.

Relationships Theory Explanations

One of the most important tasks of early childhood is the development of secure family relationships, which affect all future social relationships....

... [F]amily violence damages the development of the child's safe, reliable expectations about other people.... The relationships paradigm of children exposed to domestic violence might include the deleterious elements of domination and control in interpersonal interactions and expectations of what it means to be a man or a woman....

... The development of social relationships in children is crucial to long-term adjustment outcomes, including friendship, social skills, academic success, self-esteem and well-being. During the preschool years (ages 3 to 5), parents, and particularly mothers, are involved in facilitating the development of the child's relationships with others.... In addition, the quality of the child's relationship with the mother during this critical time period affects his or her ability to develop age-appropriate relationships with others....

... There is some preliminary evidence that children who grow up in woman-abusive families have different sets of concerns and expectations for themselves and others, relative to children who have not been exposed to such family violence. In one study of the middle childhood years (ages 6 to 12), children of battered women were more worried and concerned about the safety of their mothers and sisters, and more worried about the potential for harm by their father, than were children in comparable but less violent families....

Is there any evidence that witnessing domestic violence affects the child's relationships with peers and friends? In fact, there is some suggestive evidence on this count as well. [One] study ... found that children of battered women spend less time with their friends, were less likely to have a best friend, and had lower quality friendships than did children from non-violent families. Moreover, their worries about family members were generalized to others outside the home: Children of battered women were more worried about the safety of and potential harm to their friends than children living in non-violent families....

SUMMARY

... To recapitulate, when children are traumatized, the development of their social relationships can be impeded by the trauma symptoms they experience. Furthermore, the child may have learned inadequate coping skills or inappropriate emotional regulation strategies, which can lead to frustration and anger. The anger is expressed in social interaction with others and creates interpersonal problems, such as rejection by peers. Moreover, the traumatized child who is not able to cope well may experience trouble concentrating at school and may fall further behind academically.

... [T]he use of both theories and models allows speculation on the ways in which children's reactions to the events can be modulated and modified. By identifying protective factors, such as how the events are explained to the child, who is blamed, the quality of maternal mental health, social supports, resources in the broader community context, and so on, one may work to develop clinical and education programs and to take a preventive stance against this form of family violence....

* * *

NOTES

1. The broad range of possible consequences for children of witnessing or being exposed to violence, as well as the ways in which those consequences may vary according to the gender, age and resilience of the child, and any potentially mitigating circumstances, is likely to make it difficult to prove, in a contested legal context, that a given set of symptoms flow directly from exposure to abuse. In succeeding chapters you will see examples of arguments about whether a child's symptoms can be laid at the door of a father's abuse of his partner, rather than the stress of a parental separation, for example, or inadequate parenting by a mother. It will be important, going forward, to think about effective ways of making the link between a child's emotional distress or dysfunction, and the abuse suffered by his or her mother.

2. One of the factors mentioned by Graham–Bermann in her discussion of social learning theory is how a child interprets violent events, and the likelihood that children will be left to struggle with ascribing meaning to the violence by themselves, or even offered interpretations that will compound their feelings of guilt and responsibility for the violence. Another group of researchers offer a similar observation, and the suggestion that constructive parental interventions might do much to mitigate the impact of violence on children:

> Clearly, some comments are constructive and may facilitate the children's understanding and living with a hostile and violent father. In contrast, other explanations may serve to further terrorize a child. Similarly, children's feeling of blame and responsibility as well as control or helplessness may be influenced by maternal comments.... Thus, mothers' explanations of and interpretations about the violence may represent an important aspect of parenting and at the least warrants further investigation as a potentially important mediating influence on children's adjustment.

George W. Holden et al., *Parenting Behaviors and Beliefs of Battered Women,* CHILDREN EXPOSED TO MARITAL VIOLENCE: THEORY, RESEARCH AND APPLIED ISSUES 289, 329 (1998).

3. The following narrative concentrates on trauma as the source of a child's difficulties after witnessing his father's attack on his mother. Using Graham–Bermann's insight that the impact of exposure to violence may best be explained by bringing together social learning theory, trauma theory and relationships theory, can you point to aspects of the child's response that might be understood through social learning theory or relationships theory?

Louise Silvern and Lynn Kaersvang
The Traumatized Children of Violent Marriages, 68 Child Welfare 421, 427–30 (1989)

Long-Term Intervention—A Case Report

Jon, an eight-year-old of above average intelligence, was brought for psychotherapy by his divorced mother. She described him as a model child at home, although somewhat inhibited. Yet, teachers reported that occasionally since age five, Jon suddenly and uncontrollably kicked, punched, and sometimes dangerously choked other boys. Later, he was always remorseful, and he accepted the various punishments, lectures, and incentives that his mother and teachers tried.

Initial interviews individually with the mother and conjointly with mother and Jon revealed no glaring inadequacies in child rearing, or in the quality of attachment. The mother had a somewhat limited tolerance for normal dysphoric and angry expressions from Jon, and Jon did appear subtly protective toward his mother. Yet, this mild conflict avoidance did not appear sufficient to explain Jon's dramatic outbursts.

In initial play interviews, Jon was constricted and intent on pleasing the (woman) counselor. He claimed to have no understanding of his violence and asserted his resolve to stop it. Responses to projective testing alternated between apparently defensive and unrevealing ones and others that were full of violence, gore, and lethal snakes. Jon's potential to lose impulse control was obvious.

Jon's parents were divorced when Jon was an infant. The mother reported that he was always noncommittal about his father's sporadic visits. Since the divorce, the mother and her ex-husband sometimes argued, and he had beaten her two or three times. Jon was five the last time, when her ex-husband had choked her and she had screamed. Jon was asleep, so the mother assumed he had not heard.

Weekly individual psychotherapy (and parent counseling) was begun, because Jon's violent fantasies appeared more crucial than did immediate family dysfunction, pervasive social skills deficits, or inadequate parent management. Jon's inhibition soon gave way to excited, repetitive symbolic play. The main character was an avenging superhero who stopped bad guys from setting off violent explosions. The hero's allies were snakes that fought by choking their screaming enemies to death. Jon revealed his own fantasies of owning four boa constrictors that would take his side in fights, and he eagerly discussed techniques for taming snakes. Yet, he also revealed nightmares about snakes attacking people.

Initially, Jon avoided discussing his daily life. His secretiveness was repeatedly pointed out, along with his fears that the counselor would think badly of him. Then, after about four months, in the waiting room in front of Jon, his mother reported that he had again dangerously choked and punched a boy. In therapy, after discussing Jon's embarrassment, Jon expressed his distress and confusion about his violence.

Over the next months, mixed with continuing symbolic play, Jon began to describe his fights. The began with objectively minor provocations, such as someone bumping him. After learning that the counselor could accept his outrage, Jon acknowledged that the strength of his reactions to these provocations was unusual. Later, he accepted the comment that he reacted to the real "offenders" as if they were the bad guys in his play, that is, as evil, uncontrolled bullies who thought they could get away with "exploding'' everyone. Jon realized that during his fights he felt a little heroic, although he was genuinely regretful later.

Jon increasingly realized that however often he had promised himself to stop his violence, he experienced little control, and that the provocations for his rages were poor explanations. He admitted that a ''puzzle'' was involved. In other words, the counselor and Jon explicitly established the discontinuity between Jon's usual behavior and intentions and those that held sway during his outbursts.

About seven months into therapy, Jon described another fight. The counselor knew that Jon's father had visited recently, so she asked about the visit and if fights were more likely near visits. Jon was, as usual, noncommittal about his father, and the counselor, as usual, commented about his need to keep secrets. Later that session, in the midst of fantasy play, Jon mentioned that he had once seen his mother and father fight. Jon dismissed initial questions about the fight, saying only ''Oh, everyone fights sometimes.'' The counselor commented on his obvious anxiety and wondered if this fight was especially secret. Hesitantly, Jon explained that his father had ''hit'' his mother and she screamed. He had awakened and watched. He said that it hadn't bothered him, except that he was worried about his mother. When the counselor asked Jon if he had discussed the fight with his mother, he was appalled at the idea.

During the next two sessions, Jon wanted no part of talking. His silence was interpreted in terms of his ambivalence about having told a secret about something that ''would scare most kids.'' The third session after the disclosure, Jon drew the four boa constrictors that he like to fantasize were his pets. . . . There was discussion about the drawing, and Jon explained that the snakes got ''side by side'' so they could work together to ''choke bad guys.'' The counselor then pointed out the obvious resemblance to the four fingers of a hand—a hand choking someone. Jon appeared briefly stunned. The counselor suggested that perhaps the resemblance to a hand scared him, because he might have once seen something similar. Jon said that, maybe, it was when his mother had screamed. The counselor pointed out that the hand must have been his father's choking his mother. Shaken, Jon nodded.

In the next stage of therapy, Jon talked about the horrifying impotence and terror he had felt while his mother screamed. His self-loathing was intense, and he expressed his determination to never again just stand there ''like that.'' The many reasons for his inaction were repeatedly discussed, the most painful being that he had been scared of his father. The connection between his wish to control the choking snakes/hand and the trauma was made explicit. His rages were understood as ways of reenacting the event, but with himself in charge.

After preparation . . ., Jon's mother joined the sessions. They reviewed the traumatic event in detail and its subsequent impact on him. She also joined in the final stage of therapy, during which Jon began to sort out his protectiveness toward his mother and his ambivalence about his father. He examined his own fear and anger instead of just his initially stated worry about his mother's welfare. He also discussed his own wish to see his father, instead of just his initial statements that he tolerated the visits in order to "cooperate."

Jon productively faced his family dilemma, once the even more frightening, but protective, network of traumatic symbolization was resolved. A report one year after the termination of the 14–month therapy indicated that there had been no further recurrence of violence after Jon's initial disclosure of witnessing spousal abuse.

FIGURE 1

"Jon's" Drawing of his Boa Constrictors

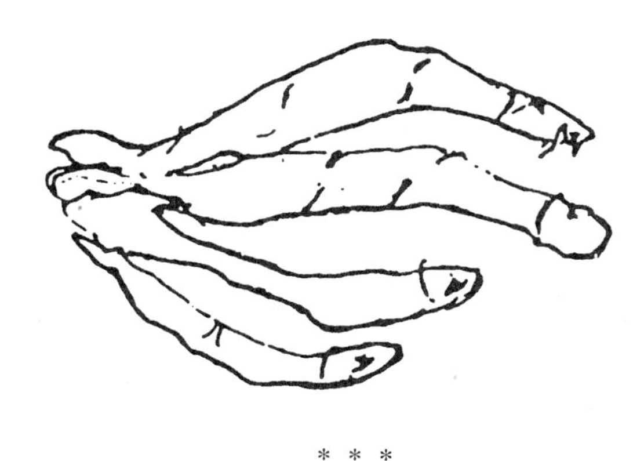

* * *

NOTES

1. Jon was helped to understand and manage his own violence in response to the abuse suffered by his mother through a relatively long-term individual therapy relationship. This is not a resource that will be available to all children, and reflects only one possible intervention. The current status of mental health treatment for children exposed to violence is summarized in the following excerpt. Lawyers working with families affected by domestic violence need to know about the goals of treatment, and about the availability of services. Because the field is still in its infancy many adults are still unaware of the consequences for their children of exposure to violence. They may well need help in identifying the problem, accessing resources, and understanding the role they themselves can play, with or without the assistance of a trained therapist, in promoting their children's recovery.

Betsy McAlister Groves
Mental Health Services for Children Who Witness Domestic Violence, 9 The Future of Children 122, 125–27 (The David and Lucile Packard Foundation, Winter 1999)

Mental health interventions for children who witness violence have traditionally been available only in battered women's shelters or from agencies providing services to battered women. However, in recent years, more programs serving these children have been established in other venues, reflecting the growing recognition that children affected by domestic violence reside outside of shelters as well, and require service availability in a broad range of settings.

Goals

A first goal of therapeutic intervention is promoting open discussion of the children's experiences. Many parents and professionals assume that it is better for the child not to dwell on the disturbing event(s), and to try to forget. The intensity of the child's terror, however, obviates the possibility of "forgetting." For many children, the process of retelling or reenacting a traumatic event in the safety of a therapeutic relationship is itself a healing experience, and a first step toward integrating the experience into their understanding of themselves and their world. In addition, the process of "breaking the silence" and speaking openly about the violent events serves to reduce the children's sense of isolation, which allows them to begin emotional healing.

Second, therapists seek to help children understand and cope with their emotional responses to the violence, while promoting their acquisition of positive behavior patterns. Strategies include assisting children with understanding why their parents fight and helping them to realize that the fighting is not their fault, and that they are not responsible for managing it. With older children, groups may also discuss violence in personal relationships, and address anger management and the use of conflict-resolution skills.

Third, mental health interventions seek to reduce the symptoms the children are experiencing in response to the violence. Most approaches strive to help the child and the nonabusing parent to link the problematic symptoms to the exposure to violence, and to teach specific strategies for managing and decreasing symptoms. For example, if the child is suffering from insomnia and nightmares, an individual therapist might work with the parent and child to build soothing and comforting rituals into bedtime routines.

Finally, therapists work to help the family create a safe, stable, and nurturing environment for the child, because children cannot begin to recover from the effects of exposure to violence so long as the exposure continues. In situations where children continue to live in a dangerous environment, therapists strive to help the nonabusing parent obtain safety for herself and her children. In accomplishing this task, the therapist must often help the family address additional stressors, such as substance abuse or housing difficulties. In situations where the child and mother are not living with the batterer, mental health intervention strives to promote the children's feelings of safety and security. Therapists work with parents to help them understand the children's needs for consistent routines. With parental permission, treatment may also include consultation with teachers or child care providers in order to develop consistent strategies for the classroom or day-care setting. In addition, therapists attempt to strengthen those emotional supports potentially available to the children, and work to reinforce the bond between the child and the nonabusing parent.

Therapy Approaches

Children who witness domestic violence may be seen in group or individual therapy. Empirical studies investigating the outcomes of these interventions are extremely limited; no controlled studies have been published. Follow-up interviews with participants, however, suggest that the therapeutic interventions have positive effects.

Group Interventions

The most widely described intervention for children who have witnessed domestic violence is group counseling. Most of these groups are time-limited, usually between 6 and 10 weeks, and use a specific psychoeducational curriculum that provides structure for discussions about family violence, personal safety, and identification of feelings. Some of the groups are held in battered women's shelters, whereas others are based in mental health clinics or social service agencies. Some settings offer concurrent groups for the mothers.

Groups generally target children between the ages of 6 and 15, typically grouping children in age spans of two to three years. Groups are less likely to be helpful for preschoolers, who are typically more impulsive, less focused, and less likely to use peer relationships to cope with stressful issues than are older children. . . . Regardless of age, groups are typically not appropriate for children who may be more severely traumatized, because such children have more complex needs and are probably better served by individual treatment. . . .

Group treatment can assist children and adolescents with important developmental tasks. Groups break the isolation and enable children to tell their stories in the presence of others who closely identify with the experience. For adolescents, groups are particularly appropriate, given the importance of the peer group for defining behavior norms. Adolescent groups may also focus on violence in dating relationships, sexism, and abuse of power. These issues are quite relevant to adolescents, whose developmental tasks include establishing intimate relationships and acquiring a sense of personal identity as they approach adulthood. . . .

A subgroup of children who witness domestic violence are also living through their parents' high-conflict divorce. Many such children feel trapped in the middle of intense and prolonged interparental conflict and experience confusing feelings of loyalty and responsibility. The goals addressed above are appropriate for these children as well. Additionally, groups can help these children to understand family members' roles in the separation and to develop their own perspectives on the conflict.

Individual Interventions

Very little has been written about theoretical models and therapeutic approaches for individual treatment of children affected by domestic violence. Some clinicians have adapted models developed to treat related phenomena, such as posttraumatic stress disorder (PTSD) in children. Not all children exposed to domestic violence display symptoms meeting the criteria for diagnosis of PTSD, but many similarities exist. In both sets of circumstances, the therapist seeks to stabilize the child's life situation, to help the child integrate the experiences of the violent event(s) in an adaptive manner, and to work with the child to manage the symptoms that resulted from the trauma.

The Child Witness to Violence Project at Boston Medical Center has developed an individual model for young children that is adapted from models for treating PTSD. . . .

The Child Trauma Research Project at San Francisco General Hospital has built upon another therapeutic model. It employs a psychodynamic approach to treat preschooler-mother pairs affected by domestic violence. This therapy program strives to help the children and mothers deal with the effects of the violence, while strengthening their abilities to function as a healthy family unit. . . .

Conclusions and Recommendations

. . .

Expansion of service-delivery locations and networks is necessary, in that available services are not sufficient to meet the needs of the population. If professionals succeed in identifying greater numbers of children affected by domestic violence, the need for such expansion will be even more pressing. Mental health providers treating children exposed to domestic violence must learn how to work with this population, developing expertise in child development and crisis intervention, and learning about the effects of trauma on individuals and appropriate assessment and treatment approaches.

* * *

NOTE

1. Groves talks about assisting adolescents who have witnessed abuse at home through groups that focus, in part, on violence in dating relationships, sexism, and abuse of power. To the extent that witnessing one parent's abuse of the other leads children to replicate patterns of relationship based on domination or control (as social learning theory would suggest), or disrupts children's development of healthy relationships with others (as relationships theory suggests), then presumably there is a real risk that these children will find themselves becoming perpetrators or victims of partner abuse in their own intimate relationships, even at a young age. We have evidence both of the startlingly high incidence of dating violence among young people, and of the connections between this violence, and young perpetrators' experiences of violence in their families of origin:

> Dating violence among individuals under the age of twenty-one is a pervasive problem. A study in one school district suggested that one in four high school students experienced violence in a dating relation-

ship either as the recipient of the violence or as the perpetrator of the violence. Other surveys of high school and college students show that an average of 28 percent of the students experienced dating violence. Overall, studies indicate that anywhere from 9 percent to 39 percent of high school students experience dating violence at some point.

. . .

The literature on teen dating violence cites various explanations for the violence. Some suggest that teens receive encouragement in the media and approval from friends for the belief that men should dominate women in relationships, including the right to use physically and sexually aggressive behavior. Others suggest that the violence is a learned behavior. One study has demonstrated, for example, that high school students whose parents had been in violent relationships had a statistically higher rate of violence in their own relationships. Although the results of studies looking at the intergenerational cycle of violence for teens are not consistent, there seems to be a correlation between experiencing abuse as a child and later perpetrating violence in a relationship.

Stacy L. Brustin, *Legal Responses to Teen Dating Violence,* 29 FAM. L. Q. 331, 335–36 (1995). The study cited by Brustin for the proposition that adolescents who have been exposed to a parent's violent relationship are more likely to become involved in a violent relationship themselves is reported in Nona O'Keefe et al., *Teen Dating Violence*, SOCIAL WORK Nov./Dec. 1986, 466, 467. In the study population, more than 51 percent of students who had seen a parent being abused were themselves involved in a violent dating relationship.

Our relative inattention to the issue of gendered violence in young people's relationships, and its connection to domestic violence in the lives of parents and other adults, is the topic of Marina Angel's article, *Abusive Boys Kill Girls Just Like Abusive Men Kill Women: Explaining the Obvious,* 8 TEMPLE POL. & CIV. RIGHTS L. REV. 283 (1999). Reacting to three school shooting incidents in 1997 and 1998, she points out that as adults talked about the "inexplicable" violence, the "mystery" of why children would kill children, and "searching for a motive," "[n]o one seemed to notice that all the killers were boys and all the dead were girls and women." Id. at 284. Pushing her analysis further, she notes that:

> all those killed by the boys were females who had power over them; women who had disciplined them or girls who had rejected them. The women were resented as authority figures; in one case a mother, in the other a teacher. In all three cases, girls who were killed or wounded had been perceived by their killers as "love objects" who had "rejected" their shooters.

Id. at 291.

By contrast with the "mystified" adults, she notes, the schoolmates and friends of the perpetrators and victims had a pretty good understanding of what had precipitated the violence. She warns that if adults fail to legitimate that understanding, and fail to address gendered violence in the homes and schools where children learn about relationships, we cannot hope to change the norms that govern relationships between girls and boys, women and men:

> Nonrecognition means that gender violence is not in the consciousness of parents, school officials, the law or society in general. These failures of perception act synergistically to perpetuate gender violence. Parents do not understand how to raise both their male and female children to abhor gender violence. Further, parents do not teach their female children to guard against gender violence. School officials are entrusted with a major role in the education and upbringing of our children. They also bear some responsibility for training against gender violence and for providing safeguards for schoolchildren.
>
> . . .
>
> By refusing to recognize the gendered nature of violence against girls and women, we teach our girls that they lack the basic human rights of safety and dignity, and we teach our boys that they can use violence and aggression against girls who do not respond in ways that satisfy them....

Id. at 294. While innovative programs addressing teen dating violence are increasingly available to middle and high schools around the country, their impact can only be minimal as long as young people are living in violent homes, and as long as their families and school communities continue to deny the presence of gendered violence both at home and at school.

D. Parenting by Battered Women

Marie Ashe and Naomi Cahn
Child Abuse: A Problem for Feminist Theory, 2 Texas Journal of Women and Law 75, 76, 84–88, 90, 93–96, 100, 104–05, 108, 111–12 (1993)

... Increased awareness of child abuse has been accompanied by popular reactions of outrage and horror and by widespread condemnation of its perpetrators.

The accounts of child abuse delivered through popular media and various types of professional literature have tended to tell the story of child abuse with a focus on the experience of child victims and have devoted only very limited attention to the realities and experiences of perpetrators of such abuse. While parents, particularly mothers, are regularly brought under the jurisdiction of trial courts in child dependency proceedings, pursuant to which children are removed temporarily or permanently from their custody, there is a surprising dearth of literature about the complexities of such parents. The developing contemporary understanding of child abuse within and without the legal system, to the degree that it focuses on perpetrators of abuse, tends to reduce to a story of "bad mothers."

. . .

Two particularly troubling pictures of "bad mothers" in popular culture have emerged over the past five years; the picture of an individual woman, Hedda Nussbaum; and the picture of a class of women, namely pregnant, drug-addicted (especially crack-addicted) women. Each has been controversial, as each has juxtaposed images of good mothers against images of bad mothers, and women as victims against women as perpetrators of abuse. The story of Hedda Nussbuam has deeply divided feminists; the question of how to respond to pregnant women who abuse drugs has created similar division.

Popular accounts of the facts of the Nussbaum case are in general agreement. Hedda Nussbaum met Joel Steinberg in 1975. Throughout their relationship, Steinberg abused Nussbaum severely, frequently causing visible bruises as well as fractured bones. In 1981, Nussbaum and Steinberg illegally adopted a two-year-old child whom they called Lisa. Six years later, Lisa died as a result of severe physical abuse, apparently perpetrated by Joel Steinberg. Although criminal charges were initially brought against Nussbaum on the basis of Lisa's death, those charges were eventually dropped, and Nussbaum testified against Steinberg during the trial at which he was convicted of first degree manslaughter. Responses by feminists to the Nussbaum issues fell into two categories. On the one hand, Nussbaum was canonized as the archetypal victim. Three hundred prominent women signed a letter requesting that the public refocus its attention onto the men responsible for domestic violence, rather than blame women victims for staying with such men. This response demonstrates an understanding of Hedda Nussbaum as a person so victimized as to be incapable of moral agency. On the other hand, there was some tendency to blame Hedda Nussbaum as a fully responsible and autonomous agent. Susan Brownmiller, a prominent feminist, suggested, for example, that "Hedda Nussbaum, far from being a passive victim, was an active participant in her own– and Lisa's–destruction."

Similarly, conflicting views have been expressed about pregnant crack-addicted mothers. Throughout the country, many prosecutors' offices have brought charges of child abuse against pregnant women who use crack. One reporter has noted that "more and more judges and lawmakers have come to view these mothers as criminals who victimize children, rather than as victims themselves." Justifying the prosecution of pregnant women by reference to the state's interest in the birth of healthy children erases not only the pregnant woman's liberty interest but also her history and her motivations.

On the other hand, some writers have urged that the problem of crack-addicted pregnant women must be put into its social context. They have further argued that a contextualized understanding should lead us away from the tendency to blame and to prosecute criminally. This perspective reflects an understanding that, to the extent that these women are morally culpable, their culpability is highly diminished. It also suggests not only that there are insufficient programs for pregnant women seeking drug treatment, but also that prosecutions have a disproportionate impact on poor and minority women.

The conflicting characterizations of "bad mothers" in popular culture, apparent in popular discussions of Hedda Nussbaum and in treatment of pregnant, drug-addicted women, seem inadequate. As perhaps most parents have reason to know, and as occasional feminist writings on motherhood have clearly stated, the gap between purportedly natural feelings of intimacy and nurturance and ostensibly unnatural feelings of aggression and rage has been enormously exaggerated. Popular simplistic and reductive interpretations of abusive mothers may constitute attempts by parents to drive away a recognition of their own tendencies toward verbal and physical violence against children. Both the model of the bad mother as the autonomous, powerful and fully responsible evildoer and the countervailing model of her as the helpless victim create barriers to our respectful understanding of women whom we experience as disturbing and challenging.

The "Bad Mother" in Psychological and Sociological Empirical Studies

Accounts of bad mothers appear not only in literature and in popular culture, but also in the stories told by the social sciences. These include both theoretical and empirical accounts. We have been surprised to discover, however, that abusive mothers are studied far less frequently than we had expected and that they are defined very tentatively by existing data. These studies, therefore, fail to provide factual information that could inform the "bad mother" stereotype.

Data show that approximately 2.5 million children are abused each year in the United States. It is difficult, however, to find accurate data on how much of the domestic abuse of children is committed by mothers as opposed to other family members. This is, presumably, because the organizations that collect data covering abuse have tended to focus on children rather than on perpetrators.... Furthermore, some data suggest that there may be a bias among child protective service workers monitoring situations of abuse to believe that the abuse is the mother's fault. Consequently, these patterns of data collection are not adequately informative concerning the amount of abuse directly perpetrated by mothers, although data from the studies discussed below do indicate that rates of abuse by women may be comparable to rates of abuse perpetrated by men.

In her historical review of the records of the Massachusetts Society for the Prevention of Cruelty to Children from 1880–1960, Linda Gordon found that mothers were reported as child abuse perpetrators in forty-six percent of cases and fathers in the remaining fifty-four percent. These raw figures are somewhat misleading because, as Gordon explains, "fathers were much more likely to abuse children in proportion to how much time they spend in child care." Gordon concluded that when the women she studied did abuse children, their violence took essentially the same form as had men's abuse.

In its analysis of national reports on child abuse and neglect between 1976–1982, the American Humane Association substantiated Gordon's claim that the caretaking parent (male or female) was more likely to abuse the child. But, contrary to Gordon, this study also found that men were more likely to have perpetrated major and minor abuse, while women were more likely to be associated with the lesser standard of neglect.

In a study that used reports from battered women who were temporarily staying in shelters during the early 1980s, Jean Giles–Sims found that 92.6 percent of women and 88.9 percent of their male partners had used a violent tactic on the child in the household during the previous year, but that the men in question had used these tactics nearly twice as often as had the women. Further, the men studied appeared to have been more likely to use more severe abusive tactics on their children than were women. Giles–Sims found that during the six-month period following their stays at battered women's shelters, all the women studied had used some form of violent tactic on one or more of their children; however, the frequency of women's use of the most violent abuse tactics showed a post-shelter stay decrease.

... The studies have not focused on sociological factors that may affect women who have committed child abuse. These accounts generally have not treated, in any depth, the politics and sociology of patriarchal society, nor have they discussed self-accounts that abused women might be able to offer. Thus they do little to displace the unexamined "bad mother" stereotype.

. . .

A very significant development in psychological literature has occurred in the last several years with the translation into English of a number of writings by Swiss psychologist Alice Miller. These works represent perhaps the strongest theoretical treatment of child abuse and its implications for human development and history....

Miller defines the mistreatment of children as "greatest crime that one human being can commit against another—causing psychological deformation in the next generation...." ... She urges that adults become consciously aware of the humiliations and losses of their own childhoods so that they will be able to avoid reproducing those injuries in the experiences of their children.

. . .

Miller's account of child abuse from the child's perspective is in some senses grandly historical and in others ahistorical. On the one hand, she sees the abuse of children as the mechanism for the perpetration of evil and destruction throughout history; on the other, she manifests no particular interest in exploring the cultural contexts within which what she defines as "abuse" occurs....

... Miller's writing can have the effect of evoking feelings of guilt in adult women (and men too, presumably) who read it and measure their care for their own children against its standards. Feminists are understandably resistant to being drawn into experiencing the kind of "parent" guilt, often reduced to "mother guilt," that Miller's writing can evoke. This is particularly the case for feminists who are struggling to make the best choices they can for themselves and their children in a culture that offers few satisfactory options. Those struggling to make do with "private" solutions to the problem of nurturing children in the absence of any available adequate "public" ones are not eager to be reminded of the inadequacies of those private attempts and of how those inadequacies occasion pain and suffering for children.

. . .

Martha Minow has proposed a partial answer to this dilemma of determining responsibility.... Minow has suggested that the context of "bad mothers," which includes complex family dynamics and a society unresponsive to domestic violence, is perhaps to blame for family violence. This proposition provides a context for understanding the mother's actions: why she did not leave the abusive situation; why she did not—or could not—prevent her partner from abusing a child; and why she herself may have abused her child. This interpretation allows us to move beyond mere blaming of the mother herself and permits our focusing on her embeddedness within systems that foster violence. While it does not entirely resolve the issue of how to understand the "bad mother" as moral agent, it reminds us of the need for examination of context, an approach to which much feminist theory has reliably directed attention....

. . .

Unlike liberal feminists, many cultural feminists have made the experience of mothering central to their theories. Many cultural feminists suggest that it is because women are mothers that they are more connected to others. Their image is of a natural mother who recognizes and appreciates her interdependence with her children. Cultural feminists celebrate women's role as nurturer. Indeed, they tend to celebrate women's positive values to a degree that erases certain negative aspects of women's experience and activity.

... [I]t is not entirely clear what a coherent cultural feminist analysis of "bad mothers" could be. The largely uncritical—and often essentialistic—emphasis by cultural feminism on caring as an attribute of women hardly leaves room for consideration of women who do not or cannot care for their children, and seems to offer no escape from the prevailing images of "bad mothers" as either utterly unnatural or utterly victimized.

. . .

Postmodernism has created a space within which new kinds of inquiry into the experiences and motivations of "bad mothers" can be undertaken. Postmodernist approaches support new directions in interpreting the intersections between violence against women and violence by women. Postmodernism legitimates stories of "bad mothers" as essential to theory. It both recognizes the difficulties of telling such stories and invites their tellings as "local knowledge." Postmodernism supports new imaginings not only by having opened up the possiblity of various "new narratives," but also by its creation of a space within which those narratives—including, for example, narratives of children as well as those of women—can intersect. Thus a specifically and explicitly postmodernist feminism may offer the greatest possibility for engagement of feminist theory with the reality of child abuse by "bad mothers."

. . . The fuller development of new narratives will require the commitment of all story-tellers to persistent inquiry and to persistent self-examination. . . .

We have suggested that such new tellings have emerged in literary fiction and other relatively isolated instances. . . . Their rarity demonstrates something that legal advocates for "bad mothers" often have occasion to note, namely, that such women are rarely able to speak effectively for themselves and of themselves, at least within the legal system. We mean not only that such women experience the violence of having to reshape the realities of their experiences to accommodate a legal discourse that demands narrowing and erasure. We mean, beyond that, that they are as constrained as are their judges and prosecutors by the ambivalences that underlie and give rise to binarisms defining "good" and "bad" motherhood. Thus, it has been our experience that women alleged to have abused or neglected their children are typically unable to self-define except by directly denying what has been alleged, by asserting its opposite. They often seem to see no alternative to reciting counterclaims: "I'm a good mother!" or "I would never hurt my child!" And these counterclaims may be no more meaningful than the original claim of "badness."

The limited ability of "bad mothers" to speak for and about themselves means that the task of representing and interpreting bad mothers will necessarily be a collaborative project. It will be one in which such women will participate in conjunction with people differently situated and, therefore, more able to begin an expansion of the relevant emotional and moral discourse. The new representations will need to examine more fully the mothers' agency, complicity, and victimization. . . .

* * *

NOTE

1. Hedda Nussbaum's tragic paralysis in the face of her adopted daughter's cruel abuse by Joel Steinberg offers a sobering reminder that we will indeed be confronted from time to time with stories of women whose own abuse has rendered them physically or emotionally incapable of parenting their children safely or well. The full telling of that story also prompts an analysis of the kind urged by Martha Minow. There were others who were aware of the mother's and the child's abuse—among them neighbors and teachers—and yet no one intervened. Nussbaum herself had made previous attempts to leave Steinberg, but had never received the level of support she needed to overcome her fears and strengthen her resolve to end the relationship. However, the following excerpt cautions that we should not be

quick to conclude that any mother who is being abused by her partner will, for that reason, be a less effective parent than her nonabused counterpart.

George W. Holden et al.
Parenting Behaviors and Beliefs of Battered Women; Children Exposed to Marital Violence: Theory, Research and Applied Issues 289, 325–30 (G.W. Holden, R. Geffner & E.N. Jouriles, eds. 1998)

... [S]tudies [conducted by the authors] point to three findings concerning the parenting of mothers who are physically abused by their spouses. The most important result concerns the diminished parenting hypothesis. These data indicate that on the vast majority of measures assessing child-rearing behavior, battered women from a shelter do not differ significantly from non-abused community mothers. Contrary to a deficiency model of battered women, no evidence was found to indicate they were less affectionate, less proactive, less likely to provide structure for the child, or more punitive.

... [V]ery little support was found for the diminished parenting hypothesis. For example, on only one index of parenting (limit setting) out of four subscales tested did the battered women show a significant difference from the other mothers. Given that most of these families are low to very low income, it appears that marital violence does not contribute over and above the effects of poverty. Nevertheless, these results are tempered by the reliance on self-report data and the finding that behavioral observations revealed some subtle interactional differences. The possibility that battered women denied, minimized, or were unaware of some of their parenting deficits cannot be ruled out.

A second general finding is that many of the mothers in violent marriages do indeed engage in aggressive behavior toward their children. However, community mothers also engage in child-directed aggression; there was relatively little difference between the battered and comparison mothers on the variable.... Furthermore, once the women leave the battering relationship, the number of women who continue to engage in aggression toward their children drops significantly. This mother-to-child aggression was found to be positively associated ... with parenting stress in all three studies.

The third major finding ... concerns the evidence for both change and stability in the mothers and the children. On several different fronts, there appears to be significant improvement for the mothers and children 6 months after leaving the batterer. Mothers reported significant decreases in the rates of stress and depressive symptoms, and they perceived their children as having fewer behavior problems. Despite this positive finding, their low self-esteem scores suggest that the considerable problems and hardships the women undoubtedly continue to face should not be forgotten. Assistance and interventions on a variety of fronts evidently are seriously needed. However, that single but monumental act of extricating oneself from the violent relationship appears to have advantageous outcomes for the mothers. On the other hand, the data indicate little change in mothers' disciplinary responses over the 6–month time period, presumably because those behaviors are based on previously developed disciplinary habits and belief systems that have not been modified.

. . .

The most surprising results of this work are that so few differences were found between battered and comparison mothers. That does not mean that all the mothers were exhibiting model parenting behavior. . . . Rather, the marital violence in itself did not appear to result in consistent group differences. Indeed, both groups engaged in some aggression directed toward children, although battered women were more likely to report doing this. As Straus and Gelles (1990) have made so clear, aggression and violence are endemic in many households.

The aggression toward the children can be partially explained by the bidirectional determinants of behavior. At least some of the child-directed aggression may be accounted for—though not excused—by the children's behavior. Just as parents respond negatively to stress, so too do their children. Given the high rate of child misbehavior and externalizing problems in many of these children, at least some mother-to-child disciplinary interactions undoubtedly escalate to the point of violence. On mother from a maritally violent home reported that her 7–year-old overactive son was becoming abusive toward others and wanted to hurt people. When asked about the characteristics she liked the best about him, she poignantly wrote: "I'm so fed up with him right now, I can't think of any." It is not difficult to imagine how conflict between the two could escalate into aggressive behavior. Fortunately, 6 months later the mother reported that her son was no longer obsessed with hurting people and had fewer behavior problems. She too was exhibiting much less aggressive behavior toward him. . . .

It should be kept in mind that parenting is not just affected by violence but can affect its consequences. As mentioned above, mothers may serve as buffers to protect children from violence or may attempt to compensate for it by providing extra warmth or support. Such evidence suggests that from the mothers' perspective, their children may not be "forgotten victims" but instead are a focal point of their attention and concern. More evidence for this view comes from the mothers who cited concerns over the negative effects on their children as the impetus for leaving the violent relationship. . . .

. . .

Future studies should collect data from other informants (e.g., child, neighbors, and even partners) to provide converging evidence about the mothers' behavior. . . . Data about and from the children's fathers are needed as well. Investigations into how different violent environments (e.g., different types of batterers) and characteristics of the mothers (e.g., post-traumatic stress disorder) may affect or interact with their parenting behavior are also needed. Such work could help to explicate relations between marital violence, parenting, and children's behavior problems. For example, women married to antisocial batterers may develop different survival skills and compensatory parenting mechanisms than wives of family-only batterers....

... Perhaps the fundamental implication of this work is that it appears researchers should revise their orientations with regard to battered women. A search for pathologies of battered women and negative qualities of their parenting seems to be the wrong direction to pursue. Rather, the focus should be shifted to one that begins to recognize and document the strengths and coping strategies of these women. Investigations are needed into the proactive, strategic, adaptive, and compensatory behaviors that many of these mothers engage in to protect or even save their children from the detrimental effects of being reared in a maritally violent home.

* * *

NOTE

1. The particular question for the lawyer or advocate to carry forward from this chapter to subsequent ones is how to utilize information about the children of battered women in the legal contexts in which mothers and children seek protection from violence, and in which fathers and/or the state seek to intervene in or usurp relationships between mothers and their children. The final reading in this chapter, however, carries the reminder that the legal system is only one of many that must be mobilized to protect children from the consequences of abuse; whether they suffer it themselves, or suffer from exposure to abuse inflicted on others. It is also a reminder that before we blame parents for their failure to protect their children from physical and emotional trauma, we must ask hard questions about the social and legal context in which we ask them to do their parenting.

David and Lucile Packard Foundation Domestic Violence and Children, 9 The Future of Children, Executive Summary 4 (Winter 1999)

RECOMMENDATION 1

- Research is needed that advances the current state of understanding of the prevalence and effects of childhood exposure to domestic violence, and the impact of resilience and risk factors, so that policymakers and practitioners can design interventions sufficient to address the size, nature and complexity of the problem.

RECOMMENDATION 2

- Stable public funding sources are needed to support comprehensive and coordinated community-based services for battered women and their children, as well as program evaluations and replication of effective interventions.

RECOMMENDATION 3

- Because the majority of children exposed to domestic violence do not have access to services through traditional avenues such as battered women's shelters, new strategies for identifying and serving these children in other venues, such as health care institutions, must be developed.

RECOMMENDATION 4

- CPS [Child Protective Services] and domestic violence service organizations must develop clear protocols for intervening with families in which both domestic violence and child maltreatment are present, offering services that provide safety and stability to the child, support to the battered woman, and treatment and sanctions for the batterer.

RECOMMENDATION 5

- Professionals who have regular contact with families and children, including teachers and child care workers, health and mental health care providers, law enforcement officers, child welfare workers, and court personnel, should receive ongoing training on domestic violence and its impact on children.

RECOMMENDATION 6

- Courts must be empowered to design and enforce protective orders that comprehensively address the safety needs of battered women and their children. All battered women must have access to affordable legal counsel, so that they can utilize available legal means to protect themselves and their children.

RECOMMENDATION 7

- In child custody and visitation cases involving domestic violence, courts should consider in their analysis of the best interests of the child the potential impact on the child of ongoing exposure to parental conflict and violence.

RECOMMENDATION 8

- In designing new laws to address the effects of childhood exposure to domestic violence, policymakers should assess the potential unintended negative consequences of these laws and weigh them against the benefits.

RECOMMENDATION 9

- Increased and ongoing public support is needed to develop effective prevention programs that address the underlying causes of domestic violence.

* * *

CHAPTER SIX

THE CHILD WELFARE SYSTEM AND CRIMINAL PROSECUTIONS FOR FAILURE TO PROTECT

A. INTRODUCTION

This poem, written by a young client of the Children's Safety Project in New York, is reprinted in Bonnie Rabin, *Violence Against Mothers Equals Violence Against Children: Understanding the Connections,* 58 ALBANY L. REV. 1109, 1109–10 (1995).

I am 17 years old
I live in a group home
I've been here for 3 years
My step-father used to beat up my mother
And he used to rape me
He didn't touch my little brothers
But he made them feel like shit
Calling them faggots assholes and shitheads
One night he beat my mother real bad
She was laying on the floor all curled up
She couldn't stop crying
She said "God give me the strength to leave him"
That's when I broke
I couldn't hold it no more
I told her he been raping me since I was 12
We both cried and screamed
She slept with me that night
He came home drunk but he left us alone
Next day she told me to tell the counselor at school
It got reported
BCW[1] told my mother she got to take us and leave
She said "How my going to do that I got nothing"
They took my brothers and me
They left my mother with him
They said my mother knew or should have

1. The Bureau of Child Welfare.

They said she was neglectful
She needed a lawyer they was charging her
We went to court so many times
Two of them she had a black eye
Nobody said nothing about that
They sent my brothers back home
Everybody acts like I'm the problem
Nobody did nothing to help my mother
It became them against me
Should have been us against him
I know in my heart
Give my mother a place to be with her kids
She would leave him for good
Tell them that

NOTE

1. The villain of this piece is the Bureau of Child Welfare, New York's child welfare agency. "It became them against me," says the poem's author, referring to the agency's decision to separate her from her family, and place her in a group home, where she has lived from the age of 14 to the age of 17. When she says, "Should have been us against him," she expresses her conviction that what the agency *should* have done was to set limits with the father who sexually abused her, physically abused her mother, and emotionally abused her brothers, and protect the rest of the family from him. As the story ends, her mother and brothers are still vulnerable to the father's abuse, and she is deprived of her mother's support, and her relationships with her brothers.

How did things go wrong? As the author describes it, the involvement of the child welfare agency was prompted by a report from a teacher—to whom the author revealed the abuse. The teacher would have had no choice in the matter; teachers are commonly mandated to report child abuse that comes to their attention. The Bureau of Child Welfare reacted by giving the mother a Hobson's choice—if she did not leave the father, taking the children with her, they would hold her responsible for the abuse. There was apparently no helpful response to her question: "How my going to do that I got nothing?" Nor was there any consideration, apparently, of a different strategy—that the mother should stay put, while the father was required to leave. The mother was then charged with neglect, and the children taken away. Indeed, having decided that the children were at risk, and having failed to provide the mother with either an alternative place to take them, or a way of keeping the father away from them, the agency was in a sense forced to bring charges—to provide a legal basis for the removal. In the subsequent legal proceedings, the focus remained stubbornly on the child who had been abused; no one is looking at the mother's black eyes, or asking whether the child could be protected by first protecting the mother.

Why did things happen this way—and is this a typical or an aberrational story? Unfortunately, the answer to the second question is that the story is a common one, for reasons that these materials attempt to illuminate. The opening section lays out, in very summary form, the workings of the child welfare system. The next section focuses on the legal standards, and the assumptions and misunderstandings that dictate their often punitive application to abused mothers of abused children. The final section looks at the historical tensions between child welfare workers and the domestic violence advocacy community, and at some recent evidence that those tensions are breaking down, and new collaborations, designed to protect both mothers and children, taking root.

B. The Workings of the Child Welfare System

Richard J. Gelles and Ira Schwartz Children and the Child Welfare System, 2 U. of Pennsylvania Journal of Constitutional Law 95, 96–99 (1999)

American law and tradition grant to parents broad discretion in how they may rear their children. In Smith v. Organization of Foster Families for Equality and Reform,[1] the Supreme Court held that the Fourteenth Amendment gave biological parents a "constitutionally recognized liberty interest" in maintaining the custody of their children "that derives from blood relationship, state law sanction, and basic human right." This interest is not absolute, however, because parens patriae duties give the state power and authority to protect citizens who cannot fend for themselves.

The state may attempt to limit or end parent-child contact and make children eligible for temporary or permanent placement or adoption when the parents: (1) abuse, neglect or abandon their children, (2) become incapacitated in their ability to be a parent, (3) refuse or are unable to remedy serious, identified problems in caring for their children, or (4) experience an extraordinarily severe breakdown in their relationship with their children (for example, breakdowns caused by a long prison sentence). Cognizant that severing the parent-child relationship is an extremely drastic measure, the Court held in Santosky v. Kramer[2] that parental rights may only be terminated if the state can demonstrate by clear and convincing evidence that a parent has failed in one of these four ways. Most state statutes also contain provisions for parents to voluntarily relinquish their rights. The state also has the authority to return a child to his or her parents. Ideally, a reunification occurs once a determination is made that it would be safe to return the child home and the child's parents would be able to provide appropriate care.

1. 431 U.S. 816 (1977).

2. 455 U.S. 745 (1982).

The family or juvenile court is involved in each step of this process. Child welfare agencies are responsible for investigating and managing cases of child maltreatment. However, the court is responsible for making the final decisions about whether children are removed from or returned to their parents, where children are to be placed, or whether to terminate parental rights and adoptions.

... Child protection is bolstered by the state's ability to seek ex parte orders or stipulations that allow a child to be removed from what is deemed an unsafe caretaking environment. State laws also allow hospitals to place "holds" of various lengths on children in order to protect the children and allow for an investigation into the children's care situations.

Ex parte orders and "holds" are short-term efforts designed to protect children. Generally, if upon conducting a medical evaluation or child protective evaluation the state concludes that a child is at risk and should be removed from the caregiving environment, the matter is placed before a juvenile or family court judge or master for a hearing. The hearing proceeds in a typical adversary style.

Before examining a child's rights and representation in a child welfare legal action, it is important to look at the institutional and cultural context of the child welfare system. For at least the last 100 years, private and public social welfare institutions and agencies—not the criminal justice system—have responded to the abuse and neglect of children....

... Despite the fact that some acts of child abuse are clearly acts of felony assault and violate criminal codes, the criminal justice system, from the police, to prosecutors, to criminal courts, are rarely directly involved in such cases (with child homicide and child sexual abuse as exceptions to this pattern).

Because social welfare institutions have authority over child welfare cases, the legal cases do not result in a true adversary proceeding pitting the state against the offenders, as would result, for example, in a case of domestic violence. Rather, the legal proceedings involve a state's, county's, or municipality's department of child welfare versus the parents or caretakers of the alleged victim.

The cultural context that led to the creation of this system and its continued support revolves around the constitutional imperative that parents should be free from undue interference in raising their children. In addition, deep cultural convictions, values and ideologies support child maltreatment as a child welfare, and not a criminal justice, issue.

* * *

NOTES

1. While this description of the child welfare system remains largely accurate, the claim that the criminal justice system is rarely involved in cases of child abuse should be treated with a little caution, particularly in the context of domestic violence. As the next section of this chapter makes

clear, there are many cases in which abused mothers of abused children are charged criminally with failure to protect their children from abuse, even in circumstances where we might hesitate to assign blame, either because the mother did in fact attempt to safeguard her children, albeit ineffectually, or because it seems unlikely that further efforts would have done anything but put her children or herself in greater danger. One commentator notes that in New York, criminal cases against parents not just for abuse but also for neglect of their children are on the rise:

> There is a growing sentiment that the police have actually expanded the "must arrest" policy used in domestic violence cases to child welfare matters as well. Regardless of whether this sentiment is true, the criminal court system has seen more cases of child neglect in recent years than it has in the past. Statistics show that while arrests for acts constituting criminal child endangerment have nearly tripled in the last eight years, the number of petitions filed in family court for neglect have not similarly increased but have instead decreased. This outcome may indicate that the increased number of arrests are not due to increased neglectful behavior, but rather increased enforcement of the criminal statute and police arrests.

Alison B. Vreeland, *The Criminalization of Child Welfare in New York City: Sparing the Child or Spoiling the Family?* 27 FORDHAM URB. L.J. 1053, 1061 (2000). For more discussion of the criminal justice system's involvement, see Section E, below.

2. Gelles and Schwartz emphasize the system's deference to the constitutional imperative that parents be free to raise their children without undue interference by the state, and charge the child welfare system with sacrificing the interests of children to that imperative. Others have leveled a different criticism, suggesting that the state accords deference to the privacy of some families, but not all; and that poor families, families of color, and female-headed households are the most likely to suffer both the intrusions of the state, and the imposition of values and norms insensitive to the economic and social realities these families confront:

> The mothers and children "served" by the public, protective system are overwhelmingly poor and disproportionately of color. Poor families are more susceptible to state intervention because they lack power and resources and because they are more directly involved with governmental agencies. For example, the state must have probable cause to enter the homes of most Americans, yet women receiving aid to families with dependent children (AFDC) are not entitled to such privacy. In addition to receiving direct public benefits (like AFDC and Medicaid), poor families lead more public lives than their middle-class counterparts: rather than visiting private doctors, poor families are more likely to attend public clinics and emergency rooms for routine medical care; rather than hiring contractors to fix their homes, poor families encounter public building inspectors; rather than using their cars to run errands, poor mothers use public transportation.
>
> Of course, the vast majority of the parents involved in the child protective system are mothers. Men are rarely brought into court, held

accountable, or viewed as resources for their children. When fathers are involved in the proceedings, they are usually subject to lower expectations and are significantly less likely to be criminally charged with neglect or passive abuse of their children.

Annette R. Appell, *Protecting Children or Punishing Mothers: Gender, Race, and Class in the Child Protection System*, 48 S.C.L. REV. 577, 584–85 (1997).

3. Before looking at some of the cases in which courts have addressed, or failed to address, the overlap between partner and child abuse, one more piece of background will be useful. The following excerpt tracks the actual process by which a child abuse investigation is launched, legal proceedings initiated, and the "case" brought to resolution.

Amy Sinden
"Why Won't Mom Cooperate?": A Critique of Informality in Child Welfare Proceedings, 11 Yale Journal of Law and Feminism 339, 344–50 (1999)

The Anatomy of a Child Welfare Case

. . . [S]tate agencies typically employ hundreds of social workers to investigate reports of suspected child abuse and neglect and work with families when such reports are substantiated. These agency social workers usually serve as case managers, contracting with other private non-profit agencies to provide particular services, such as intensive social work or foster care.

The typical case proceeds as follows. First, a hotline administered by the child welfare agency receives an anonymous report of suspected child abuse or neglect. The agency then assigns a social worker to investigate the report. The social worker begins by knocking on the family's door and attempting to interview the parent and other adults that live in the household, as well as the child who is the subject of the report. If the child attends school, the social worker may go to the school to interview her. Depending on the nature of the allegations, the social worker may also talk to school personnel, medical providers, neighbors or others who may have relevant information.

Based on her investigation, the social worker then makes one of several decisions. She may determine that the alleged abuse or neglect did not occur and close the case. Or she may determine that it did occur but did not sufficiently endanger the child to warrant removing the child from the home. In that case she will usually seek to have the family placed under agency supervision to provide those social services she thinks will help to alleviate the problem she has identified. Or, if she determines that some one in the home has perpetrated abuse or neglect sufficient to endanger the safety of the child, she may seek to have the child removed from the family and placed in foster care.

Under any of these scenarios, the social worker can seek court intervention at various stages of the case if the parent does not accede voluntarily to the social worker's plan. If, when the social worker first knocks on the family's door, the parent refuses to let her in, refuses to talk to her, or refuses to allow her to talk privately with the child, the social worker may ask the agency's attorneys to file a petition seeking a court order compelling the parent to cooperate with the investigation. If the social worker completes her investigation and determines that the family needs agency supervision and services but the parent refuses to submit to supervision or cooperate with the provision of services, the social worker may ask the agency's attorneys to file a petition seeking court-ordered supervision of the family.

Finally, if the social worker concludes that the situation warrants the removal of the child from her parents, the social worker will try to accomplish this in one of two ways. First, she will try to convince the parent to sign a voluntary placement agreement. Such an agreement will typically authorize the state to keep the child in foster care for some specified amount of time (30 days to six months), at the expiration of which a court hearing will be scheduled to determine whether the placement should continue. Second, if the parent refuses to consent to placement, the social worker will seek to have the agency's attorneys petition the court to remove the child.

Child welfare agencies will often remove children from their homes on an emergency basis. All states authorize social workers (or in some instances police) to immediately remove children form their homes where they are deemed to be in imminent danger. In some states the social worker must first obtain an ex parte order from a judicial officer, and in others the social worker acts independently in making the initial removal decision. In either case, the court holds a preliminary hearing at which the parents are entitled to appear (often called a "detention" hearing) within a prescribed period of time, generally ranging from three days to six days, but sometimes as long as two weeks. At this hearing, the court addresses only the limited issue whether the evidence warrants holding the child in foster care until a full hearing can be held.

Once in court, and following any preliminary hearing on emergency removal, cases usually proceed in two phases. At the first phase, in some states termed the "adjudicatory" hearing, the court determines whether the allegations of abuse or neglect rise to a level warranting state interference with the parent-child relationship and, if so, whether they are true. If the court finds that the state has made a sufficient showing on these issues, it makes a finding to that effect, in some jurisdictions termed an "adjudication of dependency." If the court makes such a finding, it then moves on to the second phase, usually termed the "dispositional" hearing. At this hearing the court determines where the child should be placed. Choices may include leaving the child in the home with agency supervision and provision of services, placement in foster care, or placement with a relative or friend.

... At the adjudicatory phase, the state must show parental unfitness by proving acts or omissions on the part of the parent that bring the child within the statutory definition of a "dependent" child or a "child in need of assistance." Even at the dispositional stage, after the court has already made a finding of parental unfitness, some states require a stronger showing than the best interests of the child in order to remove a child from her parents.

Following a dispositional hearing, the court reviews the case periodically, often every six months. Except in certain exceptional cases of severe abuse, once a child is placed outside the home, state agencies must make "reasonable efforts" to reunify children with their families in order to receive federal funding for foster care. Accordingly, when a child welfare agency first removes a child, the agency social worker meets with the parent and draws up a plan for reunification of the family. This plan specifies steps the parent needs to take and services the agency needs to provide to meet that goal. Tasks identified for the parent may include completing a parenting course or a program of mental health or drug treatment, or finding a suitable place to live. Services to be provided by the agency may include referrals to or payments for drug or mental health treatment or logistical or financial help finding housing.

If reunification does not occur within a certain period of time, the agency may try to have the child adopted. This requires the agency's lawyers to first petition the court for an order terminating the natural parent's rights. To obtain such an order, the agency must generally prove in court that the parent is unable or unwilling to care for the child presently and in the foreseeable future. With the passage of the Adoption and Safe Families Act of 1997, the pressures on agencies to move quickly toward termination of parental rights once removal has occurred have increased substantially. Under the Act, the agency must file a petition for termination twelve months after placement in most instances. Where the court finds "aggravated circumstances," the agency must move for termination in just 30 days.

State statutes and case law interpreting constitutional due process protections direct trial courts to conduct dependency and termination proceedings at an intermediate level of formality. These proceedings therefore include most of the standard trappings of the traditional adversarial model of dispute resolution. The state must set forth its allegations in a petition and serve it on the parent. Cases are heard by judges. Witnesses testify under oath. A court reporter transcribes the proceedings. Rules of evidence apply, with some exceptions. The parties may be represented by lawyers and may appeal adversarial decisions.

However, parents in dependency and termination proceedings do not receive many of the procedural rights that criminal defendants—even those facing minor charges—enjoy. Thus, as a matter of federal Constitutional law, an indigent parent in a dependency or termination case has no right to appointed counsel. A number of states provide a right to appointed counsel by statute, but even in those states, courts have held that parents have no right to effective assistance of counsel because the right to counsel is not constitutionally mandated. An indigent parent facing termination of parental rights has a right to a free transcript on appeal but she does not have this right in a dependency proceeding. The constitutionally required standard of proof in a termination of parental rights proceeding is the intermediate clear and convincing evidence standard. The civil "preponderance of the evidence" standard governs dependency proceedings in many states. Although termination and dependency cases generally provide the parent an opportunity to confront and cross-examine witnesses (with exceptions for child witnesses), courts in many instances apply relaxed evidentiary rules. For example, many jurisdictions allow social workers' hearsay reports to be admitted into evidence. Courts do not construe the due process rights of parents and children in dependency and termination proceedings to include rights analogous to the criminal prohibition on double jeopardy or the right against self-incrimination contained in the Fifth Amendment. Courts do not require social workers investigating reports of child abuse to comply with the Fourth Amendment's warrant and probable cause requirements before searching a home, and no exclusionary rule limits the admissibility of improperly obtained evidence.

* * *

NOTES

1. Not every call to a child welfare hotline will prompt an investigation. Trained hotline workers have the discretion to screen cases out of the system if they determine that the call is not legitimate—that it is a prank call, or is based on false accusations, or describes behavior that does not meet the state definition of child abuse or neglect.

2. Beginning in 1974, state receipt of federal funding for child protection has depended, under the Child Abuse and Prevention Act, on states mandating the reporting of acts, or failures to act, by parents or caretakers that subject children to physical or emotional harm or the imminent risk of harm. In 1996 CAPTA was amended to allow states to limit mandatory reporting to acts constituting "serious" harm or the risk of "serious" harm. This change was based on concerns that child welfare agencies were expending resources in the investigation of trivial cases, but not many states have in fact changed their standards in response to the amendment. A crucial question, which can only be answered by analysis of each state's legislation, is who qualifies as a mandated reporter. To provide an example, here is Massachusetts General Law Chapter 119 § 51A (1999):

> Any physician, medical intern, hospital personnel engaged in the examination, care or treatment of persons, medical examiner, psychologist, emergency medical technician, dentist, nurse, chiropractor, podiatrist, optometrist, osteopath, public or private school teacher, educational administrator, guidance or family counselor, day care worker or any person paid to care for or work with a child in any public or private facility, or home or program funded by the commonwealth or licensed . . . , which provides day care or residential services to children or which provides the services of child care resource and referral

> agencies, voucher management agencies, family day care systems and child care food programs, probation officer, clerk/magistrate of the district courts, parole officer, social worker, foster parent, firefighter or policeman, office for children licensor, school attendance officer, allied mental health and human services professional as licensed . . . , drug and alcoholism counselor, psychiatrist, and clinical social worker, who, in his professional capacity shall have reasonable cause to believe that a child under the age of eighteen years is suffering physical or emotional injury resulting from abuse inflicted upon him which causes substantial risk of harm to the child's health or welfare including sexual abuse, or from neglect, including malnutrition, or who is determined to be physically dependent upon an addictive drug at birth, shall immediately report such condition to the department by oral communication, and by making a written report within forty-eight hours after such oral communication.

Reports mandated by statute are not anonymous.

3. Another provision of CAPTA is that guardians ad litem (GALs) be made available to all children involved in child protection proceedings. Every state therefore has a statutory framework for at least some form of representation for all court-involved abused and neglected children. However, the guardian ad litem, while required to advocate for the child's best interests, is not bound to represent those interests as the child him- or herself understands them. He or she is not the child's "counsel;" there is no constitutional mandate requiring that children be legally represented in cases of alleged abuse and neglect; and some but not all states require that every court-involved child have a volunteer court-appointed special advocate (CASA) to represent the child's interests. In practice, therefore, dependency and termination cases can proceed with neither the parent nor the child being represented by a lawyer or advocate, while the state's lawyers argue the case on behalf of the child welfare agency.

C. How the System Works Against Battered Women

In Re Glenn G.

1154 Misc. 2d 677; 587 N.Y.S. 2d 464.
Family Court, King's County, 1992.

■ Opinion by SARA P. SCHECTER, J.

Respondent parents in the proceeding before the court are charged with sexually abusing their children—Josephine, born in 1985 and now six years of age, and Glenn, born in 1987 and now almost five years old. The definition of sex abuse in Family Court Act § 1012 (e)(iii) is cross-referenced to sections of the Penal Law. Specifically, in the instant case, father is charged with having improperly touched the genitals and rectums of both children, conduct which would constitute sexual abuse in the third degree, a violation of Penal Law § 130.55. Respondent mother is charged with having allowed the abuse, in that the acts occurred in her presence and she failed to protect the children. In addition, both respondents are charged with sexually abusing the children by having taken pornographic photographs of the children, a violation of Penal Law § 263.05, "Use of a child in a sexual performance." In the alternative, it is alleged that the children are neglected in that the foregoing conduct constitutes improper supervision of the children by the respondents.

This case came to the attention of the authorities on April 12, 1991 when the respondent mother went to the 68th Police Precinct to seek assistance after an incident of domestic violence. There she was referred to a worker with the Victim Services Agency, Barbara Anselmo. Ms. Anselmo testified that upon arrival respondent mother was pale, shaking, crying and incoherent. After about an hour, respondent mother became calm enough to speak and, in the ensuing discussion, asked if it was normal for a father to grab his children in the groin area, dance naked with them and take photos of them naked. Ms. Anselmo said, "No." After further discussion respondent mother was relocated to a battered women's shelter. The children were medically examined at Bellevue Hospital on April 19, 1991, following which a report of suspected child abuse or maltreatment (hereinafter 2221) was called in by the Bellevue social worker. The Child Welfare Administration (hereinafter CWA) was already involved, however, as a result of two 2221's it had received on April 18, 1991, relaying allegations made by the father against the mother. Upon investigation those allegations proved to be unfounded.

The CWA caseworker, Edris Juandoo, interviewed the respondent mother and the children on April 22, 1991. Josephine told the caseworker that the father plays with her and touches her in the "tushie and in the front, in the hole." Respondent mother recounted to the caseworker the same sort of touching she had described to Ms. Anselmo, and she told the caseworker that when she confronted the father about it, he threatened to kill her. . . .

. . . One photograph produced by both respondent parents depicts Glenn, who appears to be between three and four years old, lying on his back on a couch, clad in a shirt and pants. In this photo the child's underwear and jeans are pulled down to his knees, exposing him from waist to mid-thighs. He has an erection, which is conspicuous due to the angle of the photograph.

. . . The court further finds that respondent father took the lewd photograph. The child Josephine spontaneously told Dr. April Kuchuk, a psychologist who interviewed the child at Bellevue Hospital, that her father would take pictures of her and her brother with their clothes off, and specifically stated that her mother did not. Furthermore, the taking of this photo is consistent with the respondent father's over-all approach to the children as sex objects, which will be discussed further below. Accordingly, the court finds the child Glenn to have been sexually abused by the respondent father by reason of the father's having used him in a sexual performance. . . .

On the basis of the respondent mother's testimony and Josephine's out-of-court statements, which were amply corroborated by the physical findings of Dr. McHugh and the psychological findings of Dr. Kuchuk, the court finds that the respondent father sexually abused both children by touching their intimate parts for the purpose of his sexual gratification.

THE RESPONDENT MOTHER'S CULPABILITY

Respondent mother is charged with sexual abuse, and, in the alternative, neglect, based on her failure to protect the children from the father's conduct described above. She asserts as a defense that she was a battered woman during the period when the abuse was occurring and asks that the charges against herself be dismissed. CWA and the Law Guardian argue that whether the mother was a battered woman is irrelevant, since they contend that the Family Court Act child protective article is a strict liability statute. The respondent father disputes that the mother was battered. He seeks to portray her as a prime perpetrator of the child abuse, a conclusion the court rejected for the reasons already stated.

The analysis of respondent mother's defense must commence with a preliminary review of the legal responsibility of the passive parent of a child who has been sexually abused. The passive parent is guilty of child abuse when she "allows" the abuse to be inflicted. . . . Petitioner and the Law Guardian urge this court to adopt an objective standard for the conduct of the passive parent, by which the passive parent would be held to have "allowed" the abuse if she failed to act as a reasonable and prudent parent would have acted to protect the child. . . . This argument fails to distinguish between a finding of abuse and one of neglect, however, and in several of the cases cited by petitioner and the Law Guardian in support of their strict liability argument the passive parent was actually found to have neglected rather than abused the child. . . .

In a recent case which addresses the distinction between abuse and neglect it was held that when the passive parent is merely careless or negligent and inattentive, and by her failure to exercise a minimum degree of care leaves the child unprotected from the abusive parent, her conduct constitutes child neglect. . . . "Neglect," as defined by Family Court Act § 1012 (f)(i)(B) encompasses conduct which is not deliberate. Indeed, the definition of neglect includes failure to provide minimally adequate care due to the parent's mental illness or retardation, conditions for which the parent is entirely without fault. . . .

The conduct of the passive parent of a sexually abused child may range across a wide spectrum. At one extreme is the parent who actually instigates the abuse or encourages the abuser; at the other extreme is the parent who has failed to notice nonspecific symptoms in the child such as frequent rashes or recurrent urinary tract infections. In between lie countless scenarios—a child who tries to confide in the passive parent and is rebuffed, a child who does confide and is disbelieved—through endless permutations of secrecy and deception. To label such variegated behavior as monolithic "abuse" would be arbitrary and insensitive and, in many instances, would needlessly stigmatize the passive parent without providing any greater protective or dispositional alternatives than would be available upon a finding of neglect. Instead, in determining where on the abuse-neglect spectrum the liability of a particular respondent lies, the court should use two coordinates: the passive parent's knowledge or awareness of the actions of the abusive parent, and second, the passive parent's actual ability to intervene to protect the child.

The first is not in dispute in the instant case.... The issue of her ability to protect the children, however, is heavily contested. Unlike the issue of a passive parent's degree of knowledge, which has been extensively litigated, the question of the parent's ability to protect has received little judicial attention. In the case at bar, respondent mother does not claim that she was afflicted with a mental illness or physical disability which rendered her unable to protect the children. Rather, she asserts that she was unable to take appropriate action because she was suffering from "Battered Woman's Syndrome."

Respondent mother established by convincing evidence that during her relationship with respondent father she was a battered woman. She testified to an escalating pattern of abuse, which began soon after the couple began living together. In the early days the abuse consisted primarily of constant verbal abuse.... Even more upsetting than the insults and invective were what Mrs. G. called "mind games," in which Mr. G. convinced Mrs G. that he spied on her at work and actually supplied details of what she had done during the day to prove that he was having her watched. He also treated her as his personal slave....

After the birth of their first child, Mr. G. became more menacing.... The first instance of actual physical abuse occurred when Mrs. G. returned from ... an errand and found Mr. G. inappropriately touching Josephine. When she grabbed the baby away and began to yell at the father, he hit her in the mouth, causing her lip to bleed. At that point Mrs. G. realized that she should get away, and within a few weeks, in May 1987, she took Josephine and went to the home of her sister in Florida.

While in Florida she gave birth to the second child, Glenn. Mr. G., who had located the mother by phoning around to hospitals in the area ..., arrived at the mother's bedside the day after Glenn's birth. He was tearful and apologetic, said he knew the problems were his fault and that he was getting counseling. After the mother returned to her sister's house, he kept up such a campaign of telephonic harassment that the mother finally felt she was imposing on her sister. Mr. G. sent a ticket, and Mrs. G. and the children returned to New York around the end of June 1987.

Following the return to New York, the domestic situation worsened. Mrs. G. learned that Mr. G. was not in therapy and neither did he plan to be. The physical abuse became more frequent and more intense....

In November of 1990 Mrs. G. sought medical treatment in the emergency room of St. Vincent's Medical Center of Richmond for headaches, blurred vision and black lines in her left eye sustained as a result of an assault by Mr. G. Although St. Vincent's responded appropriately by giving

Mrs. G. a referral to the Victim Services Agency, she signed herself out against medical advice and failed to follow through on the referral.

Respondent mother's efforts to protect herself and the children after her return from Florida were meager. She began to call 911 once, but did not give the operator her address. She confided in her mother-in-law, who said she should just endure her situation and that Mr. G.'s father had been the same way. She stayed for days at a time at her mother-in-law's home with the children. She mentioned Josephine's frequent vaginal rashes to the pediatrician, but did not tell him of any sex abuse. She attempted to intervene when Mr. G. was behaving inappropriately with the children, but he told her, "Butt out, that's how you get hurt so much."

Respondent mother's testimony concerning Mr. G.'s abuse of her was totally credible, while Mr. G.'s denials were unworthy of belief.... The original attorney for respondent mother, the original Law Guardian, two former attorneys for respondent father and the Judge to whom this matter was originally assigned all withdrew from the case after conduct by Mr. G. which they perceived as threatening....

Respondent mother produced two expert witnesses who testified about the condition known as "Battered Woman's Syndrome." Ms. Anselmo, qualified as an expert by virtue of her experience, described the syndrome as "a breaking down of a woman's self confidence and self respect to the point where she no longer knows if she is crazy or not." She stated typically the cycle begins with psychological abuse, as it did with the Gs., builds to extreme tension followed by a violent episode, and then a "honeymoon period," in which the batterer apologizes, promises to do better and begs the woman not to leave. Mr. G.'s behavior when he found Mrs. G. in Florida is typical of the contrite phase. Over time the honeymoons get shorter and the violent periods expand. The battered woman experiences a sense of isolation, and often is socially isolated and confined to the home, which was true in Mrs. G.'s case. As the syndrome progresses, the woman loses confidence in her judgment, as Mrs. G. did, and starts to believe that she must be the one who is crazy. Based on her observations of Mrs. G. in the police station and in the days immediately following, Ms. Anselmo testified that in her opinion Mrs. G. had been a battered woman for a long period of time.

The second expert on the subject was Valerie Bryant, a certified social worker and doctoral candidate at New York University who has for six years run a therapy group for battered women....

Ms. Bryant ... stated her opinion that the role of the mother-in-law in urging Mrs. G. to "bear with it" was very instrumental in undermining respondent mother's sense of self-worth and in reinforcing her sense of helplessness, particularly because she was estranged from her own family. Mrs. G., therefore, came to see herself as having few options. She lost the ability to protect herself, and thus lost the ability to protect the children as well. Ms. Bryant also noted that Mrs. G.'s dilemma is not uncommon, as a correlation between spousal abuse and child abuse is generally recognized among professionals who work with battered women and that in her opinion the two forms of abuse share very similar psychodynamics.

Several State and Federal courts have admitted evidence concerning Battered Woman's Syndrome. Most often such evidence has been offered in support of some form of self-defense claim by a woman who assaulted or killed the man who had been battering her. Occasionally it has been used to establish a lack of criminal intent (mens rea) or to assist the jury in assessing the credibility of the battered woman's testimony, as when, for example, she may have recanted her charges against the abusive man. Although accounts have appeared from time to time in the news media of a "Battered Women's Syndrome defense" being offered in cases where a mother has been criminally charged for having failed to protect her children from an abusive father or live-in lover, these cases do not appear to have resulted in reported judicial decisions.

Although no New York decisions have been reported in which respondent asserted the Battered Woman's Syndrome defense in the context of a child protective case, there are a few such decisions from other States. The Supreme Court of Appeals in West Virginia ruled in Interest of Betty J.W. (179 W.Va. 605, 371 S.E. 2d 326 [1988]) that it was error to terminate the parental rights of a mother who had failed to protect her children from physical and sexual abuse by their father....

The court is in accord with those who have recognized that Battered Woman's Syndrome is a condition which seriously impairs the will and the judgment of the victim. The abused should not be branded as abuser. Respondent mother in the case at bar clearly did not condone the sexual abuse of the children by the respondent father, but rather, due to her affliction with Battered Woman's Syndrome, was powerless to stop it. She cannot be said to have "allowed" the abuse within the meaning of Family Court Act § 1012 (e)(iii). Accordingly, the child abuse charges against the respondent mother are dismissed. The neglect statute, however, imposes strict liability. As respondent mother's actions were manifestly inadequate to protect the children from the father's ongoing abuse, of which she was well aware, a finding of neglect must be entered against her.

NOTES AND QUESTIONS

1. The court's willingness to hear expert testimony with respect to "Battered Woman's Syndrome," and its conclusion that Mrs. G. had not "allowed" the sexual abuse of her children, and was therefore not herself guilty of child abuse, demonstrates both understanding of, and sympathy for, the battered wife and mother's situation. The CWA and the children's Law Guardian argued both that the abuse statute should be understood as creating strict liability, and that it should be read as imposing an "objective" standard; the failure to act as a reasonable and prudent parent would have acted to protect the child from abuse. Does that mean that the court, in exonerating Mrs. G. of the charge of abuse, is using a "subjective" standard? Or only that the court is applying, in the context of the abuse statute, an objective standard modified to reflect the realities of life for a mother living in a battering relationship and suffering from Battered Woman's Syndrome? Has the court, in other words, created a "reasonable

battered woman" or "reasonable battered mother" standard for use in interpreting the abuse statute?

2. If that is the case, then the next question is why the same strategy is not available in considering the charge of neglect. Here the court is quite clear that the standard is one of strict liability, and indeed, if parents who are unable to protect their children from harm because of mental illness or retardation can still be liable for neglect, it becomes hard to argue that Mrs. G. cannot. Under the strict liability standard, the statement "Mrs. G. neglected to protect her children" means nothing more than "Mrs. G. did not prevent her children from being abused." It would be possible to argue that, interpreted in this light, a finding of neglect carries no moral judgment—it is just a statement of fact. We do not usually understand neglect in this way, of course, since our legal system overwhelmingly equates negligence with unreasonableness and fault.

What makes this territory so tricky is that there is a justification for imposing strict liability in the context of the child welfare system. If our goal is to protect children, why should we care whether a parent was or was not at fault in exposing them to risk? We want steps taken to eliminate that risk; at a minimum we want services made available to the family, and if that will not ensure the child's safety, we are willing to contemplate the possibility that the child (or possibly one of the parents) should be removed. As long as we are not adjudicating criminal liability, where a strict liability standard would be considerably more problematic, why should we resist a finding of neglect if it will provide a basis for protecting a child?

One answer to that question is of course that findings of neglect, even under a strict liability standard, do still carry overtones of blame. The tendency to blame is strongly evident in child welfare investigations and adjudications, where child welfare workers and judges routinely condemn mothers for failing to save their children from abuse, not understanding or crediting the supreme difficulty of that task when the mother herself is a victim of abuse, well understands the dangers posed by her abuser, and may have experienced an increase rather than a decrease in the violence directed at both her and the children when she has tried to intervene. One of the reasons to resist findings of neglect in these circumstances, that is to say, is to combat the woman-blaming attitudes that accompany them. One commentator who has argued strongly for a "reasonable battered mother" standard in child protective proceedings is G. Kristian Miccio, in *A Reasonable Battered Mother? Redefining, Reconstructing, and Recreating the Battered Mother in Child Protective Proceedings*, 22 HARV. WMN'S L.J. 89 (1999).

Another part of the answer is the fear that a finding of neglect will lead, ultimately, to a termination of parental rights, so that a loving parent with much to offer a child will be permanently written out of that child's life, for no better reason than that the mother has not been able to keep the child safe from another's abuse. Surely this is the moment to ask who else might have helped to keep both mother and child safe, and whether we would be better off laying blame at the door of others with more resources to bring to the task of controlling the abuser's behavior. This is an issue brought to the fore by the next case excerpted below.

Is there a compromise? Can we, that is to say, invoke the system on the child's behalf without finding that the mother has either abused or neglected her child? In cases in which the abuser is also the father of the child, or a legal guardian, the answer would appear to be "yes," since the culpable party is also one against which the child welfare system has authority to proceed. In the not uncommon situation in which the abusive man is the mother's partner, but not otherwise related to or responsible for the children, the answer may be "no," since although he may be criminally liable, he is not within the jurisdiction of the child welfare authorities. A recent article offers the following thoughts on this situation:

> ... In most states, the jurisdiction of the juvenile court in child maltreatment cases is limited to those situations in which the child's parent or legal guardian has created, or failed to protect the child from, the conditions deemed by the court to be harmful to the child. Thus, in most states, the juvenile court, and thus CPS, cannot intervene in direct response to the conduct of an adult who is not the child's parent or guardian, even when the adult has regular contact with the child because of a close personal relationship with the child's parent. In situations in which such an individual is perpetrating the violence, substantiating the case by charging the nonabusive parent with failure to protect becomes the only way to obtain dependency jurisdiction over the child. Fortunately, state policies are beginning to change to address this problem. Michigan law, for example, now allows the juvenile court to assert jurisdiction and authorize CPS intervention in cases involving non-parent adults, whether or not such adults reside in the same household as the child. However, CPS has relied on the possibility of a child being removed for encouraging changes in adult behavior so that the risk of harm to the child is reduced. A violent adult who is not a custodial or biological parent may not care enough about the possible loss of the child to change his behavior. Ultimately, the CPS worker may have no choice but to use the failure-to-protect argument, if intervention is necessary to protect the child. But it should be a last resort. In situations in which the battered mother is not abusing the children, perpetrators of domestic violence should be held responsible for the violence in the household.

Janet E. Findlater and Susan Kelly, *Child Protective Services and Domestic Violence,* 9 THE FUTURE OF CHILDREN 84, 86 (1999). What do you make of the argument that even when charges could be brought directly against the abuser, the threat of removing the children from the mother may provide her with the necessary impetus for changing her situation. What strategies would you recommend CPS try, before using this strategy of last resort?

3. As child welfare agencies and courts become aware of the evidence that exposing a child to violence between parents or parent figures is itself damaging, even when the child is not physically or sexually abused, there is an increasing tendency to charge both the abusive and the nonabusive parent with neglect for allowing that exposure. While recognizing the potential injury of exposure is an important step toward safeguarding children from the consequences of domestic violence, those who work with

battered women fear that it will increase the number of cases in which women who are not themselves abusive, and even women who have managed to shield their children from physical and sexual abuse, but not from witnessing violence, will be charged with neglect, and separated from their children, temporarily or even permanently. In New York City, for example, a 1998 state court decision declared that incidents of domestic violence in the presence of a child are sufficient grounds for a charge of neglect, and the city is authorized to take children into foster care if a parent is believed to "engage in acts of domestic violence." New York Times, A1, July 8, 2000.

4. The next case involves a mother who successfully appealed the termination of her parental rights; the West Virginia case mentioned by the court in *In Re Glenn G.* The disposition of the case in the lower court illustrates the potentially devastating consequences of holding a nonabusive parent liable for a child's mistreatment by the other parent. The Supreme Court's decision, on the other hand, balances concern for the safety of the child with empathy for the plight of the mother, and respect for the mother's efforts to protect her child, despite the fact that they were insufficient to prevent the child from being abused by her father.

In re Betty J.W.

179 W.Va. 605; 371 S.E. 2d 326.
Supreme Court of Appeals of West Virginia, 1988.

Mary W. appeals from a final order ... which terminated her parental rights to her five minor children. She first assigns as error the legal insufficiency of the child abuse petition. She also contends the trial court erred in denying a statutory improvement period, in failing to adopt the least restrictive alternative appropriate to the circumstances, and in relying on her status as a victim of domestic violence as a basis for the termination of parental rights.

I. Mary W. and her husband, J.B.W., are the natural parents of five minor children, the youngest of whom is now ten years old. On June 3, 1985, the West Virginia Department of Human Services (DHS) took emergency custody of the children. In a petition to terminate parental rights filed on June 4, 1985, the DHS alleged that on April 30, 1985, the husband, J.B.W., sexually abused and assaulted his then seventeen-year-old daughter, B.J. The petition alleged that since the sexual assault, J.B.W. had been out of the marital home until June 1, 1985, when he again stayed overnight. The DHS also alleged that J.B.W. habitually physically abused his children and that Mary W. failed to protect the children from her husband's abuse.[1]

1. W. Va. Code 49-1-3(a) (1984) provides:

" 'Abused child' means a child whose health or welfare is harmed or threatened by: (1) a parent, guardian or custodian who knowingly inflicts, attempts to inflict, or knowingly allows another person to inflict, physical injury, or substantial mental or emotional injury, upon the child or another child in the home."

A hearing on the petition was held on June 10, 1985, at which all parties appeared except J.B.W., who was then a patient in St. Mary's Hospital. The court appointed a guardian ad litem for J.B.W. and a guardian ad litem for the five children. Testimony was taken, but no record was made of the proceedings. In an order entered August 1, 1985, the court denied motions for an improvement period, found no less drastic alternative than the removal of the children, ordered physical and legal custody to be placed with DHS, and scheduled a final hearing.

On September 17, 1985, at the final hearing, all parties appeared and were represented by counsel. J.B.W. and Mary W. individually requested improvement periods which the court denied. At the conclusion of the hearing, the court recited facts to be part of the final written order, which was entered on November 22, 1985. The trial court found that J.B.W. had abused his children, that Mary W. had failed to protect them, that no reasonable likelihood existed that the conditions of neglect and abuse could be substantially corrected, and that Mary W. and J.B.W. had refused and were unwilling to cooperate in the development of a plan to effectuate necessary changes. On that basis, the court concluded that there was no less drastic alternative than to terminate the parental rights of J.B.W. and Mary W.

. . .

III. Mary W . . . contends that she was unlawfully denied a statutory improvement period under W. Va. Code 49–6–2(b) (1984), before her parental rights were terminated.[2] . . .

While parents enjoy an inherent right to the care and custody of their own children, the State in its recognized role of parens patriae is the ultimate protector of the rights of minors. . . . This parens patriae interest . . . favors preservation, not severance, of natural family bonds, a proposition that is echoed in our child welfare statute. . . . The countervailing State interest in curtailing child abuse is also great. . . .

The dual nature of the State's interest is evidenced by the statute which permits a parent to move the court for an improvement period when abuse or neglect is alleged. The court must allow the improvement period unless "compelling circumstances" justify a denial. . . .

This is the thrust of Mary W.'s claim. She moved for an improvement period at the June 10, 1985 preliminary hearing. The trial court found the alleged history of abuse by her husband, J.B.W., to be a compelling circumstance justifying the denial of an improvement period. At the final

2. The text of W.Va. Code 49–6–2(b) (1984) is:

> In any proceeding under this article, the parents or custodians may, prior to final hearing, move to be allowed an improvement period of three to twelve months in order to remedy the circumstances or alleged circumstances upon which the proceeding is based. The court shall allow one such improvement period unless it finds compelling circumstances to justify a denial thereof, but may require temporary custody in the state department or other agency during the improvement period. An order granting such improvement period shall require the department to prepare and submit to the court a family case plan. . . .

hearing, Mary W. renewed her motion. The trial court again denied the improvement period, stating that to return the children to the mother, who had continued contact with the father, "would put these children at great risk again."

It appears that the trial court believed that its only option in granting an initial improvement period was to return the children to Mary W. Nothing in the record indicates the trial court gave any consideration to the possibility of granting Mary W. an improvement period without custody of the children. As previously observed, W. Va. Code 49–6–2(b) (1984) expressly permits a circuit court to grant an improvement period with temporary custody with the DHS or other appropriate agency. . . .

. . .

The failure to consider an improvement period for Mary W. was due in large part because the trial court found that she "knowingly allowed" the sexual abuse. . . .

We do not believe the record supports the trial court's legal conclusion that Mary W. "knowingly allow[ed]" the sexual abuse. Courts in other states with similar child abuse statutes, which contain a "knowingly allows" type provision, have focused on whether the parent in some sense condoned the abuse. Termination of parental rights is usually upheld only where the parent takes no action in the face of knowledge of the abuse or actually aids or protects the abusing parent. Typical is *In Interest of A.M.K.*, . . . where a mother admitted knowing that her husband had sexually abused their children. The court terminated the mother's parental rights saying "there is no evidence that the appellant attempted to make a hot-line report or to have her husband charged with child abuse." . . .

Similarly, where the mother admitted to various people that she had observed sexual abuse and had condoned it with a statement that her daughter needed to be taught about "such things" before she started dating, the court terminated the mother's parental rights for her omission to act. . . .

This case is analogous to Shapley v. Tex. Dept. of Human Resources . . ., in which the appellate court reversed the termination of a mother's parental rights where the father had physically abused their eighteen-month-old child. The mother took the child to a hospital emergency room, reported that her husband was a heavy drinker, and that he had beaten the child the night before and on one other occasion. The mother had delayed reporting the second occurrence until after her husband had gone to work. The Department of Human Resources temporarily removed the child from the home.

Three months later, the father again became intoxicated and abused the mother and the family's pet puppy. She filed suit for divorce. Witnesses who interviewed the mother after the first hearing on the abuse matter believed it unlikely that she would remain separate and apart from her husband and there was danger of future injury to the child by the father. The court held the evidence insufficient to terminate the mother's parental rights saying: "It was only because of the mother's love for her child that the beating was ever called to the attention of the authorities in the first place. Her delay could well have been caused by her own fear of her husband." . . .

Here, the evidence shows that Mary W. did not knowingly allow any sexual abuse. Her daughter told her about the sexual assault the day after it happened. She was unable to get away from her husband that day, but the following day, while her husband was absent, she paid a neighbor to take her and the children to her parents' residence. That same day she reported the abuse to DHS and requested services including a place to stay.[1] The reasons for delay in this case, as in Shapley, centered on an opportunity to get away from an abusive spouse.

There was also testimony that when J.B.W. had attempted to sexually abuse the daughter during the evening hours on the day of the assault, Mary W. had interceded and was beaten and threatened with a knife. Certainly, a parent charged with acts of omission, who takes reasonable steps to protect her child and who does not defend the abuser or condone the abusive conduct, does not "knowingly allow" the abuse.

The trial court also found that Mary W. failed to protect her children by failing to keep J.B.W. away and by not separating from him. Her perceived inability to break from the pattern of abuse was described by the court as classic spouse abuse: "Men who abuse their wives classically follow that pattern and the family follows that pattern. A man beats his wife, makes promises and they kiss and make up, and there is a period psychologists call 'the honeymoon'. At some point following the honeymoon there is a cycle of abuse and the cycle starts all over again." We recognized this syndrome, which we termed "battered woman's syndrome," in State v. Steele, 178 W.Va. 330, 359 S.E. 2d 558 (1987).[2] . . .

The court apparently believed that Mary W. would continue to reconcile with her husband, thereby exposing the children to further abuse by him. However, as we have previously pointed out, an improvement period without custody of the children would have enabled Mary W. to overcome this perceived problem.[3]

The court's decision also rested on the finding that Mary W. would not cooperate in the development of a plan to provide for the safety of her children, which would involve her separating from her husband. The

1. The court found that Mary W. obtained a warrant against her husband for the April 30, 1985 abuse.

2. In Steele, we commented on one phase of the syndrome which was that often "the abused woman in unable to free herself from her situation or report the abuse to the authorities." . . .

3. The trial court appeared to center on the week in which the husband claimed he cohabited at the family home. This was after criminal charges had been initiated for his sexual abuse of his daughter. Mary W. claimed that she was staying with friends and family members, but did return to the home to clean it. The children had been previously removed by court order and placed in temporary custody of DHS. Two neighbors who testified were somewhat equivocal. One said she saw the husband at the house in the early evening hours drinking coffee. She also stated that she was aware that Mary W. was not living there full time. Another neighbor saw both of them walk by her house. She also stated she was informed earlier by Mary W. not to disclose to J.B.W. where she was staying.

difficulty with this conclusion is that it is not borne out in the record. Prior to the child abuse incident, the DHS had not provided any regular services to the family for some two years. There was no showing that an improvement plan had been developed and had not been followed by Mary W. on the current charges.

In fact, the record indicates that Mary W. after reporting the sexual abuse incident the day after it happened to the authorities was left to fend for herself and her family. She sought refuge with relatives. There is no indication in the record that DHS acted ... to bring into play its family protective services to assist Mary W. and her family. We think it inappropriate and erroneous under these circumstances to deny Mary W. an improvement period.

For the foregoing reasons, the judgment of the Circuit Court of Mingo County is reversed, and this case is remanded for further proceedings not inconsistent with this opinion. These proceedings shall include granting an improvement period with an appropriate family case plan.... The court should decide, based on the conditions then existing, whether the children may physically reside with Mary W. during the improvement period, and should ultimately determine whether or not to reunite Mary W. and her children.

Reversed and Remanded with Directions.

NOTES AND QUESTIONS

1. Is the court's definition of child abuse, and the "knowingly allow" language of the West Virginia statute, consistent with the definition used by the New York court in *In Re Glenn G.*?

2. The lower court uses the theory of battered woman's syndrome, and the cycle of abuse, as an argument for terminating Mary W.'s parental rights, without allowing her an improvement period. How would you use the same theory to generate counterarguments?

3. If the lower court was indeed influenced in its decision by the accounts of Mary W. having been seen with her husband at or in the vicinity of their home after he had been charged with sexual assault of their daughter, do you agree that their walking or drinking coffee together was necessarily evidence of reconciliation? What other explanations can you imagine? What questions would you want to ask Mary W. to test those alternative hypotheses?

4. The Supreme Court turns the spotlight from Mary W. to DHS, noting that the agency has done nothing to support her efforts to keep her children safe with her. She has been left to "fend for herself and her family." Kristian Miccio, in her article *In the Name of Mothers and Children: Deconstructing the Myth of the Passive Battered Woman and the "Protected Child" in Child Neglect Proceedings,* 58 Albany L. Rev. 1087 (1995), argues persuasively that the tendency to ignore both women's active efforts to protect their children, and the failures and inaction of other helping systems, is a common one. She describes the case of Cynthia

D., who called the police to intervene in an incident in which she and her seven-year-old son were hurt by her husband; the boy when he tried to intercede. The police told her that while they could arrest the husband, they could not hold him unless she took the initiative in filing criminal charges. They did, however, initiate a child abuse investigation. Cynthia D. then obtained her third protective order against her husband, but when he violated the order and beat her again, the child welfare agency removed the child and brought charges against both parents, "alleging that her failure to stop the abuse and her failure to keep the father out of the home constituted neglect since it placed the child in imminent risk of physical and/or psychological harm." Id. at 1091. Miccio comments:

> The court in this case did not examine how judicial inaction shaped Mr. D.'s attitude and his conduct. There was no analysis of the nexus between systemic failure to protect Cynthia D. and the continuation of the violence. Furthermore, there was no judicial inquiry into how structural inaction (for example, failure to hold Mr. D. in contempt [for violation of the restraining orders]) created Cynthia's "inability" to exit the relationship. The court's ruling thereby obscures the nature of the violence, dismisses Cynthia D.'s attempts to get help, and minimizes the effects of systemic inaction. It is reductionism in its purest form because it distills a complex set of individual and collective interactions into a cultural and inexact stereotype—that of the passive battered woman.

Id. at 1092.

5. If you were charged with crafting a family case plan to govern the improvement period eventually granted to Mary W., what would you put in it? What would be the balance of responsibilities between Mary W. and DHS?

6. Since the passage of the federal Child Abuse and Protection Act in 1974, discussed earlier in this section, the federal government has continued to shape state child welfare policy by conditioning the receipt of federal funding by state programs on compliance with federal guidelines. The 1980 Adoption Assistance and Child Welfare Act, based on a family preservation philosophy, mandated that "reasonable efforts" to preserve the family must be made before a child was removed, even on a temporary basis, and that once a child had been removed further reasonable efforts must be made to reunify the family. In the absence of any federal definition of "reasonable efforts," states were free to develop their own guidelines, and in practice, the amount and quality of services provided to parents were limited by funding and program availability, rather than any thoughtful match between need and service. Critics suggested that "adherence to the 'reasonable efforts' requirement often encouraged states to return children to dangerous homes in their attempts to comply with the law," particularly when meaningful services were simply unavailable. Celeste Pagano, *Recent Legislation: Adoption and Foster Care*, 36 HARV. J. LEGIS. 242 (1999). In 1997, concerned that the effect of the AACWA was to prioritize family preservation at the expense of child safety, and leave too many children, for

too long, in temporary rather than permanent placements, Congress passed the Adoption and Safe Families Act, 42 U.S.C. § 671(a)(15)(A).

ASFA mandates that a child's health and safety must be the primary consideration in determining what efforts to preserve or reunify the family are reasonable. Reasonable efforts are no longer required if the parent has subjected the child to "aggravated circumstances" as those are defined by state law; if the parent has committed or aided in, conspired in, or attempted the commission of murder or voluntary manslaughter of another of the parent's children, or committed a felony assault resulting in serious bodily injury to the child or another child of the parent; or if the parent's rights with respect to a sibling have already been terminated. Furthermore, ASFA mandates that permanency planning begin immediately for children who enter the child welfare system, and that decisions about permanent placement be made in a compressed time frame. Under ASFA, states must schedule a permanency hearing within twelve months of the time a child enters foster care, rather than the previously mandated eighteen months. In addition, states must begin proceedings to terminate the parental rights of parents whose children have been in foster care for fifteen of the last 22 months.

The impact of these new requirements on women whose partners have abused both them and their children remains to be seen, but there is room for concern. If women are charged criminally, and convicted, when they fail to prevent the child abuse perpetrated by their partners, or if their failure to prevent the abuse is viewed as an "aggravated circumstance" under state law, then they may be subject to termination of parental rights without the child welfare agency ever making "reasonable efforts" to preserve their relationships with their children. This is, in effect, what the lower court did to Mary W. when it denied her an improvement period; now ASFA could be read as endorsing that result. In addition, the short time frames imposed by ASFA may be inadequate to provide meaningful services to parents wrestling with problems as complex and intractable as domestic violence. See, e.g., Jane C. Murphy and Margaret J. Potthast, *Domestic Violence, Substance Abuse and Child Welfare: The Legal System's Response*, 3 J. HEALTH CARE L. & POLICY 88, 89 (1999).

D. TRADITIONAL TENSIONS AND NEW COLLABORATIONS

There is no doubt that sensitive and informed judicial decision-making, influenced and guided by equally sensitive and informed advocacy, has a role to play in making the child welfare system more responsive to the needs, and rights, of the battered mothers of children who are themselves abused, or traumatized by witnessing violence in their homes. However, child welfare workers are vested with significant discretion in their daily practice; and only a tiny fraction of that daily practice will ever be subject to judicial oversight. Changes in the system's operation, therefore, will depend much more heavily on education and training than they will on judicial review of agency action. In changing the underlying assumptions and attitudes that guide daily practice, collaboration between those who work with battered women and those who work with children is a promising strategy. Some encouraging evidence that this collaboration is occurring, and some interesting descriptions of the different forms it may take, are contained in this next excerpt.

Janet Findlater and Susan Kelly
Child Protective Services and Domestic Violence, 9 The Future of Children 84, 87–93 (1999)

A Difficult History: Child Protection and Domestic Violence

For years, domestic violence service providers and CPS have worked with families experiencing both forms of abuse, but until recently they had not begun working together to create safe, appropriate, and effective responses to family violence. The relationship between child welfare workers and battered women's advocates has been difficult, at best. Mistrust has been common, noncollaboration the rule.

A significant obstacle to collaboration has been the tension caused by the different historical developments and missions of the domestic violence and child welfare movements.... Some battered women and their advocates viewed CPS as yet another public institution that overlooked domestic violence and the needs of battered women, or blamed battered women for the harm their batterers caused to their children.

The mistrust has existed on both sides. Because of CPS's focus on the safety of the child, caseworkers did not consider the identification of domestic violence to be important to accomplishing CPS goals. When domestic violence was identified, CPS workers have often misunderstood its dynamics and held battered mothers responsible for ending it. Furthermore, as the domestic violence movement has focused primarily on the needs of battered women, and been slower to address the needs of these women's children, CPS workers have not viewed battered women's advocates as potential allies in their efforts to protect children.

Finding Common Ground

An end to the standoff is under way, and long overdue. The reality is that many workers in both CPS and domestic violence are concerned about the safety needs of children and their battered mothers. Domestic violence service programs now seek to provide support and counseling services to the many children who go with their mothers to shelters. State CPS administrators today report that they view addressing domestic violence as important. And many CPS workers report that they develop safety plans that include protection for battered mothers.

The child welfare system and domestic violence programs in several states and local communities have begun to work together to address domestic violence and child maltreatment.... [S]urvey results show, for the most part, only the very beginning stages of cooperation. However, several collaborative strategies currently being implemented ... hold promise for more widespread collaboration in the future.

Emerging Strategies

New strategies for collaborative work between domestic violence service programs and CPS include changes in CPS policies and protocols that reflect the increasing awareness of the importance of addressing domestic violence, and training programs for domestic violence service personnel to bridge the gaps in their understanding of child protection issues. Some of the most promising collaborative efforts make child protection interventions such as family preservation services available to battered mothers and their children, or use domestic violence specialists in child protection agencies, juvenile dependency courts, and pediatric health settings. Other opportunities for greater collaboration include partnerships between community-based child protection programs and local domestic violence programs, and the participation of domestic violence specialists on CPS citizen review boards.

New Policies and Protocols in CPS

The Massachusetts Department of Social Services (DSS) was one of the first child welfare agencies to recognize that the safety of children living in homes where there is domestic violence and the safety of their battered mothers, cannot be separated. CPS workers in Massachusetts are required to screen all families for domestic violence. A protocol was developed in 1992 to serve as a guide to assist workers in investigation, risk assessment, and service planning for cases involving domestic violence. It emphasizes the need for ongoing assessment of the risk posed to children by the presence of domestic violence, and states a preference for protecting children by including mothers in safety planning and in holding domestic violence perpetrators accountable for their actions.

The development of CPS policies with regard to domestic violence centers on two critical issues: (1) whether child witnessing of domestic violence constitutes child abuse or neglect; and (2) whether and when it is appropriate to remove a child from the custody of a battered mother because she has failed to protect her child.

. . .

The Massachusetts DSS is currently revising its intake policy to provide a framework for determining which reports involving domestic violence warrant CPS intervention. The policy will not define child witnessing, in and of itself, as child maltreatment. The effects of domestic violence on the child must meet the existing definitions of child abuse and neglect. Only the most serious cases will be brought into the CPS system. Families needing less intrusive interventions will be referred to community-based services.

. . .

CPS policies that include mandatory, ongoing training for all caseworkers on domestic violence are crucial. This training should include information regarding screening for domestic violence, effective responses once it is identified, the effects of domestic violence on children, legal issues, and community-based services available for referrals.

New Policies and Protocols in Domestic Violence Programs

Domestic violence program staff are often not trained in child protection laws, policies, and court and agency practices. Nor are they provided with protocols for handling child-abuse-and-neglect cases. As a result they misunderstand the role of CPS and are uncertain about how to handle abuse or neglect cases involving the children of the battered women they serve. . . .

Domestic violence policies must require training for staff on child protection issues, including child-abuse-and-neglect law and juvenile-dependency court practice. Moreover, staff need to be informed about the range of services available from the child welfare system, and the limitations of the system. A greater understanding of child protection work will make it easier for domestic violence program staff to change their practices to better assist CPS in responding to domestic violence and accomplishing the goal of protecting children.

Trainings developed and delivered through collaborative efforts involving domestic violence prevention advocates and child protection workers are more likely to be accepted by each system and to result in changes in practice. With grant support from the U.S. Department of Health and Human Services, Michigan has developed a training institute to provide ongoing training for child welfare workers on domestic violence and for domestic violence service providers on child welfare. These trainings have fostered many informal, local partnerships between CPS and domestic violence programs. . . .

The Use of Domestic Violence Specialists

The Massachusetts DSS pioneered the placement of experienced domestic violence advocates as full-time staff in local DSS offices in 1990. Today, there are 11 domestic violence specialists and two coordinators serving 26 area offices. In addition to case consultation and direct service, the domestic violence specialists provide training on domestic violence to DSS child welfare staff and a myriad of other agencies and organizations, and serve as a liaison between DSS and domestic violence service programs. In 1998, these specialists provided consultation on more than 5,000 child welfare cases.

The presence of domestic violence specialists in child welfare offices is a constant reminder that domestic violence is a significant child protection issue and that family safety is essential to child safety. With their expertise in domestic violence and the needs of battered mothers, these specialists can assist child protection workers in identifying domestic violence and creating reasonable, supportive, and appropriate interventions. They also serve as a bridge between both systems. Having worked in shelters, they know the difficulties that domestic violence service providers face, and, as domestic violence specialists working for CPS, they understand the pressures and limitations of that system. Because of this understanding, domestic violence service providers often call on them to help battered women negotiate the CPS system.

. . .

Because the juvenile-dependency court plays such a key role in the outcome of child protection cases, it is critical that court personnel have access to domestic violence expertise. In October 1997, the Dade County, Florida, juvenile court launched a collaborative intervention program for families in which both child abuse and domestic violence are present. CPS, the court, battered women's shelters, and batterer treatment programs all participate in the project. Domestic violence advocates provide services at no cost to battered women who are referred to them by CPS or through court proceedings. Services include crisis intervention, safety planning, counseling, parenting skills training, referrals to social service agencies, and legal assistance.... Domestic violence specialists also have a key role to play in health interventions on behalf of families in which there is domestic violence and child abuse. Advocacy for Women and Kids in Emergencies (AWAKE), founded in 1986 at Children's Hospital in Boston, was the first program to link support for battered mothers with clinical services for their abused children.... The wide array of services offered includes counseling; assistance with housing; referrals for legal and medical issues; and advocacy with the criminal justice system, CPS, and other public agencies. AWAKE's advocates also provide case consultation and training to hospital staff....

Family Preservation Services

In 1988, the Michigan Department of Social Services began Families First, an intensive in-home family preservation program. Families are referred to this program when children are at risk of removal from the home because of child abuse or neglect, or delinquency. The program offers an array of services to assist families in reducing the risks of harm to their children. Families First workers handle no more than two cases at a time and are available to the families 24 hours a day.

In the early 1990s, Families First workers began to notice domestic violence in many of the homes in which they were working, and asked for training and support to address it. In response, a domestic violence training program was established for Families First staff. In addition, a demonstration project was developed to provide Families First services to battered women and their children, by direct referral from domestic violence service programs. Through this project, Families First workers have been able to support battered women in making the changes they must make to secure a safer life for themselves and their children. Workers help with safety planning, independent living issues like housing, transportation, child care, and budgeting; parenting issues; creating a social support network; and linking up with other social services.

In 1996 this demonstration project was expanded from 5 to 11 sites, which now serve 27 of Michigan's 83 counties. From August 1994 to November 1997, the program served 504 families with a total of 1,361 children. An internal evaluation of the program conducted in 1997 found that 12 months after Families First services had been provided, battered mothers and their children have been able to stay safely together in 95% of the families.

. . .

CPS Citizen Review Panels

Under a 1998 amendment to the federal Child Abuse Prevention and Treatment and Adoption Reform Act, all states receiving funding under the Act to improve their CPS system are required to establish CPS citizen review panels. These panels must meet regularly to examine the policies and procedures of state and local CPS agencies and to review CPS cases to ensure compliance with the requirements of the Act. The law also requires that panel membership include broad community representation.

Training of citizen review panel members should include information regarding domestic violence. In addition, at least one panel member should represent the domestic violence field. This is true for other CPS review boards like child fatality and foster care review panels, as well. The inclusion of individuals who have expertise in domestic violence on panels that review CPS, child fatalities, and foster care is an acknowledgment that domestic violence is a child safety issue. It also provides another forum for cooperation between the domestic violence service and child protection systems. The participation of child protection specialists on comparable domestic violence boards and councils is also important for accomplishing these goals.

* * *

NOTE

1. This last optimistic account of ways in which mothers and children can be helped to live safely with one another, out of the shadow of abuse, provides a fitting transition to the next section, which analyzes the criminal prosecutions of battered mothers who fail to protect their children from the violence of their own abusers. What function do these prosecutions serve—and do we have any evidence that they are more effective in protecting the safety and emotional wellbeing of children than the provision of services would be?

E. PROSECUTING BATTERED MOTHERS FOR FAILURE TO PROTECT

Under what circumstances will a mother who has "allowed" her child to be abused, or failed to prevent the abuse, be criminally prosecuted, rather than called to account through the child welfare system? In the last section, you read Richard Gelles' suggestion that only the death of a child, or sexual abuse, would prompt a prosecution of either the perpetrator or the perpetrator's passive partner. However, you were also introduced to the argument that, at least in New York City, there has been an increase in the "criminalization" of child neglect in recent years, perhaps prompted by a more aggressive police response to partner violence, and an increasing recognition that in homes in which there is partner violence, children are also likely to be at risk.

The irony, of course, is that the very same constituencies that welcome a heightened police response to domestic violence, and a recognition of its impact on children, are highly critical of efforts to guard the welfare of abused children by prosecuting their non-abusive, and abused, mothers. From the perspective of those who understand the dangerous and disempowering dynamics of abusive relationships, holding the abused mother accountable for failing to protect her children when she has manifestly not been able to protect herself appears profoundly unjust. This injustice is compounded when prosecutors overlook both the efforts the mother *has* made to keep her children safe or the violence directed at them at a minimum, and the failure of other helping systems to respond to the mother's or the children's needs. To blame the mother for being unable to keep her batterer away from her home when police fail to enforce the restraining order she has taken out–to give just one scenario from the reported cases–seems both hypocritical and vindictive.

Another aspect of the critique is that if we are first and foremost concerned with the wellbeing of a child, and the child is still alive, we should consider carefully whether the child's wellbeing, in the aftermath of abuse, will be better served by the foster care system, or by the mother. Both mother and child should now be safe from their abuser, assuming he is prosecuted, convicted and incarcerated. Both may well need assistance in recovering from the trauma of abuse; but if there is a bond of affection between them (and there is no reason to suppose otherwise), being able to enjoy their relationship in safety may help in that recovery. Certainly the mother understands better than most what her child has been through.

Finally, from a practical standpoint, prosecuting mothers for failure to protect provides a perverse incentive. Imagine being the woman who discovers that her child has been physically or sexually abused. Imagine knowing that making efforts to report the abuse to the authorities, or to take the child for medical care, would not only put you and the child in further danger from the abuser, but would be likely to result in the child being removed from your care, and in your being prosecuted for failure to protect. Might you not decide that the better course of action would be to continue to make whatever efforts you could to keep the child safe without "help" from the outside?

These prosecutions occur in three types of situations; where the mother was present when the child was abused and did not prevent or halt the abuse; where the mother left the child in the care of a known abuser, and where the mother failed to seek assistance for a child for abuse-related injuries. In practice, criminal justice system involvement can come about in two ways. If police respond to an incident of child or partner abuse, they may report on their findings in the home in a fashion that triggers an investigation and a prosecution, in addition to triggering an intervention by the child welfare system. Alternatively, the child welfare authorities may be the first to respond to an allegation of child abuse and neglect, but may refer the matter to a prosecutor if the circumstances seem to warrant the consideration of criminal charges. The criminal charges are likely to be charges of child abuse, neglect or endangerment; in many jurisdictions the same statutory definitions serve both to identify criminal conduct and to frame the jurisdiction of child welfare authorities. Alternatively, if the child is dead, the charges may be of murder or manslaughter.

Michelle Jacobs
Requiring Battered Women Die: Murder Liability for Mothers Under Failure to Protect Statutes, 88 Journal of Criminal Law and Criminology 579, 613–15 (1998)

Without failure to protect legislation, a state could choose to prosecute a non-abusing mother for murder, involuntary manslaughter or aggravated child abuse. The mother could be charged as an aider or abettor under each category. Each of these theories would require proof that the non-abusing mother had the requisite mens rea, as well as all other elements commonly associated with the criminal offense. People v. Novy[1] provides an example of the type of prosecution mothers face under a traditional common law crime analysis. Kimberly Novy was charged with first degree murder, aggravated battery to a child, and cruelty to a child as a result of the death of her stepson. The child died from massive internal injuries and swelling of the brain. The state prosecuted Novy on the theory that either she or the child's father was responsible for his injuries. If Novy had not inflicted the injuries herself, then she was considered accountable for the actions of Keith Novy, the boy's father. The court used twenty pages of a twenty-three page decision to recount the conflicting facts of the case. In its final pages, it upheld Novy's conviction of first degree murder and found that if she did not inflict the injuries, she knew Keith Novy inflicted the injuries. The court found it significant that: (1) she remained with the father after the point when she should have been aware of the foreseeability of injury; (2) she failed to inform the authorities of the injuries; and (3) she actively concealed some of the injuries. Novy's case is significant because under the theory of accountability, she became the first woman to be convicted of first degree murder where a failure to protect analysis formed part of the basis for her conviction. Despite the fact that Novy presented evidence that the child's abuse and neglect began at least nine months before she even met Keith Novy, she was nonetheless convicted. Keith Novy was not prosecuted.

Many states that have used traditional common law crimes as the basis for prosecution of non-abusing mothers have also adopted statutes which imposed criminal sanctions for people convicted of abusing children. The criminal abuse statutes are divided into two categories: those that punish people who actually commit the abuse, and those that seek to punish people who exposed the child to risk of danger, or neglected to perform a duty of care or protection. Purportedly, statutes seeking to criminalize passive conduct do so in order to protect children's "best interests" by compelling parents to remove their children from abusive environments....

1. 597 N.E. 2d 273 (Ill. App. Ct. 1992).

Specific failure to protect legislation can relieve the state of the burden of proving mens rea once parental responsibility for the child has been established....

* * *

NOTES

1. How unusual is it for the criminal law to punish failures to act, or omissions? In the words of Nancy Erickson:

> ... Generally the criminal law punishes only acts, not omissions. However, a failure to act may result in criminal liability if the defendant has a duty to act and fails to do so. Some examples of laws criminalizing failure to act are statutes requiring the filing of certain documents, such as tax returns, with various governmental agencies. Such cases are legally rather simple; more complex issues are raised by cases involving a duty to act based on contract, voluntary assumption of care, or a relationship between the defendant and another person, such as wife and husband or parent and child.
>
> La Fave and Scott stated in the 1972 edition of their criminal law hornbook:
>
> > Generally one has no legal duty to aid another person in peril, even when that aid can be rendered without danger or inconvenience to himself.... But there are situations which do give rise to a duty to act.... *The common law imposes affirmative duties upon persons standing in certain personal relationships to other persons—upon parents to aid their small children. ... Thus, a parent may be guilty of criminal homicide for failure to call a doctor for his sick child, a mother for failure to prevent the fatal beating of her baby by her lover.* ... Action may be required to thwart the threatened perils of nature (e.g. to combat sickness ...); or it may be required to protect against threatened acts by third persons.[1]
>
> Thus, almost twenty years ago there was already recognition of the fact that mothers were being prosecuted for failing to protect their children against the violence of others, usually husbands or boyfriends....

Nancy Erickson, *Battered Mothers of Battered Children: Using Our Knowledge of Battered Women to Defend them Against Charges of Failure to Act*, CURRENT PERSPECTIVES IN PSYCHOLOGICAL, LEGAL AND ETHICAL ISSUES, VOL. 1A, CHILDREN AND FAMILIES: ABUSE AND ENDANGERMENT 197, 198–99 (1991).

2. Separate from the question of punishing omissions is the question of what standard of liability to apply. Will the mother who fails to protect be strictly liable, liable only when she is affirmatively negligent, or liable only when she intends harm to the child. In the child welfare context, we examined the distinction between child abuse and child neglect, and discussed the justification for, and the difficulties with, imposing strict liabili-

1. Wayne LaFave and Austin Scott, *Handbook on Criminal Law* § 26, at 183–84 (1st ed. 1972)(footnotes omitted and emphasis added).

ty. The mother's civil liability for child neglect in *In Re Glenn G.* was an inevitable consequence of the strict liability standard. In the criminal context, strict liability is a rarity, usually reserved for relatively minor infractions such as exceeding the speed limit, or failing to file a tax return, and its constitutionality is regularly challenged on due process grounds. See, e.g., Alan Saltzman, *Strict Criminal Liability and the United States Constitution: Substantive Criminal Law Due Process,* 24 Wayne L. Rev. 1571 (1978); J.J. Hippard, *The Unconstitutionality of Criminal Liability Without Fault: An Argument for a Constitutional Doctrine of Mens Rea,* 10 Houston L. Rev. 1039 (1973). Yet with respect to child abuse and neglect, as Michelle Jacobs noted in the excerpt above, the strict liability imposed within the child welfare system has a tendency to spill over into the criminal context, making mothers vulnerable to prosecution even when they have not themselves abused their children, and when their failure to protect their children is not driven by any criminal intent. One commentator has summarized the situation in the following terms:

> Forty-nine states and the District of Columbia have enacted criminal child abuse legislation. All but twelve of these statutes include omissions of a duty to protect among their lists of prohibited behaviors. "Omission statutes" punish not only the perpetrators of abuse, but also any person who fails to fulfill his or her duty to protect a child from abuse.
>
> The remaining twelve states have "commission statutes" that punish only those persons who actually commit abuse. The twelve commission statutes punish any person who "willfully abuses a child," "knowingly and maliciously causes physical injury or pain to a child," or "intentionally or knowingly causes bodily harm to a child."
>
> In all fifty states, parents have an affirmative legal duty to protect and provide for their minors. Although some states with omission statutes require some knowledge or purposeful intent, most have strict liability omission statutes that require only a showing that the guardian held a duty of care or protection and that the duty was violated through inaction. Thus, the majority of omission statutes do not require a showing of an affirmative act of neglect or malevolent intent.

V. Pualani Enos, *Prosecuting Battered Mothers: State Laws' Failure to Protect Battered Women and Abused Children,* 19 Harv. Wmn's L.J. 229, 236–67 (1996).

As the following case illustrates, however, even commission statutes can be, and have been, read as imposing liability for omissions. And when they are used to prosecute failures to protect, even these commission statutes, which purportedly require a criminal intent, are applied in ways that leave defendants very little room to maneuver.

Gayle Weaver Phelps v. State

439 So.2d 727.
Court of Criminal Appeals of Alabama, 1983.

■ Sam W. Taylor, Judge.

Following the death of her twenty-month-old son, appellant was indicted and convicted for child abuse stemming from her failure to prevent harm to the boy by his stepfather, appellant's husband. The stepfather's conviction for murder was affirmed by this Court in Phelps v. State, 435 So.2d 158 (Ala.Cr.App.1983). Appellant was sentenced to five years' imprisonment.

The State's evidence established that on August 24, 1981, David Phelps caused the death of James Allen (Jamie) Weaver, Jr. by striking him in the abdomen. Dr. Thomas P. Gilchrist, forensic pathologist who performed an autopsy on the child, testified that the boy died as a result of a lacerated stomach, pancreas and mesentery which allowed the escape of air and blood into the abdominal cavity. Gilchrist gave his opinion that the injuries had been caused by a blow of "tremendous force" to the abdomen. The pathologist also noted the presence of numerous bruises on the child's body, specifically on the chest, abdomen, head, face, back, buttocks and groin areas. He stated that, in his judgment, the bruises were two to five days old, while the fatal blow had been administered only hours prior to the child's death.

> [David Phelps, Jamie's killer, became a significant figure in the family's life in January of 1981. The catalog of injuries Jamie had suffered at the hands of David Phelps by the time he died included at least: a burn on his ear; a burn on his back and a bump on his head; a hand-sized bruise on his back; marijuana smoke blown in his face; a large bruise on the side of his head and ear, and a blow that sent him "across the kitchen." As to these injuries, Gayle Phelps acknowledged that she knew of the marijuana episode, and of the time when David Phelps left his handprint on the boy's back, and testified that she had argued with her husband about his abusive behavior on both occasions. Other witnesses testified that she also knew: (1) that the burn on his ear was an injury deliberately inflicted by David Phelps and (2) about David hitting Jamie "across the kitchen," and that she had blamed herself, in conversation with others, for accidentally burning the child's back.]

Appellant stated that she and Phelps moved to Montgomery on July 10, 1981. About a week before Jamie died, her daughter Kristie complained that her leg hurt, saying that she fell in the sandbox at school. Appellant took Kristie to the hospital, the child was admitted, and appellant stayed with her daughter virtually the entire time she was hospitalized. During this period, appellant left Jamie with David Phelps. Appellant stated that because she spent all her time, during the last week of Jamie's life, in the hospital with Kristie she did not bathe or clothe Jamie and had no occasion to notice any bruises or injuries on him. When she did periodically come home from the hospital, Jamie was sleeping and she had very little contact with him.

Appellant acknowledged that Phelps had physically abused her and, immediately before they moved to Montgomery, Phelps had gotten into a violent argument with appellant's father, who lived next door to them in Autauga County. The altercation resulted in both Phelps and appellant's father having to be sewed up at the emergency room for wounds received in the fight. Appellant conceded that David Phelps had a violent temper and stated that prior to Kristie's hospitalization she had planned to take the children and leave but she "never got the opportunity."

On Monday August 24, 1981, David called her at work to tell her Jamie needed to see a doctor. She went home, called the paramedics, and gave the child mouth-to-mouth resuscitation. Appellant noticed Jamie's bruises for the first time when the paramedics cut away the boy's pajamas.

. . .

I

... The statute under which [defendant] was prosecuted, § 26–15–3, Code of Alabama 1975, provides that "A responsible person, ... who shall torture, willfully abuse, cruelly beat or otherwise willfully maltreat any child under the age of 18 years shall, on conviction, be punished by imprisonment in the penitentiary for not less than one year nor more than 10 years." ...

... [T]he grand jury of Montgomery County charged that "Gayle Weaver Phelps, ... being the natural parent ... of James Allen Weaver, Jr., a child under eighteen years of age, did torture, willfully abuse, cruelly beat or otherwise maltreat said child, by to-wit: Gayle Weaver Phelps ... did voluntarily fail to remove the child James Allen Weaver, Jr., from the custody, care or control of David Wilson Phelps who had repeatedly subjected the child James Allen Weaver, Jr., to acts of beating or burning or kicking, said omission thereby worsening or aggravating the injuries or conditions which lead to the death of James Allen Weaver, Jr., in violation of Section 26–15–3 of the Code of Alabama, ..."

... [A]ppellant maintains that the omission of the word "willfully" before the term "maltreat" in the accusation rendered the indictment fatally defective. Generally, of course, if a criminal statute makes a certain act an offense if it is done willfully, then willfulness is an essential element of the crime, and "in describing the offense it is necessary that the word 'willfully' should be used, or words equivalent in their meaning." ...

... [T]he factual averments of the indictment in the present case spelled out precisely what offense was charged and put appellant on notice that her crime was one of "fail[ure] to remove the child James Allen Weaver, Jr., from the custody, care or control of David Wilson Phelps...."

In People v. Peckens, 153 N.Y. 576, 47 N.E. 883 (1897), the New York court held that under a statute requiring the indictment to contain "[a] plain and concise statement of the act constituting the crime, without unnecessary repetition," the defendant was not harmed when the indictment omitted the term "willfully" but alleged facts necessary to constitute the offense.... Section 15–8–25, Code of Alabama 1975, is similar to § 275 of the New York Code of Criminal Procedure in that it also requires the indictment to "state the facts constituting the offense in ordinary and concise language, without prolixity or repetition, in such a manner as to enable a person of common understanding to know what is intended and with that degree of certainty which will enable the court, on conviction, to pronounce the proper judgment." ...

More importantly, the factual averment here charged that appellant voluntarily engaged in the described conduct. In our judgment, the word "voluntarily" in this context is equivalent in meaning to the word "willfully" as found in the statute. The two terms have even been used interchangeably. "Willful" has been defined as "[p]roceeding from a conscious motion of the will; voluntary." Black's Law Dictionary 1773 (rev. 4th ed. 1968).... Likewise, the word "voluntary" has been determined to mean "[p]roceeding from the free and unrestrained will of the person." Black's Law Dictionary at 1746–47.... We therefore find that the word "voluntarily" as used in the indictment is substantially equivalent to the statutory term "willfully."

. . .

It is our opinion that the language of the indictment here "necessarily import[ed] guilty knowledge" and that the term "voluntarily" substituted for the word "willfully." Any other construction would be contrary to good common sense. Moreover, in view of the detailed factual averments, there can be no serious claim that appellant was tried for an offense different from that intended by the grand jury, that she was unable to prepare her defense, or that the court was unable to pronounce judgment on the record....

III

. . .

Appellant correctly points out that for a prosecution based upon breach of her duty to prevent child abuse, venue was in the county where the duty was breached.... She claims there was no evidence that she breached a duty in Montgomery County where she was tried, and that the breach occurred in Autauga County, if at all....

. . .

[S]ection 15–2–6, Code of Alabama 1975, provides that "[w]here an offense is committed partly in one county and partly in another or the acts or effects thereof constituting or requisite to the consummation of the offense occur in two or more counties, venue is in either county."

Even if all David Phelps's abuse of Jamie had taken place in Autauga County, appellant's duty to prevent that abuse was a continuing one and was not extinguished once the family moved to Montgomery....

Contrary to appellant's assertion, the testimony regarding acts of violence committed on Jamie in Autauga County was properly admitted. It was admissible as part of a continuous pattern of ill treatment which should have put appellant on notice of the need to prevent further abuse of her son. Under the circumstances, her duty to prevent harm to Jamie could not have arisen until she was alerted to her husband's behavior. The conduct of David Phelps toward Jamie, therefore, was relevant and admissible, regardless of where it occurred, because it had a bearing on appellant's knowledge of the abuse.... Finally, the question of appellant's criminal intent was properly left to the jury to resolve. The evidence was in sharp dispute, with all the defense testimony pointing to the fact that appellant was unaware of her husband's ill treatment of her son. The testimony from State's witnesses Joy Bozeman and Mari Doyle, however, provided evidence which, if believed, would have authorized the jury to find that appellant knew of the abuse to her son and, having a duty to prevent it, did nothing to halt it. When there is legal evidence from which the factfinders can by fair inference find the accused guilty, this court will not disturb the verdict....

. . .

We have examined the issues presented on appeal and have found no error. The judgment of conviction by the Montgomery Circuit Court is due to be and is hereby affirmed.

AFFIRMED. All the Judges concur.

NOTES AND QUESTIONS

1. How credible do you find Gayle Phelps' testimony that she was ignorant of all but two of the incidents of David Phelps' abuse?

2. Given the court's interpretation of "wilfully maltreat," under Section 26–15–3 of the Code of Alabama, would you agree that the statute is a "commission" statute? How is the court able to bring "voluntarily failing to remove" within the definition of "wilfully maltreating?" Is it Gayle Phelps "guilty knowledge," in the court's words, that supplies the link? Under the court's interpretation, are there any arguments Gayle Phelps could have made to defeat the claim that she had voluntarily or wilfully maltreated her son?

3. Gayle Phelps' counsel appealed her conviction largely on technical grounds; the inadequacy of the indictment, and the choice of venue. Strikingly, she made no argument based on the abuse she herself had suffered at the hands of David Phelps. She did not argue that she was too afraid of his violence to challenge him, or to leave him, or that she feared she and the children would be at greater risk if she tried to leave him. Other women have made those arguments. This next case provides an example, in the context of a statute creating liability for "knowingly or intentionally" endangering a child.

Barrett v. State

675 N.E.2d 1112.
Court of Appeals of Indiana, 1996.

Defendant was convicted in the Morgan Superior Court, Christopher Burnham, J., of neglect of a dependent. Defendant appealed. The Court of Appeals, Baker, J., held that: (1) as a matter of first impression, expert testimony regarding battered women's syndrome was admissible to show that defendant did not have requisite intent to place dependent in dangerous situation; (2) jury instructions were proper....

Reversed and remanded.

■ Opinion by Baker, J.

In this case of first impression we are asked to determine whether testimony regarding Battered Women's Syndrome is relevant to the issue of a defendant's intent to commit a crime. Appellant-defendant Alice Barrett was convicted of Neglect of a Dependent, a Class B felony, following the death of her four-year-old child at the hands of Barrett's live-in boyfriend. Prior to trial, the trial court granted the State's motion in limine seeking to preclude Barrett from presenting evidence regarding Battered Women's Syndrome. On appeal, Barrett contends that the trial court erred for the following reasons: 1) determining that evidence of Battered Women's Syndrome was irrelevant except in cases involving a claim of self-defense; 2) refusing her tendered instructions on Battered Women's Syndrome and the definition of "knowing"....

Facts

The factual background relevant to this appeal begins many years ago in Barrett's childhood. Barrett's parents, Lorene and Daniel, divorced when Barrett was five years old. Initially, Barrett resided with Lorene; however, when Lorene lost her job, she sent Barrett to California to live with Daniel. Daniel was a heavy drinker who routinely whipped Barrett with a belt, beat her head against a wall and grabbed her by the ears....

When Barrett was fourteen years old, Daniel took her and her brother, Jeff, to the bus station and sent them back to Indiana to reside with Lorene. Soon thereafter, Lorene sent Jeff away. As a result, Barrett left Lorene's home and traveled to California. Eventually, Barrett returned to Indiana and took up residence with a family friend.

Thereafter, Barrett began a series of relationships with abusive men. First, Lorene dated Charlie, who drank heavily and abused her.... Barrett had one child with Charlie, C.J. Next, Barrett dated Perry, who was a heroin addict and who fathered two of Barrett's children, Heather and Hope.... Next, Barrett began a relationship with Johnnie, who was extremely protective and jealous.... Finally, in July 1995, Barrett began dating Steve Sherwood, who drank heavily. According to Barrett, her relationship with Sherwood was stormy in that he would often drink, become loud and angry and attempt to dominate her by following her and forcing her to stay by his side. On several occasions, Barrett attempted to leave Sherwood, only to eventually return to him.

On September 18, 1995, Sherwood telephoned Barrett at work to inform her that he had spanked Hope and had left a handprint on her buttocks. When Barrett returned from work, she did not inspect Hope's buttocks. However, three days later, when Barrett's roommate, Chris McGowan, was in the bathroom with Hope, Chris noticed that Hope's entire bottom was black and blue. Chris informed Barrett, who then confronted Sherwood. Sherwood cried and stated that he did not intend to hit Hope so hard.

Thereafter, on September 22, 1995, Barrett's mother, Lorene, contacted Barrett about babysitting Hope. During their conversation, Barrett informed Lorene of Hope's bruises. As a result, Lorene took Hope to the Fayette County Sheriff's Department to report the injuries. When Officer Jeff Griffin contacted Barrett regarding the bruises, she stated that Sherwood had admitted that he had spanked Hope and left a hand print. Barrett further reported that on another occasion Hope had fallen, hit her head and vomited and that Sherwood had yelled at Hope, grabbed her hair and pushed her face into the vomit.

Early the following morning, Barrett was awakened by Sherwood who was straddling her and holding a knife. When Barrett screamed, Sherwood threatened to kill her and Hope unless she was quiet. Sherwood then ordered Hope, who had been sleeping in Barrett's bed, to the floor and asked her if he had whipped her. When she answered affirmatively, he called her a liar. Subsequently, Sherwood and Barrett engaged in intercourse. Thereafter, Barrett called 911 and reported that Sherwood was in her home and was unwelcome. Connersville Police Officers William Rockwell and Jeffrey Locke responded to the call and removed Sherwood from Barrett's residence.

Later that day, Barrett again spoke with Officer Griffin and told him that she had been sexually abused by Sherwood that morning. Officer Griffin suggested that Barrett seek shelter at a home for battered women. Barrett declined, but took Hope with her to her brother's residence in Mitchell, Indiana. While Barrett was at her brother's house, Sherwood was charged with Battery, two counts of Criminal Confinement, Rape and Residential Entry.

The following week, Barrett and Hope returned to Connersville. Officer Griffin advised Barrett that a warrant had been issued for Sherwood's arrest, but Barrett indicated that she did not know of his whereabouts. On October 8, 1995, however, Barrett and Hope moved with Sherwood to Martinsville, Indiana, and took up residence at the Hilltop Motel. While Sherwood and Barrett worked, Michelle Fox took care of Hope. When Fox first met Hope, she noticed bruises on Hope's face. Fox questioned Barrett, who explained that Hope had been injured while riding in a truck with Sherwood. Specifically, Barrett stated that Sherwood had swerved to avoid hitting a deer and that Hope had fallen to the floor of the truck....

On October 21, 1995, Barrett reported to work at approximately 6:00 p.m. Shortly after Barrett arrived, she received a telephone call from Sherwood who stated that Hope was hot and had fainted. Barrett spoke to Hope and asked Sherwood to call her later. When Sherwood called back, he stated that Hope was fine. Barrett left work at approximately 1:00 a.m. and returned to the motel to find Hope dead. Barrett screamed at Sherwood: "What have you done?" and ran hysterically from the hotel.... When questioned by the Indiana State Police and the Morgan County Sheriff's Department, Barrett stated that she was afraid of Sherwood, was stupid to have stayed with him and that she had "paid the ultimate price for her mistake." ...

Subsequently, Barrett was charged with neglect of a dependent resulting in serious bodily injury, a class B felony.... [T]he trial court granted the State's motion in limine seeking to exclude Barrett's evidence of Battered Women's Syndrome as either a defense or as evidence of her intent, character or state of mind. Barrett was tried by a jury on December 21, 1995, and was convicted as charged. On January 19, 1996, the trial court sentenced Barrett to twenty years imprisonment. Barrett now appeals.

I. BATTERED WOMEN'S SYNDROME

Barrett contends that the trial court erred by disallowing her expert testimony regarding Battered Women's Syndrome. Prior to trial, the State filed a motion in limine seeking to preclude Barrett from introducing evidence of BWS. Following argument from the parties, the trial court granted the motion, concluding:

> The Court has researched the law in the State of Indiana and has found no case in which the "Battered Woman's Syndrome" has been recognized as a defense to the crime of Neglect of a Dependent Resulting in Serious Bodily Injury. This theory defense [sic] is inherent within a case in which the Defendant is charged with an assault upon the victim (perpetrator of the abuse) as a self-defense argument; however, this theory of defense is not available in a case in which the victim of the crime is not the perpetrator of the abuse, but instead the alleged perpetrator of abuse is a third-party ....

According to Barrett, evidence of BWS was relevant to show that she did not knowingly or intentionally neglect her child. Additionally, she claims that she was denied her right to present a defense on her own behalf because she was prevented from responding to the prosecutor's question during both opening and closing arguments regarding why she stayed with Sherwood.

. . .

In the instant case, Barrett was charged pursuant to I.C. § 35–46–1–1, which defines neglect of a dependent as:

> (a) A person having the care of a dependent, whether assumed voluntarily or because of a legal obligation, who knowingly or intentionally;
>
> (1) places the dependent in a situation that may endanger his life or health; ... commits neglect of a dependent, a Class D felony. However, ... the offense is a Class B felony if it results in serious bodily injury.

As part of its burden of proof, the State must show that the accused was subjectively aware of a high probability that she placed the dependent in a dangerous situation.... Proof of this subjective awareness requires resort to inferential reasoning to ascertain the accused's mental state.... Therefore, evidence or testimony regarding the accused's mental state is relevant to determine whether the accused knowingly or intentionally placed the dependent in a dangerous situation.

. . .

Additionally, we reject the State's contention that BWS is only relevant in cases in which self-defense is argued. Indiana courts have considered the admissibility of BWS based on the facts of each particular case, not the general nature of a case. For example, BWS has been admitted to demonstrate why a victim of abuse might recant her allegations against her abuser, Dausch v. State, 616 N.E.2d 13 (Ind.1993); to refute a defendant's testimony that he and the victim had a friendly relationship prior to her death, Isaacs, 659 N.E.2d at 1041; and as a mitigating factor for a trial court to consider when sentencing a woman for killing her abuser, Allen v. State, 566 N.E.2d 1047 (Ind.Ct.App.1991). Although this court has previously prevented the admission of BWS evidence, we did so because the evidence was not sufficient to support it, not because of the lack of a self-defense claim. Fultz v. State, 439 N.E.2d 659, 662 (Ind.Ct.App.1982) (defendant could not admit evidence of prior severe beating by victim because she failed to present appreciable evidence of victim's aggression). These cases demonstrate that the presence of a self-defense issue is not the determinative factor in deciding the admissibility of BWS. In fact, in Isaacs, our supreme court held that evidence of BWS was admissible "so long as it is relevant." Isaacs, 659 N.E.2d at 1041, citing People v. Christel, 449 Mich. 578, 537 N.W.2d 194, 201–05 (1995).

We also note that our holding today is consistent with the only other jurisdiction which has considered this issue. In State v. Mott, 183 Ariz. 191, 901 P.2d 1221 (App.1995), the defendant was convicted of child abuse and murder after her child was murdered by the defendant's boyfriend. During trial, the trial court excluded the defendant's expert testimony regarding BWS and its impact on a woman's ability to make decisions and to protect her children. Id. 901 P.2d at 1223. On appeal, the State argued that the expert's testimony was inadmissible because it was "not relevant to any recognized defense." Id. 901 P.2d at 1224. The appellate court rejected this theory, holding that the trial court erred because:

> [T]he character traits of battered women and the presence of those traits in Mott is relevant and admissible to the charged offenses because it provides evidence probative of Mott's behavior and, if accepted by the jury, would negate much of the evidence the state relied upon to show that Mott acted knowingly or intentionally.

Id. The court further found that by excluding this testimony, the trial court effectively denied the defendant the opportunity to present evidence essential to her defense. Id. 901 P.2d at 1225. For these reasons, the Arizona court set aside the defendant's convictions.

Similarly, Barrett was denied the opportunity to present evidence essential to her defense. This opportunity is mandated by the Sixth Amendment to the U.S. Constitution which guarantees defendants the right to present evidence and witnesses on their own behalf. . . .

A defendant accused of knowingly or intentionally committing a crime is entitled to present evidence in her own defense to negate that mental state. As a result, we reverse Barrett's conviction and sentence for neglect of a dependent causing serious bodily injury.

II. Jury Instructions

Next, Barrett contends that the trial court erred in instructing the jury. Specifically, Barrett argues that the court erroneously refused her tendered instruction on BWS and improperly instructed the jury on the definition of "knowing."

A trial court has the discretion to give or refuse to give a jury instruction.... We review the trial court's decision for an abuse of discretion.... When making our determination, we consider: 1) whether there is evidence to support giving the instruction; 2) whether the substance of the tendered instruction is covered by other instructions; and 3) whether the instruction is a proper statement of the law....

A. Battered Women's Syndrome Instruction

During trial, Barrett tendered the following instruction on BWS:

> It is a defense to a prosecution of neglect of a dependent resulting in serious bodily injury that at the time of the neglect there was a reasonable apprehension in the mind of the defendant that acting to stop or prevent the neglect or endangerment would result in substantial bodily harm to the defendant or the child in retaliation.

... The trial court refused the instruction on the basis that it was not authorized or justified under Indiana law.

As we determined above, BWS is relevant and admissible in a neglect of a dependent case to negate a defendant's intent to commit the crime charged. In addition, the evidence offered by Barrett's witness sufficiently supported giving an instruction on BWS. Nevertheless, the instruction tendered by Barrett is not a correct statement of the law. As we have held, evidence of BWS is relevant to establish Barrett's state of mind at the time of the offense. The evidence, however, is solely admissible to refute the State's evidence that Barrett acted knowingly or intentionally. It is not an affirmative defense to the crime charged as asserted by Barrett in her proposed instruction. As a result, while we believe that it is appropriate to instruct the jury on BWS, we cannot say that the trial court erred in refusing Barrett's tendered instruction.

B. "Knowingly" Instruction

Additionally, Barrett claims that the trial court incorrectly instructed the jury on the definition of "knowingly." Barrett offered the following instruction:

> The proof required to show that the defendant acted knowingly is based on her subjective awareness of a high probability that she placed her child in a dangerous situation. The proof is not whether a reasonable person in circumstances similar to the defendant's would have acted similarly, but rather, whether this particular defendant was

aware of a high probability that she placed her child in a dangerous situation which resulted in serious bodily injury.

. . . Over Barrett's objection, the trial court deleted the second sentence of the tendered instruction, and instructed the jury only on the first sentence. . . . According to Barrett, the trial court's instruction was incomplete in that it failed to require the jury to find that Barrett herself was aware that Sherwood would harm Hope. . . .

Although the second sentence of Barrett's tendered instruction is a correct statement of the law, we cannot say that the trial court erred in refusing to elaborate on the definition of "subjective awareness." The trial court has a duty to give definitional instructions only if the words are of a technical or legal meaning normally not understood by jurors unversed in the law. . . . Barrett has offered no evidence demonstrating that the definition of the word subjective has a technical or legal meaning beyond the comprehension of the average juror. As a result, the trial court did not err in declining to give the second part of Barrett's proposed instruction.

* * *

NOTES AND QUESTIONS

1. The court in Barrett saw BWS testimony as relevant to the defendant's state of mind, and specifically to the question of whether she "knowingly" or "intentionally" placed her child in danger, measured by a subjective standard. How might Barrett's counsel have used BWS testimony to argue that she did not have the subjective knowledge or intent to place her child in danger? Does the court's own understanding of BWS leave room for that argument?

The statute under which Barrett was convicted is rather different than the one applied to Gayle Phelps. If Barrett had been tried under the Alabama statute, do you think she would have been convicted? Could the introduction of BWS testimony in the Phelps case have altered the outcome, where the issue was not knowledge or intent, but rather whether the conduct was wilful or voluntary?

2. Barrett's counsel sought a jury instruction that would have exonerated the defendant if she reasonably feared that trying to save her child from abuse would have resulted in "substantial bodily harm to the defendant or the child in retaliation." How does that argument follow from the BWS testimony counsel sought to introduce? Why did the court reject it? Does it fit any better within an argument that the defendant's failing to protect the child was involuntary or not wilful, than within an argument that the conduct was not knowing or intentional?

3. These questions highlight the complexity of seeking to make the abuse a mother suffers legally relevant to the claim that she has failed to protect her child. The problem is actually twofold. First, the argument that she should not be held accountable must be made culturally acceptable. Translated into lay language, the "mental state" defense the court was ready to hear in Barrett had two parts: "I didn't realize she was in danger," and "I

didn't mean to put her in danger." "I didn't realize she was in danger" would have supplied a defense in Phelps as well. The Phelps court might also have accepted as a defense: "My hands were tied: there was nothing I could do to prevent what happened." If these arguments can be made persuasive at a lay level, the next question is how to translate them into a legal framework, and how to deploy BWS testimony to support recognizable legal arguments.

The next readings take on these issues. The first addresses some key assumptions and myths that drive our cultural unwillingness to exonerate mothers who "allow" their children to be abused. Subsequent readings take up the question of how to address those assumptions and misconceptions within recognized legal categories.

V. Pualani Enos
Prosecuting Battered Mothers: State Laws' Failure to Protect Battered Women and Abused Children, 19 Harvard Women's Law Journal 229, 240–46, 249–51, 253–61 (1996)

Courts rely most frequently on the following assumptions when determining the fate of battered women and their children: (1) a mother who has knowledge of abuse is always capable of doing something to prevent the abuse; (2) a battered woman's fear is exaggerated and unbelievable; and (3) parents should be treated as a unit.

. . .

A. Assumption 1: Courts Equate Knowledge of Abuse with the Ability to Stop the Abusive Behavior or Protect the Child in Some Other Way

. . .

Myth 1: The Mother Could Have Protected her Child by Taking the Child Away from the Abuser, Removing the Abuser from the Home, or Separating the Child from the Abuser by Other Means

. . .

[I]n an unreported case, Loch, decided in 1992, a Minnesota court found Janice Loch guilty of aiding and abetting her ex-boyfriend, Daniel Roethler, in the rape of her eleven-year-old daughter and in the solicitation of a child to engage in sexual conduct.

Daniel beat and threatened Janice for over two years. Janice sought help from the Minnesota CPS and the Minnesota police department, but they told her there was nothing they could do. Because these agencies do not keep records of the cases in which they fail to act, there was no documentation available for Janice to present at trial. In the meantime, Daniel refused Janice's pleas for him to stay away from Janice and her children and Daniel repeatedly forced his way into Janice's apartment by smashing her windows. Janice previously had attempted to separate herself from her attacker, planned her escape, and was awaiting one more paycheck in order to fix her car and flee without Daniel's knowledge.

In response to an attempt to obtain a Civil Protection Order (CPO), Daniel tried to attack Janice but was restrained by neighbors. Janice refrained from calling the police, remembering that Daniel had raped Janice's daughter once and Daniel had threatened to kill the daughter or Janice if Janice attempted to call the police. Janice believed that Daniel would carry through with his threats because he had done so in the past.

Daniel's violence reached its crescendo when Daniel locked both Janice and her daughter in a bedroom and Daniel raped the daughter. Janice testified that she believed that if she had tried to escape, seek help, or intervene, Daniel would have killed her or her daughter. Thus, Janice told her daughter to comply with Daniel's demands. Similarly, when Janice's son came to the door to see what was wrong, Janice sent her son away, hoping that he would notice something was wrong and call the police once he was out of Daniel's earshot. Despite the motivations behind Janice's actions, she was convicted for aiding and abetting in Daniel's rape of Janice's daughter.

Reality: Leaving the Batterer Often Increases the Danger to the Battered Woman and her Children

. . .

In some cases, leaving may be a life saving act; however, leaving the abuser is not a guarantee that physical violence, or the risk thereof, will be eliminated or reduced. On the contrary, studies indicate that in many cases, violence increases when the victim attempts to leave the home. Harassment, assaults, and threats often become more frequent and increasingly severe after the battered woman has separated from her violent partner. As in Loch, abusive men may search for women and assault, murder, or threaten them for many years after separation. . . .

. . .

Courts often "note" or "acknowledge" the fear of a battered woman but refuse to consider the reasonableness of these fears when determining the woman's culpability. . . . These judicial tendencies demonstrate the general inability by courts to understand fully the real terror of woman and child abuse.

. . .

Women often face criminal liability when attempting to remove themselves and their children from their abusive partners. For example, if a woman flees home with her children without the batterer's knowledge, she may be charged with parental kidnapping or risk the batterer finding her and abducting the children. Mothers who fail to protect their children are chastised for neglect, yet when the mothers flee with their children in order to protect them from harm, the women often are charged with acting irresponsibly. Moreover, if the battered woman flees the home without the abuser's knowledge and is unable to take the children with her, the police may charge the mother with abandonment.

. . .

Myth 2: If the Mother Wanted or Needed Help, Such Assistance Would Be Readily Available from the Police, Social Services, or the Judicial System

In State v. Jeanette Williams, the court convicted Jeanette Williams for failing to protect her daughter, who was beaten fatally by her father in the presence of her mother. Jeanette testified that she was unable to prevent the abuse because her husband also had beaten her and threatened to continue to beat her while she was pregnant. The court, however, dismissed this information as unimportant, stating that the issue was not whether Jeanette could physically prevent the abuse while it was occurring, but whether she was negligent in failing to take action to avoid foreseeable abuse or to seek help once it started. The appellate court affirmed Jeanette's conviction, agreeing that she should have been able to foresee the likelihood of the future abuse of her daughter and therefore should have sought help to prevent injury.

. . .

In In re Interest of C.P., a court terminated the parental rights of an abused mother ... because she "allowed her child to be placed in [the father's] care and custody." M.A. had maintained physical and legal custody of her child until the abusive father took the child to his home in violation of a legal order. M.A. testified that she tried to get her daughter back immediately and that she had sought help from the police and the CPS, but failed to receive assistance. The prosecution disqualified this testimony, however, because neither the CPS nor the police had records of M.A.'s calls for assistance.

. . .

Janice Loch, who had called the Minnesota CPS in order to protect her children from her boyfriend, Daniel, was told that there was nothing they could do. Similarly, when police responded to a call from Janice and found [her abuser] passed out, they claimed that "there was little [they] could do."

Reality: Both the Police and the Child Protective Services Are Often Unsupportive of and Unresponsive to the Needs of the Battered Mother and her Battered Children

The CPS deters battered women from contacting its offices because it often offers no assistance. Moreover, even when the agencies do respond, their solutions likely entail removing the children from both parents rather than protecting the child's nonabusive parent from the abuser. Courts that blame mothers for not reporting spousal abuse to CPS ignore the increased risk of losing their children that battered women face if they reveal their partner's abusive tendencies to the CPS.

The police, another institution that battered women are expected to look to for assistance, also frequently deter women from reporting spousal and child abuse. The police are infamous for their reluctance to become involved in "family disputes" and often do not treat battered women in the same manner as victims of violence who are unrelated to the assailant....

. . .

Myth 3: Family, Friends, Neighbors, and Religious Institutions Would Have Supported and Assisted the Battered Woman, if only She Truly Desired to Protect her Children

In State v. Jeanette Williams, the court chastised Jeanette Williams for not asking one of her husband's friends for assistance during an abusive incident. This friend was present during an incident where both she and her daughter were beaten by the abuser. The court deemed Jeanette's failure to ask her husband's friend for help an omission of Jeanette's duty to seek assistance in protecting her daughter, implying that the friend would have responded to Jeanette's requests for help.

Reality: Family, Friends, Neighbors, and Religious Leaders Infrequently Support Battered Women in Their Efforts to End Their Victimization

[T]he witness of Jeanette's and her daughter's beating was a friend of the abuser. The friend's failure to intervene, demonstrating an unwillingness to confront and restrain the batterer, indicates why Jeanette did not "request" the friend's assistance. Jeanette's request for help from her husband's friend likely would have further angered the abuser and caused an increase in violence.

. . .

Even if a third party acknowledges the violence, active assistance and intervention to assist the woman is rare. Outsiders usually view the problem as "none of their business" and as something that only divorce can solve.

. . .

Family members, friends, and neighbors may not only fail to support a battered woman, but many times may implicitly accept the violent behavior. Many family members advise women to remain in an abusive situation and endure the violence. Religion stresses the importance of family and encourages women to remain with their husbands for the sake of the children.

. . .

Myth 4: Battered Women Should Risk Their Lives in an Attempt to Protect Their Children from Abuse

In Loch, the court expected and implicitly required Janice to risk her life in order to prevent injury to her children. Evidence presented at trial demonstrated that Daniel posed great danger to all members of the Loch family by repeatedly threatening to hurt severely or kill Janice and her two children. Moreover, Daniel was not deterred by police and responded violently to Janice's previous attempts to separate. He broke windows when she would not let him into the apartment, and he tried to attack Janice in response to her filing a petition with the courts for a CPO.

Nevertheless, the court held that Janice should have tried to stop Daniel's rape of her child by either physically intervening or trying to get assistance. The court expected Janice to ignore all signs of danger, to disregard all of the past experiences, and to intervene while Daniel was assaulting her daughter.

. . .

Reality: A Battered Woman Is Likely to Increase the Harm to Her Children if She Attempts to Restrain the Behavior of the Abuser

It is unreasonable to require a woman to risk her life in an attempt to stop the behavior of an abuser. The courts in the Loch and Mitchell cases acknowledged the batterers' death threats, issued by the batterers to dissuade their victims from seeking help, yet still the courts based their decisions on the failure of the women to inform an outsider or seek help. This reasoning implies that a woman should act even though her action exposes her to risk of fatal retaliation by the abuser. Because thousands of women are murdered every year by their spouse or intimate partner, battered women should take seriously the threats of abusive men who have demonstrated their violent potential.

Battered women may not intervene in the batterer's abuse of his children in order to prevent the abuser from exacting more severe beatings against their children. Even a mother's intervention—sometimes life-threatening—does not guarantee protection of the mother's children. Any action the mother takes more likely will lead to an escalation of violence. The courts must permit battered women to refrain from confronting their abusers if they reasonably believe that the violent and terrifying experience will soon end with the least possible injury to all family members.

Myth 5: A Mother who Fails to Protect her Child from Harm is Responsible for that Harm, Regardless of her Efforts to Stop It

Some courts require not only that a battered mother act, but also that her actions be successful in preventing further harm to her children.

. . .

Reality: Knowledge of Abuse Does Not Automatically Empower the Mother to Protect her Children

. . .

In Loch, the prosecutor characterized Janice's failure to stop the rape as "participating, enabling and taking an active role in the abuse of her daughter." The prosecutor described the scene, suggesting that Janice "just [sat] there while her boyfriend raped [her daughter] for an hour and 45 minutes."

The prosecutor's description was a mischaracterization of what occurred and is clarified when the facts are described in context. Janice was paralyzed by fear because she was afraid her ex-boyfriend might kill her and her daughter. She told her daughter to lie still in order to protect her from additional injury and told her son not to come in the room out of fear that he might be hurt by her ex-boyfriend and in hope that he might call the police. The prosecutor characterized these acts as apathetic and malicious. In fact, these were survival tactics employed by Janice to minimize harm to her and her children. These survival tactics admittedly appear reprehensible if viewed outside of the context of domestic violence. However, within the context of trying to minimize unavoidable domestic violence, Janice's response is reasonable.

B. *Assumption 2: A Battered Woman's Fear Is Unjustified, Unbelievable, and Exaggerated*

. . .

Reality: Judges Underestimate the Grave Danger Posed by Abusive Men

. . .

Janice Loch did not have bruises or broken bones at the time of her trial, which took place several months after her abuse. She was not shaking in fear. In fact, Janice showed little emotion while on the stand except for a tinge of anger now and then.

It is difficult for a battered woman to replicate the terror and physical conditions experienced at the time of crisis. Many women, like Janice Loch, have spent months in jail, safe from their abuser, but stewing over the loss of their children and dealing with guilt and anger. During this period, bruises, cuts, and broken bones heal; the memories, however, of these injuries are long-lasting. . . .

C. *Assumption 3: Parents Should Be Treated as a Unit*

Often, no distinctions are made between an abuser and a nonabusing parent. In abuse and neglect cases, courts generally treat parents as one actor. . . . Moreover, nonabusive mothers often receive sentences similar to those sentences given to individuals who affirmatively commit an illegal act. . . .

In Loch, the court sentenced Janice Loch to seven years in prison for her inability to stop Daniel from raping her daughter. In contrast, pursuant to a plea bargain agreement, the court sentenced Daniel to ten and a half years in jail for committing the rape.

A comparison of the sentences relative to each defendant's culpability indicates that the prosecutor ignored the "control dynamic" operating between Daniel and Janice and treated the two persons as essentially one actor. The prosecutor arranged a plea bargain with the perpetrator that sentenced him to jail for half of the maximum rape sentence and vigorously prosecuted the nonacting defendant, obtaining a sentence near the maximum allowed by statute.

. . .

Reality: One Parent Should Not Be Held Responsible for the Independent Acts of the Other

The courts must distinguish the culpability of each parent when only one parent is abusive....

* * *

NOTES

1. Contrast with Enos's accounts of judicial insensitivity the statement of Justice Catherine Stone of the Texas Court of Appeals, concurring in a decision to reverse and remand the conviction of a woman for child endangerment in Elder v. State, 993 S.W.2d 229, 231 (Tx.App.Ct. 1999):

> Charges of gender bias against women have entered into the dialogue, with the complaint that the legal system expects perfection of mothers–they are to protect children from harm at all costs. A mother's failure to protect her child is deemed inexcusable. See Bonnie E. Rabin, Violence Against Mothers Equals Violence Against Children: Understanding the Connections, 58 Alb. L.Rev. 1109, 1115 (1995). As noted by one commentator, '[w]hen courts intervene to protect the child, they typically blame the mother for not removing the child from the abusive household, instead of focusing on the husband's obligation to cease the violence. This blaming is especially common where the child has been abused, and the mother has not reported the abuse.' Rebecca J. Fialk and Audrey E. Stone, Handling the Domestic Violence Case, in Estate Planning and Administration 1998, at 340 (PLI Tax Law and Estate Planning Course Handbook Series No. 271, 1998). When the mother herself is a victim of domestic violence, she is victimized further with criminal prosecution for child neglect or endangerment or with loss of parental rights.
>
> Contrary to the 'mothers as victims' construct, is the view that passive parents are not simply innocent bystanders. Had such parents taken some action, they could have prevented the fatal blow or minimized the child's damages. See Note, Punishing the Passive Parent: Ending a Cycle of Violence, U. MO. KC L.REV. 1003, 1004 (1997). This view promotes a system of 'failure to protect' and endangerment laws holding passive parents criminally accountable for permitting child abuse or failing to prevent the abuse. Id. The promoters of this 'accountability view' recognize, however, that failure to protect and endangerment laws are often inadequate to address the 'cycle of domestic violence that often plagues these families...' Id. In short, even advocates of greater accountability for passive parents realize that a battered mother may be greatly limited in choices and opportunities to protect her child.

2. However, judicial sensitivity is not enough to guarantee fair treatment for the battered mothers of abused children if exonerating arguments cannot be translated into legal arguments. What are the possibilities? Enos argues that courts should not impose what amounts to strict liability in the criminal context; that whether the court is interpreting a "commission" or an "omission" statute, liability for failure to protect a child should depend, at a minimum, on a finding of negligence–that is to say, of unreasonable conduct. Similarly, Kristian Miccio has argued, in *In the Name of Mothers and Children: Deconstructing the Myth of the Passive Battered Mother and the "Protected Child" in Child Neglect Proceedings,* 58 ALBANY L. REV. 1087, 1097 (1995) that the standard for child neglect should be one of reasonableness, measured by:

> a hybrid objective/subjective test. Under this approach, the objective "reasonably prudent parent" will be subjectively qualified by evaluating circumstances particular to the mother and the family. The "under like circumstances" provision subjectively qualifies and makes genuine the court's inquiry. The specific facts of the violence and its perpetration illustrate the environment in which the abused mother and child live and how that environment shapes the mother's steps to control and minimize harm to herself and her child. Thus, the reasonableness of the mother's response is then evaluated against the backdrop of these experiences. . . .

A different consideration is whether there are defenses that the abused mother of an abused child could deploy. In the next excerpt, Nancy Erickson suggests four, while acknowledging that in the cases she reviewed, these arguments were rarely advanced, and were unsuccessful when tried.

Nancy Erickson
Battered Mothers of Battered Children: Using Our Knowledge of Battered Women to Defend them Against Charges of Failure to Act; Current Perspectives in Psychological, Legal and Ethical Issues, Vol. 1A, Children and Families: Abuse and Endangerment 197, 204–08 (1991)

Duress. The Model Penal Code defines the duress defense as follows:

(1) It is an affirmative defense that the actor engaged in the conduct charged to constitute an offense because he was coerced to do so by the use of, or a threat to use, unlawful force against his person or the person of another, which a person of reasonable firmness in his situation would have been unable to resist.

(2) The defense provided by this Section is unavailable if the actor recklessly placed himself in a situation in which it was probable that he would be subjected to duress. The defense is also unavailable if he was negligent in placing himself in such a situation, whenever negligence suffices to establish culpability for the offense charged.[1]

1. Model Penal Code § 2.09 (Proposed Official Draft 1962).

If a mother were prevented from protecting her child against abuse by a threat from the abuser that he would beat or kill her, this would seem to fit the above definition of duress. However, in the cases we discovered of battered (or possibly battered) women convicted of homicide or assault on their children for failure to act . . ., the defendant in only one case asserted duress as a defense, and the attempt was unsuccessful.[2]

It is possible that the standard duress defense is too narrow, or has the past been interpreted too rigidly, to encompass the type of coercion experienced by the battered woman. As the Model Penal Code section indicates, the duress defense requires (1) a threat, (2) made at the time of the conduct, (3) of immediate (or imminent) death or serious bodily injury, (4) that a person of reasonable firmness would not have been able to resist. Furthermore, (5) the defendant must have had no reasonable opportunity to escape the compulsion.

A battered woman might have several problems fitting within the duress definition. First, there may have been no express threat. The batterer may never have said to her, 'If you interfere when I beat the child, or if you take the child to the doctor afterwards, I will beat or kill you or I will kill the child.' However, because of the pattern of his violence toward her, she may know that his rage is kindled if she tries to interfere with anything he is doing, especially when he is already enraged or acting out of anger or frustration, which would be the case if he was in the act of beating a child.

Second, the threat may not have been made at the time of the conduct (or failure to act) charged. She may have been threatened by him in the past when she contemplated leaving him, going to a doctor, or going to the police. It is typical of batterers that they try to keep their victims from having contact with anyone who might believe them or influence them to act, particularly the authorities, but also mere friends and relatives. Threats, of course, are only part of the arsenal of weapons batterers use to keep their victims isolated, intimidated, and compliant. If he threatened her in the past, she may view those threats as carrying over into the present, but the law might require a current threat.

Third, the abuser's threat may be of future rather than imminent harm, whereas imminent harm is required by the law. However, one might argue that, given the battered woman's perception of her situation as hopeless and her belief that no avenue of escape from him is possible, present and future harm become telescoped in her mind, and that it is her perception of danger that should govern. . . . One could also argue that, lacking any realistic source of protection against his violence, she perhaps should be excused from the requirement of immediacy.

Fourth, a jury might conclude that 'a person of reasonable firmness' would have been able to resist the batterer's coercion. The battered woman has little firmness left in her, however, and she might consider it eminently

2. United States v. Webb, 747 F. 2d 278 (5th Cir. 1984), *cert. denied*, 469 U.S. 1226 (1985).

reasonable not to interfere with his abuse of the child, fearing that interference would either increase the abuse to the child or precipitate deadly violence against her.

Fifth, the jury could view her as having 'placed [her]self in a situation in which it was probable that [s]he would be subjected to duress' by failing to remove herself and the child from the battering situation....

Sixth, and related to the fifth, the jury could believe that she could have escaped from the coercive situation when it was taking place. *United States v. Webb*, a case where a duress defense was attempted but failed, illustrates this factor. June Webb was living as the wife of Keith Webb, who beat and abused her and their six-year-old son Steve for at least three years. Finally the child died as a result of failure to get medical care for his injuries, and Keith buried him in the Texas desert. About a month later June managed to escape from his influence by claiming she had been raped by another man and asking Keith to drive her to the authorities. When she was taken into a room out of his hearing, she told the authorities of her son's death and accused Keith of causing the death. She stated that she could not report the death earlier because Keith had threatened to kill her, her other children, and her family in Delaware if she reported him.

June was charged with two counts of injury to a child for failing to obtain medical care for him.... [S]he was convicted and sentenced to ten years in prison. The court of appeals affirmed.

We do not know why the jury rejected the duress defense, but one likely explanation is that the jury believed she had a 'reasonable opportunity to escape the compulsion.' ... [T]he jurors would probably think: 'If she could get to the authorities one month after the death, why not during the time when her son was being abused?' ...

June Webb's attorneys seemed to understand that their client's circumstances did not fit neatly into the definition of duress, but they were unable either to mold the definition to fit the situation of a battered woman or to explain the battered woman's situation to the jury in a way that would convince them that the facts fit the definition....

Defenses of Impaired Mental State. Impaired mental state defenses include insanity, which is a total defense to criminal conduct, and, depending on the particular jurisdiction, partial responsibility defenses. Defense attorneys usually resort to psychiatric defenses only after everything else has failed.... [T]here are special considerations at work when the defendant is a woman. As Professors Schneider and Jordan pointed out in an article on the representation of women in self-defense situations:

> If it is necessary to use an impaired mental state defense, counsel can still accurately and fully inform the jury of the conditions and circumstances which affected the woman's state of mind. For example, when a woman has suffered years of physical ... abuse by her husband ... it is essential that her defense explain these background factors. This may be done through sociological, psychological, or psychiatric testimony, the defendant's own testimony, *or voir dire*. The defense would

suggest that the woman was driven to the breaking point by the circumstances of her situation.

In choosing an impaired mental state defense, it is important to consider that juries not only generally mistrust psychiatric defenses, but may ... apply a different standard to women. The jury may require a woman who asserts an impaired mental state defense to sound truly insane. A woman who sounds too angry or calm may not fulfill the jurors' role expectations.... This problem is particularly severe where other myths are operating as well. Prosecutors may, for example, imply that women are masochists and are themselves responsible for the preceding assaults.

Additionally, the defense attorney must be sure that the facts of the particular defendant's case fit the defense chosen.... Does ... physical abuse cause insanity or diminished capacity as those terms are defined by the legal system? If not, do we want to try to expand those definitions, or would doing so present dangers for women in other situations? As others have pointed out, a more thorough analysis of impaired capacity defenses is needed in order to more effectively represent women in these circumstances.

Physical Incapacity. '[O]ne cannot be criminally liable for failing to do an act which he is physically incapable of performing,' declare LaFave and Scott.[1] It would seem to follow, therefore, that if a mother could not have successfully prevented the batterer from battering her child, she could not be held responsible for failing to act. However, it is unclear what she would have to show in order to establish a defense of physical incapacity. Would she have to show that she was 5′4″ and wearing a cast on her leg, while he was 6′2″ and drunk? Would she have to show, in addition, that she had no gun or knife with which to impede him? What if she could have stopped him, but only by becoming his victim herself?

. . .

Lack of Causality. On causation, LaFave and Scott state:

Most of the criminal cases on omission to act deal with criminal homicide–murder or manslaughter. Homicide crimes require not only conduct ... but a certain result of conduct (the death of the victim). It must therefore be shown ... not only that the defendant had a duty to act, but also that his failure to act caused the death.

The problem of causation in omission cases has been a matter of real difficulty for many theorists. For example, it has been claimed that when a speeding train runs over a child which the father failed to rescue, the cause of death is the train and not the forbearance of the father. However, problems of this nature disappear once it is acknowledged that the question of causation is not solely a question of

1. Wayne LaFave and Austin Scott, *Handbook on Criminal Law* § 3.3(c), at 208 (2d ed. 1986).

> mechanical connection, but rather a question of policy on imputing or denying liability.
>
> Legal or 'proximate' cause, at the very least requires a showing of 'but for' causation; but for the omission the victim would not have died.[2]

Causation questions could arise both in the context of a battered woman who did nothing while a man battered the child and in the context of a mother who failed to seek medical care for a child. If the mother had attempted to stop the battering, would the child have lived? If she did seek medical care, would the child have lived? It seems as though the courts, in battered children cases, have assumed causality.... [T]he cases tend to assume that action on the mother's part would have saved the child, whereas no such assumption is made if the child is simply ill and the parent fails to seek medical help. More research needs to be done on this potential defense.

* * *

NOTES AND QUESTIONS

1. With respect to each of the defenses Erickson describes, it would be crucial to determine whether it is available only if the defendant can first establish that liability is not strict, or whether the defense is available even if liability is construed to be strict. In the child welfare context, for example, we have already seen that liability for child neglect can attach even in the face of a parent's manifest incapacity to care for a child because of mental illness or mental retardation; it would seem, by analogy, that impaired capacity or impossibility defenses would be irrelevant to a strict liability charge of failure to protect. If the mother's inaction was not the cause of harm to the child, on the other hand, because that harm would have been done regardless of any effort on the part of the mother, then an essential element of the crime is missing, and no liability should attach, even if that liability is strict.

Duress poses an interesting problem in this regard. If duress is seen as negating the existence of the requisite mens rea for a crime, then the defense might not be available for a crime which did not require any culpable mens rea–in other words, a strict liability crime. This was the approach taken by the New Mexico Supreme Court, in State v. Lucero, 647 P.2d 406 (N.M. 1982), affirming a lower court decision that the mother was strictly liable for child abuse for allowing her boyfriend to beat her son, and that the defense of duress was inapplicable. The statute at issue read:

> Abuse of a child consists of a person knowingly, intentionally or negligently, and without justifiable cause, causing or permitting a child to be:
>
> (1) placed in a situation that may endanger the child's life or health; or

2. La Fave & Scott, ... § 3.3(d), at 209–10.

(2) tortured, cruelly confined or cruelly punished....

N.M. Stat. Ann. § 30–6–1(c). In a later case, the New Mexico Supreme Court found that the "negligence" language in this statute required a showing of criminal negligence; Santillanes v. State 849 P.2d 358 (N.M. 1993); but Lucero was not overruled, leaving the overall status of the statute unclear. Liability for "knowingly" "permitting" a child to be endangered is a relatively strict liability, if a defendant is not permitted to argue that although she knew of the child's plight, she was unable to do anything about it. This was the effect of the initial decision in Barrett. A different reading of duress is that it operates to exonerate or excuse those who have acted criminally, when their only alternative is death or serious bodily injury. On this interpretation duress does not negate criminal intent, but excuses defendants otherwise guilty of crimes, whether those crimes require mens rea or not. The New Mexico Supreme Court in other contexts has held duress applicable to strict liability offenses, as have other state courts. See Heather B. Skinazi, *Not Just a "Conjured Afterthought": Using Duress as a Defense for Battered Women Who "Fail to Protect,"* 85 CAL. L. REV. 993, 1037–40 (1997).

2. Skinazi has recommended adapting the legal definition of duress for use in failure to protect cases, employing a "hybrid approach to reasonableness" based on the "reasonable battered woman" standard now used in many states in battered women's self-defense cases:

> The defense of duress is determined by considering whether, under the totality of the circumstances (including past abuse), the threat (implicit or explicit), or the use of force, was such that the actor believed she could not resist, and a reasonable person similarly situated could not resist.
>
> The core elements of this proposed standard are identical to those of traditional duress; reasonableness and coercion. Under this standard, defendants could argue that they had no genuine choice about whether to commit the criminal act because (1) their act was coerced and (2) no reasonable person could have genuinely resisted the coercion (their capitulation to the coercion was reasonable). Although sometimes it might have been physically possible for the actor to choose differently, if a reasonable person would not have, then the actor should be exonerated. By establishing that the defendant had a reasonable perception of danger, given her experience of prior battering, duress could excuse a battered woman whose fear of her batterer led to her reasonable choice of obeying him to protect her children from a worse harm that he threatened.

Heather B. Skinazi, *Not Just a "Conjured Afterthought": Using Duress as a Defense for Battered Women Who "Fail to Protect,"* 85 CAL. L. REV. 993, 1024–25 (1997). As Skinazi explains, the key differences between her proposed definition and the traditional one are that the threat made by the abuser can be implicit as well as explicit, and that the threat does not need to be one of imminent or immediate harm. Both these modifications allow jury and judge to take a longer and fuller look at the context of the abusive relationship which conditioned the mother's response to her child's abuse.

Interestingly, the "imminency" requirement was also written out of the Model Penal Code's definition of duress, despite its pedigree as a traditional element of the defense.

As further evidence of the difficulty battered defendants have claiming duress in failure to protect cases, consider the Fifth Circuit's statement in 1994: "[w]hile evidence that a defendant is suffering from the battered woman's syndrome provokes our sympathy, it is not relevant, for purposes of determining criminal responsibility, to whether the defendant acted under duress." United States v. Willis, 38 F.3d 170, 177 (5th Cir. 1994) *citing* United States v. Sixty Acres in Etowah County, 930 F.2d 857, 861 (11th Cir. 1991) (holding battered woman's generalized fear of her abuser though genuine and profound, provokes our sympathy, but cannot provoke the application of "legal standard of duress whose essential elements are absent").

3. Whether the defendant's strategy is negating criminal intent, or mounting an affirmative defense, testimony about the abuse the defendant has suffered, its impact on her, and the ways in which it has influenced her behavior, will be crucial. In all probability that testimony will be introduced under the rubric of BWS. However, the precise way in which the testimony will be presented will depend both on the court's interpretation of the scope of BWS testimony, and the particular legal context (is she arguing about whether she "knowingly" exposed her child to danger; about whether she made every reasonable effort to protect her child, under the circumstances in which she found herself; or about whether she acted, or failed to act, under duress?).

The potential difficulties with BWS testimony in this context are the same as those you have already considered in Chapter 4. Is the defendant wanting to argue a psychological impairment that (a) prevented her from seeing the danger to her child (because she had learned to protect herself by minimizing or denying her abuser's violence), or (b) made it impossible for her to act, because she was in a state of paralysis, or believed so strongly in the omnipotence of her abuser that she could not see opportunities for escape, or for invoking help, even though in fact they existed? In some cases, perhaps. But the commentary you have read in this section suggests that many if not most defendants would instead want to argue that they were not impaired in their perceptions or judgments, but faced an intractable reality. In many cases they had already tested helping systems, and found them wanting. They feared justifiably that efforts to help their children would be ineffective, and would result in potentially more severe injury to both child and mother. If their testimony alone will not be credible to a jury or judge, then the supporting expert testimony they need is testimony about the sociological reality of battering relationships, demonstrating that this defendant's perception of her situation is in line with what countless other battered women have learned through hard experience. As Mary Ann Dutton proposed in the excerpt you read in Chapter 4, above at pp. 225–33, we need a framework that allows for testimony about *both* psychological impairment *and* sociological data, and one that does not confound subjective perception and objective reality.

4. A very few jurisdictions have addressed the situation of abused mothers who fail to protect their abused children more directly; building statutory defenses into the same provisions that create criminal liability. The BWS instruction that defendant's counsel had wanted to give the jury in Barrett: "It is a defense to a prosecution of neglect of a dependent resulting in serious bodily injury that at the time of the neglect there was a reasonable apprehension in the mind of the defendant that acting to stop or prevent the neglect or endangerment would result in substantial bodily harm to the defendant or the child in retaliation," 675 N.E. 2d 1112, 1118 (1996), was drawn directly from the statutory defense enacted in Minnesota, Minn. Stat. Ann. § 609.378 Subd. 2 (West 1993). See also 21 Okl. St. Ann. § 852.1 (West 2000) and Iowa Code Ann. § 726.6 (West 1993).

Notice that the statutory defense is limited to circumstances where the defendant reasonably fears that intervening will result in substantial harm to the child or the defendant herself. This approach avoids many of the difficulties we have explored in this section. In a substantial number of cases it will forestall the imposition of strict liability. In others it will provide a helpful alternative to duress, with its rather rigid requirements. In the cases in which a defendant is, like Hedda Nussbaum, so psychologically damaged by abuse that an impaired capacity defense is more appropriate, nothing in the framing of the statutory defense proscribes exploring that alternative. In short, this is a development to be encouraged.

Nancy Erickson offers further suggestions for reform, cautioning that "the research on this issue is not sufficient to permit one to make strong, fully informed recommendations." Nancy Erickson, *Battered Mothers of Battered Children: Using Our Knowledge of Battered Women to Defend them Against Charges of Failure to Act,* Children and Families: Abuse and Endangerment, 197, 209 (Vol. 1A, Current Perspectives in Psychological, Legal and Ethical Issues, 1991):

> First, legislation should be considered that would provide that one who takes an abused child for medical treatment or who reports child abuse may not be charged with failure to act to prevent any child abuse by the same abuser in the past, or in the future until the victims are protected from the abuser. This should encourage mothers to report child abuse by others and seek medical treatment for it, because in this way they protect themselves from criminal liability....
>
> Second, attorneys and other law reformers should consider legislation providing that if the defendant proves by a preponderance of the evidence that she was battered by the abuser, she may not be convicted of failure to act unless the prosecution can prove, beyond a reasonable doubt, that fear of death or serious bodily injury at the hands of the abuser was not the cause of her failure to act. This procedure would be similar to the procedure followed in some states with regard to the insanity defense. The defendant is presumed sane, but if he or she introduced evidence creating a reasonable doubt of his or her sanity, the state must prove beyond a reasonable doubt that the defendant was sane at the time of the offense charged.

> Third, the law should provide treatment—not incarceration—for nonabusing parents charged with failure to act to protect their children from harm by others. One author suggests a pretrial diversion program for such parents. The parent would be charged under the state child abuse statute, but then 'the family would be diverted into a treatment program that would include therapy for the abused children and for the parent.' The program would also include parenting skills training for both the parent and the children, and other skills training for the parent to enable her to live independently from the abuser.... Properly funded, a program of this sort would certainly reduce the costs to the public, both in monetary and nonmonetary terms, of alternative forms of care for children whose families are broken up by the state after findings of abuse or neglect.

Id. at 209–10.

5. How different is Erickson's last suggestion from the regular operation of the child welfare system, within which officials certainly have the discretion to respond to a finding of neglect by providing services to the non-abusive members of the family, rather than taking the children out of the home? Is this an argument that if the understanding of abusive relationships reflected in these reforms were absorbed by those working within the child welfare and criminal justice systems, many of the same results could be accomplished within the existing framework by the appropriate use of prosecutorial discretion?

CHAPTER SEVEN

THE FAMILY LAW SYSTEM

A. INTRODUCTION

It could be argued that the American legal system has two family laws. One—applicable mostly to families on the lowest rungs of the socio-economic ladder—derives from the child protective system and the welfare system, while the other—applicable to all other families—derives from what we more commonly think of as "family law;" the rules governing separation, divorce, custody, visitation, support, and the division of marital property.

For the domestic violence advocate, perhaps the most frustrating thing about traditionally conceived "family law," and the family court system, is the extent to which it ignores, denies or minimizes violence between partners who come to court with a family-related legal issue. Although recent reforms are making a difference, change has to happen at two levels—in the law itself, and then in the attitudes of those who implement and enforce it. It is hard enough to change the rules, but often even harder to change attitudes. The issue may be whether an abusive husband and his partner should be required to mediate their differences, or whether the abuser should share custody of a child, or whether visitation should be supervised or unsupervised—at every level decisions continue to be made every day that ignore the power imbalance between abuser and abused, or the effects on children of being the pawns in one partner's quest for control over the other, or the necessity for a woman to make her own safety a priority, even if it means restricting her former partner's access to the children.

These problems exist even when the abuse is documented, and a matter of record. But another problem area for women in abusive relationships is the tendency for family courts to deny the reality of the abuse. At every step along the way, there is a danger that the violence will be overlooked, or misinterpreted, or discounted. Many family lawyers do not yet routinely screen their clients for domestic violence—and many clients will not bring it up unless they are explicitly invited to do so. The client who is open about her situation, and wants it presented to the court as the context in which she is requesting custody, or restricted visitation, is as likely as not to find her credibility attacked by her spouse's lawyer, undermined by a guardian ad litem or custody evaluator, and doubted by the judge. In particular, the abusive relationship is likely to be recast as a conflictual one, in which she is as much or more to blame for the violence as her partner, or in which she is fabricating or exaggerating stories of violence to gain the upper hand in struggles over children or resources.

If she argues that the abuse makes him an unfit parent, his response will be that the problems in their adult relationship have nothing to do with his relationships with his children—and that her desire to limit his access is vindictive, and against their best interests. If the children confirm their own fears, and express a desire to be with mother rather than father, she may find herself accused of "alienating" them—which suggests in turn that perhaps she is the one whose access should be restricted. She will struggle, in this legal and emotional minefield, to avoid some of the stereotypes with which women have been traditionally saddled—that they are hysterical, manipulative and deceitful.

If she loses the battle to secure a zone of safety in the aftermath of her separation from him, she and her children may be locked into a continuing relationship with her abuser, and at significant risk for further injury. If those risks materialize, and she flees from him in violation of the court's orders, the court may be more concerned about its authority having been flouted than about her, or her children's, wellbeing.

All these issues are taken up in this and subsequent sections of this chapter. The first readings in this section address the particular risks inherent in separating from a violent relationship, and the need for all family lawyers to be aware of those risks and to screen their clients to assess whether their relationships have been abusive. The final reading in this section tells one woman's story, and provides a cautionary tale about how women and children can be put at risk when those involved in the family court system—lawyers, judges and mental health professionals—fail to understand the dynamics of abuse.

The second and third sections are about the standards used by judges to regulate access to children in the aftermath of divorce, looking first at custody and then at visitation. The fourth is about the role of mediation in family court, and the particular dangers of the mediation process in the presence of abuse. The fifth addresses the role of the guardian ad litem, highlighting the need for all professionals involved in the work of the family court, not just the lawyers and judges, to be sensitive to and trained in the dynamics of abusive relationships and their impact on children. The sixth focuses on parent education at divorce, another new mechanism growing in popularity among family courts, and another context in which professionals trained in mental health rather than law have a crucial role to play. The final section deals with the complexities of parent relocation, and interstate custody disputes.

Violence and the Family A Report of the American Psychological Association Presidential Task Force on Violence and the Family, 39–41 (1996)

Understanding Abuse After Separation

When partners separate, the violence does not necessarily end. Many people still believe that the problem of battering can be solved by separation, but the risk of serious or lethal violence may actually increase after separation. The greatest risk for serious injury or death from violence is at the point of separation or at the time when the decision to separate is made. Data from a U.S. Department of Justice National Crime Victimization Survey indicate that among women who were victims of violent assault by an intimate partner, women reported that the offender was an ex-spouse almost half as many times as they reported that the offender was a spouse.

Physical separation may actually increase a man's need to control his partner and children. Women who have experienced the cycle of violence will often compromise their own safety by telling their batterers where they are. They report that they are terrified that their batterers will find them anyway, and their decision to disclose their own whereabouts to the batterer relieves the anxiety of waiting for the batterer inevitably to come and get them. Clues to the batterer's level of tension and likelihood of a new assault are best read by battered women when they are in contact with their partners.

Homicides in which a batterer is known to have killed his partner most frequently occur at the point of separation and up to two years after separation. Most homicide-suicides that occur in the United States are committed by batterers who kill their partners, sometimes their children, and then themselves. Such murders are quite rare, however, considering the large numbers of women who are battered daily.

There is no way to predict whether a specific batterer is likely to kill his partner. Even though data are available about batterers who actually commit such murders, the batterers' violent behavior does not provide enough information for accurate predictions about which batterers will go on to kill their partners. Psychotherapists can use a variety of checklists and other instruments to help determine the level of risk for a lethal incident, but these assessment devices have not been validated by empirical research.

When violence occurs during separation, it typically includes all of the usual types of violence that occurred during the relationship, in addition to new violent behaviors arising from the separation: battles over finances, custody disputes, violence at visitation, threatened or attempted child kidnaping, and stalking. Many women who reported that their batterers threatened child kidnaping also reported that the men backed up their threats of kidnaping with episodes of refusing to tell the mother where her child was or keeping the child beyond the specified time without notice.

When batterers are arrested for stalking and harassment, it is not uncommon for them to complain that they only wanted to make the woman listen to them. Most of these men do not understand that they do not have the right to force any woman to be with them.

Understanding Custody Disputes and Violence Related to Visitation

When a couple divorces, the legal system may become a symbolic battleground on which the male batterer continues his abuse. Custody and visitation may keep the battered woman in a relationship with the battering man; on the battleground, the children become the pawns. Studies of custody disputes indicate that fathers who battered the mother are twice as likely to seek sole physical custody of their children than are nonviolent fathers, and they are more likely to dispute custody if there are sons involved. If these men lose custody of their children, they are likely to continue to threaten and harass the mother with legal actions. Battering fathers also are three times as likely to be in arrears in child support, and are more likely to engage in protracted legal disputes over all aspects of the divorce.

Prolonged and bitter custody disputes are especially detrimental to children. Children from these high-conflict homes frequently maintain loyalties with only one parent, choosing either to identify with the aggressor or with the victim. When children reject their abusive fathers, it is common for the batterer and others to blame the mother for alienating the children. They often do not understand the legitimate fears of the child. Although there are no data to support the phenomenon called *parental alienation syndrome*, in which mothers are blamed for interfering with their children's attachment to their fathers, the term is still used by some evaluators and courts to discount children's fears in hostile and psychologically abusive situations.

If the mother has physical custody of the children, the father may threaten and attack her when he visits the children. Some researchers have indicated patterns of high conflict occurring during visitation. Even during supervised visitation, in which physical violence is constrained by the presence of an observer, threats as well as verbal and emotional abuse may continue. In such situations, the children often feel responsible for the violence against their mother, because the father was visiting them. A woman's attempts to protect herself may be construed by the court as an attempt to interfere with the father's visitation rights. Faced with such situations, women often describe themselves as having no real choices: If they try to protect their children, their behavior is considered alienating; if they do nothing, their behavior is considered failure to protect their children.

Understanding the Effects of Threats: Harming and Kidnaping the Children

In the breakup of a family relationship, one parent may threaten to harm or kidnap a child in an attempt to reestablish control over the other parent. This control may be directed toward restoring the relationship, or it may be aimed at generating fear and distress in the other parent. As a family breaks up, a noncustodial parent may increase the amount of time and attention that is directed toward the child, and the child then becomes more meaningful as a symbolic possession. As the battle for the child intensifies, threats to abduct the child become more frequent. Although the threats to abduct are not always carried out, the effect is to generate a climate of fear and anxiety for both the threatened parent and the child. Studies of actual kidnapings show that 55% to 69% of abductors are men.

A batterer may use threats of harming or kidnaping the children to keep a woman from leaving him or to force her to return. Many women report that they return to battering relationships to keep control of the batterer's contact with their children. For example, according to one study, more than one-third of women in shelters for battered women reported that they stayed in the relationship at least partially because they feared for their children's safety, and one-fourth of those women studied reported that they had returned to the violent relationship after threats were made against the children. Frequently, men who have not participated in the care of their children will begin to spend more time with them during their visitations. The children are often frightened of their fathers, remembering previous violence or threats, and they fear that they may be hurt or that they will not be returned to their mothers. The children's fears, in turn, add to the mother's fear that the children will be harmed.

* * *

The Crucial Role of the Family Lawyer
Clare Dalton, Domestic Violence, Domestic Torts and Divorce: Constraints and Possibilities, 31 New England Law Review 319, 352–353, 364–370 (1997)

The fact that a woman is seeking a divorce because of physical and/or emotional abuse in her marital relationship does not mean that she will spontaneously share that information with her lawyer. Shame may still be a powerful inhibitor. Further, the very boldness of the step she is considering may exacerbate her fears about her partner's potential for future abuse. She may want to minimize her present danger by minimizing the extent to which the divorce exposes his abuse. She may hope that by appeasing him, to the extent that is possible consistent with pursuing the divorce, she will be better positioned to achieve her goals, first among which are likely to be an end to the abuse, and custody of her children. Ultimately the decision about whether to disclose the abuse, first to her lawyer, and then to the court, must rest with the client. Nonetheless, there is plenty of room for the family lawyer to improve the chances that her client will at least take the first step of sharing the information with her, and plenty of reasons why working towards that initial disclosure can be crucial both to her client's safety, and to effective representation.

Are there reasons why a family lawyer may be reluctant to ask about abuse . . .?

There are injuries that are difficult to acknowledge—it is painful to think about . . . adults being victimized by their partners. Society as a whole has a tendency to deny or minimize these injuries, and to mobilize to suppress the disclosures that would erode that denial, or undercut the minimization. Disclosures can undermine our faith in humanity, or the institution of family. Sometimes they will reverberate with our own experience, stirring up emotions that we have done our best to repress. Other people's stories can make us experience vicariously their pain, their vulnerability and their powerlessness. They can also challenge us to become involved in situations in which involvement might put us personally or professionally at risk. A victim who is, quite independently, reluctant to disclose will be sensitive to cues that a listener is equally reluctant to hear....

... An additional factor, in this context, may be that the family law system has traditionally organized itself without reference to partner violence. Even in the most recent editions of family law casebooks partner violence scarcely appears as a topic, and as a consequence many family law courses still ignore it. Neither practitioners nor judges, that is to say, have traditionally learned about domestic violence in the course of their law school training.

Even more significant may be the prevailing ideology of family courts, which emphasizes the mediated resolution of conflict, the desirability of minor children continuing to have significant relationships with both parents, and the development of stable post-divorce relationships between parents in the interests of children. In this context, the partner who seeks to avoid mediation on the ground that her relationship with an abusive spouse precludes bargaining on a level playing field, and puts her at risk; or the parent who seeks to oppose shared custody or unsupervised visitation, on the grounds that it endangers her or her children, upsets the smooth functioning of the system, and is readily cast as a pariah. Such women are often suspected of manipulating the system for their own advantage, distorting the truth, or turning their children against their former partners out of vindictiveness....

Thus, while many family judges and lawyers steadfastly support the exposure of domestic violence, and the legal system's careful response to victims' rights and needs, the atmosphere in family court and within the family bar can still be hostile to claims of violence. It would not be surprising, then, if some lawyers, given a choice, would prefer not to represent victims of violence, when it means risking the ire of some of their colleagues, perhaps facing hostility from the bench, probably working harder than usual to obtain the necessary relief for a client whose needs the system is still not fully adapted to meet, and on occasion failing to obtain necessary relief in circumstances where that failure may be not just disappointing, but actually dangerous. If that is a situation to be avoided, then one way to avoid it, a strategy perhaps more unconscious than conscious, may be to avoid the questions that will reveal the abusive nature of the relationship that the client is seeking to end.

Despite all the reasons why a client may be reluctant to talk, and a lawyer reluctant to hear, the bottom line is that if a client is in fact seeking to escape from an abusive relationship, then her lawyer needs to know in order to organize the divorce process and the litigation strategy around that understanding. Without that information, the lawyer may find the client's reluctance to take certain steps, or make certain arguments, baffling, and may urge the client, against her better judgment, toward a strategy that puts her at risk. She may also misinterpret the client's insistence on certain issues—especially relating to limiting the father's access to the children—as punitive, and work toward bringing her client in line with what she thinks judicial standards of reasonable parental behavior will be, not understanding how high the stakes are. The undisclosed information then becomes a wedge between the lawyer and client, undermining the lawyer's confidence in the client, but more importantly eroding the client's trust in the lawyer. The client may begin to feel almost as powerless in this new relationship as she does in her relationship with her partner, to the point where she experiences the divorce process as revictimization. A different but equally plausible scenario involves the client who has summoned the courage to seek a divorce only by disguising from herself how violently her partner may respond to her new determination to leave him. This denial, helpful at the level of enabling her to seek help, may be dangerous if it allows her to be blind-sided by her abusive partner's response. If she has not shared the abuse with her lawyer, there is no second independent judgment available to generate hard questions about safety, and strategize with her about reducing her danger.

It should go without saying that the fully informed lawyer will be in the best position to generate the best possible outcome for her client, understanding that some goals may have to be compromised in order to accomplish others of higher priority. However, this will only be true if two further conditions are met. The first is that the lawyer not merely hear her client's story, but be educated enough about the dynamics of abusive relationships to give the facts their proper weight and significance. The second is that the lawyer respect her client's autonomy, and not use the information with which she is trusted without her client's full agreement. The vulnerability her client feels about disclosing her abuse makes it critical that the lawyer provide reassurance that the disclosure will have no consequences unless and until the client and lawyer together determine that it should....

The questions have to avoid generalities and labels that may be offputting. Asking "Has he battered you or the children," may elicit a negative answer because the woman does not accept the label "battered woman" as a description of herself or her situation, and would never admit that her children have been "battered." If the questions are more specific, they are more likely to generate useful answers: "Have you ever been afraid of him?" would be an example, or "Has he ever done anything to hurt you or your children, or to make you afraid that he would?" More useful information might be gleaned from questions like: "What makes your partner angry with you? When he is angry, what kinds of things does he do or say?" Immediately relevant will be questions like "How does your partner feel about your separating from him? Is that something you have ever talked about with him? Has he ever threatened to do anything to you, or the children, or himself, if you leave him?"

It is also important to ask question across the range of emotionally as well as physically abusive behaviors; asking questions only about physical violence may produce scant results, and the abusive context of the relationship may remain buried. It may also be easier for a woman to talk about the emotional abuse, and if she establishes a rapport with her lawyer in that context, she may then feel safe to talk about the physical or sexual abuse as well.

There will always be some questions that a lawyer finds hard to ask. For many lawyers, questions about sexual abuse fall into that category. But remembering that the lawyer's embarrassment may be read as a reluctance to hear, and provoke a reluctance to tell, she lawyer must at least try to prevent this barrier from arising. She might start out by saying, "I'd like to ask you some questions about your sexual relationship with your partner. I know these aren't easy questions to answer, in fact I even have a hard time asking them. But I'd really like to try to understand this part of your relationship, if you can manage to share it with me." Again, it is crucial in asking these questions not to rely on labels, such as "rape," or "assault," that a woman may not ever think of applying to her own situation.

Some information elicited from the client may be so arresting that the lawyer feels unable to respond. But silence by the lawyer may be taken as disapproval, and in turn silence the client. It is probably better under these circumstances to be honest about what is happening, and then to offer the client support for her strength in being able to tell her story: "I'm finding what you are telling me almost overwhelming. And then I think about what it means for you to have lived it, and still be able to relive it in telling me about it. I think that must take a lot of courage."

If it becomes clear that the client is being physically abused, or has been threatened by violence, then it will be very important for the lawyer to signal that she is aware of the risks involved and will be attentive to her client's safety. She might just want to say: "This sounds like a dangerous situation for you. I think we need to stay very focused on your safety as we plan how to go forward." Once the whole story has been told, this promise should be immediately fulfilled. The development of a safety plan should become the first item of business, whether the lawyer feels able to do that personally, or asks her client for permission to include another more experienced service provider in the planning process. This should be a priority regardless of how the client finally resolves the question of whether to go forward ... but obviously her safety needs may be different depending on the course she chooses.

* * *

NOTES

1. It is just as important for the lawyer representing an abusive partner or parent to have that information about his or her client, and not be taken by surprise. Since abusers are very likely to deny or minimize their abuse, to reframe abuse as conflict, and to shift the blame for family difficulties to their partners, it may be hard for the attorney to have a candid conversation. One strategy is to ask what "allegations" may be made by the former partner about behavior towards her or the children, This may elicit helpful information, even if the client is committed to the position that there is nothing to the allegations, or that the partner's version of the story is a

distortion. Along similar lines, if the client describes a situation in which his former partner has been abusive, or out of control, but the lawyer suspects he or she is not hearing the whole story, it may be helpful to ask: "Do you think your partner would tell this story the same way? How might her account be different, do you think?" It is a straightforward matter to explain the need for this kind of inquiry, in an adversary process in which each side has to be ready to defend its version of reality against attack from the other side.

It is also useful to establish the emotional "flavor" of the relationships between the client and his partner and children, because an abuser who is intent on concealing or denying physical abuse may be quite self-revealing in other ways. Lundy Bancroft, a Boston-based batterers' treatment counselor, has suggested a range of questions relevant to deciding whether a batterer or alleged batterer can be trusted with unsupervised rather than supervised visitation. Many of these same questions could guide a lawyer's attempts to elicit clues about whether his or her client has been abusive in the relationship which is ending, or is seeking to use the children as an ongoing way of controlling his partner. None of these questions could be asked directly, but the lawyer could decide what lines of indirect questioning, or what kinds of open-ended conversation might elicit information about:

- his level of selfishness and self-centeredness towards family members;
- his level of manipulativeness towards family members;
- his level of entitlement (expectation that his needs should always be catered to, seeing the children as personal possessions);
- his history of boundary violations towards the children;
- his history of irresponsible behavior towards the children
- his level of inability to put the children's needs ahead of his own and to leave them out of conflicts with his partner;
- the extent of his past under-involvement with the children (e.g. failing to know basic information such as the child's birth date, names of pediatricians or school teachers, or basic routines of the children's daily care);
- his level of refusal to accept the end of the relationship;
- his level of refusal to accept mother's new partner being in the children's lives;
- his level of psychological cruelty towards his partner
- whether he has been verbally degrading to his partner in front of the children
- whether he has been violent or physically frightening in front of the children

The lawyer who suspects that his or client may well have a history of abuse, even though the client has not disclosed it, or affirmatively denies it, is faced with a professionally challenging and ethically complex situation. The more the client can be persuaded to disclose, the more room the lawyer has to develop reasonable litigation strategies, or to urge a reasonable settlement, within the constraints imposed by the client's history. The more the client is adamant about a "no-holds-barred" strategy, built on a shaky foundation of denial and concealment, the more the lawyer may feel complicit in keeping relevant information from the court and contributing to an outcome that may be dangerous for the partner and children, and the more vulnerable the client may be to exposure and a negative outcome, if his partner and her lawyer are able to present a more convincing story to the court. The law can be an important ally here—the more responsive the rules and the system are to domestic violence, the greater the lawyer's ability to argue that the client's best interests lie in mitigating both his behavior and his claims, so as not to provoke adverse legal consequences.

2. Another person who has written about the need for family lawyers to identify abuse is Kathleen Waits, in *Battered Women and Family Lawyers: The Need for an Identification Protocol,* 58 ALBANY L. REV. 1027 (1995). Professor Waits is also the author of the next excerpt, which provides a sober picture of how the family court system can turn its back on the plight of battered women and their children. In this article, Professor Waits tells "Mary's story" in the first person, and then reflects on the broader implications of the story for family law and the players charged with implementing it. As you read the excerpt, which provides key pieces of Mary's story, think about the role played by her partner's lawyer, as well as the roles played by her own.

Mary's Story
Kathleen Waits, Battered Women and Their Children: Lessons from One Woman's Story, 35 Houston Law Review 29, 46–50, 52–56, 59–62 (1998)

Soon after going into hiding, I hired the first of what would be several lawyers. Overall, I am very dissatisfied with how both the lawyers and the legal system handled my situation. I feel that my lawyers did not understand what I had experienced. They did not understand because they would not or could not listen to what I had to say. They did not seem to care about what *I* wanted and why. Most had a predetermined outcome in mind and a predetermined approach of how they were going to accomplish that outcome. I could not get them to listen to me or to budge from their preconceptions.

I was always very up front with my lawyers about the abuse that had occurred. I also told them very clearly about my fears for myself and my children.

My first lawyer (I will call her Lawyer #1) was a woman and an experienced family lawyer. When I explained to her that I was very afraid of Russ, her response was completely egotistical: "just let him come after me, and I'll kick his ass." Her focus was on what *she* was going to do, not what was best for me. She also said, "You're my client, we'll screw that bastard." This was *not* what I wanted. I wanted to be safe. I didn't want to go "one on one" with Russ, and I did not want my lawyer to do that either. I felt that taking him on like this would increase the danger to me and my children. I felt that this lawyer just did not listen to me or take my concerns seriously.

Lawyer #1 was also my first introduction to how people in the legal system—people who should know better—completely dismiss abuse of women and children. At one point, after I had told her my story, she said, "So he slapped you around and beat the kids. What's your point?" She acted as if these facts were irrelevant to the divorce and custody proceedings.

Russ's lawyer said to my lawyer, "Let's sit Russ and Mary together in the pretrial conference. That'll help work things out." I strongly objected to this. I told my lawyer that sitting next to Russ would be scary and intimidating for me. My lawyer responded, "Don't be gutless like they say you are." I also asked that Russ be searched for possible weapons, but my lawyer said she would not ask for this.

This lawyer talked tough, but she spent most of her time flirting with Russ's lawyer. She did not stand up to Russ. She was also just plain incompetent; she gave away a key issue to Russ and his lawyer. When we were negotiating over money Russ and his lawyer wanted his payments to be labeled "house payments" instead of "child support." My lawyer said, "Fine, no problem." I was not happy about this, but my lawyer said to me, "money is money." I later learned, when Russ didn't make the payments, that there are special enforcement mechanisms that are available *only* for child support payments. In this context, all money is *not* the same. So the lawyer's mistake deprived me and my children of valuable rights....

Lawyer #1 demanded and received a large up front retainer fee. Then she sent me to a psychologist, which cost even more money. This psychologist was very strange and later had a mental breakdown....

Russ claimed that I was a lesbian and an alcoholic. Both of these accusations are completely false. I do not want to sound as if I believe that being a lesbian is bad; I do not. However, most judges are very homophobic, especially in a fundamentalist-dominated city like mine. Accusing a woman of being a lesbian is, unfortunately, a very effective weapon in a custody battle and a very common one. Russ also claimed that *he* had really raised the kids, which was absurdly untrue.

Russ's tactics worked. The lawyers and psychologists, as well as the judge, all concentrated on me and what I had supposedly done wrong. They let Russ off the hook.

I am really angry that the legal system allows batterers to set the agenda through their wild accusations against victims. Russ played the game of "the best defense is a good offense" to perfection. The system allowed him to put the focus on me, instead of on his abuse of me and the children. My lawyers never fought effectively against this tactic.

Eventually, I fired Lawyer #1 ... I then interviewed another female lawyer who had been recommended by HomeSafe, the local battered women's program. This lawyer told me about a specific psychologist in town who is often called as an expert witness in custody fights. The lawyer said, "We'll pay him off and he'll say what we want." I thought this was wrong and refused to hire this lawyer. This same psychologist ultimately testified for Russ in the custody hearing and ... referred to me an "airhead." I do not know if Russ and his lawyer "paid him off," but I cannot help but wonder. I hired another female lawyer (Lawyer #2) instead....

The evening of [another abusive incident] I called my lawyer (Lawyer #2) to discuss what could be done. It was clear to me that she was very intoxicated. She did not respond at all to my outrage and to my safety concerns. I fired her shortly thereafter. I was tired of paying big retainers and getting nowhere.

I then went looking for a male lawyer. I want to acknowledge that I did not yet trust women. Russ had constantly belittled women, and so I did not really believe that women professionals could be competent. I also still bought into the idea that women were natural rivals with each other. In saying this, I do not mean to excuse what my first two lawyers did. I think I was more than justified in firing them. But I think I fired them much more quickly than I would have if they had been men.

Attorney #3, a man, represented me through the trial that eventually ended in my losing custody of my son Daniel. Attorney #3 sent me to a psychologist whose attitude reminded me of Lawyer #1 ... That is, the psychologist saw this as a personal battle with Russ's psychologist. The key was for her to "win;" she did not focus on the safety or well-being of my children and me. Perhaps because she was focused on herself and not me, ultimately she was charmed by Russ and came to believe his lies. She was so self-absorbed. I can still picture her tossing her hair flirtatiously as she made remarks that destroyed me and my children.

This psychologist had a very dismissive attitude. She never really believed my story of abuse. Because I was a professional and a strong person, I think she identified with me, but that identification hurt me. I think she did not want to confront the possibility that someone like her could ever be abused, or would stay in an abusive relationship. The fact that I was a strong person seemed to make my story less credible to her....

She did not understand domestic violence at all. Like the judge who reluctantly granted my protective order, she was puzzled and troubled by the fact that I was so scared by Russ's "you're going to get the beating of your life" threat. She even asked me at one point, "When he threatened to beat you ... did he say it in a playful way?" She did not understand that physical violence is just one tool batterers use to control their victims. She did not understand the non-physical techniques (degradation, isolation, sleep deprivation) that Russ used. She did not understand that the physical violence does not have to be frequent or severe to be effective....

No one cared about Russ's ongoing intimidation of me either. During the divorce proceedings, Russ would leave angry messages on my answering machine, saying things like "I will get you." He would even threaten to kill me and make it look like a suicide. He would say, "I could do that without any problem. You know how good I am with guns." I told my family and friends over and over, "No matter how bad it gets, I'm telling you that I would never commit suicide. I would never leave my kids without a mother. If they find me dead and it looks like a suicide, don't you believe that. If that happens, make sure the police investigate Russ." I told the lawyers and psychologists about Russ's threats, but they did not take them seriously.

It also bothers me that psychologists will not investigate the true facts, yet they assert that they know the truth. I repeatedly offered to put them in touch with other witnesses who would support my story. They declined, saying that was not their job. Yet, they would claim to know what actually happened. Apparently, they felt they were such experts that they knew who was telling the truth, Russ or me. Russ, with his charming batterer's demeanor, won every time.

Both the psychologists and the judge failed to understand how the abuse affected the children. For instance, the children were scared to death of Russ. This is not surprising, given what they had seen him do to them and to me. As a result, they were very well-behaved when they were with him; they just wanted to avoid getting hurt more. Then when the kids were with me, in a comfortable, safe environment, they were often out of control. It just makes sense. They needed some place where they could safely express the trauma and stress they were experiencing. Yet, the psychologists, and ultimately the judge, held it against *me* that the kids did not always behave well when they were with me. . . . The psychologists and the judge never looked at the *causes* of the kids' problems. The never held *Russ* responsible for the behavior that was causing the kids to feel out of control in the first place.

Most fundamentally, the psychologists and judge bought the idea that Russ's abuse of me was irrelevant to child custody issues. They did not see any reason why the abuse should keep Russ from having full custody of the children. My own psychologist said, "So he's abused you. But he loves those kids." Even when I reminded her that the kids, especially Elizabeth, had seen the abuse, the psychologist responded, "She's young, she'll get over it." . . .

Overall, I found the lawyers and psychologists very self-promoting and egotistical. It seemed as if everyone was having a good time, playing the game of litigation and psychology. All the while, my life was on the line. My children and I did not matter. I also felt like the lawyers and psychologists were running a cash register business at my expense. They were a lot more interested in my money than my welfare. The first two years of my divorce proceedings cost me more than twenty-five thousand dollars.

As incredible as it might sound, *the judge who heard my custody case had an outstanding protective order against him by his ex-wife.* I also sensed very strongly that the judge did not like me. For these reasons, I told my lawyer I wanted to seek the judge's recusal. My lawyer dismissed me, saying, "You'll just get someone worse." . . .

The judge ordered that Russ be given custody of our son Daniel, then age four. The judge said that Russ was a good parent. He agreed with the psychologists that I would be a bad custodial parent because I was angry and could not get along with Russ with regard to visitation. The judge said that he was unable to determine my "sexual deviancy," thus giving credence to Russ's false claims that I was a lesbian.

To make matters worse, the judge told me that I was getting custody of Elizabeth for a six-month probationary period. I will never forget his warning from the bench: "If you do *one thing* to disrupt visitation, I'll take your daughter and give your ex-husband custody of her too."

As if losing Daniel weren't bad enough, the lawyer who accompanied me to the final hearing made it worse. My own lawyer was not there; he sent one of his associates instead. After hearing that I had lost custody of me son, I broke down in tears. The associate angrily took me into the court conference room and said, "Shut the fuck up. You'll lose the other kid."

The night that I lost custody of Daniel was the worse night of my life. I came very close to going back to Russ, just to protect my son. . . . I mean, if a parent saves two of her three children from a burning house, does she feel good about rescuing two, or terrible that she could not rescue all three? I cannot tell you how angry I am that the legal system required me to make that choice. . . .

I did not appeal the custody decision because by this point, I had no money left to pay the lawyer. It was certainly clear that the lawyer would not pursue the appeal without more up-front money. . . .

[Four or five months after Russ obtained custody of Daniel, his new girlfriend reported that Russ was abusing the four year old, and when Lawyer #3 said that it was too soon to seek a modification of the custody order, Mary fired him, and regained custody with the help of a fourth lawyer and a new psychologist. Russ continued to harass Mary by phone, and to stalk her. In March 1966, four years after Daniel returned to the custody of his mother, Russ lost visitation. Not, however, because of his abuse, but because the children were thrown out of the back of his pick up truck when he drove too fast on a bumpy road. Mary had this to say about the final outcome:]

Eliminating visitation was a proper result, and I am glad about it. Still, I cannot help but feel a little bitter that no one ever really cared about *my* safety and its affect on our children. In the court's eyes, Russ only became a bad father and a bad person when he injured the children personally and individually. . . . *My* word about his abuse of the children never counted. The court listened only after I had concrete, outside proof, such as their injuries from being thrown from the truck.

* * *

NOTE

1. In 1995, the Family Violence Project of the National Council of Juvenile and Family Court Judges issued a "call to action" to all involved in the

family court system as it affects abused parents and their children, emphasizing the many areas in which change is still essential if the system is to be responsive to their needs. As the Project's report notes: "[d]omestic violence is a pervasive problem that devastates all family members and challenges society at every level. It violates our communities' safety, health, welfare, and economy by draining billions annually in social costs such as medical expenses, psychological problems, lost productivity, and intergenerational violence. Therefore, leadership, communication, and coordination are critical among legislators, law enforcement officers, social service agency personnel, judges, attorneys, health-care personnel, advocates, and educators." The Family Violence Project of the National Council of Juvenile and Family Court Judges, *Family Violence in Child Custody Statutes: An Analysis of State Codes and Legal Practice,* 29 F.L.Q. 197, 223–224 (1995). The Project's specific recommendations included mandated formal training for attorneys in family violence; protocols and training manuals developed by local and state bar associations; making legal counsel available to currently unrepresented victims of domestic violence and their children; continuing education consistent with available national standards and recommended practices for judges, probation officers, workers in children's protective services, social workers, court-appointed special advocates, mediators and custody evaluators, and the development of specialized resources for domestic violence cases. Id. Many of these themes will be taken up, and many of these recommendations reiterated, in subsequent sections of this chapter.

B. CUSTODY

Introductory Note

This section explores the legal standards governing access to children in the aftermath of separation or divorce, and judicial application of those standards in custody determinations. These are the standards that will be used to adjudicate disputes between parents that are not resolved through mediation, which is discussed in Section D below. They also provide the backdrop to mediation, since both parties, at least if they are represented by counsel or assisted by an advocate, will understand that proposed settlement terms must be measured against the likely outcome of litigation. Finally, although a judge is likely to be influenced by the terms of an agreement reached by parents, his or her role as *parens patriae* demands at least the appearance of an independent assessment of whether those terms provide sufficient protection of the child or children's interests.

Who disputes custody, and when custody is disputed, who wins? Macoby and Mnookin, in their influential book DIVIDING THE CHILD: SOCIAL AND LEGAL DILEMMAS OF CUSTODY (1992) report that about 90% of parents settle custody through negotiation or private mediation rather than litigation. The remaining 10% take the dispute to adjudication, but many then settle before that process reaches a conclusion, whether through attorney negotiations, mediation, or with the help of a custody evaluation. It is ultimately a very tiny proportion of families—some studies suggest less than 2%—who depend on a final judicial decision to resolve the conflict.

We know that many of the families in this final group are dealing with high levels of partner conflict. *See,* W. Halikias, *The Distribution of Conflict in Child Custody Disputes*, 20 Jun. Vt. B. J. & L. Dig. 33 (1994). Unfortunately, the studies on which this conclusion is based do not distinguish between conflict and abuse, but since there is consistent data suggesting that 50% of disputed custody cases referred to court mediation programs involve partner violence, there is no reason to suppose that the abuse rate in adjudicated cases is any lower, and good reason to think it might be higher.

Studies reporting on fathers' success rates when they pursue custody through litigation yield rather inconsistent results. Macoby and Mnookin's study suggested that when both parents sought sole custody, mothers obtained it 46.2% of the time, fathers 9.6% of the time, and courts imposed joint custody 36.5% of the time. Other studies have reported greater success by fathers. Nancy Polikoff, in *Why Are Mothers Losing?*, 7 Women's Rights L. Rep. 235, 236 (1982), cites a range of studies giving fathers success rates between 38% and 63%.; Jessica Pearson and Maria A. Luchesi Ring, in *Judicial Decisionmaking in Contested Custody Cases,* 21 J. Fam. L. 703, 719 (1983), report fathers winning custody in three Colorado counties in 32.3%, 15.5% and 21.2% of cases; and Jeff Atkinson, in *Criteria for Deciding Child Custody in the Trial and Appellate Courts,* 18 F.L.Q. 1, 10–11 (1984), shows fathers winning custody in 51% of cases. If, as accumulating reports suggest, fathers who have been abusive partners are more likely than other fathers to contest custody, as a way of continuing to assert control over partner and family, then abusive fathers are in all likelihood over represented in the litigious minority, and their relative success provides legitimate grounds for concern for the ongoing safety of their children and former partners. As the family court system becomes more attuned to the presence of abuse, it should become easier to identify cases in which abusers are contesting custody, and it will be important to document and explain their success or failure under newer standards which are intended to provide greater protection to their former partners and their children.

The fundamental standard governing custody decisions is "best interests of the child," which is the first topic to be explored in this section. Judges are generally given some guidance in their interpretation of this highly discretionary and manipulable standard through a statutory list of "factors" to be weighed, but in truth these guidelines are themselves sufficiently manipulable that they impose few constraints. Over the last two decades, however, both courts and legislatures have been persuaded that in most cases the interests of children are best served by having frequent and continuing contact with both parents. Many states have adopted provisions explicitly favoring joint or shared custody arrangements, and many have also adopted so-called "friendly parent" provisions, which make one parent's willingness to share the children with the other a factor for courts to consider favorably in making custody decisions. This enthusiasm for shared parenting is the second topic covered by this section.

As long as domestic violence remained an issue invisible to or suppressed by the family court system, partner abuse tended to be discounted by, or even deemed irrelevant to, the "best interests" analysis. Further, the emphasis on the need for children to have access to both parents, and the lack of information about the impact on children of witnessing one parent's abuse of the other, meant that judges were routinely imposing shared parenting arrangements in situations where an abuser's continued access to his partner through his children put both at increased risk of ongoing physical and emotional abuse. But the most recent chapter of this story is a more encouraging one. In recent years two things have changed. First, judicial enthusiasm for shared parenting is beginning to wane as newer social science research documents the adverse consequences of such arrangements for children whose parents' relationship continues to be conflictual or abusive after the divorce. Second, legislatures and courts are waking up to the prevalence and seriousness of abuse among divorcing parents, and its impact on children, and modifying the custody framework to include consideration of abuse, whether within an open-ended "best interests" inquiry, or by means of new statutory guidelines. These guidelines may demand consideration of abuse as a "factor" in decision-making, or make proof of abuse the basis of a presumption against the award of custody. These developments, their implications, and the relationship between changing standards and changing practices, are the last topics to be explored below.

The Best Interests of the Child

The first reading in this section lays out provisions of the widely adopted *Uniform Marriage and Divorce Act*, which provide mechanisms for making the "best interests" determination, and also suggest some of the competing interests—of parents and courts—which influence both the substance and process of "best interests" determinations. The second excerpt provides a critique of the "best interests" standard, suggesting that the amount of discretion left to the decision-maker invites highly subjective decisions, and in particular allows the importation of unexamined gender-role stereotypes into the decision-making. The third reading documents legislative and judicial enthusiasm for joint custody, specifically, or shared parenting, more generally, as presumptively in the "best interests" of children whose parents divorce.

None of these first readings explicitly address domestic violence within the "best interests" framework. As you read them, you could be thinking about how issues of domestic violence might be raised under the provisions of the *Uniform Marriage and Divorce Act*, how the stereotypes identified in the second reading might impact judicial decisions in cases involving partner abuse, what other stereotypes might influence judges in cases in which abuse is alleged, and finally how presumptions favoring joint custody or assumptions about the benefits of shared parenting might put women and children at risk.

UNIFORM MARRIAGE AND DIVORCE ACT
PART IV: CUSTODY

Section 402. [Best Interest of Child].

The court shall determine custody in accordance with the best interest of the child. The court shall consider all relevant factors including:

(1) the wishes of the child's parent or parents as to his custody;

(2) the wishes of the child as to his custodian;

(3) the interaction and interrelationship of the child with his parent or parents, his siblings, and any other person who may significantly affect the child's best interest;

(4) the child's adjustment to his home, school, and community; and

(5) the mental and physical health of all individuals involved.

The court shall not consider conduct of a proposed custodian that does not affect his relationship to the child.

Section 403. [Temporary Orders].

(a) A party to a custody proceeding may move for a temporary custody order. The motion must be supported by an affidavit as provided in Section 410. The court may award temporary custody under the standards of Section 402 after a hearing, or, if there is no objection, solely on the basis of the affidavits....

Section 404. [Interviews].

(a) The court may interview the child in chambers to ascertain the child's wishes as to his custodian and as to visitation. The court may permit counsel to be present at the interview. The court shall cause a record of the interview to be made and to be part of the record in the case.

(b) The court may seek the advice of professional personnel, whether or not employed by the court on a regular basis. The advice given shall be in writing and made available by the court to counsel upon request. Counsel may examine as a witness any professional personnel consulted by the court.

Section 405. [Investigations and Reports].

(a) In contested custody proceedings, and in other custody proceedings if a parent or the child's custodian so requests, the court may order an investigation and report concerning custodial arrangements for the child. The investigation and report may be made by [the court social service agent, the staff of the juvenile court, the local probation or welfare department, or a private agency employed by the court for the purpose].

(b) In preparing his report concerning a child, the investigator may consult any person who may have information about the child and his potential custodial arrangements. Upon order of the court, the investigator may refer the child to professional personnel for diagnosis. The investigator may consult with and obtain information from medical, psychiatric, or other expert persons who have served the child in the past without obtaining the consent of the parent or the child's custodian; but the child's consent must be obtained if he has reached the age of 16, unless the court finds that he lacks mental capacity to consent. If the requirements of subsection (c) are fulfilled, the investigator's report may be received in evidence at the hearing.

(c) The court shall mail the investigator's report to counsel and to any party not represented by counsel at least 10 days prior to the hearing. The investigator shall make available to counsel and to any party not represented by counsel the investigator's file of underlying data, and reports, complete texts of diagnostic reports made to the investigator pursuant to the provisions of subsection (b), and the names and addresses of all persons whom the investigator has consulted. Any party to the proceeding may call the investigator and any person whom he has consulted for cross-examination. A party may not waive his right of cross-examination prior to the hearing.

Section 406. [Hearings].

(a) Custody proceedings shall receive priority in being set for hearing.

(b) The court may tax as costs the payment of necessary travel and other expenses incurred by any person whose presence at the hearing the court deems necessary to determine the best interest of the child.

(c) The court without a jury shall determine questions of law and fact. If it finds that a public hearing may be detrimental to the child's best interest, the court may exclude the public from a custody hearing, but may admit any person who has a direct and legitimate interest in the particular case or a legitimate educational or research interest in the work of the court.

(d) If the court finds it necessary to protect the child's welfare that the record of any interview, report, investigation, or testimony in a custody proceeding be kept secret, the court may make an appropriate order sealing the record.

Section 408. [Judicial Supervision].

(a) Except as otherwise agreed by the parties in writing at the time of the custody decree, the custodian may determine the child's upbringing, including his education, health care, and religious training, unless the court after hearing, finds, upon motion by the noncustodial parent, that in the absence of a specific limitation of the custodian's authority, the child's physical health would be endangered or his emotional development significantly impaired.

(b) If both parents or all contestants agree to the order, or if the court finds that in the absence of the order the child's physical health would be endangered or his emotional development significantly impaired, the court may order the [local probation or welfare department, court social service agent] to exercise continuing supervision over the case to assure that the custodial or visitation terms of the decree are carried out.

Section 409. [Modification].

(a) No motion to modify a custody decree may be made earlier than 2 years after its date, unless the court permits it to be made on the basis of affidavits that there is reason to believe the child's present environment may endanger seriously his physical, mental, moral, or emotional health.

(b) If a court of this State has jurisdiction pursuant to the Uniform Child Custody Jurisdiction Act, the court shall not modify a prior custody decree unless it finds, upon the basis of facts that have arisen since the prior decree or that were unknown to the court at the time of entry of the prior decree, that a change has occurred in the circumstances of the child or his custodian, and that the modification is necessary to serve the best interest of the child. In applying these standards the court shall retain the custodian appointed pursuant to the prior decree unless:

(1) the custodian agrees to the modification;

(2) the child has been integrated into the family of the petitioner with consent of the custodian; or

(3) the child's present environment endangers seriously his physical, mental, moral, or emotional health, and the harm likely to be caused by a change of environment is outweighed by its advantages to him.

(c) Attorney fees and costs shall be assessed against a party seeking modification if the court finds that the modification action is vexatious and constitutes harassment.

Section 410. [Affidavit Practice].

A party seeking a temporary custody order or modification of a custody decree shall submit together with his moving papers an affidavit setting forth facts supporting the requested order or modification and shall give notice, together with a copy of his affidavit, to other parties to the proceeding, who may file opposing affidavits. The court shall deny the motion unless it finds that adequate cause for hearing the motion is established by the affidavits, in which case it shall set a date for hearing on an order to show cause why the requested order or modification should not be granted.

* * *

NOTE

1. In this next reading, the editors of a recent (1994) casebook on family law comment on the "best interests of the child" custody standard, and its implementation. They provide valuable insights into how judges *actually* apply the "best interests" standard—what kinds of value judgments underlie custody determinations in individual cases. Remarkably, violence between the adult partners in the relationship is not even mentioned in this comment as a factor in custody determinations. The extent to which this omission is merely reflective of *judicial* failure to address violence, and the ways in which judges *do* address partner violence when it cannot be avoided, are the topics of subsequent readings.

A Comment on the "Best interests of the Child" Standard in Custody Determinations
W.O. Weyrauch, S.N. Katz and F. Olsen, Cases and Materials on Family Law: Legal Concepts and Changing Human Relationships, 838–43 (1994)

The traditional best interests standard ... is of little help in the preliminary phases of custody disputes when attorneys are making predictions, counseling their clients and negotiating with opponents. The difficulty of charting a course in these early stages is brought about by a standard which basically articulates the truism that the trial judge, in a controversy over child custody, will rule in favor of what he or she thinks is right. In actuality, and perhaps especially under no-fault divorce, the best interests standard is still concerned with the enforcement of social values, often taking implicit punitive measures against one of the parents. It also relates to finances, most blatantly in its manipulability which allows the wealthier parent to hire the more effective lawyer and expert witnesses, to promise the child a better lifestyle, and generally to present the better case. Some would argue that the best interests standard also relates to finances by openly or covertly using the child to allocate wealth.... In essence this means that children become both assets and liabilities of marriage, and, upon divorce of the parties, a rearrangement must take place that often favors one party financially over the other. While it is true that the best interests standard is indeterminate and speculative, actual adjudication poses fewer problems than is commonly assumed. In fact, the standard is not applied to bring about a result, but may serve as a convenient and useful justification for a decision reached on another level.... In reality there is a substructure of judicial guidelines that are unlikely to be published, perhaps because once fully articulated, they may be inherently objectionable.... Since they are not openly acknowledged in their totality as a cohesive body of regulations, they are relatively immune from efforts to change them....

... Over all, the mother still has preference over the father in obtaining custody of children, regardless of their age and sex, particularly if the children are of tender years and the mother has been and will continue to be the primary caretaker. The father's chances of being awarded custody of either his son or his daughter in a disputed case may not be much better than those of grandparents unless he remarries, thus providing a traditional family model. If he has not remarried he may sometimes get custody of a boy, especially a teenager. The articulated premise may be based on providing the boy with a "proper role model" (which he, as a single person, cannot do for a girl) with the unarticulated assumption that a male custodian will inculcate male values such as ambition (resulting in leadership roles), achievement, independence and competition (exemplified through academic performance and participation in sports or in boy scout activities). On some level lawyers for fathers know this and often use demonstrative evidence as a litigation strategy. They will try to show a judge a video of the father coaching a little league game, playing touch football or supervising homework. They will accompany such videos with statements about how "involved the father is" in the child's upbringing. But the subtext is one of promoting male values. A mother may be successful in winning custody of a girl for the values she will transmit. Again, while the articulated reason may be providing a "proper role model," the subtext is one of offering sexual guidance and inculcating values such as kindness, attractiveness and getting along (without being assertive). The dichotomization of gender expectations are drawn here for purposes of illustration of what happens in court and is not meant to affirm the validity of the assumptions.... Today, gender roles and expectations are not so clearly differentiated and may in fact be in the process of overlapping with one another....

A mother's moral misconduct, such as indiscriminate promiscuity, is perceived to be serious, and may negate the preference that she is often thought to have. An occasional indiscretion may be forgiven, especially if she maintains her decorum. Immorality of the mother tends to have greater weight when custody of a daughter is involved, especially if she is an impressionable age, than if custody of a boy is concerned. Perhaps, again, the reason has to do with gender expectations and the daughter's sexual safety. The father's promiscuity is often ignored. A preference for maintaining an existing situation may override any of these considerations. The child's status quo, even if it is less than ideal, is not disturbed unless the child's welfare demands it. Even when child abuse or neglect is a factor, the status quo will be disturbed only if the abuse is taken as serious, placing the child at great physical or emotional risk, and an assessment is made that the likelihood of future harm is great or that the neglectful parent is beyond rehabilitation.

A close examination of these judicial guidelines clarifies why they cannot be openly acknowledged. While they reflect arguable social values, in their totality they run counter to the demand for neutral adjudication. They violate admonitions against bias and stereotyping. But private and public acceptance of judicial decisions is facilitated because no single custody disposition is likely to offer more than a few of these justifications, which are introduced as part of the general and inconspicuous principle of best interests of the child. Indeed, the social usefulness of this principle is in its sweeping generality and positive stance. It invokes feelings that are universally shared; a palatable substitute is difficult to find. For example, no parent wants to be told that he or she was awarded custody because this was "the least detrimental alternative," although such a negatively phrased standard has been proposed in the influential book *Beyond the Best Interests of the Child* and may make sense for analytical purposes.... Nor would it be wise to tell a father that he is denied custody of his teenage daughter because of a concern for his child's sexual safety. Public sentiment, though tolerant of secret apprehensions, may find such an overt reference to the dangers of incest revolting and unfair to innocent fathers. Thus neutral phrases like "role model" are used and probably more easily acceptable to the parties.

* * *

"Best Interests" and Shared Parenting Provisions

A confluence of factors put joint custody and other forms of shared parenting on the social and legal agenda beginning in the 1970's. Explaining the shift from a view of "best interests" as most often requiring mother custody, to a view in which the father's role in parenting was given more emphasis, Martha Fineman and Anne Opie, in the excerpt which follows, provide an analysis of the context in which these reform proposals emerged.

Martha L. Fineman and Anne Opie
The Uses of Social Science Data in Legal Policymaking: Custody Determinations at Divorce, 1987 Wisconsin Law Review 107, 113, 115–117 (1987)

The ideology of equality, the discourse of women's liberation, and the father's rights movement with its corresponding backlash, have set the stage for an attack on the norm of mother custody. As the divorce rate has increased, the notion of awarding custody to the mother based on the "tender years" doctrine, has increasingly come under attack as presenting an unfair advantage to women. Perhaps ironically, the attack has in part been fueled by twentieth century feminist attacks on the cultural norms that excluded women from the market and relegated them to the home and child care. Part of the battle that these feminists fought was to break this rigid deterministic view of the lot of women and to bring men into the houses, sharing the duties so that women would be free to expend their energies at work. The rhetorical effect of such endeavors was an attempt to redefine the expectations associated with motherhood, making them merely equally dividable components of the responsibilities of "parenthood." . . .

Given the history of family relationships and the solid entrenchment of socially constructed understandings of appropriate maternal and paternal conduct, it is not too surprising that, even after the formal removal of gender specific language from the statute books, decision-makers, both judicial and non-judicial, continued to find that mothers, rather than fathers, were the preferred parents. The fact that the "rules of thumb" had for the most part accurately reflected a common sense understanding of what would be in the best interest of a child was also apparent in the way that stipulated cases were typically resolved by the parents themselves in favor of mother custody. However, this "consensus" apparently has begun to change.

During the mid 1970's, so-called "father's rights" groups began to focus on the fact that mothers continued to receive custody in the vast majority of cases. These men's groups were organizations that arose during the seventies, expressing ideas that many labeled as a backlash at some of the successes of the feminist movement. Many of these groups initially organized around the issue of child support. The problem of non-paying fathers had begun to be publicized, and the groups attempted to counter the image of the "deadbeat dad" with their own political interpretations of the situation. Custody soon became an issue for the fathers' groups, as they justified widespread non-payment of child support with the images of beleaguered fathers who were only reacting to a court system which always gave mothers custody, and treated them as nothing more than "walking wallets." . . .

The father's rights groups supported such novel arrangements as joint custody, by arguing in favor of the child's "right" to have equal access to both parents as well as the father's right to have equal control of decisions affecting the child after divorce. . . . [T]hese groups articulated a range of issues where they perceived that the law was giving women preferential treatment. Child support and custody were important targets.

* * *

NOTE

1. Parallel to the increase in divorce rates and the rise of the father's rights movement in the 1970s came a new body of popular literature favoring shared parenting. *See, e.g.,* M. Roman AND W. Haddad, THE DISPOSABLE PARENT (1978); M. Galper, CO-PARENTING: A SOURCE BOOK FOR THE SEPARATED OR DIVORCED FAMILY (1978); C. Ware, SHARING PARENTHOOD AFTER DIVORCE (1979); P. Woolley, THE CUSTODY HANDBOOK (1979); I Ricci, MOM'S HOUSE, DAD'S HOUSE: MAKING SHARED CUSTODY WORK (1980). In addition, a new body of social science literature looked at the impact of divorce on children. This literature either asserted, or was interpreted to support, two propositions, one negative and one positive. The negative proposition was that children who lost contact with their fathers after divorce were likely to experience various adaptation problems, including conduct disorders, problems with gender identification, and cognitive and learning deficits. The positive proposition was that children resisted the negative emotional fallout of their parents' divorce most successfully when they had generous ongoing access to both parents. Particularly influential in this context was a 1980 book, Judith S. Wallerstein & Joan B. Kelly, SURVIVING THE BREAKUP: HOW CHILDREN AND PARENTS COPE WITH DIVORCE.

With the ammunition provided by these new literatures, political proponents of joint custody were able to mobilize effectively in state legislatures. California was the first state to pass a statute favoring joint custody in 1980, and saw the incidence of joint custody arrangements increase from 5% to 20% by 1984. By 1990 there were at least 33 states with some form of joint custody legislation, with many of the remaining states considering bills. In assessing the impact of joint custody legislation, however, some terminological distinctions have to be made, and some quite different legislative standards considered.

First of all, joint *legal* custody, which involves parental sharing of the legal authority to make the major decisions affecting a child's life, is distinct from joint *physical* custody, which implies parental sharing of the actual physical care of and access to the child. Some advocates of joint custody mean only to endorse the concept of shared legal custody, and continue to assume that a child will have a primary physical home and primary caretaking parent. When it comes to joint physical custody, there are other terms often used interchangeably, such as "alternating," "shared," "dual" and "divided."

More important yet are the differing standards, whether created by statute or case-law, governing when joint custody is an appropriate arrangement. These are the topic of the following excerpt.

Joanne Schulman & Valerie Pitt
Second Thoughts on Joint Child Custody: Analysis of Legislation and Its Implications for Women and Children, 12 Golden Gate Law Review 538, 546–553 (1982)

1. *Joint Custody as an Option*

The simplest form of joint custody statute provides that "the order *may* include provision for joint custody of the children by the parties." ... Although a few statutes do not include reference to the "best interests" standard, most provide for joint custody as an option "if it appears to the court that joint custody would be in the best interests of the child...."

The major drawback of the "option" statute is its failure to set adequate limits or standards on the court's power to order joint custody. It permits the court to opt for joint custody as an easy out, as a means of "escap[ing] an agonizing choice, to keep from wounding the self-esteem of either parent ... to avoid the appearance of discrimination between the sexes."

Under this type of statute, it is possible for a court to force joint custody on parties who are not in agreement or who have not considered the consequences of a joint custody award and arrangement....

2. *Joint Custody as an Option Only when Parties Are In Agreement*

A few states permit a court to order joint custody only when the parties are in agreement.... This ... statute is the best of the joint custody legislation.... However, problems can arise even under this type of legislation. A parent who does not believe joint custody is in the child's best interests may be forced into accepting such an "agreement" out of fear that she or he will stand at a disadvantage and lose sole custody in a contested trial. This is particularly a problem when the custody statute requires that the court consider, as a factor in determining sole custody, which parent would provide greater access of the child to the other parent.... Because of the potential for court approval of agreements made under duress or coercion, some bar associations have actively opposed this type of legislation....

3. *Joint Custody Upon Request of One Party*

This type of statute allows the court to award joint custody "on either parent's application" or request.... This type of statute is extremely dangerous when it is coupled with a "friendly parent" provision. The parent requesting joint custody over the opposition of the other parent is given an unconscionable bargaining lever. A parent who does not believe joint custody would be in her or his child's best interests is put into a negotiating position of either "accepting" joint custody or risking the loss of custody altogether in a contested trial.... Ironically, a parent who is least fit for the custody and care of a child benefits the most from this type of statute.

4. *Joint Custody Preference/Presumption*

Joint custody "preference" statutes prioritize available custody resolutions and mandate that joint custody must be given first consideration by the courts. Under a presumption statute, joint custody is presumed by law to be in the best interests of the child. Thus, sole custody can be ordered only when the "presumption" is rebutted by evidence proving that joint custody is detrimental to the child's best interests. Many of these bills declare joint custody to be the norm, and that it is to be encouraged as an express public policy of the state. . . .

To date, most *express* joint custody presumptions are limited to those cases where parents have agreed to joint custody. However, these statutes also include provisions that (1) permit joint custody upon the request of one party, and (2) give preference in sole custody to that party requesting joint custody. The practical combined effect of these two additional provisions is an *implied* joint custody presumption in all cases.

The use of "best interests" language in "presumption" statutes is a play on words which avoids confronting the fact that the "best interests" test has in fact been supplanted.

* * *

NOTES

1. As suggested in the above excerpt, the combination of shared custody and "friendly parent" provisions is particularly troublesome when one parent has good reason to oppose shared custody, but is afraid that a judge will interpret opposition as irrational or as evidence of vindictiveness or hostility, and respond by awarding sole custody to the other parent. In 1994 the ABA Center on Children and the Law reported to the President of the ABA that:

> Although many states have recently adopted what are known as "friendly parent" provisions in their child custody laws (generally requiring courts to give custodial preference to those parents most cooperative regarding liberal visitation with the other parent), such provisions are inappropriate in cases where there has been domestic violence. Such laws should be amended accordingly.

Howard Davidson, *The Impact of Domestic Violence on Children: A Report to the President of the American Bar Association* 5 (1994).

2. As of 1995, according to the Family Violence Project of the National Council of Juvenile and Family Court Judges, ten child custody statutes included a public policy statement concerning a parent's abilities to allow an open, loving and frequent relationship between the child and the other parent, while eighteen states included such provisions in their list of factors that a court is required to consider when determining the best interest of the child. The dynamics of these provisions are explored further by Joan Zorza in her article *"Friendly Parent" Provisions in Custody Determinations*, 26 CLEARINGHOUSE REV. 921, 922–923 (1992):

> . . . [M]ental health professionals have been sadly silent in opposing either joint custody preferences or friendly parent provisions, whether before legislatures or in individual custody cases, on the erroneous assumption that they are not harmful to children. Friendly parent provisions are merely seen as the inducement to reach the goal of joint custody, which is assumed to be beneficial. . . .
>
> Attorneys report to the National Center on Women and Family Law that judges generally prefer joint custody and friendly parent provisions, presumably because they make their jobs much easier. Judges hardly need to look at what the particular child needs or how capable each parent is relative to the other in parenting. Instead, parents are effectively forced to accept some kind of joint custody arrangement; the parent who does not agree to joint custody or who contributes to the breakdown of joint custody is threatened with the complete loss of custody. Indeed, most mothers are forced to agree to joint custody or to bargain away enormous amounts of needed financial support to avoid a joint custody arrangement. This gives the party requesting joint custody an unconscionable bargaining lever over the parent opposing it.
>
> Even when a state has neither friendly parent language in its custody statutes nor any appellate court decisions favoring a friendly parent analysis, many judges still act as if their state's laws have such a provision. Indeed, such assumptions are so widely accepted, and the consequences of raising an objection to using friendly parent analysis so frightening, that few lawyers dare object when judges read friendly parent provisions into the law. Yet these provisions effectively chill the right of any parent to raise even the most meritorious claim.

3. The social science research upon which joint custody "reforms" relied was in fact never as univocal or as clear in its conclusions as political proponents of joint custody contended. In particular, the early studies of joint physical custody, which tended to reach positive conclusions, "used highly selective samples of couples who could be described as pioneers of the concept, even crusaders; they tended to be highly motivated and committed to making joint custody work for their children." Janet Johnston, *Children's Adjustment in Sole Custody Compared to Joint Custody Families and Principles for Custody Decision Making*, 33 F.C.C.R. 415 (1995). Beginning in the early eighties, and swelling in volume as the decade progressed, new studies emphasized the limitations of those early findings, and raised a series of questions:

> First, whether beneficial outcomes are due to joint custody itself, rather than the predivorce characteristics of the families (e.g., better cooperation, less conflict, and psychologically healthier parents), or to demographics like higher education and better incomes. Second, whether children of different ages, boys and girls alike, can manage and benefit from these arrangements. Third, whether mental health professionals should encourage and the courts should mandate joint custody where parents are reluctant to undertake the arrangement.

Id. at 416. This second generation of studies looked at children in different age groups, and at families where parents had varying levels of motivation to undertake joint custody after divorce. They tended to reach more negative conclusions about the impact of shared physical custody on children, but like the early studies, they too were mostly composed of small and not necessarily representative samples, generally used no control or comparison groups, and often conducted no follow-up over time.

4. From the end of the eighties into the nineties, somewhat more systematic research has explored the questions identified by the second generation of custody studies, with results that validate the concerns those studies raised. These most recent studies, and their conclusions, are summarized in this next excerpt.

Janet Johnston
Children's Adjustment in Sole Custody Compared to Joint Custody Families and Principles for Custody Decision Making, 33 Family and Conciliation Courts Review 415, 418–421 (1995)

Six Recent Studies of Different Custody Arrangements

... [T]wo of these six studies are of community samples of the broader population of divorcing families (i.e., mostly obtained from public records of divorce filings); one study was obtained from court-connected services wherein families mediated their custody plans; and three studies were of high-conflict litigated divorces, where the custody arrangement was generally imposed by recommendations or order of the court. Five of the studies were undertaken in California; the mediation study included data from Minnesota and Connecticut; and one of the litigating studies was undertaken in Michigan. The sample sizes ranged from 75 to 651 children, and families were of varied socioeconomic and ethnic status. All but one of the studies followed the families over a 2–to 4–year period.

Overview of Findings

Among those divorcing families studied ... the principal findings were that there were few, if any, significant differences in the adjustment of children in the different custody arrangements. The community studies showed that there was a tendency, over time, for a great deal of self-selection into the kind of custody arrangement that best suited the individual family: about one third of the children changed their custody arrangements over a 2–to 4–year period.... For example, there was a tendency for children in joint residential arrangements ... to drift back into the primary care of their mothers.... Thus, children who remained in the joint care of their parents did so because the arrangement suited both them and their parents. This probably explains why these children tended to be a little better adjusted as a group and felt closer to both parents. In addition, children in joint custody benefited from the fact that their parents were likely to be better educated and to have higher incomes. Interestingly, there was a tendency for emotionally and behaviorally troubled children, and those with troubled family relationships, to be deposited into the primary care of their fathers (especially during adolescence). It is perhaps not surprising, therefore, that these children's adjustment looked somewhat worse as a group. However, girls in father custody were doing more poorly than boys.

It is important to note that in the community and mediation studies, more substantial amounts of access/visitation, in itself, was associated with neither better nor worse outcomes in these children. Important predictors of good adjustment for children were, foremost, the parents' psychological functioning and the quality of the parent-child relationships. There were consistent findings that custodial parents who were anxious and depressed, and those who suffered from substantial emotional or personality disturbances, were more likely to have disturbed children. Conversely, a warm, supportive relationship with a custodial parent who was also able to maintain consistent expectations and appropriate monitoring of the child was found to protect the child's development. It was also found that during and after divorce, children benefit substantially from regular, predictable access arrangements, and from a stable social support system that includes school, social activities, and contacts with peers and extended kin. What these findings imply is that the actual physical custody and visitation arrangements are less important than is the quality of ensuing family relationships.

A small minority of divorcing parents remain in ongoing high conflict. . . . Ongoing high conflict is identified by multiple criteria, a combination of factors that tend to be, but are not always, associated with each other: intractable legal disputes, ongoing disagreement over day to day parenting practices, expressed hostility, verbal abuse, physical threats, and intermittent violence. Research findings to date indicate that high-conflict divorced parents have a relatively poor prognosis for developing cooperative coparenting arrangements without a great deal of therapeutic and legal intervention. Those parents who met the multiple criteria of high conflict at the time of divorce were likely to remain conflicted over a 2–to 3–year period. At best, they became disengaged and noncommunicative with one another; they were less likely to become more cooperative over this period of time.

The studies, as a group, consistently concluded that ongoing and unresolved conflict between divorced parents has detrimental effects on children, especially boys. Children are particularly hurt by witnessing physical violence between their parents. In divorced families where there was ongoing conflict between parents, frequent visitation arrangements and joint custody schedules were likely to result in increased levels of verbal and physical aggression between parents, compared to similar families who had sole custody arrangements, especially at the times of transitions when children moved between their parents' homes. Of even greater concern was the finding that more frequent transitions and more shared access between high-conflict parents were associated with more emotional and behavioral disturbance among children, especially girls. These children were likely to be more depressed, withdrawn and aggressive, and to suffer from physical symptoms of stress (such as stomachaches, headaches, etc.); they were also likely to have more problems getting along with their peers, compared to children with fewer transitions and typical sole custody access plans. In comparisons of sole mother custody with sole father custody in contested divorce situations, the findings were that the children fared equally well, probably because in this study the custody arrangements had been made after careful psychological evaluations of the best match between parent and child.

In summary, from the research that currently exists, there is no convincing evidence that joint custody is either more detrimental or more beneficial for the majority of children of divorce compared to mother or father sole custody arrangements. However, substantial amounts of access to both parents ... and frequent transitions between parents are generally associated with poorer children's adjustment in ... those divorced families where there is ongoing high conflict and continual disputes over the children. Where there has been a history of repeated physical violence between parents, these children are likely to be the most seriously disturbed.

* * *

"Best Interests" Revisited: Taking Partner Violence Into Account

As this last reading indicates, leading researchers in the field are increasingly reaching agreement that shared parenting after divorce is contraindicated in situations in which on-going conflict characterizes the relationship between the parents. Some of the credit for this recognition must go to the battered women's advocacy movement, which has made custody reform a priority, insisting that partner violence is relevant to custody determinations, and that joint custody is always an inappropriate, and often an unsafe, arrangement when one parent has abused the other. Confronted by new evidence, political pressure, and increasing public awareness of domestic violence and its impact on children, both the laws governing custody determinations, and judicial attitudes, have begun to change. Increasingly, they accommodate consideration of partner violence, and determinations that favor the non-abusive partner in a custody dispute. While by no means universal, the changes are undeniably significant.

The forms these changes have taken, and their implications, are explored further in subsequent readings. It is well, however, to begin with a reminder of the more traditional view that partner abuse is irrelevant to "best interests" determinations. Here that view is illustrated by Naomi Cahn with reference to cases from Maryland and Florida:

> The case of one Maryland woman provides an example of judicial treatment of this issue. The woman, who had been abused by her husband for seven years, nonetheless agreed to joint physical custody because she was "[t]errified that he would disappear with the children." Although her husband was subsequently investigated for child

abuse and neglect, the court upheld their joint custody agreement. According to the woman,

> [e]vidence regarding spousal abuse was deemed not pertinent to the issue of custody. Incredibly the judge seemed to shift responsibility for my ex-husband's uncontrollable temper to me by ruling, "A person may be violent and vindictive towards a spouse and yet be the best, most loving, caring, parent in the world. And may even in the presence of the other spouse exhibit something toward the kids that he/she wouldn't do because he/she is irritated with the other spouse."
>
> A Florida court seemed to share the above opinion when it ruled that an abusive husband did not pose a danger to his child. Though the man's violent and irrational behavior included throwing his wife to the ground, beating her when she was four months pregnant, and threatening to kill her, her father and himself, the court accepted a psychologist's conclusion that the man's "past violence was related to the deterioration of his relationship with [his wife]," and was presumably unrelated to his fitness as a parent. The court apparently dismissed the battering that occurred while the woman was pregnant.

Naomi R. Cahn, *Civil Images of Battered Women: The Impact of Domestic Violence on Child Custody Decisions,* 44 VAND L. REV. 1041, 1072–1073 (1991).

The Florida case discussed by Cahn is Collinsworth v. O'Connell, 508 So.2d 744 (Fla. Dist. Ct. App. 1987). Cahn compares this case with a case decided in West Virginia in 1982, in which a mother was accused of firing a rifle at her ex-husband when he came to visit their child. Collins v. Collins, 297 S.E.2d 901 (W. Va. 1982). Here, Cahn comments, "the court found the woman to be an unfit mother because she had "demonstrated [a] tendency to be violent as evidenced by her willingness to threaten with and to actually shoot a deadly weapon at human beings when she was upset, but not in any way threatened." The standards seemed to have changed quite drastically when the violent behavior of a woman was in question; this court looked at parental fitness instead of the best interest of the child, and appeared to have a much lower tolerance for violent behavior than courts have shown in cases involving violent men." 44 VAND. L. REV. at 1073.

Cahn also reports that State task forces addressing gender bias in state courts often hear testimony concerning, and comment on, the treatment of domestic violence in custody cases. Id., at 1072. In Nevada the task force concluded:

> The best interest of the child is rarely, if ever, served by placing a child with a parent who is physically abusive to either a child or a child's parent. In the judgment of some who addressed the Task Force, this point does not appear to be recognized by judges in making custody awards.

NEVADA SUPREME COURT GENDER BIAS TASK FORCE, JUSTICE FOR WOMEN 43 (First Report, undated). The Washington task force noted a discrepancy between the perspective of lawyers and judges, a majority of whom "agreed that judges 'usually' or 'always' give due consideration to violence whether by father or mother in an award of custody," and the perspective offered during public testimony, where "witnesses felt that the courts gave less credence to the testimony of mothers on domestic violence and sexual abuse allegations. . . ." WASHINGTON STATE TASK FORCE ON GENDER AND JUSTICE IN THE COURTS, GENDER AND JUSTICE IN THE COURTS 66, 68–69 (1989). In Maryland, a committee of the gender bias task force reported as follows:

> [L]awyers and judges were asked whether "child custody awards disregard fathers' violence against mothers." Over half (63%) of judges thought the statement was rarely or never true, indicating their belief that the father's violence against mothers usually is or should be a consideration in child custody determinations. Their opinion was shared by roughly the same percentage of male attorneys (64%), but by only a third of female attorneys (35%).
>
> . . .
>
> The most troublesome issue disclosed by the Committee's investigation is that some judges refuse to consider at all or give too little weight to violence which a mother has suffered at the hands of the father unless the child has been a victim as well or has witnessed the violence.

MARYLAND SPECIAL JOINT COMMITTEE, GENDER BIAS IN THE COURTS 31, 37 (1989).

Partner Violence as a Factor in Decision-making: Judicial Recognition

Although some courts have argued that one parent's violence towards the other is irrelevant to a custody or visitation determination, as "conduct of a proposed custodian that does not affect his relationship to the child," under Section 402 of the Uniform Marriage and Divorce Act, that argument becomes increasingly hard to justify as the consequences to children of exposure to a parent's violence are increasingly better documented and understood. For the court that does understand the connection between parental violence and child distress, the parent's violence can be incorporated into the "best interests" analysis without difficulty, as relevant to "the interaction of the child with his parent or parents . . .," to "the child's adjustment to his home, school, and community," or to "the mental and physical health of all individuals involved," all of which factors are traditional aspects of "best interests" analysis.

Massachusetts provides one example of a state that has been able to address domestic violence as a relevant factor in custody decisions, even without the benefit of explicit statutory standards. In the opinion excerpted below the Commonwealth's Supreme Judicial Court reversed a family court judge who had given primary physical custody to a father who had abused the boy's mother. The SJC followed the lead of an intermediate appellate court in demanding not only that domestic violence be a factor in the custody decision, but that a decision to award custody to an abusive parent be supported by written findings about the abuse, its impact on the child and its relevance to the parent's parenting abilities, and the appropriateness of the award in light of those other findings.

Custody of Vaughn

422 Mass. 590, 664 N.E.2d 434.
Supreme Judicial Court of Massachusetts, 1996.

■ FRIED, JUSTICE.

In 1993, a Probate and Family Court judge awarded primary physical custody of a boy (Vaughn), at the time age eleven years, to his father (Ross). The Appeals Court reversed and remanded the case to the Probate and Family Court for further consideration of evidence regarding domestic violence perpetrated by the child's father against his mother (Leslie) and the effect of the family violence on Vaughn. R.H. v. B.F., 39 Mass.App.Ct. 29, 653 N.E.2d 195 (1995). We granted Ross's application for further appellate review. We are in agreement with the Appeals Court. We reverse the judgment and remand for further findings consistent with this opinion.

I

Leslie and Ross met in Maine in 1977. Leslie, who was twice divorced, lived with her two children, a girl (Laura) then age nine years and a boy (John) age five years. Leslie worked as a real estate salesperson during the day and as a cocktail waitress at night. The Probate Court judge found that she "has been an abused person. She was abused as a child, she was divorced twice and has endured abuse because of her relationships." Ross, a former marine engineer, was working odd jobs as a carpenter and painter at the time. Shortly after they met, Ross moved into Leslie's home. They have never married. Ross is a big man, six feet five inches tall and weighing some 285 pounds. Leslie is five feet seven inches tall and weighs 150 pounds. The disparity in their size is relevant, because the relationship was fraught with anger and violence from the start. Ross had a terrible temper. The judge found that he "would fly into rages" and strike out at Leslie, once causing her to lose consciousness and requiring her to be sent to the hospital in an ambulance. According to testimony, he inflicted injuries on her on numerous other occasions. Laura and John witnessed a number of these incidents and were terrified of Ross and his rages. The testimony and findings of fact reflected that Ross was also physically and verbally abusive toward them. Both Ross and Leslie drank heavily and used marihuana. Since Leslie joined "Al–Anon" in 1978, her consumption of alcohol has diminished. The testimony is that she drinks mostly on social occasions. Ross has been alcohol free since 1985 and continues to attend Alcoholics Anonymous meetings once a week.

In 1981 the family moved to Nantucket where Leslie obtained a position as a real estate broker. Vaughn was born on July 18, 1982. After the move to Nantucket, Ross began working as a carpenter and caretaker. Leslie was successful at her work and at the time of trial was earning over $100,000 a year. Ross was much less successful financially, although he appeared to have a number of clients with second homes on Nantucket who relied on his services, and at least one of whom established a close friendship with him and Vaughn.

Ross's rages and violence toward Leslie, Laura, and John continued after Vaughn's birth. There was testimony that the police were called on approximately one dozen occasions. Ross's anger and violence, however, did not cease, and he sought psychiatric help. A psychiatrist prescribed Lithium, and there was testimony that when Ross discontinued taking it (on his own) his moods and behavior worsened. Leslie testified that on several occasions she left the house with her children to escape Ross's behavior, that many times Ross also took Vaughn from the house in the course of arguments, and that Ross used the threat of taking Vaughn from his mother as a way of keeping the mother in the relationship. Vaughn was present at many of the episodes of abuse. There was testimony that the father's disposition to use physical force was played out on the boy as well, with cuffing, pushing, knocking, and poking; he also yelled and lost his temper at the boy, as he did at every other member of the household. Laura, who is now a graduate student, further testified that, when she was a teenager, Ross kissed her on the mouth in an inappropriate manner and touched her body in an inappropriate, sexual manner.

The judge also found that Leslie engaged in taunting, provocative, and violent behavior toward Ross. On several occasions she assaulted him in a sexual and humiliating manner. It appears that for some years the parties had not shared a bedroom, and on at least one occasion Leslie without any immediate provocation taunted Ross for his sexual neglect of her. In 1986, on the occasion that received the most attention, she entered Ross's room nude and proceeded to taunt him in the grossest and most explicit terms within the boy's hearing. In 1988, in another similar incident, the judge found that Leslie, "when rejected after demanding sexual favors from [Ross] followed him from the house to the public road. She was naked and directed foul language at him. This too was done in the presence of [Vaughn]."

Until Vaughn was five years old his mother was his primary caretaker. Thereafter Ross undertook more and more responsibilities. Apparently he did the shopping and cooking for the household over the five years immediately prior to trial, and he was greatly occupied with his son's activities. Ross followed his son's progress in school, visited his teachers, attended his sporting events, and joined him in target shooting and other activities. Indeed the evidence suggests that Ross was, if anything, overly involved with his son. He embarrassed his son at times by participating in games with him or cheering with excessive enthusiasm at his team sports, and the two would shower together and would give each other massages. Ross has been very generous to Vaughn—the mother complains overly generous—buying him motorbikes and electronic equipment.

The tension and violence between the parents finally led Leslie, on October 1, 1992, to obtain an order in the District Court . . ., requiring Ross to vacate the couple's home, to surrender custody of the boy to the mother, and to remain away from the home and the mother. The next day Ross commenced this action in the Probate Court to establish paternity (which is not in dispute) and to obtain custody of Vaughn. The parties promptly entered into a temporary agreement providing for joint legal and physical custody, according to which the boy would spend part of each week with each parent. During this arrangement the father bought out the mother's share of the house in which they had been living, and the mother moved into a new home. The parties also agreed that Dr. Michael D. Abruzzese, a clinical psychologist whom they had previously consulted along with the child, should be appointed guardian ad litem to make an evaluation and report regarding custody of the child. On February 21, 1993, Dr. Abruzzese delivered his report, recommending that joint custody be continued but that the boy's primary home during the week be with his father with weekends to be spent with his mother. Thereupon the Probate Court entered a new temporary order maintaining the joint legal custody but giving the father primary physical custody and visitation rights to the mother, substantially in accord with Dr. Abruzzese's recommendations.

. . .

Leslie appealed to the Appeals Court, which reversed the judgment of the Probate Court for errors of law and remanded the case to that court. Pending a new judgment the custody arrangements in the parties' initial stipulation were ordered reinstated.

II

A. The Appeals Court based its remand to the Probate Court on the failure of that court to make findings regarding the evidence that the father had physically abused the mother throughout the relationship and the effect of this abuse on the child. The Appeals Court gave great weight to this court's Gender Bias Study of the Court System of Massachusetts (1989) and particularly to the recommendation in that study that,

> "The legislature and/or appellate courts should make it clear that abuse of any family member affects other family members and must be considered in determining the best interests of the child in connection with any order concerning custody."

The Appeals Court's remand order is designed to do just that. We endorse the Appeals Court's commitment to the propositions that physical force within the family is both intolerable and too readily tolerated, and that a child who has been either the victim or the spectator of such abuse suffers a distinctly grievous kind of harm. It might be helpful to emphasize how fundamental these propositions are. Quite simply, abuse by a family member inflicted on those who are weaker and less able to defend themselves—almost invariably a child or a woman—is a violation of the most basic human right, the most basic condition of civilized society: the right to live in physical security, free from the fear that brute force will determine the conditions of one's daily life. What our study and the growing movement against family violence and violence against women add to this fundamental insight is that, for those who are its victims, force within the family and in intimate relationships is not less but more of a threat to this basic condition of civilized security, for it destroys the security that all should enjoy in the very place and context which is supposed to be the refuge against the harshness encountered in a world of strangers. Particularly for children the sense that the place which is supposed to be the place of security is the place of greatest danger is the ultimate denial that this is a world of justice and restraint, where people have rights and are entitled to respect. The recent literature also exposes the sham and hypocrisy that condemns violence among strangers and turns a blind eye to it where its manifestations are most corrosive.

The Gender Bias Study concludes that our courts have too often failed to appreciate the fundamental wrong and the depth of the injury inflicted by family violence. In subtle and overt ways the decisions of courts fail to take these factors into account and have treated them with insufficient seriousness in making dispositions, particularly in cases involving custody of children and the realignment of family relationships in divorce and related proceedings. The Appeals Court found just such failures of attention and emphasis in the Probate Court's treatment of this case.

B. The Appeals Court was critical of the Probate Court in a number of related respects. First, the Probate Court judge "fail[ed] to make detailed and comprehensive findings of fact on the issues of domestic violence and its effect upon the child as well as upon the father's parenting ability." R.H. v. B.F., 39 Mass.App.Ct. 29, 40, 653 N.E.2d 195 (1995). Second, "because [the judge] found the mother and the father to have equally flawed parenting abilities, the relationship between the father and the child and the child's preferences weighed the scales [excessively] in the father's favor." Id. at 41, 653 N.E.2d 195. And third, the Appeals Court ruled that the Probate Court failed to consider the special risks to the child in awarding custody to a father who had committed acts of violence against the mother. Id. at 40, 653 N.E.2d 195. An important theme of all these statements was that the Probate Court had failed to give sufficient weight to the effects of domestic violence on women and their children. Id. at 36–39, 653 N.E.2d 195.

. . . The record leaves no room for doubt that Ross is a man with a poorly controlled temper, who at times threatened and inflicted violence on the mother. He has been a batterer. The Probate Court's findings clearly acknowledge that fact. The judge's findings also acknowledge the intimidation Ross imposed on John and Laura, the two older children in the household who were not Ross's children, and credit the testimony of Leslie's daughter that Ross engaged in conduct to her that can only be described as sexually abusive. These findings by the Probate Court are consistent with and indeed in some respects go beyond Leslie's proposed findings of fact and draw on the testimony at trial.

There are two sides to this sad story, and the Probate Court acknowledged both of them. There was testimony, which Leslie sought to put in context but did not deny, that she taunted and struck the father and hurt and humiliated him physically. Some, but not all of these incidents might be explained away as defensive or retaliatory. The judge found that: "Neither party exercised such conduct that would make them eligible for any awards or accolades.... They both have been physically and emotionally abusive to each other. Their conduct can be described through their profanity, vulgarity, obscenity and nudity."

The mother's expert, Dr. Peter G. Jaffe, who is a specialist in matters relating to family violence and battered women's syndrome, casts all the incidents unfavorable to Leslie as manifestations of that syndrome. Leslie had been abused as a child and in the two marriages that preceded her relationship with Ross. The judge summarized Dr. Jaffe's judgments in his findings of fact, including Dr. Jaffe's statement that children who grow up in abusive households tend to repeat that pattern in their own relationships: "Dr. Jaffe feels that children who are witnesses to violence are also victims of violence. He expressed a concern that if [Vaughn] remained in his father's physical custody, it would reinforce the acceptability of the father's behavior to [Vaughn] which has the potential to make [Vaughn] a batterer himself in the future." The judge did not, however, make any findings of fact based on Dr. Jaffe's testimony and did not say whether he considered Dr. Jaffe's testimony credible.

Rather the judge seemed moved to give particular weight to the recommendations and testimony of the guardian ad litem, Dr. Abruzzese, and less weight to the analysis and conclusions of Leslie's expert, Dr. Jaffe. Unquestionably Dr. Jaffe has impressive credentials, with very great experience in issues relating to family violence and battered women. But he was also an expert chosen by one of the parties in the context of this litigation.

Dr. Abruzzese, on the other hand, was an impartial witness whom the parties had consulted previously and who had been selected by their mutual agreement to serve as guardian ad litem. Like Dr. Jaffe, he has a doctorate in clinical psychology, though a much more recent one. His practice includes work with children, adolescents, and families. Moreover he testified that both parents had had occasion some three years earlier to bring Vaughn to Dr. Abruzzese for advice about certain difficulties he was having at school. At that time he was working as director of adolescent and child services at the town's child services agency. Dr. Abruzzese had spent many hours with Vaughn, his parents, and others. He evaluated the family with a focus on the particular circumstances of this case and the needs of this child at this time. There is no doubt that Dr. Abruzzese was particularly moved by the love and attachment the father had for Vaughn, the attachment Vaughn seemed to have for his father, and by Vaughn's wish to spend more time with him and perhaps to have his primary base at his father's house. Certainly some of this affection came across as concern for his father's welfare, and as Dr. Jaffe pointed out, may for that reason be deemed an inappropriate role reversal and one that is encountered in families with a history of violence. Be that as it may, both the affection and the preference were clearly stated. The judge was also moved by the fact that the boy appeared to be doing very well in his school work and that the father takes a great interest in his activities, meeting regularly with the boy's teachers. Finally, the Probate Court judge noted that the father, who had been a heavy drinker, had not used alcohol since 1985 and attends weekly sessions of Alcoholics Anonymous. The court also mandated that both parents should remain in therapy.

III

We agree with the Appeals Court that the judge below "fail[ed] to make detailed and comprehensive findings of fact on the issues of domestic violence and its effect upon the child as well as upon the father's parenting ability." The Probate Court failed to consider the special risks to the child in awarding custody to a father who had committed acts of violence against the mother. It is well documented that witnessing domestic violence, as well as being one of its victims, has a profound impact on children. See Note, Domestic Violence and Custody Litigation: The Need for Statutory Reform, 13 Hofstra L.Rev. 407, 417–422 (1985). There are significant reported psychological problems in children who witness domestic violence, especially during important developmental stages. See Cahn, Civil Images of Battered Women: The Impact of Domestic Violence on Child Custody Decisions, 44 Vand.L.Rev. 1041 (1991). Domestic violence is an issue too fundamental and frequently recurring to be dealt with only by implication. The very frequency of domestic violence in disputes about child custody may have the effect of inuring courts to it and thus minimizing its significance. Requiring the courts to make explicit findings about the effect of the violence on the child and the appropriateness of the custody award in light of that effect will serve to keep these matters well in the foreground of the judges' thinking....

Accordingly, we remand the case to the Probate Court for such explicit findings.... We do not by this decision require the judge to hear further testimony if he does not consider that necessary, but at the least he must hear both parties and make explicit findings on the matters set out above....

SO ORDERED

NOTES

1. The family court had determined that both parents were batterers and that both parents had been battered. The appeals court was even more direct in its criticism of those findings than the Supreme Judicial Court:

> To the extent the finding is directed to the fact that both parents used force against the other, the finding is technically correct. Although we are mindful that credibility is a "preserve of the trial judge upon which an appellate court treads with great reluctance," [citations omitted], we nonetheless conclude that the finding is inconsistent with the evidence about which the trial judge made no findings, that is, that the mother suffers from battered women's syndrome and that most of her physical acts of force were defensive.... In an area as critical as domestic violence, we are unable to conclude that the trial judge's simple finding of mutual battery implicitly rejects this evidence as incredible or irrelevant.
>
> Moreover, this suspect finding, that both parents were batterers, appears to have formed the basis for the trial judge's imprecise finding that the child "could be said to be at risk with either" of the parents. A subject of such gravity calls for a more detailed exploration and analysis of the evidence and an explication of the degree and nature of the respective risks to the child.

39 Mass. App. Ct. 29, 41; 653 N.E. 2d 195,202 (1995).

2. The Supreme Judicial Court's opinion says very little about the harm to the child of witnessing his father's abuse of his mother—largely because this was not a subject addressed by the family court. The appeals court, however, suggests that the family court record does provide evidence of harm:

> ... The mother's expert witness, a child and family forensic psychologist having a subspecialty in battered women's syndrome and expertise in the field of family violence and its impact on families, testified that the child related to him during interviews that when he was not with his father, his father would be very sad and unhappy, that he could help his father with his temper by keeping him happy and calm.... It was the psychologist's "clinical impression" that the child had taken on "an excessive sense of responsibility for his father's wellbeing. He was speaking about his father as if he was looking after his father, rather than his father looking after him."
>
> Testing of and interviews with the child by this psychologist led him to the conclusion that the child suffers from some of the emotional and behavioral problems experienced by boys who have witnessed abuse of their mothers. More specifically, the child has a "sense of depression and sadness," "some anxiety," and "an excessive sense of personal responsibility for his father." The psychologist indicated that the child revealed that "he has opinions about his mother, which is similar to boys who have witnessed violence and observed physical abuse or verbal or psychological abuse." Examples of the child's opinions are as follows: "He thought his mother exaggerates a lot. He thought that his mother was too fat. He thought that his mother had a number of difficulties." When the psychologist asked the child how he had arrived at these opinions, the child explained that "these are things that his father says about his mother."
>
> When asked his opinion about the undisputed fact that the father and the child showered together and gave each other massages with scented oil, the psychologist stated that such activity was "inappropriate and a violation of appropriate boundaries in terms of contact between a father and a son." Based upon the father's behavior toward the mother's daughter as well as his showers and massages with the child, the psychologist was of the opinion that the father had problems respecting other people's bodies.

39 Mass. App. Ct. at 36–37; 653 N.E. 2d at 199–200.

3. Justice Fried's opinion contains some descriptions of incidents which reflect poorly on the mother—suggesting, in particular, that she engaged in sexually provocative conduct toward her partner in front of the child, letting him see her naked. With respect to at least one of those incidents, the Appeals Court notes that the mother had a different account:

> It appears from the testimony of the guardian that one of the many arguments witnessed by the child was particularly upsetting to him. Based upon the child's account to him, the guardian related that

> one night the parents had been arguing, that the mother wanted to make love with the father but he refused, and that the father fled the house with the mother, naked, in pursuit. At trial, the mother did not deny running out into the yard naked. She testified that she and the father had been in their bedroom arguing, that the father walked out and went into the child's room, that he awakened him, told him of the argument, and began to dress him. Fearing that the father intended to take the child away, as he frequently threatened to do, the mother ran into the yard to remove the keys from the ignition of the father's truck. The father's version of the incident was that he intended to dress the child and take him to their "secret place," a place only he and the child knew about and to which they would sometimes go until a situation would "die down," and that the mother, yelling, swearing and naked, followed him into the child's room and out into the yard. The trial judge's finding as to this occurrence reads: "In a 1988 incident, the ... [mother], when rejected after demanding sexual favors from the ... [father], followed him from the house to the public road. She was naked, and directed foul language at him."

39 Mass. App. Ct. at 33; 653 N.E. 2d at 198.

4. The family court, court of appeals and Supreme Judicial Court all produced somewhat discrepant accounts of the facts in the *Vaughn* case, and somewhat different characterizations of both the parents and the child. We will come back to these differences when we look at problems of proof faced by battered women in custody proceedings, even when the legal standards appear to encourage disclosure of abuse, and to offer protection to its direct and indirect victims.

5. In Justice Fried's opinion, he reports on the testimony of both Dr. Peter Jaffe, the mother's expert witness and an internationally known authority on the impact of domestic violence on children, and Dr. Abruzzese, a clinical psychologist who had been appointed guardian ad litem in the case. Dr. Abruzzese recommended giving custody to the father. The mother's counsel sought to cast doubt on the value of Dr. Abruzzese's testimony, because of his lack of expertise in family violence. The Supreme Judicial Court rejected this argument:

> Although Dr. Jaffe certainly contributed valuable insights to these proceedings, we would hesitate a long time before suggesting that in cases such as these, not only must both sides produce expert witnesses, but they must be experts in family violence. A qualified clinical psychologist with experience in family matters will, as Dr. Abruzzese indicated on cross-examination, have encountered this issue in his training and, unfortunately, all too frequently in his clinical practice. Dr. Abruzzese also stated that he believed that "family violence should be a factor in family litigation."

422 Mass. at 599; 664 N.E.2d at 439. Do you agree that qualified clinical psychologists will automatically have the necessary experience and expertise to evaluate cases involving domestic violence? In 1996 a survey of psychologists from 39 states found that a history of partner violence was viewed as relevant to custody decisions by only 27.7 of respondents. Marc Ackerman and Melissa C. Ackerman, *Child Custody Evaluation Practices: a*

1996 Survey of Psychologists, 30 F.L.Q. 565 (1996). We will return to this question in looking at the role of guardians ad litem in custody cases involving domestic violence.

Partner Violence as a Factor in Decision-making: Legislative Change

As of 1999, custody provisions in more than forty states mandate consideration of domestic violence as a factor in custody decisions. Sarah M. Buel, *Domestic Violence and the Law: An Impassioned Exploration for Family Peace,* 33 F.L.Q. 719, 737 (1999).

In 1991 the National Council of Juvenile and Family Court Judges "undertook the challenge of drafting a Model State Code on Domestic and Family Violence through its Family Violence Project." As the Code's introduction goes on to say:

> [t]he Model Code was developed with the collegial and expert assistance of an advisory committee composed of leaders in the domestic violence field, including judges, prosecutors, defense attorneys, matrimonial lawyers, battered women's advocates, medical and health care professionals, law enforcement personnel, legislators, educators and others. Hard choices and necessary compromises were made during three years of intense work.... Throughout the discussions and code itself, due process and fairness were paramount. Because this is a Model Code each chapter and section can be independently assessed and accepted or modified.

The Code was approved by the Council's Board of Trustees in 1994. Its custody provisions propose presumptions against the grant of custody to an abusive parent, and contain a strong provision highlighting the relevance of domestic violence to a "best interests" analysis.

Model Code on Domestic and Family Violence National Council of Juvenile and Family Court Judges January 1994

Sec. 402. Factors in determining custody and visitation.

In addition to other factors that a court must consider in a proceeding in which the custody of a child or visitation by a parent is at issue and in which the court has made a finding of domestic or family violence:

1. The court shall consider as primary the safety and well-being of the child and of the parent who is the victim of domestic or family violence.

2. The court shall consider the perpetrator's history of causing physical harm, bodily injury, assault, or causing reasonable fear of physical harm, bodily injury, or assault, to another person.

3. If a parent is absent or relocates because of an act of domestic or family violence by the other parent, the absence or relocation is not a factor that weighs against the parent in determining custody or visitation.

COMMENTARY

This section was constructed to remedy the failure of many custody statutes to give courts direction related to appropriate consideration of domestic and family violence in contested custody cases. Subsection 1 elevates the safety and well-being of the child and abused parent above all other "best interest" factors in deliberations about custodial options in those disputed custody cases where there has been a finding of abuse by one parent of the other. It contemplates that no custodial or visitation award may properly issue that jeopardizes the safety and well-being of adult and child victims.

Subsection 2 compels courts to consider the history, both the acts and patterns, of physical abuse inflicted by the abuser on other persons, including but not limited to the child and the abused parent, as well as the fear of physical harm reasonably engendered by this conduct. It recognizes that discreet acts of abuse do not accurately convey the risk of continuing violence, the likely severity of future abuse, or the magnitude of fear precipitated by the composite picture of violent conduct.

Subsection 3 recognizes that sometimes abused adults flee the family home in order to preserve or protect their lives and sometimes do not take dependent children with them because of the emergency circumstances of flight, because they lack resources to provide for the children outside the family home, or because they conclude that the abuser will hurt the children, the abused parent, or third parties if the children are removed prior to court intervention. This provision prevents the abuser from benefitting from the violent or coercive conduct precipitating the relocation of the battered parent and affords the abused parent an affirmative defense to the allegation of child abandonment.

* * *

NOTES

1. Most state statutes requiring "consideration" of domestic violence do not, as the Model Code provision does, make safety a priority that trumps other considerations. Rather, the presence of partner abuse becomes one factor among many to be considered. Often the list of factors also includes a "friendly parent" provision, leading one commentator to conclude:

> [S]imple inclusion of domestic violence as one factor to be considered in a custody decision is not an adequate solution. Courts are free to give as much—or as little—consideration to the enumerated factors as they choose. No particular factor outweighs another, so an abusive parent could receive unrestricted visitation based on the court's perceived need of the child to have extensive contact with both parents.

Naomi Cahn, *Civil Images of Battered Women: The Impact of Domestic Violence on Child Custody Decisions*, 44 VAND. L REV. 1041, 1071 (1991). However, some 28 states, by 1995, had gone beyond the simple requirement that domestic violence be considered. Several follow the Model Code's lead in demanding separate consideration of the safety of both the children and the abused parent, even if that factor is not given the same absolute priority the Model Code accords it. *See, e.g.*, N.J. STAT. ANN. § 9:2–4 (West Supp. 1991). Some address the specific safety issue of guaranteeing confidentiality to the records and addresses of domestic violence victims. Others, including Colorado and Kentucky, have followed the Model Code's lead in providing that courts may not use as a factor militating against a grant of custody to an abused parent the fact that she left her children with the abuser when she fled her abuser. COLO. REV. STAT. § 14–10–124(4) (1989); KY. REV. STAT. ANN. § 403.270(2). *See, generally,* The Family Violence Project of the National Council of Juvenile and Family Court Judges, *Family Violence in Child Custody Statutes, An Analysis of State Codes and Legal Practice,* 29 F.L.Q. 197, 204–07 (1995).

2. Some who fear that judges will continue to decide cases without sufficient attention to issues of domestic violence, even when required to "consider" it, have argued for requiring judges to articulate, in writing, their reasons for granting custody to the parent who has abused his partner, as the Massachusetts Supreme Judicial Court did in *Custody of Vaughn*. The hope is (a) that the demand for an articulated rationale will make judges think twice about granting custody to known abusers, and (b) that the written record will facilitate appeals in cases where judges abuse their discretion in making such awards. There are two counter-arguments. One, leveled by those who represent fathers in custody litigation, is that the requirement unfairly tips the scale against fathers, because judges would rather not award custody to an abusive parent than have to articulate their reasons for doing so, even in cases in which the child would be better served by being placed with the abuser. The other, levelled by those who represent battered women, is that the requirement for an articulated rationale is easily met, given the broad discretion still entrusted to judges, and the number of factors arguably relevant to their decision. On this view, judges will use their written opinions to shore up decisions which may actually be motivated by less honorable considerations, and their decisions may become harder rather than easier to reverse.

For others critical of the "one factor among many" approach to considering domestic violence, the answer is to give priority to domestic violence by using proof of abuse to trigger a rebuttable presumption that a partner-abusing parent should not be given custody of a child.

Presumptions Favoring Non–Abusive Parents

The Family Violence Project of the National Council of Juvenile and Family Court Judges Family Violence in Child Custody Statutes: An Analysis of State Codes and Legal Practice, 29 Family Law Quarterly 197, 208–210 (1995)

[As of 1995,] [c]ustody codes in eight states establish rebuttable presumptions related to domestic violence. The codes in four states create rebuttable presumptions against the award of sole or joint custody of children to perpetrators of domestic violence. The codes in the other four states incorporate presumptions related to joint custody by providing a rebuttable presumption against joint custody if a court determines that a parent is a perpetrator of domestic violence. Also, the codes in three states articulate a presumption against unsupervised visitations when a court finds that the noncustodial parent has perpetrated domestic violence.

Finally, two statutes include an additional presumption that a child not reside with a perpetrator of domestic violence.

A provision in the Louisiana code stating the court cannot deny the abused parent custody based on the adverse effects experienced because of domestic violence is in effect a presumption. The Louisiana code also specifies that the presumption fails when the court finds that both parents have committed domestic violence, and directs the court to award sole custody to the parent "who is less likely to continue to perpetrate family violence."

Only Oklahoma's statute requires that domestic violence be established by clear and convincing evidence before the presumption is operative. Other codes trigger the presumption only upon conviction of serious crimes. The Wisconsin statute requires only evidence of a crime of interspousal battery or abuse, as defined in the civil protection order statute, to activate the presumption. North Dakota requires credible evidence of domestic violence. The remaining codes merely specify that if a court determines there has been domestic violence, the presumption arises. Furthermore, while there is little case law interpreting the "domestic violence presumption" codes, recently published and unpublished cases have tended to limit the circumstances in which the presumption is activated. Finally, some codes delineate the standard of proof or the type of evidence that must be adduced to overcome the presumption or to obtain modification of an order entered pursuant to the presumption.

* * *

NOTE

1. The eight states referred to in this passage are Delaware, Florida, Idaho, Louisiana, Minnesota, North Dakota, Oklahoma and Wisconsin. By 1997 the number had grown to fourteen, with the addition of Alabama, Hawaii, Iowa, Missouri, Nevada and New Jersey. The District of Columbia also adopted a presumption in 1997, and Massachusetts joined the list in 1998. By the year 2000 there were twenty three states on the list, with the addition of Arkansas, California, Oregon, South Dakota, Tennessee (although only when the children have been abused), Texas and Washington. Ami S. Jaeger, *A Review of the Year in Family Law: Century Ends with Unresolved Issues*, 33 F.L.Q. 908 (2000). While the precise wording of the statutes varies considerably, some states have borrowed from the language of the Model Code produced by the National Council of Juvenile and Family Court Judges.

Model Code on Domestic and Family Violence National Council of Juvenile and Family Court Judges January 1994

Sec. 401. Presumptions concerning custody.

In every proceeding where there is at issue a dispute as to the custody of a child, a determination by the court that domestic or family violence has occurred raises a rebuttable presumption that it is detrimental to the child and not in the best interest of the child to be placed in sole custody, joint legal custody, or joint physical custody with the perpetrator of family violence.

COMMENTARY

Support for the presumptions incorporated in this section, that domestic violence is detrimental to the child and that it is contrary to the child's best interest to be placed in sole or joint custody with the perpetrator thereof, is extensive. This section compels courts, attorneys, custody evaluators, and other professionals working with cases involving the custody of children to consider the impact of domestic and family violence on these children....

Sec. 403. Presumption concerning residence of child.

In every proceeding where there is at issue a dispute as to the custody of a child, a determination by a court that domestic or family violence has occurred raises a rebuttable presumption that it is in the best interest of the child to reside with the parent who is not a perpetrator of domestic or family violence in the location of that parent's choice, within or outside the state.

COMMENTARY

... [This presumption] is designed to defeat any assertion by a perpetrator of domestic or family violence that custody and residence with the abused parent should only be presumptive if the abused adult remains within the jurisdiction of the marital domicile. It recognizes that the enhanced safety, personal and social supports, and the economic opportunity available to the abused parent in another jurisdiction are not only in that parent's best interest, but are, likewise and concomitantly, in the best interest of the child.

Sec. 404. Change of circumstances.

In every proceeding in which there is at issue the modification of an order for custody or visitation of a child, the finding that domestic or family violence has occurred since the last custody determination constitutes a finding of a change of circumstances.

* * *

NOTES

1. Although Section 404 of the Model Code does not use the language of "presumption," its effect is to create a *conclusive* presumption that an incident of violence constitutes a change of circumstance sufficient to warrant a request for modification of a custody or visitation order. Unfortu-

nately, this provision does not address the two year moratorium on modifications suggested by Section 409 of the Uniform Marriage and Divorce Act, except where "the child's present environment may endanger seriously his physical, mental, moral or emotional health." In jurisdictions using Section 409 of the Uniform Act, it might be wise to add to Section 404 of the Model Code language to the effect that: "a finding that domestic or family violence has occurred since the last custody determination constitutes a finding that the child's physical, mental, moral or emotional health may be seriously endangered by his present environment." This would ensure prompt consideration of the request for modification, no matter how closely the new incident of violence follows the original custody order.

2. The National Council of Juvenile and Family Court Judges is not the only influential national organization to endorse the use of custody presumptions in the context of domestic violence. As early as 1990, Congress passed Concurrent Resolution 172, which provided in part that credible evidence of spousal abuse should create a statutory presumption against a grant of custody to the abusive parent. H.R. Con. Res. 172, 101st Cong., 2d Sess. (1990). A recent report to the President of the American Bar Association from several entities within the Association, including the Steering Committee on the Unmet Legal Needs of Children, the Children and the Law Committee of the Young Lawyers Division, the Domestic Violence Committees of the Section of Family Law and the National Conference of Special Court Judges, the Task Force on Children of the Litigation Section, and the Victims Committee of the Criminal Justice Section, has taken a similar position, supporting the creation of a presumption against awarding custody to parents who abuse their partners. Howard Davidson, *The Impact of Domestic Violence on Children, A Report to the President of the American Bar Association* 13 (1994). Similarly, a 1996 report of the American Psychological Association recommends that: "In matters of custody, preference should be given to the nonviolent parent whenever possible...." *Violence and the Family: Report of the American Psychological Association Presidential Task Force on Violence and the Family* 99 (1996).

3. More recently the American Law Institute (ALI) has also incorporated domestic violence specific provisions into its 1998 draft of model "Principles of Law Governing the Allocation of Custodial and Decisionmaking Responsibility for Children." American Law Institute, PRINCIPLES OF THE LAW OF FAMILY DISSOLUTION: ANALYSIS AND RECOMMENDATIONS (Tentative Draft No. 3, Part I, March 1998). The following excerpt describes the ALI's response, particularly as it offers relevant procedures and standards for custody decisions.

Katherine M. Reihing
Protecting Victims of Domestic Violence and Their Children After Divorce: The American Law Institute's Model, 37 Family and Conciliation Courts Review 393, 398–402 (1999)

The ALI draft defines domestic abuse as conduct "by a parent or a present or former member of the child's household against a child or another member of the household" that causes physical injury or the creation of reasonable fear thereof. The ALI definition does not include emotional abuse because of the difficulty of distinguishing abuse from the emotional problems that may occur in many intimate relationships....

Whether there is a reasonable fear of physical injury is determined by the court both subjectively and objectively. The fear must be reasonably justified. Physical injury or reasonable fear of physical injury must be established by credible evidence. This may include, but is not limited to, proof of a crime involving physical injury or threat of physical injury by the batterer. Some examples of crimes that may establish domestic violence include assault, rape, stalking and battery. However, a crime against the victim is not the only acceptable form of proof. Abuse may also be proven by credible testimony of the spouse alleging abuse, the testimony of witnesses to the abuse, or proof of a domestic abuse protection order against the batterer.

When a party is seeking a child custody or visitation order at divorce, the first thing that party must do under the ALI statute is file a proposed parenting plan with the court. It is at this stage of the process that domestic violence is initially confronted. In its parenting plan section, the statute states that when a party is filing a plan, he or she must include a number of items in an affidavit supporting the plan. One required item is a description of any circumstances involving domestic violence, such as restraining orders against either parent. If a party expresses a fear of domestic abuse, some of that party's information, such as his or her address, will be kept confidential.

The statute requires courts to develop a screening process to identify cases in which there is credible information that domestic violence or child abuse has occurred. The statute states that the goal of the screening process is to identify cases in which domestic violence is present so that the court may take a more active role in protecting both child and victim from harm and ensure that all parenting plans are voluntary. However, the statute gives no clue as to how this process would detect cases of domestic violence or exactly when the screening process would occur.

. . .

[Another] section of the statute relevant to cases involving domestic violence requires the court to order an evidentiary hearing upon the submission of a parenting agreement if there is credible information that domestic violence has occurred. The evidentiary hearing is held to determine if there are grounds to reject the parenting plan. The court may also order an evidentiary hearing, in its discretion, if it finds that the agreement is not voluntary or that it would be harmful to the child. The hearing is designed to identify cases in which there is concern about the safety of the child and to make sure any parenting agreements submitted by victims of abuse are knowing and voluntary. At this hearing, the court may also order any protective measures it deems appropriate for the victim or the child.

The court may learn of credible information substantiating domestic violence through (1) an affidavit disclosing the circumstances of the domestic violence submitted by the party with the parenting plan, (2) the screening process, (3) procedures by which the court cross-checks criminal court records, or (4) questioning the parents themselves about their understanding of the agreement and their acceptance of it.

. . .

The last section of the model statute that pertains to domestic violence allows the court to apply limiting factors to a party's parenting plan if a parent is found to have engaged in domestic violence or to be a victim of domestic violence. The section on limiting factors first provides that the court, upon request from a parent or if there is credible information, should determine "whether a parent who would otherwise be allocated responsibility under a parenting plan" has, among other things, inflicted domestic abuse or allowed another to inflict domestic abuse. If a parent is found to have engaged in abuse, the court "should impose limits that are reasonably calculated to protect the child or child's parent from harm."

The statute requires the court to consider risks to a parent's or child's safety. The court must acknowledge all forms of domestic abuse, as defined by the statute, of any degree or severity. Once the risk of domestic abuse is identified, the court may take it into account when drafting or approving a parenting plan. The court may prescribe limits to the parenting plan that are reasonably calculated to protect the child and the victim from future harm. The limits the court imposes must correspond to the severity of the abuse.

Among the limitations a court may impose are (1) an adjustment of the custodial responsibility of the parents, including the allocation of exclusive responsibility to one of them; (2) supervision by a third party during visitation; (3) exchange of the child through an intermediary or in a safe environment when it is time for visitation; (4) restrictions on the child's communication with a parent; (5) refusal of overnight visitation; (6) requiring the abusive parent to post a bond to secure the safe return of the child following visitation; (7) a requirement that a parent complete a treatment program for domestic violence; and (8) any further restraints or requirements the court finds necessary to provide the child or the parent with safety. These limitations may be ordered at any time during or after the initial allocation of custodial responsibility.

The ALI statute further states that if a parent is found to have engaged in domestic violence, the court may not award that parent custodial responsibility without making special findings that the child and the other parent will be safe from harm through the imposition of limits applied to the parenting plan. The parent found to have instigated the domestic violence has the burden of proving that the custodial responsibility he or she seeks under the parenting plan will not endanger the child or the other parent. The court's findings should be specific and should relate to the underlying situation and the risks involved.

* * *

NOTES AND QUESTIONS

1. In her *Reporter's Memorandum to the Members of the American Law Institute,* PRINCIPLES OF THE LAW OF FAMILY DISSOLUTION: ANALYSIS AND RECOMMENDATIONS xxiii (Tentative Draft No. 3, Part I, March 1998), Katherine Bartlett reports that the ALI model differs from both traditional "best interests" analysis and the newer "presumption" models; incorporating the best of each, while addressing concerns raised by, and tensions associated with, each. In what ways could it be argued that the ALI model improves upon statutes creating a presumption against the grant of custody to an abusive spouse? To what extent does the ALI framework reliably limit judicial discretion? Apart from the issue of judicial discretion, do you see other potential weaknesses in the ALI scheme?

2. When Massachusetts joined the ranks of states with a rebuttable presumption against a grant of custody to a parent who is an abusive partner, it was not without a vigorous political struggle. For several years bills were introduced into the state legislature, but effectively stalled by their opponents. In 1996 the Governor's Commission on Domestic Violence lent its weight to the reform, recommending legislation "providing that the interests of children who have been exposed to serious and chronic abuse are best served by a rebuttable presumption against an award of custody or unsupervised visitation to the perpetrator." *The Children of Domestic Violence: Report of the Governor's Commission on Domestic Violence* 4 (1996). During the 1997–98 session of the legislature, a Joint Committee on the Judiciary introduced a new version of the custody presumption, in a bill styled "An Act Protecting Children from Domestic Violence in Custody and Visitation Proceedings." It was passed by the House, and introduced into the Senate, where opponents introduced a new delaying tactic, persuading their colleagues to request the opinion of the Commonwealth's Supreme Judicial Court as to its constitutionality. However, the Supreme Judicial Court delivered a ringing endorsement of the bill, in time for proponents to secure its passage before the end of the legislative session. Excerpts of the opinion follow, providing a thorough defense of the presumption against charges that it violates the due process rights of the abusive parent.

The Supreme Judicial Court of the Commonwealth of Massachusetts
Opinion of the Justices to the Senate

SJC–07603

On March 11, 1998, the Justices submitted the following answer to a question propounded to them by the Senate.

To the Honorable the Senate of the Commonwealth of Massachusetts:

The Justices of the Supreme Judicial Court respectfully submit their answer to the question set forth in an order adopted by the Senate on November 13, 1997, and transmitted to the Justices on November 20, 1997. The order indicates that there is pending before the General Court a bill, Senate No. 2021, entitled, "An Act relative to the consideration of domestic violence in custody and visitation proceedings." ... The order recites: "[Senate No. 2021] would establish a presumption against awarding custody of a child to a parent under some circumstances; and ... would further require that, upon reaching a finding by a preponderance of the evidence [that a parent has engaged in a pattern or serious incident of abuse], the burden of proof shifts to the challenged parent to prove that it is in the best interests of a child to be placed with such parent."

The order also indicates that grave doubt exists as to the constitutionality of the bill, if enacted into law, and requests our opinion on this question:

> "Does the statutory presumption established by [Senate No. 2021] or the resulting shifting of the burden of proof violate the Due Process Clause of the Fourteenth Amendment to the United States Constitution or Article 10 of the Massachusetts Declaration of Rights by impermissibly shifting to the challenged parent the burden of proof relative to custody of a child?"

... Thus, the Justices must answer whether the establishment of a rebuttable presumption in custody disputes and the resulting shift in the burden of proof deprives the challenged parent of a liberty interest or property interest, and, if so, whether the requirements of due process have been satisfied.

The Supreme Judicial Court and the Supreme Court of the United States have recognized that parents have a fundamental interest in their relationships with their children that is constitutionally protected.... However, parents' interests ... are not absolute, because "[t]he overriding principle in determining [the right of a parent to custody] must be the best interest of the child." *C.C.* v. *A.B.*, 406 Mass. 679, 691 (1990).

There is a growing national awareness that children who witness or experience domestic violence suffer deep and profound harms. See, e.g., *Custody of Vaughn*, 422 Mass. 590, 599 (1996);.... To better protect children, many States have adopted legislation making it more difficult for an abusive parent to obtain custody of a child in a divorce proceeding.... It appears that this court is the first to advise on the constitutionality of such a presumption. In custody disputes between parents there is no constitutional or statutory entitlement to any particular form of custody.... A parent seeking custody must simply present evidence of facts which demonstrate why such an award of custody serves the child's best interests. If the other parent wishes to obtain custody, that parent must present evidence to show why he or she should be awarded custody instead. The judge weighs the evidence presented and makes a determination as to which parent can best satisfy the child's welfare and happiness.... Evidence of domestic violence is only one factor of many considered by a judge in making custody determinations.

Senate No. 2021 would change the weight that domestic violence is given in custody determinations. Instead of simply being a factor considered by the judge, it could be a determinative factor. If one parent proves by a preponderance of evidence that the other has engaged in a pattern or incident of serious abuse, then a presumption arises that it is not in the child's best interests to be in the custody of the challenged parent. The challenged parent then has the burden of proving by a preponderance of the evidence that despite evidence of abuse, it is in the child's best interests to be in his or her custody....

[T]he question is not whether the State may restrict parents' liberty interests in relating with their children, but rather, what standard of proof is constitutionally required for the State to do so. Senate No. 2021 would establish the presumption after proof by a "preponderance of the evidence." Whether this standard survives constitutional muster depends on the value society places on the affected individual's liberty, the significance of the deprivation or restriction, society's interest in avoiding erroneous deprivations or restrictions to that liberty, and the value society places on the State's interest.... This requires consideration of three distinct factors: (1) "the private interest that will be affected by the official action"; (2) "the risk of an erroneous deprivation of such interest through the procedures used, and the probable value, if any, of additional or substitute procedural safeguards"; and (3) "the Government's interest, including the function involved and the fiscal and administrative burdens that the additional or substitute procedural requirement would entail." ... We examine each of the factors to determine whether the presumption created by Senate No. 2021 meets the requirements of due process.

1. *Private Interests.* ... Creating a presumption that custody in a parent is not in the best interests of a child implicates the interest of the parent in his or her relationship with the child, as well as a child's interest in the relationship with his or her family.... The presumption also implicates the child's right to be free from abusive or neglectful behavior....

... [P]arents' interests in relating with their children are extremely important, and before the State may permanently deprive any parent of that interest, it should generally be required to meet a standard of proof higher than a preponderance of the evidence....

... [A] child's interest to be with his or her parents fluctuates with the child's interest to be free from abuse and neglect.... To allow a child to experience or witness domestic violence "is a violation of the most basic human right, the most basic condition of civilized society: the right to live in physical security, free from the fear that brute force will determine the conditions of one's daily life." *Custody of Vaughn*, supra at 595.... Because a child's interest in being free from the effects of domestic violence is extremely significant, proof by a preponderance of the evidence appears to be a sufficient standard to allow the rebuttable presumption to attach in custody disputes between parents.

2. *Risk of error.* Next we must consider the risk of an erroneous deprivation of the private interests through the procedures used, and the probable value, if any, of additional or substitute procedural safeguards....

A preponderance of the evidence standard creates a higher risk of [error] than a higher standard of proof. However, the presumption created by Senate No. 2021 "may be rebutted by a preponderance of the evidence that [a custody award to the challenged parent] is in the best interests of the child." In *Care and Protection of Robert*, [408 Mass.] at 64, the court concluded that the preponderance standard was sufficient for purposes of restricting a parent's right to custody, in part, because "further proceedings regarding the particular situation [would] be held." The protection afforded by Senate No. 2021 is even greater, because the challenged parent has an opportunity immediately to overcome the presumption based on a preponderance of the evidence.

Another issue of concern is that one parent may make false allegations of abuse to gain an advantage in custody proceedings.... However, parents acting in such a manner are clearly not acting in their child's best interests. Therefore, parents who make false allegations of abuse run the great risk that they will lose custody of their children....

... Because the risk of error is minimal, proving abuse by a preponderance of the evidence prior to the rebuttable presumption arising in custody disputes between parents is appropriate.

3. *The State's interest*.... The State, as parens patriae, has a "compelling interest in protecting the physical and psychological well-being of minors." ... Thus, the State has a significant interest in protecting a child from residing with a parent who has a history of committing acts of domestic violence, unless it is shown to be in a child's best interests.

A standard of proof stricter than the preponderance of the evidence would be inconsistent with promoting the State's interest. The burden of a stricter standard of proof would fall entirely on the parent alleging abuse.... A victim of domestic violence may not have the resources necessary to meet a higher standard of proof. One who commits domestic violence often controls a spouse by threatening to obtain custody if the spouse attempts to leave the relationship, to report abuse to the police, or otherwise to defend him or herself.... Because the purpose of Senate No. 2021 is to prevent children from witnessing or experiencing domestic violence, a standard of proof greater than a preponderance of the evidence would prevent many victims of abuse from proving the existence of domestic violence at custody proceedings, and a greater number of children could end up in the custody of a perpetrator of domestic violence.

In balancing the interests involved, the logical conclusion is that the "preponderance of the evidence" standard prescribed by Senate No. 2021 satisfies the requirements of due process under the State and Federal Constitutions. The risk of error is greatly outweighed by children's interest in being free of abuse and neglect, and the State's interest in promoting the welfare of its children. Moreover, because Senate No. 2021 only relates to custody disputes between parents, the risk of error is being shared by two individuals with equal interests. The State's interest is promoted only indirectly—through an award of custody to nonabusive parents. Therefore, the Justices conclude in response to the Senate's question, that the rebuttable presumption and resulting shift in the burden of proof established by Senate No. 2021 would not, if enacted into law, contravene that portion of art. 10 which provides that "[e]ach individual of the society has a right to be protected by it in the enjoyment of his life, liberty and property, according to standing laws,'' or the due process clause of the Fourteenth Amendment.

The answer to the question is, ''No.''

NOTES

1. Significantly, in an early version, the bill required that in any case in which the presumption was rebutted, and custody granted to a parent who had been an abusive partner, the judge must provide a written justification of that result. Fathers' rights groups objected to this provision, and the final version of the legislation requires that in any case in which the presumption is triggered by a showing of abuse, the custody award must be supported by written opinion. If the fear is that imposing the writing requirement only when custody goes to a partner-abusing parent gives an unfair advantage to the non-abusive parent, does the final form of the legislation impose an unfair burden on the abused parent who is seeking to trigger the presumption?

2. While the intent behind the creation of presumptions is to make it harder for partner-abusing parents to win custody, the impact of the presumption on actual litigation depends on several other variables. One variable is the standard of proof demanded of the party who is seeking to invoke the presumption. The Massachusetts legislation demands that the abused parent meet a ''preponderance of the evidence'' standard, but some states have set the bar higher, demanding conviction of serious crimes, while others seem to have set the bar lower, and yet others seem to have left the issue open, stating only that the presumption arises if the court determines there has been domestic violence.

One key question is whether the existence of a restraining order taken out by one parent against the other will provide a sufficient basis for the presumption. Most states have taken the position that the family court must make its own determination that the relationship between the parents is abusive. In part, this may be because many protective orders are entered by courts on the basis of an agreement between the parties, and without findings of fact about the abuse. In part it may be because of criticisms by some members of the family bar that judges are too quick to issue restraining orders on the basis of insufficient evidence. In most states, however, a conviction or plea following from a violation of a protective order will be deemed to satisfy the statutory standard. *See, generally,* The Family Violence Project of the National Council of Juvenile and Family Court Judges, *Family Violence in Child Custody Statutes, An Analysis of State Codes and Legal Practice,* 29 F.L.Q. 197, 220–21 (1995).

Another variable is the capacity and willingness of the court to investigate and consider a variety of evidentiary sources. There is a world of difference in the reliability of a determination made solely on the basis of the warring testimony of the two parents, and that of a determination buttressed by consideration of medical, court, police, and school records, and the testimony of those who have had ongoing contact with members of the family.

Some statutes are beginning to include lists of relevant categories of evidence for courts to consider in custody determinations. Arizona requires courts to consider all relevant factors, including but not limited to findings from other courts of competent jurisdiction, police and medical records, child protective service and domestic violence shelter records, school records and witness testimony. ARIZ. REV. STATE. ANN. § 25–332 (1994). The Family Code of California allows courts to require independent corroboration of one parent's abuse of the other, which corroboration can include, but is not limited to, written reports by law enforcement agencies, child protective services or other social service agencies, courts, medical facilities, or other public agencies or private non-profit organizations providing services to victims of sexual assault or domestic violence. CAL. CODE § 3011 (West 1995). Courts in Hawaii must consider evidence of spousal abuse, and make determinations as to the primary aggressor, and the frequency and degree of family violence. HAW. REV. STAT. § 571–46 (1994). *See, generally,* The Family Violence Project of the National Council of Juvenile and Family Court Judges, *Family Violence in Child Custody Statutes, An Analysis of State Codes and Legal Practice,* 29 F.L.Q. 197, 210–11 (1995).

A related question is what standard the challenged parent must meet in rebutting the presumption, once it is triggered, or what types of evidence will be relevant either to overcome the presumption, or to modify an order based on the presumption. North Dakota, for example, requires clear and convincing evidence to rebut its presumption, N.D. CENT. CODE § 14–05–22.3 (1993), whereas Louisiana, like Massachusetts, is satisfied with a showing on a "preponderance of the evidence." LA. REV. STAT. ANN. § 9:364(A) (West 1994). Delaware and Louisiana both provide that successful completion of a batterer's treatment program is one basis upon which the presumption can be overcome, as long as the award of custody can also be shown to be in the best interests of the child. DEL. CODE. ANN. Tit. 13, § 705A (1944); LA. REV. STAT. ANN. § 9:364(A) (West 1994). *See, generally,* The Family Violence Project of the National Council of Juvenile and Family Court Judges, *Family Violence in Child Custody Statutes, An Analysis of State Codes and Legal Practice,* 29 F.L.Q. 197, 210, nn. 67–68 (1995) and accompanying text.

3. More generally, the impact of these new "presumption" provisions on custody practice will depend on the readiness of lawyers to argue their applicability, of custody evaluators and guardians ad litem to recognize abuse in the parental relationships they examine, and of judges to listen with educated ears and open minds to allegations of abuse. In these crucial respects the needs of abused parents and their children are the same, whether the state offers a presumption against a grant of custody to a partner-abusing parent, or merely insists that domestic violence be a factor in any custody determination. The Family Violence Project of the National Council of Juvenile and Family Court Judges conducted a preliminary survey of participants in the initial eight "presumption" states in 1995. Its findings serve as an appropriate conclusion to this section, indicating the extent to which the real value of these recent reforms will depend on the attitudes of those practicing under them and those charged with their implementation. At the same time, it is important to note the caveat

attached by the authors, to the effect that their "report on practice in these jurisdictions is ... preliminary, at best. Further investigation and discussion is warranted." Id. at 211 n.70.

Custody Determinations: The Climate of Practice

The Family Violence Project of the National Council of Juvenile and Family Court Judges Family Violence in Child Custody Statutes: An Analysis of State Codes and Legal Practice, 29 Family Law Quarterly 197, 212–222 (1995)

1. THE PRIVATE BAR IS REMARKABLY UNINFORMED ABOUT DOMESTIC VIOLENCE, AND THE QUALITY OF REPRESENTATION AFFORDED VICTIMS BY THE BAR IS UNEVEN

... [S]ome attorneys do not consider domestic violence germane to the issues they must address in divorce or custody proceedings. Rather, many family lawyers see the civil protection or restraining order proceeding as the appropriate, and exclusive, venue for dealing with violence by one adult partner against another. This legal attitude creates strong impediments to aggressive advocacy on behalf of battered women and children.

Participants in the inquiry believe that many in the private bar are not aware that domestic violence is a pervasive social problem that affects the well-being of battered parents and children; that members of the private bar do not identify those among its clients who are victims of abuse; that they do not fully comprehend the violence inflicted by the perpetrator or the risk of continuing abuse; that they do not understand the nexus between domestic violence and child maltreatment; that they do not adduce evidence at trial to fully inform the court about the danger and the detriment posed by the perpetrator's violence both to the other parent and the child; and that they do not craft custodial recommendations that adequately safeguard the child and the abused parent from future violence.

Participants also noted that attorneys too often fail to introduce relevant evidence on domestic violence in custody cases. Moreover, participants complained that attorneys do not thoroughly identify and preserve for trial documentary evidence, including, but not limited to, protection orders, both civil and criminal; 911 tapes; voice mail tapes; police reports; medical records; criminal histories; conviction records; letters written by the perpetrator; journals kept by the victim or children; and pictures of the abused woman and children. Similarly, participants disapprovingly believe that attorneys do not interview or depose witnesses early enough in the case to properly preserve evidence and enhance negotiations. Attorneys also fail to call in experts in cases that require highly knowledgeable testimony.

Furthermore, there are disincentives related to domestic violence practice. Some participants noted that battering husbands are highly litigious. Courts often protract domestic violence custody cases, which can exhaust the resources of attorneys in solo practice or in small firms. The emotional drain of representing battered women may also be high, especially when courts are unresponsive to the risks posed by domestic violence. On the other hand, exposure to malpractice is increasing for attorneys who fail to address issues of domestic violence in custody and divorce representation.

Study participants also noted that law schools and continuing legal education programs often do not incorporate domestic violence in the curricula on custody dispute resolution. Core courses on custody infrequently address domestic violence. Those which do often employ faculty who are not expert on the subject and who offer perspectives that undercut the protective mandates of the codes.

2. LEGAL SERVICES ATTORNEYS ARE RELATIVELY WELL-INFORMED ABOUT DOMESTIC VIOLENCE.

Because legal services attorneys in many jurisdictions are knowledgeable about domestic violence, the quality of representation afforded low-income victims is better than that offered by the private bar. Numbers of legal services programs have developed specialized practice for custody cases in the context of domestic violence.

While the funding for legal services programs has sharply diminished in the last decade, slashing the numbers of poor clients that can be served, a significant number of legal services programs in "domestic violence presumption" states have prioritized domestic violence cases....

. . .

4. THE JUDICIARY IS LARGELY UNINFORMED ABOUT DOMESTIC VIOLENCE AND JUDICIAL PRACTICE IS INCONSISTENT.

Judges, like lawyers, have strong biases that conflict with the protective intent underlying "presumption" codes.... Few judges impose protective limitations on visitation in the context of domestic violence and fewer limit access to supervised visitation. Protective conditions incorporated into custody orders are often boilerplate provisions that are not crafted to the particular circumstances of the parties. Furthermore, judges almost never deny abusive parents access to their children. The paucity of case law related to these relatively new statutes and the inexperience of many custody judges must surely account for the variances in protective provisions.

Judges are no less captives of the dominant discourse on appropriate custodial arrangements than are attorneys. The "friendly parent," "frequent and continuing contact," and "joint custody preference" provisions in custody law and the social science literature about the post-separation needs of children have shaped judicial beliefs, as well as practice, for the past two decades. These stand in sharp contrast to the statutes and social science literature on domestic violence and the post-separation well-being of children and abused parents. Although a learning curve problem is apparent, bias also operates....

Participants reported that family courts have not developed administrative rules, bench guides, or practice protocols on domestic violence custody cases. However, in states that have instituted unified family courts, judges are better able to manage domestic violence cases and are more conscientious about protecting abused parents and children.

5. SPECIALIZED COURT SERVICES RELATED TO DOMESTIC VIOLENCE CUSTODY CASES ARE SORELY WANTING.

Unfortunately, few jurisdictions have instituted specialized court services for domestic violence custody cases. The exceptions are notable and worthy of replication. Court services staff members are not available in most jurisdictions to undertake risk assessment related to abduction or recurring violence toward the abused parent or child during visitation. Thus, courts are usually not able to make informed judgments based on independent risk assessment.

. . .

7. EVALUATORS AND GUARDIANS AD LITEM UTILIZED BY THE COURTS HAVE MINIMAL SPECIALIZED TRAINING ON DOMESTIC VIOLENCE.

Participants noted that custody evaluators and guardians ad litem were the professionals least trained about domestic violence of any actors in the civil justice system. While guardians ad litem are not used routinely in most "presumption" states, many judicial districts employ custody evaluators. Evaluators and guardians are heavily influenced by the social and legal policies that facilitate contact with the noncustodial parent without regard to the risks attendant upon contact or relationship. They, like mediators, are not guided as much by law as by their training and predilections about appropriate post-separation custodial arrangements. Many appear to marginalize domestic violence....

Finally, participants noted that the greater the role of custody evaluators and mediators, the less courts take responsibility for decision-making in custody cases. Consequently, they assert that decision-making deferred to nonjudicial personnel works to the detriment of battered women and children.

. . .

10. IT IS NOT YET CLEAR THAT THE "DOMESTIC VIOLENCE PRESUMPTIONS" HAVE EFFECTED AMELIORATIVE AND PROTECTIVE OUTCOMES FOR CHILDREN AND ABUSED PARENTS.

. . .

Participants gave mixed answers on the question of whether "presumption" codes better protect abused parents and children than "best interest of the child" codes that contain domestic violence as a factor courts must address in custody deliberations. Participants do believe that attorneys have litigated the issue of domestic violence more since the enactment of "presumption" codes. There is consensus among the legal community that the reformed codes that contain domestic violence as a "best interest" factor better protect abused parents and children than previous codes that did not contain such language. But it is unclear whether the reformed codes protect the victims in "presumption" states better than reformed codes protect victims in "best interest" states. The success of the battered parent in custody proceedings is a function of informed and vigorous advocacy; therefore, abused women and children fare as well under codes with a "domestic violence best interest" factor provision as under "presumption" codes. In the future, the legal community should make more assessments of both types of codes.

* * *

C. VISITATION

Introductory Note

For the parent who is given neither sole nor joint physical custody of a child in the aftermath of separation or divorce, a visitation order is the mechanism through which to seek some level of ongoing contact with the child. Like custody determinations, orders of visitation are legally governed by a "best interests of the child" standard, but heavily influenced by two other factors. The first of these is an assumption that parents have a "right" to some relationship with their minor children unless clearly unfit to exercise that right. The second is the conviction that in the overwhelming majority of cases, children will do better if they have access to both parents rather than one. This conviction, as we have already seen in the context of custody, often guides the recommendations of custody evaluators and guardians ad litem, and the decisions of judges, even in cases in which recent research would suggest that shared access is contraindicated, because of intractable conflict or violence between the parents.

Quite apart from their unquestionable authority to deny visitation to a parent who poses a risk to the physical or emotional wellbeing of a child, judges have broad discretion to structure visitation, and impose conditions on its exercise, in ways that will protect the best interests of the child. It has sometimes been argued that judges do not have the authority to limit or condition visitation solely for the purpose of protecting the custodial parent, rather than the child. There are two responses to that argument. One, which requires no change in the underlying legal standard, is that placing the custodial parent at physical or emotional risk, when a court has already decided that this individual is the most appropriate caretaker for the child, inevitably adversely affects the child's interests. The second response, which has been adopted by the National Council of Family and Juvenile Court Judges, is explicitly to expand judicial authority to take into account "the safety and well-being of the ... parent who is the victim of domestic or family violence" in making custody and visitation decisions. *See, e.g.,* Model Code on Domestic and Family Violence, Section 402, Factors in determining custody and visitation.

The first topic developed below is the variety of ways in which visitation can be structured, conditioned and managed better to protect the custodian who is a victim of domestic violence, and her children, from ongoing abuse or harassment by the other parent. The second topic is the particular promise of supervised visitation or supervised exchange in the context of domestic violence, as a means of restricting a batterer's access to his former partner, while testing his commitment to maintaining relationships with his children.

Model Code on Domestic and Family Violence National Council of Juvenile and Family Court Judges January 1994

Sec. 405. Conditions of visitation in cases involving domestic and family violence.

1. A court may award visitation by a parent who committed domestic or family violence only if the court finds that adequate provision for the safety of the child and the parent who is a victim of domestic or family violence can be made;

2. In a visitation order, a court may:

(a) Order an exchange of a child to occur in a protected setting.

(b) Order visitation supervised by another person or agency.

(c) Order the perpetrator of domestic or family violence to attend and complete, to the satisfaction of the court, a program of intervention for perpetrators or other designated counseling as a condition of the visitation.

(d) Order the perpetrator of domestic or family violence to abstain from possession or consumption of alcohol or controlled substances during the visitation and for 24 hours preceding the visitation.

(e) Order the perpetrator of domestic or family violence to pay a fee to defray the costs of supervised visitation.

(f) Prohibit overnight visitation.

(g) Require a bond from the perpetrator of domestic or family violence for the return and safety of the child.

(h) Impose any other condition that is deemed necessary to provide for the safety of the child, the victim of domestic or family violence, or other family or household member.

3. Whether or not visitation is allowed, the court may order the address of the child and the victim to be kept confidential.

4. The court may refer, but shall not order an adult who is a victim of domestic or family violence to attend counseling relating to the victim's status or behavior as a victim, individually or with the perpetrator of domestic or family violence as a condition of receiving custody of a child or as a condition of visitation.

5. If a court allows a family or household member to supervise visitation, the court shall establish conditions to be followed during visitation.

COMMENTARY

. . . The Model Code posits that where protective interventions are not accessible in a community, a court should not endanger a child or adult victim of domestic violence in order to accommodate visitation by a perpetrator of domestic or family violence. The risk of domestic violence directed both towards the child and the battered parent is frequently greater after separation than during cohabitation; this elevated risk often continues after legal interventions.

Subsection 2 lists the protective conditions most routinely imposed on visitation by the perpetrator of domestic and family violence. It is not intended to be exhaustive, nor does this subsection contemplate that each provision should be imposed on every custody order.

Subsection 3 recognizes that it may be necessary to withhold the address of the adult victim and children from the perpetrator and others in order to prevent stalking and assault of adult and child victims in their undisclosed residence. Research reveals that one of the most effective methods of averting violence is denying the abuser access to his victims, which can be facilitated by preserving the confidentiality of the victim's address.

Subsection 4 prohibits a court from ordering a victim of domestic or family violence to attend counseling related to the status or behavior as a victim as a condition of receiving custody of a child or as a condition of visitation. It does not preclude the court from ordering other types of counseling, such as substance abuse counseling or educational classes.

Subsection 5 requires a court to establish conditions to be followed if the court allows a family or household member to supervise visitation. When those supervising visitation are furnished clear guidelines related to their responsibility and authority during supervision, they are better able to protect the child should the perpetrator engage in violence or intimidating conduct toward the child or adult victim in the course of visitation.

NOTES AND QUESTIONS

1. Can you think of other conditions or restrictions generically helpful enough that they might be added to Subsection 2 of the Model Code's Section 405?

2. In each individual case, the abused parent and the children will have particular experiences of their own to draw from in thinking about how visitation might pose risks to their physical and emotional safety, and how those risks might be guarded against through language explicitly incorporated into the visitation order. The mother who has been stalked by her former partner, for example, might prefer that transfer of the children take place through a third party or at a supervised visitation center. But if those services were not available, or the judge was unwilling to insist on them, she might want the batterer's visitation privileges to be conditioned on his not using the transfer as an opportunity to follow her. This is an example of a situation where the children's interests are also directly implicated,

since they would be involved in, and would probably feel responsible for, the surveillance, and would witness any confrontation precipitated by it. Thorough discussion of safety issues between the adult victim and her advocate or counsel, and even consultation with children old enough to participate in the process, could yield a list of necessary safeguards sufficiently grounded in the prior experience of the parties to impress even a judge initially disinclined to include specific protective measures in the order. If the requested safeguards are entered into the record, they will come back to haunt the judge who ignores them, if the failure to include them in the order facilitates further abuse.

3. The specific issue of safety planning with children for unsupervised visits with a battering parent has been addressed by the Pennsylvania Coalition Against Domestic Violence. On behalf of the Coalition, long-time domestic violence advocate Barbara Hart authored the memorandum from which the following excerpts are taken. She suggests both a process by which battered women's advocates can support their clients and their children in strategizing around safety, and some specific safety strategies to consider. She ends with some caveats, detailing the risks involved in safety planning. These require careful consideration by all participants in the process.

Barbara J. Hart
Safety Planning for Children: Strategizing for Unsupervised Visits With Batterers, Pennsylvania Coalition Against Domestic Violence, 1990

... Where a batterer is potentially lethal, we believe he should not be accorded any access to the children. Where he has been violent to the children or continues to intimidate or coerce the mother, but is not thought to present a danger of death or injury to the woman or children, we suggest that supervised visitation is the most that should be awarded. And in the situation where the batterer no longer poses a substantial risk of danger to either the child or the mother, then unsupervised visitation may be appropriate. However, we would assert that the custody court should impose specific provisions on awards of supervised and unsupervised visitation to protect the child and the mother against anticipated dangers. We would also commend safety planning with the child....

Children of battered women who have witnessed their father's violence toward their mother or who have been abused themselves may be quite fearful or anxious about unsupervised visits with their fathers. Children may fear that the father will attack their mother when they are being picked up or dropped off. They may fear that their father will beat them if their mother is not around to protect them or to be the target of his violence. They may fear the unknown. They may fear that they cannot protect their mother against homicidal violence during the night if they sleep at their father's house. They may experience torn loyalties between the parents and may struggle with anger at the mother for leaving or for not having the power to stop the violence. Or they may be caught in a fantasy of family reconciliation while recognizing that their mothers cannot be safe from abuse except through separation. They may have strong feelings of love for their fathers. Even if children are only conflicted and not fearful, this conflict may create a lot of anxiety.

Planning for unsupervised visits can help children . . . manage fear or anxiety, but can also help them develop safety skills and realistic safety plans to minimize the risk of violence during visitation. The goal of safety planning is the empowerment of children. It is critical that safety planning help children identify safety issues and build problem-solving, safety skills. . . .

Skillful advocates must be careful not to aggravate the fear or anxiety that children of battered women are experiencing in anticipation of unsupervised visits. Identifying and discussing fear is not, in and of itself, beneficial to children. Once identified, children need to have skills for managing these feelings and creating safety strategies to avoid the incidents or interactions feared. . . .

Any safety plan must be realistic. It must be age appropriate. The child must be competent to undertake the strategies devised. The plan should be simple. Perhaps only children above 8 years of age can be active participants in safety strategies. For younger children, the mother and the child's advocate may have to map out safety plans that rely little on the child for implementation.

Disclaimer—No guarantees

Safety planning does not make unsupervised visitation with batterers safe. It may reduce the risks. It may empower children to act to protect themselves. It may make visitation safer by invoking community systems. . . . However, safety planning is no guarantee of safety.

And safety planning could potentially increase the risk to the child or the mother. The father who concludes that the child is exposing his violence to the mother or advocate may retaliate. The father who learns that a child is concerned about her own safety may emotionally badger the child about her lack of trust and love for the father. Thus, any safety planning must help a child deal with the possible adversity that may arise if safety planning is revealed to the batterer.

Children need to hear that the plan is no guarantee of safety and that failure of the plan is not the fault of the child. When a particular safety strategy fails, the child must clearly understand that the violence is solely and exclusively the responsibility of the battering father. However, the child needs to be aware that a safety plan can be re-designed if any component fails and that the process of safety planning involves continuing evaluations and revision.

Process of safety planning

. . . The mother can help the advocate identify critical background information, including a history of the batterer's violence towards the mother and the children, an assessment of the amount of woman abuse witnessed by the child, the child's feelings about forthcoming visitation . . ., the competence of the child to develop and execute safety plans, the safety facilitators in the context of the visitation (people, places and things that might enhance the child's safety), the mother's own feelings about visitation . . ., anticipated batterer manipulation around visitation and potential elements for a visitation contract relating to child safety and comfort.

The advocate might encourage the mother to begin a journal about visitation issues to help her in assisting the child in designing, implementing, evaluating and revising safety plans.

. . . Our goal is to facilitate the mother's empowerment and to build an alliance between the mother and child in safety planning.

. . . [A]t the first meeting with the child, the advocate should explain that the goal is to help the child develop a safety plan that meets her very special and individual needs during visitation. The child should be told that adults and children often remember important things after they leave a meeting, so the child should be aware that there will be several meetings in developing a safety plan and that at each meeting issues can be discussed several times. It will never be too late to add something to a safety plan. The first interview with the child probably should focus on the child's feelings about visitation and her father—*What is she looking forward to in visitation? What has her afraid of the visit? What does she love about her father? What about her father makes her afraid?*

At the second meeting with the child, the advocate might want to introduce the concept of journaling. If the child is too young to write, she can draw pictures in a notebook and describe the pictures to the advocate who can make titles or commentary under the picture. . . . The purpose of journaling is to identify feelings, safety issues, and proposed strategies for safety. The child can share the journal with the advocate or her mother or it can be confidential. It is a means for developing the child's own critical thinking.

Further, the child might be asked to describe the patterns of abuse the batterer has inflicted upon the mother and herself or the other children. The listing might include times, places, context and the acts of violence.

In a third meeting, the advocate could help the child identify when she fears for her own safety or the safety of her mother and siblings in relation to the batterer. She should think about the particular things that her father does that make her nervous. It may be shouting or driving recklessly or drinking or holiday depressions or sports events where his team loses, etc. The advocate can pull out how often these events occur and how dangerous the batterer is when they occur. The advocate then should ask the child to identify strategies that she has used successfully and unsuccessfully in the past to divert, minimize, or stop the father's violence toward herself or others. Some assessment about what strategies still seem useful should be made.

[In t]he next strategy session . . . [t]he advocate should help the child identify a plan for handling the interactions/situations feared. For example, the child might say that she does not want her father to drink during her visit, that she wants weapons out of the house, that she would like to have someone other than her father drive during the visit, that she will not be forced to eat during the visit, that she will not be required to talk about her mother, that anything she takes to the visit will not be withheld by the father upon her return to the mother, or that the father will not come into her bedroom or the bathroom.

The advocate should discuss the various options that the child raises to help the child consider the advantages and disadvantages of each and how to best implement the selected options. The advocate must continue to evaluate the child's competence to implement whatever safety strategies are designed. In times of great stress, the simplest strategy may be the best.

Advocates should focus on what the child thinks she could do to keep herself safe.... [She] must give the child time to come up with solutions of her own.... Adults may think of a zillion strategies. The child will probably best incorporate the one she identifies. If the child is blocked, the advocate can carefully measure out suggestions—one or two a session, assuming that there is plenty of time for development of the safety plan. The child must recognize that the planning is an on-going process and that she can engage in planning anywhere, including in the home of the batterer.

The child might also want to think of things that she could do to avoid confrontation with the batterer. Perhaps if he insists upon her attending his church, she can do so. Or if he hates her makeup or clothes, that she will dress in a way that does not irritate him. In thinking about ways that she could change her behavior in order to avoid conflict with the batterer, it is critical that she understand that it is not her obligation to do so, that these avoidance strategies may not immunize her from disputes with [the] batterer, and that any violence used by her father is solely his responsibility.

At the next meeting, the advocate might want to meet with the mother and the child together to think about the components of a safety contract with the batterer. These components then could be the subject of negotiation with the batterer, either directly or through his attorney. If negotiations fail to achieve bottom-line results, then the mother might want to forward the proposed safety conditions to the court and ask the court to impose them upon the perpetrator.[1]

Thereafter, once the mother and child know whether their contract for safety during the visit has been accepted or the court has imposed specific conditions, they can begin to make a plan about the first visit.

1. Initiation of this type of contract for safety will put the batterer "on notice" that there may be consequences for failure to act to safeguard the child. Either a contract by agreement or court-imposed conditions will help the judiciary better recognize the child's interests in safety and set clear parameters for evaluation of compliance by the batterer should the battered woman allege a violation of the visitation order. The more concrete the visitation provisions, the easier to demonstrate contempt of the visitation order.

After the first visit, there should be another meeting to evaluate the safety issues related to the visit. Perhaps the contract needs to be modified or the plan needs to be supplemented

Since the building of safety skills and plans is never completed, advocates must help children identify others outside of the domestic violence program who can assist the child in this continuing endeavor. The fundamentals of safety planning cannot be learned in one lesson. Thus, advocates need to help mothers or other committed adults learn how to assist children in the continuing process of design, implementation and evaluation of safety plans.

Possible Safety Strategies

Information.

Children need to have information to act in an empowered way. Issues likely to arise during visitation should be identified and discussed beforehand. Problem-solving about anticipated interactions or events can help the child respond with clarity about issues she has examined and thought through.

For example, batterers often use visitation to gather information about their battered partners. A father may subject a child to extensive inquiry about the activities and friends of the mother. The child is often caught in an untenable position. If she tells, she fears that the mother's safety may be jeopardized, but if she doesn't tell, she may be beaten or penalized. This interrogation about the mother is virtually certain. The child should have information that questions may be directed at her about the mother and should have the opportunity to think about how she will respond to pressure for disclosure. It is critical that she understands that it is important to put her safety first. This probably means answering her father's questions. But it can also mean that once she comes home, she may share the line of inquiry with her mother.

. . . [T]he child might be taught skills to enhance her critical thinking in crisis or emotionally-laden situations. "Self-talk" is a critical skill. "I am not responsible for my dad's drinking. . . . I am not responsible for his violence. . . . I cannot make life better for him. . . . I can and should put my safety first. . . . I can call for help if there is an emergency. . . . I can talk about how confused I feel later with my advocate. . . . I can weather this storm."

Another example of information that children need in order to strategize for unsupervised visits is an understanding of their own conflict resolution around the issue of loyalty. During a visit a father may raise and test the child's loyalty to the father. Even if he doesn't, the child may find herself struggling with feelings of guilt and ambivalence about "betrayal" of the father. The confused child will surely begin to blame herself/himself for the violence inflicted by the batterer and the break-up of the family. Thus, safety planning must squarely address the issue of torn loyalties. Safety planning should also help children figure out that their father has exclusive responsibility for the violence and that the parents are the only ones responsible for making decisions to separate or divorce.

. . . It is critical that the learning environment does not evoke fear or despair and does not mislead the child into believing that she has power or control over the batterer or his violence. Creating a balanced and empowering learning environment for children at risk is very difficult.

Avoidance.

The child can attempt to avoid a situation (place, time, circumstance) of prior violence. Avoidance can be covert or overt. For example, if the batterer has typically assaulted the child in circumstances where the child has failed to meet his expectations for excellence at video games, the child might enthusiastically suggest other activities. . . . However, if the father insists upon his own plans, perhaps the child could enlist someone in the father's extended family to share the occasion with them. The goal is to maximise safety by building a context that creates disincentives and adverse consequences for the father's violence.

Phoning Home.

Children need to know how to use a phone, which includes learning how to call long distance, how to make a credit card call, and how to achieve operator assistance. What with the recent changes in the telephone system, it is particularly important for the child to learn how to be persistent and clear with telephone operators.

The child should be taught the phone number where the mother can be reached at all times during the visit. . . . The child needs to know how to talk to an answering machine to indicate whether she is calling just to say hello and to hear her mother's reassuring voice or to report an emergency related to abuse.

Emergency Assistance.

If there is a 911 emergency number in the community, the child could be taught to dial that number and ask for assistance from the police or the emergency medical team. The child will need to be able to give the location of the place to which she is calling emergency personnel. She will also need to use language which will convince the police that she is in an emergency situation. Where a father has been criminally convicted of domestic violence and there is an outstanding protection order or the child has been found to be abused by the father by the juvenile court and the police have notice of the visit, perhaps the child will be able to persuade the police to intervene quickly and protectively. . . . Many 911 numbers now record the phone number and location of incoming calls to assist police and other emergency workers to find the location of the emergency even if there is a disconnection. It is important to find out if this display of the child's phone number occurs in the jurisdiction where she will be visiting with the father.

. . .

Escape Logistics.

A child will want to identify all of the potential escape routes from the father's house—doors and windows that the child can open, herself. She should locate all of the telephones in the home of her father and perhaps attempt to keep any cordless phone in her immediate vicinity. She might want to also locate pay telephones and fire alarms near the father's home. If there is a nearby church, she might want to learn the office hours, meet the minister and learn how to gain entrance to the church for refuge. Other escape routes should be evaluated with the child.

Managing the intoxicated father.

... [T]he child should try to keep herself between the father and routes of escape. The child should also try to remove all potential weapons from the immediate location of the intoxicated father. If there is a lot of noise from a stereo or television in the house, the child might try to turn down the noise and eliminate other stimulation such as lights, visitors, disputes with siblings, etc. The child should attempt to remain calm and speak in quiet, soothing tones. The child should try to maximise predictability and tell the father exactly what she is doing in quiet, slow speech—such as, "I'm going to walk back to the desk now and sit down."

Cooperation with an intoxicated father is generally a useful strategy except when the child's life is placed at enhanced risk by the cooperation....

... [I]t is absolutely legitimate for the child to put her life and well-being ahead of her father's if she believes that he is becoming erratic, paranoid and potentially violent. Escape must always be seen by the child as an effective option in a situation where her father is intoxicated. ...

Kidnapping.

Few battering fathers will take children and flee with them. However, if there is any notion that this might happen, the child should probably learn additional safety strategies relating to kidnapping. The child should be helped to identify her surroundings—the names of towns, restaurants, roads, schools—all those things that would help the child understand where she is. Certainly, if she is old enough to read a map, teaching the child how to use the map as a means of locating the abduction route will enable her to help those attempting to rescue her.

Children can learn to tell people dressed in police or military uniforms their names, home phone number, and how to ask for help. Children can leave notes on napkins in restrooms not likely to be used by the perpetrator. There are many ways that the child can get a message out that she is being kidnapped without disclosing her efforts to the batterer....

Since many fathers who snatch their children tell them that the mother is dead or doesn't care, the mother might tell the child that she is not to believe that the mother is dead unless a certain person (named by the mother) confirms that the mother has died. A child needs to hear that the mother loves her and will search for her diligently if there is an abduction. Abducting fathers also threaten children that they will kill the mother if the child reveals her whereabouts. The child should be told that this is not a meaningful threat, that the mother is acting to safeguard her own life and that the child should put her own safety first....

. . .

Rehearsal

Children will need rehearsal of safety plans. Much of the rehearsal should occur as an ordinary event of daily life rather than as emergency safety measures related to visiting the father. Children learn better in situations where they are not anxious.... Again, rehearsal should be done in a way that builds the child's skills without increasing her fears. This is a difficult undertaking, at best.

Mother's Supplemental Safety Planning.

The battered mother may want to consider things that she can do independent of the child to protect both the child and herself.... For example, if the mother thinks that confrontation and potential assault on her is more likely in her home, she may want to arrange for pick up and delivery of the child in a safer place—at the police station, at her brother's home, etc.

If the father changes residences or cars or license tags or promises the children magical vacations, the mother might begin to gather information about these changes and promises in order to prevent a kidnapping or to locate the children quickly. It might be helpful to obtain periodic pictures of the child and the father together. These will greatly enhance the efforts of law enforcement should there be a snatch.

To evaluate the child's safety during the visit, [the mother] might enlist the aid of some friends who could monitor the visit....

Risks of Safety Planning.

Several serious risks emerge from safety planning. The first is that the child will become fearful beyond the reality of danger and become immobilized by that fear. Another risk is that the child will feel she can stop the abuse or that she will believe she is [at] fault if the safety plan fails. Still another risk is that the battered mother who engages in this safety planning with the child will be seen by the court as an unfriendly parent for "interfering" with any reconciliation between the child and the father.

Since courts, family and friends who view the batterer as a bad partner but a good father may retaliate against the mother for encouraging safety planning, it might be better that the child engage in safety planning with an advocate or therapist in consultation with the mother. If safety planning is seen as a professional activity rather than maternal resistance, hostile attitudes from the court and community may be minimized. If domestic violence programs begin to routinely engage in safety planning with kids, the service might be viewed by the courts as essential for children of battered women, so much so that safety planning could become an integral part of every visitation order entered in favor of a battering parent.

Another risk is that the batterer's breach of a visitation order or a safety contract will be ignored by the court; the court may choose continued batterer access over child safety. Not only is there the danger that children will become angry and disillusioned with their protecting mothers and advocates in these circumstances, but the children may despair of hope for safety and autonomy, concluding that they and their protectors are powerless and that survival will best be served by carefully accommodating and deferring to the abuser....

Another risk which must be emphasized is that the battered women's movement does not have a great deal of experience in formulating safety plans for children of battered women. Certainly, we have been doing this work informally for many years, but as we formalize our practice, it may come under closer scrutiny. Therefore, safety planning should be done meticulously with the goals of teaching children safety skills and critical thinking, assisting the mother in protecting her child, and building an empowering relationship between the mother and child. Advocates should periodically consult with child development experts to evaluate whether safety planning activities adequately account for the cognitive and moral developmental capabilities of children of various ages.

* * *

NOTES

1. The idea of supervised visitation as a compromise between an abused partner and her children's fear for their safety on the one hand, and the abuser's interest in continuing contact with his children on the other, is growing in popularity. Creative programs offer a range of services; in some instances actual supervision of the visit will be necessary, while in others the goal may be just to prevent the parents from meeting face to face, so that supervised "drop off" and "pick up", or "transfer," or "exchange" will be enough.

2. In January of 1994 The National Council for Juvenile and Family Courts registered its approval of supervised visitation as a tool for families affected by domestic violence in Section 406 of its Model Code on Domestic and Family Violence, which reads:

> **Specialized visitation center for victims of domestic or family violence.**
>
> 1. The *insert appropriate state agency* shall provide for visitation centers throughout the state for victims of domestic or family violence and their children to allow court ordered visitation in a manner that protects the safety of all family members. The *state agency* shall coordinate and cooperate with local governmental agencies in providing the visitation centers.
>
> 2. A visitation center must provide:
>
> a. A secure setting and specialized procedures for supervised visitation and the transfer of children for visitation; and

b. Supervision by a person trained in security and the avoidance of domestic and family violence.

The accompanying commentary emphasizes that supervised visitation centers are "an essential component of an integrated community intervention system to eliminate abuse and protect its victims." However, the provision does not go so far as to: "mandate that the state own or operate such centers, nor that the centers be operated at public expense."

In 1994 Howard Davidson's report: *The Impact of Domestic Violence on Children, A Report to the President of the American Bar Association,* jointly sponsored by several committees of the American Bar Association, including the ABA Steering Committee on the Unmet Legal Needs of Children; the ABA Young Lawyers Division; the Children and the Law Committee; the ABA Section of Family Law; Domestic Violence Committee, the ABA Litigation Section Task Force on Children and the ABA Criminal Justice Section, Victims Committee, endorsed the proposition that state legislation should create and support appropriate supervised visitation programs. Id. at 14.

3. Two major obstacles standing in the way of broader use of supervised visitation as a means of promoting the safety of abused partners and their children are a lack of funding to support the services, and reluctance by some judges to utilize existing services. While some state legislatures have authorized the expenditure of public funds for supervised visitation (Arizona, Illinois, Massachusetts and Minnesota provide examples), others have required state agencies to provide supervised visitation when it is court-ordered, but without any accompanying appropriation of funds (New Jersey is an example). Some legislatures have tackled the issue of judicial reluctance head-on, explicitly providing judicial authority to order supervised visitation in appropriate cases, to meet any objection that such an order would exceed a judge's legitimate discretion. This is the approach followed in Section 405 of the Model Code on Domestic and Family Violence, reprinted above on p. 393. No state has gone so far as to mandate supervised visitation in appropriate classes of domestic violence cases, although both Georgia and Indiana have considered and rejected such legislation.

4. A wide range of issues raised by supervised visitation in the context of domestic violence are addressed in the excerpt which follows. The author, Robert B. Straus, directs a visitation center in Cambridge, Massachusetts, known as "Meeting Place."

Robert B. Straus
Supervised Visitation and Family Violence, 29 Family Law Quarterly 229, 230–249 (1995)

A. *The Need for Supervised Visitation*

Child protective agencies have been supervising contact between a child and one or more of the child's family members for years. When a child has been removed from the home because of abuse or neglect, regular visits are essential to maintain the child's relationships with his or her parents while interventions are made to reunify the family, or, if necessary, pending termination of parental rights. When a child's contact with a parent presents an ongoing risk, visits must be supervised.

Over the past decade, however, the major impetus for the growth of services for supervised child access has come from a rapidly expanding need for services for separated and divorced parents. . . .

The issues presented have also become more complex. The importance for a child's development of continued contact with both parents has to be balanced against the negative effects of contact if there is intractable conflict between his or her parents. Serious allegations of abuse and risk are matched by denial and counterclaims of interrupted access. Many of these cases urgently need a protected setting in which contact can occur.

. . .

B. Family Violence Cases

When allegations of physical or sexual child abuse occur, careful supervision of contact with the alleged abusive parent is necessary until a determination about the validity of the abuse has been made. If child abuse is confirmed and access is still considered useful for the child, long-term supervision is likely to be the only way to allow safe contact to continue. The central focus of this article, however, is the special risks associated with contact between children and parents when there is a history or allegations of violence between parents. . . .

. . . [T]he highest risk of violence is the period immediately following an abused woman's move to end the relationship. Other than court appearances, the drop-off and pick-up of the children for each visit is the only time a batterer has access to his former partner. Children are traumatized by screaming fights at these points. Worse, these times are also when children and their parents are injured or killed. Therefore, there exists an urgent need for protected settings for the safe transfers of children between the parents.

Risk during transfers is only one of the dangers. There is also a high degree of overlap between partner abuse and child abuse. When both child and partner abuse have occurred, the contacts with the children as well as the transfers need to be protected. Even without a history of child abuse, an abusive partner may still try to use the children manipulatively to force the abused partner to return or try to retaliate through the children. Therefore, if contact with the abusive partner is granted, the children and the custodial parent need to be protected from these manipulations.

C. The Need for Services

The volume of cases requiring supervised visitation is just beginning to be clear. Practitioners running programs know their services are swamped and have long waiting lists. Only a few formal assessments have been conducted. One is a survey of family court judges in New York City conducted by the New York City Bar Association. Over the period of one week, the judges polled saw a need for supervised visitation in 106 new cases. The eight existing visitation programs in the city can provide supervision for a total of nearly 100 cases. Most families, however, remain in a supervised visitation program for a minimum of twelve weeks. Therefore, the weekly referral estimate of 106 new cases a week means .a "demand" for supervision services over the twelve weeks of roughly 1,200 cases with programs that can only provide supervision for only 100 families at a time! Of the families referred to supervised visitation programs 50 percent involve issues of partner abuse.

Without the availability of supervised child access services, judges face untenable choices. Judges can either cut off contact between a parent and child or order continued access with the risk of physical and/or emotional abuse to the parent or child. In the New York survey, denial of visits was the most common result when supervised visitation services were not available. The second common result was unsupervised contact. Either alternative is unacceptable and dangerous.

D. *The Growth of Supervised Visitation Services*

The growth of supervised visitation services has been slow despite the pressing need. These families are difficult to work with. The expertise needed falls between the professional competencies of psychotherapists, attorneys, or mediators. Most significantly, supervised visitation is not a money-making proposition and there has been little or no public funding.

Starting with just a handful of programs in 1982 and even despite numerous obstacles, the pressure of the need has resulted in substantial growth of supervised visitation services. There are fifty-six known supervised visitation programs operating in twenty-eight different states. These statistics probably represent about a third to one-half of the existing programs. Many of these programs are small, part-time, and recently opened. . . .

1. SUPERVISED VISITATION SERVICES

Supervised visitation is actually a range of services which vary according to the degree of closeness of the observation, the training of the observer, and the site for the contacts. "One-on-one" supervision with an observer present at all times is necessary when issues of safety or parental manipulation of a child are compelling. Supervision can be less close, intermittent, or conducted in a group when the risk is lower. "Exchange supervision" is observing the transfer of child(ren) at the start and end of visits. This supervision can protect the safety of parents when a history of abusive behavior is present or when a child is upset by transfers. . . .

Virtually all supervised visitation programs provide some form of documentation of parent-child contacts. The courts or referring agencies frequently ask supervisors of visits for reports on the progress of contacts. Documentation varies from minimal recording of attendance to standardized checklists to detailed observation notes. . . .

In most cases, the visiting parent comes to the center first and is taken to the space where the visit will occur to avoid contact with the other parent. The custodial parent and child arrive later. A supervisor, who has usually met the child, brings the child from the custodial to the visiting parent. The supervisor remains present throughout the visit to observe and intervene if necessary. Visits usually last one to two hours. At the end of the visit, the process is reversed with the custodial parent and child leaving first. Then, the observer writes up observation notes.

Supervisors in different programs range from licensed mental health professionals to paraprofessionals. The only specific educational requirement usually is completion of a training program for supervising visits. In addition, a majority of programs train volunteers or student interns to supervise visits. However, training varies greatly in scope and content with each supervised visitation program.

. . .

2. FUNDING OF SUPERVISED CHILD ACCESS SERVICES

Virtually all supervised visitation programs operate as nonprofit entities. Fees for service support only part of these programs. While individual practitioners may provide supervised visitation services for a substantial fee to wealthy individuals, programs who accept referrals from the courts or public agencies must deal with a predominantly economically disadvantaged population. Therefore, all programs rely on some form of subsidy, usually a combination of support from a parent agency, foundation grants, individual contributions, or contracts with state agencies. In the absence of public funding, most programs around the country are small and struggling. In the long term, more public funding is essential to make supervised visitation services widely available.

Today, there are signs that government support for supervised visitation is moving in the right direction....

Public awareness of family violence has brought about these legislative gains. Advocates for battered women have become a potent political force promoting the need for supervised visitation services. However, responding to the risks of contact with batterers is only one of the historical functions of supervised visitation services. As discussed in the next section, the current emphasis on family violence as the primary reason for supervising visits has been the source of some tension in the development of public policy.

Differing Approaches to Supervised Visitation

. . .

For those of us who have worked with battered women or whose lives have been touched by domestic violence, the fundamental importance of the victim's perspective is compelling and primary. Those of us who are advocates for children or who have personal experience with child abuse cannot imagine any group that needs more attention. Tension between child and victim advocates has been exacerbated because child protective agencies must investigate the parents of abused children. When a family has partner abuse and child abuse, these agencies must question the care and the adequacy of protection afforded by a woman who was battered by the same man who abused the children. In these cases, women feel unfairly blamed for the actions of an abusive partner. Better understanding of family violence should lead to more sensitive assessments of battered mothers.

Supervised visitation providers need to develop inclusive approaches which balance the needs of abused women and at risk children. Attorneys and judges, aware of these differences in perspective and the issues discussed below, will choose better supervisors and craft appropriate visitation orders.

A. Contact with Abuser?

A threshold question is whether to allow contact between a parent who has abused a partner and their child. Well-documented evidence has shown the negative impact on children who are living in a home with a parent who is abused....

The first priority must be to stop the abuse. Women who are battered must be protected. Children must be removed from a situation in which abuse, either of a parent or of the children, is occurring. No contact should occur between a child and an abusive parent unless safety is assured....

Some have made powerful assertions that supervised visitation with an abusive parent is inherently damaging because the structure of supervised visitation with a supervisor acting as though things are normal during a visit implies approval of the batterer and destroys a child's sense of reality about the abuse. These are important risks if supervision is not handled well. Procedures can and should be included regularly during intake into a program, which explain the purpose of supervision for children and support their feelings and perceptions....

What about indirect negative effects? Evidence shows that children experience indirect negative effects from contact with an abusive parent because of the stresses on the custodial parent who is usually the mother. A primary factor in predicting post-divorce outcome for children is the emotional well-being of the custodial parent. After separation of an abusive couple, threats and abuse may continue if contact between the parents is maintained through child visitation. Abusive fathers use threats to litigate custody and access as instruments of control to prevent a battered partner from leaving the relationship, or to maintain control after separation. Concerns about real physical dangers to the custodial parent at transfers and the safety of the children during visits add to the stress.

Supervision of visits has its most clear impact precisely on these indirect effects. Visits occurring in a safe setting remove or greatly reduce a custodial parent's anxiety.... Experience shows that battered women feel supported and less anxious after supervised visits begin to occur. This effect is one of the stronger arguments in favor of supervised contacts.

The potential costs of maintaining contact must be balanced against the impact on the children of losing contact with the abusive parent. Children in most situations want the abuse to stop; they don't want to lose a parent. Children, particularly young children, tend to blame themselves for the loss of contact with an abusive parent. Children, both boys and girls, with a battering father who have little or no contact with him tend to repress memories of violent incidents and to long for and idealize their father. If one long-term goal is to interrupt an inter-generational cycle of dysfunction, maintaining safe contact will help a child gain a realistic assessment of his or her parent. It may also guard against identification and repetition of the abusive behaviors in the child's later adult relationships.

The impact of maintaining contact on abusive partners varies because abusers and types of abuse differ. For some abusive parents, the prognosis may be better than for chronic batterers. Anecdotal experience from supervised visitation providers is that men who are only interested in contact with their children for manipulative purposes are not able to tolerate the restrictions of an adequately run supervised visitation program. They drop out. Those abusive parents who do remain appear to have a genuine connection with their children. For these men, the connection may provide an incentive for change, particularly if the contact with their children occurs in a context that will not tolerate abuse.

. . .

The discussion of whether or not contact *should* continue between an abusive parent and the children is to some degree academic. Overwhelming evidence from the way courts currently operate show that contact *will* take place. Courts regularly order visitation even when partner abuse has clearly occurred. Therefore, it is important for practitioners to understand the differences in approaches to making contact safe.

B. *Neutrality of Visitation Programs*

. . . [T]he child visiting an abusive parent faces an immensely difficult dilemma of maintaining loyalty to one parent without losing contact with the other. For the child to feel safe during contact, the visiting parent must be able to show a willingness to care about the child no matter what the child says or believes. At a minimum, the visiting parent must not do anything that threatens a child or contradicts the child's perceptions. Meanwhile, the custodial parent needs to accept that the contact with the other parent may benefit the child. The minimum condition is that the custodial parent must not threaten a withdrawal of love if the child sees or even enjoys seeing the abusive parent. However, the question arises whether a supervised visitation program stance of neutrality between the parents is useful in promoting parental behaviors which will support the child.

Neutrality in this context does not mean that the views of each parent have equal merit. Instead, the intent is to empathize with the child's experience and to support the child's development of his or her own perceptions and feelings. A supportive program stance for the child acknowledges that the child has to maintain contact with two parents who have different views. The program prevents either parent from being negative about the other in front of the child. The visiting parent is prohibited from denying anything the child says and may not threaten the child in any way. At the same time, the program encourages the custodial parent to at least minimally support the contacts. This stance can be maintained without implying approval of prior violence. The message is that whatever has happened, things are going to work differently and safely here.

In contrast, when a program openly supports the battered parent and condemns the abuser, it is likely to recreate for the child the family conflict and the loyalty pulls. A stance of criticism of the visiting parent will also tend to have a negative impact on the quality of the visit. An authoritarian and punitive setting is likely to make abusers more defensive. It will also distract the visiting parent from paying primary attention to the interaction with the children. In addition, when a program is openly hostile to abusive parents, it can cause more dangerous reactions and risks to both staff and clients.

Nevertheless, it may turn out that children who have lived with an abusive parent do not need neutrality, but an active support of views that challenge the abuser's perceptions. From this perspective, visits that occur in a program that actively supports the abused partner and condemns the behavior of the abuser may benefit the child and allow the child to move from a compliant relationship with a feared abusive parent toward a more healthy relationship in which the child can express his or her distress at how the abusive parent has behaved. Until research provides clearer indications that either a stance of neutrality or one of advocacy for victims leads to better outcomes, policies and guidelines for practice should be broad enough to allow the development of programs with different philosophies. Therefore, courts and attorneys, before making referrals, need to be aware of the approach taken by the local supervised visitation program.

* * *

NOTES AND QUESTIONS

1. Although comprehensive evaluations of supervised access programs are not yet available, there are some preliminary findings on supervised access in Ontario reported in two articles, one of which summarizes the perspectives of parents and children, and the other the perspectives of lawyers and judges. *See,* J. Jenkins, N. Park and M. Peterson–Badali, *An Evaluation of Supervised Access II: Perspectives of Parents and Children,* 35 F.C.C.R. 51 (1997), and M. Peterson–Bedali, J. Maresca, N. Park and J. Jenkins, *An Evaluation of Supervised Access III: Perspectives From the Legal System,* 35 F.C.C.R. 66 (1997).

Both articles report satisfaction with the programs on the part of both adult and child participants, the lawyers whose clients utilize them, and the judges who incorporate supervised access into their decrees. The authors comment that the relatively high level of satisfaction with supervised access on the part of custodial and non-custodial parents contrasts sharply with their negative attitudes towards other aspects of the legal system.

2. Can you identify any potential problems with supervised visitation in the context of domestic violence—beyond the obvious one that there are as yet not nearly as many "placements" available as there are families who might benefit from the service?

One concern expressed by battered women's advocates is that where supervised visitation programs are available, lawyers may be tempted to recommend, and judges to order, their utilization in cases in which the danger posed by the battering parent makes even a highly structured program too risky. A recent tragedy in Washington State underscores the need to exercise caution:

> Far from family, her marriage a shambles, and fearing for her life, Melanie Edwards was nonetheless trying to do everything right.
>
> She and her 2–year-old daughter, Carli Fay, could have simply disappeared. Instead, she got a protection order against her abusive husband, filed for divorce, and obeyed court rulings, including a monitored visitation program that allowed the man to see his little girl.
>
> "She didn't want her daughter to live in fear," said Maureen Scott, a social worker. "She also knew her daughter loved her daddy."
>
> The same daddy, authorities say, who stalked his wife and pumped four copper-jacketed, hollow-core bullets into her head and body as she sat in her car.
>
> And a fifth into the chest of his daughter.
>
> Before police could arrive, 33–year-old Melanie and Baby Carli were dead....
>
> The day [Melanie] sought the [protective] order, she had gone with Carli to a shelter in Seattle, 40 miles from her ... home. She had also taken her husband's gun and given it to Seattle police.
>
> The next day, Carlton applied for and received ... a permit to carry a concealed weapon.
>
> The protection order was granted Nov. 2. But nine days later, Carlton obtained a court-ordered parenting plan, allowing limited visits with Carli.
>
> [A shelter-worker commented:]
>
> "You have a battered woman who is in fear for her life and her child, and she petitioned the court. And that very court awards visitation rights to a known abuser who had a gun and she ended up dead.
>
> "Big surprise."
>
> Scott, director of Common Ground [the visitation program], said she ran the Edwardses through "pretty exhaustive" interviews. They showed few danger signs—"not more than any other of our caseload."
>
> Carlton, she said, seemed depressed, subdued, almost grieving—not unusual for men whose families are breaking up....

Except for one incident in which Melanie spotted Carlton driving in the neighborhood at her arrival time, Carli's exchanges went smoothly, ... with Carlton taking his daughter home for several overnight visits.

On Wednesday, Dec. 9, Carlton brought Carli to Common Ground at 5:47 p.m. Logs showed he stayed a minute or two and left. Everything seemed as usual.

Melanie arrived half an hour later, picked up Carli and walked 50 yards to her car, parked across the street.

Neighbors told police they heard a woman's screams, quickly followed by gunshots, and saw a lone man drive off....

George Tibbets, *Washington Woman Couldn't Escape Husband,* ASSOCIATED PRESS, 12–21–98.

While there may be no degree of caution that can prevent some visitation arrangements from ending in tragedies like this one, can you think of a modification in Common Ground's rules which might have prevented the death of this mother and daughter? Would it have helped if the center had required Carlton to check in with Carli when he returned her, and to wait at the center for fifteen or thirty minutes after the little girl left with her mother?

3. It should go without saying that supervised visitation programs should not be called upon to provide formal evaluations of parents, or make recommendations about future child access arrangements. Their contacts with families are often too limited to permit program staff to reach a fully informed conclusion; program staff are often not qualified clinicians; and if program staff "take sides" in a case, the program loses the trust of the other party, jeopardizing the chances that it can continue to serve the family's needs. However, because supervised visitation is relatively inexpensive compared to the services of a formal evaluator, it can be tempting for courts, attorneys and families to pressure programs into serving an evaluation function.

Another concern expressed by advocates for abused children and for battered women is that even if program staff resist playing a formal "evaluative" role, courts will take reports of good behavior as indications that an abusive parent has "changed" and is ready for unsupervised contact. A parent's behavior with a third person in the room for a visit of short duration is clearly not reliable evidence of how that parent will behave with a child during an extended, unsupervised contact. To diminish this risk, programs can preface their reports or observation notes with the warning that these documents were generated in a highly structured setting, and should not be used to determine the appropriateness of any future arrangements for parent child contact.

A related issue is that frequent demands for program staff to appear in court as witnesses, or to substantiate their written reports, will tax the limited resources most programs have to deploy. Straus recommends that programs charge hefty additional fees if staff are required to come to court. This will discourage attorneys from subpoenaing staff unless absolutely necessary, and the fees will also help cover expenses if court appearances are required.

3. If you were assisting a client in developing a visitation plan in an area which had no organized supervised visitation program to take advantage of, how might you use what you have learned about such programs to structure a plan using other potential family and community resources? Robert Straus ends the article excerpted above with some suggestions along those lines:

1. SELECTION OF SUPERVISOR

Parents are often left by the court to come up with names of supervisors. Someone other than the parents, however, either the court or the attorneys, should exercise oversight of the selection. In particular, a battered spouse should not be left in the position of coming up with names or objecting on her own to her former partner's selections. At a minimum, a supervisor should be independent enough from the parent being supervised to properly monitor the parent's behavior. The custodial parent should have some trust in the supervisor while the visiting parent should not consider the supervisor to be antagonistic to him or her.

Accordingly, while family members are the most likely to be willing to provide the least expensive supervision, they are often inappropriate. A grandparent who is the father or mother of a visiting parent should not be used if the custodial parent has concerns. The grandparent may not report accurately, may allow the visiting parent to do whatever he or she wants, or may not be present during the whole visit. A grandparent who is the parent of the custodial parent should not be used if there is animosity between the grandparent and the visiting parent, or the grandparent is afraid of the visiting parent. Similar considerations also apply for brothers, sisters, other relatives, and friends. Supervision in the presence of a grandparent or other relative respected by both parents can work very well. However, this is unlikely to be the situation where there are concerns about family violence.

Sources of "neutral" supervisors include churches and community groups. Sometimes, they may provide supervision for free for another church or group member. Child-care facilities, schools, and child protective agencies may also have workers who will be available for a fee to supervise when off-duty. Victim services programs in some jurisdictions have been enlisted to provide supervision services. If a family has money, it could possibly hire a mental health professional for short visits at least. Child protective agencies which are inadequately staffed for supervising visits can consider training foster parents for this role.

2. UNTRAINED VOLUNTEERS

If the proposed supervisor is an untrained volunteer, the court or attorneys should investigate the person and see if this individual is adequately neutral and mature. A volunteer may be unwilling to write up observation notes of each visit. If there are no observation notes, communication between the supervisor and the parents or the attorneys about what happened during visits needs to be discussed. It should probably be assumed and stated in advance that the supervisor will talk to the custodial parent about what happened on the visit.

Volunteer supervisors are most likely to be available irregularly and for a limited number of visits. This consideration is important in drafting an access order which will avoid unnecessary difficulty when the volunteer is not available. If the parents are unable to communicate, the attorneys will need to be available to help schedule visits, often a recurrent and time-consuming task.

3. WRITTEN ARRANGEMENTS

In all cases, the arrangements for the visits and the responsibility of the supervisor should be written down, and the supervisor and the parents should have a copy. Although it may seem obvious, the supervisor should be informed of the reason for concern about contact with the visiting parent, particularly if family violence of any kind is alleged or proven. Furthermore, the supervisor's authority to intervene and to end visits should be stated clearly. If these arrangements are not included in the court order, then the attorneys should draft an agreement for signature by both parents detailing the conditions for contact.

4. VISITATION EXCHANGES

In the absence of a program center, exchanges can still be arranged so the parents do not have to have contact. The visiting parent can pick a child up directly from or return a child directly to day care or a school. Exchanges can occur at the home of a friend of the custodial parent with whom the child is comfortable. However, the day care center, school, or friend should know of and approve of the arrangement. This arrangement is not appropriate if a visiting parent has a history of being late for pick up or return.

Visitation exchanges can also occur in a public location. Courts often order exchanges in front of or at a police station. However, there are several disadvantages. Having the exchange at a police station can be scary for a child. Also, police personnel may object to having the station used this way. In fact, unless the police are supportive and aware of the arrangements, the security may not be real. At a minimum, the person making the arrangements should first check with the senior officer at the proposed police station.

If there is any history of partner abuse, exchanges should not occur unless there is a third person present. Thus, the parents can be kept physically, and preferably visually separate. If the exchange occurs at a parent's home, one parent can remain inside while the supervisor transfers the child. At a public location, the parents can be required to maintain an agreed on distance from each other.

Finally, and fundamental to all the above ideas, if supervised visitation is arranged outside an organized program, safety must be the primary criteria for whether to proceed. If there is confirmed or believable evidence of family violence, the court or other referring agency must feel that the arrangements for supervision are adequate to protect the child and parents. The unfortunate, but necessary alternative is no contact.

Robert B. Straus, *Supervised Visitation and Family Violence,* 29 F.L.Q. 229, 249–251 (1995).

D. MEDIATION IN THE CONTEXT OF ABUSE

Introductory Note

What exactly is mediation, and when is it available, or imposed, as an alternative or a precursor to more formal legal processes in the context of divorce, and contested custody or visitation issues? Given that mediation is predicated on the participants being able to negotiate with each other on a relatively equal footing, can it ever be appropriate in situations where one partner is abusing the other? Is it possible to mandate mediation, and provide an abused partner with sufficient protection that she can participate safely, and without sacrificing her legitimate goals? If not, is it possible to establish a process that can effectively screen out participants who are separating from an abusive relationship? What do we know about how legislatures are structuring mediation programs, and how courts, and mediators themselves, are handling the day to day business of mandated mediation? While all mediators, including those privately retained to assist divorcing couples settle disputed issues, must be attentive to the possibility of abuse, the question of what to do about violence is most pressing in the context of court-based programs which are either formally mandated, or so strongly encouraged by their sponsoring courts that they might as well be mandated. These programs have become increasingly popular with family courts because of their potential to reduce litigation. At the same time, "[t]here is compelling evidence that spousal abuse is present in at least one-half of custody and visitation disputes referred to family court mediation programs." Jessica Pearson, *Mediating When Domestic Violence is a Factor: Policies and Practices in Court–Based Divorce Mediation Programs,* 14 MEDIATION Q. 319 (1997).

This group of readings begins with two excerpts outlining the premises and the promise of mediation, and its potential dangers in the context of partner abuse.

Trina Grillo
The Mediation Alternative: Process Dangers for Women, 100 Yale Law Journal 1545, 1547–48, 1551–52 (1991)

There is little doubt that divorce procedure needs to be reformed, but reformed how? Presumably, any alternative should be at least as just, and at least as humane, as the current system, particularly for those who are least powerful in society. Mediation has been put forward, with much fanfare, as such an alternative. The impetus of the mediation movement has been so strong that in some states couples disputing custody are required by statute or local rule to undergo a mandatory mediation process if they are unable to reach an agreement on their own. Mediation has been embraced for a number of reasons. First, it rejects an objectivist approach to conflict resolution, and promises to consider disputes in terms of relationships and responsibility. Second, the mediation process is, at least in theory, cooperative and voluntary, not coercive. The mediator does not make a decision: rather, each party speaks for himself. Together they reach an agreement that meets the parties' mutual needs. In this manner, the process is said to enable the parties to exercise self-determination and eliminate the hierarchy of dominance that characterizes the judge/litigant and the lawyer/client relationships. Third, since in mediation there are no rules of evidence or legalistic notions of relevancy, decisions supposedly may be informed by context rather than by abstract principle. Finally, in theory at least, emotions are recognized and incorporated into the mediation process. This conception of mediation has led some commentators to characterize it as a feminist alternative to the patriarchally inspired adversary system.

. . .

The movement for voluntary mediation of divorce disputes began several decades ago as lawyers and therapists offered to help their clients settle their cases in a non-adversarial manner. Some clients reported that, by meeting together with a third party to help facilitate their communication, they were able to reach agreements that met everyone's needs and leave their marriages without the acrimony and fear they had anticipated from the adversarial divorce process.

As mediation caught on, it began to be heralded as the cure for the various ills of adversary divorce. It was touted as a process in which the parties would voluntarily cooperate to find the best manner of continuing to parent their children. Consumers, however, were not embracing the mediation cure. Whether because of lack of familiarity with the process, the hostility of the organized bar, or some more considered reluctance, few divorcing couples chose to enter mediation. In order to bypass this consumer resistance, some state legislatures established court-annexed mediation programs, requiring that couples disputing custody mediate prior to going to court.

* * *

Karla Fischer, Neil Vidmar and Rene Ellis
The Culture of Battering and the Role of Mediation in Domestic Violence Cases, 46 S.M.U. L. Rev. 2117, 2157–65 (1993)

Consider the widely quoted definition of mediation set forth by Folberg and Taylor:

> "Mediation is an alternative to violence, self-help, or litigation.... It can be defined as the process by which the participants, together with the assistance of a neutral person or persons, systematically isolate disputed issues in order to develop options, consider alternatives, and reach a consensual settlement that will accommodate their needs. Mediation is a process that emphasizes the participants' own responsibility for making decisions that affect their lives. It is therefore a self-empowering process."

The definition itself reflects what Laura Nader has labeled the "harmony ideology" underlying mediation as it is currently practiced in the alternative dispute resolution (ADR) movement. In contrast to the adversary system which is based on the notion of justice and on the understanding of power differentials, the harmony model values consensus settlement and management of disputes through "healing" processes that "minimize power differentials of class, race, economics, and gender; it articulates the notion that disputes are generated in relationships by the failure of individuals to act as they should." Nader's critique addresses the social and legal systems as a whole. She argues that the ADR movement has become increasingly coercive and "values means over ends, harmony over justice, and efficiency over due process."

Nader's critique is shared by others who have analyzed the implicit and explicit assumptions underlying mediation theory. The objections to it are brought into sharpest focus when mediation assumptions are contrasted with our analysis of the culture of battering....

... Below we consider eight purported advantages of the mediation forum and weigh them against our insights about the culture of battering.

1. IDEOLOGY OF MEDIATION: Abuse arises out of conflict
   CULTURE OF BATTERING: Conflict is only the pretext for abuse.

... [C]ulture of battering relationships are not about conflict, but rather about domination and control. To the extent that conflict is present it is only a symptom. The conflict is manufactured by the abuser in the relationship. To structure mediation sessions as if the cause of abuse is conflict is to artificially frame the problem of battering....

. . .

For divorce cases where child custody or property settlements are disputed, these conflicts may be equally likely to be manufactured by the batterer, as he may raise the issues as a pretext for regaining power in the relationship and exerting his usual system of control and domination. Martha Mahoney warned of this possibility: "[T]he custody action is part of an ongoing attempt, through physical violence and legal manipulation, to force the woman to make concessions or return to the violent partner." Because batterers use threats against the children—especially to take them away from their mothers—and abuse the children to control the woman, it is plausible to view custody "disputes" as suspicious in cases where a culture of battering has been established. Similar dynamics may operate in property settlements. Batterers use family financial resources to control their victims both physically and psychologically. Mediation sessions may simply become another forum for this coercion. Whether the issue is property or children, the mediation model of ameliorating conflict presumes, and therefore imposes, a conflict structure on a situation where these issues may not be truly disputed. The danger for battered women who have recently extracted themselves from a culture of battering is that the batterers' domination and control tactics will flourish in the mediation environment and not be recognized as such.

2. IDEOLOGY OF MEDIATION: Focus on future, not past behavior. CULTURE OF BATTERING: Ignoring past behavior denies victims' experiences of violence.

According to Bethel and Singer, "[u]nlike legal remedies, mediation is prospectively rather than retrospectively centered and is not concerned with determining rights and wrongs" but is focused on "future conduct." This component of the mediation ideology is partially responsible for the policy of many mediation centers to exclude attorneys from the mediation session even though the victim's attorney may be the primary source of support and protection for the victim's rights.

Yet, the culture of battering is ineluctably tied to an escalating history of domination and control. The batterer and the victim cannot, and should not, be separated from their history. The specific failure to consider right and wrong allows an assumption that the victim may be responsible for her plight. The mediation process then treats the victim as though she shares responsibility, in essence subtly classifying her as a perpetrator....

Consider Bethel and Singer's response to the argument for setting history aside: "[m]ediation is not therapy. Mediation's goal is to help effect behavioral change, because it is specific behavior, assaultive behavior or threatening behavior, that one or both parties cannot tolerate. Attitudinal change ... is not the paramount goal of mediation." "[F]undamental personality or attitudinal change is not required to prevent many forms of domestic violence." They go on to state that the process of mediation "requires the parties to focus on crucial rather than peripheral issues, and it allows little room for excuses."

Two interrelated problems are inherent is this aspect of mediation ideology. First, the assumption that attitude change is not a goal of mediation shifts the process away from the root cause of abuse. Second, it assumes that problem is a specific conflict or set of conflicts and that peripheral incidents are of no consequence. Yet, the peripheral matters are reflective of the total relationship between the two parties.... Being battered involves more than the specific acts of violence committed by the abuser; it means living in a relationship with a partner who systematically dominates and controls your activities, your relationships with other people, your beliefs and values, and your body. Labeling this experience as "peripheral" delegitimizes the victim's right to bring the abuse up as an issue in mediation even though it may be extremely relevant to how custody and visitation should be arranged, or how property should be divided.

3. IDEOLOGY OF MEDIATION: Each party participates equally in the search for a mutual agreement.
   CULTURE OF BATTERING: Equal participation is impossible

Another of Bethel and Singer's ideological statements addresses the process of mediation: "The parties are treated as responsible adults and in turn are expected to participate actively in the search for a mutually acceptable agreement."

This expectation ... is also problematic. Mediation theorists consistently evoke the theme that participation is a self empowering process. They assert that helping to shape the outcome that is the subject matter of the forum compels even a weak party to find new strength. However, to participate and become self empowered the weaker party must be able to articulate needs and desires. This may be extremely difficult for a victim of spousal abuse because she may not even understand her position, may have been consistently silenced by her partner, and may fear the consequences of speaking out. Further, the task of negotiating an agreement runs a grave risk of simply mimicking the battering culture. The mediation may in fact be a safe as well as powerful setting for the abuser to intimidate and control his victim through hidden symbols of impending violence. Even his mere presence may be intimidating, particularly if she is attempting to escape from the relationship; contact with the abuser is often the last thing that victims want.

The issue for battered women is consistent with the general problems that women may have when they are involved in domestic issues mediation. Trina Grillo has argued that mediation's emphasis on joint needs may push the woman away from an attempt to define herself as a person with needs and rights that are independent of the spousal relationship. The mediation process may evoke feelings of guilt and socialized tendencies to subordinate self needs to relationships with others and acquiesce in the face of social pressure. Clearly, abused women may often experience certain characteristics in the extreme, such as feelings of dependency, uncertainty about self worth, and self-censoring tendencies to deny their own needs. Thus, the mediation process, with its emphasis on compromise and healing relationships may actually serve to undo the abused woman's initial steps to find empowerment as an individual person.

Finally, the emphasis of mediation ideology on joint participation may make the mediator insensitive to the needs of an abused woman or even cause the mediator to view the woman as uncooperative....

Bethel and Singer further state that "[m]ediation relies on a rough parity in bargaining power between the parties to be successful. If one side dominates the other there is much less chance that any agreement will be truly voluntary or that it will accurately reflect the parties' needs." Indeed! And by its very nature the culture of battering makes the couple unequal in subtle and pervasive ways.

4. IDEOLOGY OF MEDIATION: Avoid blame and findings of fact.
   CULTURE OF BATTERING: Avoidance of abuse issues perpetuates status quo of victim responsibility and abuser domination.

"Mediation is an informal, participatory method of conflict resolution. The mediator ... has no higher authority to invoke, and rebuffs requests to make findings of fact or decisions about blameworthiness." If followed, this tenet of mediation ideology eschews any actions by mediators relating to the parties as anything but equals and prevents mediators from looking for elements in the relationship that might indicate a culture of battering. The tenet forces the mediator to treat spousal abuse and domination neutrally. Because batterers place the responsibility and blame for the assaults on the victim, frequently tying the abuse to her inability to live up to his rules, the status quo of the relationship is left in place when his belief system is left unchallenged. By ignoring the context of the abuse under the guise of avoiding blame, the mediator leaves behind any opportunity to learn about how the abuser might attempt to control and dominate the victim during mediation sessions.

5. IDEOLOGY OF MEDIATION: Private caucuses will encourage the victim to speak her needs.
   CULTURE OF BATTERING: Private caucuses will not assist victims who are afraid of the consequences of speaking their needs.

"The process is participatory, but the nature of the participation is controlled by the mediator...." Bethel and Singer recognize that the mediator may communicate individually, through caucuses with the parties, to develop the agreement. It is assumed that getting the victim alone will allow her to state her true feelings, wants and needs. This assumption naively ignores the fear and psychological control that develops in culture of battering relationships and extends beyond the immediate physical presence of the abuser. If the relationship has been one where the victim has been punished for having or speaking her needs, she may be justifiably afraid of the consequences of doing so, even if she is unable to articulate this fear. Spending five minutes alone with the victim ... will not substantially reduce the reality of this fear or enhance her trust of the mediators. In fact, it is absurd to believe that a five minute caucus can uncover and rectify the effects of being silenced through months or years of abuse—presuming, of course, that the mediator earns the trust of the victim who truly wishes to disclose her history and experiences.

6. IDEOLOGY OF MEDIATION: Batterers need to be coerced into mediation.
   CULTURE OF BATTERING: Batterers may coerce victims into mediation.

As explained by Erickson and McKnight, "[m]ediation is to some extent a voluntary process, but one party may participate only because it is the least objectionable of several alternatives. The prospect of court action, or further police involvement, or retaliation from the other party, may have substantial coercive effect." This assertion seems to focus on the inducements to bring the batterer to the mediation forum. It ignores the possibility that the batterer may prefer mediation because it places him in a situation where he can continue to dominate. Moreover, it clearly glosses over the pressures that may force the reluctant victim into mediation. Some women may go to mediation only because it is cheaper, or it is their only recourse because a judge or other authority has ordered it, or they cannot receive legal support unless they submit to mediation first.

7. IDEOLOGY OF MEDIATION: The novelty of a written agreement detailing the rules of the relationship will end the violence.
   CULTURE OF BATTERING: Rules in a battering relationship may justify the batterer's further abuse.

The culmination of the mediation ideology is usually a written agreement specifying the rules and obligations of the parties' relationship. Each of several examples provided by Bethel and Singer articulates rules. Yet [a culture of battering relationship] is already filled with rules imposed on the victim by the batterer. It is the violation of these rules that leads to the violence and abuse. Because the agreements place obligations on the victim as well as the batterer, any minor infraction of these rules by the victim may provide the batterer with an excuse to abandon his obligations. Moreover, he now has a written text to help justify his outrage.

8. IDEOLOGY OF MEDIATION: The process of mediation can protect battered women from future violence.
   CULTURE OF BATTERING: Battered women will not disclose abuse to mediators, during or after sessions.

. . .

The notion that the process of mediation will "heal" the relationship is anchored in the abuse-is-conflict framework. Changing the couple's communication strategies to include non-abusive ones will only be effective outside mediation if those "strategies" are the cause of the abuse. Because much of the violence in battering relationships occurs "out of the blue," or at the end of manufactured arguments, the healing power of the mediation session is likely to be limited.

The ideological statement that mediation will end the violence also has an underlying assumption that mediators will somehow know if the victim is currently being abused. The culture of battering involves an element of hiding, denying, and minimizing the abuse. Much abuse is itself hidden, leaving no visible marks: sexual assaults, emotional abuse and threats, familial abuse. Even physical abuse may not leave marks if the batterer chooses to hit where the bruises on the victim's body will not be revealed to others. The parties may cancel mediation sessions until the bruises fade away (in the event that mediation lasts for more than one session) in much the same way that battered women stay home from work or school until their injuries heal. If mediators send the message that abuse is irrelevant or peripheral, this may intensify the victim's feelings of shame, and she may be even less likely to disclose the abuse.

As a final thought on the ideology of mediation with violent couples, in cases where the couple is separated . . ., the risk for serious violence is heightened. The abuser's ability to dominate and control his partner through abuse becomes more limited as his access to her decreases. Consequently, his motivation for obtaining access to her through any means possible, including formal interaction with the legal system through court-mandated mediation sessions, is quite high. Sadly, scheduled court proceedings can lead to an opportunity to kill, as they were in one recent death for a battered woman: Shirley Lowery was killed by her estranged husband as she arrived in a Wisconsin courthouse lobby to wait for the hearing for her second order of protection. Mediators must never forget that separation is the most dangerous time for battered women, and avoid allowing the contact that the sessions require to become the abuser's safe opportunity to strike out with violence against his partner.

* * *

NOTES

1. Fischer, Vidmar and Ellis provide a comprehensive account of the mismatch between the philosophical underpinnings of mediation and the dynamics of partner abuse. To this account we need to add the flavor of actual disputes between the mediation community and the battered women's community. Battered women's advocates accuse mediators of ignorance with respect to the dynamics of abuse, and naivety with respect to abusers' efforts to manipulate the legal process. They point to mediator misconceptions about those who abuse or are abused; misconceptions which can lead to ineffective screening and inappropriate decisions about who is and who is not a suitable candidate for mediation. They are incensed by many mediators' commitment to joint custody or other shared parenting arrangements, arguing that it violates the precept of mediator neutrality, as well as endangering the women and children who, through such arrangements, become more vulnerable to further abuse.

In the arguments over both screening and shared parenting, the research and writings of Janet Johnston have been particularly influential and problematic. The excerpts below are taken from her article *Domestic Violence and Parent–Child Relationships in Families Disputing Custody*, (1995) AUST.J.FAM.L. 12, but the studies on which her conclusions are based were initially reported in J.R. Johnston & L.E.G. Campbell, IMPASSES OF DIVORCE: THE DYNAMICS AND RESOLUTION OF FAMILY CONFLICT (1988), and J.R. Johnston, *High Conflict and Violent Parents: Findings on Children's Adjustment and Proposed Guidelines for the Resolution of Custody and Visitation Disputes,* Final Report to the Judicial Council of the State of California, San Francisco (1992). *See also* J.R. Johnston & L.E.G. Campbell, *A Clinical Typology of Interparental Violence in Disputed–Custody Divorces,* 63 AM. J. ORTHOPSYCHIATRY 190 (1993).

Johnston hypothesizes, based on two preliminary studies of high-conflict and violent divorcing parents (140 couples in all) contesting the custody and care of their children, five different types of violence:

A. Ongoing/Episodic Male Battering

B. Female–Initiated Violence

C. Male–Controlling Interactive Violence

D. Separation/Divorce Trauma

E. Psychotic/Paranoid Reactions

While she adds that it is "important to acknowledge that this typology allows for mixed types or variations of a type when one considers the couple or the family as a whole," her fundamental message is that not all violence is the same when it comes to assessing practices such as mediation, or policies with respect to "reconstituting family relationships after separation/divorce." With respect to the latter, for example, she says:

> The quality of parent-child relationships, and the psychological adjustment of children can vary in important ways, depending upon the particular pattern of domestic violence. Depending upon the type of violence, the perpetrator is more or less likely to admit having a problem and to seek help. There are also different trajectories and prognoses for recovery from the psychological trauma of abuse, for the victim and witnesses. Furthermore, the potential for future violence and the conditions under which it is likely to recur also vary among these different types or patterns. For all of these reasons, domestic violence families need to be considered on an individual basis when helping them develop appropriate postdivorce parenting plans. There is no one solution that fits all.

From the perspective of many battered women's advocates, the Johnston typology plays right into the hands of those who seek (1) to deny the pervasiveness of male coercion and control in intimate relationships, (2) to blame women for male violence, and (3) to paint women as equally violent in their relationships with men. Johnston's emphasis on regular physical violence in her depiction of Type A: "Ongoing or Episodic Male Battering," for example, overlooks the many relationships in which physical violence is quite a rare occurrence, because the threat of violence, together with the use of other controlling strategies, renders more frequent physical discipline unnecessary. Johnston's Type C violence: "Male–Controlling Interactive Violence," is described as "arising primarily out of a disagreement between the spouses, which escalates from mutual verbal provocation and insults into physical struggles. Whereas either the man or the woman might initiate the physical aggression, the overriding response by the man is to assert control and prevail by dominating and overpowering the woman. These men do not beat up their spouses and do not usually employ force that is excessive to gaining the woman's compliance." Battered women's advocates note that this description does not address the nature of the "disagreement"—is it a genuine conflict, or one that grows out of one partner's refusal to "comply" with an inappropriately controlling directive issued by the other? If this is abuse masquerading as conflict, in other words, the woman's resistance to her partner's coercive control is being inappropriately labeled "mutual verbal provocation," and there seems little basis for Johnston's conclusion that "once separated and no longer able to provoke one another, there is a good prognosis for the interparental violence to cease." Rather, the separation may provide the ultimate provocation, and intensify the controlling partner's efforts to regain dominance.

In the highly charged atmosphere of the current debate between the mediation community and the domestic violence community, it becomes crucially important to register Johnston's own caveat about her work:

> My remarks ... should be viewed as exploratory hypotheses to be evaluated in future research (research that is urgently needed) rather than as established findings.

2. Despite the prevailing hostility of those who advocate for battered women toward mediation, there are some important reasons to resist the categorical conclusion that mediation is never an acceptable process for women separating from an abusive relationship. First, as Jessica Pearson reminds her readers, in her article *Mediating When Domestic Violence is a Factor,* 14 MEDIATION QUARTERLY 319, 321 (1997):

> [S]ome critics have compared the best possible litigation with the worse examples of mediation ...; many of shortcomings attributed to mediation are also present during attorney-assisted negotiations and litigation. Indeed, by encouraging parties to adopt extreme positions in negotiations or attempting to portray the other parent in the least favorable light in court documents, the judicial system can escalate and prolong conflict in ways that increase the level of danger for the victim. Because the client is usually the passive recipient of the lawyer's expertise, this can reinforce patterns of domination for women.
>
> Perhaps the most significant way the judicial system fails victims of domestic abuse is by frequently neglecting to provide them with any legal representation. Increasingly, divorcing parents are self-represented and have no attorney. The incidence of self-representation ranges from 40 percent in Alameda County, California to 90 percent in Maricopa County, Arizona. It is clearly unrealistic to compare mediation to a system of strong, assertive advocacy when the absence of advocacy is increasingly the norm.

Second, mediation and litigation are not the only two alternatives. There are other processes that may be called into play, and potentially combined with mediation or litigation to provide a richer range of options. In the same article, Pearson describes some of these possibilities:

> [S]ome high-conflict and violent couples need court interventions other than those currently available to resolve their disputes. This includes more intensive therapeutic and legal interventions that combine mediation with counseling, evaluation, and long-term therapy. Another recommended approach is arbitration, where trained and experienced mental health professionals assess issues and make binding decisions in disputes that involve children. Still a third approach to decision making used by custody evaluators in Tucson is a hybrid of evaluation and mediation wherein mental health professionals conduct an assessment, make recommendations, present them to parents and their attorneys, and use the feedback phase to stimulate parties to engage in decision-making regarding their postseparation parenting arrangements. Arbitration, case management and mediation-evaluation hybrids are less formal and stressful than litigation, are more evaluative and structured than regular mediation, and may offer more protections for victims of domestic violence.

Id. at 330. Third, mediation programs have never followed a uniform blueprint, and there is room to ask whether mediation could be reconceived and redesigned to be more attentive to the issues raised by domestic violence, and more useful to those who are separating from abusive relationships.

It is an encouraging sign that in some recent extraordinary collaborations, such as the Maine Mediation and Domestic Abuse Project (1990–1992), and the Toronto Forum on Woman Abuse and Mediation (1993), members of the mediation and domestic violence communities have begun to bridge the gulf that has traditionally separated them. In Toronto, this process was jump-started by the Ontario government, which responded to the concerns of battered women's advocates "by taking the position that unless mediators would demonstrate that mediation was *not* harmful to abused women, there would be no further funding or legislative support for family mediation. That certainly got the attention of the Ontario Association for Family Mediation!" Barbara Landau, *The Toronto Forum on Women Abuse: The Process and the Outcome*, 33 F.C.C. REV. 63, 63 (1995). As Landau, who organized the Forum, reports:

> [A]lmost one year of effort was put into organizing an agenda that women's advocates and shelter workers could say "yes" to working on, and developing a list of participants that would meet the forum's objectives. One important issue for both groups was the inclusion of women who are too often forgotten or who do not have their own voice in service delivery; namely, native women, women of color, immigrant women, and women with disabilities. Representatives of all the major family mediation organizations in North America were included and, in particular, an invitation was sent to the chairpersons of the Abuse Committees, where they existed, or to the president or president-elect where there were no such committees. A significantly greater number of women's advocates than mediators were invited so that the women's advocates would feel that they were in a relatively safe and powerful position.

The Toronto Forum Report demonstrates the progress made towards building "a real basis of trust and cooperation," and finding common ground.

Toronto Forum Report Executive Summary, 33 F.C.C.R. 63, 72–74 (1995)

INTRODUCTION

... Central to this report is the affirmation of a rebuttable presumption against the use of mediation in cases of domestic abuse.

I. WOMAN ABUSE AND THE EDUCATION AND TRAINING OF FAMILY MEDIATORS

Mediation associations ought to establish standards for the education and skills training of family mediators in the following areas:

- abuse in intimate relationships and its consequences for mediation;

- the unique needs of culturally diverse populations;
- procedures, instruments and skills to screen for abuse and assess safety risks;
- specialized skills and interventions to ensure safety and provide a specialized mediation process;
- alternatives to mediation.

Standards and qualifications for family mediation trainers also need to be established relative to domestic abuse issues.

The design of training models about abuse between intimate partners should enlist the direct participation of service providers for abused women and disadvantaged populations.

II. Pre-mediation Screening

Parties to mediation must be able to negotiate safely, voluntarily, and competently in order to reach a fair agreement. Because abuse can significantly diminish a person's ability to mediate safely and effectively, mediation should never occur without first screening for abuse.

The presumption against the use of mediation in cases of domestic abuse suggests that few cases are suitable for mediation.

Clients should be interviewed separately and in a safe environment to assess:

- the risks and/or threats of homicide and suicide;
- the safety needs of their children;
- each client's ability to mediate voluntarily and competently;
- the extent of power imbalances and their impact on the mediation process;
- the need for safe and appropriate alternatives to mediation.

As aids to assessment, screening instruments ought to be carefully designed and should not replace high levels of investigative interviewing and assessment for those cases that might proceed to specialized mediation.

Decision criteria limits need to be set for the exclusion of abuse cases or for referral to a specialized mediation process.

III. Safety and Specialized Mediation

Minimizing risk and maximizing safety ought to direct the development of protocols, interdisciplinary collaboration and research on the effectiveness of mediation and supporting services for abused persons and their children.

Provisions for client and staff safety should be in place prior to offering family mediation services. These provisions should include policies to warn and protect endangered parties and requirements to report threats of harm.

Clerical staff and/or intake workers should be trained to adapt their respective skills, functions and duties to the safety needs of clients.

Screening for abuse and maintaining safety provisions are ongoing obligations throughout the entire mediation process.

Specialized mediation for domestic abuse cases requires safety features for the mediation site as well as the development and use of specific skills and interventions to:

- ensure safety before, during and following a mediation session;
- compensate for power imbalances;
- terminate mediation safely and effectively.

IV. ALTERNATIVES TO MEDIATION

Every community should offer an array of marital dissolution models that include mediation, negotiation, facilitated settlement conferences, arbitration, and adjudication.

Jurisdictions should provide education about the benefits and risks of available alternatives and dedicate the resources necessary to assure safe and timely access by abused women to marital dissolution alternatives. Funding for the participation of community-based advocates in marital dissolution systems also should be made available.

Abused women should not be compelled into any dispute resolution system unless legal representation is authorized and economically feasible.

The need to protect and nurture children living in the context of domestic abuse should be addressed specifically in custody cases.

Courts should allow that abused persons and parents of abused children be exempted from mediation.

Courts should promulgate protocols to assure the uniform, safe, and equitable resolution of family law disputes.

The professional practice of marital dispute resolution in the context of domestic abuse should require the training and certification of intake staff, mediators, arbitrators, lawyers, guardians ad litem, court personnel, and the judiciary.

* * *

Current Mediation Practice

The next materials provide some sense of the variety of mediation practices in the United States, with a particular focus on features which make them more or less problematic for victims of abuse. Remember that the overall climate for mediation will be established by a combination of statutory requirements, court rules, program protocols, and individual mediator practices. To provide an initial orientation, here is a list of questions relevant to the individual who is being asked to mediate in the context of an abusive relationship. As you read the questions, ask yourself what the significance of the answer would be for a victim of abuse. As you look at the program descriptions that follow, keep the questions, and their significance, in mind:

- Just how mandatory is mediation?
- Is there an exemption for domestic violence? Can it be overridden if both parties request it?

- If there is no absolute exemption, are there additional safeguards provided for mediation in the context of abuse? What are they?
- What process, and what level of showing, triggers a domestic violence exemption or the additional safeguards associated with abuse? Is the process connected to a standardized screening protocol, or must it be initiated by one of the parties?
- If a screening protocol is used, does it involve the parties being interviewed separately ?
- If a decision is made that mediation would be inappropriate because the parties' relationship has been or still is violent, how is that decision communicated to the parties? Is the communication process attentive to the victim's safety?
- How effectively do the additional safeguards deployed in mediations in the context of abuse protect the safety of family members, and the integrity of the negotiating process?
- How do mediators manage the situation where a mediation has begun without any reference to abuse, but abuse is disclosed or becomes apparent as the mediation progresses?
- Are the mediators court employees, or employees in a private program with which the court contracts?
- What qualifications, if any, must the mediator have?
- Do mediators receive any training in the dynamics of domestic violence?
- Is the content of mediation sessions kept strictly confidential between the parties and the mediator, or are there circumstances when the mediator will report on the mediation to the court?
- Does the mediator maintain a strictly neutral position on each disputed issue, or does the system permit the mediator to urge certain outcomes, such as joint custody, on the parties?
- If the mediation fails to result in a settlement, is the mediator precluded from making recommendations to the court, permitted to do so, or required to do so?
- If one of the parties wishes to include an advocate or lawyer in the mediation, is that always permissible, a decision within the discretion of the mediator, or precluded? If the decision rests with the mediator, is there any information about what mediators tend to do, and is their practice consistent? Are there any special rules governing advocate and lawyer participation in cases in which domestic violence is an acknowledged issue?

a) *California: The Trendsetter*

Trina Grillo, in her article *The Mediation Alternative: Process Dangers for Women,* 100 YALE L. J. 1545, 1553–1555 (1991), describes one of the earliest mandated mediation programs:

> California's mandatory mediation law, which first became effective in 1981, requires that all custody and visitation disputes be mediated prior to being considered by the county Superior court. The mediation

is intended to "reduce acrimony" between the parties and lead to an agreement that assures the children "close and continuing contact with both parents." The court is required to appoint a mediator, who may be a member of the professional staff of a family conciliation court, probation department, or mental health services agency, or some other person or agency the court decides is appropriate. Mediators must have a master's degree in psychology, social work, or another behavioral science; experience in counseling or psychotherapy; knowledge of the California court system and family law procedure; and knowledge of adult and child psychology, including the effects of divorce on children.

In practice, the qualifications of mediators provided by the California courts vary widely. In some urban counties, there are large professional staffs of mediators, all of whom are experienced mental health professionals; in other counties, there may be only one mediator with little professional training. Similarly, some counties have extensive office facilities in which to house their mediation program and provide the opportunity to have several meetings with the mediators; in others, mediation takes place in the twenty minutes before court in a hallway. the California Judicial Council has prepared standards of practice for mediators which should increase uniformity among the counties. Nonetheless, nine years after the introduction of mandatory mediation in California, the services offered are frequently inadequate at best, even from the perspective of proponents of mandatory mediation....

In California, mediations are held in private and communications to the mediator from the parties are deemed "official information" protected from disclosure by the Evidence Code. The mediator has discretion to exclude counsel from the mediation, whether or not the parties wish to have them present.

Local courts have the option of requiring mediators to make a recommendation to the court regarding custody or visitation. If the parties do not reach an agreement, the mediator may also make a recommendation that an investigation be conducted or mutual restraining orders be issued. More than half of California counties have opted to require mediators to make such recommendations. In these counties a mediator meets with the parties and, having assured them of confidentiality, attempts to help them reach an agreement. Should they not reach an agreement, however, the mediator uses what happened in the mediation session to make a recommendation to the court. In some counties, I have observed that the recommendations of mediators are almost always accepted by the judge; indeed, some mediators disclose this fact in an effort to pressure the parties into reaching an agreement.

California does not preclude mediation in the context of abuse, but does provide for the parties to meet separately with the mediator if a party who has a protective order requests it. A mediator can also decide to meet with the parties separately when there has been a history of domestic abuse, as defined by the California Code of Civil Procedure, and separate mediation sessions have been requested.

b) *Massachusetts: Court–Created Mediation*

Andree Gagnon, in an article titled *Ending Mandatory Divorce Mediation for Battered Women,* 15 HARV. WMNS. L.J. 272, 279, 281 (1992), compares the mediation created by court policy in Massachusetts with statutory schemes in several other states. She is highly critical of the Massachusetts model:

> Mediation as practiced in the Massachusetts probate courts contains few of the elements referred to in the dispute resolution literature and no special safeguards for battered women. In most jurisdictions mediation is mandatory, and it is rarely confidential. Mediators are not neutral third parties: instead they are family service officers who may be asked to make a recommendation to the court if an agreement cannot be reached between the parties. The result is that the party with the least power and financial independence can be easily disadvantaged by the process.
>
> . . .
>
> It is unclear what kind of mediation training or background Massachusetts family service officers have. There is no mediation statute that explicitly authorizes court officers to mediate, nor are there statutory guidelines the provide for the qualifications and training of mediators.
>
> Massachusetts family service officers have indicated that there is pressure to settle cases, and that they tend to believe their job effectiveness is evaluated based on how many cases they settle. The danger of a mediation process with strong incentives to produce settlement is that power imbalances between the parties may be exploited by the mediator in order to reach agreement.

c) *Other Contemporary Schemes*

As of 1992, according to Andree Gagnon in the article cited above, more than thirty states mandated mediation of custody disputes, and only a few statutes provided exemptions for domestic violence. Furthermore, even when statutes provided for but did not mandate mediation, the courts' pro-settlement bias created a de facto mandatory regime. Since that time, increasing sensitivity to, and sophistication about, domestic violence has resulted in somewhat more generous exemption practices. As of 1993, the National Center on Women and Family Law reported 16 states with legislation exempting battered women from mediation, and the number has assuredly grown since. However, a 1993 study of 136 jurisdictions with mediation programs for custody or visitation disputes reported that mediation was mandatory, by statute or court rule, in more than 60% of programs; that approximately 20% of programs conducted no screening of referrals; that only 70% of programs reported domestic violence training, and that in a majority of programs less than 5% of cases were eliminated due to spousal abuse allegations, while in 85% of programs less than 15% of cases were eliminated. Nancy Thoennes, Peter Salem & Jessica Pearson, *Mediation and Domestic Violence: Current Policies and Practices,* 33 F.C.C.R. 6 (1995).

Exemption and Screening. In Wisconsin, any dispute about the legal custody or physical placement of a child will ordinarily go to mediation. However, the decision about whether mediation is appropriate will be made on the basis of a mandatory referral to a mediator for an initial meeting. Furthermore, a court may hold a trial or hearing without even this initial meeting if it finds that attendance at such a meeting "will cause undue hardship or would endanger the health or safety of one of the parties." In making that decision, the court is directed to look at evidence of child abuse, interspousal battery or domestic abuse, alcohol or drug abuse, or any other relevant evidence. Minnesota relies on a probable cause standard for exemption from mediation of cases with domestic abuse. If the court determines that there is probable cause that one of the parties, or a child of one of the parties, has been physically or sexually abused by the other party, exemption from the mediation process is required; nor can the court refer the parties to any other process that would require them to meet and confer. In Florida, a court "shall not refer" to mediation any case in which there has been a court finding of a "significant history of domestic abuse which would compromise the mediation process." In Colorado, the exemption from mediation requires only that one of the parties claim to have been a victim of domestic abuse at the hands of the other. Most states do not make the statutory exemption from mediation depend on the existence of a protective order, although an order is obviously a solid basis for determining that there has been abuse, and that the victim should be exempted from any mediation requirement.

One difficulty with the statutes that require judicial screening for domestic violence is that judges do not necessarily see the cases, or identify the abusive context of the parties' relationship, before they are referred to mediation. The statutes appear to assume that judges will review divorce or child custody petitions, and that a battered partner will come forward with evidence of abuse at the time a case is referred to mediation, allowing the judge to perform the screening function. But if the case is sent to mediation before a judge sees it, or the case file contains no evidence of domestic violence and the woman has not presented herself as a battered woman, then the case will probably be mediated. It would be more effective to require that the mediator be the one to screen for the presence of abuse, through an initial intake procedure involving separate interviews with each party. Despite the likelihood that cases will go to mediation without an effective judicial screening for violence, the statutes do not, with the exception of Wisconsin, provide guidelines for mediators who discover abuse during the mediation process. Wisconsin authorizes a mediator to terminate mediation if evidence of abuse emerges. In other states the understanding is that mediators will end the mediation either with a settlement, or with a report to the court that an agreement has not been reached.

Confidentiality. Most statutes specifically address the question of whether mediators can compromise their neutral role, and the confidentiality of the mediation process, by making recommendations to the court. In Wisconsin, for example, court counseling services also perform custody evaluations when mediation is not used or does not produce an agreement. However, the parties are informed that when their mediator also conducts the custody evaluation, there is no privilege of confidentiality, and must explicitly consent to the mediator serving in this dual capacity. If they do not consent, then the confidentiality privilege attached to mediation in the statute still operates. In Minnesota, mediation records are private and unavailable as evidence in related court proceedings. If the parties end a mediation without an agreement, the mediator can recommend that an investigation be conducted, but cannot be the one to conduct it. Both these schemes are significantly more protective of the parties' confidentiality than the California provisions discussed above.

d) *Summary of Changes in Recognition of Domestic Violence*

In her 1997 report, Jessica Pearson summarizes changes in mediation approaches attributable to the recognition of domestic violence, many of which would not be apparent from the governing statute:

> [V]irtually all (96 percent) court mediation programs use special techniques to address domestic violence problems. The changes that have been adopted include use of on-site metal detectors; security guards at mediation services and escort services to parking structures; written intake forms and questionnaires; individual, in-person screenings for domestic violence; use of shuttle or separate mediation techniques; the use of male-female co-mediation teams; deemphasis of agreement making in domestic violence cases; separate waiting rooms and orientations for men and women with domestic violence cases; attendance by victim advocates and other support people; termination of mediation by the mediator; and referrals to shelters and counseling programs that specialize in domestic violence. Co-mediation caucusing and security personnel are the most commonly mentioned adaptations.

e) *The Mediation Provisions of the Model Code on Domestic and Family Violence*

The Model Code's provisions governing mediation in cases involving domestic violence address the responsibilities of both mediators and judges, addressing the weakness of those statutory regimes which place the responsibility for screening on judges, but without a guarantee that the judge will in fact exercise it. The Code does not in general rule out mediation in the context of abuse, but concentrates on limiting its exercise to instances in which the victim requests it, and other safeguards are in place. One of the two alternative provisions governing judicial responsibilities does go further, and prohibits mediation when a protective order is in place.

Model Code on Domestic and Family Violence National Council of Juvenile and Family Court Judges January 1994

Sec. 407. Duty of mediator to screen for domestic violence during mediation referred or ordered by court.

1. A mediator who receives a referral or order from a court to conduct mediation shall screen for the occurrence of domestic or family violence between the parties.

2. A mediator shall not engage in mediation when it appears to the mediator or when either party asserts that domestic or family violence has occurred unless:

(a) Mediation is requested by the victim of the alleged domestic or family violence;

(b) Mediation is provided in a specialized manner that protects the safety of the victim by a certified mediator who is trained in domestic and family violence; and

(c) The victim is permitted to have in attendance at mediation, a supporting person of his or her choice including but not limited to an attorney or advocate.

The Model Code provides alternative sections concerning mediation in cases involving domestic or family violence. Both of the sections provide directives for courts hearing cases concerning the custody or visitation of children, if there is a protection order in effect and if there is an allegation of domestic or family violence. Neither of these sections prohibits the parties to such a hearing to engage in mediation of their own volition. For the majority of jurisdictions, section 408(A) is the preferred section. For the minority of jurisdictions who have developed mandatory mediation by trained, certified mediators, who follow special procedures to protect a victim of domestic or family violence from intimidation, section 408(B) is provided as an alternative.

Sec. 408(A). Mediation in cases involving domestic or family violence.

1. In a proceeding concerning the custody or visitation of a child, if an order for protection is in effect, the court shall not order mediation or refer either party to mediation.

2. In a proceeding concerning the custody or visitation of a child, if there is an allegation of domestic or family violence and an order for protection is not in effect, the court may order mediation or refer either party to mediation only if:

(a) Mediation is requested by the victim of the alleged domestic or family violence;

(b) Mediation is provided by a certified mediator who is trained in domestic and family violence in a specialized manner that protects the safety of the victim; and

(c) The victim is permitted to have in attendance at mediation a supporting person of his or her choice, including but not limited to an attorney or advocate.

Sec. 408(B). Mediation in cases involving domestic or family violence.

1. In a proceeding concerning the custody or visitation of a child, if an order for protection is in effect, the court shall not order mediation or refer either party to mediation unless the court finds that:

(a) The mediation is provided by a certified mediator who is trained in the dynamics of domestic and family violence; and

(b) The mediator or mediation service provides procedures to protect the victim from intimidation by the alleged perpetrator in accordance with subsection 2.

2. Procedures to protect the victim must include but are not limited to:

(a) Permission for the victim to have in attendance at mediation a supporting person of his or her choice, including but not limited to an attorney or advocate; and

(b) Any other procedure deemed necessary by the court to protect the victim from intimidation from the alleged perpetrator.

NOTE

Many of the new statutory protections for victims of abuse during mediation depend on the effectiveness of screening. While we have seen different models, including victim-initiated disclosure and judicial determination, the model that employs a trained mediator to conduct separate interviews with each member of the couple holds the most promise. The next reading provides a more detailed look at how that screening might be accomplished. Note that a mediator's ability to act on some of these recommendations, such as terminating the mediation if domestic abuse is identified, may depend on the statutory regime within which the mediator is operating.

Myra Sun and Laurie Woods "Domestic Abuse Screening," A Mediator's Guide to Domestic Violence (1989)

This is a screening guide for use in separate orientation caucuses with parties who have been ordered or referred to mediation. It should be used whether or not previous screening efforts have been made by attorneys or judges with whom the participants may have come into contact.

The woman should be interviewed first. If abuse is disclosed, the mediator and victim can plan for her safety while the abuser's meeting is still pending. The mediator should not disclose to either participant anything said by the other during the separate screening process.

Goals of Screening

. . . [S]creening should seek to:

IDENTIFY domestic abuse in the relationship, whether the victim uses that term to describe the parties' interaction or not; and

ASSURE that the consequences of domestic abuse for family members—for the victim and any children—are addressed *by a court*.

Few participants will make this task easy. Abusers are not likely to readily admit misconduct. Nor will all victims present the image of a bruised and passive wife, allowing the mediator to immediately identify them as domestic abuse victims.

Screening for Domestic Abuse

These screening guidelines have two components, first a document review and second, in-person screening. These can be incorporated into a routine that many mediators already follow. . . .

Document Screening

. . .

REVIEW any personal information forms or questionnaires that the participants may submit. If the mediator desires, a self-exclusion check-off may be incorporated into the personal information form. . . . However, the fact that neither party self-excludes ... should *not* halt the screening process.

EXAMINE legal documents in the case. . . . Look for:

— sworn statements from the victim or family members about domestic abuse;

— copies of police reports or medical records

— references to other legal proceedings, past and present, including proceedings for restraining orders or orders of protection. . . .

The legal documents may also disclose other conditions requiring attention, such as the participant's need for an interpreter or other special advocacy.

TERMINATE the process after document screening if a written or verbal allegation of domestic abuse is identified at this stage. . . .

In–Person Screening

The procedure outlined below should be followed if document review has not previously disclosed domestic abuse.

SCHEDULE separate orientation meetings with each participant. No appointment times except their own should be disclosed to participants, and they should be advised to arrive and leave separately.

CONDUCT face-to-face screening with each participant. . . . Questioning should be open-ended at first, and narrowed only later, if clarifying answers are needed.

EXPLORE victim concerns. If the victim has immediate safety concerns, the mediator should help her prepare a safety plan: calling on law enforcement, a friend or an advocate, or arranging for her to be accompanied to a meeting place with them. . . .

ADVISE the abuser that he will be informed in writing, at a later date, as to whether mediation is appropriate. DO NOT confront him with allegations of domestic abuse. If he does acknowledge his responsibility for domestic abuse, recommend that he seek assistance through existing community resources for abusers.

REJECT mediation if domestic abuse is identified as having occurred....

Abuser–Victim Demeanor

The abuser may be more articulate and better-prepared for the session. He may appear more believable because he is more articulate than the woman, and more reasonable because he is willing to compromise on matters at issue. For example, in a custody case, the abuser may be interested in joint custody, which is a far more favorable result for him than a custody arrangement that restricts his access to the children because his conduct is harmful to them and dangerous to the victim. He may express strong feelings for the children, but may not be willing to address issues such as the effects on them from his abusive behavior toward their mother.

The victim, by contrast, may be far less prepared to discuss matters in a businesslike way, or to immediately move toward compromise. She may appear less articulate or intelligent because her answers may be vague; she may be passive to the point of silence. Or, she may seem less reasonable because she is highly emotional, particularly if she has begun to talk about the domestic abuse. In a ... custody case, this may translate into opposition to shared care for the children, or even to visitation.

A mediator's natural response to these demeanors may be to feel some irritation with the "less cooperative" participant. However, the mediation experience often represents an important contact with the judicial system for both parties. The mediator must demonstrate concern about domestic abuse, and not appear to condone it by supporting the abuser's efforts to shift responsibility for his conduct....

Conducting the interview

1. *Discussion of the mediation process*

If the mediation program calls for voluntary participation, the mediator can begin by evaluating the participants' decision-making patterns, using their decision to mediate as an example. Even if mediation is mandatory, the mediator can still use [relevant questions], following up with questions on whether the woman has avoided the man since being ordered to mediate and why; or whether the man has tried to exert any influence over the woman, and how the woman responded.

a. How did the parties hear about mediation?

b. How was the decision to try it arrived at? Have they talked about mediation with one another? What did they decide, if anything? How did they decide it?

c. Before seeing ... [information about mediation], how did each envision the process as working?

d. Review with each participant ... [information about mediation]. Having done so, does either think mediation is not "right" for them? If not, why not?

Responses to Listen for:

From the woman:

In addition to identifying language or mental competence barriers, the mediator should be alert to any of the following responses. . . .

— he said they should try it; she was uncertain what mediation was until she saw the information sheet

— she did not talk to him about being ordered into mediation, because he gets angry at her when they try to talk

— having reviewed the information sheet on mediation, she has doubts about whether to go on (follow-up: why?)

— they talked after they got the sheet, and the man "got upset" when she expressed doubts; or he contacted her and tried to influence her views on going forward with mediation

— he abused her when she raised doubts about it

— she says she wanted mediation but does not know anything about it; or she agreed to mediation to avoid trouble (what trouble?)

— she has no attorney, and this was why she chose mediation; or

— she has an attorney who advises against mediation.

From the man:

Again, the mediator should screen for language or mental competency difficulties. In addition, while the man may not become violent, the mediator should watch for the following as possibly indicating the presence of domestic abuse:

— the man appears for the woman's meeting as well as his, either with her, or without her knowing he would be there. (The mediator should not confront him on this but should screen both with this in mind)

— his account of the decision-making process diverges greatly from hers, particularly if he perceives it to have been a joint decision, while she feels "talked into it."

— he is more sure about wanting mediation than she was

— he wants to know what she told the mediator, and questions her veracity without even being told what she said

— he becomes angry if the mediator will not tell him what she said

— he brings up incidents he thinks she mentioned, and tries to minimize any harm that occurred.

2. *Discussion of the participants' relationship in general*

Regardless of whether the previous inquiry has suggested domestic abuse, follow up with a discussion of how the two have resolved arguments in the past. The less egalitarian the decision-making process has been, the greater the possibility that one partner, more likely the man, has dominated the relationship and been abusive. The victim may talk openly about the abuse, but it is also possible that the mediator may suspect it (for example, if her answers are evasive and the man if waiting outside).

It is not likely that the man will openly acknowledge domestic abuse, so the mediator should not expect an admission. If the abuser becomes angry at the direction of the discussion, the mediator may wish to terminate the screening. Confrontation is not recommended.

a. How are the two of them getting along now?

b. What was their most recent argument about?

c. How did they resolve it?

d. What kinds of arguments did they used to have? What happened during the worst ones?

e. What happened when one got angry with the other?

f. What happened when one did not get his or her way because of something the other did?

g. Did they get physical with each other when angry?

Responses to listen for:

From the woman:

— vague hints about discord (“we just couldn't get along,” he “was always getting mad at me,” which should be followed up)

— if arguments “got bad” she left (may have gone to an abused women's shelter or gotten a restraining order)

— if she did not do something to his satisfaction (have dinner ready, or clean the house right) he withheld “rewards” from her, like refusing to let her eat or sleep, or preventing her from seeing friends

— if he disliked her friends or family, he always made a big scene when she saw them; or else she stopped seeing them in order to avoid a big scene

— if he did not like her having a particular job, she either quit or lost it because of his behavior to her or her co-workers, or because of his constantly contacting her there (variation: similar pressure on her to drop out of school or stop engaging in other activities, such as hobbies)

— if they disagreed about how to handle money, it would end up with him having control over it, her getting an allowance from him, and her request for a separate account denied

— if they disagreed about his having weapons in the house, he continued to have them there

— if, once they've separated, he has come to her separate residence when she did not want him there

— if she didn't want to have sex, he forced her to, and she felt uncomfortable about it

— specific incidents of domestic abuse, including acts that were the basis of previous criminal charges or restraining orders. (It would be typical for her to have forgotten the specific dates of arguments, to tell the story in a way that suggests she was "just as responsible" for what happened as he was, and to lack "evidence," such as medical records or a police report. However, often domestic abuse incidents occur during holidays or special events, such as family gatherings, and mentioning these may assist her in remembering.)

From the man:

— highly divergent answers about the same issues . . .

— if abuse is acknowledged, it is minimized, with an emphasis on "mitigating" circumstances: how long ago it occurred, a subsequent reconciliation that suggests that "it wasn't that bad," or provocative conduct by the woman, such as her drinking, flirting with other men or leaving the children (or him) alone

— alternative explanations for her injuries, such as accident or another assailant

— great concern with what the woman told the mediator, to the extent that he is unresponsive to screening questions

— criticism of the woman, expressing doubts about her veracity, mental stability, morality, intellectual capacity, or parenting ability

— anger or amusement with the mediator for asking the questions, coupled with refusal to answer the questions at all

— self-defense claims or claims that the woman has been abusing him (the mediator should not confront him directly, but should note height and weight differences; either partner's specialized fighting training; evidence of comparative injuries; whether the man has lost a job, dropped out of school, or given up other activities due to her conduct; whether he has been isolated from seeing his own family or his own friends due to her conduct; whether he has been without shelter or money)

3. *Checklist of Questions on Domestic Abuse*

If domestic abuse is disclosed or the mediator suspects it, it is essential to explore with the victim her concerns about the potential for imminent or severe harm to her or the children. This will allow the mediator to plan termination of the process in a way that will not exacerbate the danger to family members. . . .

Concluding the Interview

After meeting with both participants the mediator may be certain about whether domestic abuse has or has not occurred. However, some cases will present uncertainties. Because of the important issues of abuser accountability, victim safety, and the significance of the legal rights involved, all doubts should be resolved **against mediating.**

* * *

NOTE

1. In the contemporary context victims of abuse, and their advocates and lawyers, must often prepare as best they can to minimize the risks posed by mediation to their immediate safety, and their long-term wellbeing, as they participate in programs which do not incorporate the best practices identified in these pages. *A User's Checklist for Mediation,* published in 1988 by the National Center on Women and Family Law in MEDIATION AND YOU, suggests some guidelines for women to follow. They include: learning about mediation before the process begins; talking with an attorney, especially about state law and state practice with respect to mediation, mediator confidentiality, and custody and visitation decisions in domestic violence cases; meeting privately with the mediator, and being able to articulate and support your opposition to mediation; assessing the mediator's neutrality, attention to safety measures, and attitudes towards custody; taking whatever steps you can to assure your safety during the mediation; knowing how to communicate with the mediator that you wish to terminate the mediation at any time; never signing an agreement without its being reviewed by your lawyer, and making sure that any agreement that does meet your needs is adopted by the court as a court order.

E. THE ROLE OF THE GUARDIAN AD LITEM IN CASES INVOLVING DOMESTIC VIOLENCE

Introductory Note

We have already talked about the part played by judges and lawyers in the disposition of custody and visitation cases where partner abuse is at issue. There is, however, another significant player in many of these cases; the guardian ad litem (GAL) appointed as an officer of the court to investigate the case. The GAL will deliver a report, with or without explicit recommendations, to guide the judge's decision. His or her capacity to negotiate this difficult terrain: to establish procedures which will protect the confidentiality and the safety of those she or he interviews; sort out truth from fiction, particularly in the stories told by the two parents; listen attentively to what is said by children, while being sensitive to the dynamics which may inhibit their truth-telling; and decide how reliably to supplement the information supplied by the key players, will lay the basis for a sound or an unsound decision. The ways in which current GAL practice may jeopardize sound outcomes, and what kinds of changes might bring about more positive results, is the topic of this section.

Historical Background

A guardian ad litem is an individual appointed by a court to protect the interests of an incompetent person in a particular proceeding. "Ad litem" literally means "for the suit," and distinguishes this kind of guardianship from the more general and ongoing responsibilities undertaken by a permanent guardian. Guardians ad litem were first used to protect the interests of children in juvenile proceedings. Their use then extended to child abuse and neglect cases. In 1993 the federal government became involved in this class of case, through the Child Abuse Prevention and Treatment Act (P.L. 93–247, as amended by P.L. 95–266), which requires the appointment of a guardian ad litem, "or other individual whom the State recognizes as fulfilling the same functions as a guardian ad litem," "in every case involving an abused or neglected child which results in a judicial proceeding." Most recently, the use of guardians ad litem for children has extended to custody and divorce litigation.

William Halikias
The Guardian Ad Litem for Children in Divorce: Conceptualizing Duties, Roles and Consultative Services, 32 Family and Conciliation Courts Review 490, 494 (1994)

The first recorded use of a GAL in a custody case occurred in Wisconsin. In 1955, the Wisconsin Supreme Court sent back a custody dispute to the trial court with the recommendation that a GAL be appointed to represent the child. A highly unusual action at that time, this set a precedent in Wisconsin courts. In the 1960s, some Wisconsin judges argued for mandatory appointment of GALs in all divorce-related actions. Between 1965 and 1971, several bills were presented to the Wisconsin legislature that made GAL appointment mandatory, but these bills were regularly defeated. Legal professionals continued to argue for GALs and, in 1971, the Wisconsin Supreme Court invoked its rule-making power and created a statutory law mandating the use of GALs for children in contested divorce actions.

Following the Wisconsin example, with much the same rationale, was New Hampshire in 1979. By 1988, only Wisconsin and New Hampshire made GAL appointment mandatory where issues of child custody are contested. In 19 other states, statutory authority exists for judges to appoint GALs. In addition, the Uniform Marriage and Divorce Act (1983) permits a judge to appoint GALs for children in contested divorce cases, and the use of GALs for children in divorce has steadily increased.

* * *

NOTES

1. There were 1,215,000 divorces in the United States in 1992, with a slight drop to 1,187,000 in 1993. As many as half these divorces involve

minor children. Although there are no firm data on the number of divorce cases in which a GAL or the equivalent is appointed, even a conservative estimate of 5% would yield more than 1100 cases per state per year, not including appointments in third-party, modification and paternity cases where custody is also at issue. *See* Raven C. Lidman & Betsy R. Hollingsworth, *The Guardian ad Litem in Child Custody Cases: The Contours of Our Judicial System Stretched Beyond Recognition*, 6 GEO. MASON L. REV. 255 (1998). In 1994 the American Academy of Matrimonial Lawyers took the position that: "Courts should not routinely assign counsel or guardians ad litem for children in custody or visitation proceedings. Appointment of counsel or guardians should be reserved for those cases in which both parties request the appointment or the court finds after a hearing that appointment is necessary in light of the particular circumstances of the case."

2. When judges have the discretion to appoint GALs in custody or visitation proceedings, the next question is when they are likely to feel that such an appointment is desirable or necessary. That determination in turn requires exploring the function or functions that the GAL is thought to serve.

The Role and the Players

William Halikias
The Guardian Ad Litem for Children in Divorce: Conceptualizing Duties, Roles and Consultative Services, 32 Family and Conciliation Courts Review 490, 497–99 (1994)

... It is possible ... to distinguish categories around which GAL functioning can be better understood. There appear to be four categories, distributed between two continua: lawyer—psychologist, and child liberator—child saver. Most of the GAL literature falls somewhere within this four-grid matrix.

A role description is legal in the sense that it describes functions or uses language associated with an attorney. For example, Mlyniec (1977–78) describes typical legalistic roles for the GAL: "To investigate and report; to initiate contempt proceedings; to investigate and cause witnesses to appear ... to supervise support ... to determine legal rights ... to make peremptory strikes." According to Podell (1973), the GAL will "confer with the children ... locate and subpoena witnesses ... attend the hearing and put in such proof as may be necessary and desirable." Other examples of legalistic roles include "subpoena and present testimony of witnesses," "present legal arguments," and "avail themselves of pretrial discovery."

A role description is psychological in the sense that it describes an apparently clinical activity or the results of such activity, or uses language associated with mental health professionals. For example, according to Johnson (1986), the GAL assesses "the status of intellectual development and nature of home environment," and should "observe the interaction between child and parent." According to Sorkow (1981), the GAL discovers "the 'real' reason (the basic motivation) that custody is desired [and determines] the atmosphere that would be created in the proposed custodian's home." Other examples of psychologist-like functions include "perceive when the child is repressing matters," "determine the child's preference without directly asking the child," and "cut through the amassed hostility and stress of the parents to the needs of the child for attention, love and normal development." According to Flock (1983),

> "The attorney may be in the unique position of having to act as an emotional, as well as legal, counselor.... [A]lthough attorneys are not psychologists, if the attorney responds sensitively to the child and the situation, he can substantially assuage the child's emotional needs."

A second way to organize GAL roles is to classify them on the continuum between child liberator and child saver. Child liberators view children as more like than unlike adults. They favor policies to protect the autonomy of children....

Child liberators assume that the child's wishes direct the GAL's actions....

Child savers emphasize the opposite: a child's dependency, incompetence, and vulnerability. They favor policies to protect children from misuse....

Because child savers believe that children are unable to make responsible decisions, they consider their own opinions of the child's best interest to be primary. Examples in the GAL literature of this view are "persuade the child that the attorney's conception of the child's best interests is correct," ... "to recommend to the court what he thinks is in the child's best interests," ... and "to substitute their own views for those of the child as to what constitutes the best interests of the child." ...

In summary, it is possible to group GAL roles within a four-grid matrix of lawyer—psychologist, and child liberator—child saver. GAL role descriptors generally fall somewhere within this matrix. What factors determine how an individual GAL, judge or attorney position themselves within this matrix remains unclear....

Finally, although the literature makes little reference to role confusion, it is likely that this is a problem for GALs. These individuals are given a diverse array of professional, ethical, and moral models to choose from and asked to cope with impossible family conflicts. The duties of a psychologist and lawyer are sufficiently distinct that role confusion can easily occur.... Likewise, a moral or philosophical belief about minors and self-determination may be in conflict with the needs of a specific child or family.

... Some GALs may respond to role ambiguity with excessive rigidity, passivity, or indecisiveness. With some exceptions, there is little published information about ways to assist GALs to manage their various role and task demands. It is likely that these individuals require consultations, support or supervision in resolving role conflicts and stress, as well as in understanding the various psychological and legal conundrums they face.

* * *

NOTES

1. Due to the tensions described in the above excerpt, the GAL's role has been variously defined as (1) the person appointed by the court to gather information and report back recommending which parent should have custody (investigator or fact finder); (2) the lawyer appointed to represent the children; (3) an advocate for the "best interests" of the child[ren]; (4) a facilitator/mediator; and (5) some combination thereof and more. *See* Lidman & Hollingsworth, *The Guardian ad Litem in Child Custody Cases: The Contours of Our Judicial System Stretched Beyond Recognition*, 6 GEO. MASON L. REV. 255, 256–257 (1998).

2. The confusion over the GAL's role also influences decisions about who may serve as a GAL. Some states restrict the role to attorneys. Colorado provides an example, even while it acknowledges that the job is one of independent investigation and fact finding rather than representation, and that the GAL's final recommendations should be driven by the child's best interests, rather than his or her desires. The majority of states allow for both attorneys and non-attorneys to qualify as GALs, with the latter category encompassing both trained mental-health professionals, and volunteers with no formal credentials. The role of the lay volunteer GAL is well established. The national CASA (Court Appointed Special Advocate) model uses a volunteer cadre of trained individuals, both professional and lay, who assist the court by making best interest recommendations based on the investigations, interviews and information synthesis they conduct. Many courts support this model, although primarily in the context of child abuse and neglect cases, where children are placed in out-of-home settings, and federal law requires the appointment of GALs in each case.

Connected to the question of who may serve as a GAL is the question of what skills and knowledge individuals must bring to the role. If the GAL is required to have a law degree, are those legal qualifications considered enough to equip him or her for the GAL function? If successful functioning in the role is understood as importantly dependent on the kinds of skills and understandings fostered by training in the mental health field, how can attorneys or lay volunteers be expected to be effective without further training? Conversely, if the GAL is expected to participate competently in complex legal proceedings, can he or she do so without legal training? The hybrid quality of the role has led some to suggest that a "team" approach may overcome the limitations inherent in appointing any one individual. Other states are slowly but surely addressing the same issues by developing processes for screening and training GALs to increase the likelihood that they possess the right mix of skills and substantive expertise for the job.

Unlike the GAL, the custody evaluator, an individual appointed by the court for the specific purpose of investigating issues surrounding contested custody cases and making recommendations about custody and access, is in almost all cases a mental health professional. However, this greater clarity about role, and greater consensus about function, does not eliminate all of the problems associated with custody evaluation. Many of the criticisms aimed at GALs apply equally to those custody evaluators who lack specific training in domestic violence.

Tara Lea Muhlhauser & Douglas D. Knowlton
The "Best Interest Team": Exploring the Concept of a Guardian Ad Litem Team, 71 North Dakota Law Review 1021, 1023–25 (1995)

Complex cases may require the skills of an attorney to address the legal interests inherent in representing the "best interests." Understanding legal advocacy is only the beginning of the comprehensive role of a guardian ad litem. An attorney must be expected to address issues beyond this limited horizon. For many attorneys, this becomes uncomfortable or unproductive because the role requires many to work outside the "comfort zone" of skills and training they possess. Conversely, lay guardians ad litem in complex cases often request the assistance of an attorney to help with an understanding of the legal process or the legal issues that must be considered to properly fulfill their role and arrive at an informed recommendation. . . .

Balancing this array of interests while working toward the goal of presenting a recommendation can be a demanding and time consuming task that may be more efficiently managed by a "team" approach. A round table approach, where there is an opportunity for review, discourse, and the sharing of knowledge has become a synonym for efficiency, quality, and enhanced work product in education, management, corporate and medical sectors.

. . .

The concept of a team includes at least three individuals. The core of the team would be a guardian ad litem appointed by the court. . . . Given the nature of the issues present in the case, other professionals can be added to the team on an "as needed" basis. . . .

At all times, and in all team proceedings, the guardian ad litem maintains the responsibility to focus on the issue at hand and carries the traditional role that accompanies such an appointment. The guardian ad litem has an opportunity to use the skills of team members by delegating particular tasks. For instance, it is quite fitting to ask a social worker to complete a home study/social study on a family or group. Many cases require this particular task, but it is often overlooked. By delegating such tasks, the guardian ad litem can direct team members to complete tasks themselves or rely on other professionals to accomplish the tasks while team members serve as interpreters of data received from outside professionals.

... The team collaborates on a recommendation, and the guardian ad litem delivers it to the court. The guardian ad litem is the spokesperson for the team and bears the responsibility of explaining and defending the recommendation if requested or required in the legal process.

* * *

NOTES

1. One operating example of a GAL team is the GAL Project recently initiated by the Child Witness to Violence Project and the Family Advocacy Project at Boston Medical Center, the City of Boston's public hospital. Under the auspices of this project, lawyers working with the Family Advocacy Project team with clinical psychologists working with the Child Witness to Violence Project to serve the GAL function in family law cases involving domestic violence. In the limited period the GAL project has been in operation it has been increasingly called upon by local family courts to accept appointment in complex cases; both because of its sophistication in the area of family violence and its impact on children, and because of its ability to combine psychological and legal expertise.

2. In recent years several states have acknowledged the inadequacy of their guardian ad litem regulation and practice, and have promulgated new procedures and standards. While these are issues that could be taken up by a state legislature, frequently change is initiated through the mechanism by which state courts govern their own operation; usually through rules adopted by the highest court of the state. The next excerpts illustrate the kind of changes being adopted; emphasizing the questions of who can qualify to serve as a GAL, and what levels of expertise and training are required. Because these changes are coming about at the same time that family courts are being asked to pay greater attention to issues of domestic violence, new standards governing GAL practice sometimes incorporate specific directives with respect to domestic violence training or expertise.

State of Minnesota
Supreme Court Rules of Guardian Ad Litem Procedure, Effective January 1, 1999

Rule 2. [MINIMUM QUALIFICATIONS]

Before a person may be recommended for service as a guardian ad litem pursuant to Rule 4, the person must satisfy the following minimum qualifications:

(a) have an abiding interest in children and their rights and needs;

(b) have sufficient listening, speaking and writing skills in the person's primary language to successfully conduct interviews, prepare written reports, and make oral presentations;

(c) not have been involved in any conduct or activity that would interfere with the person's ability to discharge the duties assigned by the court;

(d) have knowledge and an appreciation of the ethnic, cultural and socio-economic backgrounds of the population to be served;

(e) be available for at least 18 months and have sufficient time, including evenings and weekends, to gather information, make court appearances, and otherwise discharge the duties assigned by the court;

(f) have the ability to (1) relate to a child, family members, and professionals in a careful and confidential manner; (2) exercise sound judgment and good common sense; and (3) successfully discharge the duties assigned by the court;

(g) not have been removed from a panel of approved guardians ad litem following an unsatisfactory performance evaluation pursuant to Rule 6, subdivision 2; and

(h) have satisfactorily completed the pre-service training requirements set forth in Rule 10, and demonstrated a comprehension of the responsibilities of guardians ad litem as set forth in Rule 8, subdivision 1.

. . .

Rule 10. [PRE-SERVICE TRAINING REQUIREMENTS.]

Subd. 1. [PRE-SERVICE TRAINING REQUIREMENTS FOR NEW GUARDIANS AD LITEM.] The purpose of pre-service training is to equip guardians ad litem with the skills, techniques, knowledge, and understanding necessary to effectively advocate for the best interests of children. To be listed on a panel of approved guardians ad litem maintained pursuant to Rule 3, subdivision 4, each person ... shall satisfy the following pre-service training requirements:

(a) attend a minimum of 40 hours of pre-service training and demonstrate a comprehension of the topics discussed during the training;

(b) if the person intends to serve in family court, attend an additional training course regarding family law matters and demonstrate a comprehension of the topics discussed....

Subd. 3. [INTERNSHIP REQUIREMENTS.] In addition to satisfying the pre-service training requirements ... each person who intends to serve as a guardian ad litem in family court shall make a reasonable, good faith effort to satisfy the internship requirements set forth in clauses (e) and (f), or submit to the program coordinator written proof sufficient to verify that the person has previously satisfied the requirements....

(e) Observe a variety of family court proceedings, including, but not limited to, a temporary relief hearing, a child custody hearing, and a domestic abuse hearing.

(f) Intern with an experienced guardian ad litem on at least two family court cases.

Rule 11. [Continuing Education Requirements]

Once a guardian ad litem is listed on a panel of approved guardians ad litem . . . the guardian ad litem may maintain that listing only by annually completing eight hours of continuing education.

Rule 12. [Training Curricula; Certification of Trainers]

Subd. 1. [Pre-service Training Curriculum.] The State Court Administrator, through the Office of Continuing Education in consultation with the Advisory Task Force on the Guardian Ad Litem System, shall develop a core curriculum to be used in the pre-service training of guardians ad litem and guardian ad litem program coordinators. The pre-service training curriculum should be reviewed and updated at least every three years.

* * *

Supreme Court of Missouri En Banc Standards with Comments for Guardians Ad Litem in Missouri Juvenile and Family Law Matters

STANDARD 1.0 Appointment of Guardians ad litem

Only a lawyer licensed by the Supreme Court of Missouri and, when authorized by law, a court appointed special advocate volunteer sworn in as an officer of the court shall be appointed to act as a guardian ad litem for a child. . . .

STANDARD 4.0 Volunteer Advocates

If the court appoints a court appointed special advocate volunteer, the services of a lawyer shall be obtained by the volunteer program supporting the volunteer when the volunteer has need for legal advice and assistance.

STANDARD 16.0 Training of Guardian ad litem

No person shall be appointed as guardian ad litem without first completing twelve hours of specialized training. Thereafter, to continue to be appointed as a guardian ad litem a person shall complete six hours of specialized training annually. Completion of the training hours shall be evidenced by an affidavit filed with the appointing court by July 31 of each year. . . .

The specialized training shall include, but is not limited to, the following topics:

1. Dynamics of child abuse and neglect issues

2. Factors to consider in determining the best interest of the child, including permanency planning

3. Inter-relationships between family system, legal process and the child welfare system

4. Mediation and negotiation skills

5. Federal, state and local legislation and case law affecting children
6. Cultural and ethnic diversity and gender-specific issues
7. Family and domestic violence issues
8. Available community resources and services
9. Child development issues
10. Guardian ad litem standards

Programs providing guardian ad litem training to meet the provisions of the standard shall be accredited by the Supreme Court of Missouri's judicial education committee.

COMMENT: Guardian ad litem practice is unique and complex and, as such requires special education, training and experience. The guardian ad litem needs an understanding of family dynamics and child development in order to evaluate observed and reported behaviors. The guardian ad litem must interpret lengthy case information, which may include references to stress and abuse syndromes, physical determinations of abuse, causal factors in abuse and neglect, and the concepts of treatment designed to address abusive behaviors. The guardian ad litem must be able to understand these references and see how determinations of probable cause are developed, how and why treatment programs are prescribed, and how to incorporate these references into his or her recommendations for the best interest of the child.

The guardian ad litem is not expected to make diagnostic or therapeutic recommendations but is expected to provide an information base from which to draw resources. Therefore, the guardian ad litem must have a working knowledge of family dynamics and be able to compare and relate this concept to the observations, reports and documentation received regarding the child and the child's family.

* * *

Guardians Ad Litem and Domestic Violence

Since we are, as a society, only slowly coming to understand the power and control dynamics of partner abuse, the overlap between partner and child abuse, and the impact on children of witnessing a parent's abuse, the proposition that guardians ad litem are uninformed about, and insensitive to, partner abuse in their cases is hardly a radical one. Nor will it matter, from this perspective, whether the GAL in a given case is a lay volunteer, a mental health professional, or an attorney, since professional education in both the legal and the mental health fields has traditionally paid scant attention to the issue. In 1995 the Family Violence Project of the National Council of Juvenile and Family Court Judges reported that guardians ad litem, along with custody evaluators, were "the professionals least trained about domestic violence of any actors in the civil justice system." *Family Violence in Child Custody Statutes: An Analysis of State Codes and Legal Practice,* 29 F.L.Q. 197, 220 (1995).

On the other hand, GAL inattention to partner abuse can have devastating results. As we have already seen, conflict over custody is particularly likely in cases in which the parents' marriage or relationship has been characterized by abuse. Furthermore, the tendency of abusers to deny and minimize their own abuse, while finding fault with every aspect of their partners' functioning, including their parenting, is particularly likely to result in the kind of conflicting testimony which will prompt a judge to appoint a GAL, and rely on his or her objective findings or recommendations in deciding what arrangement is in the child(ren)'s best interests.

Repeated anecdotal charges that GALs were serving children poorly in cases involving domestic violence, and putting both them and their abused parents at risk, led the Massachusetts Chapter of the National Association of Social Workers Committee on Domestic Violence and Sexual Assault to initiate a Guardian ad Litem Assessment Project in January 1996, and prepare a preliminary report in January of 1998 based on interviews with 23 providers who work with battered women (attorneys, advocates and therapists) regarding the involvement of GALs with battered women and their children in cases of contested custody and visitation. As the executive summary to the report states: "The interviews offer an explanatory and third-person perspective on the practices of GALs, their knowledge and attitudes about domestic violence. . . ."

An obvious vulnerability of the report, from a political perspective, is its exclusive reliance on reporting from those who work with and advocate for, battered women, to the exclusion of those who work with their partners, or work separately with their children. The difficulty here is in separating out legitimate and "objective" criticisms of GAL practice from the understandable but perhaps unwarranted complaints of those whose clients did not get what they wanted from the system. As you read the excerpt below, think about how these preliminary conclusions could be affirmed or bolstered in a way that would augment their credibility in the face of attacks from, for example, fathers' rights organizations, or lawyers who represent fathers in family law proceedings. Have the authors of the preliminary report already anticipated and neutralized these attacks in their future plans for the project?

Preliminary Report of the Guardian ad Litem Assessment Project Massachusetts Chapter of the National Association of Social Workers Committee on Domestic Violence and Sexual Assault, January 1998

Executive Summary

Respondents believe that GALs do not possess an adequate understanding of the issue (e.g., do not view domestic violence as serious, do not understand the implications for couples' counseling, do not realize how the courts can be used as a mechanism of control and do not understand the effects of domestic violence on victims and their parenting skills). They also agreed that a GAL's understanding of the issue affects his/her approach to working with battered women (e.g., pathologizing victims, minimizing the importance of domestic violence). Participants also felt that GALs do not always possess the clinical training that would prepare them to assess and respond to developmental and trauma issues among children they interview. They also expressed concern that the safety issues of mothers are not always considered in making recommendations for visitation and custody.... Despite participants' reported concerns about unsafe practices of GALs, few make formal complaints due to fear of retribution from the GAL or the Judge who appointed him/her. Typical issues of concern included perceived bias against the woman, manipulation of the GAL by batterers, unsafe interviewing practices with children, and recommendations without sufficiently considering the impact of violence on women and children.

Participants identified preliminary recommendations to address some of these issues. These include mandatory training for GALs on domestic violence, standardization and professionalization of the GAL role, and clarification and standardization of fee and payment arrangements. Next steps for advancing the Project were also recommended and include gathering more data through interviews with GALs, Judges, and survivors of domestic violence who have had a GAL involved in Probate Court cases.

. . .

Preliminary Recommendations

Training

Respondents felt that the current level of insight among GALs regarding the extent to which control, manipulation and intimidation are involved in battering relationships is insufficient to evaluate family dynamics accurately. When qualifying numerical responses regarding practice issues, participants made a distinction between "recognizing" or "considering" domestic violence and "understanding" how dynamics of power and control affect all family members. One respondent emphasized the need to address the subtleties of domestic violence and "how broad the coercion is, and how subtle it can be."

"Charm, cooperation and manipulation" were cited by participants as means by which batterers turn GALs and other court officials into allies, portray their former partners as villains rather than victims, deflect even substantiated charges of the physical and/or sexual abuse they have perpetrated. Participants expressed frustration when speaking about the way in which batterers' behaviors invariably sway court officials and outcomes. One respondent stated, "Men who are abusive are often charming and manipulative and successfully shift the focus of the investigation to something other than the abuse."

Most participants expressed concern regarding GALs' limited understanding of how the dynamics of intimidation and control affect children who have witnessed domestic violence. It is difficult to assess and convey children's real thoughts and experiences in a report. Interviewing children may expose them to an abuser's retribution. Limited understanding regarding the fear and control that batterers perpetuate within their families ultimately may result in poorly made recommendations for custody and visitation. One participant called "talking to children" a "minefield." One respondent noted that GALs must be sensitive to the fact that children are "always a source of the batterer's control."

In the stories participants told, visitation exposed children to repeated threats of violence and often made them messengers of these threats to their mothers. In one example, a batterer used visitation as an opportunity to coerce his child into telling the child's mother that he (the batterer) was going to kill her. Given how frequently participants cited similar occurrences, it seems unlikely that all GALs fully recognize the damage visitation may do to a child's psychological and physical well-being.

Many participants reported that battered women often lose custody of their children. Incomplete understanding of the degree of control batterers' hold over their children may lead to the misinterpretation of family dynamics and an award of custody to abusive men. As one participant explained, GALs often observe children interacting with each of their parents as a part of their investigation. Because children may be afraid and, therefore, better-behaved with the batterer, GALs mistakenly conclude that the batterer is the more capable parent. Many participants attributed misguided recommendations to GALs' limited understanding of child development as well as domestic violence.

GALs should also be trained in identifying and intervening with batterers. Almost everyone cited GALs they know who, on their own initiative, have sought additional training to better prepare them to address complex issues like domestic violence. Participants in this survey recommended making such training mandatory and standardized for all GALs. To further support this idea, participants noted the positive impact that education about domestic violence has already had within Family and Probate Courts.

* * *

NOTES AND QUESTIONS

1. The NASW report, in addition to recommending training for GALs in domestic violence, suggested standardization and professionalization of the GAL role, presumably in the direction recently taken by both Missouri and Minnesota. The Minnesota Rules are particularly thorough and detailed. In addition to the rules governing qualifications and training reproduced above, Minnesota has provided procedures for the initial recruitment and selection of GALs, and procedures for subsequent supervision, performance evaluation, removal from particular cases and more general censure. The GAL role is carefully defined, with particular attention to avoiding conflicts of interest. A GAL may not also serve as a mediator or visitation expeditor, for example, and may not, except in special circumstances, provide any direct services to the child or family. This speaks directly to one concern expressed by providers in the Massachusetts study, who complained of GALs who served as therapists to the batterers whose parenting they were

appointed to report on, or served as witnesses for those batterers in criminal trials. The rules also lay out in detail the responsibilities, rights and powers that accompany the GAL role. Significantly, the Missouri Standards acknowledge the need for GAL training in domestic violence, as do recently proposed standards of practice for GALs in Colorado.

2. If you were involved in reforming the GAL system in a state like Massachusetts, where regulation is sparse and GAL practice inconsistent in quality, how would you plan to ensure a proper sensitivity and an adequate response to issues of domestic violence? Would your emphasis be on the selection of individuals with appropriate expertise; on the initial and ongoing training of GALs; on the possibility of disciplining those who can be shown to have put children and parents at physical and emotional risk; or on the development of procedures that will promote the identification of partner abuse as an issue, and its proper consideration in determining the best interests of children? To what extent would your development of appropriate procedures for cases involving domestic violence be guided by the critique of mediation practices in such cases explored in Section D, above.

3. If you were designing a training curriculum in domestic violence for GALs, what topics would you include, and what teaching methodologies would you suggest?

F. Parent Education at Divorce

Compared to the effects of required mediation, GAL involvement, legal presumptions concerning child custody and visitation, parent relocation, or kidnaping, the impact of time-limited parent education programs upon divorcing families may seem relatively inconsequential. However, the rapid spread of court-connected parent education programs, many of them mandatory, in over fifteen hundred counties across the United States, demands that we take a closer look at this relatively new phenomenon in the divorce process and its impact upon victims of abuse. The following materials address the history, goals and content of these programs, what we know of their effectiveness, and then at the particular issues raised by offering parent education to partners whose relationship has been marked by abuse.

Historical Background

Sanford L. Braver, Peter Salem, Jessica Pearson, and Stephanie R. DeLuse
The Content of Divorce Education Programs: Results of a Survey, 34 Family and Conciliation Courts Review 41, 41–43 (1996)

One of the most recent trends in services for separating and divorcing families is the spread of parent education services. First begun in the mid-1970s in Kansas, parent education programs rapidly proliferated in the late 1980s and early 1990s....

Interest in parent education programs is spurred by several factors. One is the growing recognition of the long-term implications of postdivorce parental conflict for both families and courts. Parental conflict is often intense after divorce and has been identified in previous studies as a cause of postdivorce litigation; nonpayment of child support; visitation disputes; nonvisitation by the noncustodial parent; and poor child adjustment to divorce. Parent education programs represent a new approach—a preventive approach—to such problems. By focusing on the postdivorce needs of children and the consequences of parental conflict, these programs strive to reach parents before full-scale disputes emerge.

Another reason for the growing popularity of parent education programs is the rise in filings by parents unrepresented by attorneys. According to a recent study of domestic relations cases in 16 courts, only 29% involved two attorneys. Representation patterns in some jurisdictional districts are even more extreme.... Indeed, problems associated with *pro se* filings are the second most frequently noted problems cited by divorce court personnel.

Parent education programs are also attractive to jurisdictions that lack an extensive array of services such as court-connected mediation, custody evaluation, and visitation supervision. Many regard parent education as an affordable intervention. Similarly, courts with mediation and evaluation services regard parent education programs as a way to provide less expensive, mass-produced information to all parents and reserve more costly and time-consuming interventions for those parents who have more serious problems.

... Some professionals contend that parents who receive orientation in divorce education programs are better prepared for mediation, are more satisfied with the services, and seem better able to consider the needs of their children in negotiating parenting arrangements. Finally, for some courts with mediation services, divorce education programs are a way to expose the divorcing population to the concept of mediation.

* * *

Program Structure and Content

Karen R. Blaisure and Margie L. Geasler Results of a Survey of Court–Connected Parent Education Programs in U.S. Counties, 34 Family and Conciliation Courts Review 23, 24–35 (1996)

This article reports the results of a survey of 3,073 U.S. counties, completed in September 1994. The excitement for and number of court-connected parent education programs for divorcing parents has exponentially increased since 1992....

Survey results indicate that 541 counties are served by education programs for divorcing parents.... Connections between courts and the parenting education programs were of three types: court based, contracted, and collaborative. Court-based programs are defined here as programs administered by court officials themselves. In court-based programs, court workers either design their own programs, obtain commercially available programs, or combine materials. Contracted programs are those ... conducted by a public or private agency, an institute of higher education, or a mental health practitioner for the court.... Collaborative programs are defined as those programs with development and administrative responsibilities shared between the court and a public or private agency, institute of higher education, or mental health practitioner. Parent education programs identified here ... also serve separating parents who have not married....

Attendance Policies

Counties reported three types of attendance policies: state-or locally mandated attendance, judge-determined attendance, and invited open attendance.... Administrative orders mandating attendance for divorcing parents usually stipulated that all parents with minor children must attend divorce education programs as designated by the court; some form of mandatory attendance is required in the majority of counties with programs. In three states, Connecticut, Utah, and Vermont, all divorcing parents with minor children are required to attend ... unless a waiver is granted.... Another common mandatory attendance policy is to require parents who are in dispute over custody, child support, or visitation issues to attend parent education programs.... In some counties, the presiding judge determines, on a case-by-case basis, which parents must attend the program. Rather than mandating attendance of all parents of minor children or parents in dispute, some counties simply invited divorcing parents to attend. A few counties had interesting policies ranging, for example, from court workers deciding which parents must attend to mandated attendance for parents of 8–to 15–year olds....

. . .

Program Data

... Two thirds of county programs ... consisted of one session, and more than 75% of program sessions lasted for 2–4 hours....

* * *

NOTES

1. As part of a recent report, Blaisure and Geasler updated their 1993–1994 parent education survey, collecting similar data in 1997–1998. Their latest survey identified programs in 1,516 counties. "The survey suggests that a minimum of 49 percent of all U.S. counties offer parent education. This represents a nearly 200 percent increase in the number of programs over the past four years." Nancy Thoennes and Jessica Pearson, *Parent Education Programs in Domestic Relations Courts,* ii, 9 (Center for Policy Research, 1998).

2. As the above excerpt suggests, one key goal of parent education programs is to address the needs of children:

> [T]here is general agreement [among researchers] that parental separation precipitates a crisis for most children. The vast majority of

> youngsters are not anticipating divorce when it occurs, even when there has been considerable conflict between their parents; and only those experiencing repeated, intense conflict and family violence are relieved. The most common crisis-engendered reactions include intense anxiety about their future well-being and caretaking, sadness and acute reactive depressions, increased anger, disruptions in concentration at school, distress about the loss of contact with one parent, loyalty conflicts, and preoccupation with reconciliation. Intense conflict between parents also entails substantial risks for the development of children. Commentators have found that "ongoing high levels of [family] conflict, whether in intact or divorced homes, produce lower self-esteem, increased anxiety, and a loss of self control."... If parents place their children in a demilitarized zone, their children will be better able to cope with the emotional turmoil created by divorce and separation.

Joan B. Kelly, *Longer–Term Adjustment in Children of Divorce: Converging Findings and Implications for Practice*, 2. J. FAM. PSYCH. 119, 122 (1988).

3. Another key goal of parent education programs is "decreasing divorcing parents' reliance on the family court system." Sandford L. Braver, Melanie C. Smith, and Stephanie R. DeLuse, *Methodological Considerations in Evaluating Family Court Programs: A Primer Using Divorced Parent Education Programs as a Case Example*, 35 F.C.C.R. 9, 10 (1997). Relevant to the problem of court congestion, one group of experts estimates that the majority of divorcing adults can successfully work through the "anger, disappointment, and loss" of divorce, that one fourth to one third have "considerable difficulty doing so, and that five to ten percent 'clearly fail to attain this goal.' As a result of the high divorce rates, the 'high-conflict' group is 'clog[ging] the family courts, taking more than their share of available resources.' " Michael E. Lamb, Kathleen J. Sternberg, and Ross A. Thompson, *The Effects of Divorce and Custody Arrangements on Children's Behavior, Development, and Adjustment,* 35 F.C.C.R. 393, 396 (1997).

4. The following excerpt provides a closer look at topics that parent education programs typically cover in their curricula. It is drawn from a survey primarily of parent education program representatives from across the United States who attended the AFCC's First International Congress on Parent Education Programs in 1994.

Sanford Braver, Peter Salem, Jessica Pearson, and Stephanie R. DeLuse
The Content of Divorce Education Programs: Results of a Survey, 34 Family and Conciliation Courts Review 41, 48–50 (1996)

Most Intensively Covered Topics

Benefits of parental cooperation versus costs of parental conflict
Typical postdivorce reactions of children

Impact of "brainwashing" child, "badmouthing" other parent
Different reactions and needs of children of different ages
Responsibilities of custodials (e.g., permitting, encouraging visiting)

Topics Covered With Moderate Intensity

Conflict management skills
Parenting skills
Emotional responsibilities of noncustodials (e.g., visiting)
Typical postdivorce reactions of parents
Benefits and costs of developing a formal co-parenting plan
Additional community resources available for divorcing parents
Dispute resolution options (e.g., mediation, custody evaluation, litigation)
Custody options (e.g., joint, sole)

Least Intensively Covered Topics

Issues concerning domestic violence
Financial responsibilities of noncustodial parents (e.g., child support)
Legal rights of parents
"Nuts and bolts": How to properly file the legal paperwork, etc.
How to calculate child support under the guidelines

* * *

NOTE

1. In the handbook furnished to participants in the "Parents Apart" program, offered by the University of Massachusetts Medical Center and Family Services of Central Massachusetts, there are listed "7 Major Don'ts for Parents," including: arguing or discussing "difficult adult issues" with the other parent in front of the children, using the child as either a verbal messenger or carrier of written/printed information, discussing specifics of parents' divorce procedure, putting down or complaining about the other parent in front of the child, interfering with the child's relationship with his/her other parent, using child support as a weapon, and using contact with the children as a weapon. The section headed "Parental Pitfalls" presents as common negative parental behaviors the dynamics of "I spy," "tug of war," "messenger," "what would I do without you," and "the money game."

Do Parent Education Programs Work?

Given the ambitious topical coverage of parent education programs, the obvious question is, Do such programs work? Are they succeeding in improving children's well being and their adjustment to divorce? If reduction in court involvement by the parents is a valid indicator of success, is this occurring at a higher rate for those parents who have participated in a parent education program, when compared to those parents who have not? Judith S. Wallerstein and Julia Lewis, in *The Long–Term Impact of Divorce on Children: A First Report From a 25–Year Study,* 36 F.C.C.R. 368 (1998), stress the importance of carefully evaluating the impacts of all popular court-related agendas and programs for divorcing families, especially if these programs—and their underlying assumptions about benefits—become entrenched in the legal system.

As of the year 2000, research on the outcomes of parent education programs is minimal. As Karen Blaisure and Margie Geasler point out:

> Evaluation research on parent education programs offered in connection with court systems is in its infancy and is limited primarily to local parent surveys.... [T]he most common strategy for assessing programs was exit evaluation forms completed by participants immediately following a program. In one such study of 3,282 parental responses in Utah, 56% of parents reported feeling resentful that they were required to attend a program; however, 93% thought the program was worthwhile, and 89% thought the program should be mandatory. Additionally, 92% of the respondents agreed that the program increased their understanding of the importance of cooperative parenting, and 90% reported planning to strengthen their efforts to work with their children's other parent.

Karen R. Blaisure and Margie L. Geasler, *Results of a Survey of Court–Connected Parent Education Programs in U.S. Counties,* 34 F.C.C.R. 23, 24–35 (1996).

There are obvious limitations to what can be learned from a parent survey administered immediately after participation in a mandatory program. Can you identify factors that would tend to undermine the reliability of such findings? While evaluators acknowledge these limitations, the barriers to performing more thorough evaluations are considerable. For example, one key benefit of parent education programs often perceived to be applicable to *all* parents is the reinforcement of nurturing skills relevant to children's emotions and development. Yet numerous evaluators admit that the longitudinal study that actually tracks the children's adjustment in "parent education" families as compared to control groups, has yet to be performed. They also acknowledge the need to directly observe family members, particularly children, and to rely less on parent self-reporting. See, for example, Laurie Kramer and Christine A. Washo, *Evaluation of a Court–Mandated Prevention Program for Divorcing Parents: The Children First Program*, 42 FAMILY RELATIONS179,186 (1993).

In the absence of reliable data about the efficacy of parent education programs, why has their number continued to increase, and why do so many involved in the family court system express such enthusiasm for them? One answer may be that participants in the system experience the programs as successful, and share their enthusiasm with others; formal evaluation, which is expensive and time consuming, has just not caught up with the informal judgments of those who have seen the programs in operation. A more sceptical assessment would be that there are many within the system who stand to gain by the operation of these programs, and could be expected to encourage their adoption, at least until the evidence proved conclusively that they were not meeting their goals:

> In the case of divorced parent education programs, the possible stakeholders might include the developers of the program; other advocates for the program, which might include mothers' and fathers' groups; judges and courts; legislatures; funding agencies; domestic relations attorneys; and mental health workers of various types, including mediators, custody evaluators, and so forth. Also to be considered are divorce bureaucracies such as child support enforcement and visitation enforcement services, as well as other offices who are interested in decreasing the number of people who have to use the welfare system because of a failure to receive child support.... It is also reasonable to consider whether program evaluators themselves have a stake in the program....

Sanford L. Braver, Melanie C. Smith, and Stephanie R. DeLuse, *Methodological Considerations in Evaluating Family Court Programs: A Primer Using Divorce Parent Education Programs as a Case Example*, 35 F.C.C.R. 9, 12–13 (1997).

Many current parent education programs characterize the majority of their participants as white middle class parents. Even if the programs were to prove beneficial for this constituency, therefore, further questions would have to be asked regarding their potential effectiveness for different populations of divorcing or separating parents. For a thoughtful discussion of the complexities of responding to a range of parent constituencies—gay parents, never married parents, parents from different ethnic backgrounds, and abused parents—see Peter Salem, Andrew Shepard, and Stephen W. Schlissel, *Parent Education as a Distinct Field of Practice: The Agenda for the Future*, 34 F.C.C.R. 9, 15–16 (1996).

Parent Education and Domestic Violence

The term "high-conflict" appears to signify different things in parent education practice and literature. It can apply to couples with a high instance of motion filings, couples whose relationships are marked by instances of physical violence and verbal abuse, couples who respectively "bad mouth" their ex partners to the children, or couples who engage in more than one of these behaviors. The label "high conflict" is not infrequently used to mark couples for inclusion or exclusion in parent education programs. For example, the Children First Program has determined that high-conflict couples benefit most from attendance. In contrast, P.E.A.C.E. co-founder Andrew Schepard strongly recommends that high-conflict couples and those experiencing domestic abuse be screened out of the parent education program, leaving as ideal candidates the "moderate conflict" couple. See Laurie Kramer and Christine A. Washo, *Evaluation of a Court–Mandated Prevention Program for Divorcing Parents: The Children First Program*, 42 FAMILY RELATIONS, 179, 186 (1993); Andrew Schepard, *War and P.E.A.C.E.: A Preliminary Report and Model Statute on an Interdisciplinary Educational Program for Divorcing and Separating Parents*, 27 U. MICH. J. L. REF. 131, 182 (1993). See also Sharlene A. Wolchik at al., *The Children of Divorce Parenting Intervention: Outcome Evaluation of an Empirically Based Program*, 21 AM. J. OF COMMUNITY PSYCH. 293, 323 (1993).

Since parent education programs have neither consistently defined "high conflict," nor consistently differentiated "high conflict" and abusive relationships, they have not yet addressed questions of efficacy in the specific context of abuse. Do the children of abusive relationships fare better when their parents have participated in a parent education program? Do such parents use the court system less if they participate? Given the special needs of abuse victims and their children, are we clear that less use of the court system necessarily correlates with an increase in the well being of the parties? Although some studies make explicit reference to the need to look at parent education program efficacy with regard to abuse victims, few have attempted to measure and evaluate the impact of programs on abuse victims or their families. See, for example, Kevin M. Kramer and Donald A. Gordon: *Outcome Research: Does Program Content Make a Difference*? Congress Proceedings, AFCC Third International Congress on Parent Education Programs, Breckenridge, Colorado, 31,42 (September 1997).

Among participants in the 1994 First International Congress on Parent Education Programs (attended in 1994 by 400 people from 39 states and several foreign countries) those who were involved with children's divorce programs reported that "over fifty percent of the children who participate in their programs witness more or less severe incidents of domestic violence between their parents." Andrew Schepard, Stephen W. Schlissel, *Planning for P.E.A.C.E.: The Development of Court-Connected Education Programs for Divorcing and Separating Families*, 23 HOFSTRA L. REV. 845, 871 (1995). With such a high probability that a typical group of attendees includes many abused and abusive partners, it is indeed crucial to scrutinize the relevance of the programs for, and their impact on, this constituency.

A number of parent education program developers and evaluators have recognized this need. A survey reported by Sanford Braver, Peter Salem, Jessica Pearson, and Stephanie R. DeLuse in *The Content of Divorce Education Programs: Results of a Survey*, 34 F.C.C.R. 41, 43–55 (1996), highlights some of the issues involved:

> [I]ssues concerning domestic abuse receive limited coverage. Advocates for battered women have expressed the concern that the message of most ... programs is not appropriate for many victims of domestic abuse. Advocates are concerned that in an attempt to cooperate for the sake of their children, abused parents will risk their own or their children's unsafe exposure to batterers or compromise their interests in negotiation about property, child support, or custody.
>
> We believe that it is important that programs acknowledge and address domestic violence concerns. Many appear to have done so. Nearly 80% of programs provide at least some coverage of domestic violence issues, and 55% make "special provisions" for cases involving domestic violence. It may be that special provisions include waivers or special referrals for cases in which a finding of domestic abuse is made. This might explain the relatively limited coverage within the program per se. However, we do not know what special provisions are actually offered or what presenters say about domestic abuse. Further research is needed to determine whether this concern is being addressed ade-

quately. Providers who presently ignore this concern should consider consulting the domestic violence program in their community for assistance in being appropriately sensitive to needs of domestic violence victims.

Reviewing the common objectives of parent education programs, which ones seem most attainable by families with a history of partner abuse? A more fundamental question is whether, attainable or not, these objectives are actually beneficial to an abused partner and the children in her care. For example, lack of contact with the court by formerly abused spouses may put the abused partner at greater risk. Greater contact with the children by the noncustodial parent, without or even with structural safeguards such as supervised visitation centers, may pose chronic safety risks for the ex partner and her children. Many have begun to call attention to the apparent incongruity between the teachings and assumptions of mainstream parent education programs and the plight of domestic abuse victims, expressing concerns that such programs may be ineffective or even dangerous for victims of domestic abuse. As a result, friction has developed between those involved in parent education and those involved in providing services to abuse victims and their families.

From the point of view of domestic violence service providers, parent education can get it wrong in the following ways: failing to deal with violence as an issue in the lives of program participants and children; failing to deal with the safety issues inherent in the abuser's continued access to the children; failing to steer victims of violence towards appropriate services; failing to appreciate power differentials between parents; augmenting the power of the already powerful abuser by endorsing his demand that his partner recognize his needs—that she be flexible, cooperative, willing to negotiate; and, finally, further undermining the self-esteem of the victim of abuse by setting goals that are, for her, unattainable, and telling her that by not achieving them, she is harming her children. From the point of view of parent education providers, domestic violence advocates can get it wrong in the following ways: throwing the baby out with the bathwater by advocating that victims of domestic violence not participate in parent education, and therefore depriving them of parts of the program that would be applicable and beneficial; undermining the goal of parent education to promote what is best for *children*—leaving parents to rise to the occasion as best they can, using what works for them in their particular situation; assuming that the woman who claims to be a victim of partner violence is always telling the truth, and that she can be relied on to provide an accurate assessment of the children's relationship with their father, or the father's parenting strengths and weaknesses; and, finally, assuming that what is best for the woman will also be best for her children, even when that means that they will have no access to their father. Three different approaches have emerged as parent education programs have sought to accommodate the needs of parents and children who have been exposed to domestic violence. One alternative is to exempt parents who have been abused from participation in otherwise mandatory programs. Another is to channel parents into different programs, and to provide a targeted curriculum for parents who have been abused or abusive. A third is to adapt the mainstream curriculum to provide sufficient recognition of domestic violence, and sufficient guidance for those who have been its victims, that the program meets the objections of its critics, as outlined above.

The Waiver Option

One state's experience with the waiver option has been as follows:

> . . . In Massachusetts, a Standing Order of the Probate and Family Court allows a judge to waive the parent education attendance requirement for victims of "chronic and severe" domestic violence. A small, informal study of a Worcester, Massachusetts program suggests, however, that the waiver provision does not work very well. In a survey of 84 attendees, only 17% were aware that an attendance waiver was possible upon a showing of domestic violence. Furthermore, 14% of the parents surveyed reported chronic, serious violence in their relationships.
>
> Although the concept of waiver seems appropriate, the Massachusetts experience suggests that increased attention needs to be paid to the mechanics of its implementation. First, the availability of the waiver needs to be well publicized. Attorneys, court personnel and parents all needs to be made aware that a waiver is possible. Newspapers directed to members of the bar can publish articles about the waiver provision. Court personnel can be instructed to mention the waiver to parents who are filing divorces *pro se*. The parent education brochures that are provided to divorcing parents should highlight and emphasize the availability of the waiver.
>
> Even if the waiver were well publicized, however, obtaining a waiver requires a degree of sophistication in negotiating the legal process. In addition, victims must have made the decision that it is safe for them to pursue a waiver since it requires the victim to reveal the violence to a third party. Thus, while waivers are an important attribute of parent education programs, and while they offer one kind of protection to victims of violence, they are in no way a full solution.

Geri S. W. Fuhrmann, Joseph McGill and Mary O'Connell, *Parent Education's Second Generation: Integrating Violence Sensitivity,* 37 F.C.C.R. 24, 28–29 (1999).

In addition to the issues raised by the authors, consider the relative difficulty for a woman to make a showing sufficient to receive a waiver, if her partner engages in serious, continuing emotional abuse only periodically punctuated with physical violence. Is the court likely to acknowledge all forms of serious domestic abuse, or only that which is predominantly physical and which can be supported by ready documentation, such as emergency room records or the affidavit component of restraining order complaints?

A Targeted Curriculum

A very recent nationwide survey and in-depth study of five parent education programs points out the "need for parent education programs more specifically targeted to high conflict parents, including those with a significant past history of domestic violence." Nancy Thoennes and Jessica Pearson, Parent Education Programs in Domestic Relations Courts, Center for Policy Research, Denver, Colorado, 45 (September 1998). If both abused and abusive partners attended these sessions (although certainly not as couples), one topic of particular and joint relevance might be parallel parenting techniques, which allow parents to maintain distance from one another while still both having a role in their children's lives. Parent-to-parent contact is minimized through intermediaries and use of phone answering machines and notes or e-mail, while responsibility for the child is assigned to the parent to whose care the child is entrusted for the particular time period. Another important topic of shared concern would be the impact on children of witnessing one parent using violence against another. One difficulty with the idea of bringing abused and abusive partners together for parent education, even if not with their own partners, is that it is easy to imagine a group dynamic in which those who have been victims are silenced, and their questions and concerns overlooked.

If there were a mechanism to sort the group further, and assemble a group composed entirely of victims of abuse, additional topics such as safety planning, hypotheticals addressing conflict and safety, interventions for children (explanations to them concerning the violence, alternative modeling regarding anger management) and structural options for visitation, could be covered. However, the chief difficulty with offering a targeted curriculum is coming up with an appropriate screening mechanism, and the more refined the screening process attempts to be, the more difficulty it poses.

Fuhrmann, McGill and O'Connell describe the problem as follows:

> The advantage of a targeted approach is that messages and goals can be tailored to the particular population. The greatest problem is finding a satisfactory method of screening parents and assigning them to appropriate groups. There is no screening instrument with adequate validity and reliability to accomplish this task. Thus, there are no scientifically derived criteria for dividing the groups. Much will depend, then, on who is assigning the parents to the regular or to the specialized group.
>
> One possibility is for the court to determine which group a parent must attend. In Los Angeles and Alameda Counties in California, the courts identify high conflict parents based on a long record of court involvement. These seem to be highly successful programs, but their method precludes identification of violent or high conflict parents at an early stage of the divorce process.
>
> An alternative possibility is to assign parents to a specialized group whenever a restraining order has been issued against one parent. However, this amounts to using restraining orders in a way

never envisioned by the legislators authorizing them. Indeed, judges may become more reluctant to issue no contact orders if new implications arise from that action.

A different approach is to have parent educators assign parents to the appropriate groups. Divorce Transitions, Inc., of Fort Collins, Colorado tried this method. They found that telephone interviews intended to place parents in their proper groups regularly required an hour or more for a single screening. The method was ultimately abandoned.

Even if better screening tools and methods were developed, there is a fundamental role conflict when parent educators take on the task of evaluating those they teach. Parent educators need to remain nonjudgmental and child focused to engage the often angry class participants.

A final alternative, self-identification, may be the simplest. However, we know that victims of violence often avoid disclosing their situations for fear of retribution. Perpetrators probably also fail to identify themselves and will therefore end up in the wrong group, where they will hear an emphasis on co-operative parenting that is inappropriate to their situation.

An additional problem with targeted groups is their impact on the content of the regular program. Their existence gives the educators in the regular or non-violent group a false sense of assurance that they are teaching parents who are safe in each other's presence and who are able to co-operate in parenting their children. In fact, however, it is almost certain that both victims and perpetrators will attend the regular group despite the availability of a targeted group. In short, while targeted groups sound promising, careful consideration suggests that screening and placement issues may derail the process.

Id. at 30. Some states, such as Massachusetts, require that parents attend different parent education sessions. Would this feature remedy some of the problems identified above?

An Integrated Curriculum

If, in light of the limitations of the waiver and targeted curriculum approaches, a provider offers an integrated program—recognizing that a subpopulation of victims and perpetrators will be present—what safety, relevancy, and effectiveness issues arise? Andrew Schepard describes how New York's P.E.A.C.E. parent education program adopted features in response to the reality of domestic abuse. These include discouraging courts from referring parents with a known history of domestic violence, foregoing the requirement that parents attend together, being sure that parents are not placed in the same small discussion groups as their ex partners, providing security at program sessions in the form of court officers, and providing printed referral material to community resources that aid family members affected by domestic abuse. The program also gives the following "warnings":

All P.E.A.C.E.'s curriculum materials (the Manual, the Video, and the Parents' Handbook) contain explicit statements that:

— domestic violence may render the Program's emphasis on cooperative parenting inappropriate;

— physical safety of parent and child is the highest value;

— divorce may be an appropriate response to a violent marital relationship and may, in those circumstances, promote the well-being of a child who witnesses violence or conflict; and

— a parent who believes he or she or a child is a victim of violence should discuss the situation with counsel and bring it to the attention of the court.

Andrew Schepard, Stephen W. Schlissel, *Planning for P.E.A.C.E.: The Development of Court–Connected Educational Programs for Divorcing and Separating Families*, 23 HOFSTRA L.REV. 845, 862–863 (1995).

While the P.E.A.C.E. program in New York generally requires divorcing parents to attend the same session, foregoing that requirement only when there has been domestic violence, Massachusetts has chosen instead to assign couples to different sessions as a general rule. Fuhrmann and her co-authors, however, identify a safety problem that has arisen even in this context: "In one Massachusetts parent education program, a man calling to register was told by a receptionist that he could not attend the session he requested due to the provision prohibiting divorcing spouses from attending the same session. He was then assigned to a different session. The man's wife's car was vandalized while she was attending the session from which he had been excluded." Fuhrmann et al., supra, at 29. Security posted inside buildings can do little for abuse victims once they are outside or back home, if the act of attendance itself places them in danger.

Schepard's program takes the approach of warning victims away from irrelevant and/or potentially dangerous classroom advice. But does information about children's needs make the content of a parent education class relevant *enough* for the victims of violence in the room? Could it be made more relevant by explicitly addressing safety needs as well? The authors below are the developers of the curriculum for the Massachusetts-based "Parents Apart," program, which has been revised to acknowledge victims of abuse as program participants. How well do you feel the revised program balances the need to appeal to the entire spectrum of divorcing parents, and the need to address the particular concerns of abused partners?

Geri S. W. Fuhrmann, Joseph McGill and Mary O'Connell, Parent Education's Second Generation: Integrating Violence Sensitivity, 37 Family and Conciliation Courts Review 24, 31–32 (1999)

If we assume that victims and perpetrators of abuse and parents involved in high conflict divorces are present in the groups we teach, then our task is to offer programs that are sensitive to the issue of domestic violence but are designed for heterogeneous groups. The goal is not to eradicate domestic violence; it is far more modest. The goal is to identify and change messages that would be harmful if adopted by perpetrators and victims of domestic violence.

Example 1

Original Statement: "How well adults are able to co-operate as parents is one of the major variables in how well children adjust to divorce."

Modified Statement: "How well parents are able to cooperate as parents is a major variable affecting children's adjustment to divorce. However, in families where domestic violence has occurred, co-operation is not a goal since it could place a parent at risk. The goal for these parents should be parallel or detached parenting."

Analysis: Implied in the original statement is the message that parents who are unable to co-operate may be inadvertently harming their children. However, domestic violence in families produces an uneven playing field between the spouses, making co-operation impossible. The partner being abused should not be made to feel responsible for this situation.

Example 2

Original Statement: "It is essential that divorced parents make efforts to rebuild trust between themselves."

Modified Statement: "Parents who have a business-like relationship that is focused on the business of raising children generally fare well. For families where there has been violence, however, the business-like relationship may be best conducted through a third party such as a parent coordinator."

Analysis: The original statement here is a particularly troublesome one, of a type common to many first generation parent education programs. Rebuilding trust in one's ex-spouse is not essential to effective post divorce parenting.

Example 3

Original Statement: "Parents who allow their children to be loved and nurtured by both parents generally adapt best." **or** "Children may need encouragement and support to maintain contact with each parent."

Modified Statement: "Parents should allow children to be loved and nurtured by both parents if it is safe."

Analysis: Like many statements made by parent educators, the original statement here is accurate unless it is seen through the eyes of a victim of violence. In the original statement, children's safety is not mentioned. Parents hearing the statement are put in a double bind. If they adhere to the message they nay be compromising their child's safety. But if they do not, they are being told they are jeopardizing their child's development.

... In addition to amending or deleting statements currently in parent education materials, educators should be alert to opportunities to add statements that may be helpful to parents involved in a violent relationship. For example, many programs present the stages of loss, grief and healing following divorce. Omitted from this list of affect responses is fear. Yet, children from violent families have learned from direct experience that efforts by their parents to end a relationship have sometimes resulted in abuse. Children whose parents have recently separated may be very fearful about one parent's safety. This can be recognized and addressed with the parents by the parent education seminar.

... Parent educators can also make information about domestic violence resources in the local community available to seminar participants, another critical piece in combating domestic violence.

* * *

QUESTIONS

Based on these readings, how would you design a parent education program that addresses the needs of victims of abuse? How would you screen participants, address safety issues, and prioritize the topics of concern for this group? Would you address victims of abuse as part of a "regular" group or try to channel them into a special interest group? What kind of evaluation would you design to measure its effectiveness?

G. RELOCATION

Introductory Note

One way to seek safety from an abusive partner is to move. If the move is distant enough, it may deter further harassment and abuse, even if the batterer still knows where to find his former partner. For some women, on the other hand, only "disappearing" will end the abuse. In cases like this, women may need to go to extraordinary lengths to conceal their new locations; adopting new names, applying for new social security numbers, changing their appearances, and avoiding any careless contact with former friends or family members who might be pressured into disclosing their whereabouts. Despite the enormous social and economic disruptions involved, despite losing jobs and family and social supports, women make these moves in order to live free of fear.

But when women share young children with their abusers, moving becomes even more difficult, if not impossible, to accomplish. There are different scenarios. Imagine first the situation where a married couple has not formally separated or initiated divorce proceedings, but the violence is escalating, and the woman decides that she must leave. One possibility, if the man is not abusive towards the children, is to leave them with him, at least as a temporary measure. If the woman eventually wants to regain custody of the children, however, she will have to risk the ongoing contact with her abuser that a divorce and custody action requires, and she will have to hope that the jurisdiction in which she brings her action is one in which she will not be penalized for "abandoning" the children when she fled.

If instead she takes the children with her, then she is depriving her partner of his "share" in them, with consequences in both the family law and criminal justice arenas. Under family law, her partner can take his complaint into family court, with a request that because of his partner's abduction of the children he be granted sole custody. If his partner does not respond to the court's summons, which she may not, either because she is unaware of it, or because she is afraid to return, or because she is in a shelter with rules against residents responding to legal proceedings, then he will in all probability be awarded custody in her absence, she will be ordered to return the children to him, and she will be vulnerable to contempt charges for failing to do so. The combined effect of the federal Parental Kidnapping Prevention Act and state adoption of the Uniform Child Custody Jurisdiction Act makes it very unlikely that she will be able to persuade a court in her new location to take jurisdiction of the case. Only by returning with her children and submitting to the jurisdiction of the "home state" court, thereby making herself vulnerable to her abuser once more, can she hope to retain custody. Under the criminal law she is likely to be guilty of child kidnapping, either at the moment when she deprives her partner of his inherent right to access as a natural parent, or at the latest when she violates the court order awarding him custody. She will avoid these criminal charges only if the law in the state from which she flees recognizes flight from domestic violence as a defense against kidnapping charges, and even if such a defense is available to her, she may be subject to arrest and prosecution at the urging of her abuser, and have to establish her defense in the course of criminal proceedings.

If there has already been a formal separation or divorce, and the parents' access to the children has been regulated through custody and visitation orders, the parent who feels that her own or her children's safety is being compromised by those orders has two choices. One is to seek modification of the orders to end the abuser's access to the family through the children, and the other is simply to flee, in disregard of the orders. Modification is not an easy route, given judicial reluctance to deprive a parent of access; it becomes harder if the custodial parent wants to take the children out of the state, and harder yet if the idea is to give the abusive parent no information about the family's new location. Furthermore, the period during which the custodial parent has signaled to her abuser that she is trying to escape his control and is processing her request through the courts, a period which is likely to be protracted, is also likely to be a period of increased danger.

Fleeing, on the other hand, will put the custodial parent in legal jeopardy. She will be in violation of one or more court orders, without even the possibility of arguing that she was unaware of their existence, since they predated her departure. In these circumstances it is not uncommon for courts to transfer custody to the parent left behind, as a way of punishing the leaving parent for flouting the authority of the court, despite that fact that custody determinations are legally governed solely by a "best interests of the child" analysis. And again, the leaving parent will be vulnerable to child kidnapping charges.

This section explores many of these topics, highlighting the perils involved both in seeking to use the legal process to establish distance from an abuser, and in using the "self-help" remedy of flight in disregard of the legal process. It opens with an excerpt from an article which, in its entirety, provides an excellent introduction to these issues.

Working Within the System

Consider the Case of Deb C.
Janet M. Bowermaster, Relocation Custody Disputes Involving Domestic Violence, 46 Kansas Law Review 433, 433–435 (1998)

Consider the case of Deb C. Her husband beat her and sexually and verbally abused her. In December 1993, when he beat her in front of their four-year-old son, Deb called 911. Two sheriff's officers responded to the call. Her husband violently resisted the officers. He injured one of the officers so severely that the officer was taken to the hospital and was unable to work for three weeks. The authorities removed Deb's husband from the home and arrested him for two counts of battery against police officers, resisting arrest, battery against Deb, and domestic violence without a weapon. Deb filed for divorce ten days later and believed the horrors were behind her.

In March 1994, Deb's husband was convicted of violently resisting his December arrest. The other charges, including the charge of battery against Deb, were dropped. In April 1994, he attacked her at her bank and was arrested again. Frightened at having been attacked in public, Deb asked the court's permission to remove a restraint that prevented her from leaving the state with her son. She wanted to take her family to Florida where her parents and her brother and his wife were living. She had a job offer there starting at $42,000 a year. She had no friends or family in California, no job, and she lived in constant fear for her life. Her eighteen-year-old daughter from a prior marriage was so frightened she neither slept in her own room nor stayed in the house alone. Deb's now ex-husband had informed her daughter that he had peeked in her windows. He also had broken into their home on many occasions.

In November 1994, Deb's ex-husband pled "no contest" to the battery of Deb at the bank. But arrests, restraining orders, and incarceration were no deterrent to his bizarre, violent behavior. He was subsequently arrested for felony stalking, peeping, violation of a court order, annoying telephone calls, trespass, and felony terrorist threats. Deb and her children were chosen to participate in Sacramento County's AWARE program. The program involves an alarm system provided to "high risk" families who are considered to be in clear and present danger for their lives. In November 1995, Deb's ex-husband pled guilty to stalking and was sentenced to jail.

During this time, Deb was unable to work because of her ex-husband's death threats, batteries, and stalking. She could leave her home only when someone was with her. Because of these circumstances, her only means of support was through Aid to Families with Dependent Children (AFDC).

Pursuant to a court order, Deb's son continued to have "supervised" visits with his father. The boy's mental health suffered to the point that, at age five, he entered weekly therapy that lasted for a year and a half. The son's therapist strongly recommended he be allowed to leave the state with his mother.

During the many months that Deb feared for her life, she went to Family Court Services three different times for court-ordered mediation and still was not allowed to remove her son from the state. A psychological evaluation was ordered, which cost $6,000. The psychologist recommended Deb be allowed to take her son to Florida as soon as possible with only minimal visitation by his father. When her husband challenged the evaluation, two more follow-up evaluations were ordered. Deb's evaluation fees now totaled nearly $15,000. Each evaluator recommended Deb be allowed to take her son to Florida.

Because Deb and her ex-husband could not agree on custody, a hearing was set for November 2, 1995. Witnesses were subpoenaed and Deb's parents flew to California from Florida. On the morning of the hearing, Deb was informed that neither a courtroom nor a judge was available, and the next available trial date would be January 12,1996. Meanwhile, Deb was not allowed to move. A representative from the District Attorney's office advised her that if she took her son to Florida without the court's approval, she would be prosecuted for federal kidnapping, and her son would be returned to California and placed in his father's custody. When Deb, her parents, and her other witnesses appeared on January 12, 1996, there was another shortage of judges and courtrooms. The hearing was rescheduled again, this time for April 4, 1996. This hearing went forward as scheduled. A week later, the State of California granted Deb's request to remove her son from the state. On May 22, 1996, after a thirty-day stay, the court allowed Deb and her son to fly to safety in Florida. This finally occurred two-and-a-half years after Deb filed for divorce from her violent husband.

When Deb filed for divorce she was a successful business woman, she now owes her family law attorney $50,000, owes her parents $50,000, and has filed for bankruptcy. Yet, she considers herself fortunate to have made it out alive and with her child.

People confronted with stories like Deb's ask how such things can happen. The pervasiveness of domestic violence and its high social costs are well known. Progress in combating domestic violence has been made in many areas. In the family courts, however, stopping violence is not a priority.

* * *

NOTES

1. It would be hard to disagree with Bowermaster's conclusion that family courts often do not give priority to stopping violence, or even recognizing it. However, in the situation she describes, the criminal justice system also seems to have let Deb C. down, in allowing the initial charges of domestic violence to be dropped. The violent incident reflected in these charges was what prompted Deb C. to file for divorce, and yet when she first asked the family court for permission to leave the state, her former partner had no record of criminal convictions for domestic violence. He attacked her again in April of 1994, but then was permitted to plead "no contest" to that battery after a seven-month period during which he was free to continue his harassment. He was not incarcerated until he had been arrested, in addition, on charges of felony stalking, peeping, violation of a court order, annoying telephone calls, trespass, and felony terrorist threats. It took almost two years after his first arrest on domestic violence charges for him to be incarcerated, despite a continuous history of domestic violence offenses throughout that two year period.

Family courts, which have less direct experience with violence, often look to the criminal courts for guidance, and assume that if the criminal system has failed to convict or incarcerate a batterer, it must be because he does not pose any serious risk to his victim or their children. This assumption is often unwarranted.

2. Bowermaster locates family courts' unwillingness to allow custodial parents to relocate in an older legal tradition which accorded the husband and father the right to choose the family domicile. Conceding that "today's laws no longer give husbands the explicit right to choose their wives' domicile," she argues that "the husband's prerogative to control where his wife and children live is still embedded in the American culture." That persistent cultural assumption also underlies current judicial decisions, she suggests, even though judges talk instead about "the best interests of children after separation or divorce and the importance of keeping both parents involved in their children's lives." Id. at 442–44. See, in addition, Carol S. Bruch & Janet M. Bowermaster, *The Relocation of Children and Custodial Parents: Public Policy, Past and Present,* 30 F.L.Q. 245 (1996). In the following excerpt, Bowermaster demonstrates the inconsistency between the arguments contemporary judges use, and the consequences of their decisions. She also notes, however, that a new trend, offering more protection for the custodial family unit, may be beginning to emerge.

Rationales for Geographic Restrictions on Custodial Parents
Janet Bowermaster, Relocation Custody Disputes Involving Domestic Violence, 46 Kansas Law Review 433, 445–447 (1998)

Some courts have advanced the notion that restricting custodial parents' mobility serves children's best interests by preserving their environmental stability. While changing homes, schools, and neighborhoods is stressful for children, it seems clear that the normal incidents of moving are not at the heart of relocation disputes. Acceptable moveaway distances of 50, 100, or 150 miles specified in statutes, judgments, and separation agreements support the notion that it is not the disruptive effect of moving that is the problem in relocation disputes. Children who move even 50 miles must change homes, schools, churches, doctors, dentists, neighbors, and friends. Distance limitations protect only the ability of noncustodial parents to have convenient access to their children. Similarly, cases in which custodial parents have already resettled with their children in new communities and are ordered back to where the noncustodial parents live also belie the stated concern for the child's environmental stability.

When intact families move with their children, it is assumed that the parents have made the decision to move with the best interests of their children in mind. The only difference when a divorced, custodial parent moves with the children is that the move takes the children away from the noncustodial parent. It is the increased distance between the noncustodial parent and the child that is at the heart of relocation custody disputes.

The most widely-accepted rationale for restricting the movement of custodial parents is that children's interests are best served by ensuring frequent and continuing contact with both parents after divorce. This rationale is unconvincing for several reasons. First, the enormous sacrifices some jurisdictions require from custodial parents to keep children near noncustodial parents for visitation does not comport with the failure of those same jurisdictions to require noncustodial parents to actually exercise their visitation. Second, if the goal of frequent and continuing contact is important enough to restrict the mobility of custodial parents, it should support similar restrictions on noncustodial parents. Yet, noncustodial parents in every jurisdiction are free to relocate at will. Third, geographic restrictions do not achieve frequent and continuing contact with both parents in cases where custodial parents are unable or unwilling to remain. Custodial parents cannot constitutionally be prohibited from moving. Rather, courts try to coerce them into "voluntarily" remaining in the jurisdiction by threatening them with loss of custody if they move. When that coercion fails, changing custody does not preserve the child's frequent and continuing contact with both parents. It simply preserves the child's relationship with the noncustodial parent at the expense of the child's primary relationship with the custodial parent. Cases in which custodial parents lose custody by moving suggest that the real goal of relocation restrictions is not to ensure contact with both parents, but to protect the rights of noncustodial parents.

Why is there so much focus on noncustodial fathers' frequent visitation with and proximity to their children, sometimes in stunning disregard of the consequences to custodial mothers and their children? If the openly articulated rationales do not adequately support geographic restrictions on custodial parents, deeper unspoken influences must be at work. At least one of these influences is the cultural residue of traditional marriage laws in which unquestioned deference to the husband's choice of domicile was the law of the land.

Trend Toward Allowing Relocation

Like many other areas of family law, relocation custody law is in transition. Social science research has shed new light on children's best interests in moveaway cases. Simply put, the research literature has convincingly demonstrated the centrality of the primary caretaking relationship to the child's well-being, while finding no similar support for the visiting relationship. Research findings have failed to substantiate courts' notions that maximizing the noncustodial parent's time with the child is necessary to preserve that parent's influence and the child's welfare. So far as anyone has been able to ascertain, neither the quality of the noncustodial parent's relationship with the child nor the child's emotional well-being are influenced by the duration or frequency of visits. The opposite has been shown. Published studies by Dr. Janet Johnston indicate that when high conflict or domestic violence is present between parents, children deteriorate dramatically when subjected to frequent visitation transfers.

Noted sociologists Frank Furstenberg and Andrew Cherlin conducted a comprehensive multi-disciplinary review of large-scale national research to assess post-divorce problems. The essence of their analyses and recommendations is that because children's welfare strongly depends on the financial and emotional well-being of the custodial parent and data does not establish a comparable link between visitation and the child's well-being, support for the custodial family unit takes precedence over maintaining any particular pattern of visitation with the noncustodial parent. This means that in relocation cases in which the primary caretaker's needs conflict with the noncustodial parent's desires for more frequent visitation, the conflict should be decided in a way that supports the custodial parent's life choices, including relocation. Other prominent social science researchers have reported findings that support these conclusions.

The policy implications of this research are beginning to be recognized in the legal arena. Courts are beginning to back away from the untoward solicitude for fathers' rights that has characterized many relocation custody cases in the past. A distinct trend has emerged in recent state supreme court decisions towards more protection for the custodial family unit. While still careful to provide for noncustodial parents access to their children, courts are making it easier for custodial parents to decide where they will live without losing custody of their children.

* * *

NOTES

1. The recent research by Furstenberg and Cherlin to which Bowermaster refers, and which affirms the importance of supporting the custodial family unit, is: Frank F. Furstenberg & Andrew J. Cherlin, DIVIDED FAMILIES: WHAT HAPPENS TO CHILDREN WHEN PARENTS PART (1991).

2. For examples of the trend towards greater respect for the custodial unit, see, for example, Vachon v. Pugliese, 931 P.2d 371 (Alaska 1996); *In re* Marriage of Burgess, 913 P.2d 473 (Cal. 1996); *In re* Marriage of Francis, 919 P.2d 776 (Colo. 1996); Mize v. Mize, 621 So. 2d 417 (Fla. 1993); Lamb v. Wenning, 600 N.E.2d 96 (Ind. 1992); Silbaugh v. Silbaugh, 543 N.W.2d 639 (Minn. 1996); Bell v. Bell, 572 So. 2d 841 (Miss. 1990); *In re* Marriage of Hogstad, 914 P.2d 584 (Mont. 1996); Harder v. Harder, 524 N.W.2d 325 (Neb. 1994); Trent v. Trent 890 P.2d 1309 (Nev. 1995); Holder v. Polanski, 544 A.2d 852 (N.J. 1988); Tropea v. Tropea, 665 N.E.2d 145 (N.Y. 1996); Stout v. Stout 560 N.W.2d 903 (N.D. 1997); Fossum v. Fossum, 545 N.W.2d 828 (S.D. 1996); Fortin v. Fortin, 500 N.W.2d 229 (S.D. 1993); Aaby v. Strange, 924 S.W.2d 623 (Tenn. 1996); Lane v. Schenck, 614 A.2d 786 (Vt. 1992); Bohms v. Bohms, 424 N.W.2d 408 (Wis. 1988); Love v. Love, 851 P.2d 1283 (Wyo. 1993). *But see In re* Marriage of Eckert, 518 N.E.2d 1041 (Ill. 1988); Domingues v. Johnson, 593 A.2d 1133 (Md. 1991).

3. Not all battered women seeking to relocate with their children reap the advantages of this developing trend, however. For a very recent case in which the mother's relocation contributed to her loss of custody, see Gant v. Gant, 923 S.W.2d 527 (Mo. App. W.D. 1996). The appeals court recorded the parties' conflicting accounts of the violence in the two year marriage:

> Wife stated that husband had a violent nature and was emotionally unstable. During the course of the marriage, wife stated that husband had damaged numerous items during fits of rage, including smashing two wrist watches with a baseball bat; smashing a television set with a chair; smashing a boom box radio with a baseball bat; slicing up a baseball cap with a box cutter; smashing an alarm clock; and punching a closet door until it splintered. She testified that sometimes during arguments, husband grabbed her by the arm or "smacked up on her." According to wife, on one occasion, husband had ripped her pajamas when he grabbed her by the arm and in the process his finger poked her in the eye and broke a blood vessel. Wife also claimed that one time husband grabbed her by the face and pushed her over the arm of a couch while she was holding her six-month-old baby. She claimed that husband had often threatened her physically and threatened to kill her ten to twelve times throughout the marriage. She claimed that husband had been physically violent with at least three other men before and during the marriage. Wife claimed that husband raped her a number of times during the marriage. She further claimed that husband had told her approximately fifteen times during their relationship that he wanted to kill himself.
>
> Husband admitted to some of wife's assertions, but disputed much of wife's testimony. Husband admitted that he smashed the watches, radio, television and alarm clock. He admitted that he had gotten into some fights with other men. Husband denied wife's allegation that he threatened to kill her ten to twelve times. He admitted that on one occasion he stated that sometimes she made him want to kill her. He denied that he ever was suicidal or that he told wife he was going to kill himself. He admitted that he sometimes told wife that "he didn't

> want to be here." He stated that he made these statements because it was a way of getting her to pay attention to him. He admitted that he had poked wife in the eye, but said it was an accident. He also admitted holding wife by the jaw and tilting her back on the couch, but he claims that she was not holding their infant at the time. Husband testified that he never hit wife. He denied ever raping wife. He testified that he had changed and admitted that his past behavior was childish.

923 S.W.2d at 528–529.

The trial court concluded that "domestic violence occurred" in the marriage, but nonetheless awarded custody of the two children, who were one and three when the relationship ended, to the father. The custody statute governing the decision explicitly required the court to consider, among other factors, both: "The intention of either parent to relocate his residence outside the state," and "[w]hich parent is more likely to allow the child frequent and meaningful contact with the other parent." § 452.375.2(7) & (8), RSMo (1994). Justifying both the custody award, and the decision to limit the mother's visitation to one week in six and alternating holidays, the trial court noted that "husband was learning to exercise self-control." 923 S.W.2d at 531. The court also found that "the incidents of violence were not recent," although the significance of this finding is unclear, since by this time the parties had been separated and living in different states for two years, and that they "were not directed at the children." Id. The court chose to disbelieve the wife's "assertion that she feared husband because it was inconsistent with her actions," id. at 530, although it is not clear where the court felt the inconsistency lay. The court also concluded that "the husband was better aware of the daily needs of the children," id., based on his testimony, and the testimony of a child care provider, that he was a more attentive parent than the mother. Finally, the court was influenced by the fact that "husband showed more of a willingness to make the children available to wife for visitation than wife would for husband. Wife testified that she had moved to Minnesota. She stated that she did not have a car and that it would be difficult for her to transport the children back and forth for visitation. Wife sought sole custody, whereas husband sought joint custody." Id. The trial court also ruled that if the wife returned to Kansas City, she could have visitation every other weekend. The appeals court upheld the decision, appearing to join the trial court in minimizing the husband's violence, which it labeled only "highly improper," "wrong and childish," noting at the same time that the husband had testified that "he had changed."

For other decisions in which battered women won the right to relocate without losing custody, but only after appeal, see, e.g., Gruber v. Gruber, 583 A.2d 434 (Pa.Super. 1990); DeCamp v. Hein, 541 So.2d 708 (Fla. App. 4 Dist. 1989). In both cases, the trial courts conditioned awards of primary physical custody to the mothers on their remaining in the states in which their abusers resided. The appeals court in *DeCamp* was highly critical of the trial court's decision, concluding that it "placed an unreasonable burden" on the mother "and was, in effect, a punishment." 541 So.2d at 709. The court noted that the mother's move was not "made to defeat [the father's] visitation rights," but to "escape the violence and turmoil of her broken marriage." Id. at 711. It approved the New Jersey relocation test articulated in D'Onofrio v. D'Onofrio, 144 N.J.Super 200, 365 A.2d 27, aff'd 144 N.J.Super 352, 365 A.2d 716 (1976), and particularly the primacy given to "[t]he likelihood of the move improving the general quality of life for both the primary residential spouse and the children." Id. at 711. At the same time, the court reaffirmed the father's right to visitation: "[B]oth parents have been less than cooperative with reference to visitation during the pendency of this dissolution. This recalcitrance must cease forthwith. Generous visitation is a precious right unless one parent or the other has been found unfit." Id.

Leaving Without the Children: Is It Abandonment?

There are many reasons why an abused parent might leave without the children. If the flight is an emergency response to life-threatening violence, there may simply be no time to organize a group departure. Alternatively, the parent who leaves may lack the resources to care for her children, even in the short term. She may not be sure of finding space for her family in a shelter, and may not have the funds for food, housing, or necessary childcare. Then again, she may fear that if she takes the children, she will intensify her batterer's determination to track her down, and put herself and her children at greater risk.

Recognizing the danger that parents who leave their children behind when they flee will be accused of having abandoned them, and may be disadvantaged in any subsequent custody dispute, the National Council of Juvenile and Family Court Judges provides, in its Model Code on Domestic and Family Violence, that:

> If a parent is absent or relocates because of an act of domestic or family violence by the other parent, the absence or relocation is not a factor that weighs against the parent in determining custody or visitation.

MODEL CODE ON DOMESTIC AND FAMILY VIOLENCE, SEC. 402 (3) (1994). Several states have followed the Model Code, and enacted similar provisions. See, for example, COLO. REV. STAT. ANN. SEC. 14–10–124 (West 1994); KY. REV. STAT. ANN. SEC. 403.270 (Michie 1994); ME. REV. STAT. ANN. Tit. 15, Secs. 214, 581, 752 (West 1994).

Leaving With the Children—and Without the Court's Permission: Civil Consequences

When battered women leave with their children, they may do so either before any formal court proceedings, or in contravention of existing court orders regarding custody and visitation. However, even where no family law proceeding has been initiated prior to the flight, it is common for the abusive partner to seek an immediate judicial intervention, and to win a default custody judgment when the abused partner does not appear to defend the action. That judgment then becomes the basis for bringing the wife and children back to the "home state" for further proceedings in family court. In this context, courts take very seriously the abused partner's apparent disregard for the authority of the court, and are frequently tempted to "punish" this disregard by awarding custody to the abusive parent, even when the governing statute is clear that this is an inappropriate basis for an award. Courts of appeal quite routinely overturn these decisions, determining that they represent abuses of judicial discretion. The appeal court's opinion in Odom v. Odom, 606 So. 2d 862 (1992), illustrates this pattern.

Mr. and Mrs. Odom were married for a year between 1981 and 1982, and then remarried in 1987. They had two children, Gary, born in 1988 and Miranda, born in 1989. On April 4, 1990 Mrs. Odom left their home, with the two children, and entered a shelter. Witnesses who saw Mrs. Odom at that time observed that she had a black eye, and was bruised and battered. Eight month old Miranda also had a bruise on her head. Mrs. Odom told social workers at the shelter that Mr. Odom had struck the child while trying to hit her.

Mr. Odom immediately filed a petition for separation, and sought custody of the children. Mrs. Odom answered, alleging physical and mental abuse. She also sought a legal separation, custody of the children and child support. In May she was awarded temporary custody of the children, and the parties were ordered to attempt mediation. The mediator later told the court that the mediation was sabotaged by Mr. Odom's negative attitude.

In August Mr. Odom accused Mrs. Odom of abusing their son, and was responsible for the children being taken away from her and put in foster care while the allegations were investigated. However, neither a physician who examined the children nor the Department of Social Services found any evidence of abuse. At the end of August Mrs. Odom fled Louisiana with the children, a course of action she later explained as prompted by reliable information that Mr. Odom was planning to kidnap the children.

In October Mr. Odom filed another motion to have the children placed in foster care. A curator ad hoc was appointed by the trial court to represent Mrs. Odom, whose whereabouts were unknown. The case went forward as an uncontested proceeding, and sole custody of the children was granted to Mr. Odom. By December, Mr. Odom had found his former wife and the children living in a shelter in Missouri, and filed a petition to hold her in contempt of court for her failure to return the children. In January of 1991 Mrs. Odom filed her own petition to change custody, alleging several specific instances of physical abuse by Mr. Odom, including an incident in June of 1990 when he had attacked her while she was holding the baby Miranda. In June of 1991 Mr. Odom obtained physical custody of the children, and just one month later Mrs. Odom filed a rule for contempt, on the basis that Mr. Odom had refused to let her see the children since he had taken custody of them.

Mrs. Odom's petition for change of custody was heard in August. The parties stipulated, and the court agreed, that joint custody was not in the best interests of the children. Mrs. Odom called witnesses who testified to Mr. Odom's abuse. Mr. Odom called his mother and his pastor as witnesses. Home studies were conducted. The trial court found that neither party was psychologically unfit to have custody. The psychiatrist who had examined them gave as his opinion that the parents' problems were "intertwined with" the court proceedings. The court concluded that the hostility between the parents was so intense that an award of sole custody to either one would effectively terminate the other's parental rights, but then affirmed the previous award of sole custody to the father, granting "reasonable visitation" to the mother.

After determining that the applicable legal standard was the best interests of the children, the appeals court reviewed the testimony offered by both parties, and reversed the trial court's decision to grant sole custody to Mr. Odom. The court particularly disagreed with the lower court's conclusion that the home studies conducted would support an award of custody to either parent:

> Mrs. Odom's home study was very complimentary. The social worker found her to be cooperative and open. Due to Mr. Odom's allegations of child abuse, the agency had had prior dealings with Mrs. Odom and had always found her to be cooperative. Furthermore, investigation had found these allegations against her to be untrue. Although upset by her separation from her children, Mrs. Odom understood the need to work out custody through the court system. The social worker compiling the report found that she could make an "excellent home" for her children, was totally dedicated to her children, and had shown great strength in dealing with a stressful situation.
>
> However, we are at a loss to understand how the trial court could characterize Mr. Odom's home study as being favorable. Although the social worker stated that she did not doubt "Mr. Odom's sincere desire to be a good father and a good person" she evaluated him as being "a controlling person" who becomes "disturbed" by his inability to control the people in his life. The social worker further believed that he had "the potential for violence, but this would most likely be limited to domestic violence, as his position in the community seems important to him." When initially contacted for the home study, Mr. Odom was extremely belligerent. The social worker described him as "a very angry person with a quality of hysteria" whose accusations against the social worker had "a ring of paranoia."
>
> Furthermore, the social worker stated that if Mr. Odom were to be awarded custody of the children, she thought it unlikely "even under the best of circumstances" that he would allow them to have "any positive feelings or attachments" to Mrs. Odom because of his intense anger towards her.
>
> In order to aid the trial court, the social worker also included information gathered in April, 1990, when Mr. Odom made allegations of child abuse against his wife. An interview with a DeSoto Parish deputy sheriff familiar with the Odoms revealed a history of wife abuse in the family, and, due to the unpredictability of Mr. Odom's behavior, the deputy advised the social worker not to interview Mr. Odom alone at his residence. The social worker was unfavorably impressed by both Mr. Odom and his mother. Although they made exaggerated efforts to

> convince the social worker that Mrs. Odom was an extremely abusive parent, neither could give a satisfactory explanation of why they had not reported her alleged abuse or even sought medical aid for the children until after she left Mr. Odom. The social worker's impression was that Mr. Odom had not been "totally honest" about his role in the alleged abuse or neglect, that he was possibly hiding something, and that "his apparent immediate concern" for the children's safety was questionable.

The appeals court was also influenced by the certainty that Mr. Odom would not allow the children to have "*any* sort of relationship" with their mother, while Mrs. Odom was willing "to allow the children to develop a relationship with their father, a courtesy he obviously would not extend to her." In this context, the court felt that Mrs. Odom's flight with the children, which it accepted had been prompted by her "great fear" of Mr. Odom, should not preclude her from receiving custody. "While we cannot condone this flight, or completely ignore it," the court concluded, "we can understand it in the context of this case. Furthermore, our purpose here is to determine what is best for these children, not to use custody as a means by which to punish a parent for past misconduct." However, by granting custody to Mrs. Odom subject to the reasonable visitation of Mr. Odom, the court seems to have ignored its own further conclusion that "Mr. Odom is a manipulative and vindictive person who will not hesitate to use his children to punish his former wife," leaving the reader wondering what the outcome of the case might have been if Mrs. Odom, using those very same arguments, had opposed visitation by the father.

NOTES

1. For another recent example of an appeals court overturning a trial court custody decision on the basis that the court had inappropriately punished the wife for leaving the state and failing to return, see Marshall v. Marshall, 117 Ohio App.3d 182, 690 N.E.2d 68 (1997).

2. In Desmond v. Desmond, 134 Misc.2d 62, 509 N.Y.S.2d 979 (1986) a family court judge in New York State awarded custody to a mother who had fled the state with her children, but his opinion is a study in judicial ambivalence. While concluding that "respondent was completely justified in escaping from the marital home, with the children, to protect their respective safety and best interests," 509 N.Y.S.2d at 982, the judge elsewhere describes the same escape as "hysterical." Id. at 981. On the one hand, the judge acknowledges that the husband "has so severely abused his wife physically, emotionally, and sexually that there is little hope that their relationship can, for the forseeable future, be an umbrella of security necessary for these children's emotional peace." Id. at 982. He recognizes that "[i]n some instances the physical and emotional abuse was recklessly carried out in the presence of or with the knowledge of the children." Id., n.3. He is ready to conclude that she "had more than reasonable cause to be frightened by any prospect of her taking up residence locally after the proven history of petitioner's abuse." Id. at 982. On the other hand, he is

apparently not persuaded that she is justified in having, "secreted" the children "from their father for almost two months," id. at 981. Nor does the abuse she has suffered, and her residual fear, justify her failure "to promote the needed harmony with petitioner. For example, since August 1985 she has not sufficiently communicated with the father concerning the children's performance in school, their activities, and their health care. She failed to react appropriately against petitioner's illegal drug use in the marital home. Finally, there is insufficient evidence that respondent has actively encouraged the children to call, write, or visit their father since she left. . . . " Id. at 982.

The judge's ambivalence is also reflected in the demanding standard he ultimately articulates and applies:

> [T]his holding . . . is . . . intended to signal the acceptance by this court of the view that severely and/or repeatedly abused parents ought not to be penalized, in the context of a custody-visitation case, for seeking refuge out of the easy reach of their oppressors. On the other hand, this decision must, under no circumstances, be construed as giving a general license to parents to flee the jurisdiction with their children simply because there is some history of marital abuse. Thus, in order for such an escape to be precluded from reflecting adversely on the position of the parent who leaves the area, the level and quantum of abuse must be carefully considered together with all of the other relevant circumstances which surround the family. Such factors may, *inter alia,* include the availability of family services locally, the nearby residence of close family members of the abused parent, the severity of the abuse and the length of time it has been ongoing, the age of the children and the quality of their relationship with each parent, the presence of the children during episodes of spousal abuse and their knowledge of such misconduct, the commission of abusive acts toward any of the children, the utterance of any credible threats by the abusive spouse, the economic position of each parent, and any other factors which would significantly bear upon the children's welfare.

Id. at 982–83.

3. Compare with this standard the approach taken by the Model Code on Domestic and Family Violence, (1994) which provides that relocation because of an act of domestic or family violence will not be a factor that weighs against the parent in determining custody or visitation (§ 402 (3)), and further creates a rebuttable presumption that "it is in the best interest of the child to reside with the parent who is not a perpetrator of domestic or family violence *in the location of that parent's choice, within or outside the state*" (emphasis supplied). Id. § 403. The adoption of the Model Code approach at the state level would do much to enable abused parents to relocate without fearing that they will lose custody of their children.

However, as Janet Bowermaster points out, even protective provisions like these will not prevent abusive parents from using "the right to contest proposed relocations as a tool for continued abuse." J. Bowermaster, *Relocation Custody Disputes Involving Domestic Violence*, 46 KANSAS L. REV. 433, 460 (1998). Bowermaster advocates addressing directly the problems associated with protracted relocation litigation, and recommends for general adoption the approach used by Minnesota in moveaway cases:

> Custodial parents in Minnesota are presumptively entitled to remove their children to another state unless the party opposing removal establishes, by a preponderance of the evidence, that the move is not in the best interests of the children or is sought for the purpose of interfering with visitation. Central to this reasoning is that the custodial parent and the children are a new family unit. What is best for the children is considered in the context of what is best for this new family.... The courts thus take the view that the custodial parent's decision about where the family unit will live should be second-guessed only where it would present a "clear danger to the child's well-being."
>
> The unique aspect of the Minnesota formulation is that permission for relocation with the children may be granted without an evidentiary hearing unless the parent resisting the move makes a prima facie case against removal. Establishing that prima facie case requires more than a showing of the natural adjustments and difficulties of moving to a new community and away from one parent. It takes a showing of some unique detriment to the child involved in the move....
>
> ... Under the Minnesota approach, so long as reasonable alternative visitation can be arranged, the presumption favoring relocation requires that custodial parents be free to go where their best interests lie. Removal of the children from the jurisdiction may not be denied simply because the move may require an adjustment in the existing pattern of visitation.
>
> Permission to relocate without hearings would spare custodial parents the time, expense, and emotional trauma of defending custody challenges. This would leave them free to focus their time, energy and finances on smoothing the transition for their children to the new location. Eliminating hearings would also prevent abusive parents from being able to continue their tactics of coercion, intimidation and control through the legal system.

Id. at 461–62. See also Silbaugh v. Silbaugh, 543 N.W.2d 639 (Minn. 1996); Geiger v. Geiger, 470 N.W.2d 704, 709 (Minn. Ct. App. 1991); Auge v. Auge, 334 N.W.2d 393 (Minn. 1983).

Leaving With the Children—and Without the Court's Permission: Child Kidnapping

As the following Nevada statute illustrates, to remove a child from a parent who has custodial or visitation rights constitutes the crime of child kidnapping, even if the rights interfered with are limited in nature, and even if the "removal" is effected by someone—most commonly the other parent—who also has custodial rights to the child. These state statutes create real peril for the parent who flees abuse at the hands of a current or former partner and, by taking the children with her, prevents her partner from exercising his custodial or visitation rights. As state legislatures have become more responsive to domestic violence, many child kidnapping statutes have been revised to protect adult and child victims.

NEVADA REVISED STATUTES
TITLE 15. CRIMES AND PUNISHMENTS
CHAPTER 200. CRIMES AGAINST THE PERSON: KIDNAPING

200.359 . . .

1. A person having a limited right of custody to a child by operation of law or pursuant to an order, judgment or decree of any court, including a judgment or decree which grants another person rights to custody or visitation of the child, or any parent having no right of custody to the child, who:

(a) In violation of an order, judgment or decree of any court wilfully detains, conceals or removes the child from a parent, guardian or other person having lawful custody or a right of visitation of the child; or

(b) In the case of an order, judgment or decree of any court that does not specify when the right to physical custody or visitation is to be exercised, removes the child from the jurisdiction of the court without the consent of either the court or all persons who have the right to custody or visitation,

is guilty of a category D felony. . . .

2. A parent who has joint legal custody of a child . . . shall not willfully conceal or remove the child from the custody of the other parent with the specific intent to deprive the other parent of the parent and child relationship. A person who violates this subsection shall be punished as provided in subsection 1.

3. If the mother of a child has primary physical custody . . . , the father of the child shall not willfully conceal or remove the child from the physical custody of the mother. If the father of a child has primary physical custody . . . , the mother of the child shall not willfully conceal or remove the child from the physical custody of the father. A person who violates this subsection shall be punished as provided in subsection 1.

. . .

7. A person who aids or abets any other person to violate this section shall be punished as provided in subsection 1.

NOTES

1. The impact of this statute is softened in a number of ways. First, 200.359.4 provides that a court can only issue an arrest warrant for violation of the statute after determining that the rights of the parties could not be effectively enforced, and the best interests of the child could not be served, through a court order issued in a civil proceeding. Second,

the crime can be prosecuted as a misdemeanor rather than a felony, if either: "The defendant has no prior conviction for this offense and the child has suffered no substantial harm as a result ...," or: "The interests of justice require that the defendant be punished as for a misdemeanor." Finally, 200.359.8 specifically provides that:

> This section does not apply to a person who detains, conceals or removes a child to protect the child from the imminent danger of abuse or neglect or to protect himself from imminent physical harm, and reported the detention, concealment or removal to a law enforcement agency or an agency which provides protective services within 24 hours after detaining, concealing or removing the child, or as soon as the circumstances allowed....

The New Jersey statute similarly creates an affirmative defense to a criminal prosecution for interference with custody where

> a parent having the right of custody reasonably believed he was fleeing from imminent physical danger from the other parent, provided that the parent having custody, as soon as reasonably practicable:
>
> (1) Gives notice of the child's location to the police department of the municipality where the child resided, the office of the county prosecutor in the county where the child resided, or the Division of Youth and Family Services in the Department of Human Services, or
>
> (2) Commences an action affecting custody in an appropriate court.

N.J.S.A. 2C:13–4(d).

California requires that the parent seeking to exercise a domestic violence defense to a child abduction charge *both* notify the office of the district attorney of the county where the child resided before the action, *and* commence a custody proceeding in a court of competent jurisdiction, within a reasonable time. Cal.Penal Code § 278.7(c). A reasonable time is "at least 10 days" for the filing of the report, and "at least 30 days" for commencing the custody proceeding. Id. § 278.7(d). The report must include "the name of the person, the current address and telephone number of the child and the person, and the reasons the child was taken, enticed away, kept, withheld, or concealed," and must be updated whenever the address or telephone number of the person or the child change. Id. § 278.7(c). However, the statute also provides explicitly that the address and telephone number will remain confidential "unless released pursuant to state law or by a court order that contains appropriate safeguards to ensure the safety of the person and the child." Id. § 278.7(e).

2. There are two primary difficulties with the approach taken by jurisdictions such as Nevada, New Jersey and California. The first is that the victim of domestic violence who flees and is unaware of her obligation to file a report or commence a custody proceeding, or is too afraid to do so in the immediate aftermath of the violent incident that prompted her flight, will be deprived of a defense to the child kidnapping charge brought against her. Washington State broadens the class of legitimating acts to include "[seeking] the assistance of the police, sheriff's office, protective agencies, or the court of any state before committing the acts giving rise to the

charges or within a reasonable time thereafter...." REV. CODE WASH. § 9A.40.080(2)(a) (2000). Other jurisdictions do not impose notice requirements, but simply create an unconditional affirmative defense in situations where the "kidnapping" parent is fleeing domestic violence. Pennsylvania, for example, provides that:

> A person who removes a child from the child's known place of residence with the intent to conceal the child's whereabouts from the child's parent or guardian, unless concealment is authorized by court order or is a reasonable response to domestic violence or child abuse, commits a felony of the third degree.

18 PA.C.S.A. § 2909(a). This more generous approach strikes a different balance between the interests of victims of domestic violence, and the interests of parents who have been denied both access to their children and an opportunity to protest that deprivation, and the courts whose authority has been sidestepped.

The second difficulty is that states which require fleeing parents to initiate custody proceedings in a court of competent jurisdiction, or an "appropriate" court, are demanding either that the proceeding be initiated in the jurisdiction from which the parent is fleeing, which is difficult enough, or that the proceeding be initiated in the jurisdiction to which the parent flees, which will immediately alert her partner to her new whereabouts.

3. Increasingly state legislation specifically lists flight from domestic violence as the basis for an affirmative defense to child kidnapping charges. In addition to the Nevada statute excerpted above, see, for example, Mo. Ann. Stat. § 565.160 (West Supp. 1996) ("It shall be an absolute defense to the crimes of parental kidnapping and child abduction that (3) The person was fleeing an incident or pattern of domestic violence."), and R.I. Gen. Laws § 11–26–1.1 (1994).

Older legislation often provided an affirmative defense either in situations in which the kidnapping parent was protecting the welfare of the child, or where the defendant acted with good cause. In a significant number of jurisdictions these are still the frameworks within which battered women must justify a "kidnapping" prompted by domestic violence. For examples of the "welfare of the child" framework see Colo. Rev. Stat. § 18–3–304(3) (1986), and Md. Code Ann., Fam. Law § 9–306(a)(1) (1991). For examples of the "good cause" framework see Mont. Code. Ann. § 45–5–633 (1995), and N.M. Stat. Ann. § 30–4–4(B) (1995). As long as children's welfare is understood to include their emotional as well as physical wellbeing, the growing consensus that children who witness abuse suffer emotional injury supports the use of the defense in domestic violence cases, even where the children do not appear to be physically at risk. Similarly, our growing knowledge about the impact on children of witnessing abuse, and about the ways in which abusive parents use children as pawns in their struggles to control their partners, supports the determination that "abductions" prompted by domestic violence are "good cause" abductions.

The Impact of the UCCJA, PKPA and UCCJEA

Criminal prosecution of child kidnappers is strictly a matter for the states, and the preceding section illustrates the significant variety of approaches states have taken in addressing the problem. However, to the extent that abductions have been prompted by the desire of parents to relitigate issues of custody and visitation in a new forum, it has long been recognized that coordination among the states to prevent such relitigation might in turn diminish the appeal of abduction, and that the federal government might also have a legitimate role to play in limiting relitigation by clarifying the application of full faith and credit principles in this arena.

Kate Lee Sullivan Feeney
The Jurisdictional Juggle of Child Custody: An Analysis of the UCCJA, PKPA, UMEA, and Massachusetts Law, 16 Massachusetts Family Law Journal 35, 35–38 (1998)

An estimated 100,000 parents annually attempt to resolve their custody problems by absconding their children. Approximately 360,000 children are kidnapped per year by a parent. Additionally, many parents attempt to obtain a more favorable custody determination in a different forum, where the original court entered an unfavorable order regarding that parent. Federal and state statutes attempt to remedy the problems of parental kidnapping and forum shopping.

In 1968, the National Conference of Commissioners of Uniform State Laws ("NCCUSL") promulgated the Uniform Child Custody Jurisdiction Act ("UCCJA"). By 1981, every state enacted a version of the UCCJA. The drafters intended to create jurisdictional uniformity and prevent parental kidnapping. The UCCJA, however, failed to solve the problems of parental kidnapping and forum shopping, because not all states adopted the UCCJA. Moreover, states enacted modified versions of the UCCJA and minimized its intended uniformity. In 1981, Congress enacted the Parental Kidnapping Prevention Act ("PKPA") to provide further jurisdictional guidelines and alleviate parental abductions. The PKPA attempted to fortify the policies of the UCCJA with full faith and credit principles. Today, the PKPA and the state versions of the UCCJA represent an integral and often conflicting role in custody proceedings.

Neither the UCCJA nor the PKPA contain express provisions regarding interstate enforcement of child custody orders. The National Conference of Commissioners on Uniform State Laws recently promulgated the Uniform Child Custody Jurisdiction and Enforcement Act ("UCCJEA") as a replacement to the UCCJA. The proposed act reconciles UCCJA principles with the PKPA. Additionally, it provides interstate civil enforcement for child custody orders. The UCCJEA supports the position that jurisdictional priority belongs to the home state. The UCCJEA attempts to consolidate the provisions of the UCCJA and the PKPA and eliminate the distinctions between the two acts. The UCCJEA will be offered to the state legislatures as a substitution of the UCCJA. . . .

I. *The Uniform Interstate Child Custody Jurisdiction Act ("UCCJA")*

Today, all state statutes contain a version of the UCCJA. Jurisdiction typically remains with the state that retains the closest connection to the child, thereby providing availability of records and evidence pertaining to the child. The UCCJA allows a court capable of deciding child custody matters to exercise jurisdiction if one or more of the following prerequisites exists:

(1) the state is the home state of the child;

(2) the state has a significant connection with the child and one of the parents;

(3) the child is physically present within the jurisdiction and either has been abandoned or is threatened with child abuse or;

(4) if it appears that no other state has jurisdiction under one of the other three prerequisites, or such other state has declined to exercise jurisdiction, and it is in the best interest of the child that the forum asserts jurisdiction. An interested forum can proceed provided the state maintains a significant connection with the child and no other pending proceedings exist. This occurs even if a home state is present.

The UCCJA recommends communication between forums. A court must decline jurisdiction when a parent wrongfully removes a child from another state. As a rule, the state version of the UCCJA controls custody disputes unless a conflict exists with the PKPA. In circumstances where such a conflict exists, the PKPA provisions will supersede the state statute.

II. *The Parental Kidnapping Prevention Act ("PKPA ")*

By 1979, thirty-nine states adopted a version of the UCCJA, but problems still existed with parental seize and run tactics. In a response to this problem, Congress enacted the Parental Kidnapping Prevention Act. The PKPA requires courts to enforce any custody determination whether temporary or final, provided such orders are, "made consistent with the provisions of [the PKPA] by a court of another state." The PKPA provides five grounds for jurisdiction. Four of these jurisdictional bases parallel the UCCJA. The five jurisdictional bases of the PKPA include:

(1) home state jurisdiction;

(2) significant connection jurisdiction;

(3) emergency jurisdiction;

(4) jurisdiction when no other state would have jurisdiction under the provisions of the PKPA, or when a state with jurisdiction [by] the terms of the PKPA has declined to exercise jurisdiction; and

(5) continuing jurisdiction.

The PKPA incorporates two provisions expressly limiting the authority of state courts to construct initial custody awards. First § 738A(e) requires the parties afford notice and an opportunity to be heard regarding any custody related hearing. Second, § 1738A(g) precludes a state court from exercising jurisdiction during the pendency of custody proceedings in another state. A home state may decline to exercise jurisdiction and defer to another state with more significant connections to a child.

The PKPA affords Full Faith and Credit to custody decisions provided the order complies with the jurisdictional standards of the Act.... Once a state exercises jurisdiction consistently with the PKPA, no other state may exercise jurisdiction over the dispute, unless the original state loses or declines jurisdiction.

The state making an initial custody determination in accordance with the PKPA's standards maintains continuing jurisdiction as long as one of the five standards of jurisdiction exists and the state remains the residence of the child or any contestant. A court of another jurisdiction may modify the custody award provided the state has jurisdiction and the court of the other state no longer has jurisdiction or expressly declines jurisdiction.

III. Conflicts and Differences Between the UCCJA and the PKPA

Several major differences exist between the two statutes. First the PKPA unlike the UCCJA extends the Full Faith and Credit Clause of the United States Constitution to custody decrees.... Second, the PKPA states an explicit preference for home state jurisdiction and protects orders based on significant connections *only if* there is no home state.... [T]he UCCJEA supports the PKPA's position prioritizing home state jurisdiction. It requires deference to the home state.

Third, the PKPA provides a basis for exclusive and continuing jurisdiction in the child's home state, whereas, the UCCJA allows concurrent jurisdiction. Thus, the UCCJA permits the shifting of jurisdiction to another state. The UCCJEA, however, precludes jurisdictional shifting. The original home state retains jurisdiction provided a parent resides in the state.

Fourth, the UCCJA contains an inconvenient forum provision. The UCCJA permits a court to defer jurisdiction to a more convenient forum. The PKPA precludes any state from exercising jurisdiction where another state retains jurisdiction under the act. The PKPA allows the second state to assume jurisdiction only when the original state declines or loses jurisdiction.

Fifth, the UCCJA equalizes temporary emergency jurisdiction with its other jurisdictional grounds. The UCCJEA and the PKPA, however, limit the exercise of emergency jurisdiction. The UCCJEA permits an exercise of emergency jurisdiction for a period sufficient to secure safety of the child and to transfer to the home state or to a state with another jurisdictional basis if no home state exists. The UCCJEA provides for temporary emergency jurisdiction, which can evolve into continuing jurisdiction only if no other state with grounds for continuing jurisdiction exists, or if a state with jurisdiction declines to exercise it. The home state ordinarily remains the state with continuing jurisdiction because of the priority of the home state. The UCCJEA therefore, reinforces the PKPA's emphasis on home state jurisdiction.

... Finally, the PKPA provides parents use of the Federal Parental Locator Service.

The UCCJEA harmonizes the inconsistencies between the UCCJA and the PKPA. Additionally, the UCCJEA provides for a remedial process to enforce interstate child custody and visitation determinations.

IV. Federal Preemption

The majority of states agree that where the state jurisdictional laws conflict with the PKPA, the federal act preempts state law....

Congress enunciated PKPA preemption in its legislative findings. When enacting the PKPA, Congress listed six purposes of the Act. These six purposes include:

> (1) [to] promote cooperation between State courts to the end that a determination of custody and visitation is rendered in the State which can best decide the case in the interest of the child,
>
> (2) promote and expand the exchange of information and other forms of mutual assistance between States which are concerned with the same child,
>
> (3) facilitate the enforcement of custody visitation decrees of sister States;
>
> (4) discourage interstate controversies over child custody in the interest of greater stability of home environment and of secure relationships for the child;
>
> (5) avoid jurisdictional competition and conflict between State courts in matters of child custody and visitation which have in the past resulted in the shifting of children from State to State with harmful effects on their well being; and deter interstate abductions and other unilateral removals of children undertaken to obtain custody and visitation awards.

Congress specifically enacted the PKPA to provide national standards for the resolution of child custody jurisdiction issues.

V. Lack of Federal Courts Enforcement

Thompson v. Thompson

In 1988, the Supreme Court in *Thompson v. Thompson* 484 U.S. 174 (1988), held that the PKPA does not create an implied cause of action in federal court to determine the validity of conflicting custody orders between states. The *Thompson* decision stands for the proposition that the state courts solely determine whether a particular state's exercise of jurisdiction was proper....

VI. Declining Jurisdiction

... The tendency of some courts to refuse to decline jurisdiction even where the state maintains no substantial connection to the child unnecessarily complicates the judicial process.

In every interstate custody dispute, courts must decide two issues. First, whether the state possesses the authority under the PKPA and its own law to entertain the matter. Second, if it has the authority, whether to exercise jurisdiction or defer to a different forum. A court may not entertain custody proceedings until both determinations occur. Three situations arise supporting deference to another forum. First, where a proceeding is pending in another jurisdiction. Second, where the forum is inconvenient. Third, where the best interest of the child mandates dismissal of the proceeding by the forum....

Other factors that provide guidance to the court in determining whether or not to decline jurisdiction include: (1) where another state possesses a more significant connection to the child; (2) where a substantial amount of evidence pertaining to the child is present in another forum; and (3) where declination advances the child's best interests.

* * *

NOTES

1. Joan Zorza adds some helpful history to this account of the UCCJA and PKPA in her GUIDE TO INTERSTATE CUSTODY: A MANUAL FOR DOMESTIC VIOLENCE ADVOCATES (National Center on Women and Family Law, Inc., 1995). She says:

> Before 1968, parents were effectively rewarded for taking a child to another state and getting a custody order there. The same reward existed if a parent wrongfully held the child over after visitation and obtained a custody order in a new state. Courts saw custody orders as never final, and hence always subject to modification. The mere presence of the child in the state, for however short a time, allowed a court to accept jurisdiction of the case and make a new custody order. Of course, most of these new orders followed the wishes of the parent within the state, who was usually the only one in court. A kidnapping parent could pick which court to go to based on which state's laws or which judge would be sympathetic.
>
> A series of U.S. Supreme Court decisions beginning in 1947 refused to correct this situation. The Supreme Court refused to require other states to honor and enforce a state's custody decisions. Furthermore, as divorce became more common, the number of children whose lives were governed by court custody orders increased. Likewise, the number of children who were snatched by another parent (or sometimes a grandparent) increased. The public started realizing how harmful these snatchings were, and that the endless court battles might never be resolved except by further "self-help" snatchings.
>
> The ... UCCJA ... was drafted in 1968 ... to remedy the problem of parental kidnapping, and to partially overturn the Supreme court cases. Each state was invited to adopt the Act or its own version of it, something which each state has done....

> The PKPA was a later effort by the United States Congress to remedy the parental kidnapping problem. It was signed into law in December 1980, and, as federal law, was automatically binding on every state. Although written after some states had passed domestic violence statutes, it was written without any consideration of how domestic violence, custody and parental abductions were related. Despite its name, the *PKPA applies to every interstate child custody case,* not just cases where a parent abducted a child....
>
> The UCCJA was written primarily to protect children from child snatching. Few men got custody in the 1960's, when the UCCJA was written. Men, who were far more likely to have access to money and lawyers, often discovered that they could snatch children and file custody actions in courts which would both be more sympathetic to them and less accessible to the children's mothers. No battered women's shelters yet existed in the United States.... Indeed, we as a nation were not yet sensitive to battering as a problem.... The effort to stop parental abductions largely helped women. The drafters never foresaw that the UCCJA would become a weapon mainly used against women fleeing domestic abuse, child physical abuse and/or child sexual abuse.

Id. at 15–16, 18.

2. The UCCJEA, promulgated by the National Conference of Commissioners on Uniform State Laws in 1997, has to date been adopted in only two states, Alaska and Oklahoma, but is under consideration in many others. The text of the statute, together with extensive commentary by the reporter for the Drafting committee, Professor Robert G. Spector of the University of Oklahoma Law Center, is reprinted in 32 F.L.Q. 303 (1998). SEE ALSO, *THE ABC'S OF THE UCCJEA: INTERSTATE CHILD-CUSTODY PRACTICE UNDER THE NEW ACT,* 32 F.L.Q. 267 (1998).

Unfortunately, the potential for this new legislation to improve the situation of women fleeing abuse was limited by the requirement that its provisions be consistent with the PKPA, which would preempt any inconsistent terms. Nonetheless, the Drafting Committee paid close attention to the concerns of several organizations representing the interests of domestic violence victims, and made significant changes between the first and final drafts. The flavor of the debate is captured in the following excerpt.

Report Regarding the NCCUSL Drafting Committee for the Uniform Child Custody Jurisdiction and Enforcement Act (UCCJEA): Results of the Final Drafting Committee Meeting

by Jeff Atkinson, ABA Advisor to the Drafting Committee, March 21, 1997.

At the February meeting, the Drafting Committee spend more time on issue[s] of domestic violence than any other single issue. Between the November 1996 meeting and the February meeting, I (as the ABA advisor) received more than 40 pages of letters and memoranda regarding domestic violence issues. The two primary organizations that provided suggestions on domestic violence issues during this time period were the ABA's Commission on Domestic Violence and Ayuda, a Legal Aid advocacy group concerned with domestic violence.

Judge Martin Herman of the National Council of Juvenile and Family Court Judges also circulated materials to the Committee. In addition, the ABA's Steering Committee on the Unmet Legal Needs of Children provided input in the fall of 1996 on issues of domestic violence as well as on other issues.

The committee divided the methods of determining jurisdiction over custody cases involving domestic violence into two broad categories: (1) cases in which there was no previous custody determination prior to initiation of a custody determination in connection with a domestic violence proceeding, and (2) cases in which a custody determination already had been made and a petitioner was seeking to modify a custody order on the basis of domestic violence (or other emergency).

The committee agreed . . . that if no custody order had been issued in a case, an emergency order under Section 204 could become permanent if the state that exercised emergency jurisdiction becomes the home state of the child and if the order provides that the order shall become permanent when the state becomes the home state of the child. (A state generally becomes the home state of the child after the child has lived in the state for six months.) Under this approach, a home state from which the child is taken has a right to determine custody, provided a party files a petition for custody within six months of the child's departure. If, however, a party does not file a custody action in the state with a superior jurisdictional basis, the temporary emergency order can become a permanent order. . . .

In emergency cases where there is an existing custody order, the committee decided to apply a different rule. The rule, as reflected in Section 204(c), is that the emergency order may remain in effect for a period of time the court "considers adequate to allow a person seeking an [emergency] order to obtain an order from the State having jurisdiction under Sections 201 through 203" (which generally is a state with continuing jurisdiction). The committee felt that a state which had already entered an order in a case should have, in essence, a right-of-first-refusal to determine if permanent modification of the order is warranted.

The advocacy groups concerned with domestic violence would have preferred to allow a state to which a victim of domestic violence fled to automatically be able to enter a permanent order modifying custody. Some advocacy groups suggested that a state to which a victim of domestic violence fled with a child would immediately become the home state of the child for the purposes of custody determination.

The Drafting Committee declined to follow that recommendation for several reasons. The main reasons were: (1) the committee did not want to erode well-established concepts of home state jurisdiction and continuing jurisdiction and (2) the committee felt the state with continuing jurisdiction or traditional home state jurisdiction often would be the state with better access to the evidence, including evidence of the presence or absence of domestic violence. Committee members noted that this rationale applies both to situations in which a custodial parent goes from one state to another and seeks a new custody order as well as to situations in which a noncustodial parent retains a child after a period of visitation and claims that an "emergency" justifies modification of custody in a state other than the state with continuing jurisdiction.

Although the Drafting Committee was not willing to let a victim of domestic violence automatically obtain jurisdiction in the state of the victim's choice for the purpose of permanently modifying custody, the Drafting Committee agreed to make more explicit the provisions of the act which allow domestic violence to be a basis for one state to yield jurisdiction to another state in order to protect the parties or the child. Section 207(b) now provides that a court may decline to exercise jurisdiction on the basis of inconvenient forum after consideration of a variety of factors including: "(1) whether domestic violence has occurred and is likely to continue in the future and which State could best protect the parties and the child."

* * *

NOTES

1. Other respects in which the legislation responds to the needs of victims of domestic violence and their children include the following:

a) The definition of a "child custody proceeding" (Section 102(4)), the initiation of which will preclude another state from making a custody determination, includes proceedings for "protection from domestic violence, in which the issue may appear."

b) Temporary emergency jurisdiction is authorized under Section 204(a) not only when necessary to protect a child from direct mistreatment or abuse, but also in situations where "a sibling or parent of the child is subjected to or threatened with mistreatment or abuse."

c) Section 208 provides that the court "shall decline to exercise its jurisdiction" where the person seeking to invoke the jurisdiction has engaged in unjustifiable conduct. The commentary to this section makes explicit that: "[d]omestic violence victims should not be charged with unjustifiable conduct for conduct that occurred in the process of fleeing domestic violence, even if their conduct is technically illegal. Thus, if a parent flees with a child to escape domestic violence and in the process violates a joint custody decree, the case should not be automatically dismissed under this section. An inquiry must be made into whether the flight was justified under the circumstances of the case."

d) Section 209(a), which details information to be submitted to the court, makes the disclosure requirements "[s]ubject to local law providing for the confidentiality of procedures, addresses, and other identifying information." The comments make explicit that this provision was drafted to incorporate protections found in state domestic violence legislation, and designed to prevent abusers from tracking down their victims. Where no such protective legislation exists, Section 209(e) provides a different route for information to be sealed, on the basis of "an affidavit or a pleading under oath" alleging that disclosure would jeopardize the health, safety or liberty of a party or child. The information can then be disclosed only after a hearing in which the court decides that disclosure is in the interest of justice, even after taking into consideration the concerns alleged.

2. Prior to the UCCJEA, Joan Zorza addressed the issue of how a battered woman can prevent disclosure of her and/or her children's whereabouts, while still complying with the UCCJA's Section 9 disclosure requirements. Section 9, like the UCCJEA's Section 209, requires disclosure under oath of "the child's present address or whereabouts, the places where the child has lived during the last five years, and the names and present addresses of the persons with whom the child has lived during that period." Unlike UCCJEA Section 209, Section 9 provides no internal mechanism for securing the confidentiality of that information. Her advice remains relevant in states which have not as yet adopted the UCCJEA:

> Some states allow battered spouses to keep confidential their present address and the addresses of any shelter. Other states allow addresses to be disclosed to the court only, in order to protect an abused person's whereabouts. Where there is no statutory or court rule protecting this information, the woman should consider requesting one of the following procedures:
>
> (a) Ask the court to permit the filing of the Section 9 affidavit without names and current addresses, but with an affidavit attached stating (1) the length of time that the child has lived in each state; (2) what the history of violence has been; and (3) that disclosure would endanger the safety of the child and/or a party and/or others, so it would not be in the child's best interest;
>
> (b) Based on the violence, seek an *ex parte* order to either (1) waive disclosure, or (2) waive the filing of the affidavit;
>
> (c) Seek an *ex parte* order based on the violence to make the court seal, impound or sequester the affidavit so that it is not available to the public or to any party but only to the judge, or
>
> (d) Move that the Section 9 requirement be satisfied through an *in camera* proceeding outside of the presence of any opposing party and counsel.

Joan Zorza, GUIDE TO INTERSTATE CUSTODY: A MANUAL FOR DOMESTIC VIOLENCE ADVOCATES, 37 (National Center on Women and Family Law, Inc., 1995).

3. Unfortunately, securing the confidentiality of present and recent addresses goes only part of the way towards protecting the battered woman who has moved out of state, and is seeking to conceal her whereabouts, and the whereabouts of her children, from her abuser. The inevitable requirement, whether the governing legislation is the UCCJA, the PKPA or the UCCJEA, that she provide notice of any proceedings she files in itself gives

her abuser valuable information about her location. It immediately lets him know which state, and probably which county or district within the state, his partner has moved to, even if she is successful in keeping her actual address confidential. This may be an argument for her to litigate in the state from which she has fled, despite the obvious inconvenience and possible risks.

4. A different issue arises for the woman who is leaving one state for another, and fears that her abuser may then initiate legal proceedings of which she will not receive notice, with the result that he obtains a default judgment. Section 5 of the UCCJA, like Section 108 of the UCCJEA, governs notice, and both recognize that publication, in lieu of actual notice, may be the only option when a party's whereabouts are concealed, even though there is no guarantee that it will reach its intended recipient. Some states, in the context of providing a domestic violence affirmative defense to criminal child kidnapping charges, require fleeing victims to notify public officials; sometimes the police, sometimes the district attorney, sometimes the family court and sometimes child protective services (see pp. 482–84, above). If the clerk of the family court routinely received notice of battered partners fleeing the jurisdiction with children, and if there was a mechanism by which those partners could then supply the court with a current address or other means of reaching them, then the clerk's office could make sure they received notice of subsequent proceedings. Provision of this information to the clerk's office could then also be offered as a substitute for the more public provision of information called for by Section 9 of the UCCJA or Section 209 of the UCCJEA. Safeguards would have to be instituted to ensure that information was not carelessly, or deliberately, improperly disclosed—a problem that has plagued courts in those states which have instituted confidentiality mechanisms, only to have them undermined at the level of practice.

5. The case of Schuyler v. Ashcraft, 293 N.J.Super. 261, 680 A.2d 765 (1996), provides a dramatic example of an abusive partner seeking to manipulate the court systems of two states in his quest to maintain control over his former partner and their children. It illustrates the important role notice requirements can play. It also unfortunately illustrates the limits of the protection provided by the UCCJA or PKPA.

The parties were divorced in Florida in May of 1990. In August of 1991 the Florida court granted the mother's petition to leave the state. In that 15 month period there had been 83 entries in the family court docket. In granting the mother's petition the court said:

> The wife has presented as best she can a plan to move to California.... She has no lodging, no money and constant oppression. If the mother wants to try for a better life with the two children, the court gives her its blessing. Slavery was abolished 125 years ago and so was oppression. The mother's condition following her divorce has been analogous to that of a slave chained to false accusations, constant allegations and hatred. A human being deserves better. Id., 293 N.J.Super at 279, 680 A.2d at 774.

The 1991 Florida order also specifically refused the father's request that Florida retain jurisdiction over the matter beyond six months, the period which, under relevant state and federal statutes, would allow another state to establish custody jurisdiction. However, that was by no means the end of the story.

Before the six months expired, the father obtained ex parte orders extending Florida's jurisdiction—orders which the mother discovered only months later, never having been notified that they were being sought, or had issued. When she then tried, in 1992, to bring to the Florida court's attention the father's behavior in securing these orders, she was told that the court had "no jurisdiction" to hear her application. In 1993 the mother's counsel sought to establish plenary jurisdiction in New Jersey, by filing the 1991 Florida order with the Clerk of the Superior court of New Jersey, and notifying the Florida court and the plaintiff of the change of jurisdiction. This was not a motion, and requested no action by the Florida court. In the meantime the father had filed a new motion with the Florida court, and on the basis of this activity challenged the shift of jurisdiction to New Jersey in the New Jersey court. He also won an emergency hearing, and an order, from the Florida court denying the mother's "motion" to transfer jurisdiction, even though no such motion had been filed.

When the father then unilaterally asserted the right to take the children to Florida for visitation, the mother feared that they would not be returned, and applied to the New Jersey court for an emergency order limiting visitation to New Jersey. On April 13 New Jersey took emergency jurisdiction over the children, citing their best interests and fear of their disappearance. On April 14 the Florida court transferred custody to the father. In a June hearing in New Jersey the question was raised whether the custody and visitation provisions of the 1991 Florida order should be modified. During this hearing it became clear that the father and his Florida counsel had blatantly violated due process by failing to notify the mother, whom they knew to be unrepresented at that time, about the applications they filed and the orders they obtained from the Florida court in 1991 and 1992. The lawyer was later "admonished" by the Florida Bar for his conduct.

Throughout 1993 there were court proceedings in both states, although the father refused to cooperate with New Jersey. In March of 1994 the New Jersey and Florida judges conferred by telephone, and Florida again relinquished jurisdiction, but the father, proceeding ex parte, then had that order rescinded by a different judge who had been involved in the case in the past but was no longer even sitting in the family court, on the basis of misleading information. At this time the father also threatened, in a telephone conversation overheard by the mother's co-worker, to kill the mother and her lawyer, and to take the children. The mother obtained a restraining order, but was assaulted two blocks from the courthouse by a man who warned her to "drop the charges." The New Jersey court then terminated all the father's contact with the mother and children, and allowed the mother to unlist her telephone number. A guardian ad litem appointed for the children urged that New Jersey maintain jurisdiction over the children's custody.

The father continued to use both court systems in his campaign to regain access to the children. Although the Florida court issued an order in August staying all matters until the jurisdictional issue was resolved by New Jersey's Appellate Division or Supreme Court, the father still found judges willing to issue two orders of bodily attachment for the children. His efforts to have visitation reinstated by the New Jersey court failed.

In February of 1995 the New Jersey court ordered that it had absolute jurisdiction over the children, on the basis of the 1991 Florida order limiting Florida's ongoing jurisdiction to a six month period, and on the basis of the father's subsequent due process violations. In May, in what the New Jersey court then described as "the most bizarre incident in this history," the father successfully initiated extradition proceedings for the mother in Florida, on the basis of a representation that he had sole custody of the children, and that she was unlawfully keeping them out of the state. On July 29, 1995 she was handcuffed and arrested in front of her children. She was released on bail, and then appeared before the New Jersey criminal court, where the judge observed that: "this reads like some of the old Family Court litigation that led to the adoption of the Uniform Child Jurisdiction and Custody Act. Because this kind of thing just really hasn't happened since the 40's and the 50's."

In January of 1996 the Florida court once more ceded jurisdiction to New Jersey, and once more the father successfully sought to rescind that order by applying for a rehearing on the basis of false information, and by failing to notify the mother or her counsel of the proceedings, so that the matter was effectively heard ex parte.

New Jersey's Appellate Division had no difficulty in deciding that the 1991 order relinquishing jurisdiction after six months was the last Florida court order entitled to full faith and credit under the PKPA, because the subsequent orders failed to satisfy due process requirements. Subsequently, New Jersey had properly established jurisdiction under the terms of both the federal PKPA and the state's own version of the UCCJA. The mother's initial action in filing the 1991 Florida order with the New Jersey court merely gave the court the authority to enforce that order. However, the mother's later proceedings in New Jersey were justified under the PKPA, because Florida had ceded jurisdiction by the terms of its 1991 order, and under the state UCCJA, because the children and their mother had a significant connection to the state, and substantial evidence with respect to the children's "present or future care, protection, training, and personal relationships" was available in the state. The appellate court therefore upheld the family court's earlier decision giving sole custody to the mother, denying visitation to the father, and prohibiting any further contact between the father and the mother or the children.

Given the history of the case, it is hard to feel confident that this seemingly "tidy" resolution is in fact the end of the story.

PART THREE

HOLDING BATTERERS ACCOUNTABLE

CHAPTER EIGHT

THE CIVIL PROTECTIVE OR RESTRAINING ORDER SYSTEM

A. INTRODUCTION

For many battered women, going to court for a restraining order (RO), sometimes also called a temporary restraining order (TRO), protective order (PO) or civil protective order (CPO), is the first legal step towards ending the abuse in their relationships or separating from their abusers. As the names imply, these orders are first and foremost about "restraining" the batterer, and "protecting" the partner who is the target of abuse, but today it is a rare order that simply commands an abusive partner not to abuse. Rather, state legislatures have authorized a wide variety of protective provisions, ranging from "stay away" or "no-contact" orders which require the abusive partner to stay away from his victim's home, place of work, or other neighborhood locations, or a fixed distance from her at all times, through temporary custody and support orders designed to regulate the legal consequences of a separation on an interim basis, to miscellaneous but often crucial provisions such as giving up weapons or keys. Some legislation even authorizes the imposition of restitutionary payments for injuries inflicted or property damage done.

The entire body of law governing these protective or restraining orders has grown up since the 1970s. Until then, battered women had to initiate divorce proceedings before requesting an order, and until 1976, only two states had restraining order legislation specifically designed for battered women. However, passage of the Pennsylvania Protection from Abuse Act in 1976 marked a turning point, and by 1980 forty-five states and the District of Columbia had implemented similar legislation. At this point every state in the union offers customized relief to victims of partner abuse. Many states have by now revised their legislation several times to expand and refine the relief offered.

Another turning point came in 1994 with the passage of the Violence Against Women Act, which contains two provisions designed to strengthen the protections offered by state protective orders. The first provides that states must offer full faith and credit to protection orders issued in foreign states or tribal courts, as long as due process requirements are met at the time the order issues. The second makes the crossing of state lines to violate a protective order, or interstate violation of a protective order (as where a batterer kidnaps his partner and transports her across state lines in violation of an order), a federal crime, with penalties substantially more severe than those that would attach under state law.

The sections which follow cover numerous aspects of the civil protective order process. They look at the question of who is entitled to relief, at the range of relief offered, at issues of process and at the mechanics of enforcement. They explore the "federalization" of protective orders through the Violence Against Women Act. They address the constitutional challenges that have been raised, and largely answered, with respect to both state and federal legislation.

Since every state now offers victims of partner abuse orders of protection, since the federal government has thrown its weight behind this mechanism, and since judges around the country have largely endorsed its constitutionality, it is tempting to interpret this thirty year history as a success story. However, the story would not be complete without at least two cautionary footnotes.

First, there is as yet very little statistical evidence that restraining orders are an effective mechanism for curbing partner violence, and the data we have do not even allow us to predict with confidence when they will work, when they are likely to be ineffective, or when they may actually put their holders at greater risk. Those who work with battered women have individual success stories to share, but all of us who read the papers also know the stories of women who have died at the hands of their abusers despite, and sometimes apparently because of the restraining orders they secured. The final section of the chapter explores the limited body of social science research about the effect of restraining orders on the behavior of abusers.

Second, defendants, those who represent them, and antagonistic law enforcement personnel have not passively accepted developing restraining order legislation and practice. Although efforts to have the governing legislation declared unconstitutional have been largely unsuccessful, other strategies have proved more effective. Police officers resentful of new mandatory arrest policies have sometimes responded to incidents in which it appears that both parties have used physical force by arresting both, and recommending the issuance of mutual restraining orders, rather than seeking to determine who is the primary perpetrator. Defendants and their counsel have also sought mutual orders, or even preempted the abused partner's application for an order by filing first. The real difficulties introduced by mutual orders are addressed in Section C of this chapter.

Another battle is currently being waged around the protective order data bases increasingly maintained at the state level. Defendants argue that *ex parte* orders which are not converted into permanent orders should be immediately expunged from the system, while advocates argue that because of the many reasons victims do not return to court for permanent orders, including intimidation by their abusers, *ex parte* orders should remain in the system for some reasonable period of time. Defendants bolster their arguments with allegations that *ex parte,* and even permanent, orders are issued too readily and on scant evidence, and provide no trustworthy evidence of abuse. Although these arguments have not been accepted by the many judges who have upheld the constitutionality of restraining order legislation against attacks based on due process, they have found some resonance with state legislators who, for example, have been unwilling to allow the existence of a restraining order, by itself, to provide evidence of abuse in the family law context. Judges and those who work in the courts with victims of abuse can best address these allegations by avoiding shortcuts, and ensuring that convincing testimony supports every restraining order that issues.

The excerpt that concludes this introductory section summarizes the goals of those battered women's advocates who organized for the passage of protective order legislation at the state level.

Why Protective Orders?
Barbara Hart, State Codes on Domestic Violence: Analysis, Commentary and Recommendations, 1992 Juvenile and Family Court Journal 3, 23–24 (1992)

In the late 1960's, women's centers across the country became inundated with pleas from battered women for safe shelter and protections from violence and terrorism. With no place to refer abused women, volunteers at the centers opened up their own homes to women fleeing from violence. The demand quickly became so great that volunteers in the safe home networks concluded that shelter facilities for battered women were essential. So they went about the task of organizing their communities to open domestic violence shelters.

Advocates quickly determined that laws and social service systems offered little assistance to abused women. Contemporaneously, legal services attorneys were discovering that many of the women seeking domestic relations representation were abused by their husbands or partners. It was apparent to both advocates and legal services practitioners that short-term housing was an inadequate remedy for women whose husbands were committed to violence as a method of control and coercion, both during and after marriage.

A new remedy was needed. One that would enjoin the perpetrator from future abuse. One that would not displace the abused woman from her home but could compel relocation of the abuser. One that could constrain the abusing husband from interfering with and disrupting the life of the abused woman and children. One that could provide stability and predictability in the lives of women and children. One that would give the mother authority to act as primary caretaker of her children; limiting the risk of abduction by the father to coerce reconciliation or to penalize the abused woman for revealing the violence or terminating the relationship. One that could afford economic support so that the abused woman would not be compelled to return to the abuser to feed, clothe and house her children. One that would sharply limit the power of the battering husband or partner to coerce reconciliation. One that would advance the autonomy and independence of the battered woman from the abuser. Civil protection orders were this new remedy.

Women's advocates and their allies crafting the statutes were clear that domestic violence was intentional, instrumental behavior dedicated to control of the family. They understood that domestic violence is not impulsive, abnormal, anger-driven bursts of violence that dissipate with a short period of "cooling off" or that disappear if wives accommodate husbands' demands perfectly. They also understood that battered women may be at the most acute risk of lethal retaliation from the moment they decide to separate from the perpetrator until the time that the abuser decides not to further retaliate against the battered woman for leaving the relationship or the abuser concludes that he no longer is interested in relationship with or control over the abused woman. This period of elevated danger may last for several years. Legislators also recognized that husbands or male partners would not readily give up power accorded by their violence. Thus, the drafters of civil protection orders produced vehicles designed to provide comprehensive relief to facilitate batterer desistance and victim autonomy.

Protection order codes have proven to be tools that can significantly facilitate the achievement of the goals of safety and autonomy for abused women and children and the goals of constraint and deterrence of abusing men. The utility of protection orders depends both on the specificity of the relief ordered and the enforcement practices of the police and the courts. For orders to be effective, they must be comprehensive; crafted to the particular safety needs of the victim in each case. Providing precise conditions of relief makes the offender aware of the specific behavior prohibited. "A high degree of specificity also makes it easier for police officers and other judges to determine later whether the (perpetrator) has violated the order." Data suggest that civil protective orders increase police responsiveness to the requests of battered women for assistance.

. . .

Generally, battered women pursuing civil protection orders report that their experience of the legal process was favorable. Applicants for protection orders report that they most appreciated those judges who took their complaints seriously and encouraged them in the pursuit of safety and autonomy.

. . .

NOTE

1. Barbara Hart suggests that police are more likely to respond to domestic violence when there is a restraining order in place. This is not merely an unanticipated side benefit of the process, but was in fact one of the goals motivating those who worked for the passage of protective order legislation. At a time when police were both nonchalant about domestic incidents, and encouraged by official policy to respond more as social workers than as law enforcement representatives, it was felt that a restraining order would signal both the seriousness of the threat to the victim, and the need for a more forceful intervention. It was also hoped that if police failed to assist victims specifically designated for protection by restraining orders, they would be vulnerable to suit (under state tort law or federal or state civil

rights legislation), and not able to argue that they were simply exercising appropriate discretion in situations in which the need for their services outweighed the resources they had to commit. For a more detailed discussion of police failure to protect victims of domestic violence, and efforts to hold police accountable, see Chapter 12, below.

B. Scope of Protection

There are four dimensions to the scope of protection offered by state protective order legislation. The first important question is whom the legislation protects against—in what kinds of relationship the legislature has authorized this particular intervention. In the original drafting of protective order legislation, and in subsequent amendments, interesting assumptions are revealed about who is vulnerable to abuse, and who deserves specific protection. Early statutes were often quite limited. They saw the problem of "domestic" violence as essentially a problem of "marital," "family" or "household" violence, and some even limited relief to presently married partners on the entirely erroneous assumption that divorce would end the abuse. Failure to extend relief to cohabiting partners may have rested on the assumption that victims of abuse who were not tied to their abusers by marriage would be free to set limits without the additional assistance of a restraining order, even if they were sharing a household. Failure to include "dating" relationships may have rested on the same assumption. Alternatively, it may have been based on a failure to appreciate how early patterns of abuse can be established in intimate relationships, even among very young people, or on a reluctance to introduce such a heavy-handed tool into what were regarded as somewhat superficial relationships. The failure to include same-sex partnerships may have been the result of the relative "invisibility" of abuse in same-sex relationships when protective order legislation was first passed, or of homophobia on the part of legislators, and fears on the part of lobbyists that linking the legislation to the protection of gays and lesbians would reduce its chances of passage.

Different questions arise around whether legislation that was primarily intended to address abuse between intimate partners can be utilized by others who find themselves in power and control relationships with abusers who are not sexual partners. A piece of the answer has been that the statutes, which often talk about "household" or "family" members, or about those related by blood or marriage to their abusers, have been interpreted to include in their coverage protection for children abused by parents, parents abused by children, siblings abused by siblings, and any family member abused by another family member (a grandparent or uncle, for example, or a cousin), when the parties share the same living space. When the issue is a child being abused by a parent, questions may arise about the relationship between the protective order process and the separate mechanisms that exist for addressing child abuse, or the relationship between the protective order process and family law process around issues of custody and visitation. But in a household in which one parent poses an immediate threat both to the other parent and to the children, it may be critically important either to include the children in the protective order obtained by the adult victim, or to allow them their own orders.

Questions have also been raised about whether those who are vulnerable to abuse by caretakers, on whom they depend because they are elderly and infirm, or because of a disability, should be able to take advantage of the protective order process. If a caretaker "lives in," he or she may qualify as a "household member" under the governing statute, but this raises interesting policy questions. Should the availability of relief really depend on a criterion (co-residence) which may have no direct relevance to the vulnerability of the victim or the responsibility of the perpetrator? Is the dynamic of caretaker abuse similar enough to the dynamics of power and control in family and intimate relationships that similar mechanisms of protection should be available? Will a blanket decision to allow this vulnerable constituency to use the existing mechanism really offer meaningful protection, without further legislation which addresses the particular difficulties those with disabilities may face in enforcing their rights? These issues were discussed in greater detail in Chapter 3E, above.

Another category of people who may need protection, but may not qualify under existing legislation, are those who are exposed to the violence of the abuser because of their relationships with his present or former partner. Abusers, as we have seen, routinely threaten violence to other members of their partners' families, or to friends or others with whom their partners have contact. The threats may stem from the abuser's conviction that these relationships challenge his control over his partner; they may be used to coerce his partner into complying with his demands, or they may be triggered by concrete assistance others are offering to support the partner in her efforts to end the violence in her relationship, or to end the relationship itself. While legislatures may be unwilling to extend the protection offered by the extraordinary mechanism of the protective order so far, in some cases it may not be possible to challenge the batterer's regime of intimidation effectively without doing so.

A second way of thinking about the "scope" of protective order legislation is to examine the behavior against which it protects. What level of violence, attempted violence or threatened violence by a defendant will support the claim that a protective order should issue? How soon after the incident must the person hurt or threatened with harm seek the court's protection? If an abuser has refrained from violence or threats for the duration of an order, can it be extended on the basis of old injuries or fears, rather than new ones?

A third measure of a statute's scope is the relief it authorizes through the protective order mechanism. Some legislation is quite limited, some provides detailed and imaginative categories of relief, and some articulates only a limited range of relief, but gives judges a broad residual authority to provide other "appropriate" relief as the circumstances warrant. Judges tend to be wary of exercising this kind of unrestricted discretion, and somewhat unimaginative in their use of it, so that the legislature can perform a valuable educative function by providing a more detailed list of possibilities. A more generous catalog of available relief can also serve as a useful checklist for advocates and lawyers, as they think with their clients about what set of conditions will best secure their safety, and the safety of others threatened by the abuser's behavior. In one study:

> 30% of women said there was something they needed but did not receive in their orders. Nearly a quarter of these women wanted specifics about visitation by their partners with their shared children. One fifth wanted more specifics in the orders, such as provisions that the man not be allowed at her place of work or her parents' home, and more detail on the distance he was to keep from her.

Adele Harrell and Barbara E. Smith, *Effects of Restraining Orders on Domestic Violence Victims,* DO ARRESTS AND RESTRAINING ORDERS WORK? 214, 239 (E.S. Buzawa and C.G. Buzawa, eds. 1996).

The final question with respect to scope is the geographic reach of a protective order. Traditionally this has been a problem for women fleeing their abusers, but two relatively recent developments have made a positive difference. Even a move within the state from which the order issued traditionally necessitated alerting police in the new location to the existence and terms of the order, and more often than not victims of domestic violence were themselves responsible for supplying copies of the order to the new police precinct. As more states work to maintain computerized data bases of all restraining orders issued within the state, however, it is becoming more common for police to be able to verify the existence and terms of an order, based only on the victim's name. An even larger problem, historically, was the fact that an order issued in one state was usually not enforceable in another, leaving victims with the difficult choice of either keeping their location secret and losing the protection afforded by the order, or applying for a new order in the new state, but with the consequence that the abuser would be notified of his partner's new general location, if not her specific address. This has changed with the passage of the Violence Against Women Act, under the terms of which an order issued in one state, if it meets due process requirements, will be valid in any other, and enforceable as if it had issued in the state in which it is violated.

The following excerpts expand upon these four aspects of a protective order's scope.

Against Whom Will an Order Issue?

Nature of Relationship Between Parties for Which Protection Orders Are Available
Catherine Klein and Leslye Orloff, Providing Legal Protection for Battered Women: An Analysis of State Statutes and Case Law, 21 Hofstra Law Review 801, 814–817, 820–825, 827–841 (1993)

1. Spouses and Former Spouses

. . . Statutory protection of former, as well as current, spouses is a well-founded policy in light of the Justice Department's National Crime Survey, which revealed that seventy-five percent of all reported domestic abuse was reported by separated or divorced women. Violence is often triggered by the anger aroused by threatened loss and excessive feelings of dependency—making the period during and after separation an extremely dangerous time. Women who are divorced or separated are at higher risk of assault than married women. The risk of assault is greatest when a woman leaves or threatens to leave an abusive relationship. Nonfatal violence often escalates once a battered woman attempts to end the relationship. Furthermore, studies in Philadelphia and Chicago revealed that twenty-five percent of women murdered by their male partners were separated or divorced from their assailants. Another twenty-nine percent of women were murdered during the separation or divorce process. State statutes need to protect women and children during and after the break-up of relationships because of their continuing, and often heightened, vulnerability to violence.

2. Family Members (Parents, Siblings, Aunts, Uncles, Grandparents, and In–Laws)

Forty-seven states and the District of Columbia provide for the issuance of civil protection orders to family members. Case law has also recognized various kinds of family relationships for purposes of issuing a protection order. Protection orders may be issued to prevent violence and harassment from a sibling, a step-sibling, a parent, a step-parent, and an in-law.

3. Children

Thirty-eight states and the District of Columbia issue civil protection orders on behalf of the minor children of one or both parties. Moreover, protection orders may be issued to children as household members related by blood or marriage. In several states, emancipated minors may petition for their own protection order. Furthermore, most courts issue civil protection orders based on petitions filed by parents or other adults on behalf of children. A protection order for an abused mother may also include protection for her children, who are not abused themselves.

. . .

Case law also supports the issuance of civil protection orders based on sexual abuse of minor children. In S. v. S., the court issued a civil protection order to a minor sister against her minor brother who raped and impregnated her.

Some courts have, however, limited the forum in which civil protection orders issued *against* minors may be enforced. In *Diehl v. Drummond* [2 Pa. D. & C4th 376 (C.P. 1989)], the court issued a civil protection order against the petitioner's sixteen year old boyfriend. The *Diehl* court held that while a civil protection order may issue against a minor, enforcement of the order must occur in the juvenile court. This approach allows the courts to intervene to offer civil protection against child defendants, while placing enforcement in the court most able to protect the rights of juvenile defendants and offer juveniles appropriate sentencing alternatives. As our civil protection order issuing courts are appropriately moving toward protecting victims of dating violence and are seeing more drug-related assaults by juveniles on family members, we urge all jurisdictions to adopt this balanced approach.

Courts may also issue a civil protection order to a parent against an adult child. Courts in large cities are beginning to see greater numbers of cases in which parents seek civil protection orders against their adult or minor children who are abusing drugs. Civil protection orders can offer families experiencing these problems an opportunity to intervene to protect themselves and obtain help for their children before they might be required to turn to the criminal justice system for help. . . .

Civil protection orders are also regularly issued to adult children. Courts have issued civil protection orders based on an attempted incestuous relationship with an adult child, and for harassment of an adult child. Courts have also issued civil protection orders to an adult child who was injured as a result of an attempted assault by her step-father on her mother.

. . .

4. Parents of a Child in Common

Unmarried parties who share a child in common are frequently eligible for protection orders. Forty-one states, the District of Columbia, and Puerto Rico issue civil protection orders between parents of a child in common. A child in common between parties may also serve as a basis for issuance of a protection order between one party's child and the other party. In *Robinson v. United States* [317 A.2d 508 (D.C. 1974)], the court held that a protection order may issue on behalf of a child against the child's mother's boyfriend with whom she and the child had lived for three years and with whom the mother had two children in common.

Social science research demonstrates the importance of extending civil protection order coverage not only to parties who share a child in common, but also to pregnant women who are carrying the batterer's child. Data gathered on pregnancy and battering reveal that pregnant women face significant and increased risk of physical abuse. Recent research indicates that 37% of all obstetrical patients across race, class, and educational lines are physically abused while pregnant. Abuse often begins or escalates during pregnancy. Among battered women, 17% have been physically abused during pregnancy, with 60% of those women reporting more than one incident. The primary predictor of battering during pregnancy is prior abuse; in one study, 87.5% of women battered during the current pregnancy were physically abused prior to pregnancy. Often the worst abuse can be associated with pregnancy. Battering during pregnancy increases the risk of miscarriage and low-birth weight births. . . .

. . .

5. Unmarried Persons of Different Genders Living as Spouses

Forty-four states, the District of Columbia, and Puerto Rico will issue civil protection orders to unmarried parties who live together as spouses.

Courts look at a range of circumstances to determine whether parties "reside together" within the meaning of the domestic violence statutes. When defining "residing together," courts have interpreted the phrase to include live-in relationships of varying lengths and duration, whether or not the relationship produces children. In *Yankoskie v. Lenker* [526 A.2d 429 (Pa. Super. Ct. 1987)], the court outlined five factors which indicate that the parties are "persons living as spouses": 1) the duration of the relationship, 2) the frequency of contact, 3) the parties financial interdependence, 4) whether the parties raised children together, and 5) whether the parties engaged in tasks designed to maintain a common household.

Weighing various factors, courts have concluded that maintenance of a separate residence does not bar a finding of "residing together." In *Yankoskie,* the court held that the parties, boyfriend and girlfriend, did live as spouses even though they maintained separate residences. The parties had three children in common, he visited her apartment almost daily with her consent, and they had shared a residence in the past. In *Sapon v. Fisher* [IF 745 (D.C. Superior Court 1989)], the court found a mutual residence where a boyfriend and girlfriend alternated between sleeping at each other's apartments for some period of time, where she kept clothing at his apartment, and where her mother wrote her at his apartment. In State *v. Tripp* [795 P.2d 280 (Haw. 1990)], the court found that the parties were co-residents for purposes of the domestic violence statute where the defendant stayed with his girlfriend approximately three times a week for less than 14 weeks at a house where the victim was housesitting, where there was no certainty of continued use, where neither paid rent, where both had alternative separate residences, and where the defendant kept his clothes, did his laundry, ate his meals, and slept at the house on a continuous basis. In a criminal domestic violence case, *People v. Holifield* [252 Cal. Rptr. 729 (Cal. Ct. App. 1988)], a court interpreted "residing together" to include the respondent sleeping with and having occasional sex with the victim in the victim's hotel room for half of the three months proceeding the assault where the respondent had no regular place to stay and where he brought his belongings with him when he came.

In addition to interpreting "residing together" to include circumstances where the parties maintain separate residences, courts have held that parties were cohabitating even if they did not plan to marry, and in criminal prosecutions, even absent a finding of any sexual relationship. In *People v. Ballard* [249 Cal. Rptr. 806 (Cal. Ct. App. 1988)], the court held that for purposes of a criminal felony cohabitant abuse statute, it need not find a sexual relationship to establish jurisdiction. The court noted that "[c]ohabitation means simply to live or dwell together in the same habitation; evidence of lack of sexual relations is irrelevant."

Courts should issue civil protection orders even where the defendant will be incarcerated for the duration of the protection order. In *Maldonado v. Maldonado* [1993 D.C. App. LEXIS 227 (D.C. Ct. App. June 22, 1993)], the District of Columbia Court of Appeals reversed, as an abuse of discretion, a trial judge's decision not to extend a civil protection order based solely on the fact that the husband would be incarcerated during the duration of the civil protection order. The appellate court noted that the defendant could escape or be released prior to the expiration of the extended civil protection order and that he had the potential to continue, from jail, to threaten and harass the petitioner via the mail, telephone, or a third party. Understanding the danger release from incarceration poses to domestic violence victims, courts will issue protection orders where a defendant will soon be released from jail and pose a potential threat to the petitioner. In *Campbell v. Campbell* [584 So. 2d 125 (Fla. Dist. App. Ct. 1991)], the court issued a protection order to a petitioner where her husband was incarcerated for sexual battery of their daughter but would soon be released. The court held that the injunction was proper because the "husband had a violent temper, behaved violently in the past, blamed [the petitioner] for the arrest, and ... would soon be released from jail."

6. Intimate Partners of the Same Gender

For state civil protection order statutes to address fully the domestic violence crisis, they must recognize and combat violence in both homosexual and heterosexual intimate relationships. The civil protection order statutes of thirty-four states, Puerto Rico, and the District of Columbia extend their coverage to homosexual relationships by providing protection to those who have lived together or who have had an intimate relationship. Other jurisdictions offer this relief by case law and statutory interpretation by trial courts. In *Bryant v. Bryant* [624 A.2d 584 (N.J. 1993)], the New Jersey Supreme Court expressly interpreted their amended statute as applying to homosexual relationships which turn violent.

Ohio case law states affirmatively that its criminal domestic violence statute applies to relationships between persons of the same gender living together. In *State v. Hadinger* [573 N.E. 2d 1191 (Ohio Ct. App. 1991)], the appellate court vacated a trial court's decision to dismiss a domestic violence prosecution where one woman bit the hand of another woman with whom she was "living as a spouse," remanding the case. The appellate court focused on the fact that the parties lived together rather than on their sexual relationship, and rejected a construction of the statute which would require the parties' ability to marry under state law as a prerequisite for coverage. The court noted that since the statute defined "person living as a spouse" to include a person "who otherwise is cohabitating with the offender," it reflected the legislature's intent to protect domestic violence victims regardless of gender or gender preference.... In *Glater v. Fabianich* [625 N.E.2d 96 (Ill. Ct. App. 1993)], the appellate court upheld a decision below to grant a petition for a protection order to a man whose male roommate pushed him, choked him, and repeatedly threatened him after their intimate relationship ended. The lower court granted the protection order after an analysis of the parties' living arrangements. The petitioner had stayed at the respondent's apartment every night for three months, kept clothing there, spent 90% of his time in the apartment, and contributed to household expenses.

7. Dating Relationships

Twelve progressive state statutes in Alaska, California, Maine, Massachusetts, New Hampshire, New Mexico, North Dakota, Pennsylvania, Puerto Rico, Rhode Island, Washington, and West Virginia extend coverage of protection orders to parties in dating relationships. Courts in Wisconsin, Pennsylvania, and Oklahoma support this innovative approach of issuing civil protection orders based on a dating relationship.

Social science research that documents violence in dating relationships supports offering broader civil protection order coverage to dating partners and adolescents. A study of teen dating violence found that roughly one in four students experienced actual violence, either as victims or as perpetrators. A 1985 survey at a midwestern university found higher rates of violence in dating relationships than between married couples. Another study reported that 32% of domestic violence offenders are boyfriends or ex-boyfriends.

These studies demonstrate that the prevalence of violence in dating relationships rivals and may surpass the rate of violence between married or cohabitating couples. Authorizing the use of civil protection orders to protect against dating violence provides an important opportunity to intervene early to halt escalating violence and teach youthful offenders that violence in intimate relationships will not be tolerated. Learning this lesson while young may prevent many future cases of adult domestic violence. To address fully the domestic violence crisis, all state statutes should be amended to extend civil protection order coverage to dating relationships.

8. Persons Offering Refuge

Two forward-looking state statutes, from Hawaii and Illinois, explicitly extend civil protection order protection to persons with whom the abused party seeks refuge. California case law also supports this approach. This innovative extension of civil protection order coverage recognizes that batterers often direct violence and intimidation against persons who give aid and refuge to abused parties. Batterers may seek to control and isolate the abused party by making threats against persons who give shelter or assistance. By extending coverage to persons offering refuge and assistance, these civil protection order statutes undermine the batterer's ability to intimidate others from aiding the abused party, and reduce the abused party's reluctance to seek assistance from others.

Separated women are very vulnerable to continued abuse from their husbands or intimate partners. Violence often escalates after separation. Batterers often stalk their partners who leave them and will threaten or harass not only their intimate partner, but also the persons who shelter her. The stalking and harassment may continue for months, or even years, after separation. Many battered women will resist seeking shelter and assistance from friends and family out of fear of placing them and their children in danger from the batterer.

Perhaps most importantly, providing civil protection order protection to persons who offer refuge undermines the batterer's sense of control, alleviates the abused party's sense of isolation, and significantly improves the abused party's safety. Further, extending civil protection order coverage to persons offering refuge may also vastly improve the quality of evidence that can be presented in civil protection order contempt trials and criminal domestic violence proceedings. It may help prevent batterers from scaring off key witnesses who might otherwise assist the victim by testifying. Offering protection to persons who offer refuge to battering victims may help limit the batterer's access to them, while also calming their legitimate fears of the batterer.

9. Other Persons Covered

Progressive jurisdictions extend civil protection order coverage to other persons who are not currently family members or intimates. For example, Florida and Oklahoma protect the present spouse of the batterer's ex-spouse. Forty states and the District of Columbia protect persons who formerly lived as spouses. Thirty-seven states recognize that violence may extend to all persons living in the home when a victim is stalked and harassed by the batterer. To ensure a safe living environment for women whom shelters cannot accommodate, these states grant civil protection order coverage to unrelated household members. Four states limit this protection to unrelated household members who are present or past sexual partners. Thirty-five states extend civil protection order coverage to former unrelated household members. The New Mexico statute provides for issuance of a civil protection order to a person with whom the petitioner has a continuing relationship, and North Dakota offers protection to a member of any "sufficient" relationship with the abuser. The approach adopted by New Mexico and North Dakota allows the court to intervene and offer protection to stop violence in a broad array of cases. Under such statutes, civil protection orders may issue against stalkers or against a person who consistently pursues the petitioner with unwanted advances. Finally, Illinois recognizes the increased vulnerability of persons with disabilities, and therefore explicitly extends coverage to the assistants of dependent adults.

* * *

For What Behavior?

Qualifying Behavior
Peter Finn and Sarah Colson, Civil Protection Orders: Legislation, Current Court Practice, and Enforcement, 10–11, National Institute of Justice, March 1990

Some judges are reluctant to exercise their authority to issue an order when threats are alleged but no actual battery has occurred. For example, a judge in a state that authorized protection orders on the basis of threats grants orders only if there have been several threats and the abuser has the ability to carry out his menaces. This reluctance may in part reflect judges' uncertainty about the extent of their authority when the statutory language regarding "threat" is couched in terms of intimidating the victim. For example, the Maine statute provides that "Abuse" includes "attempting to place or placing another in fear of imminent bodily injury." Like other issues of credibility, of course, the finding of whether a threat has actually occurred is within the discretion of the court.

Statutes in [many but not all][1] states specifically include sexual assault of an adult as a ground for providing relief. For example, Oregon's statute includes "causing another to engage in involuntary sexual relations by force, threat of force or duress" within the definition of abuse. Sexual assault of a child is expressly included in the definition of abuse in [many] statutes. Moreover, in *Lucke v. Lucke*, 300 N.W.2d 231 (N.D. 1980), the North Dakota Supreme Court ruled that, although the state statute did not expressly include sexual abuse as a ground for issuing an order, the law defining abuse should be interpreted to allow relief for sexual assault.

A number of states define domestic violence to include "malicious damage to the personal property of the abused party" (Tennessee's wording). The Washington State statute provides that "Domestic violence includes but is not limited to any of the following crimes when committed by one family or household member against another":

— assault in the first, second, third, or fourth degree

— reckless endangerment

— coercion

— burglary in the first and second degree

— malicious mischief in the first, second, or third degree

— unlawful imprisonment.

Most state statutes doe not require a victim to petition for a protection order within any specified time limit, nor is there any automatic disqualification due to prolonged delay. However, although of dubious legality, many judges establish their own guidelines in this matter. For example, one judge interviewed will not issue an order unless the most recent incident occurred within the past 48 hours. That stringent a limitation does not appear to have widespread acceptance; many judges reported that they found that victims often need several days or even weeks after the incident to learn about the availability of civil protection orders; to seek encouragement from family, friends, or victim advocates to initiate legal action; and to reach an invariably difficult decision to petition for an order. As a result, judges in other jurisdictions grant orders as long as the incident did not take place more than a month before the petition was filed. Courts in Oregon are permitted by statute to consider women eligible who have been abused any time in the preceding 180 days.

* * *

NOTE

1. Despite claims on the part of defendants, those who represent them, and fathers' rights organizations, that restraining orders are not "real

1. Because this excerpt was published in 1990, and based on 1988 data, the specific numbers cited were replaced with more generic language.

evidence" of abuse, the few empirical studies that have looked in depth at what prompts women to seek restraining orders have found otherwise. In the Harrell and Smith article cited earlier in this section, the authors documented that 56% of the 355 women who sought orders had sustained physical injuries, and that first aid, medical attention, or hospitalization was necessary for 39% of those injured. 55% had suffered severe violence—being punched, choked or strangled, beat up, hurt with a weapon, run down with a car or forced to have sex, and 71% had been subjected to violence of other kinds, including 13% whose children were hurt or taken by the abuser. 31% of women had been threatened with death. Adele Harrell and Barbara E. Smith, *Effects of Restraining Orders on Domestic Violence Victims,* DO ARRESTS AND RESTRAINING ORDERS WORK? 214, 216–217 (E.S. Buzawa and C.G. Buzawa, eds. 1996). In another study, of 663 restraining orders, 64.4% were based on physical assaults on the victim, and in another third of the cases the abuser had threatened to kill or otherwise harm the complainant, her children, or another relative. The perpetrator was arrested in 10% of the incidents which gave rise to these orders. Andrew R. Klein, *Re-Abuse in a Population of Court–Restrained Male Batterers: Why Restraining Orders Don't Work,* DO ARRESTS AND RESTRAINING ORDERS WORK? 192, 194 (E.S. Buzawa & C.G.Buzawa, eds., 1996).

Available Relief

Forms of Relief
Barbara Hart, State Codes on Domestic Violence: Analysis, Commentary and Recommendations, 1992 Juvenile and Family Court Journal 3, 14–19 (1992)

The New Jersey code enumerates the most comprehensive potential relief, including any or all of the following:

— an order restraining the defendant from subjecting the victim to domestic violence;

— an order granting exclusive possession to the plaintiff of the residence or household regardless of whether the residence or household is jointly or solely owned or leased by the parties, but if it is not possible for the victim to remain in the residence;

— an order that the defendant pay the victim's rent at a residence other than the one previously shared by the parties if the defendant has a duty to support the victim;

— an order requiring the defendant to pay monetary compensation for losses suffered by the victim as a direct result of the act of domestic violence, with compensatory losses to include, but not be limited to, loss of earnings or other support, out-of pocket losses for injuries sustained, cost or repair or replacement of real or personal property damaged or destroyed or taken, cost of counseling for the victim, moving or other travel expenses, reasonable attorney's fees, court costs, and compensation for pain and suffering; an award for punitive damages, where appropriate;

— an order requiring the defendant to receive professional domestic violence counseling from a private source or a source appointed by the court and, in that event, at the court's discretion requiring the defendant to provide the court at specified intervals with documentation of attendance at the professional counseling, for which the defendant may be ordered to pay;

— an order restraining the defendant from entering the residence, property, school, or place of employment of the victim or of other family or household members of the victim and requiring the defendant to stay away from any specified place that is named in the order and is frequented regularly by the victim or other family or household members;

— an order restraining the defendant from making any communication likely to cause annoyance or alarm including but not limited to, personal, written or telephone contact with the victim or other family members, or their employers, employees, or fellow workers, or others with whom communication would be likely to cause annoyance or alarm to the victim;

— an order requiring that the defendant make rent or mortgage payments on the residence occupied by the victim if the defendant has a duty to support the victim or other dependent household members, providing this issue has not been resolved or is not being litigated between the parties in another action;

— an order granting either party temporary possession of specified personal property, such as an automobile, checkbook, documentation of health insurance, an identification document, a key and other personal effects;

— an order awarding emergency monetary relief to the victim and other dependents, if any;

— an order awarding temporary custody of a minor child (and the court shall presume that the best interests of the child are served by an award of custody to the non-abusive parent);

— an order that a law enforcement officer accompany either party to the residence to supervise the removal of personal belongings in order to ensure the personal safety of the plaintiff when a restraining order has been issued, provided the order for accompaniment is time-limited;

— an order which permits the victim and the defendant to occupy the same premises but limits the defendant's use of the premises but only if the plaintiff specifically and voluntarily requests such an order and the judge determines the request is voluntary and informed, the order conditions the defendant's access, and explicitly sets out penalties for noncompliance;

— an order granting any other appropriate relief for the plaintiff and dependent children as long as the plaintiff consents to the relief;

— an order that requires the defendant to report to the intake unit of the family court for monitoring; and

— an order prohibiting the defendant from possessing any firearm or other weapon enumerated in the code.

More typically, protection order codes authorize orders restraining the defendant from future acts of domestic violence, orders granting exclusive possession of the victim's residence to the victim and/or eviction of the perpetrator, orders awarding temporary custody to the nonabusing parent, orders for spousal or child support and stay-away or no-contact orders.

In forty-nine of the fifty-one jurisdictions, codes include injunctions against further violence. In fifty jurisdictions, codes permit exclusive use of a residence or eviction of a perpetrator from the victim's household. Awards of custody or visitation are authorized in forty-three jurisdictions. Twenty-three jurisdictions authorize the payment of child or spousal support in protection orders. Half of the codes provide for awards of attorneys fees and/or costs. About one-quarter of the state statutes permit monetary compensation other than attorneys fees and costs, which may include out-of-pocket expenses occasioned by the abuse, replacement of destroyed property, relocation expenses and/or mortgage or rental payments. Half of the codes provide that a no-contact or no-harassment order may be granted after notice and hearing. The statutes in more than forty jurisdictions allow the court to order any additional relief, as appropriate, with direction typically that the relief should be directed at protecting the victim or bringing about a cessation of the violence.

Custody and visitation orders. Apparently noting the enhanced risk posed to children by perpetrators of domestic violence in the context of visitation, several codes have included protective provisions to safeguard children. The New Jersey code pays careful attention to visitation awards issued in protection orders and specifically directs that the order "shall protect the safety and well-being of the plaintiff and minor children and shall specify the place and frequency of visitation. Visitation arrangements shall not compromise any other remedy provided by the court by requiring or encouraging contact between the plaintiff and defendant. Orders for visitation may include a designation of a place of visitation away from the plaintiff, the participation of a third party or supervised visitation. (And, further) the court shall consider a request by the plaintiff for an investigation or evaluation by the appropriate agency to assess the risk of harm to the child prior to the entry of a visitation order. Any denial of such a request must be on the record and shall only be made if the judge finds the request to be arbitrary or capricious.... The court shall consider suspension of the visitation order and hold an emergency hearing upon an application made by the plaintiff certifying under oath that the defendant's access to the child pursuant to the visitation order has threatened the safety and well-being of the child."

The Pennsylvania code is more modest but provides that a defendant shall not be granted custody or unsupervised visitation where "the court finds after a hearing ... that the defendant abused the minor children of the parties or where the defendant has been convicted of (interference with the custody of children) within two calendar years prior to the filing of the petition ... The court shall consider, and may impose on a custody award, conditions necessary to assure the safety of the plaintiff and minor children from abuse."

The Vermont code requires that if visitation rights are awarded and the court finds that visitation will result in abuse, the court must specify conditions on visitation to prevent further abuse.

Property orders. The Missouri code, among others, articulates that the court may order that "the petitioner be given temporary possession of specified personal property, such as automobiles, checkbooks, keys and other personal effects." The respondent may be prohibited "from transferring, incumbering or otherwise disposing of specified property mutually owned or leased by the parties" and that the respondent be ordered "to pay a reasonable fee for housing and other services that have been provided or that are being provided to the petitioner by a shelter for victims of domestic violence."

Electronic monitoring. The Washington code uniquely authorizes the court to require the defendant in a protection order proceeding to submit to electronic monitoring, restricting the movement of the perpetrator. The order for electronic monitoring must specify the provider of this service and the terms under which monitoring will be performed, which may include a requirement that the abuser pay the costs thereof.

* * *

Geographic Scope

Catherine F. Klein
Full Faith and Credit: Interstate Enforcement of Protection Orders Under the Violence Against Women Act of 1994, 29 Family Law Quarterly 253, 254–57, 263–66 (1995)

... Prior to the enactment of VAWA, the majority of states did not afford full faith and credit to protection orders issued in sister states....

... [I]n order to receive protection in the foreign state, a victim had to petition the foreign state's court for a new protection order. Because of due process requirements, the batterer had to be served with notice regarding pending protection proceedings, thus revealing the victim's whereabouts and putting the victim in a dangerous situation. In the absence of a full faith and credit statute, jurisdictional problems could arise. A state may not have jurisdiction to issue a new protection order unless abuse takes place within its boundaries. In addition, there are other problems that arise out of the requirement of refiling for a protective order including: additional filing fees; language barriers; the difference in each state's domestic violence laws regarding availability, duration and scope of protection; inadequate transportation; access to legal assistance; and child care facilities....

Full Faith and Credit: An Interpretation of the VAWA

The Violence Against Women Act establishes that states must grant full faith and credit to protection orders issued in foreign states or tribal courts. Any protection order issued by one state or tribe shall be treated and enforced as if it were an order of the enforcing state. The Act extends to permanent, temporary and *ex parte* protection orders. Full faith and credit is afforded during the period of time in which the order remains valid in the issuing state. Protection orders are only afforded full faith and credit under the Act, however, if the due process requirements of the issuing state were met. The Act specifies that the issuing court must have had both personal and subject matter jurisdiction, and that the respondent received reasonable notice and an opportunity to be heard. Furthermore, the full faith and credit provision applies to *ex parte* orders if notice and opportunity to be heard were provided within the issuing state's statutory requirement or within a reasonable time after the order was issued. Because the VAWA requires that due process be met before a protection order is afforded full faith and credit, it does not extend full faith and credit to mutual protection orders that do not comply with due process.

The failure to satisfy due process requirements is the only exception to the full faith and credit provision. A sister state's valid order would be accorded full faith and credit, even if the victim were ineligible for a protection order in the enforcing state. For example, a victim of abuse in a same sex relationship would be able to obtain a protection order in the District of Columbia, but might not be able to obtain one under the laws of Montana. Under the VAWA, however, Montana would have to afford full faith and credit to the order issued by the District of Columbia even though the victim would have been ineligible for protection in Montana.

The VAWA does not require the victim to register her foreign protection order in the enforcing state. Although there are advantages to registering protection orders, requiring registration could leave victims unprotected and vulnerable from the time they enter a new state until the time they become aware of and satisfy registration requirements. Under the VAWA, a victim with a valid protection order receives continuous protection until the expiration of that order, regardless of which state she has entered. Furthermore, even if a victim chooses to register a protection order in a new state, the VAWA does not require the new state to provide the respondent with additional notice. These are important considerations that provide immediate protection while ensuring confidentiality of the victim's whereabouts.

Choice of law is another consideration.... The VAWA states that a foreign order is afforded full faith and credit and is "enforced as if it were the order of the enforcing state." If, for example, a woman obtains a protection order in Maryland and later flees to Pennsylvania, which state's law would apply is a choice of law problem. Under the language of VAWA, it seems clear that Pennsylvania law would apply because the order "shall be enforced as if it were the order of the enforcing state." Thus, Pennsylvania would treat the order as if it had been issued by a court of Pennsylvania and would apply its own law....

Model Approach to Interstate Enforcement Under the VAWA

... None of the states surveyed had fees for a victim to file a protection order in a new state. It is necessary to eliminate additional economic burdens so that all victims will have adequate access to protection.

... There are reasons why registration should be encouraged: It is an excellent method of informing law enforcement officials of existing protection orders and it can relieve law enforcement officials of the burden of assessing the validity of foreign protection orders at the scene of a domestic incident. However, registration should never be a condition for enforcement of foreign protection orders. By requiring registration, the very purposes of the VAWA are undermined. A victim may not have access to or knowledge of registration procedures at the time she enters the new state. Mandatory registration leaves the victim unprotected until she is able to register.... Under the VAWA, a victim with a valid foreign protection order should be protected from the moment she crosses state lines.

An important consideration in the enforcement of foreign protection orders is police liability. Police officers play a vital role in preventing domestic violence. Many victims first learn about the rights and services available to them through police contact. More importantly, studies show that effective police responses to domestic violence can prevent future violence.... Ineffective police responses, however, serve to exacerbate the problems of domestic violence.

Police fear liability when entering into a domestic violence situation, specifically for false arrest. Because police are essential to the effective enforcement of domestic laws, they must be able to carry out their duties without threat of criminal or civil liability. Many states have explicitly provided qualified immunity for police officers acting under their state's domestic violence statute.... Police officers may also assert an immunity defense to federal actions brought under 42 U.S.C. § 1983.

Jurisdictions, concerned about the increased liability that may be faced by an officer's good faith effort to enforce an out of state order, should consider enacting qualified immunity statutes which would apply only to officers' good faith attempts to enforce protection orders, not to the failure to enforce valid orders. Oregon specifically immunizes police officers who make arrests for the violation of a foreign protection order if the officer reasonably believes that the foreign order is an accurate copy. Moreover, immunity statutes may not be necessary to provide protection to police officers, because common law has traditionally shielded state actors from liability.

Another suggested procedure for states to consider when trying to implement the full faith and credit provisions of the VAWA is to make changes to court protection order forms. The court forms should clearly inform both the respondent and law enforcement officials that the order is valid and enforceable in all fifty states, the District of Columbia, and tribal lands. The standardized protection form should clearly cite the full faith and credit provision of the VAWA as authority. Prior to having court orders changed, practitioners can put law enforcement officials and the respondent on notice by clearly stating that the order is subject to full faith and credit under the VAWA. This can be achieved by handwriting or typing a statement right on the existing court protection order form that provides notice that the order is subject to full faith and credit pursuant to the VAWA.

* * *

NOTES

1. Prior to the passage of VAWA, only seven states accorded full faith and credit to foreign orders of protection; Kentucky (KY. REV. STAT. ANN. § 426.955 (Baldwin 1993)); Nevada (NEV. REV. STAT. ANN. § 33.090 (1986)); New Hampshire (N.H. REV. STAT. ANN. § 173B:11–6 (1993)); New Mexico (N.M. STAT. ANN. § 40–13–6 (Michie Supp. 1993)); Oregon (OR. REV. STAT. § 24.185 (1993)); Rhode Island (R.I. GEN. LAWS § 15–15–8 (1994)), and West Virginia (W.VA. CODE § 48–2A–3(e) (Supp. 1993)). In addition, New Mexico afforded full faith and credit to orders of tribal courts, and Nevada accepted a foreign protection order as evidence on the basis of which to issue its own protection order.

2. The new interstate enforceability of protective orders guaranteed by VAWA, under 18 U.S.C.A. § 2265, is something for lawyers and advocates to keep in mind as they assist clients in determining what relief to ask for. A request that the defendant stay away from specific locations loses its usefulness if the petitioner is no longer at those locations, but wants equivalent protection elsewhere, without alerting her abuser as to her new whereabouts. The most "transportable" form of stay-away order will be the one that requires the defendant to stay a certain distance away from the petitioner at all times. Another alternative might be to frame the stay-away portion of the order so that it requires the defendant to stay away from the petitioner's current residence, which should be identified, for ease of enforceability, if it is already known to the defendant, but in addition from any other place where she might reside during the term of the order. Similar provisions could be crafted to cover schools attended by the children, or the petitioner's workplace.

C. ISSUES OF PROCESS

To some extent, the restraining order process mirrors the process prescribed for any other civil matter. A petition is filed in an appropriate court, a hearing date is set, and personal jurisdiction is obtained over the defendant by service of process within a specified time limit. In almost all jurisdictions the hearing is also governed by the usual civil standard of proof, requiring the complainant to demonstrate by a preponderance of the evidence that she qualifies for relief. However, in almost every respect the restraining order process is tailored to the situation it seeks to address in ways that make it unique.

Emergency, Ex Parte and Permanent Orders

Because of the emergency nature of most restraining order cases, all jurisdictions provide for temporary orders to be issued on an *ex parte* basis to complainants who come into court seeking immediate relief. For an *ex parte* order to issue, the complainant must usually submit, with her application, an affidavit which details the violence, attempted violence or threats on which the application is based. The judge will often question her further in a brief *ex parte* hearing, although it is notable that the statutory provisions governing these hearings do not explicitly demand the presence of the petitioner. To qualify for *ex parte* relief, a petitioner must substantiate the immediacy of her need, by showing, for example, "immediate and present danger" of domestic violence, or "substantial likelihood of immediate danger," or that "irreparable injury is likely or could occur." If the *ex parte* order is issued, it will generally stay in effect only until the date set for the full hearing, which will determine whether a "permanent" order will issue.[1] The defendant will receive notice of the *ex parte* order along with notice of the hearing date for the permanent order. Many jurisdictions limit the range of relief granted in this preliminary order, focusing on immediate issues of safety, but not issues such as custody or support.

In the early days of protective order legislation, constitutional challenges were brought against statutes that permitted a defendant to be excluded from a residence owned or leased by him on the basis of an *ex parte* order supported by testimony that he had no opportunity to rebut. Courts were unanimous, however, in ruling that defendants were not, in this situation, deprived of property without due process of law. In Boyle v. Boyle, 12 Pa. D. & C. 3d 767 (Pa. 1979), for example, the Pennsylvania Supreme Court, relying on the U. S. Supreme Court's decision in Fuentes v. Shevin, 407 U.S. 67 (1972), found that it was constitutionally permissible to subordinate the respondent's interest in the uninterrupted possession of the residence to the victim's right to immediate protection against abuse. Similarly, in State ex rel.Williams v. Marsh, 626 S.W.2d 223 (Mo. 1982), the Missouri Supreme Court applied the balancing test articulated in the U.S. Supreme Court's decision in Matthews v. Eldridge, 424 U.S. 319 (1976), and concluded that although the uninterrupted possession of one's own home was a significant private interest, the high incidence and severity of domestic violence made the governmental interest in preventing that violence weightier.

1. The term permanent is somewhat misleading, since very few jurisdictions provide for orders of unlimited duration. Permanent, in this context, means an order for any period up to the maximum authorized by the governing legislation.

The Missouri court also found that the *ex parte* provisions were a reasonable means to achieve the state's legitimate goal of preventing domestic violence, and afforded adequate procedural safeguards before and after any deprivation of rights. In Blazel v. Bradley, 698 F. Supp. 756 (W.D. Wisc. 1988), a case challenging the *ex parte* provisions of the Wisconsin statute, the court made a similar reference to the adequacy of the procedural safeguards built into the statute, noting that: "It is explicit in the statute that judicial participation and a verified petition containing detailed allegations are required before an ex parte order may issue, and that a prompt post-deprivation hearing must be provided." Id. at 757.

Even the *ex parte* process is not always adequate to protect a victim who requires immediate assistance during evening or weekend hours when the court is not open. A substantial number of jurisdictions have responded to this gap in service through an emergency response system. In Massachusetts, for example, police work with a designated emergency judge, who is authorized to issue orders over the phone after hearing testimony from both the responding police officer and the complainant. The complainant must then go into court the next day it is open to apply for a regular *ex parte* order, and receive a hearing date for the permanent order.

Different statutory schemes allocate the responsibility of converting an *ex parte* order into a permanent order differently. In some statutes, a defendant desiring relief from an emergency order must affirmatively request a hearing. In Oregon, for example, if the defendant does not respond to the notice that an *ex parte* order has issued by requesting a hearing, the original order will remain in effect for the maximum time permitted under statute (one year), or for whatever shorter period has been designated by the court. More commonly, however, the statutory scheme provides that the court must schedule the full hearing, or the complainant must request it, as soon as the *ex parte* order is issued. Even this full process is an expedited one; in most states the hearing is scheduled to take place within ten to twenty days after the initial application. In these states, if the defendant has been properly served but does not appear to contest the order (a not uncommon situation), the court may enter a default judgment, and issue a permanent order, with the full range of relief authorized by the statute. But if the hearing does not take place, which might be because the complainant fails to return to court, because the defendant has not been properly served, or because of administrative difficulties, the *ex parte* order will automatically expire. This can create a situation in which the complainant is forced to return several times to court, spending several hours there each time, to seek extensions of her *ex parte* order while she waits, for example, for her partner to be served. The danger inherent in this system is that the abusive partner, by avoiding service, can place his victim's employment in jeopardy or wreak havoc with her child care arrangements, and may even be able to manipulate the process so that her order expires, leaving her once more unprotected.

The obvious question is why, given the disadvantages of this system, more states do not employ the Oregon model, under which the complainant is protected unless and until the defendant appears to contest the order. One reason may be a fear that such a scheme, by laying such a heavy burden on the defendant, is vulnerable to the charge that it violates due process. Another practical disadvantage is that the defendant who never appears in court may be less likely to comply with the terms of the order—although even the defendant who receives notice of a hearing date may choose not to appear, and suffer a default judgment which he may also be inclined to ignore. A final difficulty is that even if the statute's service requirements have been met at a technical level, a defendant who has not in fact received notice may be able to invalidate the terms of the order in a subsequent challenge.

Assistance for the Victim

It is fundamental to the protective order regime that it provide victims of domestic violence with easy (and inexpensive) access to the judicial process. To that end, many protective order statutes have specifically provided for *pro se* petitioning. However, most reports on the functioning of the protective order process have emphasized that victims who approach the court without competent assistance fare less well—both in securing orders, and in securing orders containing the full range of available and appropriate relief — than those who have help. Help can come from a variety of sources; from the court clerks who serve as gatekeepers to the process, from victim witness advocates attached to the prosecutor's office, from lay advocates, or from lawyers. Lay advocates may be employed by the court or by social service or shelter organizations or they may be volunteers. Some number are currently being funded by the U.S. Department of Justice, under grants authorized by the Violence Against Women Act. Among the volunteers are many law students working in clinical programs or with student-run advocacy projects. Lawyers may be retained by individual victims, employed by a legal services program or prosecutor's office, or members of a volunteer project organized by committed individuals, law firms or local bar organizations.

The following excerpts from a 1990 report commissioned by the National Institute of Justice summarize some of the pros and cons of these different assistance mechanisms, although the report perhaps overestimates the importance of legal representation, and underestimates the value of assistance from lay advocates thoroughly trained in the restraining order process.

Assistance for the Victim
Peter Finn and Sarah Colson, Civil Protection Orders: Legislation, Current Court Practice, and Enforcement, 19–27, National Institute of Justice, March 1990

Legal Representation for the Victim

The need for legal counsel

Most judges report that even with a simplified petitioning process and energetic lay assistance to victims, those victims who are not represented by counsel are less likely to get protection orders—and, if an order is issued, it is less likely to contain all appropriate provisions regarding exclusion from the residence, temporary custody of children, child support, and protective limitations on visitation rights. Decisions in these areas may not only affect the victim and family's present well-being, but may also set precedents for subsequent protection order hearings or other domestic relations proceedings.... [D]ifficulties for victims in advocating effectively for their own rights may ... stem from the climate of emotional crisis or fear that usually precipitates seeking a protective order. Since most victims are not schooled either in the applicable law or in legal advocacy, skilled legal assistance may be crucial in obtaining adequate protection.

An attorney for the petitioner is especially important when the respondent appears with counsel. This is most likely to occur during a violation hearing, at which defendants with sufficient means have a strong incentive to hire an attorney and indigent defendants will be provided with a public defender if serving time in jail is a possible sentence. However, in Springfield,[1] where legal counsel is not generally available to many victims, defendants frequently also come to petition hearings with attorneys, forcing the victim to counter the defense attorney's rebuttals alone. In other cities, where representation of the petitioner is more common, having an attorney present has proven essential in preventing such imbalances....

Most judges in our survey also reported that evidence is generally presented more appropriately and efficiently when the petitioner is represented by counsel, rather than proceeding pro se. Many judges stated they prefer not to have to personally question petitioners in order to obtain enough information to decide whether to issue an order or what provisions to include. Several expressed concerns that such questioning might be interpreted as implying bias or might appear to violate fair procedure, although they recognized the questioning was necessary in cases in which the petitioner was without counsel.

Judges also noted that, when both parties are represented by counsel, the opposing attorneys frequently can agree to the provisions of a protection order before the hearing. In Philadelphia, attorneys at Woman Against Abuse, a woman's legal aid organization and shelter, also favor this approach. As a result, the overwhelming majority of cases in Philadelphia are resolved through a negotiated agreement between the attorneys that the judge incorporates into the protection order....

Approaches to providing counsel

While most protection order statutes do not explicitly address the issue of availability of counsel, a few do. Nebraska's statute requires the Department of Public Welfare to provide "emergency legal counseling and referral." Wyoming's statute provides that "The court may appoint an attorney to assist and advise the petitioner."

Even where not explicitly mandated or authorized by statute, judges can play a key role in promoting access to counsel.... While not so

1. Springfield, Illinois.

required by law, almost every victim who petitions for a protection order in Philadelphia is represented by an attorney, because the judge who handles civil protection order hearings has made it court policy to strongly encourage attorney representation in these cases. . . .

. . . Although legal service agencies are mandated to assist anyone who meets their eligibility criteria, resources are limited and each office establishes its own priorities. Even apparently neutral policies—such as considering the income of both spouses in determining whether a potential client is eligible financially to receive legal services—can act to deny services to a petitioner who has no realistic access to the financial resources of the abusing spouse. Judges can be influential in confronting problems such as these and encouraging legal service programs to make assisting domestic violence victims a high priority.

Bar association and pro bono service projects are another potential source for referral attorneys. . . .

Agencies and offices associated with the criminal justice system can also serve as resources in many communities. In Ithaca, New York, the Assigned Counsel Office in Family Court tries to find an attorney for every indigent petitioner. These private attorneys are paid a reduced fee by the county. Most assignments are made on an emergency basis while the victim is in court. . . .

In Chicago and Springfield, most victims who petition for an order are represented by a prosecutor, pursuant to the statutory mandate that victims may request "through the respective State's Attorney", an order of protection in a criminal proceeding during pre-trial release of a defendant or as a condition of probation, conditional discharge or supervision. These cities provide free legal counsel and expedited service in seeking a protection order if the victim files a criminal complaint at the same time she petitions for a protection order, and the prosecutor typically handles both aspects simultaneously.

. . . [P]rosecutors' offices in other states may provide services as a part of a larger mandate to control crime. In some Massachusetts courts, for example, prosecutors routinely assist protection order petitioners, but exercise prosecutorial discretion as to whether or not to also seek criminal prosecution. Since protection orders offer an opportunity to prevent future crime and enhance law enforcement, regular involvement by prosecutors, while creating an immediate time demand, may be viewed as a desirable investment in reducing future caseloads.

Judges may be able to arrange for second or third year law school students to represent victims. In structured programs with adequate training and supervision, this could provide a viable alternative to requiring petitioners to proceed pro se.

Pro Se Petitioning

. . .

Many civil protection order statutes specifically authorize and facilitate pro se petitions. . . .

The majority of victims in many jurisdictions do petition on their own. For example, during a three month period in 1987, 49 out of 61 petitioners in Nashville—80 percent—appeared at the hearing for a permanent order without an attorney. Of the other sites we studied, few victims are represented by counsel in Duluth, Colorado Springs, Seattle, and Portland, Maine, and Portland, Oregon.

In cases in which the petitioner is without legal representation . . . it is often more difficult for the court to adequately assess the need of the victim and any children for protection. However, judges in several jurisdictions respond by taking a few basic steps to learn what assistance is needed; for example, they ask questions regarding child support, alternative living arrangements, the need for shared property like a car, the need for a no-contact stipulation at places other than the residence (e.g., place of employment, local business establishments), and possible danger to the children. Some judges are careful to advise the victim at the ex parte hearing to return to the full hearing, bringing any available witnesses or other evidence. . . .

In the absence of an attorney, the likelihood that victims who proceed pro se will receive adequate protection is increased not only by the conscientiousness of judges, but also if there is competent and experienced lay assistance available. Lay help usually comes from two sources: victim advocates . . . and court clerks. . . .

Victim Advocates

Some state statutes specifically provide for the use of victim advocates to assist victims in filing for a protection order. Hawaii's statute expressly requires that "The family court shall designate an employee or appropriate non-judicial agency to assist the person is completing the petition." Georgia provides that

> Family violence shelter or social service agency staff members designated by the court may explain to all victims not represented by counsel the procedures for filling out and filing all forms and pleadings necessary for the presentation of their petition to the court.

In Duluth, Springfield and several other jurisdictions, lay advocates provide assistance to victims that extends way beyond helping them to fill out the petition forms. . . . [In Duluth], an advocate:

- determines the victim's eligibility under the statute . . . and explains the protection order process;
- assists in filling out the forms;
- explains the legal help available to the victim, the relief she can ask for, and the limitations of an order;
- joins the petitioner at the initial hearing for a temporary order;
- helps prepare the victim for the hearing for the full order; and

- attends the full hearing with the victim.

. . .

Even in Springfield and Chicago, where prosecutors represent most petitioners, victim advocates affiliated with the prosecutor's office perform an indispensable function in helping victims to prepare the petitions, and providing emotional encouragement as needed, because the state's attorneys do not have time to provide these services. A similar service is provided in many Massachusetts courts, where a victim/witness program, affiliated with the prosecutor's office, supplements the prosecutor's efforts. . . .

In many respects, a combination of legal representation and lay advocacy provides victims with the maximum protection and best enhances the court process, because victim advocates can often assist petitioners in ways that most attorneys cannot. Advocates may have a better understanding of the emotional and social impact of domestic violence and a greater ability to communicate with victims than most attorneys. They may also have more familiarity with the practical impact of common provisions in protection orders than attorneys who handle only one or two cases a year. . . .

Several judges reported that most advocates expedite court proceedings in numerous ways:

- By pre-screening petitioners for to [sic] make sure they meet the eligibility criteria under the statute, and making sure that petition forms are properly completed before the hearing;
- By accompanying distraught or intimidated victims in the courtroom, resulting in more orderly proceedings;
- By arranging to have witnesses appear with the victim, thus facilitating the orderly and complete presentation of evidence;
- By addressing petitioners' fears about appearing for the permanent hearing, or unfamiliarity with their duty to attend, thus avoiding the possible miscarriage of justice or inconvenience to the court;
- By increasing the court's ability in some cases to provide needed protection; and
- By helping to identify cases in which attorney assistance is essential.

. . .

Victim advocates do have limitations, however. Because they are not attorneys, they must be careful not to engage in the practice of law. In many jurisdictions, judges will permit advocates to sit in on the hearings but not allow them to participate. Even where advocates can participate fully in the courtroom, their effectiveness is often limited when the respondent appears with an attorney.

Court clerks

When victim advocates and attorneys are not available, assistance from court clerks is an essential last resort. In recognition of this need, several states require clerks to assist petitioners. . . .

In a few of the study sites, clerks play an extremely valuable role in assisting petitioners.... However, clerks in most jurisdictions we visited—and, reportedly, in many other parts of the country—are very cautious about providing help. In part, this hesitation reflects lack of time to undertake this new responsibility. But clerks are also concerned that they will be accused of unauthorized practice of the law. While some clerks may overreact to this threat and provide much less help than they are legally allowed to furnish, there are often good reasons for concern. Nevada's statute expressly warns that "the clerk shall not render any advice or service that requires the professional judgment of an attorney." A sign in the clerk's office in Springfield informs petitioners that "By Law, Employees Are Not Permitted to Give Legal Advice." ... The defense bar has registered complaints about clerk assistance in Chicago and in Portland, Oregon.

It is difficult to generalize regarding what clerks may or may not do because the legal definition of practice of law varies from one jurisdiction to another. However, in *Minnesota v. Errington*, 310 N.W.2d 681 (Minn. 1981), the Supreme Court of Minnesota upheld a provision in the state's civil protection order statute that requires clerks of court to assist victims in filling out protection order petition forms.... The court ruled that "the ministerial functions in question do not constitute the practice of law any more than the giving of a *Miranda* warning by a police officer to a defendant constitutes the practice of law."

Regardless of the law, clerks do at times exert substantial unsupervised influence in screening petitioners for eligibility and encouraging or discouraging them from seeking an order. In one jurisdiction, clerks mistakenly told each prospective petitioner that she was not eligible for a protection order if she had not lived with the batterer within the past year—when in fact the statute had been amended to permit order when the parties had lived together any time during the previous two years. In another site, a judge reported that only three or four protection orders are filed each year in a neighboring jurisdiction because the clerks erroneously tell every woman seeking a protection order that she must first file for divorce.

Some clerks may act out prejudices against victims of domestic violence—for example, by discouraging victims who return several times for an order. Others may act as unauthorized victim advocates; one clerk, for example, tries to persuade victims who want to have their order vacated to have it modified instead.

... The goal is to limit the role of clerks to (a) screening for statutory eligibility and (b) providing appropriate assistance in filling out the petition—in a helpful, thorough and welcoming manner.... [J]udges experienced in effective administration note that clerks need to be given adequate time to fulfil their responsibilities, regularly monitored, and rotated to prevent burnout.

* * *

NOTE

1. The report from which the above excerpt was drawn was written in part to highlight best practices among judges, courts and law enforcement personnel in the administration of the restraining order process, and encourage their emulation by others around the country. This may explain why only court clerks are singled out for explicit criticism. In many courthouses there is a messier story to be told than the excerpt suggests about the relationships among the constituencies to whom battered women look for support in obtaining their restraining orders, and about the level of support available.

For example, in many overworked prosecutors' offices, victims of domestic violence receive assistance with restraining orders, whether from prosecutors or victim advocates, only if they are simultaneously proceeding with criminal complaints against their abusers. To the extent the prosecutor's office is intent upon encouraging prosecution, linking prosecution with other assistance provides a powerful incentive to women to cooperate, but can be quite coercive. Even where prosecutors' offices genuinely lack the resources to assist all those who are seeking protective orders, they have not always welcomed an infusion of resources from other sources, leading others to question their good faith. Tension between lay advocates working in the courthouse and personnel in the prosecutor's office is commonplace. Sometimes it focuses on disagreements about the extent to which women should be encouraged to cooperate with prosecutors—with accusations that prosecutors are overly aggressive in promoting prosecution, and insufficiently attentive to safety. Sometimes it focuses on concerns that prosecutors are insufficiently experienced or aggressive, and unwilling to commit the resources necessary to build strong cases against dangerous defendants. Similar tensions exist between lay advocates and court clerks, who would often rather labor under an overload of work than have their practices open to scrutiny and criticism by advocates who may bring more experience and commitment to issues of domestic violence, but can also be insufficiently understanding of the constraints involved in working within the courthouse bureaucracy. Judges may be willing in principle to welcome advocacy programs into the courthouse, but unwilling to mediate the conflicts that arise, or even to ensure that advocates are provided with access to the clients they have come to serve.

Service of Process

Civil actions are typically commenced by service of process on the defendant; a formal delivery of papers that will detail the nature of the case, the next step to be taken (usually an answer is required from the defendant) and the timing of that next step. The plaintiff initiating the action can personally serve the defendant, or hire a professional process server to do the job. The special nature of the protective order process affects service in a number of ways. First, in the common situation in which the complainant has already received an *ex parte* order, serving the defendant is his notice that he is already subject to a court order constraining his access to his partner, as well as notification that he must defend the issuance of a permanent order. Second, because of the expedited nature of the process, the "next step" is the hearing on the permanent order, which will in most cases take place within one to three weeks of the time the *ex parte* order was granted. Third, although the restraining order is a civil mechanism, its hybrid civil/criminal status is evident in the practice of requiring law enforcement officers to serve the defendant. There are serious safety issues involved in asking the complainant to take responsibility for serving the partner she is accusing of abuse, although this is unfortunately not uncommon, and hiring professional process servers would be beyond the means of most domestic violence victims, so that the use of police is at one level a practical necessity. At the same time, it serves as a useful reminder that although the protective order is a civil remedy, its violation is in most states a criminal offense, and that any incidents of violence that have precipitated its issuance or that are incurred in its violation are themselves criminal offenses.

Serving Orders
Peter Finn and Sarah Colson, Civil Protection Orders: Legislation, Current Court Practice, and Enforcement, 60–61, National Institute of Justice, March 1990

In most jurisdictions, law enforcement officers are responsible for serving protection orders. Many officers charged with process serving read the key terms of a protection order to the defendant as part of service. For example, when the order evicts the defendant from the home, the police officer in Portland, Maine, charged with serving orders tells the respondent that he is to have absolutely no contact with his partner and is to stay away from the joint residence—even if he believes he has been invited back by the victim; a violation, the officer warns, could result in an arrest. The officer also informs the defendant of his right to a hearing and notes the hearing date. By reading the order aloud, an officer can compensate for any literacy barriers a respondent may have and can preclude future claims by a batterer that he did not understand the protection order.

Because a civil protection order is not enforceable until it has been served—and the intervening time can create serious danger of renewed or even increased violence—quick service is critical. As a result, a number of statutes have expedited service requirements, as in the Illinois statute:

> The summons . . . shall be served by a sheriff or other law enforcement officer at the earliest time and shall take precedence over other summonses except those of a similar emergency nature.

Even where a statutory mandate is provided, prompt service requires regular oversight and an appropriate allocation of resources. What may seem quick to a peace officer with numerous matters to serve may be dangerously long in light of the threat of renewed violence which prompt service can sometimes prevent. However, some sheriffs are beginning to realize the crime prevention potential prompt service can have. . . .

Judges can help insure prompt service by making sure the sheriff knows the court considers this responsibility a top priority. When a victim comes into one court for an emergency order, the judge sometimes has a staff member telephone the sheriff to have the order served within the hour. Law enforcement officers suggest that service can be expedited if the victim provides as much information as possible regarding the potential whereabouts of the respondent, including times when the batterer is likely to be at each location. To avoid giving the victim a false sense of protection, some judges make clear to petitioners that a protection order is not enforceable until it has been served.

Because of delays in service in some jurisdictions, police officers may find themselves responding to domestic violence situations in which the batterer's behavior would constitute a violation of an outstanding protection order but the order has not yet been served. State statutes or local practice may establish proper police procedures when such cases arise.... The Colorado domestic abuse statute states that:

> [I]f any person named in an order issued pursuant to this section has not been served personally with such order but has received actual notice of the existence and substance of such order from any person, any act in violation of such order may be deemed by the court a violation of such order and may be deemed sufficient to subject the person named in such order to any penalty for such violation.

Similarly, a police trainer in Nashville instructs officers that, upon verification of an outstanding protection order, *they* may inform the respondent named in the order of the existence of the order. At that point, if the offender refuses to leave despite an order prohibiting him from the household (or if he returns later), the officer can arrest the offender for violating the order. The trainer also noted that officers can make their own determination about whether or not the offender has knowledge of the protection order (for example, if the victim credibly reports that she has notified him).

Another option is for the court, at the emergency hearing, to advise victims to obtain a certified copy of the emergency order before leaving the court and keep the original and a photocopy with them at all times. Then, if the offender approaches and threatens them before being served, they will have a certified copy to hand to an officer called to the scene—who can then serve the offender.

In cases where peace officers cannot accomplish personal service, alternatives include public posting, sending the order by certified mail, or permitting personal service by other parties. For example, the Minnesota Domestic Abuse Act permits service by publication of the full notice in a qualified newspaper. The Act authorizes this alternative to personal service only if:

> the petitioner files with the court an affidavit stating that an attempt at personal service made by a sheriff was unsuccessful because the respondent is avoiding service by concealment or otherwise, and that a copy of the petition and notice of hearing has been mailed to the

respondent at the respondent's residence or that the residence is not known to the petitioner.

The Intrafamily Rules of the District of Columbia permit service by leaving copies of the order at the offender's home or usual place of abode "... with a person of suitable age and discretion then residing therein who is not a party."

* * *

NOTE

1. In the Harrell and Smith study cited in the previous section, which looked at 355 restraining orders issued between January and September of 1991 in a single state, 40% of women did not return to court for a full hearing and a permanent order after their emergency order issued. Of these, more than 40% attributed their failure to follow through to the difficulties they experienced getting the emergency order served. Adele Harris and Barbara E. Smith, *Effects of Restraining Orders on Domestic Violence Victims,* DO ARRESTS AND RESTRAINING ORDERS WORK? 214, 219 (E.S. Buzawa and C.G. Buzawa, eds. 1996).

Duration, Extension and Withdrawal or Dismissal of Orders

In a majority of states, a "permanent" order is in fact, under the governing statute, an order for any period up to a year, but not longer. In a few states (less than ten), the statute does not specify the duration of an order. Slightly more than ten states afford relief for only two through six months, and only a handful give protection for longer than a year. In Illinois and Wisconsin, the maximum duration is two years and in California and Hawaii, three years.

Almost half of the jurisdictions allow an order to be extended, requiring a hearing prior to the initial expiration date. According to Barbara Hart:

> Codes provide courts with discretion in fixing the duration of the extended order. Some codes condition an extension upon a violation of the order for protection or good cause shown and direct that extension be for a fixed period. The Massachusetts code may be the most explicit about the circumstances of extension of an order issued pursuant to notice and hearing:
>
>> Every order shall on its face state the time and date the order is to expire and shall include the date and time that the matter will again be heard. If the plaintiff appears at the court at the date and time the order is to expire, the court shall determine whether or not to extend the order for any additional time reasonably necessary to protect the plaintiff or to enter a permanent order. When the expiration date stated on the order is on a weekend day or holiday, or a date when the court is closed to business, the order shall not expire until the next date that the court is open to business. The plaintiff may appear on such next court business day at the time designated by the order to request that the order be

> extended. The court may also extend the order upon motion of the plaintiff, for such additional time as it deems necessary to protect from abuse the plaintiff or any child in the plaintiff's care or custody. The fact that abuse has not occurred during the pendency of an order shall not, in itself, constitute sufficient ground for denying or failing to extend the order, or allowing an order to expire or be vacated, or for refusing to issue a new order. [M.G.L. Ann. ch. 209A § 3 (1992).]

Barbara Hart, *State Codes on Domestic Violence: Analysis, Commentary and Recommendations,* 1992 JUVENILE AND FAMILY COURT JOURNAL 17–18 (1992).

In most jurisdictions, the legislation specifically provides that the complainant may seek to vacate the order or have it dismissed. Some statutes require the consent of all the parties, and some require a hearing before an existing order can be dismissed. The New Jersey statute is an example of legislation that seems to permit the court to deny a complainant's motion to dismiss, since the court is required to review the full record of previous hearings before ruling. In Stevenson v. Stevenson, 714 A.2d 986 (N.J. Super. Ct. Ch. Div. 1998), a New Jersey court interpreted the legislation in this way; denying a plaintiff's motion to dismiss. The court concluded that a "reasonable, objective and independent determination of the facts leads to the inescapable conclusion that a real threat of recurrence of domestic violence by the defendant upon his battered wife will exist if the Final Restraining Order is dissolved," and declined to be "an accomplice to further violence by this defendant." In practice, dismissal is generally without prejudice, but the governing legislation does not mandate this result.

The central issue in these situations is whether the complainant is seeking to have the order vacated voluntarily, or because of pressure exerted by her partner or his family, friends or other allies. It is enormously frustrating for advocates and judges to see a woman whom they believe to be at risk for physical and emotional abuse seeking to have an order vacated. It is even more frustrating, perhaps, when there are children whose wellbeing may also be affected if the order is vacated. In this context it makes good sense to impose a process which allows for careful inquiry into the petitioner's motivation in making the request, and her appreciation of the consequences, which might include, for example, the intervention of child protective services on behalf of children who will be exposed to the defendant's abuse if the protective order is lifted. Ultimately, however, it is hard to argue that the complainant should not be permitted to truncate a process which is civil in nature and which she has initiated.

In the Klein study of 663 restraining orders issued by the Quincy District Court in Massachusetts in 1990, mentioned in the previous section, almost half the women who received permanent (one year) orders returned to court to vacate them prior to the termination date. Those who had had prior restraining orders were more likely to leave the most recent order in effect until its termination date. Most interestingly, the re-abuse rate was not different for those who dropped their orders, as opposed to those who left them in effect until they expired. Andrew R. Klein, *Re-Abuse in a Population of Court–Restrained Male Batterers: Why Restraining Orders Don't Work,* DO ARRESTS AND RESTRAINING ORDERS WORK? 192, 200 (1996).

Mutual orders of protection

Imagine these three increasingly common scenarios:

(1) Police arrive at the scene of a domestic incident, having been called by a neighbor. They find a couple, both showing signs of a recent physical altercation. The woman has swelling around one eye, and bruising on her arms; the man has scratches on his face and arms. The woman complains that the man was "beating her up" accusing her of flirting with another man; the man complains that he was yelling at her, but that she "came flying at him" and he hurt her only in trying to get her to "lay off." She alleges the reverse; that he punched her in the eye when she argued with him, and she tried to defend herself. They are both very angry, swearing at one another, using provocative language, and resisting the interventions of the police. Under recent revisions in the state's abuse prevention legislation, the police have a positive responsibility to arrest anyone whom they have probable cause to believe has perpetrated domestic violence. They arrest both parties. Before long they are standing in front of a judge, who must decide whether to release them, and, if so, under what conditions. The police report indicates that each party was violent toward, and inflicted injuries on, the another.

(2) A woman obtains an *ex parte* order on the basis of an affidavit detailing an incident in which her partner threatened her with a knife. When she and her partner both appear at the hearing for the permanent order, he alleges that the violence in the relationship is mutual, and that he too needs the protection of an order.

(3) A man is arrested at the scene of a domestic incident, but later released without the imposition of any conditions, and without a restraining order being issued. The next day he appears in court and obtains an *ex parte* order on the basis of an affidavit which describes the same incident, but attributes the violence to his partner. At the hearing for the permanent order, his partner alleges that she has consistently been the target of his aggression, and that she is the one in need of a protective order.

What all of these scenarios have in common is that they provide a temptation to busy law enforcement personnel and judges to issue mutual restraining orders, on the grounds that since it is clearly best for the parties to stay out of one another's way, that goal can be accomplished as readily by two orders as by one, without the time and effort needed to sort out whether the relationship involves one perpetrator or two. However, the practice is highly problematic. First, it contributes to the arguments of those who allege that restraining orders are issued so casually that they should be given no probative value in other legal contexts. Victims of domestic violence can ill afford this "cheapening of the currency." Second, to the extent the orders are given weight in other contexts, they may unfairly prejudice the party against whom an order has issued as a matter of convenience rather than evidence. Third, mutual orders create the potential for confusion when police or the criminal justice system are later asked to enforce the orders or address violations, and may put victims of domestic violence at increased risk. Finally, the perpetrator who is successful in obtaining an order against his victim is reinforced in his tendency to place the blame for his violence on her, and deny his own responsibility.

A few state legislatures have explicitly addressed the issue of mutual protection orders. Some statutes prohibit the entry of a mutual order unless both parties have properly filed written petitions and service has been made on both parties. California has adopted language that permits mutual orders only if both parties personally appear and each party presents evidence of actionable domestic abuse. Recognizing that mutual orders of protection often leave law enforcement uncertain about enforcement, some statutes explicitly require that if a mutual order is issued, it must be "sufficiently specific to apprise any law officer as to which party has violated the order, if the parties are in or appear to be in violation of the order." Some state statutes have also addressed the problem of the perpetrator who files first, by authorizing the court to realign the designation of the parties when the court concludes that the original petitioner is the perpetrator of domestic violence.

Recently, the federal Violence Against Women Act has lent its support to those concerned about the impact of mutual orders. As described in the previous section, the Act provides in general that orders issued in one state shall be given full faith and credit in every other, so that for the first time an order issued in one state can be fully enforced in another. Where a state court has issued mutual orders, however, only the petitioner's order is accorded full faith and credit, unless the defendant has filed a separate petition or pleading seeking an order, and the court has made specific findings that the defendant, as well as the petitioner, is entitled to an order. 18 U.S.C. § 2265.

Even without the assistance of specific state or federal statutory provisions, judges at the state level can resist the demand for mutual orders by simply insisting that every protective order meet the substantive and procedural requirements laid out in the governing statute. Although there may be more work involved for law enforcement personnel and judges in sorting out competing claims of abuse, the system is ultimately best served by protecting both the integrity of the restraining order process, and the safety of those who depend on it. The following case demonstrates the appeal of mutual orders, but also documents a clear-sighted judicial response.

Deacon v. Landers

68 Ohio App.3d 26, 587 N.E.2d 395.
Court of Appeals of Ohio (1990).

■ STEPHENSON, JUDGE.

The facts pertinent to this appeal are as follows. On March 15, 1989, appellant filed, in the court below, her petition in domestic violence supported by affidavit. Therein, appellant alleged, inter alia, that she and appellee cohabited, that appellee was abusive to her, and that she was in fear of physical harm. Appellant sought both an ex parte and a permanent protection order. . . . An ex parte order was granted that day, and a full hearing was scheduled for March 23, 1989.

Due to difficulties in obtaining service on appellee, the ex parte order and hearing were continued, several times, until April 20, 1989. At that time, appellee appeared at the hearing, pro se, and consented to a protection order. Toward the end of the hearing, appellee requested that the court issue a similar protection order against appellant. Without any presentation of evidence, and over objection of counsel, the requested order was granted.

On April 27, 1989, a judgment granting a one year protection order against both parties was filed. The judgment further scheduled a subsequent hearing to determine ownership of personal property located in appellant's residence, but found, with respect to the protective orders, that there was no just reason for delay.

. . .

In her first two assignments of error, appellant advances dual arguments and, therefore, we will consider them jointly. First, appellant asserts, inter alia, that the trial court below was obligated, both statutorily and under generally accepted due process standards of notice and hearing, to afford her a proper hearing in which to defend herself before judgment could be entered against her. . . . Then appellant argues that she was denied such a hearing and, therefore, an entry of judgment against her was in error. We agree.

Generally, due process of law as guaranteed by the federal and state Constitutions requires some legal procedure in which the person proceeded against, if that person is to be bound by a judgment, must be afforded an opportunity to defend himself. . . . The fundamental requisites of due process of law are notice and an opportunity to be heard. . . .

Furthermore, as appellant asserts, the opportunity to be heard and to defend oneself is required by R.C. 3113.31 before judgment of a protection order can be entered against a party to the action. The statute provides, in pertinent part, as follows:

> (E)(1) After an ex parte or *full hearing*, the court may grant any protection order, with or without bond, or approve any consent agreement to bring about a cessation of domestic violence against the family or household members.
>
> (Emphasis added.)

Insofar as R.C. 3113.31 is concerned, and to a more general degree with regard to due process, we must determine what is meant by the phrase "full hearing," and also determine whether appellant was granted such a hearing. Initially, we note that the statute does not define "full hearing." We are also unable to find any reported decision in this state which defines the parameters of a "full hearing."

However, other jurisdictions have determined that a "full hearing" embraces not only the right to present evidence, but also a reasonable opportunity to know the claims of an opposing party and to meet them.... A "full hearing" is one in which ample opportunity is afforded to all parties to make, by evidence and argument, a showing fairly adequate to establish the propriety or impropriety of the step asking to be taken....

Without attempting to set definitive guidelines for the manner in which to conduct a "full hearing" under R.C. 3113.31, we hold that where the issuance of a protection order is contested, the court must, at the very least, allow for presentation of evidence, both direct and rebuttal, as well as arguments. In ascertaining whether such opportunity was granted to appellant, we note the following portion of the transcript:

"MR. LANDERS: I would also like for the same protection for me, that she stay away from me. Even after I've been served this petition, she's still gone and found out where I'm at and we've had lunch together and things like that. * * * I'd also like for the same protection.

"THE COURT: I'm going to have to go back to the statute. I'm not sure that this statute permits that kind of, that kind of order, although I think under the same section of the statute which grants the Court authority to grant other equitable relief, the Court would have the authority to provide for restraint against Ms. Deacon from any harassment or molestation. I don't say this, Ms. Deacon, by way of pointing a finger or agreeing with Mr. Landers, but so long as you both understand that you're just not to have any contact. Your—

"MS. KOWIESKI: Your Honor, I would object at this time to granting Mr. Landers some kind of restraining order without so much as an affidavit on his part indicating the evidence—

"THE COURT: What's the problem? You certainly don't want your client associating with him, and he doesn't want her associating with him, and I think that the bare statement is sufficient to grant restraint. I don't think it's going to be necessary, but I don't see any reason why it hurts anything. Nobody's mad at your client, Ms. Kowieski. We're just trying to be fair about this and saying that neither party should have anything to do with the other. It's a very simple matter.

"MS. KOWIESKI: No, I agree with that, Your Honor. I believe that is, would be accomplished by the—

"THE COURT: It will be accomplished by restraining your client from any contact with Mr. Landers and that will also be in the order * * *."

It is manifestly clear from this exchange that appellant was denied an opportunity to cross-examine appellee and to present rebuttal evidence. Accordingly, we hold that appellant was neither given a "full hearing" ... nor afforded an opportunity to be heard or defend herself consistent with due process of law. Appellant's first and second assignments of error are, therefore, sustained.

In her final assignment of error, appellant argues that there was insufficient evidence adduced at trial to sustain the issuance of a protection order and, thus, the court erred as a matter of law. We agree.

In Thomas v. Thomas (1988) . . . , the Franklin county Court of Appeals held that "[t]he statutory criterion to determine whether or not to grant a civil protection order pursuant to R.C. 3113.31 is *the existence or threatened existence of domestic violence*." (Emphasis added.) The only evidence offered by appellee in support of his request for a protection order was testimony that, after the petition in the action below had been served, appellant sought him out and they had lunch. Such testimony cannot support a finding of the existence, or threatened existence, of domestic violence as defined in R.C. 3113.31(A)(1) (i.e., causing, or attempting to cause bodily injury, placing another person in fear of imminent harm or abusing a child).

The decision to grant a civil protection order is within the discretion of the court. . . . An abuse of that discretion connotes more than an error of law or judgment; it implies an unreasonable, arbitrary attitude. . . . There being no evidence to support a finding of domestic violence or threat of domestic violence against appellee, we hold that the grant of a protection order against appellant constituted an abuse of discretion. Accordingly, appellant's third assignment of error is sustained.

* * *

■ GREY, JUDGE, dissenting.

I respectfully dissent. I believe we are elevating form over substance.

I agree with the majority that a court may not impose a protective order against a person without due process, but that is not what happened here. The court, based on the evidence, found that granting the order was warranted and said it would issue it. Respondent then asked, in effect, that a condition of the order be that petitioner leave him alone.

R.C. 3113.31 (E)(1)(h) says that the court may "grant other relief that the court considers equitable and fair * * *." While the order actually entered in this case did not expressly state that petitioner's obligation to leave respondent along was a condition precedent to respondent's obligation to leave petitioner alone, the entry cannot be construed in any other way. I do not regard this as error in any way.

* * *

QUESTIONS

If it were the case that defendant's request was made in good faith, a proposition that was in no way tested by the trial judge, can you think of a way of responding to it without issuing a restraining order against the petitioner? Do you think the dissenting judge was right in his analysis that the problem with the trial judge's disposition of the case was a problem of "form," or, as he said elsewhere in his opinion, "an imprecise use of words?"

D. ENFORCEMENT

> Enforcement is the Achilles heel of the civil protection process, because an order without enforcement at best offers scant protection, and at worst increases the victim's danger by creating a false sense of security. Offenders may routinely violate orders, if they believe there is no real risk of being arrested. For enforcement to work, the courts need to monitor compliance, victims must report violations, and, most of all, police, prosecutors, and judges should respond sternly to violations that are reported.

Peter Finn and Sarah Colson, CIVIL PROTECTION ORDERS: LEGISLATION, CURRENT COURT PRACTICE, AND ENFORCEMENT 4 (National Institute of Justice, 1990).

Violation

Any departure by the defendant from the terms of the restraining order is a violation, regardless of whether it involves actual violence, and regardless of whether the conduct would be criminal in its own right. Thus, a single telephone call may violate a no-contact provision, and the defendant's presence within 100 feet of the petitioner's place of work may violate the "safety zone" created by the order. If the order establishes the defendant's visitation schedule, and he returns the children an hour later than the order dictates, that too is a violation. Although this seems obvious enough, police are often reluctant to enforce the order, and particularly reluctant to exercise their arrest powers, unless the defendant's conduct is independently criminal—even when the governing legislation makes violation a criminal misdemeanor, or authorizes enforcement through criminal contempt proceedings.

What if the defendant prevails upon the petitioner to allow him back into the house the protective order demands he vacate, or the petitioner independently invites him to meet with her for coffee in violation of the "safety zone" created by the order? Frustrated by petitioners' apparent disregard for the terms of the orders they have secured, courts have on occasion ruled that the order in question is automatically vacated by the parties' reunification. Indeed, prior to a 1990 amendment to the New Jersey domestic violence statute, New Jersey courts had routinely given reunification this effect. See, for example, Mohamed v. Mohamed, 557 A.2d 696 (N.J. Super. Ct. App. Div. 1989). However, the current trend, in both legislation and case law, is to view the protective order as a matter between the respondent and the court, so that the petitioner cannot invite or excuse a violation.

As of 1995, statutes in eight states; California, Delaware, Illinois, Maine, Minnesota, New Hampshire, Pennsylvania and Texas, expressly provided that reunification of the parties does not preclude enforcement of a protective order. CAL. PENAL CODE § 13710(b) (West 1992); DEL. CODE ANN. tit. 10, § 949(d) (Interim Supp. 1993); 40 ILCS 2312/20 (Smith-Hurd 1992); ME. REV. STAT. ANN. tit. 19, § 766.8 (West Supp. 1993); N.H. REV. STAT. ANN.

§ 173B:4V (1992); 23 PA. CONST. STAT. ANN. § 6113(g) (1991); TEX. FAM. CODE ANN. § 71.16 (West Supp. 1992).

Several states, including Maine and Minnesota, have gone one step further, and confirm by statute what has become the working understanding in many jurisdictions, that a petitioner cannot be found in violation of her own order, even if she invites the defendant to ignore its terms. ME. REV. STAT. ANN. tit. 19 § 766.8 (West Supp. 1993); MINN. STAT. ANN. § 5158B.01(14)(g) (West Supp. 1993).

In Cole v. Cole, 556 N.Y.S.2d 217 (Fam. Ct. 1990), the parties had reunified for a two month period after a protection order issued that prohibited the defendant from harassing, menacing, assaulting, attempting to assault, or recklessly endangering the petitioner. After the parties broke up again, the defendant broke into the petitioner's home and sexually assaulted her. The court found that the petitioner had not waived her right to enforce the order, and that the reunification did not waive a contempt charge for marital rape:

> The validity of the court's order was in no way impaired, affected, nor nullified, by the petitioner's consensual cohabitation with the respondent after entry of the order. As stated in the order itself, the order remains in full force and effect until such time, if at all, as the order is modified or terminated by a future order of a court having competent jurisdiction.
>
> The court holds that acquiescence by a petitioner in cohabitation by a respondent after an order of protection is issued does not constitute a waiver by the petitioner of her right to be free from intrusions by the respondent after cohabiting terminates, upon either the rights of safety or the rights of privacy secured by the order. A victim of domestic violence who has procured an order of protection is entitled to the court's protection from further violence throughout the duration of an order of protection, even if the victim is desirous of pursuing a goal of voluntary reconciliation with the offender. Attempts to salvage the otherwise beneficial aspects of a relationship which is afflicted by unlawful behavior would be discouraged if the law permitted the very attempt of salvation to result in a loss of protection from the sinister aspect. The law does not impair an individual's choice to pursue a relationship with one whose prior conduct has evinced a need for judicial limits upon destructive behavior.

Id. See also, City of Reynoldsburg v. Eichenberger, No. CA–3492, 1990 Ohio App. LEXIS 5955 (Dec. 1, 1993), and People v. Townsend, 538 N.E.2d 1297 (Ill. App. Ct. 1989). New Jersey has also modified its pre–1990 stance, ruling in Torres v. Lancellotti, 607 A.2d 1375 (N.J. Super Ct. Ch. Div. 1992), that a court may not vacate a protection order on the basis of the parties' reunification without determining whether a true reconciliation occurred, and whether there is an ongoing need for protection. Attempted reconciliations of short duration do not amount to true reconciliations.

Under these new statutory and case law guidelines, there is room for complaint on the part of defendants that they may be "lured" into violations by petitioners who invite reconciliation, and then seek to enforce orders containing no-contact or stay-away provisions. An obvious precaution for a defendant who is invited and wants to reestablish contact with the petitioner is to refrain from any behavior that might prompt her to change her mind and seek to enforce the order. A safer course might be for the defendant to insist that renewed contact between them must depend on a modification of the order to allow contact; for the petitioner's safety it should still preclude further abuse. This is the approach suggested by Catherine F. Klein and Leslye E; Orloff, in *Providing Legal Protection for Battered Women: An Analysis of State Statutes and Case Law,* 21 HOFSTRA L. REV. 801, 1116–17 (1995), who go on to say:

> Simple procedures for modification should be available in all jurisdictions. Should petitioner wish to separate again and respondent refuses to comply, she may return to court to have her civil protection order modified to re-impose the stay away and no contact provisions. Evidence of post-reunification violence and petitioner's desire to have the respondent stay away from her would constitute sufficient evidence for courts to grant petitioner the modification.

As the authors point out, courts routinely grant protection orders which prohibit abuse but do not preclude contact, and, in appropriate cases, such orders have an important role to play:

> in shifting the balance of power in the relationship so as to reduce or eliminate continued violence.... In light of research that indicates that most battered women make between two and five attempts to leave a batterer before they succeed, it is very important for courts to issue civil protection orders to parties whether or not they are ready to separate permanently. Battered women should not be punished or left without protection because they have attempted to save their relationships when they seek civil protection order enforcement after parties have reconciled.

Id. at 1117.

Monitoring Compliance

In general, if a civil court order is to be enforced, the person who originally applied for the order must return to court to complain of a violation. In most jurisdictions, this is also true for orders of protection. However, in the domestic violence context there are good reasons to encourage other actors to play a role in monitoring compliance. First, many victims negotiate the restraining order process *pro se*, and may emerge with an order in hand, but with no clear understanding of how to enforce it, beyond calling the police to respond to a violation. Second, many victims suffer violations which they are afraid to report, without encouragement and support from those who can work with them to ensure their safety as they challenge the defendant's continuing violence. Third, many defendants are skilled in manipulating the system, and will engage in behaviors that appear to evade the direct prohibitions of the order, so that victims may need assistance in framing defendants' conduct as violative. Finally, if society has a stake in making the protective order system credible in order to maximize its deterrent effect, and if it is clear that orders will routinely go unenforced if their enforcement depends on victim initiative, then others need to get involved.

In their 1990 report for the National Institute of Justice, Peter Finn and Sarah Colson suggest that courts take responsibility for monitoring compliance with orders of protection, delegating that task to other appropriate agencies. The example they provide is Duluth, Minnesota:

> [J]udges in Duluth have an arrangement with the Domestic Abuse Intervention Project, which provides a counseling and education program for batterers, to monitor the behavior of respondents who are ordered into the program by the court. Monitoring occurs in three ways. Project staff review police records each day and inform the court if an incident involving a protection order violation has occurred. Project staff also contact each victim once a month to learn of any renewed violence. Finally, if an offender fails to attend counseling sessions or reports new abuses or violations, project staff request a court hearing. If the offender is found in contempt of court, he is usually sentenced to jail, but (for a first violation), given the option of completing the program while serving a probated sentence.
>
> Judges also inform victims that they should contact the Intervention Project if the defendant violates the order. To assist in this aspect of monitoring, the Duluth Women's Coalition maintains contact with victims who have used the Coalition's services, asking them to discuss any problems or violations of the order. When violations are reported during Coalition education group meetings for victims, advocates talk to victims about reporting the violation and provide support and information to do so.

Peter Finn and Sarah Colson, CIVIL PROTECTION ORDERS: LEGISLATION, CURRENT COURT PRACTICE, AND ENFORCEMENT 56–57 (National Institute of Justice, 1990). If the defendant is also on probation, whether for abuse-related or other crimes, the probation department may be another source of information, particularly if probation officers are working collaboratively with batterers' intervention programs, and if the probation department has a victim-contact policy in place.

Is there a tension here between monitoring by outside parties and victim autonomy? If external monitoring appears to be necessary to prevent under-enforcement, how do actors within the system deal with the situation where enforcement goes against the wishes of the petitioner? Should they override her desires on the theory that the order is between the defendant and the court? Or should external monitoring be used only to ensure that enforcement is accomplished in any case where it is helpful to, and desired by, the victim? These issues will be treated in much greater depth in the next chapter, in the context of criminal prosecution.

Alternative Mechanisms of Enforcement

Traditionally, civil court orders are enforced through contempt proceedings. Criminal contempt proceedings seek to punish the defendant for flouting the authority of the court, while civil contempt proceedings seek to secure future compliance. In line with this tradition, many states offer civil and/or criminal contempt mechanisms for the enforcement of protective orders. However, the primary means of enforcing a protective order today is to charge the defendant with a criminal misdemeanor. More than eighty percent of jurisdictions now make violation of an order a criminal offense. While the overwhelming majority treat the violation as a misdemeanor, a handful of states—Minnesota, Missouri, North Dakota, Ohio, Texas and Washington—have now made at least some violations a felony. In more than forty percent of jurisdictions a violation can be enforced through either criminal charges or contempt charges. In only about twenty percent of jurisdictions is the petitioner limited to contempt proceedings, and in most of those has a choice between criminal or civil contempt. In many jurisdictions police are mandated, or authorized, to arrest the defendant whom they find at the scene of a violation, or whom they have probable cause to believe has violated an order, whether the arrest is for a criminal offense or for criminal contempt. If the defendant's behavior would be criminal in and of itself, regardless of whether it violated an order of protection, then a final option is to charge the defendant with that underlying crime.

As Klein and Orloff report, "[t]he statutory trend in recent years is to augment contempt enforcement with misdemeanor charges, and to heighten the criminal classification for a violation of a protection order." Catherine F. Klein and Leslye E. Orloff, *Providing Legal Protection for Battered Women: An Analysis of State Statutes and Case Law,* 21 Hofstra L. Rev. 801, 1107–08 (1995). This trend reflects the conviction that only by classifying a protective order violation as a crime can society demonstrate its commitment to the protective order process, ensure adequate police response to violations, and impose sufficient sanctions. However, as the next section suggests, the reality of how violations are processed through the criminal justice system threatens to undercut both the message conveyed by criminalization, and its practical advantages. If most violations do not produce arrests, most arrests do not result in prosecutions, and most prosecutions result in minimal sanctions, rarely including incarceration, defendants have little reason to fear the consequences of continuing to abuse their partners. If defendants are routinely released pending trial, and trials are delayed, women remain at risk during a time of particular vulnerability, and the immediacy of the connection between the defendant's conduct and his being called to account for it is lost.

Clearly, much remains to be done to ensure that the criminalization strategy lives up to its potential. But the difficulty of changing entrenched practices and attitudes, and the need to respect the rights of defendants, which increase with the severity of the charge brought and penalty sought, suggest that other enforcement strategies should not be abandoned. In particular, the criminal contempt process may have more to recommend it than generally understood. The major disadvantages of criminal contempt as an enforcement strategy have been thought to be two. First, the maximum sentence for criminal contempt, a petty offense, is usually no more than six months. Second, police have often not been willing, even if authorized, to arrest for criminal contempt.

Since the vast majority of defendants convicted of the misdemeanor of violating a protective order do not serve as much as six months of jail time, the first concern evaporates as it meets the reality of enforcement practice. In addition, separate acts of contempt can be consolidated for hearing, and elicit separate penalties which can be aggregated without triggering a higher level of due process for the defendant or the requirement for a jury trial. As the court said in Scott v. District of Columbia, 122 A.2d 579, 581 (D.C. 1956): "[w]e see no reason why consolidation of a number of petty offenses in one information should confer upon the defendant a right he would not have had if the charges were brought in separate informations." The second concern can be met by expressly incorporating the arrest power into the legislation establishing criminal contempt as an appropriate remedy for a protective order violation, and then ensuring that police are trained to exercise that power when responding to violations. Alternatively, police training could address the extent of the arrest power authorized for criminal contempt by general legislation, and establish protocols for its use in enforcing restraining order violations.

The major advantages of criminal contempt proceedings are the speed with which they can be initiated and concluded, the simplicity of a bench rather than a jury trial, and the possibility in many jurisdictions for victims to initiate their own contempt proceedings, if the state is slow or reluctant to prosecute. For this possibility of private action to offer real advantages, of course, victims must be able to find competent and affordable representation. Although defendants in criminal contempt proceedings enjoy all the same due process rights as criminal defendants, neither the absence of a jury trial, nor pretrial detention violates those rights. On the legitimacy of pretrial detention see, for example, Commonwealth v. Allen, 486 A.2d 363 (Pa. 1984), cert. denied, 474 U.S. 842 (1985).

One commentator has made the interesting argument that criminal contempt proceedings can also be preferable to criminal prosecution for a violation because they bring the defendant back, promptly, before the very same court, and possibly even the same judge who issued the order the defendant violated:

> Granting a speedy hearing is essential because batterers are more likely to respond to a fast contempt mechanism than a slower criminal prosecution, because deterrence is generally more potent when a quick punishment follows an infraction. From a batterer's unique psychological perspective, however, contempt also offers distinct advantages. Batterers are manipulative individuals who think they can talk their way out of trouble or evade the constraints that society imposes on individual behavior. Also, because they tend to conceive relationships in terms of power, they tend to respond only to a specific threat from an identifiable person whom they perceive as more powerful. A directive from a family court judge that he or she will lock up the batterer for contempt, which is then followed by a contempt hearing before the same judge, is therefore more effective than the general threat of criminal prosecution—especially since many batterers do not regard their behavior as criminal.

David M. Zlotnick, *Empowering the Battered Woman: The Use of Criminal Contempt Sanctions to Enforce Civil Protection Orders,* 56 OHIO ST. L. J. 1153, 1201–02 (1995). Zlotnick also argues that it may be easier for police and judges to "get behind" contempt proceedings, where the focus is on the defendant's flouting the authority of the court, rather than on his behavior towards his victim: "Judges simply do not like being disobeyed, particularly when they have issued a direct order to someone, and studies suggest that judicial behavior can have profound effects on the outcome of domestic violence cases." Id. at 1204–05.

The potential inherent in the creative use of criminal contempt proceedings does not mean that contempt should be the sole enforcement mechanism. Holding a defendant in contempt is perfectly compatible with also prosecuting him for the crime of violating the order of protection, or for the underlying crimes involved in that violation. In cases in which a restraining order violation involves serious violence, it may be that a contempt proceeding would secure the victim's safety by imposing immediate pre-trial detention and a jail sentence of short duration, while the state prepared to prosecute the criminal charges—which might well be felonies rather than misdemeanors. The extent to which these combined strategies raise issues of double jeopardy is the topic of the next section.

Double Jeopardy

There are several ways in which double jeopardy issues can arise when legal proceedings are initiated in the context of domestic violence. One occurs when a complainant seeks a protective order on the basis of an abusive incident for which the state is also seeking to prosecute the perpetrator. Another occurs when a defendant violates a protective order and faces contempt proceedings, but is also subject to prosecution by the state for the underlying crimes that constituted the violation. A third situation, in which the defendant is prosecuted both for the crime of violating the order and the underlying crimes that constituted the violation is less likely to trigger a double jeopardy challenge, because the prosecutions are likely to be brought together.

In 1993, the United States Supreme Court issued its first decision ever in a domestic violence case, and the issue raised was double jeopardy. The case, U.S. v. Dixon, 509 U.S. 688, 113 S. Ct. 2849 (1993), is the second of two readings below. The first reading summarizes the state of statutory and case law in the states with respect to double jeopardy in domestic violence cases prior to the Supreme Court's decision.

Double Jeopardy
Catherine F. Klein and Leslye J. Orloff
Providing Legal Protection for Battered Women: An Analysis of State Statutes and Case Law, 51 Hofstra Law Review 801, 1122–24 (1995)

Double jeopardy does not bar a subsequent criminal prosecution for the same act for which a civil protection order is issued. Courts should not permit the existence of a criminal prosecution to delay the issuance of a civil protection order to a domestic violence victim.

Moreover, double jeopardy does not preclude a subsequent criminal prosecution for violation of a different civil protection order from that which formed the basis for a criminal contempt finding. For example, in *People v. Allen*,[1] the court held that a subsequent criminal prosecution for burglary, criminal mischief, criminal trespass, and menacing, after the defendant was held in contempt for violating a stay away protection order by breaking into the petitioner's home and threatening to kill her, did not violate double jeopardy since the proof required for the criminal offenses was greater than the proof needed to establish indirect contempt of the stay away provision.

However, both state civil protection order statutes and case law address the more difficult issue of possible double jeopardy where the state pursues a criminal prosecution based on the same incident for which the defendant was or may be held in criminal contempt of a civil protection order. A number of state domestic violence statutes specifically confirm that a civil protection order does not preclude other civil or criminal remedies. Missouri law states that enforcement of protection orders through contempt does not preclude criminal prosecution, or vice versa. Indeed, the courts have clearly identified the need for this approach. In *Commonwealth v. Smith*,[2] the court noted that to bar subsequent criminal prosecutions because of a finding of criminal contempt would gravely impair either the state's interest in punishing crime or severely undermine the practical utility of the Protection from Abuse Act in preventing physical and sexual abuse.

. . . In *United States v. Dixon*, the [Supreme] Court ruled that double jeopardy would not bar a battered woman from enforcing her civil protection order through criminal contempt while the state proceeds against her batterer criminally for his crime, as long as the contempt proceeding and the criminal prosecution each require proof of additional elements under the *Blockburger* "same elements" test. This ruling assures that battered women with civil protection orders will no longer be forced to choose between criminal prosecution and proceeding to enforce civil protection orders through criminal contempt when civil protection order respondents commit new crimes against petitioners.

. . .

NOTE

1. United States v. Dixon involved two cases raising similar issues, consolidated by the District of Columbia Court of Appeals. Dixon was arrested for murder, and released pending trial under an order warning him that he should not commit any criminal offense, and that he would be subject to prosecution for contempt of court if he violated this condition of his release. He was subsequently arrested and indicted for possession of cocaine with

1. 787 P.2d 174 (Colo. Ct. App. 1989).

2. 552 A.2d 292 (Pa. Super. Ct. 1988), *appeal denied*, 568 A.2d 1247 (Pa. 1989).

intent to distribute, held in contempt, and prosecuted. Michael Foster was the defendant in the second, domestic violence, case.

United States v. Alvin J. Dixon and Michael Foster

509 U.S. 688, 113 S. Ct. 2849.
Supreme Court of the United States, 1993.

JUSTICE SCALIA announced the judgment of the Court and delivered the opinion of the Court with respect to Parts I, II, and IV, and an opinion with respect to Parts III and V, in which JUSTICE KENNEDY joins. In both of these cases, respondents were tried for criminal contempt of court for violating court orders that prohibited them from engaging in conduct that was later the subject of a criminal prosecution. We consider whether the subsequent criminal prosecutions are barred by the Double Jeopardy Clause.

I

... Based on Foster's alleged physical attacks on her in the past, Foster's estranged wife Ana obtained a civil protection order (CPO).... The order, to which Foster consented, required that he not " 'molest, assault, or in any manner threaten or physically abuse' " Ana Foster; a separate order, not implicated here, sought to protect her mother....

Over the course of eight months, Ana Foster filed three separate motions to have her husband held in contempt for numerous violations of the CPO. Of the 16 alleged episodes, the only charges relevant here are three separate instances of threats ... and two assaults ..., in the most serious of which Foster "threw [his wife] down basement stairs, kicking her body[,] ... pushed her head into the floor causing head injuries, [and Ana Foster] lost consciousness." ...

After issuing a notice of hearing and ordering Foster to appear, the Court held a 3–day bench trial. Counsel for Ana Foster and her mother prosecuted the action; the United States was not represented at trial, although the United States Attorney was apparently aware of the action, as was the court aware of a separate grand jury proceeding on some of the alleged criminal conduct. As to the assault charges, the court stated that Ana Foster would have "to prove as an element, first that there was a Civil Protection Order, and then [that] ... the assault as defined by the criminal code, in fact occurred." ... The court found Foster guilty beyond a reasonable doubt of four counts of criminal contempt ..., but acquitted him on other counts, including the ... threats. He was sentenced to an aggregate 600 days' imprisonment....

The United States Attorney's office later obtained an indictment charging Foster with simple assault ..., threatening to injure another ..., and assault with intent to kill.... Ana Foster was the complainant in all counts; the first and last counts were based on the events for which Foster had been held in contempt, and the other three were based on the alleged events for which Foster was acquitted of contempt.... Foster filed a motion to dismiss, claiming a double jeopardy bar to all counts.... The trial court denied the double jeopardy claim.... The District of Columbia

Court of Appeals ruled that [Foster's subsequent prosecution was] barred by the Double Jeopardy Clause.... In its petition for certiorari, the Government presented the sole question "whether the Double Jeopardy Clause bars prosecution of a defendant on substantive criminal charges based upon the same conduct for which he previously has been held in criminal contempt of court." ... We granted certiorari, 503 U.S. 1004 (1992).

II

To place these cases in context, one must understand that they are the consequence of a historically anomalous use of the contempt power. In both Dixon and Foster, a court issued an order directing a particular individual not to commit criminal offenses.... That could not have occurred at common law, or in the 19th-century American judicial system.

At common law, the criminal contempt power was confined to sanctions for conduct that interfered with the orderly administration of judicial proceedings.... The 1831 amendment of the Judiciary Act still would not have given rise to orders of the sort at issue here, however, since there was a long common-law tradition against judicial orders prohibiting violation of the law.... It is not surprising, therefore, that the double jeopardy issue presented here ... did not arise at common law, or even until quite recently in American cases.... English and earlier American cases do report instances in which prosecution for criminal contempt of court—as originally understood—did not bar a subsequent prosecution for a criminal offense based on the same conduct. But those contempt prosecutions were for disruption of judicial process, in which the disruptive behavior happened also to be criminal. The Double Jeopardy Clause, whose application to this new context we are called upon to consider, provides that no person shall "be subject for the same offence to be twice put in jeopardy of life or limb." U.S. Const., AMD. 5. This protection applies both to successive punishments and to successive prosecutions for the same criminal offense.... It is well established that criminal contempt, at least the sort enforced through nonsummary proceedings, is "a crime in the ordinary sense." ...

We have held that constitutional protections for criminal defendants other than the double jeopardy provision apply in nonsummary criminal contempt prosecutions just as they do in other criminal prosecutions.... We think it obvious, and today hold, that the protection of the Double Jeopardy Clause likewise attaches.... In both the multiple punishment and multiple prosecution contexts, this court has concluded that where the two offenses for which the defendant is punished or tried cannot survive the "same-elements" test, the double jeopardy bar applies.... The same-elements test, sometimes referred to as the "Blockburger" test, inquires whether each offense contains an element not contained in the other; if not, they are the "same offence" and double jeopardy bars additional punishment and successive prosecution. In a case such as Yancy, for example, in which the contempt prosecution was for disruption of judicial business, the same-elements test would not bar subsequent prosecution for the criminal assault that was part of the disruption, because the contempt offense did not require the element of criminal conduct, and the criminal offense did not require the element of disrupting judicial business.

We recently held in Grady that in addition to passing the Blockburger test, a subsequent prosecution must satisfy a "same-conduct" test to avoid the double jeopardy bar. The Grady test provides that, "if, to establish an essential element of an offense charged in that prosecution, the government will prove conduct that constitutes an offense for which the defendant has already been prosecuted," a second prosecution may not be had. 495 U.S. at 510.

III

The first question before us today is whether Blockburger analysis permits subsequent prosecution in this new criminal contempt context, where judicial order has prohibited criminal act. If it does, we must then proceed to consider whether Grady also permits it....

... [T]his court stated long ago that criminal contempt, at least in its nonsummary form, "is a crime in every fundamental respect." ... Because Dixon's drug offense did not include any element not contained in his previous contempt offense, his subsequent prosecution violates the Double Jeopardy Clause. The foregoing analysis obviously applies as well to Count I of the indictment against Foster, charging assault ..., based on the same event that was the subject of his prior contempt conviction for violating the provision of the CPO forbidding him to commit simple assault under § 22–504.[3] The subsequent prosecution for assault fails the Blockburger test, and is barred.

The remaining four counts in Foster, assault with intent to kill (Count V ...). and threats to injure or kidnap (Counts II–IV ...), are not barred under Blockburger. As to Count V: ... that offense requires proof of specific intent to kill; simple assault does not.... Similarly, the contempt offense required proof of knowledge of the CPO, which assault with intent to kill does not. Applying the Blockburger elements test, the result is clear: These crimes were different offenses, and the subsequent prosecution did not violate the Double Jeopardy Clause.

Counts II, III, and IV of Foster's indictment are likewise not barred. These charged Foster under § 22–2307 (forbidding anyone to "threaten ... to kidnap any person or to injure the person of another or physically damage the property of any person") for his alleged threats on three separate dates. Foster's contempt prosecution included charges that, on the same dates, he violated the CPO provision ordering that he not "in any manner threaten" Ana Foster. Conviction of the contempt required willful violation of the CPO—which conviction under § 22–2307 did not; and conviction under § 22–2307 required that the threat be a threat to kidnap, to inflict bodily injury, or to damage property—which conviction of the

3. It is not obvious that the word "assault" in the CPO bore the precise meaning "assault under § 22–504." The court imposing the contempt construed it that way, however, and the point has not been contested in this litigation.

contempt ... did not. Each offense therefore contained a separate element, and the Blockburger test for double jeopardy was not met.

IV

Having found that at least some of the counts at issue here are not barred by the Blockburger test, we must consider whether they are barred by the new, additional double jeopardy test we announced three Terms ago in Grady v. Corbin. They undoubtedly are....

We have concluded, however, that Grady must be overruled. Unlike Blockburger analysis, whose definition of what prevents two crimes from being the "same offence," ... has deep historical roots and has been accepted in numerous precedents of this Court, Grady lacks constitutional roots. The "same-conduct" rule it announced is wholly inconsistent with earlier Supreme Court precedent and with the clear common-law understanding of double jeopardy....

But Grady was not only wrong in principle; it has already proved unstable in application. Less than two years after it came down ... we were forced to recognize a large exception to it. Of course, the very existence of [this] "exception" ... gave cause for concern that the rule was not an accurate expression of the law....

Having encountered today yet another situation in which the pre-Grady understanding of the Double Jeopardy Clause allows a second trial, though the "same-conduct" test would not, we think it time to acknowledge what is now, three years after Grady, compellingly clear: The case was a mistake. We do not lightly reconsider a precedent, but, because Grady contradicted an "unbroken line of decisions," contained "less than accurate" historical analysis, and has produced "confusion," we do so here.... We therefore accept the Government's invitation to overrule Grady, and Counts II, III, IV, and V of Foster's subsequent prosecution are not barred....

It is so ordered.

JUSTICE REHNQUIST, with whom JUSTICES O'CONNOR and THOMAS join, concurring in the judgment in part and dissenting in part.

I do not join Part III of Justice Scalia's opinion because I think that none of the criminal prosecutions in this case were barred under Blockburger.... I, too, think that Grady must be overruled. I therefore join Parts I, II, and IV of the court's opinion, and write separately to express my disagreement with Justice Scalia's application of Blockburger in Part III.

In my view, Blockburger's same-element test requires us to focus, not on the terms of the particular court orders involved, but on the elements of contempt of court in the ordinary sense. ... Justice Scalia rejects the traditional view—shared by every Federal Court of Appeals and State Supreme Court that addressed the issue prior to Grady—that, as a general matter, double jeopardy does not bar a subsequent prosecution based on conduct for which a defendant has been held in criminal contempt. I cannot subscribe to a reading ... that upsets this previously well-settled principle of law. Because the generic crime of contempt of court has different elements than the substantive charges in this case, I believe that they are separate offenses under Blockburger....

... Contempt of court comprises two elements: (I) a court order made known to the defendant, followed by (ii) wilful violation of that order.... Neither of those elements is necessarily satisfied by proof that a defendant has committed the substantive offenses of assault or drug distribution. Likewise, no element of either of those substantive offenses is necessarily satisfied by proof that a defendant has been found guilty of contempt of court....

Our double jeopardy cases applying Blockburger have focused on the statutory elements of the offenses charged, not on the facts that must be proved under the particular indictment at issue—an indictment being the closest analogue to the court orders in this case.... By focusing on the facts needed to show a violation of the specific court orders involved in this case, and not on the generic elements of the crime of contempt of court, Justice Scalia's double jeopardy analysis bears a striking resemblance to that found in Grady—not what one would expect in an opinion that overrules Grady....

JUSTICE WHITE, with whom JUSTICE STEVENS joins, and with whom JUSTICE SOUTER joins as to Part I, concurring in the judgment in part and dissenting in part.

I

I am convinced that the Double Jeopardy Clause bars prosecution for an offense if the defendant already has been held in contempt for its commission. Therefore, I agree with the Court's conclusion that both Dixon's prosecution for possession with intent to distribute cocaine and Foster's prosecution for simple assault were prohibited. In my view, however, Justice Scalia's opinion gives short shrift to the arguments raised by the United States. I also am uncomfortable with the reasoning underlying this holding, in particular the application of [*Blockburger*] to the facts of this case, a reasoning that betrays an overly technical interpretation of the Constitution. As a result, I concur only in the judgment in Part III–A....

Both the Government and amici submit that application of the Double Jeopardy Clause in this context carries grave practical consequences.... It would, it is argued, cripple the power to enforce court orders or, alternatively, allow individuals to escape serious punishment for statutory criminal offenses. The argument, an offshoot of the principle of necessity familiar to the law of contempt, ... is that, just as we have relaxed certain procedural requirements in contempt proceedings where time is of the essence and an immediate remedy is needed to "prevent a breakdown of the proceedings," ... so too should we exclude double jeopardy protections from this setting lest we do damage to the courts' authority. In other words, "the ability to punish disobedience to judicial orders [being] regarded as essential to ensuring that the Judiciary has a means to vindicate its own authority," ... its exercise should not be inhibited by fear that it might immunize defendants from subsequent criminal prosecution.

Adherence to double jeopardy principles in this context, however, will not seriously deter the courts from taking appropriate steps to ensure that their authority is not flouted. Courts remain free to hold transgressors in contempt and punish them as they see fit. The Government counters that this possibility will prove to be either illusory—if the prosecuting authority declines to initiate proceedings out of fear that they could jeopardize more substantial punishment for the underlying crime, or too costly—if the prosecuting authority, the risk notwithstanding, chooses to go forward. But it is not fanciful to imagine that judges and prosecutors will select a third option, which is to ensure, where necessary or advisable, that the contempt and the substantive charge be tried at the same time, in which case the double jeopardy issue "would be limited to ensuring that the total punishment did not exceed that authorized by the legislature." ...

Against this backdrop, the appeal of the principle of necessity loses much of its force. Ultimately, the urgency of punishing such contempt violations is no less, but by the same token no more, than that of punishing violations of criminal laws of general application—in which case, we simply do not question the defendant's right to the "protections worked out carefully over the years and deemed fundamental to our system of justice, ... including the protection of the Double Jeopardy Clause.... We see no sound reason in logic or policy not to apply it in the area of criminal contempt." ...

More difficult to deal with are the circumstances surrounding Foster's defiance of the court order. Realization of the scope of domestic violence—according to the American Medical Association (AMA), "the single largest cause of injury to women," ... has come with difficulty, and it has come late.

There no doubt are time delays in the operation of the criminal justice system that are frustrating; they even can be perilous when an individual is left exposed to a defendant's potential violence. That is true in the domestic context; it is true elsewhere as well. Resort to more expedient methods therefore is appealing, and in many cases permissible. Under today's decision, for instance, police officers retain the power to arrest for violation of a civil protection order. Where the offense so warrants, judges can haul the assailant before the court, charge him with criminal contempt, and hold him without bail.... Also, cooperation between the government and parties bringing contempt proceedings can be achieved. The various actors might not have thought such cooperation necessary in the past; after today's decision, I suspect they will.

Victims, understandably, would prefer to have access to a proceeding in which swift and expeditious punishment could be inflicted for that offense without prejudice to a subsequent full-blown criminal trial. The justification for such a system, however, has nothing to do with preventing disruption of a court's proceedings, or even with vindicating its authority.... No such end being invoked here, the principle of necessity cannot be summoned for the sole purpose of letting contempt proceedings achieve what, under our Constitution, other criminal trials cannot.

II

If, as the court agrees, the Double Jeopardy Clause cannot be ignored in this context, my view is that the subsequent prosecutions in both Dixon and Foster were impermissible as to all counts. I reach this conclusion because the offenses at issue in the contempt proceedings were either identical to, or lesser included offenses of, those charged in the subsequent prosecutions.... Moreover, the results to which this approach would lead are indefensible....

Take the example of Count V in Foster: For all intents and purposes, the offense for which he was convicted in the contempt proceeding was his assault against his wife. The majority, its eyes fixed on the rigid elements test, would have his fate turn on whether his subsequent prosecution charges "simple assault" or "assault with intent to kill." Yet, because the crime of "simple assault" is included within the crime of "assault with intent to kill," the reasons that bar retrial under the first hypothesis are equally present under the second: These include principles of finality, ... protecting Foster from "embarrassment" and "expense," ... and preventing the Government from gradually fine-tuning its strategy, thereby minimizing exposure to a mistaken conviction....

Analysis of the threat charges ... makes the point more clearly still. In the contempt proceeding, it will be recalled, Foster was acquitted of the—arguably lesser included—offense of threatening "in any manner." As we have stated: "The law attaches particular significance to an acquittal. To permit a second trial after an acquittal, however mistaken the acquittal might have been, would present an unacceptably high risk that the Government, with its vastly superior resources, might wear down the defendant so that 'even though innocent he may be found guilty.' " ...

To respond, as the majority appears to do, that concerns relating to the defendant's interests against repeat trials are "unjustified" because prosecutors "have little to gain and much to lose" from bringing successive prosecutions and because "the Government must be deterred from abusive, repeated prosecutions of a single offender for similar offenses by the sheer press of other demands upon prosecutorial and judicial resources," ... is to get things exactly backwards. The majority's prophesies might be correct, and double jeopardy might be a problem that will simply take care of itself. No so, however, according to the constitution, whose firm prohibition against double jeopardy cannot be satisfied by wishful thinking....

Simple assault being a lesser included offense of assault with intent to kill, ... the jury in the second prosecution would in all likelihood receive instructions on the lesser offense and could find Foster guilty of simple assault.... As I see it, Foster will have been put in jeopardy twice for simple assault. The result is as unjustifiable as it is pernicious....

JUSTICE BLACKMAN, concurring in the judgment in part and dissenting in part.

I

I cannot agree that contempt of court is the "same offence" under the Double Jeopardy Clause as either "assault with intent to kill or possession of cocaine with intent to distribute it...."

The purpose of contempt is not to punish an offense against the community at large but rather to punish the specific offense of disobeying a court order. This Court said nearly a century ago: "[A] court, enforcing obedience to its orders by proceedings for contempt, is not executing the criminal laws of the land, but only securing to suitors the rights which it has adjudged them entitled to." . . .

II

Contempt is one of the very few mechanisms available to a trial court to vindicate the authority of its orders. I fear that the Court's willingness to overlook the unique interests served by contempt proceedings not only will jeopardize the ability of trial courts to control those defendants under their supervision but will undermine their ability to respond effectively to unmistakable threats to their own authority and to those who have sought the court's protection.

This fact is poignantly stressed by the amici: "Contempt litigators and criminal prosecutors seek to further different interests. A battered woman seeks to enforce her private order to end the violence against her. In contrast, the criminal prosecutor is vindicating society's interest in enforcing its criminal law. The two interests are not the same, and to consider the contempt litigator and the criminal prosecutor as one and the same would be to adopt an absurd fiction." . . .

Justice Souter, with whom Justice Stevens joins, concurring in the judgment in part and dissenting in part. . . .

. . . Because I think that Grady was correctly decided, . . . and because, even if the decision had been wrong in the first instance, there is no warrant for overruling it now, I respectfully dissent. I join Part I of Justice White's opinion, and I would hold, as he would, both the prosecution of Dixon and the prosecution of Foster under all the counts of the indictment against him to be barred by the Double Jeopardy Clause.

* * *

NOTES AND QUESTIONS

1. Do you agree with Justice White that: "[u]ltimately, the urgency of punishing such contempt violations is no less, but by the same token no more, than that of punishing violations of criminal laws of general application?"

2. The Justices stake out three distinct positions: All the subsequent prosecutions are barred, none are barred, and some but not all are barred. Which argument do you find most persuasive? If you are attracted to the "middle position" taken by the majority, how would you respond to Justice White's scenarios in which (1) Foster is convicted in a criminal trial of the lesser offense of simple assault although charged with assault with intent to kill, and (2) Foster is convicted of threats to injure, although he had been acquitted, in the contempt proceeding, of "in any manner threaten[ing] . . ."?

3. In concluding their analysis of *Dixon,* Klein and Orloff offer the following advice:

> In those few remaining criminal assault cases where double jeopardy *may* pose a bar to the subsequent criminal action if the contempt motion goes forward before the criminal action, the court and petitioner's counsel should first determine whether the contempt action can be decided in such a fashion so as to avoid double jeopardy issues. For example, after hearing the evidence in the case, instead of finding that the respondent assaulted his wife, the trial judge could have found in *Dixon* that respondent approached petitioner in violation of the stay away provisions of the civil protection order, grabbed her, and threw her against a parked car.
>
> ... [T]here is a continuing need for cooperation and coordination between domestic violence victims bringing contempt motions and state prosecutors. Coordination will prevent poorly worded contempt findings from unwittingly precluding criminal prosecutions in some cases, as occurred on one count in *Dixon*.

Catherine F. Klein and Leslye J. Orloff, *Providing Legal Protection for Battered Women: An Analysis of State Statutes and Case Law,* 51 HOFSTRA L. REV. 801, 1128 (1995).

Does it seem at all troubling that the constitutional protections of the Double Jeopardy Clause can, in this view, be neutralized by choosing words to describe what the defendant has done to violate the protective order that avoid labeling his conduct as a criminal offense? Does this potential for manipulation make you more sympathetic towards those Justices who did not want to see *Grady* overruled? Or more sympathetic with the position of Justice Blackmun, for whom the different interests served by contempt proceedings and criminal prosecutions was the central argument against invoking the Double Jeopardy Clause in this context?

Sanctions

Sentencing
Peter Finn and Sarah Colson
Civil Protection Orders: Legislation, Current Court Practice, and Enforcement, 58, National Institute of Justice, 1990

Many judges order jail time for first-time protection order violators if they believe the severity of the abuse warrants incarceration, such as forced entry or any type of physical abuse or threats. These judges view a jail sentence as a necessary step to protect the victim from further abuse. Furthermore, they know that while this may be the first time the offender has violated the protection order, it is at least the second time he has committed assault and battery against the victim. These judges also believe it is important to impose a jail sentence because an order of the court has been held in disregard.

Most state statutes limit the length of jail sentence the judge may impose, with six months or one year the most common maximum sentence allowed.... The California statute mandates a minimum jail sentence of 48 hours if a violation involves an injury. Ohio's statute makes possible a severe sanction for multiple offenders by making a conviction of a third violation a felony of the fourth degree.

A jail sentence may also help motivate police officers to adopt or maintain a policy of arresting batterers who violate protection orders. Many police officers interviewed for the present study said one of their reasons for not arresting violators is that prosecutors and judges do not seem to take these cases seriously by following up arrests with swift and meaningful sanctions.

Especially in jurisdictions where jail crowding is a problem, judges must make sentencing determinations with several concerns in mind. Some judges decide whom to jail by weighing the greater need for jailing violent offenders ... as compared with nonviolent offenders like prostitutes, public drunks, and the perpetrators of nonserious property crimes.

Judges have also experimented with alternative sanctions for protection order violations. In Philadelphia, the judge has used intensive probation supervision and a choice between regular attendance at counseling or a jail sentence. In Portland, Maine, and in Springfield, Illinois, some cases are plea bargained down to probation and a six-or twelve-month suspended jail sentence; if no further violation occurs during that period, the case is dismissed with no criminal record.

Several judges reported on the need to consider the victim's safety between the time of the violation and the offender's appearance in court for a violation hearing. As a result, batterers arrested in Portland, Oregon, are not granted release on their own recognizance.... This position is reflected in the Pennsylvania statute: bail is usually set at $5,000. In Denver, domestic violence has been taken off the bond schedule so that suspects must stay in jail from a few hours to three days until the next court business day. In Duluth, violators are usually held overnight, allowing time for shelter advocates to contact the victim and help her obtain any assistance she needs before the batterer is released. Minnesota's statute allows jailers to hold an assailant arrested under the probable cause arrest statute for thirty-six hours if the jailer believes the assailant is likely to be a danger to the victim.

NOTE

1. This report offers a picture of the enforcement and sanctioning process as significantly more attentive both to securing victim safety and to emphasizing the seriousness of protective order violations than is the case in many jurisdictions. Where it does not reflect reality, however, it can certainly offer inspiration.

Enforcement of Restraining Orders Under the Violence Against Women Act

18 U.S.C. § 2262 Interstate Violation of Protection Order

(a) Offenses—

(1) Crossing a State line—A person who travels across a State line or enters or leaves Indian country with the intent to engage in conduct that—

(A) (i) violates the portion of a protection order that involves protection against credible threats of violence, repeated harassment, or bodily injury to the person or persons for whom the protection order was issued; or

(ii) would violate subparagraph (A) if the conduct occurred in the jurisdiction in which the order was issued; and

(B) subsequently engages in such conduct, shall be punished as provided in subsection (b).

(2) Causing the crossing of a State line—A person who causes a spouse or intimate partner to cross a State line or to enter or leave Indian country by force, coercion, duress or fraud, and, in the course or as a result of that conduct, intentionally commits an act that injures the person's spouse or intimate partner in violation of a valid protection order issued by a State shall be punished as provided in subsection (b).

(b) Penalties—A person who violates this section shall be fined under this title, imprisoned—

(1) for life or any term of years, if death of the offender's spouse or intimate partner results;

(2) for not more than 20 years if permanent disfigurement or life threatening bodily injury to the offender's spouse or intimate partner results;

(3) for not more than 10 years, if serious bodily injury to the offender's spouse or intimate partner results or if the offender uses a dangerous weapon during the offense;

(4) as provided for the applicable conduct under chapter 109A if the offense would constitute an offense under chapter 109A . . .; and

(5) for not more than 5 years, in any other case,

or both fined and imprisoned.

NOTES

1. In addition to the penalties outlined in § 2262, VAWA makes restitution mandatory for this offense:

> The court shall direct the defendant to pay the full amount of the victim's losses, including: medical expenses; physical therapy; necessary transportation, temporary housing and child care expenses; lost income; attorney's fees, including costs incurred in obtaining a restraining order; and any other losses.

18 U.S.C. § 2264(b)(3). Compliance with the restitution order is a mandatory condition of probation or supervised release. 18 U.S.C. § 2264(b)(10). The court cannot waive restitution because of the perpetrator's economic circumstances, or because the victim can claim insurance benefits for her

injuries. The defendant's economic means can be taken into consideration only in setting a payment schedule. 18 U.S.C. § 2264(b)(4). The restitution order must be enforced "by all available and reasonable means" by the U.S. Attorney, but can also be enforced civilly, by the victim. 18 U.S.C. § 2264(b)(1)(B),(b)(2).

The penalties listed in § 2262, and the restitutionary provisions contained in § 2264, also apply to the other federal crime created by the Violence Against Women Act, Interstate Domestic Violence, defined in 18 U.S.C. § 2261, and discussed in the next chapter.

2. In addition to making interstate violation of a protection order a federal offense, VAWA criminalizes the possession of a firearm by anyone who is subject to a protective order that:

> (A) was issued after a hearing of which such person received actual notice, and at which such person had an opportunity to participate;
>
> (B) restrains such person from harassing, stalking, or threatening an intimate partner of such person, or engaging in other conduct that would place an intimate partner in reasonable fear of bodily injury to the partner or child; and
>
> (C) (i) includes a finding that such person represents a credible threat to the physical safety of such intimate partner or child; or
>
>> (ii) by its terms explicitly prohibits the use, attempted use, or threatened use of physical force against such intimate partner or child that would reasonably be expected to cause bodily injury. . . .

18 U.S.C. § 922(g)(8). The maximum penalty for violating this provision is ten years in prison, a $250,000 fine, or both. 18 U.S.C. § 924(a)(2). Predictably, this provision has triggered reactions ranging from consternation to outrage among law enforcement and private security personnel whose livelihoods depend on their capacity to carry a firearm. This is one context in which the gravity of a finding that the defendant has perpetrated or is credibly threatening to perpetrate domestic violence becomes inescapably clear. Despite the fact that the federal provisions are written to guarantee the perpetrator notice of the protective order hearing and an opportunity to defend against the charges, and to limit the requirement that the perpetrator relinquish any firearm in his possession to cases in which the physical safety of a partner or child is demonstrably at risk, they have provoked widespread criticism. Protesters challenge the integrity of the restraining order process, and assert, albeit without supporting data, that restraining orders are issued on evidence insufficient to warrant potential loss of employment by defendants.

Despite the many constitutional challenges to the provision, it has survived scrutiny in all but a very few cases, and has been uniformly upheld by those circuit courts of appeal asked to review it. In one recent district court case, U.S. v. Emerson, 46 F. Supp. 2d 598 (N.D. Texas 1999), the Northern District of Texas found that 18 U.S.C. § 922(g)(8) violated the Second Amendment right to bear arms, and Fifth Amendment due process rights. But every other court asked to evaluate a Second Amendment claim has rejected it, holding that the Second Amendment confers a collective, rather than an individual, right to bear arms. See, for example, U.S. v. Henson, 55

F. Supp. 2d 528 (S.D. W. Va. 1999), and U.S. v. Spruill, 1999 WL 635697 (W.D. Tex. 1999). The court in *Spruill* noted that five Circuit Courts of Appeal have determined that the Second Amendment protects only a collective right, and held that "the Second Amendment does not prohibit the federal government from imposing some restrictions on gun ownership." Due process challenges have also routinely been rejected. In U.S. v. Meade, 175 F.3d 215 (1st Cir. 1999), for example, the First Circuit found that the statute satisfied due process, because "both the proscribed conduct and the affected class of persons are explicitly set forth."

In *Meade* the First Circuit was also asked to consider, and rejected, a Tenth Amendment challenge. The court found, as other courts have consistently done, that the provision's express jurisdictional element—forbidding the possession of firearms "shipped or transported" in interstate commerce was sufficient to satisfy the required nexus with interstate commerce, and that the provision was, therefore, a valid exercise of congressional authority. It is this expressly stated connection with interstate commerce that distinguishes 18 U.S.C. § 922(g)(8), and its partner provision 18 U.S.C. § 922(g)(9), from the civil rights remedy crafted by Congress, also contained in the Violence Against Women Act, and codified at 42 U.S.C. § 13981 (1994), but found unconstitutional by the Supreme Court in United States v. Morrison, 120 S.Ct. 1740 (2000). The civil rights remedy, and the *Morrison* case, are discussed extensively in Chapter 13, below.

18 U.S.C. § 922(g)(9), which prohibits individuals who have ever been convicted of misdemeanor crimes of domestic violence from carrying firearms, has survived similar challenges to those brought against 18 U.S.C. § 922(g)(8). However, it also raises some separate issues, which are discussed in Chapter 9, Section D, below.

Anecdotal reports from domestic violence advocates around the country suggest that in some cases judges are choosing not to issue restraining orders solely to avoid putting defendants' jobs on the line, despite the obvious risks created by leaving domestic violence victims unprotected. In some situations the victims themselves are also choosing not to apply for restraining orders where they know the likely consequence for their partners, and are either afraid of retaliation, or are economically dependent on their partners and afraid that loss of employment by their partners will create a greater risk to the wellbeing of their children or themselves than the risk of future violence. Domestic violence advocates who lobbied for these provisions are now being forced to reassess whether their net impact has been positive.

Would it be possible to rewrite these firearm provisions, perhaps by the careful framing of exceptions, to reap most if not all of the gains envisaged by those who lobbied for them, while limiting the unanticipated damage they have produced?

E. EFFICACY

There is no single answer to the apparently simple question, "Do restraining orders work?" One obvious measure is recidivism—does the defendant subject to a restraining order commit further abuse? But even here we have to ask what level of recidivism is small enough for us to decide that the protective order mechanism is a useful one—if forty percent of women who obtain restraining orders live free of violence for the duration of those orders, is that success, or failure? How does it compare with the experience of women who do not obtain protective orders in the aftermath of a violent incident?

A different measure of the efficacy of restraining orders is consumer satisfaction. Do women who obtain orders feel that they have gained by doing so? Here, while freedom from violence at the hands of a partner or former partner may be the ultimate goal, women may be more realistic than many social scientists about that probability, at least in the short term, and more ready to settle for less exacting definitions of success. In the Harrell and Smith study, for example:

> Many women thought the temporary restraining order was helpful in documenting that the abuse occurred: 86% said it was "very" helpful in this regard; 79% said it was "very" or "somewhat" helpful in sending her partner a message that his actions were wrong; and 62% said the order was "very" or "somewhat" helpful in punishing her partner for abusing her.... Also, 88% credited the judge with "doing the right thing" for her and her children.... Combined, these findings strongly suggest that the women saw the restraining order as worthwhile in significant ways.

Adele Harrell and Barbara E. Smith, *Effects of Restraining Orders on Domestic Violence Victims,* DO ARRESTS AND RESTRAINING ORDERS WORK? 214, 218 (E.S. Buzawa & C.G. Buzawa, eds. 1996). Incredibly, women had these positive reactions even though fewer than half thought the man believed that he had to obey the order. Id.

Yet another measure of the efficacy of restraining orders is whether they are in fact enforced as the governing legislation suggests they can and should be. A high rate of violations, combined with the paucity of follow-up by the criminal justice system, is what led Andrew Klein to conclude that restraining orders "don't work." Andrew R. Klein, *Re-Abuse in a Population of Court-Restrained Male Batterers: Why Restraining Orders Don't Work,* DO ARRESTS AND RESTRAINING ORDERS WORK?192 (E.S. Buzawa & C.G. Buzawa, eds. 1996). On the other hand, it seems to be the case that simply issuing a restraining order has some deterrent effect on some abusers. Thus, even though we might, with Klein, urge that enforcement be given a higher priority, we might not want to make a blanket judgment that the efficacy of an order depends, in all cases, on its enforcement.

Recidivism

There seems little doubt that in most jurisdictions at least 50% of restraining orders are violated at least once, and that many are violated multiple times. In the Harrell and Smith study, 60% of the women interviewed three months and then one year after their orders issued reported violations. *Harrell & Smith,* 240. In the Klein study, violation rates were measured not by victim interview, but by court records of new arrests for abuse

(34%), and of new restraining orders (a total of 95). By these measures, which almost certainly underestimate the actual re-abuse rate, because they fail to capture violations that did not result in either arrest or a new restraining order, 48.8% of orders were violated within 2 years after they originally issued. *Klein,* 199–200. Although Klein reported a significant drop in the violation rate after the first three months, Harrell and Smith's data looks somewhat different, as the following excerpt suggests.

Adele Harrell and Barbara E. Smith Effects of Restraining Orders on Domestic Violence Victims; Do Arrests and Restraining Orders Work? 214, 223–25 (E.S. Buzawa and C.G. Buzawa, eds. 1996)

... Threats to kill were reported by more than one fifth of the women. These threats did not seem to subside over time: 7% reported death threats only during the first 3 months, whereas more than twice that number reported death threats that continued beyond 3 months or first began after 3 months. Other acts of severe violence—kicking, strangling, beating, forcing sex, and threatening with weapons—were reported by 5% to 9% of the women. Cumulatively, these acts of severe violence affected 29% of the women who got restraining orders.

... Nearly one quarter (24%) of the women reported at least one [less severe act of violence] in the year following the initial order. One fifth were grabbed, pushed or shoved by the man, and over one tenth said the man hit or tried to hit her. With the exception of harm to pets, these violent acts were as likely to first occur more than 3 months after the order; this finding indicates the persistent nature of abuse.

Threats of violence and acts of property damage meant to threaten or intimidate were reported by 43% of the women, most of whom reported more than one type of threat. The range of threats was diverse.... [T]hreats of harm to someone important to the woman (other than her children) were reported by 25% of all the women who received restraining orders. Threats to harm the children or pets occurred in fewer cases (under 10% and under 5%, respectively). Threatening to hit her, throw or smash things, threatening to damage her property, and actually damaging her property were all reported by more than 15% of the women and represented very aggressive efforts to frighten and control the women.

Psychological abuse was by far the most prevalent type of abuse in the year after a restraining order. More than half of the women (57%) reported one of [these] behaviors.... A serious problem, now being addressed in new stalking legislation in some states, is that over 15% of all the women interviewed said the man followed her or tracked her around town. This type of behavior suggested a potentially dangerous obsession with the woman's whereabouts. Aggressive acts to control her behavior were reported by more than 10% of the women and included making her stay in the home, harassing her at work, and keeping her from using the car or the telephone. The most frequent complaints reflected continuing conflict in the relationship. Over 40% reported said the man had sworn at, screamed at, or insulted them; 35% had been humiliated or shamed in front of others.

* * *

NOTES

1. One of the most interesting findings in the two studies reported by Harrell and Smith, and by Klein, is that in many respects the level of repeat violence experienced by women who initiated the protective order process was the same regardless of whether they (a) got an *ex parte* order but did not return to court for a permanent order; (b) got a permanent order but returned to court to dismiss it before its expiration date, or (c) kept the permanent order in place until it expired. However, the Harrell and Smith study suggests that having and maintaining a permanent order did correlate with a lower incidence of psychological abuse:

> Having a permanent order did not appear to deter most types of abuse. Statistical tests showed no significant differences in the three most serious types of abuse—severe violence, other forms of physical violence, and threats or property damage—between the 212 women who had a permanent restraining order and the 143 women who did not.... The existence of a permanent order did significantly reduce the likelihood of acts of psychological abuse. The women with permanent orders were just over half as likely to experience psychological abuse....

Harrell & Smith at 229.

The stories of women who are injured or killed after they take out restraining orders make it legitimate to ask whether obtaining an order is counterproductive—creating more danger than it prevents. While that is certainly true in some cases, it is not true as a generalization. As Klein reports:

> This study gave no indication that ROs provoke more abuse. Those who maintained orders were not abused more than those who dropped them.... A third of the victims in this study had taken out at least one previous RO, and 193 (30%) took out new orders after their 1990 order expired or was dropped. If the ROs provoked more new abuse than they obviously deterred, it is unlikely that so many victims would take them out more than once.

Klein at 209.

2. Another important question is whether recidivism can be predicted, allowing victims to determine whether taking out an order is likely to protect them, and encouraging both victims and policy makers to think about supplemental or separate strategies that might work in cases where a restraining order is unlikely, by itself, to deter further violence. The studies offer some useful information.

Both Harrell and Smith and Klein report that the severity of the "presenting incident"—in other words, the incident that prompted the victim to seek an order—provides no basis for predicting reabuse. Harrell and Smith hypothesize that: "Possibly, the incidents reported to the court represent merely 'the straw that broke the camel's back' and occur at the point at which the women decide to seek protection, regardless of the severity of what happened." *Harrell & Smith* at 230. Klein found that abusers with criminal records, whether for abuse or for alcohol or drug related crimes or crimes against the person, were more likely to reabuse than those with no criminal records. Furthermore, the more extensive the criminal record, the greater the rate of reabuse. *Klein* at 202. Harrell and Smith focused on the history of abuse in the year before the restraining order issued, and found that:

> The severity of prior abuse was significantly related to the severity of abuse in the year after a restraining order. Severe violence in the year before the order predicted severe violence in the year after the order ..., and other violent behaviors in the prior year predicted other violent behaviors in the year after the order.... The duration of abuse in the relationship, however, was not significantly related to the probability of any abuse or specific types of abuse following a restraining order.
>
> The persistence in the pattern of violence, unlike the severity of the incident described in the complaint, was a predictor of risk of abuse following court action. This finding supported our interpretation that the incident that led a woman to seek a restraining order simply represented the point at which she decided to seek help, and did not measure the general level of violence in the relationship. It also pointed to the utility of screening clients for a history of severe violence to assess for potential lethality and to work with women involved in the more serious types of abuse to develop safety plans.

Harrell and Smith at 231–32.

Klein also noted that younger abusers, who were less likely to be married to their victims, were more likely to reabuse. *Klein* at 200. Harrell and Smith also reported that abusers who were living with their victims at the time of the order were less likely to reabuse than abusers who had already separated from their victims, or had never lived with them. *Harrell & Smith* at 233. Women with children, although their overall experience of reabuse was not higher than that of women without children, were especially vulnerable to violent acts of the less severe kind (70% more likely), and to threats and property damage (50% more likely). Harrell and Smith hypothesize that "these types of abuse occurred around visitation and might be indicative of a need for supervised visitation in some cases." Id.

Harrell and Smith saw a correlation between the level of resistance offered by the defendant at the restraining order hearing, and subsequent reabuse:

> As noted earlier, most men attended the permanent order hearing, and many voiced their objections, either to the evidence of abuse presented by their partners or to proposed terms of the orders. Their resistance to the orders at the time of the hearings was measured on a scale of 0 to 5, based on the number of the following things he did: denied the

> abuse, tried to get the judge not to issue the order, tried to get care and control of the children, objected to the visitation arrangements, and tried to get the judge to let him stay in the home. The level of resistance at the time of the order significantly increased the probability of severe violence ..., threats and property damage ..., and psychological abuse.... Although objection to the order is an important legal right and should not be limited in any way, it is important to note that strenuous objections voiced by the men should be treated seriously as a warning that abuse may continue. Efforts to address this risk could include firm and specific statements by the judge about the behavioral requirements of the order and the consequences of noncompliance. In addition, strenuous objections may indicate to women and their advocates the need for safety planning to minimize future exposure to risk.

Id. at 232–33.

Finally, Klein reported a curious correlation between reabuse and a "no-contact" provision in the order. If contact was allowed, reabuse was 27.3%, if not, reabuse was 35.7%. *Klein* at 202. It is significant here that Klein was measuring reabuse by a new arrest for domestic violence or a new restraining order taken out by the victim, so the statistic is not merely reflecting that no-contact orders were particularly susceptible to violation, which may also be true. Further investigation showed that this differential reabuse rate was of significance only in the group of defendants who had no prior criminal record. In other words, a defendant with no criminal history is more likely to reabuse his partner if his restraining order tells him not to contact her than if it orders him not to abuse her, but permits some contact. This finding is subject to at least two interpretation, between which Klein makes no attempt to choose. Either the frustration of being precluded from any contact with a partner precipitates more violence among this group of men, or the fact that a judge was moved to include a "no-contact" provision in a restraining order, even though the defendant had no prior criminal record, is a signal that the defendant appeared particularly aggressive or dangerous. Further research will be required to explore these two different hypotheses, both of which seem plausible.

Relationship Between Efficacy and Enforcement

Klein's study was conducted in a jurisdiction nationally recognized for its programs to stop domestic violence, and one in which violation of a restraining order is a criminal misdemeanor. Nonetheless, he criticizes the criminal justice system's response to violations of the restraining orders in his study. Although 34% of the 663 defendants were later arrested on abuse-related charges, many if not most of which must have included charges of violating the restraining order, almost 33% of the cases were then dismissed outright, and another 10% diverted without any guilty finding. More than 25% of the defendants received probation, and only 18% (42 or 43) were incarcerated for any period of time. *Klein,*at 208–09. In the Harrell and Smith study, 290 of 355 women with restraining orders sought police response to a violation, but despite a mandatory arrest provision in the relevant state law, only 59 arrests were made (20%). Very few women then went back to court to seek a violation hearing, some because they feared the defendant's retaliation, some because they thought it would not help, some because they thought the abuse would stop without court intervention, and some because they did not realize they could return to court. *Harrell & Smith* at 240.

Klein, noting that the population of abusers in his study "look like criminals, act like criminals, and reabuse like criminals" (*Klein* at 207), in no small measure because many *are* in fact criminals with prior records, suggests that it would be naive to expect that restraining orders, standing alone, would have a significant deterrent effect. This population, he points out, is "as high risk for repeat criminal behavior as any offenders generally allowed to be released to the community on probation." Id. at 209. If restraining orders are to be effective in containing abuse, he concludes, they must be supported by "vigorous prosecution and significant sanctioning of abusers." Id. at 211. Subsequent studies should test the proposition that responding more aggressively to restraining order violations will keep more women safe.

CHAPTER NINE

THE CRIMINAL JUSTICE SYSTEM

A. IT'S A CRIME

Historically, the criminal justice system has been characterized by its chronic inattention to domestic violence. It seems sensible, therefore, to open this chapter with a reminder that many of the abusive behaviors by which one partner exerts power and control over another do indeed fit the definition of traditional crimes under state law. The list provided to advocates-in-training by the Harvard Law School's Battered Women's Advocacy Project, based on the criminal law of Massachusetts, for example, includes:

- Assault (an attempted battery, where the perpetrator intends a harmful or unpermitted touching, takes an overt step towards accomplishing that intent, comes reasonably close to accomplishing it, and causes the intended victim reasonable fear that a battery is imminent)
- Assault and Battery (the perpetrator intentionally touches the victim, without any right to do so, and does it either without consent or in a fashion that is actually or potentially harmful)
- Assault and Battery on An Officer (the same elements as an assault and battery, but where the victim is an officer on duty, and the perpetrator knows that s/he is. This offense would apply where an officer responding to a domestic incident is attacked by the abusive partner)
- Assault or Assault and Battery with a Dangerous Weapon (the same elements as an assault or an assault and battery, but where the attempt, or the actual touching, is done with a dangerous weapon)
- Attempt to Commit a Crime (the perpetrator has a specific intent to commit a crime, engages in an overt act towards that end and comes reasonably close to committing the crime, but doesn't complete the crime)
- Breaking and Entering (the perpetrator breaks into the building, residential unit or vehicle of another, and enters it with an intent to commit a misdemeanor or a felony therein)
- Criminal Trespass (the perpetrator enters into or remains in or on the building, residential unit, vehicle or land of another, either without the right or the permission to be there, or after permission has been withdrawn by the person who has legal control over the space)
- Disorderly Conduct (frightening, threatening or violent behavior, involving actions that are reasonably likely to affect the public, and which

cause public inconvenience, annoyance or alarm, or recklessly create that risk)

- Disturbing the Peace (conduct which most people would find unreasonably disruptive, which is intentional, and which did in fact annoy at least one person)
- Willful and Malicious Destruction of Property (self-explanatory)
- Harassing Phone Calls (the perpetrator makes phone calls to the victim, or causes phone calls to be made to the victim, on two or more occasions, with the sole purpose of harassing, annoying or molesting the victim)
- Violation of a Restraining Order (as discussed in Chapter 8, above; where a court has issued an order of protection prohibiting the defendant from engaging in certain behavior, the order is in effect on the date the defendant engages in that prohibited behavior, and the defendant had notice of the order and its terms)
- Intimidation of a Witness (a willful endeavor through gift, offer, promise, misrepresentation, intimidation, force or threats of force to impede, obstruct, delay or interfere with any witness or informant in a criminal proceeding or investigation. This would apply whether the perpetrator was intimidating his partner, or another potential witness).

See, RESOURCE AND TRAINING MANUAL, Harvard Law School Battered Women's Advocacy Project (1996).

To this already lengthy list should be added at least the crimes of kidnapping, attempted homicide and homicide, rape and sexual assault, and the new crime of stalking. Stalking laws are the subject of a later section of this chapter. The crimes of rape and sexual assault, as applied between intimate partners, deserve a little more attention here.

Rape and Sexual Assault

The use of rape and sexual assault laws in the context of domestic violence is complicated by three factors; (a) the failure of many victims to recognize that they have the right to refuse sex with an intimate partner, (b) the reluctance of many victims to describe incidents of sexual abuse to police, prosecutors and judges, and (c) the law's slow and reluctant recognition that the marriage license is not a license to rape. That history is summarized by Joan Zorza in her article *The Criminal Law of Misdemeanor Domestic Violence, 1970–1990,* 83 J. CRIM. L. & CRIMIN. 46 (1992), at pages 50–51:

> In 1970, American law did not recognize marital rape as a crime. Although twelve percent of married women are raped by their husbands, and from thirty-four to fifty-nine percent of battered women report that their male partner rapes them, laws in most states continued to define rape as intercourse with a woman other than the rapist's wife. Marital rape is one of the strongest predictors of whether one of the spouses will kill the other. The injuries that wives receive from marital rape are more severe than those received from rape at the hands of a stranger, yet if a wife was raped by her husband before

1970, the strongest charges she could bring were assault charges or a divorce on cruelty grounds. In states like New York, where adultery was the only ground for divorce until 1966, the wife could not get a divorce regardless of how many times or how brutally her husband had raped her. Following the law, police throughout the United States largely ignored marital rape.

In 1981, the supreme courts of Massachusetts and New Jersey declared that a husband could be criminally liable for raping his wife. Several years later, New York, Florida, and Georgia followed suit. As of January 1985, twenty states permitted a wife to prosecute her husband for rape, although most of these states limited the situations in which she could do so. Even as recently as July 1991, only nineteen states had completely abolished the marital rape exemption. In those states where marital rape was not a crime, however, it was usually grounds for divorce. Furthermore, at least twenty-eight states currently specifically allow sexual abuse of a spouse as grounds for the issuance of an order for protection. These changes in the law have made police more able and willing to intervene in situations involving marital rape.

A recent Maryland case, documenting the Maryland legislature's treatment of sexual offenses, and their application as between married people, provides a good illustration of the somewhat convoluted treatment often accorded these issues. In Lane v. State, 348 Md. 272, 703 A.2d 180 (Md. Ct. App. 1997), the Court of Appeals noted:

> The relevant 1976 legislation originated with Senate Bill 358, which was the product of a legislatively created Special Committee on Rape and Related Offenses. As introduced, the bill would have repealed the common law of rape and, through new sections 462 through 464C of Article 27 of the Maryland Code, included the conduct constituting that crime in one or more new statutory sexual offenses. A major thrust of the bill, in that regard, was to treat unlawful vaginal intercourse more or less the same as other unlawful kinds of sexual assault. It also provided, in its initial form, that a person could not be prosecuted under the new subtitle "if the complainant is the person's legal spouse unless the parties are living separate and apart, pursuant to court order." In supporting that limited provision, the then-extant Governor's Commission to Study Implementation of the Equal Rights Amendment (which amendment had been added to the Maryland Constitution in 1972) noted as one of the problems with the existing law that "the word 'unlawful' in the common law definition of rape has been interpreted by the Maryland courts to mean that a person cannot rape his spouse even if the couple is living separate and apart."
>
> Ultimately, as the result of extensive amendments made to the bill by the House of Delegates, the crime of rape was retained as a statutorily defined offense but was split into two degrees, and four degrees of other sexual offenses were created. Under the law, as enacted, first degree rape (§ 462) is defined as vaginal intercourse by force or threat of force against the will and without the consent of the other person, accompanied by (1) the use or display of a dangerous

weapon, (2) suffocation, strangulation, disfigurement, or other serious physical injury, (3) placing the victim in fear that the victim or a person known to the victim will be imminently subjected to death, suffocation, strangulation, disfigurement, serious physical injury, or kidnaping, or (4) the perpetrator being aided or abetted by one or more other persons. Second degree rape (§ 463) consists of vaginal intercourse (1) by force or threat of force against the will and without the consent of the victim, or (2) with a person who is mentally defective, mentally incapacitated, or physically helpless and the perpetrator knows or should know that the victim has that condition.

The four degrees of other sexual offenses, defined in §§ 464 through 464C, are principally based on a "sexual contact" or a "sexual act" other than vaginal intercourse, accompanied by varying forms of aggravation. "Sexual contact" is defined as "the intentional touching of any part of the victim's or actor's anal or genital areas or other intimate parts for purposes of sexual arousal or gratification or for abuse of either party," including the penetration by any part of a person's body, other than the penis, mouth or tongue, into the genital or anal opening, if that penetration can be reasonably construed as being for the purpose of sexual arousal or gratification, or for the abuse of either party. § 461(f). A "sexual act" is defined to exclude vaginal intercourse but to include cunnilingus, fellatio, analingus, anal intercourse, and the penetration by any object into the genital or anal opening of another person's body. § 461(e). First and second degree sexual offenses are essentially parallels to first and second degree rape. A first degree sexual offense (§ 464) consists of engaging in a sexual *act* with another person under the same conditions that, if the act were vaginal intercourse, would constitute first degree rape; a second degree sexual offense (§ 464A) consists of engaging in a sexual *act* with another person under circumstances that, if the act were vaginal intercourse, would constitute second degree rape.

A third degree sexual offense (§ 464B) consisted of (1) a sexual *contact* against the will and without the consent of the other person accompanied by any of the other aggravating factors included as elements of first or second degree rape or first or second degree sexual offense; (2) sexual *contact* with a person who is mentally defective, mentally incapacitated, or physically helpless; (3) sexual *contact* with another person under the age of 14 if the perpetrator is four or more years older than the victim; or (4) a sexual *act* or vaginal intercourse with another person 14 or 15 years old if the perpetrator is at least 21 years of age. A fourth degree sexual offense (§ 464C) was defined as (1) a sexual *contact* against the will and without the consent of the victim, or (2) a sexual *act* or vaginal intercourse with a person 14 or 15 years old by a person at least four years older than the victim but not yet 21 years of age.

Having established and defined those substantive offenses, the General Assembly turned its attention to the marital "exemption." In § 464D, it provided that "a person may not be prosecuted under Sections 462

> [first degree rape], 463 [second degree rape], 464B [third degree sexual offense], and 464C [fourth degree sexual offense] if the victim is the person's legal spouse at the time of the commission of the alleged rape or sexual offense unless the parties are living separate and apart pursuant to a decree of divorce a mensa et thoro." With this formulation, the Legislature, on the one hand, expressly recognized and confirmed a general marital "exemption" for those offenses but, as to those offenses, chose to treat parties who were living apart pursuant to a decree of limited divorce as though they were not married at all and were, in effect, legal strangers to one another. In that limited circumstance, a husband was made subject to the same liability for engaging in the proscribed conduct against his wife as he would be if he committed it against any other woman.[1]

Id., 348 Md. at 285–89.

The court went on to note that in 1989 the Legislature had taken another look at the marital exemption, and created further important limitations on its exercise:

> The impetus for that effort was a significant and growing concern over violent sexual assaults both within the marital home and during periods of separation not sanctioned by a limited divorce.[2] House Bill 399, enacted as 1989 Md. Laws, ch. 189, amended § 464D to (1) extend the circumstances under which a person may be prosecuted for sexual offenses against his or her estranged spouse, and (2) permit a person to be prosecuted for a more limited range of sexual offenses committed against the person's spouse, even if the parties were still living together.
>
> With respect to offenses against an estranged spouse, the law kept in place, as new § 464D(d), the 1976 law allowing the prosecution of a spouse for first or second degree rape and for a third or fourth degree sexual offense when committed against a spouse who has been living separate and apart without cohabitation and without interruption pursuant to a decree of limited divorce. As a new provision, § 464D(b) permits prosecution under §§ 462(a), 463(a)(1), 464B(a)(1)(i), and 464B(1)(ii) for an offense against the person's "legal spouse" if the parties have lived separate and apart without cohabitation and without interruption pursuant to a written separation agreement or for at least

1. Section 464D made no mention of first or second degree sexual offenses, presumably because the Legislature believed that it was not necessary to do so. The marital "exemption," even as articulated by Hale, applied only to common law rape, which involved vaginal intercourse, and never applied to the kind of conduct constituting a "sexual act."

2. In supporting that reconsideration and the 1989 legislation to address the problem, the State Department of Human Resources informed the General Assembly that approximately one-third of the women seeking services through the 18 community-based battered spouse programs reported that episodes of physical violence and abuse were accompanied by forced anal or vaginal penetration, often resulting in genital or anal-genital injuries. The House of Ruth, a shelter for battered women and children, reported that, of the 987 women served by its legal clinic in the previous year, two-thirds complained of having been raped at least once during their marriage, often after separation.

> six months immediately before "the commission of the alleged rape or sexual offense." Under that provision, the person can be prosecuted for (1) first degree rape (§ 462(a)), (2) second degree rape when the vaginal intercourse is committed by force or threat of force against the will and without the consent of the victim (§ 463(a)(1)), (3) a third degree sexual offense involving sexual contact against the will and without the consent of the victim and the employment or display of a dangerous or deadly weapon or article which the victim reasonably concludes is a dangerous or deadly weapon (§ 464B(a)(1)(i)), or (4) a third degree sexual offense involving sexual contact against the will and without the consent of the victim and the infliction of suffocation, strangulation, disfigurement, or serious physical injury upon the victim or someone else in the course of committing the offense (§ 464B(a)(1)(ii)). . . .
>
> Finally, in this regard, under new § 464D(c), the Legislature authorized the prosecution of a person for those same offenses—§§ 462(a), 463(a)(1), 464B(a)(1)(I), and 464B(a)(1)(ii)—but only if the person "uses actual force [not merely the threat of force] against the will and without the consent of the person's legal spouse." . . .

Id., 348 Md. at 289–91.

Parsing these statutory provisions, how would you describe to a non lawyer the current difference between how Maryland law treats those charged with rape or sexual assault of a marital partner, and those charged with rape or sexual assault of someone not a marital partner? What explanation or justification do you suppose would be offered for the distinctions drawn? Are you personally persuaded that the distinctions are appropriate or necessary? Are there situations in which they are likely to promote more equitable treatment? Situations in which they are more likely to promote injustice? When you consider these questions, what standards are you using to gauge what is "equitable," or "just." Is the critical question whether one class of sexual offender is advantaged or disadvantaged by the application of a particular statutory provision, or whether justice is done as between the perpetrator and the victim?

Recent empirical research underscores the importance of addressing rape and sexual assault between intimate partners. In a recent special issue dedicated to wife rape, Patricia Mahoney reports that compared to other sexual assault victims, marital rape victims are more likely to be injured or seriously assaulted, but less likely to seek medical help. *High Rape Chronicity and Low Rates of Help–Seeking Among Wife Rape Survivors in a Nonclinical Sample: Implications for Research and Practice,* 5 VIOLENCE AGAINST WOMEN 993 (1999). Her findings are likely to hold true in other cases involving intimate partners, even outside of marriage. In the same issue, Jacquelyn Campbell and Karen Soeken report that men who both physically and sexually abuse their partners are considerably more dangerous than men who engage in physical but not sexual abuse. *Forced Sex and Intimate Partner Violence: Effects on Women's Risk and Women's Health,* 5 VIOLENCE AGAINST WOMEN 1017 (1999).

Partner Abuse as a Distinct Offense

In its efforts to change law enforcement attitudes and practices with respect to domestic violence, California has amended its criminal code to target partner abuse as a specific crime, making it a felony rather than the more typical domestic violence misdemeanor.

California Penal Code § 273.5 (2000)

§ 273.5. Infliction of injury on spouse, cohabitee or parent of child; Conditions of probation

—(a) Any person who willfully inflicts upon a person who is his or her spouse, former spouse, cohabitant, former cohabitant, or the mother or father of his or her child, corporal injury resulting in a traumatic condition, is guilty of a felony, and upon conviction thereof shall be punished by imprisonment in the state prison for two, three, or four years, or in a county jail for not more than one year, or by a fine of up to six thousand dollars ($6,000) or by both that fine and imprisonment.

—(b) Holding oneself out to be the husband or wife of the person with whom one is cohabiting is not necessary to constitute cohabitation as the term is used in this section.

—(c) As used in this section, "traumatic condition" means a condition of the body, such as a wound or external or internal injury, whether of a minor or serious nature, caused by a physical force.

—(d) For the purpose of this section, a person shall be considered the father or mother of another person's child if the alleged male parent is presumed the natural father under Sections 7611 and 7612 of the Family Code.

—(e) Any person convicted of violating this section for acts occurring within seven years of a previous conviction under subdivision (a), or subdivision (d) of Section 243, or Section 243.4, 244, 244.5, or 245, shall be punished by imprisonment in a county jail for not more than one year, or by imprisonment in the state prison for two, four, or five years, or by both imprisonment and a fine of up to ten thousand dollars ($10,000).

—(f) If probation is granted to any person convicted under subdivision (a), the court shall impose probation consistent with the provisions of Section 1203.097.

—(g) If probation is granted, or the execution or imposition of a sentence is suspended, for any defendant convicted under subdivision (a) who has been convicted of any prior offense specified in subdivision (e), the court shall impose one of the following conditions of probation:

—(1) If the defendant has suffered one prior conviction within the previous seven years for a violation of any offense specified in subdivision (e), it shall be a condition thereof, in addition to the provisions contained in Section 1203.097, that he or she be imprisoned in a county jail for not less than 15 days.

—(2) If the defendant has suffered two or more prior convictions within the previous seven years for a violation of any offense specified in subdivision (e), it shall be a condition of probation, in addition to the provisions contained in Section 1203.097, that he or she be imprisoned in a county jail for not less than 60 days.

—(3) The court, upon a showing of good cause, may find that the mandatory imprisonment required by this subdivision shall not be imposed and shall state on the record its reasons for finding good cause.

—(h) If probation is granted upon conviction of a violation of subdivision (a), the conditions of probation may include, consistent with the terms of probation imposed pursuant to Section 1203.97, in lieu of a fine, one or both of the following requirements:

—(1) That the defendant make payments to a battered women's shelter, up to a maximum of five thousand dollars ($5,000), pursuant to Section 1203.097.

—(2) That the defendant reimburse the victim for reasonable costs of counseling and other reasonable expenses that the court finds are the direct result of the defendant's offense.

—For any order to pay a fine, make payments to a battered women's shelter, or pay restitution as a condition of probation under this subdivision, the court shall make a determination of the defendant's ability to pay. In no event shall any order to make payments to a battered women's shelter be made if it would impair the ability of the defendant to pay direct restitution to the victim or court-ordered child support. Where the injury to a married person is caused in whole or in part by the criminal acts of his or her spouse in violation of this section, the community property may not be used to discharge the liability of the offending spouse for restitution to the injured spouse, required by Section 1203.04, as operative on or before August 2, 1995, or Section 1202.4, or to a shelter for costs with regard to the injured spouse and dependents, required by this section, until all separate property of the offending spouse is exhausted.

NOTES AND QUESTIONS

1. Section 273.5 was first passed in 1977, although it has been frequently amended since. Subsection (e) increases the penalty for someone convicted under Section 273.5 who has previously been convicted of one of a number of other crimes. Those crimes are battery, battery involving serious bodily injury, sexual battery, assault with caustic chemicals, assault with stun gun or taser, and assault with deadly weapon or by force likely to produce great bodily injury. Section 1203.097, referred to in subsections (f) and (g), governs conditions of probation for those convicted of crimes of domestic violence.

2. What do you think are the advantages and disadvantages of creating a separate crime of domestic violence? You may want to come back to this question after reading more of this chapter, particularly Sections B, C and D.

3. Other specific domestic violence crimes have been created at the federal level by the Violence Against Women Act of 1994, which makes both the interstate commission of domestic violence and the interstate violation of a restraining order federal offenses, with potentially stiffer sanctions than those typically imposed under state law, except for the most serious felony offenses. See Chapter 8D, above, and Section F of this chapter, below.

4. While it is helpful to appreciate the variety of criminal charges that can grow out of incidents of domestic violence, the fact remains that an abusive relationship is something more than the sum of crimes committed by the abusive partner. The tendency of the criminal justice system is to respond incident by incident, rather than to the abusive relationship as a whole, and to treat each incident as an isolated event, rather than interpreting it in its context. Even when partner abuse is, as in California, recognized as a distinct crime, that crime is defined as the infliction of an individual injury. This tendency contributes to the consistent inclination of police, prosecutors and judges to underestimate the danger posed by the abuser. It also contributes to the consistent failure of those same participants to understand a victim's dilemma when she is offered the resources of the criminal justice system with respect to one discrete incident of abuse, but must gauge the effect of that intervention on her long-term safety. Even more fundamentally, this tendency reflects the criminal justice system's inability, or failure, to respond to domestic violence as a pernicious form of control over, and therefore discrimination against, women. Evan Stark offers an analysis of this phenomenon in his article *Mandatory Arrest of Batterers: A Reply to Its Critics*, DO ARRESTS AND RESTRAINING ORDERS WORK? 115, 122–124 (E.S. Buzawa & C.G. Buzawa, eds. 1996):

> How does conceptualizing *battering, the social phenomenon,* in terms of sexual inequality, coercive control, and entrapment help us understand *battering, the crime?* Most notably, it highlights the contrast between criminal acts of domestic violence and the pattern of coercion and control that is not currently proscribed by law.... [H]ighlighting coercive control and entrapment moves us from an abuse model, in which otherwise legitimate authority is exercised illegitimately, to a model in which violent restraint is placed on a continuum with the normative authority men exercise over women....
>
> Because the element of control is what links the assaultive dimensions of abuse to the political fact of female inequality, there can be no hope of preventing battering simply by regulating the degree of violence. This is why we call for "zero tolerance" of force in interpersonal relationships and oppose basing police intervention on a calculus of physical harm. At the same time, no level of "treatment" (for women or men) will substantially reduce force until the political dimensions of sexual inequality are addressed....

Would it be fair to say that one of the arguments Stark is making is that responding to domestic assaults is dealing only with "the tip of the iceberg," as a response to "battering as a social phenomenon?" Beyond that, is he saying that criminal law is incapable under any circumstances of responding to "battering as a social phenomenon," or rather that we have not shaped the criminal law to respond, although it could? Would there be ways to criminalize more effectively the "sexual inequality, coercive control and entrapment" that he sees as being at the heart of battering behavior? If criminal law alone cannot provide an effective response, could other legal mechanisms fill the gap? Can civil rights law, for example, address the sexual inequality dimension of battering? This was a question answered in the affirmative by Congress in the Violence Against Women Act, which created a private civil rights action for gender-based violence against women. That provision, struck down by the Supreme Court as an unconstitutional exercise of congressional authority in United States v. Morrison, 120 S.Ct. 1740 (2000), will be a topic of discussion in Chapter 13, below. Might he instead, or also, be arguing that combating battering as a social practice will require action on many fronts, not just the engagement of the legal system?

Enforcing the Law

For women who have been physically abused, the problem has not been that their partners' behavior falls outside accepted categories of criminal conduct. Rather, the issue has been that the criminal justice system—from police and prosecutors to judges and probation officers—has turned a blind eye, refusing to respond to or take seriously criminal violations by intimate partners. A walk through the process by which a crime is identified and prosecuted, and a defendant convicted and sentenced, reveals the numerous points at which the victim may receive the message that the system is or is not concerned for her safety, and the abuser may receive the message that he will or will not be held accountable for his behavior.

When violence erupts in an intimate relationship, the first question is whether it will come to the attention of law enforcement authorities. If the victim or another witness responds by calling the police, it will, although if there is then no police response, or the police respond without ever filing a report on the incident, it will almost immediately disappear from official view. If the police are not called at the time of the incident, there is still an opportunity for the victim to instigate an official response by going to the police and filing a subsequent report. The victim will generally only do this if she is interested in prosecution, and is using the police report as her "passport" into the prosecutor's office. One further possibility is that the victim will respond to the incident by seeking a protective order, and through that process will come to the attention of the prosecutor's office. This is perhaps most likely to happen if the court where she goes for her order is one in which victim witness advocates working in the prosecutor's office are assigned to assist women with restraining orders, or one in which lay advocates working on restraining orders maintain close relationships with the prosecutor's office. However, it is also possible for the judge who issues the restraining order to bring the precipitating incident to the attention of the prosecutor, if she is concerned for the victim's safety.

If the police respond to a call, and appear at the scene of a domestic violence incident, their behavior will have an important impact on the ultimate outcome. One crucial aspect of police intervention is the writing and filing of a report. As suggested above, if police fail to enter a report, the incident will disappear from official memory, and provide no support for more aggressive intervention the next time violence is reported. It is also critical that the report be complete, detailed, and free of bias, so that it can be put to effective use in any subsequent prosecution. At the policy level, it is also important that the report carry a marker identifying the incident as one involving partner abuse, so that the state has an accurate measure of the incidence of domestic violence to justify expenditures on training or services, and any necessary substantive or procedural reforms.

A second crucial police choice is whether to arrest the perpetrator, if he is still on the premises and state law mandates or permits arrest without a warrant, or, in cases in which he has already left, whether to seek a warrant for his arrest. A related choice is whether to issue a citation, commanding the offender's later appearance in court to answer charges, but without arresting him. Finally, police response to the victim and her children—the level of immediate support provided, and the identification of other resources for the family—can dramatically affect the victim's ability and willingness to cooperate in holding her abuser accountable for his violence.

If the perpetrator is arrested, and removed from the scene, the next set of choices have to do with whether, and how, criminal charges are brought, and whether, and for how long, the perpetrator will be held before being released back into the community. If the arrest is regarded simply as a warning, and an independent decision is made by the authorities not to press charges, then the perpetrator will be released almost immediately. If the victim has chosen to obtain a restraining order, then her only ongoing protection will be the terms of that order, and the possibility of enforcing any violation. A slightly different scenario would involve the prosecutor's office consulting with the victim about the desirability of pursuing criminal action, but again, the decision not to press charges will result in the perpetrator's release, and the victim's exclusive reliance on a protective order to secure her future safety. The victim should be, but is often not, given advance notice of her perpetrator's release, so that she can take proper precautions, whether those involve moving into a shelter, staying away from her home temporarily, or simply taking whatever steps she can to secure her home against his intrusion.

If, after an arrest, a decision is made to pursue criminal misdemeanor charges, then the perpetrator will be detained for some period of time until he can be arraigned, a bail hearing held, and a trial date set. Although the primary purpose of bail proceedings is to ensure that the defendant shows up at trial, in many jurisdictions pre-trial detention can also be justified, albeit sparingly, on the grounds that the defendant poses an identifiable and serious risk to himself or others. It is also available to the hearing officer to condition release not only on the provision of a bond, but also on the defendant's consent to a protective order, or to conditions with the same effect. In volatile situations the victim's safety, or at a minimum her continued cooperation with the prosecutor, may be entirely dependent on the defendant's continuing detention, or on the conscientious and careful imposition and enforcement of conditions that keep the defendant away from her pending his trial. Again, it should be, but is not, standard practice to notify the victim before her abuser is released. If felony charges have been brought, then a grand jury proceeding will be initiated, either before or after the arraignment, and the case will proceed only on the grand jury's finding of probable cause.

The most debated issues of prosecutorial policy have been the standards governing whether or not to prosecute, and whether prosecutors should be required to prosecute domestic violence cases under "no-drop" policies even in situations where the victim is not cooperative. But another crucial choice point for the prosecutor is how to frame the charge. Should the focus be on the violation of a restraining order, which will be relatively easy to prove, but may underemphasize the level of violence involved, and result in a slap on the wrist rather than a more meaningful sanction? Should the choice be to pursue one or more criminal misdemeanor charges, which may produce a speedier resolution, or to go after felony charges which will carry more significant penalties, but will also move more slowly, and require a greater investment of prosecutorial resources, perhaps at the expense of other victims?

Even after a decision has been made to bring charges, the case may still be disposed of without a trial. If the victim proves uncooperative, and if the prosecutor's office has no expertise in or enthusiasm for presenting the case without her testimony, the charges may still be dropped. Alternatively, if the defendant or his counsel are willing to cooperate with the prosecutor, the charges may be dropped on condition that the defendant agree to the terms of a protective order, or agree to participate in a batterer's treatment program, or provide restitution, or some combination of these or other conditions. Another critical choice for prosecutors is whether to offer these "pre-trial diversion" programs, which will leave the defendant with no criminal record, or whether to insist that any such "diversion" depend on a plea-bargain which will result in a conviction, although for a lesser offense than the defendant was originally charged with. Obtaining a conviction has the advantage that the defendant can then be sentenced, with the sentence being suspended as long as he is in compliance with the terms of the "diversion" agreement. This greatly simplifies the task of holding the defendant accountable for any violation of his agreement.

These choices can in theory be made at any point between the initial charging and the trial, and often are negotiated between the prosecutor and the defendant's attorney without any judicial input. They may, on the other hand, be influenced by the judge's reaction to the case at the pretrial conference, which will usually be scheduled shortly before the trial date. Even on the day the trial is scheduled to begin, the judge, under pressure to dispose of cases as quickly as possible, may make a final effort to secure a negotiated disposition, rather than see the case go to trial.

At trial, there is, of course, always the possibility that the defendant will be acquitted. Alternatively, the case may be continued without a finding, with the threat that the trial will resume if the defendant violates the terms of the probation to which he is assigned, and the promise that if he completes the probationary period without a violation, the case will be dismissed. This poses similar risks to those created by pre-trial diversion. It will be more difficult to obtain a conviction on the original charges once any significant time has elapsed, and if the case is ultimately dismissed, there is nothing in the defendant's record to warn of his propensity for violence. Finally, if the defendant is convicted, while incarceration is increasingly a possibility, the likelihood is still that he will instead be assigned to probation, and required to comply with the terms of a protective order, as well as completing one or more treatment programs (commonly programs for alcohol and substance abuse, in addition to a batterer's treatment program). A suspended sentence may also be imposed to increase the defendant's motivation to comply with the terms of his probation.

In 1993 the U.S. Department of Justice's Bureau of Justice Assistance published a report which summarized the findings of two separate research projects, involving a total of eleven demonstration sites around the country, addressing improved justice system practices for handling domestic violence cases. The following excerpt discusses ten "critical elements" needed for an effective justice system response to family violence. As you read it, decide how those elements would affect the different choice points identified in this preliminary outline of the workings of the criminal justice system. Notice the extent to which the report advocates the participation of public and private agencies outside the justice system as part of a comprehensive effort to make the justice system responsive to victims, and hold abusers accountable. Many of the elements described here are treated in depth in later sections of this chapter, but this overview provides a good introduction to the issues they raise.

Critical Elements
Meredith Hofford and Adele V. Harrell, Family Violence: Interventions for the Justice System, 9–17, U.S. Department of Justice, 1993

Program Leadership

The long-term commitment of program leadership is critical to the success of these efforts. Unlike some other kinds of projects, which can be developed rather independently and relatively painlessly, family violence projects need to be vitally integrated into the daily workings of the court. The process of changing longstanding policies and examining ingrained personal attitudes is often quite difficult. An unfailing commitment on the part of project leadership will provide stability and continued progress when others are unable to see the light at the end of the tunnel.

Because the justice system response to family violence is the focus of the project, it is crucial that leadership come from *within* the system itself. Strong prosecutors or concerned judges, with support from their chiefs, are logical choices. Without such leadership, it is unlikely that suggestions for change and reform will be embraced by the others in the system....

In addition to the primary leadership from within the system, commitments to participate in a leadership capacity should be obtained from the following:

- The chief judge.
- The chief prosecutor.
- The public defender.
- The chief law enforcement officer.
- The court administrator.
- The juvenile court services director.
- The chief probation officer.
- The head of children's protective services.
- The director of the domestic violence coalition or battered women's shelter.
- The director of batterers treatment services.
- Members of county or State funding bodies.
- Others as determined locally.

A lead agency or office should assume the responsibility for initiating and coordinating project activities. . . . [T]he *best* location for the lead agency is within the justice system.

Early Case Identification and Response

Courts and service agencies must develop methods of identifying and responding promptly to family violence cases at the earliest possible stage of case processing. The demonstration projects found the tendency to avoid taking an active role in identifying and working with family violence cases was widespread in the justice system. The first response of many agencies was that the problem should be addressed by some other agency. As a result, many victims gave up on the system or failed to receive advocacy or services for many months after the initial incident.

The initial contact with the victim is a critical point of intervention, but may take several forms:

- *Victim-initiated actions.* Many victims need assistance in filing complaints or requests for protection orders. This assistance can be provided by specially trained clerks, victim advocates, or volunteers located at intake points in the various agencies.
- *On-scene police intervention.* Police officers called to the scene should not only arrest the offender, if appropriate, but also respond immediately to the needs of the victim and children. Several police departments employ victim advocates who can be summoned to the scene; others have arrangements to call local shelters for assistance. Police policies and concomitant forms that promote identifying cases as family violence cases and promote gathering evidence in support of prosecution, with or without victim testimony, are especially useful.

- *Calls for service.* Precinct or dispatch monitoring of repeat calls from problem families assists the police responding to calls and can be used to identify families in need of outreach services.
- *Screening by social service agencies and hospitals.* Intake staff at social service agencies and hospitals should be trained to screen for multiple abuse in families and, most importantly, to provide appropriate referrals for legal intervention on a priority basis.

Early identification and case response strategies at each of these victim contact points should include:

- Outreach efforts to identify families at high risk for repeat violence, to offer services and counseling, and to avoid renewed abuse.
- Checks on the immediate safety of the victim and other family members.
- Referral to a shelter and battered women's services.
- Information for victims about civil and criminal options and assistance, as needed, in completing forms to initiate legal action.
- Investigation of the possibility of child abuse and neglect.
- Good evidence gathering at the time of the initial report.
- Initiation of appropriate legal interventions, whether or not the victims pursue such interventions.
- Special policies and practices for family violence cases such as priority docketing, pretrial supervision of offenders, and extraordinary efforts at victim assistance and case coordination.

Designated Personnel

Each law enforcement and social service agency and each court and prosecutor's office must have personnel trained in family violence issues and specifically assigned to handle and coordinate matters related to family violence cases. Unless this occurs, cases and victims will not receive the attention they need and to which they are entitled. The designated staff is responsible for reviewing policies, ensuring compliance, and implementing changes as necessary. . . .

Coordination

A large majority of violent families have serious, multiple dysfunctions and frequently have other actions, such as divorce, custody, delinquency and child abuse cases, and restraining orders, pending elsewhere in the court system. When possible, consolidation of these cases and handling by a single court improves efficiency and effectiveness. At the very least, policies are needed that ensure case coordination. Case records should be standardized and, hopefully, computerized, and procedures should be established to allow sharing of information among courts on the status of all pending actions and orders issued in all cases involving members of a family. Such actions will facilitate consistent enforcement of court orders, monitoring of offenders, and protection of victims. . . .

Establishing a coordinating committee, council, or task force should be an early project priority. Membership should be as broad as possible to include police, sheriffs, prosecutors, court administrators, judges, probation officers, treatment agencies, and representatives of victim shelters and victim advocacy groups. . . .

Monthly meetings should be held to provide a forum for airing grievances about how cases are being handled, sharing information on new policies and practices, and building community awareness of resources and services available from the police and courts. Advocates from outside the justice system should be included to help monitor the effectiveness of the response to family violence from the perspective of those served. The heads of participating agencies need to attend initial interagency planning meetings to open lines of communication with other agencies and lend authority to the agency's commitment to change. Subsequently, a designated representative of each agency should regularly attend meetings to support ongoing coordination, problem-solving, and planning. . . .

Written Policies

Each public agency handling family violence cases should develop written policies that reflect the philosophy established by the jurisdiction. The policies should specify each agency's responsibilities for implementing the approach, for coordination, and for information sharing. New and existing policies should be regularly reviewed and revised as dictated by experience and practice. . . .

. . . Areas of friction that arise in the process of establishing new policies provide excellent opportunities to clarify and fine tune agreements between agencies. Because such cooperation is key to the success of a family violence project, each agency director should make a commitment to do this before project implementation begins.

Policies should be developed regarding:

- Arrest.
- Pretrial release.
- Prosecution.
- Availability and enforcement of protection orders.
- Docketing.
- Monitoring of offenders.
- Standards for treatment providers.
- Services and advocacy for victims.
- Case coordination and information sharing.
- Data collection.

A Vigorous, Affirmative Prosecution Effort

The policies and activities of the prosecutor's office are central to any family violence project. Without a vigorous and affirmative effort to prosecute family assaults and other family violence cases, the other components cannot work. Specifically:

- Prosecutors must have policies that do not place victims in the position of initiating and managing their own cases.
- Similarly, victims should not make the decision to proceed with or withdraw a case. Rather, investigators and prosecutors should be skilled in proving cases in court, even with a hostile or reluctant victim or witness.
- Prosecutors might even include a no-drop policy, whereby victims, who may be threatened or intimidated by the batterers, are not allowed to withdraw a complaint after it is filed.
- Many prosecutors have adopted "vertical prosecution," whereby one prosecutor is assigned to the case from start to finish, so that the victim is not working with first one person and then another.
- Prosecutors also should vigorously prosecute violations of protection orders; it may be necessary to represent victims in protection order or other civil hearings related to the violence.

Formal Entry of Court Orders

It is imperative that the facts of each case are gathered and entered into the official record as soon as possible and that some official judicial action be taken as a result of court proceedings in family violence cases. As a practical matter, diversion of a large number of cases before hearings are held to establish the facts of these cases weakens the court's ability to prosecute in other cases and discourages the good evidence-gathering necessary for formal court action. Sites that diverted cases prior to prosecution also found that reopening cases for later prosecution was difficult, as was monitoring compliance with the conditions of the original diversion.

The culmination of a successful prosecution or other appropriate disposition should be a firm official action by the court. It must be tailored and specific to the case. It should include, as appropriate, provision for punishment and treatment, as well as mechanisms for accountability and enforcement. Likewise, protection orders should be issued and served expeditiously.... In cases where petitions are denied or a criminal case is dismissed, judges should state the reasons for the record.

The need for formal entry of court orders is twofold. First, it discourages the use of informal diversion, civil compromises, reduced charges, dismissals, and suspensions that are inappropriate and inconsistent with the goals of a family violence project.... Second, it creates the necessary information base for followup intervention and victim protection. Judicial orders should be transmitted to police departments, probation departments, and treatment agencies as appropriate.

Formal Monitoring and Enforcement

Even though court orders contain specific language for monitoring offenders and enforcing court-ordered conditions, the resources must be available and the mechanisms for enforcement must be in place for effective monitoring to occur. The standard strategy for monitoring compliance in criminal cases is to place offenders on probation. However, because family violence incidents, even those involving considerable injury, are often prosecuted as misdemeanors or less serious felonies, the level of supervision by probation departments is often merely administrative, involving minimal client contact and a reliance on checks of police reports for new offenses and reports of non-compliance filed by treatment agencies. In cities with large probation caseloads and multiple treatment agencies, communication between treatment agencies and probation officers may be poor.

Thus, even if placed on formal probation, many abusers are left unsupervised because of large caseloads. This response relies heavily on the victim's willingness to notify the courts and probation officers of new incidents. Without intervention, an abusive conflict can build to a new crisis level. The high rate of recidivism of family violence offenders dictates more aggressive monitoring of offenders. This can be accomplished by setting up a special monitoring program or assigning probation cases to specially designated probation officers.

The problem of monitoring compliance with protection orders is even more acute because most court systems do not have any mechanisms in place to enforce civil court orders. In spite of the fact that violations of protection orders are very common, prosecution of perpetrators for violations . . . is only an extremely small portion of most courts' family violence caseload. Without the necessary followup, the efforts of law enforcement, prosecutors, and courts will have very little deterrent effect.

Batterers Treatment Programs

Batterers treatment programs are a mandatory part of an effective response to family violence. Such programs offer an appropriate means of intervening to remediate abusive behavior, but they must be developed with attention to protection of the victims and enforcement by the courts, and programs should be reviewed for appropriateness by professionals who are experts in treating family violence.

These programs are based on the understanding that battering is a learned behavior that can be changed by education and counseling. Batterer treatment must be specifically designed to address battering issues. Approaches that emphasize personal growth or marriage counseling and those that deal only with controlling anger without addressing the underlying issues of self-esteem, power, and control are not likely to be effective and are, therefore, inappropriate. Treatment programs should also address the lethality of violence and victim safety issues. These issues must take precedency over confidentiality issues.

Many communities have either no batterers treatment programs or do not have sufficient treatment capacity to serve court-ordered clients. As court intervention and law enforcement efforts expand, treatment caseloads expand. For this reason, continuing development of adequate and appropriate treatment tends to be an ongoing activity required on the part of family violence programs. Representatives of agencies receiving court referrals should meet regularly as a group with court monitors from the probation department or courts to discuss policies and problems.

Another continuing problem is how to address the need that many abusers have for alcohol and drug treatment. Most batterers treatment programs require the offender to attend separate substance abuse treatment prior to entering batterer treatment; a few programs address both issues. Guidelines and treatment alternatives for substance abusers need to be developed in conjunction with batterers treatment programs. . . .

Training

Training is key to solving many of the existing problems courts have with family violence cases. Current problems in responding to family violence stem in part from a lack of understanding on the part of most people as to the dynamics of domestic abuse, personal reactions and attitudes about it, and a severe dearth of information as to what effective alternative responses might be. . . .

All those individuals working directly with family violence cases or family members must receive comprehensive training on the nature of family violence. This training should provide a basic understanding of the needs of victims and the rationale behind the specific policies and practices implemented by the project. Specifically, the training should cover:

- The dynamics of family violence.
- Battered-spouse and battered-child syndromes.
- The correlation between spouse abuse, child abuse, and delinquency.
- The impact of arrest.
- Evidence gathering and prosecution techniques.
- Victim safety issues.
- Proper courtroom treatment of victims, offenders, and witnesses.
- The impact of personal attitudes and gender bias on courtroom demeanor and actions by justice system personnel.
- Sanctions available and treatment standards for offenders.
- The elements of a good protection order.
- Shelter and support services available for victims.
- Effectiveness of coordinating and consolidating services.

. . .

Finally, it cannot be noted too frequently that the high percentage of both spouse and child abuse found within these families clearly mandates the development of sound domestic violence policies and training for Departments of Social Services and Child Protection Services caseworkers. These agencies should also increase their coordination with justice system agencies addressing family violence issues.

* * *

NOTES

1. Some of these recommendations are more controversial than others. Some jurisdictions, for example, remain very committed to informal diversion programs, and would resist the recommendation that official judicial action be taken in every domestic violence case. "No-drop" prosecution policies have been the subject of heated debate, even within the battered women's advocacy community. There is as yet no clear consensus as to the relative merits of different modalities of batterers' treatment, or indeed as to the success of treatment of any kind in changing patterns of abusive behavior. These and other areas of controversy are explored in some depth in later sections of this chapter.

For accounts of jurisdictions that have attempted to implement "model" justice system responses to domestic violence, see: Linda Dakis and Laura Lazarus, *Attacking the Crime of Domestic Violence: How Dade County is Protecting the Victim and Punishing the Perpetrator*, 19–SPG FAM. ADVOC. 46 (1997); Elena Salzman, *The Quincy District Court Domestic Violence Prevention Program: A Model Legal Framework for Domestic Violence Intervention*, 74 B.U. L. REV. 329 (1994); Casey G. Gwinn and Sgt. Anne O'Dell, *Stopping the Violence: The Role of the Police Officer and the Prosecutor*, 20 WEST. ST. U. L. REV. 297 (1993); Mary E. Asmus, Tineke Ritmeester and Ellen L. Pence, *Prosecuting Domestic Abuse Cases in Duluth: Developing Effective Prosecution Strategies From Understanding the Dynamics of Abusive Relationships*, 15 HAMLINE L. REV. 115 (1991).

2. One context in which many of the "critical elements" of an effective justice system response to domestic violence have been successfully combined is the specialized domestic violence court. In the early 1980s, Cook County Illinois established the first such court to hear all domestic violence misdemeanor cases, and since then a number of other jurisdictions have followed suit. A 1997 study identified specialized courts in Dade, Lee and Broward Counties in Florida; Dallas County in Texas; Durham and Orange Counties in North Carolina; Denver County in Colorado; Dade and Marion Counties in Indiana; Kings County in Washington State; and Shelby County in Tennessee. Specialized courts were also identified in Albuquerque, New Mexico; in the Bronx, Brooklyn and Queens, New York; in Philadelphia, Pennsylvania; in Milwaukee and Chicago, Illinois; in Quincy, Massachusetts; in the District of Columbia, in thirteen jurisdictions in California, and six jurisdictions in Connecticut. S. Keilitz, H. Efkeman and P. Casey, DOMESTIC VIOLENCE COURTS: JURISDICTION, ORGANIZATION, PERFORMANCE GOALS, AND MEASURES (National Center for State Courts, 1997). Even more recently, funding under the Violence Against Women Act has supported the development of specialized courts or court sessions in the inner-city community of Dorchester, Massachusetts, in Milwaukee, Wisconsin, and in Washtenaw County, Michigan.

These specialized courts vary in the extent of their jurisdiction. Some deal only with protective orders, or only with criminal misdemeanor cases, others combine both, and the most comprehensive also have jurisdiction over related civil matters, such as paternity, child support, custody, visitation and divorce. Among the most common, and effective, features of specialized courts are their specialized intake units, which provide a range of services to victims; the allocation of dedicated calendars and specialized judges to expedite hearings and provide consistency; and integrated adjudication of abuse-related proceedings to avoid duplication and potentially inconsistent rulings from different courts.

3. Although the authors of the Department of Justice report recommend that the judiciary provide leadership in efforts to improve the criminal justice system's response to domestic violence, and although concerned judges have in fact played pivotal roles in efforts around the country, the need to preserve both the reality and the appearance of judicial impartiality in specific cases limits the extent to which, or the conditions under which, judges can participate in efforts that are manifestly "pro-victim." In Massachusetts, for example, a recent opinion of the Committee on Judicial Ethics (CJE Opinion No. 98–16), cautioned that regular attendance by a judge at a domestic violence "roundtable" convened monthly by the District Attorney's Office in his or her court would compromise the judge's appearance of neutrality. The CJE reached this conclusion even though the private (criminal defense) bar was invited to attend roundtable meetings, since representatives of the defense bar did not in fact attend. The Committee did concede that if judicial participation was occasional, and not at sessions in which substantive issues were discussed in a one-sided fashion, or was limited to sessions concerning court administration, or if the private bar was notified when the judge would be attending, then "the judge's participation would tend to signify only an interest in the subject matter and a willingness to hear any complaints or concerns about how such cases are processed, without the danger of implying an alliance with a particular side."

When, subsequent to this ruling, Dorchester District Court in Boston, Massachusetts, was chosen by the U.S. Department of Justice as a demonstration site for a new domestic violence court, representatives of the criminal defense bar were included on both the Advisory Board and the project's working committees, making it easier for the court's judges to lend their active support.

4. A developing mechanism by which law enforcement agencies and courts can work with other social service agencies and private service providers to assess the effectiveness of existing case management policies and practices and identify needed reforms is the domestic violence fatality review. The concept is borrowed from child death review teams, themselves an innovation of the late seventies. Child death reviews coordinate data from coroners, law enforcement, the court system, child protective services and health care providers. While their primary function is often investigatory—to determine the cause of a suspicious death—they have had a significant impact on case mismanagement, and the identification of interagency communication problems. See, for example, Michael J. Durfee et al., *Origins and Clinical Relevance of Death Review Teams,* 267 JAMA 3172 (1992). Like child death review teams, domestic violence fatality reviews have sometimes grown out of local and individual initiative, sometimes owe their existence to an administrative mandate, and sometimes are prompted

or supported by state legislation. In California, for example, legislation directed the Attorney General to develop protocols for the development and implementation of domestic violence death review teams. CAL. PENAL CODE § 11163.4 (2000). Both California and Nevada have also enacted general provisions permitting courts or local governments to create such teams. CAL. PENAL CODE § 11163.3 (2000). In Washington State, on the other hand, the Domestic Violence Fatality Review Project was initiated by the Department of Social and Health Services, with federal funding awarded under the Violence Against Women Act.

Domestic violence review teams typically include representatives from most or all of the following: law enforcement, social service agencies, child protective services, battered women's programs, batterers' treatment programs, probation, prosecutors, judges, medical professionals, coroners and medical examiners, and departments of health. Strict rules of confidentiality encourage open participation and protect participating agencies from the public assignment of blame, allowing the focus to remain on improving system operation in the future. It is also common, for the same reasons, for reviews to be limited to cases that are "closed," in the sense that all criminal prosecutions or civil claims arising out of the fatality have been concluded.

Domestic violence fatality reviews have tended to be either investigatory or focused instead on systems analysis. Investigatory reviews concentrate on the process of correctly identifying fatalities as the result of domestic violence. They increase public awareness of domestic violence, improve future criminal investigations by identifying "red flags" for abuse-related deaths, and fine tune epidemiological analyses of domestic violence. An investigatory review in Florida, for example, revealed that domestic fatalities for 1994, officially counted at 230 by the Florida Department of Law Enforcement, actually stood at 321. Systems analysis reviews focus instead on already identified cases, and on how the policies and practices of the different agencies that came in contact with, or could have come in contact with, the victim or the perpetrator, functioned to increase or decrease victim safety and perpetrator accountability.

It is of course possible to combine these two functions. The Washington State Review Project is primarily a systems analysis review, but incorporates the possibility of investigating deaths not initially classified as domestic violence fatalities. That initial classification includes:

(a) All homicides in which the victim was a current or former intimate partner of the perpetrator.

(b) Homicides occurring in conjunction with an attempted or completed homicide of the perpetrator's current or former intimate partner. (For example, situations in which someone kills their current/former intimate partner's friend, family, child, legal advocate....)

(c) Homicides occurring as an extension of or response to ongoing abuse between intimate partners. (For example, when an ex spouse kills the children in order to exact revenge on a former partner for leaving.)

(d) Suicides which may be a response to abuse (as determined by information indicating prior DV, or knowledge from a particular committee member/agency about the circumstances leading to the suicide).

(e) Unsolved homicides of women known to have histories of abuse.

But in addition, the Review Project criteria acknowledge that:

> In some cases a death may not fit the above criteria and/or may not be classified as homicide or DV related by the police/prosecutors or coroners/medical examiners, but members of the committee may have suspicions that the fatality is domestic violence related. In such a case, any member of the committee may request review of a particular death. In these cases, the committee will seek agreement on whether or not to include the examined death in the aggregated count of domestic violence related fatalities after the review is complete. . . .

Conclusion

The next three sections take up issues raised by police responses to domestic violence, prosecutorial policy, and sentencing, including the role of batterers' treatment programs. Although it may seem inappropriate to address a mental health intervention like batterers' treatment in the context of a chapter on the criminal justice system, the vast majority of batterers who attend counseling focused on their abusive behavior do so because a court order has mandated their attendance, or because they have agreed to participate to avoid a criminal record or a stiffer sanction. In this respect, batterers' treatment is an integral aspect of the criminal justice system's response to domestic violence.

The final two sections of the chapter address two new areas of substantive law governing abuse; stalking, and the recent development of federal domestic violence crimes, beginning with the Violence Against Women Act of 1994.

B. POLICE

Background: Police Response to Domestic Violence

Joan Zorza
The Criminal Law of Misdemeanor Violence, 1970–1990, 83 Journal Of Criminal Law and Criminology 46, 48–50 (1992)

. . . [T]hose police departments that had policies on handling domestic calls in the 1970s had a clear non-arrest policy. The Oakland Police Department's *1975 Training Bulletin on Techniques of Dispute Intervention* explicitly described:

> [t]he police role in a dispute situation [as] more often that of a mediator and peacemaker than enforcer of the law.... [T]he possibility that ... arrest will only aggravate the dispute or create a serious danger for the arresting officers due to possible efforts to resist arrest ... is most likely when a husband or father is arrested in his home.... Normally, officers should adhere to the policy that arrests shall be avoided ... but when one of the parties demands arrest, you should attempt to explain the ramifications of such action (e.g. loss of wages, bail procedures, court appearances) and encourage the parties to reason with each other.

Detroit Police commander James Bannon, in his address to the 1975 American Bar Association convention, described the manner in which his police officers respond to domestic violence calls. According to Bannon, the dispatcher would screen calls from battered women to respond only to those women who appeared in the most imminent danger. If the woman had only minor injuries when they arrived, the police became angry and would not respond quickly the next time. Women often learned to report that a stranger was attacking them or that their abuser had a gun. While such a desperate ploy might have worked once for a woman, police simply declared her not credible if they found no serious injuries. Lacking credibility, she was deemed unworthy of police protection if she called again. Police treated poor women and women of color with less concern than they did middle class and white women, even when they were severely injured.

Michigan's policy, as taught in its Police Training Academy, directed officers to:

a. Avoid arrest if possible. Appeal to their [complainants'] vanity.

b. Explain the procedure of obtaining a warrant.

   (1) Complainant must sign complaint.

   (2) Must appear in court.

   (3) Consider loss of time.

   (4) Cost of court.

c. State that your only interest is to prevent a breach of the peace.

d. Explain that attitudes usually change by court time.

e. Recommend a postponement.

   (1) Court not in session.

   (2) Judge not available.

f. Don't be too harsh or critical.

Michigan's policy also failed to provide for sufficient education. While almost half of all Michigan police calls are for domestic disturbances, only three to five out of the 240 hours of police recruit training are devoted to the manner in which police should answer these calls. Training in other police departments has been similarly inadequate. Prior to 1980, when police academies were still uncommon, those who received on-the-job training were generally assigned to those experienced officers who were seen as most successful. Unfortunately, these officers were precisely those least likely to have challenged the standard practices for responding to domestic violence incidents. Rookies looked up to their experienced partners and were rewarded for imitating them.

With the advent of police academies, new recruits were trained by men generally "chosen" as instructors, not because of their academic ability or interest in teaching, but because of their advancing age or temporary disability, or because they were on leave or special duty restriction pending departmental investigation. New officers were often trained first and foremost as men, and the ethic of masculinity was seen as being of the utmost importance. Seeing anything from a woman's perspective was, if not almost taboo, at least so completely foreign that it did not happen.

In this light, it is hardly surprising that the police who did respond to domestic violence calls almost always took the man's side. And because abusers, when they did not or could not deny their abuse, tried to shift the blame onto others, especially their victims, the police frequently joined in blaming the victim. The responding officer often admonished the woman to be a better wife or asked, or at least wondered, why she did not leave. Some officers concluded that she must enjoy the beatings, or at least not mind them. These officers conveniently ignored the fact that their failure to protect the woman, her lack of money, and the far greater risk of being beaten or killed if she tried to separate herself from her abuser all combined to make her decision logical....

* * *

NOTE

1. Criticism of police response to domestic violence has been based not only on the argument that it is inadequate—exposing victims to an unwarranted and unnecessary degree of danger—but also on the argument that it is discriminatory. Most commonly, the argument is that stranger assault is treated differently by police than domestic assault, and that since domestic assaults reported to the police disproportionately involve women victims and male perpetrators, this different treatment discriminates against women. Others have countered that police respond "situationally" to all assaults, and that what determines police response is not whether the assault is domestic, but the totality of circumstances involved in the assault. A study published in 1996, looking at one police department's responses to assaults in 1986 and 1987, set out to test that proposition, and found that even once all the surrounding circumstances were taken into account, there was evidence of discrimination against victims of domestic violence.

Eve S. Buzawa, Thomas L. Austin and Carl G. Buzawa The Role of Arrest in Domestic Versus Stranger Assault: Is There a Difference?; Do Arrests and Restraining Orders Work? 150, 153–154, 156–163, 165, 169–170 (E.S. Buzawa & C.G. Buzawa, eds. 1996)

Certainly, the concept that police base arrest decisions on the situational characteristics of an interaction is neither new nor the topic of much dispute. It is well known that police often base arrest decisions in both domestic and other forms of violence on factors unrelated to the crime itself. What are the situational characteristics of the police-citizen encounter that are most likely to lead to arrest? How do the use of these "nondiscriminatory" factors affect police performance in domestic violence cases? Initially, we noted that most police officers appear to share a common preference regarding when to make an arrest. For example, in one 1980 study of officers from 17 departments, more than 90% identified the following factors in their decisions to arrest: commission of a felony, serious victim injury, use of a weapon, violence against the police, and likelihood of future violence. Prior calls from a household and victim preference were not nearly as important....

How might these and other policy preferences affect the decision to arrest batterers and other assailants? First, in terms of their professionally defined roles and missions, most police officers believe that arrest priority should be placed on cases in which public order and authority have been challenged, with only secondary importance attached to individual victims' considerations.... Because most domestic violence cases are not "public" in nature, they would be relegated to positions of less importance....

Second, organizational imperatives at the individual officer and departmental levels drive police officers to spend time on cases that are likely to lead to convictions. The effectiveness of police officers—a key aspect of promotability—is determined, in part, by now many of their major felony arrests lead to convictions. Officers' time spent processing (largely misdemeanor) "domestics" may therefore "waste" time. Similarly, police departments seek to prove their efficacy by emphasizing the number of felony arrests and the percentage of convictions. Because most domestic violence cases are organizationally termed "misdemeanors," having officers spend time on such cases may not be warranted. Many police departments effectively create this disparity when their officers unofficially "downgrade" domestics to misdemeanor assaults even though they would otherwise fit the textbook definition of a felonious assault....

Third, the willingness of victims to assist officers and prosecutors in following the case through to conviction is an important determinant of arrest.... Domestic violence victims are notorious for dropping complaints, ostensibly because they have reconciled with their abusers. This conclusion is often erroneous. Victims drop cases for a variety of reasons. They do so because arrests have accomplished their goals of deterring future abuse, of allowing an easy separation, or of simply ratifying their status as victims.... In many instances, unique procedural hurdles and a largely impersonal bureaucracy of the police and prosecutor impel victims to drop cases.

Fourth, characteristics of police-offender interactions dramatically affect the chances of arrest, especially what offenders do *after* the officers arrive; for example, if offenders are disrespectful, arrest is justified.... Dobash and Dobash (1979) found that arrest was far more likely in domestic cases when assailants were hostile to the police. Violence in the officer's presence implies that the officer's ability to control the situation is being threatened ... or that the suspect is personally hostile to the police.... Loss of situational control is highly predictive of the threat of officer injury.... Thus viewed, arrest is a mechanism of asserting authority, rather than of protecting the victim.

. . .

Nonarrest data suggest intriguing but difficult-to-quantify differences in policing between domestic and stranger assaults. For example, according to the Bureau of Justice Statistics (1994) ... a small but consistent trend was found toward more aggressive policing in stranger assault cases when compared with intimate assault cases. According to the National Criminal Victimization Survey ... police respond within 5 minutes in 36% of cases in which the offender is a stranger and in only 24% of cases in which the offender is an intimate. Similarly, police are more likely to take a formal report if the victim is a stranger (77%), rather than an intimate (69%). Although such data suggest only minor differences between such assaults, the structure of the NCVS is likely to understate disparities in police actions. Specifically, this study used an older methodology, which has been subsequently changed ..., that counts only individuals who recognize their victimization as a crime. Many domestic violence victims, even those severely abused, have never regarded this abuse as criminal conduct. Therefore, it would not be surprising that those identifying themselves as victims were more likely the more seriously injured, which in turn would have resulted in a more rapid police response.

. . .

... We chose to study whether a department discriminates against domestic violence calls by examining whether police differentially respond to key factors in the decision to arrest. For example, complainant preferences for arrest in both domestic and stranger assaults should be studied because complainant preference for police action has been found in a variety of settings to be a consistent predictor of police behavior ... and an essential element in making domestic arrests.... Similarly, we studied whether the extent and degree of injury affects chances of arrest in cases of domestic and stranger assaults.

. . .

In using arrests, we recognize that the data might actually understate differential relationships because police may simply downgrade or not even file reports for offenses in which they do not wish to take official action.... Despite these shortcomings, we consider official measures the most reliable method of measuring police behavior. ... Nonetheless ... we included supplementary analysis of other measures for profiling and characterizing police behavior—that is, official police policies and content analysis of police reports. These measures were used to either confirm the analysis of official arrest data or cast doubt on relationships found therein. This helped us in answering whether observed practices were likely because of individual officer preferences or the result of official or unofficial policy preferences.

. . .

This research project was the outgrowth of a study conducted by one of the researchers on behalf of the plaintiffs in a lawsuit against the police department of a midsize, midwestern city. Although the study was commissioned by the plaintiffs' counsel, every effort was made to obtain unbiased data that would fairly test the premise that the department might have disparately treated victims of domestic violence.

The data set consisted of 376 assault cases from the official records of the police department. It covered all cases designated by the department as an "assault" for a period of 10 months during 1986 to 1987. . . .

Simple Effect of Type of Assault on Arrest

Assaults characterized as Acquaintance . . . were more than twice as likely to occur as either Domestic . . . or Stranger . . . assaults. Most victims experienced no injury or only minor injury, and in more than three quarters of the cases, the type of force/weapon used was the assailant's hands, arms, or feet. Witnesses were present in more than two thirds of the incidents. Similarly, in more than two thirds of the incidents, the offender was not present at the scene when the police arrived, and in about half of the cases, the victim's preference was arrest. With respect to arrest, the dependent variable, it occurs in more than one quarter of the cases.

Two findings . . . are most relevant to the current investigation. First, as the level of intimacy characterizing the relationship between the parties changes from more to less intimate, arrest becomes more likely. The relationship is statistically significant. . . . Although the modal response is to not arrest, when it does occur, incidents involving strangers result in an arrest 33% of the time, compared with 28% for acquaintances, and 18% for domestic.

The second notable finding involves the relationship between the remaining five situational variables and arrest. In all cases in which they are either evident or more certain, an arrest is more likely to occur. All five relationships are statistically significant. . . .

These bivariate findings lead to two tentative conclusions. First, although arrest is an unlikely event, it characterized stranger assaults more than domestic. Second, when an arrest does occur, it is more likely when the situational elements are present or more evident.

Additive Effects of Type of Assault on Arrest

What remains to be seen is whether the reason for fewer arrests in domestic cases is attributable to the absence of these situational factors in stranger assaults. To assess this possibility, the variables were examined by using logistic regression. . . .

. . . [A]n arrest is about 2.5 times more likely when a weapon is involved, approximately 8 times more likely when the offender is present at the scene, 2 times more likely when the victim's injury is serious, and about 3.5 times more likely when the victim's preference is arrest. Regardless of the situational variables, arrest is still more likely when the incident is characterized as a stranger assault. Compared with domestic assaults, such incidents are more than twice as likely to result in an arrest. . . .

Interactive Effects of Type of Assault on Arrest

. . .

Regardless of the type of assault, the offender's presence at the scene increases the probability of arrest, whereas the extent of injury to the victim has no effect on arrest in any of the three types of assaults. Both type of force/weapon used and presence of witnesses, however, affect the decision to arrest in domestic, but not in acquaintance or stranger, incidents. In domestic cases, when witnesses are present or the weapon used is more deadly, an arrest is more likely. Tentatively, this finding suggests that a higher standard or level of probable cause is needed for an arrest in domestic incidents. This tentative conclusion is reinforced by the finding that victim preference does not affect the decision to arrest in domestic cases, but does in cases involving acquaintances and strangers. More weight seems to be given to the victim's request in the decision to arrest when the parties are less intimately acquainted. The latter two findings support the idea of specification and suggest why arrest in less intimate incidents is more likely. Assaults involving strangers may be viewed by police as more genuine and thus do not require corroboration by outside sources. Conversely, the police may view domestic incidents as family matters and thus, by their very nature, require independent verification.

. . .

CONCLUSIONS

Perhaps of greatest significance, this study found differential treatment of domestic violence and stranger assault incidents as measured by the likelihood of arrest. Despite the relatively low level of arrests made (26%), it became clear that officers made fewer arrests for domestic assault cases than for stranger assault cases. This distinction became magnified when several relevant factors—offender presence at the scene and victim preference—were controlled. Of equal importance, victims' preferences for arrest were ignored in 75% of domestic assault cases, compared with more than 40% of stranger assault cases. Although this finding provides some confirmation for the observation that police disparately treat the problems of the largely female victims of domestic violence, we are unwilling to state that this is symptomatic of overall police behavior.

* * *

NOTES

1. The authors go on to urge further research, and the need for that research to be conducted, and interpreted, on a department by department

basis. They warn against "global constructs of police behavior" which are likely to be both "premature" and "too simplistic." Id. at 170.

2. In one respect, the authors' study underestimates the level of differential treatment exercised by the department they studied. Immediately prior to the period of the review, a domestic violence reform statute had been passed asking police departments to intervene aggressively in domestic assault cases. Presumably, therefore, the level of arrest would have been higher in cases of domestic assault than in cases of acquaintance or stranger assault, where no such policy of aggressive intervention was in place, if discrimination had not been at work. The authors criticize the "situational view of comparative arrest practices" on the same basis, arguing that it:

> largely ignores the fact that every state within the last 15 years has passed reform legislation expressly stating the policy of state ... governments to respond aggressively to domestic violence cases, including arrest. No such policy has ever been adopted or even articulated for handling cases of stranger assaults. In short, making that case that similar situational factors are used in arrests in domestic and stranger assaults implicitly concedes that many police officers simply ignore the statutory policy favoring domestic assault arrests, which is a discriminatory action in itself.

Id. at 158. A range of studies between 1977 and 1988, some pre-and some post-reform, offer estimated arrest rates for domestic assault between 3% and 14%. Id. at 152.

3. The next group of readings address strategies for increasing police responsiveness to domestic violence crimes. It is worth pausing for a moment, however, to explore more fully the range of possible explanations for the discriminatory treatment documented by Buzawa, Austin and Buzawa, because presumably the effectiveness of reform strategies will depend to no small extent on whether they address the causes of the behavior they seek to change.

If it were simply the case that discrete policing policies—like mediation, or separating abusers and their victims—needed to be changed, then dictating changes in policy through new legislation, or negotiating changes with individual police departments, should remove the barriers to change, and education and training designed to inform police of the changes should result in those changes being implemented. However, if the older policies are more consistent with (a) dominant social attitudes, (b) the world views of individual officers, and/or (c) police practices with respect to other crimes or social problems, then more resistance to change can be expected. The predictability of resistance, in turn may influence which among different possible reform policies could be most effectively implemented, and demand more attention to the steps between adoption of policy and implementation. There is a world of difference between a policy forced on a police department, where the police chief signals that he considers it politically expedient but substantively misguided, and has no intention of monitoring compliance with it, and a policy fully supported by a police chief who is committed to its implementation.

Pro-Arrest and Mandatory Arrest Policies

Beginning in the 1970s, the battered women's movement adopted as one of its top priorities increasing the responsiveness of the police to domestic violence assaults. In 1976, two groups of attorneys filed class action complaints, one in the Northern District of California, and the other in the Supreme Court of New York, alleging the failure of the police to provide protection to battered women, and seeking declaratory and injunctive relief.

The California case, Scott v. Hart (No. C–76–2395, filed October 28, 1976), alleged denial of equal protection for victims of domestic violence on the part of the Oakland Police Department. The case was settled after three years, and the settlement overseen by the court for a further three. The police department agreed to a new policy, under which its officers would respond promptly to domestic violence calls, and arrest whenever the responding officer had probable cause to believe a felony had been committed, and whenever a misdemeanor was committed in his presence. The department also acknowledged that it had an affirmative duty to enforce protective and vacate orders. Officers would be instructed not to use the threat of adverse financial consequences to justify inaction or to urge the victim not to pursue the case, They would also be instructed to inform each victim that she had the right to make a citizen's arrest, and to provide assistance to any victim who chose to do so. Finally, they would refer victims to support agencies for further assistance.

The New York case, brought on behalf of married battered women, alleged that the New York City Police Department failed to arrest husbands who battered their wives. Bruno v. Codd (90 Misc. 2d 1047, 396 N.Y.S. 2d 974 (Sup. Ct. 1977). When the trial judge denied the police department's motion to dismiss, the department entered into a consent judgment with the plaintiffs, and again the court retained jurisdiction to allow either party to apply for further relief as necessary. The judgment imposed on the police a duty to respond to every woman's request for protection against her husband if she said he was beating her or had violated an order of protection. Where a misdemeanor was committed in the officer's presence or the officer had probable cause to believe a misdemeanor had been committed, the officer should arrest, unless there was a justification for not arresting. Where the officer had probable cause to believe a felony had been committed or a protective order violated, the officer was bound to arrest. If the perpetrator had left the scene before the officer arrived, the officer must locate the husband just as with any other crime, and either effect an officer arrest or assist the wife with a civilian arrest. Officers were also mandated to help victims obtain any needed medical assistance, and to inform them of their right to obtain a protective order. The police department was ordered to develop new policies and training materials to implement the order, and supervisors were instructed to investigate and remedy promptly any violation of the order.

As a result of these cases, many police departments agreed to change their policies and practices with respect to domestic violence voluntarily, before similar suits were brought against them, and before they found themselves liable for attorneys' fees, or even civil damages. This vulnerability was made even more real by the case of Thurman v. City of Torrington, Connecticut, in which a federal jury awarded Tracey Thurman $2.3 million in damages for negligence, in compensation for the devastating injuries inflicted by her abusive husband while the police stood by and watched, after ignoring her repeated requests for protection.

Court challenges to police inaction on constitutional grounds, including the *Thurman* case, are the topic of a later chapter. Here they illustrate just one strategy among several by which battered women's advocates sought to change police policy and practice. Another strategy, as already suggested, was to use the leverage generated by success in these litigations to persuade each individual police department to develop a progressive domestic violence policy. Another more ambitious strategy was to persuade state legislatures to change the laws governing arrest to facilitate a more aggressive response. As Joan Zorza reports:

> While officers could arrest when they had probable cause to believe that a felony offense had been committed, in most, but not all, jurisdictions police could not make an arrest for a misdemeanor assault unless the assault occurred in the police officer's presence. Because most police charge domestic violence offenses only as misdemeanors, the law, in order to enable an officer to arrest the abuser when the offense was not committed in the officer's presence, has to permit the arrest without a warrant.

Joan Zorza, *The Criminal Law of Misdemeanor Domestic Violence, 1970–1990*, 83 J. CRIM. LAW & CRIMINOLOGY 46, 62 (1992). By 1983 police arrest powers in domestic violence cases had been expanded in thirty-three states. Twenty-eight states authorized arrest without a warrant where the officer had probable cause to believe that a domestic violence misdemeanor had been committed, nineteen states permitted arrest without a warrant if there was probable cause to believe a protective order had been violated, and fourteen states permitted warrantless arrest in both these situations. Id.

A different approach was taken in Oregon, where the state Coalition Against Domestic and Sexual Violence proposed, and the legislature in 1977 adopted, the first "mandatory arrest" law, requiring police to arrest when there was probable cause to believe that someone had committed an assault, or put a victim with a restraining order in fear of imminent serious physical injury. OR. REV. STAT. § 133.055(2), § 133.310(3) (1989). Originally the statute provided that police need not arrest if the victim objected, but this provision was eliminated in 1981 because it was being used by police to undermine the mandatory arrest provisions. By mid 1982 five states required police to arrest where probable cause existed to believe that a misdemeanor had been committed or a restraining order violated, and by 1992 fifteen states had adopted mandatory arrest for domestic violence misdemeanors, and nineteen for protective order violations.

What accounts for this flurry of legislative activity reversing well-established policing policy? In no small measure, the widespread adoption of mandatory arrest provisions can be attributed to a single highly influential study, conducted by Lawrence Sherman and Richard Berk, and published in 1984. Called the Minneapolis Domestic Violence Experiment, it was the first controlled, randomized test of the effectiveness of arrest for any offense, and the results showed that arrest cut in half the risk of future assaults against the same domestic violence victim during a 6 month follow up period, when measured against either separating the couple, or mediating between the partners. This study was then highlighted by the U.S. Attorney General's Task Force on Family Violence, in a 1984 report which stressed the importance of treating family violence as a criminal activity. Although the authors of the Minneapolis study themselves recommended against the adoption of mandatory arrest policies until further studies had been conducted, the momentum of these early findings overrode caution.

In 1986 and 1987, the National Institute for Justice funded six replication experiments, although none were identical to the original Minneapolis experiment. The results of these newer studies have significantly clouded the issue, to the point where Lawrence Sherman, co-author of the original study, has urged that mandatory arrest laws be repealed. The next reading documents the reasons for this change of heart. It must be remembered, however, that the relatively short-term deterrent effect of mandatory arrest is only one measure of its desirability or lack of desirability. Subsequent readings sample the vigorous debate prompted by mandatory arrest, and suggest other reasons for promoting, or opposing, mandatory arrest policies.

Janell D. Schmidt and Lawrence W. Sherman
Does Arrest Deter Domestic Violence?; Do Arrests and Restraining Orders Work? 43, 45–46, 48–49, 50–52 (E.S. Buzawa & C.G. Buzawa, eds. 1996)

What is known about the impact of police arrest policies relative to domestic assault is that the vast bulk of cases brought to police attention involve lower-income and minority-group households. One reason may be a higher rate of domestic disputes among these groups; another reason may be a lack of alternatives short of police intervention that offer immediate relief. Although arresting thousands of unemployed minority males each year may assist the goals of victim advocates and provide a brief respite for the victims, the skepticism of many police and criminologists relative to the deterrent power of arrest still remains. The key question of whether other police alternatives could prove more powerful or whether the police could be effective at all led the National Institute of Justice to fund replication studies in six major urban cities.

Beginning in 1986 and early 1987, police in Omaha (Nebraska), Milwaukee (Wisconsin), Charlotte (North Carolina), Metro–Dade County (Miami, Florida), Colorado Springs (Colorado), and Atlanta (Georgia) began controlled experiments to replicate the Minneapolis findings. Each site was afforded leeway to improve the methodology of the Minneapolis study and to design alternative nonarrest treatments to build on its theoretical foundation.... In Metro–Dade ... a sample of 907 cases was obtained so that researchers could compare arrest to no arrest, both with and without follow-up counseling by a specially trained police unit. In Colorado Springs, more than 1,600 cases were used to contrast arrest and nonarrest with immediate professional counseling at police headquarters or the issuance of an emergency protection order. In Milwaukee, police provided 1,200 cases for the researchers to test the length of time in custody—a short 2–hour arrest versus arrest with an overnight stay in jail, compared to no arrest. The experimental team in Charlotte included a citation response along with arrest, mediation, or separation treatments in its 686–case sample. Only Omaha followed the Minneapolis design with 330 cases, but added an offender-absent window of cases to test the effect of having police pursue an arrest warrant.

... Perhaps most striking is that none of the innovative treatments—namely, counseling or protective orders—produced any improvement over arrest versus no arrest. The citation used to notify offenders to appear at a future court date in Charlotte caused more violence than an arrest. Only Omaha broke ground and found an effective innovation in its offender-absent experiment. Offenders who left the scene before police arrived and whose cases were randomly assigned to the warrant group produced less repeat violence than did similarly absent offenders assigned to the nonwarrant group. The issuance of a warrant may have acted as a "sword of Damocles" hanging over an offender's head.

In short, the new experiments reported both deterrent and backfiring effects of arrest. Arrest cured some abusers but made others worse; arrest eased the pain for victims of employed abusers but increased it for those intimate with unemployed partners; arrest assisted white and Hispanic victims but fell short of deterring further violence among black victims....

One central finding is that arrest increased domestic violence recidivism among suspects in Omaha, Charlotte and Milwaukee. Although those three cities produced some evidence of a deterrent effect of arrest within the first 30 days, victims found that this protective shield quickly evaporated and that they suffered an escalation of violence over a longer period of time. None of the follow-up measures produced the 6–month deterrent effect reported in Minneapolis. Some measures showed no difference in the recidivism of offenders arrested, compared with those whom police did not arrest.

. . .

... Choosing between the lesser of two evils is best guided by the following summary of the facts and dilemmas gleaned from the domestic violence research published to date....

1. *Arrest reduces domestic violence in some cities but increases it in others.* It is not clear from current research how officials in any city can know which effect arrest is likely to have in their city. Cities that do not adopt an arrest policy may pass up an opportunity to help victims of domestic violence. But cities that do adopt arrest policies—or have them imposed by state law—may catalyze more domestic violence than would otherwise occur. Either choice entails a possible moral wrong.

2. *Arrest reduces domestic violence among employed people but increases it among unemployed people.* Mandatory arrest policies may thus protect working-class women but cause greater harm to those who are poor. Conversely, not making arrests may hurt working women but reduce violence against economically poor women. Similar trade-offs may exist on the basis of race, marriage, education and neighborhood. Thus, even in cities where arrest reduces domestic violence overall, as an unintended side effect it may increase violence against the poorest victims.

3. *Arrest reduces domestic violence in the short run but may increase it in the long run.* Three-hour arrests in Milwaukee reduced the 7% chance that a victim would be battered as soon as the police left to a 2% chance of being battered when the spouse returned from jail. But over the course of 1 year, those arrests doubled the rate of violence by the same suspects. No arrest means more danger to the victim now, whereas making an arrest may mean more danger of violence later for the same victim or for someone else.

. . .

To some, the choice between two wrongs invokes despair and inaction. Yet, policing domestic violence may not be hopeless. Careful review of the policy implications, combined with the freedom to test alternative policies, can lead to more effective solutions. Use of the best information . . . to date guides the following five policy recommendations:

1. *Repeal mandatory arrest laws.* The most compelling implication of these findings is to challenge the wisdom of mandatory arrest. States and cities that have enacted such laws should repeal them, especially if they have substantial ghetto poverty populations with high unemployment rates. These are the settings in which mandatory arrest policies are most likely to backfire. It remains possible but unlikely that mandatory arrest creates a general deterrent effect among the wider public not arrested. Even if it does, however, increased violence among unemployed persons who are arrested is a serious moral stain on the benefits of general deterrence. The argument that arrest expresses the moral outrage of the state also appears weak if the price of that outrage is increased violence against the same victims.

2. *Substitute structured police discretion.* Instead of mandating arrest in cases of misdemeanor domestic violence, state legislatures should mandate that each police agency develop its own list of approved options to be exercised at the discretion of the officer. Legislatures might also mandate 1 day of training each year to ensure that discretion is fully informed by the latest research available. The options could include allowing victims to decide whether their assailants should be arrested, transporting victims to shelters, or taking the suspects to an alcohol detoxification center.

3. *Allow warrantless arrests.* Whereas mandatory arrest has become the major issue in some states, warrantless arrest remains an issue in others. Sixteen jurisdictions have adopted mandatory arrest laws, but at last report 9 others have still not given officers full arrest powers in misdemeanor domestic violence cases that they did not witness: Alabama, California, Michigan, Mississippi, Montana, Nebraska, New York, Vermont and West

Virginia. The success of arrest in some cities suggests that every state should add this option to the police tool kit. Deciding when to use it can then become a matter of police policy based on continuing research and clinical experience, rather than on the massive effort required to change state law.

4. *Encourage issuance of arrest warrants for absent offenders.* The landmark Omaha experiment suggests that more domestic violence could be prevented by this policy than by any offender-present policy. The kinds of people who flee the scene might be more deterrable than those who stay. A prosecutor willing to issue warrants and a police agency willing to serve them can capitalize on that greater deterrability. If the Omaha warrant experiment can be replicated in other cities—a very big if—then the warrant policy might actually deter more violence than do arrests of suspects who are still present. Because it will likely be years before more research on the question is done, such policies should be adopted now. They can easily be discarded later if they are found to be harmful or ineffective.

* * *

NOTES

1. For accounts of the replication experiments see: Franklyn W. Dunford et al., *The Role of Arrest in Domestic Assault: The Omaha Police Experiment*, 28 CRIMINOLOGY 183 (1990); Lawrence W. Sherman et al., *The Variable Effects of Arrest on Criminal Careers: The Milwaukee Domestic Violence Experiment*, 83 J. CRIM. L. & CRIMINOLOGY 137 (1992); J. David Hirschel & Ira W. Hutchinson, *Female Spouse Abuse and the Police Response: The Charlotte, North Carolina Experiment*, 83 J. CRIM. L. & CRIMINOLOGY 73 (1992); Richard A. Berk et al., *A Bayesian Analysis of the Colorado Springs Abuse Experiment*, 83 J. CRIM. L. & CRIMINOLOGY 170 (1992); Antony M. Pate & Edwin E. Hamilton, *Formal and Informal Deterrents to Domestic Violence: The Dade County Spouse Assault Experiment*, 57 AM. SOC. REV. 253 (1992). The Atlanta study has yet to be published.

2. The most detailed critique of the replication studies can be found in another article by Joan Zorza. The excerpt below contains her analysis of a number of serious methodological flaws which undercut the reliability of their findings. The reading also contains the lessons she believes we can draw from the studies, despite their methodological shortcomings. As you read, compare her conclusions with those of Schmidt and Sherman.

Joan Zorza, Must We Stop Arresting Batterers?: Analysis and Policy Implications of New Police Domestic Violence Studies, 28 New England Law Review 929, 930–931, 965–967, 973–74 (1994)

... First, the studies ignored the fact that domestic violence, unchecked, usually escalates in frequency and severity. Thus, repeat offenses are to be expected, and the recidivism rate in an experimental setting should be measured not against zero but against the normal recidivism rate. Accordingly, an intervention strategy could be considered to yield a net improvement based on either an absolute decrease in abuse or a reduced degree of escalation of abuse.

Second, the experiments did not take into account the impact of decisions by prosecutors and courts subsequent to arrest. More specifically, the few studies which provided data on these responses showed very low rates of prosecution and conviction. It is likely that this failure to follow through undercut the ability of the arrest response to achieve its maximum potential for deterrence. In Milwaukee, for example, only 5% of the offenders were charged with a crime and only 1% convicted. In Charlotte, fewer than 1% of offenders were convicted and incarcerated. Thus, these experiments really studied arrest in the absence of criminal justice follow-up....

Yet another example of the flaws found in this review was the assigning of bad risks to the arrest category. All the experiments assigned offenders who misbehaved to be arrested regardless of the police response they were originally assigned and then counted them in the arrest category.

. . .

A related problem was raised by the treatment in some studies of subsequent police encounters by the same couple as initial encounters. In addition, none of the offenders were screened for police contact prior to the initial police encounter. Thus, an offender in Milwaukee who had been arrested multiple times prior to the experiment, as a result of that city's mandatory arrest policy, may have received only a warning during the actual experiment. Yet studies would [have] considered the latest contact with the police to have been the offender's first. Similarly, an offender seen twice by the police during the experiment might have received only a warning at each incident. How serious would such an offender consider the second threat of arrest, having once escaped such arrest previously? Clearly, both this abuser and his victim would understand that the subsequent warning was only empty rhetoric. Such knowledge might well make the abuser feel even more powerful and vindicated. It would also compromise the study's results.

. . .

... [I]ll-advised messages ... conveyed by the warning response in the Milwaukee study, to those victims evicted in Charlotte and Omaha, and to any couple referred to family counseling as in the Charlotte and probably Metro–Dade experiments, all acted to discourage victims from subsequently seeking police protection. Consequently, these messages may have endangered victims of domestic abuse and resulted in the production of misleading data which call the validity of these experiments into question.

. . .

The police replication experiments were framed almost entirely from the abusers' perspective in that designers assumed that the response of the victim to various policies was largely irrelevant to the outcome of the study.

That is, they assumed that the various police responses either had no effect on the victim or, if they did cause some effect, it was the abuser alone who determined whether the victim would be subsequently abused. This criticism is not meant to imply that a victim provokes her abuser or chooses to be battered, but to note that many of the victim's choices may affect whether she will be battered again. Thus, a victim who goes into shelter, who goes into hiding, or who relocates may well limit the abuser's ability to continue the violence, as well as limit the experimenter's ability to document the occurrence of continued abuse.

. . .

CONCLUSION

There may be reasons to oppose mandatory arrest, but opposition should not be based on the experiments done to replicate the original Minneapolis police domestic violence experiment. The police replication experiments do not, as they are purported to, show that mandatory arrest fails to provide any deterrent effect or one that is only effective against white employed abusers. Mandatory arrest clearly deterred white and Hispanic abusers even when they are unemployed. Even experiments that indicated that arrest may cause some escalation in domestic violence by black men showed only a slight increase in such incidents.

More to the point, the experiments do not show what mandatory arrest would accomplish as apart of a coordinated response to domestic violence. Had prosecution, conviction and punishment of the offender occurred following arrest, the deterrence effect might have been greater, particularly on those least intimidated by the arrest alone.

In addition, arrest has many purposes, not all of which are directed at the offender. When it is followed by speedy prosecution, conviction, and punishment, the arrest of a domestic abuser conveys to other members of the family and to society as a whole that certain behavior is offensive and will not be tolerated. The benefits of this message may ultimately outweigh any increase in abuse by a few batterers if it translates into greater protection for most victims.

Despite the many problems with the police replication experiments there were several hopeful developments. First, when police have probable cause to arrest, they should arrest all abusers who were not acting in self-defense, particularly those offenders identified as being most likely to be deterred: the white, employed batterers, the very group police have traditionally been reluctant to arrest.

Second, the length of time an arrested abuser is held should be no shorter than that of other offenders. Very possibly, to the extent which the law allows it, the time should be longer than that imposed in comparable offenses. And the victim should always be notified if reasonably possible before the abuser is released.

Third, when they have probable cause to arrest, police should issue an arrest warrant when they are unable to arrest an absent offender.

Fourth, arrest without more follow through by the criminal justice system may be too weak a sanction to deter many batterers, particularly the unemployed or those with prior arrest records.

Fifth, because the police replication studies showed that unemployed men are the least deterred by arrest, future studies should examine whether court-facilitated employment will lower recidivism rates for batterers. However, this should not be done at the expense of any services and employment opportunities for victims of domestic violence.

The real implication of the police replication studies are that a coordinated community response is what is needed to best eliminate domestic violence. Police, prosecutors, judges, probation officers, and those in corrections must all treat domestic violence as the serious crime that it is, giving the same strong message to the abuser without in any way blaming the victim.

Finally, any future experiments should be designed with input from those in the battered women's movement, both on the national and local levels, in order to eliminate the flaws that comprised the results of the police replication studies and actually endangered some victims.

* * *

NOTES

1. Two critical premises of mandatory arrest policies are (1) that arrest is to be encouraged (whether for its deterrent value, its short-or long-term impact on victim safety, the message it delivers to society at large or the role it plays in a larger coordinated community response to domestic violence), and (2) that mandatory arrest policies will increase the level of arrests. We have already seen that the first premise is both contestable and contested, but the second is also open to debate.

As the previous readings have demonstrated, a mandatory arrest policy is still readily manipulable by those charged with implementing it. It applies only to the perpetrator who is still on the scene when the police arrive. The speed of police response will influence what percentage of perpetrators find an opportunity to leave before the police arrive. It depends, still, on a police assessment of probable cause—to believe that a misdemeanor has been committed or a restraining order violated, and several commentators have suggested that police are less willing to find probable cause in the domestic violence context than in the context of other violent crimes. Finally, to the extent that police resent the reduction in discretion intended by mandatory arrest policies, they may find ways to subvert their implementation. One such strategy, again noted by several commentators, is the "dual arrest," where police claim to be unable to determine, on the scene, who has been the aggressor, or whether one party has used force only in self-defense. At least eight states have felt it necessary to respond to this development by enacting legislation specifically directing police to arrest only the primary physical aggressor or the party not responding in self-defense. See, e.g., ARIZ. REV. STAT. ANN. § 13–3601B (1991); Mo. Rev. Stat. § 455.085(3) (1990); R.I. Gen. Laws § 12–29–3 (C) (1991); WIS. STAT. ANN. § 968.075(3)(a) (West 1990).

There is as yet no reliable documentation of the extent to which mandatory arrest policies have increased the incidence of domestic violence arrests, or how they compare in effectiveness with pro-arrest policies (authorizing and encouraging arrest, but not mandating it) in increasing the incidence of arrest. One indication that the combination of pro-arrest and mandatory arrest policies, along with an increasing consensus that battering should be treated as a criminal activity, has resulted in more arrests being made is that between 1984 and 1989 there was a national increase of 70% in arrests for minor assaults, a category that included domestic assaults. And yet, as the reading from Buzawa, Austin and Buzawa reported, studies collecting domestic violence arrest data as late as 1988 report no more than a 14% incidence of arrest. Although more recent data is needed, it seems clear that *if* arrest is deemed a desirable aspect of domestic violence policy, more needs to be done to determine whether mandatory or proarrest policies are more effective, and to provide training and implementation to turn policy into reality.

2. It is important to recognize that those who recommend retreating from proarrest or mandatory arrest policies are in effect advocating a diminished role for the criminal justice system as a whole, since arrest is the gateway to that system. This point is forcefully made by Evan Stark:

> [O]ne can think of the proarrest strategy as a "basket of goods" that may include everything from a mere warning, handcuffing, or an arrest warrant through a weekend in jail, mandated treatment, a stalker's law, ... community intervention programs ... , real prison time, the provision of court-based advocates, and so forth.... But, of course, arrest is a precondition.... In essence, Sherman and the other critics are recommending that this keystone to reform be removed from the basket because it fails to fulfil an important policy objective—the reduction of violence. Sherman's implication ... [is] that the criminal justice system should no longer be the focal point of society's response to woman battering.

Evan Stark, *Mandatory Arrest of Batterers: A Reply to Its Critics*, DO ARRESTS AND RESTRAINING ORDERS WORK 115, 118 (E.S. Buzawa & C.G. Buzawa, eds. 1996). Given that Sherman is advocating repeal of mandatory arrest laws, but an increase in discretionary arrest authority, and an increase in the issuance of arrest warrants for absent perpetrators, is Stark fair in including him among those who would remove arrest from the "basket" of reforms?

3. In the choice between mandatory and proarrest policies, one important consideration is whether victim choice should be considered in the decision whether to arrest. This is the topic of the next reading.

Eve S. Buzawa and Carl G. Buzawa
Arrest Is No Panacea; Current Controversies on Family Violence 337, 348–351 (R.G. Gelles & D.R. Loseke, eds. 1993)

The preferred feminist image is that the victim wants her rights validated and the offender punished. This process starts with a dramatic event: an arrest. The corollary is that the primary obstacle to this vision is the obstinate failure of the police to perform their sworn duty. Reality, however, is not as clearly defined. Studies have shown that many victims of domestic violence [one in four, or one in five] do not want arrest....

In contrast, the desires of victimized women may be complex. Some desire only the cessation of violence—any other action is unwanted interference. Others desire that the police, as agents of the state, recognize their victimization. This does not necessarily equate to desire for arrest, but may mean only that they expect officers to demonstrate disapproval—perhaps by speaking sternly, making clear the victim's option to arrest, ensuring her safety, and threatening arrest upon reoccurrence. Still others desire that the police assist change in the balance of power in a relationship away from a crude measure of physical strength and violence to an emphasis on acceptable societal norms of conflict resolution. For that purpose, a warning may be sufficient. Finally, other victims may, despite violence, desire that the police act merely as mediators. For many of these scenarios, the victim may believe that arrest is inappropriate.

Treating all victimized women as a common group denigrates the real distinctions in this diverse group as well as commits the conceptual error of assuming that all batterers respond similarly to a given approach. This prevents the victim from using the criminal justice process to ensure her safety. In short, automatically assuming arrest as the preferred option forecloses an opportunity to empower victims by giving them control over the outcome of the police intervention.

We recognize that arguments have been proposed to justify the exclusion of victim preferences. When a bank is robbed or a person murdered, the criminal justice system attaches little weight to the victim's beliefs or relation to the offender. The crime itself is an acknowledged harm to society as well as to the particular victim. In addition, many advocates of battered women believe that battering may so traumatize a victim that she may be incapable of understanding her long-term interests or of judging the reality of the situation. If one believes that most victims fall into this category, mandatory arrest and other policies that expressly discount the decision-making role of the victim are justified.... Finally, some arrest advocates note that past poor performance by the police may have led victims to despair, realistically, that the police can ever effectively intervene. The use of mandatory arrest in this context might rest on a concept similar to affirmative action: It is seen as a policy necessary to right previous wrongs perpetrated by the legal system.

Despite the cogency of the arguments presented by advocates of mandatory arrest, we believe that victim preference should be honored in the decision to arrest. Despite good intentions, a policy mandating arrest is ultimately very patronizing toward battered women. The premise is that we, a highly educated, politically liberal/radical elite, can best assess the interests of disempowered victims unable to judge their own needs accurately. Conceptually, this position is as offensive as the old "patriarchy," where legal rights were all given to the male, who, by virtue of his superior intellect and logic, knew what was best for "his" women. Even assuming that we believe this elitism to be proper, where do we draw the line? ... The complete enforcement of legal rights for an individual who does not want to assert those rights and prefers a nonlegal alternative is an improper use of the legal system.

Second, mandatory arrest advocates ignore the complexity of why women may choose not to request arrest. A woman's experience may tell her that arrest is ineffective and that violence increases when the offender is freed. Although this may seem illogical, the recent replication studies suggest this *may* occur, especially in "high-risk" poor neighborhoods. Whether further research bears this out or not, we simply cannot discount that in many situations, a woman may legitimately believe that she is *more* at risk after arrest.

Further, a victim may have many other collateral reasons for not desiring arrest. An arrest may affect her family financially by leading to loss of family income or by triggering parole or probation revocation. Such a policy may also discourage women from middle or upper social classes from seeking police assistance because of the social stigma of arrest. Many small communities publish arrest records in the local newspapers, perhaps harming victims and their children more than the batterers.

In any event, there can also be little dispute that arrest does not, on balance, strengthen the relationship of the couple involved. We find it troubling that many victims' advocates presume to state categorically that this is unimportant because such a relationship is "obviously pathological." Many other societal programs are, after all, designed to salvage such relationships, by minimizing the pathology and rehabilitating the offending parties....

It is of concern that the emphasis on arrest may not necessarily have sensitized police to victim needs. Instead, official policies favoring arrest may merely change overt manifestations of behavior for pragmatic organizational reasons. In the past, avoidance may have reflected organizational realities—fear of injury, dislike of social work, lack of organizational incentives, and so on. Pro-arrest policies may now be dictated by fear of liability, political pressure, or, unfortunately, overly publicized or politicized preliminary research. Although one may state that the reasons motivating an arrest are insignificant because only behavior is relevant, this ignores the reality of policing. Despite the existence of policies limiting officer discretion, rank-and-file officers have a long, if not proud, heritage of not following the "spirit" of laws and departmental edicts the goals of which they do not share.

* * *

NOTES

1. Other commentators have also written powerfully about the needs of battered women, and the frequent incongruence between those needs and what the police have to offer. In *Irreconcilable Differences: Battered Women, Police, and the Law*, LEGAL RESPONSES TO WIFE ASSAULT 96 (N. Zoe Hilton, ed. 1993), Kathleen Ferraro and Lucille Pope argue the incompatibility of the

"culture of power" represented by police, and the "relational culture" inhabited by battered women, which they describe as follows:

> Responding to physical violence entails a wide repertoire of strategies of survival, some of which are invisible to outsiders. Women approach trusted insiders and external authority figures for assistance in defining experiences, developing strategies for change, providing tangible resources, and intervening in the abuse. Survival strategies involve scrutinizing an array of individuals and institutions for effectiveness. Within the boundaries of her relationship, the woman must evaluate each resource as making a positive or negative contribution to the safety of herself and her children. The demands of maintaining a delicate balance of outside interference add to the complexity of calculating safety. Any resource that upsets that balance threatens her survival.
>
> From this perspective, the police are only one potential resource that must be evaluated within the more complex web of resources making up the larger picture of assistance. Whether the assistance of the police officer will prove helpful must be weighed and measured in the shifting and sometimes hazy context of not only the extent of the violence but also the current status of the relationship and the short and long-term strategies for its maintenance or dissolution. To the extent that any resource, including the police, fails to provide for ultimate safety concerns, it may be abandoned by the woman. The identification and utilization of a given resource can only be framed by the woman's assessment of her needs, a frame that is at once unique and similar to the frames of other women.
>
> The expectations each woman has of helping resources will vary depending on the particular circumstances of the relationship. When women call upon the police they overlay their relational culture, within which they have vast, changeable needs, upon agents of the culture of power operating within limited boundaries with circumscribed responses. Women's needs are bounded by the culture of relationship; the police response is bounded by the culture of power.

Id. at 106–07.

Ferraro and Pope argue that police participate in the culture of power in two separate ways. First, their notions of what they are "supposed to be doing, who they are protecting from what, and the guidelines for their actions" derive from traditional liberal jurisprudence, which emphasizes maximizing private autonomy and profit and minimizing state intervention. Id. at 103–04. To the extent that the culture of liberal jurisprudence has been patriarchal, the home has been marked off as private space into which the state should not intrude, even if women's personal and property rights are being violated by their partners. Second, the culture of power offers police a basis for distinguishing between normal and deviant citizens. Id. at 105. Unfortunately, within this framework battered women are as deviant as those who abuse them: "They live with men who beat them and their children, become angry at police for trying to help them, and retract accusations of violence after arrests have been made. From the perspective of the culture of power, such actions are irrational and deviant. Women who enact them are, therefore, indistinguishable from their assailants in terms of culpability...." Id.

2. On the question of whether mandatory arrest ultimately disempowers women in abusive relationships, opinion even within the battered women's movement is divided. As you have seen, Joan Zorza, an experienced and strong advocate for battered women in both the family law and criminal law context, supports mandatory arrest. Others oppose both mandatory arrest and no-drop prosecution policies. Evan Stark acknowledges the "dilemma" posed by mandatory arrest, and yet concludes that the advantages of mandatory arrest outweigh the costs:

> The conflicting realities of coercive control and empowerment through victim preference raise what is undoubtedly the most difficult dilemma about mandatory arrest. Too often in women's lives, the question of who speaks in their name has been dealt with fatuously. For battered women, in particular, there is no more important issue in recovery than the restoration of "voice"; the essence of empowerment, we like to say, is allowing women to make the *wrong* decision. At the same time, and although all choices are constrained by an implicit calculus of costs and benefits to a certain extent, for women who are seriously injured or for those whose decisions reflect ignorance of their danger or psychological, material, economic, or racial deprivation, it is hard to see how the benefits of individual choice outweigh the social interest in stopping the use of illegitimate power. Only in situations where there are no injuries and where there is an expressed desire *not* to arrest despite probable cause to believe an assault has taken place is it likely that the arrest decision will be experienced as demeaning. Because this profile may describe the *most* as well as the least dangerous situations, I would prefer to mandate arrest than leave assessment to police.

Evan Stark, *Mandatory Arrest of Batterers: A Reply to Its Critics*, DO ARRESTS AND RESTRAINING ORDERS WORK 115, 145 (E.S. Buzawa & C.G. Buzawa, eds. 1996).

3. Another critic, Peter Manning, offers a class analysis of proarrest policies, arguing that they reflect an increasingly "market-driven" conception of policing, and play to a middle-class audience, while targeting lower-class groups. While his assessment of the older conception of policing is consistent with Ferraro and Pope's account of policing in the context of a culture of power, he argues that this framework is under attack. It is less clear whether he sees the change as one with more positive or negative potential. Manning's critique also incorporates an extreme scepticism about any claimed deterrent effect for arrest.

Peter K. Manning
The Preventive Conceit: The Black Box in Market Context; Do Arrests and Restraining Orders Work? 83, 83–84, 92–93 (E.S. Buzawa and C.G. Buzawa eds. 1996)

A belief in the deterrent effects of arrest is a "conceit" because it is mental activity organized by a misguiding metaphor that animates policy and research.... [A]dvocating an arrest policy in domestic disputes begs the question of the context of the arrest, the limits of formal social control, and the preferred role of policing in a democratic society.

... Criminalizing domestic conflict and the corollary belief in arrest as a solution to social conflict is, at least in part, a product of the reduced legitimacy of the police and their increasing vulnerability to "market pressures," "management dicta," and vaguely understood community demands....

... Concern for protection of females was dramatically associated in the media with the ideological and moral outrage of political interests, some called "feminist," seeking to control abuse mainly by men through expanding the application of criminal law. Belief in law as a democratic mechanism for producing justice was consistent with the experience of the civil rights groups who are the model for civil protest in the last part of the 20th century. As a symbolic tool, the law stands as a representation of the good, the right and the proper in the United States.... The application of law in private relations has a less consensual position. Because arrests in domestic disputes are disproportionately of lower class, minority residents of large cities ..., the policy extracts yet an additional cost, or "crime tariff," ... from them. Not all families are being policed for "violence."

The position of leaders in U.S. law enforcement since the 1930s has been that law enforcement was an objective, nondiscretionary matter unaffected by either high or low politics. The success in altering public police policy ... suggests that publicity, political forces, and movements increasingly shape policing. This has been true historically, but police were loath to admit it in an era of reformist and scientific policing.

. . .

... Growth in the demand for "law enforcement," and the transition of policing to a demand-focused "service" industry rationing its "services," is revealed in the police response to the movement to criminalize domestic conflict. Police are under pressure, some of it self-created, to make explicit their market strategy, how they differentially serve target groups and "submarkets," and manage demand. The police are moving away from an explicit egalitarian allocational and distributional function and toward a rationing, market-based corporate strategy that assumes a distributional bias. This strategy entails explicit service goals, sets differential levels of response, and seeks to manage demand. This strategy creates tensions and contradictions because the public position of 24–hour available response coupled with secret, private, discretionary rationing decisions is being replaced with reduced service, public statements of priorities, and explicit policies that ration police services. Quantitative measures of efficiency and effectiveness can become reified and be used to rationalize differentially serving needy and demanding groups.

The focus on a narrow intervention claimed to alter behavior is a change in police orientation. Anglo American policing has been incident driven, anti-intellectual, and ahistorical. It has eschewed problem-solving approaches. The controversy about intervention in domestic conflict could be a model for other policy-driven innovations, but it contains the seeds of a powerful "sting" or response. The focus is on the victim and the powerless. The audience is the middle class whose experience with police intervention in family problems is less common. The espousal of the arrest policy is a public adjustment directed to a middle class audience and lower-class target groups.

* * *

NOTES AND QUESTIONS

1. For a clear articulation of the "feminist" demand on law enforcement, consider this passage from the article by Evan Stark already excerpted above:

> Asking police to help free women from a historical process of entrapment and control by men involves them directly in the politics of gender. Even if this is not made explicit during their training, police are quite aware of the political implications of the laws against battering, just as police in the South were aware of what was involved in protecting voting rights demonstrators 30 years ago. Ethnographic descriptions of the informal codes governing how police function on the street and theoretical pictures of how policing reproduces social inequality may add substantially to other dimensions of criminal justice thinking. But they can also obscure what is, at bottom, a political process of negotiation that involves every aspect of law enforcement, from personal attitudes and departmental priorities through who sits on local police boards. Buzawa and Manning predict that the basic function and behavior of police will not change because we mandate arrest of batterers. What they miss is that implementing the mandate is inextricably linked to a range of challenges to basic police functions.... [W]e see laws against battering as part of a broad strategy of justice for women. But before we can debate the wisdom of this strategy or the role of police in its implementation, we must reach consensus that an affirmative conception of women's rights is the proper basis for reform.

Evan Stark, *Mandatory Arrest of Batterers: A Reply to Its Critics*, DO ARRESTS AND RESTRAINING ORDERS WORK 115, 124 (E.S. Buzawa & C.G. Buzawa, eds. 1996).

2. Having looked at a sampling of the empirical studies of domestic violence policing, and at a sampling of the critiques, what priorities would you now establish for empirical research in this area? What difficulties do you anticipate in finding out what you want to know? Do the mistakes others have made provide lessons for future research design, or merely demonstrate how enormously difficult it is to generate reliable data in this area?

3. At the level of policy, do you find yourself believing that mandatory arrest or proarrest policies will do more for victim safety and perpetrator accountability? If you choose proarrest, how will you answer critics who say

that merely "favoring" arrest will not be enough to counteract police tendencies to ignore or discount domestic violence crimes? If you choose mandatory arrest, how will you respond to critics who accuse you of further disempowering victims of domestic violence, and potentially exposing them to increased danger?

4. What arguments, if any, could be made for the position that all efforts to reform arrest policies and practices for domestic violence crimes were ill-advised, or that their costs exceeded their benefits?

5. You will find new voices contributing to the debate over the wisdom of imposing criminal justice interventions in domestic violence situations in the next section, which addresses issues of prosecutorial policy.

Investigation and Reporting

Another crucial police function is the investigation and reporting of incidents of domestic violence, even in cases where the perpetrator is not arrested or prosecuted. Unless an incident is reported, the victim has no back-up for any subsequent assertion that she was abused, and the city, county or state has no way to document the incidence of domestic violence, or determine what priority it should be accorded in the allocation of resources. Unless an incident is thoroughly investigated, and the report made as detailed and complete as possible, the prosecutor's task is made significantly more difficult, especially in cases where the victim is afraid to testify, or her abuser strongly contests her testimony.

Jurisdictions that have worked to develop model criminal justice responses to domestic violence have been attentive to this aspect of the police function. In Quincy, for example:

> the District Attorney's Office provides twenty hours of training to the Quincy Police Department each year. The Office trains officers on the proper procedures for incident report writing, disturbance investigation, and evidence collection.

Elena Salzman, *The Quincy District Court Domestic Violence Prevention Program: A Model Legal Framework for Domestic Violence Intervention,* 74 B.U. L. REV. 329, 344–45 (1994). San Diego provides another example, as the following reading documents.

Casey G. Gwinn and Sgt. Anne O'Dell
Stopping the Violence: The Role of the Police Officer and the Prosecutor, 20 Western State University Law Review 297, 308–09 (1993)

Law enforcement protocols which address the need for comprehensive guidelines covering initial police response, preliminary investigation, evidence gathering, follow-up investigation, training, and advocacy are slowly emerging. The most effective approach appears to focus on two questions: (1) Can We Prove This Case Without the Participation of the Victim?; and (2) If Not, Will the Victim Participate With Law Enforcement By Testifying

Truthfully? This approach allows officers to focus on how to create a case even if the victim is too frightened and confused to cooperate, while not forgetting the importance of victim advocacy. The minimum investigation must include interviewing all children and adult witnesses, recording all statements of the victim, documenting all prior incidents, and taking photographs in order to allow prosecution to proceed even if the victim later becomes uncooperative.

. . . [A] "Law Enforcement Protocol" created by workers on the Domestic Violence Task Force was used most effectively by the San Diego Police Department, one of nine law enforcement agencies in San Diego County. To insure adherence to the protocol, this department took a bold, innovative step into the future. The Department created the position of Domestic Violence Coordinator in 1990 and staffed it with a full-time sergeant. This step proved to be the critical difference in how patrol officers responded to domestic violence incidents in the field. After painstaking research into the examination of the patrol response (much of it traditional and ineffective), training needs were identified and the Domestic Violence Coordinator was designated as the trainer. In one year (1991), preliminary domestic violence reports increased by 59% citywide.

* * *

NOTE

The issue of using evidence other than the victim's direct testimony to prosecute a perpetrator of domestic violence is picked up in the next section.

C. PROSECUTION

Background and Overview

Naomi R. Cahn
Innovative Approaches to the Prosecution of Domestic Violence Crimes; Domestic Violence: The Changing Criminal Justice Response 161, 162–75 (E.S. Buzawa & C.G. Buzawa, eds. 1992)

As their underlying justification for failing to pursue aggressively domestic violence cases, prosecutors assert that they have the discretion to choose which cases to process. This discretion, which is virtually unlimited, originates in the constitutional separation of powers. . . . Prosecutors are part of the executive branch of government and, as such, have the authority to determine how laws are to be implemented or administered to obtain their goals. Although statutes or judicial review may set some outside limits on prosecutorial discretion, for the most part prosecutors have great latitude and little accountability in deciding which cases to pursue and how to pursue them.... Prosecutorial discretion is also defended for other reasons: it permits individualized treatment of defendants; it allows prosecutors to interpret statutes that may be vague; and it allows prosecutors to set priorities in handling their caseload, a necessity given the sheer number of criminal cases....

But why do prosecutors choose to exercise this discretion not to proceed in domestic violence cases? First, prosecutors have traditionally assumed that domestic violence is trivial, that women provoke the abuse against them, or even that women like being beaten.... Second, prosecutors explain that, because victims simply do not follow through in domestic violence cases, there is no need to waste precious prosecutorial resources on them. One study of the reasons that prosecutors decided not to charge domestic violence cases found that, in 45 percent of the cases, the primary reason for the failure to go forward was the victim's wishes.... Generally, because no one else has seen the violence, the victim is the only witness, making the case almost impossible to prove if she is unwilling to testify. Unfortunately, as one source explains, "[m]isunderstandings" based on the reluctance of some battered women to pursue prosecution have resulted in a systemic bias against all battered women seeking legal help....

It is true that the crime of domestic violence differs in one significant way from most other crimes, in that the lives of the aggressor and the victim are intertwined. The two may live together, be married, have been married at one time, and may have children. Consequently, unless there are special procedures to promote victim cooperation and a special unit to advocate for the victim, the victim may be unwilling to testify against the abuser and so may be an uncooperative witness.

The outcome is a vicious circle, in which prosecutors do not prosecute and victims continue to be uncomfortable with prosecutorial procedures. The resulting prosecutorial inaction, however, simply perpetuates the same problems ... and fails to protect adequately the victims of domestic violence who need action from the criminal justice system.

[Cahn goes on to document promising reforms in prosecutorial practice.]

... [P]olicies from some of the different "model prosecution" programs throughout the country ... were chosen as representative of the most innovative ..., based on recommendations from battered women's advocates. The areas for comparison are in accordance with the stages of the criminal justice system, beginning with case screening and complaint filing and proceeding through prosecutorial management policies, victim support, trial techniques, and sentencing programs. These innovations show that prosecutors who work with battered women's advocates and implement special policies to handle domestic violence cases are able to increase the number of cases prosecuted and to decrease the recidivism rate.

. . .

CASE SCREENING AND CHARGING POLICIES

Case Screening

Case screening is the first point at which a case can enter the prosecutor's office. It is the control point; if a case is screened but not filed, there can be no further action on the case. An office committed to increasing the pool of cases for prosecution must ensure that cases do not drop out at this early stage.... Thus, offices have developed different methods to ensure adequate initial processing of domestic violence cases.

Cases enter most frequently through police action, such as arrest; rarely, cases may enter through a victim-initiated procedure, as through a local citizens' complaint center. In some programs, such as Denver's, the police fill out special domestic violence incident reports, and prosecutors review these reports.... In other jurisdictions, such as Alexandria, prosecutors review all police calls to see whether there have been any domestic violence calls. The office determines which cases need further investigation. It is important that prosecutors and victim advocates work closely with the police to review domestic violence calls as soon as they occur.

When cases enter through victim initiation, the police are not involved and the prosecutor has the opportunity to interview the victim directly as a basis for an evaluation of the case. One study found that prosecutors appear to file charges less often in these cases than in cases which enter through police action, even when the cases were comparable in seriousness of injuries.... In the District of Columbia, where prosecutors hold hearings on victim-initiated complaints to determine whether there is probable cause to issue an arrest warrant, prosecutors rarely initiate arrest warrants. The District of Columbia had an estimated arrest rate of less than 5 percent in domestic violence cases ..., and prosecutors issued only 112 arrest warrants in cases referred to the local citizens' complaint center, even though they scheduled hearings in 3,650 of the cases (District of Columbia Citizens' Complaint Center 1989)....

Filing Charges

The next step is to formally charge the defendant with a crime. In the past, victims were often required to sign charges in domestic violence cases, unlike in most other cases, to show that they were willing to cooperate with the prosecution.... When the prosecutor is responsible for signing the charge, a stronger message goes to the abuser, making it clear that his action is a crime against both society and victim, not just the victim, as in any other crime. Indeed, "It is contrary to the principles of th[e criminal justice system] to even indirectly hold victims of domestic violence responsible for law enforcement in the area of their victimization".... The victim should then become like any other witness, with little control over the prosecutorial process. Accordingly, in many offices for which domestic violence crimes are a priority, it is the prosecutors who make the filing decisions, and who proceed even if this action goes against the victim's expressed wishes.... They recognize that making the filing decision the victim's responsibility provides an opportunity for the abuser to intimidate her and keep her from pursuing charges. By contrast, in Portland, Oregon, prosecutors believe that a policy that places filing responsibility on the victim has resulted in the prosecutor's office filing a comparatively low number of charges....

. . .

Detailed criteria for when to file charges and for whether to charge cases as misdemeanors or felonies are critical to improving prosecutors' response by increasing the number of charges filed. They provide a checklist that ensures that appropriate cases will be prosecuted for the actual crimes committed, and they establish accountability, so that prosecutors must explain decisions not to file. Although prosecutors still have discretion over which cases to pursue, office guidelines set up limits on this discretion, ensuring that more cases get filed. Moreover, explicit charging guidelines can help to ensure that the responsibility of whether to file is placed on the prosecutor, not on the victim.

No–Drop Policies

As part of the policy that prosecution is the prosecutor's responsibility, many offices have also decided to adopt no-drop policies, which emphasize that the prosecutors control decision-making by precluding the victim from deciding to drop charges. For example, the King County, Washington, prosecuting attorney's office explains to victims that they are witnesses for the state and that, even if they reconcile with the defendant, the state will not drop charges.... There are variations on these policies: Alexandria and Brooklyn have "soft" no-drop policies that allow victims to drop charges after counseling and appearing in front of a judge or counselor to explain why they are dropping the charges....

Proponents of strong no-drop policies assert that precluding victims from influencing prosecution forces prosecutors to take these cases seriously and establishes that domestic violence is a crime against society; opponents argue that battered women have the right to decide whether they want intervention from the criminal justice system.... The experience of Duluth with its drop policy is illuminating. Duluth initially decided not to adopt a hard no-drop policy, but to use a case-by-case approach and develop other methods to encourage prosecution.... However, after several years of experience with this policy, during which it discovered that the abuser was intimidating the victim and thereby controlling the charging decisions, Duluth adopted a hard no-drop policy.... In contrast to the Duluth experience, a controlled study in Indianapolis concluded that, in cases where the victim initiated the prosecution, recidivism decreased when victims had control over whether to drop charges and decided not to drop charges (although a victim who did drop charges was more likely to be battered again)....

Some offices have taken the no-drop policy to extremes by jailing victims for refusing to testify.... Although it is a good idea to subpoena victims, because this shows that the victim has no control over the process, it is punitive for victims who may face extreme threats and intimidation from their batterers. Thus, while offices should adopt variations on a no-drop policy and study its effects, they should also develop witness protection programs and not punish victims who refuse to testify.

PRETRIAL RELEASE

Although most domestic violence defendants are released before trial, generally on their own recognizance ..., prosecutors can ask that the court set a bail amount comparable to that of other crimes and that conditions be set on the abuser's release.... Many states allow prosecutors to impose conditions on pretrial release in domestic violence cases.... The National council of Juvenile and Family Court Judges recommends the following:

1. Setting bail consistent with other assault offenses.
2. Releasing the alleged offender conditioned upon having no contact with the victim.
3. Imposing other special conditions of release which protect and maintain victims and family members.
4. Ensuring that the victim will be notified of a pending release and that adequate provisions will be made for the victim's safety.
5. Ensuring that release conditions will be monitored and acted upon....

The most important concerns are separating the parties and protecting the victim....

The policy of the Los Angeles City Attorney is that protective orders should be sought as a condition of release in any situation where there is a reasonable likelihood that the abuser may try to harm the victim.... The office estimates that 75 to 80 percent of victims receive this type of order at arraignment. In San Francisco, the prosecutor automatically requests a stay-away order at the defendant's first appearance, unless the victim specially indicates she does not want one.... These pretrial release conditions let the batterer know that he cannot continue his behavior with impunity, and they may strengthen the victim's cooperation because she knows that the prosecutor's office will protect her. It is important that offices establish standard procedures so that they automatically seek protection orders and other appropriate pretrial release conditions.

VICTIM SUPPORT PROGRAMS

Because of the unique situation of victims of domestic violence crimes, many prosecutors work closely with outside victim advocacy programs or have established such programs internally. The goal of these programs is to provide support for victims, to encourage victim cooperation with programs, and to enhance case survival rates. Advocates at the projects may help prosecutors by getting additional information on the history of abuse and the nature of the violence; they may provide counseling to the victim; they may explain the criminal justice system to the victim; and they often accompany the victim to court.... Judges and lawyers both believe that these programs are effective in reducing dismissals.... The Los Angeles district attorney's office estimates that 70 percent of all victims cooperate with prosecution once they have the assistance of victim advocates....

There are two models for these programs: in one model, the projects are independent organizations that coordinate closely with the prosecutor's office; under the other model, the projects operate as an internal division of the prosecutor's office. The Duluth Domestic Abuse Intervention Project (DAIP) is an example of the first model. DAIP, which is actually the coordinating agency for nine criminal justice and human service agencies, trains victim advocates who are not affiliated with the prosecutor's office.... The advocates begin working with each victim at the time of initial contact with the prosecutor's office. "The role of the advocate is to assist victims in making the determination whether to press charges, to prepare the victim for the court process, to provide the prosecuting attorney with information concerning the case and assistance in evidence gathering, and to assist the prosecutor in making decisions regarding the case".... DAIP also organizes battered women's groups to provide support to help victims end the violence against them.... DAIP staff coordinates treatment programs for the abuser; and DAIP, not the victim, is responsible for monitoring the abuser's compliance with probation conditions....

Seattle and Baltimore have established victim support projects that are within the prosecuting attorneys' offices. In Baltimore, the Domestic Violence Unit is part of a citywide cooperative effort to respond to domestic violence.... The process begins after the police, commissioners, and court clerks identify domestic violence cases, when the unit sends out a letter to the victim requesting that she schedule an interview. The Baltimore unit then provides the following services:

— supportive counseling and empathic listening to meet the victim's emotional needs regarding criminal prosecution or use of the legal system.

— referral to other services such as shelter, social services and community or mental health agencies for ongoing counseling.

— information about how to obtain criminal and civil legal remedies.

— preparing victim and witnesses for court, court accompaniment.

— obtaining documentation of the crime, i.e., medical records, police reports.

— advocacy on behalf of the client within the legal system.

— communication with other agencies on behalf of the client....

. . .

There are no empirical studies of whether independent or internal programs are more effective. Both models, of course, provide victims with some of the support they need to encourage follow-through with prosecution. However, many domestic violence advocates believe that programs that are independent of prosecutors' offices can be more responsive because their primary purpose is to work with victims; internal programs have additional responsibilities, such as providing investigative and litigation support for the prosecutors....

As a final reason for providing adequate victim support, prosecutors' offices may be legally liable for injuries to victims if they establish a legally recognized "special relationship." A woman who was supposed to testify that her husband had abused their six-month-old son ... repeatedly told prosecutors that her husband had threatened—verbally and in writing—to kill her, and she even asked for an escort to the trial.... Before she could testify, her husband set her on fire. A jury awarded her $2.3 million (she can receive only a small portion of that under the state's liability cap).

CASE MANAGEMENT

Prosecutors' offices make a series of general decisions on case administration that have a significant impact on continuation of cases, including whether to use "vertical" prosecution (the case is followed from charging to sentencing by the same attorney), whether to establish a special domestic violence unit, and whether to handle misdemeanors and felonies in different offices. The decisions may be based on economic concerns or office goals. For example, prosecutors may choose to focus only on felony cases, because they are more serious crimes, or on misdemeanors, because they are more numerous and may have additional evidentiary problems and because prosecution may prevent escalation to the felony level.... The choices then have ramifications for the support provided to victims.

In Baltimore, Maryland, a special domestic violence unit handles all misdemeanor cases, although there is no comparable unit for more serious crimes. The special domestic violence unit in the State Attorney's office, which has two prosecutors and two paralegals, provided services to more than seven thousand victims in 1988–89.... However, it is simply unable, because of its limited staff, to offer special services to victims in domestic violence felony cases, and in misdemeanor cases where the defendant requests a jury trial.... Thus, while the unit offers benefits to may victims, its services are unavailable to victims who foresee lengthy trials and to those with more serious injuries (felony cases).

By contrast, in San Francisco, the Family Violence Project concentrates on felony cases, although it will take serious misdemeanor cases, such as those which were originally filed as felonies.... Because there is vertical prosecution, the same "Domestic Violence Assistant District Attorney" handles the case from arraignment through sentencing. Vertical prosecution and special domestic violence units provide case continuity for victims and also ensure that prosecutors have expertise in handling domestic violence cases....

POSTCHARGE DIVERSION OPTIONS

Diversion programs are an alternative to traditional criminal prosecution and sentencing through which case processing is suspended while the defendant completes a treatment program.... There are, essentially, two types of diversionary programs based on when the defendant is diverted out of the proceedings: (1) postcharge but pretrial, so that the batterer is referred to counseling, the charges are not otherwise prosecuted and (2) postplea, where the defendant actually enters a guilty plea, but his sentence is stayed if he complies with a counseling program (this is also called probation).

The decision as to when diversion should occur is controversial.... Proponents of pretrial diversion argue that it is a quick way to get a batterer into a counseling program and avoids problems with witness cooperation because it is so early in the proceeding. On the other hand, opponents maintain that the batterer may not take the counseling program as seriously if he has not had to admit guilt; also batterers who fail to follow through with the diversionary process are rarely prosecuted. Moreover, diversion extends the time that a case is held open so that, if there is a violation, testimony about the violence will not be as fresh. . . .

Proponents of postplea diversion argue that, because a batterer must admit guilt, diversion sends a strong message to the abuser and that prosecutors are more likely to enforce diversion agreements if an abuser violates the diversion conditions. Depending on when the abuser enters into diversion, however, postplea diversion may require much more victim cooperation, and a long time may elapse between the time when the initial charge is filed and the time when the defendant enters a diversionary program.

To prevent abuse of the diversionary process, prosecutors have developed strict eligibility guidelines for when diversion is appropriate. In San Francisco, pretrial diversion can be used only in certain misdemeanor cases:

> the defendant has no convictions for any offence involving violence within the past seven years. . . .
>
> (c). the defendant's record does not indicate that probation or parole has ever been revoked without thereafter being completed;
>
> (d). the defendant has not been diverted to domestic violence within the last five (5) years. . . .
>
> (e). the crime charged was not a corporal injury resulting in a traumatic condition . . . or an assault with a deadly [*sic*]. . . .
>
> Oppose referral where the defendant does not appear to be a suitable candidate. . . .
>
> Suitability for diversion should be evaluated in light of:
>
> (a). repeated history of violent conduct (reported or unreported within the past year but especially where medical attention was sought);
>
> (b). the victim's lack of reasonable objections;
>
> (c). the defendant's demonstrable motivation and agreement to comply with the terms and conditions of diversion. (San Francisco District Attorney, 1985).

The diversion program involves counseling once a week for a period of six months to one year. While pretrial diversion is not optimal, San Francisco has taken steps to prevent it from being used inappropriately. Guidelines can help deter prosecutors from using pretrial diversion as a means to manage their case dockets or to overcome problems with uncooperative witnesses, but it may not decrease the recidivism rate if the defendant believes that he is "getting off" his criminal charges, because he may not get the message that domestic violence is a crime. . . .

Denver has adopted postplea diversion, under which defendants must plead guilty but judgment and sentencing are deferred. . . . Defendants are first screened for eligibility (abusers with previous convictions for domestic violence cannot participate) and then are evaluated for suitability.

Given the controversy over diversion programs, the National Council of Juvenile and Family Court Judges recommends that: "diversion should only occur in extraordinary cases, and then only after an admission before a judicial officer has been entered." The organization notes that diversion is inappropriate when "it is used as a calendar management tool, when first offenders are long term abusers, when the required treatment is only of brief duration and is not monitored, and, perhaps most important, when the use of diversion is perceived as a less than serious response to the crime" (National Council of Juvenile and Family Court Judges, 1990).

. . .

TRIAL PROCEDURES

Because of the variation between states in evidentiary and procedural rules, prosecutors have developed different trial techniques where battered women are the victims to overcome evidentiary problems such as uncooperative victims and the admissibility of expert testimony.

Evidentiary Techniques

To preserve testimony when it is fresh, as well as to ensure that prosecution can proceed without testimony from the victim, the Indianapolis prosecutor videotapes the initial victim interview.... In Miami, the prosecutor obtains a sworn statement from the victim at the initial case screening. Later in the proceedings, offices use a variety of sources for additional evidence.... Los Angeles uses 911 tapes.... Other offices rely on police officer testimony, medical records, or family members who witnessed the violence as evidence when the victim is hostile. These techniques make the case stronger and decrease the office's dependence on the victim's testimony; they can also help impeach the victim's testimony if she recants on the stand.

Expert Testimony

Juries may not believe that abuse occurred if a victim returned to her abuser.... Advocates for battered women have used expert testimony on the battered women's syndrome for more than a decade ...; prosecutors are now using such testimony to help convict batterers....

In *State v. Ciskie* [1988], the prosecutor introduced expert testimony in a rape case between a former boyfriend and girlfriend to explain why the victim did not promptly report four instances of rape and why, despite the abuse, she did not leave the relationship.... In Denver, shelter personnel are called in to testify about how the battered women syndrome might cause a woman to recant earlier testimony when she appears at trial.... Similarly, Los Angeles uses shelter personnel, rather than psychologists, to testify about battered women's syndrome....

In another innovative use of expert testimony, New Hampshire prosecutors called a psychological expert to testify about the abuser, who claimed that he had assaulted his wife because of insanity (*State v. Baker* 1980). The witness explained that battered woman's syndrome might characterize the defendant's marriage and explain his actions, thus providing an alternative to mental illness as the basis for the assault. At least one California prosecutor has introduced similar testimony....

SENTENCING OPTIONS

There are two possibilities after a guilty plea or finding of guilt at trial: probation and/or fine or imprisonment. Probation conditions generally include participation in counseling or other diversionary programs.... As with pretrial diversion, offices need to set up stringent monitoring to ensure that batterers comply with their probation conditions. In Denver, if defendants are not eligible for diversion, they may still apply for probation.... An elaborate procedure for presentence investigations includes administering the Minnesota Multiphasic Personality Inventory (MMPI). The probation office then makes a recommendation, which requires at least a partially suspended jail sentence.

Too often, batterers are not imprisoned.... Prosecutors can request tougher sentences, thereby educating both the abuser and the court to the seriousness of the crime. In California, prosecutors who receive special funding for spouse abuse units must make all reasonable efforts to persuade the court to impose the most severe authorized sentence on a person convicted as a spouse abuser.

* * *

NOTES

1. Issues relating to no-drop policies, victimless prosecution, and sentencing are taken up in subsequent readings. These notes highlight a few other issues raised by Cahn's summary.

2. Cahn notes that jurisdictions focus their efforts sometimes on the prosecution of criminal misdemeanors, and sometimes on the pursuit of the most serious felony charges. This can sometimes create difficult choices in individual cases. A prosecutor may decide, for example, that a severely injured victim will be best served by charging her abuser with one or more misdemeanors, so that she can stay within the more specialized and richly resourced domestic violence unit created for misdemeanor prosecutions, even though felony charges would be appropriate, and might carry both a stronger message about the criminality of the conduct, and the possibility of stiffer penalties.

One way of "splitting the difference" is to multiply the number of misdemeanor charges to underscore the severity of the behavior, and the need for a meaningful sanction. In one reported case, a prosecutor brought fifty-two separate charges against an abusive husband who had choked, kicked, confined and raped his wife, in addition to electrocuting her by plugging an electrical cord into a socket, and shocking her repeatedly with the bare wires. The multiple charges allowed the prosecutor to document both the severity of the violence and the pattern of controlling and abusive behavior. The victim was more willing to cooperate because she was more confident that this strategy would increase the likelihood of conviction and incarceration. Martha Mahoney, *Victimization or Oppression? Women's Lives, Violence and Agency,* THE PUBLIC NATURE OF PRIVATE VIOLENCE 59, 84–85 (M.A. Fineman & R. Mykitiuk, eds. 1994).

3. Cahn talks about the choice between locating victim support services inside or outside the prosecutor's office, and the possibility that external programs can maintain a more exclusive focus on the needs of victims, where internal programs will have additional responsibilities to the prosecutors, including providing investigative and litigation support. What she does not expressly say is that there are likely to be situations in which victim support personnel hired by the prosecutor actually experience conflict between the needs of the office and the needs of individual victims. This is especially likely when the victim is disinclined to cooperate with the prosecution, and wants instead to receive counseling and support in securing her safety by other means. Another argument for locating victim advocates outside the prosecutor's office, therefore, is that independent advocates will be freer to provide a full range of information and support, unconstrained by any competing loyalty to the prosecutorial agenda. The ideal may be to have advocates both inside and outside the prosecutor's office, and to accept that while they will often be able to work together, on occasion those working relationships will be strained.

4. Cahn suggests imposing bail and pre-trial release conditions as ways of controlling a batterer's behavior between arrest and trial. Some states do, however, provide for pre-trial detention in situations where the defendant poses an explicit danger to others if released into the community. This topic is taken up in Section E, below, in the context of stalking.

No–Drop Policies

In the opening reading for this section, Naomi Cahn advocated strongly for no-drop prosecution policies, but her view is not universally shared by domestic violence specialists and advocates. Like mandatory arrest provisions, no-drop policies take control of the process away from the victim. The justification is that the perpetrator should know that he has committed a crime against the state, rather than "merely" violated his partner, that the state insists his wrong be addressed, and that he lacks the power to avoid criminal sanctions by bullying his partner into dropping charges. As participants in San Diego's innovative prosecutorial program have observed:

> In San Diego, we learned a number of years ago that abusers would become more violent and aggressive toward the victim when they learned that she controlled the outcome of the criminal prosecution. By definition, most batterers have the power in violent relationships. Thus, when the system demanded that the victim act in the role of prosecutor, in reality the batterer was being given control of the criminal case. The batterer's control over the victim is generally so

> complete that he was able to dictate whether she talked to the prosecutor, what she said, and whether she appeared in court.
>
> The solution to this vexing issue was to take the responsibility out of the hands of the victim and place it with the State where it belongs. The police officer is paid to be the police officer. The prosecutor is paid to be the prosecutor. The victim of a crime is neither trained nor emotionally able to act in the role of cop or prosecutor. Once prosecutors and police officers stop asking victims whether they want to press charges, they quickly find that victims stop asking to press charges or drop charges. The victim is able to be the victim and address her pressing issues of safety for herself and her children and the system is able to focus on the one who broke the law.

Casey G. Gwinn and Sgt. Anne O'Dell, *Stopping the Violence: The Role of the Police Officer and Prosecutor*, 20 WEST. ST. L. REV. 298, 310–11 (1993).

Nonetheless, some battered women's advocates argue that there are cases in which the victim has good reason to fear the consequences of going through with a prosecution. They express concern that in some cases women who know a no-drop policy is in effect will be deterred from seeking police assistance for fear of what may follow. They also worry that prosecutors will rely on no-drop policies to coerce victims into cooperation, rather than working to ensure that victims feel sufficiently supported by the criminal justice system, and sufficiently safe, to cooperate voluntarily. The specter of an abused woman being terrorized by her partner into withholding her cooperation, only to be jailed on contempt charges, is a haunting one. Finally, no-drop policies will backfire if they result in prosecutors taking weak cases into court, only to have them dismissed by irate judges who feel that their time is being wasted. No prosecutor likes to build a record of losses, and it is tempting then both to blame the victim for the loss, and to avoid similar cases in the future, regardless of official policy.

In more than one high profile case, the reluctant victim, compelled to testify on threat of imprisonment for contempt if she fails to appear, has changed her story and even blamed herself for the violence rather than risk the consequences of her abuser being convicted. When this results in an acquittal, the prosecutor and judge are likely to have all their victim-blaming tendencies reinforced, and the abuser still gets the message that he can control the criminal justice process just as he controls his partner.

Ultimately, the argument is not as simple as whether or not to adopt, or advocate for, a no-drop prosecution policy. No-drop policies are in reality an amalgam of policies and practices which together dictate how prosecutors will pursue domestic violence cases. Within the mix there is plenty of room to maneuver in an attempt to reap the advantages of the no-drop strategy, without putting victims of domestic violence in greater danger of private abuse, or making them newly vulnerable to abuse at the hands of the state. Various "model" programs around the country illustrate a variety of promising approaches.

Nonetheless, the question of whether a victim should be required to participate in the (perhaps rare) prosecution which cannot be won without her contribution is a question which will doubtless continue to divide those who debate it. The theoretical dilemmas it poses are the topic of the next reading. The author, Cheryl Hanna, while acknowledging the force of arguments against mandated participation, and their grounding in feminist theory, comes out in its favor, arguing that pragmatically, in the current context, battered women have more to gain than to lose from aggressive prosecution.

Cheryl Hanna
No Right To Choose: Mandated Victim Participation In Domestic Violence Prosecutions, 109 Harvard Law Review 1849, 1867, 1869–72, 1877, 1882–85, 1888, 1890–91 (1996)

My definition of a mandated participation policy is more consistent with the approaches taken in hard no-drop jurisdictions. Mandated participation must begin at the initial stage of a case and continue through final disposition. This policy can require a woman to sign statements; be photographed to document injuries; be interviewed by police, prosecutors, or advocates; provide the state with other evidence or information; produce her children if subpoenaed; and appear in court throughout the proceedings. Mandated participation may also involve forced testimony if the case proceeds to trial—although such extreme measures are unlikely given that 90% to 95% of all criminal cases end in plea bargains. Therefore, mandated participation may require the victim to play a much greater role in the early stages of the process in order to prevent the case from proceeding to trial. Nevertheless, there must be a consistent policy of requiring victim testimony if that testimony is necessary to prove the case.

. . .

A. *The Public/Private Distinction and Women's Autonomy*

Feminist theory has been the catalyst for identifying domestic violence as a public issue. Specifically, much of feminist academic discourse concerning domestic violence has centered on the argument that "private" violence must be reconceptualized as "public" in order to compel state intervention....

Much feminist work on domestic violence argues that protecting the private sphere is not a viable justification for nonintervention in domestic violence cases. Because the purpose of criminal law is to serve the greater public good, at least this strand of feminist theory seems to provide strong theoretical support for mandated participation in criminal cases.

Yet the public/private distinctions drawn in some feminist work are not always consistent with the logic of criminal law. Indeed, there is often a conflict between pursuing the traditional goals of punishing criminals and protecting society, on the one hand, and furthering the private desires and personal safety of victims, on the other....

. . . [S]tate intervention into women's lives does not necessarily promote their equality, safety, or well-being. Indeed, one of the arguments against mandated participation in criminal prosecutions is that the woman should decide for herself whether state intervention in her personal life is desirable. She may not want to send her partner to jail, break up her family, or subject herself to the criminal process. These decisions are her choices. This argument rests on the assumption that state interference in a woman's private life can be victimizing rather than liberating.

In addition, the public law model upon which our criminal justice system is based has been strongly criticized for failing to respond to the needs of crime victims generally. In the last ten years, legislation and litigation that enhance the role that crime victims play within the criminal justice system have proliferated. Given the demands on prosecutors to be more attentive to the needs of individuals whose lives have been affected by crime, is "justice" individual or community-based? The answer is increasingly less clear. . . .

These tensions pervade our thinking about the appropriate role of state intervention in women's lives. Without characterizing domestic violence as a public matter rather than a private one, little of the legal and social progress that has improved battered women's lives would have been possible. However, the shift from private to public assumes that women desire more state intervention in their lives—at least state intervention that is instrumental and positive. When this is not the case, as it is for many women who face the current criminal justice system, privacy can become a meaningful concept that women are unwilling to reject entirely.

. . .

B. *Particularity and Our Focus on the Individual*

When we reach the question whether state intervention into women's lives is "good" or "bad," much of feminist theory tends to look to the individual woman's circumstances for an answer. As Elizabeth Schneider explains, "Feminist theory rests on the fundamental notion that women's experience is the central starting point of theory: theory flows from experience in the world, and then theory refines and modifies that experience." The "particular"—the individual experiences of women who have been battered—forms the basis for the theoretical inquiry in the domestic violence context.

. . .

Work on woman abuse often ignores the "general"—the larger social costs of violence and the larger issue of women's societal subordination. Even in the context of criminal prosecution, in which the goals are more obviously associated with the "general," practice often revolves around serving the needs of individual women, even when the result of this focus is to release the batterer from criminal responsibility. How one strikes the balance between the particular and the general is not always clear.

. . .

C. *Agency/Victimization and the Tendency to Blame*

One difficulty in discussing mandated participation is distinguishing between victim-blaming arguments and arguments that call on women to overcome their victim status. In domestic violence work, this tension is often known as the "agency/victimization" dichotomy. Elizabeth Schneider explains:

> We now alternate between visions of the battered woman as agent—as cause or provocateur of the battering—and the battered woman as helpless victim. And we go back and forth between these two images without any real public engagement on the problems underlying battering. However, portraying women solely as victims or solely as agents is neither accurate nor adequate to explain the complex realities of women's lives.

The question of what the battered women's role in the prosecution process ought to be often masks an ambivalence about what her role in the abusive relationship is. Women who want to follow through with prosecution are seen either as true victims of domestic violence or as manipulators with an agenda. Women who do not want to proceed are characterized either as agents in the battering—allowing it to continue because of their lack of cooperation with the state—or as true victims who have "learned helplessness."

. . .

... If we reject mandated participation because it would be "revictimizing," we neither account for women's strength and resilience nor acknowledge the political and social context in which battering occurs. If we rationalize mandated participation on the assumption that the battered woman cannot assess her situation realistically, we reinforce her helplessness. In either case the policy can be criticized as paternalistic....

Accepting the Costs of Mandated Participation as Part of an Overall Systemic Response to Violence

. . .

At this point in history, however, the long-term benefits of mandated participation outweigh the short-term costs—costs that can be greatly diminished if we examine the issue in a pragmatic context. In particular, we need to examine the influence that mandated participation has on the effectiveness of the criminal justice system as well as the impact of such a policy on individual women....

... [W]e should be cautious not to treat victims of domestic violence differently than we would treat victims of other crimes. Most crime victims distrust the system.... Domestic violence cases are sometimes similar to other cases in which victims may believe that they have more to lose than to gain by testifying. For example, organized crime, gang-and drug-related offenses, and rape often involve witnesses who face intimidation or perceive that they will be in danger if the testify. Yet rather than allow these crimes to go unprosecuted, prosecutors have developed realistic strategies to respond to witness reluctance. Similarly, prosecutors should develop strategies for domestic violence cases that address the victim's concerns, but should never allow the victim's level of cooperation to be the sole or primary factor in deciding whether to prosecute. This approach is consistent with the criminal justice system's approach in other areas and preserves the integrity of the state's response. It is also far less paternalistic and sexist than dismissing cases based on the victim's wishes in the domestic violence context while refusing to do so in other contexts. Requiring mandated participation places domestic violence on the same level as all violent crimes and ensures the equal protection of law enforcement for women who are victimized by their intimate partners as well as for women who are victimized by strangers.

No-drop policies that do not compel victim cooperation lack credibility. When a batterer and his defense counsel know that a victim's failure to cooperate may result in case dismissal, they control the judicial process. If participation is mandated, the state takes away the batterer's ability to influence the victim's actions. Basing prosecutorial decisionmaking on witness cooperation in domestic violence cases ultimately places the victim in more danger....

In my experience as a prosecutor, the fact that the state was not likely to request a body attachment for victims who failed to appear for trial traveled very quickly by word of mouth. Defense attorneys often informed women that if they did not appear in court, they would probably not be arrested. Day after day, women would not appear and defense attorneys would request dismissals. Many times I could not locate the victim by phone or mail and did not know if the batterer or his attorney had ensured her absence. Judges rarely allowed me to postpone the case unless I had an explanation for the victim's absence.... My example illustrates that prosecutors must be willing—in at least some instances—to mandate participation, including having women picked up by police officers and brought to court if they refuse to appear. Otherwise, the state response to domestic violence is unacceptably undermined.

. . .

A prosecutor's lack of resolve also corrupts other parts of the system. When cases are dismissed because the prosecutor fails to mandate participation, police officers and other criminal justice personnel may question the legitimacy of the trial preparation process. Tremendous progress has been made in instituting preferred and mandatory arrest policies.... When police do make an appropriate arrest, only to see the case dismissed at trial because the victim did not want to proceed, their decreased confidence in the value of arrest can undermine their diligence when policing domestic violence....

* * *

NOTES AND QUESTIONS

1. San Diego has implemented a policy which is consistent with Hanna's recommendations, and yet sensitive to the issue of revictimization:

Our official policy is that we will request arrest warrants for victims who are subpoenaed and fail to appear in court. This is widely publicized in our community. The actual enforcement of the policy, however, is much more complicated. If a victim fails to appear on the day of trial for which she has been subpoenaed, a specially trained Domestic Violence Unit prosecutor will decide how to proceed. The initiative does not come from the judge or from a prosecutor insensitive to domestic violence issues. The prosecutor's decision will be impacted by whether we can prove the case without the victim's cooperation. About 60% of our cases are provable without the victim based on 911 tapes, photographs, medical records, spontaneous declarations by the victim to the officers, admissions by the defendant, neighbors' testimony, relatives' testimony, and general police officer testimony related to the case and the subsequent investigation. If the case can be proved without the victim, we will proceed to trial without requesting a warrant for the victim's arrest.

For cases that cannot be proven without the victim, the prosecutor may request a continuance and a bench warrant. This, however, is not always the case. The prosecutor may conclude the case does not merit the risk of jailing the victim. We now have legislation in California that allows us to refile the case after we locate the victim. If the prosecutor does ask for a continuance and a bench warrant, we do not let the warrant simply go into the system. We attempt to locate the victim immediately and bring her to court. In some cases, we may ask the judge to hold the warrant and continue the case for a week while we notify the victim of the pending risk of arrest. This often results in the victim contacting our victim assistance staff and agreeing to come to court.

Over the past six years, we have only had to request arrest warrants on eight cases using the policy described above. We have maintained credibility with the defense bar and we have had only two incidents where a victim has actually been jailed overnight. Our unit obtains convictions in over 2000 cases every year leading us to believe the policy is successful. . . .

Casey G. Gwinn and Sgt. Anne O'Dell, *Stopping the Violence: The Role of the Police Officer and the Prosecutor,* 20 WEST. ST. L. REV. 297, 313–14 (1993).

2. To maximize the effectiveness of law enforcement while reducing the risks of mandated participation to individual women, Cheryl Hanna, like other commentators, recommends two concurrent strategies. First, that prosecutors seek to create an environment in which women will voluntarily cooperate, both because they feel they can do so in relative safety, and because they have confidence that the prosecution will be successful, and meet their needs. The second recommended strategy is that prosecutors rely where possible not on the victim's testimony, but on other available sources of testimony. She argues that more effort needs to be put into gathering physical evidence, and into persuading courts to admit less

traditional forms of evidence. The skill of pursuing a "victimless prosecution" is the topic of the next section.

3. Is it inconsistent for battered women's advocates to argue *both* that prosecutors should not discriminate against victims of domestic violence, *and* that they should allow victims of domestic violence to exercise more control over prosecutorial decisions than victims of other crimes are traditionally permitted? Is this a fair characterization of advocates' demands of the system? Can an analogy be made to women's demands in the workplace—where they have sought both equal opportunity, and changes in workplace practices to accommodate needs more commonly experienced by women than by men?

Victimless Prosecution

As the opening reading from Naomi Cahn suggested, one critical issue for effective prosecution of domestic violence crimes is the ability of the prosecutor to proceed without the testimony, or even without the cooperation, of the victim. In the article from which the next reading is drawn, the authors advocate strongly for this approach:

> A recent training book for prosecutors and defense attorneys (written by a defense attorney) included this statement: "In domestic violence cases, the abused spouse is the main source of the evidence." This is exactly what the defense bar wants prosecutors to believe and this is how prosecutors have functioned for too long. As long as the investigation and the prosecution focus on the victim, cases will be inadequately investigated and prosecutors will fail to win convictions in large numbers of cases.

Casey G. Gwinn and Sgt. Anne O'Dell, *Stopping the Violence: The Role of the Police Officer and Prosecutor*, 20 WEST. ST. L. REV. 298, 311–12 (1993).

Casey G. Gwinn and Sgt. Anne O'Dell
Stopping the Violence: The Role of the Police Officer and Prosecutor, 20 Western State University Law Review 298, 300–303 (1993)

The handling of domestic violence cases in San Diego in early 1986 was similar to most of the country. Police officers were required to write reports but little else was mandated or encouraged. Prosecutors regularly dismissed cases if the victim refused to "press charges" or "prosecute." The familiar question, "Do you want to press charges?" was asked of victims in virtually every case. The answer often dictated what type of action the officer would take and what kind of energy would be expended in the handling of the case. While some states did have mandatory arrest statutes, California was not one of those states.

The policies of the City Attorney and the District Attorney in our county in 1986 included a refusal to file charges if the victim was uncooperative and immediate dismissal if the victim became uncooperative during the course of the case. The standard police report was two to three paragraphs and rarely were witness statements or photographs included. Simply put, domestic violence cases required little time or energy because the caseload remained extremely small. Even cases which survived and moved toward trial were generally plea-bargained for a lesser charge of disturbing the peace or creating a public nuisance and a minimal fine.

. . .

In August, 1986, we prepared a domestic violence policy bulletin for the approval of the elected city attorney. [He] endorsed the changes, put his authority behind the policies, and a new era began. The policies included the decision to file charges being made by the prosecutor rather than by the victim, no dismissals even if the victim was uncooperative, and no reduction of the charges in order to facilitate a guilty plea. For the first few months the changes were not even evident. To be sure, we began filing many more cases than we had previously been filing, but little else was noticeable until Joseph Davis was arrested on November 23, 1986.

On November 23, 1986, officers responded to a 911 call from a woman who said her boyfriend had hit her at approximately 4:30 p.m. The judge and his girlfriend lived in a condominium in an upper middle-class suburb of San Diego. When the officers arrived the judge was sitting at the kitchen table reading law books. The hysterical girlfriend was at a neighbor's house. The girlfriend's clothing was torn, there were red marks on her neck and arms, and she complained of pain from being kicked in the stomach. The girlfriend was five months pregnant. Officers, after consulting with a superior, wrote the judge a citation of arrest and released him at the scene. No photographs were taken of the condominium or of the victim. Neither the victim's daughter nor the neighbors were interviewed. The final police report was less than three pages.

Within days, the case was sent to the City Attorney's Office for review. We reviewed the case and immediately called the victim at work. She spoke to us at length about what happened and told us the judge had a terrible temper. She was very frightened and confused. She did not recant in any way but expressed a great deal of concern about the potential consequences to the judge's career. Under our new policies charges were filed on December 16, 1986. The victim was cooperative and the facts appeared straightforward.

The victim, however, sent a letter to the City Attorney soon thereafter and recanted everything. She denied the violence of the judge and said that she wanted the case dismissed. Unfortunately for Judge Davis, the City Attorney had now instituted a "no dismissal" policy. Meanwhile, the media coverage of the story was unrelenting. Television, print, and radio media stories about the case were almost daily for the first week and then continued regularly as the case proceeded. It became common knowledge that the victim was uncooperative and equally well known that the City Attorney was going to proceed irrespective of the wishes of the victim.

The new "aggressive" approach to domestic violence cases in the City Attorney's Office was not popular with judges, criminal defense attorneys, and other criminal justice professionals. It was quickly apparent that few expected us to win the case and that every one wanted to distance themselves from this ill-fated crusade to prosecute a domestic violence case without a cooperative victim.

We had a misdemeanor, minimal violence case with, at first appearance, no evidence but the victim's own testimony. We had policies but no background, training, or expertise in how to make such policies effective. Initially, we conducted a witness check and identified four neighbors who had witnessed the victim's condition after the incident and had talked to her. Second, we obtained the 911 emergency call tape from the call placed by the victim within minutes after the incident. Third, we re-interviewed the officers at the scene and obtained a great deal of detail on the condominium, the judge's demeanor and conduct, and the victim's physical and emotional state. Fourth, we located the victim's family doctor and obtained her medical records through a court order. Fifth, we learned that the victim had applied for and received a temporary restraining order the day after the incident. Sixth, we reviewed the family court records and learned that domestic violence was alleged in the judge's first marriage.

As the criminal prosecution of Judge Davis proceeded toward trial, we began to build a formidable circumstantial evidence case of domestic violence. We had a hysterical woman calling 911 saying that she had been beaten by her boyfriend. She had visible injuries as seen by the neighbors and she was five months pregnant. We were able to take photographs of the outside of the condominium and retrace with diagrams the frantic steps she took to the neighbors' house to call the police. While we still felt we would rely on the victim to a great extent, we felt we had identified corroborating evidence.

Weeks before the trial we began trying to serve the victim with a subpoena. She and the judge were still living together in the area and we felt service of a subpoena would be simple. After three or four attempts, however, we realized the victim was avoiding us. We let critical days go by as we planned how we might serve her. Finally, days before the trial we learned that the victim had disappeared. We obtained a brief continuance as we searched for her. Days before the new trial date we located her out of the country, in Mexico, and out of the jurisdiction of our subpoena.

We were thus forced to trial without a victim or an eyewitness of any kind. We, nevertheless, had built a fairly strong circumstantial evidence case against the judge.... The scene was set for an aggressive, well-prepared case-in-chief.

We did not anticipate, however, the battle we would face in seeking to have our evidence even admitted at trial. Over two days of pre-trial motions, the judge presiding over the case ruled: (1) The 911 tape was too prejudicial and could not be heard by the jury; (2) the jury could not know that the victim was pregnant; (3) all potential jurors with any knowledge of the case would be excluded; (4) the victim's doctors could not testify; (5) only one of the four neighbors would be allowed to testify; (6) any information about violence in the judge's prior marriage would be excluded; and (7) the existence of a domestic violence restraining order would be kept from the jury. With the pre-trial rulings completed, we went to trial....

The trial lasted four days. The prosecutor's case consisted of a transcript of part of the 911 call, a body diagram of the injury observed, one neighbor witness and two police officers. The defense called character witnesses for the judge and then sprung their best surprise: a self-defense theory. The judge testified on his own behalf concerning the violence of the victim toward him. He testified of his great love for her and her inability to control himself. We were dumbfounded and staggered as the trial judge continued to disallow any evidence that this woman was five months pregnant at the time of the incident. The judge was a compelling witness.

The jury deliberated nearly a day before announcing that they were hopelessly deadlocked: eleven to one for not guilty. The trial judge subsequently dismissed the entire case. We had lost. Our no-drop policy appeared discredited and the criminal defense bar looked forward to other cases set for trial.

The battle, however, was not over. [The] City Attorney ... stood behind our policies and called for continued aggressive prosecution. We had learned how to try cases without a victim. We had battled against myth, misconception, bias, and tradition. The immediate loss was devastating but the education was invaluable. Over the next six months, we tried seventeen domestic violence cases without victim participation and won all but two. We had learned how to prosecute cases without a cooperative victim, how to change the attitudes of jurors, and how to obtain evidence which had not been obtained in the original investigation. Perhaps even more significantly, the San Diego Police Department responded with strong support to the new aggressive approach from the prosecutor's office.

San Diego judges who had followed the prosecution of Judge Davis with interest were now confronted with similar legal and evidentiary issues in virtually every case brought before them. The two prosecutors assigned to domestic violence in those early months after the Davis case filed trial briefs in every case with case law authority for the admissibility of every conceivable type of evidence to prove the charge against the abuser. 911 tapes were played regularly for judges and the true emotion of the crime started to be felt in the courtrooms of San Diego as never before.

... The San Diego City Attorney's Domestic Violence unit has grown from one part-time prosecutor to twenty-one full-time staff and nine part-time and volunteer staff. Nearly 60% of our filed cases involve uncooperative or absent victims and yet we obtain convictions in 88% of our cases. The San Diego Police Department's Domestic Violence Unit has grown from one coordinating sergeant to over twenty-seven full-time staff members. While statistics must be used carefully, we have seen major reductions in our domestic violence homicide rates and in our re-arrest and re-prosecution rates for those abusers held accountable in our long-term batterers' programs. Our strategies are working to reduce violence in intimate relationships in San Diego.

* * *

NOTES

1. In addition to the evidentiary strategies detailed in the previous reading, victimless prosecutions frequently take advantage of the "excited utterance" exception to the hearsay rule to introduce statements made by the victim in the aftermath of the violence on which the prosecution is based, as this account from Minnesota explains:

> The familiar excited utterance exception to the hearsay rule offers the prosecutor another tool in seeking to present evidence of domestic abuse at trial without cooperation from the victim. For the statement to qualify as a hearsay exception under ... Minnesota Rules of Evidence, three requirements must be met. First, the statement must relate to a startling event or condition. Second, the statement must be made while the declarant was under the stress of excitement. Third, the excitement must have been caused by the startling event or condition.
>
> The admissibility of hearsay statements under this rule is grounded in the belief that excitement caused by an event insures the trustworthiness of a statement and eliminates the possibility of conscious fabrication. Though fixed guidelines for the application of the rule are impossible, the trial court must consider every relevant factor, including the length of time elapsed, the nature of the event, the physical condition of the declarant, and any possible motive to falsify.
>
> Several issues arise in applying [the] rule ... to the scenario of a typical domestic violence case. Minnesota case law provides ... relevant precedent.... In State v. Daniels, statements made within an hour of the startling event were admissible. In State v. Berrisford, statements made ninety minutes after a murder were admissible. In an Iowa domestic assault case, statements made as long as fourteen hours after the victim was severely injured were admissible. In many communities, officer response time to domestic calls and resulting investigation take place within a matter of minutes. As a result, these cases support the prosecutor's arguments for admissibility of statements made during these time periods.
>
> A second issue concerns the display of emotions necessary to establish that a declarant is under a sufficient aura of excitement so as to ensure the trustworthiness of the statement. In court decisions which have upheld the admissibility of statements such signs of excitement have included "still scared," "shaky," "very upset," "nervous," "looked unnerved," "upset," "distraught," and "in state of shock." Such indicia of excitement frequently are observed in the victims of domestic violence. This case law, however, highlights the necessity of effective police training in the area of report writing. It is crucial that police officers effectively document the emotional state of the victim, thereby providing the prosecutor with facts necessary to prepare and try the case.
>
> A third issue in applying [the] rule ... concerns whether statements qualifying as excited utterances can be made in response to

questions. Several Minnesota cases have held that such declarations are admissible. In the typical domestic violence case the victim's statement of what happened is obtained in response to questions by police officers. Consequently, this line of case law provides arguments for meeting objections to the admissibility of statements under these circumstances.

Mary E. Asmus, Tineke Ritmeester and Ellen L. Pence, *Prosecuting Domestic Abuse Cases in Duluth: Developing Effective Prosecution Strategies from Understanding the Dynamics of Abusive Relationships*, 15 HAMLINE L. REV. 115, 141–43 (1991).

2. As prosecutors become more familiar and successful with "victimless prosecutions" it is becoming increasingly apparent that for some victims, the reassurance that the case can be won without their testimony turns them from hostile witnesses to allies in the prosecution. Victimless prosecution allows them to disavow in public their interest in seeing their abuser sanctioned, while assisting the prosecutor in private. If victimless prosecution is pursued as a strategy for winning victim cooperation, it can be a crucial means of "softening" an otherwise tough no-drop policy. Obviously there is a world of difference between pursuing a no-drop policy by coercing the reluctant testimony of a victim, to the point of threatening her with incarceration if she refuses, and pursuing it by winning the case without ever asking her to take the stand. At the same time, even within the range of strategies open to the prosecutor who plans a victimless prosecution, some may be more protective of the victim than others. Using the victim's excited utterance, for example, still involves the victim's condemnation of her abuser, albeit less directly than if she were to repeat her accusation at trial. Using the independent testimony of police and neighbors, along with medical reports, goes further to distance the victim from the prosecution.

The Impact of Prosecution

Does prosecution work? As with proarrest and mandatory arrest policies, the question first needs clarification. What does "working" mean, in this context? Is it enough if prosecutorial policy generates a greater public understanding that many aspects of domestic violence are criminal, and that perpetrators are vulnerable to arrest and sanction? Might prosecutorial policy provide a general deterrent function—reducing the overall incidence of criminal acts of domestic violence? How could we even know if such a thing was occurring, let alone whether we could attribute it to prosecution policies and practices? Are we looking for specific deterrence—evidence that batterers who are prosecuted have a lower recidivism rate than ones who are not? Will we measure recidivism only with respect to the woman whose injuries generated the prosecution, or look to see if the batterer has found a new target? Over what period of time will we measure the impact of the intervention on the batterer? Can we assess the effect on the batterer of prosecution, in particular, separate from either the arrest that preceded it, or the sanction it produced—whether that was a mandatory referral to counseling or a jail sentence? How can a controlled experiment be conducted when the end result—the imposition of a sentence by a judge—cannot be controlled?

The difficulty of all these questions may explain why there is so little empirical work purporting to assess the efficacy of prosecutorial policy. The following reading describes both that paucity, and the findings from one of the few relatively large scale studies attempting to measure the impact of domestic violence prosecution, the Indianapolis Prosecution Experiment.

David A. Ford and Mary Jean Regoli The Preventive Impacts of Policies for Prosecuting Wife Batterers; Domestic Violence: The Changing Criminal Justice Response 181, 182, 184–89, 192–95, 197–205 (E.S. Buzawa and C.G. Buzawa, eds. 1992)

This [reading] describes the Indianapolis Prosecution Experiment, the first randomized field experiment to evaluate the specific preventive impacts of prosecution and adjudication in cases of wife battery. . . .

The police studies show (though with some equivocal results) that police intervention of some sort can prevent the recurrence of conjugal violence. Should we not expect an even greater impact when suspects are formally punished through prosecution with court sentencing?

THE PROSECUTION PROCESS IN INDIANAPOLIS

The range of statutory options and creative discretionary alternatives challenges our ability to evaluate all policy-relevant strategies for processing conjugal violence cases. Nevertheless, guided by policy concerns, we can categorize outcomes under four sets: no prosecution (as may occur when victims are permitted to drop charges), pretrial diversion of defendants to treatment under batterer rehabilitation programs, prosecution to conviction with sentencing to rehabilitative treatment as a condition of probation, and conviction with other conditions, including the possibility of jail.

. . . After a violent attack on a woman, someone may or may not call the police to the scene. If the police are at the scene, they are expected to investigate for evidence to support probable cause for a warrantless arrest. If it exists, they may arrest at their discretion. Upon making such an on-scene arrest, officers fill out a probable cause affidavit and slate the suspect into court for an initial hearing. When the police are not called, or if they are called but do not arrest, a victim may initiate charges on her own by going to the prosecutor's office and swearing out a probable cause affidavit with her allegation against the man. Following a judge's approval, the alleged batterer may either be summoned to court or be arrested on a warrant and taken to court for his initial hearing.

At the time of initial screening, the prosecutor determines a track for processing a case according to what outcome should be pursued. . . . A prosecutor's decisions throughout the process rely not only on legal considerations (including convictability and procedural convenience) but also on guesses about what might be in the victim's best interests. Those decisions have traditionally reflected both personal biases and prosecutorial lore....

THE INDIANAPOLIS PROSECUTION EXPERIMENT

The Indianapolis Prosecution Experiment (IPE) was designed to discover which policies work as cases move beyond the police into the realm of prosecutorial and judicial action. It examines the alternatives for processing cases ... depending on whether a case enters the criminal justice system by victim-initiated complaint or by on-scene police arrest.

The "drop-permitted" track anticipates victims dropping charges, contrary to the more widely advocated "no-drop" policy.... [T]he Marion County prosecutor's office had previously implemented a no-drop policy under the assumption that it would provide victims greater protection from continuing abuse....

The drop-permitted policy was available only to cases initiated by victim complaint to the prosecutor. When the IPE began, the law enabling warrantless probable cause arrests for misdemeanor battery had just been implemented. All agencies participating in the experiment agreed that to allow victims of on-scene arrest cases to drop charges brought by a police officer would hurt their efforts to encourage arrest.

If a woman is denied the opportunity to drop charges (or if she has permission but elects to proceed), any of three other broad prosecution policies may be activated. The first is also a "no-prosecution" alternative offered to a defendant in the form of "pre-trial diversion" to a counseling program. If he is willing to admit his guilt and to participate in an anger-control program for batterers, his trial date is deferred to allow time for him to complete the program. Successful completion of the program results in the dismissal of charges. Committing new violence or failing to abide by the terms of the agreement results in the case going to trial.

The second policy option calls for prosecuting to conviction with a request for sentencing to anger-control counseling as a condition of probation (the same batterer treatment program offered under diversion). We call this "probation with counseling." The final prosecution policy option is to seek a conviction with sentencing to fines, probation and jail, our "other" category. In practice, "other" was a residual category within which a variety of traditional sanctions might be exercised. The analyses presented hereafter use "other" as an experimental control or base category against which the remaining categories are compared.

Cases in the IPE study were selected from all cases of misdemeanor battery or criminal recklessness brought to the attention of the Marion county prosecutor's office between 30 June 1986 and 10 August 1987. To qualify for the study, a defendant had to be an adult (aged eighteen years or older) male alleged to have physically victimized a female conjugal partner.... The only cases rejected from the study were those in which the suspect fell into one or more of the following categories: he had previously been convicted of felonious violence (e.g., criminal homicide, robbery, burglary with injury, rape, arson with injury, aggravated assault); he had previously been convicted or had a warning letter sent or had a pending case for an act of violence against the same victim as in the new case; he was known to be on probation and was subject to a judgment of violation for the new offense, and the prosecutor wanted that judgment. Cases were also rejected if, prior to randomization and in the judgment of the prosecutor, the defendant posed such danger to the victim that he should be arrested immediately and given no chance of less than rigorous prosecution with harsh punishment.

A total of 678 cases were identified for study. Of those, 480 cases (71 percent) were brought by a victim's direct, in-person complaint to the prosecutor; 198 cases (29 percent) entered the prosecution process following warrantless, on-scene police arrests of suspected batterers. Within each of these "Entry Sets" (i.e., entry by victim Complaint [VC] or by On–Scene Police Arrest [OSA]), cases were randomly assigned recommendations for prosecutorial treatment (as described hereafter). In addition, the Victim Complaint cases were randomly assigned to either a warrant or a summons condition as the means of bringing a defendant to court.

The study followed each case through the prosecution process until six months following its settlement in court. Outcome measures were obtained from official records, personal interviews with victims and defendants, and direct observation in court. Victims were initially interviewed as soon as possible after the case came to the attention of the prosecutor. Each was interviewed again shortly after the case was settled in court and finally six months after settlement. Defendants were interviewed after their cases were settled. . . .

RANDOMIZATION OF RECOMMENDED PROSECUTORIAL TRACKS

The Indianapolis experiment used a "discretion-dependent" design whereby each case entering the study was randomly assigned to a treatment condition that was recommended to a deputy prosecutor for consideration as a prosecution goal. . . . The normal prosecution policy prior to the experiment was to prosecute every case to conviction with the goal of attaining presumptive sentencing, that is, fines, probation, and executed jail time. . . . With the implementation of the IPE, other less-punishing treatments were designated as possible outcomes. . . .

The experiment had remarkable success, thanks to cooperating prosecutors, in attaining near perfect agreement between randomized treatment recommendations and the prosecutor's decision, upon screening a case, to track it toward the designed outcome. In only one case did the prosecutor choose to override a randomized prosecution recommendation. That nearly 100 percent of the cases were tracked as recommended demonstrates the prosecutor's commitment to learning what prosecution policy "makes a difference."

The initial tracking decisions provide the principal basis for evaluating policy. . . . Of course, there is no guarantee that stated policy will be implemented as intended. By the time a case comes to court, some months later, a prosecutor may have reason to ignore the initial tracking recommendation. . . . A victim, a defendant, or his attorney may argue successfully against the prosecutor's recommendation.... Beyond prosecution policy, a judge may choose not to hear or to ignore a prosecutor's recommendations or request for disposing of a case. All such "failures" of policy implementation meant failures in the implementation of experimental treatments....

ANALYSIS AND FINDINGS

... A major finding emerges from initial analyses: In Indianapolis, prosecutorial action on a case, that is, accepting charges and proceeding through an initial hearing in court, significantly reduces the chance of further violence within six months of the time that the case is settled (by dismissal, by acceptance of diversion agreement, by conviction, or by a finding of not guilty).... [O]ver 85 percent of IPE victims had experienced violent episodes prior to the study incident, regardless of how the violence was measured. In the six months prior to the study incident, no less than 70 percent of the women were victimized. And when measured by the CTS [Conflict Tactics Scale], over 90 percent experienced some violence, with over 80 percent reporting severe CTS violence.

Based on rates of violence in the six months preceding the incident prosecuted, there is at least a 50 percent reduction in the prevalence of violence committed by IPE defendants in the six months following case settlement.... More notably, for cases initiated by victim complaints, there is a 66 percent reduction in general CTS violence and a 78 percent drop in severe CTS violence committed by defendants. The corresponding figures for cases entering the system by on-scene arrest are 59 percent and 68 percent. Bringing a defendant to court, even if his case is not adjudicated, provides his victim with a lower risk of recurring violence within six months of case settlement than expected, given her preprosecution experience. The preventive effect is even greater, given prior experiences with severe CTS violence.

Pre-Settlement Violence

Incredibly, victims reported that over 30 percent of the VC defendants and 20 percent of the OSA defendants facing adjudication had committed new acts of violence even before their cases had gone to trial. Can any policy reduce the chance of pre-settlement violence?

Alternative prosecution tracks create different conditions and opportunities for renewed violence, even before a case is settled. This is due in part to the amount of information available to a defendant concerning the likely outcome of his case. Under a Drop Permitted policy, a victim may acknowledge her ability to drop charges in the course of bargaining with the defendant for her security.... Under the Diversion policy, a prosecutor will generally offer the opportunity for diversion by letter or at the defendant's initial hearing in court. Other tracked outcomes may be revealed during plea negotiations. Not surprisingly, therefore, we find that the chance of pre-settlement violence varies by prosecutorial policy....

For VC cases, the Drop Permitted policy results in the lowest rate of pre-settlement violence, followed closely by Diversion.... There are no such significant differences by Prosecutorial Tracks for OSA cases.

... There are circumstances in a couple's relationship susceptible to influence by prosecutorial policy and related to violence.... The longer a case is awaiting court action, the more opportunity there is, in terms of available time, for violence. The more court appearances, the more attention, forced contact, and perhaps resentment between the victim and defendant, all of which raise the potential for violent conflict. Above all, different prosecution policies may have a direct impact on whether a couple chooses to cohabit prior to case settlement. Although cohabitation is not a necessary condition for violence, it enhances the chance of violence.... The chance is further enhanced as the length of time before case settlement is extended.

Controlling for these opportunity variables, we find that only among cases initiated by victim complaint is there any significant policy impact. In the pre-settlement time frame, allowing victims to drop charges or offering defendants the opportunity to enter a batterers' anger-control program under a diversion agreement will have a significant preventive impact prior to formal action on their respective choices....

[There is] a somewhat different pattern of effects for defendants arrested on-scene by the police. First, we see the chance of violence increasing given a longer pre-settlement time frame. But recalling that OSA cases have no Drop Permitted track, and that the other tracks were not significantly different in their effects, ... only the influence of cohabitation is significant.

Six-Month Post–Settlement Violence

Do the pre-settlement policy effects continue through the six-month period following settlement in court? Or does the court experience with its actual sanctions result in different outcomes?

As before, those women who are permitted to drop charges are least likely to experience an episode of new violence in the follow-up period. Otherwise, there is no consistent pattern of policy differences for either VC or OSA cases....

. . .

[A] woman who cohabits with her abuser for any time during the six-month follow-up period is more likely to be battered anew during that period; and a woman who has already experienced at least one new episode of violence prior to case settlement is significantly more likely to be victimized during the follow-up period.

Defendants brought into the prosecution process following victim complaints are less likely to batter again within the follow-up period when the woman is permitted to drop charges. However, if the woman is permitted to drop and does so, she is significantly more likely to be battered again during that time.... [T]he recidivism rate under a Drop Permitted policy is less than 10 percent. Put differently, victims who are permitted to drop but follow through with prosecution have less than a 10 percent chance of being battered again within six months of settlement.

. . .

... We find quite a different result for defendants who entered the system by an on-scene police arrest. After controlling for cohabitation and pre-settlement violence, only Probation with Counseling is found to have a significant impact, and its effect is in the direction of *promoting* new violence .. That is, a suspect arrested by the police at the scene of his crime who is then prosecuted with the goal of getting a conviction with sentencing to anger-control counseling is significantly more likely to batter his partner within six months of his case being settled in court than had he not been so processed.

... Although the chance of new violence associated with cohabitation appears to be somewhat lower than for VC victims, the OSA women do risk a chance of follow-up violence which approaches or exceeds 80 percent regardless of prosecution policy.

... [S]everal caveats are in order. First, our evaluation of prosecution policies does not address the actual treatments experienced by a defendant. When we describe the impact of a policy calling for prosecution to conviction, we are talking about the prosecutor's intention to seek that end. In fact, the policy may not result in prosecution at all.... "Real-world contingencies" result in misimplementation of policy, i.e., an untracking of prosecutorial plans. The finding that some policies will have low rates of implementation is itself a notable outcome.

Second, and closely related as an evaluation concern, treatment content may not be what was intended. For example, we have found that a policy calling for counseling as a condition of probation is relatively ineffective. This does not necessarily mean that counseling under probation is ineffective as a rehabilitative treatment. Even after sentencing, a defendant may never receive treatment because program space is unavailable, his probation term is less than the treatment period, or he simply fails to comply and no one pays attention.

DISCUSSION

Is prosecutorial and judicial action effective in preventing wife battery? Yes. Even if a suspected wife batterer is only brought to court for an initial hearing, the chance of his committing new violence six months after his case is settled will decrease, no matter which specific intervention he may experience. Of course, this does not mean that every defendant will be so deterred. Some may retaliate; others may be unaffected. But given the high proportion of cases with violence in the six months before intervention, we would have predicted much higher rates of new incidents than occurred in the six months after settlement.

Is prosecution tracked to adjudication more effective in preventing violence than offering victims or defendants opportunities to avoid a trial? Apparently not, except in the limited case of a woman filing charges under the Drop Permitted policy and not dropping. That she is at lower risk following adjudication than victims who could not drop suggests that the preventive policy impact derives from her power to drop rather than from judicial action.... There is a clear need for more research on the dynamics of the victim-defendant-system triad, not only to learn why those who follow through gain security but especially to learn why those who drop are at greater risk.

To that end, we speculate that victims are empowered not only by their ability to drop charges but also by their alliance with criminal justice agencies.... As long as the alliance holds, as when a victim does not drop charges, she should find protection. But the alliance must also be potent, as would be demonstrated, for example, by a decisive system response on behalf of a victim battered prior to case settlement.

A decisive system response to any violation of conditions for pre-trial release, including of course new violence, should serve notice that the victim-system alliance is strong. It tells the defendant that the victim is serious in her resolve to end the violence and that the system is unwavering in its support of her interest in securing protection. We have seen that pre-settlement violence predicts post-settlement violence. To protect victims, it is incumbent on the police, prosecutor, and courts to take such incidents seriously. The policy impacts after settlement may depend on how well agencies can control batterers while they are in the system. Control need not be effected through reactive sanctions. The prosecutor and court can remove opportunities for continuing violence through such actions as ordering conditions for child visitation and confiscating weapons.

The risk associated with cohabitation is at once obvious and distressing.... This is not to advocate that women leave their abusers. The act of separating may carry such a high risk for fatal violence that only a victim in her unique circumstances can know the impact of leaving. Our findings, however, suggest that women who have already left and have appealed to criminal justice agencies for protection should be supported for their decision and not encouraged to return.

* * *

NOTES AND QUESTIONS

1. How seriously does the authors' admission that their evaluation measures the impact of prosecution policies using "policy outcomes sought by prosecutors" as a substitute for "policies actually implemented" undermine the conclusions they seek to draw?

2. Similarly, would you want to qualify the conclusions they draw from their study based on the categories of case they excluded from their randomized assignment of cases to prosecutorial tracks? What hypotheses might you want to make about how included cases differed from excluded ones, and how that might have affected the outcomes?

3. Although the authors set out to study prosecutorial policy, the outcomes of the cases they studied were often not controlled by prosecutors, but instead driven by a judge's decision about what constituted an appropriate intervention. The subject of case disposition, and sentencing alternatives, is the subject of the next section of this chapter.

D. SENTENCING

Previous sections of this chapter have already suggested that another important variable in the management of domestic violence cases within the criminal justice system is the sentence finally imposed on a convicted offender. This decision will be driven in part by the charges the prosecutor chooses to bring, in part by applicable statutory or regulatory sentencing guidelines, in part by the type and level of resources available within the system, and in part on judicial discretion. Where the sentence involves alternatives to incarceration—notably probation and treatment—it will also depend on the discretion and resources of those in charge of supervising the offender conditionally released into the community.

Provocative hypotheses have been put forward by observers discouraged at the extent to which convicted domestic violence offenders continue to serve only minimal prison sentences, or to avoid incarceration altogether. One such hypothesis is that the criminal justice system continues to discriminate against victims of domestic violence, and covertly condone the behavior of perpetrators, by imposing more lenient sentences in these cases than in parallel stranger violence cases. Another is that the system's atypical commitment to a "treatment" paradigm in domestic violence cases reflects a continuing conviction that domestic violence is more "private" than "public," and more about "illness" than about "crime." The readings that follow acknowledge the basis for these critiques, but at the same time cast doubt on these and other easy explanations for current sentencing practices.

Discussions of sentencing in domestic violence cases must ultimately be framed by our broader understanding of the role we want criminal sanctions to play, and what experience teaches us about their efficacy. Are we trying to rehabilitate offenders? Do we know whether treatment is more effective in reshaping the attitudes and behaviors of offenders than incarceration? If we are more modest in our goals, and simply want to deter convicted abusers from reoffending, rather than rehabilitate them, do we know whether treatment, supervised probation without treatment, or incarceration is the most effective specific deterrent? Is a longer period of incarceration more effective as a deterrent than a shorter one? If our goal is even more modest, and we are simply out to "incapacitate" the offender—to deprive him of the opportunity for further violations, do we know if we can effectively do that without locking him up? Furthermore, since we do know that except in the most exceptional of circumstances he will not remain behind bars indefinitely, do we know what to predict when he is released? If we include among our goals reducing the amount of partner abuse in the society at large, and are using the criminal justice system in part as a force for public education and general deterrence, do we know whether those goals are served better by some sentencing practices than others? Finally, are batterers homogeneous enough as a group that we can assume a uniform response to different enforcement strategies, or should we be tailoring our responses to take account of important differences among categories of offender?

The first reading provides an up-to-date overview of sentencing practices, one that casts doubt on the assertion that perpetrators of domestic violence are treated more leniently by the system than other violent offenders, but confirms the bias towards treatment rather than incarceration.

A Critical Look at Sentencing Practices, Cheryl Hanna, The Paradox of Hope: The Crime and Punishment of Domestic Violence, 39 William and Mary Law Review 1505, 1513, 1517–25 (1998)

... Despite increased attention to domestic violence, there is still a deep reluctance to incarcerate domestic violence offenders. Rather, most receive probation with mandated treatment regardless of the severity of the offense or their past violent histories. This trend continues despite empirical research that questions whether there is any direct causal link between participation in a batterer treatment program and recidivism.

. . .

Unfortunately, we know surprisingly little about the outcomes of all violent crimes. Few studies compare the outcome of domestic violence with other violent offenses. Furthermore, sparse data exists on the number of domestic violence cases that arrive in the criminal justice system and what happens to them once they get there. The federal government and a majority of the states collect statistics on domestic violence, but there are wide variations in how each jurisdiction defines offenses, determines what is counted, and measures or reports incidents....

Prosecutors and judges have numerous disposition options once a domestic violence case enters the system: outright dismissal; pretrial diversion; postconviction probation with conditions, including fines; batterer treatment and/or substance abuse counseling; or incarceration. Prosecution policies nationwide are becoming more rigorous, with many jurisdictions forming specialized prosecution units and implementing "no-drop" policies. The available data, however, suggests that most of these cases still end with arrest.... Of those cases that are prosecuted, many are charged or pled down to misdemeanors despite facts that suggest the conduct constituted a felony.

When prosecutors decide to go forward, the final disposition is often a period of probation, either pre-or postconviction, contingent upon completion of a batterer treatment program. For example, in Sussex County, New Jersey, counseling and other social services for both the victim and the abuser, rather than jail time, is the preferred sentence as a matter of jurisdictional policy. There is little evidence, however, that probation departments follow up on these orders, allowing many abusers to slip through the cracks.

In addition, few batterers ever see the inside of a jail cell, even when convicted of a serious offense. A recent American Lawyer story followed all domestic violence arrests in eleven jurisdictions on June 18, 1995. Of the 140 arrests made in the eleven communities, 95 never made it to conviction, plea, or acquittal. Cases were dismissed even in jurisdictions with avowed no-drop policies. Only sixteen of the forty-four defendants who were convicted or pled no contest served any time; the vast majority received probation or a suspended sentence, including one man who sent his wife to the hospital with a broken nose and a broken rib. He received six months' probation. A man who slapped his wife in the face and tried to stab her with a kitchen knife received one year, the longest sentence given on this day. The court found that two prior felony drug convictions, not the severity of the crime, justified the length of the sentence.

What would happen to these defendants if they assaulted a stranger or acquaintance rather than a loved one? Unfortunately, we do not know. There is an abysmal lack of data comparing violent domestic and non-domestic cases. To date, no empirical evidence supports the assertion that authorities treat domestic violence offenses less seriously than other violent crimes. In fact, Kathleen Ferraro and Tascha Boychuk examined violent criminal cases in Maricopa County, Arizona from 1987 to 1988 and found that all people prosecuted for crimes of violence, whether against an intimate or a nonintimate, received relatively lenient treatment. Offenders closely related by blood or sexual ties to their victims were usually given probation or had their cases dismissed, but so too were offenders unrelated to their victims. The authors concluded that nondomestic violence receives the same treatment as domestic violence. "If incarceration is used as a measure of disapproval, few ... violent acts in these data are strongly disapproved." Given the changes in arrest and prosecution policies, as well as the increased public pressure in the ten years since Ferraro and Boychuk conducted their study, it is just as likely that domestic assault and battery cases are being treated more seriously than nondomestic assault cases, even overzealously in some instances.

Social scientists can and should do much better; comparison studies like Ferraro and Boychuk's are not difficult, yet they are vital. At the same time, feminist activists should not claim that the criminal justice system treats domestic violence differently than other violent offenders until we have further proof. Criminalization rhetoric creates a powerful illusion that the system is "getting tough" on violent crime. But many violent offenders appear to be "getting off."

* * *

NOTES AND QUESTIONS

1. Hanna opens her article with a harrowing story of a woman killed by her abusive partner after multiple interventions by the criminal justice system:

In 1995, a Chicago district court judge allowed Samuel Gutierrez to enroll in a batterer treatment program in exchange for pleading guilty to choking his girlfriend Kelly Gonzalez. This was one of nine incidents of abuse documented by Chicago police reports.

Then, in August 1996, after failing to appear for a status hearing, the police again arrested Gutierrez for beating Gonzalez. Five days later, the judge imposed, then stayed, a 120-day sentence, again ordering Gutierrez to enroll in treatment. One month later, in September 1996, the same judge continued the case. For the third time, Gutierrez was told to get counseling or face jail. In February 1997, Kelly Gonzalez's body was found; Gutierrez admitted to killing and hiding her body back in September 1996. If Gutierrez is telling the truth, then he killed Gonzalez when he should have been in treatment.

Cheryl Hanna, *The Paradox of Hope: The Crime and Punishment of Domestic Violence,* 39 WM & MARY L. REV. 1505, 1505 (1998).

Hanna writes that: [t]he criminal justice system arguably "did the right thing" in this case. The defendant was arrested, prosecuted, and sentenced to a batterer treatment program intended to aid him in unlearning his violent behavior. A probation officer even followed up to ensure that Gutierrez met his conditions of release." Id. Do you agree that the criminal justice system's response to Gutierrez was appropriate? Was probation with counseling an appropriate sentence at his initial conviction, given the nine violent incidents documented by the Chicago police? Was it appropriate, at his second conviction, to suspend his sentence and again order him to enroll in treatment, when his prior referral to treatment had not prevented him from reoffending? When a month later he was still not enrolled in a treatment program, was it appropriate to offer him yet another warning, rather than revoking his probation and incarcerating him? This level of leniency in sentencing can only fuel suspicions that judges are either minimizing the seriousness of domestic violence offenses, or dramatically underestimating the danger posed by many domestic violence offenders. It seems further that treatment, under these circumstances, is imposed not because of any real hope that it will serve a rehabilitative function, but because it serves to legitimate the choice of probation over incarceration. Responding to these kinds of concerns, the National Council of Juvenile and Family Court Judges has recommended that: "[d]iversion should only occur in extraordinary cases, and then only after an admission before a judicial officer has been entered." Diversion is inappropriate, according to the Council, when "it is used as a calendar management tool, when first offenders are long term abusers, when the required treatment is only of brief duration and has not been monitored, and perhaps most important, when the use of diversion is perceived as a less than serious response to the crime."

2. Diversion of cases to treatment without either a guilty plea or a conviction raise even more concerns, because the only leverage the criminal justice system then has over the batterer is to threaten that the case will be prosecuted if he fails to comply with the terms of the diversion agreement. Too often that is an empty threat, and if the batterer then reoffends, there

is no prior conviction to alert the court that he has a history of abusive behavior. Proponents of pretrial diversion make two arguments: first, that diversion can provide the offender with speedy access to counseling, perhaps increasing the victim's safety, and second, that some victims may be more ready to cooperate in a process that (a) follows close on the heels of an abusive incident, and (b) will not leave the abuser with a criminal record. You read Naomi Cahn's report on one pretrial diversion program that attempts to strike a balance, not ruling out pretrial diversion altogether, but establishing strict eligibility guidelines to prevent abuse, on page 618, above.

3. In 1984, the Attorney General's Task Force on Family Violence threw its significant weight behind court-mandated batterers' treatment as an appropriate response to domestic violence crimes, except for the most serious. Whether that recommendation was sound remains an open question. The next set of materials address the history and content of batterers' treatment programs. Knowing what these programs purport to deliver is a precondition both to assessing their efficacy and to evaluating them as an alternative to other criminal justice responses. The next reading describes a variety of treatment approaches, and advocates for a treatment model that combines a feminist analysis of domestic violence with a social learning analysis of aggression.

Anne L. Ganley
Integrating Feminist and Social Learning Analyses of Aggression: Creating Multiple Models for Intervention with Men Who Batter; Treating Men Who Batter: Theory, Practice, and Programs 196, 198–99, 217, 223–24 (P.L. Caesar & L.K. Hamberger, eds. 1989)

Counseling as an Intervention for Domestic Violence

Counseling as a specific intervention for domestic violence is a relatively recent phenomenon. For years, counseling theories and practice ignored domestic violence. It was not discussed in the literature until 1964, when the intrapsychic theories viewed the violence merely as a symptom of individual pathology. Too often the domestic violence was considered a symptom of the victim's pathology ... rather than a symptom of the perpetrator's pathology. Within this violence-as-symptom perspective, therapeutic efforts were misdirected at "curing" the available patient (usually the victim) of a mental disorder, in the belief that the perpetrator's violence would then disappear. The next set of therapeutic interventions to emerge was a variation of the notion that violence is merely a symptom of something else. But this time the violence was considered a symptom of a dysfunctional relationship or family rather than of a dysfunctional individual. Although this shift in perspective was viewed as a major breakthrough, since it emphasized the current interactions of the family members rather than individual personalities, intrafamily and intrapsychic conceptualizations of violence actually have the same theoretical flaws.

Alternative frameworks for understanding the occurrence of domestic violence have been developed. These frameworks name the violence as the problem and not merely as a symptom.... Furthermore, they view domestic violence as a problem fostered by social norms and institutions.... Many interventions evolved from this reconceptualization, and they focus on different dimensions of domestic violence.... The interventions developed by battered women's programs in the United States and Canada emphasize the lethal nature of domestic violence. These programs concentrate on the priority of the victim's safety and her right to control her own life. In implementing these goals, many of these programs also address the social systems (law enforcement, the legal system, religious institutions) that perpetuate domestic violence. Other battered women's programs, some traditional mental health systems, and some men's programs focus on altering the violence of individual perpetrators of abuse, using a variety of techniques and approaches.... Research measuring the effectiveness of these and similar programs is appearing as they stabilize over time.

To be effective in ending domestic violence, we must be willing to struggle with the varying theoretical frameworks, not just for the sake of abstract debate, but for the sake of developing a consistent, reliable, comprehensive theory that will allow us to explain, predict, and eliminate violence within (as well as outside) families. As practitioners we must be willing to explicate our theoretical framework so that we do not use the right technique for the wrong reason or the wrong technique for the right reason. Either may result in partial success or partial failure, which sometimes is conveniently interpreted as the client's "resistance" or "not being ready for change" rather than as a failure in our assumptions and theoretical framework....

Advantages and Disadvantages of an Integration of Feminist and Social Learning Analyses

An integration of feminist and social learning analyses not only brings together two compatible theories but also magnifies the power of each to enhance our ability to bring about change in the lives of families. Both analyses consider the roles of gender, social systems, individual attributes, and family experiences in the development of human behavior. However, a feminist analysis of domestic violence focuses on the impact of crucial variables: gender, power, and social systems. A social learning analysis of domestic violence provides us with the details of how battering is acquired and how it can be changed. Specific aspects of the learning process for aggression are outlined, allowing us to separate the process into components that can be altered to facilitate change. A social analysis considers both the variables associated with learning the pattern and the variables associated with a person's willingness to perform aggression. It makes sense out of how individuals or families with seemingly similar characteristics or dynamics may or may not have domestic violence. A social learning analysis can account for an infinite variety of individuals and situations and still provide guidance for interventions at individual, family and societal levels. This allows us to develop interventions for a wide variety of individuals and communities, rather than forcing individuals or families to fit our theories.... Whereas a feminist analysis continually reminds us to work on a social as well as on an individual level, a social learning analysis meets the hallmark of a good theory. It does more than describe dynamics and make interesting interpretations; it allows us to make predictions of behavior based on guiding principles that have been well researched....

. . .

Assumptions of Intervention Models Based on these Analyses

. . .

6. In keeping with the definition of domestic violence as a pattern of control, the goals of intervention are to stop the battering behavior in all its forms and to realign relationships from being based on the abuse of power to being based on mutuality. This involves a process of empowering victims, as well as of changing perpetrators. When the perpetrator stops the battering, success is only partial and remains fragile unless he also is able to relate in noncoercive ways. This change may occur over a long period of time, with initial success being the end of the violent behavior, but long-term change involves a process where the perpetrator acknowledges his abusive history, demonstrates noncoercive patterns of interpersonal communication, and is able to self-reward these changes rather than depending solely on the reinforcement of others.

7. [In] interventions with perpetrators based on a feminist, social learning analysis, the role of the therapist in the counseling is multifaceted: directive confronter of old patterns, active model and teacher of new patterns, and positive reinforcer of new behaviors and values. All roles require a clear conceptual framework, good assessment skills, and a willingness to take responsibility for taking an active part in the change process. This is not the type of counseling for counselors who prefer merely facilitating a context for change or, as one therapist described his work, "being the one who merely creates the opportunity for the family to have the conversation." Such a stance may be therapeutic on some issues but not in cases of family violence. Such a passive or indirect role for the counselor seems to ignore the power of the violence and its embeddedness in individuals and our culture.

. . .

Perpetrator's Accountability

Just as victim safety and empowerment are the central intervention issues for victims, client accountability is the central intervention issue for perpetrators.... A feminist, social learning analysis of battering underscores the necessity for perpetrators to become responsible for their own behaviors. Otherwise, change will not occur. For progress to be made, they must be aware of what they are doing, see it as something under their control, and use their own cognitions as regulators of their abuse. In the face of the minimization, denial, and victim blaming perpetuated by both the individuals and society, perpetrator accountability involves a process extending throughout and following the counseling intervention. Specialized programs implement this by a series of strategies: clear statements of personal responsibility for the battering, consequences for relapses, and accountability for participation in the program (attendance, homework); and avoidance of protecting perpetrators from the negative consequences of their behavior (jail, divorce, limited custody of children). Such programs often encourage the criminal justice system, family, friends, and others to hold the perpetrator accountable for his behavior. For too long, the victims have been held accountable for the perpetrator's behavior, while the perpetrator's accountability has been ignored. In doing so, social systems have colluded with the perpetrator's violence. Although it is appropriate to hold victims accountable for their own behavior, it must be done in a way that gives full recognition to the context of the power imbalance between perpetrator and victim, as well as between men and women in society. Victims have power, but within a battering relationship and within patriarchy, their power and accountability is relative rather than absolute. The perpetrator's accountability is the key to changing his behavior.

* * *

NOTE

1. Hanna notes that "most court-ordered treatment programs today treat only men," because of the extent to which couples therapy in the context of domestic violence has been "discredited." Similarly, she notes that "[m]ental health programs that focus on psychotherapy, stress management, anger control, and conflict resolution," criticized by feminists as inattentive to the gender dynamics at work in abusive relationships, "are also becoming less common." The dominant paradigm in court-ordered programs is the pro-feminist model, as practiced in Duluth Minnesota, and elsewhere:

> The Duluth model philosophy is: "Batterers, like those who intervene to help them, have been immersed in a culture that supports relationships of dominance. This cultural acceptance of dominance is rooted in the assumption that, based on differences, some people have the legitimate right to master others." The curriculum uses an educational and counseling approach, as opposed to anger-control intervention. It focuses on the use of violence by the batterer to establish power and control over his partner. Men meet in weekly groups run by a facilitator. The facilitator is not necessarily a mental health professional but is a trained lay person. Participants engage in exercises geared towards confronting their violent behavior. For example, each participant maintains a "control log" or diary that identifies their abusive behavior. Role plays based on individual experiences are used to build nonviolent skills. Videotapes, such as Profile of an Assailant, are shown to prompt discussion. Skills such as taking timeouts and recognizing women's anger are also taught. Most of these exercises preclude discussion of the particular relationship, instead focusing on the underlying issues of power and control.
>
> EMERGE in Boston is another popular feminist-inspired treatment model. The program considers itself a "collective" of men work-

ing to end violence against women. Although trained counselors run the program, sessions are conducted as supervised self-help groups. EMERGE considers itself to be part of a movement organizing men to challenge sexism in society. Battered women's shelters established other programs, like the House of Ruth in Baltimore and the Domestic Violence Project in Ann Arbor, Michigan. Shelter staff attempt to monitor both sides of the relationship and oversee both parties involved. Most programs charge the abuser a fee; many will not accept an abuser into their program unless he pleads guilty and acknowledges the underlying abusive behavior.

Cheryl Hanna, *The Paradox of Hope: The Crime and Punishment of Domestic Violence,* 39 WM & MARY L. REV. 1505, 1528–30 (1998).

The collection of techniques, including stress management and anger control, that often go by the name of "cognitive-behavioral approaches," are not necessarily incompatible with a pro-feminist analysis of domestic violence, and themselves derive from the social learning theory extolled by Ganley in the prior reading. This next excerpt provides the flavor of the cognitive-behavioral approach to treatment for batterers.

L. Kevin Hamberger and Jeffrey M. Lohr Proximal Causes of Spouse Abuse: A Theoretical Analysis for Cognitive-Behavioral Interventions; Treating Men Who Batter: Theory, Practice, and Programs 53, 57–58, 63–67, 69–71 (P.L. Caesar & L.K. Hamberger, eds. 1989)

Components of Battering

The physical contact and verbal attack of spouse abuse both involve the psychological functions of intent and consequence.... Although physical acts have the effect of compromising the health and safety of the victim, they may also result in other rewarding consequences for the perpetrator.... It can also be assumed that the behavior has been acquired because it has consistent effects and/or because it has been modeled by significant others in the past. Once learned, it may be precipitated and performed because of motivational states such as anger, fear and jealousy.

Nonphysical aspects of abuse, such as threats and disparagement, may also accompany physical violence.... Through learning, these nonphysical forms of abuse come to elicit similar types of emotional and physical responses in the victim and thus reduce the necessity of further violence. As a result, threatening words or gestures acquire punitive, controlling and dominating functions. These functions are acquired through *prior* association of the words, gestures, and so forth, with actual violence and terror, as well as through their prior association with *other* language processes associated with highly negative meaning (i.e. terror and violence).

The ability of language to control the behavior of another human being (in a battering relationship) has direct implications for the health and well-being of the victim.... The overt behaviors, with their direct effects of pain and terror, function as unconditioned stimuli for the victim. The symbolic behaviors acquire conditioned (aversive) stimulus properties and function through their association with actual aggression. We believe that an analysis of both acquired language functions (including covert language) and overt behavior patterns in battering offers a useful model for conceptualizing and intervening into battering behavior.

Cognitive-Behavioral Analysis

The interventions that follow from such an analysis have been called "cognitive-behavioral." They are behavioral in that they are structured and emphasize alteration of *functional* (intentional and consequential) aspects of behavior. They are also cognitive in that they focus upon the verbal-symbolic mediators of the battering behavior. The theory from which such procedures derive is generally known as "social learning" theory....

Language Control of Behavior

. . .

Language-Cognitive Repertoire. It is language that enables a person to communicate, reason, solve problems, plan, interpret information, and so on. The language-cognitive repertoire constitutes the knowledge that the person has. Such a repertoire also allows the person to predict events and to respond by reasoning and problem solving. Three factors are generally involved in such processes. The first is the manner in which things and events are labeled. The second involves the sequencing and organization of the labels employed. Lastly, an overt act is elicited in order to influence events, and it too is represented by verbal processes. The language-cognitive repertoire provides a means of explaining the way in which language processes maintain behavior such as battering.

Labeling repertoires are learned, beginning with concrete objects or classes of objects, proceeding to more complex labeling processes, and giving rise to grammatical classes. One example of complex labeling repertoires is social and self-labeling. Complex combinations of stimuli are labeled as anger, boredom, acting suspicious, or "whoring around." Labeling processes also have important implications for effective reasoning and problem solving. The emotional valence of the labels that are used may affect reasoning. The reasoning process is likely to be adversely affected according to the degree to which such labels are inaccurate and elicit highly negative or positive emotional responses. Adaptive behavior may be interfered with, and/or maladaptive behavior may be elicited.

The initial labeling of a stimulus situation often elicits a sequence of additional verbal responses. In this way, labels for one's own behavior function as stimuli for other behavior. The particular word association sequence elicited by a label is idiosyncratic to the person, based on his or her unique learning history. To the degree that the word association sequence is consistent with the observed events, the associated reasoning and problem solving will be facilitated. Further, if overt behavior is the end point of the reasoning, then the behavior may be appropriate or inappropriate, depending on the consistency of the reasoning sequence in relation to the actual events. In the case of battering, we suggest that the reasoning sequence is usually not consistent with respect to actual events. The basis of such faulty reasoning or problem solving can often be found in deficient labeling. For example, in the case of the female spouse coming home late, an objective event ("My spouse is late") is inappropriately labeled as "bad." The word "bad" will, in turn, elicit a negative emotional response, along with an associated verbal reasoning sequence that suggests the following train of thought: "Only loose women are out late by themselves at night" (an inaccurate premise). "My wife is late. Therefore she must be whoring around" (an inaccurate conclusion). "I'm going to have to punish and control her" (an inappropriate self-produced instruction). The likely consequence of such reasoning, then, is overt violence, verbal assault, and/or physical assault.

Language-cognitive repertoires also account for defense mechanisms observed in male batterers. For example, if the batterer minimizes his violence by labeling a fight with his wife a "slight" or "a little disagreement," he experiences much less of a negative emotional response than if he labeled his violence as "a beating" or "attempted murder." Furthermore, if the batterer considers his behavior to be under the control of his partner's actions (e.g., "If you wouldn't mess around on me, I wouldn't have to hit you"), he may further reduce his anxiety and guilt after severely beating his wife. Such verbal-cognitive constructions can also serve as reasons or justifications (excuses) for engaging in otherwise inappropriate behavior. If the batterer mislabels reality by such defensive statements, he effectively prevents the internalization of appropriate social disapproval and personal aversive consequences that might otherwise modify the problematic behavior. In this manner, the batterer contributes to his own psychological isolation—a common phenomenon observed by those who work with batterers.

Self-Control of Battering Behavior Through Language Mechanisms

One very important implication of the above discussion is that although battering may *appear* to represent a "loss of control" over "impulses," the above analysis would suggest otherwise. Indeed, by using the concept of basic behavioral repertoires, battering behavior can be clearly seen as purposeful, goal-directed, and self-produced patterns of behavior that are under the control of the batterer. Paradoxical as it may appear, the batterer not only is engaging in the control of another human being, but also is exercising a form of self-control in terms of the strategies he *decides* to use, as well as the problem-solving processes he engages in to select and execute a particular strategy. This conceptualization is consistent with profeminist theory about the purposeful nature of battering behavior.... Clinically, it is typical to observe a batterer explain a slap or a punch as a result of having "lost control." When challenged to explain why, in his state of discontrol, he did not maim or kill his partner, the batterer may explain that he had no intention (rule or strategy) of hurting her that badly.

It should be noted, in contrast, that there may exist specific deficits in basic behavioral repertoires of the batterer that also increase the probability of continued battering behavior. In studying children, for example, Camp (1977) has described what appears to be a deficiency in aggressive boys to produce nonaggressive verbal mediators or to control aggressive verbal mediators. Such boys were less likely than nonaggressive boys to tell themselves to go slowly when performing certain tasks and hence made more errors. Moreover, experimental evidence suggests that verbal stimuli can acquire the ability to direct and control such behavior.... It could be that batterers exhibit similar deficits—inaccurate labeling tendencies (i.e. they see everything as a threat) and inappropriate problem-solving strategies—in their intimate relationships and more general attitudes toward women.

Moreover, ... the ability to use self-produced verbal processes to solve problems may be related to the level of intensity of negative emotional arousal (i.e., how upset one is) in the problematic situation. The more upset one is, the less efficient and appropriate will be one's own behavior. Rosenbaum and O'Leary (1981), for example, have found that batterers are less assertive than nonbatterers. Hence, intense emotional arousal, in combination with threat-oriented labeling, maladaptive problem solving, and nonviolent skills deficits, may culminate in aggressive and assaultive behavior when other behaviors are unavailable. It should also be pointed out, however, that it is not necessary to assume that batterers uniformly exhibit skills deficits. Batterers are not constantly violent and in many situations may not be violent at all....

Treatment Implications

The therapeutic task is to assess the interaction of the various response components and to determine how they lead to battering for each individual batterer. Such an evaluation involves the identification and differentiation of response-initiating variables from response-maintaining variables.... It is with such an evaluation that precise targeting of verbal-behavioral and language-cognitive production deficits and of overt behavioral deficits and excesses can be accomplished prior to intervention....

... It is not necessary to assume that cognitive factors are either the starting point or the most influential factors in any given battering incident. However, knowledge of cognitive components and processes allow us to understand the following aspects of battering behavior. First, battering is self-produced behavior. It is neither necessary not sufficient to point to an objective, external "triggering stimulus" as a "cause" of battering.... [W]e can understand battering on the basis of unique, *learned* patterns of self-produced self-talk, overt behavior, and physiological arousal of the individual batterer, even in the absence of external variables. As such, the individual batterer is clearly responsible for his own behavior. Furthermore, he is assessed to be capable of and responsible for learning new, nonviolent behavior patterns. Simply put, nobody "made" him batter, and only he can change his behavior.

An important advantage of the present analysis is that specific direction is provided for assessment and intervention strategies. Moreover, the attention given to the multiple components of battering behavior by a cognitive-behavioral approach facilitates a flexible intervention approach based on the identification of individual abusive patterns. While the goal of all intervention is to eliminate all forms of battering behavior, the specific mechanism of such change may differ between batterers, even within the same structured treatment group.

There are some pitfalls of this approach that warrant discussion. One major disadvantage ... involves a temptation to emphasize self-talk to the detriment of attention to battering behavior. This undermines the very accomplishment that cognitive-behavioral theories have achieved in facilitating understanding of human behavior, that is, that emotions and behaviors are affected and mediated by cognitive processes. There is a tendency to focus on dysfunctional attitudes, irrational beliefs, and faulty self-statements while spending relatively little time and effort on modifying battering behavior. Although expending therapeutic effort on the cognitive components of battering behavior is important, such targets may not always be the most salient *unless,* through careful assessment, they are causally linked to the initiation and/or to the maintenance of battering behaviors (and the context in which they occur)....

The second weakness of the cognitive-behavioral model is in viewing battering as solely a problem of anger or stress management. Intervention approaches have been developed to assist with problems such as anxiety ..., depression ..., stress ... and pain ..., and anger.... Cognitive-behavioral approaches to the treatment of batterers have borrowed heavily from these systems and thus run the risk of (1) stereotyping all batterers as anger prone or "under stress" and (2) attempting to focus treatment exclusively on managing anger and/or stress.... [N]ot all batterers can be characterized as having problems with anger management. Similarly, "stress" has not been found to be differentially characteristic of batterers versus other populations. Anger management or other types of "stress management" may be seen as components of batterer treatment programs but should not comprise the entire program format, not should they be the only goals.

* * *

NOTES

1. A criticism often leveled at sentencing practices in the past was that when defendants appeared to have substance abuse problems, judges frequently assigned them to treatment programs addressing these problems rather than their abusive behavior. The misguided premise behind such dispositions was that the violence was a product of the drinking or the drugs, rather than the drinking or drugs being an accompaniment to or occasionally a facilitator of that violence, but not its root cause. On the other hand, it is unlikely that a perpetrator will be able to take advantage of a batterers' treatment program unless his substance abuse is being or

has been addressed. Many batterers' treatment programs make it a condition of enrollment that a batterer be able to show that he has no such problem, or that he is in treatment for it. Today it is more common for substance-abusing perpetrators of domestic violence to be assigned by courts simultaneously to drug or alcohol treatment and to batterers' treatment, where both resources are available.

A recent study conducted in the Dade County Domestic Violence Court has provided valuable data about the relationship between domestic violence and substance abuse, and some especially interesting data about men who have benefited from a new "integrated" approach merging substance abuse and batterer treatment:

Methods

The two-phase project took place in the specialized treatment-oriented Dade County (Florida) Domestic Violence Court. The baseline study included a review of misdemeanor cases processed in the court for a 1–year period prior to the availability of integrated batterer/substance abuse treatment.

In the experiment, misdemeanor divertees and probationers ordered to treatment for both substance abuse and battering between early June 1994 and late February 1995 were randomly assigned to either the regular dual treatment process (n=140) or the new integrated treatment program (n=210). The progress of individuals in both groups was observed for 7 months to determine treatment status and to chart reinvolvement in the criminal and civil justice systems.

Findings

Among the findings in the baseline study of immediate relevance to the followup treatment experiment were the following:

- Roughly half of misdemeanor defendants in entering cases were involved in the abuse of alcohol and/or other drugs. However, fewer than half of the defendants so involved were processed into substance abuse treatment. Many of the cases with drug or alcohol involvement were dismissed or "no-actioned."
- Slightly more than half of the defendants were diverted or placed on probation. Nearly all divertees and probationers were assigned to domestic violence treatment; about two fifths were also assigned to substance abuse evaluation and/or treatment.
- Large numbers of divertees and probationers assigned to treatment failed to appear at treatment programs.
- Higher rearrest rates were found among divertees and probationers who were not admitted to treatment. Rates of rearrest were lower for those who were admitted and "continued in process."
- Higher treatment drop-out rates were found among those substance abuse-involved divertees and probationers who were assigned to batterer treatment and substance abuse treatment in separate programs than among those assigned to batterer programs only.

The treatment experiment yielded three statistically significant findings:

- The integrated treatment approach was far more successful than the dual process in getting divertees and probationers to begin treatment (43 percent of the dual program participants never showed up for treatment after intake compared to 13 percent of the integrated program participants).
- The integrated approach was more successful than the dual process at keeping participants in treatment (median of 160 days compared to 99).
- During the 7–month followup, participants in the integrated treatment program were rearrested for same-victim domestic violence offenses at less than half the rate of those assigned to dual programs (6 percent vs. 14 percent).

John S. Goldkamp, with Doris Weiland, Mark Collins and Michael White, *Selected Findings and Implications Drawn From: The Role of Drug and Alcohol Abuse in Domestic Violence and Its Treatment: Dade County's Domestic Violence Court Experiment*, LEGAL INTERVENTIONS IN FAMILY VIOLENCE: RESEARCH FINDINGS AND POLICY IMPLICATIONS 74–75 (National Institute of Justice Research Report, July 1998).

2. Regardless of whether a batterer's intervention program emphasizes the profeminist approach to treatment exemplified by the Duluth and EMERGE programs, the cognitive-behavioral approach described in the prior reading, or a blend of the two, a separate question that arises is the suitability of treatment programs for men from different racial or cultural backgrounds. Fernando Mederos, a founder of "Common Purpose," another Boston-based batterers' treatment organization, is working to develop "culturally competent" curricula for men of color. The next reading summarizes his approach to these issues of cultural difference.

Fernando Mederos
Domestic Violence and Culture: Moving Toward More Sophisticated Encounters, 1–3, 7 (unpublished paper, 1998)

Cultural Filters and Misunderstandings

Men of color who are physically abusive frequently use their native culture as an excuse: "Where I come from everybody does it." "It's just about being a man. This is normal." "All men from (back home) beat their wives." Instead of denying their behavior, they say that their partner was disrespectful, that she argued or yelled or that she refused to do what he told her to do. Faced with these ... "scripts" European Americans often feel hopeless: What can you do with people who think it's acceptable to be violent? They also end up feeling that men of color who use these "scripts" are more violent or pathological and have less hope of changing. This causes people in the judicial system either to have lower expectations with men of color—people often back off (why bother?)—or they throw the book at these men.

What is happening in these encounters? Two factors to think about:

1. There is a universal tendency to think that "Other people are more violent—it's in their blood or their culture." When this is applied to physically abusive men, it translates into, "Our batterers are deviants, theirs are in their cultural mainstream." In reality, all cultures have ways of giving people permission to be violent. In fact, there are very high rates of perpetration of violence by men against women in mainstream Anglo culture....

2. The other element that may be behind these encounters stems from the difference in the "scripts" used by some men of color and by European American men. In general, the lopsided levels of violence by men against women that appear in many cultures are an expression of different forms of male dominance or systems of male supremacy. However, these systems change over time and are manifested in different ways. In mainstream European American culture, there is a covert or surreptitious system of male supremacy that underlies much of Anglo batterers' behavior. In mainstream Anglo culture, men do not make direct claims for women's or spouses' obedience, but they tend to react strongly when a woman does not meet their expectations. They may expect women to provide emotional caretaking, to be compliant in a lot of ways, and to do much unpaid labor in the home, and they may also expect to have a final say in many matters. Yet not many European American men directly say that their partners **have** to obey or do whatever he wants. In covert systems of male supremacy, physically abusive men tend to deny or minimize their violent behavior, claim they lost control or say their partner pushed them into it. They also engage in victim-blaming: they dwell on some instance of disappointing or hurtful behavior by their spouse as the "real" problem and the reason for their violent conduct. They also claim that their physical abuse is of no importance when compared to their spouse's transgression as if a person had to earn the right to be nonviolent. In effect, when there is a covert or veiled pattern of male supremacy, physically abusive men do not take direct responsibility for their behavior or claim they have a right to control their spouses, but their conduct has a powerful controlling and inhibiting effect nevertheless.

Also, when there is a covert system of male supremacy, as in European American society, it does not mean that men are less violent or that they use less violence or other forms of control and abuse with women. However, it is easy to believe that men who use the European American script or system of justifications are less violent—after all, they are more invested in concealing their controlling and violent behaviors or in justifying their violence as exceptional, provoked outbursts.

On the other hand, men who are imbedded in overt or direct systems of male supremacy openly expect women to subordinate themselves. They have a very strong, if not rigid, notion of gender roles and of women's position as housewives, mothers or sexualized objects who are expected to be compliant or yielding in many ways. In direct systems of male supremacy, simple disagreement by a woman may be seen as disrespectful, and if she begins a direct conflict, she may be seen as a rebellious bad wife who has turned her back on her culture and is trying to destroy her family. Women who are imbedded in a system of direct male supremacy may take longer to assert their rights when they are being battered but may feel quite determined when they take a step; they may also face enormous opposition from their families and from their communities.

Men who are from cultures where there is an overt system of male supremacy may not be more violent or less prone to change that those who grew up with a covert system. They talk about violence toward spouses in a different way, but what they do does not differ much from what Anglos do. In fact, if we take Hispanics as one example of a group where male supremacy is more directly accepted, a recently carried out national survey ... indicates that on the aggregate Hispanic men are no more violent than Anglos—there are no significant differences in the two groups. Also direct systems of male supremacy often go along with a strong sense of obligation to the family: part of "machismo," the Hispanic ideal of male supremacy, is a very strong sense of the man's duty to support his family. To fail to support one's family is to fail as a man. Finally, it is important not to confuse an overt or direct system of male supremacy with permission to be violent: men may have a "right" to subordinate their spouses, but resorting to violence is a separate matter....

Don't Misinterpret Men of Color Based on What They Say.

It is more useful to direct your attention to their level of violence (frequency, history, level of injury, impact on spouse and children and so on). This is the best indicator of dangerousness and potential to change.

. . .

Avoid Becoming Paralyzed by Fear of Destroying Someone's Culture.

Physically abusive men of color often claim that those who confront them are trying to destroy their culture or deprive them of their manhood. This is no more true for them than it is for European American offenders; to challenge someone's abusive behavior is not to destroy their culture. Instead, you can say (just as we do with Anglo batterers) that violence and abuse are never justified, and there is no way of getting off the hook about this issue. This is a legitimate cross-cultural or universal value.

. . .

Some Final Points About Culture and Domestic Violence:

... [T]here is a danger that this extended discussion of culture and domestic violence emphasizes only the parts of European American and other cultures which give people permission to be violent or encourage them to tolerate violence. This perspective pathologizes culture in general .. It is profoundly inaccurate. The reality is that all cultures have elements—values and traditions—which are protective against the use of violence and which offenders can use to shape a non-abusive identity. In European American culture, batterer intervention programs use the ideal of equality—a resonant, if not perfectly practiced value—to help men shape their change process. In Hispanic culture, the corresponding value is respect (respeto) which is also a highly resonant and not always practiced ideal.

Above all, culture is a source of healing and strength for people.

* * *

NOTE

1. Just as batterers' intervention programs have tended to overlook issues of racial or cultural difference among batterers, offering a standard curriculum no matter what the cultural context of participants, so too have they overlooked research distinguishing among "types" of batterer, even though research results strongly suggest that not all batterers will be equally amenable to treatment. One of the ways we might in the future use this research is as a basis for screening, to support the incarceration of men unlikely to benefit from treatment, and to safeguard limited and valuable treatment resources for those best able to utilize them. Under the Violence Against Women Act, both the Vermont Department of Corrections and the Colorado Office of Probation Services have received grants to research the development of risk assessment instruments for use in this context.

Unessentializing Men Who Batter
Cheryl Hanna, The Paradox of Hope: The Crime and Punishment of Domestic Violence, 39 William and Mary Law Review 1505, 1563–66 (1998)

Some of the most promising domestic violence research attempts to differentiate among batterers. Different "types" of batterers emerge from a synthesis of this research. Amy Holtzworth–Monroe and Gregory Stuart recently reviewed nineteen studies on typologies and identified three subtypes of abusive men: family-only batterers; borderline batterers; and generally violent/antisocial batterers. I rely primarily on the categories hypothesized by Holtzworth–Monroe and Stuart, but also integrate the research of Edward Gondolf, Donald Dutton, and others. Emerging typologies among different researchers are surprisingly similar: differences lie more in terminology than in concept. Family-only batterers constitute approximately fifty percent of all batterer samples. These men tend to engage in the least severe marital violence, psychological and sexual abuse. Family-only batterers are less impulsive, less likely to use weapons, and more likely to be apologetic after abusive incidents. These men may be the most deterred by the threat of criminal sanctions and the most treatable because of their ability to function normally outside of their relationships.

Borderline batterers constitute approximately twenty-five percent of batterer samples. These men tend to "engage in moderate to severe abuse, including psychological and sexual abuse." Their violence generally is confined to the family, but not always. They may evince borderline personality characteristics and may have problems associated with drugs and alcohol. Batterer treatment, as it is currently structured, is likely to be insufficient to change their behavior because many men in this group may need more intensive treatment.

Generally violent or antisocial batterers engage in moderate to severe violence, including psychological and sexual abuse. Edward Gondolf terms these batterers sociopathic. It is estimated that this group constitutes twenty-five percent of batterer samples. Uniformly, studies have found that generally violent men engage in more severe family violence than family-only men. This finding challenges the myth that abusers are only violent against family members. Generally violent batterers often have extensive criminal histories, including property, drug or alcohol offenses, and violence crimes against nonfamily victims. These men are the most impulsive, the most likely to use weapons, and feel the least amount of empathy towards their victims. Batterer treatment programs for this group are inappropriate given the high degree of danger they pose. Arguably, sociopathic batterers may be untreatable, and, in many cases, ought to be incarcerated if only to protect their potential victims.

All abusive men are not equally dangerous. Some men are frequent and severe batterers; others are not. Dr. Donald Dutton ... focuses his research on personality traits of abusive men. He distinguishes "cyclical" batterers from men who may occasionally be aggressive in their relationships, "like the distinction between a single fender bender and continual head-on collisions." Cyclical batterers constitute a subgroup of men who are violent only in their intimate relationships....

Dutton's distinction between men who are chronically abusive and those who are not has important implications for prosecutorial and sentencing decisions.... [T]he criminal justice system ought to be cautious before treating every man who engages in intimate violence as a high-risk offender. In fact, Dutton's research suggests that we may be able to identify and focus limited resources on the chronically abusive, similar to other crime control strategies that target career criminals rather than petty offenders.

* * *

NOTE

1. *Does Treatment Work?* Judicial enthusiasm for mandated batterers' treatment as a "sanction" for domestic violence is not based on any reliable findings that treatment effectively rehabilitates batterers or deters them from future violence. The studies that have been reported are plagued by methodological problems. They are generally based on very small samples. They do not randomly assign batterers to incarceration, treatment, or probation without treatment, so that the impact of treatment can be compared with the impact of alternative dispositions. Usually the men studied have all been court-mandated to attend treatment, so that the studies do not distinguish between the initial impact of legal intervention and the impact of treatment. Other variables in the participants' lives are not controlled for, so that it remains unclear what role treatment plays

compared to external factors such as social stigma, or support from one's partner, to name just two important variables. Treatment modalities vary (in content, format and length), making it impossible to generalize across programs. Finally, none of the studies are sophisticated enough to explore whether some treatment modalities are effective with some types of abuser, if not with all. For an indepth analysis of these methodological issues, see Barry D. Rosenfeld, *Court-Ordered Treatment of Spouse Abuse*, 12 CLIN. PSYCH. REV. 205 (1992). For examples of reported studies see, e.g., Melanie Shepard, *Predicting Batterer Recidivism Five Years After Community Intervention*, 7 J. FAM VIOLENCE 167 (1992); Jeffrey L Edleson & Maryann Syers, *Relative Effectiveness of Group Treatments of Men Who Batter*, SOC. WORK RESEARCH & ABSTRACTS 16 (June 1990); Huey-tsyh Chen et al., *Evaluating the Effectiveness of a Court Sponsored Abuser Treatment Program*, 4 J. FAM. VIOLENCE 309 (1989); Jeffrey L. Edleson & Roger J. Grusznski, *Treating Men Who Batter: Four Years of Outcome Data from the Domestic Abuse Project*, 12 J. SOC. SERVICE RES. 3 (1988); Donald D. Dutton, *The Outcome of Court–Mandated Treatment for Wife Assault: A Quasi–Experimental Evaluation*, 1 VIOLENCE & VICTIMS 163 (1986).

Some of the available data suggests that treatment reduces physical violence, although in many cases it neither terminates it, nor affects alternative non-physical forms of abuse. Other studies show equal rates of recidivism between men arrested and treated, and men arrested but not referred to treatment. Others find no significant difference in recidivism between men who complete a course of treatment, and men who drop out. Clearly, treatment does not work for everyone, recidivism rates among men who complete a course of treatment have varied, in some of the studies cited above, from 54% within six months, to 10% over fourteen months, to 30% in the course of a year, to 40% over a five year period.

There is room for hope that batterers' treatment will increase in sophistication and effectiveness over the next decade, and that additional research will both guide those efforts and yield more reliable data to guide the criminal justice system in its use of treatment as a sentencing option. In the meantime, it also seems clear that courts should be somewhat more cautious in mandating treatment, and somewhat more willing to use other sanctions, up to and including incarceration; putting pressure on prosecutors and probation departments to sort defendants appropriately.

In the next reading, the authors look ahead to predict how sanctions will be deployed in domestic violence cases in the future.

David A. Ford, Ruth Reichard, Stephen Goldsmith and Mary Jean Regoli
Future Directions for Criminal Justice Policy on Domestic Violence; Do Arrests and Restraining Orders Work? 243, 258–61 (E.S. Buzawa and C.G. Buzawa, eds. 1996)

Incarceration is the one sentence clearly conveying the seriousness of wife battering as a criminal offense. But, for a variety of reasons, including jail and prison overcrowding, the relative ineffectiveness of incarceration for preventing further violence, and victim reluctance to have their batterers incarcerated, judges will impose alternative sanctions. . . .

Jails and prisons . . . will be used selectively and in innovative ways as the final stages in a series of graduated sanctions to deal with wife batterers on the basis of seriousness and nature of the current charge and on the prior record and present circumstances of the offender. Incarceration will figure in future wife-battery policy primarily at the pretrial stage to protect victims, as a coercive trial outcome threatened to ensure other sanctions are fulfilled, and as a response to violations of other sanctions imposed.

Probation

After conviction, corrections will be used in a variety of ways to ensure the success of less intrusive sanctions. The most prevalent will be the use of suspended sentences in which prison terms are assessed but then suspended as long as the offender successfully completes other conditions, such as committing no further violence, paying fines and restitution to the victim, performing community service work, or completing a treatment program. Offenders with a prior record of violence or probation violations or who had trouble keeping conditions of pretrial release may be given split sentences involving a probation term preceded by a short term of incarceration to serve as a reminder to the offender of the consequences of not abiding by the conditions of probation. The incarceration term may be served all at once or intermittently, as on successive weekends, evenings, or vacations. In the future, this short jail term may be served at halfway houses for batterers where group or individual counseling can be combined with incapacitation.

Future policy will also employ corrections within the community in "intensive supervision probation" programs. Intensive supervision will provide more stringent control than usually experienced by men on probation. It allows offenders to maintain employment to pay child support and victim restitution, but still provides a substantial degree of security for the victim. Current programs usually involve some form of curfew or house arrest, with offenders being allowed to leave their homes for such purposes as work, school, community service work, probation and counseling sessions, and religious services. Future restraints on the offender's movements will be enforced by frequent contact with a probation officer and may be enhanced by some type of passive or active electronic monitoring device.

. . .

Home Detention

The improvement and expansion of electronic monitoring technology may provide the greatest security short of incarceration for victims who face continual threats of violence after separating from their offenders. A central computer stores information on the restrictions to movement for each offender. "Passive" electronic devices do not provide constant monitoring, but rather the computer generates random calls to offenders who must verify their presence through voice identification, via a video image, or by inserting a wristlet into a verification box attached to the telephone. "Active" electronic devices involve placing a transmitter on the ankle, waist, wrist, or neck of the offender. If the offender is not within a 150–foot radius of a receiving device in the home at scheduled times, the probation office is notified.... These technologies will be replaced by continuous-monitoring, satellite tracking systems so that victims can be equipped with portable receivers to detect the presence of a transmitter worn by the batterer anywhere. Victims would be instructed on appropriate measures to take if the signal indicated the batterer was within a certain distance. If necessary, the alarm will not only alert police but also locate the victim and offender anywhere in the nation. This sort of sophisticated electronic monitoring of domestic violence offenders will become commonplace with reduced costs, with the proliferation of antistalking laws, and with the shortage of prison space.

Straight prison terms will be reserved for felony battery cases and more serious misdemeanor charges, especially those involving repeat offenders. Special prison programs for violent offenders, including wife batterers, will be developed as effective rehabilitative strategies are identified. These would be therapeutic communities within the prison but with ties to outside social services and perhaps using former batterers as peer counselors.

* * *

NOTES AND QUESTIONS

1. Do you think it is significant that the authors do not identify prosecutorial and judicial attitudes towards domestic violence as a "lesser" crime among the reasons why incarceration is rare? Does this omission undermine your confidence in the remainder of their predictions? How, specifically?

2. Electronic monitoring raises the specter of the state as an Orwelllian "big brother." Is this a fair criticism, or are your concerns about the intrusiveness of monitoring mitigated by the fact that monitoring may be offered to convicted offenders, and accepted by them, as an alternative to incarceration. Is traditional incarceration more or less intrusive than some or all of the alternatives spelled out by the authors?

3. The authors mention pretrial detention as one way in which incarceration will be used in the future to protect victim safety. For a more thorough look at current practice, see Section E, below, where pretrial detention is discussed in the context of stalking.

4. On September 30, 1996, as an amendment to the Crime Control Act of 1968, President Clinton signed the Lautenberg Amendment into law. The Amendment provides that: "[i]t shall be unlawful for any person ... who has been convicted in any court of a misdemeanor crime of domestic violence, to ship or transport in interstate or foreign commerce, or possess in or affecting commerce, any firearm or ammunition; or to receive any

firearm or ammunition which has been shipped or transported in interstate or foreign commerce.'' 18 U.S.C. § 922(g)(9) (Supp. III 1997). The logic of the Amendment, as articulated by its sponsor, is that: ''[d]omestic violence, no matter how it is labeled, leads to more domestic violence, and guns in the hands of convicted wife beaters leads to death.'' 142 Cong. Rec. S10378 (1996) (statement of Sen. Lautenberg).

Under the Amendment an automatic sanction attaching to all domestic violence misdemeanor convictions is therefore the requirement that the offender surrender all firearms, and presumably his license to carry arms, since the ban is permanent. The offender does not have to be charged with a crime specifically defined as a domestic violence offense; it is enough that the crime occur in a domestic violence context. This was made clear in a letter distributed by the Bureau of Alcohol, Tobacco and Firearms following the enactment of the Amendment. Department of the Treasury, Bureau of Alcohol, Tobacco and Firearms, Open Letter to All State and Local Law Enforcement Officials (last modified Feb. 27, 1998). This was the first time in the history of Congressional gun control legislation that no exemption was provided for police, military personnel, or government officials.

The impact on offenders whose employment depends on their ability to carry a firearm has been one rallying point for critics. Others have sought, unsuccessfully, to challenge the legislation as an unconstitutional exercise of power under the Commerce Clause, on the basis of United States v. Lopez, 514 U.S. 549 (1995). See, e.g., National Association of Government Employees, Inc. v. Barrett, 968 F. Supp. 1564 (N.D. Ga. 1997); Fraternal Order of Police v. United States, 981 F.Supp. (D.D.C. 1997). For a further discussion of Lopez, and its impact on the criminal provisions of VAWA, see Section F, below. Yet others have challenged the provision on equal protection grounds, arguing that domestic violence misdemeanants should not be singled out for harsher treatment, when others convicted of violent crime do not permanently forfeit their rights to possess firearms. In the Eighth Circuit the appellant argued that strict scrutiny should be applied, because his constitutional right to bear arms was infringed by the provision. The court dismissed this argument, and held that under a rational basis standard of review the provision passed constitutional muster. United States v. Smith, 171 F.3d 617 (8th Cir. 1999). The Seventh Circuit reached a similar decision in United States v. Lewitzke, 176 F.3d 1022 (7th Cir. 1999), finding that it was not irrational for Congress to conclude that domestic violence offenders ''pose the most acute danger of turning a gun on a family member.''

The most serious constitutional challenge to the legislation has been that, as written, it applies not only to those convicted of domestic violence misdemeanors after the passage of the Amendment, but arguably also to anyone convicted of such a crime in the past, in violation of the Ex Post Facto Clause of the Constitution. U.S, Const. art. 1, §§ 9, 10. The Supreme Court has consistently applied that Clause to invalidate laws that retroactively alter the definition of a crime or increase the punishment after the act has been committed, and laws that punish as a crime an act previously innocent when committed.

Courts asked to analyze the Lautenberg Amendment have held that it is not retroactive, basing their conclusion on the Second Circuit's decision in United States v. Brady, 26 F.3d 282 (2d Cir. 1994), with respect to a new federal law prohibiting the possession of firearms by felons. In that context the court had held that:

> Regardless of the date of [the defendant's] prior conviction, the crime of being a felon in possession of a firearm was not committed until after the effective date of the statute under which he was convicted. [The defendant] had more than adequate notice that it was illegal for him to possess a firearm because of his status as a convicted felon, and he could have conformed his conduct to the requirements of the law.

Id. at 291. For similar decisions involving the Lautenberg Amendment see, e.g., United States v. Smith, 171 F.3d 617 (8th Cir. 1999); United States v. Meade, 986 F. Supp. 6, 68 (D. Mass. 1997); United States v. Hicks, 992 F. Supp. 1244, 1246 (D. Kan. 1997). As one commentator has noted, however, there is a strong argument to be made on the other side:

> [C]ourts rejecting ex post facto challenges to the Lautenberg Amendment have ignored that "it is the effect, not the form of the law that determines whether it is ex post facto." As the Supreme Court stated, "[t]he Constitution deals with substance, not shadows. Its inhibition [against ex post facto laws] was leveled [sic] at the thing, not the name. It intended that the rights of the citizen should be secure against deprivation for past conduct by legislative enactment, under any form, however disguised."
>
> Additionally, courts rejecting challenges to the Lautenberg Amendment failed to recognize that the issue is not what the defendant knew when he violated the statute, but what he did not know at the time he committed the underlying domestic violence misdemeanor. The foundation of the constitution's ex post facto prohibition is that it would be unfair to retroactively apply a law of greater severity than that in existence at the time of the defendant's conduct.

Eric Andrew Pullen, *Guns, Domestic violence, Interstate Commerce and the Lautenberg Amendment,* 39 S. TEX. L. REV. 1029, 1063 (1998).

Which side do you think has the better of this argument? Given the difficulty of enforcing the new prohibition against prior domestic violence offenders, how much would be lost if the Amendment was restricted in application to those convicted of domestic violence crimes after its enactment? Given the likelihood that retroactive application of the Amendment is particularly likely to target those who use firearms as an aspect of their public sector employment (because they are more easily identified as violators), that this constituency is already incensed at losing its traditional exemption from firearm controls, and that it is a politically vocal and influential lobby, would it make political sense to abandon efforts at retroactive application in favor of securing the Amendment from ongoing challenges in courts and in Congress? Notably, five bills were introduced in the House and Senate in 1997, aimed at the Amendment's repeal or modification. None were successful, but it would be premature to assume that these challenges will be the last.

E. STALKING AND DOMESTIC VIOLENCE

Introductory Note

In 1990 California became the first State to pass legislation making stalking a crime. Since then all the states, as well as the District of Columbia, have enacted anti-stalking laws, and in 1996 a federal law was passed making it a crime for stalkers to travel across state lines in pursuit of their targets. While the most publicized cases prompting these legislative initiatives have usually involved celebrities rather than victims of domestic violence, battered women's advocates have heralded the new legislation as one more tool in the arsenal of those seeking to hold batterers accountable for their tactics of intimidation.

The following sections look first at the nature of stalking behavior, and data about who stalks and who is stalked, with what consequences; second at the shape of state and federal legislation and the constitutional challenges that have been mounted against that legislation; and third at law enforcement initiatives and proposals that seek to make good on the promise inherent in legislation prohibiting stalking.

Stalking as Social Phenomenon

What is stalking? As defined in *Stalking and Domestic Violence: The Third Annual Report to Congress under the Violence Against Women Act*, published by the U.S. Department of Justice in 1998, it is:

> harassing or threatening behavior that an individual engages in repeatedly, such as following a person, appearing at a person's home or place of business, making harassing phone calls, leaving written messages or objects, or vandalizing a person's property. These actions may or may not be accompanied by a credible threat of serious crime, and they may or may not be precursors to an assault or murder.

The recent National Violence Against Women Survey, jointly sponsored by the National Institute of Justice and the Centers for Disease Control and Prevention and summarized in the same *Third Annual Report*, is based on interviews with 8,000 American women and 8,000 American men. Extrapolating from this sample, the researchers, Pat Tjaden and Nancy Thoennes of the Center for Policy Research, conclude that at least one million women and 370,000 men are stalked annually—almost five times as many as previously estimated. (The definition of stalking used in the survey required the victim to fear bodily harm from his or her stalker.) 94% of the stalkers identified by women victims and 60% of the stalkers identified by men were men, so that 87% of stalkers overall were men. The average stalking lasted more than eighteen months, and all but six percent of victims were forced to alter their lives significantly in response to their stalkers' tactics. 59% of women victims, compared with 30% of male victims, were stalked by current or former husbands, cohabiting partners or former dates or boy-or girlfriends rather than by strangers. Interestingly, 21% of women victims reported that the stalking had occurred before the relationship ended, while 43% said it started only after the relationship ended, and 36% said it occurred both during and after the relationship ended. Others have estimated that as many as ninety percent of women murdered by present or ex-boyfriends or husbands have been stalked prior to their deaths.

Developing scholarship on stalking has begun to differentiate among categories of stalkers in a way that clarifies the relationship between stalking and domestic violence. One study, published in 1993, examined case files collected by the Threat Management Unit of the Los Angeles Police Department of men and women with a history of "obsessional pursuit." The authors of the study found that the cases could be divided into three separate groups: erotomanic, love obsessional and simple obsessional. The erotomanic and love obsessional groups harbored deluded beliefs that their victims, with whom they had had either no contact, or only superficial contact, loved them passionately. They made frequent attempts to contact their victims, believing that only some external influence prevented those victims from admitting their passion, or responding to their advances. The simple obsessional group, by contrast, was one in which prior relationships had existed between the stalkers and their victims. These relationships were often romantic or intimate relationships that had ended, leaving the pursuers feeling wronged or mistreated. This is the type of stalking case that relates most closely to domestic violence.

In part because of the emphasis in early studies of stalking on erotomania, and the deluded thinking that characterizes it, there has been a tendency to assume that stalking is a product of mental illness, perhaps even to the point where the stalker cannot be held legally responsible for his, or her, conduct. However, available evidence suggests that only a minority of stalkers are, by prevailing standards, incompetent to stand trial. One study of 25 cases in which alleged stalkers had been ordered by Missouri courts to undergo pretrial mental evaluations reported that only 35% of this group were diagnosed as psychotic and delusional, and only one subject was specifically diagnosed as suffering from erotomania. Furthermore, nonpsychotic subjects most often pursued former intimates, while psychotic subjects most often pursued individuals with whom they had never had intimate relations.

The authors of this study summarize their findings as follows:

> . . . [T]he stalking pattern of psychotic subjects is dominated by delusional beliefs about the activities and motives of the victim. The nonpsychotic subjects, on the other hand, are best described as personality disordered, and their pursuit of the victim is characterized by obsessional ideation, dependency, narcissism, projection, and uncontrolled anger. These differences between psychotic and nonpsychotic stalkers have important consequences.
>
> . . .

> ... [N]onpsychotic stalkers made threats significantly more often than psychotic stalkers. This finding may be explained by the fact that nonpsychotic stalkers threatened and pursued former intimate partners more often than psychotic stalkers....
>
> ... [N]onpsychotic stalkers acted out violently and used weapons more often than the psychotic stalkers. While seven (41%) of the nonpsychotic stalkers physically harmed the victim (two murdered the victim) and/or physically harmed a significant other of the victim, only one (13%) of the psychotic stalkers physically harmed the victim. While eight (47%) of the nonpsychotic stalkers had possession of a weapon ... when stalking, only one (13%) psychotic subject had a weapon....

Kristine K. Kienlen et al., *A Comparative Study of Psychotic and Nonpsychotic Stalking,* 25 J. Am. Acad. Psych. & Law Bull. 317, 333–34 (1997)

Consistent with these findings, the 1993 study mentioned earlier reported that the simple obsessional stalkers—those with a prior relationship to their victims—had committed a variety of stalking behaviors. 65% of them had made telephone contact with their targets, and 34% had written letters. 34% had gone to their victims' homes to find them, 31% had looked for them in other locations, and 22% had actually had person-to-person contact. Compared with stalkers in the other groups, the simple obsessional group made more contacts, and were more likely to make threats. Only the simple obsessional stalkers in the study sample actually caused bodily injury to their victims or destroyed their property. See, Michael A. Zona, Kaushal K. Sharma and John Lane, *A Comparative Study of Erotomanic and Obsessional Subjects in a Forensic Sample,* 38 J. of Forensic Sc. 894 (1993).

Another 1997 study focussed on stalking among undergraduate psychology students. The female subjects were divided into three groups; a control group who reported that they had never experienced repeated unwanted attention from a former partner following a break-up; a "harassed" group who had experienced such attention but who believed that the attention was not intended to harm or frighten them, were not afraid for their physical safety, and who reported that the attention did not become more threatening or violent over time; and a "stalked" group for whom the unwanted attention was frightening, or who felt that it was intended to harm or frighten, or who had experienced an escalation in the level of threat or violence over time. Subjects in the stalked group had not only experienced more harassing and violent behaviors from their former partners after the break-up of their relationships, but also reported more abusive behavior by their partners prior to the break-ups. As the author concludes: "These results suggest that men who are verbally or physically abusive during relationships are more likely to pursue their partners in a harassing or violent manner after the relationships have dissolved." Frances L. Coleman, *Stalking Behavior and the Cycle of Domestic Violence,* 12 J. of Interpersonal Violence 420 (1997). Similarly, the National Violence Against Women Survey reported that ex-husbands who stalked (either before or after the relationship ended) were more likely than ex-husbands who did not stalk to engage in emotionally abusive and controlling behaviors towards their partners.

Among the National Violence Against Women Survey subjects only 55% of women victims and 48% of men victims reported the stalking to the police. The three reasons most often cited by those who did not report were that it was not a police matter, that the police couldn't do anything, or that the victims were afraid of reprisals by the stalker. When victims did report to police, they gave the police a 50/50 approval rating, with those whose stalkers had been arrested expressing much more enthusiasm than those whose stalkers had not. Police were more likely to arrest or detain a suspect in cases involving women victims, and they were more likely to refer women victims to services. Of the cases in which police reports were generated, 24% of women victims and 19% of male victims reported that there was a subsequent prosecution; when stalkers were prosecuted 54% were convicted of some crime, and of those convicted 63% had served some jail or prison time. Women victims were much more likely than men to obtain restraining orders (28% as opposed to 10%), but 69% of women and 81% of men who received restraining orders reported that the stalker had subsequently violated the order. Victims were more likely to believe that informal justice system interventions—such as a warning from police—had helped to stop the stalking, than to believe that formal interventions had had that effect. This is significant, but not surprising, given the relative infrequency of formal interventions such as arrest and prosecution, or issuance and enforcement of restraining orders, in stalking cases.

Although the average stalking lasts for 1.8 years, about two-thirds last a year or less, some 23% last between two and five years, and about 10% last for more than five years. National Violence Against Women Survey subjects who were no longer being stalked were asked why they thought the stalking had stopped; 19% said it was because they had moved away, 18% thought it was because the stalker had a new partner, 15% said it was because the stalker had been warned by the police, and only 9% said it was because the stalker was arrested. Less than 2% thought that a conviction or a restraining order had ended the stalking.

State Legislation

Those who oppose stalking statutes argue that they are unnecessary—that any truly criminal behavior involved in stalking is reachable under existing provisions of the criminal law. The opponents argue that to the extent stalking legislation reaches conduct not previously considered criminal, it is likely to be unconstitutional—so broad and ill-defined that it imposes too burdensome a curb on individual liberties of speech and movement.

Proponents, on the other hand, argue that subtle regimes of harassment, using tactics that instill fear only because of the target's past experience with her harasser, are likely to escape the cut and dried requirements of crimes like battery or assault. How many stalking victims, in the past, have sought police protection, only to be told that nothing can be done until the stalker is threatening "imminent" violence? By that time, of course, police intervention may come too late to prevent the destruction of property, physical injury or even lethal violence to which a campaign of stalking can lead.

The tension between deflecting constitutional challenge while offering real protection to stalking victims is captured in the next readings, which describe a variety of approaches to defining and responding to stalking, and some of the (generally unsuccessful) constitutional challenges that have been brought. Despite an effort sponsored by the National Institute of Justice to promote a Model Anti–Stalking Code, there remain significant differences among the states, with some states lagging behind the protections advocated in the Model Code, while others move beyond the Model Code to sweep more conduct into the prohibited realm, enhance penalties, or focus on specific classes of perpetrator or victim.

Project to Develop a Model Anti–Stalking Code for the States: A Research Report of the National Institute of Justice (October 1993)

The model anti-stalking code development project has sought to formulate a constitutional and enforceable legal framework for addressing the problem of stalking.

The model code encourages legislators to make stalking a felony offense; to establish penalties for stalking that reflect and are commensurate with the seriousness of the crime; and to provide criminal justice officials with the authority and legal tools to arrest, prosecute, and sentence stalkers.

. . .

Section 1. For purposes of this code:

(a) "Course of conduct" means repeatedly maintaining a visual or physical proximity to a person or repeatedly conveying verbal or written threats or threats implied by conduct or a combination thereof directed at or toward a person;

(b) "Repeatedly" means on two or more occasions;

(c) "Immediate family" means a spouse, parent, child, sibling, or any other person who regularly resides in the household or who within the prior six months regularly resided in the household.

Section 2. Any person who:

(a) purposefully engages in a course of conduct directed at a specific person that would cause a reasonable person to fear bodily injury to himself or herself or a member of his or her immediate family or to fear the death of himself or herself or a member of his or her immediate family; and

(b) has knowledge or should have knowledge that the specific person will be placed in reasonable fear of bodily injury to himself or herself or a member of his or her immediate family or will be placed in reasonable fear of the death of himself or herself or a member of his or her immediate family; and

(c) whose acts induce fear in the specific person of bodily injury to himself or herself or a member of his or her immediate family or induce fear in the specific person of the death of himself or herself or a member of his or her immediate family;

is guilty of stalking.

Analysis and Commentary on Code Language

Prohibited Acts

Unlike many state stalking statutes, the model code does not list specific types of actions that could be construed as "stalking." Examples of specific acts frequently proscribed in existing stalking statutes include following, non-consensual communication, harassing, and trespassing.

Some courts have ruled that if a statute includes a specific list, the list is exclusive. The model code, therefore, does not list specifically proscribed acts because ingenuity on the part of an alleged stalker should not permit him to skirt the law. Instead, the model code prohibits defendants from engaging in a "course of conduct" that would cause a reasonable person fear.

Credible Threat

Unlike many state stalking statutes, the model code does not use the language "credible threat." Stalking defendants often will not threaten their victims verbally or in writing but will instead engage in conduct which, taken in context, would cause a reasonable person fear. The model code is intended to apply to such "threats implied by conduct." Therefore the "credible threat" language, which might be construed as requiring an actual verbal or written threat, was not used in the model code.

"Immediate Family"

A stalking defendant may, in addition to threatening the primary victim, threaten to harm members of the primary victim's family. Under the provisions of the model code, such a threat to harm an immediate family member could be used as evidence of stalking in the prosecution for stalking of the primary victim.

The model code uses a definition of "immediate family" . . . broader than the traditional nuclear family, encompassing "any other person who regularly resides in the household or who within the prior six months regularly resided in the household."

If states want to consider further expanding the definition of "immediate family," they should be aware that broadening it too much may lead to challenges that the statute is overly broad.

Classification as a Felony

States should consider creating a stalking felony to address serious, persistent, and obsessive behavior that causes a victim to fear bodily injury or death. The felony statute could be used to handle the most egregious cases of stalking-type behavior. Less egregious cases could be handled under existing harassment or intimidation statutes. As an alternative, states may wish to consider adopting both misdemeanor and felony stalking statutes.

Since stalking defendants' behavior often is characterized by a series of increasingly serious acts, states should consider establishing a continuum of charges that could be used by law enforcement officials to intervene at various stages. Initially, defendants may engage in behavior that causes a victim emotional distress but does not cause the victim to fear bodily injury or death. For example, a defendant may make frequent but non-threatening telephone calls. Existing harassment or intimidation statutes could be used to address this type of behavior. States also may want to consider enacting aggravated harassment or intimidation statutes that could be used in situations in which a defendant persistently engages in annoying behavior. The enactment of a felony stalking statute would allow law enforcement officials to intervene in situations that may pose an imminent and serious danger to a potential victim.

Classification as a felony would assist in the development of the public's understanding of stalking as a unique crime, as well as permit the imposition of penalties that would punish appropriately the defendant and provide protection for the victim.

Of utmost importance is a state's decision to require the criminal justice system and related disciplines to take stalking incidents seriously. A state's decision on how to classify stalking and how to establish its continuum of charges is of less importance.

"Conduct Directed at a Specific Person"

Under the model code's language, the stalking conduct must be directed at a "specific person." Threatening behavior not aimed at a specific individual would not be punishable under a statute similar to the model code. For example, a teenager who regularly drives at high speed through a neighborhood, scaring the residents, could not be charged under a stalking statute based upon the model code.

Fear of Sexual Assault

The model code language does not apply if the victim fears sexual assault but does not fear bodily injury. It is likely that victims who fear that a defendant may sexually assault them most likely also fear that the defendant would physically injure them if they resisted. Furthermore, since the human immunodeficiency virus (HIV), which causes acquired immunodeficiency syndrome (AIDS), could be contracted through a sexual assault, a victim is more likely to fear bodily injury or death, as well as psychological injury. Nevertheless, due to the nature of stalking offenses, states may want to consider expanding the language of their felony stalking statutes to include explicitly behavior that would cause a reasonable person to fear sexual assault in addition to behavior that would cause a reasonable person to fear bodily injury or death.

Intent Element

... [I]f a defendant consciously engages in conduct that he knows or should know would cause fear in the person at whom the conduct is directed, the intent element of the model code is satisfied.

A suspected stalker often suffers under a delusion that the victim actually is in love with him or that, if properly pursued, the victim will begin to love him. Therefore, a stalking defendant actually may not intend to cause fear; he instead may intend to establish a relationship with his victim. Nevertheless, the suspected stalker's actions cause fear in his victim. As long as a stalking defendant knows or should know that his actions cause fear, the alleged stalker can be prosecuted for stalking. Protection orders can serve as notice to a defendant that his behavior is unwanted and that it is causing the victim to fear.

Fear Element

Since stalking statutes criminalize what otherwise would be legitimate behavior based upon the fact that the behavior induces fear, the level of fear induced in a stalking victim is a crucial element of the stalking offense. The model code, which treats stalking as a felony, requires a high level of fear—fear of bodily injury or death. Acts that induce annoyance or emotional distress would be punishable under statutes such as harassment or trespassing, that do not rise to the felony level and carry less severe penalties.

In some instances, a defendant may be aware, through a past relationship with the victim, of an unusual phobia of the victim's and use this knowledge to cause fear in the victim. In order for such a defendant to be charged under provisions similar to those in the model code, the victim actually must fear bodily injury or death as a result of the defendant's behavior and a jury must determine that the victim's fear was reasonable under the circumstances.

* * *

NOTES

1. In *Stalking and Domestic Violence: The Third Annual Report to Congress under the Violence Against Women Act,* 26 (U.S. Department of Justice, 1998), the authors put stalking laws into the broader context of criminal laws addressing behaviors that are commonly components of stalking:

- Harassment laws have been adopted in 25 states and the territory of Guam. In three of these States, harassment may be a felony. In 3 other States, a second harassment offense may also be a felony. In the remainder of the States, harassment is either a misdemeanor or a summary offense (one State).
- Threatening or intimidating behavior is a statutory crime in 35 States, the District of Columbia, Guam, and Puerto Rico. In 17 of

these States and Guam, threatening or intimidation may be a felony offense. Two States call for enhanced penalties for repeat offenses.

- Laws specifically directed at telephone threats or harassment have been adopted in 43 States, Guam, and the Virgin Islands. Of these jurisdictions, only two States' laws provide felony sentences. An additional six States make a repeat telephone threat or harassment offense a felony crime.
- Letter threats are the subject of 21 States' and the Virgin Islands' criminal laws. Five of these States make letter threats a felony offense. One State provides misdemeanor penalties for "written" forms of harassment.
- With respect to other stalking-related crimes, one State criminalized threats by facsimile. Three other States have make stalking by e-mail or fax elements of their definition of a stalking crime. The territory of Guam forbids harassment by fax.

2. Many states, as the commentary to the model code suggests, define more precisely than the code the categories of conduct that may constitute stalking. Often, "following" is on the list, as is "harassment." Harassment, in turn, is often defined as "conduct directed toward a victim that includes, but is not limited to, repeated or continuing unconsented contact that would cause a reasonable individual to suffer emotional distress and that actually causes the victim to suffer emotional distress. Harassment does not include constitutionally protected activity or conduct that serves a legitimate purpose." See, e.g., MICHIGAN COMPILED LAWS § 750.411h(1)(c) (1999). "Unconsented contact" is defined, in Michigan and elsewhere, as:

> any contact with another individual that is initiated or continued without that individual's consent or in disregard of that individual's expressed desire that the contact be avoided or discontinued. Unconsented contact includes, but is not limited to, any of the following:
>
> (i) Following or appearing within the sight of that individual.
>
> (ii) Approaching or confronting that individual in a public place or on private property.
>
> (iii) Appearing at that individual's workplace or residence.
>
> (iv) Entering onto or remaining on property owned, leased, or occupied by that individual.
>
> (v) Contacting that individual by telephone.
>
> (vi) Sending mail or electronic communications to that individual.
>
> (vii) Placing an object on, or delivering an object to, property owned, leased, or occupied by that individual.

MICHIGAN COMPILED LAWS § 750.411h(1)(e) (1999); see also 21 OKL. ST. § 1173.F.4 (1998).

Notice that these definitions of unconsented contact include "cyberstalking"—a stalker's use of the internet to harass a victim.

3. The commentary to the model code explains that using language of "threat" in defining stalking may lead courts to require an explicit verbal or written threat, rather than understanding that conduct, in context, can imply a threat. Only a relatively small number of states—perhaps a dozen—explicitly define "threat" to include implied threats, although a number of others use the language of threat only in the context of a longer list, such as "terrorized, frightened, intimidated, threatened, harassed, or molested," which gives the implementing court plenty of flexibility. See, e.g. 21 OKL. ST. § 1173.A.2 (1998).

4. The model code does not demand that defendants "intend" the result proscribed by the legislation (to make victims fear bodily injury or death for themselves or for members of their immediate family). A majority of states (at least thirty) do require that the defendant intend the proscribed result, or that the stalking be "wilful" or "malicious," although some soften that requirement by adding, as Hawaii does, that it is enough for the defendant to act in "reckless disregard" of the consequences of his actions. HAWAII REV. ST. § 711–1106.5(1) (1999). Another group of states (about fifteen) follow the lead of the model code in requiring that the defendant's behavior be purposeful, which means that the conduct must be intended, even though the results of that conduct are not, or cannot be proved to be, intended. In those states, it is enough that the defendant intends to engage in the stalking behavior (has not accidentally encountered the victim in a grocery store, for example, rather than planning the encounter), and that the behavior is enough to cause a reasonable person fear, which in turn suggests that the defendant should have predicted that result. Although this suggests that there are a handful of states in which neither intent nor purposeful conduct is required, in fact these states appear to require that the defendant make an actual threat, which in essence supplies the element of intent.

5. The model code's recommendation that even a first stalking offense be treated as a felony is not the approach adopted in a majority of states. In fact, as of 1998 only sixteen states provided that a first simple stalking offense could be a felony, although another 16 provided felony penalties for first stalking offenses if the stalking involved certain "aggravating" features, such as bodily injury to the victim, the use or carrying of a weapon, or the violation of a protective order. Of the remaining 18 states, sixteen made repeat stalking a felony. Nine states provided enhanced penalties for stalking or harassing minors; with five states using sixteen as the cutoff, three using eighteen, and the ninth using twelve. *Stalking and Domestic Violence: The Third Annual Report to Congress under the Violence Against Women Act,* 24–25 (U.S. Department of Justice, 1998).

6. As noted in the introduction to this section, stalking laws have been subject to a myriad of constitutional challenges on the grounds of vagueness and overbreadth, with challengers asserting that stalking statutes impinge on constitutional freedoms of speech and movement. Increasingly, stalking legislation has survived these challenges. In 1997, for example, 20 cases were brought in 13 states, and in every one of those cases the stalking provisions at issue were upheld. The following case, decided by the Court of

Appeals of Alaska in 1996, provides the flavor of this body of litigation, and its judicial disposition. The case is of particular interest because it consolidates three cases involving three quite different stalking scenarios. The statute at issue, AS 11.41.270, defines stalking, in Subsection (a), as: "knowingly engag[ing] in a course of conduct that recklessly places another person in fear of death or physical injury, or in fear of the death or physical injury of a family member. Subsections (b)(1) and (b)(3) of the statute further define 'course of conduct' as 'repeated acts of nonconsensual contact involving the victim or a family member'," and define nonconsensual contact in the same language as that used in the Michigan statute cited above.

Petersen et al. v. State of Alaska

930 P.2d 414.
Court of Appeals of Alaska, 1996

■ MANHEIMER, JUDGE

In these consolidated appeals, the three defendants challenge the constitutionality of Alaska's stalking statutes.... As explained below, we conclude that the statutes do not violate the Constitution, and thus we affirm the defendants' convictions.

Facts of the Case: Petersen

[Gary Petersen began receiving massage therapy at a health center in Anchorage in 1989, and developed an interest in R.H., an apprentice massage therapist who worked there. He followed her, as a client, to another health center when she had completed her apprenticeship. In June of 1990 she married, but for a while maintained a somewhat friendly relationship with him, although she began to feel "annoyed and intruded upon" when Peterson kept showing up at her workplace as she was leaving work. Over time she became more and more clear with him that she wanted no further relationship. Both she and her employer told him she would no longer accept him as a client. He continued to seek her out at public events, and to demand explanations for her unwillingness to continue a relationship with him.

Throughout 1991 and 1992 Petersen continued his surveillance of her at her workplace and elsewhere, frequently following her in his car, and sometimes parking in her driveway. He received a formal warning from the health center that police action would be taken if he did not stop harassing R.H., and the police also told him to stay away from her. Early in 1992 he was convicted of trespass for parking in her driveway, his sentence was suspended, and as a condition of probation he was ordered not to go near R.H.'s residence. Nonetheless his surveillance continued. In January of 1993 he tried to ram her car at an intersection, and then chased her home in his car. For that, in April of 1993 he was convicted of assault, placed on five years probation, and ordered to have no contact with her.

After several more incidents in which Petersen approached her in public places between May and July of 1993, a police officer again found him in R.H.'s driveway. This time he was arrested, charged with first degree stalking, and convicted following a jury trial. He told the police officer who arrested him that: "he loved R.H. and that he had come to her house only because he wanted to 'explain some things to her.' "]

Facts of the Case: Larson

Bruce Larson, Jr., was involved in a romantic relationship with I.H.; he lived in Unalaska with I.H. and her daughter. In May of 1994 Larson was convicted of assaulting I.H., and a restraining order was entered that prohibited Larson from having any contact with her. Larson was later convicted of violating the restraining order. However, despite these difficulties, I.H. and Larson resumed their relationship.

On December 1, 1994, Larson ... returned to Unalaska from over a month at sea. Almost immediately, the relationship between [them] began to deteriorate. On December 3rd, Larson and I.H. went out to the UniSea Bar in Dutch Harbor. Larson made several remarks that prompted I.H. to leave without him. She handed Larson the keys to her car and told him she would be leaving with friends. As I.H. walked across the parking lot, Larson ran up from behind her and "slammed" into her back. Larson then took hold of I.H. She told him, "Please don't touch me; leave me along." Larson screamed at I.H., calling her a "fucking bitch."

I.H. got into her friends' car and they started to drive.... Larson chased them, tailgating their car in a dangerous manner. Because of Larson's actions, I.H. asked her friends to take her to the Unalaska police station. Larson followed them most of the way, then made a u-turn and left. At the police station, I.H. explained that Larson had her keys and that she no longer wanted him to stay at her apartment. She asked the police to accompany her home and to assist her in removing Larson's belongings.

The police and I.H. went to her apartment.... Larson was not in I.H.'s apartment, but the officers found him in the upper floor of the apartment building. Larson relinquished his key to I.H.'s apartment and removed his personal possessions from the apartment. I.H. told Larson not to come back, and the police also instructed him to stay away. However, when the police checked the area a short time later, they found Larson hiding under a car. They again directed him to leave the area.

Later that night, Larson telephoned I.H. approximately fifteen times. During one of these calls, Larson informed I.H. that he was going to pick up I.H.'s daughter from the babysitter and take her. In response, I.H. telephoned the police and again asked for their assistance: an officer stood guard as I.H. went to the babysitter and picked up her child.

The next day (December 4th), Larson telephoned I.H. to tell her that she needn't go to work because he had "trashed" her office. (It turned out that this was not true.) On December 8th, Larson appeared at I.H.'s door at 1:00 a.m. and asked her to talk with him; when I.H. declined, Larson sat in a truck outside I.H.'s apartment building until the police came and asked him to leave.

On December 10th, Larson repeatedly called I.H. at work. Later that day, he confronted her at the Unisea bar (where she was seated with a group of friends). Using vulgar language, Larson accused several of the men in the group of having had sex with I.H. When I.H. asked Larson to leave, he told her, "Don't bother driving the car tonight; it won't start." He also told her, "I'm going to ruin your night. I'm going to screw up your life. You're a bitch."

I.H. took a cab back to her apartment. As she was putting her key in the lock, she became aware that Larson was behind her. Larson said, "You fucking bitch, I'm going to kill you. You're the next Nicole Simpson." Although I.H. was scared she shoved Larson away; then she finished unlocking the door and went inside. Once inside the apartment, she had a friend call the police. When the police arrived, they found Larson at a nearby phone booth; they arrested him.

Larson was indicted for first-degree stalking under two theories: first, that he had previously been convicted of violating a restraining order, ... and second, that he had previously been convicted of assaulting I.H.,.... Under a subsequent plea agreement, Larson pleaded no contest to a reduced charge of second-degree stalking, reserving his right to attack the constitutionality of the statute....

Facts of the Case: Colbry

Donald Colbry was married to E.H. for several years.... After the birth of their daughter, Colbry began drinking and manifested a tendency toward violence. In May of 1993 E.H. asked Colbry to agree to a dissolution. Colbry initially agreed, but he delayed leaving the house. He finally moved out in August 1993.

During September 1993, Colbry telephoned E.H. three or four times a day, both at home and at work. He threatened to fight for custody of their daughter and to "take [E.H.] for everything [she] had." Colbry also threatened J.L., a man whom he suspected of being romantically involved with E.H .. Toward the end of September, Colbry assaulted E.H.; she called the troopers, who took Colbry away, but no criminal charges were filed....

Two weeks later, on October 10, 1993 Colbry again assaulted E.H ..... Accompanied by J.L., she went to the courthouse and obtained a domestic violence restraining order against Colbry. The magistrate who issued the order telephoned Colbry from court and informed him that he was forbidden from contacting E.H.

E.H. and J.L. left the courthouse in separate cars. Colbry drove past in the opposite direction; seeing their cars, Colbry turned around and began to pursue J.L. at high speed. J.L. drove to the State Trooper headquarters.... As J.L. was telling the troopers about Colbry's actions, Colbry drove up and told the troopers that J.L. had tried to run him off the road. Then, in the trooper's presence, Colbry informed J.L. that he was going to kill him.

When Colbry drove away from this encounter, he went to E.H.'s home. Ignoring the no-contact provision of the ... restraining order (which had been issued only hours before), Colbry barged into E.H.'s house and began to scream at E.H.... When E.H. tried to reach to telephone, Colbry grabbed her by the neck and pulled her away. The police were summoned by the couple's daughter, who had run to a neighbor's house to make the call. By the time the police arrived, Colbry was gone.

In the ensuing weeks, Colbry frequently appeared at E.H.'s workplace and followed E.H. home from work. In December 1993, Colbry used his key to enter E.H.'s residence without permission. When he began to yell at E.H., she called the police. The police dispatcher spoke with Colbry and convinced him to leave, but after Colbry finished speaking with the dispatcher, he grabbed E.H. and threw her against the wall before he left.

[In January and in March Colbry was convicted of assault and trespass, based on the October 10 and December incidents at E.H.'s house. However, in both instances he was not incarcerated, but merely put on probation, and again ordered to have no contact with E.H. This despite the fact that between January and March Colbry continued to telephone E.H.'s home, and threaten to harm or kill J.L., with whom E.H. was now living.]

On June 7, 1994, after E.H. informed the police that Colbry had again violated the restraining order, the police prepared to monitor and record Colbry's next telephone call. Colbry called E.H.'s house later that day; J.L. answered the phone. During the ensuing conversation, Colbry made numerous threats to injure or kill J.L.

In August 1994, Colbry was indicted for first-degree stalking.... Colbry ultimately pleaded no-contest to a single consolidated count that charged him with first-degree stalking ... (because his acts of stalking were violations of both the domestic violence restraining order and his condition of probation ..., [and] because he had previously been convicted of assaulting E.H.). Colbry reserved the right to challenge the constitutionality of the statute.

The Definition of "Stalking" and a General Discussion of the Defendants' Constitutional Claims

In the present appeals, the defendants assert that the statutory definition of stalking is unconstitutionally "vague". However, their primary argument is that the statute criminalizes "innocent behavior protected by [the] rights of association and the freedom a citizen [possesses] to go about his daily behavior".... Properly understood, this is a substantive due process claim or an overbreadth claim rather than a vagueness claim.

A statute is unconstitutionally vague if its wording is so imprecise "that people of common intelligence would be relegated to differing guesses about its meaning".... Such a statute offends constitutional values in two major ways: by failing to give people "adequate notice of the conduct that is prohibited", and by placing a power of arbitrary or discriminatory enforcement in the hands of police, prosecutors, and ultimately judges and juries....

The defendants do level a cursory vagueness attack on a few of the terms used in the definition of stalking. The defendants assert in conclusory fashion, without providing any supporting argument or citation to legal authority, that the terms "follow" and "approach", as well as the phrase "appear within the sight of", are all too vague to be understood by people of common intelligence.

The stalking statutes require the State to prove that the defendant acted knowingly. We believe that people of common intelligence would readily understand the meaning of "knowingly follow another person", "knowingly approach another person", and "knowingly appear within the sight of another person".... Given the apparent clarity of these terms, the defendants' conclusory assertions of vagueness are not sufficient to preserve their claims....

The defendants also claim that the word "repeated" is too vague to be understood. However, this court has interpreted "repeated" to mean "more than once", and has held that this term is not vague....

... As indicated above, the defendants' main argument is not that the statutory definition of stalking is incapable of being understood. Rather, they argue that the definition of the crime manifestly includes too much. The defendants contend that the definition of stalking includes innocent conduct—blameless personal activities that can not properly be criminalized by the legislature. Essentially, the defendants are making a substantive due process claim: they assert that the legislature has exceeded its proper law-making authority.

Alternatively, one could characterize the defendants' argument as a claim that the statutory definition of stalking is "overbroad" because it punishes conduct that people have a constitutional right to engage in. Although courts often discuss overbreadth as an aspect of vagueness, these two concepts are distinct. "[A] statute may be invalid for being overbroad [even though its working is] clear and precise if it prohibits constitutionally protected conduct." ...

This recasting of the defendants' argument does not alter the importance of the concerns the defendants raise. If anything, it heightens those concerns: for between two laws, the first one worded so ambiguously that it might proscribe innocent behavior, and the second one worded precisely to achieve this unlawful aim, society might justifiably condemn the second law more strongly. We thus turn to the merits of the defendants' challenges to the definition of stalking.

The definition of "nonconsensual contact" contained in [the statute] is quite broad. [It] includes such acts as approaching another person, appearing within sight of another person, initiating a conversation, calling someone on the telephone, or sending a letter to someone if these acts are done "without that person's consent". The [statutory] wording ... suggests that the phrase "without that person's consent" is not limited to instances in which the other person has previously expressed a desire not to be contacted. Rather, it appears that this phrase covers all contacts that are not expressly authorized beforehand. Defined in this fashion, "nonconsensual contact" could include such everyday activities as making telephone solicitations for businesses or charities, sending advertising brochures in the mail, or walking up to someone to ask them to sign a political petition or contribute to a social cause. These activities could all be "nonconsensual contact" if the recipient of these attentions was not in an agreeable mood.

The other side of the coin is that, even when the recipient of these contacts has previously expressed a desire not to be contacted, there may be situations in which a defendant's right to continue the contact is constitutionally guaranteed. For instance, the definition of "nonconsensual contact" is broad enough to include a defendant who repeatedly pickets a government office building or who makes repeated telephone calls to a government office to protest an official's actions.

Nevertheless, the crime of stalking requires proof of more than repeated acts of nonconsensual contact.... [T]he State must prove (1) that the defendant "knowingly" engaged in repeated acts of nonconsensual contact, (2) that the defendant's conduct placed another person in fear of injury or death (or in fear of the injury or death of a "family member") ... and (3) that the defendant acted "recklessly" with regard to this result. The question, then, is whether these three additional elements are sufficient to make the definition of stalking constitutional.

Public Encounters

Defendants Petersen and Larson point out that ... stalking includes the acts of "approaching [another] person in a public place" and even "appearing within the sight of that person" in a public place. The defendants suggest that these provisions of the statute are so broad as to effectively forbid people from attending public events, taking public transportation, going to restaurants, engaging in normal shopping, or even walking down the street for business or pleasure—because if the person were by chance to encounter or appear within sight of the alleged stalking victim, the State could charge them with recklessly disregarding the possibility that the other person would be there too.

However, as explained above, the crime of stalking requires proof that the defendant knowingly engaged in repeated acts of nonconsensual contact.... [T]o prove that a person "knowingly" engaged in conduct, the government must establish that the person "[was] aware that [his or her] conduct [was] of that nature". This provides one answer to the defendants' contention that a person might be prosecuted for happening to attend the same public function as the victim or happening to patronize a restaurant or grocery at the same time as the victim. A defendant who inadvertently encounters another person in a public place has not "knowingly" approached or appeared within sight of that person.

This, however, is only a partial answer to the defendants' argument. There may be times when the defendant knows before hand that the other person will be attending a public function (say, a music festival or a municipal assembly meeting) that the defendant also has a legitimate interest in attending. If the defendant attends the festival or assembly meeting and the other person is there as expected, the defendant will have "knowingly" come within the sight of the other person.

Additionally, the defendants suggest the hypothetical situation of a person who, in the course of promoting a political or social cause, knowingly initiates contact with other people without their consent, either by approaching them on the street, or by telephoning them, or by coming to their home or workplace. For example, a person seeking signatures for a political petition might come door-to-door or might approach people at public gatherings. If the defendant's cause was unpopular, the defendant might reasonably anticipate that most people would not welcome his or her approach.

These objections lose their force when a defendant is charged with first-degree stalking under ... provisions that speak to acts of stalking committed while the defendant is under a court order or a parole condition that prohibits the defendant from having contact with the other person in the first place. The defendants in the present appeals do not challenge the constitutionality of domestic violence restraining orders or the constitutionality of no-contact orders imposed as a condition of bail, probation, or parole. Nor have the defendants suggested any reason to believe that the constitution forbids the legislature from enacting a criminal statute that addresses a defendant's repeated knowing violations of a no-contact order.

... [S]ome of the acts charged against Petersen consisted of approaching R.H. in public places. Because of this, the existence of no-contact orders is significant in Petersen's case.

. . .

Because Petersen was under court order to have no contact with his victim, and because he does not challenge the lawfulness of this condition of probation, we conclude that Petersen had no constitutional right to knowingly approach or follow R.H., even in public places or at public events. Even if these portions of the definition of stalking might be unconstitutionally broad when applied generally, Petersen was under a no-contact order, and the State's proof of this additional element in Petersen's case means that he has no claim.

Colbry, like Petersen, was under a court order not to contact his victim. Moreover, even if the stalking statutes posed constitutional problems with respect to public encounters, these problems would not affect Colbry's case. The acts of nonconsensual contact charged against Colbry were not public encounters, but rather physical assaults and threatening telephone calls.

Defendant Larson's case is distinguishable from Petersen's and Colbry's because Larson was convicted of second-degree stalking; the State did not assert that Larson's conduct violated any court order or parole condition. Thus, in Larson's case we must address the contention that the definition of stalking is unconstitutional because it allows a person to be prosecuted for encountering someone else in a public place when that other person does not wish to have contact with him.

Here we confront again the hypothetical situations of a political protester who knowingly engages in repeated nonconsensual contacts with a government official to protest the government's actions or policies—for example by picketing the building where the official works, or by making repeated telephone calls to her office, or by sending her vituperative letters of protest. However, as already noted, these actions do not constitute the crime of stalking unless the State proves that the defendant recklessly placed another person in fear of injury or death. That is, the State must establish that the defendant's actions actually caused another person to fear injury or death, that the defendant consciously disregarded a substantial and unjustifiable risk that his actions would have this effect, and that the defendant's disregard of this risk constituted a gross deviation from the standard of care that a reasonable person would exercise in that situation.

The government clearly possesses the authority to prosecute a person for recklessly causing another to fear imminent injury or death....

... Still, it is unclear whether this is a total answer to the defendants' First Amendment arguments. It is possible to imagine troublesome cases brought under the stalking statute. For instance, protesters might repeatedly picket an abortion clinic or the office of the Ku Klux Klan, committing acts of "nonconsensual contact" against the people who work there.... Depending upon the emotion and the rhetoric of the protesters, the people working inside might fear injury or death because of the protesters' actions, and there might be close questions as to (1) whether that fear was reasonable, and (2) whether, even if the fear was reasonable, the protesters' actions should still be protected by the First Amendment.

Besides these overbreadth issues ..., the stalking statutes also present substantive due process issues. Leaving aside the realm of constitutionally protected activities, there are still limits to a legislature's power to regulate or criminalize conduct.... The stalking statutes pose due process problems because they potentially apply to situations where defendants engage in no activity other than going about their daily lives.

For instance, a group of skinheads may routinely ride the municipal bus. Their appearance, their language, and the demeanor may cause other regular bus riders to fear for their safety. The skinheads know that the other bus riders are afraid of them, but they continue to ride the bus. Have the skinheads committed stalking?

Or, to take another example, a person paroled from prison after serving a sentence for sexual abuse of children may be employed at the check-out counter of a grocery. Parents who patronize the grocery become aware of the parolee's background. Although the parents would prefer not to come into contact with the parolee, they inevitably do. Moreover, because of the parolee's background, these parents are afraid for the safety of their children who sometimes stop at the grocery after school to buy snacks. The parolee learns that the parents are afraid, but he continues to work at his job. Has the parolee committed stalking?

In both of these hypothetical situations, the government could plausibly claim that the defendant, through repeated acts of nonconsensual contact ... has place another person in fear of injury or death (either for themselves or for a family member). Further, the government could plausibly claim that the defendant consciously disregarded a substantial and unjustifiable risk that his conduct would have this result. Yet the defendant's conduct was not directed at anyone; that conduct consisted of nothing more than riding the bus or pursuing a livelihood.

Thus, the definition of stalking may present troubling cases. However, when a constitutional challenge is leveled against a statute whose main concern is conduct rather than speech, "the possibility of difficult or borderline cases will not invalidate a statute" if there is a "hard core of cases to which ... the statute unquestionably applies".... See Broadrick v. Oklahoma, 413 U.S. 601 ... (1973) (Before a statute will be invalidated for overbreadth "where conduct and not merely speech is involved, ... the overbreadth of [the]statute must be substantial[,] ... judged in relation to the statute's legitimate sweep. [If not], whatever overbreadth may exist should be cured through case-by-case analysis[.]")

. . .

The facts of Larson's case do not raise the constitutional concerns argued in the defendants' briefs. Larson was charged with physically assaulting I.H., threatening to kill her, threatening to kidnap her child, and chasing and tailgating I.H.'s vehicle. In his motion to dismiss, Larson did not deny any of this conduct, nor did he claim that he had a constitutional right to engage in any of this conduct.

... Even supposing that the First Amendment gave Larson the right to approach I.H. in a public place and insult her, he had no right to come to her residence and threaten to kill her.

More generally, none of the cases presently before the court are "borderline" cases....

Accordingly, we are convinced that the potential due process and overbreadth problems in the definition of stalking do not require invalidation of the stalking statutes. Rather, those problems should be resolved on a case-by-case basis, if and when we face litigation that actually presents those problems. We hold that, as applied to these three defendants, the portions of the stalking statutes dealing with public encounters are constitutional.

Constitutionality of the Stalking Statutes: Summary

The constitutional arguments raised by the defendants are not trivial. As we noted at the beginning of this section, the stalking statutes' definition of "nonconsensual contact" covers a wide spectrum of social interaction. This definition is undoubtedly the Alaska Legislature's most comprehensive codification of a person's right to be free from unwanted contact. Yet even though our society values and protects individual autonomy and privacy, our society at the same time recognizes a person's right to engage in uncomfortable, distasteful, and annoying contacts—even abrasive confrontations—with other citizens. Such interactions are not merely tolerated; they are explicitly protected by our Constitution.

However, the Constitution does not guarantee a right to threaten other people. When a person's words or actions constitute an assault—when they cause other people to reasonably fear for their own safety or the safety of those close to them—the Constitution no longer provides a refuge. We conclude that Alaska's stalking statutes are constitutional because, in essence, they outlaw assaultive conduct....

As we indicated above, the stalking statutes may present difficult constitutional questions in particular hypothetical situations. However, the conduct of the defendants in these three appeals falls within the core of the statutory definition—assaultive conduct with no constitutional justification. We therefore reject the defendants' challenges to the statute.

* * *

NOTES AND QUESTIONS

1. Do you agree with the Alaska court that law enforcement officials in Alaska might "plausibly claim" that the skinheads who used the municipal bus, or the paroled child molester at the grocery cash register, were acting "recklessly" with respect to the risk that they might be instilling fear of bodily injury or death in others. If acting "recklessly" means acting in conscious disregard of a "substantial and unjustifiable risk," is there room to argue that the skinheads' right to use public transportation "justifies" the risk their appearance poses to others, as long as they stop short of more explicitly threatening behavior? Does the situation change if those riding the bus have witnessed, or know of, prior altercations between the skinheads and other passengers? Does the addition of this factor make the case more like that of the paroled child molester? Can an individual "stalk" when he or she makes no move to initiate contact with the person who claims to be a victim, but waits for the victim to come to him or her? Does the Alaska statute answer this question?

Notice that the Model Anti–Stalking Code excerpted above solves the problem posed by the skinhead and parolee hypotheticals by requiring that stalking conduct be directed at a "specific person." Behavior that is threatening, but does not have a specific target, would not constitute stalking under legislation based on the code.

2. The Alaska court concludes that the statutes at issue are constitutional because "in essence, they outlaw assaultive conduct." If that is the case, does the stalking legislation render any conduct criminal that would not already have been criminal under existing legislation? Looking at the facts of the three cases, do you see alternative charges that might have been brought? Why do you think the prosecutors chose to bring the cases as stalking cases?

3. How effective did you think the police were in responding to the stalking histories involved in the three cases? Should they have taken more definitive action—by arresting the defendant, for example—sooner? Could they have done so? If you are uncertain, what more would you need to know about Alaska's restraining order legislation or criminal law and process before you could answer?

Federal Legislation

In 1996 Congress added an interstate stalking provision to the federal domestic violence crimes created by the 1994 Violence Against Women Act. 18 U.S.C. § 2261A provides:

> Whoever travels across a State line or within the special maritime and territorial jurisdiction of the United States with the intent to injure or harass another person, and in the course of, or as a result of, such travel places that person in reasonable fear of the death of, or serious bodily injury . . . to, that person or a member of that person's immediate family . . . shall be punished as provided in Section 2261 of this Title.

P.L. 104–201, Div A, Title X, Subtitle F, § 1069 (a), 110 Stat. 2655 (September 23, 1996).

Section 2261, discussed further below, defines and prohibits interstate domestic violence, and provides for a maximum penalty of 5 years in a case involving no aggravating factors; a maximum penalty of 10 years if the offender uses a dangerous weapon or causes serious bodily injury; a maximum penalty of 20 years if the victim is permanently disfigured or suffers a life-threatening injury, and a maximum penalty of life if death results. 18 U.S.C. § 2261. The federal sentencing guidelines provide that the base offense level for interstate domestic violence, and therefore for interstate stalking, is 14, which carries a sentence of between 15 and 21 months. But the level of the offense is raised to 16 if it involves one aggravating factor, and to 18 if it involves more than one. At 18, the sentence would be between 57 and 71 months. Aggravating factors include bodily injury, possession or threatened use of a dangerous weapon, the violation of a restraining order, or "a pattern of activity involving stalking, threatening, harassing, or assaulting the same victim."

It is notable that the federal legislation outlaws even a single instance of stalking, in contrast to legislation in many states that requires a pattern or course of conduct, or repeated instances of nonconsensual contact. At the same time the federal sentencing guidelines, by imposing increased penalties on repeat offenders, adopt a strategy similar to that adopted by those states in which a second offense is a more serious crime, with correspondingly stiffer sanctions.

Law Enforcement Issues

Despite the wealth of state stalking legislation, stalking prosecutions and convictions appear to be somewhat rare. Some of the reasons for this lack of activity, and ways in which more activity could be encouraged, are explored in the next reading.

State Stalking Codes and Sentencing Stalking and Domestic Violence: The Third Annual Report to Congress under the Violence Against Women Act, 39–45, U.S. Department of Justice, 1998

. . . [C]riminal justice officials interviewed for this report indicated that, in their collective experience, most persons convicted in cases involving stalking behavior are sentenced under statutes other than stalking laws, even when stalking was among the original charges brought in the case. Andrew R. Klein, former chief probation officer for the Quincy (Massachusetts) District Court, said that between 1995 and 1996, only 5 of 400 cases involving stalking behavior that came before the Quincy District Court were prosecuted under the State's stalking statute.

Judge John Rowley of the Ithaca (New York) City Court said that none of the cases involving stalking that have come before his court have been charged under the State's stalking statute. The cases involving stalking that he sees "usually are connected" to domestic violence and therefore "always [are handled] in the domestic violence arena." ...

Gwen P. Wilkinson, Tompkins County (New York) domestic violence prevention coordinator and a former Tompkins Country assistant district attorney, said that in her 5 years with the District Attorney's Office, no cases were prosecuted under the State's stalking statute.... Most stalking offenders were sentenced for violations of protection orders that had been issued by the court in domestic violence cases, she added.

. . .

Proving the Stalking Case

George E. Wattendorf, city prosecutor with the Dover (New Hampshire) Police Department's Prosecution unit ... said that New Hampshire currently is examining its stalking law to consider changes that would allow "indirect contact" between the offender and the victim and prior acts to be admitted as evidence in support of a charge of stalking. Wattendorf said that it is "difficult under the current law to show that the victim is in fear."

Paziotopolous of the Cook County State's Attorney's Office said that her division prosecutes numerous stalking cases.... While certainly underscoring the seriousness of the crime, the felony status of a stalking offense creates a number of evidentiary problems that complicate the development and prosecution of stalking cases, Paziotopolous noted. She added that often it is difficult to convince a judge or a jury of the potential dangerousness of the stalking behavior. "We are not able to get prior acts admitted," she said, and therefore are unable to meet the burden of proving a "course of conduct" that is required....

. . .

Roxann Ryan of the Iowa Attorney General's Office said that judges' attitudes toward stalking vary widely across the State, but she agreed with Rowley and Paziotopolous that many judges do not appreciate the dangerousness of stalking behavior. Ryan said many judges see stalking as a "trendy crime" instead of a real crime. They don't understand the terror that the victim feels, Ryan said. "They think, 'this is harassment, a civil case; the victim is overreacting.' "

Because of evidentiary issues involved in proving stalking under existing law, Wattendorf of the Dover Police Department said criminal justice officials in New Hampshire ... often opt to prosecute cases involving stalking behavior under the State's protection order statute. Wattendorf explained that ... a lesser standard of proof applies under the State's protection order statute. A violation of a protection order is an act of contempt against the court....

Training

Steven R. Siegel of the Denver District Attorney's Office acknowledged, "We need to do a better job about training in [handling] stalking cases." ...

For police and prosecutors, handling stalking cases may require departures from traditional ways of carrying out their respective responsibilities. "Cops are afraid that they will have to put 24 hour guards on stalkers," Siegel said. Prosecutors may see stalking cases as unwinnable, he observed. "Prosecutors generally get trained in how to win a case. When a case doesn't look winnable in the traditional sense, when essential elements of the case are missing, they say 'Let's not try the case.'" Because of this, Siegel especially emphasized the need for training prosecutors. "Prosecutors really understand an aggravated robbery," Siegel observed. "They need to develop that [same] understanding of stalking." Prosecutors need training about the specific dynamics of stalking and on protocols for handling stalking cases that are based on interdisciplinary cross-training, Siegel said.

Paziotopolous ... underscored the need for training judges on stalking to help them understand the complexities and potential dangerousness of cases involving stalking behavior. "We need to make sure that training for judges includes a separate section on stalking," Paziotopolous said. "Stalking needs to be explored separately [from domestic violence]."

Black of the Colorado Springs Police Department also believes that police, prosecutors, and judges need training in handling stalking cases. "We're just not doing a good job in this country in investigating and prosecuting stalking cases," Black said. He added, "We don't understand stalking" or appreciate that handling stalking cases can be expensive and time-consuming. Stalking cases "can be easy to prosecute if we do a better job on their investigation," Black said.

* * *

NOTES

1. In the last reading, prosecutors from both Dover, New Hampshire and Cook County noted that they had difficulty getting "prior acts" into evidence in stalking cases. If the statute requires "repeated" behaviors, or a "course of conduct," then evidence of a sequence of events, some more recent than others, is essential, and it hard to see how a judge could rule that evidence inadmissible. However, if the prosecution is trying instead to introduce evidence of past abuse, rather than stalking, then it is easier to understand how a judge might find that the evidence was highly prejudicial

to the defendant, and be inclined to exclude it, just as judges routinely used to exclude evidence of past abuse in cases where women who killed their batterers argued that they killed in self-defense. In both situations, however, the evidence is in fact highly relevant, and often essential. Only by introducing the fact finder to the defendant's prior abuse of the victim can the prosecution demonstrate that the defendant's most recent conduct made the victim fearful, and that her fear was reasonable. In the stalking context, evidence of prior abuse will also support the claim that the defendant had reason to know he was frightening the victim, even in the absence of explicit threats. This evidentiary issue is taken up again, in the context of battered women's self-defense claims, in Chapter 10.

2. Even if an offender is prosecuted and convicted, either under a stalking statute or under a domestic violence or general criminal statute for conduct related to stalking, there are serious questions about whether the management and disposition of the average case will provide an appropriate sanction, or enhance the victim's safety. Judge Rowley, of the Ithaca City Court, told his interviewers that probation is the most likely sentence in stalking cases that result in convictions in his court, and that the maximum sentence imposed is a year. This is not atypical. An assistant attorney general from Iowa reported that some stalking offenders would receive a little jail time, or be placed in a halfway house, but that most, as in Ithaca, would be sentenced to supervised release (in other words, probation). In Colorado Springs, where a Domestic Violence Enhanced Response Team has been addressing criminal justice responses to domestic violence, some longer sentences (including one of 2.5 years and another of 2 years) have been imposed in stalking cases. The very first stalking case prosecuted under this DVERT program, on the other hand, involved an offender who had been arrested 24 times for domestic violence, and yet the sentence he received was only 18 months.

3. In any time period following an arrest when a stalker is not detained, whether because he has been released pre-trial, released between conviction and sentencing, or sentenced to probation, the target of his stalking may be particularly vulnerable. As Steven Siegel puts it, an arrest in a stalking case "light[s] a fuse. Every stage is a dangerous time." In the pre-trial period, or the period between conviction and sentencing, the offender may feel that he is looking at his last window of opportunity to plead his case with, or settle his score with, his victim. A representative of the Westchester County Probation Department reported that she and her colleagues are "just beginning to get a sense of the amount of harassment going on between adjudication of guilt and the sentencing hearing," and are discovering that when there is violence in this period, it is "very severe." After conviction, the stalker who is put on probation without any initial period of incarceration, and without a suspended sentence hanging over his head, may receive the message that his behavior, if not entirely condoned, is not regarded as seriously problematic, and may interpret that as a license to reoffend. Presumably that message is dramatically reinforced if, as in the Colbry case, subsequent offenses again bring no sanction more onerous than probation. The management and disposition of stalking cases must

therefore take into account not just offender accountability, but also victim safety. Supervision of the offender is a critical factor in this equation.

One means of facilitating supervision is for law enforcement to encourage the stalking victim to obtain a restraining order with clear no-contact provisions as soon as the criminal process is initiated, if she has not already done so. A violation of this order will then provide additional mechanisms for policing the stalker, including warrantless arrest powers. There are two problems with this approach. The first is that the onus for reporting violations rests entirely with the victim; law enforcement personnel are not offering surveillance, but only, at most, an enhanced response to reported conduct in violation of the order. The second is that a simplified restraining order mechanism will only be available to victims who have been in family, household or intimate relationships with their stalkers under the definitions provided by state restraining order legislation. In this regard individuals who are stalked by strangers have fewer protections available to them.

The other means of supervising stalkers during and after the disposition of their cases involves the imposition of conditions on their bail, pre-sentence or post-conviction release. Again, imposing conditions is of limited assistance if there is no surveillance mechanism attached, but if compliance with those conditions is supervised by the probation department, some of the burden is shifted from the victim to the criminal justice system, although supervision will be most effective if they work together. Once there has been a conviction there is no legal impediment to attaching conditions to the offender's release; the difficulties lie in crafting an effective set of constraints, and monitoring the offender's compliance. Prior to conviction, however, any conditions imposed on the offender must be attached to bail, which raises a different set of questions. The following reading, drawn from the National Institute of Justice's Research Report of 1993, addresses those questions, as well as the issue of whether stalkers can be detained pending trial, consistent with constitutional guarantees and the presumption of innocence.

Pretrial Release: Supervising Accused Stalkers Project to Develop a Model Anti–Stalking Code for the States: A Research Report of the National Institute of Justice (October 1993)

Pretrial Detention

Presumption of innocence is a basic tenet of American jurisprudence and, accordingly, the right to pretrial release is guarded carefully in state constitutions and statutes. Regardless of the charge, pretrial detention is precluded unless the proof is evident or the presumption great that the defendant committed the offense charged. Thirty states allow for the denial of pretrial release only for persons charged with capital offenses or offenses that could result in life imprisonment. In 21 of these states, the limitations are constitutional. In several, even a defendant charged with a capital offense cannot be detained before trial unless there is a specific judicial finding that no release conditions can assure appearance or ensure public safety.

The other 20 states extend restrictions on the opportunity for pretrial release to people charged with offenses other than capital and life imprisonment crimes; however, with few exceptions, release is precluded only if the offense charged is a violent and/or felony offense and if the accused was on bail, probation, or parole for a violent or felony offense at the time of arrest or had previously been convicted of a related felony or violent crime. About half of these states also require a judicial finding of dangerousness or likelihood of nonappearance that no conditions of release can abate. Only Illinois has a specific statutory provision designating stalking as a non-bailable offense.

While stalking often may portend violence, states are unlikely to make detention exceptions for stalking that they have been unwilling to make for other crimes generally considered more serious. Moreover, they are unlikely to make exceptions for stalking when it is accompanied by violence. States with more restrictive pretrial release policies already have decided that charges of violent offenses other than capital and life imprisonment offenses do not warrant exceptions. Most other states can use existing exceptions for violent offenses.

Pretrial Release Conditions

Even if states are unlikely to make stalking a non-bailable offense, they should consider developing appropriate conditions of release for stalking defendants. The bail laws of most states and the District of Columbia explicitly declare one or more of the purposes for release conditions. In each of these states at least one purpose is to ensure the defendant's appearance. In addition, about one half explicitly provide that conditions may be imposed to protect the public or certain members of the public. . . .

Authorizing judicial authorities to impose reasonable conditions of release to reduce the likelihood of danger to the public does not deny defendants their fundamental right to release. Accordingly, states that currently do not allow conditions of release for such purposes should consider doing so.

Virtually all states authorize the pretrial release of people accused of bailable crimes based on their promise to appear when required. Individuals who promise to appear when required are "released on their own recognizance" (ROR). Over half of the states mandate ROR under certain circumstances. For example, 16 require ROR if there is a likelihood of appearance; eight require ROR if there is a likelihood of appearance and the defendant presents no danger; and three require ROR if there is a likelihood of appearance, no danger, and no likely impairment of judicial integrity.

States should consider eliminating ROR for stalking cases. While money bail may not be necessary, states should consider, at a minimum, making it a condition of release that the accused refrain from deliberately contacting the victim and, if appropriate, members of the victim's immediate family. This requirement poses no undue hardship on the defendant; in fact, it may impose considerably less hardship than money bail. Furthermore, it is essential to the victim's security and peace of mind.

Most states' pretrial release laws already enumerate factors for the court to consider in setting release conditions for individuals arrested for bailable offenses in general. Examples of factors states might want to consider include the nature and circumstances of the charge; the background of the accused, including family and community ties, employment, education, and financial resources; the character and mental condition of the accused; the accused's willingness to seek counseling, if appropriate; the probability of the accused's future appearance at court proceedings; the accused's previous criminal record and current status with respect to bail, probation, and parole; the likelihood of the accused endangering the alleged victim, members of the alleged victim's immediate family, or other named individuals; the existence of or application for orders of protection from the accused by the alleged victim or another individual; evidence of the alleged victim's attempts to terminate a relationship with the accused, including but not limited to initiation of separation or divorce proceedings; the accused's use or possession of firearms or other weapons; the accused's use of controlled substances; the likelihood that the accused will violate conditions of release; evidence of past threats by the accused, including but not limited to threats to the alleged victim, members of the alleged victim's family, or witnesses in court proceedings; the extent and nature of available pretrial supervision; and such other considerations that may be relevant to protection of the alleged victim and members of the alleged victim's immediate family....

Pretrial release laws generally enumerate specific conditions of release that the judicial authority may impose on the accused. States should consider authorizing the imposition of specific conditions of pretrial release in stalking cases. Examples of possible conditions of release include subjecting the accused to the custody of a person or organization agreeing to provide adequate supervision; restrictions on movements of the accused, including house arrest with or without electronic monitoring; prohibition on the possession of weapons; prohibition on use and possession of drugs and alcohol; prohibition on contact or other communication with the victim, members of the victim's family, or other named individuals, either directly or through an intermediary; drug treatment and testing; mental health testing and treatment; specified curfew; prohibition on intentionally following the victim; prohibition on going to or near the residence, place of employment, or business of the victim or a member of the victim's immediate family; prohibition on going to or near a school, day-care facility, or similar facility where a dependent child of the victim is in attendance; and other such conditions that may be necessary to ensure the protection of the victim and the victim's immediate family.

. . .

Bail Hearings

Because of the dangers stalkers pose, it is important that the judicial authority be aware of the circumstances of individual cases before releasing alleged stalkers. Conditions of release can best be tailored to the needs of the accused and the victim alike at a formal hearing at which both are present and heard. While release determinations should take place in as timely a fashion as possible, slight delays to enable victim participation are appropriate. If it is impractical for the victim to participate or if the victim chooses not to participate, relevant information about any specific dangers to the victim and efforts by the victim to stop the alleged stalking should be conveyed to the court by the police, pretrial service agency personnel, or other appropriate officials.

Victim Notification

Few pretrial release or bail statutes, as opposed to a number of victims' rights statutes, require victims to be notified of the pretrial release of their alleged perpetrators. An exception is Montana's bail statute: " . . . Whenever a person accused of [stalking] is admitted to bail, the court shall, as soon as possible under the circumstances, make one and if necessary more reasonable attempts, by means that include but are not limited to certified mail, to notify the alleged victim or, if the alleged victim is a minor, the alleged victim's parent or guardian of the accused's release." Under Georgia law, the law enforcement agency, prosecutor, or court directly involved with the victim at the outset of a criminal prosecution for stalking must notify the victim that the victim may provide a telephone number to be used by the custodian of the accused to inform the victim of the defendant's release from custody.

Stalking victims have an obvious concern about the release of their alleged stalkers as well as in any release conditions relevant to their own safety. Such awareness enables victims to plan their own lives accordingly. It also enhances their ability to report violations and, as a consequence, improves the likelihood of compliance. Therefore, states should consider including provisions in their pretrial release or bail laws requiring authorities to make reasonable efforts to provide victims with copies of relevant pretrial release orders together with information about how and to whom to report alleged violations and the sanctions for violations. Notification can be made contingent upon the victim providing a current address or telephone number or upon the victim's request for such notice if there is a means whereby the victim is informed of such requirements.

* * *

NOTES AND QUESTIONS

1. Reluctance on the part of many states to make "dangerousness" a grounds for pretrial detention stems from the fear that it will be used as a catch-all category, and applied in a discriminatory fashion. This fear grows out of the difficulty of knowing, in most cases, whether the defendant, even if ultimately found guilty of the charges being brought against him, poses further risks to his current victims, or to others. Can an argument be made that in stalking cases, or indeed in other domestic violence cases, the continuing danger to victims, and potentially to their family members,

friends and helpers, is more likely than in other cases to reach a level of probability that justifies detention? Within the current framework, the limited availability of pretrial detention, and its restriction to cases involving the most serious allegations of violence, should encourage prosecutors to charge defendants with the most serious crimes their conduct warrants in cases in which pretrial release will jeopardize victims' safety and even their lives.

Massachusetts is an example of a state that has recently incorporated a dangerousness standard into its bail statute. The statute originally provided for release on personal recognizance unless release would "not reasonably assure the appearance of the prisoner before the court." M.G.L. c.276, § 58 (1992). An initial attempt by the legislature to allow courts to consider risk of danger in granting or denying bail, inspired in part by advocacy from the battered women's community, was held unconstitutional in Aime v. Commonwealth, 414 Mass. 667, 611 N.E.2d 204 (1993). A second reform effort built in due process safeguards by requiring a dangerousness hearing before a defendant is detained pretrial on dangerousness grounds. This legislation survived constitutional scrutiny in Mendoza v. Commonwealth, 423 Mass. 771, 673 N.E.2d 22 (1996).

2. For further reading on stalking and domestic violence, see J. Reid Meloy, THE PSYCHOLOGY OF STALKING: CLINICAL AND FORENSIC PERSPECTIVES (1998); Robert L. Snow, STOPPING A STALKER: A COP'S GUIDE TO MAKING THE SYSTEM WORK FOR YOU (1998); George Lardner, THE STALKING OF KRISTIN (1996); Elaine Landau, STALKING (1995); Kenneth R. Thomas, ANTI-STALKING STATUTES: BACKGROUND AND CONSTITUTIONAL ANALYSIS (1992); Leslie J. Kurt, *Stalking as a Variant of Domestic Violence,* 23 AM. ACAD. PSYCH. & LAW BULL. 219 (1995); Robert P. Faulkner & Douglas H. Hsiao, *And Where You Go I'll Follow: The Constitutionality of Antistalking Laws and Proposed Model Legislation,* 31 HARV. J. LEG. 1 (1994); Silvia A. Strikis, *Stopping Stalking,* 81 GEO. L. J. 2771 (1994).

F. DOMESTIC VIOLENCE AS A FEDERAL CRIME

Introductory Note

In the previous chapter, and in this, reference has already been made to the federal role in policing domestic violence. The Violence Against Women Act of 1994, part of the larger Violent Crime Control and Law Enforcement Act of 1994, Pub. L. No. 103–322, 108 Stat. 1796 (codified as amended in scattered sections of 42 U.S.C.), federalized the enforcement of restraining orders by requiring that states provide full faith and credit to orders issued by sister states, but also criminalized interstate violations of restraining orders. (See Chapter 8D, above). In addition, the act made "interstate domestic violence" a federal crime. The definition of "interstate domestic violence" will be explored further in this section. As the previous section of this chapter described, interstate stalking was added to the list of federal domestic violence crimes in 1996. 18 U.S.C. § 2261A. Finally, offenses relating to the transportation or possession of firearms by state and federal domestic violence offenders are incorporated both in the original Violence Against Women Act (for those subject to valid restraining orders), 18 U.S.C. § 922 (g)(8), and in the later and more controversial Lautenberg Amendment (for those convicted of a domestic violence misdemeanor), 18 U.S.C. § 922(g)(9). See Chapters 8D and 9D, above.

These recent criminal provisions are still in the early stages of interpretive refinement in the federal district courts and courts of appeal. In addition, they have faced robust challenges on constitutional and policy grounds, not only by defendants anxious to escape the consequences of federal prosecution, but by scholar and participant observers who worry about the growing role of federal law enforcement in areas traditionally left to the states. This section opens with an excerpt that introduces the interstate domestic violence provision, but also provides a reminder of how the criminal provisions of the Violence Against Women Act fit into the broader context of that legislation. The next readings address interpretive issues arising out of the interstate domestic violence provision. Readers are referred back to Chapter 8D, above, for a parallel discussion of the interstate violation of a restraining order provision. Next, the section addresses the (predominantly unsuccessful) constitutional challenges brought against the criminal provisions. The section closes with arguments for and against the creation of federal crimes from a policy, rather than a constitutional, perspective.

Michelle W. Easterling
For Better or Worse: The Federalization of Domestic Violence, 98 West Virginia Law Review 933, 933–38, 940–43 (1996)

On December 1, 1994, Christopher Jarett Bailey carried his comatose wife Sonya into a Corbin, Kentucky emergency room. The Kentucky physicians discovered a large open wound on Sonya's forehead, two black eyes, bruises on her neck, chin, and forearms, as well as signs of rope burns on her wrists and ankles. Upon inspection of the couple's car, police discovered that the trunk lid was dented on the inside, there were scratch marks around the lock, and there was a pool of blood and urine. The couple had last been seen arguing in a bar on November 25, 1994. Bailey had beaten his wife into unconsciousness at their home in St. Albans, West Virginia. Bailey then began an aimless six-day drive in and out of West Virginia and Kentucky. Sonya had spent at least part of that journey in the trunk. When Bailey finally carried Sonya into a Kentucky hospital, doctors discovered that she had suffered a severe head injury and was near death from the loss of blood, fluids and oxygen. Sonya Bailey's doctors predict that she will spend the remainder of a normal life expectancy comatose in a nursing home. Christopher Bailey, convicted of kidnapping and interstate domestic violence, will spend the remainder of his life in a federal prison. On May 23, 1995, after only two and one-half hours of deliberations, Bailey became the first person convicted under ... the Federal Violence Against Women Act of 1994.

The [Act] ... created two new federal criminal offenses: interstate domestic violence and interstate violation of a protective order....

[The] new [interstate domestic violence] offense allows for the federal prosecution of a person who travels across a state line with the intent to injure, harass, or intimidate his or her spouse, and who intentionally commits a crime of violence causing bodily injury to that spouse. One is also subject to federal prosecution if he or she, like Bailey, causes a spouse to cross a state line by force, coercion, duress, or fraud and in the course or as a result of that conduct intentionally commits a crime of violence causing injury to his or her spouse. The Act calls for the defendants convicted of interstate domestic violence to be sentenced as according to the extent of injuries to the victim. If the victim dies, the offender can be sentenced to life or any term of years. If permanent disfigurement or life threatening bodily injury results, the offender may be sentenced to a maximum of twenty years in prison. If the victim suffers serious bodily injury, or if the offender uses a dangerous weapon when committing the offense, imprisonment can not exceed ten years. Otherwise, sentencing is allowed ... for not more than five years. The VAWA also directs the court to order restitution to be paid to the victim.... Other provisions of the VAWA call for law enforcement and prosecution grants to aid in the reduction of violent crimes against women. Section 2263 allows the victim of domestic violence an opportunity to be heard about the danger posed by the defendant when determining pre-trial release conditions.

. . .

The Violence Against Women Act ... was only enacted after extensive congressional hearings concerning domestic violence statistics and testimonials about domestic abuse. The resulting Act was intended to be a comprehensive piece of legislation in order to prevent, punish, and deter spousal abusers.

. . .

Congress, alarmed by the startling statistics, was apparently convinced that the states were not solving the domestic violence problem, and that the federal government's involvement was needed. Senator Kennedy said that "the bill provides funds to train and educate police, prosecutors and judges so that violence within the family will be taken seriously and treated as the crime that it is." Representative Moakley urged the House that "(d)omestic violence is no longer an issue that we, in society, can ignore or simply dismiss as a lover's quarrel."

. . .

Perhaps the most straightforward remarks were made by Representative Schumer from New York:

> (t)here is a dirty little secret hidden here, and that secret is that our legal system is all too indifferent to this violence. Our legal system looks the other way, tolerating the daily battering and abuse of women.... A woman is raped; she goes to the police and is told, "You aren't really hurt. Just try and forget about it." Another victim is told

by the prosecutor, "I won't bring this case because you were wearing a short skirt." A woman has her nose broken by her husband. When the police finally come they say, "You two work out your problems together." A woman goes before a judge asking for a protection order from a husband she has tried to leave, and the judge says, "Why are you two wasting our time with marital squabbles?"

. . .

Congress responded to the terrifying testimonials and statistics with the VAWA. The Act was intended to be a comprehensive arsenal to fight a war against gender-motivated violence. The VAWA was designed to deter, punish and rehabilitate offenders in order to prevent domestic abuse. Senator Biden explained that the bill would make women substantially safer because of the increased number of battered women's shelters, the education of prosecutors and judges, and the creation of both criminal and civil causes of actions. Grants were included to train and educate police, prosecutors and judges so that domestic violence "would be taken seriously." Funds were also allotted to assist law enforcement, support counselors and shelters, and restore a national toll-free domestic violence hotline.

As passed, the VAWA provided for $1.62 billion to be given to the states over the next six years for funding community programs to battle violence against women and provide battered women with support. Each state was to receive $500,000 a year, with additional funds to be provided to states with higher populations. In 1995, Congress allotted $426,000 for each state. After the states submitted plans to the Department of Justice, the government planned to release the remainder of the funds. For example, West Virginia's general plan includes training and cross-training between law enforcement, courts, and those who provide direct services to abuse victims. The plan also contains more legal advocates to aid victims and a computerized system to allow officers to track protective orders across county lines. It extends direct services to all fifty-five West Virginia counties and provides awareness about local resources which would help women in abusive situations.

Finally, the VAWA also called for several studies to be conducted by various branches of government to examine gender bias in courts, campus sexual assaults, battered women's syndrome, the confidentiality of victims' addresses, and domestic violence related recordkeeping. These studies were designed to gain a clear understanding of the origins and extent of women's issues and to provide recommendations for further reform.

* * *

NOTE

1. Although Easterling uses the word "spouse" in her account of the interstate domestic violence provision, the language of the statute actually encompasses all "intimate partners":

18 U.S.C. § 2261 Interstate Domestic Violence

(a) Offenses—

(1) Crossing a State line—A person who travels across a State line or enters or leaves Indian country with the intent to injure, harass, or intimidate that person's spouse or intimate partner, and who, in the course of or as a result of such travel, intentionally commits a crime of violence and thereby causes bodily injury to such spouse or intimate partner, shall be punished as provided in subsection (b).

(2) Causing the crossing of a State line—A person who causes a spouse or intimate partner to cross a State line or to enter or leave Indian country by force, coercion, duress, or fraud and, in the course or as a result of that conduct, intentionally commits a crime of violence and thereby causes bodily injury to the person's spouse or intimate partner, shall be punished as provided in subsection (b).

Subsection (b) contains the schedule of penalties outlined by Easterling in the excerpt above. It is the same schedule that applies to interstate violations of restraining orders, discussed in the previous chapter, and interstate stalking, discussed in the previous section of this chapter.

Interpretive Issues

In United States v. Bailey, 112 F. 3d 758 (4th Cir. 1997), the Fourth Circuit Court of Appeals upheld Christopher Bailey's conviction for interstate domestic violence under the jurisdictional trigger identified in § 2261(2); injuring a partner by a crime of violence in the course of causing him or her to cross a State line by force, coercion, duress or fraud. A similar conviction was obtained in United States v. Hornsby, 88 F.3d 336 (5th Cir. 1996), in which the principal issue raised by the defendant on appeal was application of the federal sentencing guidelines. The court had only this to say about the defendant's conduct: "On June 13, 1995, in Brookeland Texas, Horsby approached his former girlfriend and asked to speak to her. When she refused, Hornsby choked her until she was unconscious, placed her in an automobile, and took her to Louisiana, where he was apprehended." Id. at 338.

In a third case, United States v. Page, the defendant objected that his violence toward his girlfriend had ended before he caused her to cross a state line, and that § 2261(2) did not properly apply. The defendant was convicted in the District Court for the Southern District of Ohio after a jury trial. On appeal the Sixth Circuit reversed and remanded, finding that:

> "this statute does not criminalize domestic violence that occurs prior to interstate travel. Rather, the statute only covers domestic violence occurring 'in the course or as a result of' such travel. Interpreted in this way, the statute criminalizes the aggravation of injuries inflicted before interstate travel only so long as the worsening of the injuries was caused by intentional violent conduct during interstate travel. Because the jury was not instructed on the proper interpretation of the statute, we reverse the defendant's conviction and remand for retrial."

136 F.3d 481, 483 (1998). The United States then obtained a rehearing en banc, and when the sixteen members of the plenary panel were equally divided in their vote, the defendant's conviction and sentence were restored. A petition for certiorari was filed on May 21, 1999. The following excerpts from opinions in the case both supporting and opposing the conviction address the interpretive question raised.

United States v. Page

167 F.3d 325.
United States Court of Appeals for the Sixth Circuit, 1999.

■ KAREN NELSON MOORE, CIRCUIT JUDGE, concurring in the order.

. . .

Derek Page, the defendant in this case, was convicted under 18 U.S.C. § 2261(a)(2).... On appeal, he raises the questions whether physical violence that occurs before interstate travel begins can satisfy the "in the course ... of that conduct" requirement of § 2261(a)(2) and whether a threat of violence that results in the aggravation of pre-existing injuries can be a "crime of violence" causing "bodily injury" for purposes of the statute. I would answer both questions in the affirmative and conclude that there was sufficient evidence for the jury to convict Page under either theory....

I. BACKGROUND

[All citations to the record have been omitted.]

The facts of this case are not unlike the stories of many women who attempt to leave abusive relationships. Carla Scrivens's relationship with Page started out on fairly blissful terms. Yet, Page soon became controlling, possessive, and even physically abusive, demanding that Scrivens stop associating with her friends and family, controlling what she could wear and eat, and on one occasion even punishing her disobedience with a stun gun and mace. In light of the deterioration of their relationship, after less than three months together, Scrivens told Page that she was moving out and ending their relationship.

The planned attack against Scrivens took place when she attempted to retrieve her belongings, all of which were still in Page's condominium in Columbus, Ohio. Upon Scrivens's arrival, Page pushed her down, dragged her away from the door when she attempted to leave, and tried to spray her with mace. He then beat her with his fists, a claw hammer, and a pipe wrench over the course of several hours. Scrivens also testified that Page used a stun gun during the assault. After the beating, Page carried his victim, who could not walk on her battered feet and legs, and who had fallen into unconsciousness several times during the attack, and placed her into his car under threat of further violence from his stun gun. Page then drove around for approximately four hours, crossing state lines through West Virginia into Pennsylvania and intentionally passing several local hospitals on the way even though Scrivens pleaded with him to stop for medical treatment at either Riverside or Ohio State University, two hospitals in the Columbus area. During this time, Scrivens continued to bleed, and painful swelling from her injuries increased. Page eventually left her at a hospital in Washington, Pennsylvania, where, after she realized that Page would not return, Scrivens told emergency room personnel that Page had attacked her, and agreed to report the incident to the police.

II. Statutory Scope

Page's conduct, as presented to the jury, falls within the scope of § 2261(a)(2) under at least two theories of liability. The evidence showed that he committed interstate domestic violence both: (1) when, by beating his ex-girlfriend into a state of semi-consciousness over the course of several hours, he was enabled to and did force her across state lines against her will in an attempt to evade the law, and (2) when he forced her to travel interstate under threat of violence, intentionally preventing her from obtaining medical treatment, thereby causing aggravation of her pre-existing injuries.

A. *"In the Course of": Infliction of Bodily Injury Integrally Related to the Forcible Transportation of a Victim Across State Lines*

In order to escape liability under § 2261(a)(2), Page argues that "in the course ... of that conduct" as used in the statute refers to the narrow act of "crossing a State line" rather than to all conduct involved in "causing a spouse or intimate partner to cross a State line ... by force, coercion, duress, or fraud." ... This construction not only distorts the plain language of the statute but also makes little sense given the reality of the crime and the very reasons why Congress believed federal involvement was necessary in this area that has traditionally been left to the states.

The crime of violence that took place inside Page's condominium—the beating and the use of a stun gun and mace—is precisely what enabled Page to force Scrivens to travel across state lines. The beating subdued his victim, rendered her in no condition to resist him physically as she was being placed into his car, and frightened her so severely that she agreed not to make any "commotion" that might attract attention and aid from others once they left his condominium. The attack also allowed Page to retain control over Scrivens during the forcible transportation. Not surprisingly, a person who has just been beaten in the manner Scrivens had been is far less capable physically and emotionally of attempting an escape, formulating a method of escape, or eliciting aid from others. The beating was an integral part of the forcible transportation since it enabled Page to force Scrivens on an unwilling four-hour journey the destination of which was not revealed to Scrivens until much later. Consequently, the beating that took place inside Page's condominium clearly occurred "in the course" of Page forcibly "causing" Scrivens "to cross a State line."

Furthermore, evidence presented to the jury showed that Page removed Scrivens from the local area precisely because he feared the consequences of his having harmed her and knew that interstate travel would make it more difficult for police authorities to hold him liable for his crime. It is difficult to believe that Congress intended to exclude from this statute's purview the beating of an intimate partner by a batterer who then forcibly transports his victim across state lines under threat of further violence in order to avoid detection from the law. Gaps and inadequacies of state law enforcement were among the main reasons for which federal legislation dealing with domestic violence was thought to be necessary. The VAWA was intended to deal with the problem of batterers who make their crimes more difficult to discover and prosecute by carrying or forcing their intimate partners across state lines. *See* S. REP. NO. 103–138, at 43, 62; *see also Gluzman,* 953 F. Supp. at 87. Those who enacted the VAWA's interstate domestic violence provision recognized that batterers were using interstate travel as a loophole in the system of state law enforcement and that such crimes, "because of their interstate nature, transcend the abilities of State law enforcement agencies." S. REP. NO. 103–138, at 62. When batterers take their victims across state lines, local prosecutors often encounter difficulties subpoenaing hospital documents and witnesses from other states. Multi-state jurisdiction is also valuable during the investigative stage, in which local police officers encounter similar barriers.... As it has often done, Congress used the VAWA "to 'come to the aid of the states in detecting and punishing criminals whose offenses are complete under state law, but who utilize the channels of interstate commerce to make a successful getaway and thus make the state's detecting and punitive processes impotent.' " ... Page's crabbed interpretation would prevent the statute from reaching precisely the type of situation for which a federal domestic violence statute would be needed and that § 2261(a)(2) was intended to cover.

... To assume that Congress intended to criminalize only those beatings occurring precisely during travel but not those occurring inside a home that are integrally related to forcible interstate travel would be to suggest that Congress somehow missed the boat.

The text of § 2261(a)(2) refers to violence that occurs in a course of "conduct." Its neighboring statutes demonstrate that Congress knew how to say in the course of "travel" when it wanted to. In addition to interstate domestic violence, Congress has created the federal crimes of interstate stalking and interstate violation of a protection order. *See* 18 U.S.C. § § 2261A (interstate stalking), 2262 (interstate violation of protection order). All three of these statutes require interstate travel as an element of the crime, but only § 2261(a)(2) and § 2262(a)(2) involve forcing another person to cross state lines. Sections 2261 and 2262 are parallel, prohibiting interstate domestic violence and interstate violation of a protection order, respectively. Subsection (a)(1) of each section prohibits interstate travel with the intent to commit domestic violence or violate a protection order, respectively. In these provisions—and in § 2261A, which prohibits travel with the intent to harass—coverage is clearly limited to violence or harassment that occurs during or after interstate travel: the statutes refer to actions that occur "subsequent[]" to interstate travel or "in the course of or as a result of such travel." See 18 U.S.C. § § 2261(a)(1), 2261A, 2262(a)(1)(B). In contrast, subsection (a)(2) of both § 2261 and § 2262 specifically addresses violations that involve forcing another person to travel, and only these two subsections, of all the VAWA crimes, refer to "that conduct." This is a sensible distinction that should not be read out of the statute.

B. "In the Course of": Aggravation of Injuries During Forced Interstate Travel

The government argues that Page's threats during the trip to Pennsylvania resulted in "bodily injury" to the extent that they kept Scrivens from receiving medical treatment sooner and aggravated her preexisting wounds. I agree that threats can be a "crime of violence," that aggravation of preexisting injuries can be "bodily injury," and that there was sufficient evidence to convict Page under this theory.

A "crime of violence" includes "an offense that has as an element the use, attempted use, or threatened use of physical force against the person or property of another." 18 U.S.C. § 16(a). It may also be an offense "that is a felony and that, by its nature, involves a substantial risk that physical force against the person or property of another may be used in the course of committing the offense." 18 U.S.C. § 16(b). To meet this definition, the government was required to prove that Page committed some state or federal "offense" and that this offense was of a type described in § 16(a) or (b). The two offenses that the jury considered were kidnaping and assault. . . .

In addition to proving that Page committed a kidnaping or an assault during the actual travel, in order to obtain a conviction under its aggravation-of-injury theory, the government had to prove that the kidnaping or assault caused Scrivens to suffer bodily injury. . . .

Nowhere does the statute suggest that the bodily injury must be an injury newly inflicted, completely distinct from the prior criminal actions of the batterer. Such a limitation would make little sense. If we were to require that an injury be "fresh" in order to satisfy the statute, Page's actions would not constitute a crime of interstate domestic violence even if Scrivens had bled to death or gone into shock during and as a result of the forcible transportation. Page's interpretation would also prevent the statute from reaching the conduct at issue in United States v. Bailey, 112 F.3d 758 (4th Cir.), cert. denied, 522 U.S. 896, 118 S. Ct. 240, 139 L. Ed. 2d 170 (1997). The defendant in *Bailey* severely injured his wife, put her in a car, and drove around West Virginia and Kentucky for five days before taking her to a hospital. The victim suffered further injuries—including blood loss, which led to permanent brain damage, and dehydration, which led to renal failure—due to the defendant's failure to obtain medical care or provide adequate food and water. There was no question in *Bailey* that the statute applied. Yet, there is no relevant distinction between a person who forcibly prevents his intimate partner from obtaining medical care, causing her to bleed to death; a person who forcibly prevents his diabetic intimate partner from obtaining insulin shots, causing her to fall into a coma; and a person who forcibly prevents his intimate partner from obtaining food and water for several days, causing her to suffer renal failure. Any prior criminal actions of these batterers should in no way weaken or negate the observation that these three situations are analogous and that in all of these scenarios the batterer has committed a crime of violence causing bodily harm.

■ KENNEDY, CIRCUIT JUDGE, dissenting in the order.

. . .

Preceded by a descriptive caption, one sentence containing four separate elements defines the federal domestic violence crime in question:

Causing the crossing of a State line.—A person who [1] *causes* a spouse or intimate partner *to cross a State line* or to enter or leave Indian country by force, coercion, duress, or fraud [2] *and, in the course or as a result of that conduct,* [3] intentionally commits a crime of violence [4] *and thereby causes bodily injury* to the person's spouse or intimate partner, shall be punished as provided in subsection (b). 18 U.S.C. § 2261(a)(2) (Emphasis and numbering added).

A literal or precise reading of the words of the sentence, and the sequence of elements described there, requires me to find that Page should not be punished under this statute for the criminal assault that occurred before he began to cause Scrivens to cross a state line. That result is necessary because an offender is covered by the statute only if he "causes" the victim "to cross a state line" by force, coercion, duress, or fraud, and "causes bodily injury" to the victim "in the course ... of that conduct;" that conduct of causing the victim "to cross a state line" by force, coercion, duress, or fraud. The literal meaning of the words does not allow punishment of a man who beats a woman before the journey begins *unless of course his purpose in inflicting bodily injury is to cause her to cross state lines*. The provision therefore criminalizes an act of domestic violence that occurs before interstate travel actually begins only if the violence is the same "force" that the attacker employs to cause his victim to cross state lines against her will *and* the attacker's purpose at the time he inflicts the injury is to transport his victim across state lines.

The construction I have described above appears to be the obvious meaning of the statute. In criminal law, we should not strain to give a broad construction to a penal statute. For centuries in Anglo–American law, the rule of lenity has required a strict construction of criminal statutes.... As Judge Merritt explained in the original panel's opinion in this case, "we must enforce the statute according to the words that Congress actually adopted and not according to our own view of what might be a better or more comprehensive statutory policy on domestic violence against women." United States v. Page, 136 F.3d 481, 484 (6th Cir. 1998).

Judge Moore concludes that because Scrivens was completely incapacitated by the attack, she was under Page's control continuously from the time she entered the condominium until she crossed state lines, and that this somehow permitted the jury to find that the injuries she suffered in the attack in the condominium were inflicted in the course of causing her to cross state lines. While I agree that injuries inflicted before any travel begins can be found to be a part of "that conduct" if inflicted to cause the victim to cross state lines, there is no evidence here that such intent caused any of the injuries Scrivens sustained before she was placed in the car.

Were the evidence in this case such that the jury could conclude that the *severity* of the attack was to enable Page to take Scrivens across state lines to a distant hospital, then I could agree that conduct was covered by the statute. . . .

If there were some evidence that any of the *particular injuries* inflicted on Scrivens were inflicted not merely to prevent her escape from the condominium, but specifically in order to make it easier to transport her across state lines, . . . I could then agree that Page's attack is covered by the statute. While causing someone to cross state lines encompasses broader conduct than simply traveling across state lines, still there must be some evidence from which the jury could find the connection between the earlier violence and "causing" the victim to travel. . . .

In sum, the plain language of section 2261(a)(2) shows that Congress did not intend the statute to apply to those attacks where, after the fact, the defendant decides to use interstate travel to conceal his wrongdoing. By no means do I suggest that Congress should not have criminalized such conduct. Indeed, the particularly disturbing facts of cases such as *Page* and United States v. Bailey suggest that it would not have been illogical to criminalize flight across state lines to avoid apprehension. As enacted by Congress, however, the Act requires the attacker to intend to cause interstate travel. The provision at issue applies to situations where "force, coercion, duress or fraud" on the part of the defendant triggers the interstate travel, and then sometime in the course or as a result of *causing* the victim to travel, the defendant commits a crime of violence and inflicts bodily injury on the victim. Sadly, Congress simply did not draft the statute to cover the situation in which an attacker first beats an intimate partner, and only later develops the intent to transport her across state lines in order to hamstring law enforcement efforts or conceal evidence. If Congress intends to criminalize such conduct, Congress should state so clearly. Accordingly, I would reverse the judgment and the conviction.

I agree with Judge Moore that the evidence would permit the jury to find that the further injuries Scrivens suffered while the defendant was causing her to cross state lines would sustain a guilty verdict. However, the case was neither argued to the jury nor submitted on instructions on that theory. I would, therefore remand the case for a new trial on that theory.

* * *

NOTES AND QUESTIONS

1. In United States v. Helem, 186 F.3d 449 (4th Cir. 1999), the Fourth Circuit followed the reasoning of Circuit Judge Moore in the Page case, upholding the defendant's conviction in District court in a case very similar to Page. The defendant viciously assaulted his wife in their Maryland apartment, as she was packing to leave him, and then drove her through Virginia to North Carolina. Eventually he took her to a hospital, where he "hovered over her" and told medical personnel she had been in a car

accident. She was able to communicate what had happened to her, and the defendant was arrested. The court concluded:

> The evidence showed that Helem committed interstate domestic violence both (1) when, by beating his wife into a state of semi-consciousness, he was enabled to and did force her across state lines against her will in an attempt to evade the law, and (2) when he forced her to travel across state lines under threat of violence, intentionally preventing her from obtaining medical treatment, thereby exacerbating her injuries.

Id. at 455. On November 15, 1999 the Supreme Court denied certiorari in *Page,* 120 S.Ct. 496, 145 L.Ed. 382, 68 U.S.L.W. 3325 (1999). If the Court had granted certiorari, which party do you think would have had the stronger argument on this issue? If it had decided against the United States, would the decision in Bailey also be vulnerable, or are the facts in Bailey distinguishable?

Constitutional Challenges

The criminal provisions of the Violence Against Women Act rest on Congress's authority to regulate interstate commerce under the Commerce Clause. Historically, this power has been far reaching. The Supreme Court has traditionally upheld federal statutes demonstrating only the most tenuous links to interstate commerce, and for decades those convicted of federal crimes have been unsuccessful in challenging, under the Commerce Clause, the criminal statutes on which their convictions were based.

However, with its decision in United States v. Lopez, 514 U.S. 549 (1995), the Supreme Court signalled its willingness to reconsider its interpretation of congressional Commerce Clause authority. The defendant in Lopez successfully challenged a provision of the Gun–Free School Zone Act (GFSZA) of 1990, on the grounds that the prohibited conduct—knowingly possessing a firearm within 1000 feet of a school—had an insufficient connection to interstate commerce. In the years since Lopez was decided, litigation has tested the new limits on congressional authority, only to discover that the changes heralded by Lopez were less than many imagined they might be.

On the strength of Lopez, defendants in cases brought under VAWA's criminal provisions challenged Congress's authority to regulate interstate domestic violence (and interstate violations of restraining orders) under the Commerce Clause. With one exception, United States v. Wright, 965 F.Supp. 1307 (D.Neb. 1997), rev'd on appeal, 128 F.3d 1274 (8th Cir. 1997), the courts have distinguished Lopez and the GFSZA, and upheld the validity of both § 2261 and § 2262. A thorough analysis is provided by the Southern District of New York, in United States v. Gluzman, 953 F.Supp. 84 (S.D.N.Y. 1997), in an opinion adopted wholesale by the Second Circuit, which described the analysis as "admirable." 154 F.3d 49, 50 (2d Cir. 1998). For another Circuit Court of Appeals decision upholding the interstate domestic violence provision of VAWA, see United States v. Bailey, 112 F. 3d 758 (4th Cir. 1997), and for a parallel decision upholding the interstate violation of a restraining order provision see United States v. Von Foelkel, 136 F.3d 339 (3d Cir. 1998).

United States v. Gluzman

953 F. Supp. 84.
United States District Court for the Southern District of New York, 1997.

■ PARKER, DISTRICT JUDGE.

On April 25, 1996, defendant Rita Gluzman ... was indicted for conspiring to commit interstate domestic violence and for committing interstate domestic violence in violation of 18 U.S.C. § 2261 (1996). Gluzman moves to dismiss the indictment on the ground that Congress, when it enacted section 2261, exceeded its authority under the Commerce Clause. See U.S. Const., Art. I, § 8, cl. 3. For the reasons stated below, I find the challenged provision to be a constitutional exercise of Congress' power to regulate interstate commerce. Accordingly, the motion to dismiss is denied.

. . .

Gluzman argues ... that the legislative history of 18 U.S.C. § 2261 fails to indicate that the statute as finally enacted was based on any findings in that history that the interstate travel in furtherance of spousal abuse was activity that affected interstate commerce. She further contends that section 2261 neither regulates a commercial activity nor contains a requirement that the activity in question be connected to interstate commerce, and therefore its enactment exceeded the authority of Congress to legislate under the Commerce Clause.

The challenged statutory provision arose in an area in which Congressional power is exceedingly broad....

Review of the legislative history of the section, although sparse, indicates that Congress had a rational basis for concluding that the regulation of interstate domestic violence was "reasonably adapted to [an] end permitted by the Constitution." ... Congress, in enacting section 2261, alluded to the substantial toll of domestic violence on the physical and economic welfare of individuals directly affected by such violence as well as the public generally.... Although gender-based violence, particularly when it is targeted against women, was clearly of primary concern to Congress, it was not the exclusive motive for the VAWA in its entirety. As previously noted, when addressing section 2261, the Committee considered, in nongender specific terms, "the health care, criminal justice, and other social costs of domestic violence," ... and crafted what it believed to be an "appropriate response to the problem[s] of domestic violence which, because of their interstate nature, transcend the abilities of State law enforcement agencies." ...

Having determined that a rational basis exists, "the only remaining question for judicial inquiry is whether the 'means chosen by [Congress] [are] reasonably adapted to the end permitted by the Constitution.'" ...

Gluzman suggests that the Supreme Court's recent decision in United States v. Lopez, ... compels the conclusion that they are not.

... In defining the contours of the Commerce Clause, the Lopez Court identified three broad categories of activity that Congress may regulate under its commerce power: (1) the use of the channels of interstate commerce; (2) the instrumentalities of interstate commerce or persons or things in interstate commerce, even though the threat comes only from intrastate activity; and (3) intrastate activities that have a substantial relation to interstate commerce.... Lopez, however, was concerned only with the third category of activity, and did not purport to affect Congress' exercise of its commerce power with regard to the regulation of the use of the channels or instrumentalities of commerce.

Unlike the statute at issue in Lopez, section 2261 does not regulate purely local activity, but, instead, is an exercise of Congress' power under the first category of cases articulated by the Lopez Court—the authority to regulate the use of channels of commerce. Furthermore, the statute clearly requires an identifiable interstate nexus, namely, the crossing of a state line with the criminal intent to commit domestic violence against one's spouse and the actual commission of such violence. See 18 U.S.C. § 2261(a). Section 2261 therefore avoids the constitutional deficiencies identified in Lopez where the interstate nexus was non-existent and the activity to be regulated was purely local. Thus, whatever limitation Lopez may have recognized with respect to congressional power over intrastate activities that may affect commerce, the decision did not speak to the broad power of Congress to regulate the channels of interstate commerce, an area occupied by section 2261 as well as numerous other criminal statutes. See, e.g., 18 U.S.C. § 1073 (criminalizing travel in interstate commerce to avoid prosecution); 18 U.S.C. § 1201 (criminalizing kidnaping if the victim is transported in interstate commerce); 18 U.S.C. § 1952 (prohibiting travel in interstate commerce to carry on certain specified unlawful activities including, inter alia, extortion, bribery or arson); 18 U.S.C. § 2314 (prohibiting the transportation or transfer in interstate commerce of stolen property).

Congress' authority "to keep the channels of interstate commerce free from immoral or injurious uses has been frequently sustained, and is no longer open to question." ... Thus, courts consistently have upheld federal criminal statutes that regulate the crossing of state lines by persons or things in a manner incident to some criminal activity....

Gluzman contends, nonetheless, that Congress exceeded the scope of its authority under the Commerce Clause by attempting to regulate an activity that was not commercial. According to the defendant, for statutory enactments under Lopez categories one and two to pass constitutional muster, such regulations must involve "economic activity" or must expressly require movement "in interstate commerce" as grounds for jurisdiction. In other words, in order to affect the channels of interstate commerce as a basis for regulation, the conduct sought to be criminalized must involve the transportation of something—e.g. pornography or goods—from state to state or at a minimum some other commercial activity that has a clearly identifiable connection with commerce.

While these contentions might carry some weight if the analysis concerns whether local activities substantially affect interstate commerce, they are wide of the mark where, as here, the statute regulates conduct in interstate commerce. Five days after Lopez was decided, in United States v. Robertson, 514 U.S. 669 ... (1995) (per curiam), the Supreme Court reaffirmed the distinction between activities in interstate commerce and local activities that substantially affect interstate commerce. There, the Court concluded that it was not necessary to prove that an Alaskan gold mine "affect[ed]" interstate commerce to bring it under the Racketeer Influenced and Corrupt Organizations Act (RICO); it was sufficient merely to prove that the gold mine was an "enterprise ... engaged in ... interstate or foreign commerce." ... The Court made clear that "[t]he 'affecting commerce' test was developed [] to define the extent of Congress' power over purely intra state commercial activities that nonetheless have substantial inter state effect." ...

As the Ninth Circuit recently stated, the Supreme court in Robertson "explained that the[] three bases of congressional authority [identified in Lopez] are analytically distinct." ... Thus, to the extent that Congress seeks to regulate persons or things in interstate commerce—as opposed to local activities that affect interstate commerce—its power to do so was not changed by Lopez.

It has long been established that Congress can not only regulate activities that involve interstate or international transportation of goods and people, but it can do so "regardless of whether the transportation is motivated by a 'commercial purpose.' " ... Congress has long exercised the authority to keep the channels of interstate commerce free from injurious noncommercial uses, including, among others, the transportation of firearms for private use, ... pornography for private use, ... liquor for private use, ... and obscene materials for private use.... The Court has also upheld the Mann Act's application to interstate transportation of persons for an immoral purpose—polygamy—on the ground that the statute, "while primarily aimed at the use of interstate commerce for the purpose of commercialized sex, is not restricted to that end." ...

Moreover, this Court cannot glean, as Gluzman urges, any principled distinction between Congress' power to prohibit one from transporting an article or another person and its power to prohibit the use of commerce by the illegal actor herself. Indeed, statutes regulating persons who cross state lines harboring the intent to commit an unlawful activity have consistently been upheld as within Congress' authority under the commerce clause.

. . .

Section 2261 has the requisite relation to interstate commerce as defined under controlling law since it is triggered only if an individual crosses a state line with the intent to injure, harass, or intimidate his or her spouse or intimate partner, and that travel actually results in the intentional commission of a crime of violence that causes bodily injury to such spouse or intimate partner. See 18 U.S.C. § 2261. As was previously noted, it is a "well settled principle that Congress may impose relevant conditions and requirements on those who use the channels of interstate commerce in order that those channels will not become the means of promoting or spreading evil, whether physical, moral, or economic in mature." . . .

* * *

Broader Federalization Concerns

Sections 2261 and 2262 may well survive all constitutional challenges based on the scope of the powers accorded to Congress under the Commerce Clause, as the prior analysis suggests. Nonetheless, there are those who oppose the creation of these, and many other, federal crimes, on broader policy grounds. The following two excerpts provide a concise summary of these objections, and of the arguments mounted by those with a more positive view of the federal role in this and other arenas. The authors of the second piece were, at the time they delivered their remarks at a symposium at Hastings College of Law, the Deputy Attorney General and a Deputy Assistant Attorney General, respectively, with the U.S. Department of Justice.

Anti–Federalization Arguments
Michelle Easterling, For Better or Worse: The Federalization of Domestic Violence, 98 West Virginia Law Review 933, 944–946 (1996)

The primary argument against the federalization of criminal offenses is that it would swell the federal judicial docket. The increased workload is said to reduce the quality of adjudication by decreasing the time and attention judges spend on each individual case. Expanding the federal docket with cases that can be handled effectively by the states is considered a misallocation of resources. Many of these problems are blamed on the Speedy Trial Act requirements, which are accused of pushing "civil cases off the docket altogether" or causing "such severe backlogs as to result in dismissals of serious criminal cases." With more than 3,000 federal crimes now on the books, many of those sharing jurisdiction with nearly identical state crimes, the concern for overwhelming the federal courts is widespread. . . .

Another prevalent de-federalization argument is that the federalization of criminal statutes is a blatant usurpation of states' rights. The states traditionally were left with primary jurisdiction over criminal problems because they were largely of local interest and impact. As Congress creates more and more federal criminal offenses, it shows less and less regard for the states. For example, by enacting the death penalty for dozens of federal crimes, Congress has encroached upon the will of several states and the District of Columbia which have banned capital punishment.

One reason proffered for federalization is that it achieves uniformity in the law. This uniformity ordinarily involves stiffer sentencing, often ten to twenty times higher. However, criminal offenders committing identical crimes can now receive radically different treatment depending on who prosecutes them. For example, Christopher Bailey, convicted of kidnapping and interstate domestic violence, received life in prison and cannot seek parole for thirty-five years (when he reaches age 70). If he had been prosecuted and convicted for his crimes against Sonya by the state of West Virginia, he would have been sentenced to between two and ten years in prison for malicious assault. Even more alarming than the sentencing disparity is that in some cases double jeopardy does not bar an offender being tried by both federal and state prosecutors.

The primary problem with the stiffer sentencing is the arbitrariness by which a defendant is subjected to federal criminal prosecution, so arbitrary in fact that it has been called "a cruel lottery." While the United States Attorney's manual contains general guidelines to aid in the decision of whether to prosecute, the manual does not mandate that the federal prosecutors try the case. The lack of set guidelines has given rise to unusual forms of prosecutorial discretion such as "Federal Day" in the Southern District of New York. "Federal Day" is one random day each week on which all street-level drug offenders apprehended by police are tried in federal court, with the stiffer federal penalties, in an attempt to create a Russian–Roulette type of deterrence. Much of the prosecutorial discretion in federal cases is exercised with a similar motive. . . .

After being convicted in federal court, the offenders have no equal protection challenge to the disparity in sentencing, even if the prosecutor's decision to try the case was motivated by the harsher sentence itself. Those opposed to federalization note that the sentencing disparity between identical federal and state crimes is contrary to federal sentencing policy. The Sentencing Reform Act of 1984 states that one of the factors to be considered in sentencing is the avoidance of disparities among similar defendants with similar records found guilty of similar conduct. In some cases, rather than promoting uniformity, prosecutors have seized the disparity and used the tougher federal sentence as a threat so that a defendant will take a plea bargain and sentence from state court. The disparate treatment of offenders, as well as the arbitrariness in choosing a forum, lead many to criticize the federalization of criminal law.

* * *

Jamie Gorelick and Harry Litman
Prosecutorial Discretion and the Federalization Debate, 46 Hastings Law Journal 967, 968–77 (1995)

. . . [P]roposals for the creation of new federal crimes have drawn fire on a number of grounds. Some claim that the continuing federalization of crime will swamp the federal courts with "local" crimes, thereby preventing them from fulfilling a traditional role of adjudicating distinctively federal matters. Other critics believe that some of the recently enacted federal crimes inappropriately infringe on federalism interests by taking matters traditionally of local concern out of the hands of local officials. Still others believe that the new federal criminal laws are political gimmicks that will do nothing to address the nation's real crime problems.

Many scholars and judges have attempted to address these concerns with proposals that call on Congress to maintain strict subject matter limits on the business of the federal courts....

At least two ideas animate such proposals. The first is that the federal courts are a scarce resource with specialized functions that cannot be fully performed in the state courts. The second is that matters of public concern can be neatly divided into fixed spheres of federal and of state responsibility so that it is possible and useful to divide criminal jurisdiction generally into "inherently state areas" and "inherently federal areas."

The Department wholeheartedly subscribes to the first of these two ideas: for a number of well-known reasons, the federal courts must be viewed as a scarce resource whose specialized functions should be carefully safeguarded. Federal judges have life tenure, have a distinguished record as guardians of individual liberties, and are few in number. By virtue of sheer numbers, the federal courts can handle only a small fraction of the criminal business of the nation's courts: today, well over ninety-five percent of criminal prosecutions take place in the state courts.... Adding criminal cases indiscriminately to the docket of the federal courts would squander a valuable resource that, if wisely deployed, could make a significant difference in the nation's struggle with crime. At the same time, indiscriminate expansion of the federal criminal docket would impair the ability of the federal courts to fulfill their important responsibilities in the civil realm.

For these reasons, we agree that it is vital to identify where the potential lies for a distinctively federal contribution to the fight against crime and to ensure that, as in other areas of the law, the federal government's role is designed to exploit its peculiar advantages.

But the Department does not agree that the principle for identifying a distinctively federal contribution should—or can—be framed in terms of fixed spheres of federal and state activity.... That approach has significant failings.

First, such a limiting principle cannot be squared with the historical development of the federal courts' jurisdiction. Large sections of the federal criminal code—including offenses that today are universally accepted as core federal court matters—originally represented an extension of the federal law into areas traditionally and concurrently subject to state jurisdiction.... Even civil rights offenses—often cited as the paradigm of proper federal criminal jurisdiction—are clearly appropriate for prosecution under state law. Indeed, a strict application of the "fixed-spheres" approach would leave no room for the Department to respond to state prosecutions that leave compelling federal interests unvindicated, as in the Rodney King or Crown Heights cases....

... [C]ases in which a state is completely unable to prosecute because of, for example, jurisdictional problems or the inability of the state to protect witnesses are only the most extreme examples of cases in which the federal government has a demonstrable advantage in dealing with certain aspects of a crime problem.... [A] federal response may [also] be needed so secure full justice in other cases. Federal legal and investigative advantages in some instances permit the federal government to undertake a complete and efficient prosecution where a state could not. But such full justice will not be possible unless the federal government is able to assert a concurrent jurisdiction over the kind of criminal conduct at issue....

Our view on the scope of federal criminal jurisdiction is that it is appropriate for Congress to provide for federal involvement in a particular criminal area where: (1) there is a pressing problem of national concern; (2) state criminal jurisdiction is inadequate to solve significant aspects of the problem; and (3) the federal government—by virtue of its investigative, prosecutorial or legal resources—is positioned to make a qualitative difference to the solution of the problem....

... It is exceedingly difficult to draft a statute in a way that includes only those crimes that are sophisticated, inter-jurisdictional, or sensitive enough to require a federal solution. In order to allow sufficient flexibility to bring a federal prosecution when an aspect of a law enforcement problem requires it, federal criminal jurisdiction will inevitably have to be overinclusive. It will have to be drafted in a way that includes criminal activities that state and local criminal justice systems can handle, as well as activities that they cannot.

... The exercise of prosecutorial discretion, then, becomes the most important and effective brake on the federalization of crime.

In prosecuting only a small percentage of conduct falling under federal criminal legislation, the Department is not thwarting congressional will or shirking its duty vigorously to enforce the laws. The selective exercise of federal jurisdiction is an essential and unavoidable incident of our criminal justice system. A brief reflection of the potential federal jurisdiction under just one statute, the Hobbs Act, confirms this fact: If the Department was not highly restrained in its exercise of prosecutorial discretion under the Hobbs Act, which makes it a federal crime to interfere with interstate commerce by threat or violence and thus potentially federalizes any convenience store holdup, the criminal business of the federal courts would more than quadruple overnight. Thus, Congress's passage of new criminal legislation incorporates the expectations that the Department will continue to be highly selective in bringing federal charges, particularly in areas of concurrent jurisdiction.

. . .

... If, in a particular arena, the federal system is able to add no more than the states could achieve with the same commitment of resources, the case for federalization has not been made. For example, a proposal in last year's Crime Bill would have made it a federal offense to use a gun that had passed in interstate commerce in any crime of violence. It would have federalized, in other words, virtually any crime committed with a gun. The Department opposed that measure on explicit federalism grounds, and it was defeated. The proposal, in addition to being breathtaking in scope, could have authorized a federal presence where there is not distinctive federal contribution to make, or any reason to believe that the proposed statute addresses a problem that cannot be adequately handled by the states....

The Child Support Recovery Act provides an example of how our approach to federalization works in practice. We deliberately select a difficult example that has created substantial controversy. The Act, passed in 1992, makes it a federal crime willfully to fail to pay more than $5,000 in court-ordered support for a child living in another state. Those who approach the federalization issue from a fixed-spheres perspective will view this statute as a flagrantly inappropriate expansion of the federal courts' jurisdiction.... It is certainly true that the great run of deadbeat parents cases are properly prosecuted in the state courts. Consider, however, that over $35 billion of court-ordered child support remains uncollected. An important, and limited aspect of that large problem arises from a relatively small number of egregious offenders who intentionally exploit states' jurisdictional limitations to elude their child support responsibilities. The federal government is uniquely positioned to prosecute these few offenders. So the question is whether to reach these offenders through "federalization" of child support violations combined with a highly selective enforcement policy, or not to reach them at all....

. . .

During fiscal year 1993, the most recent year for which comprehensive statistics are available, the Northern District of California disposed of 671 criminal cases and 5,659 civil cases. This works out to about 10 federal criminal dispositions per 100,000 population. By way of comparison, during that same year, the crime index in this jurisdiction—the FBI's survey of seven major crimes—totaled 424,358, which figures out to 6,374 per 100,000 population. The judges in the Northern District on average disposed of about 35 criminal cases each, as compared with a national average for federal district court judges of about 50 cases....

If we go back ten years to try to assess the relative impact of new federal criminal jurisdiction, the numbers indicate that the criminal workload of the federal courts in the Northern District of California has actually tailed off in recent years.... During the last five years, criminal filings dropped nearly a third from the previous five-year period.... These statistics indicate that in the overall scheme of things, the growth in federal criminal jurisdiction cannot be singled out as the cause of a grave crisis in the federal judicial workload. The reason is that, while federal criminal jurisdiction has expanded significantly, the Department's exercise of concurrent jurisdiction has remained highly selective.

. . .

The Department's prosecutorial policy emphasizes two elements: (1) allocation of criminal justice resources according to the comparative advantage of the federal, state, and local governments; and (2) cooperation between federal and state or local law enforcement officials to promote the most efficient use of criminal justice resources.

The comparative advantage approach rests on the idea that each agency or level of government should handle those aspects of a law enforcement problem that it is best equipped to handle. The federal government's advantages may vary according to the case, but they typically include inter-jurisdictional investigative capabilities, victim-and witness-assistance programs, expertise in traditionally federal areas of law such as organized crime or environmental crime, and favorable procedures, such as preventive detention. The availability of stiffer penalties in the federal system is also a potential comparative advantage, particularly in multiple-offender cases, where the prospect of a long sentence may induce a low-level figure to plead guilty and cooperate in the prosecution of the most culpable offenders.

The comparative advantage approach does not imply that a federal prosecution should be brought whenever the federal government has a comparative advantage. Rather, federal law enforcement resources should be deployed in the way that federal, state, and local actors jointly believe would be most effective. For example, federal investigative resources or witness-and victim-protection programs can be made available to state authorities in cases in which a state prosecution is brought. This approach can maximize the effectiveness of state and federal criminal justice resources.

* * *

NOTES AND QUESTIONS

1. Gorelick and Litman argue that the availability in the federal system of preventive detention, or a longer sentence, can be a legitimate reason for a federal as opposed to a state prosecution. Professor Steven Clymer, on the other hand, lists these two features of the federal system along with three others—less access to pretrial discovery; fewer opportunities to suppress evidence, and lack of parole eligibility—that he argues make federal prosecution decisions vulnerable on equal protection grounds:

> The federalization of substantive criminal law and the disparity between treatment received in federal and state criminal justice systems have created . . . a 'cruel lottery,' in which some unfortunate offenders are subject to dramatically harsher treatment than similarly situated others. Equal protection, which requires that government actors have a rational basis for imposing differential treatment—even in contexts in which there is far less at stake than in the criminal justice system—should impose the same obligations on prosecutors. It compels federal prosecutors, whose selection decisions can mean the difference between pretrial release and detention, dismissal and conviction, or a slap on the wrist and a lengthy prison term, to use principled methods of determining which eligible offenders will be subject to

> federal rather than state prosecution. To ensure rational charging decisions, the Department of Justice should amend its 'Principles of Federal Prosecution' to require that federal prosecutors not only avoid bad reasons for making charging decisions, but that they have good ones for treating federally prosecuted offenders differently than those charged in state court.
>
> If faced with evidence that arbitrary selection is routine and unchecked by administrative policy, courts should reconsider their reluctance to review charging decisions absent proof of improper discrimination. Considerations that counsel judicial restraint are not convincing barriers to limited judicial oversight of the rationality of federal prosecutors' decisions to bring charges under duplicative federal statutes. Although such review would rarely result in a finding of an equal protection violation and the need to grant a remedy, it would prompt federal prosecutors to make principled selection decisions.

Steven D. Clymer, *Unequal Justice: The Federalization of Criminal Law,* 70 S. CAL. L. REV. 643, 739 (1997).

2. Using Gorelick and Litman's guidelines, when do you think federal prosecutors should become involved in interstate domestic violence, or interstate violation of restraining order cases? Are you confident that the criteria you have settled on would survive an equal protection scrutiny of the kind suggested by Clymer?

PART FOUR

Self Defense and Beyond: Battered Women as Criminal Defendants

CHAPTER TEN

Defenses Available to Battered Women Defendants

Introductory Note

This chapter deals with the legal problems that face battered women as criminal defendants, particularly women who assault or kill the men who batter or threaten them. This area of work began in the 1970's with efforts to address the special problems of gender-bias that faced women in these circumstances. The opening section documents some of the early cases in which judges were persuaded to put women's violence into the specific social and psychological context of violence *against* women, and to allow lawyers to educate juries about the nature of battering relationships before they addressed the question whether any particular woman had acted reasonably in defending herself against her batterer. It also explains the form this reform movement took–dealing especially with arguments about the need for expert testimony, and addressing precisely how that expert testimony was supposed to help decision-makers apply the law of self-defense accurately and fairly to battered women's cases. Finally, it analyzes the limitations of this strategy, limitations that have become more apparent over time. Unfortunately, those limitations are apparent not only in judicial decisions, but also in some of the special legislation that has been introduced at the state level to ensure the admissibility of expert testimony about battering in cases in which it may be relevant to women's criminal defenses. This section also presents some more recent and hopeful material, suggesting that both policy makers and judges are developing a more sophisticated understanding of the dynamics of battering relationships, and the functions that can be served by expert testimony.

The next set of materials carry the analysis beyond self defense, into other criminal cases in which battered women defendants seek to use evidence of their abuse to eliminate or mitigate their responsibility for the crimes for which they are charged.

The final section takes us beyond the moment at which the battered woman is convicted of the crime with which she is charged, and asks whether, and how, that conviction can be challenged, in circumstances in which her trial was tainted by the failure of her lawyer to address her situation as a battered woman, or by the failure of the criminal process more generally to incorporate that perspective into her trial. The issues addressed here are not whether a successful appeal can be brought, but whether the battered woman defendant can argue ineffective assistance of counsel, or step outside the criminal justice system to seek clemency.

A. Women's Self-Defense Claims: Gender Bias and the Role of Expert Testimony

Battered Women Who Kill
Elizabeth M. Schneider, Battered Women and Feminist Lawmaking, 112–140 (2000)

Legal reform for battered women who kill has been one of the most significant areas of feminist lawmaking on domestic violence. In courtrooms around the United States, lawyers have challenged assumptions about battered women in general, and battered women who kill their assailants in particular. Lawyers have raised issues concerning gender bias in criminal defenses that have begun to make it possible for battered women to obtain what I have called "equal rights to trial." Nevertheless, backlash continues to plague this work....

Claims made by battered women to explain their actions as shaped by their experiences of abuse are commonly perceived as "special pleading." There is a deep societal resistance to perceiving the circumstances of battered women, and particularly the circumstances of battered women who kill their assailants, as a problem of gender equality.

This resistance is evident not only among the public and in media commentary, but also in legal representation, judicial treatment, and scholarly analysis. Many lawyers who handle these challenging cases fail to place them within an equal-rights framework and are not sufficiently thoughtful in grappling with the legal issues these cases present....

The Problem of Equal Rights to Trial

The insight that first generated legal work on this issue was that, for a variety of reasons, women who were battered and faced criminal charges for homicide or assault of their assailant were likely to be denied equal rights to trial—that is, equal rights to present the circumstances of their acts within the framework of the criminal law. The equal-rights problem in this context flows from an equal-rights problem in criminal law generally: what Stephen Schulhofer has described as the fact that "the criminal justice system is dominated (incontrovertibly so) by a preoccupation with men and male perspectives."

The equal-rights problem for battered women who kill has many sources: widespread views of women who act violently, particularly against intimates, as "monsters"; commonly held misconceptions about battered women (that they "ask for" or provoke the violence, for example); gender bias in the concept of reasonableness; societal misconceptions about self-defense and application of the legal standards of imminent danger and proportionality; and deeply held cultural attitudes that pathologize women generally and battered women particularly. Moreover, the law has traditionally viewed husband-killing as a special crime that strikes at the root of all civil government, threatening basic conceptions of traditional society. Long ago, William Blackstone observed that a woman who killed her husband was committing "treason": "If the baron kills his feme it is the same as if he had killed a stranger, or any other person; but if the feme kills her baron, it is regarded by the laws as a much more atrocious crime, as she not only breaks through the restraints of humanity and conjugal affection, but throws off all subjection to the authority of her husband. And therefore, the law denominates her crime a species of treason, and condemns her to the same punishment as if she had killed the king. And for every species of treason ... the sentence of women was to be drawn and burnt alive." Based on the confluence of these factors, the equal-rights argument holds that battered women who kill are more likely to be viewed as crazy than reasonable; thus they are likely to face substantial hurdles in asserting self-defense and to be limited in the range of defense options available at trial.

The goal of this work has been to expand defense options in order to equalize women's rights to trial and afford women equal opportunity to present an effective defense. It has not rested on the claim that all battered women are entitled to self-defense, or that there should be a special defense for battered women, either as self-defense or as a special "battered woman defense." To the contrary, the argument is that battered women, like all criminal defendants, had to be included within the traditional framework of the criminal law in order to guarantee their equal rights to trial.

Those insights have generated much legal scholarship, case law, and statutory reform. Nevertheless, much of this work is premised on a fundamental misunderstanding of the original arguments, and is based on the assumption that pleas of self-defense or a special "battered woman defense" are appropriate in all cases of battered women who kill their assailants. These efforts miss the crucial insight that has shaped this work: that the particular facts and circumstances of each case must be evaluated in light of the general problem of gender bias in order to ensure an individual woman's equal right to trial....

With respect to battered women who kill, gender bias pervades the entire criminal process. It permeates perceptions of appropriate self-defense and the legal standard of self-defense, the broader problem of choice of defense, and the need for expert testimony on battering, all of which are interrelated. Lawyers' failure to appreciate the problem of gender bias in the law of self-defense and in judicial application of the law of self-defense can lead to problematic judgments concerning the choice of defense in any particular case, as well as all decisions that flow from this (such as expert testimony that might be proffered in support of that defense), since the defense necessarily shapes the content of all testimony at trial.

... Scholars have amply documented that situations involving battered women who kill fall within traditional frameworks of defenses or excusable action, but are nonetheless viewed as different or exceptional by judges who apply the law to these cases, and that battered women of color face particular hurdles in this regard....

Despite this overwhelming record, there has been little change in attitudes among legal scholars, lawyers, judges, the media, and the public at large. Legal arguments in battered women's cases are routinely viewed as claims for special and undeservedly lenient treatment for battered women. Indeed, some well-intentioned lawyers, legislators, legal scholars, and judges have made legal arguments, developed legislation, and written articles and judicial opinions that assert "battered women's" or "battered woman syndrome" defenses or claims, whether as the basis for claims of self-defense, for admissibility of expert testimony, or for a special cause of action in tort. This dilemma is a familiar one when gender discrimination claims are made, because the tension between equal treatment and special treatment is inherent to the problem of equality generally, and it is particularly endemic in claims of gender equality. But in the context of criminal cases involving battered women as defendants, the mischaracterization of claims of equal treatment as pleas for special treatment is especially problematic. Battered women's actions in these cases are widely perceived to be outside the traditional justification framework of the criminal law. As a result, the problem of gender bias is not only neither addressed nor remedied; it is exacerbated.

The Legal Framework

Homicide is generally divided into first-and second-degree murder, manslaughter, and justifiable or excusable homicide. If a homicide is justifiable or excusable, it is because special circumstances exist that the law recognizes as justifying or excusing the defendant's acts from criminal liability. Proof that a killing occurred in a sudden, provoked "heat of passion"—upon provocation that would cause a "reasonable man to lose his self-control"—is considered in most jurisdictions to indicate manslaughter. Manslaughter is an "intermediate" crime between murder and justifiable homicide; it means that the homicidal act is not "justifiable" but, because of the circumstances of the individual, is "understandable" or "excusable" and therefore deserving of some mitigation in punishment. Alternatively, where a defendant's belief in the need to use force to defend herself is "reasonable," and she is not the initial aggressor, self-defense is a "complete" defense and results in acquittal. Where a defendant's belief is found to be honest but "unreasonable," some jurisdictions recognize "imperfect" self-defense, permitting a reduction from murder to manslaughter.

Although the law of self-defense is purportedly universally applicable, it is widely recognized that social concepts of justification have been shaped by male experience. Familiar images of self-defense are a soldier; a man protecting his home, his family, or the chastity of his wife; or a man fighting off an assailant. Yet the circumstances in which women kill in self-defense are usually related to physical or sexual abuse by an intimate, not to the conventional barroom brawl or fist fight with a stranger that shapes male experience with self-defense. Society, through its prosecutors, juries, and judges, has more readily excused a man for killing his wife's lover than a woman for killing a rapist. The acts of men and women are subject to a different set of legal expectations and standards. The man's act, while not always legally condoned, is viewed sympathetically. He is not forgiven, but his motivation is understood by those sitting in judgment. The law, however, has never protected a wife who killed her husband after finding him with another woman. A woman's husband simply does not belong to her in the same way that she belongs to him.

The man who kills his wife after finding her with another man is the paradigmatic example of provocation; his conduct is widely perceived to deserve more lenient treatment than other kinds of killings under the law. In a Maryland case involving a man who shot and killed his wife four hours after coming home and finding her in bed with another man, the judge sentenced the man to only eighteen months in a work release program, stating that he could imagine nothing that would provoke "an uncontrollable rage greater than this: for someone who is happily married to be betrayed in your personal life, when you're out working to support the spouse.... I seriously wonder how many men married five, four years ... would have the strength to walk away without inflicting some corporal punishment." Although many homicides of women committed by men are now recognized as occurring in a context of domestic violence, men's killings of their wives are, as Donna Coker has put it, "seldom recognized as belonging to the universe of 'domestic violence' killings." Conversely, women who have killed their husbands in response to battering have raised considerable controversy and are perceived to deserve harsher treatment under the law.

Consequently, it is not generally acknowledged that women defendants face substantial hurdles in pleading self-defense. Battered women defendants experience serious problems in meeting the judicial application of the standard of reasonableness and elements of the law of self-defense; the requirement of temporal proximity of the danger perceived by the defendant; the requirement of equal proportionality of force used by the defendant to that used against her by the batterer; and the duty to retreat.

Alternatives to self-defense are the insanity defense and the range of partial responsibility or impaired mental state defenses, which vary among jurisdictions. If a defendant pleads insanity, she claims that, owing to her mental condition at the time of the act, she is not guilty because she either did not know what she was doing or did not know that it was wrong. The insanity defense is usually a "complete" defense, in the sense that the defendant is not legally responsible for the act committed. However, a finding of not guilty by reason of insanity most often results in institutionalization for an indefinite period of time. Some, but not all, jurisdictions recognize partial responsibility or impaired mental state defenses, such as heat-of-passion and intoxication, where a successful defense will mitigate the act and reduce a charge from murder to manslaughter.

The Goals of Equal Rights to Trial

When the theoretical framework of gender bias in the law of self-defense was developed more than twenty years ago, relatively little was known about the problem of domestic violence. The public and the judiciary had little consciousness even of the existence of battered women who killed their assailants, much less of the nature of the battering these women had experienced. The equal rights framework developed from the experiences of battered women, whose stories, though hardly new, had rarely been told or heard. Lawyers and social scientists who were sensitive to the subtleties of gender bias listened to the experiences of women who had been battered and who killed their assailants. The theory was based on the particular experiences of women who were battered, the social context of battering, and the broader problems of gender subordination within which the particular problem of battering had to be understood.

. . .

Early work on equal rights to trial focused first on choice of defense, for the threshold issue for defense lawyers who represent battered women who kill is to interpret the facts and the law in order to choose a defense. The argument was that lawyers were more likely to rely on partial responsibility and insanity defenses for battered women rather than on self-defense, because lawyers would be more likely to see battered women as irrational. The assumption was that battered women who kill are likely to be seen as either bad or mad or both, but in any case as inappropriate claimants of self-defense, and the judge and jury may share these stereotypes.

... The crux of self-defense is the concept of reasonableness. In order for a defense lawyer to believe that a battered woman has a credible claim of self-defense, the lawyer will first have to overcome sex-based stereotypes of reasonableness, understand enough about the experiences of battered women to be able to consider whether the woman's actions are reasonable, and, in a manner sensitive to the problems of gender-bias, be able to listen to the woman's experiences. Early work on women's self-defense asserted that in many cases of women charged with homicide, particularly battered women, self-defense was likely to be overlooked by defense counsel, but might be appropriate and should be considered. The goal was to ensure that the full range of defenses were available and explored for battered women defendants, just as they should be available for all other criminal defendants.

The next step was to make sure that battered women's experiences were heard—first by defense lawyers in the process of representation and choice of defense, and then in the courtroom—regardless of what defense was chosen. Admission of evidence on battering was considered crucial, first from the woman and others who might have observed or known about the violence, and then from experts who might be able to explain those experiences and assist fact finders to overcome misconceptions that might impede their determination. Evidence concerning the history and experience of abuse was not only relevant, but essential to determining guilt. The goal was not to have every battered woman on trial plead self-defense, but to improve the rationality of the fact-finding process....

* * *

NOTES

1. How specifically might gender bias interact with self-defense doctrine to prejudice battered women defendants? Elizabeth Schneider mentions

four specific areas. One is the "reasonableness" of the defendant's determination that force was necessary, and the extent to which a reasoned judgment can draw on the defendant's experiences as a woman, or a battered woman. This theme is amply elaborated on in the pages that follow. A second is the "temporal proximity" between the threat against the defendant and her use of violence to deflect it. Some jurisdictions require that the threat be "imminent," while others use "immediacy," which in general requires closer proximity, as the standard. Whichever standard is used, the critical issue for battered women is whether the jury will be invited to look at the question of proximate threat from the perspective of someone who has suffered abuse from this perpetrator before, and reads the signals of impending violence differently from someone with no prior exposure. A third is the "proportionality" of the violence threatened, and the violence used in self-defense. For women, this sometimes raises the question of when their smaller stature, or lack of physical training, permits them to use a weapon, when it would not be appropriate for a man to use one in similar circumstances. This was part of the court's analysis in the *Wanrow* case, which follows. But "proportionality" also involves assessing the level of threat posed by the assailant who is then injured or killed by his intended victim, and here again the question will be whether the woman can share with the jury her experience with her abuser, which informs her assessment.

A fourth relevant aspect of the doctrine of self-defense is the so-called duty to retreat, by which some, but not all, jurisdictions require someone threatened by violence to retreat rather than counterattack *if they can safely do so*. Traditionally, jurisdictions that did impose such a duty (it was more common in Northeastern states than in the frontier territories of the South and West) created an exemption, permitting individuals to stand their ground when they were threatened in their own homes. However, some of these jurisdictions then limited the exemption, holding that it would not apply in situations in which the attacker was a cohabitant, or in which the person claiming self defense had struck the first blow. The "cohabitant" rule limits the use of self defense by those attacked in their homes by intimate partners, and therefore has a clearly disparate impact on women and children, who more often than men bear the brunt of those attacks. More generally, however, there is a danger that judges and juries will confuse the question of whether the defendant had a duty to retreat in the specific incident which led to her prosecution with the more general question of why she did not leave her abuser. They may then blame her for putting herself in the way of violence rather than avoiding it, in ways that prejudice their conclusions about the case, even if they do not technically decide that she has violated a duty to retreat. For a very recent case in this area see Weiand v. State, 732 So. 2d 1044 (Fla. 1999), in which the Florida Supreme Court retreated from an earlier (1982) decision imposing a duty to retreat on co-occupants. The court based its change of heart on increased knowledge about domestic violence, and an evolution in the public policy of the state. The new standard adopted by the court still requires retreat within the home, to the extent reasonably possible without increasing the danger, but does not require an attacked co-occupant to flee the residence before resorting to force in self defense.

2. Yvonne Wanrow, the defendant in the case you will next read, did not kill her batterer. Rather, she killed a man whom she barely knew, but whom she perceived as dangerous, and who appeared to be threatening her. Decided in 1977, the case provides a valuable introduction to issues of potential gender bias in the application of self-defense doctrine.

State of Washington v. Yvonne L. Wanrow

88 Wn.2d 221, 559 P.2d 548.
Supreme Court of Washington, 1977.

■ UTTER, JUDGE.

Yvonne Wanrow was convicted by a jury of second-degree murder and first-degree assault. She appealed her conviction to the Court of Appeals. The Court of Appeals reversed and remanded the case.... State v. Wanrow, 14 Wn. App. 115, 538 P.2d 849 (1975). We granted review and affirm the Court of Appeals.

We order a reversal of the conviction on two grounds.... The second ground is error committed by the trial court in improperly instructing the jury on the law of self-defense as it related to the defendant.

On the afternoon of August 11, 1972, defendant's (respondent's) two children were staying at the home of Ms. Hooper, a friend of defendant. Defendant's son was playing in the neighborhood and came back to Ms. Hooper's house and told her that a man tried to pull him off his bicycle and drag him into a house. Some months earlier, Ms. Hooper's 7-year-old daughter had developed a rash on her body which was diagnosed as venereal disease. Ms. Hooper had been unable to persuade her daughter to tell her who had molested her. It was not until the night of the shooting that Ms. Hooper discovered it was William Wesler (decedent) who allegedly had violated her daughter. A few minutes after the defendant's son related his story to Ms. Hooper about the man who tried to detain him, Mr. Wesler appeared on the porch of the Hooper house and stated through the door, "I didn't touch the kid, I didn't touch the kid." At that moment, the Hooper girl, seeing Wesler at the door, indicated to her mother that Wesler was the man who had molested her. Joseph Fah, Ms. Hooper's landlord, saw Wesler as he was leaving and informed Shirley Hooper that Wesler had tried to molest a young boy who had earlier lived in the same house, and that Wesler had previously been committed to the Eastern State Hospital for the mentally ill. Immediately after this revelation from Mr. Fah, Ms. Hooper called the police who, upon their arrival at the Hooper residence, were informed of all the events which had transpired that day. Ms. Hooper requested that Wesler be arrested then and there, but the police stated, "We can't, until Monday morning." Ms. Hooper was urged by the police officer to go to the police station Monday morning and "swear out a warrant." Ms. Hooper's landlord, who was present during the conversation, suggested that Ms. Hooper get a baseball bat located at the corner of the house and "conk him over the head" should Wesler try to enter the house uninvited during the weekend. To this suggestion, the policeman replied, "Yes, but wait until he gets in the house." (A week before this incident Shirley Hooper had noticed someone prowling around her house at night. Two days before the shooting someone had attempted to get into Ms. Hooper's bedroom and had slashed the window screen. She suspected that such person was Wesler.)

That evening, Ms. Hooper called the defendant and asked her to spend the night with her in the Hooper house. At that time she related to Ms. Wanrow the facts we have previously set forth. The defendant arrived sometime after 6 p.m. with a pistol in her handbag. The two women ultimately determined that they were too afraid to stay alone and decided to ask some friends to come over for added protection. The two women then called the defendant's sister and brother-in-law, Angie and Chuck Michel. The four adults did not go to bed that evening, but remained awake talking and watching for any possible prowlers. There were eight young children in the house with them. At around 5 a.m., Chuck Michel, without the knowledge of the women in the house, went to Wesler's house, carrying a baseball bat. Upon arriving at the Wesler residence, Mr. Michel accused Wesler of molesting little children. Mr. Wesler then suggested that they go over to the Hooper residence and get the whole thing straightened out. Another man, one David Kelly, was also present, and together the three men went over to the Hooper house. Mr. Michel and Mr. Kelly remained outside while Wesler entered the residence.

The testimony as to what next took place is considerably less precise. It appears that Wesler, a large man who was visibly intoxicated, entered the home and when told to leave declined to do so. A good deal of shouting and confusion then arose, and a young child, asleep on the couch, awoke crying. The testimony indicates that Wesler then approached this child, stating, "My what a cute little boy," or words to that effect, and that the child's mother, Ms. Michel, stepped between Wesler and the child. By this time Hooper was screaming for Wesler to get out. Ms. Wanrow, a 5–foot 4–inch woman who at the time had a broken leg and was using a crutch, testified that she then went to the front door to enlist the aid of Chuck Michel. She stated that she shouted for him and, upon turning around to reenter the living room, found Wesler standing directly behind her. She testified to being gravely startled by this situation and to having then shot Wesler in what amounted to a reflex action.

After Wesler was shot, Ms. Hooper called the police via a Spokane crime check emergency phone number, stating, "There's a guy broke in, and my girlfriend shot him." The defendant later took the phone and engaged in a conversation with the police operator. . . .

. . .

Reversal of respondent's conviction is required by a . . . serious error committed by the trial court. Instruction No. 10, setting forth the law of self-defense, incorrectly limited the jury's consideration of acts and circumstances pertinent to respondent's perception of the alleged threat to her person. An examination of the record of the testimony and of the colloquys which took place with regard to the instructions on self-defense indicate the critical importance of these instructions to the respondent's theory of the case. Based upon the evidence we have already set out, it is obviously crucial that the jury be precisely instructed as to the defense of justification.

In the opening paragraph of instruction No. 10, the jury, in evaluating the gravity of the danger to the respondent, was directed to consider only those acts and circumstances occurring "at or immediately before the killing. . . ."[1] This is not now, and never has been, the law of self-defense in Washington. On the contrary, the justification of self-defense is to be evaluated in light of all the facts and circumstances known to the defendant, including those known substantially before the killing.

In State v. Ellis, 30 Wash. 369, 70 P. 963 (1902), this court reversed a first-degree murder conviction obtained under self-defense instructions quite similar to that in the present case. The defendant sought to show that the deceased had a reputation and habit of carrying and using deadly weapons when engaged in quarrels. The trial court instructed that threats were insufficient justification unless " 'at the time of the alleged killing the deceased was making or immediately preceding the killing had committed some overt act ... ' " ... This court found the instruction "defective and misleading", stating "the apparent facts should all be taken together to illustrate the motives and good faith of the defendant ..." ....

> [I]t is apparent that a man who habitually carries and uses such weapons in quarrels must cause greater apprehension of danger than one who does not bear such reputation ... The vital question is the reasonableness of the defendant's apprehension of danger ... The jury are [sic] entitled to stand as nearly as practicable in the shoes of defendant, and from this point of view determine the character of the act.

... Thus, circumstances predating the killing by weeks and months were deemed entirely proper, and in fact essential, to a proper disposition of the claim of self-defense.

Similarly, in State v. Churchill, 52 Wash. 210, 100 P. 309 (1909), the court upheld self-defense instructions directing the jury to consider all

1. Instruction No. 10 reads:

"To justify killing in self-defense, there need be no actual or real danger to the life or person of the party killing, but there must be, or reasonably appear to be, at or immediately before the killing, some overt act, or some circumstances which would reasonably indicate to the party killing that the person slain, is, at the time, endeavoring to kill him or inflict upon him great bodily harm.

"However, when there is no reasonable ground for the person attacked to believe that his person is in imminent danger of death or great bodily harm, and it appears to him that only an ordinary battery is all that is intended, and all that he has reasonable grounds to fear from his assailant, he has a right to stand his ground and repel such threatened assault, yet he has no right to repel a threatened assault with naked hands, by the use of a deadly weapon in a deadly manner, unless he believes, and has reasonable grounds to believe, that he is in imminent danger of death or great bodily harm."

relevant facts and circumstances, including those preceding the homicide. The trial court's instructions referred to an overt act of the person killed " 'at or immediately before the killing . . . which, either by itself, or coupled with words, facts or circumstances, then or theretofore occurring,' " may establish a reasonable belief of imminent danger.... The instruction further requested the jury to " 'take into consideration all the facts and circumstances bearing on the question and surrounding defendant and existing at or prior to the time of the alleged shooting . . .' " . . . This court found these instructions "clear, apt, and comprehensive" and free from error. . . .

State v. Tribett, 74 Wash. 125, 132 P. 875 (1913), is in accord. There this court approved an instruction which twice directed the jury to evaluate the reasonableness of the defendant's actions in defense of himself " 'in the light of all the circumstances'." . . . Such circumstances included those existing and known long before the killing, such as the reputation of the place of the killing for lawlessness. This court stated with reference to the self-defense instruction:

> All of these facts and circumstances should have been placed before the jury, to the end that they could put themselves in the place of the appellant, get the point of view which he had at the time of the tragedy, and view the conduct of the [deceased] with all its pertinent sidelights as the appellant was warranted in viewing it. In no other way could the jury safely say what a reasonably prudent man similarly situated would have done.

. . . The rule firmly established by these cases has never been disapproved and is still followed today. "It is clear the jury is entitled to consider all of the circumstances surrounding the incident in determining whether [the] defendant had reasonable grounds to believe grievous bodily harm was about to be inflicted." State v. Lewis, 6 Wn. App. 38, 41, 491 P.2d 1062 (1971). By limiting the jury's consideration of the surrounding acts and circumstances to those occurring "at or immediately before the killing," instruction No. 10 in the present case was an erroneous statement of the applicable law on the critical focal point of the defendant's case.

The State attempts to minimize this deficiency in instruction No. 10 by invoking the rule that an instruction is "sufficient" if counsel may satisfactorily argue his or her theory of the case. This is a mistaken application of the rule and will cause widespread mischief in civil as well as criminal cases if adopted here.... [T]he test of an instruction's sufficiency is an additional safeguard to be applied only where the instruction given is first found to be an accurate statement of the law. Furthermore, it would be illogical to apply such a test to erroneous instructions—of what significance is it that counsel may or may not be able to argue his theory to the jury when the jury has been misinformed about the law to be applied?

More importantly, there is a test for reviewing instructions that is clearly designed for and consistently applied to cases in which the instruction given is an erroneous statement of the law.

> When the record discloses an error in an instruction given on behalf of the party in whose favor the verdict was returned, the error is presumed to have been prejudicial, and to furnish ground for reversal, unless it affirmatively appears that it was harmless....
>
> A harmless error is an error which is trivial, or formal, or merely academic, and was not prejudicial to the substantial rights of the party assigning it, and in no way affected the final outcome of the case.

State v. Golladay, 78 Wn.2d 121, 139, 470 P.2d 191 (1970)....

As shown by the discussion above, instruction No. 10 erred in limiting the acts and circumstances which the jury could consider in evaluating the nature of the threat of harm as perceived by respondent. Under the well-established rule, this error is presumed to have been prejudicial. Moreover, far from affirmatively showing that the error was harmless, the record demonstrates the limitation to circumstances "at or immediately before the killing" was of crucial importance in the present case. Respondent's knowledge of the victim's reputation for aggressive acts was gained many hours before the killing and was based upon events which occurred over a period of years. Under the law of this state, the jury should have been allowed to consider this information in making the critical determination of the " 'degree of force which ... a reasonable person in the same situation ... seeing what [s]he sees and knowing what [s]he knows, then would believe to be necessary.' " State v. Dunning, 8 Wn. App. 340, 342, 506 P.2d 321 (1973). ...

Instruction No. 10 also may not be salvaged by asserting any deficiency in it to have been cured by instruction No. 12, through reliance upon the general rule that, if the instructions, when considered as a whole, properly state the law, they are sufficient. The only language in instruction No. 12 which could conceivably be viewed as curing the defect in instruction No. 10 informs the jury that they may "consider the words and actions of the deceased prior to the homicide ... together with any and all factors which in your judgment may bear upon [self-defense]." This language does not cure the statements in instruction No. 10 which are here challenged. At best, the two instructions are inconsistent, instruction No. 10 containing a patent misstatement of the law applicable to the defendant's theory of the case.

. . .

When instructions are inconsistent, it is the duty of the reviewing court to determine whether "the jury was misled as to its function and responsibilities under the law" by that inconsistency. ... It follows from the cases previously cited, that where such an inconsistency is the result of a clear misstatement of the law, the misstatement must be presumed to have misled the jury in a manner prejudicial to the defendant.

The second paragraph of instruction No. 10 contains an equally erroneous and prejudicial statement of the law. That portion of the instruction reads:

However, when there is no reasonable ground for the person attacked to believe that his person is in imminent danger of death or great bodily harm, and it appears to him that only an ordinary battery is all that is intended, and all that he has reasonable grounds to fear from his assailant, he has a right to stand his ground and repel such threatened assault, yet he has no right to repel a threatened assault with naked hands, by the use of a deadly weapon in a deadly manner, unless he believes, and has reasonable grounds to believe, that he is in imminent danger of death or great bodily harm.

In our society women suffer from a conspicuous lack of access to training in and the means of developing those skills necessary to effectively repel a male assailant without resorting to the use of deadly weapons.[1] Instruction No. 12 does indicate that the "relative size and strength of the persons involved" may be considered; however, it does not make clear that the defendant's actions are to be judged against her own subjective impressions and not those which a detached jury might determine to be objectively reasonable.... The applicable rule of law is clearly stated in Miller at page 105:

If the appellants, at the time of the alleged assault upon them, as reasonably and ordinarily cautious and prudent men, honestly believed that they were in danger of great bodily harm, they would have the right to resort to self defense, and their conduct is to be judged by the condition appearing to them at the time, not by the condition as it might appear to the jury in the light of testimony before it.

The second paragraph of instruction No. 10 not only establishes an objective standard, but through the persistent use of the masculine gender leaves the jury with the impression the objective standard to be applied is that applicable to an altercation between two men. The impression created—that a 5–foot 4–inch woman with a cast on her leg and using a crutch must, under the law, somehow repel an assault by a 6–foot 2–inch intoxicated man without employing weapons in her defense, unless the jury finds her determination of the degree of danger to be objectively reasonable—constitutes a separate and distinct misstatement of the law and, in the context of this case, violates the respondent's right to equal protection of the law. The respondent was entitled to have the jury consider her actions in the light of her own perceptions of the situation, including those perceptions which were the product of our nation's "long and unfortunate history of sex discrimination." Frontiero v. Richardson, 411 U.S. 677, 684, 36 L. Ed. 2d 583, 93 S. Ct. 1764 (1973). Until such time as the effects of that history are eradicated, care must be taken to assure that our self-defense instructions afford women the right to have their conduct judged in light of the individual physical handicaps which are the product of sex discrimination. To fail to do so is to deny the right of the individual woman involved to trial by the same rules which are applicable to male defendants.... The portion of the instruction above quoted misstates our law in

1. See B. Babcock, A. Freedman, E. Norton & S. Ross, Sex Discrimination and the Law: Causes and Remedies 943–1070 (1975); S. Brownmiller, Against our Will: Men, Women and Rape (1975).

creating an objective standard of "reasonableness." It then compounds that error by utilizing language suggesting that the respondent's conduct must be measured against that of a reasonable male individual finding himself in the same circumstances. We conclude that the instruction here in question contains an improper statement of the law on a vital issue in the case, is inconsistent, misleading, and prejudicial when read in conjunction with other instructions pertaining to the same issue, and therefore is a proper basis for a finding of reversible error.

. . .

In light of the errors in admission of evidence and instruction of the jury, the decision of the Court of Appeals is affirmed, the conviction reversed, and the case remanded for a new trial.

NOTES

1. The arguments first raised in *Wanrow* and accepted by a plurality of the Washington Supreme Court rest on several assumptions that have gradually won wider and wider acceptance: first that women act in self-defense under different circumstances and in different ways than men; second, that the traditional law of self-defense, as applied, incorporates sex bias; and third, that sex-based stereotypes of women generally, and battered or raped women specifically, interfere with jurors' assessments of women's claims of self-defense. *Wanrow* and the substantial work on women's self-defense that followed it resulted from efforts to have the reasonableness standard of self-defense expand to include women's different experience.

On the level of practice, *Wanrow* and subsequent women's self-defense work sought to expand the legal options available to women defending against charges of homicide or assault for killing men who battered or raped them. Through explanations of the circumstances in which women acted to save their own lives, women's acts that had previously been viewed as outside the purview of self-defense but appropriate for insanity, diminished capacity or heat of passion defenses could now be seen as legitimately within the province of self-defense. Violence used in self defense is justified violence; justification rests on a determination that the act was right because of its circumstances. In contrast, violence prompted by insanity, diminished capacity or the heat of passion is still wrong, although we may excuse it (and treat it less harshly) because of the actor's particular characteristics or state of mind. Traditionally, women's acts of violence were not understood as reasonable, and could not, therefore, be justified. Instead, the inquiry shifted to excuse. Women's self-defense work, beginning with *Wanrow*, has attempted to redraw the lines between justification and excuse, and to challenge the stereotypes that might prevent women's acts from being seen as justified.

2. The value of the decision in *Wanrow* to other women seeking to develop self-defense claims was limited in one important respect. Washington State had a subjective, individualized, standard of self defense, so that all Yvonne

Wanrow was required to prove was that she honestly believed in the necessity of using lethal force to protect herself. In fact, of course, the proof Wanrow and her counsel offered went further than that. The content of the individualized perspective that *Wanrow* illuminated was not simply psychological, but clearly social; Yvonne Wanrow's individual perspective as shaped by her experience as a woman within the collective and historical experience of sex discrimination. Elizabeth Schneider, who was involved in the *Wanrow* case, comments that "[a]t the time, it seemed difficult enough to convince a jury that the woman might be reasonable even when applying a standard emphasizing the woman's own perspective. It was even more difficult to imagine arguing that the woman's experience was objectively reasonable." Elizabeth M. Schneider, BATTERED WOMEN AND FEMINIST LAWMAKING 139 (2000). Nonetheless, the self-defense standard in most jurisdictions requires a showing not only that the defendant honestly believed that force was necessary, but also that the use of force was objectively reasonable under the circumstances in which the defendant found him or herself. Lawyers representing battered women who killed in self defense therefore had, in most cases, to take on the harder task of showing that the defendant's violence met an objective standard of reasonableness.

3. The next case, State v. Kelly, provides an early example of the use of expert testimony to support a defendant's claim that her use of violence was objectively reasonable. At the same time, the case demonstrates some of the dangers inherent in this strategy, and particularly in the use of the label "battered women's syndrome" to describe the content of the expert testimony.

The question of the admissibility of expert testimony on battered woman syndrome has been the primary legal issue that appellate courts have addressed in the area of women's self-defense work. There are several reasons for this. First, most women's self-defense cases have involved battered women. The Women's Self–Defense Law Project, which began legal work in this field, had stressed the particular utility of expert testimony in this context, depending on the facts of the case. Many lawyers defending women have sought to introduce expert testimony on "battered woman syndrome" at trial. Although trial judges appear to have admitted this testimony in the majority of cases, where courts have excluded it and the women have been convicted, the question of the admissibility of expert testimony has frequently become the major issue on appeal. As a consequence, the question of expert testimony has received a great deal of attention from courts and commentators. Legal commentators have almost unanimously supported admissibility. Significantly, the majority of appellate courts that have ruled on the trial court's exclusion of expert testimony have determined that expert testimony on battered woman syndrome is relevant to a claim of self-defense. Even where it is found relevant, however, the trial court must find that it has met the general standard for admissibility of expert testimony. In several cases, this requirement has proven to be a substantial hurdle. Moreover, even if the trial court admits the expert testimony proffered by the defense, the prosecution may be permitted to have an expert testify to counter the assertion that the woman is battered or has suffered from battered woman syndrome.

Expert testimony on battering has had a substantial impact on the criminal process. At this point it has been admitted in cases involving battered women defendants in all fifty states and the District of Columbia, and not only in those involving claims of self-defense. Defense lawyers have also proffered it in response to other criminal charges, and at other stages of the criminal process, such as before the grand jury, on motions to dismiss, and at sentencing. Where expert testimony on battering has been held inadmissible, courts have largely ruled simply that there was an insufficient basis on which to find it admissible in the particular context or on the facts presented. These cases have demonstrated judicial recognition of the depth and severity of the problems of sex stereotyping in the criminal process for battered women.

State of New Jersey v. Gladys Kelly

97 N.J. 178, 478 A.2d 364.
Supreme Court of New Jersey, 1984.

■ WILENTZ, JUDGE.

The central issue before us is whether expert testimony about the battered-woman's syndrome is admissible to help establish a claim of self-defense in a homicide case. The question is one of first impression in this state. We hold, based on the limited record before us (the State not having had a full opportunity to prove the contrary), that the battered-woman's syndrome is an appropriate subject for expert testimony; that the experts' conclusions, despite the relative newness of the field, are sufficiently reliable under New Jersey's standards for scientific testimony; and that defendant's expert was sufficiently qualified. Accordingly, we reverse and remand for a new trial. If on retrial after a full examination of these issues the evidence continues to support these conclusions, the expert's testimony on the battered-woman's syndrome shall be admitted as relevant to the honesty and reasonableness of defendant's belief that deadly force was necessary to protect her against death or serious bodily harm.

I.

On May 24, 1980, defendant, Gladys Kelly, stabbed her husband, Ernest, with a pair of scissors. He died shortly thereafter at a nearby hospital. The couple had been married for seven years, during which time Ernest had periodically attacked Gladys. According to Ms. Kelly, he assaulted her that afternoon, and she stabbed him in self-defense, fearing that he would kill her if she did not act.

Ms. Kelly was indicted for murder. At trial, she did not deny stabbing her husband, but asserted that her action was in self-defense. To establish the requisite state of mind for her self-defense claim, Ms. Kelly called Dr. Lois Veronen as an expert witness to testify about the battered-woman's syndrome. After hearing a lengthy voir dire examination of Dr. Veronen, the trial court ruled that expert testimony concerning the syndrome was inadmissible on the self-defense issue . . . . Apparently the court believed that the sole purpose of this testimony was to explain and justify defendant's perception of the danger rather than to show the objective reasonableness of that perception.

Ms. Kelly was convicted of reckless manslaughter. In an unreported decision relying in part on Bess, the Appellate Division affirmed the conviction. We granted certification, . . . and now reverse.

II.

The Kellys had a stormy marriage. Some of the details of their relationship, especially the stabbing, are disputed. The following is Ms. Kelly's version of what happened—a version that the jury could have accepted and, if they had, a version that would make the proffered expert testimony not only relevant, but critical.

The day after the marriage, Mr. Kelly got drunk and knocked Ms. Kelly down. Although a period of calm followed the initial attack, the next seven years were accompanied by periodic and frequent beatings, sometimes as often as once a week. During the attacks, which generally occurred when Mr. Kelly was drunk, he threatened to kill Ms. Kelly and to cut off parts of her body if she tried to leave him. Mr. Kelly often moved out of the house after an attack, later returning with a promise that he would change his ways. Until the day of the homicide, only one of the attacks had taken place in public.

The day before the stabbing, Gladys and Ernest went shopping. They did not have enough money to buy food for the entire week, so Ernest said he would give his wife more money the next day.

The following morning he left for work. Ms. Kelly next saw her husband late that afternoon at a friend's house. She had gone there with her daughter, Annette, to ask Ernest for money to buy food. He told her to wait until they got home, and shortly thereafter the Kellys left. After walking past several houses, Mr. Kelly, who was drunk, angrily asked "What the hell did you come around here for?" He then grabbed the collar of her dress, and the two fell to the ground. He choked her by pushing his fingers against her throat, punched or hit her face, and bit her leg.

A crowd gathered on the street. Two men from the crowd separated them, just as Gladys felt that she was "passing out" from being choked. Fearing that Annette had been pushed around in the crowd, Gladys then left to look for her. Upon finding Annette, defendant noticed that Annette had defendant's pocketbook. Gladys had dropped it during the fight. Annette had retrieved it and gave her mother the pocketbook.

After finding her daughter, Ms. Kelly then observed Mr. Kelly running toward her with his hands raised. Within seconds he was right next to her. Unsure of whether he had armed himself while she was looking for their daughter, and thinking that he had come back to kill her, she grabbed a pair of scissors from her pocketbook. She tried to scare him away, but instead stabbed him.[1]

1. This version of the homicide—with a drunk Mr. Kelly as the aggressor both in pushing Ms. Kelly to the ground and again in rushing at her with his hands in a threaten-

III.

The central question in this case is whether the trial court erred in its exclusion of expert testimony on the battered-woman's syndrome. That testimony was intended to explain defendant's state of mind and bolster her claim of self-defense. We shall first examine the nature of the battered-woman's syndrome and then consider the expert testimony proffered in this case and its relevancy.

In the past decade social scientists and the legal community began to examine the forces that generate and perpetuate wife beating and violence in the family. What has been revealed is that the problem affects many more people than had been thought and that the victims of the violence are not only the battered family members (almost always either the wife or the children). There are also many other strangers to the family who feel the devastating impact, often in the form of violence, of the psychological damage suffered by the victims.

. . .

While common law notions that assigned an inferior status to women, and to wives in particular, no longer represent the state of the law as reflected in statutes and cases, many commentators assert that a bias against battered women still exists, institutionalized in the attitudes of law enforcement agencies unwilling to pursue or uninterested in pursuing wife beating cases. . . .

Another problem is the currency enjoyed by stereotypes and myths concerning the characteristics of battered women and their reasons for staying in battering relationships. Some popular misconceptions about battered women include the beliefs that they are masochistic and actually enjoy their beatings, that they purposely provoke their husbands into violent behavior, and, most critically, as we shall soon see, that women who remain in battering relationships are free to leave their abusers at any time. See L. Walker, The Battered Woman at 19–31 (1979).

As these cases so tragically suggest, not only do many women suffer physical abuse at the hands of their mates, but a significant number of women kill (or are killed by) their husbands. In 1978, murders between husband and wife or girlfriend and boyfriend constituted 13% of all murders committed in the United States. Undoubtedly some of these arose from battering incidents. Federal Bureau of Investigation, Crime in the United States 1978 (1978). Men were the victims in 48% of these killings. Id.

As the problem of battered women has begun to receive more attention, sociologists and psychologists have begun to focus on the effects a sustained pattern of physical and psychological abuse can have on a

ing position after the two had been separated—is sharply disputed by the State. The prosecution presented testimony intended to show that the initial scuffle was started by Gladys; that upon disentanglement, while she was restrained by bystanders, she stated that she intended to kill Ernest; that she then chased after him, and upon catching up with him stabbed him with a pair of scissors taken from her pocketbook.

woman. The effects of such abuse are what some scientific observers have termed "the battered-woman's syndrome," a series of common characteristics that appear in women who are abused physically and psychologically over an extended period of time by the dominant male figure in their lives....

According to Dr. Walker, relationships characterized by physical abuse tend to develop battering cycles. Violent behavior directed at the woman occurs in three distinct and repetitive stages that vary both in duration and intensity depending on the individuals involved....

. . .

[The judge then described the "tension-building," "acute battering incident" and "contrition" phases of the "cycle of violence," as presented in Lenore Walker's early work.]

. . .

The cyclical nature of battering behavior helps explain why more women simply do not leave their abusers. The loving behavior demonstrated by the batterer during phase three reinforces whatever hopes these women might have for their mate's reform and keeps them bound to the relationship....

Some women may even perceive the battering cycle as normal, especially if they grew up in a violent household.... Or they may simply not wish to acknowledge the reality of their situation....

Other women, however, become so demoralized and degraded by the fact that they cannot predict or control the violence that they sink into a state of psychological paralysis and become unable to take any action at all to improve or alter the situation. There is a tendency in battered women to believe in the omnipotence or strength of their battering husbands and thus to feel that any attempt to resist them is hopeless....

In addition to these psychological impacts, external social and economic factors often make it difficult for some women to extricate themselves from battering relationships. A woman without independent financial resources who wishes to leave her husband often finds it difficult to do so because of a lack of material and social resources.

Even with the progress of the last decade, women typically make less money and hold less prestigious jobs than men, and are more responsible for child care. Thus, in a violent confrontation where the first reaction might be to flee, women realize soon that there may be no place to go. Moreover, the stigma that attaches to a woman who leaves the family unit without her children undoubtedly acts as a further deterrent to moving out.

In addition, battered women, when they want to leave the relationship, are typically unwilling to reach out and confide in their friends, family, or the police, either out of shame and humiliation, fear of reprisal by their husband, or the feeling they will not be believed.

Dr. Walker and other commentators have identified several common personality traits of the battered woman: low self-esteem, traditional beliefs about the home, the family, and the female sex role, tremendous feelings of guilt that their marriages are failing, and the tendency to accept responsibility for the batterer's actions. . . .

Finally, battered women are often hesitant to leave a battering relationship because, in addition to their hope of reform on the part of their spouse, they harbor a deep concern about the possible response leaving might provoke in their mates. They literally become trapped by their own fear. Case histories are replete with instances in which a battered wife left her husband only to have him pursue her and subject her to an even more brutal attack. . . . The combination of all these symptoms—resulting from sustained psychological and physical trauma compounded by aggravating social and economic factors—constitutes the battered-woman's syndrome. Only by understanding these unique pressures that force battered women to remain with their mates, despite their long-standing and reasonable fear of severe bodily harm and the isolation that being a battered woman creates, can a battered woman's state of mind be accurately and fairly understood.

The voir dire testimony of Dr. Veronen, sought to be introduced by defendant Gladys Kelly, conformed essentially to this outline of the battered-woman's syndrome. . . .

. . .

Dr. Veronen described the various psychological tests and examinations she had performed in connection with her independent research. These tests and their methodology, including their interpretation, are, according to Dr. Veronen, widely accepted by clinical psychologists. Applying this methodology to defendant (who was subjected to all of the tests, including a five-hour interview), Dr. Veronen concluded that defendant was a battered woman and subject to the battered-woman's syndrome.

In addition, Dr. Veronen was prepared to testify as to how, as a battered woman, Gladys Kelly perceived her situation at the time of the stabbing, and why, in her opinion, defendant did not leave her husband despite the constant beatings she endured.

IV.

Whether expert testimony on the battered-woman's syndrome should be admitted in this case depends on whether it is relevant to defendant's claim of self-defense, and, in any event, on whether the proffer meets the standards for admission of expert testimony in this state. We examine first the law of self-defense and consider whether the expert testimony is relevant.

The present rules governing the use of force in self-defense are set out in the justification section of the Code of Criminal Justice. The use of force against another in self-defense is justifiable "when the actor reasonably believes that such force is immediately necessary for the purpose of protecting himself against the use of unlawful force by such other person on the present occasion." N.J.S.A. 2C:3–4(a). Further limitations exist when deadly force is used in self-defense. The use of such deadly force is not justifiable unless the actor reasonably believes that such force is necessary to protect himself against death or serious bodily harm.... [N.J.S.A. 2C:3–4(b)(2)].

. . .

Self-defense exonerates a person who kills in the reasonable belief that such action was necessary to prevent his or her death or serious injury, even though this belief was later proven mistaken. "Detached reflection cannot be demanded in the presence of an uplifted knife," Justice Holmes aptly said, Brown v. United States, 256 U.S. 335, 343, 41 S.Ct. 501, 502, 65 L.Ed. 961, 963 (1921); and the law accordingly requires only a reasonable, not necessarily a correct, judgment....

While it is not imperative that actual necessity exist, a valid plea of self-defense will not lie absent an actual (that is, honest) belief on the part of the defendant in the necessity of using force.... Ultimately, of course, it is for the jury to determine if the defendant actually did believe in the necessity of acting with deadly force to prevent an imminent, grave attack....

Honesty alone, however, does not suffice. A defendant claiming the privilege of self-defense must also establish that her belief in the necessity to use force was reasonable. ... As originally proposed, the new Code of Criminal Justice would have eliminated the reasonableness requirement, allowing self-defense whenever the defendant honestly believed in the imminent need to act.... This proposed change in the law was not accepted by the Legislature. N.J.S.A. 2C:3–4 as finally enacted retains the requirement that the defendant's belief be reasonable.

Thus, even when the defendant's belief in the need to kill in self-defense is conceded to be sincere, if it is found to have been unreasonable under the circumstances, such a belief cannot be held to constitute complete justification for a homicide. As with the determination of the existence of the defendant's belief, the question of the reasonableness of this belief "is to be determined by the jury, not the defendant, in light of the circumstances existing at the time of the homicide." ... It is perhaps worth emphasizing here that for defendant to prevail, the jury need not find beyond a reasonable doubt that the defendant's belief was honest and reasonable. Rather, if any evidence raising the issue of self-defense is adduced, either in the State's or the defendant's case, then the jury must be instructed that the State is required to prove beyond a reasonable doubt that the self-defense claim does not accord with the facts; acquittal is required if there remains a reasonable doubt whether the defendant acted in self-defense. ...

With the foregoing standards in mind, we turn to an examination of the relevance of the proffered expert testimony to Gladys Kelly's claim of self-defense.

V.

Gladys Kelly claims that she stabbed her husband in self-defense, believing he was about to kill her. The gist of the State's case was that

Gladys Kelly was the aggressor, that she consciously intended to kill her husband, and that she certainly was not acting in self-defense.

The credibility of Gladys Kelly is a critical issue in this case. If the jury does not believe Gladys Kelly's account, it cannot find she acted in self-defense. The expert testimony offered was directly relevant to one of the critical elements of that account, namely, what Gladys Kelly believed at the time of the stabbing, and was thus material to establish the honesty of her stated belief that she was in imminent danger of death.

The State argues that there is no need to bolster defendant's credibility with expert testimony concerning the battering because the State did not attempt to undermine defendant's testimony concerning her prior mistreatment at the hands of her husband. The State's claim is simply untrue. In her summation, the prosecutor suggested that had Ernest Kelly lived, he might have told a different story from the one Gladys told. (In its brief, the State argues that evidence in the case suggests that Gladys Kelly's claims of abuse could have been contradicted by her husband.) This is obviously a direct attempt to undermine defendant's testimony about her prior mistreatment.

Moreover, defendant's credibility was also attacked in other ways. Gladys Kelly's prior conviction for conspiracy to commit robbery was admitted into evidence for the express purpose of impeachment, even though this conviction had occurred nine years before the stabbing. Other questions, about Gladys Kelly's use of alcohol and drugs and about her premarital sexual conduct, were clearly efforts to impeach credibility.

As can be seen from our discussion of the expert testimony, Dr. Veronen would have bolstered Gladys Kelly's credibility. Specifically, by showing that her experience, although concededly difficult to comprehend, was common to that of other women who had been in similarly abusive relationships, Dr. Veronen would have helped the jury understand that Gladys Kelly could have honestly feared that she would suffer serious bodily harm from her husband's attacks, yet still remain with him. This, in turn, would support Ms. Kelly's testimony about her state of mind (that is, that she honestly feared serious bodily harm) at the time of the stabbing.

On the facts in this case, we find that the expert testimony was relevant to Gladys Kelly's state of mind, namely, it was admissible to show she honestly believed she was in imminent danger of death.... Moreover, we find that because this testimony was central to the defendant's claim of self-defense, its exclusion, if otherwise admissible, cannot be held to be harmless error.

We also find the expert testimony relevant to the reasonableness of defendant's belief that she was in imminent danger of death or serious injury. We do not mean that the expert's testimony could be used to show that it was understandable that a battered woman might believe that her life was in danger when indeed it was not and when a reasonable person would not have so believed.... Expert testimony in that direction would be relevant solely to the honesty of defendant's belief, not its objective reasonableness. Rather, our conclusion is that the expert's testimony, if accepted by the jury, would have aided it in determining whether, under the circumstances, a reasonable person would have believed there was imminent danger to her life.

At the heart of the claim of self-defense was defendant's story that she had been repeatedly subjected to "beatings" over the course of her marriage. While defendant's testimony was somewhat lacking in detail, a juror could infer from the use of the word "beatings," as well as the detail given concerning some of these events (the choking, the biting, the use of fists), that these physical assaults posed a risk of serious injury or death. When that regular pattern of serious physical abuse is combined with defendant's claim that the decedent sometimes threatened to kill her, defendant's statement that on this occasion she thought she might be killed when she saw Mr. Kelly running toward her could be found to reflect a reasonable fear; that is, it could so be found if the jury believed Gladys Kelly's story of the prior beatings, if it believed her story of the prior threats, and, of course, if it believed her story of the events of that particular day.

The crucial issue of fact on which this expert's testimony would bear is why, given such allegedly severe and constant beatings, combined with threats to kill, defendant had not long ago left decedent. Whether raised by the prosecutor as a factual issue or not, our own common knowledge tells us that most of us, including the ordinary juror, would ask himself or herself just such a question. And our knowledge is bolstered by the experts' knowledge, for the experts point out that one of the common myths, apparently believed by most people, is that battered wives are free to leave. To some, this misconception is followed by the observation that the battered wife is masochistic, proven by her refusal to leave despite the severe beatings; to others, however, the fact that the battered wife stays on unquestionably suggests that the "beatings" could not have been too bad for if they had been, she certainly would have left. The expert could clear up these myths, by explaining that one of the common characteristics of a battered wife is her inability to leave despite such constant beatings; her "learned helplessness"; her lack of anywhere to go; her feeling that if she tried to leave, she would be subjected to even more merciless treatment; her belief in the omnipotence of her battering husband; and sometimes her hope that her husband will change his ways.

Unfortunately, in this case the State reinforced the myths about battered women. On cross-examination, when discussing an occasion when Mr. Kelly temporarily moved out of the house, the State repeatedly asked Ms. Kelly: "You wanted him back, didn't you?" The implication was clear: domestic life could not have been too bad if she wanted him back. In its closing argument, the State trivialized the severity of the beatings, saying: I'm not going to say they happened or they didn't happen, but life isn't pretty. Life is not a bowl of cherries. We each and every person who takes a breath has problems. Defense counsel says bruised and battered. Is there any one of us who hasn't been battered by life in some manner or means?

Even had the State not taken this approach, however, expert testimony would be essential to rebut the general misconceptions regarding battered women.

The difficulty with the expert's testimony is that it sounds as if an expert is giving knowledge to a jury about something the jury knows as well as anyone else, namely, the reasonableness of a person's fear of imminent serious danger. That is not at all, however, what this testimony is directly aimed at. It is aimed at an area where the purported common knowledge of the jury may be very much mistaken, an area where jurors' logic, drawn from their own experience, may lead to a wholly incorrect conclusion, an area where expert knowledge would enable the jurors to disregard their prior conclusions as being common myths rather than common knowledge. After hearing the expert, instead of saying Gladys Kelly could not have been beaten up so badly for if she had, she certainly would have left, the jury could conclude that her failure to leave was very much part and parcel of her life as a battered wife. The jury could conclude that instead of casting doubt on the accuracy of her testimony about the severity and frequency of prior beatings, her failure to leave actually reinforced her credibility.

Since a retrial is necessary, we think it advisable to indicate the limit of the expert's testimony on this issue of reasonableness.... No expert is needed ... to tell the jury the logical conclusion, namely, that a person who has in fact been severely and continuously beaten might very well reasonably fear that the imminent beating she was about to suffer could be either life-threatening or pose a risk of serious injury. What the expert could state was that defendant had the battered-woman's syndrome, and could explain that syndrome in detail, relating its characteristics to defendant, but only to enable the jury better to determine the honesty and reasonableness of defendant's belief. Depending on its content, the expert's testimony might also enable the jury to find that the battered wife, because of the prior beatings, numerous beatings, as often as once a week, for seven years, from the day they were married to the day he died, is particularly able to predict accurately the likely extent of violence in any attack on her. That conclusion could significantly affect the jury's evaluation of the reasonableness of defendant's fear for her life.[1]

VI.

Having determined that testimony about the battered-woman's syndrome is relevant, we now consider whether Dr. Veronen's testimony satisfies the limitations placed on expert testimony.... Evidence Rule 56(2) provides that an expert may testify "as to matters requiring scientific, technical or other specialized knowledge if such testimony will assist the trier of fact to understand the evidence or determine a fact in issue." In effect, this Rule imposes three basic requirements for the admission of expert testimony: (1) the intended testimony must concern a subject matter

1. ...

Defendant's counsel at oral argument made it clear that defendant's basic contention was that her belief in the immediate need to use deadly force was both honest and reasonable; and that the evidence concerning the battered-woman's syndrome was being offered solely on that issue. We therefore are not faced with any claim that a battered woman's honest belief in the need to use deadly force, even if objectively unreasonable, constitutes justification so long as its unreasonableness results from the psychological impact of the beatings....

that is beyond the ken of the average juror; (2) the field testified to must be at a state of the art such that an expert's testimony could be sufficiently reliable; and (3) the witness must have sufficient expertise to offer the intended testimony....[1]

. . .

... [T]he record before us reveals that the battered woman's syndrome has a sufficient scientific basis to produce uniform and reasonably reliable results.... The numerous books, articles and papers referred to earlier indicate the presence of a growing field of study and research about the battered woman's syndrome and recognition of the syndrome in the scientific field. However, while the record before us could require such a ruling, we refrain from conclusively ruling that Dr. Veronen's proffered testimony about the battered-woman's syndrome would satisfy New Jersey's standard of acceptability for scientific evidence. This is because the State was not given a full opportunity in the trial court to question Dr. Veronen's methodology in studying battered women or her implicit assertion that the battered-woman's syndrome has been accepted by the relevant scientific community.

. . .

We have concluded that the appropriate disposal of this appeal is to reverse and remand for a new trial....

. . .

■ HANDLER, JUDGE, concurring in part and dissenting in part.

The record in this case persuasively establishes the professional acceptance and scientific reliability of the clinical psychological condition referred to as the "battered women's syndrome." Therefore, I would rule that expert evidence of the battered women's syndrome is both competent and relevant as related to the defense of self-defense. Consequently, no further expert testimony or evidence concerning the admissibility of this doctrine should be required on a retrial of this case. I would also allow into evidence on the retrial the testimony of defendant's expert that defendant was suffering battered women's syndrome when she killed her husband. That testimony was unquestionably relevant to defendant's claim of self-defense. In addition, the evidence in this case indicates that repeated sexual and physical victimization of a woman's children may, in conjunction with her own abused treatment, contribute to the development of battered women's syndrome. I therefore concur in the majority's determination to allow on a retrial evidence of the decedent's sexual assaults upon defen-

1. Of course, expert testimony that meets these three criteria is still subject to other rules of evidence. For example, the probative value of the testimony must not be substantially outweighed by the risk that its admission would necessitate undue consumption of time or create substantial danger of undue prejudice or of confusing the issues or of misleading the jury.... The danger of undue prejudice would be only slightly greater if expert testimony on the battered-woman's syndrome is introduced than without it, however, because the jury, even without it, will certainly hear about the past beatings from lay witnesses.

dant's daughter as related to the issue of the battered women's syndrome and defendant's defense of self-defense.

The Court in this case takes a major stride in recognizing the scientific authenticity of the battered women's syndrome and its legal and factual significance in the trial of certain criminal cases. My difference with the Court is quite narrow. I believe that defendant Gladys Kelly has demonstrated at her trial by sufficient expert evidence her entitlement to the use of the battered women's syndrome in connection with her defense of self-defense. I would therefore not require this issue—the admissibility of the battered women's syndrome—to be tried again.

. . .

For the reasons expressed, I dissent in part from the Court's decision.

NOTES AND QUESTIONS

1. On remand, Gladys Kelly was convicted, and the expert testimony of Dr. Veronen was again excluded, this time on the basis that battered women's syndrome lacked the necessary level of acceptance in the relevant scientific community.

Result in Kelly case

It is important to remember that even when battered women defendants are successful in introducing expert testimony in their trials, that testimony by no means guarantees their acquittal. In the 1995 study conducted by the National Clearinghouse for the Defense of Battered Women for the U.S. Departments of Justice and Health and Human Services, which looked at the appeals of 152 battered women defendants in state courts, 63 percent resulted in affirmance of the woman's conviction or sentence, even though expert testimony was admitted or found admissible in 71 percent of the affirmances. *The Validity and Use of Evidence Concerning Battering and Its Effects in Criminal Trials,* REPORT RESPONDING TO SECTION 40507 OF THE VIOLENCE AGAINST WOMEN ACT, NCJ 160972, *Overview and Highlights* at 5–6 (May 1996).

2. If Gladys Kelly had not been married to the man she killed, do you think she would have had difficulty establishing that she acted in self defense, if the jury accepted her version of the events leading up to the killing? What is it precisely about her prior relationship with the decedent that makes the self defense claim so problematic, and suggests the necessity for expert testimony? Is it the "imminence" requirement; the requirement that the force she use be proportional to the level of threat against her; her motivation for the killing, or more than one of these elements that might be affected by her relationship? Judge Wilenz suggests that the most important function of the expert testimony may be to explain to the jury why Gladys Kelly had not walked out on Ernest before the events that led to his death. Why is that, do you suppose?

In his own explanation of why Gladys Kelly, or any other battered woman, might not leave her batterer, even though she was subjected to serious abuse, and afraid for her safety or even her life, Wilenz mentions both internal and external factors. On the one hand, he talks about the "psychological paralysis'' women can sink into; their tendency to believe that their husbands are omnipotent, and that attempts to escape will be futile; and their capacity to be ''trapped by their own fear.'' On the other, he talks about the practical difficulties encountered by women who lack the material and social resources to support themselves and their children; the social stigma attached to women who abandon their children, and the real prospect that leaving will provoke increased violence. Unfortunately, as you have discovered earlier in this book, lumping all these factors together under the heading ''battered woman's syndrome'' frequently leads to judicial emphasis on the ''internal'' rather than the ''external'' factors, and the term ''syndrome'' also calls into question whether the defendant's ''state of mind'' is indeed reasonable, so that her violence is justified, or whether instead her violence is ''excusable,'' on the basis that her state of mind is disordered, for reasons that lead us to conclude she should be not be held fully accountable for her actions. Although Judge Wilenz himself emphasizes the value of the testimony as offering grounds for the conclusion that the defendant acted reasonably, it is easy to see how other less careful interpreters of the testimony (both lawyers and judges) have been led in a different direction. The battered women's perspective that too many courts are hearing and to which they are responding is that of damaged women, not of women who perceive themselves to be, and in fact are, acting competently and rationally in light of the alternatives.

3. At another point in his opinion, Wilenz offers a different analysis, and one that is consistent with a view of women as competent, rational, and capable of exercising sound judgment about the need to use force in self defense. He notes that the battered partner in a relationship may, because of her prior experience with her partner, be more sensitive to his signals of impending or escalating violence, and better able than an outsider ''to predict the likely extent of violence in any attack on her.'' If the jury were to draw this conclusion about a defendant's knowledge of her abusive partner, Wilenz goes on to say, it could clearly influence the jury's evaluation of the reasonableness of defendant's fear for her life. In this analysis the defendant is essentially presented as an ''expert'' in her partner's violence, rather than someone's whose perceptions have been distorted by her experience. The contrast between these two images is quite stark.

In a recent California case, People v. Humphrey, 13 Cal. 4th 1073 (Cal. 1996), Judge Brown, concurring in a judgment holding that battered women's syndrome testimony may be relevant to the objective reasonableness of a defendant's decision to use force in self defense, elaborated on the expertise victims of domestic violence develop in predicting their partners' behavior:

> Despite the extensive and vivid, even lurid, details of battering relationships, the literature and published opinions contain relatively limited discussion, even on an anecdotal basis, of BWS directly relating to objective reasonableness. The single most pertinent aspect, which defendant here invokes, is the hypervigilance generated by the cycles of abuse that mark these relationships. As the commentators explain: ''[T]he battered woman's familiarity with her husband's violence may

> enable her to recognize the subtle signs that usually precede a severe beating.... Moreover, even if the woman kills her husband when he is only threatening her, rather than actually beating her, she knows from past experience that he is not merely making idle comments but is fully capable of carrying out his threats. Thus, the battered woman may reasonably fear imminent danger from her husband when others unfamiliar with the history of abuse would not." (Kinports, Defending Battered Women's Self-Defense Claims (1988) 67 Or. L.Rev. 393, 423–424, fns. omitted; Crocker, The Meaning of Equality for Battered Women Who Kill Men in Self-Defense (1985) 8 Harv. Women's L.J. 121, 141, 143; Walker, Battered Women Syndrome and Self-Defense (1992) 6 Notre Dame J.L. Ethics & Pub. Pol'y 321, 324, 328.) "[E]xperts testify that, because a battered woman is attuned to her abuser's pattern of attacks, she learns to recognize subtle gestures or threats that distinguish the severity of attacks and that lead her to believe a particular attack will seriously threaten her survival." (Developments in the Law–Legal Responses to Domestic Violence (1993) 106 Harv. L.Rev. 1498, 1582, fn. omitted.)
>
> In a related vein, researchers also note that "[w]hen a woman kills her batterer, the abuse almost always will have escalated both in frequency and intensity in the period immediately preceding the killing." (Rosen, On Self-Defense, Imminence, and Women Who Kill Their Batterers (1993) 71 N.C. L.Rev. 371, 401, fn. omitted; see Walker et al., Beyond the Juror's Ken: Battered Women (1982) 7 Vt. L.Rev. 1, 3; Browne, When Battered Women Kill (1987) pp. 68–69, 105–107.) "Expert testimony [shows] that among battered women who kill, the final incident that precipitates the killing is viewed by the battered woman as 'more severe and more life-threatening than prior incidents.' [Citation.]" (Commonwealth v. Stonehouse (1989) 521 Pa. 41, 63 [555 A.2d 772, 784], fn. omitted.) On the basis of her experience, a battered woman may thus be "better able to predict the likely degree of violence in any particular battering incident" (Ewing, Battered Women Who Kill (1987) p. 55) and in turn may more precisely assess the measure and speed of force necessary to resist. (People v. Aris, supra, 215 Cal.App.3d at p. 1194.)

Id. at 1096–97.

4. Despite the sophistication demonstrated by judges such as Judge Brown in *Humphrey*, and indeed by the entire California Supreme Court in its decision in that case, excerpted later in this chapter, there is still a present danger that battered women's syndrome testimony is operating to create a new stereotype, fostering the view that the "real" battered woman is one who is dependent, passive, psychologically as well as physically damaged by the abuse, and helpless. This stereotype is crowding out the competing image of the battered woman who saves her own life by making a reasonable and informed judgment that she has no alternative but to use violence against her abuser. This in turn creates the risk that women who do not conform to the helpless stereotype may be unable to benefit from expert testimony about battering, and may even be precluded from arguing

that they acted in self defense, even though their decisions to use violence are indistinguishable from the decisions made by those who defend themselves against the violence of strangers. You might want at this point to revisit the excerpt from Mary Ann Dutton's article, *Understanding Women's Responses to Domestic Violence: A Redefinition of Battered Women's Syndrome,* 21 HOFSTRA L. REV. 1191 (1993), in Chapter 4, above, and the notes which followed it. As you may remember, a recent report prepared for the U.S. Departments of Justice and Health and Human Services sounded the same cautionary note, while concluding at the same time that expert testimony had served a valuable function in increasing recognition of the problem of domestic violence in the nation's courtrooms, educating judges and juries, and dispelling common myths and stereotypes about battered women. *The Validity and Use of Evidence Concerning Battering and Its Effects in Criminal Trials,* REPORT RESPONDING TO SECTION 40507 OF THE VIOLENCE AGAINST WOMEN ACT, NCJ 160972 (May 1996).

The same issue is tackled head on by Judge L'Heureux Dubé of Canada's Supreme Court, in the case of Malott v. Her Majesty the Queen, 1998 Can. Sup. Ct. LEXIS 7 (1998). The *Lavallee* case discussed by Dubé is an earlier decision in which the court recognized the importance of admitting expert testimony in battered women's self defense cases. R. v. Lavallee, [1990] 1 S.C.R. 852. In *Malott*, Judge Dubé commented:

> . . . Concerns have been expressed that the treatment of expert evidence on battered woman syndrome, which is itself admissible in order to combat the myths and stereotypes which society has about battered women, has led to a new stereotype of the "battered woman." . . .
>
> It is possible that those women who are unable to fit themselves within the stereotype of a victimized, passive, helpless, dependent, battered woman will not have their claims to self-defence fairly decided. For instance, women who have demonstrated too much strength or initiative, women of colour, women who are professionals, or women who might have fought back against their abusers on previous occasions, should not be penalized for failing to accord with the stereotypical image of the archetypal battered women. . . . Needless to say, women with these characteristics are still entitled to have their claims of self-defence fairly adjudicated, and they are also still entitled to have their experiences as battered women inform the analysis. Professor Grant . . . warns against allowing the law to develop such that a woman accused of killing her abuser must either have been "reasonable 'like a man' or reasonable 'like a battered women'." I agree that this must be avoided. The "reasonable women" must not be forgotten in the analysis, and deserves to be as much a part of the objective standard of the reasonable person as does the "reasonable man."
>
> How should the courts combat the "syndromization" of battered women who act in self-defense? The legal inquiry into the moral culpability of a woman who is, for instance, claiming self-defence must focus on the *reasonableness* of her actions in the context of her personal experiences, and her experiences as a woman, not on her status as a battered woman and her entitlement to claim that she is

suffering from "battered woman syndrome." ... By emphasizing a woman's "learned helplessness," her dependence, her victimization, and her low self-esteem, in order to establish that she suffers from "battered woman syndrome" the legal debate shifts from the objective rationality of her actions to preserve her own life to those personal inadequacies which apparently explain her failure to flee from her abuser. Such an emphasis comports too well with society's stereotypes about women. Therefore, it should be scrupulously avoided because it only serves to undermine the important advancements achieved by the decision in *Lavallee.*

There are other elements of a women's social context which help to explain her inability to leave her abuser, and which do not focus on those characteristics most consistent with traditional stereotypes. As Wilson J. herself recognized in *Lavallee*, ... "environmental factors may also impair the woman's ability to leave—lack of job skills, the presence of children to care for, fear of retaliation by the man, etc. may each have a role to play in some cases." To this list of factors I would add a woman's need to protect her children from abuse, a fear of losing custody of her children, pressures to keep the family together, weaknesses of social and financial support for battered women, and no guarantee that the violence would cease simply because she left. The considerations necessarily inform the reasonableness of a woman's beliefs or perceptions of, for instance, her lack of an alternative to the use of deadly force to preserve herself from death or grievous bodily harm.

How should these principles be given practical effect in the context of a jury trial of a woman accused of murdering her abuser? To fully accord with the spirit of Lavallee, where the reasonableness of a battered woman's belief is at issue in a criminal case, a judge and jury should be made to appreciate that a battered woman's experiences are both individualized, based on her own history and relationships, as well as shared with other women, within the context of a society and a legal system which has historically undervalued women's experiences. A judge and jury should be told that a battered woman's experiences are generally outside the common understanding of the average judge and juror, and that they should seek to understand the evidence being presented to them in order to overcome the myths and stereotypes which we all share. Finally, all of this should be presented in such a way as to focus on the reasonableness of the woman's actions, without relying on old or new stereotypes about battered women.

Id. at 28.

In this opinion, Judge L'Heureux Dubé ties together the need for expert testimony to address reasonableness, the interplay between the individual and the social, and the hurdles of "syndromization." She highlights the possibilities and dilemmas of expert testimony on battering, details the obstacles to fair consideration, and illuminates the profound challenge that feminist lawmaking poses to judges.

5. In the 1995 study discussed above, *The Validity and Use of Evidence Concerning Battering and Its Effects in Criminal Trials,* REPORT RESPONDING TO SECTION 40507 OF THE VIOLENCE AGAINST WOMEN ACT, NCJ 160972 (May 1996), the National Clearinghouse for the Defense of Battered Women studied and summarized state practice regarding the admissibility of expert testimony:

> Although there is significant consensus among the courts as to the issues on which expert testimony on battering and its effects is relevant and admissible, case-by-case variations also exist within a given jurisdiction that depend on the nature of the case, the specific facts of the case, or the specific issues raised by the defendant on appeal.
>
> 1. Over three quarters of the states have found expert testimony admissible to prove the defendant is a battered woman or that she "suffers from 'battered woman syndrome,'" Almost 70 percent of the states have found "generic" expert testimony admissible in order to explain battering and its effects generally, without reference to a specific defendant. Twenty percent of the states, however, explicitly preclude experts from testifying that the defendant is a battered woman or "suffering from 'battered woman syndrome.'"
>
> 2. Nearly 70% of the states have found expert testimony relevant to supporting a self-defense claim; nearly 70% of the states also agree that expert testimony is relevant to the issue of the defendant's state of mind at the time of the charged crime.
>
> 3. Two-thirds of the states consider expert testimony on battering and its effects relevant to the question of why the defendant did not leave the battering relationship or to explain other conduct, such as acts performed under duress. A similar proportion of the federal courts have found the testimony relevant for these purposes.
>
> 4. A significant minority of the states have explicitly noted that the testimony is admissible to rebut common myths and misperceptions about battered women (33 percent), to prove a defendant's diminished capacity or lack of intent (30 percent), to bolster the defendant's credibility (25 percent), or to show the existence of mitigating factors in the defendant's favor at the sentencing phase of the trial (20 percent). A similar proportion of the federal courts admitting such expert testimony have also found it relevant for these purposes.

Id., *Overview and Highlights* at 5.

4. While many states initially admitted expert testimony about battered women's experiences, or battered women's syndrome, by judicial decision, and have allowed the standards for admissibility to evolve in the same way, other jurisdictions chose to address the issue through special legislation. By 1995 12 states had taken this step, as reported in the same 1995 study. Id., *Trend Analysis* at 9–10. In most if not all states the legislation was

introduced out of frustration with judicial inaction, and a desire to ensure that battered women would not go to trial without the benefit of expert testimony. However, the legislative route has its problems, as the following excerpt suggests.

The Impact of "Special" Legislation Elizabeth M. Schneider, Battered Women and Feminist Lawmaking, 143–144 (2000)

... Statutes that focus exclusively on battered women, largely centering around admissibility of expert testimony, are problematic for several reasons. First, they tend to single out problems of battered women as though they are "special" and should not be understood within the general framework of the criminal law. For example, a statute that makes evidence of battered woman syndrome admissible suggests that this evidence would not otherwise be admissible. Second, it is questionable whether wholesale legislative reforms are the best solution to the problem of unequal treatment of battered woman defendants, since many problems result from unequal application of the law. Third, experience demonstrates that the language used in these statutes may be too limiting and will restrict their utility.

Two examples are a Maryland statute that permits evidence of abuse of the defendant and expert testimony on "battered spouse syndrome," and two Ohio statutes that authorize expert testimony on "battered-woman syndrome" in self-defense and insanity defenses. MD. CODE ANN., CTS. & JUD. PROC. § 10–916 (1999); OHIO REV. CODE ANN. § 2901.06 (1999); OHIO REV. CODE ANN. § 2945.32 (1999). The Ohio statutes permit the introduction of expert testimony only to support either the imminence element of a self-defense claim or "to establish the requisite impairment of the Defendant's reason necessary for finding that the Defendant is not guilty by reason of insanity." OHIO REV. CODE ANN. § 2901.06 (1999); OHIO REV. CODE ANN. § 2945.392 (1999). Both the Ohio statutes and the Maryland statute assume that this evidence would not be otherwise admissible. This assumption can create the impression that a separate defense for battered women has been codified.

The need for special legislation concerning battering may also be questioned on other grounds. Depending on the particular state, it may be the legal standard of self-defense or the law governing the admissibility of evidence of battering that is problematic and needs reform, or it may be simply that judges apply these laws in gender-biased fashion. In many states, special legislation has been rushed through as a "quick fix" to the problem of domestic violence, without careful analysis of the particular state's criminal-law statutory scheme and of case law on procedural issues, such as burden of proof on self-defense.

If special legislation to admit expert testimony is developed, it is important that the statutory language be as inclusive as possible to admit evidence of battering generally. One example is a Texas statute which states that, in all prosecutions for murder, the defendant shall be permitted to offer "relevant evidence that the defendant had been the victim of acts of family violence committed by the deceased and relevant expert testimony regarding the condition of [her] mind ... [including] relevant facts and circumstances relating to family violence that are the basis of experts' opinions." Similarly, in Louisiana, the relevant statute does not refer at all to "battered woman syndrome" but provides simply that "an expert's opinion as to the effects of the prior assaultive acts on the accused's state of mind is admissible." A Massachusetts statute provides for admissibility of evidence "that the defendant is or has been the victim of acts of physical, sexual or psychological harm or abuse" in a wide range of circumstances, including self-defense, defense of another, duress or coercion, or "accidental harm."

* * *

NOTES AND QUESTIONS

1. Half of the twelve statutory provisions in place by 1995 referred specifically to expert testimony on "battered woman syndrome," or "battered spouse syndrome," while the other half used more generic language, referring to the nature and effects of domestic violence, family violence or physical, sexual or psychological abuse on the beliefs, perceptions and behaviors of the person being abused. *The Validity and Use of Evidence Concerning Battering and Its Effects in Criminal Trials,* REPORT RESPONDING TO SECTION 40507 OF THE VIOLENCE AGAINST WOMEN ACT, NCJ 160972, *Trend Analysis* at 14 (May 1996). In Missouri as well as Ohio, the statutory provisions have been interpreted as limiting the admissibility of expert testimony to self-defense cases, even though they do not expressly preclude introduction of relevant expert testimony in other cases involving battered women. Id. In eight of the states the statutes use mandatory language, while in four (Georgia, Maryland, Ohio and Wyoming) the language is permissive.

2. Mindful of Elizabeth Schneider's critique, how would you evaluate the following California statute?

> *Battered women's syndrome; expert testimony in criminal actions; exception; sufficiency of foundation; abuse and domestic violence; applicability to Penal Code*
>
> (a) In a criminal action, expert testimony is admissible by either the prosecution or the defense regarding battered women's syndrome, including the physical, emotional, or mental effects upon the beliefs, perceptions, or behavior of victims of domestic violence, except when offered against a criminal defendant to prove the occurrence of the act or acts of abuse which form the basis of the criminal charge.
>
> (b) The foundation shall be sufficient for admission of this expert testimony if the proponent of the evidence establishes its relevancy and the proper qualification of the expert witness. Expert opinion testimo-

ny on battered women's syndrome shall not be considered a new scientific technique whose reliability is unproven.

(c) For purposes of this section, "abuse" is defined in Section 6203 of the Family Code and "domestic violence" is defined in section 6211 of the Family Code.

(d) This section is intended as a rule of evidence only and no substantive change affecting the Penal Code is intended.

California Evidence Code § 1107 (West 2000)

Even though the language of the statute appears generous in its scope, several California courts interpreted it to approve the introduction of expert testimony only for the purpose of assisting the jury in determining whether the battered woman defendant *actually* (subjectively) believed it was necessary to defend herself with force, and not in determining whether that belief was reasonable. The ruling in one such case, People v. Humphrey, was upheld by a Court of Appeal, but reversed by the Supreme Court of California in People v. Humphrey, 13 Cal. 4th 1073 (Cal. 1996). The court held that:

> The instruction was erroneous. Because evidence of battered women's syndrome may help the jury understand the circumstances in which the defendant found herself at the time of the killing, it is relevant to the reasonableness of her belief. Moreover, because defendant testified, the evidence was relevant to her credibility. The trial court should have allowed the jury to consider this testimony in deciding the reasonableness as well as the existence of defendant's belief that killing was necessary.

Id. at 1076–77. How do you explain the trial court's ruling? In its critique, the California Supreme Court emphasized that a determination of objective reasonableness is not an abstract determination, but one that requires consideration of the defendant's prior knowledge, and her particular circumstances. The Court also noted that while it could not avoid use of the term "battered women's syndrome" to describe the testimony, since the legislation incorporated it, it was no longer the preferred term for describing "expert testimony about battering," or "expert testimony on battered women's experiences." The following excerpts from the opinion contain both the majority's account of how battered women's syndrome testimony can, in general terms, be relevant to the issue of reasonableness, and a concurring judge's detailed analysis of the relevance of the testimony in this particular case.

People v. Evelyn Humphrey

13 Cal. 4th 1073.
Supreme Court of California, 1996.

■ CHIN, JUDGE.

. . .

I. THE FACTS

. . .

B. Defense Evidence

Defendant claimed she shot Hampton in self-defense. To support the claim, the defense presented first expert testimony and then nonexpert testimony, including that of defendant herself.

1. Expert Testimony

Dr. Lee Bowker testified as an expert on battered women's syndrome. The syndrome, he testified, "is not just a psychological construction, but it's a term for a wide variety of controlling mechanisms that the man or it can be a woman, but in general for this syndrome it's a man, uses against the woman, and for the effect that those control mechanisms have."

Dr. Bowker had studied about 1,000 battered women and found them often inaccurately portrayed "as cardboard figures, paper-thin punching bags who merely absorb the violence but didn't do anything about it." He found that battered women often employ strategies to stop the beatings, including hiding, running away, counterviolence, seeking the help of friends and family, going to a shelter, and contacting police. Nevertheless, many battered women remain in the relationship because of lack of money, social isolation, lack of self-confidence, inadequate police response, and a fear (often justified) of reprisals by the batterer. "The battering man will make the battered woman depend on him and generally succeed at least for a time." A battered woman often feels responsible for the abusive relationship, and "she just can't figure out a way to please him better so he'll stop beating her." In sum, "It really is the physical control of the woman through economics and through relative social isolation combined with the psychological techniques that make her so dependent."

Many battered women go from one abusive relationship to another and seek a strong man to protect them from the previous abuser. "[W]ith each successful victimization, the person becomes less able to avoid the next one." The violence can gradually escalate, as the batterer keeps control using ever more severe actions, including rape, torture, violence against the woman's loved ones or pets, and death threats. Battered women sense this escalation. In Dr. Bowker's "experience with battered women who kill in self-defense their abusers, it's always related to their perceived change of what's going on in a relationship. They become very sensitive to what sets off batterers. They watch for this stuff very carefully.... Anybody who is abused over a period of time becomes sensitive to the abuser's behavior and when she sees a change acceleration begin in that behavior, it tells them something is going to happen...."

Dr. Bowker interviewed defendant for a full day. He believed she suffered not only from battered women's syndrome, but also from being the child of an alcoholic and an incest victim. He testified that all three of defendant's partners before Hampton were abusive and significantly older than she.

Dr. Bowker described defendant's relationship with Hampton. Hampton was a 49–year-old man who weighed almost twice as much as defendant. The two had a battering relationship that Dr. Bowker characterized as a "traditional cycle of violence." The cycle included phases of tension building, violence, and then forgiveness-seeking in which Hampton would promise not to batter defendant any more and she would believe him. During this period, there would be occasional good times. For example, defendant told Dr. Bowker that Hampton would give her a rose. "That's one of the things that hooks people in. Intermittent reinforcement is the key." But after a while, the violence would begin again. The violence would recur because "basically ... the woman doesn't perfectly obey. That's the bottom line." For example, defendant would talk to another man, or fail to clean house "just so."

The situation worsened over time, especially when Hampton got off parole shortly before his death. He became more physically and emotionally abusive, repeatedly threatened defendant's life, and even shot at her the night before his death. Hampton often allowed defendant to go out, but she was afraid to flee because she felt he would find her as he had in the past. "He enforced her belief that she can never escape him." Dr. Bowker testified that unless her injuries were so severe that "something absolutely had to be treated," he would not expect her to seek medical treatment. "That's the pattern of her life.... "

Dr. Bowker believed defendant's description of her experiences. In his opinion, she suffered from battered women's syndrome in "about as extreme a pattern as you could find."

2. Nonexpert Testimony

Defendant confirmed many of the details of her life and relationship with Hampton underlying Dr. Bowker's opinion. She testified that her father forcefully molested her from the time she was seven years old until she was fifteen. She described her relationship with another abusive man as being like "Nightmare on Elm Street." Regarding Hampton, she testified that they often argued and that he beat her regularly. Both were heavy drinkers. Hampton once threw a can of beer at her face, breaking her nose. Her dental plates hurt because Hampton hit her so often. He often kicked her, but usually hit her in the back of the head because, he told her, it "won't leave bruises." Hampton sometimes threatened to kill her, and often said she "would live to regret it." Matters got worse towards the end.

The evening before the shooting, March 27, 1992, Hampton arrived home "very drunk." He yelled at her and called her names. At one point when she was standing by the bedroom window, he fired his .357 magnum revolver at her. She testified, "He didn't miss me by much either." She was "real scared."

The next day, the two drove into the mountains. They argued, and Hampton continually hit her. While returning, he said that their location would be a good place to kill her because "they wouldn't find [her] for a while." She took it as a joke, although she feared him. When they returned, the arguing continued. He hit her again, then entered the kitchen. He threatened, "This time, bitch, when I shoot at you, I won't miss." He came from the kitchen and reached for the gun on the living room table. She grabbed it first, pointed it at him, and told him "that he wasn't going to hit [her]." She backed Hampton into the kitchen. He was saying something, but she did not know what. He reached for her hand and she shot him. She believed he was reaching for the gun and was going to shoot her.

Several other witnesses testified about defendant's relationship with Hampton, his abusive conduct in general, and his physical abuse of, and threats to, defendant in particular. This testimony generally corroborated defendant's. A neighbor testified that the night before the shooting, she heard a gunshot. The next morning, defendant told the neighbor that Hampton had shot at her, and that she was afraid of him. After the shooting, investigators found a bullet hole through the frame of the bedroom window and a bullet embedded in a tree in line with the window. Another neighbor testified that shortly before hearing the shot that killed Hampton, she heard defendant say, "Stop it, Albert. Stop it."

. . .

C. Procedural History

Defendant was charged with murder with personal use of a firearm. At the end of the prosecution's case-in-chief, the court granted defendant's motion under Penal Code section 1118.1 for acquittal of first degree murder.

The court instructed the jury on second degree murder and both voluntary and involuntary manslaughter. It also instructed on self-defense, explaining that an actual and reasonable belief that the killing was necessary was a complete defense; an actual but unreasonable belief was a defense to murder, but not to voluntary manslaughter. In determining reasonableness, the jury was to consider what "would appear to be necessary to a reasonable person in a similar situation and with similar knowledge."

The court also instructed:

> "Evidence regarding Battered Women's Syndrome has been introduced in this case. Such evidence, if believed, may be considered by you only for the purpose of determining whether or not the defendant held the necessary subjective honest [belief] which is a requirement for both perfect and imperfect self-defense. However, that same evidence regarding Battered Women's Syndrome may not be considered or used by you in evaluating the objective reasonableness requirement for perfect self-defense.
>
> "Battered Women's Syndrome seeks to describe and explain common reactions of women to that experience. Thus, you may consider the evidence concerning the syndrome and its effects only for the limited purpose of showing, if it does show, that the defendant's reactions, as demonstrated by the evidence, are not inconsistent with her having been physically abused or the beliefs, perceptions, or behavior of victims of domestic violence."

During deliberations, the jury asked for and received clarification of the terms "subjectively honest and objectively unreasonable." It found defendant guilty of voluntary manslaughter with personal use of a firearm. The court sentenced defendant to prison for eight years, consisting of the lower term of three years for manslaughter, plus the upper term of five years for firearm use. The Court of Appeal remanded for resentencing on the use enhancement, but otherwise affirmed the judgment.

We granted defendant's petition for review.

II. DISCUSSION

. . .

B. Battered Women's Syndrome[1]

Battered women's syndrome "has been defined as 'a series of common characteristics that appear in women who are abused physically and psychologically over an extended period of time by the dominant male figure in their lives'." (State v. Kelly (1984) 97 N.J. 178, 193. . . .)

The trial court allowed the jury to consider the battered women's syndrome evidence in deciding whether defendant actually believed she needed to kill in self-defense. The question here is whether the evidence was also relevant on the reasonableness of that belief. Two Court of Appeal decisions have considered the relevance of battered women's syndrome evidence to a claim of self-defense.

People v. Aris, supra, 215 Cal.App.3d at page 1185, applied "the law of self-defense in the context of a battered woman killing the batterer while he slept after he had beaten the killer and threatened serious bodily injury and death when he awoke." There, unlike here, the trial court refused to instruct the jury on perfect self-defense, but it did instruct on imperfect self-defense. The appellate court upheld the refusal, finding that "defendant presented no substantial evidence that a reasonable person under the same circumstances would have perceived imminent danger and a need to kill in self-defense." (Id. at p. 1192.) . . .

Although the trial court did not instruct on perfect self-defense, the appellate court first concluded that battered women's syndrome evidence is not relevant to the reasonableness element. "[T]he questions of the reasonableness of a defendant's belief that self-defense is necessary and of the reasonableness of the actions taken in self-defense do not call for an

1. We use the term "battered women's syndrome" because Evidence Code section 1107 and the cases use that term. We note, however, that according to amici curiae California Alliance Against Domestic Violence et al., ". . . the preferred term among many experts today is 'expert testimony on battering and its effects' or 'expert testimony on battered women's experiences.' Domestic violence experts have critiqued the phrase 'battered women's syndrome' because (1) it implies that there is one syndrome which all battered women develop, (2) it has pathological connotations which suggest that battered women suffer from some sort of sickness, (3) expert testimony on domestic violence refers to more than women's psychological reactions to violence, (4) it focuses attention on the battered woman rather than on the batterer's coercive and controlling behavior and (5) it creates an image of battered women as suffering victims rather than as active survivors." (Fns. omitted.)

evaluation of the defendant's subjective state of mind, but for an objective evaluation of the defendant's assertedly defensive acts. California law expresses the criterion for this evaluation in the objective terms of whether a reasonable person, as opposed to the defendant, would have believed and acted as the defendant did. We hold that expert testimony about a defendant's state of mind is not relevant to the reasonableness of the defendant's self-defense." (People v. Aris, supra, 215 Cal. App. 3d at p. 1196.)

The court then found the evidence "highly relevant to the first element of self-defense—defendant's actual, subjective perception that she was in danger and that she had to kill her husband to avoid that danger.... The relevance to the defendant's actual perception lies in the opinion's explanation of how such a perception would reasonably follow from the defendant's experience as a battered woman. This relates to the prosecution's argument that such a perception of imminent danger makes no sense when the victim is asleep and a way of escape open and, therefore, she did not actually have that perception." (People v. Aris, supra, 215 Cal.App.3d at p. 1197.) The trial court thus erred in not admitting the testimony to show "how the defendant's particular experiences as a battered woman affected her perceptions of danger, its imminence, and what actions were necessary to protect herself." (Id. at p. 1198.)

Concerned "that the jury in a particular case may misuse such evidence to establish the reasonableness requirement for perfect self-defense, for which purpose it is irrelevant," the Aris court stated that, "upon request whenever the jury is instructed on perfect self-defense, trial courts should instruct that such testimony is relevant only to prove the honest belief requirement for both perfect and imperfect self-defense, not to prove the reasonableness requirement for perfect self-defense." (People v. Aris, supra, 215 Cal.App.3d at p. 1199.) The trial court gave such an instruction here, thus creating the issue before us.

In People v. Day (1992) 2 Cal.App.4th 405, the defendant moved for a new trial following her conviction of involuntary manslaughter. Supported by an affidavit by Dr. Bowker, she argued that her attorney should have presented evidence of battered women's syndrome to aid her claim of self-defense. Relying on Aris, the appellate court first found that the evidence would not have been relevant to show the objective reasonableness of the defendant's actions.... It also found, however, that the evidence would have been admissible to rehabilitate the defendant's credibility as a witness.... Finding that counsel's failure to present the evidence was prejudicial, the court reversed the judgment....

The Attorney General argues that People v. Aris, supra, 215 Cal. App.3d 1178, and People v. Day, supra, 2 Cal.App.4th 405, were correct that evidence of battered women's syndrome is irrelevant to reasonableness. We disagree. Those cases too narrowly interpreted the reasonableness element. Aris and Day failed to consider that the jury, in determining objective reasonableness, must view the situation from the defendant's perspective. Here, for example, Dr. Bowker testified that the violence can escalate and that a battered woman can become increasingly sensitive to the abuser's behavior, testimony relevant to determining whether defendant reasonably believed when she fired the gun that this time the threat to her life was imminent. Indeed, the prosecutor argued that, "from an objective, reasonable man's standard, there was no reason for her to go get that gun. This threat that she says he made was like so many threats before. There was no reason for her to react that way." Dr. Bowker's testimony supplied a response that the jury might not otherwise receive. As violence increases over time, and threats gain credibility, a battered person might become sensitized and thus able reasonably to discern when danger is real and when it is not. "[T]he expert's testimony might also enable the jury to find that the battered [woman] ... is particularly able to predict accurately the likely extent of violence in any attack on her. That conclusion could significantly affect the jury's evaluation of the reasonableness of defendant's fear for her life." (State v. Kelly (1984) 97 N.J. 178.)

. . .

Contrary to the Attorney General's argument, we are not changing the standard from objective to subjective, or replacing the reasonable "person" standard with a reasonable "battered woman" standard. Our decision would not, in another context, compel adoption of a " 'reasonable gang member' standard." Evidence Code section 1107 states "a rule of evidence only" and makes "no substantive change." (Evid. Code, § 1107, subd. (d).) The jury must consider defendant's situation and knowledge, which makes the evidence relevant, but the ultimate question is whether a reasonable person, not a reasonable battered woman, would believe in the need to kill to prevent imminent harm. Moreover, it is the jury, not the expert, that determines whether defendant's belief and, ultimately, her actions, were objectively reasonable.

Battered women's syndrome evidence was also relevant to defendant's credibility. It "would have assisted the jury in objectively analyzing [defendant's] claim of self-defense by dispelling many of the commonly held misconceptions about battered women." (People v. Day, supra, 2 Cal. App.4th at p. 416.) For example, in urging the jury not to believe defendant's testimony that Hampton shot at her the night before the killing, the prosecutor argued that "if this defendant truly believed that [Hampton] had shot at her, on that night, I mean she would have left.... If she really believed that he had tried to shoot her, she would not have stayed." Dr. Bowker's testimony " 'would help dispel the ordinary lay person's perception that a woman in a battering relationship is free to leave at any time. The expert evidence would counter any "common sense" conclusions by the jury that if the beatings were really that bad the woman would have left her husband much earlier. Popular misconceptions about battered women would be put to rest....' "

. . .

We do not hold that Dr. Bowker's entire testimony was relevant to both prongs of perfect self-defense. Just as many types of evidence may be relevant to some disputed issues but not all, some of the expert evidence was no doubt relevant only to the subjective existence of defendant's belief. Evidence merely showing that a person's use of deadly force is scientifically explainable or empirically common does not, in itself, show it was objectively reasonable. To dispel any possible confusion, it might be appropriate for the court, on request, to clarify that, in assessing reasonableness, the question is whether a reasonable person in the defendant's circumstances would have perceived a threat of imminent injury or death, and not whether killing the abuser was reasonable in the sense of being an understandable response to ongoing abuse; and that, therefore, in making that assessment, the jury may not consider evidence merely showing that an abused person's use of force against the abuser is understandable.[1]

We also emphasize that, as with any evidence, the jury may give this testimony whatever weight it deems appropriate in light of the evidence as a whole. The ultimate judgment of reasonableness is solely for the jury. We simply hold that evidence of battered women's syndrome is generally relevant to the reasonableness, as well as the subjective existence, of defendant's belief in the need to defend, and, to the extent it is relevant, the jury may consider it in deciding both questions. The court's contrary instruction was erroneous. We disapprove of People v. Aris, supra, 215 Cal.App.3d 1178, and People v. Day, supra, 2 Cal.App.4th 405, to the extent they are inconsistent with this conclusion.

. . .

■ Brown, Judge, concurring in the order.

. . .

Turning to the facts of this case, for the most part defendant's account of events leading to the shooting did not require the filter of an expert's opinion to assist in determining the question of reasonableness. She presented a relatively straightforward claim of self-defense the jury could either accept or reject as such. According to defendant, Hampton had been physically and verbally abusive for most of the year they lived together. His threats and acts of violence had been increasing for several weeks prior to the fateful evening. Although he liked guns and owned several, he had never shot at her until the previous night. On the way home from the mountains the next day, he pointed out what he thought would be a good place to kill her because no one would find the body for awhile. Just minutes before the shooting with the gun lying within easy reach, he told her "[t]his time" he would not miss. She then grabbed the weapon as he appeared about to do the same. While she was holding him at bay, he reached for her arm at which point she apparently shot him. On their face, nothing in these facts lies beyond the experience of the average reasonable person or the ken of the average juror. (See State v. Griffiths, supra, 610 P.2d at p. 524.)

1. If the prosecution offers the battered women's syndrome evidence, an additional limiting instruction might also be appropriate on request, given the statutory prohibition against use of this evidence "to prove the occurrence of the act or acts of abuse which form the basis of the criminal charge." (Evid. Code, § 1107, subd. (a); see CALJIC No. 9.35.01)(1996 new)(5th ed. Supp.).)

At the same time, defendant also testified to facts implicating characteristics of BWS that correspond to the objective element of self-defense. Consistent with his threats, Hampton began hitting her more frequently when he got off parole. The night before, he was "getting crazy" asking for the gun, which he then shot in her direction narrowly missing her. At that moment, he had a "look on his face" that defendant had seen before "but not this bad"; he "wasn't the same person." As to events surrounding Hampton's death, defendant related that shortly before she grabbed the gun, the two were screaming and arguing; "then all of a sudden, he got quiet for a minute or two, and, then, he just snapped." A few moments later, he moved from the kitchen toward the gun saying, "This time, bitch, when I shoot at you, I won't miss." At this point, she "knew he would shoot me" and was "scared to death" not only because of Hampton's threats and prior violence but also because of his "very, very heavy" walk indicating he was "mad." She had no doubt he would kill her if she did not kill him first. As they confronted each other in the kitchen, he "looked crazy." She assumed he was going for the gun when he reached for her arm and shot him.

As relevant to this testimony, Dr. Bowker explained generally that with the cycles of violence typifying BWS the "severity tends to escalate over time." Battered women develop a heightened awareness of this escalation as threats and physical abuse become increasingly menacing. A sense of the batterer's omnipotence due to his dominance may augment this hypervigilance, causing the woman to believe all the more he will act on his threats of violence.

Bowker also discussed some specifics arguably relating to defendant's objective perception of imminent harm: "[T]he escalation had been such, particularly the night before, where [Hampton] actually shot at her that it would be pretty hard to doubt the seriousness." "A difference, I think, [between Hampton's last threat and previous ones] is that [defendant] felt for the first time that he really intended to do it and, you know, my experience with battered women who kill in self-defense their abusers, it's always related to their perceived change of what's going on in a relationship. They become very sensitive to what sets off batterers. They watch for this stuff very carefully. Anybody who is abused over a period of time becomes sensitive to the abuser's behavior and when she sees a change acceleration begin in that behavior, it tells them something is going to happen and usually the abuser said things specifically like 'I'm really going to kill you this time,' and, you know, they don't admit to that something happens that there's a label put on it by the abuser which was certainly true in Albert's case and that's intensification or an acceleration of the process is what leads to some self-defensive action which is beyond anything that the woman has ever done before."

This testimony could assist the jury in determining whether a reasonable person in defendant's situation would have perceived from the totality of the circumstances imminent peril of serious bodily injury or death. Absent the expert's explanation, the average juror might be unduly skeptical that a look, footstep, or tone of voice could in fact signal impending grave harm or that a reasonable person would be able accurately to assess the need to take self-defensive action on that basis. (State v. Kelly, supra, 478 A.2d at p. 378.) Accordingly, the trial court erred in categorically precluding consideration of evidence relevant to this purpose rather than giving a properly worded limiting instruction.

. . .

NOTE

1. One scholar who has been critical of targeted legislation governing the admissibility of expert testimony on battering is Holly Maguigan. The next reading is an excerpt from her article *Battered Women and Self-Defense: Myths and Misconceptions in Current Reform Proposals*, 140 U. PA. L. REV. 379 (1991). Maguigan argues that the problems faced by battered women criminal defendants in the courts have more to do with biased application of the rules than with deficiencies in the rules themselves. If judicial bias, or ignorance, is the real problem, then supplementing the body of law judges are required to interpret and apply is a strategy as likely to backfire as to produce real change. It could certainly be argued that the *Aris* and *Day* cases in California, and the trial court decision in the *Humphrey* case, confirm her hypothesis; nothing in the language of the governing statute mandated the narrow interpretation embodied in those decisions. In addition, however, Maguigan worries that many legislative initiatives in this area are incorporating restrictions that add rather than remove barriers to the admission of relevant expert testimony, and will make it available to "only a small percentage of battered women":

> Expert testimony about the effects of a history of abuse has been ruled admissible by the vast majority of appellate courts that have confronted the question, generally because it is deemed relevant to a self-defense claim for the broad purposes of explaining a defendant's state of mind and of rebutting myths and misconceptions about battered women, and generally after a defendant claims self-defense and introduces evidence of a history of abuse. Many enacted and proposed reforms contain provisions that are significantly more restrictive than the existing law in most jurisdictions. For instance, some legislators have undertaken to define the content of expert testimony in a way that is not only narrower than the current definition in their jurisdictions, but is also inconsistent with the findings of social scientists. An illustrative example is the statutory definition of "battered person syndrome" proposed but not introduced in Washington and modeled closely on an enacted Missouri provision:
>
> > "Battered person syndrome" means a group of concurrent psychological and behavioral characteristics resulting from repeated victimization by family violence or threat of family violence, including:
> >
> > (a) An extreme level of anxiety or depression;
> >
> > (b) Repeated unsuccessful attempts to stop, decrease, or escape from acts or threats of family violence;

(c) Extreme fearfulness of the family violence perpetrator and constant anticipation of future acts of violence; or

(d) Loss of belief in one's ability to take effective action for self-protection.[1]

Neither Missouri's earlier statute nor Washington's existing common-law evidentiary rule contained any attempt to limit the *content* of expert testimony. The definition quoted above, even though its four "included" factors are arguably disjunctive, is one with which many experts would not agree....

. . .

In some of the statutes and proposals limiting admission of expert testimony to cases involving self-defense claims, there are even more refined limitations on the purpose and scope of expert testimony. These statutes and proposals limit the testimony to the reasonableness of a defendant's belief that the use of force was immediately necessary, or that danger was imminent. These provisions may be read to exclude the presently admissible testimony on state of mind, on myths and misconceptions, and on the question why the defendant did not leave the abusive relationship. Further, some legislative language creates an additional hurdle to the admissibility of expert testimony in the form of a written notice requirement and a mandatory court-ordered pre-trial psychiatric or psychological examination of the defendant. The risk of such provisions is not only that they subject a self-defense claim to the procedural rules governing insanity defenses, but also that they appear by their terms and have been interpreted by trial judges to provide for a pre-trial factual determination whether the defendant meets the statutory definition of a person who experiences the battered woman syndrome.

Id. at 452–55.

In the excerpt that follows Maguigan debunks two assumptions that have guided legislative reform efforts, and argues that traditional self-defense jurisprudence, fairly applied, within a facilitative procedural framework, should, in most cases, protect the interests of battered women defendants.

Holly Maguigan
Battered Women and Self-Defense: Myths and Misconceptions in Current Reform Proposals, 140 University of Pennsylvania Law Review 279, 382–87, 439–43 (1991)

The impetus in current reform efforts toward redefinition of substantive criminal law and of evidentiary rules comes from two related, and incorrect, assumptions. The first incorrect assumption is that jury verdicts

1. MO. ANN. STAT. § 563.001(1)(b) (Vernon Supp. 1991).

convicting battered women result from the "fact" that most battered women do not kill in circumstances traditionally defined as "confrontations," but rather that they kill during a lull in the violence, or when the man is asleep, or by hiring someone else to kill him.... [T]he appellate decisions do not support the commonly encountered assertion that most battered women kill in nonconfrontational situations.

The reformers' second incorrect assumption is that existing doctrine is defined in a narrow and male-identified fashion to encompass one-time-only and time-bounded encounters between men of roughly equal size and strength. Using these assumptions, critics argue that the law by definition refuses to take into account the social context of a battered-woman defendant's act, even in those cases that involve traditionally defined confrontations. In the legal literature the basis of this assumption is, again, the body of opinions issued on appeals from homicide convictions. A survey of those opinions, however, does not support the view that existing definitions exclude consideration of social context.

Proceeding from these two unsupported and incorrect empirical assumptions, most proponents of reform are asking the wrong question. They ask not whether, but how substantive and evidentiary law should be redefined to guarantee the fair-trial rights of battered women who kill, and they describe "fair trials" either not at all or as those that result in not guilty verdicts. I will suggest that the proper inquiry requires a definition of fair trial that is not outcome-oriented and a careful evaluation of the appropriate definition's substantive-law, evidentiary-rule, and procedural-provision determinants. Reformers must decide carefully what is broken before setting out to make repairs.

Fair trials should be defined as those in which a defendant is able to put her case fully before the finder of fact, to "get to the jury" both the evidence of the social context of her action and legal instructions on the relevance of that context to her claim of entitlement to act in self-defense. My conclusion, after review of the cases from that perspective, is that the most common impediments to fair trials for battered women are the result not of the structure or content of existing law but of its application by trial judges.

. . .

The work of sociologists and criminologists demonstrates, even with the most conservative reading of representative empirical studies, that over seventy percent of all battered women who kill do so when faced with either an ongoing attack or the imminent threat of death or serious bodily injury; and some studies suggest that the figure may be closer to ninety percent. These estimates are consistent with the results of [my] analysis of appeals from battered women's homicide convictions, a sample that is likely to contain an overrepresentation of non-confrontation cases: at least three-quarters of the cases involve confrontations.... [M]ost homicide convictions of battered women do not result from the fact that circumstances of the killings were outside the traditional definition of self-defense.

... [T]he second incorrect assumption—which similarly dominates current scholarship and legislative efforts—[is] that existing legal definitions are insufficient to accommodate the self-defense claims of battered women, even those who kill during confrontational situations. It is true that the law of self-defense has developed in a context in which the overwhelming majority of defendants were men. It is not true, however, that the law by definition ignores the context of a woman defendant's actions.

In the area of substantive law, most scholars focus on four aspects of self-defense jurisprudence: the definitions of the standard for measuring the reasonableness of the defendant's actions, of the temporal proximity of danger facing the defendant, of the proportionality of force used to meet the threatened harm, and of the defendant's duty to retreat. These factors are not in fact generally defined in a way that excludes consideration of the circumstances in which battered women kill. In most jurisdictions, the standard of reasonableness against which the necessity of a defendant's act is measured explicitly includes consideration of the characteristics and history of the defendant on trial; her acts are measured in light of her own perceptions and experience. The definitions of the required temporal proximity of that harm is, again in most jurisdictions, broader than the particular instant of the defendant's action; the definition includes its context—the circumstances surrounding the action, including past events. Only a minority of jurisdictions impose a duty to retreat, if safe retreat is possible, before using deadly force, and most of that minority exempt a person attacked in her home from the duty to retreat. No jurisdiction has a per se rule prohibiting use of a weapon against an unarmed attacker; rather, the proportionality of force is measured on a case-by-case basis, taking into consideration the relative sizes, ages, and physical conditions of the decedent and defendant, as well as any history of violence between them.

A similar pattern exists in the law of evidence, which is the focus of legislative reform efforts. The existing evidentiary law in every jurisdiction provides that testimony about a defendant's history of abuse by the decedent is admissible. Expert testimony regarding the effects of a history of abuse, usually in the form of testimony about the "battered woman syndrome," is admissible in the overwhelming majority of the states whose appellate courts have addressed the question. In all but two of these states, the testimony has been ruled admissible on the basis of existing evidentiary provisions, without the necessity of special legislation.

To say that existing definitions can accommodate the self-defense claims of battered women and can provide for their evaluation in the relevant social context is not to say that trial courts apply those definitions when the defendants are battered women.... [T]o the extent that there is a problem getting to the jury, it is generally the result not of definitions, but of the application of the law at the trial level. That conclusion is supported by the disparity between reversal rates in these cases and in other homicides. Forty percent of the battered women's convictions [in the sample of 223 appellate cases analyzed by Maguigan] were reversed on the ground of trial errors. Only 16% of the reversals were because of errors dealing with expert testimony. The rest were reversed on the basis of the same errors (in roughly the same proportion) as in other homicides, where the reversal rate was only 8.5%. The conclusion is reinforced by the tone of the reversal opinions, many of which explicitly criticize trial courts for failing to apply to these defendants long-standing principles developed in the context of a jurisdiction's ruling on appeals involving male appellants. It is further corroborated by the appellate opinions from the jurisdictions that have adopted special substantive-law standards to measure the necessity of the defendant's act against a "reasonable battered woman" definition. In those states, there are both trial and appellate judges who, despite the redefinition of reasonableness, apply that definition in a way that precludes defendants from getting to the jury.

... [T]he operation of procedural rules (the crucial importance of which is ignored by most commentators) ... set the standards by which trial judges are to measure the defendant's evidence for the purpose of determining whether she is entitled to any self-defense instruction at all. When the rules are defined in a way that entitles judges to make credibility judgments as part of their assessment of the sufficiency of the defense evidence, they often have the effect of encouraging disparate application of self-defense standards and of permitting directed verdicts of guilt in battered women's cases.

. . .

... A jurisdiction's definition of the evidentiary showing that is a precondition to entitlement to the instruction is the single most important determinant of the defendant's ability to get an instruction on self-defense. The content of a self-defense instruction is only relevant if the rules do not block a defendant from receiving one, and the significance of evidence of a defendant's social context is clear to jurors only when a judge tells them to consider its significance to her claim of self-defense. The definition and application of the rules that govern a judge's decision on whether to allow the jury to consider self-defense illustrates the enormous power of trial judges to make outcome-determinative decisions in cases involving battered women defendants. Substantive and evidentiary law proposals must be analyzed in the context of the operation of this definitional requirement.

The most basic of the get-to-the-jury inquiries is this: what criteria must a defendant satisfy before the judge will instruct the jury to consider whether she acted in self-defense? The inquiry has four parts. The first, called the quantum of evidence ..., defines the amount of evidence on the self-defense claim the defendant must offer and have admitted. The conclusions reached in various jurisdictions range from (a) "slight" or "any," through (b) enough to raise the (even insubstantial) possibility of a reasonable doubt, to (c) "appreciable" or "substantial." The second definition involves the source of the evidence, whether it may come from any witness (including evidence developed during direct and cross-examination of the prosecution's witnesses), or whether it must be offered through a witness or witnesses called by the defense. The third inquiry is the scope—or the required extent—of the evidence: does the defendant get a self-defense instruction if she produces evidence of any element of the claim, or must she satisfy the trial judge that she has produced evidence (at the required quantum, from the required source) on each element of the self-defense claim? The final inquiry, called the quality of the evidence . . ., is whether the trial judge, whatever the quantum of evidence required and whatever its required source and scope, exercises his or her own determination about the credibility of the evidence of self-defense.

A rule whose definition of the last part of the test includes the judge's duty to evaluate credibility puts defendants most at risk of judicial misapplication of substantive and evidentiary standards, regardless of the standards' definitions. A judge vested with the power to make credibility determinations on the sufficiency of defense evidence has license to direct a verdict against a defendant.

The appellate opinions resolving battered women's complaints on appeal that no self-defense instruction was given demonstrate the critical importance of the definition of this standard. Although courts in various jurisdictions reversed trial judges' resolutions of each of the other inquiries, no trial-level ruling denying a self-defense instruction was reversed in any jurisdiction that permitted credibility determinations. A different result was reached in jurisdictions where the rules limited the judge's credibility-determining role, even where high standards were used in other parts of the test.

In a proper formulation of the showing-necessary requirement the required quantum of evidence is "any" or "slight." The evidence may come from any source, whether introduced during the prosecution's case on direct or cross-examination or during the defendant's case. The defendant does not have the burden of satisfying the judge that she has produced the requisite evidence on each element of the defense; rather, the jury is instructed on the jurisdiction's definition of each element and on its obligation to determine whether the defendant's evidence satisfies it. Finally, the judge makes no credibility determination regarding the sufficiency of the evidence.

* * *

NOTES AND QUESTIONS

1. Elsewhere in her article Maguigan does endorse specific substantive standards and evidentiary rules. She approves, for example, of a standard of reasonableness like that adopted in the *Humphrey* case—one that combines objective and subjective elements. With respect to evidentiary rules, she says the following:

> First, when a defendant claims to have acted in self-defense, both evidence of the history of abuse and of a history of other violence [by the decedent], where offered, should be admissible without a prior showing of an overt act on the part of the decedent. Second, once that testimony is received, it should be a sufficient predicate for receipt of expert testimony. The expert testimony should be admitted to explain

> the effects of a history of abuse on a defendant's behavior and perceptions and to rebut popular myths and misconceptions about battered women. There should be no requirement of a judicial determination either pre-trial or at trial that the defendant "established" herself as a battered woman.

Id. at 457–58. However, she warns that unless the procedural requirements are attended to, "substantive law standards proposed by scholars, like the special evidentiary provisions presented to legislatures, will be applied in high threshold-showing jurisdictions to prevent defendants from introducing context evidence and from receiving self-defense instructions." Id. at 459.

2. One interesting feature of the procedural reforms suggested by Holly Maguigan is that they would presumably be general in nature, and applicable to all self-defense cases rather than limited to cases involving battered women defendants. Would that make them easier or harder to procure, do you think?

3. If you were now approached by a group of criminal defense lawyers from a particular state, concerned that battered women prosecuted for assaulting or killing their abusers were not receiving justice, how would you go about determining what aspect of the process was not working for them? What substantive, evidentiary and procedural standards would you need to "audit" to make this determination? If they were eager to introduce legislative reform, what counsel would you offer about the most helpful way to frame that legislation, and the most obvious pitfalls to avoid?

4. As you have already seen in several cases, and as Maguigan's account underscores, jury instructions often provide the basis for the appeals brought by battered women who have killed their batterers when they are convicted at the trial level. *Wanrow* involved the issue of jury instructions and in *Humphrey* it was the jury instruction that provided an opportunity for the California Supreme Court to clarify its self-defense standard. Jury instructions must track both the theory of the defense in the particular case, and the governing law; they provide an opportunity to educate the jury about the law and its potential application to the facts of the case. The next case demonstrates the perils involved in shaping appropriate jury instructions in this complex and evolving area of law. Note that the substantive self-defense standard in Ohio is a subjective one, like the standard that governed the *Wanrow* decision.

State of Ohio v. Susan M. Daws

104 Ohio App. 3d 448.
Court of Appeals of Ohio, 1994.

■ WOLFF, JUDGE.

I. THE TRIAL COURT ERRED IN INSTRUCTING THE JURY.

In this assignment of error, Susan asserts that the trial court erred in failing to instruct the jury on the battered woman syndrome. Given the extensive testimony on the battered woman syndrome during trial, Susan contends that a jury instruction tailored to the syndrome was essential to assist the jury in applying that evidence to her claim of self-defense.

In response, the State argues that . . . the failure to give the instruction presented by defense counsel was neither prejudicial nor plain error because the instruction requested was not a correct statement of the law and because the trial court's instruction on self-defense was sufficient.

. . .

Susan's proffered instructions were as follows:

> [1] You have heard evidence that the Defendant suffers from Battered Woman Syndrome. In determining if this is true you must consider the following factors:
>
> a. The nature and length of her relationship with the deceased;
>
> b. The history of physical abuse between the couple including, but not limited to, previous reports to the police, physicians, counselors, family or friends; and
>
> c. The status of the Defendant that is, did she have small children to care for, the psychological assessment of her by the experts who testified in this case.
>
> [2] If you find from all of your deliberations that evidence presented shows the Defendant suffered from Battered Woman syndrome, you must consider that fact in assessing her state of mind at the time of the homicide.
>
> [3] If you find from all of your deliberations that she did not so suffer then you must not consider that fact in assessing her state of mind at time of the homicide.
>
> [4] A person is justified in the use of force when and to the extent that she reasonably believes that such conduct is necessary to defend herself against the imminent use of force.
>
> [5] However, a person is justified in the use of (sic) which is intended or likely to cause death or great bodily harm only if she reasonably believes as a Battered Woman that such force is necessary to prevent imminent death or great bodily harm to herself or the commission of a forcible felony.
>
> [6] A person who suffers from the Battered Woman syndrome may reasonably believe such force is necessary at a threshold lower than that which a person (sic) does not so suffer would consider reasonable.
>
> [7] You have heard evidence that the victim in this case has committed certain violent acts against the Defendant. If, after your consideration of the evidence, you believe this to be true, you must consider that fact in assessing whether the Defendant was in fear at the time of the homicide.

Our review of these proposed jury instructions indicates that they are improper for several reasons. First, paragraph one mandates that the jury consider three factors in determining whether Susan was a battered woman. However, this list of factors is not exhaustive of the factors relevant to this determination nor are the factors given necessarily the most important considerations in determining whether Susan was a battered woman. Thus, this instruction incorrectly highlights certain evidentiary factors to the jury and improperly limits the jury's deliberation to those factors. Second, paragraphs four and five, which attempt to explain the law of self-defense, were also improper in this case. Paragraph four explains when the use of force against another is justified. However, it does not explain when the use of deadly force is justified and is thus not relevant to a homicide case in which the accused claims that she acted in self-defense. Paragraph five, on the other hand, does contain the pertinent law of this case and explains to the jury what circumstances justify the use of deadly force. However, in instructing the jury to consider what Susan "reasonably believes as a Battered Woman," paragraph five implies that Susan's status as a battered woman could justify her use of force. Thus, this instruction tends to elevate the battered woman syndrome to the level of an independent affirmative defense, rather than informing the jury that evidence of the syndrome is merely one factor to consider in evaluating Susan's self-defense claim. Therefore, paragraph five does not accurately inform the jury as to the proper use of evidence relating to the battered woman syndrome. . . . Finally, paragraph six is misleading in informing the jury that a battered woman may reasonably believe that force is necessary at a threshold lower than others who do not suffer from the syndrome. As stated supra, Ohio has a subjective test in self-defense cases. Therefore, the reasonableness of the accused's beliefs and actions are determined on a case by case basis, and there are no objective "thresholds" or "reasonable person" standard. A woman's status as a battered woman does not alter her evidentiary burden in establishing her self-defense claim. Any instruction suggesting otherwise would be improper. Although paragraph six, taken in isolation, may be a correct abstract statement, it tends to invite the jury to excuse unreasonable behavior.

However, we do believe that given the complexity of the syndrome itself and its limited applicability to the defense, some specific instruction with respect to the battered woman syndrome would have been appropriate. For instance, the jury should have been instructed that the battered woman syndrome is not a defense in and of itself and that evidence of it is only offered to assist the jury in determining whether the defendant acted out of a reasonable belief that she was in imminent danger of death or great bodily harm and that the use of force was her only means of escaping that danger. Additionally, the jury should have been instructed that it could only consider the evidence of the battered woman syndrome if it found that the Defendant was a battered woman.

Accordingly, we agree with Susan that an instruction tailored to the battered woman syndrome was warranted in this case. However, as discussed supra, the proposed jury instructions were not limited to matters of law and did not accurately reflect the law of Ohio. Therefore, we must conclude that the trial court did not err in refusing to accept them.

The . . . assignment of error is overruled.

NOTES AND QUESTIONS

1. How would you write a self-defense instruction that would have satisfied the court in the *Daws* case? How would you then adapt that instruction for use in the larger number of jurisdictions that use an objective standard of reasonableness?

2. Focusing on instructions to the jury leads to the prior question about who the jurors will be, and what control the defendant may be able to exercise over their selection. Voir dire is the process by which attorneys elicit information from prospective jurors in order to determine how their attitudes, experiences and personality are likely to influence their reactions to the evidence, witnesses, and testimony in the case on trial. Voir dire is also an opportunity for attorneys to begin to educate jurors about the law and their duties and responsibilities. In preparation for trial, attorneys formulate voir dire questions in language that is easy for laypersons to understand, and design them to reveal attitudes and experiences that are relevant to the theory of the case. Areas for voir dire questions of particular import for battered women's self-defense cases include the ability to accept the legal concept of self-defense, jurors' exposure to violence, exposure to pretrial publicity about the case or media coverage about domestic violence more generally, attitudes about women's roles in society, racism, attitudes about psychiatric opinions, possible responses to gruesome evidence, and attitudes about unflattering facts that may come out about the defendant at trial, such as use of drugs or alcohol, or possession or use of a weapon. The following excerpt provides examples of voir dire questions attorneys have used in women's self-defense cases. Clearly, however, many would be appropriate in any case involving the use of expert testimony on behalf of a battered woman defendant, and many would be appropriate in any case involving issues of domestic violence, even when no expert testimony is at issue.

Liza Lawrence and Lisa Kugler Selected Voir Dire Questions; Women's Self–Defense Cases: Theory and Practice, 256–265 (E. Bochnak, ed. 1981)

The areas for voir dire and the specific questions suggested below have been used in cases in jurisdictions around the country. They are by no means exhaustive, but are offered to provide examples and stimulate creative thinking in designing appropriate questions for any particular case.

When these questions are used, the wording should be modified to conform with the speaking style of the attorney conducting the voir dire, being sure to preserve the open-ended format.

Voir dire conditions affect the manner in which questions are asked. In some jurisdictions it may be extremely difficult to persuade a judge to allow some of these questions. Nevertheless, it is always worthwhile to prepare explanations for the need for each question prior to voir dire and assume that it will be possible to persuade a judge to allow unfamiliar questions.

Some of the questions are applicable to group voir dire situations and some are only applicable to individual questioning. Before using any of them, it is wise to anticipate probable responses to ascertain the appropriate setting for asking the question.

Standard questions on criminal justice issues and ability to follow judge's instruction have not been included; nor have questions concerning jurors' background. In-depth background questions covering: occupation, religious affiliation and church attendance, marital status, education, military experience, community activities and similar questions regarding jurors' spouse and children, provide crucial information during voir dire and should not be overlooked....

I. Exposure to Publicity

1. Have you heard of this case before you came to court today?
2. What impressions do you have about it from reading the newspapers? (*or*: from what was said on the radio? *or*: from what was said in that conversation?)
3. When you were called for jury duty did you think you might sit on this case? If yes: How did that make you feel?
4. Do you think you might have some difficulty keeping any impressions or opinions that you have about the case out of your mind?

II. Battering

A. DEFINITION OF THE PROBLEM

1. Do you feel that wife abuse (battering) is a problem in your community? Why? Why not?
2. Have your heard that this is a problem in some communities?
3. How common a problem do you think it is?
4. Do you think that battering is a personal problem which should be handled within the family, or do you think it's a problem which requires outside assistance?
5. Do you think a man is ever justified in hitting a woman? Why? Why not?
6. Do you think that a man is ever justified in hitting his wife? Under what circumstances?
7. Do you think that use of physical force, such as hitting or shoving, is an assault when it happens between members of a family? Why? Why not?
8. Some people think that a woman who is beaten over and over again has only herself to blame. What do you think about that?

9. What sort of psychological effect do you think physical abuse would have on a woman?

B. EXPOSURE TO THE PROBLEM

1. Do you know any women who have been physically abused? What happened? What did you think about it?
2. Have you ever read anything in the newspapers or seen any TV programs about women who have been battered? What have you read or seen? What did you think about it?

C. NOT LEAVING

1. Some people think that a woman has an obligation to stay with her husband no matter what. What do you think?
2. Why do you think a woman might feel that she is unable to leave a situation where her husband is beating her?
3. Have you ever known a person who was unable to leave an unhappy marriage (or relationship)? Why do you think he/she was unable to leave? What were your feelings about that situation?
4. Do you know people who have problems in their marriage? Have they discussed the situation with you?
5. Do you think that sometimes people believe what they want to believe? Why is that? Why not?
6. Have you and your spouse ever argued?

III. Self-defense

A. PERSONAL DEFINITION

1. In your own words, can you tell me what self-defense means to you?
2. What comes to mind when you hear the term self-defense?
3. Everyone has his own idea about what self-defense is. The judge will tell you what the law says, but I'm just interested in what you think self-defense means?
4. Do you think that shooting/killing another person can ever be justified? Under what circumstances?
5. Do you have any religious or moral convictions that a person does not have the right to kill another person, even in self-defense?
6. Do you think that a person who shoots and kills another person should be punished for that act, no matter what the circumstances?

B. PERSONAL EXPERIENCE

1. Have you ever been physically afraid of someone? What happened? Did you feel you were able to defend yourself? Why not?
2. If someone were hitting you, how would you defend yourself?

3. If you were attacked by someone much larger or stronger than yourself do you feel you would be able to defend yourself?
4. Could you use a weapon in self-defense?
5. What if you were attacked by someone you knew. How do you think you would defend yourself?
6. Can you imagine a situation in which you might be overcome by fear or anger?
7. Have you ever been frightened by a person who was acting crazy or irrational? If yes: What were the circumstances? If no: How do you think you would deal with that sort of situation?

C. THE LAW

1. The judge will tell you that the law states that a person is justified in using force to defend herself against the threat of death or serious bodily harm, if her action seemed reasonable under the circumstances. Do you think you will be able to consider the circumstances from [defendant's] point of view?
2. The judge will tell you that the law states that there is no duty to retreat from one's own home when under attack. A person can stand and defend herself. If you find that [defendant] was in danger of death or serious harm and had a right to defend herself, would you acquit her if you thought there was some possibility of escape?
3. Do you understand that you are not being asked to approve of [defendant's] action, but only to decide whether or not she acted in self-defense?
4. The law recognizes that there are certain circumstances where it is justified to kill someone. Do you feel that there are circumstances where it is justified to kill someone?
5. If after hearing the evidence, you determine that [defendant] acted in self-defense, could you vote for acquittal regardless of your own feelings about her having shot/killed someone?

D. THE DEFENDANT'S CREDIBILITY

1. How do you feel about [defendant], knowing that she is on trial for murder? Why is that?
2. Do you feel that you would give her testimony the same serious consideration as any other witness?
3. Do you think that because [defendant] was married to/living with/involved with [deceased] it is likely that she acted intentionally rather than in self-defense?

IV. Stereotypes Based on Sex

1. To men: Have you ever been beaten in an arm wrestle? Have you ever arm-wrestled with a woman?

2. To women: Have you ever arm-wrestled with a man? Have you ever won? Do you think you could win?
3. Do you think it is harder for a woman to defend herself from an attack than it would be for a man to defend himself? Why? Why not?
4. Do you think it might be reasonable for a woman to use a weapon to defend herself in a situation in which a man might not need a weapon? Why is that?
5. Have you heard the expression "a man's home is his castle"? Why do you think people say that? Do you agree with it? Why? Why not?
6. Do you think the same is true for a woman, that her home is her castle? Why? Why not?

V. Memory Loss

1. Do you think that someone might experience some memory loss after a particularly stressful or traumatic situation? Why do you think that would happen?
2. Do you think that sometimes people remember what they want to remember?
3. Some people who have been in accidents have found out later from other people that they did things they never thought themselves capable of. How do you think that kind of reaction can be explained? Have you ever been a situation like that?

VI. Exposure to Violence and Guns

1. Have you ever been involved in an argument where physical force was used?
2. Have you ever seen someone hit another person? What were the circumstances? What did you think at that time?
3. Have you ever seen someone who had been beaten? What were the circumstances? What did you think at that time?
4. Do you or any members of your family own any guns?
5. Do you know how to use a gun?
6. Have you ever fired a gun?
7. How do you feel about guns?
8. What is your opinion about people having guns in their home for home protection?
9. Can you imagine yourself in a situation where you would use a gun to protect yourself?

VII. Lifestyle

Whenever there will be evidence at trial about the defendant's lifestyle, it is wise to explore the jurors' reactions to these facts during voir dire. For example:

1. [Defendant] has two children. The deceased was their father. There will be testimony in this trial that [defendant] and [deceased] lived together on and off for five years and never married. What are your opinions about people who live together and have children without being married?
2. [Defendant] has been receiving welfare assistance to help support her children since 1976. What is your opinion about people who receive welfare? Do you have any opinions or feelings that people on welfare are more likely than other people to end up in violent situations?
3. If you are seated as a juror in this case you will learn that on the day of this incident [defendant] purchased cocaine. Knowing that she may have used illegal drugs that day, do you think you might discount [defendant's] testimony that she acted in fear for her life?

VIII. Drinking

1. Do you drink occasionally?
2. Do you ever go to a bar to drink?
3. Do you have any moral or religious feelings about people who drink alcohol?
4. Have you ever observed a change in the personality of someone who is drinking? What was the change? What were the circumstances?
5. How would the fact that [defendant and/or deceased] were drinking affect your opinion of the incident?
6. How difficult do you think it is for one person to persuade another person to stop drinking?

IX. Gruesome Evidence

1. In the course of this trial you may be shown items of blood-stained clothing worn by [defendant] and/or [deceased] when [deceased] was shot/stabbed. How do you think this kind of evidence will affect you?
2. You may also be shown pictures of [deceased] after he was shot/stabbed and of the room where the incident occurred. Do you think that this type of evidence, aside from the facts of this case, will affect your decision in this matter?
3. Knowing that this kind of evidence will be presented in this trial, do you think you might have some difficulty sitting as a juror on this case?

X. Psychological or Psychiatric Testimony

1. Have you or anyone you know ever used the services of a psychiatrist or a psychologist? What were the circumstances?
2. Do you know anyone who is a psychiatrist or psychologist?
3. Do you feel a psychiatrist or psychologist can be helpful in treating or helping a person overcome mental problems or mental illness?
4. Do you think psychiatrists/psychologists can give us insights into why people react in certain situations, and the reasons for their actions?

5. Do you think that psychiatry and psychology are sciences?
6. We know that some sciences, like physics or mathematics, can give us very precise answers to questions. Some people say that medicine in general, and psychiatry in particular are an imprecise science? What does this mean to you?
7. Can psychiatrists/psychologists give scientific answers, or just educated guesses?

XI. Racial Attitudes

1. What contact do you have with minority people (at your job, in your neighborhood, at your church)?
2. Do you know any people who are prejudiced against people of other races? Why do you think they are prejudiced?
3. Some people think that Black/Indian/Hispanic people are more violent than white people. Have you ever heard someone say this? What do you think?
4. Do you think that Indian/Black/Hispanic people are treated differently by the police than white people are?
5. Can you think of anything about your feelings about Black people which might affect your view of this case, and the basis on which you would form your opinions?

* * *

B. BEYOND SELF-DEFENSE: FURTHER USES FOR EXPERT TESTIMONY ON BEHALF OF BATTERED WOMEN

The materials you have just read highlighted the issue of self defense for battered women who kill their assailants. But there are other contexts in which battered women face criminal charges that may be related to the abuse they have experienced. You have in fact already looked at one other context in which battered women faced criminal charges; cases in which their children were injured or killed by their batterers and they were tried for murder, or for criminal child abuse, or criminal neglect, or child endangerment, or for aiding and abetting their abusers in the commission of one or more of these crimes. See Chapter 6E, above. But in addition, women not infrequently find themselves involved in other criminal activity because they are coerced by their batterers to engage in criminal conduct, forced to participate *with* their batterers in criminal conduct, or witness their batterers' criminal conduct without attempting to intervene, leave the scene, or alert law enforcement. Beth Richie, in her book COMPELLED TO CRIME, 149 (1996), reports that in her study of women incarcerated for a variety of criminal offenses, it was particularly true of the African American women that their criminal activity (whether illegal drug use, illegal sex work, or economic or even violent crime) grew out of their entrapment in violent relationships:

> Given the broader social conditions that the African American battered women lived in, staying *for them* meant participating in illegal activity. From their perspective—created by their experience of abuse and their marginalized social location—becoming involved in crime was a reasonable behavioral response to abuse—it was a part of their survival strategy.... Their participation in illegal activities takes on a new meaning when analyzed from within this context.

It therefore becomes important to ask whether, and under what conditions, expert testimony about battered women's experiences can be introduced into cases in which battered women defendants are charged with crimes other than assaulting or killing their abusers. As Judge Dubé reasoned in *Malott:*

> The expert evidence is admissible, and necessary, in order to understand the reasonableness of a battered women's perceptions.... Accordingly, the utility of such evidence in criminal cases is not limited to instances where a battered woman is pleading self-defense, but is potentially relevant to other situations where the reasonableness of a battered women's actions or perceptions is at issue (e.g. provocation, duress or necessity).

Malott v. Her Majesty the Queen, 1998 Can. Sup. Ct. LEXIS 7, 29 (1998).

Most commonly, the defense with which such testimony is associated is duress, because duress expresses the law's understanding that a defendant should not, as a general matter, be responsible for an action that is not chosen, but is coerced. But matters are not as simple as this sketch suggests. First, the law has traditionally defined duress very narrowly, as you have already seen, in Chapter 6E, above, in cases where women have argued that their incapacity to intervene on behalf of their children was based on their fear for the safety of their children and themselves. At present, therefore, the legal doctrine of duress may not, even with the introduction of expert testimony, capture the full range of coercive behaviors that prompt abused women to crime. Second, even before we introduce the complexities of battering and expert testimony, there is disagreement about the precise nature of the duress defense; whether it "wipes the slate clean" by depriving the defendant of the intent that is a necessary element of the crime, or whether instead it acts as an "affirmative defense," justifying or excusing the conduct even though it is criminal. If the question is whether duress can eliminate intent, the answer may depend on what level of intent is required for the crime in question. If we are choosing between duress as justifying criminal conduct, and duress as excusing criminal conduct, what rides on the distinction?

A different argument that might be put forward by a battered woman defendant is that the impact of the abuse on her is such that she should have the benefit of an insanity or diminished responsibility defense. As soon as we acknowledge that some women will be arguing: "I did the only thing open to me to do," while others may need to argue "I didn't know what I was doing," we can see the parallels between the issues raised by the introduction of expert testimony in self-defense cases, and the issues raised by defenses in other criminal cases. Is the testimony supporting a claim of psychological damage or a claim of reasonableness tied to the specific context of a battering relationship? It only adds to the confusion to recognize that to say a particular defendant lacked the necessary intent to commit the crime could either be an argument that her capacity for rational judgment was impaired by her experience of abuse, or an argument that she made a rational decision to allow her abuser's will to override her own, so that her act was not voluntary.

The next reading lays out the elements of a duress defense, elaborates on the similarities and differences between the theoretical underpinnings of duress and self-defense, and argues that admission of evidence of past abuse, and expert testimony about abuse, is as relevant in the duress context as it is in the self-defense context. Subsequent materials explore the often erratic ways in which both state and federal courts have responded to requests that such testimony be admitted to support a battered woman's defense to criminal charges, usually but not always in the context of duress.

Beth I.Z. Boland
Battered Women Who Act Under Duress, 28 New England Law Review 603, 623–27, 629–34(1994)

To establish a *prima facie* defense of duress under the common law, the defendant charged with a crime other than murder must introduce evidence sufficient to prove that she reasonably believed the only way to avoid imminent death or serious bodily injury to herself or another person was to engage in criminal conduct, and that the unlawful threat legally "caused" her to engage in that conduct. As in claims of self-defense, duress at common law requires a "present, immediate and impending threat" of such a nature as to induce a well-founded fear of death or serious bodily injury. Similarly, a claim of duress requires that the circumstances be such that the actor has no reasonable chance of escape.

A significant minority of states have adopted in whole or in substantial part the Model Penal Code (MPC) definition of duress, which applies to a defendant who committed a crime "because he was coerced to do so by the use of, or a threat to use, unlawful force . . . that a person of reasonable firmness in his situation would have been unable to resist." The MPC differs from the common-law rule in several key respects: (1) it eliminates the requirement of imminency; (2) it eliminates the requirement of deadly force; (3) it is available as a defense even to homicide; and (4) it covers cases where the defendant was "brainwashed" upon the coercer's *prior* use of force.

Scholars have also debated whether duress acts as an excuse or as a justification for otherwise criminal activity. If considered a justification, the defense's success depends upon whether the harm avoided (i.e., the harm threatened by the batterer) is greater than the harm committed (i.e., the criminal activity). If seen as an excuse, the defendant ostensibly need only show that her free will was overcome such that she was not acting voluntarily, regardless of the heinousness of the crime committed while under duress.

Whether utilizing the common law or the MPC standard, or whether viewing duress as an excuse or as a justification, in each case the defendant's credibility and her state of mind—including whether she honestly and reasonably believed she was in imminent danger from her batterer—will be placed directly before the jury. In addition, the jurors must also make a moral judgment regarding the defendant's blameworthiness, whether in the context of determining that the threats "caused" the criminal activity (under the common law), or whether the defendant maintained "reasonable firmness" in the face of the threats (under the MPC).

In any event, evidence of past abuse should be relevant and admissible on the issues of the defendant's state of mind and her credibility in order to allow the jury to make a reasoned and informed decision about the defendant's culpability. In fact, the inquiry into the defendant's apprehension of danger in the context of a duress claim is virtually identical to that used for self-defense. A woman who views her circumstances through the eyes of one who has already suffered abuse at the hands of the coercer may see imminent danger even though some time may pass between the threat and her subsequent criminal act, and even though others may see no serious threat at all. There is no reason why the defendant's perception, altered through a cycle of battering, of the imminence of the threat should be any less informative in a case of coerced conduct than where the defendant acted in self-defense. And, in the same way that evidence of past abuse may affect the jury's perception of the defendant's credibility in cases of self-defense, so, too, does it apply in duress cases.

Finally, evidence of past abuse is relevant in assessing the blameworthiness of the defendant's decision to engage in criminal activity rather than to risk the physical abuse she faces. As noted above, the defendant's precise mental state at the hands of her coercer can be viewed in one of two ways: either the defendant's free will was overcome by the threat of harm to her, so that she had no criminal intent, or she voluntarily acted to avoid what she perceived to be the lesser of two evils (i.e., committing the unlawful act versus being beaten), so that she should be excused from criminal culpability. In either event, the relevance of evidence of past abuse seems clear.

In the former inquiry, the strength of the defendant's will in the face of her batterer's threats is in large part a function of the level of abuse—and particularly the level of physical and psychological abuse—that she suffered in the past. Expert testimony regarding the effect of a seemingly minimal level of threats upon a woman who has been "beaten down" over long periods of time would undoubtedly go far in educating the jury as to the point at which the defendant's will may be overcome. Thus, to the extent the defendant can show, through her own testimony and/or that of an expert, that her ability to resist the batterer was precipitously low to begin with, the greater the chances are that the jury will conclude that it was overcome by the particular threats at issue.

Evidence of past abuse also relates directly to the reasonableness of the defendant's choice between being beaten and committing the criminal activity. In exploring the nature of this choice, legal theorists have suggested that juries undertake a kind of balancing test and an assessment of how much sacrifice an individual should be expected to make before "giving in" to the threat. Notably, this balancing test is similar to the test utilized by the jury in determining whether the force used by the defendant against her batterer was reasonable when weighed against the force threatened by her batterer against her. The introduction of evidence concerning past abuse inflicted upon the defendant does not suggest that the defendant was fundamentally incapable of recognizing the wrongness of her acts, but asks the jury to believe that she made a reasonable choice in favor of self-preservation, given the alternatives posed to her by the coercer. Even where the jury is asked to apply solely an objective, rather than a subjective, standard, evidence of past abuse may nevertheless be informative on the totality of the circumstances in which the defendant finds herself when faced with such a choice.

. . .

It has been said that all criminal defenses revolve around three fundamental principles: necessity, proportionality, and fault. Both self-defense and duress require the jury essentially to perform a balancing test among these three principles. . . .

Yet the balancing process is somewhat different when the defendant claims she acted under duress rather than in self-defense. Although her perception of the threat posed by her batterer does not change from one context to the other, the decisions she makes in response to that threat do. For example, how should the jury deal with the fact that a duress defense generally involves criminal activity directed at a wholly innocent third party, whereas self-defense involves violence directed against the person who initiated the violence? And how exactly should the jury balance the harm inflicted upon the third party against the harm threatened against the defendant by her batterer? Finally, does the fact that a claim of duress more closely resembles a claim of mental impairment or insanity than it does a claim of self-defense affect the admissibility of evidence of past abuse? Although ultimately none of these factors dictates that evidence of past abuse should not be admitted in cases of duress, they do require consideration before blindly concluding that such evidence be equally admissible for duress claims as for claims of self-defense.

1. Necessity—Alternatives to Fighting Back

As discussed above, to the extent that the defendant seeks to argue she acted out of "necessity" because of the threat imposed upon her by her batterer, evidence of past abuse should be admissible to support a claim of duress in the same way it is admissible to support a claim of self-defense. This part of the inquiry focuses entirely upon the defendant's perception of the threat, and whether her perception was reasonable and/or sincere. . . .

. . .

... Without expert testimony, the jury will almost certainly misread the level of necessity perceived by the defendant, and thereby disrupt the entire process of determining whether the threats "caused" her to act as she did (under the common law) or whether she possessed the requisite "moral firmness" (under the MPC).

2. Proportionality and Fault—The Lack of an "In–Kind" Response to the Batterer's Threats, and the "Innocent Victim" Problem

In the case of self-defense, proportionality is maintained by the requirement that lethal force can only be used when one is threatened with like force, and only against the person initially making such a threat. When translated to the defense of duress, however, the equation changes dramatically: not only is the threat of physical force not always met with physical force in return, but the defendant's activities are directed away from the batterer and onto an innocent third party. The question then becomes whether the admission of evidence of past abuse to support a claim of duress unfairly shifts the balance on behalf of the defendant further than is desirable.

The beauty and simplicity of a self-defense claim lies in the apparent symmetry with which the defendant responds to the threat presented to her: the defendant is threatened by her batterer with physical force and responds directly in kind against her batterer with physical force. As such, self-defense appears to maintain the boundaries of communication and interaction within the relationship: the woman injures her batterer, and her response travels in the same medium and in the same direction as the threat.

By contrast, a defendant claiming duress requests forgiveness for an act (which may or may not involve physical violence) against an innocent third party.... If the jury accepts the reasonableness of the defendant's trade-off, it must also conclude that it was reasonable for her to put her self-interest ahead of that of an innocent third party, and to do so in a way that bears little direct relation to the threat she perceives to herself. Thus, duress on the surface raises far more troubling questions of proportionality and fault for the jury....

. . .

... What is important for purposes of the discussion here is that the lack of proportionality in the defendant's response does not *detract* from the usefulness of evidence of past abuse to interpret other aspects of the balancing equation, such as the reasonableness of the defendant's perception of danger.

Underlying the above discussion is the question of whether it is fair and just that we punish a defendant who acts not out of criminal malice, but out of fear of abuse. When presented with a claim of self-defense, the jury essentially faces a "two-dimensional" apportionment of fault: as between the batterer and the defendant, who is more to blame for the defendant's decision to fight back? When presented with a claim of duress, however, the decision is complicated by the presence of an additional party: the wholly innocent victim of the defendant's criminal acts. In such cases, the jury must decide how much burden to place on each of the three parties in order to reach a fair and equitable result for all.

It is clear from the start that a large measure of fault should lay against the batterer for his threats against the defendant; whether or not a defendant successfully invokes a claim of duress, the batterer can still be held liable for aiding and abetting or for conspiracy to commit the crime.... The real question, then, is the extent to which any fault should lie with the defendant herself, and the extent to which the innocent victim must forsake retribution against the defendant in favor of punishment of the defendant's batterer.

Perhaps the nub of any potential reluctance to admit evidence of past abuse in cases of duress may lie in the fear that the evidence will be used to achieve acquittal from crimes which severely victimize an innocent third party merely by painting the defendant in a more sympathetic light—i.e., that the prejudicial value of the evidence would outweigh its probative value. Some states have thus tipped the balance to prohibit introduction of a defense of duress against a charge of homicide, even though the principles of proportionality and necessity are satisfied by the defendant's reasonable fear that she would otherwise be killed.

. . .

Yet the problem of undue sympathy is always present whenever a defendant—and in particular a battered woman defendant—raises a claim of self-defense. This alone, however, has not prevented the admissibility of evidence of past abuse to support such a claim. Moreover, this alone has not prevented juries from convicting battered women who actually present evidence of the effects of past abuse.

* * *

NOTES

1. Model Penal Code § 2.09 reads, in relevant part, as follows:

   (1) It is an affirmative defense that the actor engaged in the conduct charged to constitute an offense because he was coerced to do so by the use of, or a threat to use, unlawful force against his person or the person of another, which a person of reasonable firmness in his situation would have been unable to resist.

   (2) The defense provided by this Section is unavailable if the actor recklessly placed himself in a situation in which it was probable that he would be subjected to duress. The defense is also unavailable if he was negligent in placing himself in such a situation, whenever negligence suffices to establish culpability for the offense charged.

2. At common law, a wife who could show that her husband commanded her to commit a crime could create a presumption of duress. The modern view, embraced by the Model Penal Code, is that coercion of a wife by a husband should be treated no differently than coercion in any other situation. Model Penal Code § 2.09(3). Some jurisdictions follow the lead of

the Model Penal Code in accepting threats against a person other than the defendant as part of a duress claim, especially family members.

3. In *The Validity and Use of Evidence Concerning Battering and Its Effects in Criminal Trials,* REPORT RESPONDING TO SECTION 40507 OF THE VIOLENCE AGAINST WOMEN ACT, NCJ 160972, *Trend Analysis* at 18–19 (May 1996), the National Clearinghouse for the Defense of Battered Women reported that as of 1995 eight states had admitted expert testimony about battering in duress cases, while 5 had refused to do so. Seven states had admitted testimony in cases in which battered women had committed crimes against third parties but did not claim duress, and two had refused to do so. Eleven out of sixteen federal courts that had ever admitted expert testimony had done so in a duress case, while three federal courts had refused to admit testimony in duress cases. (Federal courts rarely have jurisdiction of battered women's self-defense cases.)

4. In the next case, a California appeals court considered the relevance of expert testimony about battered women's experiences to a duress defense, and determined that defense counsel's failure to offer such testimony amounted to ineffective assistance of counsel.

People v. Romero

26 Cal. App. 4th 315, 13 Cal. Rptr. 2d 332.
Court of Appeal of California, Second Appellate District, 1992.

OPINION:

Debra Romero and Terrance Romero were both charged with one count of second degree robbery and four counts of attempted robbery. Debra's defense was duress. She admitted the crimes but claimed she participated because she was afraid Terrance would kill her if she didn't do as he demanded. The jury apparently didn't believe Debra and she was convicted as charged. She now petitions for a writ of habeas corpus, contending her lawyer was ineffective because he failed to present expert testimony explaining Battered Woman Syndrome. We agree.

FACTS

Debra and Terrance are not married but they began living together (with Terrance's two minor children and his father) in March 1989. About six weeks after Debra moved in, Terrance began hitting her if she didn't get money when he told her to do so (they are both cocaine addicts and he needed the money to support his habit) and, from that point on, he hit her "almost every day." Debra left Terrance on several occasions but he would always find her and persuade her to return. When he became angry, he would rip screens off windows, throw things out of windows and, when she would try to leave, he would threaten her, telling her that he would kill her and that, "If I can't have you, nobody else can." At one point, Debra's father obtained a restraining order against Terrance because he had been throwing things through her father's windows. On another occasion, Debra was hospitalized after she attempted to jump through a window to get away from Terrance. The window fell on her and she was badly cut (she required 23 stitches). Debra did not tell the police about Terrance's beatings.

On May 28, 1989, Debra, posing as a prostitute, was picked up by Gary Shortridge. Following Debra's instructions, Shortridge drove into an alley where he was confronted by Terrance, who drove his car to block Shortridge's car. Debra asked Shortridge to give her some money so Terrance wouldn't hurt her. Shortridge responded by ramming Terrance's car and driving away at high speed with Debra still in his car. Debra screamed at Shortridge to stop and pleaded with him to give her money so Terrance wouldn't hurt her ("He'll be happy with that, and he won't hurt me"). Shortridge waited until he saw a policeman and then stopped.

On July 11, 1989, Terrance (with Debra as a passenger) pulled up to Grace De Vos's car in a Bank of America parking lot, Debra got out, and Terrance told De Vos to give Debra all of her money. De Vos explained that she didn't have any and attempted to start her car, at which point Terrance pointed a gun at her and said, "Start the car and I'll shoot you." Debra then looked in De Vos's car and reported to Terrance that there was a briefcase. Terrance told De Vos to give the briefcase to Debra but at that point someone walked into the lot, Debra got back into Terrance's car and Terrance drove away.

On July 12, 1989, Terrance (with Debra as a passenger) drove up alongside Wilda King's van in a Lucky's market parking lot. Debra got out of the car and King, thinking they needed help, walked over to Terrance's car and asked if they needed directions. Terrance pointed a gun at King and said, "No, I want your purse." Debra appeared nervous and hesitant and just stood there, without doing anything. King said "No" and Terrance said "Please" and King said "No" again and started backing away. King ran to some people who were standing nearby and Terrance drove away.

On July 19, 1989, Terrance (with Debra as a passenger) drove his car head-on at Sarah McClain's car as she was driving out of a Lucky's market parking lot and into an alley. As McClain pulled to the right and stopped to let Terrance pass, Terrance stopped his car, pointed a gun at her and asked for money. McClain gave Terrance her change purse. Terrance took the change (about $1.50), returned the purse to McClain, and told Debra to go see whether McClain had anything else in her purse. Debra got out of Terrance's car and McClain showed her that all she had was checks, no cash. Debra got back into Terrance's car and Terrance then asked McClain if she had any jewelery. McClain said she couldn't get her rings off and Terrance drove off. This incident, with a total take of $1.50, constitutes the only completed robbery.

On July 23, 1989, James Stratton was stopped at a light on Pacific Coast Highway when Debra approached the passenger side of his van and said she had been beaten and robbed. She appeared hysterical and had her hand over her left eye. She tried the door handle, found it was locked, then reached through the open window, opened the door, and got into the van. Her face was bruised and puffy and she looked as though she had been hit. At that point, Terrance drove up on the left side of Stratton's van and pointed a gun at Stratton. Debra grabbed the key to turn off Stratton's engine and Terrance told Stratton to give his money to Debra. Debra said, "He has a gun. Give him all the money." Stratton panicked, knocked Debra's hand off the ignition key and drove off, followed by Terrance. Debra screamed at him, pleading to be let out of the car. Stratton eventually stopped, when he could no longer see Terrance in his rear view mirror, and Debra got out.[1] Debra and Terrance were charged with one count of second degree robbery and four counts of attempted robbery. Enhancement allegations charged Terrance with the personal use of a handgun and Debra with participating in crimes in which a principal was armed with a handgun. They both pleaded not guilty and were able to make bail. While they were awaiting trial, Debra continued to see Terrance and he continued to beat her.

At trial, Debra testified to the facts stated above, agreeing with the victims' testimony and simply adding her explanation for why she did what she did. Terrance also testified on his own behalf, telling the jury that he met Debra when he picked her up on a street corner and offered her money for sex and that she moved in with him about a year later. Not withstanding that he was identified by all five victims (not to mention Debra's testimony), Terrance said he was not involved in any of the incidents and never saw any of the victims prior to the court proceedings. Terrance also testified that he is "very much in love" with Debra, he has never threatened her and he has never hit her. On the night she tried to jump out the window, it was because he was trying to stop her from going out to buy more cocaine. Debra wrote to him while he was incarcerated and her letters expressed her love.

Debra was convicted of all five charges and the enhancement allegations were found true as to three counts (Wilda King, Sarah McClain and Grace De Vos) but not true as to the other two counts (James Stratton and Gary Shortridge). Debra was sentenced to state prison for a term of five years, eight months.

DISCUSSION

Debra contends she was denied the effective assistance of counsel because her trial attorney failed to present expert testimony about Battered Woman Syndrome to corroborate her duress defense. As indicated at the outset, we agree.

. . .

1. Debra testified that she had argued with Terrance earlier that day. Her father had called the police to report Terrance's treatment of her and she told Terrance she was leaving. She went to her father's house and Terrance called her there. She finally agreed to meet Terrance and he picked her up at her father's. She once again agreed to help Terrance try to get some money but when her efforts proved unsuccessful, Terrance beat her, hitting her nose and her eye. Terrance dragged her to his van but she got away from him.

The officer who arrested Debra that night testified that she appeared to have been beaten. Although he could not recall prior contacts with her, his report for July 23 notes that "on each of these occasions and during this arrest, [Debra] had showed [*sic*] severe beating on her face with her eyes swollen and was bruising much [*sic*] on her face."

D. When a woman kills her batterer and pleads self-defense, expert testimony about BWS is admissible to explain how her particular experiences as a battered woman affected her perceptions of danger and her honest belief in its imminence (People v. Aris, supra, 215 Cal.App.3d at p. 1198) and also to rehabilitate her credibility when the prosecutor has attempted to impeach her by urging that her conduct is inconsistent with her claim of self-defense (People v. Day, supra, 2 Cal.App.4th at p. 415).

E. If BWS testimony is relevant to credibility when a woman kills her batterer, it is a fortiori relevant to her credibility when she participates in robberies at her batterer's insistence.[1] To paraphrase People v. Day, supra, 2 Cal.App.4th at pages 416–418, "BWS evidence" would have deflected the prosecutor's [and Terrance's] challenge to [Debra's] credibility. Such evidence would have assisted the jury in objectively analyzing [Debra's] claim of [duress] by dispelling many of the commonly held misconceptions about battered women. As the record reflects, the prosecutor [and Terrance] exploited several of these misconceptions in urging the jury to reject [Debra's duress] claim....

" 'Expert testimony on the battered woman syndrome would help dispel the ordinary lay person's perception that a woman in a battering relationship is free to leave at any time. The expert evidence would counter any 'common sense' conclusions by the jury that if the beatings were really that bad the woman would have left her [batterer] much earlier. Popular misconceptions about battered women would be put to rest, including the beliefs the women are masochistic and enjoy the beatings and that they intentionally provoke their [batterers] into fits of rage.' " (Ibid....)

As relevant to this case, the defense of duress is the same as self-defense—in both, the key issue is whether the defendant reasonably and honestly believed she was in imminent danger of great bodily harm or death. To establish duress, a defendant must raise a reasonable doubt that she acted in the exercise of her free will ... by showing she committed the charged crime under threats or menaces sufficient to create a good faith, objectively reasonable belief that there was an imminent threat of danger to her life. Fear of great bodily harm is sufficient and, except as to homicide, duress is available as a defense to any crime....

For purposes of this opinion ... self-defense has two requirements. First, the defendant's acts must have been motivated by an actual, genuine or honest belief or perception that (a) the defendant was in imminent

1. Debra was tried in 1990. In 1991, the Legislature added section 1107 to the Evidence Code, to provide that, "[i]n a criminal action, expert testimony is admissible by either the prosecution or the defense regarding battered women's syndrome, including the physical, emotional, or mental effects upon the beliefs, perceptions, or behavior of victims of domestic violence, except when offered against a criminal defendant to prove the occurrence of the act or acts of abuse which form the basis of the criminal charge." (Stats. 1991, ch. 812, § 1.) There is nothing in the language of the statute suggesting a legislative intent to limit its application to cases involving a claim of self-defense. To the contrary, section 1107 appears to make expert testimony admissible in *any* criminal case, regardless of the charges or defenses, except a case in which the batterer is prosecuted for his acts of abuse and the evidence is offered to prove that he committed those acts.

danger of death or great bodily injury from an unlawful attack or threat by the victim and (b) the defendant's acts were necessary to prevent injury. Second, it must appear that a reasonable person in the same circumstances would have had the same perception and done the same acts.

With the two defenses thus juxtaposed, it is clear that a rule permitting expert testimony about BWS in a self-defense case must necessarily permit it in a case where duress is claimed as a defense. In both cases, the evidence is relevant to the woman's credibility and to support her testimony that she entertained a good faith objectively reasonable and honest belief that her act was necessary to prevent an imminent threat of greater harm. . . .

F. Debra's claim that trial counsel's assistance was so ineffective as to require reversal of her conviction has two components. First, she must show that counsel's performance was deficient. Second, she must show prejudice—that there is a reasonable probability that, but for counsel's mistake, the result of her trial would have been different. . . .

. . .

This is not a case in which there can be any doubt about whether trial counsel's failure to conduct a careful investigation withdrew an obviously crucial defense from his client's case. Berger admitted to Anyon that he recognized the possibility that Debra suffered from BWS and considered offering BWS evidence to support Debra's duress defense. Indeed, he obtained the name of a BWS expert who could evaluate Debra and testify at trial. But that's all he did. When he was unable to reach the expert before trial, he simply dropped the ball and his failure to provide a declaration explaining his conduct (notwithstanding several requests from Anyon) permits us to presume the absence of a satisfactory explanation. . . . At the risk of understating the obvious, we conclude that Berger neither carefully nor sufficiently investigated an obviously crucial defense. . . . We agree with Debra that there is a reasonable probability that presentation of expert testimony about BWS would have bolstered her credibility and persuaded the jury to accept the defense of duress. . . .

Debra admitted that she committed all of the charged offenses and her sole defense was duress. Although substantial evidence established that Debra was frequently and severely beaten by Terrance and that he threatened her with further harm and even death if she left or did not do what he wanted her to do . . . there was no mention at all of BWS. There was no explanation for Debra's failure simply to walk away from Terrance or for her continued participation in the robberies or for her apparently inconsistent behavior after they were arrested, when she wrote loving letters to him while he was still incarcerated.

. . .

Evidence of BWS would have explained a behavior pattern that might otherwise (and obviously did) appear unreasonable to the jurors. Evidence of BWS not only explains how a battered woman might think, react, or behave, it also places the behavior in an understandable light. "One of the most commonly made argument[s] by prosecutors in urging rejection of a defense is that the person's behavior is inconsistent with that defense.... Jurors are told to evaluate and react to evidence by what a reasonable person would do or not do. Frequently, conduct appears unreasonable to those who have not been exposed to the same circumstances.... It is only natural that people might speculate as to how they would react and yet be totally wrong about how most people in fact react." (People v. Day, supra, 2 Cal.App.4th at p. 419.)

That is precisely what happened here. The prosecutor argued that, assuming Debra wasn't lying about the whole thing, she could have run away and that she was not really in any imminent danger. An expert could have helped persuade the jury that Debra was not lying and also could have explained that battered women are afraid to run away because they are convinced their batterers will find them and beat them again or even kill them. (Walker, Terrifying Love, *supra*, at p. 47 [the greatest risk of harm to a battered woman is when she tries to leave].) An expert could have explained that Terrance's threat—"If I can't have you, nobody else can"—is the threat most commonly made by battering males. An expert could have explained a battered woman's heightened awareness of danger and the jury could have considered that circumstance in deciding whether Debra believed she was in imminent danger. And Terrance's lawyer's suggestion that Debra would have reported the beatings to the police or to her family if, in fact, they had really occurred could have been met with an expert's explanation that only about one in ten incidents of battering are reported because shame and fear of reprisals frequently keep battered women from calling the police....

Expert testimony explaining BWS would have given the jurors an ability to understand why a battered woman acts as she does and, with that information, the jury could have fairly decided the ultimate questions about whether Debra was, in fact, suffering from BWS and, if so, whether she was acting under duress. Since the presentation of BWS evidence would have given Debra's attorney something affirmative to argue while at the same time eliminating much of the prosecutor's ability to attack her defense, the conclusion is unavoidable that the failure to present this evidence was prejudicial....

DISPOSITION

The petition for writ of habeas corpus is granted. The judgment is vacated, and Debra Romero is remanded to the Superior Court of Los Angeles County for a new trial. The appeal is dismissed.

NOTES

1. The California Supreme Court reversed the appeal court's decision in *Romero*, but on grounds unrelated to the admission of expert testimony, in People v. Romero, 8 Cal. 4th 728, 883 P.2d 388 (Cal. 1994).

2. Other courts have not been as clear or as cogent in their analysis. In United States v. Johnson, 956 F.2d 894 (9th Cir. 1992), for example, female

defendants appealed their convictions of low-level activity in a drug ring operated by a "violent drug lord." The defendants offered evidence that they were battered by their intimate partners, and that their response of acquiescence to the threats and abuse of the drug lord was therefore reasonable. The Ninth Circuit held that evidence of battering was not relevant to duress, because the "reasonable firmness" test imposed an objective standard. The evidence was considered relevant, however, under the Federal Sentencing Guidelines, for a downward departure at sentencing. The court therefore remanded the women's cases for reconsideration of their sentences. Id. at 907. The Eighth Circuit and the Eastern District of New York are two other federal courts that have permitted the use of expert testimony in the sentencing phase of the trial.

In United States v. Willis, 38 F.3d 170 (5th Cir. 1994), the Fifth Circuit held that evidence of battering was not relevant to a duress defense. Kathy Evelyn Willis appealed her conviction for carrying a firearm during and in relation to the commission of a drug trafficking crime, based on the trial court's exclusion of expert testimony on battering she offered at trial as relevant to her defense of duress, on an erroneous jury instruction on duress, and on ineffective assistance of counsel.

The court laid out the four traditional common law requirements for a complete duress defense: (i) present, imminent, and impending threat inducing a well-grounded apprehension of death or great bodily injury, (ii) that the defendant did not recklessly or negligently place herself in a situation where she was likely to be coerced into criminal acts, (iii) that the defendant had no opportunity to escape or other reasonable opportunity to avoid the threatened harm, and (iv) a direct causal relationship between the criminal act and the avoidance of the threatened harm. 38 F.3d at 175. Although the court articulated each requirement of the law of duress as though it were at least to some degree a subjective test, it then went on to say that this formulation of the law of duress is "in harmony with the analysis of duress in the Model Penal code which . . . [states that] 'a person of reasonable firmness in his [or her] situation would have been unable to resist.' " Id. The court then concluded, citing Johnson, that evidence of battering is not relevant to the objective test for the law of duress:

> [e]vidence that the defendant is suffering from the battered woman's syndrome is inherently subjective . . . such evidence is usually consulted to explain why this particular defendant succumbed when a reasonable person without a background of being battered might not have. Specifically, battered woman's syndrome evidence seeks to establish that, because of her psychological condition, the defendant is unusually susceptible to the coercion.

Id. Neither the Ninth nor the Fifth Circuit appears to have understood the role of expert testimony about battering in educating the jury about the objective reality of battering relationships.

Duress cases involving battered women also appear at the state level. In a number of states, as noted earlier, evidence of battering has been held to be relevant to duress. It would seem that battered women might fare better in states that have, following the Model Penal Code, eliminated the requirement that the defendant be subject to an "imminent" threat. However, in Pennsylvania, the absence of an imminence requirement persuaded at least one court that testimony about battering was entirely irrelevant to a duress defense. In Commonwealth v. Ely, 578 A.2d 540 (Pa. Super. Ct.1990) a developmentally disabled woman appealed her conviction in a bench trial of endangering the welfare of children, indecent assault, indecent exposure, incest, and corruption of minors, based on ineffective assistance of counsel. The court, in denying her appeal, noted that:

> the controversial aspect of the battered woman's syndrome theory of self-defense case is not controversial in duress cases. The stumbling block in battered woman's syndrome self-defense cases is the legislative requirement that there be an immediate or imminent threat of serious bodily injury when the deadly force was used; the battered woman's syndrome theory of self-defense (even if accepted) merely establishes that the accused reasonably perceived an immediate or imminent threat which did not actually exist . . . Immediacy or imminence is not a requirement of duress, as it is of self-defense. Consequently, acceptance of the battered woman's syndrome theory of self-defense in Pennsylvania would add little, if anything, to the existing law that the existence of duress is to be determined by considering whether under the totality of the circumstances . . . the threat . . . or use of force was such that a person of reasonable firmness would have been unable to resist.

578 A.2d at 542. It is hard to explain why the court adopted such a limited definition of the function served by testimony about battering.

3. Another puzzling case is that of Dunn v. Roberts, excerpted below. Lisa Dunn was convicted of aiding and abetting her former boyfriend, Daniel Remeta, in a crime spree that included kidnapping, murder, and armed robbery. After consistently high academic performance in high school, Lisa began to have troubles at home and in school at the age of 15, including problems with drugs and alcohol. At 17, she left home and was raped in Florida. Because she did not cooperate with the district attorney, her rapists were never prosecuted. Shortly after returning home to a stormy relationship with her parents, she met Remeta. When he decided to jump bail for a charge of breaking into a car, she went with him to Florida, taking with her one of her father's guns.

Lisa J. Dunn v. Raymond Roberts

963 F.2d 308.
Tenth Circuit Court of Appeals, 1992.

■ McKAY, CHIEF JUDGE.

This cross-appeal involves a challenge to a District Court judgment granting Petitioner habeas corpus relief from a state conviction. Petitioner and Respondent raise several issues on appeal. We need only address one of these issues, however, because we find it dispositive of whether Petitioner is entitled to a new trial. The sole question we address is whether the state trial court denied Petitioner due process when it refused Petitioner's request for funds to employ a psychiatric expert to assist in her defense.

Petitioner is an inmate at the Kansas Correctional Institute. She was convicted as an aider and abettor in 1985 of two counts of felony murder, two counts of aggravated kidnaping, one count of aggravated battery on a law enforcement officer, one count of aggravated robbery, and one count of aggravated battery....

Petitioner was eighteen years old when she met Daniel Remeta in Michigan in December of 1984. In January of 1985, Daniel Remeta, Petitioner, and another individual decided to travel to Florida. Before leaving Michigan, Petitioner took a .357 magnum pistol from her father's gun collection at Daniel Remeta's request.

According to Petitioner's trial testimony, she first became aware of Daniel Remeta's prison record and cruel nature during the drive to Florida. Petitioner stated that when she expressed a desire to return home to Michigan, Daniel Remeta threatened her with the .357 magnum. Petitioner testified that, as the trio continued their travels from Florida to Kansas, Daniel Remeta repeatedly threatened to harm Petitioner or her family if she left him. Daniel Remeta testified that Petitioner had no choice regarding her whereabouts and affirmed that he would have carried out his threats had Petitioner attempted to leave him. Petitioner testified further that Daniel Remeta's erratic and violent behavior intensified and he exerted more and more control over her as the trip continued.

On February 13, 1985, the trio picked up a hitchhiker north of Wichita, Kansas. Shortly thereafter, Daniel Remeta verbally threatened the hitchhiker and fired shots out of the car window. Near Levant, Kansas, the group was stopped by a sheriff driving a patrol car. Daniel Remeta exited his vehicle and shot the sheriff a number of times.

The group then drove to a grain elevator in Levant. At the grain elevator, Daniel Remeta forced two individuals into the back of a pickup truck at gunpoint. Daniel Remeta also shot and wounded another individual who was attempting to call the police. The group then drove in the pickup truck to a point near Colby, Kansas. Here Daniel Remeta shot the two hostages with the .357 magnum and left their bodies by the side of the road. Shortly thereafter, the group was captured after a gun battle. Petitioner was charged with a number of crimes relating to the events discussed above.

Prior to trial, Petitioner moved the court ... for $1800 to employ a psychological expert to assist in developing her defense. At the hearing, Petitioner's counsel presented the testimony of a jail chaplain who had spent approximately fourteen hours talking with Petitioner. The chaplain testified that Petitioner had told him that Daniel Remeta had threatened her with a gun, had choked her and had repeatedly threatened to kill her family if she left him or didn't do what he wanted her to do....

Petitioner's counsel then discussed statements Daniel Remeta had made to the media regarding his abusive treatment of Petitioner. Petitioner's counsel related Daniel Remeta's admissions that he had threatened to kill Petitioner many times, that he had subjected her to Russian Roulette with the .357 magnum, and that he had advised her that her family or other innocent parties would be in danger if she contemplated leaving him....

Petitioner's counsel stated that he had discussed the case with both a Michigan psychologist who had evaluated Daniel Remeta and a forensic psychiatrist from the Menninger Foundation.... Counsel said that both had suggested he investigate whether Petitioner suffered from battered woman's syndrome and dissociative response when she was with Daniel Remeta. See id. Counsel related his belief that such evidence was relevant to Petitioner's mental state at the time the crimes were committed.... He explained that such evidence would be important because the state's case cast Petitioner as an aider and abettor of Daniel Remeta's crimes and that specific intent to assist, rather than mere presence, was a necessary element of the crime of aiding and abetting.... Counsel stated that he was not competent to investigate and develop such evidence....

In requesting the funds, Petitioner's counsel explicitly stated that the assistance sought did not relate to the defense of compulsion but, rather, lack of intent.... Counsel then invoked the United States Supreme Court case of Ake v. Oklahoma, 470 U.S. 68, 84 L. Ed. 2d 53, 105 S. Ct. 1087 (1985). He said:

> The issue there was whether the constitution requires the indigent defendant to have access to a psychiatric examination and assistance to provide effective defense on a mental condition when sanity is in question. I believe we can put in "mental state" is in question. It's definitely in question in this matter, Your Honor.
>
> . . .
>
> The ... mental state of my client has been made relevant because they alleged that she was an intentional active participant in this matter by aiding and abetting. I believe we've shown the threshold showing that mental state is a significant factor at trial in this matter.

... The trial court rejected Petitioner's request, stating basically that Petitioner would have to convince the jury of her lack of intent without the assistance of an expert.... Petitioner renewed her request twice more, but the trial court denied each motion.

At trial, witnesses for the state and the defense offered conflicting evidence concerning Petitioner's participation in the crimes. None of the witnesses identified Petitioner as having a weapon or personally engaging in violence at any time. The only evidence offered of any direct participation by Petitioner was the testimony of four witnesses who said they saw Petitioner or someone with Petitioner's hair color driving the pickup after the elevator robbery. Daniel Remeta, the hitchhiker, and Petitioner all testified that Petitioner did not drive the truck. Another witness testified that she had seen another member of the group driving the truck. Thus, the State's principal arguments in support if its aiding and abetting theory relied heavily on Petitioner's presence with Daniel Remeta at the time the crimes were committed.

The jury found Petitioner guilty of aiding and abetting Daniel Remeta's crimes pursuant to the following instruction:

> A person who, either, before or during its commission, intentionally aids or abets another to commit a crime with intent to promote or assist in its commission is criminally responsible for the crime committed regardless of the extent of the defendant's participation, if any, in the actual commission of the crime.

Record, Vol. V, Kansas Vol. II, at 83. Petitioner was originally sentenced to four consecutive terms of 15 years to life. These terms were later modified to be served concurrently.

On direct appeal to the Kansas Supreme Court, Petitioner contended, in pertinent part, that the trial court's refusal to provide funds for a forensic psychiatrist violated her right to due process under Ake v. Oklahoma. The Kansas Supreme Court affirmed Petitioner's conviction, however. That court, in relevant part, determined that Petitioner could not have made a sufficient showing to the trial court that her mental condition would be a significant issue at trial as required by Ake v. Oklahoma. Thus, it rejected Petitioner's due process contention.

The Kansas Supreme Court's determination on this issue was inextricably linked to its conclusion that Petitioner was not entitled to raise the affirmative defense of compulsion. The Kansas Supreme Court noted that the Petitioner could not avail herself of a compulsion defense unless she made a threshold showing that the compulsion was continuous and that there was no reasonable opportunity to escape the compulsion without committing the crime. The Kansas Supreme Court found that Petitioner had numerous opportunities to escape Daniel Remeta and, thus, could not invoke a compulsion defense. The Kansas Supreme Court seemed to reason that because the defense of compulsion was unavailable to Petitioner, the evidence Petitioner sought to develop using an expert regarding battered woman's syndrome was irrelevant to her case. Thus, the Kansas Supreme Court determined, Petitioner had not made a sufficient showing that her mental condition would be a significant issue at trial.

Petitioner filed for a writ of habeas corpus in federal district court pursuant to 28 U.S.C. 2254(d). The District Court granted the writ after determining, in relevant part, that the state trial court erred in refusing Petitioner's request for funds for expert services. The District Court determined that Petitioner had sufficiently shown the trial court that her mental condition would be a significant issue at trial and Petitioner was unable to effectively present her defense without access to expert services. Thus, the District Court concluded that the trial court's refusal of Petitioner's motion resulted in a deprivation of due process and granted Petitioner a new trial. The state now challenges the District Court's disposition of this issue.

When the state brings criminal charges against an indigent defendant, it must take steps to insure that the accused has a meaningful chance to present her defense. .... While the state need not provide the indigent with all the tools the wealthy may buy, it must provide the defendant with the "basic tools of an adequate defense." Britt v. North Carolina, 404 U.S. 226, 227, 30 L. Ed. 2d 400, 92 S. Ct. 431 (1971). In Ake v. Oklahoma, 470 U.S. 68, 84 L. Ed. 2d 53, 105 S. Ct. 1087 (1985), the United States Supreme Court identified as one of these "basic tools" the appointment of a psychiatric expert when a defendant makes a threshold showing that her mental condition at the time of an offense is likely to be a "significant factor" at trial. ... In such a case, denying access to the assistance of a psychiatric expert to perform an examination relevant to defense issues and to assist in developing the defense would be a deprivation of due process....

. . .

The record indicates that the state trial judge was made aware in general terms of Daniel Remeta's threats against and physical abuse of Petitioner and that evidence of battered woman's syndrome would likely have bearing on whether Petitioner had the state of mind necessary to commit the crime of aiding and abetting. Petitioner's counsel explained clearly that the state's case against Petitioner rested heavily on an aiding and abetting theory; that specific intent to assist, rather than mere presence, is a necessary element of the crime of aiding and abetting; that Petitioner's case rested on her ability to show that she lacked the requisite intent; and that Petitioner could not develop an effective rebuttal of that element without the assistance of an expert. We conclude that Petitioner made a compelling showing that her mental state would be a central issue at trial. Given the facts before the state trial judge and the defense counsel's explanation for requesting expert assistance, we conclude the state trial court should have known that a refusal of Petitioner's request for expert assistance would deny Petitioner an adequate opportunity to prepare and present her defense.

... Because specific intent is an essential element of the offense for which Petitioner was tried, the state was required to prove beyond a reasonable doubt that Petitioner entertained a specific mental objective to assist Daniel Remeta in committing the crimes. If the jury found that Petitioner, for any reason, did not entertain that particular mental state, it could not convict Petitioner of that crime. Thus, Petitioner's mental condition was squarely at issue in this case.

The state's theory of aiding and abetting rested heavily on Petitioner's presence with Daniel Remeta at the time the crimes were committed. From Petitioner's presence, the jury was asked to infer that Petitioner specifically intended to participate in Daniel Remeta's crimes. In light of the state's overwhelming emphasis on Petitioner's presence, it is clear that an expert would have aided Petitioner in her defense by supporting her assertion that she did not have the required specific intent.

The mystery in this case, as in all battered woman cases, is why Petitioner remained with Daniel Remeta despite repeated abuse. An expert could have explained to the jury the nature of battered woman's syndrome and given an opinion on whether Petitioner suffered from the syndrome. This is an area where expert opinion is particularly useful and oftentimes necessary to interpret for the jury a situation beyond average experience and common understanding. The effect of the expert testimony would be to explain why a defendant suffering from the battered woman syndrome wouldn't leave her batterer.... Thus, such evidence could have provided an alternative reason for Petitioner's continued presence with Daniel Remeta. We agree with the District Court that this evidence should have been "considered by the jury in evaluating whether Petitioner had the requisite intent to participate in the crimes of which she was charged." Dunn v. Roberts, 768 F. Supp. 1442, 1448 (D. Kan. 1991). This would not be the first case in which psychiatric testimony was considered crucial to the issue of intent.... By refusing Petitioner the funds for expert assistance, the state trial court effectively prohibited Petitioner from presenting relevant information directly bearing on an essential element of the crime of which she was convicted. Without that assistance, Petitioner was deprived of the fair trial due process demands....

For the foregoing reasons, we conclude that Petitioner is entitled to a new trial with the assistance of an expert in the preparation and presentation of her defense. Accordingly, we AFFIRM the judgment of the District Court that Petitioner be released from custody unless, within 120 days of the issuance of this order, a new trial outside of Thomas County, Kansas, is commenced.

NOTES AND QUESTIONS

1. On the specific issue before the court in *Dunn*—whether the trial court should have provided funding for an expert to testify—the Tenth Circuit's decision is unusual. In five states; Georgia, Kansas, Mississippi, Montana and Tennessee, state courts have determined that there was no violation of due process involved in denying such funds. It was the Kansas decision that was successfully appealed in *Dunn*. Ironically, Tennessee has also found counsel ineffective for not presenting expert testimony in battered women's cases, suggesting a "Catch-22" when counsel cannot obtain funding for an indigent client to have the testimony to which they are entitled. *The Validity and Use of Evidence Concerning Battering and Its Effects in Criminal Trials,* REPORT RESPONDING TO SECTION 40507 OF THE VIOLENCE AGAINST WOMEN ACT, NCJ 160972, *Trend Analysis* at 21 (May 1996).

2. Dunn's counsel argued that the testimony was relevant, not to a claim of duress, but to a claim of lack of intent. Why did the lawyer take that approach? Do you agree that the case is not one of duress? Why did the Kansas Supreme court decide that Dunn was not entitled to raise a defense based on duress, or compulsion? Is there a parallel between the requirement of a "threshold showing" here, and the role of procedural hurdles critiqued by Holly Maguigan in the self-defense context? What is the crime with which Lisa Dunn is charged, and what level of intent does it require? Did her counsel want to argue (a) that she was psychologically impaired, and incapable of forming the necessary intent, or (b) that she participated in her abuser's crime spree only under compulsion, or (c) that the testimony would simply suggest that she had no intent to assist or encourage him,

but that there was an alternative explanation for her accompanying him? What consequences might flow from choosing one or another of these theories?

C. POST-CONVICTION RELIEF AND CLEMENCY

Ineffective Assistance of Counsel and Clemency Elizabeth M. Schneider, Battered Women and Feminist Lawmaking, 144–147 (2000)

[M]isconceptions about battered women who kill have led to considerable confusion in judicial opinions, legal scholarship, and in more "public" sources of information, such as the media. Issues of admissibility of evidence and expert testimony on battering are confused with "special" defenses for battered women; the term "battered woman syndrome" becomes the short-hand for both. Not surprisingly, it appears that homicide cases involving battered women have a substantially higher appellate reversal rate than other comparable cases. Two final areas of law reform for battered women who kill underscore these problems: ineffective assistance of counsel cases, and the host of clemency cases that have surfaced around the country.

Over the past several years, battered women defendants have initiated post-conviction efforts to claim ineffective assistance of counsel against lawyers who represented them at trial. These cases are notoriously difficult to win, for the standard for ineffectiveness set by the Supreme Court requires egregious error resulting in prejudice to the defendant; at trial the defendant has the burden of proof to show such error, and anything that may be characterized as a tactical decision by the trial attorney is non-reviewable.

Of the many claims of ineffective assistance of counsel that have been brought by battered women who have been convicted at trial, a majority tend to fall into the category of claimed attorney error that courts rarely review, particularly if they are based on an attorney's failure to interview possible defense witnesses, or to otherwise investigate sources of information which could possibly be helpful to the defense. Among cases involving battered women defendants where ineffective assistance of counsel claims have been successful, the most common ground appears to be faulty advice, either in the plea-bargaining process or regarding whether the defendant should testify. Courts have also found ineffective assistance based on the attorney's failure to adduce evidence or examine witnesses at trial. Generally, the attorney's failure in either of these areas has resulted in no evidence of battering being offered at trial from such sources as medical reports, lay witnesses, family members, or the defendant's own testimony, or in no expert testimony on battering being offered.

From the number of claims of ineffective assistance of counsel based on faulty advice regarding plea bargains or the defendant testifying, and on attorney failure to present evidence and testimony that could have assisted the jury to understand and eradicate the very same misconceptions apparently held by counsel, it is apparent that attorneys are susceptible to misconceptions about battered women. Cases involving claims of ineffective assistance based on counsel's failure to offer jury instructions on battering suggest that many attorneys lack knowledge about the particular complexities of representing battered women. Nevertheless, because many of the judges who rule on ineffective assistance of counsel claims also lack knowledge about domestic violence, and have not been sensitive to the complex issues of choice of defense and admission of evidence, they may not be particularly thoughtful or rigorous in evaluating these claims.

Clemency efforts for battered women in many states suggest a widespread recognition of the problems battered women charged with homicide face at trial. One of the major arguments advanced by proponents of clemency for battered women have been that clemency is necessary and will continue to be necessary so long as individual battered women are denied their rights to present an adequate defense at trial and until society responds adequately to the problem of woman abuse. The "clemency movement" first gained national recognition in October 1990, when Richard Celeste, then governor of Ohio, issued a mass clemency, just before leaving office, of twenty-five battered women who had been convicted of killing or assaulting their batterers. Shortly after this highly publicized act, Governor William Schaefer of Maryland granted clemency to eight battered women incarcerated in that state for killing their batterers. Governors in several other states, including Jim Edgar of Illinois, Lawton Chiles of Florida, and Pete Wilson of California, have granted clemency to battered women convicted of killing or assaulting their batterers. In 1998, Colorado Governor Roy Romer granted clemency to four battered women, and six women were granted clemency in Florida. International human rights appeals for clemency for battered women outside the United States have also begun.

Of the nearly forty thousand women in prison in the United States, roughly two thousand are incarcerated for killing a husband, ex-husband, or boyfriend–a number that constitutes around one-third of all women in prison for homicide. Studies have concluded that at least 45 percent and perhaps as many as 97 percent of incarcerated women who killed a partner were abused by the person they killed. We do not know exactly how many of these women may not have gone to trial, consenting to plea-bargain arrangements on the advice of attorneys who were unaware that their clients were battered, or who were ignorant of the possible legal significance of evidence of battering. Many of those women who did go to trial may have received unfair trials, either because of attorney ineffectiveness or judicial error in applying the law where evidence of battering was present. Because clemency petitions can be based on many different grounds, including attorney error or ineffectiveness, or judicial error that was not appealed or affirmed on appeal, we can only speculate about the number of cases in which clemency might be sought. Nonetheless, the number of cases of women in prison for killing their batterers in which clemency has been sought, and the number in which clemency might be sought, suggest that attorney and judicial conduct has had a substantial impact on women's lives and on the criminal justice system.

Resistance to Equality

The premise of the work seeking to ensure battered women equal rights to trial has been the radical idea that battered women's experiences had to be articulated, genuinely heard, and taken into account in reshaping the law. Recognizing the social context—women's experiences of battering and society's response to battering—was crucial, because without understanding the social context and the social circumstances of battering, the facts of a particular case could not be understood. As in all legal cases, the critical struggle is who gets to define the facts. Without first listening to women's experiences, and without understanding the social framework and experience of battering, it was simply not possible for lawyers to fairly represent battered women in these circumstances. Truly listening to women who have been hurt and traumatized, who may not have words to express their pain, who may not trust that anyone will listen, who may be viewed as "difficult" because they are angry, or whose gender, racial, cultural, or class experiences may be different from the lawyer's, judge's, or juror's, is not easy. But listening to the women's experiences in these cases is not only subversive; it can mean the difference between life and death. For battered women who kill, these experiences, whether told to defense lawyers, in court, on clemency petitions, or in other contexts, as Jody Armour puts it, "is their social reality, constitute[s] their social identity, and vindicate[s] their social existence." The stakes attached to the telling of this narrative are high; this "explains much of the stubborn resistance to this work."

Resistance to equality takes many forms. First, there is the resistance of lawyers who may find it hard to listen to the voices and experiences of battered women, even when they can be surfaced and articulated, and who then must thoughtfully consider the implications of these stories for the defenses that may be available within an equal rights framework. Resistance to hearing these experiences as complex and nuanced is explicit in the crude characterization of "abuse excuse." Judges' resistance may lead them to engage in a process of gender construction in which women's experiences are considered "in the form of sexist stereotypes (of women as "bad" or "mad") which reinforce the oppression and control of women in general." Finally, because this work argues for affirmative recognition of the significance of social context, and social responsibility, it challenges fundamental assumptions about "free will" in the criminal law, and triggers considerable resistance for some criminal law scholars. All these aspects of resistance are forms of resistance to equality. The legal problems of battered women who kill demonstrate the devastating impact of the social failure to link violence to equality.

* * *

Ineffective Assistance of Counsel

The *Romero* case, above, has already introduced you to claims of ineffective assistance of counsel in the domestic violence context. The Sixth Amendment guarantees the right of criminal defendants "to have the assistance of counsel for [their] defence." U.S. Const. Am. VI. This right has been understood to function to "assure fairness in the adversary process." U.S. v. Cronic, 466 U.S. 648, 656 (1984) [citing U.S. v. Morrison, 449 U.S. 361, 364 (1981)]. Thus, the rights of the accused have not been met where either interference by the state in the form of court orders or statutes, or the defense attorney's own actions or omissions, cause the trial process to lose "its character as a confrontation between adversaries." Id. at 657. Since the function of the right to counsel is to "assure fairness in the adversary process," id. at 656, when a criminal defendant is not represented by her attorney in a manner that subjects the prosecution's case to the "crucible of meaningful adversary testing," id., she has received ineffective assistance of counsel, and her Sixth Amendment rights have been violated.

Strickland v. Washington, 466 U.S. 668 (1984), resolved a split among lower courts on the standards to be applied in ineffective assistance of counsel cases. *Strickland* held that, in order to establish ineffective assistance of counsel to reverse a conviction, the criminal defendant has the burden of proof to show both that (1) "counsel made errors so serious that counsel was not functioning as 'counsel' guaranteed ... by the Sixth Amendment," and (2) that the "deficient performance prejudiced the defense." Id. at 687. *Strickland* also enunciated standards for measuring attorney performance and prejudice. The *Strickland* attorney performance standard is a deferential one: "reasonably effective assistance," guided by "prevailing professional norms," and consideration of "all the circumstances," relevant to counsel's performance. The Court noted that more specific guidelines in applying the standard for attorney performance are "not appropriate." Id. at 687–88.

Proving ineffective assistance of counsel is challenging for most defendants. The prejudice prong is not easily satisfied unless the defendant can show that "counsel's unprofessional errors rendered the proceeding fundamentally unfair." Long v. Krenke, 138 F.3d 1160 (7th Cir. 1998). Generally, such a showing requires evidence not readily available to a convicted defendant who is incarcerated. There are many cases, for example, where the defendant claims ineffective assistance based on counsel's failure to adequately investigate, in which courts give the standard response that there has been no showing of prejudice because the defendant has failed to establish what specific further evidence existed that the trial attorney could have adduced. *See, e.g.* Commonwealth v. Ely, 578 A. 2d 540, 542 (Pa. Super. Ct. 1990) (noting in the case of a defendant who claimed ineffective assistance due to counsel's failure to present evidence of battering that "it is incumbent upon an appellant claiming ineffective assistance of counsel on such grounds to proffer specific, admissible evidence to be presented at an evidentiary hearing in order to even warrant a hearing on such a claim"). Moreover, the same attorney who represented the defendant at trial may represent her on appeal, and may not want to bring certain acts or omissions on her part to the attention of the court, if she is willing to base an appeal on a claim of her own ineffective assistance at all. Courts do not require attorneys' performance to be flawless. Thus, a defendant is more likely to win a claim of ineffective assistance where she can point to a laundry list of errors that suggest a lack of diligence, rather than one mistake which could be the result of human error.

Claims involving failure to interview possible defense witnesses or otherwise investigate sources of information which could possibly be helpful to the defense are among the most difficult for courts to evaluate. *See* Burger v. Kemp, 483 U.S. 1056 (1987). This is because a "fair assessment of attorney performance requires every effort be made to eliminate the distorting effects of hindsight." *Strickland*, at 680. Other areas where attorney incompetency is difficult to challenge because they require "hindsight," are (1) claims based largely on the attorney's decision to pursue a particular line of defense over other possibilities, where the attorney appears to have investigated other defenses; (2) failure to call a witness who offers to give favorable testimony; (3) the attorney's decision to relinquish a certain defense right where he had exercised various other rights; and (4) failure to advance additional supporting arguments or rebut counter-arguments to a legal objection the attorney has made and developed previously.

As domestic violence has inundated the courts with cases in recent years, there has been an increase in the number of ineffective assistance claims brought by battered women defendants. However, many of the most common areas of attorney performance complained of by these women fall into the especially-difficult-to-prove categories discussed above. Battered women face additional difficulties related to their particular experiences and widespread ignorance about the phenomenon of intimate violence in showing ineffective assistance of counsel. For example, in *Strickland*, the Court noted that special attention must be given in claims based on attorney failure to investigate the "information supplied [to counsel] by the defendant." Id. at 691. Because we know that women who have killed their partners frequently suffer memory lapse and confusion following the incident, an attorney representing a battered woman who kills in self-defense is likely not to get accurate or adequate information from the defendant alone to develop an effective defense. Commonwealth v. Stonehouse, 555 A.2d 772, 780 (Pa.1989).

Claims of ineffective assistance of counsel by battered women defendants fall into seven categories: (1) failure to investigate adequately; (2) improper legal advice (generally regarding plea bargaining or whether or not defendant should testify); (3) choice and application of defenses (frequently a focus on or misunderstanding of the law of self-defense that eclipses the attorney's exploration of provocation, heat of passion, or other available defenses); (4) faulty opening statements (often promising evidence of battering that is not adequately delivered); (5) failure to adduce evidence or examine witnesses at trial (almost always including a failure to present expert testimony on battering, and often a failure to present medical records, witnesses, and the defendant's own testimony that could have demonstrated the existence of domestic violence and its impact on the defendant); (6) failure to request jury instructions about battering (particularly in terms of how it is relevant to the law of self-defense); and (7) other acts or omissions (including failure to obtain exculpatory reports regarding battering, failure to object to prosecution's closing remarks, and advancing the interests of counsel over the client's interests in making tactical decisions). All but the last two of the categories of attorney ineffectiveness complained of by battered women are included in the list, discussed in the previous section, of areas where courts are loathe to find incompetence because investigation into these actions or omissions by attorneys most often requires the "hindsight" discouraged in *Strickland*.

Among the cases involving battered women defendants where ineffective assistance has been found, the most common complaint appears to be faulty advice (either in the plea bargaining process or regarding whether the defendant should testify). State v. Zimmerman, 823 S.W.2d 220 (Tenn. Crim. App.1991); State v. Scott, 1989 WL 90613 (Del. Super. 1989); Larson v. State, 766 P.2d 261 (Nev.1988); State v. Gfeller, 1987 WL 14328 (Tenn. Crim. App. 1987). The second most common complaint in these cases is the attorney's failure to adduce evidence or examine witnesses at trial. Commonwealth v. Miller, 634 A.2d 614 (Pa. Super. Ct.1993); People v. Day, 2 Cal. Rptr.2d 916 (Ca. Ct. App.1992); State v. Zimmerman, 823 S.W.2d 220; Commonwealth v. Stonehouse, 555 A.2d 772 (Pa.1989); Martin v. State, 501 So. 2d 1313 (Fl. Dist. Ct. App.1986). Generally, attorney failure in either of these areas results in either no expert testimony on battering being offered at trial, or no evidence of battering being offered from other available sources, including medical reports, lay witnesses, family members, or the defendant's own testimony. Cases where ineffective assistance of counsel has been found also include complaints that the attorney failed to investigate evidence of battering, People v. Rollock, 557 N.Y.S.2d 90, 91 (1991), the attorney's choice and use of available defenses, State v. Adkinson, 236 Ga. App. 270 (Ga. Ct. App. 1999), the attorney's opening statements indicating a defense involving evidence of battering which was not followed with any such evidence, State v. Zimmerman, 823 S.W.2d 220, and the attorney's self-interest interfering with the effectiveness of his performance, Larson v. State, 766 P.2d 261 (Nev.1988). Among the cases where ineffective assistance has not been found, the most common area complained of by far appears to be the attorney's failure to adduce evidence or examine witnesses regarding battering at trial.

Mistakes made by attorneys in their representation of battered women as criminal defendants frequently appear to be based on the same kinds of myths and misconceptions so many courts have recognized that juries are likely to have about battered women. That attorneys are susceptible to the same types of misconceptions about battered women is apparent from the number of claims of ineffective assistance of counsel based on faulty advice regarding plea bargains or the defendant testifying, and on attorney failure to present evidence and testimony that could have assisted the jury to understand and eradicate those very misconceptions apparently held by counsel. Cases involving claims of ineffective assistance based on counsel's failure to offer jury instructions on battering also raise the issue of attorney ignorance about the particularities of representing battered women. *See, e.g.,* Commonwealth v. Stonehouse, 555 A.2d 772; Commonwealth v. Singh, 539 A.2d 1314 (Pa. Super.Ct.1988); Commonwealth v. Tyson, 526 A.2d 395 (Pa. Super. Court 1987).

Ironically, then, even though criminal defense work on behalf of battered woman was one of the earliest priorities of lawyers allied with the battered women's movement, it may well be the case that around the country today prosecutors are better educated and trained in the handling of domestic violence cases than the criminal defense bar. Strategic and comprehensive efforts to increase the competence of defense lawyers in this area are long overdue.

Clemency for Battered Women

The first national recognition of what has since been named the "clemency movement" occurred in October, 1990, when the former Governor of Ohio, Richard Celeste, just before he left office, issued a mass clemency of twenty-five battered women who had been convicted of killing or assaulting their batterers. For background reading about the clemency movement, see, for example, Patricia Gagne, BATTERED WOMEN'S JUSTICE: THE MOVEMENT FOR CLEMENCY AND THE POLITICS OF SELF-DEFENSE (1998); Leslie Friedman Goldstein, CONTEMPORARY CASES IN WOMEN'S RIGHTS 276 (1994), and Linda L. Ammons, *Discretionary Justice: A Legal and Policy Analysis of a Governor's Use of the Clemency Power in the Cases of Incarcerated Battered Women,* 3 J. L. & POLICY 2 (1994). The experience of women incarcerated in Maryland for killing their abusers is captured in the 1990 documentary film *A Plea for Justice*, and both the film and the women's subsequent petition for clemency is discussed in Jane C. Murphy, *Lawyering for Social Change: The Power of the Narrative in Domestic Violence Law Reform,* 21 HOFSTRA L. REV. 1243 (1993).

Executive clemency is the power of the executive branch of government (the President or Governor) to mitigate the consequence of a sentence. It is a remedy that is grounded in the United States Constitution, but it also exists in some form in every major nation but China. Comments of Cookie Ridolfi in *Courtroom, Code and Clemency: Reform in Self Defense Jurisprudence for Battered Women* (panel discussion), 23 GOLDEN GATE U. L. REV. 829, 833 (1994). The major political criticism of clemency is that it violates the principle of separation of powers because it appears to allow the executive branch to interfere with and override decisions about criminal liability and punishment properly made by the judicial and legislative branches of government. However, the Federalist Papers make clear that the power was specifically included in the constitution to balance and complement the other two powers in the area of criminal law. Because no justice system can predict every case that may come before it, no system can mete out perfect justice. There will always be cases in which the rules say a person is guilty and must be punished, even though most people would agree that this is an unjust result. For this reason, the clemency power is an "essential safety net for the public good." Id. at 837.

Cookie Ridolfi, a defense attorney who has represented many battered women and contributed to women's self-defense work for the last two decades, says there are essentially three types of situations where clemency is appropriate: 1. situations where the convicted person is factually innocent; 2. situations in which the convicted person is technically guilty, but mitigating factors exist which argue for leniency; and 3. situations in which the convicted person is technically guilty, but morally innocent. The third case is frequently the most accurate description of what has happened to a formerly battered woman who fought back against her batterer. Essentially, the argument goes that but for imperfections in the law as it existed at the time of her trial, or as it currently exists, or trial factors such as jury bias or improper jury instructions, the person would have not have been convicted. This third case is strongest when the law has changed, since the defendant was convicted, in a direction that makes it unlikely they would be convicted again if retried under contemporary standards. It is easier, that is to say, for the executive branch to challenge decisions that either the legislative or judicial branch of government has already acknowledged were based on a flawed vision of justice.

Clemency may take the form of commutation, pardon, reprieve, or amnesty. A pardon implies forgiveness or acknowledgement of the convicted person's actual or moral innocence. Generally, pardon restores rights lost by being convicted of a crime, such as the right to vote or to serve on a jury. It may be granted after release from prison and/or after parole supervision has ended. It may be conditional. A reprieve suspends execution of sentence, usually to allow time for further investigation or an appeal. Reprieves are most common in death penalty cases. Amnesty excuses groups of convicted persons, usually where the crimes with which they were charged were political acts.

Finally, commutation is the substitution of a less severe punishment than the one imposed by the court at sentencing. It usually implies not that the person is actually or morally innocent, but that the punishment is overly harsh, given the circumstances of crime, some inequity in the law, or circumstances that have occurred since sentencing (being diagnosed with a terminal illness, for example, so that a five year sentence becomes a de facto life sentence, or a subsequent change in the law so that the defendant might well not be found guilty if retried under the new regime). It may lead to parole and does not restore civil rights. Commutation may reduce a death sentence to life imprisonment, shorten a sentence of imprisonment, reduce the minimum sentence so that the parole eligibility date is advanced, or reduce the maximum sentence (either shortening probation time after parole or reducing the time served in prison). A commutation to time served will make the defendant eligible for immediate release. Even when a person is granted a commutation, they may still need to apply for and be granted parole. Commutation is the appropriate form of clemency in most cases of battered women who kill their assailants, because they are usually not facing a death penalty, have usually not been released, and are not considered political prisoners.

Executive clemency is at the discretion of the governor or president. An advisory board, usually the Parole Board, may be authorized to advise and make recommendations to the executive officer. Typically, executive officers follow the recommendations of their advisory boards. Therefore, appeals to this body are an important part of the clemency process. Generally, the petitioner must exhaust all administrative remedies before applying for commutation. Usually, the clemency process involves several levels. First, the petition must meet basic requirements or be changed to comply with such requirements. Second, an investigation is conducted into the petitioner's criminal, social, and institutional histories. Third, the advisory or parole board makes a recommendation to the executive officer, based upon which the officer makes her determination. Finally, where commutation is granted, there is usually a review conducted under the auspices of the executive officer, sometimes including another hearing. Because executive officers, as well as many executive advisory or parole board members, are elected to office, they are particularly susceptible to public opinion. Community education about battering and identifying support by the community are therefore also very important parts of the clemency process.

There is a connection between clemency and "special" legislation. Policy makers often think that legislation making expert testimony admissible in the trials of battered women who kill their batterers is the key to battered women staying out of prison. For this reason, they may focus their efforts on creating "special" legislation for battered women. Along with other problems associated with special treatment (including pathologizing women or presenting them as passive victims), such measures can obstruct the possibility of clemency for women by creating the illusion that clemency is no longer necessary. "A statute allowing Battered Woman Syndrome evidence is not necessarily going to prevent convictions, but policy makers may feel that there is no longer a problem." Comments of Rebecca Isaacs in *Courtroom, Code and Clemency: Reform in Self Defense Jurisprudence for Battered Women* (panel discussion), 23 GOLDEN GATE U. L. REV. 829, 833 (1994). Moreover, the absence of "special" statutes is often cited in support of clemency. In Ohio, for example, Governor Celeste justified clemency for battered women on the grounds that a state Supreme Court decision specifically barred expert testimony about battering until 1990. In Maryland, clemency activism was also based on the inadmissibility of evidence of battering. Finally, and perhaps problematically, in Florida the parole board has adopted a rule making battered women's syndrome a criterion for consideration of clemency. Rita Thaemert, *Till Violence Do Us Part,* STATE LEGISLATURES, March 1993, at 26.

The role of public education in creating a climate within which elected officials can grant clemency to convicted "killers" without fearing adverse political consequences is well captured in the following reading, which describes efforts by a coalition of battered women's advocates in Maryland to change the context within which battered women's self-defense claims were heard and understood.

Jane C. Murphy
Lawyering for Social Change: The Power of the Narrative in Domestic Violence Law Reform, 21 Hofstra Law Review 1243, 1278–79, 1284–86 (1993)

... Creative new strategies were needed. The coalition shifted the focus [away from litigation and legislation] to storytelling—having victims who had killed or attempted to kill their abusers tell the grim stories of their lives with their abusers—in a variety of ways, to a number of audiences.... First, the Domestic Violence Task Force arranged for the financing and production of a videotape, *A Plea for Justice.* The objective of the videotape was to have victims tell their stories to a wide audience....

In May 1990, the thirty-minute videotape, one of the first of its kind, was completed and premiered to a large audience in Baltimore. Representatives from the coalition interviewed thirty women who had killed or attempted to kill their abusers and were serving time at Maryland's only women's prison, the Maryland Correctional Institution for Women (the "MCIW"). From these interviews, the stories of four Baltimore women—serving sentences ranging from fifteen years to life for killing their partners—were selected to feature in the film. With the exception of the narrator, a battered woman herself, and brief statements from psychologist Lenore Walker and former Attorney General Benjamin Civiletti, the voices in the film are those of the women telling their stories.

The stories were classic examples of domestic violence. All of the women were the product of abusive homes, and all had initially sought a haven within their relationships. The batterers began as "intense" and "passionate" partners. Later, this passion turned to violence and isolation, making the women totally dependent upon their abusers. The details of the stories vary, yet paint a horrifying picture of lives that led these women to believe that killing their abusers was their only chance to live.

. . .

The targeted audience for the film included: the Governor of Maryland, who could grant clemency or recommend parole to the Parole Commission; the Parole Commission; the Maryland Legislature, which in 1990 had rejected a bill that would have required the admission of battered spouse syndrome testimony, and would consider another version of the bill in 1991; the Maryland Congressional Delegation; and the general public.

The Governor of Maryland, William Donald Schaefer, was one of the first legal decisionmakers targeted. During his sixteen years as Mayor of the City of Baltimore and his first four-year term as Governor, Schaefer had never actively supported legislation or policies designed to improve the plight of domestic violence victims. The Governor viewed the film with key members of his staff. Moved by what he saw, he asked to meet with the women in the film. He met with those women and others for over two hours at the MCIW, and he listened to their stories. When Governor Schaefer emerged from that meeting, he told reporters how the experience had changed his understanding of the plight of battered women:

> You read a newspaper: "Mary Jones shot her husband." When you see Mary Jones and understand how she got there, it is a little different.... [The women told] stories of a lack of self-esteem, abuse, hoping things get better, things don't get better, and finally a point where the women break.

Later, testifying before a congressional subcommittee that was considering legislation intended to strengthen training for judges who deal with domestic violence and to encourage the enactment of state laws allowing the introduction of testimony of abuse and battered spouse syndrome, Schaefer commented:

> I never focused on the issue of domestic violence until two years ago. I had no interest in it at all and I started off unsympathetic. After hearing the women's stories I decided they should be given a chance to say how they were treated.

The third and final piece of the storytelling campaign was the filing in January, 1991, of a 300–page petition seeking clemency on behalf of twelve inmates at the MCIW who were serving sentences from fifteen years to life for killing or attempting to kill their abusers. The petition, entitled *Twice Imprisoned*, described the components of battered spouse syndrome, analyzed the law in Maryland and around the country with regard to the admissibility and use of this testimony, and described the clemency options available to the Governor. At the heart of the petition, however, are the stories of the four women featured in the videotape, and the stories of eight other women as well. The stories, called *Inmate Profiles*, included a careful review of the development of domestic violence in each relationship, a discussion of the specific circumstances surrounding the crime, a review of the woman's institutional record and achievements, a commentary on her family and educational background, and a brief summary of the woman's plans if released. Most, if not all, of this information was not before the court at trial or at sentencing, nor was it in the inmates' institutional parole files.

As a result of the storytelling in all its forms, in February, 1991, the Governor signed executive orders commuting the sentences of eight women.... Although the women became eligible for immediate release, they would be subject to supervised probation for the balance of their sentences. In announcing this decision, the governor's press secretary noted that the governor had met with several of the women and was "very impressed by the circumstances that led to their imprisonment," and "sympathize[d] with the difficulty they have had in the courts trying to explain their circumstances that led to the crime...." It was a historic and dramatic conclusion to the first phase of a successful campaign in which storytelling had played a central role.

* * *

*

PART FIVE

NEWER LEGAL FRAMEWORKS

CHAPTER **11** Domestic Violence and the Law of Torts

CHAPTER **12** Third Party Liability for Abuse

CHAPTER **13** Domestic Violence as a Violation of Women's Civil Rights

CHAPTER **14** Domestic Violence as a Violation of Women's International Human Rights

CHAPTER ELEVEN

Domestic Violence and the Law of Torts

Introductory Note

This chapter addresses tort actions available to those who suffer, physically and/or emotionally, at the hands of abusive partners. While many abused women do not have the resources to bring tort actions, and many of their abusers are virtually judgment-proof, there are still situations in which a tort claim is a potential source of redress, and of vindication, for someone who has been abused. The symbolic value of such cases also goes well beyond their practical impact—they send a clear message to those batterers with substantial resources that their behavior is not merely condemned by law, but may be costly as well.

This area of law is still in its infancy, for several reasons. Most generally, the problem of accidental injury, and the choice between negligence and strict liability in that arena, has been the central concern of modern tort law. Intentional torts have not, by and large, captured the intellectual interest or imagination of torts theorists. This has begun to change, with the development of the relatively new tort of intentional infliction of emotional distress or outrage, and the realization that it has a potentially significant role to play in addressing issues of contemporary concern, such as discrimination and harassment in the workplace, and domestic violence. But the change is recent, and the field still underdeveloped.

More specifically, despite the fact that not all tort suits based on abuse are between married partners, the development of domestic tort law has been significantly slowed by the tradition of interspousal tort immunity, and more recently by confusion and conflict about the relationship between domestic tort actions and divorce proceedings. In 1992 one researcher reported:

> Among approximately 2600 reported cases of battery, assault, or both, from 1981 through 1990, only fifty-three involved adult parties in domestic relationships. Similarly, during the same time frame, only four reported federal cases involved a claim or counterclaim between adult parties in a domestic relationship. From 1958 through 1990 slightly more than 6000 intentional infliction of emotional distress cases were reported from all state and federal courts. Evaluation of these cases revealed a total of eighteen in which courts have applied the tort action to a domestic abuse fact pattern.

Douglas D. Scherer, *Tort Remedies for Victims of Domestic Abuse,* 43 S.C. L. Rev. 543, 565 (1992). The fact that reform has been focused on the threshold issue of access to the tort system has meant that the system has been slow to adapt to the needs of 'domestic' claimants:

> Their somewhat specialized experiences of injury and violation were previously excluded from the courts, remaining unheard and unconsidered by the judges who built modern tort law, necessarily, out of the cases that came before them. A parallel could be drawn here with women's experiences in the workplace. The first goal of reformers was to overcome the discrimination that kept women out of so many work environments. The second phase of reform has been to work for change in those environments to make them practically, rather than merely theoretically, accessible to women. In both cases the first step must, of necessity, precede the second, and has enormous symbolic importance. But in both cases the second step may turn out to be the harder struggle, requiring a level of change that stirs up resistance, and offers resisters many fronts on which to fight.

Clare Dalton, *Domestic Violence, Domestic Torts and Divorce: Constraints and Possibilities,* 31 NEW. ENG. L. REV. 319, 329–30 (1997).

The succeeding sections look first at interspousal immunity, and its slow demise; then at existing causes of action that might be applicable in the context of a battering relationship; then at the very considerable barriers to those claims imposed by statutes of limitation; and then at the question of whether a new cause of action for "partner abuse" might ease the way for victims seeking compensation for abuse. The final section looks at the vexed relationship between tort actions and divorce proceedings.

A. INTERSPOUSAL TORT IMMUNITY

In Chapter One you read an excerpt from Reva Siegel's *"The Rule of Love": Wife Beating as Prerogative and Privacy*, 105 YALE L. J. 2117 (1996), in which she used the evolution of rules and rhetoric restricting the freedom of women to sue their partners to demonstrate how apparent "reforms" can serve to disguise the perpetuation of status hierarchy, and the subordination of women. You also read Townsend v. Townsend, 708 S.W.2d 646 (Mo. 1986), in which the Supreme Court of Missouri finally abolished interspousal immunity for intentional torts and documented Missouri's long history of avoiding that step by shifting the grounds on which the immunity supposedly rested. Missouri's prevarication provides a perfect illustration of the process Siegel describes. You might want at this point to reread those materials.

This section adds just a little more background on the gradual demise of interspousal immunity, and the surprising resilience of some of the more contemporary policy arguments offered in its support.

Domestic Torts in Historical Perspective
Clare Dalton, Domestic Violence, Domestic Torts, and Divorce: Constraints and Possibilities, 31 New England Law Review 319, 324–30 (1997)

From the perspective of many modern commentators, interspousal tort immunity has long seemed an anachronism. This has perhaps obscured from modern audiences just how durable the immunity has proved to be in many states, and how very recent its demise. Georgia and Louisiana are still hanging on stubbornly to their immunities. Florida's Supreme court capitulated, finally, to the demand for its total abolition only in 1993. In the same year Delaware abolished the immunity for negligence cases, with the implication that cases involving intentional torts would be treated similarly, and Hawaii passed legislation generally abolishing the immunity. Missouri made the move only in 1986.... Other states could be added to this list of late and reluctant abolitionists, while still others, like Massachusetts, have taken confusingly piecemeal steps toward reform, with the first steps coming early, but the last coming late. When you add to this the crucial fact that not many domestic tort suits are brought, for some obvious and some not-so-obvious reasons, it becomes apparent that there has been relatively little opportunity for state courts to "develop" their domestic tort law to fit current understandings and needs, or to tinker creatively with the fit between tort litigation and divorce proceedings, even if inclined to do so.

... Back in the nineteenth century the immunity was understood to flow from the even earlier idea that a woman was merged with her husband in marriage, so that as an indivisible marital unit, neither partner could sue the other on any cause of action, tortious or otherwise. The husband, of course, was the legal representative of this marital unit, and the only partner endowed with legal capacity to pursue its goals or protect its interests in court. This highly legalized explanation served to distance the legal profession from another enduring ideology—that as head of the household, the husband, father and master was in fact privileged to discipline those under his sovereignty, whether wife, children or servants, which privilege extended to the use of reasonable physical "chastisement."

By the end of the nineteenth century, however, the Married Women's Property Acts and Earnings Acts, supported by an energetic women's movement, had made significant inroads on the "marital unity" ideology, endowing women with legal personality and capacity, and thereby recognizing their individuality....

While it was possible to hang on to interspousal tort immunity simply through obdurately restrictive interpretations of Married Women's Property Acts or related legislation, reformulated policy arguments were usually brought in to provide a second line of defense. The two most crucial arguments, often used in tandem, were the "domestic harmony" argument and the "privacy" argument. Domestic harmony, the argument goes, requires that a state committed to the institution of marriage—as all states are—should encourage the maintenance of marital relationships, and not provide discontented partners with opportunities for blowing their domestic grievances out of all proportion, exacting revenge for minor slights and injuries, rather than kissing and making up. Family life, the privacy argument goes, is an essential feature of society, but at the same time fragile, requiring protection from the incursions of the state. To some extent, both arguments propose, we are better off tolerating abuses within that private sphere than we would be trying to micromanage family relationships.

Both domestic harmony and privacy arguments have proved vulnerable, over time, to the feminist critique that they privilege men over women in relationships in which privacy can too easily become a license for abuse, and in which the illusion of "harmony" is too frequently maintained by male dominance and female subservience. In the often extreme cases in which state Supreme Courts have done away with interspousal tort immunity, it would have been preposterous to argue that there was any "harmony" left to preserve, and recognizing the "privacy" argument would have made a mockery of the state's power to protect its citizens against private predation. Nonetheless, these arguments, unlike the older "marital unity" argument, still exert residual influence on the legal system, just as they do on popular thinking, complicating the impetus for reform.

* * *

NOTES

1. Political theorist Carole Pateman said in 1989: "The dichotomy between the private and the public is central to almost two centuries of feminist writing and struggle; it is, ultimately, what the feminist movement is about." Carole Pateman, THE DISORDER OF WOMEN: DEMOCRACY, FEMINISM AND POLITICAL THEORY 118 (1989). For a survey of feminist analysis of the public/private distinction, and its role in the subordination of women, see, for example, Frances Olsen, *Constitutional law: Feminist Critiques of the Public/Private Distinction,* 10 CONST. COMMENT. 319 (1993), and Ruth Gavison, *Feminism and the Public/Private Distinction,* 45 STAN. L. REV. 1 (1992). Catharine MacKinnon points out that privacy arguments do more than simply deprive women of remedies for the violence that subordinates them. Such arguments actually exacerbate women's situation. The "right to privacy is a right of men 'to be let alone' to oppress women one at a time." Catharine MacKinnon, TOWARDS A FEMINIST THEORY OF THE STATE 194 (1989).

Most recently, arguments about 'public' responses to 'private' violence against women have centered around the contested constitutionality of the federal civil rights provision enacted as part of the 1994 Violence Against Women Act, and codified at 42 U.S.C. § 13981(1994). See, for example, Sally F. Goldfarb, *Violence Against Women and the Persistence of Privacy,* 61 OHIO ST. L.J. 1 (2000). This provision receives extensive discussion in Chapter 13, below.

2. Georgia most recently addressed a proposal to abolish interspousal tort immunity in New v. Hubbard, 426 S.E.2d 379, 379–80 (Ga. Ct. App. 1992), a third party action growing out of an automobile accident:

> ... In 1983, the Georgia legislature codified interspousal immunity doctrine: "Interspousal tort immunity, as it existed immediately prior to July 1, 1983, shall continue to exist on and after July 1, 1983."
> ...

> ... Appellees argued below, and the trial court apparently concluded, that interspousal immunity nonetheless should not bar appellees' third-party action because the doctrine is antiquated and, to the extent its purposes—preservation of marital harmony and prevention of collusive tort actions—still apply at all, they do not apply in the context of third-party actions. We recognize that the majority of jurisdictions have abrogated interspousal immunity. However, it is still the rule in Georgia; and it has been reaffirmed as such numerous times since the national trend away from the doctrine has been recognized....
>
> ... Now that the doctrine has been codified, judicial intervention to invalidate it on the grounds that interspousal immunity and the policy concerns underlying it are "antiquated" would clearly be improper. Id.

The situation in Louisiana is different. In Duplechin v. Toce, 497 So.2d 763, 765 (La. Ct. App. 1986), the court held that the immunity only suspended the right to sue until the parties were legally separated or divorced. Ironically, this intermediate position may provide better protection for some women than outright abrogation of the immunity, because it allows more time after separation for a suit to be brought.

3. Florida had abolished the immunity for battery by statute in 1986. Fla. Stat. ch. 741.235 (1986 & Supp. 1997). Judicial consideration was required in the 1993 case of Waite v. Waite, 618 So.2d 1360, 1361 (Fla. 1993) because the events involved in that case—Joyce Waite and other members of her family were attacked by her husband with a machete—occurred in 1984, prior to the passage of the legislation.

4. The list of "late and reluctant abolitionists" includes Colorado, which abolished the immunity for intentional torts only in 1988, in Simmons v. Simmons, 773 P.2d 602, 604–05 (Colo. Ct. App. 1988); Mississippi, which did the same in the same year in Burns v. Burns, 518 So.2d 1205, 1209 (Miss. 1988) and Kansas, which climbed on the bandwagon in 1987, with Flag v. Loy, 734 P.2d 1183, 1186, 1189–90 (Kan. 1987). Rhode Island abolished the immunity through legislation in 1989, R.I. GEN. LAWS § 1504017 (1997), and Illinois did the same a few years earlier in 1986, 750 Ill. COMP. STAT. ANN. 60/225 (West 1993 & Supp. 1996). In Vermont, Nevada and Alaska the immunity has been abolished for negligence actions, but whether that ruling also applies to intentional torts is still not entirely clear, while in Utah the immunity has been abolished for intentional torts, but may still be in place for negligence actions.

5. The marital rape immunity, shielding rape within marriage from criminal liability, has proven even more resistant to change than the interspousal tort immunity. While some (surprisingly small) number of states have done away with it altogether, many others retain significant distinctions between rape and sexual assault inside and outside of marriage. For an up to date account, see Jill Elaine Hasday, *Contest and Consent: A Legal History of Marital Rape,* 88 CAL. L. REV. 1373 (2000).

A separate question is whether the existence of a criminal immunity will affect civil liability for rape or sexual assault of a spouse. In their treatise, DOMESTIC TORTS, FAMILY VIOLENCE, CONFLICT AND SEXUAL ABUSE (1989 & Supp. 1996), the authors, Karp and Karp, suggest:

> In jurisdictions that have abrogated the marital rape exemption in criminal cases, there should now be no impediment to bringing a tort case in a civil action based upon the rape. Moreover, regardless of whether the jurisdiction in question has abrogated the marital rape exemption, in criminal cases, one should always consider a civil action for assault and battery, as these jurisdictions may not necessarily preclude the civil action.

Id. at 38.

The Maryland case of Lusby v. Lusby, excerpted below, provides support for the proposition that the existence of a criminal marital rape exemption will not bar a civil action based on the same conduct. The marital rape exemption was still in force in the state, except where the parties were separated under a decree of limited divorce or written separation agreement, when Gerald Lee Lusby raped his wife. MD. ANN. CODE art. 27 § 464 (D) (1976). The trial court dismissed the wife's tort claim, but the Maryland Court of Appeals chose this case as the vehicle to declare that Maryland's interspousal tort immunity had never been applied to bar an action involving "intentional, outrageous conduct" of the sort alleged here.

Lusby v. Lusby

283 Md. 334; 390 A.2d 77.
Court of Appeals of Maryland, 1978.

■ Opinion by: SMITH, J.

We shall here hold that under the facts and circumstances of this case, amounting to an outrageous, intentional tort, a wife may sue her husband for damages—a holding which represents somewhat of a departure from the earlier decisions of this Court.

Appellant, Diane R. Lusby (the wife), brought an action in the Circuit Court for Prince George's County against John Doe, Richard Roe, and Gerald lee Lusby (the husband). She alleged that while she was operating her motor vehicle on a public highway the husband "pulled alongside of [her] in his pick-up truck and pointed a highpowered rifle at her." She attempted to flee by increasing the speed of her car. She claimed that then "another truck occupied by two (2) men, whose identities are unknown to [her] ... cut and forced her off the road, nearly causing a collision." ... After she stopped the car, the husband "approached her automobile with a rifle pointed at her, opened her left door, ordered her to move over, forced his way into the automobile and began to drive the automobile." They were followed by Doe in the husband's truck and Roe in the second truck. Thereafter, the wife "was forced to enter [the husband's] truck with [the husband] and Richard Roe." John Doe drove the wife's vehicle and the second truck was left parked. She alleged that her husband then struck her, "tore [her] clothes off and did forcefully and violently, despite [her] desperate attempts to protect herself, carnally know [her] against her will and without her consent." She further claimed that, with the aid and assistance of her husband, both Doe and Roe attempted to rape her. She said that following these events her husband "and his two companions released [her] and [her husband] told [her] that he would kill her if she informed anyone of the aforesaid events; and that he has continued to harass and threaten [her]."

The husband demurred to the declaration on several grounds including the fact that the parties were married at the time and that, notwithstanding Maryland Code (1957, 1971 Repl. Vol., 1975 Cum. Supp.) Art. 45, § 5, Maryland "law is unequivocal . . . that a husband and a wife, as the case may be, may not sue the other for a tort committed by the other upon and/or against his or her person; this is a principle that dates from the common law."

. . .

We can conceive of no sound public policy in the latter half of the 20th-century which would prevent one spouse from recovering from another for the outrageous conduct here alleged. There certainly can be no domestic tranquility to be preserved in the face of allegations such as we have before us. It will be recalled that in Gregg, 199 Md. at 667, Chief Justice Marbury said for the Court, "After discord, suspicion and distrust have entered the home, it is idle to say that one of the parties shall not be allowed to sue the other because of fear of bringing in what is already there." It will further be recalled that he labeled as "artificial" the theory that "the identity of husband and wife persists in its original vigor until it has been completely dissolved by express legislative mandate. . . ."

. . . None of our prior cases has involved an intentional tort. We find nothing in our prior cases or elsewhere to indicate that under the common law of Maryland a wife was not permitted to recover from her husband in tort when she alleged and proved the type of outrageous, intentional conduct here alleged. Note that under the common law in England as reflected in Blackstone it was under "the old common law" that a husband "might give his wife *moderate* correction" (Emphasis added.) The type of action in the case at bar not being forbidden by the common law of this State or any statute of this State, it follows that the trial court erred.

Judgment reversed; costs to abide the final result.

NOTES AND QUESTIONS

1. How likely is it, do you think, that a state court in a state which has definitively overruled interspousal immunity for intentional torts would preclude a civil action based on spousal rape, because of a criminal marital rape immunity? What arguments would you make to support the proposition that the criminal immunity is irrelevant to the issue of civil liability? Could you go further and argue that criminal immunity is a *reason* for imposing civil liability? Would it be strategically wiser to use intentional

infliction of emotional distress rather than sexual assault or battery as the basis for the tort claim? Are there countervailing arguments for treating marital rape consistently in the criminal and civil law?

2. When *Lusby* was decided, the Maryland legislature had just recently revisited its criminal provisions relating to "sexual offenses." You read a brief account of that legislation, and of the marital rape exemption contained in it, as described in the decision in Lane v. State, 348 Md. 272, 703 A.2d 180 (Md. Ct. App. 1997), in Chapter 9A, above. The Legislature had nothing to say, in either 1976 or 1989, about any relationship between the narrowing criminal immunity for marital rape and sexual assault, and the capacity of one spouse to sue another civilly for the same conduct.

3. As in the *Townsend* decision, the Maryland courts had been offered many opportunities to abolish the state's interspousal immunity prior to the *Lusby* case. As in Missouri, however, the state's 1898 statute granting married women the right to sue and be sued, in contract, tort, and with respect to property rights, "as fully as if they were unmarried," was restrictively interpreted to preclude husbands and wives from suing one another. As late as 1932 the Court of Appeals was basing this restriction not solely on the grounds of legislative intent, but also: "upon the broader sociological and political ground that it would introduce into the home, the basic unit of organized society, discord, suspicion and distrust, and would be inconsistent with the common welfare." David v. David, 161 Md. 532, 535, 157 A. 755 (1932). Beginning in 1952, the Court repeatedly urged the Legislature to address the question whether this "omission should be repaired." Gregg v. Gregg, 199 Md. 662, 87 A.2d 581 (1952). However, as of 1978 the Legislature had failed to address the issue, and the Court, in Lusby, therefore found itself forced to engage in remedial lawmaking. It disguised the fact that it was treading on ground it had previously marked off as belonging to the legislature by concluding that no clear prior authority, legislative or judicial, established an immunity for intentional torts.

4. Most states have abolished their interspousal tort immunities through legislation, or through decisions in which the highest court of the state has exercised its prerogative to adapt the common law to changing social conditions, or to rectify the mistakes of earlier courts. For most litigants, therefore, there has been no need to invoke constitutional doctrine to support the argument that interspousal tort immunities have no place in late twentieth century tort jurisprudence. However, it can certainly be argued that interspousal tort immunities discriminate against married people in violation of the equal protection guarantees of the Fourteenth Amendment. In 1984 the Seventh Circuit invalidated Illinois' immunity on that basis. Note that because the discrimination is, on its face, between married and unmarried people, and not between men and women (although we might argue that its impact is disproportionately felt by women), the lowest level of equal protection scrutiny, "rational basis" scrutiny, is applied, rather than the intermediate level of scrutiny adopted by the Supreme Court for gender-based discrimination. Nonetheless, the immunity was held to flunk even this least stringent of tests.

Moran v. Beyer

734 F.2d 1245.
Seventh Circuit Court of Appeals, 1984.

■ JUDGES: BAUER, FLAUM, CIRCUIT JUDGES, and EVANS, DISTRICT JUDGE.[1]

■ Opinion by: EVANS, DISTRICT JUDGE.

At issue on this appeal is the constitutionality of Illinois' interspousal tort immunity statute. The district court, on a motion for summary judgment, rejected the constitutional challenge to the statute and dismissed those portions of Deborah Moran's suit against her husband in which she alleged that he had beaten her. We reverse.

I.

Ms. Moran alleges in her complaint that, a short time after she was married to Daniel Beyer, he became increasingly hostile towards her. Her complaint details a number of disputes between the two which ended in physical injury to her. The injuries included cuts, bruises and a broken nose. Beyer's answer admits his part in the violence Moran describes, but replies that his actions were justified. He claims extreme provocation and self-defense. By Christmas of the year after the marriage, Moran had moved away from Beyer. At the time this action was commenced, the two were no longer married. In her suit, Moran alleged one count of assault and battery and one count of intentional infliction of emotional distress. Beyer counterclaimed, alleging the same.

Had the paths of these two individuals crossed under any circumstances other than marriage, the district court would have proceeded to weigh their allegations and decide who, on the basis of the evidence, should win the case. However, since Moran and Beyer were married, the district court was confronted with Ill. Rev. Stat., ch. 40, § 1001 (1980), which was controlling at that time, and which commanded that:

> A married woman may, in all cases, sue and be sued without joining her husband with her, to the same extent as if she were unmarried; provided, that neither husband nor wife may sue the other for a tort to the person committed during coverture.[2]

Beyer moved for summary judgment on the ground that Moran's action was barred by this provision of Illinois law. The trial court was persuaded, summary judgment was granted in Beyer's favor, and this appeal was commenced. The thrust of Moran's appeal is that her Four-

1. The Honorable Terence T. Evans, Judge of the United States District Court for the Eastern District of Wisconsin, is sitting by designation.

2. The statute has since been altered to abrogate interspousal immunity in cases of intentional tort. In 1981, the Illinois Domestic Violence Act, Pub. Act 82–621, 1981 Ill. Laws 3200 (1981), effective March 1, 1982, amended the statute to read:

> A married woman may, in all cases, sue and be sued without joining her husband with her, to the same extent as if she were unmarried; provided that neither husband nor wife may sue the other for a tort to the person committed during coverture, except for an intentional tort where the spouse inflicted physical harm.

Id. at § 403; Codified as Ill. Rev. Stat., ch. 40, § 1001 (1982).

teenth Amendment right to equal protection of the laws is violated by a statute which prohibits a married person from pursuing the same remedy for the same kind of injuries which an unmarried person is free to pursue.

II.

In evaluating ch. 40, § 1001 under the Equal Protection Clause, "we must first determine what burden of justification the classification created thereby must meet, by looking to the nature of the classification and the individual interests affected." Memorial Hospital v. Maricopa County, 415 U.S. 250, 253, 39 L. Ed. 2d 306, 94 S. Ct. 1076 (1974). Moran argues that the statute is constitutionally suspect under both the "strict judicial scrutiny" standard and the less rigorous "rational relationship" test. *See* San Antonio School District v. Rodriguez, 411 U.S. 1, 17, 36 L. Ed. 2d 16, 93 S. Ct. 1278 (1973).

A. We decline the invitation to declare that the interests upon which ch. 40, § 1001 impinges are so fundamental that they justify the protections of strict judicial scrutiny. It is true, as Moran argues, that the courts have come to confer this heightened protection upon certain decisions relating to marriage....

However, not every choice made in the context of marriage implicates the privacy and family interests which make certain marital decisions fundamentally important.... The decision to bring suit against a spouse does not so strategically advance privacy or family interests that the decision itself accedes to the status of a fundamental right. Nor does a statute limiting the exercise of this choice constitute a direct legal obstacle to marriage. Also, the statute does not so significantly discourage marriage that it merits the "rigorous scrutiny" which has been applied to other regulations qualifying marital rights.... Accordingly, strict scrutiny of the statute is not required.

B. Thus, we turn to Moran's second line of argument. She contends that there is no rational relationship between the statutory classification and the Illinois legislature's purpose in enacting it. The pertinent inquiry is whether the scheme, which prevents a married person from seeking a remedy which is available to an unmarried person, "advances a reasonable and identifiable governmental objective." Schweiker v. Wilson, 450 U.S. 221, 235, 67 L. Ed. 2d 186, 101 S. Ct. 1074 (1981). The analysis breaks down into two questions: (1) whether the statute's purpose is reasonable, and (2) whether the statute rationally advances that purpose.

Without question the purpose behind creating interspousal tort immunity is reasonable. Maintaining marital harmony is an admirable goal, especially considering the numerous social problems to which marital strife gives rise.[1]

1. Moran submits that marital harmony is not the actual purpose behind the statute, but rather a *post hoc* justification. Moran's argument traces the statute to its archaic common law roots, where husband and wife were treated as a legal unit, incapable of suing itself. Without disputing the considerable authority supporting this position, we choose to give the benefit of the doubt to the purpose put forth by contemporary defenders of the statute.

However, we cannot agree with the district court that ch. 40, § 1001, is rationally related to this goal. It truly would take "something more than the exercise of strained imagination," Logan v. Zimmerman Brush Co., 455 U.S. 422, 442, 71 L. Ed. 2d 265, 102 S. Ct. 1148 (1982) (Blackmun, J., concurring), to find some objective basis for believing that depriving a physically battered spouse of a civil remedy for her injuries will advance some sense of "harmony" with the person who inflicted the injury. Dean Prosser eloquently dismantled this justification when he observed that the "domestic harmony" rationale rests upon

> the bald theory that after a husband has beaten his wife, there is a state of peace and harmony left to be disturbed; that if she is sufficiently injured or angry to sue him for it, she will be soothed and deterred from reprisals by denying her the legal remedy—and even though she has left him or divorced him for that very ground[.]

Prosser, TORTS, 863 (4th ed. 1972). The immunity rule confuses cause and effect. Because the immunity rule leaves unchecked the actual cause of marital discord—such as the assault and battery committed in this case—it can do absolutely nothing to further marital harmony. Indeed, for a knowledgeable couple leery of marriage, the statute may do more to retard the institution than further it: unmarried persons living together can still resort to the courts for protection from a "partner", while a married person has no such protection against his or her spouse. Finally, added to these inconsistencies is the fact that nothing in the statute prevents one spouse from undermining domestic tranquility altogether by swearing out a criminal complaint against the other.

. . .

For his part, Beyer urges us to yield to the wisdom of the Illinois legislature. This is the restrained position which Illinois courts have taken in construing ch. 40, § 1001. See Steffa v. Stanley, 39 Ill.App.3d 915, 350 N.E.2d 886 (1979). We do not share the reluctance of these state courts. To begin with, we are faced with facts of a more egregious character than *Steffa*, which arose out of an automobile accident. Furthermore, we cannot find it at all rational to believe that the Illinois legislature's desire to protect marital harmony is fulfilled by ch. 40, § 1001, which does little more than grant one spouse almost unconditional license to make his marriage partner a sparring partner. We are, therefore, compelled to declare it unconstitutional.

Accordingly, the decision of the District Court is reversed, the judgment entered on behalf of Beyer is vacated, and this action is remanded to the district court for further proceedings.

B. EXISTING CAUSES OF ACTION

Now that tort actions are more freely available between married people, it is important to think creatively about precisely which causes of action may be effective in the context of partner violence. An enormously valuable resource on this topic is Frederica L. Lehrman's DOMESTIC VIOLENCE PRACTICE AND PROCEDURE, 2–1 to 2–236 (1996).

Assault and battery are obvious candidates for the battered litigant; they were the claims, for example, argued in both *Townsend* and *Moran*. When they are not available it is often because the applicable statute of limitations, usually quite short, has run. The relatively new tort of intentional infliction of emotional distress is also an important candidate for consideration, especially for cases in which an abuser has relied more on psychological and emotional abuse than physical abuse, or in which the major injuries are the consequence of emotional rather than physical abuse. This cause of action receives extensive coverage below.

Wrongful or false imprisonment is a less obvious choice, but may fit the reality of battering relationships in which the battered partner is essentially held prisoner by her abuser, isolated from friends and family, and able to leave the house or apartment only with, or with the permission of, her abuser.

In Lorange v. Hays, 69 Idaho 440, 209 P2d 733 (1949), a husband forcibly removed his wife of 23 years from her automobile, and without any legal authority, took her, over her protests and objections, to the state hospital for the insane, where she remained confined for more than three months. The court found that the now ex-husband could appropriately be named as the defendant in a wrongful arrest and imprisonment case. This case epitomizes the "total restraint" usually required in wrongful imprisonment cases.

In an article by Jane Murphy, *Lawyering for Social Change: The Power of the Narrative in Domestic Violence Law Reform*, 21 HOFSTRA L. REV. 1243 (1994), the author recounts the stories of Maryland women incarcerated for killing their abusers, drawing from the documentary film, *A Plea for Justice,* which supported their pleas for clemency. Two passages in her account describe the experiences of women essentially "imprisoned" by their obsessively jealous abusers. Might a false imprisonment claim be available to one or both of them? What more information would you want in order to make that decision?

> And he had popped the question to me and said, look, you don't have to work; I make enough money to take care of me and you both. That's every girl's dream. I'm 19 years old and somebody's telling me I don't have to work and he's going to take of me. I was like, girl, my boyfriend told me I don't have to work, he's going to take care of me so I don't have to go to work nowhere. I didn't know he was in the process of putting me in his own little prison, my own little world. I agreed. I quit my job. And I stayed home. And I never had any friends. With him keeping me within my apartment, one bedroom, one kitchen, and one dining room and den hooked together, I was really restricted to what I could do, where I could go, who I could see, who could come and see me and I was like within my own prison within my own home.

> I would never go to the hospital. I would stay in my house since I was home all the time anyway. I would just doctor on myself, heal myself. He beat me up so bad and blackened both my eyes at once, but I knew he loved me and I loved him and whatever came with loving him was all right with me.

Statement of Gale A. Hawking, reproduced in Jane Murphy, *Lawyering for Social Change: The Power of the Narrative in Domestic Violence Law Reform*, 21 HOFSTRA L. REV. 1243, 1282 (1994).

> Soon after we started dating I had noticed that he was kind of possessive and he was very jealous. But I didn't really count it as out of the ordinary; it kind of flattered me to be honest. I kind of thought, well, he loves me this much that he cares, he don't want me speaking to this one or he don't want me going there without him. And I kind of thought that was really kind of nice, so I must have been something really special.
>
> There was something about him that frightened me because he was getting more and more abusive and he got more and more demanding and he kept isolating me and isolating me. I couldn't talk to my family. I couldn't talk to my friends. Wherever I went, I had to be by his side. If we traveled in the car, I had to look at the floorboards, I couldn't look out the window.

Statement of Joyce Danna, id., at 1280.

Other causes of action may also be available. When an abuser verbally humiliates his partner in public, making false accusations of infidelity or substance abuse, or when he tries to poison his partner's professional relationship with a school or an employer by blackening her reputation, she may have an action in defamation. Illegal wiretapping may be civilly actionable. If children are themselves abused or threatened, physically or sexually, they have their own assault and battery claims. If they witness a parent's violence, the psychological consequences for them may provide a basis for a claim of negligent, reckless or intentional infliction of emotional distress. If their access to one parent is manipulated by the other as part of his campaign to control or terrorize his partner, there may be claims, called by various names in different jurisdictions, such as child snatching, obstruction of visitation rights, or interference with custody. A child hurt accidentally by violence aimed at his or her parent can pursue a straightforward negligence action.

Would there be circumstances where a battered partner might sue in negligence rather than battery for physical injury? Why might she want to? Chiefly because negligence claims may find a deeper pocket than the batterer's own—if injuries negligently inflicted are covered by a household or an automobile insurance policy, as they usually are, while intentionally inflicted injuries are not, as is also common. Is it then worth a woman's while to argue that when her husband drove down the driveway, pinning her to the garage door, he was driving negligently, while the insurance company argues that his violence was deliberate, and therefore beyond the terms of the policy? If compensation is the priority, this may be a strategy to consider in some cases. However, it is hard to feel enthusiasm for tort recovery that depends on the plaintiff's participation in a "cover-up." "Covering-up," after all, is what most victims of domestic violence have done for too long before they are able to take action to challenge their abusers. In addition, all too often their abusers have tried to persuade them, after the fact, that they were hurt by accident, rather than deliberately. There is a good deal unsavory about a legal process that mimics this same distortion of reality.

Survival and Wrongful Death Actions

Survival and wrongful death actions are possible in cases in which the abuse has ended in the victim's death. In the case of a wrongful death action, there must also be qualified survivors—most often the victim's minor children. In the survival action the victim herself is the plaintiff, although the suit is brought on her behalf by a representative of her estate. Recovery is for injuries and losses the victim experienced between the time of her injury and the time of her death. In a wrongful death action, on the other hand, others sue for their derivative losses; the financial support they are now deprived of, the services the deceased can no longer perform for them, and, in a minority of states, the loss of companionship or other emotional damages.

A number of state courts authorized wrongful death actions against batterers, or the estates of batterers, even before any more general abolition of interspousal tort immunity. More than one of these cases involved a situation in which the abusive partner had killed his wife and then himself, which is why the suit was brought against his estate, rather than against him personally. For some courts, the critical consideration was that the suit, while it depended on the primary claim of the dead spouse, was protecting the interests of others—almost always the victim's children. For other courts the critical consideration was that whatever arguments could be made about protecting domestic harmony or the privacy of the relationship while the husband and wife lived, those arguments plainly had no bearing in a situation in which one or both of the partners was dead. The next case illustrates these lines of reasoning.

Jones v. Pledger

363 F.2d 986; U.S. App. D.C. 254.
United States Court of Appeals for the District of Columbia Circuit, 1966.

■ Opinion: FAHY, CIRCUIT JUDGE.

The administratrix of the estate of Zelma Mae Pledger sued the administrator of the Estate of John Pledger. John Pledger was the husband of Zelma Mae Pledger. The complaint alleged that the husband intentionally shot his wife, inflicting injuries from which she died, and that thereafter on the same day he took his own life. The husband and wife had separated and there was a decree of limited divorce, but the bonds of marriage had not been severed completely. The wife's sole heir and next of kin, it is alleged, is the minor son of the marriage, for whom plaintiff is guardian.

The minor, it is also alleged, was dependent in part upon his mother for support and was in her sole custody. The suit is to recover damages alleged to be due the minor, and is brought under the Wrongful Death Act, D.C. Code § 16–1201....

The defendant administrator answered and moved for summary judgment, which was granted on the ground that "a wife may not maintain a personal injury suit against her husband for injuries which occurred during coverture" and, therefore, after her death there can be no action by her representative under the Wrongful Death Act because had she lived the husband, by reason solely of the doctrine of interspousal immunity, could not be sued in tort by his wife. The court thought that this followed from the terms of the Wrongful Death Act. We do not agree. The Act provides, in pertinent part:

> Whenever * * * the death of a person shall be caused by the wrongful act * * * of any person * * * and the act * * * is such as would, if death had not ensued, have entitled the party injured, * * * to maintain an action and recover damages, the person who * * * would have been liable if death had not ensued shall be liable to an action for damages for such death * * * and such damages shall be assessed with reference to the injury resulting from such act * * * to the spouse and next of kin of the deceased person * * *.

D.C. Code § 16–1201 (1961 ed.).

The interspousal immunity upon which the District Court relied has prevailed in this jurisdiction. This is so notwithstanding the Married Women's Act.... The important respects in which this Act eliminated a wife's disability did not go so far, the Court held in Thompson,[1] as to enable her to sue her husband for a tort committed by him upon her person....

Thompson, however, involved only the question whether the Married Women's Act should be construed to have abrogated by statute the husband's immunity. The Court was not concerned with whether the doctrine of interspousal immunity in tort could be changed in this jurisdiction by evolution of the common law through judicial decision in the light of changed conditions. Since for reasons to be stated we hold that the doctrine does not apply to the facts of the present case we do not face that problem.

. . .

At common law there was no right of action for wrongfully causing the death of another.... The right of action exists in the District of Columbia by virtue of our statute....

Such a statute is said to create a right derivative in nature. The cases divide on whether the right is derived from a right of action or from a cause of action.... Some courts hold that the right to maintain the action derives from the one whose death is caused by the wrongful act, and therefore an action by the legal representative of the deceased is subject to defenses that

1. Thompson v. Thompson, 218 U.S. 611, 31 Sp. Ct. 111, 54 L. Ed. 1180 (1910).

would have been good against the deceased. Others hold that it derives from the cause of action arising from the operative facts of the wrong, a new right of action being created to enable a person other than the one physically injured to seek compensatory damages. Such damages in our case is for harm to the child attributable to the wrong which resulted in the loss of his mother.

We agree with the view that the Wrongful Death Act creates such a new right of action in the next of kin. It derives from the cause of action which stems from the wrongful cause of the death. The right to pursue this cause of action by suit is in the legal representative here, acting for the minor. This determination that the right of action resides in the legal representative bears directly upon the question whether it is barred by the interspousal tort immunity.... The administratrix, while she may be said to stand in the shoes of the deceased in some respects, for the purposes of the Wrongful Death Act is the agent of the beneficiary of the action, here the minor son. The beneficiary labors under no personal disability by reason of interspousal immunity. Such a personal defense is not available to defeat the action brought on his behalf.

Even if the right of action is not created as we have explained in the next of kin but is derived from the deceased wife at her death, the immunity would not bar this action. The reasons for the immunity have completely disappeared and it should be given no effect. In an identical factual situation, Justice Schaefer, speaking for the Supreme Court of Illinois, said:

> Today the immunity can be based solely upon the ground that domestic tranquility is fostered by the prohibition of actions by a wife against her husband. An immunity based upon the preservation of marital harmony can have no pertinence in this case, for here the marriage has been terminated, husband and wife are both dead, and the action is brought for the benefit of a third person.

Welch v. Davis, [410 Ill.130, 134; 101 N.E.2d 547, 549 (1961)].

We conclude that the action is not barred by the doctrine of interspousal immunity....

Reversed and remanded for proceedings not inconsistent with this opinion.

Concur: Prettyman, Senior Circuit Judge (concurring in the result):

I heartily support the interspousal immunity doctrine in respect to torts, but, where the couple had a limited decree of divorce and the tort was the murder of the wife by the husband coupled with his own suicide, the doctrine has no factual substance on which to rest, and I see no reason to give effectiveness to its fiction. Especially is this so in an action brought on behalf of a minor child of the marriage against the estate of the parent who destroyed his sole support and security.

NOTES

1. In addition to the *Welch* case cited by the *Jones* court, see Apitz v. Dames, 205 Or. 242, 287 P.2d 585 (1955), another case in which the

husband killed both his wife and himself, and the Supreme Court of Oregon permitted a wrongful death action to proceed against his estate. In Maestas v. Overton, 87 N.M. 213, 531 P.2d 947 (1975) the New Mexico Supreme Court allowed a wrongful death action in a case in which the husband killed himself and his wife by crashing the plane he was piloting. In 1976 the Supreme Court of Illinois went a step further than it had in *Welch,* and allowed a wrongful death action to proceed against a still-living husband responsible for his wife's death. Herget National Bank v. Bernardi, 64 Ill. 2d 467, 356 N.E2d 529 (1976).

2. The *Thompson* case cited by the *Jones* court was one in which the Supreme Court of the United States, interpreting the District of Columbia's Married Women's Act, narrowed its application in much the same way that you have seen state courts do in Maryland and Missouri. Thompson v. Thompson, 218 U.S. 611, 31 Sp. Ct. 111, 54 L. Ed. 1180 (1910).

3. After O.J. Simpson was acquitted of the murders of Nicole Brown Simpson and Ronald Goldman, the Brown and Goldman families brought survival and wrongful death actions against him, seeking both compensatory and punitive damages. Under the civil "preponderance of the evidence" standard, the jury found O.J. Simpson responsible for the deaths, and brought back substantial verdicts; $8,500,000 for the wrongful death claim brought by the survivors of Ronald Goldman, and punitive damage awards of $12,500,000 in each of the survival actions. The punitive damage award to the estate of Ronald Goldman was attached to property damages in the amount of $100, and the award to the estate of Nicole Brown Simpson was attached to property damages in the amount of $250. Judgment on Jury Verdict in Favor of Plaintiff Louis H. Brown as Executor and Personal Representative of the Estate of Nicole Brown Simpson, Against Orenthal James Simpson [C.C.P. § 664], 1997 WL 114570 (Cal. Super. Doc.); Judgment on Jury Verdict in Favor of Plaintiff Fredric Goldman and Against Defendant Orenthal James Simpson [C.C.P. § 664], 1997 WL 114574 (Cal. Super. Doc.).

Intentional Infliction of Emotional Distress

Douglas Scherer
Tort Remedies for Victims of Domestic Abuse, 43 South Carolina Law Review 543, 557–62 (1992)

Domestic abuse ... typically involves purposeful infliction of severe emotional harm and presents a prototype setting for use of the tort action of intentional infliction of emotional distress. This tort received recognition as an actionable form of conduct in section 46 of the Restatement (Second) of Torts. A comprehensive revision of this section appeared in the 1965 Restatement (Second) of Torts, which requires intentional or reckless conduct, extreme and outrageous in nature, that results in severe emotional distress. Normally, a plaintiff must prove that the defendant had an intent to inflict severe emotional distress; however, courts occasionally rely on a recklessness standard rather than an actual intent standard. Although courts require proof of severe emotional distress, juries may consider the character of the defendant's conduct to determine whether the plaintiff suffered emotional harm. Therefore, evidence of physical or objective manifestations of emotional distress is not technically required, but it has significant probative value. Despite the arguably vague phrase "extreme and outrageous conduct," courts and juries in different jurisdictions have acted with substantial uniformity in distinguishing between actionable conduct and "mere insults, indignities, threats, annoyances, petty oppressions, or other trivialities." Comment d to section 46 supports this position.

> Liability has been found only where the conduct has been so outrageous in character, and so extreme in degree, as to go beyond all possible bounds of decency, and to be regarded as atrocious, and utterly intolerable in a civilized community. Generally, the case is one in which the recitation of the facts to an average member of the community would arouse his resentment against the actor, and lead him to exclaim, "Outrageous!"

Applying this extreme and outrageous conduct standard, courts and juries have uniformly denied recovery for emotional distress when the claim is based on wrongful discharge of an employee, failure by an insurance company to pay claims, false arrest by police officers, and financial, commercial, and real estate disputes. Recovery is likely, however, in cases that involve sexual abuse of children, sexual assault against adults, sexual harassment of employees, threats against a person's life, serious interference with visitation or custody rights of parents, extreme forms of harassment by debt collectors, interference with funeral services, forcible and illegal eviction of tenants, transmission of genital herpes, extortion, repeated obscene phone calls, continuous and highly insulting or threatening behavior, beatings, and threats of future beatings.

Subsection 46(2) of the Restatement addresses liability for harm to one person because of conduct directed at another person. This derivative liability is limited by the requirement that the plaintiff must actually suffer severe emotional distress. Most of the cases that have permitted recovery derived from harm to a third party have involved sexual abuse of a child or sexual assault upon a spouse. Finally, comment e to section 46 notes that "[t]he extreme and outrageous character of the conduct may arise from an abuse by the actor of a position, or relation with the other, which gives him actual or apparent authority over the other, or power to affect his interests."

. . .

The four interchangeable names used to describe the tort are intentional infliction of emotional distress, intentional infliction of mental distress, tort of outrage, and tort of outrageous conduct. The name intentional infliction of emotional distress predominates, especially in recent cases. Regardless of the name used by the state courts, however, the elements of the tort remain the same.

* * *

NOTE

1. The following two cases illustrate two very different judicial approaches to the standard of "outrageousness" demanded by the tort of intentional infliction of emotional distress, in the context of an abusive intimate relationship. The first, Davis v. Bostick, represents an early example of judicial recognition of the tort in the context of domestic abuse; the second, Hakkila v. Hakkila, although more recent, demonstrates a far less sympathetic attitude.

Davis v. Bostick

282 Or. 667, 580 P.2d 544.
Supreme Court of Oregon, 1978.

■ Opinion by JOSEPH, JUSTICE PRO TEM.

Plaintiff brought this action against her former husband, alleging that he had "engaged in an intentional course of conduct designed to inflict emotional stress and mental anguish." The conduct complained of consisted of 10 incidents, some of which were individual acts and some of which were groups of substantially identical acts committed at different times. The jury returned a verdict for $7,500 general damages and $10,000 punitive damages. Defendant appeals from the judgment.

The parties separated in May, 1973, after a nine-year marriage. The first of the incidents occurred shortly afterwards as they were returning to Eugene from an outing in Portland with their children when defendant struck plaintiff and broke her nose. Later in that year (in addition to initiating a series of threatening and abusive phone calls of varying frequency to her home and place of business which continued through 1975) he choked her and threatened to kill her and her male friends. During 1974 he accused her of being in the hospital for an abortion and told others the same thing, again threatened to kill her and destroyed some of her personal property. During 1975 he destroyed some more of her personal property, acted toward her in a threatening manner with a loaded pistol, damaged her boyfriend's pickup, told plaintiff and others she had a fatal mental illness, called her mother-in-law-to-be obscene names, harassed her mother and once more threatened to kill her.

Defendant acknowledges there was evidence to support conclusions that defendant did each and every one of those things, and they encompass all of the acts alleged to have constituted the course of conduct. Indeed, there was also considerable evidence that around, between, during, in preparation for and as constituent parts of the specific or collective acts recited defendant behaved in a manner that was, to put it mildly, outrageous in the extreme. There was substantial evidence that individually and as a whole the defendant's actions caused plaintiff to suffer emotional (as well as physical and economic) injury.

The parties were divorced in December, 1974, or January, 1975. Defendant remarried in April 1975, and plaintiff remarried in November. This action was filed in August, 1976, more than two years after the acts which occurred in 1973 and more than two years after at least two of the acts which occurred in 1974.

Two assignments of error relate to acts which occurred in 1973 and 1974. The first is a claim that the court should not have submitted to the jury any of the acts that took place during the parties' marriage. Acknowledging that Apitz v. Dames, 205 Or. 242, 287 P.2d 585 (1955), abolished the rule of interspousal immunity in cases of intentional tort, defendant argues that where no physical injury is alleged[1] there ought to be immunity. The argued basis for that assertion is that otherwise a great many dissolutions of marriage will carry in their train an action like this one. An implication of that rationale is that the law ought to treat the dissolution of a marriage as a new beginning for both parties, with the aggressor free to go his (or her) way with at worst possibly a burden of guilt and the victim free to go her (or his) way with the burden of the emotional and mental scars.

We decline to carve out that exception to the destruction of interspousal immunity for intentional torts. Apitz did not create a flood of litigation, even though it is a fair guess that the deterioration of many marriages since 1955 has been accompanied by the rendering by one spouse to another of physical injury. While injuries of a psychic nature as proved here are very likely much more common than physical injury, we see no virtue in basing a rule of law on a speculative fear of increased litigation. We prefer to rely upon the burden of proof as the best protection against unwarranted, meretricious or merely vindictive litigation. As we said in Rockhill v. Pollard, ... "the conduct must be outrageous in the extreme and it must have produced severe emotional distress." Where a jury could reach those conclusions, as it fairly could and did here, the conduct ought to be actionable and not protected by an assumption that too much justice might be demanded by injured persons. As Dean Prosser has said ...:

> "It is the business of the law to remedy wrongs that deserve it, even at the expense of a 'flood of litigation,' and it is a pitiful confession of incompetence on the part of any court of justice to deny relief on such grounds."

NOTES AND QUESTIONS

1. Why do you think the plaintiff did not seek to recover for her physical injuries and economic damage? Might it have undermined her intentional infliction of emotional distress claim by accentuating the discrete episodes of abuse and harassment, rather than the "course of conduct" that provided the basis for the emotional distress claim?

It seems that the plaintiff's exclusive reliance on an emotional distress claim was indeed strategic. Some of the defendant's abusive behavior had occurred in 1973 and early 1974, more than two years before the suit was filed. The defendant pleaded the two-year statute of limitations as to that conduct, but the trial court struck the defense on the ground that a

1. The evidence indicated that plaintiff did in fact suffer some physical injuries of a temporary nature and economic damage, but the complaint alleged only "emotional stress and mental anguish."

continuous tort was alleged. The jury was therefore told that it could award plaintiff damages for "any emotional distress and anxiety which she has suffered."

The appeals court saw matters differently. It agreed that the statute of limitations "might well not begin to run on this sort of cause of action 'until the defendant's conduct has culminated into the plaintiff's severe emotional distress'." However, the court also felt that the defendant's behavior in 1973 and 1974 had already produced that level of distress; that it was, therefore, separately actionable, and that the plaintiff was barred by the statute of limitations from wrapping it into her current claim:

> The plaintiff, or witnesses on her behalf, testified that each of the incidents caused her severe distress and anguish at the time. The only testimony that might be said to have gone to a cumulative effect was that she always felt harassed by the defendant's conduct and she is now a nervous person. On the facts proven there can be no doubt that defendant's abusive behavior was all of a piece in intent and content without substantial letup for three years and with almost diabolical variety. But there can also be no doubt that the acts of assault and battery and the death threat in 1973 and the defamatory abortion talk and death threat in early 1974 were separately actionable because they caused harm.
>
> Plaintiff's assertion that no cause of action accrued for those incidents cannot be accepted.... Polin v. Dun & Bradstreet, Inc., 511 F.2d 875 (10th Cir. 1975), cert. den. 423 U.S. 895 (1975), is cited by plaintiff, but it is a more limited case. It concluded that the harm complained of (invasion of privacy) might have reached the level of actionability only at the end of the series of publications, the first of which was beyond the statute of limitations. As we have said, this defendant's conduct repeatedly reached the level of actionability.

Id., 282 Or. at 672, 580 P.2d at 547.

Do you agree with the court's analysis? Is it enough to say that the earlier conduct was "actionable," or do we need to distinguish whether the action is being brought in assault and battery, or defamation, or instead as an intentional infliction of emotional distress claim? Does it help the analysis to know that courts have, in other contexts, been reluctant to find intentional infliction of emotional distress where the plaintiff is complaining about a single incident of abuse or harassment, however severe?

2. In *Davis,* therefore, the court is willing to recognize claims for emotional distress in the context of partner violence, but because it is not willing to characterise the tort as a continuing one, the impact of its decision is severely curtailed. The jury is also left with the unenviable task of sorting out which injuries belong to the time-barred claims, and which to the timely claims. In the next case the court is hostile to the claim altogether. Both decisions should then be contrasted with Curtis v. Firth, which both recognizes a cause of action for intentional infliction of emotional distress in the context of partner abuse, and recognizes its 'continuing' and 'cumulative' character.

Hakkila v. Hakkila

112 N.M. 172, 812 P.2d 1320.
Court of Appeals of New Mexico, 1991.

■ Opinion by HARTZ, J.

In response to the petition of E. Arnold Hakkila (husband) for dissolution of marriage, Peggy J. Hakkila (wife) counter-petitioned for damages arising from alleged intentional infliction of emotional distress. Husband appeals from the judgment entered against him on the tort claim and from the award of attorney's fees in the divorce proceeding. We reverse the damage award and remand for further proceedings with respect to the award of attorney's fees.

I. FACTS

Husband and wife were married on October 29, 1975. Each had been married before. They permanently separated in February 1985. Husband filed his petition for dissolution of marriage the following month. Husband, who holds a Ph.D. in chemistry, had been employed at Los Alamos National Laboratory throughout the marriage. Wife, a high school graduate with credit hours toward a baccalaureate degree in chemistry and a vocational degree as a chemical technician, had been employed at the laboratory as a secretary for seven years and as a chemical technician for about seven and one half years. She voluntarily terminated her employment in December 1979.

. . .

Finding No. 22 summarized husband's intentional misconduct:

The manner in which [husband] treated [wife] during the marriage and which resulted in her disability and impairment is as follows. [Husband] on occasions throughout the marriage and continuing until the separation[:]

a. assaulted and battered [wife],

b. insulted [wife] in the presence of guests, friends, relatives and foreign dignitaries,

c. screamed at [wife] in home and in the presence of others,

d. on one occasion locked [wife] out of the residence over night in the dead of winter while she had nothing on but a robe,

e. made repeated demeaning remarks regarding [wife's] sexuality,

f. continuously stated to [wife] that she was crazy, insane, and incompetent,

g. refused to allow [wife] to pursue schooling and hobbies,

h. refused to participate in normal marital relationship with [wife] which ultimately resulted in only having sexual relations with [wife] on four occasions in the last three years of the marriage,

i. blamed his sexual inadequacies upon [wife].

Finding No. 26 stated:

> [Husband's] acts in intentionally inflicting severe emotional distress upon [wife] was so outrageous in character and so extreme in degree as to be beyond all possible bounds of decency and were atrocious and utterly intolerable.

The district court also found:

> 31. [Wife] has been sufficiently legally incompetent since 1981 to be unable to file a lawsuit against [husband] for damages, and any statute of limitations which may have run prior to the filing of [wife's] counterclaim for the period from 1981 to the date of the filing of the countersuit were tolled because of such disability.

a. There was evidence of several incidents of assault and battery. In late 1984 when wife was pushing her finger in husband's chest, he grabbed her wrist and twisted it severely. In 1981 during an argument in their home husband grabbed wife and threw her face down across the room, into a pot full of dirt. In 1978 when wife was putting groceries in the camper, husband slammed part of the camper shell down on her head and the trunk lid on her hands. In 1976 and "sometimes thereafter" during consensual sexual intercourse husband would use excessive force in attempting to stimulate wife with his hands.

b. The one incident in which husband insulted wife in the presence of others was at a friend's Christmas party. At about 11:00 p.m. wife approached husband, who was "weaving back and forth with his hands in his pockets," and suggested that they go home. Husband began screaming, "You f___ bitch, leave me alone." Wife excused herself and walked home alone.

c. Wife also testified that when she and husband were home alone he would go into rages and scream at her. There was no evidence of his screaming at her in the presence of others except for the incident described in "b."

d. The locking-out incident occurred after husband returned from a trip. Wife had been at a friend's home where she had eaten dinner and had some wine. During an argument that had ensued when he returned, she grabbed his shirt and popped all the buttons off. She went downstairs and stepped outside. He closed and locked the door. She went across the street to a home of neighbors, who let her in. He then threw his clothes into a camper and drove off for the night. When he returned the next morning, they made up and made love.

e. On several occasions husband told wife that "you prefer women to men." He did not use the word "lesbian." He testified that he meant only that wife preferred the company of other women to his company. She did not testify that his remarks had sexual connotations.

f. Throughout the marriage husband made remarks such as, "You're just plain sick, you're just stupid, you're just insane."

g. With respect to the finding that husband "refused to allow [wife] to pursue schooling and hobbies," husband's brief-in-chief contends that no evidence supports the finding. Wife's answer brief does not respond to the contention, so we will not consider that finding as support for the judgment.

h., i. With respect to the final two items in the finding, husband acknowledges that their sexual relationship atrophied and that wife testified that (1) it was his decision not to engage in sexual relationships more frequently, and (2) he blamed her for their poor sexual relationship.

II. SHOULD WE RECOGNIZE THE TORT OF INTENTIONAL INFLICTION OF EMOTIONAL DISTRESS IN THE MARITAL CONTEXT?

A. Introduction

Husband argues that as a matter of public policy one spouse should have no cause of action against the other spouse for intentional infliction of emotional distress. Wife responds that husband's argument is foreclosed in this court by the New Mexico Supreme Court's recognition of the tort.

We reject, at least for the time being, the husband's suggestion. Nevertheless, the policy grounds opposing recognition of the tort in this context counsel caution in permitting lawsuits of this nature.

Wife contends that we must recognize the tort when committed by one spouse against the other because New Mexico has abandoned immunity for interspousal torts. . . .

Yet the abolition of immunity does not mean that the existence of the marriage must be ignored in determining the scope of liability. After explaining the reasons for abolition of interspousal immunity, the commentary to Restatement Section 895F points out:

> The intimacy of the family relationship may . . . involve some relaxation in the application of the concept of reasonable care, particularly in the confines of the home. Thus, if one spouse in undressing leaves shoes out where the other stumbles over them in the dark, or if one spouse spills coffee on the other while they are both still sleepy, this may well be treated as not negligence.

Id., comment h. The comment refers to Section 895G comment k, which explains that despite abolition of parental immunity:

The intimacies of family life also involve intended physical contacts that would be actionable between strangers but may be commonplace and expected within the family. Family romping, even roughhouse play and momentary flares of temper not producing serious hurt, may be normal in many households, to the point that the privilege arising from consent becomes analogous.

Thus, the family relationship can be an important consideration in analyzing intrafamilial torts, both negligent and intentional. Despite the abolition of interspousal immunity, we must still evaluate wife's claims in light of the marital context in which they arose. . . .

To appreciate the importance of the marital context to the tort of outrage, one must examine the policy considerations underlying restrictions on the scope of the tort. Perhaps the most striking aspect of the tort is that liability does not flow from every act that intends to cause, and does cause, emotional distress. One restriction on the tort is the limitation that the conduct be "extreme and outrageous." . . .

. . . Courts must recognize that we are not yet as civilized as we might wish. Many, if not all, of us need some freedom to vent emotions in order to maintain our mental health. The law should not require a degree of civility beyond our capacity. Indeed, it has been suggested that because of pervasive incivility in our society, judicial resources would be taxed if a cause of action were permitted for every intentional infliction of emotional distress. Givelber, The Right to Minimum Social Decency and the Limits of Evenhandedness: Intentional Infliction of Emotional Distress by Outrageous Conduct, 82 Colum. L. Rev. 42, 57 (1982).

Intentionally making another person unhappy or upset may also serve useful purposes besides simply preserving the mental health of the perpetrator. Professor Givelber notes, such conduct may be "justified either in pursuit of one's legal rights (e.g., debt collection) or in service of a greater social good (e.g., cross-examination at trial) or for the [recipient's] 'own good' (e.g., basic training)." Id. (footnote omitted). . . .

An additional reason for restricting the scope of the tort is that there may be a protected liberty interest in conduct that would otherwise be tortious. As Dean Prosser wrote, "There is still, in this country, such a thing as liberty to express an unflattering opinion of another, however wounding it may be to his feelings * * * ". . . . Similarly, the interest in personal autonomy apparently has led courts to reject a cause of action when a person intentionally causes emotional distress by engaging in an extramarital relationship. . . .

. . .

D. Application of the Tort to Interspousal Conduct

Considerations that justify limiting liability for intentional infliction of emotional distress to only outrageous conduct also suggest a very limited scope for the tort in the marital context.

Conduct intentionally or recklessly causing emotional distress to one's spouse is prevalent in our society. This is unfortunate but perhaps not surprising, given the length and intensity of the marital relationship. Yet even when the conduct of feuding spouses is not particularly unusual, high emotions can readily cause an offended spouse to view the other's misconduct as "extreme and outrageous." Thus, if the tort of outrage is construed loosely or broadly, claims of outrage may be tacked on in typical marital disputes, taxing judicial resources.

In addition, a spouse's most distressing conduct is likely to be privileged. Partners who are pledged to live together for a lifetime have a right to criticize each other's behavior. . . . Even though one may question the utility of such comments, spouses are also free to express negative opinions of one another. "You look awful" or even "I don't love you" can be very wounding, but these statements cannot justify liability. See Restatement § 46 illustration 13 (you look "like a hippopotamus").

Not only should intramarital activity ordinarily not be the basis for tort liability, it should also be protected against disclosure in tort litigation. Although the spouse who raises a claim of outrage has no right to complain of the exposure of matters relevant to the claim, courts must be sensitive to the interests of the defending spouse. Any litigation of a claim is certain to require exposure of the intimacies of married life. This feature of the tort distinguishes it from intramarital torts already recognized in New Mexico. For example, a suit by one spouse against another arising out of an automobile accident poses no such risk. Nor does one ordinarily think of exposure of an incident of battery as implicating legitimate privacy interests. In contrast, in this case the judge found that it was extreme and outrageous conduct for husband to refuse sexual relations with wife. Should we really use this tort as a basis for inquiry into a matter of such intimacy? Cf. Thompson v. Chapman, 93 N.M. 356, 600 P.2d 302 (Ct. App. 1979) (actions for alienation of affections engender more harm than good). In determining the scope of the tort of outrage in the marital context, it is necessary to consider the privacy interests of the accused spouse.

Moreover, because so much interspousal communication is privileged (not in the evidentiary sense, but in the sense that it cannot be the basis for liability), a reliable determination of causation is difficult if not impossible when outrage is alleged in this context. The connection between the outrageousness of the conduct of one spouse and the severe emotional distress of the other will likely be obscure. Although the victim spouse may well be suffering severe emotional distress, was it caused by the outrageousness of the conduct or by the implied (and privileged) message of antipathy? What could be more devastating to one's spouse than to say, "I don't love you any more"—a statement that could not form the basis for a cause of action? Rejection alone can create severe emotional distress. Suicides by jilted lovers are legion. Every adult knows individuals who have sunk into disabling depression when a spouse seeks divorce. As a result, litigation of an interspousal claim of outrage could easily degenerate into a battle of self-proclaimed experts performing psychological autopsies to "discover" whether the cause of the emotional distress was some particular despicable conduct or simply rejection by a loved one. Of course, no such problem arises in the context of previously recognized intramarital torts. If one spouse commits battery on another or causes an accident by driving negligently, the injuries to the other spouse can readily be tied to the tortious conduct.

In summary, concerns that necessitate limiting the tort of intentional infliction of emotional distress to "extreme and outrageous" conduct—(1) preventing burdensome litigation of the commonplace, (2) protecting privileged conduct and (3) avoiding groundless allegations of causation—argue strongly in favor of extreme care in recognizing intramarital claims of outrage.

A cautious approach to the tort of intramarital outrage also finds support in the public policy of New Mexico to avoid inquiry into what went wrong in a marriage. New Mexico was the first state to provide for no-fault divorce on the ground of incompatibility.... New Mexico apportions community property without regard to fault, ... and grants alimony without consideration of punishment to either spouse....

In addition, although the tort has not been formally abolished, our courts have expressed dissatisfaction with the tort of alienation of affection, which has features similar to the tort of outrage in the marital context....

E. Conclusion

Consequently, in determining when the tort of outrage should be recognized in the marital setting, the threshold of outrageousness should be set high enough—or the circumstances in which the tort is recognized should be described precisely enough, e.g., child snatching, ... —that the social good from recognizing the tort will not be outweighed by unseemly and invasive litigation of meritless claims.

Some jurisdictions have apparently set the threshold of outrageousness so high in the marital context as to bar all suits. See Whittington v. Whittington, 766 S.W. 2d 73 (Ky. Ct. App. 1989) (no tort of outrage for adultery and fraud by spouse): Wiener v. Wiener, 84 A.D. 2d 814, 444 N.Y.S.2d 130 (1981); Pickering v. Pickering, 434 N.W. 2d 758 (S.D. 1989) (barring tort of intentional infliction of emotional distress if predicated on conduct which leads to dissolution of marriage ...).

Thus far, however, New Mexico has not witnessed an onslaught of claims of outrage by one spouse against the other. There is no need at this time to adopt husband's recommendation that all such claims be barred.

III. DID WIFE PROVE OUTRAGE?

We now move to the specifics of the case before us. The merits of wife's claims can be disposed of summarily. Husband's insults and outbursts fail to meet the legal standard of outrageousness.... Restatement § 46, illustration 4 ("A makes a telephone call but is unable to get his number. In the course of an altercation with the telephone operator, A calls her a God damned woman, a God damned liar and says that if he were there he would break her God damned neck."); illustration 13 (you look "like a hippopotamus"). He was privileged to refrain from intercourse. There was no evidence that the other conduct caused severe emotional distress, as opposed to transient pain or discomfort....

Indeed, this case illustrates the risk of opening the door too wide to claims of this nature. Despite the claim's lack of merit, husband was subjected to a six-day trial, to say nothing of discovery and other preparation, surveying the rights and wrongs of a ten-year marriage. Motions for summary judgment should be viewed sympathetically in similar cases. If the potential harms from this kind of litigation are too frequently realized, it may be necessary to reconsider husband's suggestion that the tort of outrage be denied in the interspousal context.

We reverse the decision in favor of wife on her claim of intentional infliction of emotional distress.

NOTES AND QUESTIONS

1. Notice Judge Hartz's continuing reliance on an ideology of privacy in expressing his reservations about recognizing the tort of intentional infliction of emotional distress in the marital context.

2. The judge also expresses concern that domestic tort claims will undermine the policies promoted by no-fault divorce. In Ira Mark Ellman and Stephen D. Sugarman's article, *Spousal Emotional Abuse as a Tort*, 55 MD. L. REV. 1268, 1285–86 (1996), the authors share that concern:

> [A]nyone who favors no-fault divorce, believing that the legal process should not focus on recriminations and assigning blame, should oppose joining a spousal suit for outrageous marital conduct with the divorce action. Even if the suit is brought separately from the divorce action, it is likely that lawyers, as well as their clients, will be battling simultaneously over the tort suit and the divorce settlement, connecting them psychologically and strategically if not procedurally. Routine use of IIED tort claims would thus undermine one important rationale often offered for no-fault divorce.

There are two possible ways of responding to that argument. One is to question whether the policies underlying no-fault divorce should be given priority when the marriage leaves one partner damaged by abuse. The other is to argue that where possible the dissolution action should indeed retain its no-fault character, not least because that would usually be the desire of the abused as well as the abusive partner, but that a separate tort action should also be permitted, preferably after the divorce is final. The extent to which courts have found this argument troubling is discussed in Section D, below.

3. What do you make of the contrast between Judge Hartz's comfort in recognizing the tort of battery between spouses, and his discomfort in recognizing the tort of intentional infliction of emotional distress? How should we then understand his failure to consider the physical abuse in the Hakkilas' relationship as both one potent source of emotional distress, and an indicator that Mr. Hakkila's behavior has crossed the line between "rejecting" his wife, or making her unhappy, and engaging in "outrageous" conduct? What about his use of the telephone operator and "hippopotamus" examples from the Restatement? Do you get the sense that he has understood the abusive nature of Mr. Hakkila's relationship with his wife?

Interestingly, Ellman and Sugarman, in the article mentioned in the last note, follow Hartz's lead in describing *Hakkila* as a case that is about a "bullying," but not a physically abusive, relationship. Id. at 1312–18. They would go further than Hartz, and recognize not only spousal battery but intentional infliction of emotional distress in the context of physical abuse, but their inability, and the judge's, to recognize that *Hakkila* is such a case raises doubts about the workability of that distinction. *Their* concern is that going further, and allowing claims between spouses based "solely" on emotional abuse, will leave courts imposing value-laden and inconsistent standards of marital conduct, and invite "virtually all discontented, divorcing spouses to try their chance at the lottery." Id. at 1321. Do you share this concern? Are there ways to guard against it, other than restricting IIED recovery between intimates to cases in which it is linked to physical abuse? Later in their article Ellman and Sugarman suggest that perhaps recovery for IIED should depend on the defendant's conduct being criminal. Id. at 1135. Is that a significantly different or better standard?

3. There is no indication in the *Hakkila* opinion that expert testimony was introduced to support Mrs. Hakkila's claims. With the benefit of hindsight, do you think such testimony might have been useful? What should the expert have been asked to cover in that testimony?

Some answers to those questions can be found in the next case, Curtis v. Firth, which is a plaintiff's success story, and provides a striking contrast to *Hakkila*. Sandra Firth was the first woman to collect damages from an abuser in the State of Idaho. The case was also the first in the state to use battered women's syndrome testimony in a civil matter. The Supreme Court of Idaho not only recognized the tort of intentional infliction of emotional distress within a marriage-like relationship, but defined it as a continuing tort for purposes of the relevant statute of limitations. The fact that the parties had never married made it unnecessary for the court to wrestle with any relationship between the tort action and an action for divorce.

Curtis v. Firth

123 Idaho 598, 850 P.2d 749.
Supreme Court of Idaho, 1993.

■ Opinion by TROUT, J.

BACKGROUND AND PRIOR PROCEEDINGS

This appeal arose from a district court action for personal injury and a cross action for collection of a promissory note, which was the culmination of ongoing litigation between a man and a woman who had shared a home and intimate relations over a period of ten years. Appellant Carl Curtis and respondent Sandra Firth . . . began living together in Curtis' home in May of 1978. While the relationship began as a very loving one, the periods of happiness became less prevalent over time and were replaced by antagonism and violence. The couple's behavior was characterized by cycles of violence which commenced with Curtis becoming irritated and angry; then turning to verbal and sometimes physical abuse, and finally ending with him becoming loving again. Throughout much of this time, both Curtis and Firth turned to alcohol and drugs for entertainment or solace. Although the parties participated in counseling in an attempt to resolve their problems, the relationship continued to deteriorate. In 1988, while Firth was vacationing in California, Curtis evicted her from his home.

In the initial phase of this litigation, Firth sought to establish a common law marriage, and brought an action for divorce and the division of all marital property. After a trial on the merits, the trial court determined that no common law marriage had been established because the parties had not held themselves out in the community as husband and wife.

Although the court denied Firth an interest in Curtis' personal and real property, Curtis was ordered to pay significant financial support for rehabilitative purposes as well as Firth's attorney fees.

In a subsequent phase of the litigation, Firth brought a personal injury action seeking damages for battery and intentional infliction of emotional distress. She also sought punitive damages. At trial, she presented extensive expert testimony regarding Battered Wife Syndrome and Post Traumatic Stress Disorder. The jury returned a verdict in favor of Firth, awarding her $50,000 in compensatory damages for battery, $225,000 for intentional infliction of emotional distress, and $725,000 in punitive damages. Curtis appealed.

. . .

II. Trial Issues

Intentional Infliction of Emotional Distress

Curtis contends that Firth's claim for intentional infliction of emotional distress must fail because there was an insufficient showing of an accompanying physical injury or manifestation.

Unlike a claim for negligent infliction of emotional distress which requires a showing of physical injury or manifestation, . . . a claim for intentional infliction of emotional distress has no such requirement. As we [have] noted . . .:

> The four elements which a plaintiff must show to be able to recover for intentional infliction of emotional distress are: 1) the conduct must be intentional or reckless; 2) the conduct must be extreme and outrageous; 3) there must be a causal connection between the wrongful conduct and the emotional distress; and 4) the emotional distress must be severe.

. . .

Although evidence of physical harm may bear on the severity of emotional harm, . . . it is clear that evidence of physical injury or manifestation is not a required element for the claim of intentional infliction of emotional distress. . . . [A]ccordingly, Curtis' argument in this regard is without merit.

Statute of Limitations

Curtis asserts that much of Firth's claim for intentional infliction of emotional distress was barred by the statute of limitations, and that the trial court's failure to instruct the jury on the defense was reversible error. It is well established that a party asserting the affirmative defense of statute of limitations has the burden of proving the applicability of the statute. . . .

Regarding Curtis' claim, the trial court remarked in its memorandum decision:

> With respect to the court's decision to omit the statute of limitations instruction, the court notes at the outset that the proposed instruction was not even submitted by the [appellant]. Prior to the instruction conference, the court ruled that the tort of intentional or reckless infliction of emotional distress is a continuing tort. On that basis, the instruction was refused. The court is still of the opinion that refusal of the instruction was proper and as a result sees no basis for a new trial.

In Page v. United States, 729 F.2d 818, 821–22 (D.C. Cir. 1984), the court succinctly described the theory of continuing tort:

> It is well-settled that "[w]hen a tort involves continuing injury, the cause of action accrues, and the limitation period begins to run, at the time the tortious conduct ceases." Since usually no single incident in a continuous chain of tortious activity can "fairly or realistically be identified as the cause of significant harm," it seems proper to regard the cumulative effect of the conduct as actionable. Moreover, since "one should not be allowed to acquire a right to continue the tortious conduct," it follows logically that statutes of limitation should not run prior to its cessation.

Page involved allegations by a veteran that the Veteran's Administration subjected him to harmful drugs over a period of years. The court reviewed a number of cases in which the courts recognized the continuing tort doctrine where the tortious acts were ongoing, as distinguished from cases where the injuries continue after the tortious acts cease. The court held:

> We view the injury claimed by Page as gradual, resulting from the cumulative impact of years of allegedly tortious drug treatment. To us it seems unrealistic to regard each prescription of drugs as the cause of a separate injury, or as a separate tortious act triggering a new limitation period. Page charges precisely the sort of continuous conduct accreting physical and mental injury that justifies characterization as a continuing tort. Resultingly, the cause of action Page stakes on continuous drug treatment did not accrue, and the statutory limitations did not come into play, until the allegedly tortious conduct came to a halt in 1980.

As we have indicated previously, the definition of intentional infliction of emotional distress requires that there must be a causal connection between the wrongful conduct and the emotional distress, and the emotional distress must be severe.... By its very nature this tort will often involve a series of acts over a period of time, rather than one single act causing severe emotional distress. For that reason we recognize the concept of continuing tort ... should be extended to apply in other limited contexts, including particularly intentional infliction of emotional distress. We note, however, that embracing this concept in the area of intentional or negligent infliction of emotional distress does not throw open the doors to permit filing these actions at any time. The courts which have adopted this continuing tort theory have generally stated that the statute of limitations is only held in abeyance until the tortious acts cease.... At that point the statute begins to run. If at some point after the statute has run the tortious acts begin again, a new cause of action may arise, but only as to those damages which have accrued since the new tortious conduct began.

In applying the concept of continuing tort to the case before us we note at the outset that there was no objection by Curtis at trial to the testimony of Firth and others concerning the ongoing abusive actions of Curtis which began as early as 1980 and continued throughout their relationship. This is not a case where the wrongful acts, severe emotional distress and damages occurred at the same time and suit could have been brought when the actions first took place.

There was testimony that it was not until 1986 that the more severe psychological injuries were beginning according to Dr. Walker. Roberta Sawyer Betts, a marriage and family counselor who counseled both Curtis and Firth periodically between August 1986 and May, 1990, also testifies at trial that Firth's symptoms were excessive and not what she would normally expect to see when people go through a difficult divorce. All witnesses agree that the tortious acts ceased when Curtis evicted Firth from his home in early 1988. As this litigation was commenced shortly thereafter, it clearly falls within the two year statute of limitations for this action.

When there is no substantial evidence to support a claim, the trial court may withdraw that issue and not instruct the jury on it.... We believe that there was no substantial evidence to support Curtis' claim that the intentional infliction of emotional distress action was barred by the statute of limitations and we, therefore, affirm the trial court's refusal to so instruct.

Submission of Punitive Damages to the Jury

Curtis asserts that punitive damages were not warranted in this case, and that the trial court erred by submitting the issue of punitive damages to the jury. It is well established that punitive damages are not favored in the law and should be awarded in the most compelling and unusual circumstances, and are to be awarded cautiously and within narrow limits....

The decision of whether to submit the question of punitive damages to a jury rests with the sound discretion of the trial court.... In reviewing the trial court's decision we examine the sufficiency of the evidence and determine whether the record contains substantial evidence to support an award of punitive damages....:

> An award of punitive damages will be sustained on appeal only when it is shown that the defendant acted in a manner that was "an extreme deviation from reasonable standards of conduct, and that the act was performed by the defendant with an understanding of or disregard for its likely consequences." The justification for punitive damages must be that the defendant acted with an extremely harmful state of mind, whether that state be termed "malice, oppression, fraud or gross negligence"; "malice, oppression, wantonness"; or simply "deliberate or willful." ...

. . . In the instant case, we are satisfied that the trial court did not abuse its discretion in presenting the issue of punitive damages to the jury. As discussed later in this opinion, there was extensive evidence presented at trial concerning Curtis' conduct toward Firth during their ten years together. We believe that there was substantial evidence presented on which a jury could have found Curtis' conduct to be an extreme deviation from reasonable standards of conduct. Similarly, the jury could have found that Curtis acted with malice, oppression, wantonness, or gross negligence. Accordingly, we hold that the trial court did not err in submitting the issue of punitive damages to the jury.

III. Post-Trial Motions

Judgment Notwithstanding the Verdict

At the risk of subjecting the parties to additional public scrutiny of their private lives, it is necessary to recount some of the testimony which relates to this issue. Several witnesses attested to Firth's conservative attitudes regarding sex and substance abuse prior to her relationship with Curtis. They further testified that she was very family oriented, and even took her younger brother in and raised him after their mother died. She was portrayed as a kind, good-hearted, hard-working woman who would do anything for family or friends. After she quit her job and moved in with Curtis, witnesses told of her continuing efforts to try and please him. She learned to cook the way he liked, she organized parties for his friends, she decorated the new house he built and worried about spending too much money on household expenses.

Firth also testified at length about the efforts she made to get along with Curtis. Despite those efforts, Curtis was an almost constant source of criticism. He complained that his socks were not in his drawer, his shirts were not cleaned, his bathroom sink was not cleaned, the tags were not clipped off his shirts, his food was poorly prepared and that Firth spent too much money. All of these criticisms might pass as the trials of everyday life between two cohabiting people, for which Curtis argues we should expect tolerance. . . . There was more to this relationship, though, than might be expected as part of daily existence.

The testimony of Firth and Dr. Walker reflected a relationship between the parties which became progressively more depraved. While Curtis' sexual appetite was known to Firth from the beginning of their relationship, the type of sexual practices in which he chose to engage changed over time. Even though she was sickened at the nature of his activities, Firth chose to drug herself and participate in an effort to please and get along with Curtis. She testified to being videotaped during sexual activities, being forced to engage in sexual acts which she found repugnant and to being sexually assaulted.

There was also extensive testimony about mental abuse which Curtis inflicted on Firth. She and several witnesses testified that on numerous occasions Curtis would publicly and loudly scream at Firth if she displeased him. On some occasions she could identify the conduct which displeased him, such as Curtis not liking her cooking; but frequently she had no idea what made him angry or when he might start using profanities toward her. She also identified incidents where Curtis physically shook her so hard she feared she would fall off a boat dock, placed his foot in her back and kicked her out of bed, slapped her on the buttocks hard enough to leave a hand print, and pulled her hair as he threw her against the sink. Dr. Walker testified, without objection, to these incidents as well as to Curtis' anally raping Firth.

These incidents were sufficient to lead Dr. Walker, a well known specialist in dealing with battered women, to diagnose Firth as suffering from Post Traumatic Stress Disorder. In so doing, she distinguished between a dysfunctional marriage relationship and an actual battering relationship. We find there was evidence to support the conclusion that these actions by Curtis went far beyond the acceptable trials and tribulations of daily life and into the area of severe, extreme and outrageous conduct. We believe there was sufficient evidence by which the jury could conclude that Curtis' conduct was beyond that which a reasonable person should be expected to tolerate or endure.

Curtis' defense to the allegations seems to be that Firth enjoyed these activities and was a willing participant. It is obvious from the testimony and jury verdict, that the jury chose not to believe him and instead chose to believe Firth. Curtis now asks us to second guess the jury and to place more weight on his testimony. This is not the standard for reviewing a trial court's ruling on a motion for judgment notwithstanding the verdict. Based upon the foregoing, we find that there was sufficient evidence upon which the jury could arrive at a verdict in favor of Firth and the trial court committed no error in so concluding.

. . .

NOTES

1. When Sandra Firth's lawyers first began talking with her about her dispute with Carl Curtis, she did not identify abuse as an issue. Her original action was a request for a divorce from a common law marriage, and for property division. Quite early, however, her lawyers began to suspect that she was a battered woman, and, with her permission, arranged for an assessment. In a second round of litigation, she filed the tort action. An initial award of $1,000,000; $50,000 for battery, $225,000 for intentional infliction of emotional distress, and $725,000 in punitive damages, was reaffirmed by the trial court after remand for rehearing and additional findings, and upheld by the Supreme Court in the opinion you have just read.

Dr. Lenore Walker's "assessment" of Sandra Firth was a crucial step in freeing her up to talk about the abuse she had suffered, first in the relationship of trust built with Walker, then with her lawyers, and finally in open court. The trial court also allowed Walker to recount the abuse as Firth had shared it with her, reinforcing its impact on the judge and jury.

In the description of Walker's testimony that follows, the quotations are taken from the trial transcript.[1]

In meeting the requirement that the conduct productive of emotional distress be "outrageous," Walker likened Curtis' treatment of Firth to psychological torture, as defined by Amnesty International:

> [The definition] includes nine different psychologically abusive or nine different ways of being psychologically abusive, and I'll list them here.
>
> The first one is one that they call verbal degradation. That's put-downs, name calling, using words to be verbally aggressive and to make somebody feel very bad about themselves
>
> The second one is called the denial of powers. And those are also ... psychological cruelty, [by] telling someone that they don't do things right: That they don't cook right, that they don't clean right, that they don't take care of the children properly, that they're not very good at what they're supposed to do. They don't do sex right , whatever it is. And so those are the kinds of comments that come into denial of powers.
>
> The third one is isolation, and that's a systematic isolating a woman from a support system. Sometimes putting wedges between herself and her family, oftentimes making her not have as many friends, commenting on her friendships and increasing amounts of time that she spends with the batterer, so that she has less of a support system [from] outside.
>
> Now, that is also connected with the next one, which is called monopolizing her perceptions or making her think the way he thinks. And that, to some extent, also comes under ... trying to have mind control....
>
> The fifth one is one they call hypnosis. But you can also call it just mind control itself. Hypnosis is really just the intense focus and concentration in a particular area. And if you're monopolizing someone's perceptions, you're isolating them....
>
> The next one are [sic] threats to kill, and they're often direct and indirect kinds of threats to kill. Sometimes it's simply implied, that the woman knows he could kill her at any time.
>
> The next one is what's called induced debility. That means doing things that makes the woman feel that she's less strong physically. Sometimes it's doing it [directly], like waking her up in the middle of the night and haranguing her or forcing her into long hours of sex. Sometimes it's not letting her eat well. Sometimes it's not directly preventing her from eating but so much distress around mealtime that she's unable to eat. And oftentimes it's increasing the stress and the pressure when she begins to develop some physical kinds of symptoms and stress-related symptoms.

1. This note draws extensively on an unpublished student paper written in 1994 by Sara Shepard, of American University's Washington College of Law.

> Now the eighth one are [sic] drugs and alcohol. . . .
>
> . . .
>
> And then the last one were [sic] occasional indulgences. So that you couldn't have it all bad in order to create the effect, you needed to have some of the positive effects or indulgences.

Despite the power of this testimony, the opinion by Justice Trout suggests that the court may have been especially influenced by the details of the sexual abuse suffered by Firth, and the "depraved" nature of the sexual demands made by Curtis. Verbal abuse alone, the court indicates, "might pass as the trials of everyday life between two co-habiting people." This is a troublesome note in an otherwise sensitive opinion.

On the issue of the severity of the distress suffered by Firth, Walker was able to make effective use of objective assessment tools. She used the Minnesota Multiphasic Personality Inventory to plot Firth's emotional state on a scale, and compare it to the emotional state characteristic of the overall population. By this measure, Firth's "scores" were clinically significant. While her answers were within the normal range on the three scales used by test-givers to demonstrate the validity or credibility of a test-taker's answers, her scores on six of the remaining ten scales were "clinically significant," or within the top two percent of the population. These scales measure: 1) body symptoms or somatic complaints, 2) depression, 3) hysteria or need to demonstrate distress, 4) anger and family discord, 5) traditional male/female stereotypes, 6) suspiciousness and paranoid ideation, 7) rumination and obsessive thinking, 8) schizophrenia or confused thinking, 9) mania or anxiety, and 10) sociability.

Looking at a chart of Firth's results, Walker testified:

> Now, this particular profile, if you just looked at this with one graph and you looked at the clinical scales, you see one, two, three, four, five, six out of ten clinical scales that are above a seventy. If you only looked at this MMPI and you did not . . . have a history, which is not, of course, a recommended way to do it, but if you just looked at it, anybody who looked at it would probably say that this is a profile of somebody who was demonstrating an extreme level of emotional disturbance, such an extreme level that we might even suggest that this person was totally psychotic and ought to be hospitalized because so many clinical scales were elevated.
>
> . . .
>
> And of course when I evaluated Sandra Firth she was not [psychotic]. . . .
>
> . . . And then you have to say: Okay, if that's true, why would these profiles, why would these particular clinical scales, be elevated? . . .

In answer to her own question, the expert suggests that Firth's results are consistent with the conclusion that she is suffering from posttraumatic stress disorder. As Walker related the symptoms that play a part in the diagnosis of PTSD, she is also giving the jury a detailed listing of some of the damage done by Curtis:

> [T]here are recurrent and intrusive memories, ... they just pop into your head. Sometimes it's associated with something and sometimes it may not be. You may be sitting very calmly and all of a sudden you get a flashback or something that pops into your head. And in this particular case, that did occur.
>
> . . .
>
> ... [S]omeone suddenly acts or feels like they are reexperiencing the whole trauma all over again, so it's not just the intrusive memory but it's actually thinking it's happening when you know better, you know it's not....
>
> And we know a lot about flashbacks from ... the literature on Vietnam veterans, where they might be out ... and hear a helicopter and think they're back in Vietnam again.
>
> So, in this particular case, we do have dissociations. We did have flashbacks.
>
> . . .
>
> [Another symptom] is avoiding thoughts or feelings about the trauma or about the battering, and that did take place. In fact there was a great deal of minimization and denial when Sandra first came in at the beginning of the evaluation. She had a great deal of difficulty in even talking about or remembering some of the incidents....
>
> . . .
>
> There was also psychogenic amnesia. That means that your mind just simply forgets some part of the abuse because it's just too much to have to remember all of it. And that was present.
>
> There was also marked diminished ... interest in significant activities.
>
> And that was also true. Sandra began to do less and less, giving up more and more things to try and make that relationship work.
>
> There was also a feeling of detached [sic] or estrangement from other people. Her relationships with others changed and still is changed. That's one of the areas that has, I think, been permanently damaged. It's much more difficult for Sandra to trust other people and to make relationships with people.
>
> . . .
>
> And then a sense of foreshortened future, a belief that you won't live without this relationship and you won't live with the relationship, just this sense that life is ... that you're going to die, somehow. That life is not going to go well. And indeed, that did happen during this relationship. And at the time of my evaluation I still saw some of that, including some serious suicidal thoughts that Sandra had.

... [I]n the middle of the night she would call me, very suicidal, and would need some reassurance, some connection with somebody else so that she would not feel as though she was going to die.

And that was part of it. She would have nightmares. She'd get into extreme anxiety attacks and panic attacks and believe that she was going to die. And some of the suicide was, she wanted to have more control over it. If she was going to die anyhow, she might as well do it herself. And that is still a serious problem for her.

. . .

... And then [there] are the arousal symptoms....

... We're talking about anxiety.... Where the organism is aroused to protect itself.

That there's danger that's perceived all the time.... Sandra's sleep was interfered with. It was interfered with both by the sexual abuse and by her difficulty with anxiety, from very high anxiety and from nightmares and night terrors, that she had difficulty in both falling asleep and in staying asleep.

. . .

I also saw difficulty in concentrating. It was harder for her to think because there were so many other things interfering with her ability to think. She certainly has the intellectual ability, but it's interfered with by the emotional factors.

And that's still true today. She's been going back to school and taking courses. She's doing all right with them but it's a real struggle for her because she's not consistently able to concentrate, as you often need to. She has periods where she is very efficient and other periods where she's not.

Hypervigilance to cues of danger is an important characteristic for battered woman syndrome. Here, women, because they've been through this repeatedly, learn a lot of coping strategies. And they learn how to sense before a battering incident is going to occur....

And Sandra still is very hypervigilant to cues of danger and is easily scared at times, ... she sees it [faster] than other people do.... It's not unreasonable.

The exaggerated startle response also goes with that. And she's much more easily spooked, much more nervous about things.

. . .

... When I saw her [the symptoms] were still in existence. And today, two years even after I saw her and little over two and a half years ... or so after the relationship broke up, there are still a number of those characteristics, indicating some long lasting or maybe permanent damage from the trauma.

The cumulative effect of this testimony is to establish beyond challenge that Firth has suffered severe emotional distress. To complete her task, however, Walker must also confront the doubt often expressed by judges, and presumably experienced by juries, about whether distress resulting from abuse can properly be separated from distress caused by the termination of a long-term relationship. Curtis had presented expert testimony to the effect that what Firth was experiencing was distress over the breakup of their relationship. Walker discusses this causation issue from two different angles in the course of her testimony. First, she suggests, it is possible to ascertain causation by examining the levels of distress experienced by Firth. Second, it is possible to ascertain causation by examining the kinds of conduct which might be used to produce those levels of distress. Again, the objective assessment tools available to Walker provide a reassuringly "scientific" basis for her conclusion that Firth's symptoms are explicable only as the result of severe and continuing abuse:

> For example, ... when you're trying to diagnose whether it's simply a marriage that's falling apart, a dysfunctional marriage relationship, you want to differentiate between the two. And that particular chart helps you to do that. The rating scale goes from a zero to a six. The highest is a six....
>
> . . .
>
> ... [A] marital separation would be a three on that chart, or a moderate level of stress.
>
> ... We would expect a certain amount of distress from people who separate and leave a marital or marriage-like relationship, as this one was. But [Sandra Firth's stress is] a level five, or extreme ... which would be the stress that would be expected from ongoing physical and/or sexual abuse in a marriage.
>
> . . .
>
> Q: So if I understand this testimony, are you saying, then, if you reach five or six, then, more likely than not, the problem that she's experiencing is not due to leaving the relationship but it's due to something more serious, like the PTSD?
>
> A: That's correct. That's correct.

Finally, Walker's account of the cumulative damage done by Curtis' abuse over an extended period of time lends credibility to the argument that the conduct at issue amounted to a continuing tort. As Firth's brief stated:

> This is a case where the only way of presenting it is on the 'continuing tort' theory because that is exactly what we have. This case is a claim for damages for Intentional Infliction of Emotional Distress. That emotional distress was caused by the inducement of Post Traumatic Stress Disorder which by definition is a disorder which usually is induced by repeated acts of trauma over a long period of time.

By happenstance, Walker testified on the first day of the trial, because she would otherwise have been unavailable and the court was willing to accommodate her schedule. Firth's lawyers feel that this distinctly helped her case—the expert was able to dispel some illusions and create a framework within which Sandra Firth's own testimony could be heard in an unbiased and even sympathetic way. This offers a useful strategic lesson—the order in which testimony is heard may be almost as important as whether it is heard at all.

2. The success of cases like *Curtis* makes it seem that perhaps intentional infliction of emotional distress can provide a safe home for tort actions based on partner violence, as long as judges and juries can be educated about the difference between an unhappy relationship and an abusive one, and about the high emotional costs of sustained abuse. The willingness of courts to treat intentional infliction as a continuing tort, and look at the cumulative effect of patterns of behavior, seems to offer a way around the common road blocks imposed by statutes of limitation. However, this strategy does leave in the air the question of recovery for physical injury and property damage. If these claims could be brought within the relatively short limitation periods traditionally attached to battery and conversion, of course, they would pose no particular problem. More typically, however, the partner does not sue until she has already endured years of abuse, and risks being told that she is too late to recover for her injuries, for any resulting physical disability, and for the possessions he has destroyed, or the repairs she has had to pay for.

There are essentially three possible ways around this problem. The first is to ground the claim as one for intentional infliction of emotional distress, but use a punitive damage claim as a substitute for concrete losses that cannot be recouped. Arguably this was the strategy employed in *Curtis*. The second is to develop an argument that the statute of limitations should be "tolled." The last and most risky is to ask the court to create a new "continuing "tort of domestic abuse, and recognize the accumulating injuries, physical, economic and emotional, that have been inflicted over the course of the relationship. Statutes of limitation and tolling arguments are the topic of the next section, and tentative movements in the direction of creating a new tort are taken up in the following one.

C. STATUTES OF LIMITATION AND TOLLING

In cases in which a victim of partner abuse has been in a long-term relationship with her abuser, she is highly unlikely to sue until she is leaving or has left him. At this point, the statute of limitations may already have run with respect to many of the incidents of abuse in which she suffered injury. Actions for battery or assault must usually be brought within one or two years. Sometimes emotional distress claims carry the same limitations period, and sometimes a longer one; the range is between one and six years. The more standard period for negligence actions is three years. The reasons for these distinctions are generally not articulated, and not obvious; their variability from state to state suggests that the choice of period may in fact be quite arbitrary.

Ironically, while interspousal tort immunity was still the rule, reformist courts could argue that the immunity ended with the end of the marriage, and that the statute of limitations was also tolled until that time. Once the immunity is abolished, the abused partner has no technical reason to postpone suit, and may lose the advantage of that tolling rule. From a policy perspective, this may be a mistake:

> [T]o the extent victims remain in abusive relationships out of the desire to make them work—seeking to end the violence without ending the relationship—they are expressing the very values that supported the old interspousal tort immunity. In essence, they are seeking to restore marital harmony to a relationship disrupted by violence. The immunity was flawed in imposing that value on marital partners, whether or not they shared it. But to the extent an abused partner embraces that value as her own, we should not penalize her by jeopardizing her ability to recover for her injuries if her efforts are sabotaged by further abuse. Rather, the legal system should recognize her efforts by preserving her right to sue.

Clare Dalton, *Domestic Violence, Domestic Torts and Divorce: Constraints and Possibilities,* 31 NEW ENG. L. REV. 321, 360 (1997).

Parties to recent suits have tried in a variety of ways to overcome the substantial barriers created by restrictive limitation periods. One strategy, discussed above, is to use an emotional distress claim and downplay the availability of other claims, taking advantage of the widespread recognition that the infliction of emotional distress is a continuing tort, so that the statute of limitations does not begin to run until the abuse ends. The strategy of arguing for recognition of a new cause of action for a continuing tort of abuse (both emotional and physical) is reserved for discussion in the next section. Here we describe other possible tolling arguments, in particular duress and insanity.

Duress

If an abused partner fails to take action against her abuser because she is afraid of him, her argument for tolling applicable statutes of limitation is an argument based on duress. Even if her abuser does not say in so many words: "Sue me and you are dead," or: "Tell anyone what I've done to you and you'll pay for it," the underlying theory is the same. She fears, with reason, that any action taken to separate herself from her abuser, or confront him with his abuse, will result in serious injury or death to her, and for the time being she chooses what appears to be the lesser of two evils. In the New Jersey case of Giovine v. Giovine, 284 N.J. Super. 3; 663 A.2d 109 (N.J. Super. App. Div. 1995), the court recognized a new continuing tort of partner abuse (infliction of battered woman's syndrome). In its opinion, however, the court also endorsed tolling in the context of duress, when the duress "is either an element of or inherent in the underlying cause of action." Id., 663 A.2d at 116. The court stated that "within certain limits, a prospective defendant's coercive acts and threats may rise to such a level of duress as to deprive the plaintiff of his freedom of will and thereby toll the statute of limitations." Id.

You have read enough of battered women's attempts to invoke duress in both the child welfare context (Chapter 6, above) and the criminal justice context (Chapter 10, above), to know that judges and juries often require express threats of imminent violence before they will exonerate battered women of criminal wrongdoing on the basis of duress. The more subtle and pervasive atmosphere of terror created by an abusive partner often fails to meet standards for duress established in cases of the "gun to the head" model of coercion. So too in this different context; it is often hard for women to persuade judges that their fear was both strong and imminent enough, over an extended period of time, to prevent them from filing suit. This difficulty is exacerbated when the woman continues to delay the filing of a suit, even after she has separated from her abuser.

Perhaps because of these difficulties, it is hard to find cases in which victims of domestic violence argue duress as a basis for tolling a statute of limitations. This next case, however, decided in the rather different context of childhood sexual abuse, illustrates the potential for duress arguments in both situations.

Jones v. Jones

242 N.J. Super. 195; 576 A.2d 316.
Superior Court of New Jersey, Appellate Division, 1990.

■ Opinion by: Baime, J.A.D.

... Plaintiff Susan Jones (Susan) ... instituted this action seeking compensatory and punitive damages against her parents, alleging that her father, Robert Jones (Robert), with the connivance of her mother, Sarah Jones (Sarah), sexually abused her over a protracted period of time.... The Law Division judge granted summary judgment, ... finding that the two-year statute of limitations had expired under N.J.S.A. 2A:14–2.

At issue is whether the mental trauma suffered by plaintiff as the result of her father's alleged sexual misconduct serves to toll the statute of limitations. Closely intertwined with this question is whether the duress allegedly exerted by plaintiff's father had the effect of extending the limitations period.

We hold that factual questions were presented with respect to whether the psychological sequelae flowing from the alleged acts of sexual abuse were so severe as to constitute "insanity" under N.J.S.A. 2A:14–21, thereby extending the period of limitations. We also conclude that genuine issues of material fact were raised as to whether defendants' allegedly coercive acts and threats were such as to deprive plaintiff of her free will and whether such duress was so compelling as to toll the statute of limitations

Our recital of the facts is derived from the pleadings as well as the certifications and affidavits submitted by plaintiff in opposition to defendants' motion for summary judgment. Defendants Robert and Sarah are the natural parents of Susan....

We need not recount at length the sordid facts relating to Robert's alleged sexual misconduct. According to Susan, her father commenced this course when she was approximately 11 years old. Initially, Robert allegedly found various excuses to have Susan sleep in his bed with him. During this period, Robert is alleged to have perpetrated several acts of sexual abuse short of penetration, repeatedly impressing upon Susan the need for secrecy. Susan claims that the two ultimately engaged in sexual intercourse and continued this pattern on a regular basis "at least once a week."

According to Susan, she "lived in terror of Robert" throughout the years of abuse. Fearful of continuation of the incestuous relationship, Susan claims that she was even more panicked over the prospect of disclosure. "Racked with guilt and shame and terrified lest anyone learn of her secret," Susan asserts that she ultimately repressed all awareness of her incestuous relationship with her father.

Susan contends that Robert repeatedly threatened to kill her if she were to disclose his acts of abuse. According to Susan, her father regularly beat her in order to reinforce these threats. On several occasions, Robert allegedly attempted to suffocate her. Susan claims that these acts continued until the early months of 1983. In her certification, Susan alleged that she "still ha[s] nightmares" after which she awakes "sweating and shaking," thinking that her father "is coming after [her]."

According to Susan, the sexual abuse, which in its later stages is said to have taken the form of forcible rape, continued unabated over the years. In 1983, however, Susan began to receive counselling from Jean Heller, a psychiatric social worker at Riverview Hospital. Heller's notes for August 21, 1984 indicate that Susan, for the first time, revealed her father's alleged acts of sexual abuse. Susan claims that in September 1984 she "finally broke loose from the prison of mental and physical dependence" and was able to recount the details of her incestuous relationship with her father.

On October 4, 1984 Susan filed a criminal complaint, alleging Robert's sexual assaults. As a result, Robert was arrested.... Susan's allegations of sexual abuse were presented to a grand jury which returned a "no bill," apparently because the statute of limitations had expired.

. . .

On October 11, 1985 Susan ... commenced the present action. Factually, the allegations contained in the complaint are crystal clear. Susan contends that beginning in her childhood, her father embarked upon a course of sexual abuse which continued into her adulthood and culminated in the birth of [a daughter,] Jane. In a legal sense, the complaint is inartfully drafted by original counsel. Apparently, Susan seeks compensatory and punitive damages based upon legal theories of battery, intentional infliction of emotional distress, "wrongful birth" with respect to her independent claim, and "wrongful life" as to the cause of action asserted on behalf of Jane. We need not probe further into the substance of the causes of action alleged since the sole issue presented here pertains to the statute of limitations.

In this respect, we note that it is essentially undisputed that the last acts of alleged sexual abuse occurred in January 1983, when Susan left her parents' home. As we mentioned earlier, Jane was born in 1976. The complaint was thus filed two years and nine months from the date of the last act of alleged sexual misconduct and some nine years following Jane's birth. Defendants moved for summary judgment, claiming that the statute of limitations had expired.

... With respect to her independent claims, Susan did not differentiate between her causes of action for battery, infliction of emotional distress and wrongful birth. As to all of her claims, Susan asserted that the limitations period was tolled by reason of her "insanity." More specifically, Susan claimed that the mental trauma caused by her father's sexual abuse was so disabling as to impair her ability to institute her action prior to the expiration of the statute of limitations.

In support of her assertion, Susan presented the treatment notes of her psychologist, who was seriously ill and thus unable to provide a personal certification. Susan also submitted the affidavit of Howard Silverman, a psychologist. Although Dr. Silverman had not examined Susan, it was his opinion that individuals subjected to childhood sexual abuse often find it impossible to communicate and describe such misconduct. According to Dr. Silverman, "psychological disability on the part of the victims [is] common."

Susan further claimed that her father's coercive acts, physical assaults and explicit threats served to excuse her failure to institute suit in a timely fashion. She asserted that the duress exerted by defendants was so compelling as to prevent her from filing suit within the limitations period.

The Law Division judge granted defendants' motion for summary judgment, finding as a matter of law, that Susan was able to file a complaint at least as of the date she left her parents' home in January 1983. Since two years and nine months had passed from that date, the judge determined that Susan's independent causes of action were time-barred....

We are convinced that the issues raised by Susan's allegations of mental impairment and duress should not have been resolved in summary fashion. Instead, a plenary hearing should have been conducted.

We reach this conclusion notwithstanding our recognition of the salutary purposes served by a statute of limitations. The most important of these purposes is the security and stability of human affairs created by eventual repose.... Separate from the interest of repose is the prospective defendants' ability to respond to allegations made against them. By penalizing unreasonable delay, "such statutes induce litigants to pursue their claims diligently so that answering parties will have a fair opportunity to defend." ... So too, statutes of limitations "spare the courts from litigation of stale claims." ... "Once memories fade, witnesses become unavailable, and evidence is lost, courts no longer possess the capacity to distinguish valid claims from those which are frivolous or vexatious." ...

We emphasize, however, that the effect of a statute of limitations is to deny access to our courts. Unswerving, mechanistic application of statutes of limitations would at times "inflict obvious and unnecessary harm upon individual plaintiffs" without materially advancing the objectives they are designed to serve.... The legislative and judicial response to such inequities has been to provide certain statutory exceptions and fashion equitable remedies to avoid the injustice which would result from a literal reading of the general statutory language.... We are concerned here with two such exemptions, one statutorily created, insanity, and the other judicially devised, duress.

A. *Insanity*

[An excerpt from this portion of the opinion appears below at pp. 858–59.]

B. *Duress*

We are ... satisfied that Susan's allegations of duress raised genuine questions of material fact not amenable to summary disposition. Unlike insanity, we have found no statutory provision tolling the limitations period in cases of duress. So too, our research discloses no reported New Jersey opinion dealing with this issue.

However, we in New Jersey have a "long history of instances where equity has interposed to bar the statute of limitations ... where some conduct on the part of the defendant ... has rendered it inequitable that he be allowed to avail himself of the defense." Lopez v. Swyer, 62 N.J. 267, 275 n.2, 300 A.2d 563 (1973). This principle is bottomed on equitable considerations and, hence, the exact contours of the doctrine defy rigid definition. Suffice it to say, the rule has been applied in a variety of factual and legal settings....

We do not suggest that the decisions we have cited should be applied uncritically whenever a plaintiff claims that his or her failure to initiate suit in a timely fashion was caused by a defendant's wrongful act. We are, nevertheless, of the view that, within certain limits, a prospective defendant's coercive acts and threats may rise to such a level of duress as to deprive the plaintiff of his freedom of will and thereby toll the statute of limitations.

As we have pointed out, the question presented here has not been the subject of any reported New Jersey opinion. Decisions in other jurisdictions have generally accepted the theory that duress tolls the statute of limitations, at least, when, as here, it is either an element of or inherent in the underlying cause of action. See, e.g., Cullen v. Margiotta, 811 F.2d 698, 722 (2nd Cir.1987); Pahlavi v. Palandjian, 809 F.2d 938, 942–943 (1st Cir.1987); Ross v. United States, 574 F.Supp. 536, 542 (S.D.N.Y.1983); Clary v. Stack Steel and Supply Co., 611 P.2d 80, 83 (Ala.1980); Day v. General Elec. Credit Corp., 15 Conn.App. 677, 685–86, 546 A.2d 315, 319 (Conn.App.Ct. 1988), certif. den. 209 Conn. 819, 551 A.2d 755 (1988); Babco Industries, Inc., et al. v. New England Mer. Nat. Bank, 6 Mass.App. 929, 380 N.E.2d 1327, 1328 (Mass.App.Ct.1978); Baratta v. Kozlowski, 94 A.D.2d 454, 458–459, 464 N.Y.S.2d 803, 806 (2d Dep't 1983); Pacchiana v. Pacchiana, 94 A.D.2d 721, 723, 462 N.Y.S.2d 256, 257 (2d Dep't 1983); Haggard v. Studie, 610 P.2d 1228, 1231 (Okl.App.Ct.1980); Whatley v. National Bank of Commerce, 555 S.W.2d 500, 505 (Tex.Civ.App.Ct.1977). While we have found no cases discussing the point, we add the requirement that both a subjective and an objective standard must be satisfied in order for the plaintiff to prevail. Specifically, the duress and coercion exerted by the prospective defendant must have been such as to have actually deprived the plaintiff of his freedom of will to institute suit in a timely fashion, and it must have risen to such a level that a person of reasonable firmness in the plaintiff's situation would have been unable to resist....

Applying these principles, we are convinced that plaintiff's submissions raised unresolved factual issues which can be decided only by way of a plenary hearing. Because of the nature of plaintiff's allegations, we repeat that our function on appeal from a summary judgment is not to resolve factual disputes. To reverse and remand, it is sufficient to conclude from the record, as we do, that genuine issues of material fact exist.

Accordingly, the order granting defendant's motion for summary judgment is reversed and the matter is remanded for further proceedings consistent with this opinion.

NOTES AND QUESTIONS

1. An important feature of the court's opinion was its unwillingness to endorse, without further fact finding, the view of the lower court that Susan Jones was free to sue her parents as of the time she moved out of their home. Rather, the appeals court was willing to entertain the idea that her parents' coercion, and her own fear, might reasonably have restrained her from bringing suit for almost an additional three years. In a case in which an abused partner separates from her abuser, but delays bringing a civil suit, for how long do you think a duress claim might continue to be credible, in the absence of renewed threats, or abuse?

2. In Overall v. Estate of Klotz, 53 F.3d 398 (2d Cir. 1995), the Second Circuit refused to entertain a tolling argument based on duress when the childhood abuse suffered by the victim stopped in 1949, and she filed suit in 1992. Her primary argument was that she had repressed all memories of the abuse for more than forty years, and sued in a timely fashion following her "discovery" of the abuse. However, since New York had already rejected tolling based on memory suppression and delayed discovery, she sought the unlikely protection of a tolling argument based on duress. In denying her relief the court articulates an understanding of duress that is at once more narrow than that expressed by the *Jones* court, and probably more widely shared.

As you read the decision, ask yourself under what circumstances an abused partner, separated from her abuser, who sues to recover damages more than two or three years after the separation, might meet the test formulated by the court.

Overall v. Estate of Klotz

53 F.3d 398.
Second Circuit Court of Appeals, 1995.

■ Opinion: JOSE A. CABRANES, CIRCUIT JUDGE.

Carol Overall claims that her father abused her sexually, emotionally and physically from 1947 until 1949, and that the abuse was so severe that she repressed all memories of it for more than forty years. We are not called upon to decide whether Overall is telling the truth. Instead, we must decide whether in 1992, more than forty-three years after she claims her father struck the last blow and uttered the last threat, it was too late for her to ask the courts to force her father, or more precisely his estate, to pay for this alleged abuse.

... Because we cannot expect a child to file a lawsuit to protect his legal rights—certainly not against an abuser—New York common law has long provided that a statute of limitations will not start running until the child becomes an adult. The courts have carved out another general exception to the statute of limitations, the "duress tolling" exception. One important application of this doctrine is to children who continue to suffer at the hands of their abusers even after they reach the legal age of majority. As long as these victims remain subject to "duress" (that is, the abuse), the courts treat them as suffering from a "continuous wrong." For these victims, the statute of limitations clock starts ticking only when the abuse finally ends.

Overall asks this court to extend the period within which she can file suit by forty-one years, relying primarily on the "duress tolling" theory. She argues that because she repressed all memories of childhood abuse until 1991, she has been subjected to a "continuous wrong" for all these years—despite the fact that her father did not threaten or abuse her after 1949.

This is not the first time New York courts have faced lawsuits brought by persons who claim to have recently unearthed long-hidden memories of child abuse. In other repressed-memory child abuse cases, New York has consistently refused to toll the statute of limitations on the theory that the abuse victim's memory loss constituted insanity, that the abuser was somehow profiting from his own wrongdoing (equitable estoppel), or that the limitations period should begin after the abuse was "discovered" through psychotherapy. We conclude that, in the circumstances presented here, the "duress tolling" doctrine is equally unavailing.

. . .

I. Background

. . .

On March 26, 1992, Overall filed the complaint in this action. She brought three claims against her father: (1) assault and battery; (2) false imprisonment; and (3) intentional infliction of emotional distress. Leopold Klotz died on November 20, 1993, and his estate was substituted as the defendant.

. . .

The district court granted summary judgment for the defendant, reasoning that New York law required the plaintiff to suffer conscious fear in order to trigger tolling by duress....

Overall appeals from that decision.

II. DISCUSSION

. . .

In order to determine the scope of duress tolling, we bear in mind that New York construes tolling doctrines as narrowly as possible.... We must also remember that it is only one of several tolling doctrines, each developed in Chancery to remedy a different inequity. We can say with confidence that equity generally favors blameless plaintiffs and punishes blameworthy defendants. But because these laudable goals of fairness undergird all tolling doctrines—particularly equitable estoppel and duress—they cannot explain all the differences between these doctrines.

In order to invoke equitable estoppel, a plaintiff must show that the defendant "wrongfully induced the plaintiff to refrain from timely commencing an action by deception, concealment, threats or other misconduct." Zoe G. v. Frederick F.G., 208 A.D.2d 675, 617 N.Y.S.2d 370, 371 (2d Dep't 1994).... Because a person who seeks equity must do equity, a plaintiff invoking estoppel must show that he brought his action "within a reasonable time after the facts giving rise to the estoppel have ceased to be operational." ... Equitable estoppel, therefore, looks at the parties' conduct only to determine their relative blameworthiness in delaying the commencement of suit.

Duress tolling, on the other hand, examines the parties' conduct only to determine whether that conduct constitutes a continuation of the underlying tort. New York law requires that a plaintiff be subjected to a "continuous wrong" for duress tolling to be appropriate. ...

"Duress" involves both threats or force by the defendant, and the submission of the plaintiff's free will to those threats. Both elements of duress must continue in order for a duress-based tort to persist as a "continuous wrong." As shorthand for this rule, courts have explained that duress tolling is available only when duress is an element of the cause of action alleged. ...

Duress tolling is not triggered, however, simply because duress constitutes an element of the underlying tort. In order to constitute a "continuous wrong" that tolls the limitations period, *the tortious conduct itself must continue.* ... Furthermore, the tortious conduct must continue uninterrupted. In the seminal case of Piper v. Hoard, 107 N.Y. 67, 71, 13 N.E. 632 (1887), for example, the New York Court of Appeals would not permit tolling for duress where the defendant coerced the plaintiff into signing over a deed, and later forced him into forgoing a lawsuit to rescind the deed. Because the two episodes of coercion were separate, the limitations period as to the first was not by the second tolled. ...

The rationale behind duress tolling is that certain torts occur over a stretch of time, not just at the single identifiable moment when the cause of action accrues. When a plaintiff is subject to a "continuous wrong," the moment of accrual still determines when judicial relief is first available, but equity begins to run the limitations period from when the tortious conduct ceases. We presume that a plaintiff is unable to file suit so long as—but no longer than—she is subjected to a duress-based tort. . . .

. . .

The district court assumed for the purposes of deciding the summary judgment motion that duress constituted an element of each of Overall's claims. Although in some sense each of her tort claims contains an element of "duress," the precise injury that she purportedly suffered until 1991—memory suppression—does not alone constitute actionable duress *within the meaning of those torts*. In other words, Overall has not alleged that she was continually subjected to the tortious conduct which constitutes false imprisonment, assault, or intentional infliction of emotional distress since 1949. Accordingly, she has not suffered from a "continuous wrong" within the meaning of the duress tolling doctrine since she left her father's home in Texas, and we cannot toll the limitations period for duress beyond 1949.

. . .

Assault and battery. Plaintiff also argues that "duress" is an element of her claims of assault and battery, because her father forced her through threats and violence to undergo an unwanted touching. However, she was not subjected to the threat of an unwanted touching (that is, the duress that constitutes an element of assault and battery) after 1949. Even if Overall suffered memory repression resulting from a series of assaults committed between 1947 and 1949, she was not subjected to continuous assaults through 1991. Again, the continuing duress (in the form of threats and violence) that Overall allegedly endured while she lived in Texas tolled the statute of limitations as to her earlier claims of assault, but only until 1949.

Intentional infliction of emotional distress. Plaintiff argues that she suffered emotional distress as the direct result of her father's physical and emotional abuse. As with Overall's other claims, however, the *infliction* of that duress concededly ended in 1949. That Overall still bears scars from abuse inflicted more than forty years ago speaks to the severity of that duress, but not to its continuing nature. Furthermore, it would make little sense to permit indefinite tolling for this tort *solely* on the grounds that the effects of the distress have persisted for 45 years, when (for example) a person whose hand was chopped off in an accident 45 years ago cannot similarly maintain suit on the grounds that he still suffers the effects of that injury. Yet that would be the logical result of characterizing her father's abuse as a "continuous wrong."

. . .

Accordingly, we affirm.

Insanity

In Giovine v. Giovine, 284 N.J. Super. 3, 663 A.2d 109 (N.J. Super.App.Div. 1995), in addition to the duress analogy discussed earlier, the court analogized the plaintiff's situation to others in which "insanity," induced by the defendant's conduct, has been held enough to toll a statute of limitation. "Insanity," according to the court, meant "such a condition of mental derangement as actually prevents the sufferer from understanding his [or her] legal rights or instituting legal action," and was a concept broad enough to encompass "the status of a victim of repeated violence within the marital setting, who may 'sink into a state of psychological paralysis and become unable to take any action at all to improve or alter the situation.' " Id., 663 A.2d at 115–16. While this may be an argument applicable to the situation of some women, as the next case demonstrates, it should not be used to the exclusion of duress, which recognizes constraint without attaching a potentially pejorative label to its victim.

In 1988 Hedda Nussbaum sued her abuser, Joel Steinberg, for assault, battery, and intentional infliction of emotional distress, on the basis of his conduct toward her between 1978 and 1987. At the time she sued him, he was incarcerated for the murder of Lisa Steinberg, the young girl whom they had unofficially adopted. The relevant period of limitations for all Nussbaum's claims was one year. She argued that the statute should be tolled on the grounds of insanity. As in *Giovine*, the standard she had to meet was high. It required a showing that she was, prior to 1988, so incapacitated by Steinberg's abuse that she was "incapable of effectively functioning in society," and "precluded ... from protecting her legal rights." In 1997 the special referee assigned to the case determined that she met the standard, and allowed her case to go forward. That decision was subsequently upheld on appeal, Nussbaum v. Steinberg, 703 N.Y.S.2d 32 (N.Y.App. Div. 2000). An excerpt from the referee's decision follows.

Hedda Nussbaum v. Joel Steinberg

Supreme Court of the State of New York
County of New York: IA Part 36R
Index No. 23416/88

■ STEVEN E. LIEBMAN, SPECIAL REFEREE.

. . .

It must be recognized that domestic violence, by its very nature, is much more insidious and complex than even other intentional torts or crimes involving assault, or other abuse, in that the abuser and the victim are generally found to be in a close or intimate relationship. The destructive impact of violence in such an intimate relationship may be so complete that the victim is rendered incapable of independent judgment even to save one's own life. In various forms, the victim may very well turn to the tormentor for connection and support. Significantly, because of the usual close proximity and/or relationship of the domestic violence abuser and the victim, the abused and battered person is often less able than other intentional tort victims to obtain legal protection or recourse after being abused or assaulted. The emotional commitments and the psychological attachments that domestic violence victims usually have to their abusers provides a significant impediment to the victims being capable of seeking help or assistance, even where the abuser does not appear to be actively restraining them from seeking aid. These factors, in various combinations, confirm the devastating effect that such prolonged psychological and physical abuse can have on the victims; including a demonstration that such a person would be clearly incapacitated and incapable of recognizing or asserting their legal rights. In instances where a batterer's primary goal is often absolute control over every aspect of the victim's life, the combination of such extensive control and violence may disable one's independent judgment and functioning so as to place that person within the insanity definition. . . .

Plaintiff testified on her own behalf detailing, through her own testimony, her story of her relationship with Joel Steinberg for over a ten year period, that only ended because of the intervening and tragic death of Lisa Steinberg. Plaintiff's testimony recounted the years of the horrific physical abuse and violence and total emotional and psychological domination over every aspect of her life and being. The magnitude of this traumatic, brutal and destructive relationship was dramatically illustrated by the New York City Police Department videotape of the plaintiff, shortly after her arrest, evidencing physical injuries to virtually every part of her body. . . . No less evident than the condition of her ravaged and mutilated body were her significant psychological disorders and mental defects that undoubtedly were the consequences of her relationship with Joel Steinberg.

Plaintiff also offered the testimony of her treating psychiatrist Dr. Samuel C. Klagsbrun and a prominent expert in psychological trauma Professor Bessel van der Kolk, M.D. The defendant relied on the offer of the expert testimony of Dr. Daniel Schwartz, a retired forensic psychiatrist.

Dr. Schwartz offered his opinion that throughout the entire period of 1975 through 1987, the plaintiff never became incapable of protecting her legal rights or functioning overall in society. Dr. Schwartz characterized plaintiff as having made bad choices or used very poor judgment, but that she still retained the ability to exercise her free will and make decisions. Dr. Schwartz described his former practice as primarily examining criminal defendants to establish their competency to stand trial. . . . He admitted that he had no clinical knowledge about the psychology or life experience of battered women, nor received any training in physical or psychological trauma. Dr. Schwartz conceded that he had never worked with any professionals who treated victims of domestic violence; and he was unaware of his own former institution's protocols for the treatment of battered women. He eventually concluded that plaintiff suffered from what he described as a dependent personality disorder, and that she retained power to extricate herself from the control of the defendant if she wanted to.

The testimony offered by Dr. Klagsbrun and Dr. van der Kolk confirmed their respective expert opinions that Hedda Nussbaum decisively demonstrated that her behavior was consistent with prolonged and extensive psychological and physical abuse. The result of such exposure, they concluded, made the plaintiff incapable of functioning independently of the defendant to the extent of making her unable to make her own judgments about her life or the protection of her interests. Dr. Klagsbrun testified that at the time the plaintiff was admitted to his hospital for treatment she was still delusional and still suffering from a psychotic disorder. He also described Ms. Nussbaum as continuing to display "robotic" impaired functioning and to even talk about the defendant in an adoring manner. Dr. Klagsbrun further stated that the plaintiff believed that she was responsible for the abuse; a perception confirmed as common among trauma victims by Dr. van der Kolk. The testimony of Dr. Klagsbrun emphasized that the impact on Hedda of the defendant's violence so impaired her judgment that she was unable to make judgments and decisions which were basic to human life. Dr. van der Kolk concluded that the plaintiff had even lost her capacity to escape or take independent action; and for all intents and purposes, the plaintiff was "dead to the world." Both physicians maintained that the plaintiff's process to recovery was slow and painful. Notwithstanding the opinion of Dr. Schwartz in this case, it appears that every competent psychiatrist who had examined the plaintiff found that she was not functioning in society, and that this incapacity was the result of chronic trauma inflicted upon her by the defendant.

It was only after plaintiff separated from the defendant that she began to first experience, as reported by Dr. Klagsbrun, conflicting feelings about the defendant. It was not until May 1988, that plaintiff made known that she was experiencing these conflicting feelings. Dr. van der Kolk testified that the ties are so strong that it can take from six months to a year for a battered woman to develop enough strength to remain away from her abuser permanently. In the professional opinions of the plaintiff's experts, Hedda Nussbaum lacked the capacity to function overall in society to the extent of being out of the control and influence of the defendant to at least October 1988. Both doctors conjectured that the earliest the plaintiff had any real ability to function without her incapacity was September 1988, but that she still lacked such ability in August 1988. Dr. Klagsbrun stated that even in October 1988, when Hedda Nussbaum instituted the instant action against Joel Steinberg, there was still significant concern about the plaintiff's capacity to see it through.

. . .

Accordingly, I hereby report my findings that the plaintiff, Hedda Nussbaum, was under a disability because of insanity within the meaning of CPLR § 208 through the period of September 1988, thereby rendering her underlying action timely upon the appropriate application of the tolling statute. I herein order that the defendant's underlying motion for summary judgment to dismiss the Complaint, as time-barred by the Statute of Limitations and held in abeyance, is denied and plaintiff is permitted to proceed on her causes of action alleged in her Complaint. . . .

. . .

This constitutes the decision and order of the court.

Dated: March 6, 1997

NOTES AND QUESTIONS

1. In many cases battered women, while clearly continuing to suffer the emotional sequelae of sustained abuse, will not be able to meet the demanding definition of "insanity" articulated in the *Nussbaum* case. They may well continue for some period of time to be confused about the nature of their relationships with their abusers, and about who properly bears the responsibility for the abuse they have suffered. They may well be too fearful of further interactions with their abusers to bring suit. However, they may otherwise be rebuilding their lives and managing their affairs. They may have won, or be seeking, custody of their children, and unwilling to claim a disability that would seem incompatible with competent parenting. The question therefore arises whether an incapacity short of insanity, or a more accommodating definition of insanity, might be recognized as justifying the tolling of a statute of limitations.

The *Jones* decision, excerpted above to illustrate the application of duress, offers a more accommodating definition of insanity, but it should be recognized that its position is not one widely shared among state courts:

> We first consider plaintiff's claim that the limitations period was tolled by reason of her insanity. The operative statute, N.J.S.A. 2A:14–21, provides "[i]f any person ... shall be, at the time of any such cause of action ... accruing ... insane, such person may commence such action ... within such time as limited by such sections, after his coming ... of sane mind." ...
>
> Despite its ancient lineage, the statute has been cited in relatively few published opinions.... [O]ur Supreme Court, after tracing the statute's historical antecedents, held that N.J.S.A. 2A:14–21 "foreclose[d] a tolling of the running of the [limitations period] unless plaintiff was [insane] at the time the cause of action accrued.... " The Court carved out an equitable exception, however, where the defendant's "negligent act brings about [a] plaintiff's insanity." ... In that instance, the Court said the defendant "should not be permitted to cloak himself with the protective garb of the statute of limitations." ... The Court directed the trial judge to conduct a hearing without a jury and "determine (1) whether insanity developed on or subsequent to the date of the alleged act of defendant and within the period of limitations and if so, whether that insanity resulted from the defendant's bad acts; and (2) whether plaintiff's suit was started within a reasonable time after restoration of sanity.... " In this context, the Court concluded that the word "insane" in the statute of limitations "means such a condition of mental derangement as actually prevents the sufferer from understanding his legal rights or instituting legal action." ...
>
> In Sobin v. M. Frisch & Sons, 108 N.J.Super. 99, 260 A.2d 228 (App.Div.1969), certif. den. 55 N.J. 448, 262 A.2d 702 (1970), we addressed the question whether the plaintiff's extended period of

unconsciousness and semi-consciousness allegedly resulting from the defendant's negligent act was encompassed by the word "insane" as used in N.J.S.A. 2A:14–21. In the course of our opinion, we rejected the defendant's argument that the statutory language should be construed narrowly so as to encompass only those forms of mental illness that require commitment and institutionalization.... Instead, we held that the "aim of N.J.S.A. 2A:14–21 is to relieve from the strict time restrictions any person who actually lacks the ability and capacity, due to mental affliction, to pursue his lawful rights." ...

Against this backdrop, we are satisfied that mental trauma resulting from a pattern of incestuous sexual abuse may constitute insanity under N.J.S.A. 2A:14–21, so as to toll the statute of limitations. We are also convinced that plaintiff's submissions in opposition to defendants' motion for summary judgment raised genuine issues of material fact concerning whether she had the ability and capacity, due to mental affliction allegedly caused by defendants' conduct, to assert her lawful rights. We note that a plethora of recent studies has revealed the disabling psychological impact of incestuous sexual abuse. [Citations omitted.] The gist of these studies, as recounted in Dr. Silverman's affidavit, is that "often even long after the cycle of abuse itself has been broken, the victim will repress and deny, even to himself or herself, what has happened." According to Dr. Silverman, "[i]n many instances, this repression is so complete that the secret inside the victim becomes hidden even from [himself or herself] and can be discovered only through therapy or as a result of subsequent events which trigger off the first conscious recollection of the trauma."

Of course, we offer no opinion with respect to the truth of Susan's allegations. We stress, however, that resolution of the question presented depends critically upon a determination of plaintiff's state of mind. In that context, we have repeatedly held that issues hinging upon a party's mental state are not appropriate for resolution by way of summary judgment. This principle is particularly applicable in light of the lack of any clear precedent bearing upon the precise question presented. We thus conclude that the Law Division judge erred by granting summary judgment.

Jones v. Jones, 242 N.J. Super. 195, 204–07; 576 A.2d 316, 320–22 (N.J. Super. Ct. App. Div. 1990).

2. A related but somewhat different argument, one that in a sense "splits the difference" between insanity and duress, is that the abuser's continuing psychological hold on his partner may prevent her from being able to frame her abuse as a wrong for which he is responsible, and from seeking to hold him accountable. Like the sexual abuse victim of a therapist, she needs distance from this inherently unequal relationship to see the exploitation for what it is and to summon the independence to challenge it.

The analogy to sexual abuse by therapists is not a perfect one, because those courts that have allowed tolling in this context, usually by applying a "discovery" rule (the period of limitations begins to run at the point where the plaintiff is capable of recognizing the wrongful nature of the therapist's conduct, and acting on it), have emphasized the professional "tools" that make the patient vulnerable to exploitation (the phenomena of transference and counter-transference). However, the equally effective "tools" of the batterer could be viewed as giving his victim's claim just as much force. For decisions favoring tolling in cases involving sexual abuse by therapists, see Simmons v. United States, 805 F.2d 1363 (9th Cir. 1986); Greenberg v. McCabe, 453 F. Supp. 765 (E.D. Pa. 1978), aff'd 594 F.2d. 854 (3d Cir. 1979); Riley v. Presnell, 565 N.E.2d 780 (Mass. 1991).

The other problem with relying on an analogy to cases involving sexual abuse by therapists is that many courts have refused to toll statutes of limitation in this context. Adult survivors of childhood sexual abuse have had similarly mixed success in arguing for tolling under the various common law doctrines and equitable principles you have been introduced to in the last pages. Some states have responded with tolling legislation specific to suits based on childhood sexual abuse. It is therefore worth considering whether the plight of battered partners who need a period of healing before pursuing legal remedies is one that should be addressed by state legislatures rather than, or in addition to, state courts.

3. If you were crafting such legislation, how would you frame it? What would be the benefits of arguing for a fixed additional term during which someone emerging from a battering relationship might bring suit? What would be the appropriate term—five years, or three, or seven? Would it be better to leave the term undefined, but articulate the circumstances under which the running of the statute of limitations would be suspended? Would this new legislation preclude the plaintiff from arguing any other applicable tolling rule or principle, or simply provide additional ammunition? From a political perspective, what choices would give your legislation the best chance of being adopted?

The New Tort of Spouse, Domestic or Partner Abuse

The recognition of a new cause of action for abuse has been proposed by commentators, and endorsed by courts in New Jersey and the state of Washington, in decisions described and discussed below. For two representative articles, see Rhonda Kohler, *The Battered Woman and Tort Law: A New Approach to Fighting Domestic Violence,* 25 LOY. L.A. L. REV. 1025, 1068 (1992), and Clare Dalton, *Domestic Violence, Domestic Torts and Divorce: Constraints and Possibilities,* 31 NEW ENG. L. REV. 319, 344–46 (1997). The Superior Court of the District of Columbia, however, took a different position in this next case.

de la Croix de Lafayette v. de la Croix de Lafayette

15 Family Law Reporter (BNA) 1501.
D.C. Super. Ct. Fam. Div., Nos. 88 CA–6337 & –2641, 1989.

Digest of Opinion:

. . .

The question arises as to which statute of limitation applies. The amicus (National Organization for Victims' Assistance) asks this court to find that spouse abuse is a separate identifiable tort. Presumably such a tort would differ from the individual torts of which it was made up in that the statute of limitations otherwise applicable to the individual acts would be tolled during the continued occurrence of spouse abuse. In this respect it would resemble conspiracy. As spouse abuse is not specifically addressed in [the statute governing periods of limitation for torts actions], it would fall under the catch-all provision . . . of three years. The statute would begin to run upon the last instance of abuse, and not lapse until three years thereafter.

The parties have not presented nor has the court found any cases holding that spouse abuse is a tort in its own right as described above. . . . The Supreme court of Utah has held that a catch-all count which makes a general allegation of abusive behavior throughout the course of a marriage should be defined, for purposes of a statute of limitations argument, in terms of specific allegations: *Lord v. Shaw*, 665 P.2d 1288 (1983).

Nothing in this record suggests that a new tort of a continuous nature is required to adequately address the occurrences between these parties. Instead, each act of abuse gives rise to a claim that is subject to its own statute of limitations. This is consistent with the need for finality in the context of an unstable marital relationship, where the decision whether to divorce or not should be made in an environment as free of extraneous financial and fault considerations as possible.

. . .

As to allegations of intentional infliction of emotional distress arising from assault and various forms of psychological abuse, the complaint states a claim upon which relief could be granted. However, some of the claims are subject to a statute of limitations defense.

Section 12–301 does not provide a specific limitation for the tort of intentional infliction of emotional distress. The amicus asks this court to find that the general three year period applies. This is the rule in Maryland, . . . but in the District of Columbia, what statute of limitations applies to an action for intentional infliction of emotional distress depends upon the underlying acts. . . .

The plaintiff alleges that the defendant has intentionally inflicted emotional distress on the plaintiff through various acts, including sexually assaulting the parties' daughter. Any allegations stemming from incidents of assault and battery are subject to the one year statute of limitations.

Whether the plaintiff may maintain an action for intentional infliction of emotional distress for acts committed upon her daughter raises a different issue. Generally, a party seeking damages for intentional infliction of emotional distress for conduct directed at third parties must be a member of the immediate family and have been present at the time the act was committed. Allegations of sexual assault upon the parties' child out of the plaintiff's presence do not constitute an actionable claim for emotional distress in the District of Columbia.

Even assuming a cause of action was recognized in these circumstances, plaintiff's claim is barred by the statute of limitations. The underlying tort of plaintiff's claim for intentional infliction of emotional distress is an assault and battery that occurred in November 1986. The applicable limitation period is one year. This action was filed July 7, 1988.

As to other allegations of physical violence and psychological harassment against the plaintiff directly, this court finds that they are sufficiently pled to establish a claim of intentional infliction of emotional distress, with respect to those acts alleged to have occurred since July 7, 1987.—King, J.

NOTES

1. The *de la Croix de Lafayette* case makes clear the connection between urging a new cause of action and the need to avoid the application of traditional statutes of limitation. Can you articulate other reasons, however, why recognition of a new tort might be advantageous to plaintiffs seeking redress for domestic abuse? Could you use the *de la Croix de Lafayette* case to illustrate the potential advantages, by focusing on how the plaintiff in that case was *disadvantaged* by her inability to present the story of her abuse as a coherent narrative, rather than a collection of discrete incidents?

2. It is significant that Judge King cited no authority for his assertion that no claim for intentional infliction of emotional distress would lie for the distress caused the mother by the father's sexual assault on their daughter. The restrictions he cites are those attached to "witness" claims for *negligent* infliction of emotional distress, in situations where the defendant has no intent to harm those who witness the injury his negligence causes the primary victim. There is no reason to impose those same restrictions in situations where the defendant *intends,* by his assault on one person, to traumatize another. "Intending," in this context, means desiring that result, or knowing or believing, with substantial certainty, that it will occur. Section 46(2) of the Restatement Second of Torts specifically provides for the action to lie in these circumstances.

3. A superior court in Spokane County, in the state of Washington, may have been the first to recognize a specific cause of action for domestic violence, or battered women's (or battered woman) syndrome (BWS). This terminology is a little awkward; what is meant is that the cause of action is based on the plaintiff's having developed BWS as a result of the defendant's course of conduct. The case, Jewett v. Jewett, No. 93 2018465 (Wash. Super Ct. Spokane County Apr. 21, 1993), is unreported, but described in detail in the following account, which makes clear how much the final result was influenced by the proactive stance of the judge who heard the defendant's motion to dismiss, and denied it on June 16, 1994.

Casenote: A New Tort: Domestic Violence Gets the Status it Deserves in Jewett v. Jewett, No. 93 2018465 (Wash. Super Ct. Spokane County, Apr. 21, 1993), 21 Southern Illinois University Law Journal 355, 356–57, 376–79 (1997)

Over a period of about five years, Michael Jewett caused permanent physical and emotional injury to Teresa Jewett. On one occasion, she suffered permanent scarring from an attack in which he threw her into a coffee table and then beat her until she became unconscious, breaking her facial bones so that reconstructive surgery was necessary to reposition her cheekbone. Teresa also suffered disfigurement and disc damage to her neck and back as a result of an attack during which Michael hyperextended her neck while in bed and again later over the headrest of her car. Michael subjected Teresa to extreme emotional trauma by continually threatening to harm others close to her, including his own mother, if she attempted to leave him.

Teresa filed suit for assault and battery, intentional infliction of emotional distress, outrage, and battered women's syndrome/domestic violence. The defendant, Michael, answered the complaint with affirmative defenses and a motion to dismiss the action for battered women's syndrome for failing to state a claim for which relief could be granted. He claimed that the plaintiff's damages, if any, were the proximate result of her own conduct and that her claim was barred by the statute of limitations and by the doctrines of estoppel and/or waiver. To aid in its ruling on the motion to dismiss, the court heard arguments from counsel and considered an amicus curiae brief from Spokane Legal Services Center....

. . .

... The court asked that the Center "provide information to the court regarding the alleged cause of action relating to battered women's syndrome." The brief focused on "the availability of a comprehensive civil remedy to victims of domestic violence generally ... but took no position with regard to the availability of the remedies presented and their applicability to the facts of the present case."

In summary, the amicus curiae concluded that existing tort law fails to adequately compensate the victim for the harm incurred through domestic violence. The amicus curiae went on to describe the continuous nature of the violence and the incapacity of the victim from the unusual dependency which characterizes the relationship. It recommended that to fully recognize and compensate victims of domestic violence, the court could either 1) toll the statutes of limitation until the violence stops so that the victim could get full recovery, or 2) recognize a separate tort of domestic violence that would allow full recovery for injuries.

The elements that would define the new tort of domestic violence were also included in the amicus curiae brief as follows:

(1) a pattern of volitional acts, which include physical acts and gestures, as well as statements, threats or verbal utterances;

(2) which is reasonably calculated to create fear or anxiety or to establish perceptions of fear or anxiety for the victim's self or family;

(3) that is continuous in nature, and, occurs over a period of time;

(4) that could reasonably have been foreseen to, and that in fact did cause;

(5) physical injury, emotional distress, or a state of emotional dependency that renders a victim unable to effectively maintain an action against her abuser.

The amicus curiae further suggested that "the court's role is to insure that the threshold showing is both broad enough to provide a meaningful opportunity for redress and sufficiently narrow to effectively discourage lawsuits for each and every insult uttered in a domestic relationship."

In the defendant's response to the amicus curiae brief, the stated issue was "whether the trial court should recognize the tort of domestic violence or toll the statutes of limitations for alleged victims of domestic violence, based upon theories of continuous tort and subjective incapacity of the victim." Defendant's brief concluded that the legislature was the appropriate forum to create a domestic violence tort,.... The plaintiff's proposal to toll the statute of limitations was also rejected in defendant's brief.... "No civilized society could lay claim to an enlightened judicial system which puts no limits on the time in which a person can be compelled to defend against claims brought in good faith, much less whatever stale, illusory, false, fraudulent or malicious accusations of civil wrong might be leveled against him."

The court, after hearing arguments from both sides and from the amicus curiae, rejected defendant's arguments and denied his motion ... and granted the plaintiff leave to amend her complaint to comply with the ruling. The court explained that it took judicial notice of the "extreme form of dependence" that characterized those living in a relationship marked by domestic violence. It concluded that:

> Their [the couple's] interaction encourages not only the continuance of the relationship but also the violence within it. Once caught in the cycle, traditional remedies under the law, including the right to file civil actions for assault, battery and intentional infliction of emotional distress [outrage], for all practical purposes are not available because the statutes of limitation prevent the victim from fully asserting her rights.

The court went on to recognize that the number of victims would only increase if we continue to send the message that it is the abuser who is protected by law, rather than the victim. The court stated that those injured by domestic violence must have a "meaningful opportunity, through the court system, to recover for injuries." It was found "appropriate and necessary to recognize a separate civil cause of action for damages incurred during the pendency of a dependent domestic relationship which is marked by a pattern of domestic violence."

The elements adopted by the court for the cause of action of domestic violence were those set forth in the amicus brief. The court ruled that the tort will allow "all individual, cumulative, and continuing injuries suffered by the victim," and will be governed by the two year statute of limitations which will begin to run at the cessation of the tortious activity.... The pattern of abuse may end through divorce or separation, as was the case in Jewett.

The court declined to rule that there were no set of facts under which the plaintiff could prevail under the new claim; therefore, it did not grant the defendant's motion to dismiss. Instead, the court acknowledged that the facts that the plaintiff alleged in her complaint, if proven, would state a cause of action for the tort of domestic violence....[1]

* * *

NOTES

1. Hard on the heels of the ruling in Jewett, another Superior Court, this time in Bergen County, New Jersey, also recognized a new cause of action based on battered woman's syndrome. In Cusseaux v. Pickett, 279 N.J. Super 335, 652 A.2d 789 (1994), a good portion of the opinion was dedicated to recapitulating the New Jersey Supreme Court's description of battered woman syndrome in the *Kelly* case, which you read in Chapter 10. Then Judge Napolitano went on to say:

> It is well established in this state that an injured party may sustain a cause of action for serious personal and emotional injuries that are directly and causally related to the actions of another person.... As discussed above, the Legislature has specifically found domestic violence to be a serious crime against society.... More importantly, in enacting the Prevention of Domestic Violence Act, the Legislature recognized that our judicial and law enforcement system was insufficient to address the problem. If this Act had never become law, the ubiquitous deficiency of our legal system would continue in spite of the fact that the acts listed among those classified as "domestic violence" under the statute were already criminal offenses.
>
> ... As is the case with the domestic violence statute where existing criminal statutes were inadequate, so too are the civil laws of assault and battery insufficient to redress the harms suffered as a result of domestic violence. Domestic violence is a plague on our social structure and a frontal assault on the institution of the family. The battered-woman's syndrome is but one of the pernicious symptoms of that plague. Though the courts would be hard-pressed to prescribe a panacea for all domestic violence, they are entrusted with the power to fashion a palliative when necessary. The underpinning of our common law and public policy demand that, where the Legislature has not gone far enough, the courts must fill the interstices. As the Legislature stated,
>
> > it is the responsibility of the courts to protect victims of violence that occurs in a family or family-like setting by providing access to

1. Following Judge Eitzen's order denying Michael Jewett's motion to dismiss, Teresa Jewett submitted an amended complaint, and the case was ultimately won by default. As to the issue of damages, the case was finally settled with an award of $125,000 going to Teresa Jewett.

> both emergent and long-term civil and criminal remedies and sanctions....
>
> . . .
>
> Thus, this court will recognize the battered-woman's syndrome as an affirmative cause of action under the laws of New Jersey.
>
> In order to state a cause of action for the battered-woman's syndrome, the plaintiff must allege the following elements. The plaintiff must show 1) involvement in a marital or marital-like intimate relationship; and 2) physical or psychological abuse perpetrated by the dominant partner to the relationship over an extended period of time; and 3) the aforestated abuse has caused recurring physical or psychological injury over the course of the relationship; and 4) a past or present inability to take any action to improve or alter the situation unilaterally.
>
> ... The mate who is responsible for creating the condition suffered by the battered victim must be made to account for his actions—all of his actions. Failure to allow affirmative recovery under these circumstances would be tantamount to the courts condoning the continued abusive treatment of women in the domestic sphere. This the courts cannot and will never do.

Id., 279 N.J. Super. at 342–45, 652 A.2d at 793–94.

Subsequently, a New Jersey appeals court upheld Cusseaux, while imposing on battered women plaintiffs the requirement that they support their claims with expert testimony:

> We agree with the premise espoused in Cusseaux and conclude that a wife diagnosed with battered woman's syndrome should be permitted to sue her spouse in tort for the physical and emotional injuries sustained by continuous acts of battering during the course of the marriage, provided there is medical, psychiatric, or psychological expert testimony establishing that the wife was caused to have an "inability to take any action to improve or alter the situation unilaterally." Ibid. In the absence of expert proof, the wife cannot be deemed to be suffering from battered woman's syndrome, and each act of abuse during the marriage would constitute a separate and distinct cause of action in tort, subject to the statute of limitations....
>
> . . .
>
> We do not adopt the conclusion in Cusseaux that battered woman's syndrome is itself a continuous tort. Battered woman's syndrome is more correctly the medical condition resulting from continued acts of physical or psychological misconduct. Because the resulting psychological state, composed of varied but identifiable characteristics, is the product of at least two separate and discrete physical or psychological acts occurring at different times, to overcome the statute of limitations, it is imperative that the tortious conduct giving rise to the medical condition be considered a continuous tort....

Giovine v. Giovine, 284 N.J. Super. 3, 10–13; 663 A.2d 109, 114–15 (1995).

The appeals court endorsed the Cusseaux court's finding that this new cause of action was a continuing tort, but held in addition that the statute of limitations for the continuing tort might be tolled for as long as the woman remained incapacitated as a consequence of the abuse she had suffered, and unable "to take any action to improve or alter the circumstances in her marriage unilaterally. . . ." The court drew on prior decisions tolling statutes of limitation in the context of both insanity and duress, including the *Jones* case discussed above.

2. Although *Cusseaux* emphasized abuse in the marital context, the court was careful to acknowledge that the tort it was creating could occur in any intimate relationship. Presumably, the court therefore understands battered woman's syndrome as a condition not necessarily limited to women. We have talked elsewhere about the dangers of conditioning legal relief for victims of domestic violence on any rigid definition of battered woman's syndrome; this is yet one more context in which a flexible understanding of how abuse affects those who suffer it, and how not all victims respond in the same way, will be critical. If other states are inclined to follow New Jersey's example and create a new tort for this class of victims, it might therefore be wiser to label it the tort of "partner abuse," rather than risk inhibiting its application by tying it too closely to battered woman's syndrome. Similarly, the expert testimony required to support the claim should be understood broadly as evidence about battered women and their experiences, rather than more narrowly as evidence about battered woman's syndrome, even though clinical descriptions of the psychological impact of abuse will be an important part of the testimony.

D. THE RELATIONSHIP BETWEEN TORT ACTIONS AND DIVORCE PROCEEDINGS

In many abusive relationships, the first time the abused partner will be able even to contemplate a tort action is when she decides to separate from her abuser. At this moment, something has happened to tip the balance, to make separation feel either safe, or in any event less dangerous, physically and emotionally, than trying to maintain the relationship. Perhaps the level of violence has become life-threatening. Perhaps it is spilling over onto the children. Perhaps the police have come to the house, and through a restraining order or criminal process the woman has made contact with an advocate who has expanded her sense of the options available to her. Perhaps a friend's patient insistence that she does not deserve to be beaten has eroded her partner's hold on her. For whatever reason, she has shifted from efforts to minimize and contain the abuse, to invoking the legal system to help her put it behind her. If she has, in addition, retained the services of a family lawyer, she also has, or should have, access to new information, not only about the dissolution of her marriage, if she *is* married, but also about her rights and options with respect to a tort claim.

On the other hand, the barriers to suit we have already identified are still there. And if she has been married to her partner, a new set of questions about the relationship between the divorce proceedings and any cause of action in tort will have to be answered. Thus far, courts around the country have responded in a bewildering variety of ways to the question of whether, and under what circumstances, the civil cause of action can be pursued simultaneously with, or subsequent to, the divorce. And even when a tort action is a possibility, the lawyer and her client will have to decide whether it provides a useful supplemental or alternative mechanism for sorting out her financial claims—measured against the financial settlement that will accompany the divorce.

The Divorce/Tort Interface
Clare Dalton, Domestic Violence, Domestic Torts and Divorce: Constraints and Possibilities, 31 New England Law Review 319, 374–94 (1997)

1. *Together or Apart?*

New Jersey provides an example of a state that insists on divorce and tort claims being joined, on the grounds that "all claims between the same parties arising out of or relating to the same transactional circumstances [should] be joined in a single action."[1] In New Jersey, it seems that an intentional tort committed by one spouse against the other is considered a "constituent element" of the divorce action, even when the divorce is not fault-based. New Jersey's position, which subsequent caselaw has revealed to be less than absolute,[2] is surely influenced by the fact that, under state law, wrongful marital conduct can be considered in a divorce case, and an award made for that conduct. New Jersey courts have also been careful to preserve a claimant's right to jury trial where her tort claims are sufficiently divisible from the other claims in the divorce proceeding. Nonetheless, the courts' reasoning seems insufficiently attentive to the reality of divorce proceedings in the context of abusive relationships, as the remainder of this discussion will clarify.

A number of states, among them Arizona, Colorado, New Hampshire, Illinois, Utah and Vermont, forbid joining a tort claim with a divorce action. These states see tort actions and divorce proceedings as fundamentally distinct.[3] Some emphasize that divorce statutes do not provide courts

1. Brown v. Brown, 208 N.J. Super. 372, 506 A.2d 29, 32 (1986)....

2. See, e.g., Brown v. Brown, 506 A.2d 29, 32–33 (N.J. Super. Ct. App. Div. 1986), in which the court found that the defense of preclusion could be waived under appropriate circumstances.

3. *See, e.g.,* Aubert v. Aubert, 529 A.2d 909, 911 (N.H. 1987): "a civil action in tort is fundamentally different from a divorce proceeding, and ... the respective issues are entirely distinct." *See also* Heacock v. Heacock, 520 N.E.2d 151, 153 (Mass. 1988), a case in which the court was dealing with the issue of res judicata rather than compulsory joinder, but gave a thoughtful account of the differences between tort and divorce actions: "A tort action is not based on the same underlying claim as an action for divorce. The purpose of a tort action is to redress a

with the authority to award a spouse a money judgment for an intentional tort committed by the other. Divorce is about terminating the relationship, and allocating resources, generally on a no-fault basis. Torts are about compensation for an identified wrong. Moreover, divorce proceedings are equitable and tort claims legal; either a tort claimant forced into family court might lose her right to jury trial, or the very equitable nature of the divorce proceedings might be compromised by the inclusion of "matters of law." Yet other states, including Alaska, Arkansas, Idaho, Texas and Wisconsin, take the view that the tort claim may be combined with the divorce, but need not be. The same reasons articulated by courts which have forbidden joinder appear to guide those courts which permit but do not require it.

2. *Simultaneous or Subsequent?*

Typically, the issue of joinder arises when an abused partner seeks to bring a tort action after the divorce, and the defendant seeks to have the action dismissed, on the grounds that the divorce settlement has already provided a full and final disposition of all claims between the former partners. If joinder is required, as in New Jersey, the later tort claim will almost inevitably be dismissed. The most crucial consequence of allowing the claims to be brought separately is therefore that it opens the way for a subsequently filed tort claim. But not all such claims will be permitted to go forward. Courts have variously used doctrines of res judicata, equitable estoppel and waiver to bar certain tort actions when brought by one divorced partner against the other.

If joinder is forbidden, it is hardly possible for the defendant in the tort action to argue res judicata.... How can a claim which cannot be made in the context of the divorce proceeding be resolved by it? But arguments may still be advanced either that the plaintiff is equitably estopped from pursuing the claim, or that the divorce judgment or settlement contained an express or implied waiver of the claim.... In those states which neither mandate nor prohibit joinder as a blanket rule, on the other hand, courts will inevitably be asked to determine whether principles of res judicata preclude some number of tort actions brought subsequent to divorce proceedings in which a partner's abuse was arguably already addressed. Issues of waiver or equitable estoppel will be relevant in this context as well.

Res Judicata

There are a number of decisions in which res judicata has been used to bar plaintiffs from bringing tort actions after their divorces on the grounds that the issue of their partners' abuse was fully addressed in the context of the divorce. The crucial question here is how ready a court will be to reach that conclusion. In the 1987 Tennessee case of Kemp v. Kemp,[1] for

legal wrong in damages; that of a divorce action is to sever the marital relationship between the parties, and, where appropriate, to fix the parties' respective rights and obligations with regard to alimony and support, and to divide the marital estate."

1. 723 S.W.2d 138, 139–40 (Tenn. Ct. App. 1986).

example, a Court of Appeals applied res judicata to bar an abused wife's tort claim, because the divorce court had ordered the husband to pay the past and future medical bills associated with his abuse. The court admitted that the two causes of action were not the same, but concluded that because of this award she had "in effect ... prevailed on a tort claim." While the court stopped short of saying that all tort actions must be joined to divorce actions when the injuries occur during marriage, it nonetheless espoused a broad application of res judicata, suggesting that "principles of res judicata apply not only to issues actually raised and finally adjudicated in prior litigation, but to 'all claims and issues which were relevant and which could reasonably have been litigated in a prior action.'" ...

On the other hand, the Eleventh Circuit, applying Alabama law in a 1989 case, found that a subsequent tort suit for battery, intentional infliction of emotional distress and outrage was not barred when the husband's abuse was not the basis of the no-fault divorce, even though the injunctive terms of an earlier protective order obtained by the wife were merged with the divorce decree.[1] In 1988 a Michigan Court of Appeals refused to bar a later-filed assault and battery and intentional infliction of emotional distress claim even though the divorce court had divided marital property according to the parties' fault.[2] Also in 1988 the Idaho Supreme Court allowed a subsequent tort action, concluding that even though Idaho trial courts have the jurisdiction to address and resolve issues of intentional wrongful conduct occurring in the course of a marriage in the context of dissolution proceedings, an exception to the court's traditional interpretation of res judicata should be recognized in cases involving abuse.[3] And in the same year the Massachusetts Supreme Court declined to apply res judicata in a tort action in which evidence of the husband's abuse and the wife's resultant injuries were introduced during the earlier divorce proceedings, when the divorce was granted based on irretrievable breakdown of the marriage, and the probate judge did not specify what factors had influenced his award of alimony and his division of marital property.[4]

Equitable Estoppel

Massachusetts, while roundly rejecting a mandatory joinder approach, and appearing sympathetic to arguments against the application of res judicata to subsequently filed tort suits, has nonetheless used the doctrine of equitable estoppel to create strong incentives for lawyers to bring divorce and tort suits simultaneously. This is the practical result of two defining decisions. In the first, *Heacock I*, the Supreme Court rejected the defendant's argument that his former wife's tort claim was precluded by their earlier divorce. On remand, however, the trial court found that the abusive husband had been disadvantaged by not knowing, at the time of his divorce, that his wife was planning the later tort claim. The claim was

1. Abbott v. Williams, 888 F.2d 1550, 1552–55 (11th cir. 1989).

2. McCoy v. Cooke, 419 N.W.2d 44, 46 (Mich Ct. App. 1988)....

3. Nash v. Overholser, 757 P.2d 1180, 1180 (Idaho, 1988).

4. Heacock v. Heacock (Heacock I), 520 N.E. 2d 151,152 (Mass. 1988)....

therefore disallowed, on the grounds of equitable estoppel, and this ruling was upheld on appeal, in a case known as *Heacock II*.[1]

Members of the Massachusetts family bar have sensibly determined that the best advice they can give their clients in the aftermath of these two decisions is to file the claims at the same time, although the decision depended heavily on the particular facts of the case, and its reach cannot be determined without further testing in the courts. It is noteable that Mrs. Heacock did not allege that her delay in prosecuting the tort action was caused by fear of Mr. Heacock, and what he might do in response. Rather, her lawyer asserted that he wanted "to work up more potent evidence that Carla's epileptic seizures had been brought on by Gregg's battery." The appellate court was unconvinced, and repeatedly used language expressing its conviction that Mrs. Heacock's lawyer had been attempting to gain an unfair tactical advantage, by seeking evidence "on the sly," and keeping both the defendant and the probate court "in the dark."

Mr. Heacock argued that after the divorce judgment became final he destroyed evidence that might have helped him defend against the tort action. Further, his lawyer was able to suggest a variety of ways in which Mr. Heacock's interests could have been better protected had the tort claim been disclosed. He would have moved, he asserted, to consolidate the two actions, or to stay the divorce action until the tort suit was adjudicated. He would at a minimum have filed a notice of appeal from the probate court judgment in order to obtain findings from the judge who presided over the divorce, which findings might have had an issue preclusion effect on some of the factual matters involved in the tort action. He would also have "attempted to obtain an independent evaluation of Carla's medical condition and would have taken 'steps to locate and preserve the testimony of all those persons who could corroborate Mr. Heacock's version of [the alleged violence].' "

. . .

A dramatic contrast to *Heacock II* is provided by a 1987 Wisconsin case, in which an abused wife brought a tort suit for assault, battery and intentional infliction of emotional distress three months following the conclusion of a no-fault divorce proceeding.[2] The divorce and the division of the marital estate were based on a stipulation that there had been "a full disclosure of all assets, debts, and other ramifications of the marriage." As in *Heacock II*, the husband argued that the wife's failure to mention her potential tort claims in the context of the divorce proceeding should preclude the suit on the basis of res judicata, waiver and equitable estoppel. The trial court agreed, concluding that it was " 'absolutely unconscionable'

1. Heacock v. Heacock (Heacock II), 568 N.E. 2d 621 (Mass. App. Ct. 1991). The court noted that:

> A judge of the Superior Court ... decided: (1) that Carla's delay in serving the complaint was not excusable, (2) that the delay had deliberately been contrived for tactical advantage; and (3) that the delay had prejudiced Gregg's ability to defend against the tort action. Having so concluded, the judge ... dismissed Carla's action, with prejudice.... We affirm.

Id. at 622.

2. Stuart v. Stuart, 410 N.W. 2d 632, 634 (Wis. Ct. App. 1987).

that she would negotiate her divorce, and advise the court that it was based upon full disclosure, when she knew a civil lawsuit would be filed immediately after the divorce was granted." So strong was the trial court's reaction that it described the tort suit as "an abuse of the judicial system," and agreed with the husband that it was "brought in bad faith and solely for the purposes of harassment and malicious injury." On this basis that the claim was frivolous, the court awarded the husband $10,000 for his legal expenses in responding to it.

The appeals court saw the case entirely differently. It saw no basis for the application of res judicata. The issues litigated in the divorce proceedings were: "the termination of the marriage and the equitable division of the marital estate," without regard to the fault of the parties. "Consequently, in making the financial allocation between the parties, the court could not consider one spouse's tortious conduct or, based upon that conduct, award the injured spouse punitive damages or compensatory damages for past pain, suffering, and emotional distress." Since "divorce and tort actions do not easily fit within the framework of a single trial," the objectives of res judicata, which the court identified as "judicial economy and the conservation of those resources parties would expend in repeated and needless litigation," would not be met by demanding a single trial in these circumstances. In addition, the appeals court felt that it would be fundamentally unfair to the wife to apply res judicata, since the divorce proceeding "did not provide an opportunity for a full and fair determination of [her] tort claim."

The appeals court was equally unimpressed with the equitable estoppel argument. "Failing to disclose a tort claim," it concluded, "cannot be interpreted as a representation that no such claim exists." Nor was there any evidence that the husband relied to his detriment on any such representation "in achieving the divorce stipulation and the division of the marital estate," since those were "achieved according to the dictates of state law." The Supreme Court of Wisconsin affirmed the appeals court, adopting its reasoning wholesale.

Waiver

The appeals court in *Stuart* was also clear that neither the wife's decision to pursue divorce proceedings, nor her failure to mention her tort claim in those proceedings, could be construed as a waiver—a voluntary and intentional relinquishment—of her right to pursue the tort action subsequent to her divorce. There was no evidence of any such intent on the part of the wife, the court concluded, and the law of Wisconsin "will not force one party to a marriage to choose between commencing an action to terminate a marriage or one to recover compensation for injuries sustained as a result of spousal abuse." Nor could her stipulation that she had disclosed all "assets, debts and other ramifications of the marriage" be interpreted as a waiver of the tort claim, even though the court felt that the claim was indeed an asset that should have been disclosed.

While the requirement that waiver be both intentional and voluntary argues strongly against any findings of implied waiver in this context, a more difficult question is whether to interpret release clauses, which are routinely included in settlement agreements, and subsequently incorporated into divorce decrees, as explicit waivers of later tort claims. Many courts have so found, but the language of these releases is not uniform, and decisions about their scope must be made on a case-by-case basis.

In a federal district court case in Kentucky in 1990, a tort claim brought after a divorce was barred, on the strength of a release claim which provided that "[e]ach party hereby releases and discharges the other from all obligations of support, and from all other claims, rights, and duties arising or growing out of said marital relationship."[1] In South Dakota in 1995, on the other hand, the Supreme Court decided that a similarly worded release did not bar a claim based on abuse which occurred after the divorce. The court was clear that the goal of a release in the context of a divorce is to extinguish other claims, rights and responsibilities existing prior to the signing of the agreement, not those which arise subsequently.[2]

The language of other release clauses is even broader. A striking example is the clause at issue in the 1995 *Cerniglia* decision by a Florida court of appeals.[3] The settlement agreement provided that it was "a full and complete settlement ... of claims of any nature whatsoever that each party may have against the other," that all parties "mutually renounce and relinquish all claims of whatever nature each may have," and that the agreement "shall constitute a complete, general, and mutual release of all claims whatsoever." The court barred a later tort suit by the wife against her former husband. An earlier decision by an Alabama court of appeals in 1984 found that a "boilerplate" clause in an agreement, providing that the agreement was "a full, final and complete settlement of all property matters and other matters between the parties" operated to bar a later tort claim....

Notably, none of these decisions come from jurisdictions in which joinder of tort claims with divorce actions is barred. Courts in those states might be more hesitant to decide that a tort claim was a claim arising or growing out of a marital relationship, since they view the marriage, and issues surrounding its termination, as fundamentally distinct from any tort claim either partner might have against the other. It might be harder to resist the interpretation that a release as broadly framed as the one in the *Cerniglia* case does indeed preclude a later tort action. There is no reason, on the other hand, to follow the Alabama Supreme Court's reasoning, and presume that a release clause precludes a subsequent tort action unless one of the partners expressly preserves the right to bring one. Given the very compelling safety reasons why an abused partner may want to preserve that right without drawing attention to it until the divorce proceedings are concluded, the burden should be placed squarely on the partner who has reason to fear being sued to protect his interests by seeking an appropriately specific release.

1. Overberg v. Lusby, 727 F. Supp. 1091, 1093 (E.D. Ky. 1990).

2. Henry v. Henry, 534 N.W. 2d 844, 847 (S.D. 1995).

3. 655 So.2d 172, 174 (Fla. Dist. Ct. App. 1995).

The lesson here for lawyers representing clients in divorce proceedings is that much may ride on the language of release provisions. Those representing marital partners who have been abused must be cautious not to give away too much; those representing partners who may have been abusive have every incentive to make the release as all-inclusive as possible. There is an inherent tension between an abused partner's desire not to signal her intention to bring a later tort suit, and her need to protect that possibility by insisting on language, or refusing to accede to language, that may give her away. The courts will eventually be faced with the question whether a release which precludes a subsequent suit should be invalidated as "involuntary," when the abused partner's fear of further violence is what prevented her from objecting to its inclusion in the settlement.

Later is Better

An increasing number of jurisdictions are allowing former marital partners to bring tort claims after divorce proceedings are concluded, resisting the application of any of the restrictive doctrines discussed above. In recent years the Supreme Courts of both Maine and Connecticut have written strong and thoughtful opinions in support of this position. In the 1993 case of Henricksen v. Cameron,[1] the Supreme Court of Maine allowed a later-filed tort claim to go forward, even though the parties' divorce was based on the husband's cruel and abusive treatment of his wife. The court noted that: "Maine courts are prohibited from considering fault in dividing marital property ... or in awarding alimony, and stressed that raising tort claims in a divorce action "would undermine the policy premises of no-fault divorce. In addition the court worried that "requiring joinder of tort claims in a divorce action could unduly lengthen the period of time before a spouse could obtain a divorce and result in such adverse consequences as delayed child custody and support determinations."

The 1996 Connecticut case, Delahunty v. Mass. Mutual Life Insurance Co.,[2] involved fraud on the part of the husband, rather than abuse. Nonetheless, the court rendered an opinion which summarizes the many arguments advanced by other courts in the context of abuse. In particular, the court emphasized the danger of giving marital partners an incentive

> to raise and litigate [in their divorce proceedings] every marital grievance that might later form the basis of a possible tort action, for fear of forfeiting the ability to do so later in the form of a tort action. ... This in turn would tend to make contested dissolution actions even lengthier and more acrimonious and expensive than they already are ... contrary to our established policy to foster amicable marital dissolutions whenever possible.

The most crucial argument in favor of allowing a woman to wait until her divorce is resolved before she brings a tort action against her abuser is that unless the legal system preserves this option, a tort remedy will be foreclosed altogether for any woman who feels that pursuing a claim is simply too dangerous, until such time as her separation from her abuser

1. 622 A.2d 1135 (Me. 1993).

2. 674 A.2d 1290 (Conn. 1996).

has been successfully accomplished, and a structure has been put in place that sets limits to his interactions with her and her children. If she is forced to pursue the tort claim together with the divorce, or even to notify the probate court that she is bringing it, or plans to bring it, in another court, she may well forfeit the claim to buy her safety. But if the legal system encourages or facilitates this choice, it rewards her abuser; reinforcing his belief that violence, or the threat of violence, is an effective strategy to secure his interests. As the court in *Delahunty* concluded: "The doctrines of preclusion ... should be flexible and must give way when their mechanical application would frustrate other social policies based on values equally or more important than the convenience afforded by finality in legal controversies." The values furthered by allowing the abused partner to recover for her injuries, and holding the abuser accountable for his abuse, must weigh heavily in the balance.

Courts have not always acknowledged the unique constraints faced by a victim of abuse as she embarks upon the difficult and dangerous task of challenging her abuser's control, and breaking free of the coercive relationship in which she is trapped. Many courts have noted that separating out tort claims from dissolution proceedings will reduce the level of acrimony attending the divorce, consistent with the goals of a no-fault system. Fewer have paused to consider what that may mean in the context of an abusive relationship. In the *Stuart* case, however, the Wisconsin appeals court, in a portion of its opinion specifically endorsed by the Supreme Court, did pay attention to this reality:

> "If an abused spouse cannot commence a tort action subsequent to a divorce, the spouse will be forced to elect between three equally unacceptable alternatives: (1) Commence a tort action during the marriage and possibly endure additional abuse; (2) join a tort claim in a divorce action and waive the right to jury trial on the tort claim; or (3) commence an action to terminate the marriage, forego the tort claim, and surrender the right to recover damages arising from spousal abuse. To enforce such an election would require an abused spouse to surrender both the constitutional right to a jury trial and valuable property rights to preserve his or her wellbeing. This the law will not do."[1]

Similarly, in the *Nash* case, the Idaho Supreme Court reasoned that a divorce proceeding should not serve as a catalyst for additional abuse, and the Connecticut Supreme Court in *Delahunty* approvingly cited both.

3. *Managing the Money*

As courts have repeatedly emphasized, a divorce proceeding is usually not a suitable forum in which to present detailed accounts of abuse, with specific price-tags attached. Further, while the distribution of marital assets *may* be governed by a set of criteria broad enough to respond to past abuse, and support obligations *may* also be structured to account for

1. Stuart v. Stuart, 421 N.W.2d 505, 508 (Wis. 1988) (quoting Stuart v. Stuart, 410 N.W.2d 632, 637–38 (Wis. Ct. App. 1987)).

continuing needs and disabilities, both physical and emotional, that are the consequence of abuse, both distribution and support decisions may legitimately be made on the basis of such an array of "factors," that the abuser never fully pays the bill associated with his abuse. This is problematic from both the perspective of justice, and the perspective of accountability. Furthermore, with respect to support, an award may be subsequently modified for reasons that have nothing to do with one partner's wrongdoing toward the other, or her legitimate claim for redress—seriously undercutting the message that he is responsible because of his past conduct, and the injuries he has inflicted. There is the further danger that in the context of a divorce proceeding an abuser will use the leverage of access to the children to make his partner scale down her financial claims. This is, of course, a charge against the family law system not limited to those interested in the issue of domestic violence—but it has particular poignancy in a context in which a woman may be very legitimately concerned for the physical safety of her children.

For all these reasons the tort system may offer a more satisfactory process for collecting compensation. Here the only issues are the perpetrator's wrongdoing, and the injuries, physical and emotional, he has inflicted. The award can recognize pain and suffering, as well as more tangible elements such as medical expenses and lost earnings, and punitive damages are also a possibility. However, some difficult questions remain about the precise relationship between the financial settlement, or judgment, that comes out of the divorce proceeding, and a tort recovery.

Courts that have insisted that the claims be joined, or at least brought simultaneously, have sometimes suggested that the divorce proceeding, which would normally be concluded before the tort action, should be stayed, so that any tort recovery by the abused partner can be taken into account in distributing the marital estate and awarding support. The defendant in *Heacock II* claimed that his former wife's failure to disclose the tort action until the divorce was final disadvantaged him precisely because it left him unable to employ this strategy. An appellate court in a New York case in 1991, allowing joinder of a tort claim for the transmission of genital herpes with equitable distribution and support claims, said that the divorce court must wait to determine the divorce issues until a jury had rendered a verdict on the tort claim. The court felt that success on the part of the injured spouse would significantly affect the parties' future financial situations, which would in turn affect the maintenance and distribution decisions.[1]

One problem with this approach is the delay it imposes with respect to the divorce. Quite apart from the psychological importance of closure, which may provide some peace of mind for the abused partner, and an important message to the abuser that his claim on his victim has been finally and firmly annulled, there is a practical need to settle both the financial issues and issues about the custody and support of minor children. Courts which have forbidden joinder have frequently argued that this need

1. Maharam v. Maharam, 575 N.Y.S.2d 846, 847 (N.Y. App. 1991).

for closure militates against tying the two claims together, and having the divorce be hostage to the timing of the tort claim.

An even more serious problem with this approach is the possibility that the abuser will be "rescued" from full responsibility for his abuse, if a court, looking at the issue of distribution subsequent to the tort award, when he is relatively poorer and his partner relatively richer, divides the marital estate in a fashion that favors him. This was recognized by another New York court in 1993. The court there insisted that the parties' assets be distributed prior to any award for personal injuries, so that the wife's damages, if any, would be paid from his separated assets, and not from the marital estate.[1] The Wisconsin appeals court in the *Stuart* case took the same position, arguing that any "damages Ronald Stuart would be obligated to pay as a result of the alleged tort are to be satisfied from his individual property or from his interest in the marital property."

If the tort action is brought simultaneously with, but concluded after, the divorce proceedings, the question will be how the probate court should address any potential overlap between the two judgments. One issue is whether the divorce court should try to factor the pending claim into the distribution, as an "asset" belonging to the abused partner, even though its value is uncertain. Some courts have opted for that strategy, while others have declined, on the theory that the value of an unliquidated claim is simply too speculative to warrant inclusion in the calculations. Again, the argument could be couched in terms of justice—why should the distribution favor the abuser, when his potential liability for the injuries he has caused is designed either to compensate his partner (not to make her richer, but only to make her whole) or, in the case of punitive damages, to punish him for egregious behavior. The impact of those damages is surely cushioned in a troubling way if he is given more, by way of the distribution, to pay for them.

If the jurisdiction is one in which marital misconduct can be taken into account in the distribution, the probate judge who knows a tort claim is pending might choose not to use fault as one of the factors guiding his allocation, on the theory that liability for the abuse will be better addressed in the tort action. Or he might want to use fault as one among the many relevant criteria, but indicate what influence it had on his decision, allowing the court in which the tort claim is tried to reduce its award to the abused partner by that amount, to prevent any double recovery.

If the probate court does not know that a tort claim will be filed, because the abused partner has chosen to say nothing until after the divorce is concluded, the judge's options are somewhat different. The abuse may or may not be apparent. If the abused partner has chosen to disclose the abuse, and the jurisdiction allows the judge to use that conduct in calculating the distribution, then it would be safer for the judgment to specify how the abuse had influenced the outcome, on the theory that a tort suit might be brought subsequently. If the abuse is not disclosed, then it cannot explicitly influence the distribution, and the problem disappears

1. Clemente v. Clemente, 19 Fam. L. Rep. (BNA) 1156 (Feb. 2, 1993).

from the probate court's view. It may resurface in the later tort action, if the abusive partner claims that a need-based distribution was in fact responsive to needs created by his abuse, and was, to that extent, compensatory. The best answer to this problem may be that it is the responsibility of the partner who knows, or should, that he may be vulnerable to a later tort claim to seek clarification from the probate court about the basis of the property allocation, if he wishes to preserve the possibility of reducing the tort award on a double recovery theory.

The support obligation raises no double recovery concern, because it can be modified in the face of material changes in circumstance. This enables an abusive partner to go back into probate court seeking a downward modification of his support obligation in the event that his former mate receives a substantial award in her tort case. Thus, if the woman's claim in the divorce proceedings is that she is unable to support herself financially, either out of her share of the marital estate, or by her own efforts, because of a temporary or permanent disability caused by her partner's abuse, her support award should reflect that current need. If the tort award then provides her with a lump sum reflecting that same disability, her former partner can seek to have his support obligations reduced or eliminated. It is clearly preferable to modify the support award, rather than reduce the tort award to reflect support payments, because of the lesser security provided by a support obligation—which can be changed for a variety of reasons having nothing to do with her need. It is also clearly preferable to leave the support order in place until the tort award is safely in the bank, since support payments are often substantially easier to collect.

As long as we have safeguards in place to deal with the limited kinds of double recovery issues which might arise, and which are precisely the same for the subsequently filed tort suit as they are for the suit filed simultaneously but concluded subsequently, there is little to support the idea that the Mr. Heacocks of the world are prejudiced by not anticipating a later tort action when they finalize their divorces Could we not move to view the situation as one in which an abusive partner should be aware of that possibility as a matter of course, especially if his partner has not agreed, in the context of the divorce proceedings, to waive any other rights she may have against him? Given the prevalence of abuse, should not every divorcing partner be counseled to disclose any potential allegations of abuse against him, so that his lawyer can attend to the potential consequences of those allegations? Hopefully more and more courts will follow the lead of those which have already declared the legitimacy of the "divorce first, tort last" strategy, and those which have "managed the money" so that the abused partner can be fully compensated for the injuries she has suffered, while her partner is held fully accountable for his abuse.

* * *

NOTES AND QUESTIONS

1. If you were a family lawyer advising a client who had been abused about the wisdom of pursuing a tort claim as well as a divorce, what

research would you do into the law of the relevant jurisdiction before laying out her options? What you want to know from her about her relationship, her current circumstances and her future plans as you continued to explore those options together?

2. In this chapter, we have dealt exclusively with tort claims brought against abusers by their abused partners. In the next we continue to address tort claims, but this time claims against third parties who arguably had responsibilities to prevent the abuse from occurring, or to limit the damage done, and failed to fulfil them.

CHAPTER TWELVE

THIRD PARTY LIABILITY FOR ABUSE

Introductory Note

This chapter looks at two contexts that have generated claims by victims of domestic violence against third parties. The first involves police or other law enforcement officers or agencies who fail to protect women from their abusers. The second involves situations in which abuse follows women to work, and employers become implicated, either by their failure to offer protection, or by taking adverse action against victimized employees. In the first context, it is fair to say that recent cases demonstrate increasing reluctance to impose liability, at both the federal and the state level. In the second, the parameters of potential liability are only now being worked out.

Both contexts present complex doctrinal questions. Failures of law enforcement can be challenged under federal civil rights law, as constitutional torts—violations of constitutional guarantees of due process or equal protection. However, constrictive interpretations of the substantive due process owed by state actors to those threatened by private violence, and demanding levels of proof of discrimination have created significant barriers for plaintiffs. Alternatively, failures of law enforcement can be challenged under state tort law, as breaches of a duty of care owed to those threatened by violence. But issues of sovereign immunity, coupled with judicial reluctance to recognize specific duties of protection, make this road equally difficult.

In the workplace context, those seeking redress from employers must grapple with a variety of regulatory schemes, and risk that their claims will fall through the cracks. Workers' compensation schemes generally provide an exclusive remedy for claims arising out of and in the course of employment. While these "no-fault" schemes offer compensation without any proof of fault on the employer's part, recovery is usually significantly less generous than it would be in a comparable tort claim. Depending on the state's interpretation of its workers' compensation statute, and the precise circumstances of the case, a plaintiff may find herself shut out of the statutory scheme, and then may or may not find that she has an alternative remedy under state tort law. If her abuser is a fellow employee, there is even a possibility that Title VII's guarantees against gender discrimination and sexual harassment may come into play. If her employer takes adverse action against her, and her workplace is unionized, her claim is likely to be processed through a grievance procedure and decided by an arbitrator under federal labor relations law. Outside the union context, her only recourse against adverse action by an employer because of her status as a victim of partner abuse is under state contract law, which is likely to offer only very limited protection.

A. WHEN LAW ENFORCEMENT FAILS TO PROTECT

Challenges to police inaction in the face of domestic violence have a venerable history within the battered women's movement; they were among the earliest strategies deployed by lawyers working with battered women to change policing policy and force public recognition of the criminal, and often lethal, nature of partner abuse. In this first reading, Joan Zorza describes the early challenges, and their impact.

Joan Zorza
The Criminal Law of Misdemeanor Violence, 1970–1990, 83 Journal of Criminal Law and Criminology 46, 53–60 (1992)

In the 1970s, Americans gradually became aware that millions of women were being brutally abused by their husbands. A few women had started organizing around the issue of battered women. Some opened their homes to victims or started shelters. Others proposed legislation to assist battered women. It was clear, however, that neither of these approaches would have much effect if the police did not enforce the new laws. As women [became] increasing[ly] frustrated by the failure of police to arrest even husbands who committed even felony assaults, it became clear that they needed to concentrate their efforts on forcing the police to enforce the few laws that did exist to help battered women.

In 1972, the executor of Ruth Bunnell's estate filed a wrongful death action against the San Jose Police Department.[1] Mrs. Bunnell had called the police at least twenty times in the year before her death to complain that her husband was abusing both her and her two daughters. Only once did they arrest her husband. In September of 1972, she called the police for help, telling them that her husband was on his way to the house to kill her. They told her to wait until he arrived. By the time police came in response to a neighbor's call, her husband had stabbed her to death. The California Court of Appeals upheld the trial court's dismissal of the case, reasoning that the police had never "induced decedent's reliance on a promise, express or implied, that they would provide her with protection."

Legal aid and legal service lawyers, who had always known that the vast majority of their female divorce clients were being violently abused by their husbands, were experiencing the same frustrations. Fearing that another tort action for damages against the police would probably meet with little success, two groups of legal services lawyers on opposite shores of the country decided to adopt a different approach. They filed for declaratory and injunctive relief against the police in order to force them to do what the law empowered them to do to protect battered women.

1. Hartzler v. City of San Jose, 46 Cal. App. 3d 6, 120 Cal. Rptr. 5 (1975).

The first to file suit was a group of five attorneys in the Legal Aid Society of Alameda County in Oakland. They filed a complaint in October of 1976 in the Northern District of California.[2] The suit which was captioned *Scott v. Hart,* was in the form of a class action against George T. Hart, Chief of the Oakland Police Department. They filed on behalf of "women in general and black women in particular who are victims of domestic violence." All five of the named plaintiffs were black women who had repeatedly called the Oakland police for protection when they were beaten up by their husbands, ex-husbands or boyfriends. The officers had either failed to respond or had responded in an ineffectual or, in one case, a threatening manner. By bringing their suit on behalf of black victims of domestic violence who were getting less adequate police responses than were white victims, the legal aid lawyers were able to allege a denial of the equal protection mandated by the Fourteenth Amendment. They also claimed that the police had breached their duty to arrest the abusers "when a felony [had] been committed such as felony wife beating" and that a "police policy that de-emphasizes and discourages arresting assailants . . . is arbitrary, capricious, discriminatory, and deprives plaintiffs and the plaintiff class of the right to equal protection of the laws." The complaint asked the court to: (1) permanently enjoin the police from refusing to respond adequately to battered women's calls; (2) affirmatively order the police to respond adequately; (3) order the police "to arrest when they know that a felony has been committed or when the woman requests the arrest of the assailant"; (4) order the police to "advise women of their right to make citizens' arrests and [of the fact] that the police [will] effectuate those arrests by taking the assailant into custody"; (5) order the police to "take assailants to a mental facility for 72–hour observation" when appropriate; (6) order the police to train officers in "how to best handle these incidents"; (7) order the police to start a batterer treatment program; (8) order the city to establish a shelter for women; and (9) force defendants to pay plaintiffs' "court costs, expenditures and reasonable attorneys fees."

The first hurdle which plaintiffs needed to overcome was posed by the Supreme Court's ruling in *Rizzo v. Goode*.[1] In that case, the Court held that supervisory officials must have actual knowledge of and responsibility for promulgating discriminatory polices before an aggrieved party could get injunctive relief in federal court. This hurdle, however, proved to be not much of an obstacle in *Scott.* The existence within the Oakland Police Department of a clear arrest-avoidance policy which was known to the watch commanders and other supervisors persuaded the court to allow the case to survive a motion to dismiss. Not until November 14, 1979, however, more than three years after the class had filed its complaint, did the parties agree to a settlement. The settlement granted most of the plaintiffs' requested relief: the police agreed to a new policy in which they would respond quickly to domestic violence calls. The police also agreed to make an arrest whenever an officer had probable cause to believe that a felonious assault had occurred or that a misdemeanor had been committed in his

2. Scott v. Hart, No. C–76–2395 (N.D. Cal., filed Oct. 28, 1976).

1. Rizzo v. Goode, 423 U.S. 364 (1976).

presence. This new policy required the police to make their arrest decisions without looking to factors traditionally used to justify inaction. The police also agreed not to use the threat of adverse financial consequences for the couple to justify inaction or to urge the victim not to pursue the case. The settlement also required police to inform each battered woman that she had a right to make a citizen's arrest, and required police to help her to do so. Officers would thereafter refer victims to supportive agencies for counseling and other assistance. Furthermore, the department acknowledged that it had an affirmative duty to enforce civil restraining and "kick out" orders. While Oakland was not required to provide a shelter and counseling for victims (or assailants), the city agreed to apply for federal funding for any support services available to battered women, and to pay the plaintiffs' attorney fees and court costs.

. . .

In December 1976, approximately six weeks after the *Scott* case was filed, three New York legal services programs and the Center for Constitutional Rights filed a similar class action suit on behalf of married battered women against the New York City Police Department and the New York Family Court. In their complaint, captioned *Bruno v. Codd,*[1] twelve named plaintiffs alleged that the police failed to arrest husbands who battered their wives and that New York Family Court personnel denied battered wives access to the court. The complaint, filed in the Supreme Court of the State of New York, named the New York City Police Department, the Family Court, the Probation Department, and sixteen others as defendants. They claimed thirteen causes of action on behalf of battered wives who had repeatedly been denied police protection or given endless runarounds. During the pendency of the case, affidavits from forty-eight more women were received, supporting all of the charges.

Thirteen months before the complaint was filed, two New York lawyers had decided to "institute a lawsuit challenging the legal system's treatment of battered wives" there. They interviewed numerous battered wives and collected information about the policies of the New York City Police Department. The affidavits that they collected showed a blatant disregard for women's welfare. The affidavits also showed that the women were desperate to stop the abuse, had tried numerous times to do so, and had failed due only to the system's faults. The women explained in their affidavits the economic and societal pressures that kept them from leaving their husbands. They outlined the obstacles each encountered, such as a lack of day care, shelter beds or housing, and increased violence from their husbands, which, along with the absence of police protection, combined to prevent them from leaving their husbands. They described how, even when women managed to obtain orders of protection, the police refused to enforce them.

The Administrative Judge of the Family Court stated to the *Bruno* court that he was unaware of the problems described in the plaintiffs' complaint, and that the Family Court had a right to address the changes

1. . . . Bruno v. Codd, 90 Misc 2d 1047, 396 N.Y.S. 2d 974 (Sup. Ct. 1977). . . .

which the plaintiffs' sought. The Director of the New York City Probation Department issued an order setting forth procedures for processing oral or written complaints against any probation employee who failed to advise women of their right to reject offers of mediation and instead appear immediately before a judge on a petition for an order of protection. In addition, the legislature amended of the Family Court Act to prohibit officials from discouraging or preventing anyone wishing to file for a protective order from having access to the courts for such purposes. Accordingly, the New York Court of Appeals dismissed the causes of action against the Family Court and Probation Department. Even in dismissing the causes of action against the Family Court, however, New York's highest court praised "the welcome efforts of plaintiff's counsel" to alert and sensitize the courts to their responsibility to respond to the brutality inflicted upon battered women.

After the Court of Appeals dismissed the counts against the Family Court and the Probation Department, several counts against the Police Department remained pending in the trial court. Judge Gellinoff, the trial judge, was troubled by the allegations supporting these counts. "For too long," he wrote in denying a motion to dismiss,

> Anglo–American laws treated a man's physical abuse of his wife as different from any other assault and, indeed as an acceptable practice. If the allegations of the instant complaint—buttressed by hundreds of pages of affidavits—are true, only the written law has changed; in reality, wife beating is still condoned, if not approved, by some of those charged with protecting its victims.[1]

The police department, concerned that the ruling on the motion to dismiss was a precursor of things to come, entered into a consent judgment with the plaintiffs. The judgment provided that the police would thenceforth have a duty to respond and would respond to every woman's request for protection against someone she alleged to be her husband if she said he was beating her or had violated an order of protection. If the officer has reasonable cause "to believe that a husband has committed a misdemeanor against his wife or has committed a violation against his wife in the officer's presence, the officer shall not refrain from making an officer arrest of the husband without justification." When the officer has reasonable cause to believe that a husband committed a felony against his wife or violated an order of protection, the officer must arrest him and should not attempt to reconcile the parties or mediate. When a husband who allegedly committed a crime against her is not present when the police arrive and the wife wants him arrested or to make a civilian arrest, the officer must locate the husband just as with any other crime. Officers must hereafter assist the wife in obtaining any needed medical assistance, and inform her of her right to get a protective order from the family court. The police department must promulgate new policies and training materials in conformance with the decree, and a supervising officer must promptly investigate any allegation that a provision of the consent decree was violated and,

1. Bruno v. Codd, 90 Misc. 2d 1047, 396 N.Y.S. 2d 974 (Sup. Ct. 1977)....

if it was, cause it to be immediately complied with as soon as possible. The court retained jurisdiction of the police action and allowed either party to apply for further relief as may be necessary or appropriate.

The Oakland and New York City lawsuits made clear to police departments throughout the United States that they were vulnerable to being sued if they failed to protect the rights of battered women. Battered women's advocates soon learned how many police chiefs knew that both of the departments had "lost." As a result, police departments in many towns and cities agreed to revamp their policies and practices without any suit having to be filed. The possibility that the town or city might be liable for attorney fees and even for damages in a case by injured women became a persuasive bargaining chip to many battered women's lawyers and advocates.

The caselaw took one more important step forward in *Thurman v. City of Torrington, Conn.,*[2] where a federal jury awarded Tracey Thurman and her son $2.3 million because the police were negligent in failing to protect her from her abusive husband. The court found that Torrington's policy of indifference amounted to sex discrimination.

The effect of the case was dramatic. As one commentator observed,

> The Thurman case was widely reported in the popular press and in academic journals. It graphically confirmed the extreme financial penalty that could be imposed on police departments when they abjectly fail to perform their duties. In addition, it confirmed that in appropriate cases, these massive liability awards would be upheld.

Many police departments that did not get the message from *Scott* and *Bruno* were forced by *Thurman's* threat of huge liability to change their policies.

* * *

Federal Civil Rights Claims under 42 U.S.C. § 1983

42 U.S.C. § 1983, the federal civil rights law on which some of these early challenges were based, provides a cause of action against government officials whose actions deprive individuals of a constitutionally protected right. It was originally enacted as part of the Ku Klux Klan Act of 1871 as a federal response to state inaction in the face of private racially-motivated violence—in particular the violence of the Klan's nightriders against former slaves. In the 1960s, after decades of disuse, § 1983 was reinvigorated to protect against police misconduct. See Monroe v. Pape, 365 U.S. 167, 5 L. Ed. 2d 492, 81 S. Ct. 473 (1961).

To establish a claim, a plaintiff must show: (1) that the conduct complained of was committed by a person acting under color of state law; (2) that the conduct deprived the plaintiff of a constitutional right; and (3) that the deprivation proximately caused the plaintiff's injury. The defendant may be an individual, or a municipality or municipal agency, such as a police department. States and state agencies can be sued only for prospective

2. 595 F. Supp. 1521 (Dist.Conn. 1984).

relief, not damages, because of state sovereign immunity under the Eleventh Amendment. Individual state employees can be sued for damages, but only in their personal rather than their official capacities, so that any judgment against them will be satisfied out of their personal assets. Municipalities are not vicariously liable for the actions of their employees under § 1983, but only for their own policies or practices. Individual municipal employees can be sued in either their personal or their official capacities. If they are sued in their official capacities, any judgment against them will be satisfied by their employer. Individual defendants are also protected by certain immunities. Judges and prosecutors have absolute immunity for acts within the scope of their official duties. Police officers and other officials have qualified immunity for discretionary actions, meaning that they are protected from individual liability unless their conduct violates clearly established law, and is unreasonable, based on the knowledge they had at the time.

Plaintiffs in § 1983 actions can recover attorneys' fees, compensatory damages, punitive damages for reckless or callously indifferent conduct, and declaratory or injunctive relief.

As Joan Zorza comments, the *Thurman* case may be the high watermark of § 1983 jurisprudence in the context of challenges to inadequate law enforcement against domestic violence perpetrators.

Tracey Thurman, et al. v. City of Torrington, et al.

595 F. Supp. 1521.
United States District Court for the District of Connecticut, 1984.

■ Blumenfeld, Senior District Judge.

The plaintiffs have brought this action pursuant to 42 U.S.C. §§ 1983, 1985, 1986 and 1988, as well as the fifth, ninth, and fourteenth amendments to the Constitution, alleging that their constitutional rights were violated by the nonperformance or malperformance of official duties by the defendant police officers. In addition, the plaintiffs seek to hold liable the defendant City of Torrington (hereinafter, the "City"). The defendant City has filed a motion to dismiss the plaintiffs' complaint....

... A complaint should not be dismissed unless it appears that the plaintiff could prove no set of facts in support of her claim which would entitle her to relief.... Furthermore, it is well settled that for purposes of a motion to dismiss, the well pleaded material allegations of the complaint are taken as true....

Between early October 1982 and June 10, 1983, the plaintiff, Tracey Thurman, a woman living in the City of Torrington, and others on her behalf, notified the defendant City through the defendant police officers of the City of repeated threats upon her life and the life of her child, the plaintiff Charles J. Thurman, Jr., made by her estranged husband, Charles Thurman. Attempts to file complaints by plaintiff Tracey Thurman against her estranged husband in response to his threats of death and maiming were ignored or rejected by the named defendants and the defendant City.

An abbreviated chronology of the plaintiff's attempted and actual notifications of the threats made against her and her son by her estranged husband to the defendant City and police officers is appropriate for consideration of this motion.

In October 1982, Charles Thurman attacked plaintiff Tracey Thurman at the home of Judy Bentley and Richard St. Hilaire in the City of Torrington. Mr. St. Hilaire and Ms. Bentley made a formal complaint of the attack to one of the unnamed defendant police officers and requested efforts to keep the plaintiff's husband, Charles Thurman, off their property.

On or about November 5, 1982, Charles Thurman returned to the St. Hilaire–Bentley residence and using physical force took the plaintiff Charles J. Thurman, Jr. from said residence. Plaintiff Tracey Thurman and Mr. St. Hilaire went to Torrington police headquarters to make a formal complaint. At that point, unnamed defendant police officers of the City of Torrington refused to accept a complaint from Mr. St. Hilaire even as to trespassing.

On or about November 9, 1982, Charles Thurman screamed threats at Tracey while she was sitting in her car. Defendant police officer Neil Gemelli stood on the street watching Charles Thurman scream threats at Tracey until Charles Thurman broke the windshield of plaintiff Tracey Thurman's car while she was inside the vehicle. Charles Thurman was arrested after he broke the windshield, and on the next day, November 10, 1982, he was convicted of breach of peace. He received a suspended sentence of six months and a two-year "conditional discharge," during which he was ordered to stay completely away from the plaintiff Tracey Thurman and the Bentley–St. Hilaire residence and to commit no further crimes. The court imposing probation informed the defendants of this sentence.

On December 31, 1982, while plaintiff Tracey Thurman was at the Bentley–St. Hilaire residence, Charles Thurman returned to said residence and once again threatened her. She called the Torrington Police Department. One of the unnamed police officer defendants took the call, and, although informed of the violation of the conditional discharge, made no attempt to ascertain Charles Thurman's whereabouts or to arrest him.

Between January 1, 1983 and May 4, 1983, numerous telephone complaints to the Torrington Police Department were taken by various unnamed police officers, in which repeated threats of violence to the plaintiffs by Charles Thurman were reported and his arrest on account of the threats and violation of the terms of his probation was requested.

On May 4 and 5, 1983, the plaintiff Tracey Thurman and Ms. Bentley reported to the Torrington Police Department that Charles Thurman had said that he would shoot the plaintiffs. Defendant police officer Storrs took the written complaint of plaintiff Tracey Thurman who was seeking an arrest warrant for her husband because of his death threat and violation of his "conditional discharge." Defendant Storrs refused to take the complaint of Ms. Bentley. Plaintiff Tracey Thurman was told to return three weeks later on June 1, 1983 when defendant Storrs or some other person connected with the police department of the defendant City would seek a warrant for the arrest of her husband.

On May 6, 1983, Tracey filed an application for a restraining order against Charles Thurman in the Litchfield Superior Court. That day, the court issued an ex parte restraining order forbidding Charles Thurman from assaulting, threatening, and harassing Tracey Thurman. The defendant City was informed of this order.

On May 27, 1983, Tracey Thurman requested police protection in order to get to the Torrington Police Department, and she requested a warrant for her husband's arrest upon her arrival at headquarters after being taken there by one of the unnamed defendant police officers. She was told that she would have to wait until after the Memorial Day holiday weekend and was advised to call on Tuesday, May 31, to pursue the warrant request.

On May 31, 1983, Tracey Thurman appeared once again at the Torrington Police Department to pursue the warrant request. She was then advised by one of the unnamed defendant police officers that defendant Schapp was the only policeman who could help her and that he was on vacation. She was told that she would have to wait until he returned. That same day, Tracey's brother-in-law, Joseph Kocsis, called the Torrington Police Department to protest the lack of action taken on Tracey's complaint. Although Mr. Kocsis was advised that Charles Thurman would be arrested on June 8, 1983, no such arrest took place.

On June 10, 1983, Charles Thurman appeared at the Bentley–St. Hilaire residence in the early afternoon and demanded to speak to Tracey. Tracey, remaining indoors, called the defendant police department asking that Charles be picked up for violation of his probation. After about 15 minutes, Tracey went outside to speak to her husband in an effort to persuade him not to take or hurt Charles Jr. Soon thereafter, Charles began to stab Tracey repeatedly in the chest, neck and throat.

Approximately 25 minutes after Tracey's call to the Torrington Police Department and after her stabbing, a single police officer, the defendant Petrovits, arrived on the scene. Upon the arrival of Officer Petrovits at the scene of the stabbing, Charles Thurman was holding a bloody knife. Charles then dropped the knife and, in the presence of Petrovits, kicked the plaintiff Tracey Thurman in the head and ran into the Bentley–St. Hilaire residence. Charles returned from within the residence holding the plaintiff Charles Thurman, Jr. and dropped the child on his wounded mother. Charles then kicked Tracey in the head a second time. Soon thereafter, defendants DeAngelo, Nukirk, and Columbia arrived on the scene but still permitted Charles Thurman to wander about the crowd and to continue to threaten Tracey. Finally, upon approaching Tracey once again, this time while she was lying on a stretcher, Charles Thurman was arrested and taken into custody.

It is also alleged that at all times mentioned above, except for approximately two weeks following his conviction and sentencing on November 10, 1982, Charles Thurman resided in Torrington and worked there as a counterman and short order cook at Skie's Diner. There he served many members of the Torrington Police Department including some of the named and unnamed defendants in this case. In the course of his employment Charles Thurman boasted to the defendant police officer patrons that he intended to "get" his wife and that he intended to kill her.

I. *Motion to Dismiss the Claims of Tracey Thurman*

The defendant City now brings a motion to dismiss the claims against it. The City first argues that the plaintiff's complaint should be dismissed for failure to allege the deprivation of a constitutional right. Though the complaint alleges that the actions of the defendants deprived the plaintiff Tracey Thurman of her constitutional right to equal protection of the laws, the defendant City argues that the equal protection clause of the fourteenth amendment "does not guarantee equal application of social services." ... Rather, the defendant City argues that the equal protection clause "only prohibits intentional discrimination that is racially motivated"....

The defendant City's argument is clearly a misstatement of the law. The application of the equal protection clause is not limited to racial classifications or racially motivated discrimination.... Classifications on the basis of gender will be held invalid under the equal protection clause unless they are substantially related to an important governmental objective, Craig v. Boren, 429 U.S. 190, 197, 50 L. Ed. 2d 397, 97 S. Ct. 451 (1976), reh'g denied, 429 U.S. 1124, 51 L. Ed. 2d 574, 97 S. Ct. 1161 (1977). And lastly, the equal protection clause will be applied to strike down classifications which are not rationally related to a legitimate governmental purpose. San Antonio School Dist. v. Rodriguez, 411 U.S. 1, 55, 36 L. Ed. 2d 16, 93 S. Ct. 1278, reh'g denied, 411 U.S. 959, 36 L. Ed. 2d 418, 93 S. Ct. 1919 (1973).

In the instant case, the plaintiffs allege that the defendants use an administrative classification that manifests itself in discriminatory treatment violative of the equal protection clause. Police protection in the City of Torrington, they argue, is fully provided to persons abused by someone with whom the victim has no domestic relationship. But the Torrington police have consistently afforded lesser protection, plaintiffs allege, when the victim is (1) a woman abused or assaulted by a spouse or boyfriend, or (2) a child abused by a father or stepfather. The issue to be decided, then, is whether the plaintiffs have properly alleged a violation of the equal protection clause of the fourteenth amendment.

Police action is subject to the equal protection clause and section 1983 whether in the form of commission of violative acts or omission to perform required acts pursuant to the police officer's duty to protect. ... City officials and police officers are under an affirmative duty to preserve law and order, and to protect the personal safety of persons in the community.... This duty applies equally to women whose personal safety is threatened by individuals with whom they have or have had a domestic relationship as well as to all other persons whose personal safety is threatened, including women not involved in domestic relationships. If officials have notice of the possibility of attacks on women in domestic relationships or other persons, they are under an affirmative duty to take reasonable measures to protect the personal safety of such persons in the community. Failure to perform this duty would constitute a denial of equal protection of the laws.

Although the plaintiffs point to no law which on its face discriminates against victims abused by someone with whom they have a domestic relationship, the plaintiffs have alleged that there is an administrative classification used to implement the law in a discriminatory fashion. It is well settled that the equal protection clause is applicable not only to discriminatory legislative action, but also to discriminatory governmental action in administration and enforcement of the law.... Here the plaintiffs were threatened with assault in violation of Connecticut law. Over the course of eight months the police failed to afford the plaintiffs protection against such assaults, and failed to take action to arrest the perpetrator of these assaults. The plaintiffs have alleged that this failure to act was pursuant to a pattern or practice of affording inadequate protection, or no protection at all, to women who have complained of having been abused by their husbands or others with whom they have had close relations.... Such a practice is tantamount to an administrative classification used to implement the law in a discriminatory fashion.

If the City wishes to discriminate against women who are the victims of domestic violence, it must articulate an important governmental interest for doing so.... In its memorandum and at oral argument the City has failed to put forward any justification for its disparate treatment of women.[1] Such a practice was at one time sanctioned by law....

Today, however, any notion of a husband's prerogative to physically discipline his wife is an "increasingly outdated misconception." *Craig v. Boren*, 429 U.S. at 198–99. As such it must join other "archaic and overbroad" premises which have been rejected as unconstitutional....

A man is not allowed to physically abuse or endanger a woman merely because he is her husband. Concomitantly, a police officer may not knowingly refrain from interference in such violence, and may not "automatically decline to make an arrest simply because the assaulter and his victim are married to each other." *Bruno v. Codd*.... Such inaction on the part of the officer is a denial of the equal protection of the laws.

In addition, any notion that defendants' practice can be justified as a means of promoting domestic harmony by refraining from interference in marital disputes, has no place in the case at hand. Rather than evidencing a desire to work out her problems with her husband privately, Tracey pleaded with the police to offer her at least some measure of protection. Further, she sought and received a restraining order to keep her husband at a distance. Finally, it is important to recall here the Supreme Court's

1. It may develop that the classification in the instant case is not one based on gender, but instead consists of all spouses who are victims of domestic violence—male and female. At this stage of the proceedings, however, plaintiffs' allegations of gender-based discrimination will be taken as true. In one study of interspousal abuse it is claimed that "in 29 out of every 30 such cases the husband stands accused of abusing his wife." ... cited in *Bruno v. Codd*, 47 N.Y.2d 582, 419 N.Y.S.2d 901, 902 n.2, 393 N.E.2d 976.

dictum in *Reed v. Reed,* 404 U.S. at 77, that "whatever may be said as to the positive values of avoiding intrafamily controversy, the choice in this context may not lawfully be mandated solely on the basis of sex." Accordingly, the defendant City of Torrington's motion to dismiss the plaintiff Tracey Thurman's complaint on the basis of failure to allege violation of a constitutional right is denied.

II. *Motion to Dismiss the Claims of Charles Thurman, Jr.*

Plaintiff Charles Thurman, Jr. also claims that the City of Torrington denied him the equal protection of the laws. He alleges that the defendants fail to protect children against the domestic violence of fathers and stepfathers. This claim fails on several grounds. Other than the June 10, 1983 assault, Charles Thurman, Jr. has alleged no attacks made against him.... Thus Charles Thurman Jr. did not suffer from a continuous failure of the police to provide him protection as did his mother, Tracey Thurman. The isolated failure of the defendants to prevent the June 10, 1983 assault on Charles Thurman, Jr. does not violate any constitutional rights....

III. *Have the Plaintiffs Properly Alleged a Custom or Policy on the Part of the City of Torrington?*

The plaintiffs have alleged in paragraph 13 of their complaint as follows:

> During the period of time described herein, and for a long time prior thereto, the defendant City of Torrington acting through its Police Department, condoned a pattern or practice of affording inadequate protection, or no protection at all, to women who have complained of having been abused by their husbands or others with whom they have had close relations. Said pattern, custom or policy, well known to the individual defendants, was the basis on which they ignored said numerous complaints and reports of threats to the plaintiffs with impunity.

While a municipality is not liable for the constitutional torts of its employees on a *respondeat superior* theory, a municipality may be sued for damages under section 1983 when "the action that is alleged to be unconstitutional implements or executes a policy statement, ordinance, regulation, or decision officially adopted and promulgated by the body's officers" or is "visited pursuant to governmental 'custom' even though such a custom has not received formal approval through the body's official decisionmaking channels." Monell v. New York City Department of Social Services, 436 U.S. 658, 690, 56 L. Ed. 2d 611, 98 S. Ct. 2018 (1978).

Some degree of specificity is required in the pleading of a custom or policy on the part of a municipality. Mere conclusory allegations devoid of factual content will not suffice.... As this court has pointed out, a plaintiff must typically point to facts outside his own case to support his allegation of a policy on the part of a municipality. ...

In the instant case, however, the plaintiff Tracey Thurman has specifically alleged in her statement of facts a series of acts and omissions on the part of the defendant police officers and police department that took place over the course of eight months. From this particularized pleading a pattern emerges that evidences deliberate indifference on the part of the police department to the complaints of the plaintiff Tracey Thurman and to its duty to protect her. Such an ongoing pattern of deliberate indifference raises an inference of "custom" or "policy" on the part of the municipality.... Furthermore, this pattern of inaction climaxed on June 10, 1983 in an incident so brutal that under the law of the Second Circuit that "single brutal incident may be sufficient to suggest a link between a violation of constitutional rights and a pattern of police misconduct." Owens v. Haas, 601 F.2d 1242, 1246 (2d Cir.), cert. denied, 444 U.S. 980, 100 S. Ct. 483, 62 L. Ed. 2d 407 (1979).... Accordingly, defendant City of Torrington's motion to dismiss the plaintiffs claims against it, on the ground that the plaintiffs failed to properly allege a custom or policy on the part of the municipality, is denied.

IV. *The Unidentified Police Officers*

Defendant City of Torrington has moved to dismiss the claims against the unidentified police officers claiming that this court lacks jurisdiction over these parties as they have not been properly served. At this stage of the proceedings, such a dismissal would be inappropriate:

> at this time, before plaintiff has had an opportunity to engage in discovery which could disclose the exact identity of the officers whom plaintiff presently is able to partially identify ..., the Court discerns no purpose in dismissal of the "John Doe" defendants.

... Hence, defendant's motion, to the extent that it suggests dismissal of the unidentified defendants, is denied without prejudice to its renewal at a later date.

. . .

SO ORDERED

NOTES AND QUESTIONS

1. Tracey Thurman's claim resulted in a jury award of $2.3 million. Subsequent efforts to invoke equal protection as the basis for challenges to police inaction, however, have fared less well. To succeed, the plaintiff must demonstrate: (1) the existence of a policy or a practice which leads police to respond differently to domestic violence situations than they do to other similar incidents of violence, affording victims of domestic violence less protection; and (2) that the policy or practice purposefully, or intentionally, discriminates against women. As the court in *Thurman* suggested, there will often be a question whether the policy or practice in question discriminates between women and men, or rather between domestic violence and other victims. If the discrimination is not gender-based, it will be subject only to a deferential "rational basis" scrutiny. See, for example, Cellini v. City of Sterling Heights, 856 F. Supp. 1215, 1219 (E.D. Mich. 1994), in which the court applied a rational relationship test because even though the complaint alleged gender discrimination, the plaintiff's response to a summary judgment motion only articulated discrimination against domestic violence victims. Similarly, the Second Circuit in Eagleston v. Guido, 41

F.3d 865 (2d Cir. 1994) noted that there were differences between domestic disputes and nondomestic disputes that could reasonably result in disparate treatment, without discriminatory intent. More recently, the First Circuit ruled that the testimony of officers that they "shied away from" domestic violence cases established a discriminatory policy, but not gender discrimination. Soto v. Flores, 103 F.3d 1056 (1st. Cir 1997), cert. den. 118 S. Ct. 71 (U.S. 1997).

2. Proving an intent to discriminate on the basis of gender has become increasingly difficult in the context of § 1983 actions, as it has in equal protection challenges more generally, and also in Title VII cases. Courts generally require evidence beyond the facts of plaintiff's own case, contrary to the finding in *Thurman* that a sufficient history in a single case, or even a single brutal incident, could at least raise an inference of a discriminatory custom or policy. On the other hand, in Balistreri v. Pacifica Police Department, 901 F.2d 696 (9th Cir. 1990), where the police officer who responded to the plaintiff made disparaging remarks, the Ninth Circuit found those remarks enough to suggest an equal protection violation, an intent to treat domestic violence less seriously than other assaults, and an animus against abused women.

It would seem that statistics, aggregating information about police handling of different classes of case, could support the argument that the plaintiff's treatment was not aberrant, but was indeed part of a pattern of discriminatory conduct. However, the statistics are unlikely to do more than prove that domestic disputes receive different treatment than nondomestic disputes, which is not enough, as noted above, to demonstrate denial of equal protection. Furthermore, courts have in a number of cases found fault with the statistical testimony offered by the plaintiff. In McKee v. City of Rockwall, 877 F.2d 409, 415 (5th Cir. 1989), for example, the Fifth Circuit found that the statistics proferred by the plaintiff were mathematically inaccurate, and that even if they had been accurate they would not have accounted for a wide variety of factors that might influence the likelihood of arrest. In a more recent district court case, Soto v. Carrasquillo, 878 F.Supp. 324, 330 (D.P.R. 1995) the statistics offered were insufficient, because the expert did not explain how they had been compiled, and because the plaintiff did not compare arrest rates under the domestic violence law with arrest rates for other cases of abuse or violence.

The difficulties of proof are illustrated in this excerpt from the opinion in Ricketts v. City of Columbia, 36 F.3d 775, 781–82 (8th Cir. 1994):

> When a widespread custom of a municipality impacts disproportionately on one gender, an equal protection violation arises "only if that impact can be traced to a discriminatory purpose." Personnel Admin. of Mass. v. Feeney, 442 U.S. 256, 272, 60 L. Ed. 2d 870, 99 S. Ct. 2282 (1979). The disproportionate impact is only relevant to the extent that it "reflects a discriminatory purpose." Washington v. Davis, 426 U.S. 229, 239, 48 L. Ed. 2d 597, 96 S. Ct. 2040 (1976). A discriminatory purpose is more than a mere "awareness of the consequences." *Feeney,* 442 U.S. at 279. The law or custom must be found to

have been implemented "at least in part 'because of,' not merely 'in spite of,' its adverse effects upon an identifiable group." Id.

When a municipal custom employs a facially neutral classification and its disproportionate impact on one gender is not susceptible to a neutral explanation, "impact itself would signal that the real classification made by the law was in fact not neutral." *Feeney,* 442 U.S. at 275. However, in only a few cases, where a facially neutral policy impacted exclusively against one suspect class and that impact was unexplainable on neutral grounds, has the impact alone signalled a discriminatory purpose. See Gomillion v. Lightfoot, 364 U.S. 339, 5 L. Ed. 2d 110, 81 S. Ct. 125 (1960); Yick Wo v. Hopkins, 118 U.S. 356, 30 L. Ed. 220, 6 S. Ct. 1064 (1886). When there is a rational, neutral explanation for the adverse impact and the law or custom disadvantages both men and women, then an inference of discriminatory purpose is not permitted. See *Feeney,* 442 U.S. at 275.

> When the adverse consequences of a law [or custom] upon an identifiable group are as inevitable as the gender-based consequences ... a strong inference that the adverse effects were desired can reasonably be drawn. But in this inquiry—made as it is under the Constitution—an inference is a working tool, not a synonym for proof. When, as here, the impact is essentially an unavoidable consequence of a [legitimate neutral policy or custom] the inference simply fails to ripen into proof.

Id. at 279, n.25. In sum, when determining whether there is a showing of discriminatory intent, disproportionate impact is but one factor to consider along with the inferences that rationally may be drawn from the totality of the other relevant facts....

The plaintiffs offered the expert testimony of Dr. Eve Buzawa who had gathered statistics indicating that the Columbia police department makes fewer arrests in domestic abuse cases than in nondomestic cases. Dr. Buzawa's opinion was based upon assault reports from portions of the previous year. Dr. Buzawa testified that the custom of disparate treatment for victims of domestic abuse adversely impacts women to a greater extent than men because over 90% of the victims of domestic abuse are women. The disproportionate impact is not exclusively suffered by women, however, because the classification itself is facially neutral and includes male victims of domestic abuse. There is no evidence that male victims of domestic abuse are treated differently than female victims of domestic abuse.

We must discern whether there is a rational explanation for the disparate impact on women. Because of the inherent differences between domestic disputes and nondomestic disputes, legitimately different factors may affect a police officer's decision to arrest or not to arrest in any given situation. Dr. Buzawa's statistics took into account some of the variables that affect a decision to arrest in domestic disputes, but we believe that not all of the differences that enter into the discretionary decision of whether to arrest can be properly assessed and quantified through statistics.... Police "discretion is essential to the criminal justice process." *McCleskey,* 481 U.S. at 297. "Where the discretion that is fundamental to our criminal process is involved, we decline to assume that what is unexplained is invidious." Id. at 313.

Because the statistical disparity alone does not signal an intent to discriminate against women, we look to whether the plaintiffs submitted any other evidence of a discriminatory intent. The plaintiffs introduced hearsay statements from members of the Ricketts family, but this evidence is insufficient. Kimberly's sister-in-law testified to statements allegedly made by a police officer to the effect that one man accused of domestic abuse should have been arrested before but was not. Kimberly's father testified that he heard that one officer had been instructed not to arrest Sonny because Kimberly had gone back to him before and probably would again.... These statements are unreliable hearsay. More importantly, while they might offer support for a discriminatory intent toward domestic disputes, they do not evidence an intent to discriminate against women.

The plaintiffs also offered evidence of a historic tolerance of domestic abuse in society and of one fairly recent newspaper statement. A Columbia officer was quoted as blaming a woman victim of domestic abuse for bringing on the assault herself. The officer explained that the context of the statement related only to one particular case where he had seen that happen.

... These were the only factors directly bearing on gender discrimination, and they do not combine to create a submissible inference of a discriminatory animus toward women by the Columbia police department. Although we are sympathetic to the plaintiffs and we acknowledge that they have suffered greatly from the criminal acts of Sonny Stephens, we conclude that the plaintiffs have failed to present evidence of an equal protection violation on the basis of gender.

3. See also Hynson v. City of Chester Legal Department, 864 F.2d 1026 (3d Cir. 1988), and Watson v. City of Kansas City, 857 F.2d 690 (10th Cir. 1988). Based on your reading of these materials, what do you think might qualify as proper evidence of a discriminatory intent underlying police inaction in domestic violence cases? How likely do you think it is that an individual plaintiff could offer that proof?

4. Early challenges to police inaction were also brought on substantive due process grounds, by plaintiffs who claimed that they were wrongfully deprived of a protected interest in life, liberty or property when police failed to protect them from their abusers. These cases are described in the next reading.

Caitlin E. Borgmann
Battered Women's Substantive Due Process Claims: Can Orders of Protection Deflect DeShaney?, 65 New York University Law Review 1280, 1290–1293 (1990)

Prior to the Supreme Court's decision in *DeShaney,* courts deciding battered women's section 1983 substantive due process claims looked to whether a "special relationship," necessary to create an affirmative duty on the part of the state, existed between the state and the battered woman. These analyses yielded confusing results. Two federal courts upheld battered women's substantive due process claims, finding that the existence of an order of protection, together with certain other state contacts, could give rise to a special relationship between the woman and the state. Two other federal courts denied battered women's substantive due process claims, one of them finding that no special relationship existed despite the woman's order of protection.

In its original ... opinion in *Balistreri v. Pacifica Police Department,*[1] the Ninth Circuit upheld a section 1983 claim by a battered woman who had obtained an order of protection enjoining her former husband from "harassing, annoying or having any contact with her." Despite this order, Balistreri's estranged husband continued to harass her for several years and, on one occasion, threw a firebomb through the window of her house. She consistently reported these incidents to the police, who either failed entirely to respond to the reports or responded slowly.

In her complaint, Balistreri alleged that the police department's actions and failures to act had deprived her of her right to due process of law. The district court, on defendants' motion, dismissed Balistreri's complaint with prejudice, finding that Balistreri had failed to show that a special relationship might have existed between her and the state. The Ninth Circuit Court of Appeals reversed and reinstated the claim, holding that a jury could find that the state had a constitutional duty to protect Balistreri.

While the court agreed that the state's awareness of a victim's plight will not by itself create a special relationship, it nonetheless decided for the plaintiff. The court found that, in this case, the state's awareness that Balistreri was in danger, coupled with the possibility that the state had committed itself affirmatively to protect her by granting an order of protection, could satisfy the requirements for a special relationship. The factors it considered in determining whether a special relationship could exist included: (1) whether the state had assumed a custodial relationship with the victim; (2) whether the state was aware of a specific risk of harm to the victim; (3) whether the state affirmatively placed the victim in danger; and (4) whether the state affirmatively committed itself to protecting the victim.

Similarly, in *Dudosh v. City of Allentown,*[2] the District Court for the Eastern District of Pennsylvania allowed a due process claim brought by the administrator of the estate of a battered woman who was murdered by her former boyfriend. An order of protection, which had been issued against the boyfriend, required the police to remove him if the woman reported that he had violated the order. The woman had made repeated reports to the police of her boyfriend's continued threats and harassment, including one report shortly before her death. The court found that the

1. 855 F.2d 1421 (9th Cir. 1988), amended and superceded, 901 F.2d 696 (9th Cir. 1990).

2. 665 F. Supp. 381 (E.D. Pa 1987), rehearing denied sub nom Dudosh v. Warg, 668 F. Supp. 944 (E.D. Pa. 1987).

existence of the order, in conjunction with the woman's contacts with the police, "placed an affirmative duty upon the police department to protect the deceased."

Prior to *DeShaney,* at least one court of appeals and one district court looked with disfavor upon due process claims by battered women. In *Estate of Gilmore v. Buckley,*[1] in which a battered woman had been kidnapped and murdered by her estranged boyfriend, the First Circuit affirmed the district court's dismissal of the substantive due process claim brought by the deceased woman's estate, finding that the state's knowledge that the woman was in danger did not create a special relationship of constitutional dimensions. Because the court seems not to have considered whether the woman had obtained an order of protection, however, the precedential and analytical relevance of this case ... is limited. The court simply based its decision on the grounds that, as a general matter, where the state neither plays a part in creating the danger to the victim nor takes her into its custody, it has no special relationship with the victim.

In *Turner v. City of North Charlestown,*[2] a South Carolina district court also rejected a claim by a battered woman who alleged deprivation of her substantive due process rights under section 1983. In *Turner,* the woman had obtained an order of protection and had notified the police several times that her estranged husband was threatening her in violation of the order. The husband later shot her in the head several times. Nevertheless, the court found that there was no special relationship between the state and the victim to trigger an affirmative duty on the part of the state to protect her. Reasoning that "the [South Carolina domestic violence statute] is addressed to follow-up procedures rather than to any affirmative duty to protect a person prior to a domestic abuse incident," the court found that police officials had no affirmative duty under the statute to protect the claimant. In relying solely on the state statute to reach its holding, however, the court failed to address the question of whether an order of protection in and of itself gives rise to a special relationship.

The disparate results in these four cases demonstrate the lack of uniformity among the federal courts as to when an order of protection may trigger a state duty to protect a battered woman.

* * *

NOTES AND QUESTIONS

1. In 1989, in DeShaney v. Winnebago County Department of Social Services, 489 U.S. 189 (1999), the Supreme Court addressed the question of what constitutes a 'special relationship' for purposes of substantive due process claims under § 1983. Indeed, the Court explained that it had granted certiorari "[b]ecause of the inconsistent approaches taken by the lower courts in determining when, if ever, the failure of a state or local

1. 787 F.2d 714 (1st Cir.), cert. den. 479 U.S. 882 (1986).

2. 675 F. Supp. 314 (D.S.C. 1987).

governmental entity or its agents to provide an individual with adequate protective services constitutes a violation of the individual's due process rights." The court's decision left many lower courts believing that battered women, even those with restraining orders against their abusers, would no longer qualify for relief under § 1983 on due process grounds. The Ninth Circuit amended its decision in *Balistreri*, continuing to uphold the plaintiff's right to argue that she had been denied equal protection, but dismissing her due process claim on the basis of *DeShaney:*

> The heart of Balistreri's due process claim is that the Pacifica police failed to take steps to respond to the continued threats, harassment and violence towards Balistreri by her estranged husband. There is, in general, no constitutional duty of state officials to protect members of the public at large from crime. ... However, such a duty may arise by virtue of a "special relationship" between state officials and a particular member of the public....
>
> As the district court noted, Balistreri alleged neither that the state had created or assumed a custodial relationship over her, nor that the state actors had somehow affirmatively placed her in danger. There were no allegations that the defendants had done anything to "ratify, condone or in any way instigate" the actions of Balistreri's ex-husband.... However, Balistreri did allege that state actors knew of her plight and affirmatively committed to protect her. Specifically, she alleged that the state committed to protect her when it issued her a restraining order.
>
> In the recent case of *DeShaney* ..., however, the Supreme Court limited the circumstances giving rise to "a special relationship." Joshua DeShaney fell into a life-threatening coma after he was severely beaten by his father. Prior to this beating, the social services agency recorded multiple incidents indicating that someone in the DeShaney household was physically abusing Joshua and temporarily placed Joshua in the custody of the juvenile court. In the course of explaining its holding that Joshua DeShaney and his mother failed to make out an actionable § 1983 claim, the Court explained that its previous decisions recognizing "affirmative [constitutional] duties of care and protection.... stand only for the proposition that when the State takes a person into its custody and hold him there against his will, the Constitution imposes upon it a corresponding duty to assume some responsibility for his safety and general wellbeing.... The affirmative duty to protect arises not from the State's knowledge of the individual's predicament or from its expressions of intent to help him, but from the limitation which it has imposed on his freedom to act on his own behalf." ... We conclude that the state's knowledge of DeShaney's plight and its expressions of intent to help him were no greater than its knowledge of Balistreri's plight and its expressions of intent to help her. *See id.* at 1010–11 (Brennan, J., dissenting) ("Wisconsin law invites—indeed, directs—citizens and other governmental entities to depend on local departments of social services such as respondent to protect children from abuse.... Through its child-protection program,

> the State actively intervened in Joshua's life and, by virtue of this intervention, acquired ever more certain knowledge that Joshua was in grave danger."). *DeShaney* is therefore controlling in Balistreri's case. Accordingly, we hold that Balistreri failed to allege "a special relationship" and affirm the district court's dismissal of Balistreri's due process claim.

901 F.2d 696, 699–700 (9th Cir.1990).

The Supreme Court in *DeShaney* also stressed that the department of social services had not affirmatively put Joshua at risk; rather, the risk was created by his abusive father, and the state was guilty only of inaction, in failing to rescue him. 489 U.S. 189, 195–96 (1989).

2. Caitlin Borgmann, whose article excerpted above, has argued that the situation of a battered woman with a restraining order can be distinguished from the situation of Joshua DeShaney. She suggests first that an order of protection does involve the state in a custodial relationship with its holder, because that individual must remain within the sphere of protection created by the order in order to secure her safety. Caitlin E. Borgmann, *Battered Women's Substantive Due Process Claims: Can Orders of Protection Deflect DeShaney?* 65 N. Y. U. L. REV. 1280, 1304–07 (1990). Unfortunately, this argument has been undermined by the Violence Against Women Act, which essentially makes orders of protection national in scope by requiring that each state give full faith and credit to a sister state's orders. 18 U.S.C.A. § 2265. In one case, a court found no custodial relationship where a domestic violence victim was killed by her estranged husband outside a courtroom, even though the court mandated her attendance, and had offered her specific assurances of safety. Duong v. County of Arapahoe, 837 P.2d 226 (Colo. App. 1992). In Losinski v. County of Trempealeau, 946 F.2d 544 (7th Cir. 1991), the Seventh Circuit found that a woman was not in protective custody for purposes of § 1983 when a deputy accompanied her to her home, since she had not been coerced or persuaded to accept protection.

Second, Borgmann argues that when a state issues a protective order and fails to enforce it, it creates an affirmative danger:

> In cases in which the state has granted an order of protection to a battered woman, the state affirmatively "play[s] a part" in the creation of a dangerous situation. Thus, a state's conduct in granting an order of protection to a battered woman gives rise to an affirmative duty to protect her. The requirement of causation, namely that the state played a role in causing the woman's danger, may be satisfied in two ways when an order of protection goes unenforced. First, the state gives the woman reason to forgo self-defense and other self-help remedies in reliance on the order. Second, the issuance of an order of protection results in a high likelihood of retaliation by the batterer.

Borgmann, supra, at 1307–08. How would you assess the strength of these arguments? Does she make her case that these factors differentiate the battered woman from the abused child in whose case a Department of

Social Services makes a preliminary intervention, but then fails to prevent further abuse?

Since *DeShaney,* substantive due process claims brought by battered women have focused on showing that the state increased the danger they faced from their batterers, rather than just failing to protect them from violence. Suppose, for example, that the state promised to put or keep an abuser in custody, or to notify his victim before his release; that the promise was relied upon by the victim in her own safety planning, and then broken. In this situation the argument that the state's actions increased the victim's vulnerability seems a strong one. Unfortunately, this very scenario was found insufficient to ground a due process claim in Pinder v. Johnson, 54 F.3d 1169 (4th Cir. 1995). In *Pinder* an officer assured a woman that her abuser, who had been arrested, would not be released until the following day. The officer provided this information in response to her specific question whether it would be safe for her to return to work, leaving her three children in the house. After she had gone back to work the officer was persuaded by the abuser to release him on his own recognizance. The abuser promptly returned to the plaintiff's house and set it on fire, killing her three children.

Another scenario that has led to litigation is where the abuser is himself a law enforcement officer, and his peers or inferiors, out of solidarity or fear of the consequences of intervention, fail to provide appropriate protection to his victim. Substantive due process claims along these lines survived motions to dismiss in Wright v. Village of Phoenix, 2000 WL 246266 (N.D. Ill. 2000), and Freeman v. Ferguson, 911 F.2d 52 (8th Cir. 1990).

It could also be argued that where police reinforce the batterer's behavior by failing to take his victim's complaints seriously, or to hold him accountable, they increase his sense of entitlement, and correspondingly increase his victim's danger. This argument was successful in defeating a summary judgment motion in Smith v. City of Elyria, 857 F. Supp. 1203 (N.D. Ohio 1994). However, in Ricketts v. City of Columbia, 36 F.3d 775 (8th Cir. 1994), the Eighth Circuit found the argument that the police had repeatedly failed to arrest the defendant, and had therefore "emboldened" him to continue his campaign of violence, insufficient to show a proper causal connection between the conduct of the police and the ultimate injury to the plaintiff.

State Tort Claims

Another possible route for domestic violence plaintiffs complaining of police inaction is the state tort system—and the importance of this alternative has increased as the availability of relief under § 1983 has diminished. If an action is available, it will lie in negligence, and depend on a showing that the defendant or defendants owed the plaintiff a duty of care, and breached that duty, causing the plaintiff injury. There are two preliminary obstacles to suit that a plaintiff will have to overcome. The first is sovereign immunity, addressed in this next reading.

Issues of Immunity
Fredrica L. Lehrman, Domestic Violence Practice and Procedure, §§ 6:23–6:26 (1997)

Common law sovereign immunity protected government entities from tort liability. Traditional blanket sovereign immunity has been limited or abrogated in many states through judicial and legislative action. Each state defines the source and scope of its current immunity law. A state may provide immunity for a discretionary act, as opposed to a ministerial one; for all suits against the government that are not included in a tort claims act; or for any specific act granted immunity by statute.

. . .

—Discretionary Government Acts

Some states grant sovereign immunity for *discretionary* government acts, but not for *ministerial* acts. The purpose of this distinction is to prevent the judiciary from intervening in basic policy determinations that are exclusively within the realm of the executive or legislative branches, and to prevent lawsuits from chilling zealous enforcement of the law.

A tort claim challenging the amount of police resources directed towards domestic violence prevention could be blocked under this doctrine because allocation of resources is considered a discretionary government function. An action against an officer for failing to arrest a domestic abuser might be barred if the decision whether to arrest is determined to fall within the officer's discretion. However, even if the decision to act is immunized, the method of action may not be. Once choosing a course of action, an officer is obligated to carry out that choice with reasonable care.

To overcome a defense of discretionary immunity, the practitioner should evaluate whether the police officer acted pursuant to law that restricted discretion. A domestic violence statute that mandates arrest limits police discretion. Subsequent failure to arrest could be a ministerial error for which there is no immunity.

—Police Conduct

Some states have codified municipal immunity for police failure to protect. State legislatures may grant immunity as part of a general grant of good faith immunity for police, a tort claims act, or a domestic violence act.

Tort claims acts delineate government liability. Sovereign immunity is waived for some acts and established for others.... The plaintiff must establish that the offense falls within an area for which sovereign immunity has been waived. For example, analysis of liability in Texas is a two-step process. A claim must arise under one of three specific provisions of the Texas Tort Claims Act; then it must not fall within an exception to the waiver of sovereign immunity. In Illinois, however, immunity under a tort claims act may be trumped by a showing that a special relationship existed between the police and the plaintiff creating a special duty to protect.

The scope of any statutory grant of immunity is subject to the vagaries of statutory interpretation. Rather than find blanket immunity for the actions of police, courts will make a determination based on the facts at hand in conjunction with the statutory requirements.

—Clauses in Domestic Violence Acts

An arrest statute may contain a clause providing immunity to police and their municipal employers, for actions taken or omissions made in good faith under the statute. These immunization clauses should not provide absolute immunity for police failure to arrest. Some courts have recognized that this interpretation would defeat the purpose of the statute and that an immunity clause should be read in harmony with the intent of the domestic violence act of which it is a part. The purpose of a domestic violence act may be implicit or explicitly stated in the act and/or the legislative history. These purposes include protecting victims of domestic violence and requiring police to enforce laws to that end. Effective enforcement and protection is defeated if there is no liability for failure to abide by the law.

* * *

NOTES

1. In connection with domestic violence arrest laws, some states only immunize officers from liability when they do, in good faith, and in the exercise of due care, make an arrest. See, for example, ARK. CODE § 16–81–113(3); MINN. ST. § 629.341(2). Other states have gone further, and immunized officers with respect to good faith decisions either to arrest or not to arrest. See, for example, N.J. ST. § 2C:25–22; WISC. ST. § 968.075(6m). For a decision noting that a broad interpretation of immunity language contained in a statute would undermine the purpose of the domestic violence act, see Roy v. City of Everett, 118 Wash. 2d 352, 823 P.2d 1084 (1992).

2. The second major barrier to tort liability under state law is the traditional "public duty" or "no duty" common law doctrine, under which law enforcement officers and agencies have a general duty to the public to provide protection, but no specific duty to safeguard any individual, unless the case falls within a recognized exception to the rule. The rationale for the rule is the same as the rationale for sovereign immunity; the importance of preserving separation of powers, and not allowing the judicial branch to question allocative and policy decisions made by the legislative or executive branches. Nonetheless, in most jurisdictions the two bodies of law are distinct; the plaintiff must establish *both* that the conduct of the state and its agents is not immunized from liability, *and* that the case falls within an exception to the public duty rule. The following opinion develops fully the arguments both for and against the public duty rule.

Linda Riss v. City of New York

22 N.Y.2d 579; 240 N.E.2d 860; 293 N.Y.S.2d 897.
Court of Appeals of New York, 1968.

■ CHIEF JUDGE FULD and JUDGES BURKE, SCILEPPI, BERGAN and JASEN concur with JUDGE BREITEL; JUDGE KEATING dissents and votes to reverse in a separate opinion.

■ Opinion by: Breitel

This appeal presents, in a very sympathetic framework, the issue of the liability of a municipality for failure to provide special protection to a member of the public who was repeatedly threatened with personal harm and eventually suffered dire personal injuries for lack of such protection. The facts are amply described in the dissenting opinion and no useful purpose would be served by repetition. The issue arises upon the affirmance by a divided Appellate Division of a dismissal of the complaint, after both sides had rested but before submission to the jury.

. . .

... [T]his case involves the provision of a governmental service to protect the public generally from external hazards and particularly to control the activities of criminal wrongdoers.... The amount of protection that may be provided is limited by the resources of the community and by a considered legislative-executive decision as to how those resources may be deployed. For the courts to proclaim a new and general duty of protection in the law of tort, even to those who may be the particular seekers of protection based on specific hazards, could and would inevitably determine how the limited police resources of the community should be allocated and without predictable limits. This is quite different from the predictable allocation of resources and liabilities when public hospitals, rapid transit systems, or even highways are provided.

. . .

When one considers the greatly increased amount of crime committed throughout the cities, but especially in certain portions of them, with a repetitive and predictable pattern, it is easy to see the consequences of fixing municipal liability upon a showing of probable need for and request for protection. To be sure these are grave problems at the present time, exciting high priority activity on the part of the national, State and local governments, to which the answers are neither simple, known, or presently within reasonable controls. To foist a presumed cure for these problems by judicial innovation of a new kind of liability in tort would be foolhardy indeed and an assumption of judicial wisdom and power not possessed by the courts.

. . .

For all of these reasons, there is no warrant in judicial tradition or in the proper allocation of the powers of government for the courts, in the absence of legislation, to carve out an area of tort liability for police protection to members of the public. Quite distinguishable, of course, is the situation where the police authorities undertake responsibilities to particular members of the public and expose them, without adequate protection, to the risks which then materialize into actual losses (Schuster v. City of New York, 5 N.Y.2d 75).

Accordingly, the order of the Appellate Division affirming the judgment of dismissal should be affirmed.

■ KEATING, J. (dissenting).

Certainly, the record in this case, sound legal analysis, relevant policy considerations and even precedent cannot account for or sustain the result which the majority have here reached. For the result is premised upon a legal rule which long ago should have been abandoned, having lost any justification it might once have had. Despite almost universal condemnation by legal scholars, the rule survives, finding its continuing strength, not in its power to persuade, but in its ability to arouse unwarranted judicial fears of the consequences of overturning it.

Linda Riss, an attractive young woman, was for more than six months terrorized by a rejected suitor well known to the courts of this State, one Burton Pugach. This miscreant, masquerading as a respectable attorney, repeatedly threatened to have Linda killed or maimed if she did not yield to him: "If I can't have you, no one else will have you, and when I get through with you, no one else will want you". In fear for her life, she went to those charged by law with the duty of preserving and safeguarding the lives of the citizens and residents of this State. Linda's repeated and almost pathetic pleas for aid were received with little more than indifference. Whatever help she was given was not commensurate with the identifiable danger. On June 14, 1959 Linda became engaged to another man. At a party held to celebrate the event, she received a phone call warning her that it was her "last chance". Completely distraught, she called the police, begging for help, but was refused. The next day Pugach carried out his dire threats in the very manner he had foretold by having a hired thug throw lye in Linda's face. Linda was blinded in one eye, lost a good portion of her vision in the other, and her face was permanently scarred. After the assault the authorities concluded that there was some basis for Linda's fears, and for the next three and one-half years, she was given around-the-clock protection.

No one questions the proposition that the first duty of government is to assure its citizens the opportunity to live in personal security. And no one who reads the record of Linda's ordeal can reach a conclusion other than that the City of New York, acting through its agents, completely and negligently failed to fulfill this obligation to Linda.

Linda has turned to the courts of this State for redress, asking that the city be held liable in damages for its negligent failure to protect her from harm. With compelling logic, she can point out that, if a stranger, who had absolutely no obligation to aid her, had offered her assistance, and thereafter Burton Pugach was able to injure her as a result of the negligence of the volunteer, the courts would certainly require him to pay damages. (Restatement, 2d, Torts, § 323.) Why then should the city, whose duties are imposed by law and include the prevention of crime . . . and, consequently, extend far beyond that of the Good Samaritan, not be responsible? If a private detective acts carelessly, no one would deny that a jury could find such conduct unacceptable. Why then is the city not required to live up to at least the same minimal standards of professional competence which would be demanded of a private detective?

Linda's reasoning seems so eminently sensible that surely it must come as a shock to her and to every citizen to hear the city argue and to learn that this court decides that the city has no duty to provide police protection to any given individual. What makes the city's position particularly difficult to understand is that, in conformity to the dictates of the law, Linda did not carry any weapon for self-defense.... Thus, by a rather bitter irony she was required to rely for protection on the City of New York which now denies all responsibility to her.

It is not a distortion to summarize the essence of the city's case here in the following language: "Because we owe a duty to everybody, we owe it to nobody." Were it not for the fact that this position has been hallowed by much ancient and revered precedent, we would surely dismiss it as preposterous. To say that there is no duty is, of course, to start with the conclusion. The question is whether or not there should be liability for the negligent failure to provide adequate police protection.

The foremost justification repeatedly urged for the existing rule is the claim that the State and the municipalities will be exposed to limitless liability. The city invokes the specter of a "crushing burden" ... if we should depart from the existing rule and enunciate even the limited proposition that the State and its municipalities can be held liable for the negligent acts of their police employees in executing whatever police services they do in fact provide....

The fear of financial disaster is a myth. The same argument was made a generation ago in opposition to proposals that the State waive its defense of "sovereign immunity". The prophecy proved false then, and it would now.... Thus, in the past four or five years, New York City has been presented with an average of some 10,000 claims each year. The figure would sound ominous except for the fact the city has been paying out less than $8,000,000 on tort claims each year and this amount includes all those sidewalk defect and snow and ice cases about which the courts fret so often.... Court delay has reduced the figure paid somewhat, but not substantially. Certainly this is a slight burden in a budget of more than six billion dollars (less than two tenths of 1%) and of no importance as compared to the injustice of permitting unredressed wrongs to continue to go unrepaired. That Linda Riss should be asked to bear the loss, which should properly fall on the city if we assume, as we must, in the present posture of the case, that her injuries resulted from the city's failure to provide sufficient police to protect Linda is contrary to the most elementary notions of justice.

The statement in the majority opinion that there are no predictable limits to the potential liability for failure to provide adequate police protection as compared to other areas of municipal liability is, of course, untenable. When immunity in other areas of governmental activity was removed, the same lack of predictable limits existed. Yet, disaster did not ensue.

Another variation of the "crushing burden" argument is the contention that, every time a crime is committed, the city will be sued and the claim will be made that it resulted from inadequate police protection....

The argument is ... made as if there were no such legal principles as fault, proximate cause or foreseeability, all of which operate to keep liability within reasonable bounds. No one is contending that the police must be at the scene of every potential crime or must provide a personal bodyguard to every person who walks into a police station and claims to have been threatened. They need only act as a reasonable man would under the circumstances. At first there would be a duty to inquire. If the inquiry indicates nothing to substantiate the alleged threat, the matter may be put aside and other matters attended to. If, however, the claims prove to have some basis, appropriate steps would be necessary.

. . .

In dismissing the complaint, the trial court noted that there are many crimes being committed daily and the police force is inadequate to deal with its "tremendous responsibilities". The point is not addressed to the facts of this case. Even if it were, however, a distinction must be made.... If the police force of the City of New York is so understaffed that it is unable to cope with the everyday problem posed by the relatively few cases where single, known individuals threaten the lives of other persons, then indeed we have reached the danger line and the lives of all of us are in peril. If the police department is in such a deplorable state that the city, because of insufficient manpower, is truly unable to protect persons in Linda Riss' position, then liability not only should, but must be imposed. It will act as an effective inducement for public officials to provide at least a minimally adequate number of police. If local officials are not willing to meet even such a low standard, I see no reason for the courts to abet such irresponsibility.

It is also contended that liability for inadequate police protection will make the courts the arbiters of decisions taken by the Police Commissioner in allocating his manpower and his resources. We are not dealing here with a situation where the injury or loss occurred as a result of a conscious choice of policy made by those exercising high administrative responsibility after a complete and thorough deliberation of various alternatives.... Linda Riss' tragedy resulted not from high policy or inadequate manpower, but plain negligence on the part of persons with whom Linda dealt....

More significant, however, is the fundamental flaw in the reasoning behind the argument alleging judicial interference. It is a complete oversimplification of the problem of municipal tort liability. What it ignores is the fact that indirectly courts are reviewing administrative practices in almost every tort case against the State or a municipality, including even decisions of the Police Commissioner. Every time a municipal hospital is held liable for malpractice resulting from inadequate record-keeping, the courts are in effect making a determination that the municipality should have hired or assigned more clerical help or more competent help to medical records or should have done something to improve its record-keeping procedures so that the particular injury would not have occurred. Every time a municipality is held liable for a defective sidewalk, it is as if the courts are saying that more money and resources should have been allocated to sidewalk repair, instead of to other public services.

The situation is nowise different in the case of police protection. Whatever effects there may be on police administration will be one of degree, not kind. In McCrink v. City of New York (296 N. Y. 99) we held the city liable where a drunken policeman, while off duty, shot and killed a citizen in an unprovoked assault. The policeman had a long history of being a troublemaker, having been brought up before the Police Commissioner on drunkenness charges on three prior occasions. In imposing liability on the city, were we not in effect overruling the Commissioner's judgment in retaining the policeman on the force and saying his decision was so unreasonable that the city should be required to pay damages? . . .

The truth of the matter, however, is that the courts are not making policy decisions for public officials. In all these municipal negligence cases, the courts are doing two things. First, they apply the principles of vicarious liability to the operations of government. Courts would not insulate the city from liability for the ordinary negligence of members of the highway department. There is no basis for treating the members of the police department differently.

Second, and most important, to the extent that the injury results from the failure to allocate sufficient funds and resources to meet a minimum standard of public administration, public officials are presented with two alternatives: either improve public administration or accept the cost of compensating injured persons. . . . Perhaps officials will find it less costly to choose the alternative of paying damages than changing their existing practices. That may be well and good, but the price for the refusal to provide for an adequate police force should not be borne by Linda Riss and all the other innocent victims of such decisions.

What has existed until now is that the City of New York and other municipalities have been able to engage in a sort of false bookkeeping in which the real costs of inadequate or incompetent police protection have been hidden by charging the expenditures to the individuals who have sustained often catastrophic losses rather than to the community where it belongs, because the latter had the power to prevent the losses.

Although in modern times the compensatory nature of tort law has generally been the one most emphasized, one of its most important functions has been and is its normative aspect. It sets forth standards of conduct which ought to be followed. The penalty for failing to do so is to pay pecuniary damages. At one time the government was completely immunized from this salutary control. This is much less so now, and the imposition of liability has had healthy side effects. . . . Thus, every reason used to sustain the rule that there is no duty to offer police protection to any individual turns out on close analysis to be of little substance.

. . .

No doubt in the future we shall have to draw limitations just as we have done in the area of private litigation, and no doubt some of these limitations will be unique to municipal liability because the problems will not have any counterpart in private tort law. But if the lines are to be drawn, let them be delineated on candid considerations of policy and fairness and not on the fictions or relics of the doctrine of "sovereign immunity".

. . .

Perhaps, on a fuller record after a true trial on the merits, the city's position will not appear so damaging as it does now. But with actual notice of danger and ample opportunity to confirm and take reasonable remedial steps, a jury could find that the persons involved acted unreasonably and negligently. Linda Riss is entitled to have a jury determine the issue of the city's liability. This right should not be terminated by the adoption of a question-begging conclusion that there is no duty owed to her. The order of the Appellate Division should be reversed and a new trial granted.

NOTES

1. Despite the eloquence of Judge Keating's dissent in *Riss*, the public duty doctrine remains firmly in place. In litigation, the question therefore becomes whether the circumstances of an individual case can fit within one of the exceptions to that doctrine. The exceptions can all be viewed as answers to the question: "What is special about the relationship between this plaintiff, and the public actors who failed to keep her safe?" In this respect there is a close parallel between case law at the state level developing exceptions to the public duty rule, and case law at the federal level developing exceptions to the rule that state *inaction* is insufficient to ground a substantive due process claim under § 1983. However, in many jurisdictions the exceptions to the public duty rule are more generously framed than the "special relationship" test articulated by the Supreme Court in the *DeShaney* case.

In New York, for example, where public duty doctrine is still governed by *Riss,* a special relationship requires (a) a promise made to the plaintiff that affirmative action will be taken on her behalf; (b) the plaintiff's action in reliance on that commitment; (c) direct contact between the plaintiff and those who make the commitment, and (d) knowledge on the part of those making the commitment that a failure to follow through could lead to harm. Cuffy v. City of New York, 69 N.Y.2d 255, 513 N.Y.S.2d 372, 505 N.E.2d 937 (1987). It is hard to imagine that the plaintiff in Pinder v. Johnson, 54 F.3d 1169 (4th Cir. 1995), discussed above at page 900, would not have met this test, although she was unable to persuade the Fourth Circuit that she had a due process claim.

2. In the domestic violence arena, special relationships are not uncommonly created by statute; by mandatory arrest laws, for example, which require specific action on the part of police, or even by abuse prevention legislation. In another New York case, Sorichetti v. City of New York, 65 N.Y.2d 461, 492 N.Y.S.2d 591, 482 N.E.2d 70 (1985), the court found a special relationship where police had knowledge of and failed to enforce a valid order of protection, and where, in addition, they knew the level of danger potentially posed by the abuser. The Illinois Supreme Court reached

a similar decision in 1995, in Calloway v. Kinkelaar, 168 Ill.2d 312, 213 Ill. Dec. 675, 659 N.E.2d 1322 (1995):

> To give effect to the legislature's purposes and intent in enacting the Domestic Violence Act, we believe judicial recognition of a right of action for civil damages is necessary, provided that the injured party can establish that he or she is a person in need of protection under the Act, the statutory law enforcement duties owed to him or her were breached by the willful and wanton acts or omissions of law enforcement officers, and such conduct proximately caused plaintiff's injuries.

Id. 168 Ill.2d at 324. The Domestic Violence Act itself had limited the liability of public officials, requiring a showing of willful or wanton negligence, rather than simple negligence.

In Simpson v. City of Miami, 700 So.2d 87 (Fla. Dist. App. 1997), an abuser who had violated a protective order was detained at his victim's home by a police officer, but then released after promising to leave the plaintiff alone. The following day he returned and shot her. The trial court dismissed the complaint on the basis of sovereign immunity (arguing that the officer's decision to release the perpetrator was a discretionary one), and the lack of any special relationship between the plaintiff and the police. In a per curiam opinion, the court of appeals reversed and remanded, in order to allow the plaintiff to amend her complaint to allege that the officer's initial detention of the perpetrator was an arrest. If she could do that, the court said, the officer's subsequent decision to release the abuser violated a clear statutory directive to hold the violator in custody until he could be brought before a court. FLA. ST. § 741.30(9)(b) (1993). Presumably the court felt that the statute would operate both to defeat the argument that the officer had discretion, and to create the necessary special relationship. A concurring opinion instead grounded the special relationship in Florida's abuse prevention legislation more generally:

> Although the legislature, perhaps unadvisedly, did not expressly state that police officers have an affirmative duty to arrest domestic violence injunction violators, it created a special category of crime victim and established a special relationship between the decedent in this case and the responsible governmental entity.

Id. at 89. The concurring judge also noted that the Miami Police Department was well aware of the "discordant relations" between the plaintiff and her abuser, having responded to previous calls.

3. Some jurisdictions recognize separate exceptions to the public duty rule in situations in which the public actor affirmatively puts the plaintiff in danger, or increases her danger; or commits to act on her behalf and then carries out his or her duties in a negligent way. Other jurisdictions incorporate these scenarios into the 'special relationship' exception, and indeed they often contain the same elements as those listed in the *Cuffy* case. In Hutcherson v. City of Phoenix, 192 Ariz. 51, 961 P.2d 449 (Ariz. 1998), for example, the plaintiffs recovered well in excess of $1 million from the City of Phoenix, when negligent handling of a 911 call resulted in the deaths of the perpetrator's ex-partner and her new boyfriend. The 911

operator told the victim that an officer would be sent to her apartment, but gave the lowest priority rating to the call, even though the operator was told that the abuser had threatened lethal violence, that he was on his way to the apartment, and that he was less than five minutes away. Twenty-two minutes after the 911 call, the damage was done. When witnesses of the shootings called 911 to report them, the police arrived within seven minutes. This case meets the *Cuffy* criteria: there was direct contact between one of the victims and the operator, enough information for the operator to understand that the situation was serious, a specific commitment on the part of the operator, and a basis to believe that the victims of the shooting might have acted differently (by leaving the apartment, for example) if they had known that the police were not going to arrive. But the case can also be framed as one in which the operator increased the danger to the victims by promising protection that did not materialize, or as one in which an intervention was begun (the call taken, and action promised), and then negligently continued.

4. If a plaintiff is able to surmount the hurdles created by sovereign immunity and the public duty doctrine, it will remain to establish actual and proximate cause, as in any other negligence action. Significantly, respondeat superior, which does not apply in § 1983 actions, is applicable in state tort actions, so that police departments or other governmental entities will be liable for the negligence of their employees.

B. Domestic Violence at the Workplace

Introductory Note

According to a report published by the Bureau of National Affairs, domestic abuse is costing businesses between 3 and 5 billion dollars annually in lost productivity in the forms of higher health care costs, lost wages, sick leave, absenteeism and higher turnover rates, and liability for injuries inflicted in the workplace by abusers on their partners or co-workers. One small pilot study of employed battered women found that more than half missed three days of work each month because of abuse. Lucy Friedman and Sarah Cooper, *The Costs of Domestic Violence*, (New York Victim Services Agency, 1987). In another study of domestic violence victims, 96% of those who were employed reporting experiencing severe problems in the workplace as a result of their abuse or abuser; 60% were often late, more than 50% missed work; 70% had difficulty performing job-related tasks; 60% were reprimanded for problems associated with the abuse, and 30% lost their jobs. *Domestic Violence: An Occupational Impact Study* (Domestic Violence Intervention Services, Inc., Tulsa, Oklahoma, July 27, 1992). In addition, domestic violence threatens the physical safety of victims and victims' co-workers on the job. In the New York study referenced above, 75% of women said they had been harassed by their batterers while at work. In 17% of the cases in which women are murdered at work, the alleged assailant is a current or former husband or boyfriend.

Employers are not unaware that domestic violence is costing them. In a recent study of senior executives of Fortune 1000 companies, 47% said that domestic violence has a harmful effect on employee attendance, and 44% said that it increases insurance and medical costs. Liz Claiborne, Inc., *Addressing Domestic Violence: A Corporate Response* (Roper Starch Worldwide, 1994). However, only 12% of those surveyed said that corporations should play a significant role in addressing the issue, while 96% said that responsibility should ideally fall to the family. In the minds of most business leaders, therefore, domestic violence is still a private matter. A 1997 study supported by the National Institute of Justice found that only 14% of larger U.S. companies addressed domestic violence in their workplace policies or guidelines, although 75% had policies or guidelines addressing workplace violence more generally. The study, which surveyed employee assistance professionals as well as counselors in internal and external Employee Assistance Programs (EAPs), found that a large majority of providers had dealt with specific partner abuse scenarios within the previous year, including employees with restraining orders and employees being stalked at work. Nancy Isaac, *Corporate Sector Responses to Domestic Violence,* VIOLENCE AGAINST WOMEN ACT NEWS, Volume II, No.3 (U.S. Department of Justice, Violence Against Women Office, June/July 1997).

The materials that follow include: (1) some information about proactive employer responses to partner violence among their employees; (2) a look at potential employer liability to employees who are injured or killed by their abusive partners at work; (3) limits on employers' freedom to discipline or fire employees because of their involvement in abusive relationships; and (4) some steps being taken by employers and professional organizations to discipline employees and members who are perpetrators of abuse.

Affirmative Corporate Responses to Victims of Abuse

A few companies have taken the lead in addressing domestic violence as it affects their employees. Polaroid, for example, has adopted a number of initiatives. It has developed a leave policy that gives women time to seek shelter, arrange new housing, and find legal representation or resolve pressing legal issues. It offers flexible work hours, short-term paid leaves, and long-term unpaid leaves with a guarantee that an employee will still have a job when she returns. The company's EAP has been expanded to offer employees counseling, support groups and referrals to local domestic violence agencies. If an employee obtains a restraining order, the company provides security personnel with a picture of the batterer, and provides similar information to the Police Department. When batterers seek to harass their victims at work, Polaroid has on occasion sought its own restraining orders to keep them off the premises. Polaroid has also supported domestic violence initiatives outside the company; providing financial support, donating cameras to facilitate the documentation of abuse-related injuries, participating in research on how EAPs might most effectively assist victims of abuse, and starting the "Chief Executive Officer's Project." The Project encourages businesses across Massachusetts to provide training for their managers and supervisors, develop a family violence protocol for employees, and support a local battered women's service agency.

Liz Claiborne, Inc. is another leader in responding to the needs of battered women at work. In 1993 the company's "Women's Work" project focused exclusively on domestic violence. In addition to featuring radio campaigns, educational posters and brochures, and a series of commemorative products to benefit domestic violence programs, it commissioned a survey of business leaders to determine their understanding and perceptions of domestic violence. The company also worked to create an internal environment supportive of the needs of battered women. EAP counselors were trained to handle domestic violence cases and provide counseling and referrals. Personnel in the Human Resources, Health Services and Security Departments were also trained to respond to domestic violence. Employees may take the time they need to seek safety or services, to attend court appearances, and to arrange for new housing. Like Polaroid, Liz Claiborne Inc. also provides flexible hours, short-term paid leaves and extended leaves without pay.

A 1999 Bill introduced into the U.S. Senate by Senators Wellstone, Murray and Schumer, proposing the adoption of a "Battered Women's Economic Security and Safety Act," offered a tax credit to companies who that implemented workplace safety programs to combat violence against women. S. 1069, Title II, Subtitle C (106 Cong. 1st Sess. 1999). The list of expenses for which the credit could be claimed serves as a useful summary of steps an employer could take to address the domestic violence that affects its workforce:

(i) the hiring of new security personnel in order to address violent crimes against women,

(ii) the creation of buddy systems or escort systems for walking employees to parking lots, parked cars, subway stations, or bus stops ...

(iii) the purchase or installation of new security equipment, including surveillance equipment, lighting fixtures, cardkey access systems, and identification systems

. . .

(iv) the establishment of an employee assistance line or other employee assistance services ...

(v) the retention of an attorney to provide legal services to employees seeking restraining orders or other legal recourse ...

(vi) the establishment of medical services addressing the medical needs of employees who are victims of violent crimes against women,

(vii) the retention of a financial expert or an accountant to provide financial counseling to employees seeking to escape ...

(viii) the establishment of an education program for employees, consisting of seminars or training sessions about violent crimes against women undertaken in consultation and coordination with national, State, or local domestic violence and sexual assault coalitions or programs,

(ix) studies of the cost, impact or extent of violent crimes against women at the employer's place of business, if such studies are made available to the public and protect the identity of employees included in the study,

(x) the publication of a regularly disseminated newsletter or other regularly disseminated materials about violent crimes against women,

(xi) the implementation of leave policies for the purpose of allowing or accommodating the needs of victims of violent crimes against women to pursue legal redress against assailants, including leave from work to attend meetings with attorneys, to give evidentiary statements or depositions, and to attend hearings or trials in court,

(xii) the implementation of flexible work policies for the purpose of allowing or accommodating the needs of employees who are victims of violent crimes against women, or employees at risk with respect to such crimes, to avoid assailants,

(xiii) the implementation of transfer policies for the purpose of allowing or accommodating the needs of employees ... to change office locations within the company in order to avoid assailants or to allow the transfer of an employee who has perpetrated violent crimes against women in order to protect the victim, including payment of costs for the transfer and relocations of an employee to another city, county, State, or country for the purpose of maintaining an employee's safety ...

(xiv) the provision of any of the services described ... to the spouses or dependents of employees.

Subtitle A of S1069 authorized the grant of a total of $2.5 million over five years to a National Clearinghouse on Domestic Violence and Sexual Assault in the Workplace, to provide information and assistance to employers, labor organizations and advocates in developing and implementing appropriate responses to victims. Subtitle D, Employment Protection for Battered Women, provided for unemployment compensation for women forced to leave their employment because of partner violence, and for the use of available leave, both paid and unpaid, to respond to individual and family needs created by partner violence. Subtitle B, Victims' Employment Rights, which proposed to protect women from discrimination on the basis of their status as victims of domestic violence, will be discussed below, in the context of adverse action taken by employers against victims of domestic violence. Although S1069 did not become law, it is likely that similar measures will be reintroduced at the federal level, and that the bill will provide a model for state legislation in the future.

Employer Liability for Abuse at Work

The model employment practices described above contrast starkly with some of the experiences of battered women who have been victimized at work:

> Because it is easy to assume that domestic violence is a private family problem, one reaction of employers confronted with battered employees may be to tell them to leave their personal problems behind when they come to work. This is exactly the response one Chicago woman got when she went to her boss for help. Although she had received harassing phone calls from her boyfriend while at work, her boss informed her that her situation was not a company problem and that she should deal with it herself. However, it became a company problem that evening when her boyfriend appeared in the company parking garage and opened fire. He injured her, killed a parking attendant, and then killed himself.
>
> All too often it is not only the battered employee, but also her coworkers and supervisors that may be in the line of fire when an abuser shows up at the office. For example, an owner of an answering service was shot in the face when an employee's former boyfriend showed up at work. He had been stalking the employee up to the very day that he found her at work and killed her. A coworker who tried to stop him was also killed. In California, a woman was at work when her ex-husband arrived. He killed three of her coworkers and badly injured six others. She had previously informed her employer that her ex-husband threatened to find her at work and kill her. The employer failed to take action. . . . In yet another case, two employees were killed and nine employees were injured when a coworker's husband showed up at the office, assembled a shotgun, and opened fire. . . . Although the building owners and occupants had knowledge that the husband had made threats to kill his wife at work, they refused to tighten security at their offices.

Stephanie L. Perin, *Note: Employers May Have to Pay When Domestic Violence Goes to Work*, 18 REV. LITIG. 265, 367–68 (1999).

In cases in which harm to an employee or coworker results because an employer has not shielded an employee threatened by partner violence, what liability may attach? In every state, the vast majority of on-the-job injuries are channeled through a statutory workers' compensation scheme which supplants tort recovery. On the one hand, recovery under worker's compensation does not depend on finding the employer at fault, but on the other hand, recovery is less generous than in the tort system. Notably, neither punitive damages nor pain and suffering are recoverable. In almost every state, injuries are governed by the Workers' Compensation Act if they arise out of and in the course of employment. The first question, therefore, is whether the harm inflicted by a violent partner or ex-partner at the victim's workplace fits that definition. Most courts have answered that question in the negative, as the following case illustrates.

Epperson v. Industrial Commission of Arizona

549 P.2d 247; 26 Ariz. App. 467.
Court of Appeals of Arizona, 1976.

■ NELSON, J.

The primary question presented by this appeal is whether the assault upon Billie Epperson (Mrs. Epperson) on April 28, 1973, arose out of and occurred in the course of her employment with respondent Mountain Bell. The hearing officer found, and affirmed on review, that while the assault occurred during the course of petitioner's employment, it did not arise out of that employment, and was therefore not compensable under the Workmen's Compensation Act of Arizona. We agree with this conclusion and therefore affirm the award.

Mrs. Epperson sustained a gunshot wound while on the premises of Mountain Bell. She was married to the assailant, Willie Epperson (Mr. Epperson). Their stormy marriage of over 20 years had been plagued by violent fights, often precipitated by Mr. Epperson's frequent intoxication and extreme jealousy.

On Friday, April 27, 1973, petitioner and her husband had a serious quarrel at home. Shortly thereafter, Mrs. Epperson left the house and went to work at Mountain Bell. That night she stayed in a motel with three of her four children. Mrs. Epperson went to work a little early on Saturday in hopes of avoiding a confrontation with her husband, who was familiar with her time schedule. Upon entering the employer's premises, petitioner told the security guard that she was having some personal difficulties with her husband and did not wish to see him if he should come to the building.

Mr. Epperson was angered by his wife's failure to return home Friday night. On Saturday morning he drank two bottles of beer and some Scotch, hid a gun under his shirt, and went looking for his wife. He arrived at the Mountain Bell building at approximately 10:30 a.m. .... [H]e was standing at the security guard's desk when his wife appeared in that area after returning from the cafeteria. Mr. Epperson approached Mrs. Epperson, and for approximately five to ten minutes conversed with her in an unthreatening manner and in a normal tone of voice.

Mr. Epperson urged his wife to talk with him; she insisted that she had to return to work. During this time petitioner did not address the security guard, nor did he speak to her. She testified that she walked in front of the guard to enable him to see anything that transpired. Mr. Epperson subsequently turned his back to the security guard, reached under his shirt, grabbed his gun, disarmed the guard, and shot his wife. Soon thereafter the police arrived and subdued Mr. Epperson.

In order for an injury to be compensable, it must "arise out of" the employment and be sustained "in the course of" the employment. ... The term "arising out of" is said to refer to the origin or cause of the injury, while "in the course of" refers to the time, place and circumstances of the accident in relation to the employment. The hearing officer specifically found that the accident occurred in the course of Mrs. Epperson's employment. We agree with that finding. It thus becomes necessary to inquire whether the assault in question "arose out of" Mrs. Epperson's employment.

If the motivating cause of an assault is purely personal, compensation is ordinarily denied ... This Court has stated that:

> When the animosity or dispute that culminates in an assault is imported into the employment from claimant's domestic or private life, *and is not exacerbated by the employment,* the assault does not arise out of the employment under any test.

Wyckoff v. The Industrial Commission of Arizona, 14 Ariz.App. 288, 482 P.2d 897 (1971). (Emphasis added)

. . .

Petitioner contends that her injuries resulted from an assault which arose out of her employment in that the assault was exacerbated by the employment. She points to three specific occurrences as having exacerbated the assault: "The act of flirtation; the ending of her coffee break; and the reliance upon the security guard for protection." We hold that none of these circumstances constituted an exacerbation of the assault by the employment so as to bring the assault within the meaning of the Workmen's Compensation Act.

There was no evidence of any act of flirtation on the part of either the security guard or Mrs. Epperson. We reject this argument summarily.

The issue of suspected flirtation as an exacerbation of the employment situation has recently been treated in Robbins v. Nicholson, 281 N.C. 234, 188 S.E.2d 350 (1972).... In analyzing the issue of causal relation, the Court determined that the risk of murder by a jealous spouse was not an incident of employment. Similarly, marital friction and difficulties were not deemed to be risks arising out of the nature of the employment in question.

Mrs. Epperson next points to the fact that she angered her husband by telling him that she had to return to work after her break. She contends that this shows further exacerbation of the assault by her employment. This argument also fails to convince us that her work exacerbated the assault. The evidence supports the conclusion that Mr. Epperson's anger was stirred by the fact that she finally quit talking to him and walked away, rather than that she was going to return to work.

The third respect in which Mrs. Epperson contends that the assault was exacerbated by her employment is her reliance upon the security guard for protection. While the security guard had knowledge of the marital conflict and Mrs. Epperson's desire to have her husband denied admission to the building, the guard was not informed of Mr. Epperson's violent nature or the fact that he might be armed. Mr. Epperson was stopped at the door. It was not until his wife appeared in that area that he actually entered the building. The discussion between them was conducted in a normal voice. There was no request or indication of a need for assistance. From these facts one is not compelled to conclude that the guard knew of Mrs. Epperson's danger or that she had conveyed her fears sufficiently to justify any reliance upon the guard for protection.

Petitioner argues that Carter v. Penney Tire and Recapping Company, 261 S.C. 341, 200 S.E.2d 64 (1973) is apposite to the determination of this case. That case allowed an award of compensation because (1) the employer had been aware of some danger of assault to petitioner; (2) the employer required the workman to work in the face of that danger. There is no evidence in the record as to what Mountain Bell would have required had it been made aware of the existence of a danger to petitioner, hence this Court will not apply the *Carter* decision to the instant case.

Mrs. Epperson next argues that the "arising out of" element is unnecessary in this case. She contends that A.R.S. § 23–901(9) only requires that the "in the course of employment" element be established in cases involving the willful act of a third person. We disagree. In cases involving assaults, Arizona courts have consistently held that one must prove that the assault occurred in the course of employment *and* that it arose out of the employment....

. . .

The award is affirmed.

NOTES AND QUESTIONS

1. The Washington State workers' compensation statute provides compensation for any injury sustained in the course of employment, without any additional requirement that the injury "arise out of" the employment. WASH. REV. CODE § 51.32.010. In Maryland, injuries caused by an assault by a third party are compensable if they occur in the course of employment. MD. LAB. & EMPL. Code Ann. § 9–101(b)(2). IN BOTH THESE STATES, THEREFORE, THE OUTCOME IN *EPPERSON* WOULD HAVE BEEN DIFFERENT.

2. In some states, the *Epperson* case would have been decided in the same way, but on the basis of an express statutory defense, providing that employees will not be compensated for assaults at the workplace if they stem from personal disputes. Alabama, Georgia, Iowa, Minnesota, Pennsylvania and Texas all have such defenses. Similarly, Delaware provides that an assault by a coworker will not be compensable if the assault is motivated by personal grievances, DEL. CODE. ANN. TIT. 19, § 2301(15)(b), and Missouri provides that injuries will not be compensable if they arise from a risk unrelated to employment, to which the employee would be equally exposed in his or her life outside the workplace. MO. REV. STAT. § 287.020(3)(2). In those states that have considered this issue without the benefit of express statutory provisions, most, like Arizona, have concluded that injuries sustained at work, but arising out of an abusive personal relationship, are not compensable under workers' compensation schemes. For examples more recent than *Epperson,* see, e.g., Peavler v. Mitchell & Scott Machine Co., 638 N.E.2d 879 (Ind. App. 1994); Robinson v. Village of Catskill Police Department, 209 A.D.2d 748, 617 N.Y.S.2d 975 (1994).

3. What if the person hurt in *Epperson* had been the security guard? What if, instead, it had been a coworker who sought to restrain Mrs. Epperson's abusive husband? Could those injuries be said to "arise out of" the coworker's employment? Would they be covered by the express statutory defenses described in the previous note? Would the Missouri statute generate a different result than the others? In one disturbing case in North Carolina, an employee was being harassed at work by her violent boyfriend.

Responding to concerns expressed by other employees who were afraid for their own safety, the employer decided to monitor the abused employee's performance, in order to justify firing her. A co-worker was given the task of keeping a record of the victim's working hours, and because of that assignment was injured by the boyfriend when he appeared at the workplace and shot and killed his partner. The Court of Appeals decided that his injury was not compensable, because it was caused by the criminal act of a third party that did not arise out of employment. Hemric v. Reed and Prince Manufacturing Co., 54 N.C. App. 314, 283 S.E.2d 436 (1981). The court's error lay in shifting the focus from whether the *injury* arose out of the coworker's employment, to whether the boyfriend's violent *act* arose out of the employment. If the abused partner had been the plaintiff, it would have been unsurprising for the court to hold that her death did not arise out of her employment, but out of her private relationship. But the coworker had no private relationship with his assailant, and was in the line of fire solely because of workplace responsibilities imposed by his employer.

4. Mrs. Epperson's claim that her vulnerability to assault was "exacerbated" by her employment was rejected by the court. Given what we know about abusive relationships it seems likely that Mr. Epperson would have suspected her of flirting with fellow employees, even if that were not in fact the case. It also seems likely that her employment was a threat to him. It gave her a measure of independence by providing an arena in which he could not control her behavior. It also imposed obligations on her that were not compatible with his demands. When he shot her, he wanted her to stay and talk to him, while she felt she needed to return to work. Was the court wrong to decide that her employment was not an "exacerbating" factor? Would a decision for Mrs. Epperson mean that any victim of partner violence at work could make the same argument?

In Guillory v. Interstate Gas Station, 653 So.2d 1152 (La. 1995), a Louisiana court held that a gas station employee who was shot by her husband while she was at work could not recover workers' compensation benefits because her injuries arose out of a non-employment related dispute. The employee had filed for a divorce from her husband and taken out a restraining order. She was afraid for her life, and had asked her employer both whether she could keep a gun with her at work, and whether she could work the day shift rather than her customary evening shift, so that she would be less accessible to her husband. Her employer refused both these requests. Could you make the argument that her vulnerability to her husband's assault was exacerbated by her employment?

The argument that the victim's employment is an exacerbating factor in her injury is more commonly used when the assault is perpetrated by a fellow employee, whose attentions, and violence, cannot be evaded because the employment environment forces victim and perpetrator into proximity, or precipitates the violent incident. See, for example, Torres v. Triangle Handbag Manufacturing, 13 A.D.2d 559, 211 N.Y.S.2d 992 (1961).

5. It is important to remember that a finding that an injury is not compensable under the applicable workers' compensation statute may leave

a victim uncompensated, but may instead open the door to a substantially greater award of damages through the mechanism of a tort claim.

In Massie v. Godfather's Pizza, Inc., 844 F.2d 1414, 1420–21 (10th Cir. 1988), the plaintiff sued her employer, seeking to hold it vicariously liable for the negligence of a fellow employee. The Tenth Circuit first addressed the question whether the employee, who had been raped and sexually assaulted by robbers, was precluded by the Workers' Compensation statute from suing in tort. It then went on to examine whether a tort action could lie against the employer for injuries inflicted through the criminal conduct of a third party. The alleged negligence was the fellow employee's failure to follow the company's robbery policy, which was to comply promptly with any demands made by robbers. The plaintiff argued that if her coworker had immediately opened the store safe, as the robbers requested, her injuries would have been avoided.

The jury had found that the injuries to plaintiff did not arise out of or in the course of her employment, even though the assault happened at her workplace, and was threatened, and then perpetrated, to coerce the plaintiff's coworker to assist in the robbery. The court reviewed cases cited by the defendant, but determined that the issue was properly left to the jury:

> The issue of the applicability of the workmen's compensation law was presented for jury determination in this manner:
>
> > "The defendant has asserted as an affirmative defense in this case that the plaintiff's injuries arose out of or in the course of her employment with defendant. It has the burden of proving this by a preponderance of the evidence. If you find such claim to be true, plaintiff is barred in this action from any recovery against the defendant because of the Worker's Compensation Act. In making this determination as to whether the incident arose out of or was within the scope of plaintiff's employment with defendant, you should focus on the factual situation and plaintiff's relationship thereto as it existed at the time of the incident. In determining whether plaintiff was in the course of her employment at the time, you need not find that she was doing a particular task which constituted her main duties. Rather, you should focus on whether her injuries suffered in such incident may be said to arise out of or in the course of her employment, and that such incident resulted from a risk reasonably incident to her employment." . . .
>
> . . .
>
> Our review of the record establishes that the facts surrounding plaintiff's employment situation at the time of the assault presented a classic jury question, and that question was properly submitted to the jury.
>
> Defendant next contends that if plaintiff was not within an employment situation, then in effect, it had no duty at all toward plaintiff since no duty is imposed in law upon a proprietor of a business establishment to comply with a demand of a robber. This precise argument was presented to—and rejected by—the trial court at the

close of plaintiff's evidence, . . . and the case was submitted to the jury upon general principles of common law negligence, which required an element of "foreseeable harm."

Under Utah law, Godfather's had a duty to act reasonably under the circumstances. In Utah, the possessor of land may be liable when harm is caused by the negligent or intentional acts of third parties, if the landowner failed to exercise reasonable care to discover that such acts were being, or were likely to be done. The rule applies, even though criminal conduct by third persons is involved, if such conduct is foreseeable. Mitchell v. Pearson Enterprises, 697 P.2d 240 (Utah 1985).

In *Pagan*, the Utah rule was stated in this manner, 460 P.2d at 834:

> "A possessor of land who holds it open to the public for business purposes is subject to liability for injuries to members of the public where harm is caused by negligent or intentional acts of third persons provided the possessor of the land failed to exercise reasonable care to discover that such acts are being done or likely to be done, or to give a warning adequate to enable visitors to avoid harm."

The trial court ruled, and the evidence established, that Godfather's had recognized foreseeable harm, and created its own duty to the public when it established [a] written "robbery policy,". . . . There was no error in the submission of the question to the jury, under the instructions of the court which are quoted above.

6. In the next case, the plaintiff represents the estate of a woman killed at work by her husband, and the court deals squarely with the question of the foreseeability of the harm. Unlike the Tenth Circuit in *Massie,* the Supreme Court of Alabama is not content to leave the issue to the jury, but determines as a matter of law that the plaintiff has no claim. As you read the decision, ask yourself not just whether you think the court was right to decide that the harm was not foreseeable, but whether you think it was right to take this issue away from the jury.

Carroll v. Shoney's, Inc., d/b/a Captain D's Restaurant

2000 WL 236348.
Supreme Court of Alabama, 2000.

■ MADDOX, J.

Willie Gene Carroll, as administrator of the estate of Mildred K. Harris, deceased, filed a wrongful-death action against Shoney's Inc., d/b/a Captain D's Restaurant (hereinafter "Captain D's"), and Ronnie Harris, Mildred Harris's husband. Willie Gene Carroll is Mildred Harris's father. The trial judge dismissed the claim against Ronnie Harris, and entered a summary judgment for Captain D's.

Ms. Harris, an employee of Captain D's, died as a result of a gunshot wound inflicted by Ronnie Harris while she was working at the Captain D's restaurant. The legal issue presented is whether Captain D's can be held liable for Ms. Harris's death, which resulted from a criminal act of a third party—her husband. The trial judge ruled that it could not, and entered a summary judgment in favor of Captain D's. Carroll appeals from that summary judgment, arguing that in a similar case this Court held that these facts present a jury question. After thoroughly reviewing the record and the applicable law, we hold that the trial judge properly entered the summary judgment in favor of Captain D's; consequently, we affirm.

FACTS

The facts, viewed in the light most favorable to Carroll, as the nonmovant, suggest the following: On the evening of September 22, 1995, Mildred Harris was working at Captain D's. Adrian Edwards, the relief manager, was also working that evening. Ms. Harris told Edwards that, the night before, her husband, Ronnie Harris, had beaten and choked her and that he had threatened her. Ms. Harris told Edwards that she was afraid of Ronnie Harris and that she did not want to talk to him. Ms. Harris asked Edwards to telephone the police if Ronnie Harris appeared at the restaurant that evening.

Around 10 o'clock that evening, while Ms. Harris was working in the rear of the restaurant, Ronnie Harris came in. He pushed his way past Edwards and went to the back of the restaurant, where he confronted Ms. Harris. He told Ms. Harris that he was going to "get her." Edwards and another employee repeatedly told Ronnie Harris to leave, but he continued yelling at Ms. Harris. Edwards telephoned the police; the officer who responded to the call escorted Ronnie Harris from the restaurant. The police detained him briefly; they released him after learning that Captain D's was not going to press charges. Evidence was presented indicating that after that confrontation Ms. Harris asked employees of Captain D's to help her hide from her husband; there was evidence indicating that she was taken to a motel in Montgomery and that her fellow employees lent her enough money to pay for the motel room.

The next day, September 23, 1995, Edwards reported for work and told the restaurant manager, Rhonda Jones, about the incident that had occurred the night before, i.e., that Ronnie Harris had threatened Ms. Harris, and that the police had to be called to remove Ronnie Harris from the restaurant. Edwards also told Jones that Ms. Harris had said that she was afraid to return to work. At some point after the conversation, Ms. Harris telephoned Jones and asked to be excused from work that evening. Ms. Harris told Jones that she and her husband had been fighting and that she was afraid of him. Jones told Ms. Harris to come into work; and she also told Ms. Harris that if Ronnie Harris showed up, she would telephone the police. Ms. Harris went to work that evening, and was working at the front counter. At some point during her shift, Ronnie Harris walked into the restaurant, pulled out a pistol, and shot Ms. Harris in the back of the head. Ms. Harris died as a result of the gunshot wound.

I.

A summary judgment is appropriate when there is no genuine issue of material fact and the nonmovant is entitled to a judgment as a matter of law.... When a party moving for a summary judgment makes a prima facie showing that there is no genuine issue of material fact ... the burden shifts to the nonmovant to present substantial evidence creating a genuine issue of material fact. ... Substantial evidence is "evidence of such weight and quality that fair-minded persons in the exercise of impartial judgment can reasonably infer the existence of the fact sought to be proved." ... In reviewing a ruling on a motion for a summary judgment, this Court views the evidence in the light most favorable to the nonmovant and entertains such reasonable inferences as the jury would have been free to draw. ...

II.

The general rule is that an employer is not liable to its employees for criminal acts committed by third persons against an employee. Gaskin v. Republic Steel Corp., 420 So. 2d 37 (Ala. 1982). Carroll contends, however, that this case falls within an exception to that rule, i.e., when a special relationship or special circumstances create a duty to protect an invitee or an employee from the criminal acts of a third party. Such a duty arises where the criminal conduct was foreseeable.... The plaintiff argues that the facts of this case are "strikingly" similar to the facts set out in Thetford v. City of Clanton, 605 So. 2d 835, 841 (Ala. 1992). In Thetford, the trial court entered a summary judgment for the defendants in a wrongful-death action. In that case, the wife, after telephoning the sheriff's department because her husband had allegedly abused her, checked into a Holiday Inn motel, under a fictitious name. She requested that her husband not be allowed to enter her room. Two days later, her husband arrived and asked the manager to let him into her room. The manager used his pass key to open the door and then cut the chain off the door to admit the husband. The wife was beaten to death several hours later at a different motel. A majority of this Court reversed the summary judgment for Holiday Inn and the manager, holding that foreseeability of harm was a jury question based on the facts of that case. Carroll contends that, in light of the circumstances and the relationship that existed between Captain D's and its employee Mildred Harris the exception to the general rule is applicable. Carroll argues that he presented substantial evidence in opposition to the motion for summary judgment creating a genuine issue of material fact as to whether the fatal shooting of Mildred Harris by her husband was foreseeable. We disagree.

III.

It is well settled that absent a special relationship or special circumstances a person has no duty to protect another from criminal acts of a third person....

We recognize, of course, that this Court has held that "there is a singular exception to this general rule, which arises where 'the particular criminal conduct was foreseeable.'" ... This Court has also recognized that this exception can apply to employers in certain circumstances. See Parham v. Taylor, 402 So. 2d 884, 885 (Ala. 1981) ("In certain circumstances an employer may have a civil liability to his employees for the criminal acts of third persons: ... However ... 'employers should not be saddled with such liability except in the most extraordinary and highly unusual circumstances.' " ...) Parham involved an action by a convenience-store clerk who had been shot during a robbery at the store, at which previous robberies had occurred.

We believe that Carroll has failed to show how this case falls outside the general rule that a person has no duty to protect another from criminal acts of a third person. Alabama law requires a plaintiff to show three elements to establish a duty that would be the basis for a cause of action such as the one presented in this case.... First, the particular criminal conduct must have been foreseeable. Second, the defendant must have possessed "specialized knowledge" of the criminal activity. Third, the criminal conduct must have been a probability.[1]

Viewing the facts most favorably to Carroll, as we are required to do, and applying the law to those facts, we conclude that the plaintiff has not presented evidence creating a genuine issue of material fact as to Captain D's liability. The particular criminal conduct in this case was a murder.... [T]here was no evidence in this case that any employee of Captain D's was told, or should have reasonably foreseen, that Ronnie Harris would enter the Captain D's restaurant and murder his wife. Admittedly, there was evidence that Mildred Harris and her husband had been fighting, and that she had requested permission to be away from work for that reason, but the evidence also indicated that she had made similar requests on other occasions for the same reason. During his deposition, Carroll, who is Mildred Harris's father, admitted that he had no reason to think that Ronnie Harris would shoot Mildred Harris. Based on the foregoing, we fail to see how Captain D's can be held responsible for Ms. Harris's death. Consequently, we affirm the judgment of the trial court.

■ JOHNSTONE, JUSTICE (dissenting).

The crucial issue is not whether the murder was foreseeable, but whether violence and injury, fatal or not, were foreseeable. Had the husband slapped the deceased, would anyone say the slapping was not foreseeable? If he had blackened her eye or broken her nose or knocked her

1. "It is [the] recognition of the harsh reality that crime can and does occur despite society's best efforts to prevent it that explains this Court's requirement that the particular conduct be foreseeable and that the defendant have 'specialized knowledge' that criminal activity which could endanger an invitee was a probability." *Moye,* 499 So. 2d at 1372. Cf. Guerrero v. Memorial Medical Center of East Texas, 938 S.W.2d 789 (Tex. App. 1997). In Guerrero, a woman was killed by her estranged husband while she was at work. The facts of that case are similar to the facts here: The husband came to the employer's premises, took the victim by the arm, and tried to get her to leave with him. The supervisor reported the incident to security, and the security officer ordered the husband to leave the premises. The following day, the wife telephoned her supervisor and requested that the supervisor meet her in the parking lot, because she was afraid her husband would be waiting for her. The supervisor asked security to escort the wife into the building, which it did. About two hours later, one of the officers saw the husband, took him by the arm, told him to leave the premises, and threatened to file criminal trespass charges against him if he refused. Within 20 minutes the husband returned and shot and killed the wife on the employer's premises. The trial court entered a summary judgment for the employer, and the appellate court affirmed, holding that the husband's criminal act was not foreseeable and that the employer had no duty to protect the wife from her husband.

teeth down her throat, would anyone say any of these batterings was not foreseeable? Is the defendant less liable because the husband killed her? "[A plaintiff] is not required to prove 'that the particular consequence should have been anticipated, but rather that some general harm or consequence could have been anticipated.' " Hail v. Regency Terrace Owners Ass'n, [Ms. 1981397, December 22, 1999]....

On the day of the killing, the defendant's manager Rhonda Jones was, at all pertinent times, acting within the line and scope of her agency for the defendant itself. Jones was informed of the decedent's husband's angry trespass into the back of the restaurant and angry threat against the deceased during the preceding night. Jones was informed that the incident was so bad the restaurant personnel needed to call the police in order to remove the husband. Jones was informed that the deceased had told her coworkers that her husband had beaten her two days earlier and that she thought that he would kill her. Nonetheless, Jones refused the deceased's plea to be excused from work, ordered the deceased to report to work, and promised to protect the deceased at work. Jones then assigned the deceased to work at the counter, where she was more exposed to violence from her husband than she would have been on virtually any other assignment within the restaurant. The husband's injuring the deceased was not just foreseeable but was expectable.

. . .

... As already discussed, violence by the husband was so obviously foreseeable that the manager of the restaurant expressly promised to protect the deceased from the husband. Second, the manager had specialized knowledge of the husband's trespass, abuse, and threat the preceding night, the battery he had committed on the deceased two days earlier, and the deceased's perception of the danger he posed. Third, the husband's criminal conduct was a probability if not a certainty: the night before, he had pushed his way past a restaurant employee and trespassed into the back of the store in order to threaten the deceased that he was going to "get her."

To absolve the defendant of liability, the main opinion cites the rationale of Moye, supra, "that crime can and does occur despite society's best efforts to prevent it." ... Society did not exert its best efforts to prevent the crime committed on the deceased in the case before us. Rather the defendant, through its managerial personnel, demonstrated a preoccupation with the logistics of fast food and an irresponsible disregard for the notorious dangers of spouse abuse and the public policy of this state, expressed in a number of recent statutes, against spouse abuse.

Foreseeability is a matter of common sense. The decision of this Court in this case will send a message whether we think common sense entails recognizing the danger of demonstrated spouse abuse.

NOTES AND QUESTIONS

1. Who do you think has the better of this argument, the majority, or the dissent? Does it seem surprising, given all the society has learned about the

nature of abusive relationships, that a court would find violence unforeseeable to an employer, even when the employer has witnessed threatening conduct? In the *Guerrero* case cited by the majority there was no evidence that the victim had ever informed her employer of her partner's physical abuse, or that his behavior in the workplace prior to the shooting provided any indication of his violent propensities. Do you agree with the majority's assessment that the facts in *Guerrero* are similar to the facts in *Carroll*?

2. The claim against Shoney's was essentially a negligent security claim, analogous to well-established lines of cases brought by tenants against landlords, and customers against store owners. In all these cases the focus is on the foreseeability of the risk created by criminal third parties to the class of people represented by the plaintiff, and on whether the defendant has the kind of control over the environment that puts it in the best position to guard against the risk. Although the focus of these materials is on an employer's responsibilities towards its employees, it is worth noting that the same arguments could be used by victims of domestic violence terrorized in schools and on college campuses, in hospitals, and while using public transportation. To the extent these facilities are run by public rather than private entities, issues of sovereign immunity may complicate the analysis.

In none of these contexts do defendants have an obligation to guarantee the safety of their tenants, customers, employees, students or patients. Once the foreseeability of the risk establishes that a duty of care is owed, the next question will be whether the steps taken by the defendant were reasonable, or whether the plaintiff is right to claim that they were inadequate. When you look at the facts of *Guerrero,* as recited by the majority in *Carroll*, do you think the defendant Memorial Medical Center acted reasonably, given what it knew about the situation? Is that another basis for distinguishing *Guerrero* from *Carroll*?

3. Different tort theories of liability may come into play if the perpetrator of workplace violence is another employee, or a supervisor. If the conduct is intentional, as it almost certainly will be, the employer will not be liable on a respondeat superior basis. However, the employer could potentially be liable for negligent hiring, negligent supervision, or negligent retention of the abusive employee. A negligent hiring claim focuses on whether the employer properly investigated the employee's background prior to hiring him or her; a negligent supervision claim focuses on whether the employer has exercised appropriate control over the employee's conduct on the job; and a negligent retention claim focuses on whether, as problems come to light, the employer has taken appropriate action to investigate charges of misconduct, reassign an employee who is causing trouble for a specific fellow worker, or terminate the employment. In all these actions the key questions will again be whether the risk created by the employer was foreseeable, and whether, under the specific circumstances of the case, the employer's conduct was or was not reasonable.

4. An employee who is threatened, harassed or assaulted by another employee or a supervisor at work may also be able to invoke Title VII of the Civil Rights Act of 1964, 42 U.S.C. § 2000e–2, claiming sexual harassment

as a form of gender discrimination. Title VII claims are not precluded by workers' compensation schemes. Remediable sexual harassment in the workplace falls into two categories. The first is quid pro quo harassment—unwelcome conduct on the basis of an employee's sex affecting a term or condition of employment. Classic examples are making a promotion or favorable assignment conditional on the employee's granting sexual favors, or threatening discharge or demotion if those favors are withheld. The second category is hostile work environment harassment, which requires that an employee show she was was subject to unwelcome conduct based on her gender sufficiently severe or pervasive that it affected the conditions of her employment and created an abusive working environment. It seems likely that partner abuse would more often manifest itself in the workplace in this second way.

In order to recover, the employee must show that the employer knew or had reason to know about the harassment, and failed to take appropriate action to end it. In Title VII cases the perpetrator of the abusive or harassing behavior is usually a fellow employee, over whose behavior the employer has control. However, there have been cases in which employers have been held liable for failing to protect employees from harassment by customers, so that some precedent exists for bringing a Title VII claim when the primary perpetrator is not employed by the defendant. For a more thorough discussion of Title VII suits in the context of partner violence, see Fredrica L. Lehrman, DOMESTIC VIOLENCE PRACTICE AND PROCEDURE, §§ 10:19–10:21 (1997 & SUPP. 1999).

In some jurisdictions, courts have used the existence of Title VII or parallel state civil rights legislation to preclude tort actions based on sexual or racial harassment. Illinois, for example, requires that all claims based on intentionally discriminatory conduct must be brought under the state's Human Rights Act, rather than in tort. Daulo v. Commonwealth Edison, 938 F. Supp. 1388 (N.D. Ill. 1996). Similarly, a federal district court in New York has held that under New York law no tort claim for negligent hiring and retention will lie when the gravamen of the claim is racial harassment by a coworker. Brown v. Bronx Cross County Medical Group, 834 F. Supp. 105 (S.D.N.Y. 1993). Other courts have allowed discrimination-based negligence actions to go forward. See, for example, Cox v. Brazo, 165 Ga. App. 888, 303 S.E.2d 71 (1983), judgment affirmed 251 Ga. 491, 307 S.E.2d 474 (1983); Kerans v. Porter Paint Co., 61 Ohio St.3d 486, 575 N.E.2d 428 (1991). See also Fredrica L. Lehrman, DOMESTIC VIOLENCE PRACTICE AND PROCEDURE, §§ 10:21.3 (Supp. 1999). In the context of partner violence at work, the practical response to this problem may be to frame the claim squarely as a negligence claim, without reference to discrimination, in those states in which the discrimination framework may preclude other alternatives.

5. Since 1993, the Federal Occupational Safety and Health Administration (OSHA) has been issuing citations to employers, charging that incidents of workplace violence involve employer violations of the Occupational Safety and Health Act's "general duty clause." The general duty clause requires each employer covered by the Act to "furnish to each of his employees

employment and place of employment which are free from recognized hazards that are causing or are likely to cause death or serious physical harm." 29 U.S.C. § 654. In 1996 OSHA further demonstrated its concern with workplace violence by issuing guidelines for preventing violent acts in the health care and social service sectors, the two industries in which violent acts are most prevalent. Occupational Safety and Health Admin., U.S. Dept. of Labor, Guidelines for Preventing Workplace Violence for Health Care and Social Service Workers (1996). The guidelines suggest a prevention program that includes: "(1) management commitment and employee involvement, (2) worksite analysis, (3) hazard prevention and control, and (4) safety and health training."

In 1995, however, The Occupational Safety and Health Review Commission dismissed a citation involving workplace violence, noting that when the Act was passed, it was not contemplated that it would be used to combat this type of "hazard." The OSHRC, finding that third party violence introduces a "wild card" into the analysis, held that before an employer can be liable, a high standard of proof must be met to show that the employer recognized the potential danger posed by third parties. The employee's fear of violence, even if known to the employer, is not sufficient proof; nor is the fact that employees have been subject to violence on prior occasions. *Workplace Violence: General Duty Citation for Assaults Against Workers Dismissed by Law Judge*. DLR, July 6, 1995 at A–3. An additional limitation of this approach is that the Act does not create a private cause of action for employees; employers who violate its mandates are subject only to limited administrative penalties, including relatively modest fines. However, tort claimants can use Occupational Safety and Health Act violations as evidence of negligence, or even negligence per se. See John P. Luddington, *Annotation, Violation of OSHA Regulation as Affecting Tort Liability*, 70 A.L.R. 3d 962 (1978).

6. When the abusive partner is the employer himself, injuries inflicted by his intentional conduct will not be compensable under workers' compensation schemes, but can be addressed under the rubric of a variety of intentional torts, as described in Chapter 11, above.

When Employers Sanction Victims

When an employee's abusive partner sets out to sabotage her ability to perform her job, or carries his campaign of harassment to her workplace, he frequently jeopardizes her employment. Sometimes employers are simply unaware that the reason their employee is late, distracted or unreliable is that she is coping with violence at home. Sometimes they know, but simply decide that the problem is one personal to the employee. If the abusive partner begins to make his presence felt at work; either by appearing at the worksite, or by making harassing calls, other employees may begin to worry about their own safety, or have their own work performance disrupted. In all too many situations, the result is that the employee loses her job, or suffers other adverse job action. The question in this section of the materials is whether she has any recourse against the employer who seeks to punish her for her abuser's behavior.

Twenty five states have laws on the books that make it illegal for an employer to fire, or otherwise discriminate against, any victim of a crime who takes time off from work to testify in a criminal proceeding, pursuant to a subpoena. This protection, albeit somewhat limited, would certainly extend to victims of domestic violence in those states, if they were cooperating in criminal proceedings against their batterers. Three states, Rhode Island, California and Maine, offer more targeted protection to domestic violence victims. Maine provides job-protected leave to employees who need time to obtain a restraining order, and forbids employers from discriminating against those who exercise that right. Rhode Island and California also prohibit employers from discharging or discriminating against employees because they seek or obtain protective orders. R.I. GEN. LAWS § 12-28-11 (1998); CAL. LAB. CODE § 230 (1999). The California legislation offers the same protection if the employee is seeking any "other relief for domestic violence," and the Rhode Island legislation covers not only current employees, but those seeking employment, who may not be turned away because they are seeking or have obtained a protective order. Employers in New York may not fire employees for pursuing their rights under the New York Family Court Act.

Proposed federal legislation goes much further. Senate Bill 1069 (106th Cong. 1st Sess. 1999), introduced by Senators Wellstone, Murry and Schumer but not enacted, proposed a Battered Women's Economic Security and Safety Act. Subtitle B of Title II addressed Victims' Employment Rights, and proposed the following provisions:

SEC. 2024. PROHIBITED DISCRIMINATORY ACTS.

An employer shall not fail to hire, refuse to hire, or discharge any individual, or otherwise discriminate against any individual with respect to compensation, terms, conditions or privileges of employment, of the individual (including retaliation in any form or manner) because—

(1) the individual—

(A) is or is perceived to be a victim of domestic violence, sexual assault, or stalking;

(B) attended, participated in, or prepared for, or requested leave to attend, participate in or prepare for a criminal or civil court proceeding relating to an incident of domestic violence, sexual assault, or stalking of which the employee, or the son or daughter or parent of the employee, was a victim; or

(C) requested an adjustment to a job structure or workplace facility, including a transfer, reassignment, or modified schedule, leave, a changed telephone number or seating assignment, or installation of a lock or implementation of a safety procedure, in response to actual or threatened domestic violence, sexual assault, or stalking, regardless of whether the request was granted; or

(2) the action of a person whom the employee states has committed or threatened to commit domestic violence, sexual assault, or

stalking against the employee, or the son or daughter or parent of the employee, disrupted the workplace.

SEC. 2025. ENFORCEMENT.

(a) CIVIL ACTION BY EMPLOYEES.—

(1) LIABILITY.—Any employer who violates section 2024 shall be liable to any employee affected for—

(A) damages equal to the amount of wages, salary, employment benefits . . ., or other compensation denied to or lost by such employee by reason of the violation, and the interest on that amount calculated at the prevailing rate;

(B) compensatory damages, including damages for future pecuniary losses, emotional pain, suffering, inconvenience, mental anguish, loss of enjoyment or life, and other nonpecuniary losses;

(C) such punitive damages, up to 3 times the amount of actual damages sustained, as the court described in paragraph (2) shall determine to be appropriate; and

(D) such equitable relief as may be appropriate, including employment, reinstatement, and promotion.

(2) RIGHT OF ACTION.—An action to recover the damages or equitable relief prescribed in paragraph (1) may be maintained against any employer (including a public agency) in any Federal or State court of competent jurisdiction by any 1 or more employees.

(b) ACTION BY DEPARTMENT OF JUSTICE.—The Attorney General may bring a civil action in any Federal or State court of competent jurisdiction to recover the damages or equitable relief described in subsection (a)(1).

Subtitle B also provides for the payment of attorneys' fees.

What do you make of these provisions? Do they place too heavy a burden on employers? How would they apply to the employer who reluctantly, after a long period of time, terminates the employment of a worker who has missed so much time on the job because of her partner's abuse that the employer is forced to hire another employee to do her work? Can that employer claim that he let his employee go not because she was a victim of partner violence, but because, even with reasonable accommodations, she was unable to fulfil her job responsibilities?

The following descriptions of current employer response to victims of domestic violence provide some indication of the sea change that legislation securing victims' employment rights would demand. The excerpt presents four cases involving union employees, all of whom invoked grievance procedures to challenge adverse actions taken against them by their employers because of their involvement in abusive relationships. Every case resulted in an arbitration decision favoring the employee. The author remains critical of how the cases were handled, not only by the employers, but also by the employees' unions, and the arbitrators. As you read, however, imagine how much less protection there might currently be for the more than 90% of American workers who are not union members.

Jennifer Atterbury
Employment Protection and Domestic Violence: Addressing Abuse in the Labor Grievance Process, 1998 Journal of Dispute Resolution 165, 169–74 (1998)

... In re ITT Higbie Manufacturing Company, Fulton Division and International Association of Machinists and Aerospace Workers, Local Lodge 956 ... involved an employee who was a victim of abuse.[1] She had separated from her husband and was seeking a divorce when she returned to work from her lunch break and encountered her husband in her employer's parking lot. He grabbed her arm and punched her in the mouth, causing a severe cut. The company immediately suspended the woman for "fighting on the premises," and she filed a grievance.

The arbitrator determined the employee was improperly suspended for "fighting." The grievant was not disciplined because she did not provoke the fight, but rather was the victim. The arbitrator did not apply the "fighting" policy to the victims of the attacks, and noted that the employee's attempt to retreat to the facility demonstrated that she was not the aggressor. Similarly, the arbitrator noted that the employee was not responsible for the attacker's actions, although the arbitrator did not state what constituted provocative behavior. The arbitrator awarded the employee wages for the day she was attacked pursuant to a contract provision awarding back pay when harmed [sic] on the premises. She did not receive back pay for the overtime she missed the following day because the collective bargaining agreement provided that employees would only be compensated for regular eight-hour shifts. This loss of overtime was significant because such compensation is usually twice the amount of a regular wage.

The second arbitration is an unpublished opinion between Company and Union. An employee of Company was abused by a former boyfriend who had fathered her daughter. During a late shift, her abuser came to the work premises and company personnel allowed him into the facility. He asked the employee where their baby was, became loud and abusive, and ultimately knocked off her glasses, pushed her, and threatened to kill her. Two plant managers witnessed the incident and did not intervene. The woman had previously obtained an order of protection and went to the police station to press charges following this incident. The company took no legal action against the abuser.

The abuser continued to stalk, harass and threaten the employee at her home despite her attempts to enforce her order of protection. One morning, the abuser called the victim and threatened to kill her, so she took a gun to work. When she arrived at work, her abuser drove into the

1. 85 Lab. Arb. (BNA) 859 (1985) (Shanker, Arb.).

parking lot and sped directly toward her. She fired two shots at the car, stopping him from hitting her.

She was indefinitely suspended for bringing firearms onto the work premises in violation of a Company rule. After a hearing, Company discharged the employee for knowingly violating this rule. The suspension caused the employee to file a grievance. Company maintained that the grievant should have defended herself by avoiding the car on foot. Company also asserted that its past actions gave the employee no sense that it would not protect her. Company also claimed that the abuser's intentions were "noble" in that he entered the premises to inquire about his daughter.

The arbitrator addressed the nature and impact of domestic violence. He found the employee legitimately feared for her life and reasonably believed that neither Company nor the police would protect her. The arbitrator reinstated the employee but declined to award thirteen months of back pay because the employee knowingly violated Company's rules. The arbitrator noted that the employee would be immediately discharged if she brought a gun on the premises again.

In In re State of Ohio [Southern Ohio Correctional Facility] and Ohio Civil Service Employees Association an employer fired a woman for repeated absenteeism caused by her husband's serious and continuous abuse.[1] The employee received over ten letters of reprimand and confirmations of suspensions. She was suspended for one, five, ten and then fifteen days for absenteeism. On several occasions, the employee was disciplined because she notified her employer that she was sick and subsequently failed to provide a physician's verification. Throughout the course of her employment, the employee was provided with fliers in her paycheck alerting her to the Employee Assistance Program (EAP). Based on these findings, the arbitrator determined that the employee would be terminated if she did not enroll in the EAP within thirty days. The arbitrator stated that if the employee voluntarily attended EAP counseling she would be reinstated without back pay. Although the employer had properly enforced the collective bargaining contract, the employee was not immediately terminated because of continuing spousal abuse. The arbitrator also criticized the employee for not alerting her employer to the abuse and not utilizing the EAP.

Similarly, in In re Smith Fiberglass Products, Inc., Little Rock, Arkansas and Local 6904 United Steelworkers of America, an employee was absent for ten days when she erroneously believed she was granted personal leave.[2] The employee had previously requested a short medical leave for a skin rash. Soon after, the employee and her manager discussed giving the employee more leave. The employee and her manager met at the guard house by the parking lot. The employee was in her car filled with her belongings, and she informed her manager that she was looking for a place to stay because her husband was abusive and had previously entered the work premises to find her. She assumed her manager knew she was hiding

1. 106 Lab. Arb. (BNA) 914 (1996) (Feldman, Arb.).

2. 108 Lab. Arb. (BNA) 225 (1997) (Allen, Arb.).

from her husband; however, he assumed she was requesting additional medical leave. The employment contract allowed the employer to fire an employee who failed to appear at work for three consecutive days. The employee assumed her manager had granted her personal leave, did not contact work for ten days, and was subsequently terminated. The employee then filed a grievance.

The arbitrator determined the grievant was improperly terminated, but he only awarded her six weeks back pay despite her nine month suspension pending investigation. He justified this penalty by concluding that the employee was at fault for not notifying her employer of her whereabouts and not making certain that her manager had authorized her personal leave.

. . .

All the abused employees were reinstated, but no grievant received full back pay. In all the opinions, battered women were disciplined or terminated because abuse either entered the workplace or inhibited job performance. In only one opinion did the arbitrator educate himself about domestic violence. The four opinions demonstrate the need for arbitrators, unions and employers to be educated about domestic violence so as to prevent absenteeism and violence in the workplace before the labor grievance process is initiated. The opinions demonstrate that once grievances reach arbitration abused employees have already suffered financial loss and adverse job consequences while suspended pending a hearing. Arbitration rarely diminishes the effects of abuse and arguably exacerbates domestic violence by placing greater financial burdens on abused women.

* * *

NOTES AND QUESTIONS

1. What would you identify as the most troubling aspects of the arbitrators' decisions in these cases? What features of their decisions lead you to doubt their grasp of the nature of abusive relationships and of women's, and society's, responses to abuse?

2. In the non-union context, most workers are employed "at will," meaning that both they, and their employers, can terminate the employment arrangement for any reason, or no reason, by giving reasonable notice. The common law doctrine of "wrongful discharge" sets limits to the employer's freedom to fire, in three situations: (1) where the firing violates an express oral commitment to the employee, or a commitment implicit in the employer's conduct, or a commitment made in an employee policy or handbook; (2) where the firing violates established public policy; and (3) where the firing breaches the covenant of good faith and fair dealing implied in all contracts as a matter of law. Each state has developed its own body of precedent interpreting these three exceptions, and states differ widely in their willingness to encroach upon the employer's freedom to dismiss its employees.

As Fredrica Lehrman has suggested, the "public policy" theory of wrongful discharge may be potentially the most helpful to employees seeking relief from adverse action by their employers because domestic violence has encroached on their workplaces, or on their ability to perform their jobs. However, the theory tends to be narrowly construed:

> The elements of this tort have been described as:
>
> - Clear public policy existed and was manifested in a state or federal constitution, statute or administrative regulation, or in the common law.
> - Dismissing employees under circumstances like those involved in the plaintiff's dismissal would jeopardize the public policy.
> - The plaintiff's dismissal was motivated by conduct related to the public policy.
>
> The biggest obstacle for the employee bringing this cause of action is identifying a clear public policy that is violated by the employee's termination, because courts typically demand that the public policy come from a specific source such as state statutes, constitutional provisions, common-law causes of action, or recognized professional standards.
>
> In a situation in which an employee is assaulted at work by a battering partner, the employee can attempt to pursue a wrongful discharge claim based on the violation of public policies articulated in criminal statutes penalizing the batterer's actions or in state statutes enabling victims of domestic violence to obtain restraining orders against batterers to protect the injured person from further violence or intimidation. However, if the statute does not expressly protect an employee from being fired, a court may not be willing to infer a policy from the statute.

Fredrica L. Lehrman, DOMESTIC VIOLENCE PRACTICE AND PROCEDURE, §§ 10:18 (1997).

The difficulties suggested by Lehrman are well illustrated by this next case.

Green v. Bryant

887 F. Supp. 798.
United States District Court for the Eastern District of Pennsylvania, 1995.

■ DITTER, J.

The primary question in this case is whether Pennsylvania's public policy protects an at-will employee who is the victim of spousal abuse from discharge by her employer. For the reasons stated below, I find that it does not.

I. FACTS

Defendant, Dr. Winston Murphy Bryant, employed plaintiff, Philloria Green, from December 1992 through August 1993. Plaintiff asserts that during her last week of work, her estranged husband raped and severely beat her with a pipe at gun point. She received medical treatment and returned to work shortly thereafter. Ms. Green informed another doctor in the office about the attack. The doctor informed defendant, who then terminated plaintiff's employment. Ms. Green asserts that Dr. Bryant told her that the discharge had nothing to do with plaintiff's performance at work, but was based solely upon her being the victim of a violent crime.[1] ... She also alleges that she has suffered migraine headaches and post-traumatic stress disorder as a result of her being fired.

Plaintiff's amended complaint alleges five causes of action.... Count II alleges a claim for wrongful discharge. Counts III and IV assert that defendant is liable, respectively, for negligent and intentional infliction of emotional distress. Count V alleges that defendant breached an implied covenant of good faith and fair dealing. Defendant has moved to dismiss counts II through V pursuant to Federal Rule of Civil Procedure 12(b)(6) on the ground that they fail to state a claim upon which relief can be granted.

II. PLAINTIFF'S STATE-LAW CLAIMS

A. Wrongful Discharge

Plaintiff asserts in count II that defendant wrongfully discharged her from employment in violation of Pennsylvania public policy. Plaintiff admits she was an at-will employee of Dr. Bryant's. The general rule in Pennsylvania is that an at-will employee may be dismissed with or without cause, for good reason, bad reason, or no reason. ... Some courts have recognized a narrow exception, "in only the most limited of circumstances," where discharge of an at-will employee would threaten clear mandates of public policy.... The cases in Pennsylvania where the public policy exception has been recognized all involve a constitutionally or legislatively established prohibition, requirement, or privilege; e.g., firing an employee who made a nuclear safety report required by law, not hiring someone whose criminal conviction had been pardoned, and firing an employee who was absent due to jury duty. ... In addition, terminated plaintiffs have been successful when fired for refusing to serve alcohol to an intoxicated patron, refusing to participate in lobbying, refusing to engage in antitrust violations, and refusing to take a polygraph test. ... In sum, the exception is most frequently applied when the discharge results from an employee's compliance with or refusal to violate the law, or where the employee did something he or she was privileged to do. Id. As the Third Circuit has stated, the public policy exception does not exist to protect the employee. ... Rather, it protects society from public harm or vindicates fundamental individual rights....

Ms. Green argues that her dismissal violates dual public policies: protecting an employee's right to privacy and protecting victims of crime or spousal abuse.[1] In support of her first contention, plaintiff notes that the

1. Presumably, defendant's concerns stemmed from the physical or emotional danger to other employees or patients if plaintiff's estranged husband came to the workplace and engaged in further violent behavior directed primarily at plaintiff.

1. Plaintiff's complaint also mentions "protection of employment of crime victims

Third Circuit has recognized a strong policy favoring a right to privacy.... In this case, plaintiff states that she revealed to another employee, Dr. Brown, that she had been raped and severely beaten. There is no allegation that defendant initiated the conversation, required disclosure of the information, questioned plaintiff about her marital situation, inquired into personal or private details, or in any way sought to intrude upon plaintiff's privacy in a substantial and highly offensive manner.... I find that defendant's discharge of plaintiff did not violate the public policy favoring a right to privacy.Plaintiff also argues that her discharge is in violation of Pennsylvania's policy to protect victims of crime and domestic abuse, as embodied in the state's criminal code, Protection from Abuse Act, 23 Pa. C.S.A. § 6101 et seq., and the establishment of the Crime Victim's Compensation Board, 71 P.S. § 180–7 et seq. The flaw in plaintiff's argument is that while these statutes provide certain procedures and protections, they do not thereby create a protected employment class. In the statutes to which plaintiff refers, the legislature included certain programs or safety measures, but excluded others. For example, the Protection from Abuse Act specifies that a defendant may be directed to pay a plaintiff for economic losses incurred as a result of the abuse. 23 Pa.C.S.A. § 6108(a)(8). It does not, however, say that a complainant is entitled to any kind of employment rights or benefits. Similarly, a crime victim may be eligible for compensation pursuant to 71 P.S. § 180–7.3, but the statute does not create employment rights or privileges. It might be a different case, and a closer question as to the public policy exception, if plaintiff alleged that she was discharged because she had applied for victim compensation or had sought a protective order. That, however, is not her allegation. Plaintiff was not discharged because she refused to violate the law, because she complied with the law, or because she exercised a right or privilege granted by the law. Therefore, in the absence of any indication that Pennsylvania has established a clear mandate that crime victims generally, or spousal abuse victims specifically, are entitled to benefits or privileges beyond those enumerated in the laws, I must conclude that plaintiff's dismissal was not in violation of public policy. Because plaintiff has not alleged facts sufficient to state a claim that her discharge from at-will employment was in violation of public policy, defendant's motion to dismiss count II must be granted.

B. Negligent Infliction of Emotional Distress

... As the Supreme Court of Pennsylvania has pointed out, the first point of inquiry is whether the defendant owed plaintiff a duty of care.... One panel of the Superior Court of Pennsylvania implicitly found such a duty in an employee-employer context when it reversed a lower court's order sustaining preliminary objections to plaintiff's allegations of NIED. See Crivellaro v. Pennsylvania Power & Light Co., 341 Pa. Super. 173, 491 A.2d 207, 208, 210 (Pa. Super. 1985) (court focused on whether plaintiff had sufficiently pleaded physical injury). I do not read Crivellaro, however,

and witnesses." She has not, however, alleged any facts indicating that she was fired for appearing as a witness or for participating in court proceedings against her assailant.

as establishing that an employer owes a duty to an employee not to discharge her. The emotional distress alleged in Crivellaro involved not the firing of an employee, but rather, an employer's corralling an employee into a 30–day residential treatment program at a psychiatric facility.... Ms. Green's situation is far removed from that of the plaintiff in Crivellaro, and I do not think that the higher courts of Pennsylvania would recognize a claim for NIED derived from an employer's discharging an employee.... While Crivellaro suggests, and Armstrong echoes, that there is a pre-existing duty between an employer and employee, the cases do not imply that simply terminating a worker's employment breaches that duty.... Therefore, because plaintiff has not alleged that defendant breached any duty to her, and because I found above that defendant committed no wrong in discharging plaintiff, I find that Ms. Green has not sufficiently alleged a claim for NIED. Defendant's motion to dismiss count III must be granted.

C. Intentional Infliction of Emotional Distress

... Under Pennsylvania law, the conduct complained of in a claim for IIED must be extreme or clearly outrageous, a determination initially made by the court. ... It is rare within the employment context that the conduct will reach a sufficient level of outrageousness.... Ms. Green asserts that because of her status as an abused spouse, Dr. Bryant's termination of her employment was extreme and outrageous. While I can contemplate circumstances where this might be the case, Ms. Green's complaint does not allege such a circumstance. Rather, she alleges only that she was fired because she was the victim of a violent crime. Although any involuntary discharge from employment is unpleasant, defendant's conduct was not so outrageous in character or extreme in degree as to exceed all bounds of decency. See McMahon v. Impact Sys., Inc., [1992 WL 95920] (E.D. Pa. Apr. 5, 1992) (plaintiff's discharge from employment paled in comparison to hit and run driver burying victim's body without notifying authorities, defendant fabricating report that plaintiff had caused the death of third person, or falsely telling the press that person had an incurable disease (citations omitted)). Because plaintiff has not alleged facts that would support a claim for IIED, defendant's motion to dismiss count IV must be granted. D. Breach of Covenant of Good Faith and Fair Dealing

Finally, plaintiff alleges in count V that defendant has breached the implied covenant of good faith and fair dealing, arguing that "all employment contracts, including those construed to be at-will, contain an implied covenant of good faith." ... In this case, it is unnecessary to explore the boundaries of employer-employee good faith in the at-will context. It is sufficient to say that there is no bad faith when an employer discharges an at-will employee for good reason, bad reason, or no reason at all, as long as no statute or public policy is implicated. Defendant's motion to dismiss count V (numbered as a second count IV) must therefore be granted.

III. CONCLUSION

Plaintiff's discharge from at-will employment was not in violation of public policy. Dr. Bryant breached no duty that would give rise to a claim for negligent infliction of emotional distress, and his conduct was not sufficiently extreme or outrageous to support a claim for intentional infliction of emotional distress. Finally, it was not bad faith for defendant to terminate plaintiff's employment. Defendant's motion to dismiss counts II, III, IV, and V of plaintiff's complaint must therefore be granted.

NOTES

1. Notice how the court's decision that the employer had the right to fire the plaintiff operates to undermine the rest of her claims. If he has the right to terminate her employment, his conduct cannot be construed as outrageous or unreasonable, for purposes of her emotional distress claims (unless, perhaps, he communicated that decision in a particularly outrageous or unreasonable way). Nor can he breach a covenant of good faith, if he is acting within his legal rights.

2. For further analysis, see Deitrich, *Domestic Violence in the Workplace: Exploring Employee Rights and Remedies,* 28 CLEARINGHOUSE REVIEW 467 (1994).

Employment-based Discipline of Abusers

As employers and professional organizations become more sensitive to issues of partner violence, and more willing to participate in broader societal responses, some have focused not only on providing assistance to victims, but also on disciplining perpetrators. The easiest case is presented by the abusive employee who is harassing a co-worker on the job. Here the employer's responsibility is clear, and failure to act may expose the employer to substantial liability, whether under a workers' compensation scheme, through tort litigation, or through a Title VII action. On the other hand, employers must still be attentive to their employees' rights. Where the abuse is perpetrated by the employee outside the workplace, the issues become still more complex. In the following excerpt, Fredrica Lehrman summarizes the possible challenges an employee might bring against the employer who disciplines him for abuse either at work or at home.

Liability to Employees Who Commit Domestic Violence Fredrica Lehrman, Domestic Violence Practice and Procedure §§ 10:26–10:30 (Supp. 1999)

Employers who act rashly against employees suspected of engaging in acts of domestic violence can find themselves liable to these employees. Employees discharged or disciplined for committing acts of domestic violence may attempt to sue the employer for any number of torts, including defamation, wrongful discharge, invasion of privacy. The employer may be liable under the Americans with Disabilities Act. Employers should take appropriate sanctions against employees who perpetrate acts of domestic violence; however, employers need to respect the legal rights of these employees.

Defamation

An employer who accuses an employee suspected of committing domestic violence [of being] a "wifebeater" or sexual harasser or any other socially-charged, derogatory name may find itself liable for defamation. Employee meetings, internal memos, conversations with clients or customers, and post-employment references all can be the backdrop of a defamatory statement. To prove liability, the defamed employee must show:

1. The employer made a false and defamatory statement about the employee;
2. An unprivileged publication to a third party;
3. Fault amounting to at least negligence on the part of the publisher; and
4. Either actionability of the statement regardless of special harm or the existence of special harm caused by the publication.

To be published, a statement simply must be made to a third party. The statement published by the employer must be false. Truth is an absolute defense to a claim of defamation. However, the publication of a truthful statement can lead to lawsuits under other tort theories, including intentional infliction of emotional distress, invasion of privacy, or interference with contractual relations.

Employers have a qualified privilege in the area of defamation. This qualified privilege allows an employer to publish a false and defamatory statement about an employee if the employer can show that the statement:

1. Was made with a good faith belief in its truth;
2. Served a business interest or had a business purpose;
3. Was limited to a business interest or purpose to be served; and
4. Was made on a proper occasion.

Additionally, the employer must properly verify the facts underlying the defamatory statement. If an employer abuses its qualified privilege, it is likely to lose the privilege. Thus, the employer must keep confidential all inquiries into an employee's possible commission of domestic violence, informing other employees on a need-to-know basis only.

Some jurisdictions have recognized the tort of "self-defamation" or "compelled defamation." Compelled defamation arises when an employee is discharged on false or defamatory ground and must explain the grounds for termination to potential future employers. In these jurisdictions, an employer can find itself liable when it knew or should have foreseen that the discharged employee would be compelled to repeat the defamatory statement.

Wrongful Discharge

An employee who is fired because he or she committed an act of domestic violence may argue that he or she was wrongfully discharged.... A wrongful discharge claim can arise when an employee is fired in contravention of public policy; a covenant of good faith and fair dealing; or promises made orally, through a course of performance, or in employer policies or handbooks.

Invasion of Privacy

An employer who investigates charges that an employee has engaged in acts of domestic violence should do so with the employee's privacy rights in mind. State courts have recognized four different types of invasion of privacy torts:

- appropriation of another's name or likeness;
- false light publicity;
- public disclosure of private facts;
- intrusion upon seclusion.

The first type ... will probably not be at issue in the case of an employee discharged for committing an act of domestic violence. The others, however, may be implicated.

False light publicity is similar to defamation. A plaintiff in a defamation action seeks to vindicate his or her reputation; however, in a false light invasion of privacy tort, a plaintiff seeks to protect his or her right to be left alone. An employer can be held liable for placing an employee in a false light if the false light into which the employee was placed was highly offensive to a reasonable person, and the employer acted in a reckless disregard of the falseness of the publicized matter. To be actionable, the statement or statements in question must be communicated to the public at large so as to become a matter of public knowledge.

An employer also could be sued for public disclosure of private facts if the matter publicized would be highly offensive to a reasonable person and is not of legitimate concern to a reasonable person. As with the false light tort, this tort requires a public disclosure, not a mere communication to a third party, as in defamation.

Intrusion upon seclusion, the final type of privacy tort, occurs when one intentionally intrudes, physically or otherwise, on the seclusion of another, or on the other's private affairs or concerns, if the intrusion would be offensive to a reasonable person. As with defamation, an employer has a qualified privilege in privacy tort cases.

Americans with Disabilities Act

The Americans with Disabilities Act (ADA) prohibits employers from discriminating against a qualified individual with a disability on the basis of the disability. An employee who commits an act of domestic violence against a coworker or other intimate partner may claim that such behavior is the result of a mental illness. Mental illnesses, such as depression, can qualify as disabilities for the purposes of the ADA. However, the ADA does not require the employment of a disabled individual if that individual poses a direct threat to the health and safety of others. Therefore, an employer must evaluate carefully the employee's conduct and determine appropriate remedial measures to take in light of a claim of disability. If there is no direct threat, the employer may be required to make reasonable accommodations for the mentally ill employee. Examples of such accommodations include providing for leave or flexibility in scheduling, job restructuring, part-time work, working from home, reassignment to a vacant position, providing for or monitoring medication.

* * *

NOTES

1. Clearly the best protection for an employer is to ensure that any information about an employee's abusive behavior that is shared with others inside or outside the workplace is accurate, and that the information is disseminated only to those who have a need to know. Beyond these parameters, to what extent do you think an employee should be able to claim that his abusive behavior outside the workplace is a "private" matter? Is the claim that it is "private" based on the nature of the relationship within which it occurs, it's lack of relevance, arguably, to the employee's job performance, or simply the fact that until the information was publicized by the employer, no one in the employee's work environment knew about it? Does it make a difference whether there were witnesses to any of the incidents of abuse, whether police reports exist, or whether a protection order has issued? In other words, are there situations in which it could be said that an individual has waived his privacy rights by drawing public attention to his abuse? Or is the stronger argument that the lesson of the last twenty-five years is precisely that domestic violence is no longer a private issue, even when it happens behind closed doors?

2. In Chesser v. City of Hammond, 725 N.E.2d 926 (Ind. Ct. App. 2000), the Court of Appeals of Indiana upheld the dismissal of a police officer for abuse of his wife. At the time of the incident Chesser was on probation following a citizen complaint about his use of violent force, and had been ordered not to violate any rules or regulations of the police department. During that period, however, police responded to a report of domestic violence at his home, and found his wife with scratches and red marks on her neck and lumps on her head. Chesser was dismissed even though the charge of domestic battery against him was dropped when Mrs. Chesser chose not to proceed, and even though she testified at his disciplinary hearing that she had attacked him, and inflicted her injuries on herself. The court found that Mr. Chesser had been accorded due process, and that the evidence was sufficient to support his dismissal.

3. In recent years state bar associations and state courts have been asked with increasing frequency to discipline lawyers who abuse their partners, and lawyers have been subject to a wide range of sanctions, from reprimand to suspension to disbarment. In one Indiana case, in which the disciplined attorney was both a prosecutor and a private practitioner, the Supreme Court addressed directly the attorney's claim that his conduct was "private":

> Respondent urges this Court to conclude that no professional misconduct occurred. His argument is that the physical altercation was

the culmination of a private, adult relationship, and that the battery "arose instantaneously" after provocation.

The circumstances presented by the findings reveal an act of domestic violence. This admittedly criminal conduct is not and did not remain a private matter. We are not persuaded by the claim of provocation, nor are we comforted by the fact that the grievant's daughter, also a victim of Respondent's conduct, recovered after some counselling sessions. Respondent's position as deputy prosecutor requires even stricter scrutiny of this conduct.... Respondent's duty to conform his behavior to the law does not arise solely out of his status as an attorney. As an officer charged with the administration of the law, Respondent's behavior has the capacity to bolster or damage public esteem for the system. Where those whose job it is to enforce the law break it instead, the public rightfully questions whether the system itself is worthy of respect. The damage this incident has undoubtedly brought to the public's esteem will be addressed only if Respondent is held accountable. We conclude that, as a prosecuting attorney, Respondent engaged in conduct prejudicial to the administration of justice in violation of Rule 8.4(d).

Also, Respondent's conduct reflects upon his fitness as a lawyer and constitutes a violation of Rule 8.4(b). Not every violation of the penal code reflects upon an attorney's suitability as a practitioner.... The issue is whether there exists a nexus between the misconduct and the Respondent's duties to his clients, the courts, or the legal system.... Another important assessment is the impact of the conduct on the public's perception of Respondent's fitness as a lawyer.... As a part-time prosecutor, Respondent inevitably encounters domestic assaults, and this incident calls into question his ability to zealously prosecute or to effectively work with the victims of such crimes. As a part-time practitioner, Respondent's effectiveness with his own clients or with adversaries in situations involving issues of domestic violence is compromised by his own contribution to this escalating societal problem. In both his capacities, we believe the perception of his fitness is tainted.

Matter of Walker, 597 N.E.2d 1271, 1271–72 (Ind. 1992). Walker was suspended from practice for 60 days. The rules referenced in the opinion are drawn from the Rules of Professional Conduct for Attorneys at Law.

For two cases in which attorneys were disbarred for their abuse, see In re Nevill, 39 Cal.3d 729, 217 Cal. Rptr. 841, 704 P.2d 1332 (1985), in which the attorney was convicted of manslaughter after shooting his wife ten times; and Matter of Runyon, 491 N.E.2d 189 (Ind. 1986), in which the attorney had forced his way into his former wife's apartment, struck her with a club, and held her at gunpoint. On the other hand, in Matter of Margrabia, 150 N.J. 198, 695 A.2d 1378 (1997), an attorney was suspended for two years rather than being disbarred, even though he had violated the protection order taken out by his wife more than fifteen times, served several jail terms for those violations, and on at least one occasion threatened to break down her door and shoot her. One important issue in these cases is whether the court imposes suspension with an automatic reinstatement once the period has run, or continues to monitor the situation, requiring the attorney to petition for reinstatement, and demonstrate that he is no longer abusing his partner, or that he has completed a batterers' treatment program. This was the approach taken by the Colorado Supreme Court in People v. Musick, 960 P.2d 89 (Colo. 1998).

CHAPTER THIRTEEN

DOMESTIC VIOLENCE AS A VIOLATION OF WOMEN'S CIVIL RIGHTS

Introductory Note

Our starting point in Chapter One was that domestic violence, like other forms of violence against women, has historically been, and is still, a public practice as well as a private practice. It is public in the sense that it has historically enforced, and still enforces, broadly accepted or tolerated norms about what women are for, where they belong, and what they may and may not do, even as it exacts a terrible and often excruciatingly private price from individual women.

If we were looking for support for the idea that private violence is still attached to ideas about male entitlement and power, we might note how often it continues by other means restrictions on women that in the not too distant past were legally sanctioned or enforced, such as the exclusion of women from participation in the professions and many other forms of employment, or the legal subordination of women to men in marriage. John Stuart Mill, writing about the subjection of women in 1869, saw a progression from the exercise of brute force against women to the more legally-based restrictions of his own day. John Stuart Mill, THE SUBJECTION OF WOMEN 11–12 (S.M. Okin ed. 1988). As we do away with this overt, state-sanctioned machinery of women's subordination, it seems we are leaving to private enforcers the last ditch efforts to sustain the old order.

To the extent that practices of violence against women, including domestic violence, still function to subordinate women to men, public failure to curb that violence has particular consequences. First, as long as "the state" in its official capacity, and society more generally, continue to tolerate private violence, women are not, in reality, the full and equal citizens the constitution and laws promise they will be; the full and equal citizens we tend to imagine, for the most part, they are. They are not, in other words, receiving their full "due" from the state. At the same time, violence against women, in its daily and mundane exercise, concretely impedes women's participation in civic and political life, and diminishes their contribution to it. Women are not in a position, in other words, to give the full measure of what they have to offer to society. This may in turn explain why we are not, as a society, making faster progress towards eradicating practices of violence against women.

Feminist scholars have consistently stressed this political and public aspect of women's private oppression, offering frameworks that reflect both the richness of feminist legal interpretations of battering and the expressive dimensions of rights claims. Within this literature, domestic violence has been interpreted as a perpetuation of coverture, as a denial of equal protection, as involuntary servitude, and as terrorism and torture. All these formulations underscore the problem of woman abuse as political, and identify the underlying issues of liberty, autonomy, equality and women's citizenship, which have become important in feminist social theory. The use of political imagery highlights the degree to which domestic violence is understood within a broader public-private dichotomy and challenges this dichotomy to describe the "personal" and "domestic" problem of partner violence as a problem of public dimension, implicating issues of citizenship and political rights.

Significantly, no sooner does law confront one of the contested arenas in which "private" violence against women still flourishes, and begin to elaborate new norms, or make new demands on behalf of women, than these efforts are discredited, ridiculed and attacked, in a highly public and political way. It could be that this is because the efforts are consistently wrongheaded, or misdirected, or clumsy, or trample on "rights" of higher priority than women's full and equal participation as citizens in society. It may surely be the case that individual initiatives on behalf of women sometimes miss the mark, or prove blunt instruments in need of refinement or adjustment. But the intensity of the opposition may have much more to do with the fact that as a society we do still resist, at a fundamental level, the idea that women's concerns, their needs, their perceptions and even their rights are as valid, as legitimate, as deserving of recognition and protection, as men's. The intensity of that resistance may not have changed much since J.S. Mill wrote about it in 1869:

> So long as an opinion is strongly rooted in the feelings, it gains rather than loses in stability by having a preponderating weight of argument against it. For if it were accepted as a result of argument, the refutation of the argument might shake the solidity of the conviction; but when it rests solely on feeling, the worse it fares in argumentative contest, the more persuaded its adherents are that their feeling must have some deeper ground, which the arguments do not reach; and while the feeling remains, it is always throwing up fresh intrenchments of argument to repair any breach made in the old. And there are so many causes tending to make the feelings connected with this subject the most intense and most deeply rooted of all those which gather round and protect old institutions and customs, that we need not wonder to find them as yet less undermined and loosened than any of the rest by the progress of the great modern spiritual and social transition; nor suppose that the barbarisms to which men cling longest must be less barbarous than those which they earlier shake off.

Id. at 1.

The opening section of this chapter introduces some scholarly theorizing about the political and public nature of domestic violence. Section B traces the history of the first federal effort to define violence against women as a violation of women's civil rights. In the opposition to the provision's passage, in the compromises reached in order to secure its enactment, and in the subsequent legal challenges which resulted in the Supreme Court's decision that Congress had no power to enact it, you will see replayed the contest over what is public and what private, and the contest over whether we are willing to reorder our priorities to give precedence to women's freedom from violence. The final materials in this section offer a glimpse of how the next round of the contest may be shaping up. A concluding section provides some thoughts about the full implications of gender equality for the society at large.

A. VIOLENCE, EQUALITY AND CITIZENSHIP

Isabel Marcus has argued, as the next reading illustrates, that abusive relationships continue the practice of coverture; the legal structure which denied the separate legal existence of married women, and merged their identities with those of their husbands, who had exclusive control of their property and earnings, and exclusive authority over the children of the marriage.

Isabel Marcus
Reframing "Domestic Violence": Terrorism in the Home; The Public Nature of Private Violence 11, 20–23 (M.A. Fineman and R. Mykitiuk, eds. 1994)

Coverture was a designation of limitation and exclusion. It encoded beliefs regarding women's capacity and competence to act in the world. It confirmed and validated a sex-based locus of virtually unaccountable control in a marital relationship. It was a manifestation of cultural consciousness and a statement about the condition of citizenship....

Both political and economic theory reinforced the theologically ordained structure of family. Political theory identified the family as the building block or basis of society and the state, though women, even as family members, are virtually absent from the works of Western political theorists. Like a polity, a family must possess a hierarchical structure. Logically, there must be one designated head for a family whose will prevails by virtue of an assigned place in the structure. The absence of a clear rule designating a head would create disharmony and strife in the family and, consequently, both in the polity and in the market which were best served by *a priori* clear—that is—sex-based—designations of competence in civic matters and in commercial transactions.

Separately, or in combination, these beliefs spoke to the self-evident "naturalness" of the family structure of coverture. Even a skeptic might be convinced by the array of theology, political theory, and economics which proffered dire predictions of societal disorder and chaos in the wake of any proposed separate legal identity for married women. No wonder that contesting this seemingly closed belief system was the first important task of nineteenth-century American feminism.

While the most economically disempowering aspects of the doctrine of coverture were officially abolished by the end of the nineteenth century, it was not until the final quarter of the twentieth century that the last formal vestiges of the doctrine in a commercial setting were eliminated....

The demise of the formal doctrine of coverture did not signal the eradication of beliefs regarding the "naturalness" or appropriateness of sex-based power in marital relationships and the use of coercive means, including violence and abuse ..., for securing or maintaining that power. In the interval between the formal elimination of coverture and the present, there is no reason to believe that the violence abated.

When the second wave of feminism began to interrogate the status of women ..., emphasis was placed initially on pay equity, sexuality, and personal freedom. With the emergence in the seventies of rape and pornography as issues, contemporary feminists rediscovered battered women, and the, at times, lethal level of resistance on the part of men to efforts to divest them of privilege. I argue that the continuation of the violence, and the widespread failure of the state to address and punish it, are contemporary manifestations of the practice of coverture in the United States; the men who abuse or batter their spouse or partner practice that domination and control which is the *sine qua non* of coverture. I recognize that this claim is open to several challenges: ahistoricism, or at least the blurring or conflating of historical boundaries, or, worse yet, engagement in a mere semantic dispute. My answer is that this response is shortsighted and parochial. In no other relationship established and "privileged" by law or contract is such physical violence condoned; in no other relationship enjoying the protection of the state is such physical violence minimized or denied. Simply put, coverture cannot be said to have disappeared when its essential enforcement mechanism is available and widely used to maintain power and control in a marriage. That the structures of subordination persist in reshaped form is not unique to women's subordination in families. Critical race theorists understand well the premise that "contemporary inequalities and social institutional practices are linked to earlier periods in which the intent and cultural meaning of such practices were clear."[1]

* * *

NOTES

1. Marcus argues further that modern day coverture is imposed by a strategy that approximates terrorism:

> Regimes or groups seeking to terrorize populations utilize three tactics to enhance their credibility: unannounced and seemingly random but actually calculated attacks of violence; psychological as well as physical warfare aimed at silencing protests and minimizing retaliatory

1. Mari J. Matsuda et al. WORDS THAT WOUND: CRITICAL RACE THEORY, ASSAULTIVE SPEECH AND THE FIRST AMENDMENT 6 (1993).

> responses from the targets of violence; and the creation of an atmosphere of intimidation in which there is no safe place of escape....
>
> There are strong and striking parallels and similarities between terrorism as a strategy used to destabilize a community or society consisting both of women and men, and the abuse and violence perpetrated against women in intimate or partnering situations. Like terror directed at a community, violence against women is designed to maintain domination and control, to enhance or reinforce advantages, and to defend privileges. Like other individuals or communities who experience politically motivated terrorism, women whose partnering and intimate relationships are marked by violence directed against them live in a world similarly punctuated by traumatic and or catastrophic events, such as threats and humiliation, stalking and surveillance, coercion and physical violence.

Id. at 31–32. There is a powerful connection between Marcus's suggestion that modern-day enforcers of coverture are terrorists, and the terrorism practiced in the post Civil War era by those unwilling to yield the privileges of slave ownership.

2. Joyce McConnell, in the article from which the next reading is drawn, likens the situation of abused women to the plight of those relieved from "involuntary servitude" by the passage of the Thirteenth Amendment. While she properly resists the analogy to slavery, calling it both inaccurate and inherently racist, she suggests multiple ways in which the life of an abused woman parallels a life under involuntary servitude: the creation of slave-like conditions through the private use of force; the control of all aspects of the woman's life; the forced performance, not only of economic production and domestic tasks, but of personal services such as sex and reproduction; the abuser's controlling of food, water, medicinal care, movement, formal education, religion and familial affiliation; deprivation, beatings, maimings, whippings, rape, murder, torture, starvation, and the ever present threat of any of them, and the constant threat and actual separation of mothers from children, and other family members from one another.

Joyce McConnell
Beyond Metaphor: Battered Women, Involuntary Servitude and the Thirteenth Amendment, 4 Yale Journal of Law and Feminism 207, 207–09, 219–20 (1992)

When Congress debated the Thirteenth Amendment and its prohibitions against slavery and involuntary servitude, anxious members inquired whether it would alter the traditional relationship of husband and wife. Their concern materialized out of a political context in which those who sought abolition of African American chattel slavery and the establishment of women's rights were applying the norm of individual freedom beyond the narrow scope of landed white men. At that time, the metaphor "women are slaves" had rhetorical currency, and suggested that white women shared with African American men and women a similar legal and social status of non-identity and disability. No matter how rhetorically useful this metaphor may have seemed then or may seem now, it was and remains grossly inaccurate and inherently racist. It obscured the fact that white women were slaveholders or beneficiaries of the slave system. It failed to recognize that even though there were significant political and social constraints on white women, they did not as a class suffer in the way that African Americans did under slavery. Finally, it ignored the fact that African American women were slaves and that other women were not, no matter what their subordinate legal or socio-economic status. So, the metaphor was and is fundamentally flawed both by its generality and its exclusion.

It was not slavery, as metaphor or term, however, that evoked the concern of some Congressmen that their dominant positions in their families were in jeopardy. Rather, their uneasy recognition of the Amendment's potential to reach into marital relationships was sparked by the term "involuntary servitude," which was explicitly included in the Thirteenth Amendment to prohibit the creation of slave-like conditions through the private use of force. Although the Congressmen's anxiety was treated as absurd by sponsors of the Amendment, an examination of the Thirteenth Amendment's prohibition against involuntary servitude in the context of the conditions to which women who are battered in intimate relationships such as marriage are subjected reveals that their anxiety was well-founded....

. . .

To fully understand the potential reach of the Thirteenth Amendment's prohibition, it is best to dispense, if only for a minute, with the mind's attempt to define slavery and to permit the soul to explore the horror of what it meant to be owned as human property. The owner of human chattel could freely use this human property as she or he would any other piece of property, animate or inanimate. Although there were some legal sanctions against some egregious acts, such as unjustified murder of a slave, they were seldom enforced and had little if any impact on slaveholders' conduct. Their freedom was essentially unbridled.

As important as legal ownership was, the slaveholders' belief in their moral right of ownership, in their natural superiority, and in the African–Americans' natural inferiority provided the justification for daily degradation and subjugation. Thus, the system of American slavery is best understood as the absolute control by white slaveholders over all aspects of the lives of their slaves. This is not to diminish the ways in which the slaves manifested their free will, but rather to acknowledge the legal right and the power of the slaveholders to attempt to break it and to supplant it with their own. Understood in this way, the concept of the servitude contemplated by slavery as being just like that exchanged by the free worker for wages becomes absurd. The owner of humans was free to demand whatever he or she pleased, and what pleased was not confined to existing market equivalents. Thus, along with forced economic production and domestic tasks, with their obvious counterparts in the free wage-labor system, came other personal services such as sex and reproduction.

Furthermore, there were services demanded through coercion that should be categorized as such, but which are more typically thought of as aspects of the coercion itself. For example, splitting families, removing children, controlling food, water, medical care, movement, formal education, religion and familial affiliation are all coercive techniques. They involve services of the body, mind, heart and spirit, all outside the bounds of the free marketplace, but completely and legitimately within the private sphere of the master/slave relationship. Viewed in historical context, the concept of the servitude embodied in the Thirteenth Amendment is an expansive one with roots in both the public and private spheres.

Congress recognized that the system of absolute control existing in slavery flowed from the legal status of slaves as chattel. Thus, when Congress prohibited slavery, it started from the premise that one person should not be permitted by law to own another. But Congress also recognized that, even without the imprimatur of the state, an evil similar to slavery could exist. The system of chattel slavery provided proof of the abuses springing from the actual ownership of, or the belief in the right of domination over, other human beings. The nature and level of coercion used against slaves was violent and horrific. It included deprivation, beatings, maimings, whippings, rape, murder, torture, starvation, and the ever present threat of any or all of them. In addition, it included the constant threat and actual separation of mothers from children and other family members from one another.

Congress sought to abolish not just slavery, but the characteristics of slavery created through coercion. Thus, in adopting the Thirteenth Amendment, Congress not only forbade the legal ownership of human chattel (slavery) but prohibited anyone from treating another as if such ownership existed (involuntary servitude). The Thirteenth Amendment sought to preserve the tenet of free will and prohibited the use of coercion sufficient to break it.

* * *

NOTE

1. A third theorist, Robin West, looks not at the Thirteenth Amendment but the Fourteenth. The passage of the Thirteenth Amendment was not enough, as a practical matter, to abolish slavery: the continued enforced subordination of former slaves through economic coercion and private violence allowed the continuation of slavery by other means, and law enforcement, at the state level, turned a blind eye. The passage of the Fourteenth Amendment, she argues, was viewed as a necessary next step; enabling the federal government to step in and ensure that state authority was not complicit in upholding the private authority of former slave owners.

Robin West argues that, historically, the equal protection clause was understood as challenging the "dual sovereignty" under which slaves lived, and that the situation of women subject to violence at the hands of their partners, and deprived of legal remedy, can also be understood as a situation of dual sovereignty. She urges that the Fourteenth Amendment should be interpreted to allow those deprived of meaningful state protection against private violence to challenge this public inaction, while acknowledging that Fourteenth Amendment jurisprudence has strayed far from this original "abolitionist" interpretation.

Robin West
Toward an Abolitionist Interpretation of the Fourteenth Amendment, 94 West Virginia Law Review 111, 129–32, 140–44, 146–47 (1991)

... [T]he citizen lives under the rule of only one sovereign—the state—while the slave lives under the rule of at least two sovereigns—the state and the master—the commands of both to be endured under the threat of unchecked violence. The citizen must abide by the commands of the state if he wishes to avoid its violent sanctions, but must not abide the commands of any other. He is protected by the state and more specifically by its criminal law against all non-state violence: this protection is certainly a part of what it means to have rights. The slave, in marked contrast, must abide by the commands of two sovereigns, the state and the master, if he wishes to avoid violence or deprivation: this is *what it is* to be denied the protection of the state's law. Where one citizen, but not others, is denied protection, then protection is obviously unequal. The inequality of *protection*, unlike the unequal application of general laws ..., gives rise not only to the evil of formal injustice but to the much more concrete, pervasive, and pernicious evil of slavery.

. . .

... [T]he plainest possible meaning of the Fourteenth Amendment mandate ... is that no state may deny to any citizen the protection of its criminal and civil law against private violence and private violation. Put differently, no state may, through denials of protection, permit any citizen to live in a state of "dual sovereignty." ... Only the state shall have access to the use of unchecked and uncheckable violence to effectuate its will (and then, of course, only with due process). No citizen shall be subject to uncheckable violence by anyone other than the state; no citizen shall be under the will and command of anyone other than the state. Inversely, no entity, no individual, no group, no race, no gender, and no class other than the state shall have recourse to uncheckable violence as a means of effectuating his, her, or its will. No one other than the state shall have the power, backed by the credible threat of violence, to command and dominate the will of others.... Any relationship of sovereignty between a subject and master, other than that between state and citizen, that exists through state acquiescence—a refusal of the state to deter the credible threat of violence on which sovereignty depends—is evidence that the state has violated this guarantee of protection.

. . .

... The abolitionists, above all else, understood that it was precisely a denial of the protection of the state against private violence and private violation of trust that facilitated and even defined the status of the slave. After the passage of the Thirteenth Amendment, it became apparent to the abolitionists, their advocates, and fellow travelers in Congress that although a denial of equal protection is a necessary condition of slavery, eradication of slavery is not tantamount to a guarantee of equal protection. The wave of Ku Klux Klan violence of whites against blacks and abolitionists, the refusal of the southern states (and in many instances the northern states), to punish, check or deter that violence, and the states' refusal to extend to the freed slaves the legal forms of contract and property that were essential to their participation in the community's economic life ... engendered precisely the relationship of sovereign and subject, dominance and subservience, command and obedience, which the unchecked violence and violation of one group against another can predictably insure....

Thus, the need for yet another amendment: one outlawing not just the symptom of slavery but the disease itself—the denial of the protection of the state against private violence and violation, of which slavery is one, but only one, possible manifestation. The equal protection clause of the Fourteenth Amendment was thus intended by the abolitionists, and at least some of its proponents, to abolish not only slavery *per se*, but also the "dual sovereignty" which facilitates it....

As far as I can tell, this particular history is not controversial; indeed, this can fairly be called the *uncontested* meaning of the Fourteenth Amendment.

. . .

... [T]he marital rape exemption still in force, albeit in an attenuated form, in several states, constitutes as literal a modern withdrawal of the states' protection against violent assault as did the states' failure to protect against murder during the heyday of Klan violence. The consequences are also not dissimilar. A woman who can be forcibly and physically intruded upon without recourse to legal protection or remedy is not a victim of crime, with the remedies and rights pertinent thereto; rather, she is, and will most likely regard herself, as subject to the sovereign whim of he who can, without fear of state reprisal, coerce her consent through legitimate threats of force and violence. Such a woman ... lives under the will of two sovereigns rather than one: the state and her husband against whose violence there is no recourse. Consequently, the husband's commands must be obeyed if violence is to be avoided. The marital rape "exemption" is in a very literal sense a denial of the state's promise of protection against violent assault and, as such, given an abolitionist understanding of the phrase, is clearly and unproblematically unconstitutional.

. . .

... [I]t follows that a number of the [Supreme] Court's recent decisions, whether grounded in the Fourteenth Amendment's equal protection clause or not, are wrong, or, if not wrong in their outcome, wrong in some aspect of their reasoning. The major premise of the Court's recent decision in *DeShaney v. Winnebago County Department of Social Services,* and the sizeable number of similar cases that followed and preceded it, that there is no constitutional right to a police force, is squarely wrong. The right to a police force, or, more specifically, the right to the state's protection against the subjugating effects of private violence, are the paradigm Fourteenth Amendment rights. It is precisely these rights which make us "equal" in the eyes of the law. Given our right to police protection against private violence, we are equally subject to the commands of only one sovereign, the rule of law, and given that right we are equally free because we are equally free of subjection to the commands of any other. It follows that little Joshua DeShaney, brutally, repeatedly, and privately assaulted by his father, suffering massive and permanent brain damage as a result, did indeed suffer a constitutional deprivation. This violation was not *because* the state had sufficiently intervened into the family's life so as to satisfy the state action requirement as (indirectly) argued by the dissent, but, rather, because it did not intervene *enough*. Through its inaction, not its action, the state failed to provide equal protection of the law.

. . .

It also follows from the abolitionists' minimalist understanding of equal protection that the so-called "state action" requirement, at least as presently understood by the court, and according to some of its various definitions, is drastically misconceived. The equal protection clause, under an abolitionist interpretation, targets states' refusal to protect citizens against profoundly private action which results in subordination or enslavement. The "state action," then, which is the object of the Amendment, is the breach of an affirmative duty to protect the rights of citizens to be free, minimally, of the subordinating, enslaving violence of other citizens.... The state breach that constitutes the violation may take the form either of action or inaction, feasance or malfeasance: the state may simply fail to protect one group from the violence of others (as in the case of unpunished and undeterred Klan or domestic violence), or the state may do something far more visible, such as pass legislation explicitly removing one group from the reach of the state's protection against the violence of others (such as in the case of marital rape exemption laws). Whether the state's failure to protect constitutes an action or inaction, however, is not determinative. What is determinative are the consequences of the state's conduct: whether by virtue of the state's action or inaction there exists a separate state of sovereignty in which one citizen is subjected to the will of another citizen as well as to the sovereignty of the state.

* * *

NOTES

1. You have encountered equal protection claims, successful and unsuccessful, elsewhere in this book. Remember the case of Moran v. Beyer, 734 F.2d 1245 (7th Cir. 1984), excerpted in Chapter 11 A, above, in which the Seventh Circuit struck down Illinois' interspousal tort immunity as viola-

tive of equal protection for married people. Remember also the constitutional tort claims based on police failures to protect abused women, discussed in Chapter 12A. To what extent might these claims have been more successful had Robin West's proposed abolitionist interpretation of the Fourteenth Amendment guided the development of Fourteenth Amendment jurisprudence? Are there other contexts in which this interpretation might support litigation against state action or inaction in response to domestic violence?

2. Another scholar, Reva Siegel, has suggested that women have been handicapped in their quest for equality under the Constitution by the necessity of relying on the Fourteenth Amendment, which offers no legislative history specific to issues of gender. She wonders whether the debates surrounding the passage of the Nineteenth Amendment might have more to offer than is commonly appreciated. We understand the Nineteenth Amendment as doing nothing more than guaranteeing women the right to vote. Her argument is that read in the light of its history, that Amendment could instead be understood as incorporating a sex-equality norm bearing on a wide range of institutions and practices. "In particular," she suggests, "those who advocated and opposed enfranchising women understood woman suffrage to raise questions concerning the family, and the link between voting and family structure shaped debates over enfranchising women as a matter of state and federal law." Reva B. Siegel, *Collective Memory and the Nineteenth Amendment: Reasoning About "the Woman Question" in the Discourse of Sex Discrimination,* HISTORY, MEMORY AND THE LAW 131–182 (A. Sarat & T. Kearns, eds. 1999).

3. One very recent context in which the connections between "private" violence against women and women's political and civil rights have again been debated is the civil rights provision of the 1994 federal Violence Against Women Act. This is the topic of the next section.

B. THE CIVIL RIGHTS REMEDY CREATED BY THE VIOLENCE AGAINST WOMEN ACT OF 1994

In 1994, the Violence Against Women Act passed by Congress included a civil rights provision. Many women's rights and civil rights organizations and domestic advocacy groups around the country worked to develop this legislation and struggled mightily for many years to achieve its passage. The provision was controversial, and as soon as it was invoked as the basis for litigation, it was challenged on constitutional grounds. In May 2000, the United States Supreme Court held the provision unconstitutional in United States v. Morrison, 120 S.Ct. 1740 (2000).

This section examines the history and meaning of the VAWA federal civil rights provision, and its demise. The section begins with a statement made prior to the provision's passage by the NOW Legal Defense Fund, one of the legislation's major proponents, and a discussion of the concerns and compromises that shaped the legislative process. The section continues with the provision as it was ultimately enacted, looks at commentary on the significance of the controversies surrounding the provision and the constitutional challenges it faced, and ends with an excerpt from the Supreme Court's opinion in *Morrison*. The following section turns to the future of alternative federal and state civil rights provisions in light of *Morrison*.

Statement of the Now Legal Defense and Education Fund on the Violence Against Women Act, H.R. 1133, Before the Subcommittee on Civil and Constitutional Rights, Committee of the Judiciary, House of Representatives, United States Congress, Presented November 16, 1993 by Sally Goldfarb, Senior Staff Attorney

. . .

The Violence Against Women Act's Civil Rights Provision

The versions of the Violence Against Women Act that are under consideration in the House (H.R. 1133) and the Senate (S. 11) both contain a civil rights provision in Title III. Both would declare that crimes of violence motivated by gender are discriminatory and violate the victim's civil rights under federal law. Both provide a civil cause of action for deprivation of this right. A person who proves that a crime of violence was motivated by gender is eligible to receive compensatory damages, punitive damages, injunctive relief and declaratory relief.

However, there are differences between the two bills. In May of this year, the Senate bill was narrowed in several significant ways in an effort to clarify and limit the cause of action provided. These changes were adopted after extensive discussions with federal judges, civil liberties groups, and others concerned about the scope of the proposed civil rights remedy. As a result, Title III of the Senate bill now provides that only crimes against a person, and crimes against property that pose a risk of physical injury to a person, are covered; deletes a presumption that rape and sexual assault are motivated by gender; and adds a requirement that, in order to meet the definition of "crime of violence motivated by gender," the plaintiff must prove that the crime was due, at least in part, to an animus based on gender.

The NOW Legal Defense and Education Fund strongly supports Title III of H.R. 1133 in its present form. We feel that the definition of "crime of violence motivated by gender" furnished in the bill is clear, workable, and sound public policy. However, we have also endorsed the Senate bill S. 11. Therefore, if it is necessary to modify the House bill along the lines already adopted in the Senate, NOW LDEF will continue to support the legislation. If the term "animus" is adopted, it would be helpful to clarify that the term means simply intent or purpose, as it was originally used in the case *Griffin v. Breckenridge*, 403 U.S. 88 (1971).

Several important limitations already appear in both H.R. 1133 and S. 11. Both bills contain an explicit statement that the Violence Against

Women Act does not confer jurisdiction on federal courts to decide divorce or domestic relations cases. In addition, the civil rights remedy extends only to acts that would rise to the level of a felony under state or federal law. It does not cover random acts of violence unrelated to gender. Thus it is amply clear that not every crime against a women would qualify. Indeed, the civil rights remedy is gender-neutral and is available to male or female victims of serious gender-motivated crimes.

The burden rests on the plaintiff to prove by a preponderance of the evidence that the crime was motivated by gender. Proving that a crime was gender-motivated under the new law will presumably be analogous to proving that a crime was racially motivated under existing laws. Evidence typically presented in civil rights cases alleging racial violence include: racially derogatory epithets used by the assailant, membership of the victim in a different racial group than the assailant, a history of similar attacks by the assailant against other members of the victim's racial group, a pattern of attacks against victims of a certain race in a certain neighborhood and time period, lack of provocation, use of force that is excessive in light of the absence of other motivations, etc. By substituting "gender" for "race" in the foregoing list, it becomes apparent that many—but not all—crimes against women will qualify as crimes of violence motivated by gender.

Recognizing the gender-discriminatory element in some violent crimes is not radical or unprecedented. Not only does federal law already contain civil remedies for racially-discriminatory violence, but the Hate Crimes Sentencing Enhancement Act of 1993 (H.R. 1152), passed by the House in September and under consideration as part of the Senate crime bill, provides increased sentences for defendants convicted in federal court of having selected a victim because of gender. The Violence Against Women Act simply takes this principle and applies it to a civil, rather than criminal, remedy. Moreover, unlike the Hate Crimes Sentencing Enhancement Act, application of the Violence Against Women Act is not limited to crimes occurring on federal lands.

To the extent that questions remain about how this cause of action will work in practice, this is to be expected with any cutting-edge legislation. As Judge Stanley Marcus, chair of the U.S. Judicial Conference Ad Hoc Committee on Gender–Based Violence, has helpfully pointed out, it is inevitable that there are some questions about legislation that cannot be answered until cases are litigated and judges have the opportunity to apply the law to specific facts.

What Title III Will Accomplish

Because of gender-based violence, American women and girls are relegated to a form of second-class citizenship. Just as a democratic society cannot tolerate violence motived by the victim's membership in a minority racial group, and must pass special laws to combat such oppression, so too we need effective federal laws to combat violent crimes motivated by the victim's gender.

The enactment of civil rights legislation would convey a powerful message: that violence motivated by gender is not merely an individual crime or a personal injury, but is a form of discrimination, an assault on a publicly-shared ideal of equality. When half of our citizens are not safe at home or on the streets because of their sex, our entire society is diminished.

The impact of the legislation would not be purely symbolic, however. Federal recognition that gender-based violence is a form of discrimination is likely to alter the way both men and women regard sexual assault and domestic violence. The impact of this attitudinal change will be felt in homes, streets, and workplaces. It will also be felt in courtrooms. Currently, jury studies and research on gender bias in the judiciary have shown that the "boys will be boys"/ "she must have asked for it" mentality that prevails in most sectors of our society has a direct, measurable effect on the outcome of cases involving sexual assault, domestic violence, and a host of other issues where men's violence toward women is directly or tangentially involved. Thus, the educational power of the VAW Act is of immense practical importance to the development of American law.

In addition, many victims who are currently unable to succeed in state criminal and civil proceedings would, for the first time, have access to legal redress.

It is not true that all men who beat or rape women lack the resources to pay damages. In fact, violence against women is found at every socioeconomic level in America. For some victims, even a damages judgment that cannot be collected (or a judgment granting only declaratory or injunctive relief) will be seen as an immensely valuable vindication of their rights.

Enactment of the Violence Against Women Act will not eliminate rape, domestic violence, and other sex-based attacks on women, any more than passage of the civil rights legislation of the 19th century and the mid–20th century has eliminated racism. Nevertheless, the power of this proposed federal civil rights law to improve the prospects for social justice and equality are substantial.

State Criminal and Civil Laws Are Not Adequate to Protect Victims of Gender–Motivated Crime

The existence of state criminal and tort laws covering rape and domestic violence does not do away with the need for a federal civil rights remedy. First, a federal civil rights law would redress a different injury than the injuries that are at issue in state criminal and tort proceedings.

In addition, gender-motivated crimes are currently not being adequately addressed in state courts.

- A woman is forcibly raped by her husband. In over half the states he is immune from prosecution under many or most circumstances–for example, if the couple is living together and no divorce or separation papers have been filed.
- A young woman is sexually assaulted by her boyfriend. Several states have statutes exempting cohabitants and dating companions from sexual assault laws.

- A man brutally beats his wife, causing her severe injuries. Interspousal immunity doctrines in at least seven states prevent her from suing him to recover damages for her medical expenses and pain and suffering.
- A teenage girl is subjected to incestuous sexual abuse by her father. In some states, strict statutes of limitations require her to bring suit within a few years–which is virtually impossible for an emotionally and economically dependent young person–or else lose forever the chance to pursue a civil legal remedy.
- It was recently revealed that the Oakland, California Police Department closed over 200 rape cases with little or not investigation in 1989 and 1990. The complaints involved rapes of prostitutes and drug users, as well as allegations of acquaintance rape.
- A recent Senate Judiciary Committee study showed that only one in 100 forcible rapes results in a sentence of more than one year in prison.
- State rape shield laws do not apply in civil cases. Thus, women bringing tort actions for sexual assault are routinely subjected to intrusive questions about consensual sexual activity unrelated to the attack.

The laws on the books are only part of the problem. In states throughout the country, prosecutors, juries, and judges routinely subject female victims of rape and domestic violence to a wide range of unfair and degrading treatment that contributes to the low rates of reporting and conviction that characterize these crimes. Although federal courts are not immune from these problems, the fact that federal judges are not elected, are subjected to a more rigorous selection process, and typically exercise greater control over courtroom procedures such as jury voir dire help to minimize these problems.

Federal civil rights laws passed since the mid-19th century have typically prohibited acts that were already illegal under state law. The reason for this is that federal remedies are needed to reinforce state remedies and to provide a "back-up" when the state justice system is unable to protect victims' rights adequately. In an eloquent testimony to the need for federal intervention, 41 state attorneys general have signed a letter to members of this House urging passage of the Violence Against Women Act.

The Violence Against Women Act Builds on and Complements Existing Federal Civil Rights Laws

Currently, American women are being attacked and killed because they are women. Over 100 years ago, following the Civil War, Congress responded to an epidemic of race-based violence by passing a series of federal laws to provide remedies against private individuals who deprive citizens of their civil rights. Similar legislation is needed today to protect citizens from an epidemic of gender-based violence.

Title III of the Violence Against Women Act is modeled on well-established federal civil rights laws. For example, the key phrase "because of . . . gender or on the basis of gender," which describes crimes of violence that are covered, is modeled on language found in Title VII of the Civil Rights Act of 1964, which is the leading federal statute prohibiting discrimination in employment.

Similarly, the basic concept of Title III resembles that of the Reconstruction-era civil rights laws. Like those earlier laws (42 U.S.C. §§ 1981, 1982, and 1985(3)), the Violence Against Women Act provides a federal civil remedy for deprivation of certain rights. The "animus" requirement, which has been added to S. 11, is derived from caselaw decided under 42 U.S.C. § 1985(3). Title III is not identical to its predecessors, however. Each law has different technical legal requirements. For example, unlike § 1983, Title III does not require that the challenged actions were taken "under color of state law," and unlike § 1985(3), it does not require more than one wrongdoer. While Title III is thus broader in some respects than other civil rights laws, it is far narrower in some other respects: it protects *only* against gender-motivated crimes of violence that rise to the level of a felony, whereas 42 U.S.C. §§ 1983 and 1985(3) protect disadvantaged groups from virtually any deprivations of rights, privileges and immunities.

The differences between Title III of the Violence Against Women Act and the nineteenth-century federal civil rights laws are necessary because gender-based violence typically differs from the types of racial violence directed against men. For instance, § 1985(3) was drafted to combat the Ku Klux Klan and similar conspiracies. The dangers confronting women of all races are often quite different. Conspiratorial group attacks on women are not the primary cause of gender violence. In fact, *women are six times more likely than men to suffer a crime at the hands of someone they know.*

The Reconstruction-era civil rights laws were not designed with women in mind. For 120 years since they were passed, "women of all races have lacked a meaningful civil rights remedy to protect them from pervasive anti-female violence." While §§ 1983 and 1985(3) fall short of providing ideal protection against discrimination based on race, religion, or national origin, they at least provide a meaningful remedy for a significant percentage of such cases. The fact that these two statutes require the plaintiff to prove conspiracy or color of state law virtually eliminates the possibility that women of any race can redress what is arguably the most common and most damaging form of gender discrimination: acts of gender-motivated violence committed by private individuals.

This defect in existing civil rights laws has meant, among other things, that rape by individual white men acting in a private capacity, which has historically been a widespread form of oppression of African-American women, has never been actionable under the civil rights laws ostensibly designed to protect all African-Americans from racial terrorism. In short, most of the victimization that women experience because of their gender alone, or because of their gender in combination with their race, remains ignored by the federal civil rights laws currently on the books.

. . .

The Impact of Title III on the Courts

Some have suggested that lawsuits brought under the Violence Against Women Act will overwhelm the federal courts. In fact, the legislation will provide a significant new remedy without generating a large number of new cases.

... The inhospitality of state courts to such claims (see above) is doubtless one reason why this figure is so low, but there are other reasons that would be equally applicable to cases brought under federal law.... Women do not now, and will not in the future, rush to proclaim themselves as victims of sex crimes or of violence inflicted by family members.

Sexual harassment provides a useful analogy. A major study by the U.S. Merit Systems Protection Board found that 42% of women employed by the federal government had experienced sexual harassment, but despite the availability of legal remedies, only 5% of those who had been sexually harassed made any kind of formal complaint (including complaints in the workplace); an even smaller number actually filed a legal action.

Moreover, a certain number of potential VAW Act defendants (though by no means all) are indigent, and many women and their attorneys may be unwilling to bring suit if there is no hope of collecting damages. And of course, a large number of violent gender-motivated crimes are committed by assailants who are never caught. As Prof. Cass Sunstein has pointed out, the fact that few cases will probably be filed under Title III of the VAW Act does not detract from its importance as an addition to the civil rights legal arsenal.

The fact that a bill to enhance the rights of women is met with a concern for overloading the federal courts adds a disturbing note of sexism to the debate. In recent decades, when Congress was considering the Americans With Disabilities Act and other civil rights legislation that created private rights of action, this concern was heard only from staunch opponents of civil rights. In any event, the fact that violence against women is widespread would seem to argue in favor of, not against, passing legislation to remedy it.

The true burdens on the federal courts are a heavy criminal caseload, particularly drug-related cases, together with a large number of vacant judgeships. Keeping civil rights cases out of federal court will not solve these problems.

It should be noted that in March 1993, the U.S. Judicial Conference revoked its previous opposition to the Violence Against Women Act and specifically adopted a position of neutrality on this bill, with the exception that the organization now actively supports the portions of the bill regarding task forces on gender bias in the courts. The National Association of Women Judges also supports the principles of Title III. A recent Congressional Budget Office report estimates the cost of Title III to be far lower than previously projected.

. . .

Congress Has Constitutional Authority to Enact This Legislation

Federal legislation to remedy gender-based crime is amply justified by Congress's obligation to advance principles of equal rights under section 5 of the Fourteenth Amendment. Constitutional authority to enact this legislation is also conferred by the Commerce Clause, due to the damaging impact of gender-based crime on the national economy.

- On a national level, domestic violence costs employers 3 to 5 billion dollars annually due to worker absenteeism.
- 30 percent of all women seeking treatment in hospital emergency rooms are victims of battering by a husband or boyfriend. Medical costs related to domestic abuse are estimated at $100 million a year.
- High rates of rape and other crimes deter women from taking many types of jobs, including high-paying night jobs that would require travel on unsafe streets and public transportation. For instance, one rape survivor reported in testimony to the U.S. Senate Judiciary Committee that she had to give up plans for a career in real estate sales because she was afraid to be alone in an empty house with a stranger.
- Homicide is the leading cause of death on the job for women. (For men, the leading cause is accidents.)
- More than half of all homeless women have lost their housing because they are fleeing domestic violence.

Leading scholars of constitutional law have testified in support of Congressional power to enact the Violence Against Women Act.

Conclusion

The Congress has a historic opportunity to play a crucial role in the effort to reduce crime and combat discrimination against women. This long overdue legislation will recognize that violence motivated by gender is a deprivation of civil rights. We urge you to support the Violence Against Women Act. Thank you.

* * *

NOTE

1. Implicit in this carefully crafted advocacy statement is the argument that violence against women is a "public" issue—one that implicates society's commitment to gender equality, and to women's full participation in society. In the next reading, Sally Goldfarb elaborates on the role of "public-private dichotomies in the debate over the Violence Against Women Act," providing a richer and more robust account of the arguments advanced by the provision's proponents, and also by its opponents.

Sally F. Goldfarb
Violence Against Women and the Persistence of Privacy, 61 Ohio State Law Journal 1, 7–8, 46–54 (2000)

When VAWA was pending in Congress, the civil rights provision was its most controversial aspect. To attain its passage, supporters of the legislation had to overcome opposition based on the longstanding attitude that violence against women is a private matter, not a suitable subject for federal judicial attention. During congressional deliberations on the Act, the controversy over the civil rights provision focused in large part on whether federal courts should concern themselves with violence committed by private individuals—particularly when such violence takes place in the context of family relationships. The bill's opponents, including organizations representing the federal and state judiciaries, advanced arguments that relied heavily on traditional concepts of the split between the market and family and the split between the state and civil society. In fact, one of the primary goals of supporters of the Act was to overcome centuries of assumptions about the public and private spheres that have operated to deny women full equality under the law. Passage of VAWA seemed to signal a major victory for feminist efforts to bring violence against women out from behind the veil of privacy.

. . .

A. Rhetoric of Public and Private Among Supporters of VAWA

. . .

... The first report on the legislation by the Senate Judiciary Committee described its purpose as bringing domestic violence out from "behind closed doors." In its report a year later, the Committee stated:

> Historically, crimes against women have been perceived as anything but crime—as a "family" problem, as a "private" matter, as sexual miscommunication.... Vast numbers of these crimes [rape and domestic violence] are left unreported to police or other authorities. Both literally and figuratively, these crimes remain hidden from public view.

A House of Representatives subcommittee hearing on the bill was entitled "Domestic Violence: Not Just a Family Matter." Similar themes were sounded by the bill's co-sponsors and by witnesses who testified in support of the legislation.

Proponents of the legislation directly attacked the legal legacy of the market-family dichotomy as reflected in state law. For example, in congressional testimony supporting the legislation, the NOW Legal Defense and Education Fund (NOW LDEF) argued that federal intervention was necessary in light of trends in the state courts that denied justice to victims of domestic violence and rape. Among the trends cited by NOW LDEF were judges who trivialized domestic violence with comments like "Let's kiss and make up and get out of my court"; criminal court judges who denied relief for domestic violence on the ground that it is "merely a domestic problem that belongs in family court"; rape immunities for husbands, cohabitants, and social companions; interspousal and parental tort immunity doctrines; the unwillingness of police to enforce orders of protection; and judicial reluctance to take nonstranger rape seriously. As we have seen, all of these trends are traceable to the split between market and family and the concomitant assumption that the law should not interfere in the domestic sphere.

VAWA's supporters also attempted to counter the view that violence against women is purely a domestic matter by proving the massive effects of such violence on interstate commerce. The Senate Judiciary Committee noted that domestic violence alone is estimated to cost society between five and ten billion dollars a year. Congress heard extensive testimony on the effect of violence on women's workforce participation and productivity, income, health care expenses, consumer spending, and interstate travel. Based on the evidence before it, the Senate Judiciary Committee concluded that gender-based violence bars women from full participation in the national economy. According to the Committee, the experience of gender-based violence interferes with women's ability to obtain and keep employment, travel, and engage in other economic activities, and the fear of gender-motivated violence has a deterrent effect that prevents women from taking available, well-paying jobs.

In addition to helping establish Congress's constitutional authority to enact the civil rights provision under the Commerce Clause, this economic evidence was a direct challenge to the conventional view that domestic matters, including domestic violence, have no impact on the public sphere of the marketplace. By indicating that violence against women has a prominent place in the market, VAWA's supporters sought to show that violence against women also deserves to have a prominent place in the law.

In another indication of the relevance of the market-family split to the debate over VAWA, the bill's supporters repeatedly emphasized that the civil rights provision would not create a federal domestic relations law. This strategy was necessitated by two ways in which the market-family dichotomy is reflected in federal law: first, the federal judiciary's staunch resistance to hearing family-related cases, and second, the tendency to assume that all cases concerning women are really about the family.

Another way in which supporters of the civil rights remedy positioned violence against women as a public issue was by emphasizing that gender-motivated violence is a group-based denial of equality. Patricia Ireland, president of the National Organization for Women, testified:

> It's very clear to all of us who see the bombings of NAACP offices, the vandalizing of synagogues, that these are more clearly political and public violence. But because so much of the violence against women is behind closed doors, is ... private violence, ... the political aspect of it has often been ignored. It's not just a problem that an individual woman faces ... but rather a systemic problem that all women face.

Echoing this analysis, the Senate Judiciary Committee described violence motivated by gender as "not merely an individual crime or a personal injury, but ... a form of discrimination," "an assault on a publicly shared ideal of equality." The Committee characterized the civil rights provision as "an effective anti-discrimination remedy for violently expressed prejudice."

In addition to highlighting the discriminatory impact of individual acts of gender-motivated violence, the bill's supporters also emphasized the discrimination inherent in the state legal systems' responses to such violence. Testimony of individual witnesses and committee reports repeatedly stressed the fact that states have condoned violence against women through legal doctrines that treat crimes against women less seriously than crimes against men; through inadequate enforcement of existing laws by police, prosecutors, and judges; and through overtly discriminatory treatment of female crime victims. Thus, the bill's supporters identified causes of violence against women in the public sphere of the state, not merely in the private sphere of civil society. After reviewing a series of reports from official state task forces on gender bias in the courts, the Senate Judiciary Committee concluded that there was "overwhelming evidence that gender bias permeates the court system and that women are most often its victims."

. . .

B. Rhetoric of Public and Private Among Opponents of VAWA

While VAWA was pending in Congress, much of the opposition to the civil rights provision was premised on a group of attitudes associated with orthodox adherence to the public-private distinctions: the idealization of family privacy and legal nonintervention in the family; the tendency to equate women with the domestic sphere; the belief that matters involving the family belong only in state court; and resistance to the recent trend of applying federal constitutional and civil rights to nonstate actors. The clearest expressions of these attitudes came from the judiciary, who lobbied actively against the bill. An examination of statements made by VAWA's opponents reveals the lingering influence of traditional conceptions of public and private.

In a particularly striking evocation of the ideology of legal nonintervention in the family, the Conference of Chief Justices, which represents the state judiciary, criticized VAWA's civil rights provision on the ground that it would conflict with the marital rape exemption. Similarly, lawyer Bruce Fein, who testified against the legislation, specifically objected to the fact that VAWA would interfere with a state's choice not to criminalize spousal rape—a choice that, according to Fein, states should be free to make based on "local customs." Although the marital rape exemption survives, it is rare to see it openly defended; the fact that VAWA's opponents did so reveals the depth of their immersion in the world view of the market-family split.

Much of the opposition to the civil rights provision took the form of assertions that federal courts should not interfere in the private, domestic sphere. Chief Justice Rehnquist, for example, used his 1991 Year–End Report on the Federal Judiciary to urge Congress not to pass the Violence Against Women Act because it would create an influx of "domestic relations disputes" into the federal courts. Similarly, the Conference of Chief Justices opposed the statute on the basis that it would constitute an unwarranted federal intrusion into the domain of the state courts. Like its state counterpart, the Judicial Conference of the United States, representing the federal judiciary, adopted a resolution in 1991 opposing VAWA's civil rights provision because of "its potential to disrupt traditional jurisdictional boundaries between the federal and state courts."

Implicit in these objections are the familiar assumptions that all violence against women is "domestic" and that domestic issues do not belong in federal court. In fact, VAWA's scope encompasses any "crime of violence motivated by gender"; the fact that an act of violence took place in the home or among family members is neither necessary nor sufficient to make out a cause of action. Viewed objectively, VAWA is not a domestic relations law. It explicitly does not confer pendent jurisdiction over state law claims seeking establishment of divorce, alimony, marital property, and custody decrees. VAWA is a civil rights law, modeled on other federal civil laws....

Both the Conference of Chief Justices and the Judicial Conference of the United States expressed concern that women would use VAWA as a bargaining chip to extort larger settlements in divorces. The President of the Conference of Chief Justices complained that VAWA "would add a new count to many if not most divorce and other domestic relations cases, further complicating their adjudication and making them more difficult to settle peacefully." This emphasis on "peaceful[ ]" settlement of domestic relations cases echoes nineteenth-century cases arguing against judicial intrusion in the marriage relationship. Settlement, like mediation, is a way to keep family disputes out of court even when legal recourse is technically available.

In addition to raising arguments based on the split between market and family and corresponding assumptions about federal and state jurisdiction, the Conference of Chief Justices also invoked the split between the state and civil society. The Conference objected that VAWA's civil rights provision "appears to eliminate, or at least vitiate, the 'state action' requirement for civil rights litigation." Because VAWA's scope is not limited to actions taken under color of state law, the Conference argued, it is inconsistent with existing federal civil rights laws. In other words, civil rights statutes can protect private individuals only from the state, not from each other. As noted earlier, the preceding three decades had seen a proliferation of federal cases and statutes prohibiting discrimination by private actors. The fact that the organization representing the leading state jurists in the country argued repeatedly and forcefully that federal civil rights laws apply exclusively to state actors, without acknowledging the growing number of exceptions to that general rule, demonstrates the lingering power of the state-civil society dichotomy over the judicial imagination.

* * *

NOTE

1. Ultimately, as indicated by the NOW LDEF statement excerpted above, the Judicial Conference of the United States withdrew its opposition to the legislation, and adopted a position of neutrality. In essence, the Conference allowed its concerns about "federalizing" "private" arenas of violence against women to be allayed by compromises that limited the scope of the legislation: making explicit that nothing in the provision would give federal

courts jurisdiction over domestic relations law; requiring that violence must be at the level of a felony to trigger the provision, and adding a gender animus requirement. The text of the provision, as enacted, follows.

Violence Against Women: Civil Rights for Women 42 USCS § 13981 (2000)

(a) Purpose. Pursuant to the affirmative power of Congress to enact this subtitle under section 5 of the Fourteenth Amendment to the Constitution, as well as under section 8 of Article I of the Constitution, it is the purpose of this subtitle to protect the civil rights of victims of gender motivated violence and to promote public safety, health, and activities affecting interstate commerce by establishing a Federal civil rights cause of action for victims of crimes of violence motivated by gender.

(b) Right to be free from crimes of violence. All persons within the United States shall have the right to be free from crimes of violence motivated by gender (as defined in subsection (d)).

(c) Cause of action. A person (including a person who acts under color of any statute, ordinance, regulation, custom, or usage of any State) who commits a crime of violence motivated by gender and thus deprives another of the right declared in subsection (b) shall be liable to the party injured, in an action for the recovery of compensatory and punitive damages, injunctive and declaratory relief, and such other relief as a court may deem appropriate.

(d) Definitions. For purposes of this section—

(1) the term "crime of violence motivated by gender" means a crime of violence committed because of gender or on the basis of gender, and due, at least in part, to an animus based on the victim's gender; and

(2) the term "crime of violence" means—

(A) an act or series of acts that would constitute a felony against the person or that would constitute a felony against property if the conduct presents a serious risk of physical injury to another, and that would come within the meaning of State or Federal offenses described in section 16 of title 18, United States Code, whether or not those acts have actually resulted in criminal charges, prosecution, or conviction and whether or not those acts were committed in the special maritime, territorial, or prison jurisdiction of the United States; and

(B) includes an act or series of acts that would constitute a felony described in subparagraph (A) but for the relationship between the person who takes such action and the individual against whom such action is taken.

(e) Limitation and procedures.

(1) Limitation. Nothing in this section entitles a person to a cause of action under subsection (c) for random acts of violence unrelated to

gender or for acts that cannot be demonstrated, by a preponderance of the evidence, to be motivated by gender (within the meaning of subsection (d)).

(2) No prior criminal action. Nothing in this section requires a prior criminal complaint, prosecution, or conviction to establish the elements of a cause of action under subsection (c).

(3) Concurrent jurisdiction. The Federal and State courts shall have concurrent jurisdiction over actions brought pursuant to this subtitle.

(4) Supplemental jurisdiction. Neither section 1367 of title 28, United States Code, nor subsection (c) of this section shall be construed, by reason of a claim arising under such subsection, to confer on the courts of the United States jurisdiction over any State law claim seeking the establishment of a divorce, alimony, equitable distribution of marital property, or child custody decree.

(5) [Omitted]

NOTES

1. The passage of the Violence Against Women Act, and specifically of the civil rights provision, was greeted with jubilation by feminist activists and scholars. In the words, again, of Sally Goldfarb:

> The passage of this legislation had great practical and symbolic value. On a practical level, VAWA offers a remedy that in some cases is the only source of legal redress for violence against women and in many others is vastly superior to other available legal options. VAWA avoids the restrictive effects of state tort immunities, marital rape exemptions, and unduly short statutes of limitations. Unlike most previous federal civil rights laws, VAWA does not require a showing of action taken under color of state law or proof of a conspiracy to deny the plaintiff an independent, federally protected right. VAWA civil rights claims brought in federal court are covered by Rule 412 of the Federal Rules of Evidence which, as amended elsewhere in VAWA, extends rape shield protections to civil cases; few states offer such protections. For cases of gender-motivated violence in the workplace, VAWA provides a desirable alternative to Title VII because it permits unlimited awards of compensatory and punitive damages; has a far longer statute of limitations; does not require exhaustion of administrative remedies; and applies to workplaces with fewer than fifteen employees. As a civil rather than criminal action, VAWA empowers women by placing control over the litigation in their own hands and sidesteps the obstacles of gender bias among police and prosecutors. Also, unlike criminal cases, VAWA permits plaintiffs to collect money damages and applies the preponderance of the evidence standard rather than the more onerous standard of beyond a reasonable doubt.
>
> On a symbolic level, VAWA was a major victory for women's equality and seemed to displace rigid conceptions of privacy that had for so long hidden violence against women from public recognition and

public response. A federal civil rights remedy places the issue of violence against women squarely in the domain of public law rather than relegating it to private law remedies or no legal remedies at all. Notably, VAWA's challenge to traditional distinctions between public and private was applauded by a range of feminist writers whose views on privacy otherwise differ profoundly, from those who have emphasized the negative impact of privacy ideology on women to those who have celebrated privacy as a potential source of freedom and autonomy for women. If indeed the public-private distinction is what the feminist movement is all about, it would seem that the enactment of VAWA's civil rights remedy advanced the movement's agenda significantly.

Sally F. Goldfarb, *Violence Against Women and the Persistence of Privacy*, 61 OHIO ST. L.J. 1, 55–57 (2000).

2. Despite the jubilation, however, no one expected that the provision would go unchallenged. As Sally Goldfarb put it: "There was still the danger that despite VAWA's successful journey through the legislative process, the judiciary's privacy-based opposition would reassert itself in interpretations of the statute." Id. at 57. There were, however, two different schools of thought about the form those challenges would take. In the following reading, Reva Siegel, in 1996, was predicting that the struggle would be over the definition of "crime motivated by gender," as adversaries of civil rights for women victimized by violence shifted their ground from the federalism arguments that characterized debate over the passage of the statute to the interpretive arguments that would limit its impact. In fact, as the subsequent readings demonstrate, the attack was instead framed as an assault on the constitutionality of the provision, an assault in which arguments about the limits of federal authority were again predominant. Precisely because federalism continues to limit women's quest for freedom from violence, Siegel's analysis, which provides a rich historical account of the connection between federalism and women's subordination within marriage, remains relevant to the contemporary debate—more relevant even than she imagined it would be.

Reva B. Siegel
The Rule of Love: Wife Beating as Prerogative, 105 Yale Law Journal 2117, 2197–2206 (1996)

While VAWA's civil rights remedy drew many critics, not one critic of the civil rights remedy disparaged the statute's goal of protecting women from rape and domestic violence. Rather, critics argued that creating a federal cause of action to vindicate such injuries usurped a traditional regulatory interest of the states and threatened to flood the federal courts with cases the federal judiciary was ill-equipped to handle.

For example, in January of 1991, the Conference of Chief Justices announced its opposition to Title III on the grounds that the provision could "cause major state-federal jurisdictional problems and disruptions in the processing of domestic relations cases in state courts." The state chief justices reasoned that the "right will be invoked as a bargaining tool within the context of divorce negotiations and add a major complicating factor to an environment which is often acrimonious as it is." They continued:

> The issue of inter-spousal litigation goes to the very core of familial relationships and is a very sensitive policy issue in most states. It does not appear that S. 15 is meant to plunge the federal government into this complex area which has been traditionally reserved to the states, but this might well be the result if the current language stands. It should be noted that the volume of domestic relations litigation in state courts is enormous.
>
> *It should also be noted that the very nature of marriage as a sexual union raises the possibility that every form of violence can be interpreted as gender-based.*[1]

Observing that "the federal cause of action ... would impair the ability of state courts to manage criminal and family law matters traditionally entrusted to the states," the Conference of Chief Justices resolved that the provision should be eliminated.

By September of 1991, the Judicial Conference of the United States joined the Conference of Chief Justices in opposing Title III. The federal judges complained that the new civil rights remedy would burden an already overcrowded federal docket; they also echoed the concern voiced by the state judges that the civil rights cause of action " 'will be invoked as a bargaining tool within the context of divorce negotiations [complicating] an environment which is often acrimonious as it is.' " The Judicial Conference then observed that the "subject of violence based on gender and possible responses is extremely complex," and promised to work with Congress "to fashion an appropriate response to violence directed against women." It was in this context that Chief Justice Rehnquist raised his objections to Title III, complaining that the "new private right of action [is] so sweeping that the legislation could involve the federal courts in a whole host of domestic relations disputes."

Facing opposition to Title III, VAWA's original sponsor, Senate Judiciary Committee Chairman Senator Joseph Biden, joined with Senator Orrin Hatch (then ranking minority member of the Committee) to draft a version of the civil rights remedy that could allay the federalism concerns voiced by the bill's critics. In order to defer to the states' traditional role in regulating matters of marriage and divorce and to shield federal dockets from overcrowding, Senator Hatch sought to limit the range of assaults that might fall within the ambit of Title III's protections.

. . .

1. Crimes of Violence Motivated by Gender: Hearing Before the Subcomm. On Civil and Constitutional Rights of the House Comm. on the Judiciary, 103rd Cong., 1st Sess. 80–81 (emphasis added) (statement by Conference of Chief Justices on S.15, Violence Against Women Act of 1991, adopted by the State–Federal Relations Committee of the Conference of Chief Justices at meeting in Scottsdale, Arizona on Jan. 31, 1991).

The same federalism concerns that critics raised in opposition to the civil rights remedy presumably will shape its interpretation, as courts attempt to identify which acts of violence are "gender-motivated" within the meaning of the act, and which are not. But how is it that courts are to determine which acts of rape and domestic violence are "gender-motivated" and which are not? Here the meaning given the phrase "an animus based on the victim's gender" will be pivotal in the interpretation of the new civil rights remedy. Will courts construe "animus" to mean something akin to "*purpose*" or "*malice*"? Those, such as Senator Hatch, who seek a more restrictive construction of the civil rights remedy will argue that animus means malice, while those more receptive to a federal role in remedying violence against women will construe animus as a form of purpose. To appreciate how the interpretive struggle will unfold in more concrete terms, it is helpful to consider how Senator Hatch described for the *New Republic* the injuries the statute covers:

> "We're not opening the federal doors to all gender-motivated crimes. Say you have a man who believes a woman is attractive. He feels encouraged by her and he's so motivated by that encouragement that he rips her clothes off and has sex with her against her will. Now let's say you have another man who grabs a woman off some lonely road and in the process of raping her says words like, 'You're wearing a skirt! You're a woman! I hate women! I'm going to show you, you woman!' Now, the first one's terrible. But the other's much worse. *If a man rapes a woman while telling her he loves her, that's a far cry from saying he hates her. A lust factor does not spring from animus.*" [Emphasis added.]

. . .

In the controversy over the scope of VAWA's civil rights remedy, we can see the law of intimate assault undergoing modernization. The bill's proponents sought to provide women relief from intimate assault, treating it as a form of sex discrimination—as "gender-motivated violence." The bill's opponents raised a series of federalism objections to the cause of action, first resisting and then accepting with reservations, the antidiscrimination framework of the statute. Although both groups now espouse a commitment to ending gender-motivated violence, their understanding of what that violence is differs. Accordingly, there will be a struggle over the scope of the civil rights remedy, focusing on the meaning of "crime of violence motivated by gender." What is "a crime of violence committed because of gender or on the basis of gender, and due, at least in part, to an animus based on the victim's gender"? The answer to this question will depend in part on the weight given the federalism arguments raised by critics of the civil rights remedy. If we examine these federalism objections, it is possible to see how they gain persuasive power as they draw on the discourse of affective privacy, using it as a basis for restricting the meaning of "gender motivated violence," and thus the protections afforded women by the Act. In short, the struggle over VAWA's civil rights remedy resembles the struggle over the tort provisions of the married women's property acts, not only in structure, but in substance: Federalism objections to the civil rights remedy acquire persuasive power as they draw on the traditional modes of reasoning about intimate assault.

There are several levels at which we can discern the discourse of affective privacy operating in disputes over the civil rights remedy. The first involves the characterization question on which the whole federalism dispute hinges. Suppose a man rapes, beats, or knifes his wife. Does a woman's ability to secure relief for such injuries bear on her status as an equal citizen of this nation? Or is this question properly of local concern, implicating matters of family law and criminal law, but not matters of sex discrimination or equal protection? The assertion that VAWA interferes with traditional state regulatory concerns implicitly, and explicitly, adopts the latter view. In these objections the issue of gender bias that prompted VAWA's enactment recedes from view, and sexualized assault appears as a problem concerning "family matters." As Chief Justice Rehnquist succinctly expressed his objections to the civil rights remedy, the statute "could involve the federal courts *in a whole host of domestic relations disputes*." [Emphasis added.] When the Conference of Chief Justices asserted that "the issue of inter-spousal litigation goes to the very core of familial relationships and is a very sensitive policy issue in most states," it was characterizing intimate assaults in the idiom of the interspousal immunity doctrine.... It is only by virtue of this historical tradition that significant audiences of lawmakers and jurists find it at all persuasive to characterize acts of rape or battery as matters of "domestic relations" law, or the stuff of "acrimonious" "divorce negotiations," or as "sensitive policy issues," or "matters traditionally entrusted to the states." In short, it is because critics of the civil rights remedy are still reasoning within the common law tradition the statute seeks to disestablish that they can characterize VAWA as intruding in regulatory domains that are not properly of federal concern.

Just as history plays a role in characterizations of VAWA's regulatory objectives, it also plays a role in the federalism story that characterization sets in motion. Under our system of federalism, states have historically regulated matters of family law. And in federalism claims about the family, that history typically assumes dispositive weight: Congress should not disturb the allocation of regulatory responsibilities that this nation has forged under the federal constitutional system. But as the paradigm case of slavery teaches us, before we defer to the weight of tradition in such matters, we need at least to consider the normative underpinnings of that initial allocation of federal and state regulatory responsibilities. In the case of family law, uncritical perpetuation of past practice is likely to prove normatively problematic for reasons that, upon reflection, are not terribly surprising: Federalism discourses about the family grew up in intimate entanglement with the common law of marital status. Indeed, as we examine the claim that marriage is a state-law concern, it begins to appear that federalism discourses about marriage bear strong family resemblances to common law privacy discourses about marriage, and in some instances are even direct descendants of the discourse of affective privacy.

The claim that marriage is properly a matter of state-law concern has important roots in nineteenth-century deliberations of Congress and the

Court. One prominent source of this notion is the "domestic-relations exception" to federal diversity jurisdiction, announced in the 1858 case of Barber v. Barber.[1] But if we read *Barber* closely, it turns out that *the claim that husband and wife cannot be diverse for federal jurisdictional purposes was itself an outgrowth of the doctrine of marital unity.* Under the common law of marital status, a wife's domicile was her husband's; thus, following the logic of the common law, the Supreme Court reasoned that husband and wife could not be diverse (i.e., citizens of different states) for federal jurisdictional purposes. Both the majority and dissenting opinions in *Barber* affirm that proposition. The *Barber* dissent then goes on to translate that precept of marital unity doctrine into the discourse of affective privacy:

> *It is not in accordance with the design and operation of a Government having its origin in causes and necessities, political, general, and external, that it should assume to regulate the domestic relations of society; should, with a kind of inquisitorial authority, enter the habitations and even into the chambers and nurseries of private families, and inquire into and pronounce upon the morals and habits and affections or antipathies of the members of every household....* The Federal tribunals can have no power to control the duties or the habits of the different members of private families in their domestic intercourse. This power belongs exclusively to the particular communities of which those families form parts, and is essential to the order and to the very existence of such communities. [Emphasis added.]

This passage from *Barber* should sound somewhat familiar. It discusses the role of the federal and state government in regulating domestic relations much as the *Rhodes* opinion discussed the role of state government and "family government" in regulating domestic relations. As this passage from *Barber* might suggest, much of the idiom used to designate marriage as a "local" matter within discourses of federalism either echoes or can be traced to ... common law doctrines of marital privacy....

The conviction that marriage is a matter for states to regulate can also be traced to efforts to protect the common law of marital status from reform in the aftermath of the Civil War, an era when Congress was first beginning to exercise its new power to regulate race discrimination in the states. As several historians have recounted, Congress sought to draft the Fourteenth Amendment and the 1866 Civil Rights Act so as to protect emancipated slaves from race discrimination while shielding from reform certain features of gender status law: specifically, restrictions on woman suffrage and the marital status doctrines that, for example, prohibited wives from forming contracts, filing suit, or otherwise exercising legal capacity independently of their husbands.

1. 62 U.S. 582, 584 (1858) (announcing that "[w]e disclaim altogether any jurisdiction in the courts of the United States upon the subject of divorce, or for the allowance of alimony"). Judith Resnick offers a detailed account of the domestic-relations exception to federal diversity jurisdiction in her study of the gendered premises of federal jurisdiction. *See* Judith Resnik, *"Naturally" Without Gender: Women, Jurisdiction and the Federal Courts,* 66 N.Y.U. L. Rev. 1682, 1739–50 (1991).

Thus, the notion that family law is a matter of state, not federal, concern can be traced to gendered domicile rules of the common law of marital status, as well as to efforts to preserve other gender-specific aspects of the common law of marital status—law that is now deemed unconstitutional. In addition, as our examination of *Barber* reveals, the claim that marriage is a state-law concern acquires persuasive force at least in part because it draws upon discourses of affective privacy that grew out of the doctrine of marital unity. Claims about federal intervention in domestic relations reiterate more generalized anxieties about governmental interference in family life.

Thus far I have shown how traditions of common law reasoning have shaped federalism claims about regulating domestic relations raised by critics of VAWA's civil rights remedy. But the discourse of affective privacy plays another important role in disputes over the scope of the civil rights remedy, supplying normative criteria for identifying the types of assaults to which the cause of action applies. Here historical connection is by no means as direct, and yet some notion of affection in intimate relationships seems to be regulating intuitions about what kinds of sexualized assaults are "gender-motivated" within the meaning of the Act. It is easier to appreciate this connection once we examine the narratives that Senator Hatch and others employ to separate the acts of rape and domestic violence considered of "local" regulatory concern from those properly considered of "federal" regulatory concern.

Senator Hatch differentiates the roles of federal and state government in regulating intimate assaults by looking to the motivation animating the conduct. When such acts are motivated by hate, he reasons, they are properly matters of federal concern, but when they are motivated by love, they are not. As Senator Hatch succinctly put it: "If a man rapes a woman while telling her he loves her, that's a far cry from saying he hates her. A lust factor does not spring from animus." Restating this distinction, those acts of rape and domestic violence that are motivated by hate properly concern women's status as equal citizens of the United States, while those acts of rape and domestic violence that are motivated by love (or lust) are matters of purely local concern having no bearing on women's status as federal citizens or persons entitled to equal protection of the laws. The structure of this claim depends in part on an assumption that gender bias will manifest itself as race discrimination manifests itself: in an emotional state called "hate." But the claim also draws force from specifically gendered assumptions about intimate relations of the sort manifested in the discursive tradition of affective privacy. As in the nineteenth-century interspousal immunity cases, assertions about love and intimacy in a relationship rhetorically efface the violence of sexualized assault. We might distill the logic of this tradition to the following maxim: Where love is, law need not be. Intimacy occurs in a domain having no bearing on matters of citizenship.

I believe that federalism claims about VAWA's civil rights remedy are persuasive in significant part because they perpetuate traditional discourses of marital status in new idiomatic form. But one need not trace the lineage of these federalism claims to appreciate how the controversy over regulation of "gender-motivated violence" that we are examining will function to modernize discourses of gender status. A civil rights initiative intended to dismantle elements of a centuries-old status regime declares that violence against women is a form of sex discrimination, and soon thereafter becomes the object of political controversy. Those who wish to prevent enactment of the law raise a series of objections to it, couched in "legitimate, nondiscriminatory" reasons. They prevail to the extent of imposing an as yet indeterminate limit on the reach of the new antidiscrimination statute. Now courts are about to implement a law that requires them to determine which acts of rape and domestic violence are gender-motivated, hence violative of women's civil rights as equal citizens of this nation, and which acts of rape and domestic violence are purely local, presumably personal matters, attributable to love or lust, but not gender-based animus. The very struggle over the interpretation of VAWA's civil rights remedy will, of necessity, modernize gender status discourse, altering the rules and rhetoric governing intimate assaults in such a way as to make the distinctions VAWA draws "reasonable" for our day. Considered in larger historical perspective, controversy over the civil rights remedy contained in the Violence Against Women Act has set in motion a legal regime that will restate sexual assault law in the gender mores of American society at the dawn of the twenty-first century.

* * *

NOTES

1. After VAWA was enacted in 1994, plaintiffs brought claims under the new civil rights provision alleging various types of gender-motivated violence, including rape, sexual assault, nonsexual assault, sexual abuse of minors, partner abuse, and murder. For examples of cases involving domestic violence, see: Kuhn v. Kuhn, 1999 WL 519326 (N.D. Ill. 1999) (physical and sexual abuse by husband); Bergeron v. Bergeron, 48 F. Supp. 2d 628 (M.D. La. 1999) (battery, assault and attempted rape by husband); Wright v. Wright, No. Civ. 98–572–A (W.D. Okla. Apr. 27, 1999) (physical violence by defendant against both wife and daughter); Culberson v. Doan, 65 F. Supp. 2d 701 (S.D. Ohio 1999) (beating murder of girlfriend); Ziegler v. Ziegler, 28 F. Supp. 2d 601 (E.D. Wash. 1998) (assault, threats and harassment by husband); Timm v. Delong, 59 F. Supp. 2d 944 (D. Neb. 1998) (physical and sexual abuse by husband); Seaton v. Seaton, 971 F. Supp. 1188 (E.D. Tenn. 1997) (physical and sexual abuse by husband); Doe v. Doe, 929 F. Supp. 608 (D. Conn. 1996) (physical and mental abuse by husband). In all these cases except *Bergeron*, the civil rights provision was found to be a constitutional exercise of the Commerce Clause. In *Wright* and *Timm*, the courts also found the provision constitutional under section 5 of the Fourteenth Amendment.

2. In response to the early claims brought under VAWA's civil rights provision, a growing number of defendants challenged its constitutionality.

These challenges revived the public-private distinctions that VAWA itself was designed to transcend:

> First, the challenges claim that the civil rights provision is not a legitimate exercise of Congress's Commerce Clause power because violence against women does not have sufficiently close ties to the market. Second, they argue that Congress lacked authority to enact the civil rights remedy under section 5 of the Fourteenth Amendment because violence against women does not have sufficiently close ties to the state. These constitutional challenges, by invoking the image of an irreconcilable division between family and market and between civil society and the state, simply recapitulate the public-private split in both its forms. Relying on the familiar public-private dichotomies, the defendants bringing these challenges, and the judges who agree with them, would isolate violence against women in the private sphere and thereby exclude those injuries from federal civil rights relief. In addition, the litigants and judges who embrace these arguments bring to bear a set of assumptions that, as we have seen, arise naturally from rigid adherence to conventional rubrics of public and private, such as the assumptions that women exist only in the domestic sphere and that cases affecting the family belong exclusively in state courts. Their arguments, in short, echo the judiciary's unsuccessful opposition to VAWA during the legislative process.

Sally F. Goldfarb, *Violence Against Women and the Persistence of Privacy*, 61 OHIO ST. L.J. 1, 59 (2000).

The first constitutional challenge to reach a federal court of appeals was Brzonkala v. Virginia Polytechnic Institute & State University, 169 F.3d 820 (4th Cir., en banc 1999). The Fourth Circuit issued an en banc decision striking the provision down as unconstitutional under both the Commerce Clause and section 5 of the Fourteenth Amendment. The Supreme Court granted certiorari, and affirmed the Fourth Circuit in the decision that follows.

United States v. Antonio J. Morrison, et al. and Christy Brzonkala v. Antonio J. Morrison, et al.

120 S.Ct. 1740.
Supreme Court of the United States, (2000).

■ REHNQUIST, C. J., delivered the opinion of the Court, in which O'CONNOR, SCALIA, KENNEDY, and THOMAS, JJ., joined. THOMAS, J., filed a concurring opinion. SOUTER, J., filed a dissenting opinion, in which STEVENS, GINSBURG, and BREYER, JJ., joined. BREYER, J., filed a dissenting opinion, in which STEVENS, J., joined, and in which SOUTER and GINSBURG, JJ., joined as to Part I–A.

■ CHIEF JUSTICE REHNQUIST delivered the opinion of the Court. . . .

I.

Petitioner Christy Brzonkala enrolled at Virginia Polytechnic Institute (Virginia Tech) in the fall of 1994. In September of that year, Brzonkala met respondents Antonio Morrison and James Crawford, who were both students at Virginia Tech and members of its varsity football team. Brzonkala alleges that, within 30 minutes of meeting Morrison and Crawford, they assaulted and repeatedly raped her. After the attack, Morrison allegedly told Brzonkala, "You better not have any . . . diseases." Complaint P22. In the months following the rape, Morrison also allegedly announced in the dormitory's dining room that he " 'liked' to get girls drunk and. . . ." Id., P31. The omitted portions, quoted verbatim in the briefs on file with this Court, consist of boasting, debased remarks about what Morrison would do to women, vulgar remarks that cannot fail to shock and offend.

Brzonkala alleges that this attack caused her to become severely emotionally disturbed and depressed. She sought assistance from a university psychiatrist, who prescribed antidepressant medication. Shortly after the rape Brzonkala stopped attending classes and withdrew from the university.

In early 1995, Brzonkala filed a complaint against respondents under Virginia Tech's Sexual Assault Policy. During the school-conducted hearing on her complaint, Morrison admitted having sexual contact with her despite the fact that she had twice told him "no." After the hearing, Virginia Tech's Judicial Committee found insufficient evidence to punish Crawford, but found Morrison guilty of sexual assault and sentenced him to immediate suspension for two semesters.

Virginia Tech's dean of students upheld the judicial committee's sentence. However, in July 1995, Virginia Tech informed Brzonkala that Morrison intended to initiate a court challenge to his conviction under the Sexual Assault Policy. University officials told her that a second hearing would be necessary to remedy the school's error in prosecuting her complaint under that policy, which had not been widely circulated to students. The university therefore conducted a second hearing under its Abusive Conduct Policy, which was in force prior to the dissemination of the Sexual Assault Policy. Following this second hearing the Judicial Committee again found Morrison guilty and sentenced him to an identical 2–semester suspension. This time, however, the description of Morrison's offense was, without explanation, changed from "sexual assault" to "using abusive language."

Morrison appealed his second conviction through the university's administrative system. On August 21, 1995, Virginia Tech's senior vice president and provost set aside Morrison's punishment. She concluded that it was " 'excessive when compared with other cases where there has been a finding of violation of the Abusive Conduct Policy,' " 132 F.3d 949, 955 (CA4 1997). Virginia Tech did not inform Brzonkala of this decision. After learning from a newspaper that Morrison would be returning to Virginia Tech for the fall 1995 semester, she dropped out of the university.

In December 1995, Brzonkala sued Morrison, Crawford, and Virginia Tech in the United States District Court for the Western District of Virginia. Her complaint alleged that Morrison's and Crawford's attack violated § 13981 and that Virginia Tech's handling of her complaint violated Title IX of the Education Amendments of 1972. Morrison and

Crawford moved to dismiss this complaint on the grounds that it failed to state a claim and that § 13981's civil remedy is unconstitutional. The United States, petitioner in No. 99–5, intervened to defend § 13981's constitutionality.

[The lower courts granted defendants' motion to dismiss the VAWA claims on the ground that the law exceeded Congress's authority under either the Commerce Clause or the Fourteenth Amendment.]

. . .

II.

. . .

As we observed in [United States v. Lopez, 514 U.S. 549 (1995) (holding that Congress does not have constitutional authority to criminalize possession of firearms near schools)], modern Commerce Clause jurisprudence has "identified three broad categories of activity that Congress may regulate under its commerce power." "First, Congress may regulate the use of the channels of interstate commerce." *Lopez*. "Second, Congress is empowered to regulate and protect the instrumentalities of interstate commerce, or persons or things in interstate commerce, even though the threat may come only from intrastate activities." ... "Finally, Congress' commerce authority includes the power to regulate those activities having a substantial relation to interstate commerce, ... *i.e.*, those activities that substantially affect interstate commerce." ...

[Petitioners United States and Brzonkala argued that § 13981 fell under the third category, which was also the focus of *Lopez*.]

... [A] fair reading of *Lopez* shows that the noneconomic, criminal nature of the conduct at issue was central to our decision in that case.... *Lopez*'s review of Commerce Clause case law demonstrates that in those cases where we have sustained federal regulation of intrastate activity based upon the activity's substantial effects on interstate commerce, the activity in question has been some sort of economic endeavor....

The second consideration that we found important in analyzing [the statute at issue in Lopez] was that the statute contained "no express jurisdictional element which might limit its reach to a discrete set of firearm possessions that additionally have an explicit connection with or effect on interstate commerce." ... Such a jurisdictional element may establish that the enactment is in pursuance of Congress' regulation of interstate commerce.

Third, we noted that neither [the statute] " 'nor its legislative history contains express congressional findings regarding the effects upon interstate commerce of gun possession in a school zone.' " ... While "Congress normally is not required to make formal findings as to the substantial burdens that an activity has on interstate commerce," ... the existence of such findings may "enable us to evaluate the legislative judgment that the activity in question substantially affects interstate commerce, even though no such substantial effect [is] visible to the naked eye." ...

Finally, our decision in *Lopez* rested in part on the fact that the link between gun possession and a substantial effect on interstate commerce was attenuated.... The United States argued that the possession of guns may lead to violent crime, and that violent crime "can be expected to affect the functioning of the national economy in two ways. First, the costs of violent crime are substantial, and, through the mechanism of insurance, those costs are spread throughout the population. Second, violent crime reduces the willingness of individuals to travel to areas within the country that are perceived to be unsafe." ... The Government also argued that the presence of guns at schools poses a threat to the educational process, which in turn threatens to produce a less efficient and productive workforce, which will negatively affect national productivity and thus interstate commerce. ...

We rejected these "costs of crime" and "national productivity" arguments because they would permit Congress to "regulate not only all violent crime, but all activities that might lead to violent crime, regardless of how tenuously they relate to interstate commerce." ... We noted that, under this but-for reasoning:

> "Congress could regulate any activity that it found was related to the economic productivity of individual citizens: family law (including marriage, divorce, and child custody), for example. Under these theories ..., it is difficult to perceive any limitation on federal power, even in areas such as criminal law enforcement or education where States historically have been sovereign. Thus, if we were to accept the Government's arguments, we are hard pressed to posit any activity by an individual that Congress is without power to regulate." ...

With these principles underlying our Commerce Clause jurisprudence as reference points, the proper resolution of the present cases is clear. Gender-motivated crimes of violence are not, in any sense of the phrase, economic activity. While we need not adopt a categorical rule against aggregating the effects of any noneconomic activity in order to decide these cases, thus far in our Nation's history our cases have upheld Commerce Clause regulation of intrastate activity only where that activity is economic in nature....

. . .

In contrast with the lack of congressional findings that we faced in *Lopez*, § 13981 *is* supported by numerous findings regarding the serious impact that gender-motivated violence has on victims and their families. But the existence of congressional findings is not sufficient, by itself, to sustain the constitutionality of Commerce Clause legislation....

In these cases, Congress' findings are substantially weakened by the fact that they rely so heavily on a method of reasoning that we have already rejected as unworkable if we are to maintain the Constitution's enumeration of powers. Congress found that gender-motivated violence affects interstate commerce:

> "by deterring potential victims from traveling interstate, from engaging in employment in interstate business, and from transacting

with business, and in places involved in interstate commerce; ... by diminishing national productivity, increasing medical and other costs, and decreasing the supply of and the demand for interstate products."

H.R. Conf. Rep. No. 103–711, at 385....

Given these findings and petitioners' arguments, the concern that we expressed in *Lopez* that Congress might use the Commerce Clause to completely obliterate the Constitution's distinction between national and local authority seems well founded. See *Lopez, supra,* at 564. The reasoning that petitioners advance seeks to follow the but-for causal chain from the initial occurrence of violent crime (the suppression of which has always been the prime object of the States' police power) to every attenuated effect upon interstate commerce. If accepted, petitioners' reasoning would allow Congress to regulate any crime as long as the nationwide, aggregated impact of that crime has substantial effects on employment, production, transit, or consumption. Indeed, if Congress may regulate gender-motivated violence, it would be able to regulate murder or any other type of violence since gender-motivated violence, as a subset of all violent crime, is certain to have lesser economic impacts than the larger class of which it is a part.

Petitioners' reasoning, moreover, will not limit Congress to regulating violence but may, as we suggested in *Lopez*, be applied equally as well to family law and other areas of traditional state regulation since the aggregate effect of marriage, divorce, and childrearing on the national economy is undoubtedly significant. Congress may have recognized this specter when it expressly precluded § 13981 from being used in the family law context. See 42 U.S.C. § 13981(e)(4). Under our written Constitution, however, the limitation of congressional authority is not solely a matter of legislative grace....

We accordingly reject the argument that Congress may regulate noneconomic, violent criminal conduct based solely on that conduct's aggregate effect on interstate commerce. The Constitution requires a distinction between what is truly national and what is truly local.... In recognizing this fact we preserve one of the few principles that has been consistent since the Clause was adopted. The regulation and punishment of intrastate violence that is not directed at the instrumentalities, channels, or goods involved in interstate commerce has always been the province of the States.... Indeed, we can think of no better example of the police power, which the Founders denied the National Government and reposed in the States, than the suppression of violent crime and vindication of its victims....

III.

[Because the Court rejected Congress's Commerce Clause authority, it also considered, but rejected the claim that § 5 of the Fourteenth Amendment provided constitutional authority for § 13981.]

Petitioners' § 5 argument is founded on an assertion that there is pervasive bias in various state justice systems against victims of gender-motivated violence. This assertion is supported by a voluminous congressional record. Specifically, Congress received evidence that many participants in state justice systems are perpetuating an array of erroneous stereotypes and assumptions. Congress concluded that these discriminatory stereotypes often result in insufficient investigation and prosecution of gender-motivated crime, inappropriate focus on the behavior and credibility of the victims of that crime, and unacceptably lenient punishments for those who are actually convicted of gender-motivated violence.... Petitioners contend that this bias denies victims of gender-motivated violence the equal protection of the laws and that Congress therefore acted appropriately in enacting a private civil remedy against the perpetrators of gender-motivated violence to both remedy the States' bias and deter future instances of discrimination in the state courts.

As our cases have established, state-sponsored gender discrimination violates equal protection unless it " 'serves "important governmental objectives and ... the discriminatory means employed" are "substantially related to the achievement of those objectives." ' " United States v. Virginia, 518 U.S. 515, 533, 135 L. Ed. 2d 735, 116 S. Ct. 2264 (1996)... However, the language and purpose of the Fourteenth Amendment place certain limitations on the manner in which Congress may attack discriminatory conduct. These limitations are necessary to prevent the Fourteenth Amendment from obliterating the Framers' carefully crafted balance of power between the States and the National Government. See *Flores,* 521 U.S. at 520–524 (reviewing the history of the Fourteenth Amendment's enactment and discussing the contemporary belief that the Amendment "does not concentrate power in the general government for any purpose of police government within the States").... Foremost among these limitations is the time-honored principle that the Fourteenth Amendment, by its very terms, prohibits only state action. The principle has become firmly embedded in our constitutional law that the action inhibited by the first section of the Fourteenth Amendment is only such action as may fairly be said to be that of the States. That Amendment erects no shield against merely private conduct, however discriminatory or wrongful....

Shortly after the Fourteenth Amendment was adopted, we decided two cases interpreting the Amendment's provisions, United States v. Harris, 106 U.S. 629, 27 L. Ed. 290, 1 S. Ct. 601 (1883), and the Civil Rights Cases, 109 U.S. 3, 27 L. Ed. 835, 3 S. Ct. 18 (1883). In *Harris*, the Court considered a challenge to § 2 of the Civil Rights Act of 1871. That section sought to punish "private persons" for "conspiring to deprive any one of the equal protection of the laws enacted by the State." 106 U.S. at 639. We concluded that this law exceeded Congress' § 5 power because the law was "directed exclusively against the action of private persons, without reference to the laws of the State, or their administration by her officers." 106 U.S. at 640....

We reached a similar conclusion in the *Civil Rights Cases*. In those consolidated cases, we held that the public accommodation provisions of the Civil Rights Act of 1875, which applied to purely private conduct, were beyond the scope of the § 5 enforcement power. 109 U.S. at 11 ("Individual invasion" of individual rights is not the subject-matter of the [Fourteenth] Amendment.)

[Rejecting a broad reading of United States v. Guest, 338 U.S. 745 (1966), the Court dismissed the petitioners' argument that the Fourteenth Amendment could justify federal regulation of private actions.]

Petitioners alternatively argue that, unlike the situation in the Civil Rights Cases, here there has been gender-based disparate treatment by state authorities, whereas in those cases there was no indication of such state action. There is abundant evidence, however, to show that the Congresses that enacted the Civil Rights Acts of 1871 and 1875 had a purpose similar to that of Congress in enacting § 13981: There were state laws on the books bespeaking equality of treatment, but in the administration of these laws there was discrimination against newly freed slaves....

But even if that distinction were valid, we do not believe it would save § 13981's civil remedy. For the remedy is simply not "corrective in its character, adapted to counteract and redress the operation of such prohibited state laws or proceedings of state officers." ... Section 13981 is not aimed at proscribing discrimination by officials which the Fourteenth Amendment might not itself proscribe; it is directed not at any State or state actor, but at individuals who have committed criminal acts motivated by gender bias.

In the present cases, for example, § 13981 visits no consequence whatever on any Virginia public official involved in investigating or prosecuting Brzonkala's assault. The section is, therefore, unlike any of the § 5 remedies that we have previously upheld. For example, in Katzenbach v. Morgan, 384 U.S. 641, 16 L. Ed. 2d 828, 86 S. Ct. 1717 (1966), Congress prohibited New York from imposing literacy tests as a prerequisite for voting because it found that such a requirement disenfranchised thousands of Puerto Rican immigrants who had been educated in the Spanish language of their home territory. That law, which we upheld, was directed at New York officials who administered the State's election law and prohibited them from using a provision of that law. In South Carolina v. Katzenbach, 383 U.S. 301, 15 L. Ed. 2d 769, 86 S. Ct. 803 (1966), Congress imposed voting rights requirements on States that, Congress found, had a history of discriminating against blacks in voting. The remedy was also directed at state officials in those States. Similarly, in Ex parte Virginia, 100 U.S. 339, 25 L. Ed. 676 (1880), Congress criminally punished state officials who intentionally discriminated in jury selection; again, the remedy was directed to the culpable state official.

Section 13981 is also different from these previously upheld remedies in that it applies uniformly throughout the Nation. Congress' findings indicate that the problem of discrimination against the victims of gender-motivated crimes does not exist in all States, or even most States. By contrast, the § 5 remedy upheld in Katzenbach v. Morgan, supra, was directed only to the State where the evil found by Congress existed, and in

South Carolina v. Katzenbach, supra, the remedy was directed only to those States in which Congress found that there had been discrimination.

. . .

IV

Petitioner Brzonkala's complaint alleges that she was the victim of a brutal assault. But Congress' effort in § 13981 to provide a federal civil remedy can be sustained neither under the Commerce Clause nor under § 5 of the Fourteenth Amendment. If the allegations here are true, no civilized system of justice could fail to provide her a remedy for the conduct of respondent Morrison. But under our federal system that remedy must be provided by the Commonwealth of Virginia, and not by the United States. The judgment of the Court of Appeals is

Affirmed.

■ JUSTICE SOUTER, with whom JUSTICE STEVENS, JUSTICE GINSBURG, and JUSTICE BREYER join, dissenting.

DISSENT

. . .

The Court says both that it leaves Commerce Clause precedent undisturbed and that the Civil Rights Remedy of the Violence Against Women Act of 1994, 42 U.S.C. § 13981, exceeds Congress's power under that Clause. I find the claims irreconcilable and respectfully dissent.

I.

Our cases, which remain at least nominally undisturbed, stand for the following propositions. Congress has the power to legislate with regard to activity that, in the aggregate, has a substantial effect on interstate commerce. See Wickard v. Filburn, 317 U.S. 111, 124–128, 87 L. Ed. 122, 63 S. Ct. 82 (1942).... The fact of such a substantial effect is not an issue for the courts in the first instance, ... but for the Congress, whose institutional capacity for gathering evidence and taking testimony far exceeds ours. By passing legislation, Congress indicates its conclusion, whether explicitly or not, that facts support its exercise of the commerce power. The business of the courts is to review the congressional assessment, not for soundness but simply for the rationality of concluding that a jurisdictional basis exists in fact.... Any explicit findings that Congress chooses to make, though not dispositive of the question of rationality, may advance judicial review by identifying factual authority on which Congress relied. Applying those propositions in these cases can lead to only one conclusion.

One obvious difference from United States v. Lopez, 514 U.S. 549, 131 L. Ed. 2d 626, 115 S. Ct. 1624 (1995), is the mountain of data assembled by Congress, here showing the effects of violence against women on interstate commerce. Passage of the Act in 1994 was preceded by four years of hearings, which included testimony from physicians and law professors; from survivors of rape and domestic violence; and from representatives of state law enforcement and private business. The record includes reports on gender bias from task forces in 21 States, and we have the benefit of specific factual findings in the eight separate Reports issued by Congress and its committees over the long course leading to enactment. Compare *Hodel,* 452 U.S. at 278–279 (noting "extended hearings," "vast amounts of testimony and documentary evidence," and "years of the most thorough legislative consideration").

With respect to domestic violence, Congress received evidence for the following findings:

"Three out of four American women will be victims of violent crimes sometime during their life." H. R. Rep. No. 103–395 p. 25 (1993) (citing U.S. Dept. of Justice, Report to the Nation on Crime and Justice 29 (2d ed. 1988)).

"Violence is the leading cause of injuries to women ages 15 to 44. . . ." S. Rep. No. 103–138, p. 38 (1993) (citing Surgeon General Antonia Novello, From the Surgeon General, U.S. Public Health Services, 267 JAMA 3132 (1992)).

"As many as 50 percent of homeless women and children are fleeing domestic violence." S. Rep. No. 101–545, p. 37 (1990) (citing E. Schneider, Legal Reform Efforts for Battered Women: Past, Present, and Future (July 1990)).

"Since 1974, the assault rate against women has outstripped the rate for men by at least twice for some age groups and far more for others." S. Rep. No. 101–545, at 30 (citing Bureau of Justice Statistics, Criminal Victimization in the United States (1974) (Table 5)).

"Battering 'is the single largest cause of injury to women in the United States.' " S. Rep. No. 101–545, at 37 (quoting Van Hightower & McManus, Limits of State Constitutional Guarantees: Lessons from Efforts to Implement Domestic Violence Policies, 49 Pub. Admin. Rev. 269 (May/June 1989)).

"An estimated 4 million American women are battered each year by their husbands or partners." H. R. Rep. No. 103–395, at 26 (citing Council on Scientific Affairs, American Medical Assn., Violence Against Women: Relevance for Medical Practitioners, 267 JAMA 3184, 3185 (1992)).

"Over 1 million women in the United States seek medical assistance each year for injuries sustained [from] their husbands or other partners." S. Rep. No. 101–545, at 37 (citing Stark & Flitcraft, Medical Therapy as Repression: The Case of the Battered Woman, Health & Medicine (Summer/Fall 1982).)

"Between 2,000 and 4,000 women die every year from [domestic] abuse." S. Rep. No. 101–545, at 36 (citing Schneider, *supra*).

"Arrest rates may be as low as 1 for every 100 domestic assaults." S. Rep. No. 101–545, at 38 (citing Dutton, Profiling of Wife Assaulters: Preliminary Evidence for Trimodal Analysis, 3 Violence and Victims 5–30 (1988)).

"Partial estimates show that violent crime against women costs this country at least 3 billion—not million, but billion—dollars a year." S. Rep. No. 101–545, at 33 (citing Schneider, *supra*, at 4).

"Estimates suggest that we spend $5 to $10 billion a year on health care, criminal justice, and other social costs of domestic violence." S. Rep. No. 103–138, at 41 (citing Biden, Domestic Violence: A Crime, Not a Quarrel, Trial 56 (June 1993)).

The evidence as to rape was similarly extensive, supporting these conclusions:

"[The incidence of] rape rose four times as fast as the total national crime rate over the past 10 years." S. Rep. No. 101–545, at 30 (citing Federal Bureau of Investigation Uniform Crime Reports (1988)).

"According to one study, close to half a million girls now in high school will be raped before they graduate." S. Rep. No. 101–545, at 31 (citing R. Warshaw, I Never Called it Rape 117 (1988)).

"[One hundred twenty-five thousand] college women can expect to be raped during this—or any—year." S. Rep. No. 101–545, at 43 (citing testimony of Dr. Mary Koss before the Senate Judiciary Committee, Aug. 29, 1990).

"Three-quarters of women never go to the movies alone after dark because of the fear of rape and nearly 50 percent do not use public transit alone after dark for the same reason." S. Rep. No. 102–197, p. 38 (1991) (citing M. Gordon & S. Riger, The Female Fear 15 (1989)).

"[Forty-one] percent of judges surveyed believed that juries give sexual assault victims less credibility than other crime victims." S. Rep. No. 102–197, at 47 (citing Colorado Supreme Court Task Force on Gender Bias in the Courts, Gender Justice in the Colorado Courts 91 (1990)).

"Less than 1 percent of all [rape] victims have collected damages." S. Rep. No. 102–197, at 44 (citing report by Jury Verdict Research, Inc.).

" 'An individual who commits rape has only about 4 chances in 100 of being arrested, prosecuted, and found guilty of any offense.' " S. Rep. No. 101–545, at 33, n. 30 (quoting H. Feild & L. Bienen, Jurors and Rape: A Study in Psychology and Law 95 (1980)).

"Almost one-quarter of convicted rapists never go to prison and another quarter received sentences in local jails where the average sentence is 11 months." S. Rep. No. 103–138, at 38 (citing Majority Staff Report of Senate Committee on the Judiciary, The Response to Rape: Detours on the Road to Equal Justice, 103d Cong., 1st Sess., 2 (Comm. Print 1993)).

"Almost 50 percent of rape victims lose their jobs or are forced to quit because of the crime's severity." S. Rep. No. 102–197, at 53 (citing Ellis, Atkeson, & Calhoun, An Assessment of Long–Term Reaction to Rape, 90 J. Abnormal Psych., No. 3, p. 264 (1981)).

Based on the data thus partially summarized, Congress found that:

"crimes of violence motivated by gender have a substantial adverse effect on interstate commerce, by deterring potential victims from traveling interstate, from engaging in employment in interstate business, and from transacting with business, and in places involved, in interstate commerce ... [,] by diminishing national productivity, increasing medical and other costs, and decreasing the supply of and the demand for interstate products. . . ." H. R. Conf. Rep. No. 103–711, p. 385 (1994).

Congress thereby explicitly stated the predicate for the exercise of its Commerce Clause power. Is its conclusion irrational in view of the data amassed? True, the methodology of particular studies may be challenged, and some of the figures arrived at may be disputed. But the sufficiency of the evidence before Congress to provide a rational basis for the finding cannot seriously be questioned.

Indeed, the legislative record here is far more voluminous than the record compiled by Congress and found sufficient in two prior cases upholding Title II of the Civil Rights Act of 1964 against Commerce Clause challenges. In Heart of Atlanta Motel, Inc. v. United States, 379 U.S. 241 (1964), and Katzenbach v. McClung, 379 U.S. 294 (1964), the Court referred to evidence showing the consequences of racial discrimination by motels and restaurants on interstate commerce. Congress had relied on compelling anecdotal reports that individual instances of segregation cost thousands to millions of dollars. Congress also had evidence that the average black family spent substantially less than the average white family in the same income range on public accommodations, and that discrimination accounted for much of the difference.

While Congress did not, to my knowledge, calculate aggregate dollar values for the nationwide effects of racial discrimination in 1964, in 1994 it did rely on evidence of the harms caused by domestic violence and sexual assault, citing annual costs of $3 billion in 1990, see S. Rep. 101–545, and $5 to $10 billion in 1993, see S. Rep. No. 103–138, at 41. Equally important, though, gender-based violence in the 1990's was shown to operate in a manner similar to racial discrimination in the 1960's in reducing the mobility of employees and their production and consumption of goods shipped in interstate commerce. Like racial discrimination, "gender-based violence bars its most likely targets—women—from full participation in the national economy." ...

If the analogy to the Civil Rights Act of 1964 is not plain enough, one can always look back a bit further. In *Wickard*, we upheld the application of the Agricultural Adjustment Act to the planting and consumption of homegrown wheat. The effect on interstate commerce in that case followed from the possibility that wheat grown at home for personal consumption could either be drawn into the market by rising prices, or relieve its grower of any need to purchase wheat in the market. . . . The Commerce Clause predicate was simply the effect of the production of wheat for home consumption on supply and demand in interstate commerce. Supply and demand for goods in interstate commerce will also be affected by the deaths of 2,000 to 4,000 women annually at the hands of domestic abusers, ... and by the reduction in the work force by the 100,000 or more rape victims who lose their jobs each year or are forced to quit. . . . Violence against women may be found to affect interstate commerce and affect it substantially.

II

The Act would have passed muster at any time between *Wickard* in 1942 and *Lopez* in 1995, a period in which the law enjoyed a stable understanding that congressional power under the Commerce Clause, complemented by the authority of the Necessary and Proper Clause, Art. I. § 8 cl.18, extended to all activity that, when aggregated, has a substantial effect on interstate commerce. As already noted, this understanding was secure even against the turmoil at the passage of the Civil Rights Act of 1964, in the aftermath of which the Court not only reaffirmed the cumulative effects and rational basis features of the substantial effects test ... but declined to limit the commerce power through a formal distinction between legislation focused on "commerce" and statutes addressing "moral and social wrongs," ....

The fact that the Act does not pass muster before the Court today is therefore proof, to a degree that *Lopez* was not, that the Court's nominal adherence to the substantial effects test is merely that. Although a new jurisprudence has not emerged with any distinctness, it is clear that some congressional conclusions about obviously substantial, cumulative effects on commerce are being assigned lesser values than the once-stable doctrine would assign them. These devaluations are accomplished not by any express repudiation of the substantial effects test or its application through the aggregation of individual conduct, but by supplanting rational basis scrutiny with a new criterion of review.

. . .

A.

. . .

If we now ask why the formalistic economic/noneconomic distinction might matter today, after its rejection in *Wickard*, the answer is not that the majority fails to see causal connections in an integrated economic world. The answer is that in the minds of the majority there is a new animating theory that makes categorical formalism seem useful again. Just as the old formalism had value in the service of an economic conception, the new one is useful in serving a conception of federalism. It is the instrument by which assertions of national power are to be limited in favor of preserving a supposedly discernible, proper sphere of state autonomy to legislate or refrain from legislating as the individual States see fit. The legitimacy of the Court's current emphasis on the noncommercial nature of regulated activity, then, does not turn on any logic serving the text of the Commerce Clause or on the realism of the majority's view of the national economy. The essential issue is rather the strength of the majority's claim to have a constitutional warrant for its current conception of a federal relationship enforceable by this Court through limits on otherwise plenary commerce power. This conception is the subject of the majority's second categorical discount applied today to the facts bearing on the substantial effects test.

B.

The Court finds it relevant that the statute addresses conduct traditionally subject to state prohibition under domestic criminal law, a fact said to have some heightened significance when the violent conduct in question is not itself aimed directly at interstate commerce or its instrumentalities. ... Again, history seems to be recycling, for the theory of traditional state concern as grounding a limiting principle has been rejected previously, and more than once....

. . .

C.

... Today's majority ... finds no significance whatever in the state support for the Act based upon the States' acknowledged failure to deal adequately with gender-based violence in state courts, and the belief of their own law enforcement agencies that national action is essential.

The National Association of Attorneys General supported the Act unanimously, ... and Attorneys General from 38 States urged Congress to enact the Civil Rights Remedy, representing that "the current system for dealing with violence against women is inadequate,".... It was against this record of failure at the state level that the Act was passed to provide the choice of a federal forum in place of the state-court systems found inadequate to stop gender-biased violence.... The Act accordingly offers a federal civil rights remedy aimed exactly at violence against women, as an alternative to the generic state tort causes of action found to be poor tools of action by the state task forces. See S. Rep. No. 101–545, at 45 (noting difficulty of fitting gender-motivated crimes into common-law categories). As the 1993 Senate Report put it, "The Violence Against Women Act is intended to respond both to the underlying attitude that this violence is somehow less serious than other crime and to the resulting failure of our criminal justice system to address such violence. Its goals are both symbolic and practical...." ...

The collective opinion of state officials that the Act was needed continues virtually unchanged, and when the Civil Rights Remedy was challenged in court, the States came to its defense. Thirty-six of them and the Commonwealth of Puerto Rico have filed an *amicus* brief in support of petitioners in these cases, and only one State has taken respondents' side. It is, then, not the least irony of these cases that the States will be forced to enjoy the new federalism whether they want it or not. For with the Court's decision today, Antonio Morrison, like *Carter Coal*'s James Carter before him, has "won the states' rights plea against the states themselves." R. Jackson, The Struggle for Judicial Supremacy 160 (1941).

III

All of this convinces me that today's ebb of the commerce power rests on error, and at the same time leads me to doubt that the majority's view will prove to be enduring law....

■ JUSTICE BREYER, with whom JUSTICE STEVENS joins, . . . dissenting.

[The portion of the dissent addressing the Commerce Clause, and joined also by Justices Souter and Ginsburg is omitted.]

II.

Given my conclusion on the Commerce Clause question, I need not consider Congress' authority under § 5 of the Fourteenth Amendment. Nonetheless, I doubt the Court's reasoning rejecting that source of authority. The Court points out that . . . § 5 does not authorize Congress to use the Fourteenth Amendment as a source of power to remedy the conduct of *private persons*. That is certainly so. The Federal Government's argument, however, is that Congress used § 5 to remedy the actions of *state actors*, namely, those States which, through discriminatory design or the discriminatory conduct of their officials, failed to provide adequate (or any) state remedies for women injured by gender-motivated violence—a failure that the States, and Congress, documented in depth.

Neither *Harris* nor the *Civil Rights Cases* considered this kind of claim. The Court in *Harris* specifically said that it treated the federal laws in question as "directed *exclusively* against the action of private persons, without reference to the laws of the State, or their administration by her officers." 106 U.S. at 640 (emphasis added); see also *Civil Rights Cases,* 109 U.S. at 14 (observing that the statute did "not profess to be corrective of any constitutional wrong committed by the States" and that it established "rules for the conduct of individuals in society towards each other, . . . without referring in any manner to any supposed action of the State or its authorities").

The Court responds directly to the relevant "state actor" claim by finding that the present law lacks " 'congruence and proportionality' " to the state discrimination that it purports to remedy. *Ante*, at 26; see City of Boerne v. Flores, 521 U.S. 507, 526, 138 L. Ed. 2d 624, 117 S. Ct. 2157 (1997). That is because the law, unlike federal laws prohibiting literacy tests for voting, imposing voting rights requirements, or punishing state officials who intentionally discriminated in jury selection, . . . is not "directed . . . at any State or state actor." . . .

But why can Congress not provide a remedy against private actors? Those private actors, of course, did not themselves violate the Constitution. But this Court has held that Congress at least sometimes can enact remedial "legislation . . . [that] prohibits conduct which is not itself unconstitutional." *Flores,* 521 U.S. at 518; see also Katzenbach v. Morgan, *supra,* at 651; South Carolina v. Katzenbach, *supra,* at 308. The statutory remedy does not in any sense purport to "determine what constitutes a constitutional violation." *Flores, supra,* at 519. It intrudes little upon either States or private parties. It may lead state actors to improve their own remedial systems, primarily through example. It restricts private actors only by imposing liability for private conduct that is, in the main, already forbidden by state law. Why is the remedy "disproportionate"? And given the relation between remedy and violation—the creation of a federal remedy to substitute for constitutionally inadequate state remedies—where is the lack of "congruence"?

The majority adds that Congress found that the problem of inadequacy of state remedies "does not exist in all States, or even most States." *Ante*, at 27. But Congress had before it the task force reports of at least 21 States documenting constitutional violations. And it made its own findings about pervasive gender-based stereotypes hampering many state legal systems, sometimes unconstitutionally so.... The record nowhere reveals a congressional finding that the problem "does not exist" elsewhere. Why can Congress not take the evidence before it as evidence of a national problem? This Court has not previously held that Congress must document the existence of a problem in every State prior to proposing a national solution. And the deference this Court gives to Congress' chosen remedy under § 5, *Flores, supra,* at 536, suggests that any such requirement would be inappropriate.

Despite my doubts about the majority's § 5 reasoning, I need not, and do not, answer the § 5 question, which I would leave for more thorough analysis if necessary on another occasion. Rather, in my view, the Commerce Clause provides an adequate basis for the statute before us. And I would uphold its constitutionality as the "necessary and proper" exercise of legislative power granted to Congress by that Clause

NOTES AND QUESTIONS

1. Do you find yourself more persuaded by Rehnquist's opinion for the Court, or by the dissenters? Do you think the outcome in *Morrison* was predetermined by the Court's earlier decision in *Lopez*? Does the fact that *Lopez* preceded *Morrison* persuade you that the Court had an agenda (the reassertion of limits on federal authority) quite distinct from any concern about framing violence against women as a public rather than a private issue?

2. In the aftermath of *Morrison,* new civil rights legislation has already been introduced in Congress. The Violence Against Women Civil Rights Restoration Act of 2000, H.R. 5021, 106th Cong. (2000), amends Section 40302 of the Violence Against Women Act, 42 U.S.C. 13981, in two critical respects. First, it adds a requirement that, in connection with the crime of violence for which the victim seeks redress, EITHER:

> (A) the defendant or the victim travels in interstate or foreign commerce;
>
> (B) the defendant or the victim uses a facility or instrumentality of interstate or foreign commerce; or
>
> (C) the defendant employs a firearm, explosive, incendiary device, or other weapon, or a narcotic or drug listed pursuant to section 202 of the Controlled Substances Act, or other noxious or dangerous substance, that has traveled in interstate or foreign commerce;
>
> OR:

(2) the offense interferes with commercial or other economic activity in which the victim is engaged at the time of the conduct;

OR:

(3) the offense was committed with intent to interfere with the victim's commercial or other economic activity.

Second, the bill adds an entirely new provision:

DISCRETIONARY AUTHORITY OF ATTORNEY GENERAL—Whenever the Attorney General has reasonable cause to believe that any State or political subdivision of a State, official, employee, or agent thereof, or other person acting on behalf of a State or political subdivision of a State has discriminated on the basis of gender in the investigation or prosecution of gender-based crimes and that discrimination is pursuant to a pattern or practice of resistance to investigating or prosecuting gender-based crimes, the Attorney General, for or in the name of the United States, may institute a civil action in any appropriate United States district court against such party for such equitable relief as may be appropriate to ensure the elimination of such discriminatory practices.

Based on a careful reading of Rehnquist's opinion for the Court in *Morrison*, do you believe the new provisions will pass constitutional muster? Do they impose significant limits on the scope of the redress provided? Has the cause of action against "state actors" been included with the expectation that such suits would actually be brought, or simply to shore up the claim that the legislation is designed to address discrimination that women experience when they pursue their claims at the state level?

3. Civil rights legislation modeled on VAWA's original civil rights provision has also been introduced at the state level. New York Senate Bill S.7903 (May 22, 2000), for example, follows 42 U.S.C. § 13981 closely, except that it does not restrict the cause of action to those who can show that a felony was committed against them. Rather, the action lies whenever a crime against the person, or against property, is committed because of gender, or on the basis of gender, and due at least in part to an animus based on the victim's gender. Treble damages, punitive damages, and attorneys fees are available, as well as declaratory and injunctive relief.

Bills have also been introduced in state legislatures in Arizona and Illinois. The Arizona bill is similar to the New York provision but is entitled "Actions Relating to Domestic Violence." Arizona, SB 1535 (2000). The Illinois bill, entitled the "Gender Violence Act," provides that "any person who has been subjected to sex discrimination may bring a civil action for damages, an injunction or appropriate relief against the person who committed that act." Illinois, HB 4407 (2000). What do you think about the relative merits of each of these formulations?

4. More fundamentally, what are the advantages and disadvantages of enacting civil rights legislation at the state rather than the federal level? If the federal legislation was prompted in part by the inadequacy of state responses to violence against women, will additional legislation, which must

still be interpreted and implemented by state courts, produce significant changes in the climate within which women seek redress?

C. CONCLUSION

When Sally Goldfarb represented the position of NOW LDEF on the Violence Against Women Act civil rights provision, she was careful to point out that the legislation was in fact gender-neutral—it offered men as well as women the prospect of suing those who used violence against them when that violence was motivated by gender animus. It is not our experience, however, that men are the targets of violence because they are men—except, perhaps, when men are victimized by other men because they fail to conform to "manly" stereotypes (because they are effeminate, or gay, or transsexual, or in their behavior or dress otherwise fail to observe gender boundaries). Ironically, our gender-discrimination jurisprudence has not as yet recognized that this male-on-male violence *is* gender-motivated; these cases tend to be viewed as cases involving discrimination based on sexuality rather than gender, and as such they fall outside the scope of protection offered by gender discrimination laws.

There is another way, however, in which civil rights legislation addressing discrimination against women, or more narrowly violence against women, benefits men as well as women, and therefore society at large. John Stuart Mill said it as well as anyone, in describing the costs to society of inequality, and the corresponding gains associated with eradicating that inequality:

> The example afforded, and the education given to the sentiments, by laying the foundation of domestic existence upon a relation contradictory to the first principles of social justice, must, from the very nature of man, have a perverting influence of such magnitude, that it is hardly possible with our present experience to raise our imaginations to the conception of so great a change for the better as would be made by its removal. All that education and civilization are doing to efface the influences on character of the law of force, and replace them by those of justice, remains merely on the surface, as long as the citadel of the enemy is not attacked.... If no authority, not in its nature temporary, were allowed to one human being over another, society would not be employed in building up propensities with one hand which it has to curb with the other. The child would really, for the first time in man's existence on earth, be trained in the way he should go, and when he was old there would be a chance that he would not depart from it. But so long as the right of the strong to power over the weak rules in the very heart of society, the attempt to make the equal right of the weak the principle of its outward actions will always be an uphill struggle; for the law of justice ... will never get possession of men's innermost sentiments; they will be working against it, even when bending to it.
>
> . . .

> . . . The love of power and the love of liberty are in eternal antagonism. Where there is least liberty, the passion for power is the most ardent and unscrupulous. The desire of power over others can only cease to be a depraving agency among mankind, when each of them individually is able to do without it: which can only be where respect for liberty in the personal concerns of each is an established principle.

John Stuart Mill, THE SUBJECTION OF WOMEN 88–89, 105 (S.M. Okin ed. 1988).

Jane Maslow Cohen puts the same thought in more contemporary language:

> [N]othing about the model of patriarchy even begins to suggest how the mothers into whose care the males of our society entrust our future citizens can likely inculcate in them a love of the liberty and equality that these same women have been denied. . . . [I]t is remarkable that the young of this society ever grow up to be democrats. . . . From a practical standpoint, therefore, it can be nothing other than a mistake for democracy to be married to patriarchy, since patriarchy is barren of democratic values and cannot, therefore, reproduce them.

Jane Maslow Cohen, *Private Violence and Public Obligation: The Fulcrum of Reason,* THE PUBLIC NATURE OF PRIVATE VIOLENCE 349, 367 (M.A. Fineman and R. Mykitiuk, eds. 1994).

When women are full civic participants in both the senses discussed in these pages; when they both receive their full due from the state, and are free to make their maximum contribution to it, we will have left far behind the notion that power is society's first organizing principle, and be well on our way to embracing respect, the foundation of democratic governance, as its replacement. While civil rights legislation is only one of the many tools available to move society towards this goal, it does have the advantage of framing the debate in a fashion that clarifies what is at stake.

CHAPTER FOURTEEN

Domestic Violence as a Violation of International Human Rights

Introductory Note

This chapter addresses the issue of domestic violence as a violation of international human rights. Like many other areas that we have explored, developments in this chapter are very recent. It is only in the last decade that the human rights of women have emerged as a major focus of international advocacy efforts. Largely due to the work of a developing global women's movement, what international human rights lawyer and scholar Rhonda Copelon has called "the coalescence of women as a global presence," there are new efforts to expand the scope of protection of international treaties and covenants to victims of domestic violence. Important accomplishments, such as the appointment of a Special Rapporteur on Violence Against Women in 1994, testify to the progress that has been made.

Framing violence against women as a violation of international human rights raises issues parallel to those explored in the last chapter, which looked at domestic violence as a violation of women's civil rights. The human rights effort seeks to persuade the international community that violence against women is a public issue, and an issue of state dereliction of responsibility toward its citizenry, rather than a purely or merely private problem faced by individual women in their relationships with individual men. On the other hand, whereas the ill-fated civil rights remedy enacted as part of the Violence Against Women Act gave victims private rights of action against perpetrators, the international efforts are aimed at increasing state responsiveness to the needs of women. As with any other international regulatory effort, however, the issue of enforcement is crucial. Do any of the increasingly specific international mandates in this area have any teeth? This chapter documents the history of the inclusion of women's concerns in the international arena and suggest the extent of the barriers that still exist.

The chapter begins with two articles that develop theoretical frameworks for understanding domestic violence as a violation of international human rights. In the first, Dorothy Thomas and Michele Beasley provide an historical overview of the arguments that paved the way for women's international human rights advocacy and offer examples of early advocacy efforts. In the second, Rhonda Copelon argues that domestic violence can be understood within one of the most important and conventional frameworks of international human rights, the prohibition against torture. We then turn to examination of some of the basic international human rights documents relevant to intimate partner violence: the Convention on the Elimination of All Forms of Discrimination Against Women (CEDAW); CEDAW Committee General Recommendation Number 19, specifically addressing violence; the General Assembly Resolution "Declaration on the Elimination of Violence Against Women;" Reports of the Special Rapporteur on Violence Against Women, and an excerpt of a contemporary report on Violence from the Women's Section of Human Rights Watch. An excerpt from Elizabeth Schneider's book Battered Women and Feminist Lawmaking considers the significance of international human rights work for, and its impact on, domestic violence advocacy in the United States.

Finally we turn briefly to a related issue—the question of whether women who have been subjected to violence in their countries of origin, and claim international human rights violations, can successfully seek asylum in the United States.

A. Domestic Violence as a Violation of International Human Rights

Dorothy Q. Thomas and Michele E. Beasley Domestic Violence As a Human Rights Issue, 58 Albany Law Review 1119, 1119–33, 1140–47 (1995)

Maria was brutally assaulted in her own kitchen in England by a man wielding two knives. He held one of the weapons at her throat, while raping her with the other. After he finished, the man doused her with alcohol and set her alight with a blow torch. Maria lived through the assault to prosecute the man, although seventy percent of her body is now covered with scars. But because they were married, he could not be charged with rape. He received a ten-year sentence for bodily injury, of which he will serve only five years.

Between 1988 and 1990 in the Brazilian state of Maranhio, women registered at the main police station over 4,000 complaints of battery and sexual abuse in the home. Of those complaints, only 300—less than eight percent—were forwarded to the court for processing, and only two men were ever convicted and sent to prison.

In Pakistan, Muhammad Younis killed his wife, claiming that he found her in the act of adultery. The court found his defense untrue, in part because the woman was fully dressed when she was killed, and sentenced him to life imprisonment. However, on appeal the Lahore High Court reduced his sentence to ten years at hard labor stating that the "accused had two children from his deceased wife and when accused took the extreme step of taking her life by giving her repeated knife blows on different parts of her body she must have done something unusual to enrage him to that extent."

It has been observed that "the concept of human rights is one of the few moral visions ascribed to internationally." Domestic violence violates the principles that lie at the heart of this moral vision: the inherent dignity and worth of all members of the human family, the inalienable right to freedom from fear and want, and the equal rights of men and women. Yet until recently, it has been difficult to conceive of domestic violence as a human rights issue under international law. We would like to explore some of the reasons why such a conceptualization has been so problematic, and how difficulties are beginning to be resolved through a combination of theory and practice. We stress that the methods of combating domestic violence under international law are still emerging and that the strategies set forth [here] mark only one step in this process.

. . .

I. Problems with Understanding Domestic Violence as a Human Rights Issue

A. The Scope of International Human Rights Law

The concept of human rights developed largely from Western political theory of the rights of the individual to autonomy and freedom. International human rights law evolved in order to protect those individual rights from limitations that might be imposed on them by states. States are bound by international law to respect the individual rights of each and every person and are thus accountable for abuses of those rights. The aim of the human rights movement is to enforce states' obligations in this regard by denouncing violations of their duties under international law. The exclusive focus on the behavior of states confines the operation of international human rights law entirely within the public sphere.

B. Gender-Neutral Law, Gender-Biased Application

International human rights law is facially gender neutral. The rights embodied in the Universal Declaration of Human Rights are defined as belonging to "all human beings," not just to men. All the major human rights instruments include sex as one of the grounds upon which states may not discriminate in enforcing the rights set forth.

Although international law is gender neutral in theory, in practice it interacts with gender-biased domestic laws and social structures that relegate women and men to separate spheres of existence: private and public. Men exist as public, legal entities in all countries, and, barring an overt abuse by the state, participate in public life and enjoy the full extent of whatever civil and political rights exist. Women, however, are in every country socially and economically disadvantaged in practice and in fact and in many places by law. Therefore, their capacity to participate in public life is routinely circumscribed. This gender bias, if unchallenged, becomes so embedded in the social structure that it often assumes the form of a social or cultural norm seemingly beyond the purview of the state's responsibility, rather than a violation of women's human rights for which the state is accountable. In some cases, even civil and political rights violations committed directly by state actors have been shrugged off as acceptable....

. . . In past human rights practice, organizations often have not challenged the relegation of women and what happens to them in the private sphere, whether in law or in practice, and have allowed social or cultural justifications to deter them from denouncing restrictions on women's capacity to participate in public life. Even where abuses against women have occurred in realms they traditionally monitor, such as police custody, they have not consistently reported them. For example, only very recently have human rights organizations begun to report on rape of women prisoners as a form of torture. Thus, in the absence of a challenge to states' consistent relegation of women to the private sphere, application of international law can have the effect of reinforcing, and to some extent replicating, the exclusion of women's rights abuses from the public sphere and therefore from the state's international obligations. . . .

Nowhere is the effect on international human rights practice of the public/private split more evident than in the case of domestic violence which literally happens "in private." States dismiss blatant and frequent crimes, including murder, rape, and physical abuse of women in the home, as private, family matters, upon which they routinely take no action. Moreover, the state's failure to prosecute violence against women equally with other similar crimes or to guarantee women the fundamental civil and political right to equal protection of the law without regard to sex have largely escaped international condemnation.

At least four interrelated factors have caused the exclusion of domestic violence in particular from international human rights practice: (1) traditional concepts of state responsibility under international law and practice, (2) misconceptions about the nature and extent of domestic violence and states' responses to it, (3) the neglect of equality before and equal protection of the law without regard to sex as a governing human rights principle, and (4) the failure of states to recognize their affirmative obligation to provide remedies for domestic violence crimes. These factors, independently and in relationship to one another, are beginning to change and, with them, so is the treatment of domestic violence under international law. . . .

C. The Concept of State Responsibility

The concept of state responsibility defines the limits of a government's accountability for human rights abuses under international law. Of course, all acts are done by real people, individually or with others, and not by the fictive "person" of the state. Therefore, responsibility is generally understood to arise only when an act by a real person or persons can be imputed to the state. . . .

More recently, however, the concept of state responsibility has expanded to include not only actions directly committed by states, but also states' systematic failure to prosecute acts committed either by low-level or para-state agents or by private actors. In these situations, although the state does not actually commit the primary abuse, its failure to prosecute the abuse amounts to complicity in it. . . .

. . . To hold a state accountable for the actions of state actors, one of two things must be shown: (1) the state explicitly authorized the act (i.e., a senior official committed or authorized it), or (2) the state systematically failed to prosecute abuses committed by its agent, whether or not these acts were ordered by senior officials. In the latter case, one must usually show a pattern of non-prosecution of acts that violate human rights, and that the state has agreed to enforce those human rights. For example, the state is responsible if it fails systematically to prohibit or prosecute torture, because the right to be free from torture is guaranteed under international law. Governments have agreed not to torture people themselves and have undertaken to ensure that no one else in the state tortures. If the state failed to prosecute torturers, it would violate its international obligations.

The test is different when the actors are private....

. . .

... The state's international obligation with regard to the acts of private individuals is to ensure that where it does protect people's lives, liberty, and security against private depredations, it must do so without discrimination on prohibited grounds. Therefore, there would have to be systematic, discriminatory non-enforcement of the domestic criminal law against murder or assault for domestic violence to constitute a human rights issue, not merely a showing that the victims' lives ended or their bodies were harmed.

The expansion of state responsibility to include accountability for some acts of private individuals as defined above is one of the factors necessary to permit analysis of domestic violence as a human rights violation. However, in many cases it is also necessary to show a pattern of discriminatory nonprosecution which amounts to a failure to guarantee equal protection of the law to women victims. The following section is an overview of new information about the vast extent of violence experienced by women and the frequency of its non- or discriminatory prosecution, which was revealed as a general characteristic, not merely a rare anomaly of domestic criminal law.

D. Widespread Violence and a Pattern of Non-prosecution

. . .

New information on domestic violence has surfaced as a result of a long international campaign by women's rights groups to raise consciousness about women's issues. After successfully pushing for the inclusion of a commitment to equal rights for women in the U.N. Charter and Universal Declaration of Human Rights, women's organizations worked for the establishment of the U.N. Commission on the Status of Women and other formal mechanisms for the advancement of women's status. The Commission and affiliated non-governmental organizations (NGOs) drafted a variety of conventions to combat discrimination against women internationally and pressed for the General Assembly to declare a Decade for Women program. It was the international resurgence of women's activism in the 1960s and 1970s, and the pressure generated by women's organizations internationally, that made the U.N. Decade for Women (1975–1985) a reality. As the Decade unfolded, women's rights activists coordinated international efforts to study the position of women in all societies and the reasons for their subordinate status....

In 1989, the U.N. Commission on the Status of Women in Vienna compiled a mass of domestic violence statistics and analyses by women's rights activists and academics, and published its report, Violence Against Women in the Family. The report's author reviewed over 250 articles, books, and studies of various aspects of domestic violence, of which only ten had been published earlier than 1971....

Domestic violence has been revealed as widespread and gender specific. For example, in the United States a 1984 National Crime Survey found that women were victims of family violence at a rate three times that of men, and that of all spousal violence crimes, ninety-one percent were victimizations of women by their husbands or ex-husbands. In Colombia during 1982 and 1983, the Forensic Institute of Bogota found that out of 1,170 cases of bodily injury, twenty percent were due to marital violence against women. The Forensic Institute also determined that ninety-four percent of persons hospitalized in bodily injury cases were battered women. In Thailand, a study in Bangkok revealed that more than fifty percent of married women were beaten regularly by their husbands. And the reported number of women killed in dowry disputes in India almost doubled between 1985 and 1987, rising from 999 reports to 1,786 reports per year.

This is only a small sampling of the information emerging on domestic violence. Certain characteristics of the problem become clear from the overall research: domestic violence is not unusual or an exception to normal private family life; the vast majority of crimes against women occur in the home and are usually committed by a spouse or relative in the form of murder, battery, or rape; and, domestic violence is endemic to all societies....

If violence against women in the home is inherent in all societies, then it can no longer be dismissed as something private and beyond the scope of state responsibility.... The widespread absence of state intervention in crimes against women is not merely the result of governments' failure to criminalize a class of behavior (since the violent acts themselves usually are crimes), but rather is the result of governments' failure to enforce laws equitably across gender lines....

E. The Underlying Right to Equal Protection of the Law

... [E]ven though increased research into and understanding of domestic violence indicated that states were discriminating against women in the enforcement of criminal laws, gender discrimination under international law was not a central human rights concern.

Until recently, sex discrimination has been visibly absent from the agendas of most governmental and non-governmental bodies concerned with human rights, with the exception of the Committee on the Elimination of All Forms of Discrimination Against Women, the U.N. body which monitors state conduct under the Convention on the Elimination of All Forms of Discrimination Against Women. The Committee and the other women's rights bodies located in Vienna have undertaken landmark work in holding governments accountable for discrimination on the basis of sex, whether by commission or omission. These organizations have made notable progress despite insufficient resources and limited enforcement mechanisms in the instruments they oversee.

However and more importantly for the purposes of this Article, the mainstream Geneva-based human rights bodies, which oversee instruments that have stronger protective mechanisms, have used the existence of this separate women's human rights regime as an excuse to marginalize sex discrimination and most other women's human rights violations, which nonetheless fall clearly within their own mandates. Within the cumulative human rights practice of governments and governmental bodies, sex discrimination has been de-emphasized and placed outside the rubric of central human rights concerns. International non-governmental human rights organizations, including the two largest groups, Amnesty International and Human Rights Watch, have until recently reflected and perpetuated this trend.

. . .

Ultimately, women's rights activists internationally condemned many of the international governmental and non-governmental human rights bodies for gender bias and, among other things, for their failure to adequately promote and protect women's rights to nondiscrimination and equal protection of the law. Largely as a result of this increasing pressure from women's rights activists internationally, and heightened awareness of the extent of violence against women and government tolerance of it, the non-governmental human rights organizations of nations began to highlight these issues within their overall human rights practice.

These separate but interrelated developments have allowed domestic violence to be placed within the context of international human rights law and practice. Developments in the concept of state responsibility, new information about the gender-specific nature of domestic violence, its pervasiveness and frequent non- or discriminatory prosecution by governments, and a new emphasis on equal protection of the law as a central human rights concern have made it possible to conceptualize domestic violence as a human rights issue and to hold governments accountable for the pervasive abuse of women worldwide....

. . .

III. Conclusions: The Limits and Value of the Equal Protection Human Rights Approach to Combating Domestic Violence

A. Practical Problems

Human rights practice is a method of reporting facts to promote change. The influence of non-governmental human rights organizations is intimately linked to the rigor of their research methodology. One typical method of reporting human rights violations in specific countries is to investigate individual cases of human rights violations through interviews with victims and witnesses, supported by information about the abuse from other credible sources.

Analysis of domestic violence as a human rights abuse depends not only on proving a pattern of violence, but also on demonstrating a systematic failure by the state to afford women equal protection of the law against that violence. Without detailed statistical information concerning both the incidence of wife-murder, battery, and rape, and the criminal justice system's response to those crimes, it can be difficult to make a solid case against a government for its failure to guarantee equal protection of the law. And inadequate documentation of human rights abuses against women is common to countries throughout the world.

... Inadequate documentation is a function of another practical problem which is equally common internationally: the lack of cooperation between women's rights and human rights groups on both national and international levels. In Brazil, for example, the human rights and women's rights groups had no history at all of working together and, in fact, often saw their aims as antagonistic. For example, efforts to emphasize the equal rights of women in the context of the struggle against military dictatorship were often perceived by the human rights community as divisive and marginal to the central issue of creating a non-oppressive (and in this case, democratic) form of government. As a result of this split, human rights organizations lack information pertaining to violations of women's rights, and women's rights organizations often have neither the training nor the resources to document abuses as required to make a case under international law.

One of the important practical advances resulting from field work on women's human rights was the realization that to address abuses against women adequately in the context of international human rights practice, women's rights organizations and human rights organizations at national and international levels need to work together to locate and develop the data and methods necessary for the rigorous fact-finding and analysis on which human rights reporting is based.

. . .

B. Methodological Limitations

In addition to the quality of its facts, the efficacy of the human rights method depends on the solidity of the legal principles on which arguments are made that governments are in violation of their international obligations and should change their practices. Consequently, changes in methodology must be developed from those legal principles or they will be ineffective to condemn states.

The most general methodological problem with applying human rights to domestic violence is not specific to domestic violence per se, but is a function of the general focus of human rights law: international human rights law is law that binds states, not law that binds individuals. As was discussed at length in Part I, the focus of human rights law on states and the fact that domestic violence, and other abuses of women's human rights, are often committed by private individuals at present necessitate a complicated analysis to demonstrate state accountability....

Another limitation is that human rights practice tends to focus on individual acts (whether by state or non-state actors) and not on the causes of those acts. Documentation of a government's failure to prosecute domestic violence does not directly address the causes of that violence, which are rooted in social, economic, and legal structures that discriminate against women, and in widely-held attitudes about women's lesser status. The inability, in current human rights practice, to hold governments accountable for the broad economic and social inequities that underlie domestic violence has at least two consequences. First, it may lead governments to the false conclusion that all they need to do to eliminate domestic violence is prosecute aggressors equally with other violent criminals. Second, it largely limits human rights organizations to denouncing abuses after they have already occurred, when the victim is hurt or dead.

Put another way, it is very difficult to use the human rights approach to prevent domestic violence. Positive state responsibilities such as education or economic support programs, which might help eliminate the causes of domestic violence, are less clearly prescribed by international law than prohibitions against certain abuses, even where the state may be domestically obligated to undertake certain functions. It is one thing for a human rights organization to address the state's discriminatory application of law; it is quite another to direct a state to adopt a particular social program to change discriminatory attitudes. The first instance is, in a sense, a "negative" injunction, one to stop violations of international human rights law; the second is a "positive" exhortation to adopt a particular policy. The latter statement has a more amorphous basis in international legal principles and requires a less straightforward remedy. It is more difficult for an international human rights organization to be persuasive positively than negatively.

Increasingly, the positive responsibilities of states are being incorporated into international human rights law and practice. The Convention on the Elimination of All Forms of Discrimination Against Women (CEDAW), for example, requires governments to take positive measures to end legal, social, and economic gender inequality.... [A]s the concept of state responsibility in international law evolves further, human rights organizations may more easily hold governments accountable for failing actively to counter the social, economic, and attitudinal biases which underpin and perpetuate domestic violence.

Finally, and perhaps most importantly, the current human rights approach to domestic violence and state responsibility only addresses the problem of equal protection; it usually cannot hold governments accountable for the domestic violence itself, just as it could not hold governments accountable internationally for other violent crimes committed by private individuals....

Addressing the state's responsibility for domestic violence per se would entail investigating in more detail the particular characteristics of domestic violence, as distinguished from other violent crime. To some extent domestic violence is not random, that is, it is directed at women because they are women and is committed to impede women from exercising their rights. As such, it is an essential factor in maintaining women's subordinate status, as well as in the resulting domestic and international privatization of gender-specific abuse.... In this sense, domestic violence is different from other violent crimes.... The norm of gender neutrality itself, embodied in the human rights treaties and international customary law, may unintentionally reinforce gender bias in the law's application and obscure the fact that human rights laws ought to deal directly with gender-specific abuse, and not just gender-specific failures to provide equal protection. The gender-neutral norm may appear to require only identical treatment of men and women, when in fact, equal treatment in many cases is not adequate.

. . .

C. Value of the Human Rights Approach

... [T]o understand the limits of the human rights approach is also to clarify the particular contributions it can make as part of broader local and international efforts to combat domestic violence.

... [N]ongovernmental international human rights organizations have great prestige and influence. Heads of state pay significant attention to the findings and recommendations of such NGOs, even if only to deny their validity, and states regularly monitor whether other states have successfully met their international obligations to uphold their citizens' human rights. Human rights activists have shown the effectiveness of prompting governments to curb human rights violations by aiming the spotlight of public scrutiny on the depredations....

Therefore, the potential power of the human rights machinery to combat domestic violence is a strong incentive to use this approach.

The human rights approach employs a preexisting international system to bring pressure to bear on governments that routinely fail to prosecute domestic violence equally with other similar crimes. This provides an opportunity for local institutions and activists to supplement their efforts with support from the international community. The effect is twofold: local struggles are enhanced and domestic protections available to women may improve....

The human rights approach to domestic violence may also have the effect of improving international protections for women. Although, until recently, "women's issues" have been seen as marginal to the "real" issues of human rights, placing domestic violence within the mainstream of the theory and practice of international human rights draws attention to the extent and seriousness of the problem. This not only points out the past failure of the human rights community adequately to counter the problem, but brings to light the urgent need for the international human rights system to function more effectively on behalf of women.

The most compelling advantage to utilizing a human rights approach to oppose domestic violence may be that it simultaneously raises women's issues in the mainstream of human rights practice, while it broadens the mainstream's perceived scope.... Together with developments in other areas of law and activism, this dynamic ultimately may help transform the international human rights system so that it honors the Universal Declaration of Human Rights and protects more than just the rights of man.

* * *

NOTE

1. As Dorothy Thomas and Michele Beasley describe, traditional human rights analysis failed to address violence against women because human rights guarantees, such as those established by the Universal Declaration of Human Rights, were applied in gender-biased ways, despite their facial gender-neutrality or universality. This explains the perceived necessity for gender-specific initiatives such as the Convention for the Elimination of All Forms of Discrimination Against Women, or the General Assembly's Declaration on the Elimination of Violence Against Women. Is there a parallel here to the situation in the United States, where dissatisfaction with the protection accorded women under the Fourteenth Amendment led to the (ultimately unsuccessful) campaign to ratify a separate Equal Rights Amendment?

Current efforts on the part of human rights activists and scholars are not limited, however, to pursuing new remedies for women. In addition, these reformers are revisiting traditional human rights doctrine, and arguing that unbiased analysis demands its application to certain harms suffered by women. This tension between seeking to frame women's claims within existing structures, and seeking to establish new ones, has been a theme running through much of what you have read in prior chapters. It is not surprising to see it resurface in this new context.

In the next reading, Rhonda Copelon argues that domestic violence can, and should, be understood as a form of torture, a practice traditionally condemned by international law.

DV understood in torture framework

Rhonda Copelon
Recognizing the Egregious in the Everyday: Domestic Violence as Torture, 25 Columbia Human Rights Law Review 291, 292–98, 306–15, 319 (1994)

Gender-based violence is nearly universal, affecting women of every class, race, ethnicity and social background in all the pursuits of life and at every phase of the life cycle. The number of its victims exceeds those of war and the most brutal dictatorships of our time. And yet, to speak of it as a violation of women's human rights has been, until recently, treated as absurd or heretical. The egregiousness of gender-based violence has been matched only by its absence from human rights discourse.

Since 1985, a global women's campaign, built upon national and regional initiatives, has begun to transform significantly the place of women and the status of gender based violence within the human rights discourse. United Nations bodies charged with women's concerns have taken up the issue of gender-based violence. Women's issues—with a focus on gender violence—entered the mainstream at the 1993 World Conference on Human Rights in Vienna. The horror of the mass rape of women as a tactic of "ethnic cleansing" in the wars in the former Yugoslavia, combined with the presence of a global women's caucus, made it impossible for the world community to continue to keep gender-violence outside the circle of urgent human rights issues. The Vienna Declaration thus recognized a broad range of gender-based violence—both private and official—as among "human rights concerns."

Notwithstanding these major steps towards a reconceptualization of gender violence as a human rights violation, it remains an open question whether privately inflicted gender violence will be treated unequivocally as a human rights violation, and as one giving rise to enforceable as opposed to precatory state responsibility to prevent it. International condemnation, in the form of the Vienna Declaration and the United Nations Declaration on the Elimination of Violence Against Women, is, of course, profoundly important: it undermines the plausibility of state denials of gender-based violence and simultaneously begins to undermine the enculturation of men to use violence and of women to endure it. It focuses attention on the need for reform and provides women a basis for demanding resources and support for their protection and empowerment, politically, economically, socially and culturally. But condemnation has little sustained effect in most contexts, unless it also gives rise to accountability.

This article—begun when the recent advances were considered, even by some human rights proponents, to be foolish if not dangerous ravings—seeks to push the boundaries of women's human rights further. It addresses what is perhaps the most common and dangerous form of gender-based violence—the battering and sexual abuse of women by their partners. It argues that such violence must be understood as torture, giving rise to obligatory international and national responsibilities. Through a conventional human rights lens this appears as a "hard case"; from women's experience, however, it is an obvious one.

There are two major obstacles to the recognition of intimate violence against women as a human rights violation. One is the role of the public/private dichotomy in international law. The second, which is the focus of this piece, is the persistent trivialization of violence against women. Intimate violence—with the exception of some of its more sensationalized and culture-specific examples—has not been considered violence. Seen as "personal" or "private," a "domestic" or "family" matter, its goals and consequences have been obscured and its use justified as chastisement or discipline. My thesis is that, when stripped of privatization, sexism and sentimentality, private gender-based violence is no less grave than other forms of inhumane and subordinating official violence that have been prohibited by treaty and customary law and recognized by the international community as jus cogens, or peremptory norms.

To elucidate the egregiousness of gender-based violence, I have chosen to examine commonplace domestic violence against women partners in light of the evolving international legal understanding of torture. The analogy is neither original nor new. Women survivors and activists from around the globe—particularly from societies where torture was or is a state practice—commonly speak of domestic violence as torture. Feminist researchers have elucidated this analogy through their study of battered women and political prisoners. The analogy is not popular with leading torture experts, however. Edward Peters, a leading historian of torture, calls the comparison "sentimental," insisting that the essence of torture is its public character. And Nigel Rodley, the United Nations Commission on Human Rights Special Rapporteur on Torture and former Legal Advisor to Amnesty International, has stated that he might consider private gender violence within his mandate only if it had the explicit imprimatur of the state.

The insistence on state involvement ignores the role and function of male violence—and especially intimate violence—in women's lives. It can no longer be justified as simply a reflection of a neutral or traditional state-centered ordering of international law; rather, it is rooted in and perpetuates the culture as well as the structure of the patriarchal state. The basis is simple but durable: what is public concerns the world of men and is, therefore, important; the private is female and, therefore, not important. In the realm of intimacy and sexuality, the tendency to discount the integrity of women and the gravity of violence and coercion is multiplied. The public/private dichotomy thus justifies the partial or total impunity enjoyed by the perpetrators of violence against women. This, in turn, constitutes men as a de facto absolutist state in women's lives. Moreover, the insistence on explicit state involvement does not explain the continuing reluctance unequivocally to characterize official rape as torture. It is also inconsistent with the permeability of the public/private dichotomy in the treaties governing torture which hold the state responsible for passive complicity in privately inflicted torture.

Hopefully, the comparison between domestic violence and torture will be influential in deepening the awareness of the atrocity of domestic violence, its role in women's lives, and the urgency of unequivocal international condemnation and accountability. Torture, accepted as jus cogens or a peremptory norm of international law, illustrates what renders violence exceptional and heinous, and thereby provides a framework for assessing the gravity of gender-based violence. The definition and practice of torture illuminate the nature and purposes of severe and deliberately inflicted violence—violence as an assault on the body, the mind and the dignity of the person; violence as an instrument of repression and subordination of the individual, group or society. When examined through the lens of torture, domestic violence against women emerges as a disturbingly comparable system of terror. And if violence in intimate relationships can be understood as a violation of international human rights, then other forms of gender-based violence, whether universal or particular in their incidence or form, should merit the same recognition.

. . .

II. DOMESTIC VIOLENCE THROUGH THE LENS OF TORTURE

A. A Brief History of Torture

Over the centuries torture has evolved in the West from a judicial or quasi-judicial method of eliciting or testing truth into a weapon of terror.

Significantly, the terroristic use of torture common today was initiated in the Inquisition and reached its apogee in the European witch-craze of the sixteenth and seventeenth centuries.... It persisted in the United States as an unregulated, low visibility police practice and elsewhere as an instrument of nationalism, fascism and Stalinism. In Nazi Germany, torture was industrialized, reaching unprecedented levels of sophistication and horror.

Revulsion against Nazi atrocities led to the prohibition of torture and cruel, inhuman and degrading treatment in the Universal Declaration of Human Rights, the International Covenant on Civil and Political Rights (ICCPR) and the Geneva Conventions. Recent decades have seen a resurgence of torture in many parts of the world, both North and South, as well as a campaign against torture, spearheaded by Amnesty International and other human rights groups. These phenomena have inspired the adoption of increasingly detailed and binding instruments on both an international and regional level. Investigatory and adjudicatory bodies have further elaborated these instruments....

B. The Elements of Torture As Applied to Domestic Violence

... As defined in the binding instruments, torture involves four elements: (1) severe physical and/or mental pain and suffering; (2) intentional infliction; (3) specified purposes; and (4) some degree of official or quasi-official involvement, whether active or passive....

1. Severe Physical and/or Mental Pain and Suffering

The classic notion of torture in western history and imagination focuses on gross physical invasion of the body. Derived from the Latin tortura, the word "torture" literally means "twisting," "writhing" or "torment." But to treat physical brutality as the sine qua non of torture obscures the essential goals of modern official torture: the breaking of the will and the spread of terror. It obfuscates the relationships between acts of violence and the larger context of torture, between physical pain and mental stress, and between mental integrity and human dignity. It ignores the facts that abuse of the body is humiliating as well as searing, and that the body is abused and controlled not only for obscene sadistic reasons but ultimately as a pathway to the mind and spirit.

. . .

Thus, while it is possible to identify both physical and psychological methods of torture and their analogues in the context of domestic violence, it is critical to recognize the futility of segregating them in terms of either goals or effects in practice.

a. The Physical Component

According to Amnesty International, the infliction of physical pain is common in the practice of official torture. Some methods are ancient—the falanga, the thumbscrew, pulling out of fingernails, and near-drowning submersion in foul water. With the exception of electroshock, however, the most common forms of physical torture involve no special equipment. They include beating, kicking and the infliction of pain with ordinary objects such as canes, knives, and cigarettes. For women, sexual abuse, rape and the forcing of instruments or animals into the vagina are common and devastating forms of torture. Sexual violence also takes the form of forced undressing, pawing, threats of rape, or being forced to perform sexual acts. In other words, torture is very frequently inflicted through means available in everyday life; the commonplace is transformed into official brutality.

Like torture, domestic violence usually involves some form of physical brutality, which often escalates over time. The methods of intimate violence resemble the common methods of torture. They include beating with hands or objects, biting, spitting, punching, kicking, stabbing, strangling, scalding, burning and attempted drowning. The consequences include physical and mental pain and suffering, disfigurement, miscarriage, maiming and death. Rape is likewise a common concomitant of battering. Sexual abuse takes many forms, including "the insertion of objects into the woman's vagina, forced anal or oral sex, bondage, forced sex with others, and sex with animals." Some women are threatened with mutilation of their breasts or genitals and suffer permanent disfigurement.... Domestic violence also causes women to fear for their lives, and with good reason. It is a leading cause of death among women.

b. The Psychological Component

The psychological component of torture consists of anguish, humiliation, debilitation and fear caused by physical brutality, rape and sexual abuse and abuse of children, partners, other family members or associates; by threats of such brutalities and of death; and by methods of sensory deprivation, stress and manipulation designed to break the will of the tortured.

Often among the most insidious forms of torture are those that do not involve overt brutality. Anguish and disintegration of the self can be accomplished through methods that passively as well as actively attack the body. Such hybrid techniques include forcing prisoners to assume positions such as wall-standing for prolonged periods, thereby causing agonizing pain without directly administering it. Not only do these methods leave no marks, but they create in the prisoner the bizarre sense that the pain is self-induced. Sensory deprivation techniques, which create anxiety and disorientation, include exposure to continuous loud noises, hooding, alternating darkness with blinding light, sleep deprivation, starvation and dehydration. Loss of control of bodily functions and forced and observed nudity—particularly with women, trained in modesty, degraded as sex objects, and fearing assault—are intended not only to terrify but also to humiliate and destroy all sense of autonomy.

Some methods rely wholly on the psychological. Threats to kill, mutilate or torture the person, her family members or her friends create terror. Torturers stage mock executions and force people to listen to the screams of others being tortured. With women, threats to abuse their children or abuse the women in front of their children, as well as observing or hearing the rape of other women, are especially effective.

Torturers use even more subtle methods to break the prisoner's will: isolation, arbitrary and unpredictable punishments, and intermittent rewards. The alternation of active and passive brutality with kindness is one of the most effective means to undermine the prisoner's morale-sustaining hatred of the torturer and convert the torturer into savior. All these methods, which are designed to exhaust endurance and manipulate dependency, underscore the significance of the psychological in torture: torture is a context and process of domination and not simply, or even necessarily, a distinct set of brutal acts.

. . .

... [P]sychologists and advocates for battered women have analogized the condition of POWs to that of battered women. Batterers manipulate and create stress in much the same way as official torturers. ... women are isolated from family, friends and others, which is a form of "house arrest." They are subjected to verbal insult, sexual denigration and abuse. Their lives and those of their loved ones are threatened and they are made to fear the loss of their children. At the same time, at least early in the battering cycle, they are occasionally showered with apologies, promises and kindness. Even so, the possibility of explosion over the smallest domestic detail places battered women in a condition of severe and unremitting dread. For some women the psychological terror is the worst part.

. . .

In regard to psychological suffering, the comparison between survivors of official torture and imprisonment and battered women makes clear that submission is not a particularity of women's pathology. Rather, it is a consequence of terroristic efforts at domination. And, just as we do not excuse torture that fails to accomplish the complete submission of the victim, neither must battering result in complete surrender to violate international law. As we condemn the practitioners of terror, we must recognize the heroism of women's efforts to endure and survive, just as we have begun to recognize that of POWs and victims of dictatorships.

* * *

NOTE

1. Treating domestic violence as torture has significance in a number of ways. If domestic violence were classified as torture under the United Nations Convention Against Torture, states would have to act to prevent domestic violence through training, investigation and prosecution or extradition of offenders. In addition, victims would have the right to be free from retaliation and to receive fair and adequate compensation. Aggressors could still be prosecuted, even if they left the country. Finally, a victim would not be faced with expulsion, return or extradition to another state where it was probable she would be subject to further torture. States ratifying the U.N. Convention Against Torture make their own decisions about how to fulfil their obligations under the Convention, and what legislative measures may

be necessary to implement it. However, those obligations are certainly more specific and more robust than any obligations attendant on the Convention for the Elimination of All Forms of Discrimination Against Women, discussed below.

In the United States, for example, both civil and criminal causes of action for torture are available. A victim of torture, who has minimum contacts with the U.S. (either through residence or a current visit) can bring a civil suit against the perpetrator in federal court under the Torture Victim Protection Act of 1991, 28 U.S.C. § 1350. S.Rep. 102–249, pt.(iv)(c)(1991). Actions brought under the Torture Victim Protection Act may only be brought against an individual, not a state. Further, the Act does not allow actions against former leaders "merely because an isolated act of torture occurred somewhere in that country." S. Rep. 102–249, pt.(iv)(E)(1991). Torture is also a criminal offense in the United States under the Torture Convention Implementing Legislation, 18 U.S.C. §§ 2340–2340B (2000). Under this authority, federal courts have jurisdiction for torture committed outside the U.S. so long as the alleged perpetrator is a U.S. national or is in the U.S. 18 U.S.C. § 2340A (2000). Neither the alleged victim nor offender need be citizens of the U.S. for the court to have jurisdiction.

B. International Human Rights Documents and Reports on Domestic Violence

Advocacy efforts concerning women's human rights have had a significant impact on institutional responses. The subject of women's human rights received prominent attention in the Declaration and Programme of Action adopted at the United Nations World Conference on Human Rights in Vienna in 1993. In 1994, the U.N. Commission on Human Rights appointed a Special Rapporteur on Violence Against Women and in 1995, the United Nations sponsored a World Conference on Women in Beijing. Out of that conference came the Beijing Declaration and Platform for Action, and a Beijing + 5 meeting, planned for and held in the year 2000.

The first international document that dealt specifically with gender-based discrimination was a special treaty, the Convention on the Elimination of All Forms of Discrimination Against Women, ("Women's Convention" or CEDAW). The Women's Convention was adopted by the United Nations General Assembly in 1979, and entered into force two years later. In order for a treaty like CEDAW to have effect, States must ratify it. Some States, however, are uncomfortable with ratifying treaties as they stand. In order to both ratify the treaty and assuage their fears, States often make reservations to a treaty. Reservations qualify or negate any provisions in the treaty that the State sees as undesirable. A State will consider a treaty, decide which provisions pose a problem and make reservations to deal with them. The State will then ratify the treaty with those reservations. Reservations are unilateral—only the obligations of the State making the reservation are affected. Other States parties to the same treaty are not affected by another State's reservations. See Vienna Convention on the Law of

Treaties, art. 2(1)(d). CEDAW is notorious for having the most reservations of any human rights treaty.

Despite the fact the President Carter signed CEDAW in 1979, the U.S. Senate has still not ratified the treaty. Efforts to gain Senate ratification in 1980, 1994 and, most recently, in 2000 did not meet with success. The House International Relations Committee held a hearing on CEDAW in May 2000 (in order to introduce a resolution urging the Senate to ratify CEDAW); at this hearing, various representatives emphasized that passing CEDAW was necessary to gain credibility within the international human rights community. Rep. Lynn Woolsey (D–CA) stated that:

> CEDAW is ratified by 165 countries, all of our allies. I'm disappointed that the Senate's inaction puts the U.S. in the company of North Korea, Sudan, Somalia, and Iran. I'm certain, and I know you will agree, that the U.S. does not belong in this company, particularly when it comes to women's rights. The U.S. played a major role in drafting CEDAW, and now we should live up to our commitment and we must ratify it.

International Efforts to End Discrimination Against Women, Hearing before the House International Relations Committee, 106th Cong. (2000)(statement of Rep. Lynn Woolsey).

The State Department has emphasized in its testimony (both in 1994 and in 2000) that CEDAW is well within the bounds of already established U.S. law and that any provisions exceeding these bounds have been contained by the U.S. proposed reservations, understandings and declarations (RUDS). *See, International Efforts to End Discrimination Against Women: Hearing before the House International Relations Committee,* 106th Cong. (2000)(statement of Theresa Loar, Director, President's Interagency Council on Women, Department of State). *See also Convention on the Elimination of All Forms of Discrimination Against Women: Hearing before the Senate Foreign Relations Committee,* 103rd Cong. (1994)(statement of Jamison S. Borek, Deputy Legal Adviser, Department of State). The U.S. has, for example, proposed a reservation which states that ratifying CEDAW will not obligate the U.S. to pass legislation mandating equal pay for women. Also among the RUDS proposed by the U.S. is a non-self executing declaration which would bar the use of CEDAW as an independent cause of action in U.S. federal court. Malvina Halberstam argues that CEDAW "would, in fact, be without any legal effect whatsoever domestically if ratified with the present RUDS." Malvina Halberstam, *United States Ratification of the Convention on the Elimination of All Forms of Discrimination Against Women,* 31 GEO. WASH. J. INT'L L. & ECON. 49, 75 (1997).

The Committee on the Elimination of Discrimination Against Women (CEDAW Committee) is the treaty body that monitors States parties' compliance with the Women's Convention. The Committee's primary means of supervising compliance is through consideration of reports that States parties are required to submit on a periodic basis. Traditionally, the powers and procedures of this Committee have been weak, when compared with other Committees, but in 1999 the U.N. Commission on the Status of

Women adopted an Optional Protocol to CEDAW, which could expand the Committee's supervisory powers if it enters into force.

Article 1 of CEDAW defines discrimination against women as "any distinction, exclusion or restriction made on the basis of sex which has the effect or purpose of impairing or nullifying the recognition, enjoyment or exercise by women, irrespective of their marital status, on a basis of equality of men and women, of human rights and fundamental freedoms in the political, economic, social, cultural, civil or any other field." Article 3 requires States parties to take all appropriate measures "to ensure the full development and advancement of women." Article 5(a) requires States parties "(t)o modify the social and cultural patterns of conduct of men and women, with a view to achieving the elimination of prejudices and customary and all other practices which are based on the inferiority or superiority of either of the sexes or on stereotyped roles for men and women."

Although the text of CEDAW is silent about violence, the Committee has interpreted the Convention to prohibit violence against women. In 1992, the Committee adopted General Recommendations on Violence Against Women, excerpted below.

General Recommendation No. 19: Violence Against Women, CEDAW Committee, U.N. Doc. A/47/38 (1992)

1. Gender-based violence is a form of discrimination that seriously inhibits women's ability to enjoy rights and freedoms on a basis of equality with men.

. . .

4. . . . The full implementation of the Convention require(s) States to take positive measures to eliminate all forms of violence against women.

. . .

6. The Convention in article 1 defines discrimination against women. The definition of discrimination includes gender-based violence, that is, violence that is directed against a woman because she is a woman or that affects women disproportionately. It includes acts that inflict physical, mental or sexual harm or suffering, threats of such acts, coercion and other deprivations of liberty. Gender-based violence may breach specific provisions of the Convention, regardless of whether those provisions expressly mention violence.

7. Gender-based violence, which impairs or nullifies the enjoyment by women of human rights and fundamental freedoms under general international law or under human rights conventions, is discrimination within the meaning of article 1 of the Convention. These rights and freedoms include:

(a) The right to life;

(b) The right not to be subject to torture or to cruel, inhuman or degrading treatment or punishment;

(c) The right to equal protection according to humanitarian norms in time of international or internal armed conflict;

(d) The right to liberty and security of person;

(e) The right to equal protection under the law;

(f) The right to equality in the family;

(g) The right to the highest standard attainable of physical and mental health;

(h) The right to just and favourable conditions of work.

8. The Convention applies to violence perpetrated by public authorities. Such acts of violence may breach that State's obligations under general international human rights law and under other conventions, in addition to breaching this Convention.

9. It is emphasized, however, that discrimination under the Convention is not restricted to action by or on behalf of Governments (see articles 2(e), 2(f) and 5). For example, under article 2(e) the Convention calls on States parties to take all appropriate measures to eliminate discrimination against women by any person, organization or enterprise. Under general international law and specific human rights covenants, States may also be responsible for private acts if they fail to act with due diligence to prevent violations of rights or to investigate and punish acts of violence, and for providing compensation.

. . .

11. Traditional attitudes by which women are regarded as subordinate to men or as having stereotyped roles perpetuate widespread practices involving violence or coercion, such as family violence and abuse, forced marriage, dowry deaths, acid attacks and female circumcision. Such prejudices and practices may justify gender-based violence as a form of protection or control of women. The effect of such violence on the physical and mental integrity of women is to deprive them the equal enjoyment, exercise and knowledge of human rights and fundamental freedoms. While this comment addresses mainly actual or threatened violence, the underlying consequences of these forms of gender-based violence help to maintain women in subordinate roles and contribute to the low level of political participation and to their lower level of education, skills and work opportunities.

. . .

23. Family violence is one of the most insidious forms of violence against women. It is prevalent in all societies. Within family relationships women of all ages are subjected to violence of all kinds, including battering, rape, other forms of sexual assault, mental and other forms of violence, which are perpetuated by traditional attitudes. Lack of economic independence forces many women to stay in violent relationships. The abrogation of their family responsibilities by men can be a form of violence, and coercion. These forms of violence put women's health at risk and impair their ability to participate in family life and public life on a basis of equality.

Specific recommendation

24. In light of these comments, the Committee on the Elimination of Discrimination against Women recommends that:

(a) States parties should take appropriate and effective measures to overcome all forms of gender-based violence, whether by public or private act;

(b) States parties should ensure that laws against family violence and abuse, rape, sexual assault and other gender-based violence give adequate protection to all women, and respect their integrity and dignity. Appropriate protective and support services should be provided for victims. Gender-sensitive training of judicial and law enforcement officers and other public officials is essential for the effective implementation of the Convention;

(c) States parties should encourage the compilation of statistics and research on the extent, causes and effects of violence, and on the effectiveness of measures to prevent and deal with violence;

(d) Effective measures should be taken to ensure that the media respect and promote respect for women;

(e) States parties in their reports should identify the nature and extent of attitudes, customs and practices that perpetuate violence against women and the kinds of violence that result. They should report on the measures that they have undertaken to overcome violence and the effect of those measures;

(f) Effective measures should be taken to overcome these attitudes and practices. States should introduce education and public information programmes to help eliminate prejudices that hinder women's equality;

. . .

(k) States parties should establish or support services for victims of family violence, rape, sexual assault and other forms of gender-based violence, including refuges, specially trained health workers, rehabilitation and counselling;

. . .

(n) States parties in their reports should state the extent of these problems and should indicate the measures that have been taken and their effect;

(o) States parties should ensure that services for victims of violence are accessible to rural women and that where necessary special services are provided to isolated communities;

(p) Measures to protect them from violence should include training and employment opportunities and the monitoring of the employment conditions of domestic workers;

(q) States parties should report on the risks to rural women, the extent and nature of violence and abuse to which they are subject, their need for and access to support and other services and the effectiveness of measures to overcome violence;

(r) Measures that are necessary to overcome family violence should include:

(i) Criminal penalties where necessary and civil remedies in cases of domestic violence;

(ii) Legislation to remove the defence of honour in regard to the assault or murder of a female family member;

(iii) Services to ensure the safety and security of victims of family violence, including refuges, counselling and rehabilitation programmes;

(iv) Rehabilitation programmes for perpetrators of domestic violence;

(v) Support services for families where incest or sexual abuse has occurred;

(s) States parties should report on the extent of domestic violence and sexual abuse, and on the preventive, punitive and remedial measures that have been taken;

(t) States parties should take all legal and other measures that are necessary to provide effective protection of women against gender-based violence, including, inter alia:

(i) Effective legal measures, including penal sanctions, civil remedies and compensatory provisions to protect women against all kinds of violence, including inter alia violence and abuse in the family, sexual assault and sexual harassment in the workplace;

(ii) Preventive measures, including public information and education programmes to change attitudes concerning the roles and status of men and women;

(iii) Protective measures, including refuges, counselling, rehabilitation and support services for women who are the victims of violence or who are at risk of violence;

(u) States parties should report on all forms of gender-based violence, and such reports should include all available data on the incidence of each form of violence and on the effects of such violence on the women who are victims;

(v) The reports of States parties should include information on the legal, preventive and protective measures that have been taken to overcome violence against women, and on the effectiveness of such measures.

* * *

Declaration on the Elimination of Violence Against Women, General Assembly Resolution, U.N.Doc. A/RES/48/104 (1994)

DEVAW

The General Assembly,

Recognizing the urgent need for the universal application to women of the rights and principles with regard to equality, security, liberty, integrity and dignity of all human beings,

Noting that those rights and principles are enshrined in international instruments, including the Universal Declaration of Human Rights, the International Covenant on Civil and Political Rights, the International Covenant on Economic, Social and Cultural Rights, the Convention on the Elimination of All Forms of Discrimination against Woman and the Convention against Torture and Other Cruel, Inhuman or Degrading Treatment or Punishment,

Recognizing that effective implementation of the Convention on the Elimination of All Forms of Discrimination against Women would contribute to the elimination of violence against women and that the Declaration on the Elimination of Violence against Women, set forth in the present resolution, will strengthen and complement that process,

Concerned that violence against women is an obstacle to the achievement of equality, development and peace . . . and to the full implementation of the Convention on the Elimination of All Forms of Discrimination against Women,

Affirming that violence against women constitutes a violation of the rights and fundamental freedoms of women and impairs or nullifies their enjoyment of those rights and freedoms, and concerned about the long-standing failure to protect and promote those rights and freedoms in the case of violence against women,

Recognizing that violence against women is a manifestation of historically unequal power relations between men and women, which have led to domination over and discrimination against women by men and to the prevention of the full advancement of women, and that violence against women is one of the crucial social mechanisms by which women are forced into a subordinate position compared with men,

Concerned that some groups of women, such as women belonging to minority groups, indigenous women, refugee women, migrant women, women living in rural or remote communities, destitute women, women in institutions or in detention, female children, women with disabilities, elderly women and women in situations of armed conflict, are especially vulnerable to violence,

Recalling the conclusion in paragraph 23 of the annex to Economic and Social Council resolution 1990/15 of 24 May 1990 that the recognition that violence against women in the family and society was pervasive and cut across lines of income, class and culture had to be matched by urgent and effective steps to eliminate its incidence,

Recalling also Economic and Social Council resolution 1991/18 of 30 May 1991, in which the Council recommended the development of a framework for an international instrument that would address explicitly the issue of violence against women,

Welcoming the role that women's movements are playing in drawing increasing attention to the nature, severity and magnitude of the problem of violence against women,

Alarmed that opportunities for women to achieve legal, social, political and economic equality in society are limited, inter alia, by continuing and endemic violence,

Convinced that in the light of the above there is a need for a clear and comprehensive definition of violence against women, a clear statement of the rights to be applied to ensure the elimination of violence against women in all its forms, a commitment by States in respect of their responsibilities, and a commitment by the international community at large to the elimination of violence against women,

Solemnly proclaims the following Declaration on the Elimination of Violence against Women and urges that every effort be made so that it becomes generally known and respected:

Article 1

For the purposes of this Declaration, the term "violence against women" means any act of gender-based violence that results in, or is likely to result in, physical, sexual or psychological harm or suffering to women, including threats of such acts, coercion or arbitrary deprivation of liberty, whether occurring in public or in private life.

Article 2

Violence against women shall be understood to encompass, but not be limited to, the following:

(a) Physical, sexual and psychological violence occurring in the family, including battering, sexual abuse of female children in the household, dowry-related violence, marital rape, female genital mutilation and other traditional practices harmful to women, non-spousal violence and violence related to exploitation;

(b) Physical, sexual and psychological violence occurring within the general community, including rape, sexual abuse, sexual harassment and intimidation at work, in educational institutions and elsewhere, trafficking in women and forced prostitution;

(c) Physical, sexual and psychological violence perpetrated or condoned by the State, wherever it occurs.

Article 3

Women are entitled to the equal enjoyment and protection of all human rights and fundamental freedoms in the political, economic, social, cultural, civil or any other field. These rights include, inter alia:

(a) The right to life;

(b) The right to equality;

(c) The right to liberty and security of person;

(d) The right to equal protection under the law;

(e) The right to be free from all forms of discrimination;

(f) The right to the highest standard attainable of physical and mental health;

(g) The right to just and favourable conditions of work;

(h) The right not to be subjected to torture, or other cruel, inhuman or degrading treatment or punishment.

Article 4

States should condemn violence against women and should not invoke any custom, tradition or religious consideration to avoid their obligations with respect to its elimination. States should pursue by all appropriate means and without delay a policy of eliminating violence against women and, to this end, should:

(a) Consider, where they have not yet done so, ratifying or acceding to the Convention on the Elimination of All Forms of Discrimination against Women or withdrawing reservations to that Convention;

(b) Refrain from engaging in violence against women;

(c) Exercise due diligence to prevent, investigate and, in accordance with national legislation, punish acts of violence against women, whether those acts are perpetrated by the State or by private persons;

(d) Develop penal, civil, labour and administrative sanctions in domestic legislation to punish and redress the wrongs caused to women who are subjected to violence; women who are subjected to violence should be provided with access to the mechanisms of justice and, as provided for by national legislation, to just and effective remedies for the harm that they have suffered; States should also inform women of their rights in seeking redress through such mechanisms;

(e) Consider the possibility of developing national plans of action to promote the protection of women against any form of violence, or to include provisions for that purpose in plans already existing, taking into account, as appropriate, such cooperation as can be provided by non-governmental organizations, particularly those concerned with the issue of violence against women;

(f) Develop, in a comprehensive way, preventive approaches and all those measures of a legal, political, administrative and cultural nature that promote the protection of women against any form of violence, and ensure that the re-victimization of women does not occur because of laws insensitive to gender considerations, enforcement practices or other interventions;

(g) Work to ensure, to the maximum extent feasible in the light of their available resources and, where needed, within the framework of international cooperation, that women subjected to violence and, where appropriate, their children have specialized assistance, such as rehabilitation, assistance in child care and maintenance, treatment, counselling, and health and social services, facilities and programmes, as well as support structures, and should take all other appropriate measures to promote their safety and physical and psychological rehabilitation;

(h) Include in government budgets adequate resources for their activities related to the elimination of violence against women;

(i) Take measures to ensure that law enforcement officers and public officials responsible for implementing policies to prevent, investigate and punish violence against women receive training to sensitize them to the needs of women;

(j) Adopt all appropriate measures, especially in the field of education, to modify the social and cultural patterns of conduct of men and women and to eliminate prejudices, customary practices and all other practices based on the idea of the inferiority or superiority of either of the sexes and on stereotyped roles for men and women;

(k) Promote research, collect data and compile statistics, especially concerning domestic violence, relating to the prevalence of different forms of violence against women and encourage research on the causes, nature, seriousness and consequences of violence against women and on the effectiveness of measures implemented to prevent and redress violence against women; those statistics and findings of the research will be made public;

(l) Adopt measures directed towards the elimination of violence against women who are especially vulnerable to violence;

(m) Include, in submitting reports as required under relevant human rights instruments of the United Nations, information pertaining to violence against women and measures taken to implement the present Declaration;

(n) Encourage the development of appropriate guidelines to assist in the implementation of the principles set forth in the present Declaration;

(o) Recognize the important role of the women's movement and non-governmental organizations world wide in raising awareness and alleviating the problem of violence against women;

(p) Facilitate and enhance the work of the women's movement and non-governmental organizations and cooperate with them at local, national and regional levels;

(q) Encourage intergovernmental regional organizations of which they are members to include the elimination of violence against women in their programmes, as appropriate.

Article 5

The organs and specialized agencies of the United Nations system should, within their respective fields of competence, contribute to the recognition and realization of the rights and the principles set forth in the present Declaration and, to this end, should, inter alia:

(a) Foster international and regional cooperation with a view to defining regional strategies for combating violence, exchanging experiences and financing programmes relating to the elimination of violence against women;

(b) Promote meetings and seminars with the aim of creating and raising awareness among all persons of the issue of the elimination of violence against women;

(c) Foster coordination and exchange within the United Nations system between human rights treaty bodies to address the issue of violence against women effectively;

(d) Include in analyses prepared by organizations and bodies of the United Nations system of social trends and problems, such as the periodic reports on the world social situation, examination of trends in violence against women;

(e) Encourage coordination between organizations and bodies of the United Nations system to incorporate the issue of violence against women into ongoing programmes, especially with reference to groups of women particularly vulnerable to violence;

(f) Promote the formulation of guidelines or manuals relating to violence against women, taking into account the measures referred to in the present Declaration;

(g) Consider the issue of the elimination of violence against women, as appropriate, in fulfilling their mandates with respect to the implementation of human rights instruments;

(h) Cooperate with non-governmental organizations in addressing the issue of violence against women.

Article 6

Nothing in the present Declaration shall affect any provision that is more conducive to the elimination of violence against women that may be contained in the legislation of a State or in any international convention, treaty or other instrument in force in a State.

NOTES

1. What is the power of a General Assembly Resolution? Here is an analysis by Oscar Schachter, from his article *United Nations Law*, 88 A.L.I.L. 1, 3–4 (1994):

> The legal arguments that resolutions may be authoritative evidence of binding international law usually rest on characterizing them as (1) "authentic" interpretations of the UN Charter agreed by all the parties, (2) affirmations of recognized customary law, or (3) expressions of general principles of law accepted by states. These reasons fit into the three sources of international law contained in Article 38 of the Statute of the International Court of Justice. The Court itself has recognized the legal force of several UN declarations in some of its advisory opinions. But some caution is called for. Even a UN declaration adopted unanimously will have diminished authority as law if it is not observed by states particularly affected. Negative votes by a few concerned states to a declaratory resolution also cast doubt on its authority as presumptive evidence of existing law. We cannot apply a categorical rule to all cases; distinctions must be drawn that take into account the nature and importance of the legal rule in question. Declarations that affirm the prohibitions against aggression, genocide,

torture or systematic racial discrimination would not be deprived of their legal value because they were not uniformly observed. On the other hand, declarations asserting or affirming legal rules of a less peremptory character would not prevail over evidence that such rules were not generally observed by affected states.

UN recourse to recommendatory authority to declare law is a reflection of the perceived need for more law in many fields. The traditional case-by-case process of customary law cannot meet the necessity for common action to deal with the numerous problems raised by technological developments, demographic and environmental impacts, changing attitudes as to social justice, or the many requirements of international business. While all of these matters could be dealt with by multilateral treaties, the treaty processes are often complicated and slow. In contrast, UN resolutions can be more readily attained. As we have noted, the curious result is that new law is often considered as "custom" or as based on already-recognized general principles. The law-declaring resolutions are not only a response to felt needs; they are also a consequence of the opportunity afforded by voting rules in the UN system. Weaker states, which constitute a majority in UN bodies, use their voting strength for lawmaking to improve their position vis-a-vis the more powerful states. However, these efforts are often limited by the realities of power and politics. It has come to be recognized that resolutions by majorities on economic matters are likely to remain "paper" declarations without much effect unless genuinely accepted by states with the requisite resources to carry them out.

Do you think that the U.N. Declaration on the Elimination of Violence Against Women might, like resolutions on economic matters, remain a "paper" declaration? What might make you think so? Is there an argument to be made that this Declaration is likely to have a greater impact?

2. Only one treaty directly addresses violence against women. In June 1994, the Organization of American States adopted the Inter-American Convention on the Prevention, Punishment and Eradication of Violence Against Women (effective March 1995, with 29 States parties as of March 2000). Like the U.N. Declaration, the preamble recognizes that violence against women is "a manifestation of the historically unequal power relations between women and men." This Convention defines violence more broadly, in Article 2 it encompasses "physical, sexual and psychological violence." Article 3 specifies that a woman's rights are "to be free from violence in both the public and private sphere." Under Article 7, States agree "to pursue, by all appropriate means and without delay, policies to prevent, punish and eradicate such violence."

3. Also in 1994, the U.N. Economic and Social Council endorsed the resolution of the U.N. Human Rights Commission to appoint for a three-year term a Special Rapporteur on violence against women, its causes and consequences. Radhika Coomaraswamy from Sri Lanka was appointed to this post and continues to hold it. The significance of this development is that the Human Rights Commission is the U.N. body with traditional

jurisdiction over human rights issues; the appointment of the Special Rapporteur is therefore an acknowledgment that violence against women falls within that jurisdiction. The Special Rapporteur has the power to engage in field missions, to work with other rapporteurs and working groups, to seek and to receive information from governments, other treaty bodies, specialized agencies of the U.N. and NGO's; and to consult with the CEDAW Committee. Significantly, her reports go beyond the information provided by states themselves pursuant to their obligations under the Women's Convention. Coomaraswamy has submitted annual reports to the Commission since 1994; excerpts from two of these reports follow. The first, from the earliest report, grounds violence against women in a political understanding of women's subordination. The second focuses specifically on domestic violence.

Preliminary Report by the Special Rapporteur on Violence Against Women, Its Causes and Consequences, Ms. Radhika Coomaraswamy, Commission on Human Rights, U.N. Doc. E/CN.4/1995/42 (1994)

49. ... [V]iolence against women is a manifestation of historically unequal power relations between men and women. Violence is part of a historical process and is not natural or born of biological determinism. The system of male dominance has historical roots and its functions and manifestations change over time.... The oppression of women is therefore a question of politics, requiring an analysis of the institutions of the State and society, the conditioning and socialization of individuals, and the nature of economic and social exploitation. The use of force against women is only one aspect of this phenomenon, which relies on intimidation and fear to subordinate women.

50. Women are subject to certain universal forms of abuse.... It is argued that any attempt to universalize women's experience is to conceal other forms of oppression such as those based on race, class or nationality. This reservation must be noted and acknowledged. And yet it must be accepted that there are patterns of patriarchal domination which are universal, though this domination takes a number of different forms as a result of particular and different historical experiences.

. . .

54. The institution of the family is ... an arena where historical power relations are often played out. On the one hand, the family can be the source of positive nurturing and caring values where individuals bond through mutual respect and love. On the other hand, it can be a social institution where labour is exploited, where male sexual power is violently expressed and where a certain type of socialization disempowers women. Female sexual identity is often created by the family environment. The negative images of the self which often inhibit women from realizing their full potential may be linked to familial expectation. The family is, therefore,

the source of positive humane values, yet in some instances it is the site for violence against women and a socialization process which may result in justifying violence against women.

. . .

57. In the context of the historical power relations between men and women, women must also confront the problem that men control the knowledge systems of the world. Whether it be in the field of science, culture, religion or language, men control the accompanying discourse. Women have been excluded from the enterprise of creating symbolic systems or interpreting historical experience. It is this lack of control over knowledge systems which allows them not only to be victims of violence, but to be part of a discourse which often legitimizes or trivializes violence against women. . . .

. . .

64. The ideologies which justify the use of violence against women base their discussion on a particular construction of sexual identity. The construction of masculinity often requires that manhood be equated with the ability to exert power over others, especially through the use of force. Masculinity gives man power to control the lives of those around him, especially women. The construction of femininity in these ideologies often requires women to be passive and submissive, to accept violence as part of a woman's estate. Such ideologies also link a woman's identity and self-esteem to her relationship to her father, husband or son. An independent woman is often denied expression in feminine terms. In addition, standards of beauty, defined by women, often require women to mutilate themselves or damage their health, whether with regard to foot binding, anorexia nervosa and bulimia. It is important to reinvent creatively these categories of masculinity and femininity, devoid of the use of force and ensuring the full development of human potential.

. . .

67. Certain customary practices and some aspects of tradition are often the cause of violence against women. Besides female genital mutilation, a whole host of practices violate female dignity. Foot binding, male preference, early marriage, virginity tests, dowry deaths, sati, female infanticide and malnutrition are among the many practices which violate a woman's human rights. Blind adherence to these practices and State inaction with regard to these customs and traditions have made possible large-scale violence against women. States are enacting new laws and regulations with regard to the development of a modern economy and modern technology and to developing practices which suit a modern democracy, yet it seems that in the area of women's rights change is slow to be accepted.

* * *

Report by the Special Rapporteur on Violence Against Women, Its Causes and Consequences, Ms. Radhika Coomaraswamy, Commission on Human Rights, U.N. Doc. E/CN.4/1999/68/Add.4 (1999)

Introduction

1. The Commission on Human Rights, at its fifty-fourth session, in resolution 1998/52, welcomed the report of the Special Rapporteur on violence against women, its causes and consequences (E/CN.4/1998/54 and Add.1) and commended her for her analysis of violence in the family, violence in the community, and violence as perpetrated and/or condoned by the State.

. . .

I. WORKING METHODS AND ACTIVITIES

3. In an attempt to provide a systematic review of States' compliance with their international obligations with respect to domestic violence, the Special Rapporteur requested Governments to provide her with a written account and copies of the measures taken since 1994, in the context of those which existed prior to that time, to bring State policy and practice into compliance with the recommendations.

4. In particular, the Special Rapporteur sought the following information, first from Governments and subsequently from NGOs:

> "1. National plans of action: Because of the nature of domestic violence, its prevalence, persistence and high incidence throughout the world, States must develop comprehensive strategies to combat domestic violence and provide remedies for victims of domestic violence. The Special Rapporteur seeks information on the strategies that have been adopted to address domestic violence.
>
> "2. Statistics: In order to evaluate the impact of law and policies on the incidence of domestic violence and reporting, up-to-date statistical data should be collected and recorded in a public forum. The Special Rapporteur seeks copies of official statistics compiled by the State in relation to domestic violence.
>
> "3. Training: Training must be instituted for the police, prosecutors, forensic experts and the judiciary in order to combat the traditional insensitivity of the criminal justice system in addressing complaints of domestic violence. The Special Rapporteur seeks information regarding the training programmes that have been instituted to train and sensitize more adequately the various components of the criminal justice system on the issue of domestic violence.
>
> "4. Support services for victims: In addition to criminalizing domestic violence, services must be provided to meet the many needs, including safety, economic, housing, employment and child-care needs, of the

victim. The Special Rapporteur requests information regarding victim support services provided by either the State or NGOs."

. . .

II. FAMILY AND VIOLENCE: DEFINITIONS

6. Defined in both international and national law as the natural and fundamental unit of society, the family has been the focus of very little scrutiny under international law. This is largely a consequence of the traditional division between the public and private spheres and the emphasis in human rights discourse on public sphere violations. Increasingly, however, this is changing. No longer are human rights guarantees restricted solely to the public sphere. They likewise apply to the private realm, including within the family, and oblige the State to act with due diligence to prevent, investigate and punish violations therein.

7. The State, through legal and moral regulation, plays an important role in family life, as well as an important role in determining the status, rights and remedies of individual family actors. Women's traditional familial roles are enshrined in secular and religious laws on, inter alia, sexuality, violence (including marital rape or the lack thereof), privacy, divorce, adultery, property, succession, employment, and child custody. Such laws validate and entrench the dominant ideology of the traditional family and the woman's position within it. Familial ideology is often Janus faced. On the one hand, it offers private space for nurturing and intimacy. On the other hand, it is often the site of violence against women and social constructions of women's role in society that are disempowering.

8. Throughout the world, there exist divisions between the dominant, normative ideal of the family and the empirical realities of family forms. Whether the ideal is the nuclear family or a variation of the joint or extended family, such ideals in many cases are not wholly consistent with the realities of modern family forms. These family forms include, in increasingly large numbers, female-headed households in which women live alone or with their children because of choice (including sexual and employment choices), widowhood, abandonment, displacement or militarization....

9. Despite such differences, however, the culturally-specific, ideologically dominant family form in any given society shapes both the norm and that which is defined as existing outside of the norm and, hence, classified as deviant.... The extent to which such concepts apply to and have an impact upon women's lives is mediated by class, caste, race, ethnicity, access to resources and other ways in which women are marginalized. The dominance of familial ideology both within and outside the walls of the family home entrenches women's roles as wives and mothers and impedes women's access to non-traditional roles. Such ideology exposes women to violence both within and outside the home by enforcing women's dependent status, particularly among poor and working class women, and by exposing those women who do not fit within or ascribe to traditional sex roles to gender-based hate crimes.

10. It is important to understand that feminist critiques of the oppressive and violent aspects of traditional family forms are neither "anti-family" nor an attempt to destroy the family. Increasingly women's human rights defenders are coming under attack for, among other things, challenging traditional notions of the family. Public denouncements, accusations, harassment and physical violence are increasingly employed against women's human rights defenders. Commentators argue that in order to ensure that women's human rights are protected in both public and private life, the acceptance of non-traditional family forms is necessary. It is essential to recognize the potential for and work to prevent violence against women and the oppression of women within all family forms.

. . .

16. ... The Special Rapporteur has adopted an expansive definition of violence in the family to include "violence perpetrated in the domestic sphere which targets women because of their role within that sphere or as violence which is intended to impact, directly and negatively, on women within the domestic sphere. Such violence may be carried out by both private and public actors and agents. This conceptual framework intentionally departs from traditional definitions of domestic violence, which address violence perpetrated by intimates against intimates, or equates domestic violence with woman-battering"....

17. Violence within the family comprises, inter alia, woman-battering, marital rape, incest, forced prostitution, violence against domestic workers, violence against girls, sex-selective abortions and female infanticide, traditional violent practices against women including forced marriage, son preference, female genital mutilation and honour crimes.

18. Honour crimes were not addressed in the Special Rapporteur's earlier report. Since then numerous communications have been sent to her concerning such crimes against women, whereby the family kills a female relative deemed to have defiled the honour of the family. Reportedly, honour crimes are legal in Lebanon. Honour is defined in terms of women's assigned sexual and familial roles as dictated by traditional family ideology. Thus, adultery, premarital relationships (which may or may not include sexual relations), rape and falling in love with an "inappropriate" person may constitute violations of family honour. In many cases, as in cases reported to the Special Rapporteur from Turkey, the male members of the family meet to decide on the execution of the woman. Once this has been decided, the family will often give the woman the opportunity to commit suicide. If she refuses to kill herself, one of the male family members will be forced to kill her. Adolescent boys are often compelled to commit the murder because they will receive a light sentence. The Special Rapporteur is gravely concerned about the practice of honour killing and is seeking additional information about such violence and measures that are being undertaken to combat it.

III. AN EVOLVING LEGAL FRAMEWORK

. . .

22. Violence against women in the family raises the jurisprudential issue of State responsibility for private, non-State actors. In her previous report on violence in the family the Special Rapporteur outlined three doctrines put forward by scholars and experts in international law in attempting to deal with this issue of violence against women by private actors. The first, taken from the international law doctrine of State responsibility, was that States have a due diligence duty to prevent, investigate and punish international law violations and pay just compensation. The second doctrine is related to the question of equality and equal protection. If it can be shown that law enforcement discriminates against the victims in cases involving violence against women, then States may be held liable for violating international human rights standards of equality. Finally, scholars have also argued that domestic violence is a form of torture and should be dealt with accordingly.

23. The principle of "due diligence" is gaining international recognition. In accordance with article 4 of the Declaration on the Elimination of Violence against Women, States must "exercise due diligence to prevent, investigate and, in accordance with national legislation, punish acts of violence against women, whether those acts are perpetrated by the State or by private persons." General Recommendation 19 of CEDAW states that "under general international law and specific human rights covenants, States may also be responsible for private acts if they fail to act with due diligence to prevent violations of rights, or to investigate and punish acts of violence, and for providing compensation."

24. The due diligence standard of State responsibility for private actors was discussed in detail by the Inter–American Court of Human Rights in the judgement of the Velasquez–Rodriguez case handed down on 29 July 1988. In that case, the Government of Honduras was held responsible for violating human rights in the case of disappearances. The Court found that:

> An illegal act which violates human rights and which is initially not directly imputable to the State (for example, because it is the act of a private person or because the person responsible has not been identified) can lead to international responsibility of the State, not because of the act itself but because of the lack of due diligence to prevent the violation or to respond to it as required by the Convention.

Further, the Court held that:

> The State has a legal duty to take reasonable steps to prevent human rights violations and to use the means at its disposal to carry out a serious investigation of violations committed within its jurisdiction, to identify those responsible, to impose the appropriate punishment and to ensure the victim adequate compensation. This obligation implies the duty of State parties to organize the governmental apparatus and, in general, all the structures through which public power is exercised, so that they are capable of juridically ensuring the free and full enjoyment of human rights.

25. On her field visits concerning violence against women by private actors, the Special Rapporteur has attempted to assess State adherence to the due diligence standard. In so doing, she has relied upon the Declaration on the Elimination of Violence against Women and upon General Recommendation 19 of CEDAW and has considered information provided in response to the following questions:

(i) Has the State Party ratified all the international human rights instruments including the Convention on the Elimination of All Forms of Discrimination against Women?

(ii) Is there constitutional authority guaranteeing equality for women or the prohibition of violence against women?

(iii) Is there national legislation and/or administrative sanctions providing adequate redress for women victims of violence?

(iv) Are there executive policies or plans of action that attempt to deal with the question of violence against women?

(v) Is the criminal justice system sensitive to the issues of violence against women? In this regard, what is police practice? How many cases are investigated by the police? How are victims dealt with by the police? How many cases are prosecuted? What type of judgements are given in such cases? Are the health professionals who assist the prosecution sensitive to issues of violence against women?

(vi) Do women who are victims of violence have support services such as shelters, legal and psychological counselling, specialized assistance and rehabilitation provided either by the Government or by non-governmental organizations?

(vii) Have appropriate measures been taken in the field of education and the media to raise awareness of violence against women as a human rights violation and to modify practices that discriminate against women?

(viii) Are data and statistics being collected in a manner that ensures that the problem of violence against women is not invisible?

26. In 1998 the first case raising the issue of domestic violence as a violation of human rights was brought before an international tribunal, the Inter-American Commission on Human Rights. According to the arguments made in the Pamela Ramjattan case, the Government of Trinidad and Tobago breached Ms. Ramjattan's rights when it convicted her of murder and sentenced her to death after failing to consider mitigating factors specific to Ms. Ramjattan's experience as a battered woman. Ms. Ramjattan testified at her trial and has subsequently given sworn evidence that she was subjected to severe forms of domestic violence throughout her eight year common-law marriage. Reportedly, the police, legal aid lawyers, prison authorities, the courts and the Government of Trinidad and Tobago failed to consider the violent abuse which Ms. Ramjattan and her children were subjected to, and the effect of the abuse on her state of mind and her actions.

27. Under the Declaration, Recommendation 19 of CEDAW (Trinidad and Tobago ratified the Convention on the Elimination of All Forms of Discrimination against Women in 1990), the American Convention on Human Rights and the Inter–American Convention on the Prevention, Punishment and Eradication of Violence against Women, Ms. Ramjattan's right to life, fair trial, equal protection of the law and non-discrimination on the grounds of sex were reportedly violated. Although the Commission has not yet reached a conclusion in the case, the fact that it has been brought before the Commission is, in itself, an important step in the international movement to guarantee women's human rights. The Special Rapporteur remains concerned about Ms. Ramjattan and is watching the case with interest.

IV. Findings

A. General trends

28. In the Spring of 1998, the Special Rapporteur sent a note verbale to Governments, requesting them to provide her with information about initiatives taken with regard to violence against women in the family. Subsequently, she sought the same information from non-governmental sources. In both governmental and non-governmental responses, there were common trends, positive and negative. Overwhelmingly, Governments presented a picture which suggested that they are taking steps, as small as they may sometimes be, to address violence in the family. Governments have begun to acknowledge that violence against women in the family is a serious social issue that should be confronted. Formal provisions and policies have been adopted in many States.

29. The Special Rapporteur would like to highlight the encouraging trend in Latin America and the Caribbean to adopt specific legislation on domestic or intra-family violence. Thus far in the 1990s, 12 Latin American and Caribbean countries have adopted such legislation. The Special Rapporteur welcomes these initiatives and encourages Governments to ensure effective implementation.

30. Generally, as testified to in non-governmental submissions from all regions, however, there is a lack of coordination between the State and civil society in working towards the effective implementation of formal provisions and policies. While some States make an active attempt to consult and include civil society representatives in the process of developing and implementing laws and policies, others have maintained a distant and, at times, antagonistic relationship with NGOs. Overwhelmingly, Governments lack the necessary expertise to develop and implement policy relating to violence against women. Government actors generally, and those within the criminal justice system in particular, continue to subscribe to outdated myths about the role of women in society and the family, and about causes of violence in the family. Systematic training and gender awareness programmes are essential if policies are to be implemented by the criminal justice system.

31. Many States continue to make the erroneous link between alcohol and violence. While alcohol does in many cases exacerbate violence, alcohol

does not itself cause violence against women. The focus on alcohol or drugs, rather than on male patriarchal ideology, which has as its ultimate expression male violence against women, undermines the anti-violence movement....

32. Increasingly, States are using cultural relativist claims to avoid responsibility for positive, anti-violence action. The recognition of heterogeneous or multicultural communities is not at odds with developing comprehensive and multifaceted strategies to combat domestic violence. In all communities, the root causes of domestic violence are similar, even when the justifications for such violence or the forms of such violence vary.

33. Many Governments continue to classify women, children, the elderly, the disabled or any combination of these together as one social group. This arises from the paternal nature of the State, which seeks to protect "vulnerable" groups. While distinct measures must be developed to combat violence against women and provide remedies and support to victim-survivors, the emphasis must be on empowerment rather than care—on social justice rather than social welfare. Women must be treated, in fact and in law, as full citizens, endowed with rights and reason.

34. There is a continuing emphasis on mediation and counselling by police or mediation boards in cases of violence in the family. Police efforts to counsel victims in such cases, which often includes mediation between victim and perpetrator, may serve to undermine the seriousness of crimes of violence against women and, in many instances, may heighten the risk for the victim.

* * *

NOTES

1. The activities of women's rights activists have often been criticized as inappropriate applications of Western values to other cultures or even worse, cultural imperialism. Activists themselves are acutely aware of this tension and have long debated how to balance the feminist valuation of difference with efforts to advance women's rights internationally. Tracy Higgins, *Anti–Essentialism, Relativism, and Human Rights*, 19 HARV. WOMEN'S L.J. 89, 90 (1996). At the same time, they have made the argument that cultural justifications are used selectively to preserve State power and further argue that culture is not the monolithic, static force that States might claim. Id. at 111. Notice that Paragraph 50 of Coomaraswamy's 1994 report makes an effort to address the tension between the universalist nature of women's rights and cultural relativism. Coomaraswamy addresses this issue even more explicitly in Paragraph 32 of her 1999 report, which you have just read.

2. Despite the increasing recognition of women's human rights claims, and the increase in "official" monitoring of violence against women around the world by a variety of international agencies, there has been widespread criticism of the lack of concrete results of women's human rights advocacy. The U.N. Commission on the Status of Women has recommended that a

Special Session be convened in June 2000 "to Review and Appraise the Achievements of the U.N. Decade for Women and of the Beijing Platform of Action from the Fourth World Conference on Women in 1995," in order to focus on the need for more U.N. resources, and for the reallocation of existing resources to women's rights. In her 1999 report, Coomaraswamy criticized governments for "lack of strategies of implementation on commitments to eradicate violence." Although she observed that many countries have "acknowledged domestic violence as an important human rights issue," she concluded that states have "overwhelmingly" failed in their international obligations to prevent, investigate, and prosecute domestic abuse. Hilary Charlesworth, a leading feminist legal scholar on women's international human rights, concurs, concluding that "the human rights system appears to have learned that the art of politically correct rhetoric is an effective tool in silencing potential critics. It finds it very hard, however, to institute significant change."

3. In the face of recalcitrance on the part of state governments, the role of NGOs, who may be less inhibited in their denunciation of violence and state participation in violence, remains a crucial one. In 1991 the Women's Rights Project of Human Rights Watch joined with Americas Watch to send a delegation to Brazil, to assess the government's response to domestic violence. The subsequent report was the first issued by an international human rights organization to analyze systematic non-prosecution of domestic violence crimes by the state as a violation of equal protection under human rights law. Dorothy Thomas and Michele Beasley describe the report's findings as follows:

> Information indicates that wife-murder is a common crime in Brazil, and reveals a pattern of impunity or undue mitigation of sentence in homicides where the victim is a woman. In cases of spousal murder, men are able to obtain an acquittal based on the theory that the killing was justified to defend the man's "honor" after the wife's alleged adultery. The reverse is rarely true. The honor defense is rooted in proprietary attitudes towards women; many Brazilians believe that any action by a woman has the potential to so mortally offend her husband that he is within his rights to execute her, in what is interpreted by the courts as an act of self-defense. And, in general, a defendant will not be held accountable for a homicide if, among other things, it was committed in legitimate self-defense.
>
> . . .
>
> Even when the honor defense is not invoked, ample evidence indicates that Brazilian courts treat defendants in wife-murder cases more leniently than others tried for murder, largely through misuse of a "violent emotion" defence which allows sentence mitigation. In wife-murder cases, Brazilian courts ignored evidence of premeditation and intent to kill, and focused instead on the behavior of the victim. The same was not true where a wife murdered her husband. Evidence also indicated that men who murdered their wives were often arraigned on reduced charges, although information about this problem was scarce. Even when the murderer is not exculpated, the notion that the victim

"provoked" the murder frequently results in unduly short prison terms for wife-murderers, irrespective of the degree of premeditation involved. In cases where wife-murderers are prosecuted their crime is often reclassified as a less serious charge, and defendants, who are usually first-time offenders, receive preferential treatment from the courts despite the extreme gravity of their crimes.

Like spousal murder, punishment of domestic abuse of women that falls short of death is also the exception rather than the rule in Brazil. Brazil's 1988 census, the first to collect data by gender on incidents of physical abuse, found that between October 1987 and September 1988, over 1.1 million people declared that they had been victims of physical abuse. Of that number, forty percent were women and the violence they experienced was markedly different from that suffered by men. Available statistics show that over seventy percent of all reported incidents of violence against women in Brazil take place in the home, versus ten percent for men.

Despite the prevalence of violence in the home, police rarely investigated such crimes prior to 1985. Studies from 1981 and 1983 show that "when [women] tried to report aggressions" to the police, the police often turned them away on the grounds that domestic violence was "a private problem." When the police did register domestic abuse crimes they frequently failed to follow standard procedures, leaving out pertinent information about the circumstances of the abuse or subjecting the victim to abusive treatment aimed at implicating her in the crime. These biased police attitudes greatly deterred women from seeking the government's protection.

Some positive steps were taken to address the issue in 1985. After a nationwide campaign by the women's rights movement, the government instituted women's police stations—delegacias—to deal exclusively with crimes of violence against women. Reports of violence against women immediately increased and police treatment of female victims markedly improved. However, although the delegacias have been successful in raising social consciousness of domestic abuse as a crime they have been less successful in changing institutional attitudes necessary to criminalize the abuse, even in police stations run by women.

The work of the delegacias is further inhibited by the fact that abuse of women, even if investigated, is rarely prosecuted. The chief of the women's police station in Rio de Janeiro stated that of the more than 2,000 battery cases she investigated in 1990, none resulted in punishment of the accused. In the main delegacia in So Luis, Maranho, of over 4,000 battery complaints registered by women from 1988 to 1990, only 300 were forwarded for processing by the court and only two men were convicted and sent to prison. These figures indicate the persistent failure by the judiciary to see violence against women in the home as a crime, rather than as a mere "domestic dispute" in which the government should not interfere.

Dorothy Q. Thomas and Michele E. Beasley, *Domestic Violence As a Human Rights Issue,* 58 ALBANY L. REV. 1119, 1135–38 (1995).

In the words of these authors, the Brazil report mobilized the "persuasive force of public embarrassment" to direct attention to the problem of domestic violence as a human rights issue and promote the enforcement of human rights guarantees. As the following excerpt from a more recent report demonstrates, Human Rights Watch continues to play that role.

Human Rights Watch
Women's Human Rights, World Report 2000

... Domestic violence remained a critical issue for women worldwide. The World Health Organization asserted that violence against women causes more death and disability among women aged fifteen to forty-four than cancer, malaria, traffic accidents, and war. In particular, sexual violence, including marital rape, was denounced as a major cause of the rapid spread of HIV/AIDS among women. In Kenya, for example, the U.N. estimated that 42 percent of women were battered by husbands or partners. Kenyan laws do not specifically criminalize domestic violence, and offenders were seldom punished. In Pakistan, estimates of spousal abuse ranged as high as 90 percent of all married women. Despite occasional signs of progress—Egypt this year repealed a law allowing rapists to go free if they married their victims, and Peru passed legislation requiring prosecutors to pursue rape cases—everyday violence and discrimination against women remained among the most flagrant and overlooked of human rights abuses.

Where women organized against such injustice, they often did so under threat. In Pakistan, government officials denounced women's rights organizations as purveyors of immorality as part of a broad attack on nongovernmental organizations. In Egypt, the government used a new law regulating NGOs to halt the creation of the Egyptian Women's Union and denied that working on women's issues was a legitimate pursuit.

... Our investigations and monitoring throughout the year showed that violence and discrimination against women as committed and tolerated by states remained the norm in the countries in which we worked. Reports from activists and press in other countries confirmed the pattern of abuse of women's rights and underscored the need for urgent attention to the problem.

. . .

In 1999, Human Rights Watch continued to investigate the state response to sexual assault and domestic violence against women in Peru, Russia, South Africa, and Pakistan. We also monitored the state response to "honor killings" in Jordan and to the sexual abuse of female prisoners in the United States. Despite some positive efforts by state and non-state actors, abuses against women were carried out frequently and with virtual impunity, as states largely failed to fulfill their obligations to prevent and provide redress for such crimes. States were particularly negligent in addressing violence in the family. This problem received widespread international attention in recent years, but concrete action was slow in coming.

Japan, for example, only began to consider specific legislation and support services to combat domestic violence in mid–1999. There were also disturbing indications that such violence was increasing. UNICEF reported in 1999 that violence against women was rising in post-communist countries as economic crises increased women's financial dependence upon men. In many of these states, domestic violence was not prohibited by law and marital rape was not recognized as a crime. Speaking on a more global level, in her 1999 report to the U.N. Commission on Human Rights, the special rapporteur on violence against women noted the "growing prevalence of violence against women generally and domestic violence specifically," and concluded that "[o]verwhelmingly, States are failing in their international obligations to prevent, investigate and prosecute violence against women in the family."

... In Russia, where women continued to be subject to domestic violence, attempts to pass national legislation on the topic failed, and little was done to improve the state response to the abuse. The federal government did not make financial resources available for combating violence against women. Activists, expressing frustration with the lack of progress nationally, focused their attention on local level initiatives, establishing cooperative links with local law enforcement, city officials, and journalists. The number of nongovernmental crisis centers grew across the country, while the few existing government-sponsored centers and shelters closed due to budget cuts. Crisis center leaders traveled throughout Russia, training judges, police, and activists on rape and domestic violence issues. The Russian Association of Crisis Centers for Women officially registered in 1999 and held a national meeting in September to coordinate its activities. But according to crisis center workers, despite educational campaigns and continuing advocacy, police still failed to report cases of rape and domestic violence, and few such cases made it to court.

As South Africa celebrated its fifth year of democratic rule, it continued to face staggering levels of domestic and sexual violence against women. In a 1999 study by the South African Medical Council, 25 percent of the women interviewed in three rural provinces had been assaulted by an intimate partner. Victims of rape and domestic violence confronted significant obstacles to legal redress. Even at a handful of new one-stop rape crisis centers, women were often unable to receive adequate examinations by forensic doctors, whose reports were needed for a legal case. These doctors were criticized—by NGOs and the head of forensic medicine at a leading South African medical school—for being poorly trained and often biased against rape victims. Proposals for reform of the forensic medical service moved forward only slowly. On National Women's Day, President Mbeki tied judgment of the country's progress toward total liberation to advancement in combating violence against women. Still, to the dismay of women's groups, South Africa's ground-breaking 1998 Domestic Violence Act languished, its implementation delayed, according to the government, by the cost of drafting regulations and training personnel to implement the legislation in the courts. At this writing, the government was still using a flawed 1993 domestic violence law.

In Pakistan, it was estimated that eight women were raped every twenty-four hours and 70 to 95 percent of women had experienced domestic or familial violence. Extreme forms of familial violence included so-called honor killings and bride burnings, with both practices claiming the lives of hundreds of women every year. In April 1999, Samia Sarwar was gunned down in a much publicized honor killing at the behest of her parents for seeking a divorce. Other women were attacked, by or at the instigation of family members, for choosing their spouses. The government appeared uninterested in combating impunity for these acts. Women victims of violence who turned to the criminal justice system confronted a discriminatory legal regime, venal and abusive police, untrained doctors, incompetent prosecutors, and skeptical judges. As a result, few women reported crimes of violence, and fewer still saw their attackers punished. In the case of Sarwar's murder, a police report was registered, but as of October 1999 her killers remained free despite exceptionally strong and credible evidence against them. In August 1999, Pakistan's Senate refused even to consider a resolution sparked by Sarwar's murder condemning the practice of honor killing, sending a clear message of government acquiescence in the climate of impunity surrounding acts of violence against women.

Honor killings continued to plague women in Jordan, too, where seventeen women were killed in the name of "family honor" from January to mid-October 1999. According to Jordanian government statistics, since 1994 there were on average between twenty-five and thirty honor killings annually, constituting approximately one third of the country's homicides. Articles 340 and 98 of the Jordanian Penal Code exempted or reduced the punishment for murder when a woman was killed in the name of honor, and this legal bias was compounded by inadequate investigations and lenient sentences. In July 1999 a Ministry of Justice committee recommended to the Cabinet elimination of article 340 of the Penal Code, and in September 1999 the Cabinet approved the proposed amendment from the Ministry of Justice sending the proposal to Parliament for review. In addition official sources indicated that article 98 would be amended to eliminate the exemption from prosecution it offered to males who killed in the name of family honor.

While activists welcomed these legal reforms, they continued to organize to demand greater and more immediate accountability for these crimes. For example, in August 1999 Jordanian activists launched a national campaign in which they gathered over 8,000 signatures to call for the government to abolish laws protecting men who kill female family members in the name of honor. Activists also called for the government to adopt better means of protecting women from honor crimes. Official efforts to protect women threatened by their families consisted of placing them into the protective custody of prisons or other corrections facilities. Official statistics indicated that fifty to sixty women were placed in administrative detention each year for periods ranging from a few months to over three years. Treated as minors, these women were prohibited from leaving the facility. In 1998, the government established a family protection unit within the Public Security Directorate to handle crimes committed within the family, including crimes of honor. But more than one year later it operated only one office and remained largely unknown to the public.

* * *

NOTES

1. The report was also critical of the United States, but with respect to custodial sexual misconduct in state and federal prisons, not with respect to its response to domestic violence.

2. As with the VAWA civil rights remedy examined in the last chapter, the international human rights perspective presented here links violence explicitly with issues of gender discrimination and women's equality. Within this framework, violence against women is inextricably linked with issues of reproductive choice and sexual equality, workplace discrimination, wage equity, child care and health care. Some have argued that in the aftermath of *Morrison*, domestic violence advocates in the United States need "to bring Beijing home," in the words of Rhonda Copelon, and work harder to promote an understanding of domestic violence as just one among many practices that enforce women's continuing subordination in American society. The next materials explore these links between the work of international and national activists and scholars.

C. Linking the International to the Domestic

Elizabeth M. Schneider
Battered Women and Feminist Lawmaking, 53–56 (2000)

International human rights work on gender violence provides an example of rights claims as grand theory. Compared with the history of women's rights struggles in the United States and around the world, the development of feminist approaches to international human rights is a recent phenomenon, but women's international human rights work has enriched and internationalized feminist legal theory, discourse, and law reform. Women's international human rights work challenges our more conventional understandings of women's rights and provides new opportunities for feminist legal work generally, and particularly on woman abuse. Most important, this work demonstrates the liberatory possibilities of rights claims.

. . .

... First, feminist challenge to the dichotomy of public and private is expanded by experiences of globalization. There is an extraordinary proliferation of all sorts of non-state groupings, subnational groupings based on regional and ethnic identity, as well as international regulatory agencies. This requires us to understand much more about the interrelationship between public and private. In international human rights work we are also examining broader notions of state responsibility and complicity. This important theoretical development has consequences for international law, for feminist law reform, and for legal theory.

Second, this work highlights the indivisibility of violence, reproductive choice and sexual equality, workplace conditions, wage equity, child care and health care, and economic and social rights. Over the past several years I have done legal work in South Africa assisting lawyers and judges with the development of the new South African Constitution and training lawyers, judges, and advocates in issues of violence against women. The struggle to have social and economic rights included in their Constitution was extraordinary; in the end, these rights, not just civil and political rights, were explicitly incorporated into the South African Constitution. The particular situation of women's rights within the framework of international human rights and globalization underscores the need for economic and social rights to be integrated into this broader perspective. Economic and social rights guarantees are an important antidote to the problems of both women's international human rights and globalization.

Globalization also presents concrete opportunities for connection. The internationalization of this work has already had a considerable political and psychological impact. The concept of an international "non-governmental organization" did not exist twenty-five years ago. Globalization and internationalization, then, provide an extraordinary opportunity for change.

Technology underscores this opportunity. The Internet has made information about faraway places accessible. In preparation for a workshop on domestic violence that I was to conduct in South Africa, for example, I was able to obtain activist materials from South Africa through an online organization, Women's Net, that linked women's organizations throughout the world. It collected documents, programs for action, and lists of organizations, and it provided extraordinary access to information. The new possibilities of internationalism that flow from this technology cannot be minimized.

The concept of universal human rights also enriches simple domestic understandings of rights. In South Africa I participated in a workshop assisting local activists to document cases of woman abuse as international human rights violations. One of the things we talked about was what difference it made to women who were already doing activist work on violence against women within South Africa under South African law to perceive these issues within a framework of international human rights. For these women, the concept of universalization was implicit in the notion of international human rights and connected their experience in South Africa with struggles of women around the world. The concept of international human rights took what was previously understood as trivial and invisible and gave it larger meaning; it transformed simple domestic rights claims into "human rights" claims and "international" claims. Power and organizing potential are inherent in experiencing oneself as linked to what Aihwa Ong has called a "strategic sisterhood of women activists around the globe."

This international work also has transformed potential for activist work within North America. Legal treatment of pregnant workers in the *maquiladora,* U.S. manufacturing export zones in northern Mexico, has received considerable international human rights attention. In the United States, exclusion of pregnant women from workplaces because of reproductive hazards is not new. Pregnancy exclusion and even forced sterilization policies have been widespread. Many years ago I was involved with litigation challenging the sterilization policy at the American Cyanamid plant in West Virginia, and despite the Supreme Court's subsequent decision in *Johnson Controls,* U.S. workplaces continue to have exclusionary policies respecting reproduction. What difference does it make to have these issues raised in a global context? In the United States we have not had large protests or activist efforts concerning reproductive hazards in the workplace for many years, so global pressure could make a big difference. Another example is international human rights concern about the use of the "honor" defense in Muslim countries to punish, control, and kill women who have been adulterous or promiscuous. Yet in the United States, the analogous "defense" has a long history; only a few years ago it was the basis for a Maryland judge's expression of empathy for a man who had killed his wife after finding her in bed with another man. If part of what happens as a result of the internationalization of global problems is a renewed attention to these issues both domestically *and* around the world, so much the better.

These understandings of a new "publicness," of a new internationalism, of perspectives on woman abuse that cross borders, are important. Through lawmaking on international human rights we have broadened our vision, deepened our understanding of the links between gender and violence, and reshaped feminist analysis. This work has given us a sense of new and renewed possibilities for activism. Ideally, these efforts can strengthen both our international work and our understanding of the inextricable link between violence and equality in the United States.

* * *

NOTES

1. One example of the way in which international human rights advocacy on violence can enrich domestic efforts and assist in struggles against violence in the United States is the amicus curiae brief filed by International Law Scholars and Human Rights Experts in the *Morrison* case discussed in the previous chapter. This brief argued that Congress had the authority to enact legislation such as the Civil Rights remedy of the Violence Against Women Act to meet both international treaty obligations and customary law obligations. In particular, the brief argued that U.S. ratification of the International Covenant on Civil and Political Rights (ICCPR) and other treaties meant that the U.S. was required to provide protection from gender-based violence from both private person and public officials. For other examples of the ways in which international human rights argumentation can assist in U.S. domestic struggles see Martin A. Geer, *Human*

Rights and Wrongs In Our Own Backyard: Incorporating International Human Rights Protections Under Domestic Civil Rights Law—A Case Study of Women in United States Prisons, 13 HARV. HUM. RTS. J. 71 (2000).

2. International human rights meetings organized by groups such as the Global Human Rights Program at Rutgers University have resulted in the generation and sharing of strategies to support advocacy in the United States. Going one step further, the Women's Rights Network in Boston was specifically founded to provide international resources to U.S. domestic violence advocates. See Carrie Cuthbert and Kim Slote, *Bridging the Gap Between Battered Women's Advocates in the US and Abroad,* 6 TEX. J. WMN & L. 287 (1997).

D. ASYLUM

Finally we turn to the related question of asylum. If a woman from outside the United States claims that she has been beaten, and that her country has failed to protect her, can she claim refugee status in this country? Women's rights activists have criticized a June 11, 1999 decision by the United States Board of Immigration Appeals (BIA), In Re R–A–, which denied asylum to a domestic violence victim from Guatemala. The Guatemalan woman sought asylum to escape brutal spousal violence from which she claimed the Guatemalan government had failed to protect her. The BIA overturned a grant of asylum on the grounds that, despite her undisputed suffering, she did not meet the legal standards for refugee status and establish that she was persecuted on account of her membership in a social group or her political opinion.

In reaching its decision, the BIA refused to recognize a social group based on gender, relationship to an abusive partner, and the asylum seeker's opposition to domestic violence. The BIA also failed to credit her claim that her husband's abuse was at least in part in response to her political opinion that her husband had no right to beat her—reversing the immigration judge's finding that her husband's violence had escalated in response to her resistance and futile attempts to seek official aid.

In Re R–A–, Respondent
Interim Decision 3403
Board of Immigration Appeals, 1999

Opinion:

In a decision dated September 20, 1996, an Immigration Judge granted the respondent's application for asylum under section 208(a) of the Immigration and Nationality Act, 8 U.S.C. § 1158(a) (1994). The Immigration and Naturalization Service has timely appealed the grant of asylum. The Service's request for oral argument before the Board has been withdrawn. The appeal will be sustained.

I. ISSUES

The question before us is whether the respondent qualifies as a "refugee" as a result of the heinous abuse she suffered and still fears from her husband in Guatemala. Specifically, we address whether the repeated spouse abuse inflicted on the respondent makes her eligible for asylum as an alien who has been persecuted on account of her membership in a particular social group or her political opinion. We find that the group identified by the Immigration Judge has not adequately been shown to be a "particular social group" for asylum purposes. We further find that the respondent has failed to show that her husband was motivated to harm her, even in part, because of her membership in a particular social group or because of an actual or imputed political opinion. Our review is de novo with regard to the issues on appeal. . . .

II. FACTUAL BACKGROUND

A. *Testimony and Statements of Abuse*

The respondent is a native and citizen of Guatemala. She married at age 16. Her husband was then 21 years old. He currently resides in Guatemala, as do their two children. Immediately after their marriage, the respondent and her husband moved to Guatemala City. From the beginning of the marriage, her husband engaged in acts of physical and sexual abuse against the respondent. He was domineering and violent. The respondent testified that her husband "always mistreated me from the moment we were married, he was always . . . aggressive."

Her husband would insist that the respondent accompany him wherever he went, except when he was working. He escorted the respondent to her workplace, and he would often wait to direct her home. To scare her, he would tell the respondent stories of having killed babies and the elderly while he served in the army. Oftentimes, he would take the respondent to cantinas where he would become inebriated. When the respondent would complain about his drinking, her husband would yell at her. On one occasion, he grasped her hand to the point of pain and continued to drink until he passed out. When she left a cantina before him, he would strike her. As their marriage proceeded, the level and frequency of his rage increased concomitantly with the seeming senselessness and irrationality of his motives. He dislocated the respondent's jaw bone when her menstrual period was 15 days late. When she refused to abort her 3- to 4-month-old fetus, he kicked her violently in her spine. He would hit or kick the respondent "whenever he felt like it, wherever he happened to be: in the house, on the street, on the bus." The respondent stated that "as time went on, he hit me for no reason at all."

The respondent's husband raped her repeatedly. He would beat her before and during the unwanted sex. When the respondent resisted, he would accuse her of seeing other men and threaten her with death. The rapes occurred "almost daily," and they caused her severe pain. He passed on a sexually transmitted disease to the respondent from his sexual relations outside their marriage. Once, he kicked the respondent in her genitalia, apparently for no reason, causing the respondent to bleed severely for 8 days. The respondent suffered the most severe pain when he forcefully sodomized her. When she protested, he responded, as he often did, "You're my woman, you do what I say."

The respondent ran away to her brother's and parents' homes, but her husband always found her. Around December 1994, the respondent attempted to flee with her children outside the city, but her husband found her again. He appeared at her door, drunk, and as she turned to leave, he struck her in the back of her head causing her to lose consciousness. When she awoke, he kicked her and dragged her by her hair into another room and beat her to unconsciousness.

After 2 months away, her husband pleaded for the respondent's return, and she agreed because her children were asking for him. One night, he woke the respondent, struck her face, whipped her with an electrical cord, pulled out a machete and threatened to deface her, to cut off her arms and legs, and to leave her in a wheelchair if she ever tried to leave him. He warned her that he would be able to find her wherever she was. The violence continued. When the respondent could not give 5,000 quetzales to him when he asked for it, he broke windows and a mirror with her head. Whenever he could not find something, he would grab her head and strike furniture with it. Once, he pistol-whipped her. When she asked for his motivation, he broke into a familiar refrain, "I can do it if I want to."

Once, her husband entered the kitchen where the respondent was and, for no apparent reason, threw a machete toward her hands, barely missing them. He would often come home late and drunk. When the respondent noted his tardiness, he punched her. Once, he asked where the respondent had been. When she responded that she had been home waiting for him, he became enraged, struck her face, grabbed her by her hair, and dragged her down the street. One night, the respondent attempted to commit suicide. Her husband told her, "If you want to die, go ahead. But from here, you are not going to leave."

When asked on cross-examination, the respondent at first indicated that she had no opinion of why her husband acted the way he did. She supposed, however, that it was because he had been mistreated when he was in the army and, as he had told her, he treated her the way he had been treated. The respondent believed he would abuse any woman who was his wife. She testified that he "was a repugnant man without any education," and that he saw her "as something that belonged to him and he could do anything he wanted" with her.

The respondent's pleas to Guatemalan police did not gain her protection. On three occasions, the police issued summons for her husband to appear, but he ignored them, and the police did not take further action. Twice, the respondent called the police, but they never responded. When the respondent appeared before a judge, he told her that he would not interfere in domestic disputes. Her husband told the respondent that, because of his former military service, calling the police would be futile as he was familiar with law enforcement officials. The respondent knew of no shelters or other organizations in Guatemala that could protect her. The abuse began "from the moment [they] were married," and continued until the respondent fled Guatemala in May 1995. One morning in May 1995, the respondent decided to leave permanently. With help, the respondent was able to flee Guatemala, and she arrived in Brownsville, Texas, 2 days later.

A witness, testifying for the respondent, stated that she learned through the respondent's sister that the respondent's husband was "going to hunt her down and kill her if she comes back to Guatemala."

We struggle to describe how deplorable we find the husband's conduct to have been.

B. Country Conditions

Dr. Doris Bersing testified that spouse abuse is common in Latin American countries and that she was not aware of social or legal resources for battered women in Guatemala. Women in Guatemala, according to Dr. Bersing, have other problems related to general conditions in that country, and she suggested that such women could leave abusive partners but that they would face other problems such as poverty. Dr. Bersing further testified that the respondent was different from other battered women she had seen in that the respondent possessed an extraordinary fear of her husband and her abuse had been extremely severe.

Dr. Bersing noted that spouse abuse was a problem in many countries throughout the world, but she said it was a particular problem in Latin America, especially in Guatemala and Nicaragua. As we understand her testimony, its roots lie in such things as the Latin American patriarchal culture, the militaristic and violent nature of societies undergoing civil war, alcoholism, and sexual abuse in general. Nevertheless, she testified that husbands are supposed to honor, respect, and take care of their wives, and that spouse abuse is something that is present "underground" or "underneath in the culture." But if a woman chooses the wrong husband her options are few in countries such as Guatemala, which lack effective methods for dealing with the problem.

The Department of State issued an advisory opinion as to the respondent's asylum request. The opinion states that the respondent's alleged mistreatment could have occurred given its understanding of country conditions in Guatemala. The opinion further indicates:

> Spousal abuse complaints by husbands have increased from 30 to 120 a month due to increased nationwide educational programs, which have encouraged women to seek assistance. Family court judges may issue injunctions against abusive spouses, which police are charged with enforcing. The [Human Rights Ombudsman,] women's rights department and various non-governmental organizations provide medical and legal assistance.

The respondent has submitted numerous articles and reports regarding violence against women in Guatemala and other Latin American countries. One article, prepared by Canada's Immigration and Refugee Board, indicates that Guatemala has laws against domestic violence, that it has taken some additional steps recently to begin to address the problem, and that "functionaries" in the legal system tend to view domestic violence as a violation of women's rights. Nevertheless, the article indicates that Guatemalan society still tends to view domestic violence as a family matter, that women are often not aware of available legal avenues, and that the pursuit of legal remedies can often prove ineffective.

III. IMMIGRATION JUDGE'S DECISION

The Immigration Judge found the respondent to be credible, and she concluded that the respondent suffered harm that rose to the level of past persecution. The Immigration Judge also held that the Guatemalan Government was either unwilling or unable to control the respondent's husband. The balance of her decision addressed the issue of whether the respondent's harm was on account of a protected ground.

The Immigration Judge first concluded that the respondent was persecuted because of her membership in the particular social group of "Guatemalan women who have been involved intimately with Guatemalan male companions, who believe that women are to live under male domination." She found that such a group was cognizable and cohesive, as members shared the common and immutable characteristics of gender and the experience of having been intimately involved with a male companion who practices male domination through violence. The Immigration Judge then held that members of such a group are targeted for persecution by the men who seek to dominate and control them.

The Immigration Judge further found that, through the respondent's resistance to his acts of violence, her husband imputed to the respondent the political opinion that women should not be dominated by men, and he was motivated to commit the abuse because of the political opinion he believed her to hold.

IV. ARGUMENTS ON APPEAL

On appeal, the Service argues that "Guatemalan women who have been involved intimately with Guatemalan male companions, who believe that women are to live under male domination" is not a particular social group, and that the respondent was not harmed because she belonged to such a group. The Service also contends that the respondent's husband did not persecute the respondent because of an imputed political opinion.

The respondent's brief supports the Immigration Judge's conclusions and advances additional arguments. The Refugee Law Center and the International Human Rights and Migration Project filed a joint amicus curiae brief. The thorough and well-prepared amicus brief argues that the Immigration Judge's decision is supported not only by United States asylum law, but also by international human rights laws, and that the respondent's asylum claims should be analyzed against the fundamental purpose of refugee law: to provide surrogate international protection when there is a fundamental breakdown in state protection resulting in serious human rights violations tied to civil and political status.

V. The Law

An asylum applicant bears the burden of proof and persuasion of showing that he or she is a refugee.... The term "refugee" refers to:

> any person who is outside any country of such person's nationality ... and who is unable or unwilling to return to, and is unable or unwilling to avail himself or herself of the protection of, that country because of persecution or a well-founded fear of persecution on account of race, religion, nationality, membership in a particular social group, or political opinion....

[8 U.S.C. § 1101(a)(42)(A) (1994)]; see also INS v. Cardoza–Fonseca, 480 U.S. 421, 441 (1987).

We have held that members of a particular social group share a "common, immutable characteristic" that they either cannot change, or should not be required to change because such characteristic is fundamental to their individual identities.... The United States Court of Appeals for the Ninth Circuit, the circuit within which this case arises, defines a particular social group as:

> a collection of people closely affiliated with each other, who are actuated by some common impulse or interest. Of central concern is the existence of a voluntary associational relationship among the purported members, which impart some common characteristic that is fundamental to their identity as a member of that discrete social group.

Sanchez–Trujillo v. INS, 801 F.2d 1571, 1576 (9th Cir. 1986)....

The asylum applicant bears the burden of providing evidence, either direct or circumstantial, from which it is reasonable to conclude that her persecutor harmed her at least in part because of a protected ground. See INS v. Elias–Zacarias, 502 U.S. 478, 483 (1992).... The Court in Elias–Zacarias pointed out that overcoming or punishing a protected characteristic of the victim, and not the persecutor's own generalized goals, must be the motivation for the persecution....

VI. Analysis

... [W]e agree with the Immigration Judge that the severe injuries sustained by the respondent rise to the level of harm sufficient (and more than sufficient) to constitute "persecution." We also credit the respondent's testimony in general and specifically her account of being unsuccessful in obtaining meaningful assistance from the authorities in Guatemala. Accordingly, we find that she has adequately established on this record that she was unable to avail herself of the protection of the Government of Guatemala in connection with the abuse inflicted by her husband. The determinative issue, as correctly identified by the Immigration Judge, is whether the harm experienced by the respondent was, or in the future may be, inflicted "on account of" a statutorily protected ground.

It is not possible to review this record without having great sympathy for the respondent and extreme contempt for the actions of her husband.

The questions before us, however, are not whether some equitable or prosecutorial authority ought to be invoked to prevent the respondent's deportation to Guatemala. Indeed, the Service has adequate authority in the form of "deferred action" to accomplish that result if it deems it appropriate. Rather, the questions before us concern the respondent's eligibility for relief under our refugee and asylum laws. And, as explained below, we do not agree with the Immigration Judge that the respondent was harmed on account of either actual or imputed political opinion or membership in a particular social group.

A. Imputed Political Opinion

The record indicates that the respondent's husband harmed the respondent regardless of what she actually believed or what he thought she believed. The respondent testified that the abuse began "from the moment [they] were married." Even after the respondent "learned through experience" to acquiesce to his demands, he still abused her. The abuse took place before she left him initially, and it continued after she returned to him. In fact, he said he "didn't care" what she did to escape because he would find her. He also hurt her before her first call to the police and after her last plea for help.

The respondent's account of what her husband told her may well reflect his own view of women and, in particular, his view of the respondent as his property to do with as he pleased. It does not, however, reflect that he had any understanding of the respondent's perspective or that he even cared what the respondent's perspective may have been. According to the respondent, he told her, "You're my woman and I can do whatever I want," and "You're my woman, you do what I say." In fact, she stated that "as time went on, he hit me for no reason at all," and that he "would hit or kick me whenever he felt like it."

Nowhere in the record does the respondent recount her husband saying anything relating to what he thought her political views to be, or that the violence towards her was attributable to her actual or imputed beliefs. Moreover, this is not a case where there is meaningful evidence that this respondent held or evinced a political opinion, unless one assumes that the common human desire not to be harmed or abused is in itself a "political opinion." The record before us simply does not indicate that the harm arose in response to any objections made by the respondent to her husband's domination over her. Nor does it suggest that his abusive behavior was dependent in any way on the views held by the respondent. Indeed, his senseless actions started at the beginning of their marriage and continued whether or not the respondent acquiesced in his demands. The record reflects that, once having entered into this marriage, there was nothing the respondent could have done or thought that would have spared her (or indeed would have spared any other woman unfortunate enough to have married him) from the violence he inflicted.

. . .

. . . The respondent's husband, it seems, must have had some reason or reasons for treating the respondent as he did. And it is possible that his own view of men and women played a role in his brutality, as may have been the case with the brutality that he himself experienced and witnessed. What we find lacking in this respondent's showing, however, is any meaningful evidence that her husband's behavior was influenced at all by his perception of the respondent's opinion.

. . .

As we understand the respondent's rationale, it would seem that virtually any victim of repeated violence who offers some resistance could qualify for asylum, particularly where the government did not control the assailant. Under this approach, the perpetrator is presumed to impute to the victim a political opinion, in opposition to the perpetrator's authority, stemming simply from an act of resistance. Then, notwithstanding any other motivation for the original violence, the imputed political opinion becomes the assumed basis for the infliction of more harm.

It is certainly logical and only human to presume that no victim of violence desires to be such a victim and will resist in some manner. But it is another matter to presume that the perpetrator of the violence inflicts it because the perpetrator believes the victim opposes either the abuse or the authority of the abuser. We do not find that the second proposition necessarily follows from the first. . . .

As for the record here, there has been no showing that the respondent's husband targeted any other women in Guatemala, even though we may reasonably presume that they, too, did not all share his view of male domination. The respondent was unable to set forth an accurate time frame for the great majority of the incidents she described. We are thus unable in general to link the incidents to acts of resistance in a way that might tend to support the respondent's theory. Moreover, the myriad situations in which the abuse occurred and the various unsuccessful responses adopted by the respondent point strongly away from it having a genesis in her husband's perception of the respondent's political opinion. Put another way, it is difficult to conclude on the actual record before us that there is any "opinion" the respondent could have held, or convinced her husband she held, that would have prevented the abuse she experienced.

. . .

B. Particular Social Group

1. Cognizableness

Initially, we find that "Guatemalan women who have been involved intimately with Guatemalan male companions, who believe that women are to live under male domination" is not a particular social group. Absent from this group's makeup is "a voluntary associational relationship" that is of "central concern" in the Ninth Circuit. . . .

Moreover, regardless of Ninth Circuit law, we find that the respondent's claimed social group fails under our own independent assessment of what constitutes a qualifying social group. We find it questionable that the social group adopted by the Immigration Judge appears to have been defined principally, if not exclusively, for purposes of this asylum case, and without regard to the question of whether anyone in Guatemala perceives this group to exist in any form whatsoever. The respondent fits within the proposed group. But the group is defined largely in the abstract. It seems to bear little or no relation to the way in which Guatemalans might identify subdivisions within their own society or otherwise might perceive individuals either to possess or to lack an important characteristic or trait. The proposed group may satisfy the basic requirement of containing an immutable or fundamental individual characteristic. But, for the group to be viable for asylum purposes, we believe there must also be some showing of how the characteristic is understood in the alien's society, such that we in turn may understand that the potential persecutors in fact see persons sharing the characteristic as warranting suppression or the infliction of harm.

Our administrative precedents do not require a voluntary associational relationship as a social group attribute. But we have ruled that the term "particular social group" is to be construed in keeping with the other four statutory characteristics that are the focus of persecution: race, religion, nationality, and political opinion.... These other four characteristics are ones that typically separate various factions within countries. They frequently are recognized groupings in a particular society. The members of the group generally understand their own affiliation with the grouping, as do other persons in the particular society.

In the present case, the respondent has shown that women living with abusive partners face a variety of legal and practical problems in obtaining protection or in leaving the abusive relationship. But the respondent has not shown that "Guatemalan women who have been involved intimately with Guatemalan male companions, who believe that women are to live under male domination" is a group that is recognized and understood to be a societal faction, or is otherwise a recognized segment of the population, within Guatemala. The respondent has shown neither that the victims of spouse abuse view themselves as members of this group, nor, most importantly, that their male oppressors see their victimized companions as part of this group.

. . .

On the record before us, we find that the respondent has not adequately established that we should recognize, under our law, the particular social group identified by the Immigration Judge.[1]

1. Other "social group" definitions potentially covering the respondent were suggested below or in the appeal briefs, such as "Guatemalan women" and "battered spouses." We need not now address whether there are any circumstances under which the various alternative proposals might qualify as a "particular social group," as each of them fails on this record under the "on account of," or nexus, requirement of the statute, for the reasons we identify below with regard to the group adopted by the Immigration Judge....

2. Nexus

. . .

In this case, even if we were to accept as a particular social group "Guatemalan women who have been involved intimately with Guatemalan male companions, who believe that women are to live under male domination," the respondent has not established that her husband has targeted and harmed the respondent because he perceived her to be a member of this particular social group. The record indicates that he has targeted only the respondent. The respondent's husband has not shown an interest in any member of this group other than the respondent herself. The respondent fails to show how other members of the group may be at risk of harm from him. If group membership were the motivation behind his abuse, one would expect to see some evidence of it manifested in actions toward other members of the same group. . . .

The Immigration Judge's nexus analysis fails to limit consistently the source of persecution to the respondent's husband. At one point, the Immigration Judge seems to identify all Guatemalan males who abuse their partners as the persecutors, but the record indicates that the respondent suffered and feared intimate violence only from her own husband. When the Immigration Judge correctly identifies the husband as the persecutor whom the Guatemalan Government failed to control, her nexus finding is both too broad and too narrow. It is too broad in that he did not target all (or indeed any other) Guatemalan women intimate with abusive Guatemalan men. It is too narrow in that the record strongly indicates that he would have abused any woman, regardless of nationality, to whom he was married.

Indeed, the record does not reflect that the respondent's husband bore any particular animosity toward women who were intimate with abusive partners, women who had previously suffered abuse, or women who happened to have been born in, or were actually living in, Guatemala. There is little doubt that the respondent's spouse believed that married women should be subservient to their own husbands. But beyond this, we have scant information on how he personally viewed other married women in Guatemala, let alone women in general. On the basis of this record, we perceive that the husband's focus was on the respondent because she was his wife, not because she was a member of some broader collection of women, however defined, whom he believed warranted the infliction of harm.

The respondent's statements regarding her husband's motivation also undercut the nexus claims. He harmed her, when he was drunk and when he was sober, for not getting an abortion, for his belief that she was seeing other men, for not having her family get money for him, for not being able to find something in the house, for leaving a cantina before him, for leaving him, for reasons related to his mistreatment in the army, and "for no reason at all." Of all these apparent reasons for abuse, none was "on account of" a protected ground, and the arbitrary nature of the attacks further suggests it was not the respondent's claimed social group characteristics that he sought to overcome. The record indicates that there is nothing the respondent could have done to have satisfied her husband and prevented further abuse. Her own supposition is that he abused her because he was abused himself in the military.

The respondent was not at particular risk of abuse from her husband until she married him, at which point, given the nature of his focus, she was in a "group" by herself of women presently married to that particular man. Such a group, however, would fail to qualify as a "particular social group" under the Act....

The Immigration Judge nevertheless found, and the respondent argues on appeal, that her various possible group memberships account for her plight, in large measure because the social climate and the Government of Guatemala afford her no protection from her husband's abuse. Societal attitudes and the concomitant effectiveness (or lack thereof) of governmental intervention very well may have contributed to the ability of the respondent's husband to carry out his abusive actions over a period of many years. But this argument takes us away from looking at the motivation of the husband and focuses instead on the failure of the government to offer protection.

Focusing on societal attitudes and a particular government's response to the infliction of injury is frequently appropriate in the adjudication of asylum cases. It is most warranted when the harm is being inflicted by elements within the government or by private organizations that target minority factions within a society. But governmental inaction is not a reliable indicator of the motivations behind the actions of private parties. And this is not a case in which it has been shown that the Government of Guatemala encourages its male citizens to abuse its female citizens, nor in which the Government has suddenly and unreasonably withdrawn protection from a segment of the population in the expectation that a third party will inflict harm and thereby indirectly achieve a governmental objective.

The record in this case reflects that the views of society and of many governmental institutions in Guatemala can result in the tolerance of spouse abuse at levels we find appalling. But the record also shows that abusive marriages are not viewed as desirable, that spouse abuse is recognized as a problem, and that some measures have been pursued in an attempt to respond to this acknowledged problem. In this context, we are not convinced that the absence of an effective governmental reaction to the respondent's abuse translates into a finding that her husband inflicted the abuse because she was a member of a particular social group. The record does not support such a conclusion, as a matter of fact, when the husband's own behavior is examined. And Guatemala's societal and governmental attitudes and actions do not warrant our declaring this to be the case as a matter of law.

The Immigration Judge's decision relies heavily on the absence of governmental protection in its finding that the respondent was targeted for harm on account of her claimed group membership. The respondent takes this even further on appeal, arguing that governments can be deemed responsible for private acts of violence against women by virtue of the failure to afford protection. She also contends that she should be considered a "refugee" simply because she is not adequately protected by her own government.

We do not know whether enforcement measures would have deterred the abusive behavior of the respondent's husband in this case. But we do know that spouse abuse takes place even in communities with strong enforcement mechanisms. Varying levels of governmental tolerance of, or vigorous enforcement measures against, abuse can reasonably be expected to affect the incidence of spouse abuse within particular communities. It does not necessarily follow, however, that antagonism toward a "particular social group" is the motivation for the harm that husbands inflict upon their wives in those communities which afford little or no protection, even if certain societal attitudes may be seen as contributing to the absence of effective enforcement.

The adequacy of state protection is obviously an essential inquiry in asylum cases. But its bearing on the "on account of" test for refugee status depends on the facts of the case and the context in which it arises. In this case, the independent actions of the respondent's husband may have been tolerated. But, as previously explained, this record does not show that his actions represent desired behavior within Guatemala or that the Guatemalan Government encourages domestic abuse.

Importantly, construing private acts of violence to be qualifying governmental persecution, by virtue of the inadequacy of protection, would obviate, perhaps entirely, the "on account of" requirement in the statute. We understand the "on account of" test to direct an inquiry into the motives of the entity actually inflicting the harm.... Further, the adoption of such an approach would represent a fundamental change in the analysis of refugee claims. We see no principled basis for restricting such an approach to cases involving violence against women. The absence of adequate governmental protection, it would seem, should equally translate into refugee status for other categories of persons unable to protect themselves.

. . .

We reject the approach advocated by the respondent in view of the existing statutory language and the body of case law construing it. Consequently, the respondent must show more than a lack of protection or the existence of societal attitudes favoring male domination. She must make a showing from which it is reasonable to conclude that her husband was motivated to harm her, at least in part, by her asserted group membership.

In the end, we find that the respondent has failed to show a sufficient nexus between her husband's abuse of her and the particular social group the Immigration Judge announced, or any of the other proffered groups.

3. The Kasinga Decision

Our decision in Matter of Kasinga, [Interim Decision 3278 (BIA 1996)], does not prescribe a different result. In that case, the alien belonged to the Tchamba–Kunsuntu tribe in Togo in which young women normally underwent female genital mutilation ("FGM") before the age of 15. Under tribal custom, the alien's aunt and husband planned to force her to submit to FGM before she was to be married. Following her escape from Togo, the Togolese police were looking for her. The record included a letter from a cultural anthropologist indicating that women from the Tchamba people probably would be expected to undergo FGM prior to marriage. A Department of State report in the record indicated that FGM was practiced by some Togo ethnic groups, that as many as 50% of Togolese females may have been mutilated, and that violence against women in Togo occurs with little police intervention. We held that FGM was persecution, that "young women of the Tchamba–Kunsuntu Tribe who have not had FGM, as practiced by that tribe, and who oppose the practice" constitute a particular social group, that the alien was a member of such a group, and that she possessed a well-founded fear of persecution on account of her membership in that group.

In contrast to our ruling in Matter of Kasinga, supra, the Immigration Judge in the instant case has not articulated a viable social group. The common characteristic of not having undergone FGM was one that was identified by Kasinga's tribe, and motivated both her family and the tribe to enforce the practice on Kasinga and other young women. Indeed, the tribe expected or required FGM of women prior to marriage, signifying the importance of the practice within that tribal society. The record in Kasinga indicated that African women faced threats or acts of violence or social ostracization for either refusing the practice or attempting to protect female children from FGM. Moreover, although the source of Kasinga's fear of physical harm was limited to her aunt and husband, she established that FGM was so pervasive that her tribal society targeted "young women of the Tchamba–Kunsuntu Tribe who have not had FGM, as practiced by that tribe, and who oppose the practice."

The respondent in this case has not demonstrated that domestic violence is as pervasive in Guatemala as FGM is among the Tchamba–Kunsuntu Tribe, or, more importantly, that domestic violence is a practice encouraged and viewed as societally important in Guatemala. She has not shown that women are expected to undergo abuse from their husbands, or that husbands who do not abuse their wives, or the nonabused wives themselves, face social ostracization or other threats to make them conform to a societal expectation of abuse. While the respondent here found no source of official protection in Guatemala, the young woman in Kasinga testified that the police in Togo were looking for her and would return her to her family to undergo FGM. Matter of Kasinga, supra, at 4.

. . .

VII. CONCLUSION

In sum, we find that the respondent has been the victim of tragic and severe spouse abuse. We further find that her husband's motivation, to the extent it can be ascertained, has varied; some abuse occurred because of his warped perception of and reaction to her behavior, while some likely arose out of psychological disorder, pure meanness, or no apparent reason at all. Absent other evidence, we accept the respondent's own assessment that the foundations of the abuse she suffered lay in the abuse her husband had experienced in his own life. We are not persuaded that the abuse occurred because of her membership in a particular social group or because of an actual or imputed political opinion. . . .

The respondent in this case has been terribly abused and has a genuine and reasonable fear of returning to Guatemala. Whether the district director may, at his discretion, grant the respondent relief upon humanitarian grounds—relief beyond the jurisdiction of the Immigration Judge and this Board—is a matter the parties can explore outside the present proceedings. We further note that Congress has legislated various forms of relief for abused spouses and children. The issue of whether our asylum laws (or some other legislative provision) should be amended to include additional protection for abused women, such as this respondent, is a matter to be addressed by Congress. In our judgment, however, Congress did not intend the "social group" category to be an all-encompassing residual category for persons facing genuine social ills that governments do not remedy. The solution to the respondent's plight does not lie in our asylum laws as they are currently formulated.

. . .

ORDER: The appeal of the Immigration and Naturalization Service is sustained and the Immigration Judge's order of September 20, 1996, is vacated.

FURTHER ORDER: In lieu of an order of deportation the respondent is allowed to depart voluntarily, without expense to the Government, within 30 days from the date of this order or any extension beyond that time as may be granted by the district director and under such conditions as he may direct. In the event of the respondent's failure so to depart, the respondent shall be deported to Guatemala.

DISSENT:

I respectfully dissent. I agree with the thorough and well-reasoned decision of the Immigration Judge that the respondent has demonstrated past persecution and a well-founded fear of future persecution based on her membership in a particular social group and upon her express and imputed political opinion.[2]

I. Issues Presented

This case presents two questions: (1) whether a woman trapped in a long-term relationship with an abusive spouse, in a country in which such abuse is tolerated by society and ignored by governmental officials, is a member of a particular social group entitled to the protection of asylum law; and, (2) whether the domestic abuse in the instant case was at least partially motivated by an actual or imputed political opinion.

2. The briefs of amici curiae, the Refugee Law Center and the International Human Rights/Migration Projects, and the respondent's brief to the Board also provide persuasive arguments in support of the Immigration Judge's decision.

II. Overview

This is not merely a case of domestic violence involving criminal conduct. The respondent's husband engaged in a prolonged and persistent pattern of abuse designed to dominate the respondent and to overcome any effort on her part to assert her independence or to resist his abuse. His mistreatment and persecution of her in private and in public was founded, as the majority states, on his view that it was his right to treat his wife as "his property to do as he pleased." He acted with the knowledge that no one would interfere. His horrific conduct, both initially and in response to her opposition to it, was not that of an individual acting at variance with societal norms, but one who recognized that he was acting in accordance with them.

The harm to the respondent occurred in the context of egregious governmental acquiescence. When the respondent sought the aid and assistance of government officials and institutions, she was told that they could do nothing for her. This is not a case in which the government tried, but failed, to afford protection. Here the government made no effort and showed no interest in protecting the respondent from her abusive spouse. Thus, when the respondent went to the police or to the court to seek relief from threats, physical violence, broken bones, rape, and sodomy inflicted by her husband, Guatemalan police officials and the judge refused to intervene.

The record confirms the Immigration Judge's finding that in Guatemala there are "institutional biases against women that prevent female victims of domestic violence from receiving protection from their male companions or spouses." The Immigration Judge found that these institutional biases "appear to stem from a pervasive belief, common in patriarchal societies, that a man should be able to control a wife or female companion by any means he sees fit: including rape, torture, and beatings." Because of the principle that men should control women with whom they are intimately involved and the belief that domestic abuse is a family matter in which others must not intervene, women are not protected when they complain of domestic violence, and men who inflict such violence are not prosecuted. The respondent's husband told her that because of his connections to the military, the police and courts would not support her against him, and consistent with his threats, when she sought governmental intervention, her pleas fell on deaf ears and she was told she could not divorce him because her husband's consent was needed. No one, neither society nor the government, was able or willing to protect the respondent from her husband.

The majority's insistence that the respondent's husband was not motivated to harm her, "even in part, because of her membership in a particular social group or because of an actual or imputed political opinion," cannot be reconciled either with the reality of the respondent's situation in Guatemala, or with United States law. . . .

III. Persecution on Account of Membership in a Particular Social Group

. . . The respondent has a fundamental right to protection from abuse based on gender. When domestic abuse based on gender occurs, as here, with state acquiescence, the respondent should be afforded the protection of asylum law.

A. The Immigration Judge's Finding of a Particular Social Group is Consistent With Board Precedent

The Immigration Judge found that the respondent was a member of a social group comprised of "Guatemalan women, who have been involved intimately with Guatemalan male companions, who believe that women are to live under male domination." In so finding, she carefully analyzed the facts of the case and correctly applied the law as set forth in Matter of Acosta, 19 I. & N. Dec. 211 (BIA 1985), modified on other grounds, Matter of Mogharrabi, 19 I. & N. Dec. 439 (BIA 1987), and, most recently, in Matter of Kasinga, Interim Decision 3278 (BIA 1996).

We first set forth the requirements for a particular social group in Matter of Acosta, supra. There we interpreted the phrase "membership in a particular social group" in a manner consistent with the other enumerated grounds for asylum. As each of the other grounds (race, religion, nationality, and political opinion) refers to a common, immutable characteristic which a person either cannot change, or should not be required to change, because it is "fundamental to individual identity or conscience," we determined that the phrase "particular social group" also should be defined by this type of characteristic. Id. at 233–34. The shared immutable characteristic "might be an innate one such as sex, color, or kinship ties, or in some circumstances it might be a shared past experience such as former military leadership or land ownership." Id. We concluded that such determinations must be made on a case-by-case basis. Applying this test to the record in Acosta, we found that members of a taxi cooperative and persons engaged in the transportation industry of El Salvador did not constitute a particular social group, because the characteristics defining the group were not immutable. . . .

Under Acosta, then, immutability is of the essence. In a number of decisions, we have applied the Acosta immutability standard to recognize particular social groups. In each case, we recognized an immutable trait or past experience shared by the members of the social group. The shared past experience of former members of the national police force in El Salvador, for example, has been recognized as an immutable characteristic which makes such individuals members of a particular social group for asylum purposes. . . . Similarly, gay men and lesbians in Cuba have been found to constitute a particular social group. . . .

In Matter of Kasinga, supra, a case involving a young Togolese woman who fled her country to avoid the practice of female genital mutilation practiced by her tribe, we considered a social group partly defined by gender. We found that the applicant had a well-founded fear of persecution based on her membership in the social group of young women of the Tchamba–Kunsuntu tribe who have not been mutilated and who oppose the practice. In so holding, we ruled that Ms. Kasinga's gender and ethnic affiliation were characteristics she could not change, and the characteristic of having intact genitalia was so fundamental that she should not be required to change it. Id. at 13–14.

The Immigration Judge decided the case before her consistent with our precedent decision in Kasinga. In both cases, the social group was defined by reference to gender in combination with one or more additional factors. In Kasinga, the social group was defined by gender, ethnic affiliation, and opposition to female genital mutilation ("FGM"). In the instant case, the social group is based on gender, relationship to an abusive partner, and opposition to domestic violence. As the Immigration Judge below correctly observed, the respondent's relationship to, and association with, her husband is something she cannot change. It is an immutable characteristic under the Acosta guidelines, which we affirmed in Kasinga. Id. at 13.

There are a number of other striking similarities between the instant case and Kasinga. Both cases involve a form of persecution inflicted by private parties upon family members. In both cases, the victims opposed and resisted a practice which was ingrained in the culture, broadly sanctioned by the community, and unprotected by the state. In both cases, the overarching societal objective underlying the cultural norm was the assurance of male domination. Kasinga lost the protection of her father when he died; Kasinga experienced strong indicators (i.e., her forced marriage to a polygamist) that she would be forced to undergo the procedure in the future; and Kasinga was unable to escape her own ethnicity and live within another tribal society within Togo. See Matter of Kasinga, supra. In the instant case, the respondent lost the protection of her family when, at the age of 15, she married her would-be persecutor; the harm suffered by the respondent in the past is a clear indicator that the harm would continue in the future, and perhaps become more severe; and, finally, the respondent was unable, within the borders of Guatemala, to obtain governmental protection from her persecutor.

In attempting to distinguish this case from Kasinga, the majority contends that domestic violence in Guatemala, unlike FGM in Togo, is not so pervasive or "societally important" that the respondent will face "social ostracization" for refusing to submit to the harm. The majority's distinction is flawed. The facts of Kasinga did not suggest that Kasinga would face severe social ostracization for her refusal to submit to FGM; rather, as a member of a social group defined by her unique circumstances, she faced harm only because she lost the protection of her father. In Kasinga, a family member, Kasinga's aunt, targeted her after the death of her father who, as the primary authority figure in her family, had previously protected her from FGM. In other words, the practice was not so pervasive in Togo that her father, also a member of the ethnic group which had targeted her, had been unable to identify the practice as harmful. Some persons within Togo viewed FGM as an acceptable practice; other persons, even those within the same ethnic group (such as Kasinga's father, mother, and sister), did not. We extended asylum protection to Kasinga not because she faced societal ostracization, but because she demonstrated a well-founded fear of harm on account of her membership in a group composed of persons sharing her specific circumstances.

In the end, there are no meaningful distinctions that justify recognizing the social group claim in Kasinga while refusing to recognize such a social group claim in the instant case. The gender-based characteristics shared by the members of each group are immutable, the form of abuse resisted in both cases was considered culturally normative and was broadly sanctioned by the community, and the persecution imposed occurred without possibility of state protection.

B. The Instant Case Involves More Than Mere Membership in a Statistical Group

The finding of the United States Court of Appeals for the Ninth Circuit in Sanchez–Trujillo v. INS, 801 F.2d 1571, 1573 (9th Cir. 1986), that "young, urban, working class males of military age who had never served in the military or otherwise expressed support for the government of El Salvador" were not members of a particular social group because they lacked a "voluntary associational relationship," does not compel a different conclusion.

First, the instant case does not involve the type of all-encompassing grouping posited in Sanchez–Trujillo, which arose in the context of country-wide civil strife and anarchy. Here, the circumstances of group members who share the immutable traits of gender and a relationship to an abusive partner are distinct from those of other members of society who may fear general civil strife, criminal assault or other social disorder.

. . .

In addition, in the intervening decade since Sanchez–Trujillo was decided, most courts outside the Ninth Circuit have applied Acosta's immutability standard, rather than a "voluntariness" standard, in deciding whether a group is cognizable under the Act. See, e.g., Lwin v. INS, 144 F.3d 505, 511–12 (7th Cir. 1998) (adopting Acosta standard in accepting a group described as "parents of Burmese student dissidents"). The First and Third Circuits have also endorsed the immutability/fundamental identity approach in determining what constitutes a particular social group. See Fatin v. INS, 12 F.3d 1233, 1239–41 (3d Cir. 1993) (observing that an Iranian woman who refused to conform to the Iranian Government's gender-specific laws and social norms may well satisfy the Acosta definition "simply because she [was] a woman"); Ananeh–Firempong v. INS, 766 F.2d 621 (1st Cir. 1985) (noting that individuals associated with the former government of Ghana could comprise a social group because their fears arose from characteristics beyond their power to change); see also Meguenine v. INS, 139 F.3d 25, 28 n.2 (1st Cir. 1998) (approving a social group definition that requires "some immutable trait (such as an ethnic group) or a mutable trait which a member of that group should not, in good conscience, be required to change (such as a religious adherent's beliefs)").

Although the Eighth Circuit Court of Appeals acknowledged the Sanchez–Trujillo approach in Safaie v. INS, 25 F.3d 636, 640 (8th Cir. 1994), concluding that a group comprised of all Iranian women was too broad to constitute a particular social group, the court noted its agreement with the Third Circuit's observation in Fatin v. INS, supra, in stating that "a group of women, who refuse to conform and whose opposition is so profound that they would choose to suffer the severe consequences of noncompliance," may well qualify as a particular social group. See also Fisher v. INS, 79 F.3d 955, 966 (9th Cir. 1996) (Canby, J., concurring) (noting that it remains an open question in the Ninth Circuit "whether persecution of women because they are women is a ground for asylum under the Act").

Social groups may be defined more or less broadly depending upon the level of generality of the defining characteristics. In the instant case, the Immigration Judge used a fairly precise and narrow focus. She could have legitimately broadened the perspective to include all Guatemalan women or, possibly, all married Guatemalan women as the particular social group. See, in this regard, the discussion in Islam (A.P.) v. Secretary of State for the Home Dept., App. Cas. (Mar. 25, 1999), ... (opinion of Lord Steyn, recognizing a particular social group consisting of all Pakistani women and, in the alternative, a particular social group consisting of women suspected by their husbands of adultery who would be unprotected by the Government of Pakistan). Whether defined broadly or narrowly, an independent contextual evaluation of the respondent's claim in the instant case demonstrates a particular social group.

C. Gender–Related Social Group Claims, Like Those Involving Race, Religion, Nationality, and Political Opinion, Implicate Fundamental Human Rights

The international community has recognized that gender-based violence, such as domestic violence, is not merely a random crime or a private matter; rather, such violence is a violation of fundamental human rights. In recognition of the special issues confronting female victims of violence, international bodies have responded accordingly....

Domestic bodies have also responded. The Department of Justice has addressed asylum claims involving violence against women in guidelines promulgated in 1995. See Phyllis Coven, U.S. Dept., of Justice, Considerations for Asylum Officers Adjudicating Claims from Women (1995) ("DOJ Guidelines"). The DOJ Guidelines announce the principle that "women's rights are human rights, and women's rights are universal." Id. at 2. They explicitly state that "rape ... sexual abuse and domestic violence, infanticide and genital mutilation are forms of mistreatment primarily directed at girls and women and they may serve as evidence of past persecution on account of one or more of the five grounds." Id. at 4. The DOJ Guidelines advise that claims to asylum should be analyzed against the background of the fundamental purpose of refugee law: to provide surrogate international protection where there is a fundamental breakdown in state protection. The DOJ Guidelines go on to state that domestic violence exemplifies just such a breakdown:

> This principle becomes crucial where the applicant alleges private actions—such as domestic violence—that the state will not protect against. In such situations, the officer must explore the extent to which the government can or does offer protection or redress resulting in serious human rights violations tied to civil and political status.

DOJ Guidelines, supra, at 16 (emphasis added). The DOJ Guidelines explicitly state that "the evaluation of gender-based claims must be viewed within the framework provided by existing international human rights instruments and the interpretation of those instruments by international organizations." Id. These statements are persuasive evidence that our asylum laws, as they are currently formulated, provide a sound basis for providing protection to this respondent.

Canada has promulgated similar guidelines. See Immigration and Refugee Board of Canada, Guideline 4: Women Refugee Claimants Fearing Gender–Related Persecution: Update 3 (1996). Moreover, Canadian appellate courts have extended protection to a victim of domestic violence on the basis of her membership in a particular social group. In Mayers v. Canada, 97 D.L.R.4th 729 (C.A. 1992), the Canadian Court of Appeals recognized a social group defined as "Trinidadian women subject to wife abuse." . . .

More recently, in conjoined appeals involving women seeking asylum protection in the United Kingdom for domestic violence in Pakistan, the House of Lords found "women in Pakistan" to constitute a particular social group under the Convention's refugee definition, Islam (A.P.) v. Secretary of State for the Home Dept., supra. Lord Steyn found "women in Pakistan" to be a "logical application of the seminal reasoning" of Acosta. Lord Hoffman recognized the importance of context in deciding whether a social group has been identified: "While persecutory conduct cannot define the social group, the actions of the persecutors may serve to identify or even cause the creation of a particular social group." Id. Citing the example of a Jew whose business was destroyed by a competitor in Nazi Germany, Lord Hoffman recognized that a persecutor's knowledge that he could act with impunity "for reasons of" (i.e., "on account of") his victim's religion went to the heart of the analysis of why the harm occurred. Id.

D. The Respondent Was Harmed and Has a Well–Founded Fear of Harm on Account of Membership in a Particular Social Group

. . .

. . . [T]o assess motivation, it is appropriate to consider the factual circumstances surrounding the violence. The factual record reflects quite clearly that the severe beatings were directed at the respondent by her husband to dominate and subdue her, precisely because of her gender, as he inflicted his harm directly on her vagina, sought to abort her pregnancy, and raped her.

Second, the very incomprehensibleness of the husband's motives supports the respondent's claim that the harm is "on account of" a protected ground. This is not a case of simple assault. Nor is this a case where the factors motivating the harm arguably are limited only to some comprehensible criminal motive.... Rather, this is a case where the respondent's husband treated her merely as his property, to do with as he pleased. Under these circumstances, to place undue emphasis on the respondent's explanations for her husband's motives misses the obvious point that no good reason could exist for such behavior....

Third, we should attempt to identify why such horrific violence occurs at all. In Kasinga, we determined that FGM exists as a means of controlling women's sexuality. So too does domestic violence exist as a means by which men may systematically destroy the power of women, a form of violence rooted in the economic, social, and cultural subordination of women.... The fundamental purpose of domestic violence is to punish, humiliate, and exercise power over the victim on account of her gender....

. . .

It is reasonable to believe, on the basis of the record before us, that the husband was motivated, at least in part, "on account of" the respondent's membership in a particular social group that is defined by her gender, her relationship to him, and her opposition to domestic violence....

IV. Persecution on Account of Actual or Imputed Opinion Opposing Domestic Abuse and Violence Against Women

. . .

Opposition to male domination and violence against women, and support for gender equity, constitutes a political opinion.... Such opposition is not restricted to those who have not been victims of domestic violence, but constitutes a political opinion that may also be held by victims of domestic violence themselves. Both the respondent's status as a battered spouse in an intimate relationship with a man who imposes such domination and her actual or perceived opinion opposing domestic violence trigger continuing abuse from the persecutor who seeks to dominate her.

A. Resistance to Domestic Violence As an Actual or Imputed Political Opinion

... The Ninth Circuit recently held unequivocally that "under our case law, and unchanged by Elias–Zacarias, an applicant can establish his political opinion on the basis of his own affirmative political views, his political neutrality, or a political opinion imputed to him by his persecutors." Id. (emphasis added)....

In order to establish her political opinion, an asylum-seeker may testify about her political beliefs, ... or provide evidence of her past activities.... As the Ninth Circuit reiterated in Meza–Menay v. INS, 139 F.3d 759, 763 (9th Cir. 1998), "An asylum petitioner may hold a political opinion within the meaning of the INA even if the petitioner did not participate in organized political activities." ... The respondent's political opinion opposing male domination and domestic violence imposed upon her by her husband is clearly stated in the record—both in her statements and her actions. As he persisted in subjecting her to persecution that would affirm his dominance over her, she resisted him, tried to flee, sought governmental intervention, and filed legal actions against him.

The respondent may, in addition, establish a "political opinion" by demonstrating that such an opinion has been attributed to her by her persecutors.... Opposition to male domination and violence against women may be imputed to a victim of domestic violence who protests, resists, or seeks to escape such domination and violence....

In establishing an imputed political opinion, the focus of inquiry turns away from the views of the victim to the views of the persecutor. Sangha v. INS, [103 F.3d 1482 (9th Cir. 1994)] , at 1489. As the Ninth Circuit makes clear, "If the persecutor attributed a political opinion to the victim, and acted upon the attribution, this imputed view becomes the applicant's political opinion as required under the Act." Id.; see also Nasseri v. Moschorak, [34 F.3d 723 (9th Cir. 1994)] at 730 (holding that "regardless of how her attackers came to view her as a threat [to the fundamentalist cause], it is clear that they took action against her on account of opinions they imputed to her ... [and] are likely to harm her in the future because of political opinions they believe she possesses").

. . .

B. Evaluation of the Harm Suffered by the Respondent on Account of Political Opinion

The notion that the "heinous abuse" suffered by the respondent, who opposed her husband's abuse, challenged his dominance, attempted to leave him, and sought relief from the government, was only personal and does not constitute anything more than illegitimate criminal conduct unprotected under the Act is unacceptable.... This type of differentiation between the supposedly more private forms of persecution, typically suffered by women, and the more public forms of persecution, typically suffered by men, is exactly the type of outdated and improper distinction that the DOJ Guidelines were intended to overcome....

... The record reflects that the respondent not only holds an actual opinion opposing her husband's violence, but it is apparent that her husband believed that her resistance to his domination and abuse, particularly as reflected in her seeking assistance from governmental authorities, constituted an opinion opposing his male dominance. Imputing this opinion to her, he sought to overcome her opposition by escalating his abuse of her. The legal interpretation of such a course of events—which undisputedly has occurred in the respondent's case—is classic. It corresponds to our longstanding analysis of the elements that must be present to support a finding of persecution on account of a protected ground....

. . .

... [T]he record before us reflects that the abuser is motivated to continue and even escalate his abuse in order to stifle and overcome his victim's opposition to it. As the majority notes, the rage, abuse, and violence against the respondent escalated as the marriage progressed. This is illustrated by the respondent's credible and corroborated account in the record of the persistent, brutal physical and mental abuse inflicted by her husband....

. . .

The majority insists that the respondent's husband persecuted her regardless of what she believed or what he thought she believed, claiming that the record does not reflect he was motivated by gender animus generally. The majority contends that the abuser was not, even in part, motivated by the respondent's resistance to his domination, even though he had told her he viewed women as property to be treated brutally in order to sustain his domination. This is contrary to fact, law, and logic. To reach such a conclusion, the majority must ignore entirely the mixed motive doctrine, which not only constitutes a well-established basis for asylum in cases arising before the Ninth Circuit, but also constitutes a basis for asylum in claims made before this Board.... Furthermore, as we stated in conjunction with our consideration of the respondent as a member of a particular social group, illegitimate motives triggering persecution raise an inference that the harm has occurred on account of a statutorily enumerated ground....

. . .

Had the respondent been subjected to such heinous abuse due to political opposition to communism, imputed as a result of her family's economic class or political activities, the majority would recognize her situation as one of persecution on account of political opinion.... She is not less eligible or entitled to protection on account of her political opinion opposing male domination expressed through the abuse of women by their husbands, or the political opinion attributed to her, than were the comparably qualifying applicants to whom we have granted asylum.

V. CONCLUSION

For the foregoing reasons, I would dismiss the Service's appeal. The Immigration Judge was correct in determining that the respondent is eligible for asylum pursuant to section 208 of the Act, 8 U.S.C. § 1158 (1994). I, therefore, respectfully dissent.

NOTES AND QUESTIONS

1. Asylum advocates have now sought certification and reversal of the decision from US Attorney General Janet Reno. As of October 2000 she has not acted.

2. The dissent accuses the majority of making an "unacceptable," as well as "outdated and improper" distinction between the "supposedly" more private forms of persecution suffered by women and the more public forms of persecution suffered by men. Does the majority or the dissent have the better of this argument? How does the dissent frame domestic violence as a "political" and "public" matter? How exactly does the majority consign domestic violence to the private sphere? As both opinions make clear, the abuse suffered by an applicant can provide a basis for asylum if it is inflicted on either of two grounds: membership in a particular social group, or an actual or imputed political opinion. The majority finds that R–A- qualifies on neither ground, while the dissent argues that she qualifies on both. Do you find one basis more persuasive than the other?

3. Does the Supreme Court's decision in United States v. Morrison, 120 S. St. 1740 (2000), reproduced and discussed at length in Chapter 13, above,

undermine the arguments of those who seek asylum in the United States on the basis of state-condoned domestic violence in another country? Can you generate arguments on both sides of that question?

4. For further discussion of the issues raised by the application of asylum doctrine in the context of domestic or other gender-based violence, see Deborah Anker et al., *Women Whose Governments are Unable or Unwilling to Provide Reasonable Protection from Domestic Violence May Qualify as Refugees Under United States Asylum Law,* 11 GEO. IMMIGR. L.J. 709, 713 (1997); Kristin E. Kandt, *United States Asylum Law: Recognizing Persecution Based on Gender Using Canada as a Comparison,* 9 GEO. IMMIGR. L.J. 137, 145 (1995); Nancy Kelly, *Gender-Related Persecution: Assessing the Asylum Claims of Women,* 26 CORNELL INT'L L.J. 625 (1993); Pamela Goldberg, *Anyplace But Home: Asylum in the United States for Women Fleeing Intimate Violence,* 26 CORNELL INT'L L.J. 565, 591–92 (1993).

PART SIX

CONCLUSION

CHAPTER **15** Doing the Work

CHAPTER FIFTEEN

DOING THE WORK

Introduction

Often in the preceding chapters you have encountered situations in which lawyers and advocates have failed their battered women clients. You have read about family lawyers who have not taken their clients' abuse seriously, or advocated effectively for their safety or the safety of their children; about prosecutors who have failed to understand why victims might have difficulty cooperating with law enforcement, and failed to hold batterers accountable; and about criminal defense lawyers who have not understood how to use testimony about abuse to present a strong self-defense claim. Some of these failures of representation are lodged in failures of strategy, and some in failures of relationship. The failures of strategy often reflect a lack of understanding; of the dynamics of abusive relationships, of those who perpetrate and those who live with abuse, of what legal interventions are appropriate, and of how to procure them. Unfortunately, these failures of understanding have characterized not only traditional approaches to violence in intimate relationships, but even some of the newer approaches advocated by feminist activists and theorists; think back, for example, on the controversy surrounding new policies of mandatory arrest and no-drop prosecution. The failures of relationship can result either from the inadequacies of the model of lawyer-client relationship within which a particular lawyer or advocate is working, or from more specific difficulties introduced by the experiences a particular client brings to the relationship, and the responses those experiences evoke.

The first section of this chapter takes on these failures of representation, at the levels of both strategy and relationship. It explores their causes and consequences, and also the question of what it takes to provide effective representation in the context of abuse. This involves looking not only at how to meet the needs of a battered client, but also at how the lawyers and advocates who work with battered clients can take care of their own needs, and sustain themselves in this very challenging work.

The second section of the chapter expands the inquiry, and looks at the broader context within which lawyers and advocates are doing their work at the start of the twenty-first century. The theme of this section is that recent developments in the field, and particularly the increasing focus on coordinated and multidisciplinary responses to domestic violence, offers new opportunities for lawyers and advocates to serve their clients and to sustain themselves. Legal mechanisms will only ever provide a partial solution to the social problems created by partner violence; paradoxically, lawyers and advocates who recognize their limitations are likely to be more effective in their work than those who assume too much responsibility.

A. Representing Battered Clients

Since the nineteen seventies, activists, advocates and lawyers have been working to transform the legal system's responses to intimate partner violence, and the attitudes towards victims of violence that guided those responses. Specifically, as you have read, the goal was to dislodge old stereotypes of women as provocateurs of violence, as masochistic participants in their own abuse, or as deceitful manipulators who fabricate tales of abuse to achieve other ends. Although those stereotypes are slow to die, the work of the last thirty years has created competing images that have been successful in prompting legal reform, and have resulted in many women receiving more sympathetic treatment within the legal system. The accomplishments of the battered women's movement, and the many committed individuals who have contributed to these changes, should not be minimized. However, within the last decade we have begun to see new tendencies toward stereotype, and to appreciate the limitations of the reform strategies that guided work in the seventies and eighties. You have seen these new stereotypes at work, and discussed, earlier in this book, but this next reading provides a useful summary.

Ann Shalleck
Theory and Experience in Constructing the Relationship between Lawyer and Client: Representing Women Who Have Been Abused, 64 Tennessee Law Review 1019, 1023–1027 (1997)

Without rejecting the importance of many of the cultural, social, political and legal developments of the last quarter century, or the recognition of the oppression of women underlying the efforts to secure these changes, some feminist theorists and activists have identified limitations, contradictions and dangers embedded in the theoretical constructs that have dominated both the discourse about, and the institutional developments affecting, the experience of abused women in an intimate relationship. They have seen the harms women who have been abused suffer under the legal regime resulting from the changes that have been implemented, and confronted the conceptual problems revealed in the actualization of the new legal landscape. Against this background, these feminist theorists and activists have begun to articulate new ways to conceive and approach the issue of abuse of women in intimate relationships. Although not all of those who have engaged in this critique embrace all of the following elements, several overlapping and intersecting themes characterize this emerging feminist critique.

First, these theorists see the construct of the "battered woman" as essentializing. It makes one characteristic of a woman's experience define her entire identity, thereby marginalizing or trivializing other aspects of her identity. Those aspects of her life that she may have insulated from the impact of the violence in her life become invisible. Her strengths and her accomplishments become submerged under the label of "battered woman." Her relationship with a violent person entirely defines her.

Second, these critics also view the construct of "battering" as essentializing because this framework treats intimate abuse as a single, uniform experience. Within dominant theories of domestic violence, the "cycle of violence" is presented as having a powerful, internal dynamic that, of necessity, replicates itself in all battered women's lives. Experiences that do not fit into the cycle are denied, diminished, or interpreted to make them fit into the model. If a woman's experience does not fit the cycle, it must not be "battering." In addition, this view of "battering" is constructed out of the experiences of primarily white, heterosexual women. "Battering" of women of color or of lesbians is understood as a variant of the dominant model. Their experiences of intimate abuse and their understanding of those experiences are not used to alter the model or to challenge its validity, but are assimilated into it.

Third, "battered women" are portrayed as victims, as powerless and passive objects of another's violence, helpless to free themselves from the constraints imposed by the "batterer." Women whose actions seem to fit into the stereotypical portrait are denied affirmation of their attempts to resist, to survive, to protect their children, or to create space to maneuver within the constraints they face. The reasonableness of the choices made within the constraints they face is obliterated. In addition, the stereotype of "battered women" as passive victims might secure them help or protection in one context, but may boomerang to harm them in another. Other women, whose actions challenge the stereotypical portrait, who wish to assert their capacity to shape or control the violent situation in some way, are often left outside of the sphere of protection offered by the legal developments regarding domestic violence.

Fourth, the power of the construct of the "battered woman" tends to put the focus on the woman, rather than the man who is violent. This focus has two consequences. First, the common question asked about abused women is "Why didn't she leave?" This question tends to obscure the inquiry about why she had to face the violence at all. Second, the twin constructs of "battering" and "battered woman" are dependent upon the demonization of the "batterer." Seen solely as the instrument or incarnation of violence, he is rarely a real, complex human being for whom a woman might have felt or still feel affection. When differences among men who abuse women are minimized or the complexities of a particular woman's history with a man are invisible, women's differential responses to varying situations are more difficult to comprehend. Therefore, women's efforts to find help for or to protect the person who has abused them are understood, at best, as misguided and, at worst, demented. Other women's efforts to protect their children's relationship with a parent who may be loving, or at least adequate, by staying in an abusive situation or resisting punishment of an abusive partner are demeaned, ignored, or treated as irrational.

Fifth, these four characteristics of the concepts of "battering" and "battered woman" lead many women not to recognize themselves or their experiences in the standard narrative of domestic violence. In order to secure what legal protections exist, they often must violate their own understanding of themselves and conform to the dominant stereotype. In making this strategic maneuver, a woman can feel additional powerlessness at her inability to explain her own situation as she experienced it. If she refuses to participate in this violation of her self-understanding, a woman may forego the limited protections that the legal system offers. She may decide to withdraw from the legal system that seems to demand adherence to the stereotype, incurring the wrath or the pity of many participants in that system. She may even end up jailed or punished for failing to play her appointed role. Alternatively, if she proceeds in the legal system but refuses to adopt the standard story, she may find herself denied the protection that she sought.

Sixth, using legal remedies may create additional dangers for women who have been abused rather than ensuring or even increasing their safety or the safety of their children. This feminist critique is directed not just at the partial nature of most legal tools, but also at the site of the decision about whether to use available legal mechanisms. Beyond the debates about whether or not civil protection orders, arrests, criminal prosecutions and incarceration actually decrease the incidence or level of violence in the aggregate, these critics are concerned that those who work with or counsel the women, initiate legal actions, or make decisions in those cases disregard and belittle an individual woman's evaluation of the danger she or her children face when she participates in legal action.

These feminist theorists and activists seek first to reveal and challenge the assumptions behind and consequences of legal reforms, many of which they themselves originally sought. Second, they attempt to place these reforms in a historical and political perspective, in order to further our understanding of how visions implicit in legal reforms may not be apparent until those reforms are realized and how the consequences of legal change may not be predictable or intended. Third, these theorists and activists are engaged in a search for new legal strategies that provide abused women with legal accounts of abuse by an intimate partner that resonate with their own experiences, that create additional space for successfully challenging that abuse, and that do not separate social policies regarding domestic violence from the complex and multiple realities of women who must find ways to cope with violence in their intimate relationships.

* * *

NOTES AND QUESTIONS

1. It is worth pausing to consider how much of the "backfiring" of legal reforms designed to address partner abuse has been due to mistakes of characterization or conceptualization on the part of activists and theorists, and how much has been due to the translation process by which accurate and nuanced characterizations and conceptualizations are filtered through mainstream cultural assumptions and attitudes before being integrated into the legal system. You might decide, for example, that it is legal readings of Lenore Walker's early work that have created problems for battered women who do not fit the "helpless" stereotype, rather than the

work itself. On the other hand, it does seem that policies like mandatory arrest and no-drop prosecution have been guided by an "essentializing" and paternalistic (or perhaps in this case maternalistic) impulse that it is *always* better for women if their batterers are held accountable for their abuse within the criminal justice system, even if the women themselves resist that outcome.

2. Is it ever appropriate for those working in the domestic violence field, whether as theorists, activists, advocates or lawyers, to claim that they know what is best for victims of partner violence, either in the aggregate, or individually? At the policy level it is of course necessary to advocate for solutions at a generic level, even knowing that they will not serve every individual equally, and that there may be individuals who are not helped at all, and may even be hurt, by proposed reform. Responsible policy advocacy consists of careful listening, study and learning, so that proposals grow out of a wide and solid base of information, and aim for solutions flexible enough to accommodate the needs of the vast majority of those who will be affected by them. Even after more than twenty years of study, the body of empirical research on the impact of reforms in the domestic violence arena is dangerously thin; there is too much room, still, for advocacy based more on conviction than knowledge.

At the level of individual representation, can lawyers or advocates know what is best for their clients, and should they ever act on that conviction, if it does not accord with the client's own understanding? What counts as effective representation in this context? The next reading provides a summary of what has been written on this subject, again drawn from the work of Ann Shalleck. Her account draws from articles by Susan Bryant and Maria Arias, *Case Study: A Battered Women's Rights Clinic: Designing a Clinical Program Which Encourages a Problem–Solving Vision of Lawyering that Empowers Clients and Community,* 42 WASH. U. J. URB. & CONTEMP. L. 207 (1992); Leslie G. Espinoza, *Legal Narratives, Therapeutic Narratives: The Invisibility and Omnipresence of Race and Gender,* 95 MICH. L. REV. 901 (1997), Peter Margulies, *Representation of Domestic Violence Survivors as a New Paradigm of Poverty Law: In Search of Access, Connection and Voice,* 93 GEO. WASH. L. REV. 1071 (1995); Joan S. Meier, *Notes From the Underground: Integrating Psychological and Legal Perspectives on Domestic Violence in Theory and Practice,* 21 HOFSTRA L. REV. 1295 (1993); Linda Mills, *Intuition and Insight: A New Job Description for the Battered Woman's Prosecutor and Other More Modest Proposals,* 7 U.C.L.A. WOMEN'S L. J. 183 (1997); and Linda Mills, *On the Other Side of Silence: Affective Lawyering for Intimate Abuse,* 81 CORNELL L. REV. 1225 (1996).

Ann Shalleck
Theory and Experience in Constructing the Relationship between Lawyer and Client: Representing Women Who Have Been Abused, 64 Tennessee Law Review, 1019, 1028–38 (1997)

Several theorists of practice have identified elements that they think are essential to effective representation of women who have been abused.

Although these various efforts ... have differences, certain recurring characteristics emerge from these models. Identifying these characteristics can be helpful in increasing our awareness of the assumptions we bring to representation for women who have been abused, evaluating our emerging conceptions of this representation, fashioning alternative models, identifying lawyering practices through which the models can be realized, and exploring pedagogical methods that would enable students to learn how to provide and critique the practices that the aspirational models describe.

In different ways, these theorists of practice are particularly attentive to the affective components of the lawyer-client relationship. Two of them, Peter Margulies and Linda Mills, have explicitly characterized their models as "affective." A third, Leslie Espinoza, has characterized hers as "therapeutic." A fourth, Joan Meier, in the creation of a model integrating both legal and psychological theory and practice, has made the affective component central to her vision of lawyering. Finally, while Susan Bryant and Maria Arias are deeply concerned abut making a client's understanding of her situation and definition of her needs a critical component in the interaction between lawyer and client, they also stress the importance of other aspects of client representation....

A. Reflection on Experience

First, these models of lawyering encourage lawyers representing women who have been abused to identify and reflect upon, both before and during their representation, their own experiences of and feelings about violence or powerlessness in intimate relationships. This reflection is needed for three interrelated reasons. First, understanding his or her own vulnerability and powerlessness within intimate relationships is part of a lawyer's ability to experience empathy with the client's situation. Although the lawyer may not have gone through the same type of experience as the client, the lawyer needs to find within his or her own experience a basis for beginning to understand the situation of a client on an emotional level. For these theorists, the discovery of common experiential ground is necessary, not primarily for instrumental reasons of gaining the trust of or increasing rapport with a client, but for the construction of a relationship built explicitly on the shared recognition of the similarities and differences in their situations. From a relationship characterized by this sort of understanding comes the lawyer's abilities to act effectively with and for the client.

For these theorists, self-reflection is important for more than empathic understanding, however. Reflection by the lawyer on his or her own experiences is part of the process of understanding the pervasive nature and complex dynamics of intimate violence. The lawyer needs to see intimate abuse not as a single category within which one fits or not, but as a complex mixture of experiences involving not just physical violence, but also coercive behavior and the exercise of power and control, as well as other, yet unnamed, forms of domination and dependency. From this identification of commonalities of experience, lawyers can see that abuse is not a problem of the "other," but a shared experience, even if the experience is different.

Within these models, reflection by the lawyer furthers a third goal. Only with reflection can the lawyer respond respectfully to both the client's understanding of, and the decision-making affecting, her life. Lawyers must confront and overcome any barriers in their own reactions to and understanding of a client that could prompt them to disregard or overwhelm a client's own thoughts and decisions about how to proceed in a case. For these theorists, the lawyer's ability to not impose his or her own assumptions, ways of thinking, stereotypes, or biases on a client is grounded in reflection on the lawyer's own experience. A lawyer's views of and feelings about intimate abuse cannot just be left outside the door to the lawyer's office. A lawyer can "shed" those attitudes only by reaching into his or her own experience and finding commonalities, as well as differences, with the client. The lawyer, by appreciating, or at least sensing, the ways in which he or she shares in the vulnerabilities of the client ... may avoid judging the client. As the lawyer perhaps becomes increasingly uncertain about what he or she would have done if in the client's situation, the lawyer becomes less likely to impose on the client a course of action that arises from the lawyer's imposition of his or her own framework of understanding on the client.

As with the development of empathy, the process of not judging the client is a part of understanding the nature of intimate violence. For these theorists, the uni-dimensional conception of "battering" within the dominant theories of domestic violence has masked the complexities and contradictions of the interactional structures within which intimate violence occurs. It has permitted and even encouraged participants in all parts of the legal system to judge harshly women who have experienced abuse. By failing to see and respect an individual woman's sometimes shifting and contradictory ways of dealing with and interpreting the violence in her relationship, a lawyer may easily impose his or her own understanding of the violence on the client as the client makes the multiple decisions involved in taking any legal action at all, including meeting with a lawyer. The lawyer can come to understand the dynamics involved in continuing in an intimate relationship in which there is abuse only if he or she accepts the conflicted and unstable accounts that the woman has of her relationships and experiences.

B. Recognition of the Fluidity of the Lawyer–Client Relationship

The second characteristic of these models of lawyering is their explicit recognition of the fluidity of the lawyer-client relationship. A woman who is or has been in an abusive relationship and has entered the legal system is often in a long process of coming to understand the relationship and herself within that relationship. As her understanding of the complex dynamics of the relationship changes, and her vision of herself alters over time, she can bring great instability to the relationship with her lawyer. In addition, the relationship between the client and her lawyer can become an element affecting her concepts of her life and herself. Therefore, the lawyer needs to see his or her role not as furthering a stable goal of the client, but as creating an opportunity for a client to explore multiple possibilities, as well as her own changing desires to further any of them.

The fluid character of the lawyer-client relationship, therefore, has two components of particular importance for women who have been in abusive relationships. First, it helps to affirm within the process of representation the non-judgmental attitude of the lawyer. If the woman can experience a space within which she can examine multiple possibilities and shift among them freely without fear of being judged as unstable or indecisive, she is then better able to figure out, within the contours of that relationship, what she thinks is best for her to do. If most people in the legal system are telling her that she ought to leave, she has at least one place where the desirability of leaving is not assumed and the complexities of separating are acknowledged not just in words, but throughout the multiple aspects of the lawyer-client interactions.

Second, by explicitly recognizing the unstable character of the client's goal, the lawyer is better able to accept the seemingly non-instrumental character of the representation. The purpose of the representation is not just to help the client achieve what she wants, but to work with the client to help her figure out what she wants. The client's ambivalence is not a moment to be confronted and worked through, but an important and continuing aspect of a case. The process of deciding what she wants may even be bound up for the client with the process of attempting to bring about an articulated goal. When concrete actions are taken to move towards a goal, a client may see that the goal is not what she understood it to be abstractly, or that the goal has consequences she did not foresee. As the client shifts in what she wants, the lawyer can come to understand the multiple meanings that each step within the legal system has for a woman who is abused within an intimate relationship.

C. Working Collaboratively with Clients

The lawyer and client operate collaboratively within these models of lawyering. This collaboration is grounded in two principles. First, this model rejects the pre-eminence of legal solutions for women who are abused in their intimate relationships. Not only are legal remedies limited in their effectiveness in stopping or reducing violence, but they can interfere with a woman's ability to develop for herself both an understanding of the violence in her intimate relationships and responses that enable her to alter the situation in ways that meet her changing needs. At their worst, legal actions can further harm women. If the lawyer treats legal understanding of violence and legal remedies as not better than any other possible understanding or response, and if the lawyer views a woman's decision to pursue a legal remedy as constantly fluid, then the lawyer has no special claims to expertise. Within this framework, a client must be treated as an equal participant in shaping both the understanding of what type of action should be taken and how it should be pursued.

Second, the lawyer's ability to act effectively for his or her client is dependent upon a relationship within which lawyer and client recognize each other as jointly involved in a common enterprise. For some of the theorists of this model of lawyering, the lawyer not only takes on a client's goal, but participates with the client in achieving a goal that has significance for both of them. For some advocates of this model of lawyering, this collaboration entails at least some form of self-disclosure by the lawyer. Advocates of this approach stress the importance of the respect and shared commitment that come from mutual self-disclosure that is part of a collaborative effort despite the dangers of manipulation, imposition of a lawyer's understandings and responses on a client, and the inequality that may be part of the lawyer's having and exercising discretion about how and when to disclose aspects of his or her life to the client.

D. Developing Responses that Enable Clients to Take Steps that Are Viable Within Their Particular Situations

This model of lawyering is particularly attentive to the limitations of remedies available through the legal system to women who have been in abusive relationships. Even the legal system's more innovative efforts of the last few years fail to respond to the needs of most women who are attempting to figure out ways to deal with the violence in their intimate relationships. Because of the legal system's emphasis upon eradicating violence rather than understanding it or helping women find ways to address the intimate violence in their own lives, as well as the system's emphasis upon the termination of a woman's relationship with the person who has abused her, the remedies available through the legal system often do not provide women an opportunity to make the changes in their lives that they need. When the inadequacies of these remedies are combined with the need to conform to the stereotypical image of a "battered woman" that the legal system reinforces, many women seek to escape from the system once they enter it or are deterred from even approaching it at all.

Within this legal context, lawyers for women who have been abused face several challenging tasks in their relationship with a client. The lawyer needs to work with the client to develop a variety of actions that both fit within the client's sense of her own capacity for acting and respond to the shifting and conflicting needs that the client feels. Also, the lawyer needs to explore with the client how each of those responses might work if implemented. Each response might or might not have a legal component to it. The lawyer needs to respect the client's judgments about the dangers that any action might pose, as well as the disruption of the client's life that each action could entail. In identifying and explaining various legal actions that could be part of a client's plan, the lawyer needs to be particularly careful not to favor legal action over other kinds of actions, either implicitly or explicitly. Furthermore, in describing the nature of the legal actions, as well as the multiple consequences that might flow from them, the lawyer needs to draw upon his or her understanding of the client in anticipating the meaning that those consequences could have for the client in her own struggle to deal with the violence in her relationship.

E. Making Time

Often, for lawyers, time assumes the quality of a commodity. While it feels like the most precious thing we have, it also feels like the one over which we have the least control. Lawyers can feel that they are constantly in a responsive mode, answering to multiple demands.... Against this backdrop, lawyering in this model requires that lawyers recognize the centrality of time in the process of representing women who have been in abusive relationships. Each of the elements of lawyering identified above demands significant and often unpredictable allocations of time. In order to be self-reflective in a serious and meaningful way, the lawyer must set aside time to explore his or her own feelings and experiences. Developing empathic understanding of the relationships surrounding the violence in someone's life involves becoming familiar with the details and texture of her experiences and thoughts. Accepting the constant changes in a client's desires regarding her situation requires patience and attention to the reasons for the shifts in understanding and decisions. The mutual recognition of shared understanding and mutual projects that characterizes a collaborative relationship comes only after multiple interactions and much exploration in the search for common ground. Developing with a client creative and specifically tailored responses to her situation is a process that results only after lawyer and client have imagined and explored multiple possibilities.

* * *

NOTE

1. As Ann Shalleck suggests, the model of lawyering with and on behalf of victims of domestic violence she describes is deeply informed by psychological theory and insight. One of the most helpful theorists in the domestic violence field is psychiatrist Judith Lewis Herman. In her pathbreaking 1992 book TRAUMA AND RECOVERY, Herman draws on the experiences of combat veterans, prisoners of war and battered women to explain the consequences of prolonged and chronic exposure to violence and abuse for those who suffer it, and also for those who work with survivors:

> This is a book about restoring connections: between the public and private worlds, between the individual and the community, between men and women. It is a book about commonalities: between rape survivors and combat veterans, between battered women and political prisoners, between the survivors of vast concentration camps and the survivors of small, hidden concentration camps created by tyrants who rule their homes.

Id. at 2–3. An important focus for Herman is the survivor's path to recovery, and the ways in which helping professionals can assist, or hinder, that process. The next reading is an excerpt from the chapter of Herman's book called *A Healing Relationship*, which focuses on the work of therapy, and the task of the therapist, in the context of abuse. Lawyers and advocates are not therapists, and there are obviously important distinctions between the types of assistance and support they can provide a survivor of domestic violence. Nonetheless, much of what Herman says about the client-therapist relationship may have application to the lawyer-client, or advocate-client, relationship. As you read the next pages, ask yourself what aspects of Herman's analysis have relevance for the lawyer or advocate, and how many of her admonitions and recommendations have value, even in the different context of legal advocacy. One way to do that is to ask to what extent her analysis supports the model of lawyering described in the previous reading by Ann Shalleck.

A Healing Relationship Judith Lewis Herman, Trauma and Recovery, 133–54 (1992)

The core experiences of psychological trauma are disempowerment and disconnection from others. Recovery, therefore, is based upon the empowerment of the survivor and the creation of new connections. Recovery can take place only within the context of relationships; it cannot occur in isolation. In her renewed connections with other people, the survivor re-creates the psychological faculties that were damaged or deformed by the traumatic experience. These faculties include the basic capacities for trust, autonomy, initiative, competence, identity and intimacy....

The first principle of recovery is the empowerment of the survivor. She must be the author and arbiter of her own recovery. Others may offer advice, support, assistance, affection and care, but not cure. Many benevolent and well-intentioned attempts to assist the survivor founder because this fundamental principle of empowerment is not observed. No intervention that takes power away from the survivor can possibly foster her recovery, no matter how much it appears to be in her immediate best interest....

... In exceptional circumstances, where the survivor has totally abdicated responsibility for her own self-care or threatens immediate harm to herself or to others, rapid intervention is required with or without her consent. But even then, there is no need for unilateral action; the survivor should still be consulted about her wishes and offered as much choice as is compatible with the preservation of safety.

. . .

The therapy relationship is unique in several respects. First, its sole purpose is to promote the recovery of the patient. In the furtherance of this goal, the therapist becomes the patient's ally, placing all the resources of her knowledge, skill and experience at the patient's disposal. Second, the therapy relationship is unique because of the contract between patient and therapist regarding the use of power.... It is the therapist's responsibility to use the power that has been conferred upon her only to foster the recovery of the patient, resisting all temptations to abuse. This promise, which is central to the integrity of any therapeutic relationship, is of special importance to patients who are already suffering as the result of another's arbitrary and exploitative exercise of power.

In entering the treatment relationship, the therapist promises to respect the patient's autonomy by remaining disinterested and neutral.

"Disinterested" means that the therapist abstains from using her power over the patient to gratify her personal needs. "Neutral" means that the therapist does not take sides in the patient's inner conflicts or try to direct the patient's life decisions. Constantly reminding herself that the patient is in charge of her own life, the therapist refrains from advancing a personal agenda. The disinterested and neutral stance is an ideal to be striven for, never perfectly attained.

The technical neutrality of the therapist is not the same as moral neutrality. Working with victimized people requires a committed moral stance. The therapist is called upon to bear witness to a crime. She must affirm a position of solidarity with the victim. This does not mean a simplistic notion that the victim can do no wrong, rather, it involves an understanding of the fundamental injustice of the traumatic experience and the need for a resolution that restores some sense of justice. This affirmation expresses itself in the therapist's daily practice, in her language, and above all in her moral commitment to truth-telling without evasion or disguise. Yael Danieli, a psychologist who works with survivors of the Nazi Holocaust, assumes this moral stance even in the routine process of taking a family history. When survivors speak of their relatives who "died," she affirms that they were, rather, "murdered." ... "The use of the word 'death' ... appears to be a defense against acknowledging murder as possibly the most crucial reality of the Holocaust."

The therapist's role is both intellectual and relational, fostering both insight and empathic connection.... The psychoanalyst Otto Kernberg makes similar observations on the treatment of patients with borderline personality disorder: "The therapist's empathic attitude, derived from his emotional understanding of himself and from his transitory identification with and concern for the patient, has elements in common with the empathy of the 'good-enough mother' with her infant.... There is, however, also a totally rational, cognitive, almost ascetic aspect to the therapist's work with the patient which gives their relation a completely different quality."

The alliance of therapy cannot be taken for granted; it must be painstakingly built by the effort of both patient and therapist. Therapy requires a collaborative working relationship in which both partners act on the basis of their implicit confidence in the value and efficacy of persuasion rather than coercion, ideas rather than force, mutuality rather than authoritarian control. These are precisely the beliefs that have been shattered by the traumatic experience. Trauma damages the patient's ability to enter into a trusting relationship; it also has an indirect but powerful impact on the therapist. As a result, both patient and therapist will have predictable difficulties coming to a working alliance. These difficulties must be understood and anticipated from the outset.

TRAUMATIC TRANSFERENCE

Patients who suffer from a traumatic syndrome form a characteristic type of transference in the therapy relationship. Their emotional responses to any person in a position of authority have been deformed by the experience of terror. For this reason, traumatic transference reactions have an intense, life-or-death quality unparalleled in ordinary therapeutic experience.... Some of the most astute observations on the vicissitudes of traumatic transference appear in the classic accounts of the treatment of borderline personality disorder, written when the traumatic origin of the disorder was not yet known. In these accounts, a destructive force appears to intrude repeatedly into the relationship between therapist and patient.... The psychiatrist Eric Lister remarks that ... "The terror is as though the patient and therapist convene in the presence of yet another person. The third image is the victimizer, who ... demanded silence and whose command is now being broken."

The traumatic transference reflects not only the experience of terror but also the experience of helplessness.... The greater the patient's emotional conviction of helplessness and abandonment, the more desperately she feels the need for an omnipotent rescuer. Often she casts the therapist in this role. She may develop intensely idealized expectations of the therapist. The idealization of the therapist protects the patient, in fantasy, against reliving the terror of the trauma. In one successful case both patient and therapist came to understand the terror at the source of the patient's demand for rescue: "The therapist remarked, 'It's frightening to need someone so much and not be able to control them.' The patient was moved and continued this thought: 'It's frightening because you can kill me with what you say ... or by not caring or [by] leaving.' The therapist then added, 'We can see why you need me to be perfect.' "

When the therapist fails to live up to these idealized expectations—as she inevitably will fail—the patient is often overcome with fury. Because the patient feels as though her life depends upon her rescuer, she cannot afford to be tolerant; there is no room for human error....

... Many traumatized people feel ... rage at the caregivers who try to help them and harbor ... fantasies of revenge. In these fantasies they wish to reduce the disappointing, envied therapist to the same unbearable condition of terror, helplessness and shame that they themselves have suffered.

Though the traumatized patient feels a desperate need to rely on the integrity and competence of the therapist, she cannot do so, for her capacity to trust has been damaged by the traumatic experience.... The patient enters the therapeutic relationship prey to every sort of doubt and suspicion. She generally assumes that the therapist is either unable or unwilling to help. Until proven otherwise, she assumes that the therapist cannot bear to hear the true story of the trauma. Combat veterans will not form a trusting relationship until they are convinced that the therapist can stand to hear the details of the war story. Rape survivors, hostages, political prisoners, battered women, and Holocaust survivors feel a similar mistrust of the therapist's ability to listen. In the words of one incest survivor, "These therapists sound like they have all the answers, but they back away from the real shitty stuff."

At the same time, however, the patient mistrusts the motives of any therapist who does not back away. She may attribute to the therapist many of the same motives as the perpetrator. She often suspects the therapist of exploitative or voyeuristic intentions.... Patients who have been subjected to chronic trauma and therefore suffer from a complex post-traumatic syndrome also have complex transference reactions. The protracted involvement with the perpetrator has altered the patient's relational style, so that she not only fears repeated victimization, but also seems unable to protect herself from it, or even appears to invite it. The dynamics of dominance and submission are reenacted in all subsequent relationships, including the therapy.

Chronically traumatized patients have an exquisite attunement to unconscious and nonverbal communication. Accustomed over a long time to reading their captors' emotional and cognitive states, survivors bring this ability into the therapy relationship....

The patient scrutinizes the therapist's every word and gesture, in an attempt to protect herself from the hostile reactions she expects. Because she has no confidence in the therapist's benign intentions, she persistently misinterprets the therapist's motives and reactions. The therapist may eventually react to these hostile attributions in unaccustomed ways. Drawn into the dynamics of dominance and submission, the therapist may inadvertently reenact aspects of the abusive relationship....

The reenactment of the relationship with the perpetrator is most evident in the sexualized transference that sometimes emerges in survivors of prolonged childhood sexual abuse. The patient may assume that the only value she can possibly have in the eyes of another, especially in the eyes of a powerful person, is as a sexual object....

Patients may be quite direct about their desire for a sexual relationship. A few patients may actually demand such a relationship as the only convincing proof of the therapist's caring. At the same time, even these patients dread a reenactment of the sexual relationship in therapy; such a reenactment simply confirms the patient's belief that all human relationships are corrupt.

. . .

TRAUMATIC COUNTERTRANSFERENCE

Trauma is contagious. In the role of witness to disaster or atrocity, the therapist at times is emotionally overwhelmed. She experiences, to a lesser degree, the same terror, rage, and despair as the patient. This phenomenon is known as "traumatic countertransference" or "vicarious traumatization." The therapist may begin to experience symptoms of post-traumatic stress disorder. Hearing the patient's trauma story is bound to revive any personal traumatic experiences that they therapist may have suffered in the past. She may also notice imagery associated with the patient's story intruding into her own waking fantasies or dreams....

Engagement in this work thus poses some risk to the therapist's own psychological health. The therapist's adverse reactions, unless understood and contained, also predictably lead to disruptions in the therapeutic alliance with patients and to conflict with professional colleagues. Therapists who work with traumatized people require an ongoing support system to deal with these intense reactions. Just as no survivor can recover alone, no therapist can work with trauma alone.

Traumatic countertransference includes the entire range of the therapist's emotional reactions to the survivor and to the traumatic event itself. . . . This interpretation recognizes the shadow presence of the perpetrator in the relationship between patient and therapist and traces the countertransference, like the transference, to its original source outside of a simple dyadic relationship.

In addition to suffering vicarious symptoms of post-traumatic stress disorder, the therapist has to struggle with the same disruptions in relationship as the patient. Repeated exposure to stories of human rapacity and cruelty inevitably challenges the therapist's basic faith. It also heightens her sense of personal vulnerability. She may become more fearful of other people in general and more distrustful even in close relationships. She may find herself becoming increasingly cynical about the motives of others and pessimistic about the human condition.

The therapist also empathetically shares the patient's experience of helplessness. This may lead the therapist to underestimate the value of her own knowledge and skill, or to lose sight of the patient's strengths and resources. Under the sway of countertransference helplessness, the therapist may also lose confidence in the power of the psychotherapy relationship. It is not uncommon for experienced therapists to feel suddenly incompetent and hopeless in the face of a traumatized patient. Putnam describes experienced therapists as feeling intimidated and "deskilled" when they encounter a patient with multiple personality disorder. Similar feelings arise among those who work with survivors of extreme political violence and repression. The case of Irene, a victim of sexual terrorism, illustrates a temporary therapeutic stalemate occasioned by the therapist's loss of confidence:

> . . .
>
> The therapist identified with Irene's frustration and helplessness. Doubting that psychotherapy had anything to offer, he found himself offering practical advice instead. Irene despondently rejected all of his suggestions, just as she had rejected suggestions from friends, family and the police. She felt sure that the perpetrator would defeat anything she tried. Therapy was not helping her either; her symptoms worsened, and she began to report thoughts of suicide.
>
> Reviewing the case in supervision, the therapist realized that he, like Irene, had been overwhelmed with a feeling of helplessness. Consequently, he had lost confidence in the utility of listening, his basic skill. In the next session, he asked whether Irene had ever told anyone the whole story of what happened to her. Irene said that no one wanted to hear about it; people just wanted her to shape up and get back to normal. The therapist remarked that Irene must feel really alone, and wondered if she felt she could not confide in him either.

Irene burst into tears. She had indeed felt that the therapist did not want to listen.

In subsequent sessions, as Irene told her story, her symptoms gradually abated. She began to take more action to protect herself, mobilizing her friends and family, and finding more effective ways to get help from the police. Though she reviewed her new strategies with her therapist, she developed them primarily on her own initiative.

As a defense against the unbearable feeling of helplessness, the therapist may try to assume the role of a rescuer. The therapist may take on more and more of an advocacy role for the patient. By so doing, she implies that the patient is not capable of acting for herself. The more the therapist accepts the idea that the patient is helpless, the more she perpetuates the traumatic transference and disempowers the patient.

Many seasoned and experienced therapists, who are ordinarily scrupulously observant of the limits of the therapy relationship, find themselves violating the bounds of therapy and assuming the role of a rescuer, under the intense pressures of traumatic transference and countertransference. The therapist may feel obliged to extend the limits of therapy sessions or to allow frequent emergency contacts between sessions. She may find herself answering phone calls late at night, on weekends, or even on vacations. Rarely do these extraordinary measures result in improvement; on the contrary, the more helpless, dependent, and incompetent the patient feels, generally the worse her symptoms become.

Carried to its logical extreme, the therapist's defense against feelings of helplessness leads to a stance of grandiose specialness or omnipotence. Unless this tendency is analyzed and controlled, the potential for corrupting the therapy relationship is great. All sorts of extreme boundary violations, up to and including sexual intimacy, are frequently rationalized on the basis of the patient's desperate need for rescue and the therapist's extraordinary gifts as a rescuer....

In addition to identifying with the victim's helplessness, the therapist identifies with the victim's rage.... This anger may be directed not only at the perpetrator but also at bystanders who failed to intercede, at colleagues who fail to understand, and generally at the larger society. Through empathic identification, the therapist may also become aware of the depths of the patient's rage and may become fearful of the patient. Once again, this countertransference reaction, if unanalyzed, can lead to actions that disempower the patient. At one extreme, the therapist may preempt the patient's anger with her own, or at the other extreme, she may become too deferential toward the patient's anger....

The therapist also identifies with the patient through the experience of profound grief. The therapist may feel as though she herself is in mourning.... Unless the therapist has adequate support to bear this grief, she will not be able to fulfill her promise to bear witness and will withdraw emotionally from the therapeutic alliance....

Emotional identification with the experience of the victim does not exhaust the range of the therapist's traumatic countertransference. In her role as a witness, the therapist is caught in a conflict between victim and perpetrator. She comes to identify not only with the feelings of the victim but also with those of the perpetrator. While the emotions of identification with the victim may be extremely painful for the therapist, those of identification with the perpetrator may be more horrifying to her, for they represent a profound challenge to her identity as a caring person. . . .

Identification with the perpetrator may take many forms. The therapist may find herself becoming highly skeptical of the patient's story, or she may begin to minimize or rationalize the abuse. The therapist may feel revulsion and disgust at the patient's behavior, or she may become extremely judgmental and censorious when the patient fails to live up to some idealized notion of how a "good" victim ought to behave. She may begin to feel contempt for the patient's helplessness or paranoid fear of the patient's vindictive rage. She may have moments of frank hate and wish to be rid of the patient. Finally, the therapist may experience voyeuristic excitement, fascination, and even sexual arousal. Sexualized countertransference is a common experience, particularly for male therapists working with female patients who have been subjected to sexual violence. . . .

Finally, the therapist's emotional reactions include not only those identified with victim and perpetrator but also those exclusive to the role of the unharmed bystander. The most profound and universal of these reactions is a form of "witness guilt," similar to the patient's "survivor guilt." . . . The therapist may simply feel guilty for the fact that she was spared the suffering that the patient had to endure. In consequence, she may have difficulty enjoying the ordinary comforts and pleasures of her own life. Additionally, she may feel that her own actions are faulty or inadequate. She may judge herself harshly for insufficient therapeutic zeal or social commitment, and come to feel that only a limitless dedication can compensate for her shortcomings.

If the therapist's bystander guilt is not properly understood and contained, she runs the risk of ignoring her own legitimate interests. In the therapy relationship she may assume too much personal responsibility for the patient's life, thus once again patronizing and disempowering the patient. In her work environment she may similarly take on excessive responsibility, with the attendant risk of eventual burnout.

The therapist may also feel guilty for causing the patient to reexperience the pain of the trauma in the course of treatment. . . . As a result, the therapist may shy away from exploring the trauma, even when the patient is ready to do this.

Additional complications of countertransference are to be expected with patients who have a complex post-traumatic syndrome. Especially with survivors of prolonged, repeated abuse in childhood, the therapist may initially respond more to the damaged relational style of the survivor than to the trauma itself. . . .

The therapist may also feel completely bewildered by the rapid fluctuations in the patient's moods or style of relating. . . . Reenactment of the dynamics of victim and perpetrator in the therapy relationship can become extremely complicated. Sometimes the therapist ends up feeling like the patient's victim. Therapists often complain of feeling threatened, manipulated, exploited, or duped. One therapist, faced with his patient's unremmiting suicidal threats, described feeling "like having a loaded gun at my head."

. . .

Traumatic transference and countertransference reactions are inevitable. Inevitably, too, these reactions interfere with the development of a good working relationship. Certain protections are required for the safety of both participants. The two most important guarantees of safety are the goals, rules and boundaries of the therapeutic contract and the support system of the therapist.

THE THERAPY CONTRACT

The alliance between patient and therapist develops through shared work. The work of therapy is both a labor of love and a collaborative commitment. Though the therapeutic alliance partakes of the customs of everyday contractual negotiations, it is not a simple business arrangement. And though it evokes all the passions of human attachment, it is not a love affair or a parent-child relationship. It is a relationship of existential engagement, in which both partners commit themselves to the task of recovery.

This commitment takes the form of a therapy contract. The terms of this contract are those required to promote a working alliance. Both parties are responsible for the relationship. Some of the tasks are the same for both patient and therapist, such as keeping appointments faithfully. Some tasks are different and complementary: the therapist contributes knowledge and skill, while the patient pays a fee for treatment; the therapist promises confidentiality, while the patient agrees to self-disclosure; the therapist promises to listen and bear witness, while the patient promises to tell the truth. The therapy contract should be explained to the patient explicitly and in detail.

From the outset, the therapist should place great emphasis on the importance of truth-telling and full disclosure, since the patient is likely to have many secrets, including secrets from herself. . . .

In addition to the fundamental rule of truth-telling, it is important to emphasize the cooperative nature of the work. The psychologist Jessica Wolfe describes the therapeutic contract that she works out with combat veterans: "It's clearly spelled out as a partnership, so as to avoid any repetition of the loss of control in the trauma. We [therapists] are people who know something about it, but really they know much more, and it's a sharing arrangement. In some of the things we might be recommending, we would be serving as a guide." . . .

The patient enters the therapy relationship with severe damage to her capacity for appropriate trust. Since trust is not present at the outset of the treatment, both therapist and patient should be prepared for repeated testing, disruption, and rebuilding of the therapeutic relationship. As the patient becomes involved, she inevitably reexperiences the intense longing for rescue that she felt at the time of the trauma. The therapist may also wish, consciously or unconsciously, to compensate for the atrocious experiences the patient has endured. Impossible expectations are inevitably aroused, and inevitably disappointed. The rageful struggles that follow upon disappointment may replicate the initial, abusive situation, compounding the original harm.

Careful attention to the boundaries of the therapeutic relationship provides the best protection against excessive, unmanageable transference and countertransference reactions. Secure boundaries create a safe arena where the work of recovery can proceed. The therapist agrees to be available to the patient within limits that are clear, reasonable, and tolerable for both. The boundaries of therapy exist for the benefit and protection of both parties and are based upon a recognition of both the therapist's and the patient's legitimate needs. These boundaries include an explicit understanding that the therapy contract precludes any other form of social relationship, a clear definition of the frequency and duration of therapy sessions, and clear ground rules regarding emergency contact outside of regularly scheduled sessions.

Decisions on limits are made based on whether they empower the patient and foster a good working relationship, not on whether the patient ought to be indulged or frustrated. The therapist does not insist upon clear boundaries in order to control, ration, or deprive the patient. Rather, the therapist acknowledges from the outset that she is a limited, fallible human being, who requires certain conditions in order to remain in an emotionally demanding relationship. . . .

. . . Therapists usually discover that some degree of flexibility is also necessary; mutually acceptable boundaries are not created by fiat but rather result from a process of negotiation and may evolve to some degree over time. A patient describes her view of the process: "My psychiatrist has what he calls 'rules,' which I have defined as 'moving targets.' The boundaries he has set between us seem flexible, and I often try to bend and stretch them. Sometimes he struggles with these boundaries, trying to balance his rules against his respect for me as a human being. As I watch him struggle, I learn how to struggle with my own boundaries, not just the ones between him and me, but those between me and everyone I deal with in the real world."

. . .

Because of the conflicting requirements for flexibility and boundaries, the therapist can expect repeatedly to feel put on the spot. Distinguishing when to be rigid and when to be pliable is a constant challenge. Beginner and seasoned therapists alike often have the feeling of relying on intuition, or "flying by the seat of the pants." When in doubt, therapists should not hesitate to seek consultation.

THE THERAPIST'S SUPPORT SYSTEM

The dialectic of trauma constantly challenges the therapist's emotional balance. The therapist, like the patient, may defend against overwhelming feelings by withdrawal or by impulsive, intrusive action. The most common forms of action are rescue attempts, boundary violations, or attempts to control the patient. The most common constrictive responses are doubting or denial of the patient's reality, dissociation or numbing, minimization or avoidance of the traumatic material, professional distancing, or frank abandonment of the patient. Some degree of intrusion or numbing is probably inevitable. The therapist should expect to lose her balance from time to time with such patients. She is not infallible. The guarantee of her integrity is not her omnipotence but her capacity to trust others. The work of recovery requires a secure and reliable support system for the therapist.

Ideally, the therapist's support system should include a safe, structured, and regular forum for reviewing her clinical work. This might be a supervisory relationship or a peer support group, preferably both. The setting must offer permission to express emotional reactions as well as technical or intellectual concerns related to the treatment of patients with histories of trauma.

Unfortunately, because of the history of denial within the mental health professions, many therapists find themselves trying to work with traumatized patients in the absence of a supportive context. Therapists who work with traumatized patients have to struggle to overcome their own denial. When they encounter the same denial in colleagues, they often feel discredited and silenced, just as victims do. In the words of Jean Goodwin: "My patients don't always believe fully that they exist, nor, much less, that I do.... This is made all the worse when my fellow psychiatrist treats me and my patients as though we don't exist. This last is done subtly, without overt brutality.... If it were only one time, I would not worry about being extinguished, but it is one hundred and one hundred hundreds, one thousand thousand tiny acts of erasure."

Inevitably, therapists who work with survivors come into conflict with their colleagues. Some therapists find themselves drawn into vituperative intellectual debates over the credibility of the traumatic syndromes in general or of one patient's story in particular. Countertransference responses to traumatized patients often become fragmented and polarized, so that one therapist may take the position of the patient's rescuer, for example, while another may take a doubting, judgmental, or punitive position toward the patient. In institutional settings the problem of "staff splitting," or intense conflict over the treatment of a difficult patient, frequently arises. Almost always the subject of the dispute turns out to have a history of trauma. The quarrel among colleagues reflects the unwitting reenactment of the dialectic of trauma.

Intimidated or infuriated by such conflicts, many therapists treating survivors elect to withdraw rather than to engage in what feels like fruitless debate. Their practice goes underground. Torn, like their patients, between the official orthodoxy of their profession and the reality of their own experience, they choose to honor the reality at the expense of the orthodoxy. They begin, like their patients, to have a secret life. As one therapist puts it, "we believe our patients; we just don't tell our supervisors."

. . . Unless the therapist is able to find others who understand and support her work, she will eventually find her world narrowing, leaving her alone with the patient. The therapist may come to feel that she is the only one who understands the patient, and she may become increasingly arrogant and adversarial with skeptical colleagues. As she feels increasingly isolated and helpless, the temptations of either grandiosity or flight become irresistible. Sooner or later she will indeed make serious errors. It cannot be reiterated too often: *no one can face trauma alone.* If a therapist finds herself isolated in her professional practice, she should discontinue working with traumatized patients until she has secured an adequate support system.

In addition to professional support, the therapist must attend to the balance in her own professional and personal life, paying respect and attention to her own needs. Confronted with the daily reality of patients in need of care, the therapist is in constant danger of professional overcommitment. The role of a professional support system is not simply to focus on the tasks of treatment but also to remind the therapist of her own realistic limits and to insist that she take as good care of herself as she does of others.

The therapist who commits herself to working with survivors commits herself to an ongoing contention with herself, in which she must rely on the help of others and call upon her most mature coping abilities. Sublimation, altruism and humor are the therapist's saving graces. . . .

The reward of engagement is the sense of an enriched life. Therapists who work with survivors report appreciating life more fully, taking life more seriously, having a greater scope of understanding of others and themselves, forming new friendships and deeper intimate relationships, and feeling inspired by the daily examples of their patients' courage, determination and hope. This is particularly true of those who, as a result of their work with patients, become involved in social action. These therapists report a sense of higher purpose in life and a sense of camaraderie that allows them to maintain a kind of cheerfulness in the face of horror.

By constantly fostering the capacity for integration, in themselves and their patients, engaged therapists deepen their own integrity. Just as basic trust is the developmental achievement of earliest life, integrity is the developmental achievement of maturity. . . .

Integrity is the capacity to affirm the value of life in the face of death, to be reconciled with the finite limits of one's own life and the tragic limitations of the human condition, and to accept these realities without despair. Integrity is the foundation upon which trust in relationships is originally formed, and upon which shattered trust may be restored. The interlocking of integrity and trust in caretaking relationships completes the cycle of generations and regenerates the sense of human community which trauma destroys.

* * *

NOTES AND QUESTIONS

1. In suggesting that the first principle of recovery for survivors is empowerment, Herman acknowledges that: "Caregivers schooled in a medical model of treatment often have difficulty grasping this fundamental principle and putting it into practice." Id. at 133. Do you think lawyers would have more or less difficulty than doctors? What about non-lawyer advocates? What has your legal education taught you so far about the nature of the relationships with clients you should anticipate, or work toward?

2. Herman states very categorically that: "no intervention that takes power away from the survivor can possibly foster her recovery." She then suggests that there may be exceptional cases where the survivor's safety, or the safety of others, may justify overriding the principle of empowerment. Might there be situations when a lawyer or advocate would similarly be justified in overriding a client's autonomy? What would those situations be? Should they be as exceptional in the legal context as Herman argues they should be in the context of therapy?

3. Herman argues that the ideal stance of the therapist is one of disinterest and neutrality. Taken out of context, those characteristics sound unappealing, and even inappropriate. How would you explain their meaning, and their importance, to someone who had not read Herman's account?

4. How much of what Herman has to say about the therapist-patient relationship do you think is relevant to the lawyer-client, or advocate-client relationship? If you believe that the dynamics of the relationships are similar enough in some respects that the lawyer or advocate should expect to experience some of the same difficulties as the therapist, are Herman's prescriptions realistic for the lawyer or advocate? Is there a difference in this regard between the professional who works exclusively, or almost exclusively, with battered women, and the family lawyer, prosecutor or criminal defense lawyer who works on occasion with a survivor of partner violence, but does not maintain a specialized practice?

In the next reading Joan Meier suggests ways in which the roles of psychological and legal professionals are similar and different, and what the differences may imply for how those roles will play out.

Joan Meier
Notes From the Underground: Integrating Psychological and Legal Perspectives on Domestic Violence in Theory and Practice, 121 Hofstra L. Rev. 1295, 1361–65 (1993)

... The analogy between therapists and lawyers stems from their common commitment to "helping" or serving individuals who are their clients. This commonality is profound; indeed, the lawyer's role as "advocate" for the client is probably the most essential aspect of her role, and the fundamental attribute of the therapeutic role is the therapist's unconditional acceptance of and commitment to the patient on a psychological level. Nonetheless, the methods which lawyers and therapists use to help their clients differ profoundly. At root, the lawyer's role is to act as an advocate for the client vis a vis other people and institutions in the world. The therapist's role is characterized primarily by his or her limitation to private, confidential communication only with the patient, as a supportive listener in an isolated one-on-one interaction, without communication or advocacy in the larger world on the patient's behalf. . . .

From this fundamental difference flow several potential differences in the way the professional roles must be played out with clients.

a. Goals and Methods of Information–Gathering

First, the difference in methods means that psychologists and lawyers need information for different purposes. Psychological professionals need information to a large extent as an end in itself. . . . Lawyers, on the other hand, need information so that they may take legal action on the client's behalf in the legal system to achieve the client's goals. . . .

. . .

In short, the lawyer's role in "interviewing" the client is both narrower and broader than the therapist's role. It is narrower, in that only a limited portion of the client's life, feelings, or concerns are relevant to the legal matter. It is broader in that the lawyer needs to go beyond the client, to explore other sources of information.

. . .

With respect to the broader aspect, i.e., the lawyer's need to search for "proof," corroboration, and contradictions of the client's point of view, the lawyer's investigations into the external facts is potentially more alienating to the client than the ideal therapeutic exchange. . . . [I]n the legal context, unlike the therapeutic context, confrontations of the client (albeit sympathetic and gentle ones) are often necessary. . . .

b. The Need for Lawyers to Take Action on Behalf of Clients

. . . Insofar as the lawyer's role requires her to act "expressively" on behalf of the client, in ways that both affect her own reputation and professional relationships, and also affect third parties, she is personally involved in and affected by client decisions far more than the typical therapist. The lawyer thus must frequently discuss decisions, actions, and tactics with clients, sometimes engaging in persuasion or expressing her own views. In addition, the morally engaged lawyer may need to engage the client in "moral dialogue" with respect to actions desired by the client but about which the lawyer feels moral qualms.

. . .

c. The Need for Clients to Make Decisions

The action orientation of legal representation also means that a central part of the lawyer-client relationship entails assisting clients in making decisions, often quickly. This is in complete contrast to the therapeutic relationship in which decisions regarding action by the client are, if not discouraged, certainly not considered an integral element of most mainstream types of psychotherapy. Most directly, this means that the lawyer-client relationship typically entails far more "counseling" or input by the lawyer, than the typical therapist-patient relationship. Lawyers must, at a minimum, describe and interpret legal procedures and options, and the risks and consequences of different tactics, so the client can make a timely "informed" choice about these actions. Stephen Ellman suggests that one consequence of this greater involvement of the professional in client decisions is that overt expression of "approval" may be more appropriate and beneficial in the lawyer-client relationship than it has traditionally been considered to be in the therapeutic relationship. It may be posited that another consequence is, very simply, the need for greater input by the legal professional than the psychological professional. In short, lawyers must learn how to "advise" clients. This means they must develop their own abilities to assess legal options and consequences, but also means developing a sensitivity to the boundaries between appropriate "informing," "counseling" or "advising" and inappropriate control over decisions which should be made by the client.

* * *

NOTES AND QUESTIONS

1. Do you agree with this assessment of the differences between the roles of therapist and lawyer or advocate? To the extent you do, do you think the differences affect the applicability of the principles outlined by Judith Herman to good legal advocacy on behalf of battered women clients? How would Herman react, do you think, to the idea of a lawyer or advocate explicitly "approving" a client's decision?

2. Herman comments that battered women may approach relationships with helping professionals "prey to every sort of doubt and suspicion." In the legal arena, those doubts and suspicions are too often based in a recalcitrant reality. However, Herman's insight makes it easier to understand why women who have been victims of abuse might abandon their efforts to secure help from the legal system, or law enforcement, after just one negative experience—where individuals who have a greater capacity for trust might persist in their help-seeking efforts. On the other hand, Herman also notes that victims' "intense perceptiveness," when combined with doubt and suspicion, can result in misinterpretations of a helping professional's motives and reactions. It might be valuable at this point to revisit Mary's story, at the start of Chapter 7. Rereading her indictment of the family lawyers who failed to support her in her litigation against her abusive husband, in light of Herman's analysis, is there room to believe that she was overly critical, or expected too much of them? Or, does Herman's analysis offer some new insights into where and how their representation failed?

3. The final reading in this section is drawn from a manual used at Northeastern University School of Law in a clinical program training law students to advocate for battered women. As you read it, ask yourself whether it implements Judith Herman's vision of a client-empowering relationship, and incorporates the lessons she teaches about the impact of trauma.

Client-Centered Interviewing and Counseling Skills
Lois H. Kanter & V. Pualani Enos
Domestic Violence Manual: Volume One, 159–66 (Domestic Violence Institute, NUSL, 1999)[1]

1. *Client Empowering Interviewing Skills for the Battered Women's Advocate*

Many women will readily talk about the violence if they feel safe and supported. The purpose of this section is to aid the interviewer in creating a safe and supportive environment in which to assist the woman in exploring her options while respecting her right to self-determination. It is crucial that the interviewer consistently remind the woman that violence is unacceptable and that she is not to blame. In order to empower and assist her in making an informed choice, the following steps are suggested:

. . .

a. Validating the woman's experience:

Empathize with her and validate her feelings. Because the abuser blames her for the violence and because society frequently does nothing to stop the assaults, many battered women feel that they are responsible for the violence. The advocate needs to take a stand against the violence and make alliance with the battered woman so that she can talk about her confusion, fear, guilt, anger and pain. The advocate must also articulate a clear set of beliefs about the unacceptability of violence. However, it is important to remember that you cannot define the experience for her or suggest that you know more about this than she does.

Take some time to explain the interview process to her and to let her know that she should stop you at any point to ask questions, make comments or simply tell you that she's not comfortable continuing the interview. You'll be asking her some very personal questions dealing with experiences that she may not even have revealed to those closest to her. Talking about the violence and coercion can be embarrassing, humiliating and even frightening and you are virtually a stranger to her. Therefore, it's important that you take the time necessary to make her feel as comfortable with you as possible.

However, to reassure the novice interviewer, we've found that once your initial explanations are made, the simple statement "I'm here because

1. This material is adapted from an earlier version authored by Chris Butler and Mary Bow, which in turn drew on an unpublished work by Susan Schechter.

I am most concerned about your safety. Can you explain to me what happened to bring you to here (to the court, to the office, etc.) today?" is often an easy way to begin a two-way conversation. Thereafter, by asking short, simple questions which encourage the woman to "think aloud" about her situation, her concerns and her objectives, the novice will frequently discover that the task of exploring options while respecting the client's right to make decisions is not quite as difficult as it first appears.

It is important to listen carefully to what she says and to make no assumptions. Give her plenty of time to answer each of your questions and to ask her own. Understand that some of the information will be very difficult for her to convey.

Ask her directly about the violence, If the advocate avoids talking about it, so will the woman.... Do not lapse into "legalese." Support her for telling her story. If English is not her native language, and she feels more comfortable speaking in her native language, consider asking her to bring a friend to interpret or arrange for an interpreter if possible....

Convey that you do not believe that she is responsible for the violence. No matter what she's done, including striking back, drinking or taking drugs, the assailant is responsible for the abuse. Advocates need to reiterate that the violence is criminal and wrong, and no one deserves to be abused.

Universalize the information. Let her know that she's not alone, that many women have been trapped in violent relationships feeling isolated, discouraged and ashamed....

b. Reminding her of and building her strengths:

Many women who are battered have extremely poor or no self-esteem. Anyone who is consistently and repeatedly told that he or she is worthless, while being isolated from other people who could contradict this information, will in time doubt his or her own worth. Since women in our society are often treated less respectfully to begin with, a woman is even more vulnerable to attacks on her self-confidence and self-worth.

Battered women, though doubting themselves, are actually strong and courageous, but they need to be reminded of this. Battered women are not passive recipients of abuse. Rather, they constantly try to stop the violence and protect themselves and their children. Their thoughtfulness is often invisible to the outsider because frequently, in the face of erratic and irrational assault, it is best to proceed very cautiously and by means tailored to meet the needs of the individual woman's situation.

Acknowledge her strengths, the specific ways that she has protected herself and her children, methods she used to leave the abuse or maintain her sanity, the courage she demonstrates by telling you about the violence or calling for help.

c. Avoiding victim-blaming:

One of the most common and damaging mistakes an advocate can make is to frame a question or statement in such a way as to appear to be blaming the victim for the violence. Questions that suggest that her behavior can trigger the violence or that she is in any way responsible for the violence are offensive, inappropriate and even dangerous; they can help to perpetuate the woman's feeling that she should take partial (or even sole) responsibility for the violence.

Do not ask questions that blame the victim like "What keeps you with a man like that? Do you get something out of the violence? Is all this worth the financial security? What did you do at that moment that caused him to hit you? What could you have done to de-escalate the situation? Is there any way you participate in the escalation of the violence?"

If the children have been abused as well or were witnesses to her abuse, do not blame her for his abuse even indirectly. Avoid questions such as "How can you keep your children in this situation? How can you allow your children to go through this? How could you not know what was happening to your child?, or How could you let him do that to your child?"

d. Exploring her options while advocating for her safety:

1. *Identifying Support Systems:* Ask her about support she may have from friends, relatives or co-workers. Are there people who would help her in terms of temporary housing, child care or even appearing in court as a witness on her behalf. Find out if she knows about shelters and/or support groups in her area. Give her referral numbers to these programs if she doesn't already have them....

2. *Identifying Legal Options:* The advocate should explain both criminal and civil options available so that the woman can make an informed choice about how she wants to proceed if she chooses to use the legal system.

3. *Assistance If She Chooses to Take No Legal Action*: It is important to tell every battered woman that you are concerned about her safety and to plan together for her protection. Remember that *she is an expert about the batterer*, and that she, not you, must live with her choices. Do not choose for her. Rather, help her assess her options and the potential consequences of her decisions. When battered women choose to live with their partners, safety is still a priority. If you are not developing a formal safety plan with her, ask some of the following questions as you discuss safety:

- How can we help ensure safety? What do you feel you need in order to be safe?
- Can I safely call you? How should I identify myself when I call? What should I do if the abuser answers the telephone?
- If the violence escalates, can you leave for a few days? Do you have a place to go and the telephone numbers for shelters?
- Is there a car available; have you a hidden set of keys? Do you have any money that you can hide in case of emergency?
- Can you run to a neighbor's or work out a signal so that the neighbor calls the police?

- Do you understand how you can request protective orders on an emergency basis in the evening or on weekends?

e. Respecting her right to self-determination:

Once the advocate has explored with the battered woman the options available to her, the woman must make a choice as to what course of action she wishes to take. Sometimes the choice will be to do nothing. While it is the advocate's role to lay out the options available to her, and even, if asked, to recommend a course of action, once the woman has made her choice the advocate must respect it. It is inappropriate, for instance, to communicate even indirectly or nonverbally that you are disappointed or dissatisfied with her choice.

Battered women are adults who are making virtually impossible choices under extremely difficult circumstances. They must be allowed to make decisions for themselves. Be sure that you are sensitive to this and keep the following suggestions in mind during your conversations with her:

- Do not bully the woman or mandate conditions for your help. Do not say things such as "I can't do anything for you unless you leave him." Instead, ask questions like: "In what way can I be helpful to you?" and "What do you want to do?"
- Allow women to talk about their ambivalence toward the batterer. No one gives up a relationship without a struggle. "How will it feel if he moves out?" and "Is it sad to think about not being with him?"
- Respect her pace in the process. Frequently we urge the impossible. By pressuring her, we may do more damage than good by making her feel out of control in the process and, therefore, more vulnerable, or by placing her in a position of greater danger because we haven't listened to her assessment of what action is safe and appropriate. Encourage her to trust her gut by saying things like, "You seem to make choices which are good for you and your kids," and "It's OK to take it one step at a time." Also remember that some battered women leave and return to their partners several times. Then it is important to say, "Someone will always be available to talk if you want to."
- Accept that each woman must find solutions that she can live with.... Be sensitive and respectful of cultural, class and religious differences which may affect the choices she makes.

Conclusion: Many of the interviewing techniques described above are appropriate and helpful in any legal interview. However, in cases involving battered women, these techniques are even more crucial because of the level of danger involved and the vulnerability of the women being interviewed. It is absolutely critical that the woman feel as comfortable and safe as possible in order to ensure that she can discuss every aspect of her case, even those experiences which are painful, humiliating and extremely intimate. Good interviewing skills can make a tremendous difference in the case in the long run and are worth the extra time and sensitivity required.

2. *Additional Tips Applicable to Interviewing Battered Women*

. . .

Listening and Giving Support

- Be real. People in crisis are very sensitive to others; they will catch you hiding behind a role.
- You need to decide when to set limits. You can set them by bartering or by standing firm on your own determination. Trust your gut.
- A woman may need space to freak out before calming down and talking.
- A lot of crisis counseling is bearing witness to her pain—allowing her to go through it but staying with her.
- Maintain eye contact, even if she doesn't she will be aware of it.
- Maintain a respectful, non-judgmental attitude toward the woman (not necessarily toward her actions).
- Give criticism in a form of "I feel ... when you do...."
- Show empathy by feeding back what you hear. Paraphrase.
- Look for subtitles—e.g., "I am so tired of it all" may be subtitled "I want to kill myself"; figure out what is behind what she is talking about, especially if time is a problem.
- Take all she said and make it simpler, classify and present it back to her.
- Prioritize together; decide what needs to be dealt with first and start with that. Either deal with items in turn or give some idea of when others might be dealt with.
- Try to present options. People in crisis often think they don't have options.
- Don't get into "why" during crisis, it may avoid getting to closure.
- Watch when she seems to have gone through the needed crisis and is holding onto crisis. Use your own sense of fatigue or boredom. Lay it out that you are tired and need to set limits.
- Make sure you get back to her, touch base again within the next few days.
- Take part in peer supervision; get feedback on your own process, feelings, places you felt you did well or not well.

Contradict the Batterer

Frequently battered women come to us with messages their partners have worked hard to instill. These messages may be supported by the media and other members of the community. Every interaction with a survivor provides an opportunity to provide an alternative message, one which encourages help-seeking and supports the skills women do have. The following are examples of ways in which an advocate can contradict the batterer's disempowering and abusive messages:

Batterer says: "No one cares about you"

We say: "I AM WORRIED ABOUT YOU"
"IS THERE ANYTHING YOU WANT TO TALK ABOUT"

Batterer says: "This is all your fault. If only you didn't . . ."

We say: "NO ONE DESERVES TO BE HURT. YOU DIDN'T DO ANYTHING TO CAUSE THIS"

Batterer says: "No one will believe you"

We say: "IT SOUNDS LIKE YOU HAD VERY GOOD REASON TO BE AFRAID"
"I AGREE THAT WHAT HE DID WAS VERY DANGEROUS"
"I AM VERY CONCERNED FOR YOUR SAFETY"
"I KNOW HOW DIFFICULT IT IS TO TALK ABOUT THESE ISSUES. THANK YOU FOR TRUSTING ME WITH SOMETHING SO IMPORTANT"

Batterer says: "If you leave me, you'll have nowhere to go"

We say: "THERE IS SOMEONE HERE FOR YOU TO TALK TO BOTH DURING THE DAY AND AT NIGHT. YOU CAN COME ANYTIME"
"WE CAN TELL YOU ABOUT OTHER RESOURCES AND SERVICES AND SUPPORT YOU TO ACCESS THEM"

Batterer says: "You are crazy"

We say: "ANYONE FACING THOSE CIRCUMSTANCES WOULD HAVE FELT AND REACTED THE WAY YOU DID"

Batterer says: "You are stupid. You need me. You wouldn't survive without me"

We say: "I TRUST YOU TO MAKE THE RIGHT DECISIONS"
"I BELIEVE THAT YOU KNOW WHAT IS BEST FOR YOU"
"I HAVE FAITH IN YOUR ABILITY TO MAKE DECISIONS AND ACT ON YOUR OWN BEHALF"

Batterer says: "You are weak"

We say: . . . "WE ADMIRE YOUR STRENGTH AND COURAGE"

Batterer says: "You will do as I say or you will suffer"

We say: "WE WILL SUPPORT ANY DECISIONS YOU MAKE"
"WE RESPECT YOUR RIGHT TO CHOOSE"

* * *

NOTE

1. Judith Herman is adamant about the need for professionals working with those who have experienced trauma to engage in "self-care." Specifically, she talks about setting appropriate limits with clients, about guarding against over-commitment, about finding room in one's life for relaxation and pleasure, and about working in an environment in which there is sufficient support, ideally among peers, but at a minimum from a clinical supervisor. These conditions may be harder for lawyers and legal advocates

to secure than for those working in the mental health field, where concepts of self-care are better established, and clinical supervision traditionally includes attention to the clinician's own emotional state. Ironically, lawyers and legal advocates working with domestic violence victims may have chosen their work in part because it gave them the freedom to reject overly distanced and professionalized models of lawyering—they may, that is to say, be particularly vulnerable to the temptations of doing too much for their clients and not maintaining appropriate boundaries.

On the other hand, anyone who has worked in this field has either experienced, or witnessed, burnout, and Herman offers a compelling explanation both of why this happens, and of what to do to guard against it. She is also clear that self-care by professionals enhances rather than detracts from the service they provide to their clients. It is worth careful attention, therefore, on the part of students, advocates and lawyers in the many different settings in which they work, to the ways in which they can create and maintain a working environment sufficiently attentive to their own needs.

B. LEGAL ADVOCACY: A CHANGED AND CHANGING LANDSCAPE

Author Ann Jones concludes her recent book NEXT TIME SHE'LL BE DEAD: BATTERING AND HOW TO STOP IT (2d ed. 2000) with a grim assessment, and a call to action. Looking at recent manifestations of society's attitudes towards battering, and its victims, she concedes that there has been change, but questions whether that change genuinely reflects a desire to put an end to intimate partner violence, or to keep its victims safe. The other disturbing possibility, she suggests, is that society still depends on battered women, carefully defined as "other," to absorb male violence—imagining, or fearing, that the violence might otherwise spill out and find other (more vulnerable or less deserving) targets. Perhaps, Jones argues, we do not, despite our protestations to the contrary, want to disturb the status quo. This provocative thesis is the topic of the first reading below.

If we reject that hypothesis, then Jones asserts that we could, and should, demonstrate the sincerity of our commitment to ending domestic violence by making substantially greater progress towards that goal. The goal is not out of reach, she argues; we need only to intensify our efforts, and in some instances redirect or refocus them. Her suggestions for how that could and should be done provide a springboard for the rest of this section, which looks at some of the key components of a broadly based societal response to domestic violence.

The emphasis here is not on substantive law reform; the previous chapters have already highlighted many areas where the law as written, or as applied, could offer more protection to victims of partner violence. To the extent the legal profession is under scrutiny in these final pages, the questions are, instead, (1) how we educate lawyers and future lawyers, judges and future judges, to address domestic violence in their practices and their dockets, and (2) how the legal community works with other institutions and actors, recognizing that no single profession holds 'the answer' to the problem, but that the greatest promise lies in a multidisciplinary and coordinated response.

Ann Jones
Next Time She'll Be Dead: Battering and How to Stop It, 199–206 (2000)

To measure change, it helps to take the long view of history. Then one can see that in the last century and a half public opinion about battered women has undergone a fundamental shift. During the nineteenth century and a good part of this one, when a woman left her husband, the public asked: Why did she leave? The question was not merely inquisitive but judgmental, suggesting other loaded questions: What kind of woman walks out on her husband and family, the sacred duty entrusted to her by God and nature? How could she abandon her obligations, her destiny? Throw away her life? Her children's happiness? Is she deranged? Irreligious? Unnatural?

Today, family, friends, clergy, courts and counselors still urge a woman's duty upon her, but when a woman complains too loudly, or some "real" trouble occurs—a homicide, perhaps, or the battery of a child—the public wants to know: Why didn't she leave? A century ago a dutiful wife's place was with her husband, even a brutal one, though she herself was blameless. Today she is still supposed to stand by her man, but only up to a point—a point always more easily discerned in retrospect, and by others. Then, as we saw in the case of Hedda Nussbaum, if he is "really" abusive and she stays, whatever happens is said to be her own fault.

It is also clear that today in the mainstream culture of this country a woman's duty to her child is supposed to take precedence over her duty to her husband. This judgment too represents a fundamental shift away from an older, purely patriarchal order which valued nothing so much as the privilege of the patriarch himself. Marilyn French tells an old story from India, one of those instructive moral tales designed to teach women how they are supposed to *be*. French writes: "The story presenting an exemplary Indian wife tells of a woman sitting with her sleeping husband's head in her lap, watching over him and her baby playing in front of the fire. The baby wanders near the fire, but the woman does not move lest she disturb her sleeping lord. When the child actually enters the flames, she prays, begging Agni not to harm the baby. Agni rewards her wifely devotion by letting the child sit among the flames unscathed." As French observes, the Indian wife is "a model for Hedda Nussbaum." But as we've seen, the model no longer applies—except perhaps in the minds of men like Joel Steinberg who still feel entitled to all the powers and privileges of the sleeping lord. Today, in this country, the exemplary wife is supposed to stand up and rescue her child from the flames, and if need be, from her "lord" himself.

Thus it happens that the big question—Why didn't she leave?—cuts two ways. On one hand, it shifts the blame from the "nature" of men in general and the societal attitudes and institutions that abet male violence to the character of the individual victim; it blames the victim for the abuse she suffers. On the other hand, it suggests that women now have more options and should make use of them. It implies a widespread belief that women *should* leave abusers, that living with brutality (or, as some would say, "excessive" brutality) is no longer a good wife's duty. Taken in the context of a century and a half of struggle, this is progress.

Yet nothing makes it easy for a woman to leave. Many factors—from low wages and inadequate child care to the unresponsive criminal justice system and a Congress unwilling adequately to fund victim services—conspire to keep the abused woman in her place within the "traditional" family. Abused women leave anyway, but often they are strictly on their own. Many flee one problem—battering—only to become part of another: "the feminization of poverty." These days 65 percent of black children live in a family headed by a single mother, and 45 percent of all American families headed by a single mother live in poverty. When Aid to Families with Dependent Children benefits were suspended in 1996, 60 percent of the poor women receiving them were victims of "domestic violence." Dan Quayle pointed to abortion, divorce, and these single-parent families as grevious *causes* of "the disintegration of the American family." But we can attribute this "disintegration" in part to violence, just as we can attribute the "feminization of poverty" in part to woman and child abuse, a cause economists and politicians never cite. Today experts name battery as a "major cause" of homelessness; large numbers of the nation's growing band of homeless are women on their own with children—women and children who, despite the social and economic obstacles, ran from male violence at home. (Reflect for a moment on conventional explanations for the feminization of poverty—*her* youth, *her* lack of education, *her* lack of job skills, *her* sexual activity, *her* insistence upon becoming a single mother, heedless of Quayle's righteous admonitions—and you'll see that we blame the victim for poverty too. Men, especially men of color, are blamed for "abandoning" women and children—but not for the violence that drives women and children away.) Today most people recognize that women have a right—even a responsibility—to leave abusive men, and many individuals feel an impulse to help them, but we don't yet recognize our responsibility as a society to rise to their aid: our duty as a society to safeguard the right of every woman to be free from bodily harm.

Our public attitude—damned if you don't leave, damned if you do—is not simple hypocrisy. Two conflicting views come down to us from nineteenth-century debates, and we've never sorted them out. To radical women in the mid-nineteenth century, questions of marriage and divorce were, as Elizabeth Cady Stanton put it, "at the very foundation of all progress" on women's rights. After all, as Stanton wrote in 1860 in a letter to the editor of the *New York Tribune:* "We decide the whole question of slavery by settling the sacred rights of the individual. We assert that man cannot hold property in man, and reject the whole code of laws that conflicts with the self-evident truth of the assertion." How then can man hold property in woman? Has woman no sacred rights as an individual?

As Stanton and her colleague Susan B. Anthony saw it, marriage was an institution devised by men, and backed by all the authority of church and state, to give husbands absolute authority over wives.... Fundamental to Stanton's "radical" view, of course, is the assumption (never shared by American law) that women and men are equal beings in the eyes of God and should enjoy equal rights and responsibilities in all things.

For women in the nineteenth century the catch was this: marriage made in heaven maintained on earth the rights and privileges of the husband, the man, as Stanton correctly said, and so did all other social institutions. Divorce might be the way out of domestic tyranny, but for most women it looked like a dead end, depriving them as it did at the time of their children, home, livelihood, reputation and prospects. Consequently, more conservative advocates of women's rights tried not to get women out of marriage but to protect them within it. Temperance leaders battled drunkenness, always considered a cause of brutality and violence, while moral reformers sought to curb male "animal" lust and to "improve" men with an infusion of female "purity." More to the point, Lucy Stone and her husband Henry Blackwell campaigned in Massachusetts from 1879 to 1891 for legislation modeled on laws already passed in England in response to Frances Power Cobbe's revelations about "wife-torture." The new legislation provided legal separation (not divorce) and financial maintenance for wives whose husbands were convicted of assaulting them; but even that modest proposal, seen as an attack upon the family, failed.

The same attitudes persist today, both within the family and outside it. Some battered women are as dedicated as any conservative congressman to keeping the family, their own family, together; they want only to stop the violence. Other battered women are ready to strike out for freedom and self-determination, for themselves and their kids. All these women, whether they struggle under the banner of *Family Values,* the flag of *Women's Rights,* or the colors of *Women's Liberation,* need protection from violence, and institutional supports to help them.

In the public arena, "radical" feminists go on arguing for the rights of women, though we live in what conservatives wishfully call a "postfeminist" age. Never mind that for a pile of economic and social reasons the "traditional" family is as scarce these days as the blue whale. Never mind Elizabeth Cady Stanton's observation that "A legislative act cannot make a unit of a divided family." Policy makers and legislators backed by custom, the church and "modern" psychology, and beholden to the far right, still try to keep "the family" alive. Consequently, our economic and social arrangements still impede a woman's departure, especially if she has children. Some federal reimbursement programs require child welfare agencies to try to keep "families" intact; and although most such agencies now consider a woman and her children to *be* "a family," some abused women may be pressured to enter counseling or mediation with their assailants, while their abused children may be left at his mercy, sometimes in his household. If a woman reports that her husband or boyfriend abuses the children, she may see them removed not only from his custody but from hers to be placed in a *family* of foster parents. If she and the kids set up their own household, they may get poorer, while the abusive husband (unless he is trapped in poverty himself) is likely to get relatively richer. And even the prospect of that supposedly inevitable financial decline, much trumpeted in the media, serves to intimidate the woman who considers setting out on her own. On the other hand, the battered woman who wants to help to stop the violence while preserving her marriage and family may find the proffered alternatives—arrest, prosecution, shelter—of no use at all.

Nevertheless, today's battered woman has options her sisters struggled in the last century and in this to win for her. She may not be formally married at all. If married, she can divorce, provided her religion and her pocketbook permit. She may get custody of her children, if she can afford the lawyers she'll need to persuade a judge that a violent man is not fit to be a custodial parent. She can work, albeit for lower wages than a man doing the same job—that is, if she can find a job. She may even get some public assistance, though only for a short term. And she hears, as her nineteenth-century sister did not, the nagging question: "Why doesn't she leave?"

The danger now is that we overestimate society's changes. Implicit in the question, "Why doesn't she leave?" is the assumption that social supports are already in place to help the woman who walks out: a shelter in every town, a cop on every beat eager to make that mandatory arrest, a judge in every courtroom passing out well-enforced restraining orders and packing batterers off to jail and effective re-education programs, legal services, social services, health care, child care, child support, affordable housing, convenient public transportation, a decent job free of sexual harassment, a living wage. The abused woman, wanting to leave, encouraged to think she will find help, yet finding only obstacles at every turn, may grow disheartened and doubt herself. If it's supposed to be so easy, and it's *this* hard, she must be doing something wrong. What seemed to be a social problem—judging by all the reports about "domestic violence" in the news—becomes a personal problem after all. For the abused woman, it's just one more turn of the screw.

Public opinion, too, can easily turn backward—without even changing the dialogue. When we ask "Why doesn't she leave?" do we mean to be helpful, encouraging, cognizant of her rights, and ready with our support? Or do we mean once again to blame her for her failure to avail herself of all the assistance we mistakenly think our society provides? Lucy Stone and Henry Blackwell thought wife abuse would cease when women got the vote—because women would vote off the bench judges who failed to punish wife beaters. That didn't work. The battered women's movement has organized for more than twenty-five years against "domestic violence," yet the violence continues. Could it be that individual women are to blame after all?

Or could it be rather that battered women play some indispensable part in this society that we've overlooked? Could it be that battered women have some function, some role or social utility we haven't taken into account? Thus far ... we've looked at the problem from the point of view of battered women—women who almost invariably ask for help. But perhaps we should look again from the point of view of "society"—if we can try for a moment to imagine that this many-headed abstraction has something like a point of view. Perhaps we should put a different question: What are battered women *for?*

Asking a different question puts a new light on the problem right away: battered women are *for battering*. The battered woman is a woman who may be beaten; she is a *beatable* woman; If you doubt that society views battered women as, by definition, "beatable," then how do you explain the fact that we almost always put responsibility for woman beating on the woman? Why else would we probe her psyche to reveal the secret self within, yearning for abuse, if not to set her apart as a *beatable* woman, unlike ourselves? In our society there are millions of these beatable women. Many of them live within "the family" which entitles only the "head" of the family to beat them. Many others live outside "the family"—in which case anyone may beat them who will. Many live and work in industries that rent or sell beatable women and children to the male "public"—prostitution, for example, and pornography. A few beatable women, like Hedda Nussbaum, become public figures whom everyone can assail.

In the aggregate, battered women are to sexism what the poor are to capitalism—always with us. They are a source of cheap labor and sexual service to those with the power to buy and control them, a "problem" for the righteous to lament, a topic to provide employment for academic researchers, a sponge to soak up the surplus violence of men, a conduit to carry off the political energy of other women who must care for them, an exemplum of what awaits all women who don't behave as prescribed, and a pariah group to amplify by contrast our good opinion of ourselves. And for all their social utility, they remain largely, and conveniently, invisible.

* * *

NOTES

1. As Jones' excerpt suggests, and as many prior discussions in this book have confirmed, the ineffectiveness of reform measures often has to do with the attitudes or the ignorance of those charged with implementing them. Attitudes hostile to women's autonomy, and women's claims, are still deeply embedded in our culture; passed from one generation to another in our families, confirmed by our peers in educational and work environments, and reinforced by our exposure to the music, television, movies, newspapers and magazines that comprise our popular culture. Ann Jones offers harsh criticism of the media, and their contribution to societal perceptions of domestic violence:

> The murders of Nicole Brown Simpson and Ron Goldman in June 1994 and the indictment of O.J. Simpson prompted a flood of calls to the new National Resource Center on Domestic Violence from journalists

> nationwide, many of whom subsequently produced informative background stories on domestic violence. That early coverage of the Simpson case—before the trial started and the case went up in sensational smoke—surely raised public awareness of the issue. It is a good example of the role responsible journalism can play in stimulating, informing, and elevating public discourse on social issues. But too often reporters covering domestic violence assaults, femicides, and trials, pressed by deadlines, fall back on sexist cliches and readymade sexist sex-and-violence scenarios to get their copy out. It happens so easily, so "naturally'; they may not even realize that instead of investigating and accurately reporting the facts, they've masked rape and battering in the language of "love." They quote police and lawyers as authoritative sources but rarely consult battered women's advocates who could provide valuable background information, a different perspective, and an alternative scenario. Sometimes journalists seem willfully to throw fairness and balance to the winds.... [A]s long as routine press coverage presents rape, assault, and femicide from the perspective of the offender, the press will be part of the problem women and children are up against.

Ann Jones, NEXT TIME SHE'LL BE DEAD: BATTERING AND HOW TO STOP IT, 244 (2000).

2. The helping professions—legal, mental health and medical—have a special opportunity, and a special obligation, to educate their members. For all members of the legal profession, the need to understand the nature of abusive relationships, and law's relationship to abuse, is acute. In its 1997 report, WHEN WILL THEY EVER LEARN? EDUCATING TO END DOMESTIC VIOLENCE, the ABA Commission on Domestic Violence summarized the current situation as follows:

> Domestic violence has a tremendous impact on the legal profession. Whether or not lawyers recognize it, domestic violence permeates the practice of law in almost every field. Corporate lawyers, bankruptcy lawyers, tort lawyers, real property lawyers, criminal defense lawyers, and family lawyers, regularly represent victims or perpetrators of domestic violence. Criminal and civil judges preside over a range of cases involving domestic violence as an underlying or a hotly contested issue. Failure to fully understand domestic violence legal issues threatens the competency of individual lawyers and judge, as well as the legal profession as a whole.
>
> Legal professionals who are uninformed about domestic violence issues may endanger the safety of victims or contribute to a society which has historically condoned the abuse of intimate partners. In Maryland, for example, a victim was killed by her intimate partner after a judge refused to grant her a civil protection order. Recently, another judge expunged a batterer's criminal record for wife abuse in order to allow him to join a country club; the judge reversed his ruling only in response to public outcry. Still another judge modified a custody order and awarded custody of the child to the child's father,

> despite the fact that the father had abused the child's mother, and had been convicted of murdering his first wife.
>
> The vast majority of telephone calls received by the American Bar Association Commission on Domestic Violence indicate that lawyers, too, are not representing victims of domestic violence according to the standards dictated by the profession. Callers report that many family and criminal lawyers fail to address a client's safety needs where there is a history of domestic violence or refuse to introduce evidence of the violence in court, despite the legal consequences. This hesitation to handle domestic violence cases, or to address domestic violence issues when they arise, stems in part from lack of legal training. It is time for law schools to fill this desperate gap in legal education by incorporating domestic violence law into core curricula courses, upper level courses, and clinical programs.

When Will They Ever Learn? Educating to End Domestic Violence: A Law School Report I–5—I–6 (ABA Commission on Domestic Violence, 1997).

Legal education in domestic violence needs to begin, as the ABA Commission concluded, in law school. Certainly much progress has been made on that front in the last decade. When Mithra Merryman conducted the first national survey in 1993, she found only one school offering a seminar on domestic violence on an annual basis—Boalt Hall School of Law at the University of California–Berkeley. There were more schools offering clinical courses; a total of thirteen courses at twelve schools. Mithra Merryman, *A Survey of Domestic Violence Programs in Legal Education*, 28 New Eng. L. Rev. 383 (1993). By 1997, when the ABA Commission conducted a similar survey, it found twenty-two schools offering an upper-level seminar or course, and a grand total of forty-two schools offering clinical programs either dedicated exclusively to serving victims of domestic violence, or offering a substantial amount of domestic violence casework. An additional two schools were reported as offering entirely student-run programs representing battered women; there may be more schools in this category who were not counted in the survey. Nine schools offered both a specialized course and clinical education in domestic violence, and two schools offered more than one clinical opportunity. The development of domestic violence clinics has been assisted by funding authorized by the Violence Against Women Act, and administered through the U.S. Department of Justice.

Much harder to gauge is the extent to which education in domestic violence issues has permeated into the mainstream law school curriculum, and is being addressed in both core courses (in the first year and beyond), and relevant specialty courses. The ABA Commission recommends that all law students should be taught to screen for domestic violence, and to conduct safety planning with victims. It also suggests ways in which domestic violence issues can be introduced into criminal law, civil procedure, torts, property, contracts, constitutional law, professional responsibility, legal research and writing, trial advocacy and moot court. "While domestic violence issues could be raised in virtually every course," the Report continues, it is "vital" that they be included in evidence, family law, and advanced criminal courses. In the year 2000 is is also hard to imagine teaching either welfare law or immigration law without reference to domestic violence, given the new developments in those fields discussed in Chapter 3, above. The advantages of integrating domestic violence throughout the curriculum are clear; every law student will be exposed, and there will be multiple opportunities to refine and extend the student's learning. There are also disadvantages, however; the time given to the subject may be insufficient to help students acquire sufficient knowledge, or to overcome their preconceptions, and teachers may themselves be unprepared to offer a thorough or accurate description or analysis of the issue at hand.

Analyses of casebooks available in two of the "vital" fields identified by the ABA Commission suggest that much work remains to be done in providing students with the material they need to foster discussion and learning about domestic violence. In 1984, for example, Catherine Klein, then Director of the Family Abuse Project at Columbus School of Law, Catholic University of America, conducted an informal survey of family-law casebooks, and discovered that only one raised the issue of spouse abuse. A more recent survey revealed the following:

> In WALTER WEYRAUCH ET AL., CASES AND MATERIALS ON FAMILY LAW: LEGAL CONCEPTS AND CHANGING HUMAN RELATIONSHIPS 341–46 (1994) ... six pages are devoted to "physical safety." The primary case involves the abolition of a marital rape exemption, and the comment, less than a page in length, discusses battering. ... An additional three pages is devoted to stalking, under the heading "Freedom of Movement." ... There is no discussion of partner violence in the custody materials.... The entire book is some 1500 pages in length. In JUDITH AREEN, FAMILY LAW: CASES AND MATERIALS (3d ed. 1992), there is somewhat more coverage. A section on "Encroachments on the Doctrine of Family Privacy" contains 23 pages on "Tort and Criminal Law." ... Those pages include cases dealing with marital rape immunity, battered women's self-defense claims, police failure to protect, a case on the constitutionality of protective order legislation, and a note on the criminal justice response to domestic violence.... But there is no reference to parental violence as a factor in the section on "Applying the 'Best Interests' Standard" in the custody chapter.... This text is approximately 1650 pages in length. In LESLIE HARRIS ET AL., FAMILY LAW (1996), 24 of approximately 1500 pages are devoted to "Violence Between Spouses." ... Only six of these pages deal with tort liability, and one of the two cases included is a 1982 Florida case that upheld spousal immunity, but was overturned in 1993, a fact which is not mentioned. The remainder of the materials in this section deal with criminal liability, the criminal justice response, and possible constitutional arguments challenging police inaction. The section on "Standards for Custody Determinations" contains subsections on the "best interests" standard, maternal preference, the primary caretaker, and religion, sexual behavior and race, but not parental violence....

Clare Dalton, *Domestic Violence, Domestic Torts and Divorce: Constraints and Possibilities,* 31 NEW ENG. L. REV. 319, 364–65, n.133 (1997). None of these texts, in the editions then current, talked about screening clients for domestic violence, or about safety planning.

In Nancy Erickson and Mary Ann Lamanna, *Sex-Bias Topics in the Criminal Law Course: A Survey of Criminal Law Professors,* 24 U. Mich. J. L. Ref. 189 (1990), the authors report on a survey of 238 criminal law professors. 81% taught self defense by battered women, dedicating an average of 85 minutes of class time to the issue, and 70% discussed other issues related to domestic violence, for an average of 86 minutes. The authors conclude that:

> Self-defense by battered women falls into the most frequently taught grouping of gender-related topics (81%). Other issues related to conjugal violence are covered by two thirds of responding professors. Coverage of conjugal violence represents an important modification of the criminal law curriculum, reflecting increasing societal awareness of spouse abuse.

Id. at 222. Significantly, more female than male professors incorporated spouse abuse into their criminal law courses, although female teachers comprised only 15% of the total sample. However, without knowing more about the content of these discussions, it is hard to know how much they may have contributed to an understanding of abusive relationships. As we have seen, battered women's self defense claims and the use of expert testimony about battered women's syndrome present complex issues. In the wrong hands, discussion may reinforce existing stereotypes and perpetuate misunderstanding.

Professional education for lawyers does not stop with a law school diploma, and much has already been said in preceding chapters about the proliferation of domestic violence "trainings" offered to lawyers and judges. For lawyers in private practice, the primary vehicle for this ongoing training will be voluntary participation in continuing legal education. For lawyers employed within a court system, and for judges, training may be mandatory. In either case, the major question will be whether the product being delivered is a quality product; one capable of engaging and challenging participants, and fostering growth rather than resistance. Again, the American Bar Association Commission on Domestic Violence has taken a leading role in emphasizing the need for lawyers to be informed about domestic violence issues, producing a "Lawyer's Handbook" in 1996 titled The Impact of Domestic Violence on Your Legal Practice.

3. Milestones in the response of the mental health professions to domestic violence include a report, *Violence and the Family*, published by a Presidential Task Force of the American Psychological Association (APA) in 1996, and the APA's subsequent publication of a *Resolution on Male Violence Against Women* in 1999. In Edward W. Gondolf, Assessing Woman Battering in Mental Health Services (1998), the author specifically addresses the need to bridge the gap between mental health clinicians and battered women's advocates. The extent of that gap was discussed in some depth in Chapters 6 and 7, above, in the context of the child protective service and family law systems, where mental health professionals play such an influential role.

4. With the exception of a few innovative but isolated programs, the medical profession has also been slow to respond to new knowledge about abusive relationships and the needs of victims. It was not until 1992 that the Joint Commission on Accreditation of Healthcare Organizations (JCAHO) imposed a requirement that hospital emergency services develop written policies and procedures governing the screening of patients for abuse, the documentation of abuse, the provision of referrals to other services, and the training of appropriate staff in identifying and treating victims of abuse. 1992 was also a banner year for the American Medical Association. The January issue of American Medical News was dedicated to family violence; two complete issues of the Journal of the American Medical Association (JAMA) were dedicated to interpersonal violence in June, and all nine AMA Archives journals concurrently dedicated all or most of their pages to violence and trauma. In addition, the AMA issued its *Diagnostic and Treatment Guidelines on Domestic Violence,* recommending "routine screening of all women patients in emergency, surgical, primary care, pediatric, prenatal, and mental health settings." The Guidelines were thorough, providing information about abuse; suggestions for conducting the screening; a lengthy list of physical and emotional conditions, and behaviors, that might be associated with abuse; an introduction to potentially helpful interventions, and a documentation protocol. They also introduced physicians to legal developments in the area of domestic violence.

The following excerpt sets these encouraging developments in the context of the medical profession's longer history of inattention to the intimate sources of women's injuries

Anne Flitcraft, MD
The AMA Guidelines One Year Later; Preventing Violence to Women: Integrating the Health and Legal Communities, 21–24 (Conference Report, 1993)

UNCOVERING THE SCOPE OF VIOLENCE

Within the health community during the 1970s a small research group began to outline the health dimensions of violence against women. We discovered that violence against women is more than the sum of its parts. When we looked at the epidemiology of injury to women, we discovered that homicide and near homicide represented only the very tip of the iceberg of injuries that women presented regularly to hospitals across the country. Women came to emergency departments not once, not twice, but dozens of times with injuries. Many of these injuries were medically insignificant, required few stitches, and passed invisibly through the medical gauge.

But when we accumulated these recurrent trauma episodes over time, we discovered that domestic violence was the leading cause of injury to women—more common, more prevalent than automobile accidents, muggings and rapes combined.

But the whole is greater than the sum of its parts and injury is only one part of living within a violent relationship. Our teachers within the battered women's movement shared with us the terror, the ongoing threats that undermined any moment of peace and security. Women returned to the hospitals and clinics with traumatic stress symptoms—headaches, abdominal pains, sleeplessness, sexual dysfunction, depression, a host of vague medical complaints—like those of soldiers. But unlike our soldier colleagues who came home from the war, women lived daily within the war.

So responding with tranquilizing medicine, sleeping medications, pain medications and inappropriate referrals, medicine became, with law and police, religion and education, a vehicle for maintaining women's isolation in violent relationships.

The cost in individual and social terms becomes clear. Nearly half of all female alcoholism emerges in the context of domestic violence. We cannot talk seriously about drug use among women unless we talk about ongoing violence in their intimate relationships, nor pretend to address crack cocaine during pregnancy without talking about violence during pregnancy.

Mental Illness, Child Abuse and Violence

One out of every four suicide attempts among women takes place in the context of a violent relationship, and we have found that about 7 percent of battered women were eventually committed to state hospitals for psychotic and depressive illness. The whole picture of domestic violence is indeed greater than the sum of its parts.

For years researchers and service workers in the field of child abuse did not recognize violence against women as an important codeterminant of child abuse. We as a society have invested in a virtual army of legal, social and health providers to intervene in child abuse, yet never recognized the women within those homes who were also victimized by those same perpetrators.

When we look at the health consequences of violence against women, it is much larger than the sum of its parts. Such violence extends to recurrent injury, illness, our own imposed isolation of battered women and, finally, some of the most serious and vexing health problems to date. There is virtually no major health issue on the current agenda that can be substantially addressed without simultaneously addressing the role of violence against women in perpetuating the very conditions upon which illness thrives in this society.

Developing Programs to Deal with Violence

In the 1980s model programs of domestic violence intervention began in health settings. These were experiments. They included programs at Brigham and Women's Hospital in Boston, where nurses put together a team similar to that of the rape crisis team to address the broader issue of violence against women. AWAKE (Advocacy for Women and Kids in Emergencies), developed by Susan Schechter, was designed to address and meet the challenges of concurrent child abuse and domestic violence. Womankind, Susan Hadley's program in Minnesota, demonstrated that the hospital can serve as a true point of advocacy for women.

Surgeon General C. Everett Koop first addressed domestic violence as a public health problem in 1985.

The AMA Guidelines emerged against this backdrop of activism, research and policy consideration....

We see across the country the emergence of initiatives at the state and local levels to articulate a real role for medicine in the struggle to eliminate domestic violence and to provide sanctuary and safety for victims of violence. I am very pleased because people recognize that we need to take the guidelines, sit down with the state and local community and say: "What does this mean to me? What does this mean in my state, in my hospital organization, in my community?"

For instance, the Massachusetts State Medical Association has developed guidelines for the state and a program of physician education. This may provide the basis for a model curriculum within the Boston area medical schools.

The Ohio Medical Society has put together a wonderful program called Trust Talk. The very title suggests the level of change we are talking about in medicine. This is not about a new pill we prescribe; this is about a new set of relationships between physicians and patients. The notion of Trust Talk reflects the extent to which we are struggling to articulate this new relationship.

In Connecticut we are developing a program called Project SAFE, which in some sense takes the opposite tack. While all physicians have a responsibility to understand how to identify domestic violence, not all physicians will be able to incorporate advocacy into their daily work. Project SAFE outlines basic safety assessment skills for physicians and calls for routine assessment in all medical encounters.

The surest sign of the significance of the AMA Guidelines is the adaptation of the spirit—not only the letter of the guidelines—at the local level.

* * *

NOTES

1. Despite further activity on the part of the AMA; the formation of a National Advisory Council on Family Violence in 1992, the sponsorship of the National Coalition of Physicians Against Family Violence in 1993, and the adoption of a 1996 resolution advocating that all medical schools and graduate medical education programs provide training in screening patients for abuse, and information about available community resources, progress has been disappointingly slow. A 1999 article in JAMA reported that fewer than one in ten primary care physicians are routinely screening patients for partner abuse. Michael A. Rodriguez et al., *Screening and Intervention for Intimate Partner Abuse: Practices and Attitudes of Primary Care Physicians,* 282 JAMA 468 (1999). The next reading also illuminates the distance

between the language of the JCAHO requirement and its implementation in hospital emergency departments.

2. While much remains to be done within each profession to educate practitioners and students about partner violence, and about appropriate standards of practice in situations involving partner violence, it is also critical for the professions to cross disciplinary lines, and collaborate in designing and implementing interventions that will serve the needs of battered women and their children. Recent research is revealing that although women know where to go for abuse-related services, they tend not to seek help from "official" sources when they are victimized. Battered women's advocates from around the country, as well as victims themselves, confirm that help-seeking can itself be a perilous enterprise. Sometimes the problem is a single unresponsive, insensitive or incompetent caregiver, but often the problem comes when women "fall between the cracks" as they are referred from one caregiver to another for help with the multiplicity of issues that abuse brings in its wake. Interdisciplinary collaboration begins to address this issue by ensuring that victims are supported in their transitions from one service to another.

Collaboration brings new challenges, as professionals seek to overcome the barriers to cooperation created by their different perspectives, training and priorities. It can also provide new education even for those who have a good understanding of domestic violence from the perspective of their own discipline. A project which demonstrates both the inevitability of interdisciplinary tensions, and the value of collaboration, is the subject of the next reading. The project, which was guided by a partnership of seasoned practitioners from the legal, medical and social work communities, was a research collaboration looking at the documentation of domestic violence in medical records. The immediate goal was to measure the potential value of medical records in a variety of legal proceedings in which victims of abuse might be involved. However, the researchers' conclusions and recommendations were actually broader in scope, addressing limitations in both medical and legal spheres, as well as in the interface between them. The excerpt which follows is drawn from the Executive Summary of the authors' final report.

Nancy E. Isaac and Pualani Enos
Medical Records as Legal Evidence of Domestic Violence, 5–8 (National Institute of Justice, May 2000)

This study sought to describe, from a legal perspective, how domestic violence is being documented in abused women's medical charts. In total, 96 medical charts of 86 abused women covering 772 visits were reviewed. For 184 of these visits (24%), detailed information was abstracted ... because there was an indication of domestic violence, an injury of some type, or both.

. . .

Based on the work of this practitioner-researcher partnership and the review of abused women's medical charts, we conclude the following:

- The legal and medical communities hold many misperceptions of one another's roles in responding to domestic violence. Many barriers to collaboration are based on these misperceptions and false assumptions.
- The work of the interdisciplinary partnership demonstrates that a common meaningful goal, respect for one another's professional expertise, and willingness to view a problem from a new perspective, can provide the context for productive medical/legal collaborations on the issue of domestic violence.
- Some legal advocates do not utilize medical records regularly in civil contexts or to their full potential in criminal contexts. Reasons for not using medical records include: difficulty and expense in obtaining them; their illegibility, incompleteness or inaccuracy; the possibility that the information in them, due to these flaws, may be more harmful than helpful.
- Many if not most health care providers are confused about whether, how and why to record information about domestic violence in medical charts.
- In an effort to be "neutral" regarding abuse situations, some health care providers are using language that is likely to harm an abused woman's legal case and aids her abuser (in a legal context).
- Though physicians' poor handwriting is often the subject of jokes, it can in fact prevent use of the medical chart in court. In this study, among medical visits that contained some indication of abuse or an injury, one-third of the notes from doctors or nurses contained vital information that was illegible.
- With minor modifications to documentation practices, many more abused women's medical charts would contain the elements necessary to allow their statements about abuse to be introduced in court as "excited utterances." Such evidence can allow a prosecution to proceed even when the woman is unwilling to testify against her abuser in court due to fear or other reasons. The element needed for excited utterance exceptions that was most frequently missing from medical records was a description of the patient's demeanor.
- Many providers are recording significant details regarding injuries and health conditions in abused women's charts. If these practices were consistent, and symbols and abbreviations were standardized, this type of documentation could act as effective corroborative evidence in court.
- Emergency medical services (EMS) personnel may be an underutilized source of legal documentation of domestic violence. It appears that EMS providers may already be recording patient statements quite often; with additional training, the legal utility of these data could be greatly increased. This is especially true given the proximity of these providers (in time and space) to the actual violent events.
- Though many if not most protocols on healthcare response to domestic violence call for documenting injuries on body maps, this study found

such maps or any types of drawing of injuries in only a handful of medical visits.

- Photographs, the "sine qua non" of evidence regarding abuse-related injuries, were almost never present in the charts reviewed in this study. Only one of the 93 visits involving an injury contained a photograph. The medical records also did not mention photographs stored in other locations, e.g., with local police.
- Although the partnership discussions and prior focus group research had both identified inappropriate, derogatory statements about abused patients as one current problem with medical documentation, such comments were found in physician or nurses' notes in only five instances, and in social work or psychiatry notes in four cases.

This research also identified some relatively minor changes in documentation practices that would be likely to improve the usefulness of abused women's medical records in legal contexts. Such changes may help health care providers to "work smarter, not harder" on behalf of their abused patients. Some recommended changes for clinicians include the following:

- Clinicians should, when at all feasible, take photographs of injuries that are known or suspected to have resulted from interpersonal violence. Optimally, there should be at least one photo each of the full body, the injury itself, and the patient's face.
- Clinicians should take care to write legible notes. Clinician training should emphasize that illegible notes may negatively impact health care and are likely to hinder a woman's ability to obtain legal remedies to address her abuse. . . .
- As often as possible, clinicians should use quotation marks or the phrases "patient states . . ." or "patient reports . . ." to indicate that the information being recorded is coming directly from the patient.
- Clinicians should stay away from words that imply doubt about the patient's reliability ("patient claims . . .", "patient alleges . . . "). Alleges is a legal term. It implies the statement following it is unproven and may not have occurred. Providers should instead use quotes around statements made by the patient. If the clinician's direct observations are in conflict with the patient's description of events, the clinician's reasons for doubt should be stated explicitly.
- Clinicians should not use legal terms such as "alleged perpetrator," "assailant," "assault," etc. All legal terms are defined with great detail by federal or state statute and case law. Typically, such terms are used by lay persons to mean something more ambiguous or larger in scope. By using legal terms, providers may convey an unintended meaning. For example, assault is defined as an attempt to cause an unwanted touching, whether or not the touching actually occurred. Naming the person who has injured the patient as her "assailant" or "perpetrator" after the patient has identified the person who has hurt her as a husband, boyfriend, father of her child or by name, is likely to be interpreted in a legal setting as the provider's doubting the patient's credibility. These

terms are used regularly by attorneys seeking to raise doubt as to who committed an act.

- Optimally, providers should describe and name the person who hurt the patient in quotes exactly as the patient has identified him. This prevents the abuser from obscuring his responsibility by accusing the victim of having multiple partners.
- Practitioners should avoid summarizing a patient's report of abuse in conclusory terms such as "patient is a battered woman," "assault and battery," or "rape" because conclusions without sufficient accompanying factual information are inadmissible in court. Instead, providers should document the factual information reported by the patient that leads them to conclude abuse occurred.
- Placing the term "domestic violence" or abbreviations such as "DV" in the diagnosis fields of medical records is of no benefit to the patient in legal contexts. This practice should be reconsidered unless there are other clear benefits with respect to medical treatment.
- Clinicians should include words that describe a patient's demeanor, such as: crying, shaking, upset, calm, angry, agitated, happy. Clinicians should describe what they observe, even if they find the demeanor to be confusing given statements of abuse.
- Clinicians should record the time of day in their record, and (ideally) some indication of how much time has passed since the incident (e.g., "patient states that *early this morning* her boyfriend, Robert Jones, hit her . . .").

Though these changes would go a long way to improve medical documentation of abuse, the research findings also imply that changes will be needed at the institutional level if the use of medical records in domestic violence cases is to improve. Specifically it appears that:

- The importance of photographing traumatic injuries needs to be re-emphasized in training programs on medical response to domestic violence. Research should determine the most common barriers to taking photographs. Interventions that aim at increasing the frequency of taking photographs should be developed and evaluated.
- Medical units that handle abuse cases routinely (e.g., emergency medicine, social work) should have cameras stored in a secure but easy to access location. Resources should be allocated to buy cameras and film, and to train providers in their use. Each institution's policy on response to domestic violence should include details on where the camera can be found, how to photograph injuries, where to store photographs, and how to document the existence and location of these photographs in the medical record.
- Non-clinical health professionals (medical records managers, administrators, risk managers) should work with domestic violence legal and clinical experts to examine changes that might facilitate the accessibility of medical records for legal use without compromising patient confidentiality.

- Training regarding current health care response to domestic violence should be provided to judges who hear domestic violence cases regularly.
- Domestic violence training programs and materials for health care providers should clarify that a failure to document domestic violence completely when treating an abused patient does not constitute taking a "neutral" stance about the incident. It will almost always convey a legal advantage to the abuser. In medical terms, it constitutes poor preventive medicine.

* * *

NOTES AND QUESTIONS

1. The National Institute of Justice has funded a second, follow-up project that will train providers in two hospitals and an emergency medical services organization in a new documentation protocol, and evaluate the extent to which this intervention improves their documentation practices.

2. The recommendation that physicians not hesitate to record patient demeanor reflects the discovery of an important rift between health care providers and lawyers. Health care providers had assumed that it was more helpful to bolster their patients' credibility by *not* revealing that they were "upset" "shaking" or "hysterical." Lawyers, on the other hand, recognized that it was exactly these descriptions of emotional state that might qualify patient statements as "excited utterances," and allow them to be introduced as evidence despite the hearsay rule. Can you find other examples of documentation practice that reflect medical providers' mistaken assumptions about legal matters? When clinicians hedge their descriptions with language like: "the patient claims ..." or "the alleged assailant ..." are they perhaps worrying about their own vulnerability to a defamation suit by the perpetrator? Is that a real worry, or one that good legal advice would help set to rest?

3. Do you find yourself surprised by the level of detail the researchers' feel it is necessary to include in a documentation policy? Would it be realistic to expect a healthcare institution to generate a policy that detailed without input from "outsiders"—whether those outsiders are lawyers, or battered women's advocates?

4. Interdisciplinary collaborations constitute a modest step towards what it now viewed as the most promising approach to partner violence and those victimized by it—the coordinated community response. Here is Ann Jones on the subject:

> To change things, we must see to it that those who staff our institutions are schooled in the causes and consequences of violence against women and children and trained to intervene effectively. What's more, we must see to it that *all* our community institutions change, for piecemeal change may be worse than no change at all. If police arrest offenders and judges release them without punishment, for example, the result is offenders who feel licensed by the court to carry on, and to scoff at the police as well. If social workers or journalists encourage

women to take the dangerous step of running from batterers and no shelter is available, the result is homeless women doubly endangered. If judges issue restraining orders but police do not enforce them, the result is often another headline femicide: "Murdered Wife Had Protection Order."

Sometimes, with the best intentions, institutions work at cross purposes and do more harm than good. Social workers charged with child protection, for example, may place abused children in foster care, heedless of the fact that their battered mother would protect herself and them if the batterer were held to account for his violence. On the other hand, some judges, determined to keep the nuclear family intact, may pressure battered women into marital counseling, mediation, or child custody and visitation arrangements that are debilitating and profoundly dangerous to the women and their children. For their part, women who fear that they will lose their children or be bound into some continuing legal relationship with the offender may not report child abuse or even seek help themselves.

To avoid such mistakes, and to plan an effective, coordinated community program, Schechter suggests that *every* institution establish "policies, standards, training programs and practices" to meet *one set of goals:*

- to identify and respond sensitively to every victim in the family;
- to protect and empower abused women so that they in turn may protect their children;
- to make it safe for women and children to seek help;
- to stop further harm by holding offenders, rather their victims, accountable for maltreatment;
- to ensure that every agency in the community adheres to these standards and works cooperatively to achieve them.

To plan a coordinated community program, members of every community agency, public and private, must sit down together. That includes not just police and prosecutors and battered women's advocates, but agencies and institutions that may think they have no role to play in helping battered women: the housing authority, for example, the vocational school, the credit union. They must build into their design specific ways to monitor one another's work, collaborate on reviewing and revising programs, hold one another accountable for ineffective policies and practices, provide mutual support, and work to overcome institutionalized sexism, racism, and homophobia. Ideally, they should hire a full-time coordinator to monitor and promote their continued collaboration. Every aspect of the coordinated community program should aim to protect victims, to hold offenders accountable, and to recognize that these are only the first steps toward securing economic and social justice for women.

Ann Jones, NEXT TIME SHE'LL BE DEAD: BATTERING AND HOW TO STOP IT, 218–19 (2d ed. 2000)

If interdisciplinary work surfaces tensions between partners, imagine the difficulty and complexity of a collaboration that seeks to include multiple community partners, with radically different institutional cultures and priorities. One of the earliest such collaborations in the domestic violence field was the Duluth Domestic Abuse Intervention Project. In their introduction to Coordinating Community Responses to Domestic Violence: Lessons from Duluth and Beyond, 3–4, 16 (Melanie F. Shepard & Ellen L. Pence, eds. 1999), Shepard and Pence describe the DAIP, and offer an account of eight key components of a community intervention project:

> The Domestic Abuse Intervention Project (DAIP), located in Duluth, Minnesota, was initiated in 1980 after legal advocates in other cities had effected changes in every aspect of criminal court interention, from dispatching to sentencing. The DAIP gained national recognition as the first community-based reform project to successfully negotiate an agreement with the key intervening legal agencies to coordinate their interventions through a series of written policies and protocols that limited individual discretion on the handling of cases and subjected practitioners to minimum standards of response.... The Duluth project's most well-known accomplishments have been its work with the Duluth Police Department to develop a mandatory arrest policy in the early 1980s and the creation of an educational curriculum for batterers that focuses on power and control as the purpose and function of battering....
>
> Many domestic violence agencies have adopted what has been termed the *Duluth model*. ...
>
> . . .
>
> *Eight Key Components of Community Intervention Projects*
>
> Community intervention projects engage in a fairly complex set of activities that occur simultaneously. The staff of the Duluth DAIP have identified eight key components that comprise a community intervention project:
>
> 1. Creating a coherent philosophical approach centralizing victim safety
> 2. Developing "best practice" policies and protocols for intervention agencies that are part of an integrated response
> 3. Enhancing networking among service providers
> 4. Building monitoring and tracking into the system
> 5. Ensuring a supportive community infrastructure for battered women
> 6. Providing sanctions and rehabilitation opportunities for abusers
> 7. Undoing the harm violence to women does to children
> 8. Evaluating the coordinated community response from the standpoint of victim safety

Denise Gamache and Mary Asmus
Enhancing Networking Among Service Providers: Elements of Successful Coordination Strategies; Coordinating Community Responses to Domestic Violence: Lessons From Duluth and Beyond 65, 73–86 (Melanie F. Shepard & Ellen L. Pence, eds. 1999)

Key Elements of Successful Networking On Domestic Violence Cases

Greater coordination among community agencies is a concept that has been embraced and encouraged by several national organizations–notably, the National Council of Juvenile and Family Court Judges, the American Prosecutor's Research Institute, the American Bar Association, and the American Medical Association. All of these organizations have urged the formation of "coordinating councils".... *[C]oordinating council* denotes any model in which a committee is created to lead the coordinating effort. The membership consists of representatives–usually leaders at a policy-making level–from agencies, departments, and community groups dealing with domestic violence. Its stated purpose is to increase communication and improve coordination among the member agencies so that incidents of domestic violence are reduced and prevented. Within this broad goal, a range of activities are planned. Most large councils eventually develop a system of subcommittees to accomplish their work. Leadership of the council varies but is often a judge or prosecutor and sometimes the head of a local organization or governmental unit. Councils often focus on coordinating the justice system response with social services to victims, batterers, and their families. However, in many jurisdictions, the council has defined its role as much broader and concerns itself with the entire community response to domestic violence, including representatives from medical facilities, public schools, public health nurses, religious institutions, and local businesses. Although some states have also set up coordinating bodies to guide statewide plans, this discussion relates more to coordination issues on the local level.

Several points distinguish the coordinating council model from the DAIP approach: There is not an external monitoring agency focused on institutional advocacy guiding the process, the council model emphasizes the participation and leadership of personnel at the policy-making level of institutions, and the recommended council structure does not necessarily facilitate ways to overcome the existing power dynamics in the criminal justice system that can impede the work of the council. Over the past years, different communities have experienced varying levels of success when adopting either networking model. An analysis of the key elements of successful coordination efforts provides important guidance for communities that are initiating coordination efforts or those attempting to revive an ailing or ineffective project.

. . .

Because the DAIP has always considered battered women to be its primary constituency, its coordination efforts have been directed toward the goal of victim safety....

The importance of maintaining a commitment to this priority is clear when conflicting goals arise in discussions of proposed reforms. For example, a local coordinating council was considering a proposal from the court administrator, who was responsible for assisting victims in writing up protection orders. She was concerned that the criminal acts described in the orders, some of which were extremely serious, were not often being charged in criminal court. She proposed that procedures be implemented to automatically refer the protection order forms to the appropriate police department so they could initiate charges based on the information on criminal acts contained in the orders. Her intent was to hold these abusers accountable for their criminal acts, a common goal of coordination efforts. However, in discussing the idea, the former victims and advocates on the council were unanimous in arguing that this change could be harmful to victims in several ways. Victims choose not to pursue criminal charges for different reasons, but often they feel that this process may endanger them. The protection order process allows victims different remedies from those available in the criminal courts, such as removal of the abuser from the home or temporary custody arrangements. A victim who feels that these remedies are more helpful to her should be allowed to seek them without being forced into other legal proceedings that she is not interested in pursuing. Most important, many felt that this change would keep women from applying for protection orders, thus blocking access to a significant legal option. The council's priority on victim safety led them to reject the proposal. Similar concerns are present in the current debate over the public policy in some states that requires mandatory reporting by medical personnel of patients who disclose domestic assaults. Should patients be thrust into the legal system when seeking medical aid, even when they do not wish to involve the criminal courts? Will this practice keep women from obtaining critical medical attention and further endanger their lives? Only recently have studies been initiated to evaluate the impact of this policy on victims of domestic violence.

Another example highlights the difficulty of adhering to this priority, even when all parties share a strong commitment to it. The DAIP's experience with the development of a domestic violence prosecution policy has been a struggle to safeguard victim safety in a context of ambiguous circumstances and conflicting goals. In its original interagency agreement, the city prosecutor's policy was to vigorously pursue domestic assault cases, to subpoena victims to appear, and to proceed to trial if necessary. . . . The theory behind this approach was that the state was trying to shift the burden of confronting the abuser from the shoulders of the victim. The state understood that the victim's relationship with the abuser resulted in her reluctance to participate in the process. However, to place sanctions on the abuser that would aim to deter future violence, the prosecutor proceeded with the case. After several years, the prosecutor and advocates expressed concern about the policy's impact on the safety of reluctant victims and the sense that the trials were revictimizing the victims. Since the policy had been implemented, guilty pleas had decreased and the defense bar brought more cases to trial. The prosecutor found that these trials were often lost or, if won, felt like hollow victories if the victim was so anguished by the proceedings. After many discussions about these concerns, the policy was shifted, and the prosecutor's office was more willing to negotiate pleas to lesser charges or possibly dismiss a case if a victim clearly desired it. However, experience with this policy resulted in the belief that the new approach also was compromising victim safety. If the reluctance of a victim stemmed from the abuser's control over her outside of the court, the dismissal only reinforced his sense of power by rewarding his ability to escape sanctions by manipulating her and the courts. The prosecutor began to see repeat offenders enter the courts and felt that the justice system lacked any controls over their behavior. Again, the prosecutor, advocates, and the DAIP staff reviewed the policy and sought ways to sanction the abuser but safeguard the victim from retaliation. The prosecutor refocused his or her trial strategy on proving the case without the victim's testimony, which led to a new cooperative training effort with the policy department that enhanced policy investigation and evidence gathering in ways that strengthened the prosecutor's ability to try the case. As a result, more trials were successful, and the prosecutor's ability to obtain guilty pleas and spare the victim from court proceedings was improved.

In some of the articles about coordinating councils, the first step of organizing a council is described as "decide on a common goal." However, without a clear commitment to the priority of victim safety, it is more likely that the council will propose changes in policy that cause additional problems for victims or actually endanger them. It is important that coordination not be seen as an end in itself but as a means to achieve the overall goal. For example, in response to internal case-processing concerns, a local coordinating council recommended changes to the court calendar that sped up the processing of misdemeanor cases. As a result, a large number of victims failed to appear at hearings, and record numbers of cases were dismissed. The shortened time frame made it impossible for court staff and advocates to contact or work with victims. Although the calendar change solved a court personnel problem, the failure to evaluate the proposal from the viewpoint of its impact on victims had serious negative consequences.

In addition, the institutions represented on the council have roles and interests in the justice system that can sometimes compete with the priority of victim safety. A prosecutor who puts a high priority on obtaining convictions may seek to institute policies that punish victims who refuse to cooperate. A police department may resist enforcing violations of protection orders if it takes the view that the victims are to blame for the offenders' return to the residence. Projects such as the DAIP and early coordinating committees or task forces were organized by advocates or practitioners who already had a strong commitment to victims. The "core group" kept the priority of victim safety clearly in focus as it involved others in its work or established a formal council structure. However, with the promotion of the coordinating council model around the country, a formal council structure may be adopted as a starting point for coordination efforts, rather than having formed organically over time. The resulting group often lacks a shared understanding of domestic violence and a core group that will maintain a focus on victim safety as the cornerstone of the project. One of the most difficult challenges for these councils is the development of a shared philosophical base that centralizes victim safety and maintains this priority over time.

The centralization of victim safety is ensured through the composition of the coordinating body and by instituting various means by which activities are evaluated from this perspective. To repeat an important concept noted in the previous chapter: Without some kind of significant input from victim advocates and victims in this process, the outcome of the justice reform effort is unlikely to actually centralize issues of victim safety. The involvement of these two groups is invaluable to a coordination effort because they have firsthand knowledge of the handling of the case from police intervention through probation in criminal court and through related proceedings in civil court, unlike justice system practitioners who must pass cases along to the next intervening agency in the system. Advocates often have the best opportunity to gather information on the overall impact of the system's intervention on victims. Successful coordination efforts using different structures, such as Duluth, San Diego, Pittsburgh, and Seattle, have been inclusive in their approach and actively sought the participation of numbers of advocates and victims.

The composition of the coordinating body should facilitate the participation of all existing advocacy programs in a community. In Duluth, the DAIP staff and shelter advocates are involved in all coordination activities. In San Diego, the large domestic violence council has numerous representatives from the local advocacy programs who are also active on all of its subcommittees. The Los Angeles County Domestic Violence Council also has taken a unique approach to this issue. Half of the council's membership comprises representatives from the relevant city and county departments who have contact with domestic violence victims, and half of the members represent advocacy programs and shelters. In addition, battered women's agencies are represented by two voting representatives, and public agencies have only one. In a statement explaining their structure, Alana Bowman (1993), then council chair, wrote,

> Until the Council created this bold structure, battered women and their advocates were too frequently outnumbered during policy meetings in which one or two advocates met with many representatives from government agencies ... Without this commitment to strong representation by domestic violence programs, county agencies can numerically overwhelm the true experts on the Council, those community-based agencies whose sole purpose is to represent battered women's interests. When only a single shelter exists in a county, that single representative voice can easily become viewed as just another member of the Council, and the focus can become diffused, addressing instead other agency priorities. The concerns of battered women's representatives can become just one of the voices on the panel, rather than the necessary controlling force.... This distinction is important and should become the model for all proposed domestic violence coordinating agencies which may be created....

Too many communities have instituted councils that exclude significant input from advocates or victims. The example of the court calendar fiasco cited earlier was a decision of a council that had been constituted to deliberately exclude all but one advocacy group in its large metropolitan area In addition, the inclusion of all groups serving victims increases the input of racial or ethnic minorities within a community and other groups who have particular issues related to their treatment by the justice system, such as gays and lesbians or immigrant and refugee women. This is not to say that victim advocates do not also propose ideas that are misguided or that they should not be challenged by justice system practitioners. However, the deliberate limitation of this input raises the likelihood that reforms will fail to account for the safety of all victims in a community.

It also must be acknowledged that not all advocacy programs in local communities are prepared to assume the key role that is necessary for coordination to be effective. Some have limited experience in community organizing or working with the justice system in their community; many lack the resources that would allow them to devote staff to this function. Once a coordination council is established, the time required to participate effectively sometimes has overwhelmed small advocacy programs, leaving the governmental agencies frustrated by their absence. As communities develop coordination plans and apply for additional financial resources, it is important that funds be designated to local advocacy programs so that they can hire staff capable of fulfilling these coordinating functions. With the additional funds now available through the Violence Against Women Act to support collaborative initiatives, communities have a unique opportunity to improve the effectiveness of their coordination efforts, regardless of the model they have adopted, by supporting the expansion of their local advocacy programs.

In addition to the meaningful inclusion of victim advocates, the coordinating body should institute ways to actively gather feedback from victims to monitor the impact of their activities on victim safety....

The coordinating body takes account of the existing power dynamics in the justice system and the community when developing decision making procedures and strategies for resolving problems and conflicts. As described in the examples previously cited, the DAIP customizes its coordination efforts to fit the issue under consideration. A major reason for this approach is an acknowledgment of the power dynamics and politics operating within the justice system and the community at large. In the early development of the project, it became clear to the staff that discussions were more open and honest, with much less defensiveness when conducted in private meetings with an agency or with only the agencies involved in the problem. In more public forums, agency staff tended to defend their practices or personnel and avoid any detailed discussion of possible problems. The power relationships within the justice system also impeded honest interchanges. The police department deflected any suggestion that they were not conducting good investigations in front of the prosecutor or judge. Due to the adversarial nature of the justice system, the prosecutor's office avoided discussion of their protocols when defense attorneys were present. Advocates and practitioners found it difficult to discuss problems with the judiciary when they were likely to appear before the same judges on individual cases. Therefore, large public meetings with all of the cooperating agencies were reserved for keeping agency leaders informed about the impact of the coordinated response and more general discussion of their views on future project activities. Later, in-depth discussions of these plans were held in more informal settings with the individual leaders of the affected agencies.

A coordinating council often duplicates the makeup of the justice system and the existing power relationships. The meetings are public, with many councils now including other community institutions outside of the justice system. This structure presents serious impediment to open discussion. Time for in-depth analysis is often limited. Difficult issues or conflicts are unlikely to surface in this type of public forum unless organizers develop additional strategies to identify and resolve them. In fact, a common complaint about councils is that they have tended to stagnate after the more obvious coordination problems have been resolved. Several large councils, such as the Domestic Violence Council in San Diego, have assigned the bulk of their work to subcommittees composed of advocates and related practitioners who are able to work out conflicts without involving the entire body or to prepare proposals for the full council. Clearly, staff from the concerned agencies need to be involved in a decision that affects their work, and others should be involved when it becomes clear that they are affected or that the strategy for solving the problem involves them. A flexible approach, employing a variety of customized and timely problem-solving strategies, is an important element of successful coordination efforts.

Another way to improve effectiveness is to maximize the participation of middle managers and frontline workers in problem-solving discussions. Although the participation of agency leaders has the advantage of engaging the staff who have the power to adopt policy changes, leaders may lack information on the day-to-day experiences of the agency, unlike the staff who directly handle these cases. When analyzing the actual practices in an agency, this is precisely the level of information needed. Here again, power dynamics have to be respected. Putting line staff into discussion groups with their own supervisors can stifle their willingness to openly discuss internal problems or disagree publicly with their supervisor's views.

Last, additional questions have been raised about the participation of judges on coordinating councils. This has been encouraged for different reasons: Judges have a unique perspective on the ways courts operate, control how parties have access to judicial intervention, and play a major role in holding offenders accountable by imposing sanctions or controls on their behavior. Some judges have also acknowledged that they as a group are in need of education on domestic violence. In Santa Clara, the judges claimed that by their participation, they learned a great deal about the different ways that domestic violence cases are processed through the court system and made significant administrative changes as a result. . . . However, these benefits are counterbalanced by concerns about separation of powers and the impact of participation on judicial impartiality.

. . . Should judges participate in setting police policy when they may be asked to rule on evidence that arises from that policy? Should they participate in setting policies for prosecutors or defense attorneys? Could the perception arise that a judge's decision in an individual case was prejudiced by his or her public agreement with the manner in which the case was presented to the court? Was it appropriate for the judicial branch of government to be involved in setting policies of the executive branch? In [one particular] situation, these concerns were exacerbated by a lack of clear decision-making procedures for the council. The judge had convened the council and acted as chair; no further discussion of how decisions would be reached had occurred. This omission resulted in the appearance that the judge was in a position of authority over other council members, even if this was not intended.

In a model such as the DAIP, these concerns have not arisen because the judges are not asked to be involved in the policy making of other agencies. They have been invited and have attended educational training sessions on domestic violence and related issues. They have attended informational meetings about the project's progress or evaluation results, which provided the victims' perspective on the impact of the combined intervention. Staff have met with judges to address issues related to court procedures that were important to the coordinated case response, such as their initial agreement to order presentence investigations for all misdemeanor domestic crimes, not a standard practice at that time. The DAIP approach preserves judicial impartiality and sidesteps separation of powers issues.

In discussions of these issues around the country, a range of opinions have been expressed. At least one judiciary ethics committee (Judicial Qualifications Commission, 1995) has issued an opinion defining some limitations on judicial participation in certain aspects of the work of state commissions and local task forces. Certainly, further debate and guidance on this topic are needed. In the meantime, it would probably be wise for councils that include judges to discuss this issue and formulate their own guidelines about limitations on judicial participation, if the group feels they are warranted. Clear definitions of the council's mission and the adoption of democratic decision-making procedures also can facilitate the open participation of all members of the council.

The cooperating agencies agree to exchange information that not only improves the response to individual cases but also allows the coordinating body to monitor adherence to interagency agreements and evaluate the impact of the coordinated effort. To reduce fragmentation in the response to individual domestic violence cases, most coordination efforts institute new ways to communicate vital case information to each professional intervening in the case. The lack of these linkages is often one of the most obvious problems in the justice system response. In the early stages of many coordination efforts, attention has focused on the development of new sources of case information, such as reports provided by advocates with the victim's permission and on the improvement of data exchange among the intervening agencies, such as the inclusion of civil court data on existing protection orders in the case file of a defendant appearing in criminal court. Data privacy laws must be taken into account when proposing new data exchanges, but most communities find it possible to introduce many improvements fully within these guidelines.

Increasingly, data exchanges are being facilitated by the computerization of databases and the introduction of computer networks, but many improvements can be accomplished manually with the dedication of resources to the task. For example, in Duluth, the protection order files are located in the same building as the probation office, yet for years, neither probation officers, prosecutors, nor judges were routinely checking these files before making decisions in criminal domestic assault cases. Once this problem was identified, funds were raised to allow the police department to contract with the DAIP for a staff position whose role was to ensure that information from this source and others is routinely included in each case file and provided to all of the intervening agencies in accordance with interagency agreements on data sharing. Only recently has this information exchange been computerized.

However, to evaluate the effectiveness of these and all other changes instituted as part of a coordinated effort, the coordinating body must be able to monitor the actual compliance of the cooperating agencies with the protocols they have adopted. Lacking this information, conclusions cannot be accurately drawn about the success or failures resulting from the effort. Without access to police reports, how can a coordinating body be assured that arrest policies are being implemented properly? If a probation department has agreed that certain actions by offenders should result in violations of probation that are reported to the court, how can the coordinating body ascertain that this is happening without access to probation records? To be able to demonstrate its success, a coordinating body must be able to identify the information necessary to monitor and evaluate its progress. Then, it must obtain agreements to provide access to this information from the cooperating agencies. A clear plan for how the evaluative information will be relayed to the agencies and how it will be shared with the public facilitates the process of negotiating these agreements.

Over time, normal institutional processes, such as staff turnover, can erode compliance with agency policies. It is important to continue to randomly assess performance so that any resulting problems can be identified and resolved.... Over the past 2 years, the DAIP has developed and used a method of institutional analysis, titled a "safety and accountability audit," to examine all agency practices in depth. The audit team of advocates and justice professionals observed and interviewed workers in each agency and randomly surveyed case records as to their compliance with agency policies. They developed more than 60 recommendations for additional changes to agency practices, even after 18 years of successful collaboration and reform. For communities to continue to make in-depth improvements in the justice response to domestic violence cases, each cooperating agency needs to subject its practice to the scrutiny of its partners and to participate fully in the discussion of how problems can be resolved.

The coordination role is assumed by persons who possess exceptional negotiation skills and who are able to devote the time and resources necessary to adequately fulfill these responsibilities. Successful coordination efforts of either model have been initiated by extraordinary individuals with exceptional organizational and leadership skills. These leaders, whether justice practitioners or advocates, have possessed key qualities needed to build a successful collaboration: strong analytical and problem-solving skills, highly developed inter-personal skills, exceptional ability to negotiate agreements and resolve conflicts with diverse groups of people, and a passionate commitment to this work. When communities adopt a council structure with appointed members, the resulting group may or may not include individuals with these skills.

This problem may be remedied to some degree if skilled staff can be employed to implement the coordinating effort. Some communities effectively use subcommittees to enable greater participation of community members in the actual coordination effort, another strategy that increases involvement by people committed to this issue. An organization attempting to adopt the DAIP's networking approach also needs to hire community organizers of this type. Although some individuals just seem blessed with these qualities, it is also true that most of us can improve our abilities in these areas with effective training. However, the education of many justice professionals and advocates prepares them only to fulfill their individual roles in the system and may not necessarily provide them with the skills needed to lead successful collaborations. Communities that intend to shift their entire justice response to a more open, collaborative process must plan to provide training in collaboration skills to the staff charged with this task.

The success of both coordination models has been greatly facilitated by the availability of adequate numbers of staff who are able to devote their time to coordination activities rather than other agency functions. Although initial efforts may succeed with the participating agencies donating staff time, it becomes increasingly difficult to sustain these activities or initiate the monitoring or evaluations necessary to measure the impact of the project without additional resources. Although it is true that many of the policy changes enacted by these projects may not entail additional expenditures, the communication and time necessary to identify issues and create these solutions do. Currently, available federal funding can assist local communities in supporting the additional staff needed to organize effective coordination efforts.

* * *

NOTES AND QUESTIONS

1. Thinking back on all the issues we have covered in this book, as well as learning from the Duluth experience, what partners would you seek to

bring to the table if you were the grant-funded Executive Director of a coordinated community response project? Remember that you have to decide not only which organizations are going to be represented, but at what level—are you going to invite the City Police Chief, for example, or the domestic violence detective from your particular precinct? Or will you structure your Roundtable, or Coordinating Council, or Advisory Board, so that different representatives are involved in different ways? Other than law enforcement, which legal institutions will you seek to involve?

2. If we take seriously all the admonitions and advice contained in this book about what it takes to work as a lawyer with victims of domestic violence, the job seems a daunting one indeed. It requires a thorough grounding in the psychological dynamics of abuse, and how those can affect the lawyer's relationship with the women she seeks to assist. It requires resisting the comfort and sense of control that can attach to "paternalistic" or even "maternalistic" lawyering, in favor of partnerships with women whose control over their own lives is tenuous, and whose lives may even be at risk. It requires a broad interdisciplinary education as well as a careful and intensive legal education. It requires working within a legal system in which a lawyer who advocates for victims of partner violence may still encounter hostility and resistance, and experience attacks on her credibility and competence that uncannily resemble the parallel attacks on her client's reliability and integrity. It requires crossing disciplinary boundaries; working with and depending on other professionals who will not always be welcoming or responsive. And it involves participation in the often bewildering politics of community organization.

Of course, not every lawyer-in-training who seeks to educate him or herself about domestic violence will practice in that field. For those who do not, there will be ample opportunities, commensurate with whatever resources they have to give, to contribute to a profession, and a society, in which the needs of victims are understood and met. It may be as simple as setting someone straight about battered women's self-defense claims at a dinner party, or advocating for a firm's pro bono practice to include work on behalf of adult and child victims of domestic violence, and making sure that the firm provides adequate training. It may be standing ready to advise a corporate client or employer about developing a responsible policy to govern those situations where domestic violence comes to work. It may be as personal, and as sensitive, as seeking out a friend or a colleague who is showing the signs of abuse, to offer support.

For those who do decide that this work is their vocation, there will be rewards that match the demands; indeed the rewards are inextricably bound up with the demands. Involvement with community partners and colleagues from other disciplines makes the work less lonely, and adds a public and policy dimension to a practice that might otherwise be too consistently close to other people's pain. Engagement with other service providers also helps the lawyer remind herself, or himself, that the responsibility for the safety of clients is one lawyers share with others, and neither can nor should shoulder alone. A grounding in the psychological and emotional dimensions of the work demands a level of self-knowledge, self-awareness and self-care that will stand the lawyer in good stead not only in his or her work with clients, but in every aspect of his or her life. And then finally there is the reward of knowing that the work, done well, contributes both to the safety and wellbeing of those in need, and to a future, to paraphrase John Stuart Mill, in which the love of liberty has overtaken the love of power as the organizing principle of our society. "The reward of engagement," as Judith Herman has said, "is the sense of an enriched life."

INDEX

References are to Pages

†

1–56662–480–0
90000
9 781566 624800